T0186769

ENCYCLOPEDIA OF
Information Assurance

VOLUME II

Encyclopedias from Taylor & Francis Group

Agriculture Titles

Dekker Agropedia Collection (Eleven Volume Set)
ISBN: 978-0-8247-2194-7   Cat. No.: DK803X

Encyclopedia of Agricultural, Food, and Biological Engineering, Second Edition (Two Volume Set)
Edited by Dennis R. Heldman and Carmen I. Moraru
ISBN: 978-1-4398-1111-5   Cat. No.: K10554

Encyclopedia of Animal Science, Second Edition (Two Volume Set)
Edited by Duane E. Ullrey, Charlotte Kirk Baer, and Wilson G. Pond
ISBN: 978-1-4398-0932-7   Cat. No.: K10463

Encyclopedia of Biotechnology in Agriculture and Food
Edited by Dennis R. Heldman
ISBN: 978-0-8493-5027-6   Cat. No.: DK271X

Encyclopedia of Pest Management
Edited by David Pimentel
ISBN: 978-0-8247-0632-6   Cat. No.: DK6323

Encyclopedia of Pest Management, Volume II
Edited by David Pimentel
ISBN: 978-1-4200-5361-6   Cat. No.: 53612

Encyclopedia of Plant and Crop Science
Edited by Robert M. Goodman
ISBN: 978-0-8247-0944-0   Cat. No.: DK1190

Encyclopedia of Soil Science, Second Edition (Two Volume Set)
Edited by Rattan Lal
ISBN: 978-0-8493-3830-4   Cat. No.: DK830X

Encyclopedia of Water Science, Second Edition (Two Volume Set)
Edited by Stanley W. Trimble
ISBN: 978-0-8493-9627-4   Cat. No.: DK9627

Chemistry Titles

Encyclopedia of Chromatography, Third Edition (Three Volume Set)
Edited by Jack Cazes
ISBN: 978-1-4200-8459-7   Cat. No.: 84593

Encyclopedia of Supramolecular Chemistry (Two Volume Set)
Edited by Jerry L. Atwood and Jonathan W. Steed
ISBN: 978-0-8247-5056-5   Cat. No.: DK056X

Encyclopedia of Surface and Colloid Science, Second Edition (Eight Volume Set)
Edited by P. Somasundaran
ISBN: 978-0-8493-9615-1   Cat. No.: DK9615

Engineering Titles

Encyclopedia of Chemical Processing (Five Volume Set)
Edited by Sunggyu Lee
ISBN: 978-0-8247-5563-8   Cat. No.: DK2

Encyclopedia of Corrosion Technology, Second Edition
Edited by Philip A. Schweitzer, P.E.
ISBN: 978-0-8247-4878-4   Cat. No.: DK1

Encyclopedia of Energy Engineering and Technology (Three Volume Set)
Edited by Barney L. Capehart
ISBN: 978-0-8493-3653-9   Cat. No.: DK65

Dekker Encyclopedia of Nanoscience and Nanotechnology, Second Edition (Six Volume Set)
Edited by Cristian I. Contescu and Karol Putyera
ISBN: 978-0-8493-9639-7   Cat. No.: DK9

Encyclopedia of Optical Engineering (Three Volume Set)
Edited by Ronald G. Driggers
ISBN: 978-0-8247-0940-2   Cat. No.: DK9

Business Titles

Encyclopedia of Information Assurance
Edited by Rebecca Herold and Marcus K. Rogers
ISBN: 978-1-4200-6620-3   Cat. No.: AU66

Encyclopedia of Library and Information Science, Third Edition (Seven Volume Set)
Edited by Marcia J. Bates and Mary Niles Maack
ISBN: 978-0-8493-9712-7   Cat. No.: DK97

Encyclopedia of Public Administration and Public Policy, Second Edition (Three Volume Set)
Edited by Evan M. Berman
ISBN: 978-0-4200-5275-6   Cat. No.: AU52

Encyclopedia of Software Engineering
Edited by Phillip A. Laplante
ISBN: 978-1-4200-5977-9   Cat. No.: AU59

Encyclopedia of Wireless and Mobile Communications (Three Volume Set)
Edited by Borko Furht
ISBN: 978-0-4200-4326-6   Cat. No.: AU43

These titles are available both in print and online. To order, visit:
www.crcpress.com
Telephone: 1-800-272-7737
Fax: 1-800-374-3401
E-Mail: orders@taylorandfrancis.com

ENCYCLOPEDIA OF
Information
Assurance

VOLUME II

EDITED BY
Rebecca Herold
Marcus K. Rogers

CRC Press
Taylor & Francis Group
Boca Raton   London   New York

CRC Press is an imprint of the
Taylor & Francis Group, an **informa** business

AN AUERBACH BOOK

Auerbach Publications
Taylor & Francis Group
6000 Broken Sound Parkway NW, Suite 300
Boca Raton, FL 33487-2742

© 2011 by Taylor and Francis Group, LLC
Auerbach Publications is an imprint of Taylor & Francis Group, an Informa business

No claim to original U.S. Government works

Printed in the United States of America on acid-free paper
10 9 8 7 6 5 4 3 2 1

International Standard Book Number: 978-1-4200-6739-2 (Hardback)

This book contains information obtained from authentic and highly regarded sources. Reasonable efforts have been made to publish reliable data and information, but the author and publisher cannot assume responsibility for the validity of all materials or the consequences of their use. The authors and publishers have attempted to trace the copyright holders of all material reproduced in this publication and apologize to copyright holders if permission to publish in this form has not been obtained. If any copyright material has not been acknowledged please write and let us know so we may rectify in any future reprint.

Except as permitted under U.S. Copyright Law, no part of this book may be reprinted, reproduced, transmitted, or utilized in any form by any electronic, mechanical, or other means, now known or hereafter invented, including photocopying, microfilming, and recording, or in any information storage or retrieval system, without written permission from the publishers.

For permission to photocopy or use material electronically from this work, please access www.copyright.com (http://www.copyright.com/) or contact the Copyright Clearance Center, Inc. (CCC), 222 Rosewood Drive, Danvers, MA 01923, 978-750-8400. CCC is a not-for-profit organization that provides licenses and registration for a variety of users. For organizations that have been granted a photocopy license by the CCC, a separate system of payment has been arranged.

Trademark Notice: Product or corporate names may be trademarks or registered trademarks, and are used only for identification and explanation without intent to infringe.

Visit the Taylor & Francis Web site at
http://www.taylorandfrancis.com

and the Auerbach Web site at
http://www.auerbach-publications.com

This work is dedicated to June, Jillian and Jordan.
Without the love and support of my family, any success would be but a hollow shell.

—Marc

Many thanks go to my husband, Tom, and sons, Heath and Noah, for their understanding
and support while I spent significant amounts of time working and writing when they
would rather I join them for some family fun. I want to dedicate my work also to my late parents,
Harold and Mary Ann Flint, who always encouraged me to write, explore, and never
set limits on what was possible.

—Rebecca

We would both like to dedicate this work to the memory of our late friend and Auerbach editor,
Ray O'Connell, who brought us together to create this encyclopedia and made sure it continued
to move forward throughout some challenging times.

Contributors

Thomas Akin, CISSP / *Founding Director and Chairman, Board of Advisors, Southeast Cybercrime Institute, Marietta, Georgia, U.S.A.*

Mandy Andress, CISSP, SSCP, CPA, CISA / *Founder and President, ArcSec Technologies, Pleasanton, California, U.S.A.*

Jim Appleyard / *Senior Security Consultant, IBM Security and Privacy Services, Charlotte, North Carolina, U.S.A.*

Sandy Bacik / *Information Security Professional, Fuquay Varina, North Carolina, U.S.A.*

Dencho N. Batanov / *School of Advanced Technologies, Asian Institute of Technology, Pathumthani, Thailand*

Robert B. Batie, Jr., CISSP-ISSAP, ISSEP, ISSMP, CAP / *Cyber Defense Solutions, Network Centric Systems, Raytheon Company, Largo, Florida, U.S.A.*

Ioana V. Bazavan, CISSP / *Global Security, Accenture, Livermore, California, U.S.A.*

Mark Bell / *Independent Consultant, U.S.A.*

Kenneth F. Belva / *Manager, Information Security Risk Management Program, Bank of New York, Melville, New York, U.S.A.*

Al Berg / *Global Head of Security and Risk Management, Liquidnet Holdings Inc., New York, New York, U.S.A.*

Alan Berman / *IT Security Professional, Los Angeles, California, U.S.A.*

Chuck Bianco, FTTR, CISA, CISSP / *IT Examination Manager, Office of Thrift Supervision, Department of the Treasury, Dallas, Texas, U.S.A.*

Christina M. Bird, Ph.D., CISSP / *Senior Security Analyst, Counterpane Internet Security, San Jose, California, U.S.A.*

Steven F. Blanding, CIA, CISA, CSP, CFE, CQA / *Former Regional Director of Technology, Arthur Andersen, Houston, Texas, U.S.A.*

David Bonewell, CISSP, CISSP/EP, CISA / *President, Accomac Consulting LLC, Cincinnati, Ohio, U.S.A.*

William C. Boni / *Chief Information Security Officer, Motorola Information Protection Services, Bartlett, Illinois, U.S.A.*

Kate Borten, CISSP / *President, Marblehead Group, Marblehead, Massachusetts, U.S.A.*

Dan M. Bowers, CISSP / *Consulting Engineer, Author, and Inventor, Red Lion, Pennsylvania, U.S.A.*

Gerald Bowman / *North American Director of ACE and Advanced Technologies, SYSTIMAX® Solutions, Columbus, Ohio, U.S.A.*

D. K. Bradley / *Insight Global, Inc., Raleigh, North Carolina, U.S.A.*

Robert Braun / *Partner, Corporate Department, Jeffer, Mangles, Butler & Marmaro, LLP, California, U.S.A.*

Thomas J. Bray, CISSP / *Principal Security Consultant, SecureImpact, Atlanta, Georgia, U.S.A.*

Al Bredenberg / *Writer, Web Developer, and Internet Marketing Consultant, Orem, Utah, U.S.A.*

Anthony Bruno, CCIE #2738, SISSP, CIPTSS, CCDP / *Senior Principal Consultant, International Network Services (INS), Pearland, Texas, U.S.A.*

Alan Brusewitz, CISSP, CBCP / *Consultant, Huntington Beach, California, U.S.A.*

Graham Bucholz / *Computer Security Researcher, Baltimore, Maryland, U.S.A.*

Mike Buglewicz, MsIA, CISSP / *Microsoft Corporation, Redmond, Washington, U.S.A.*

Mike Buglewicz, MsIA, CISSP / *Norwich University, Northfield, Vermont, U.S.A.*

Roxanne E. Burkey / *Nortel Networks, Dallas, Texas, U.S.A.*

Carl Burney, CISSP / *Senior Internet Security Analyst, IBM, Salt Lake City, Utah, U.S.A.*

Dean Bushmiller / *Expanding Security LLC, Austin, Texas, U.S.A.*

Ken Buszta, CISSP / *Chief Information Security Officer, City of Cincinnati, Cincinnati, Ohio, U.S.A.*

James Cannady / *Research Scientist, Georgia Tech Research Institute, Atlanta, Georgia, U.S.A.*

Mark Carey / *Partner, Deloitte & Touche, Alpine, Utah, U.S.A.*

Tom Carlson / *ISMS Practice Lead, Orange Parachute, Sioux City, Iowa, U.S.A.*

Kevin Castellow / *Senior Technical Architect, AT&T, Marietta, Georgia, U.S.A.*

Glenn Cater, CISSP / *Director, IT Risk Consulting, Aon Consulting, Inc., Freehold, New Jersey, U.S.A.*

Samuel W. Chun, CISSP / *Director of Information and Risk Assurance Services, TechTeam Global Government Solutions Inc., Burke, Virginia, U.S.A.*

Anton Chuvakin, Ph.D., GCIA, GCIH, GCFA / *LogLogic, Inc., San Jose, California, U.S.A.*

Ian Clark / *Security Portfolio Manager, Business Infrastructure, Nokia, Leeds, U.K.*

Douglas G. Conorich / *Global Solutions Manager, Managed Security Services, IBM Global Service, Clearfield, Utah, U.S.A.*

Michael J. Corby, CISSP / *Director, META Group Consulting, Leichester, Massachusetts, U.S.A.*

Mignona Cote, CISA, CISM / *Senior Vice President, Information Security Executive, Card Services, Bank of America, Dallas, Texas, U.S.A.*

Steven P. Craig / *Venture Resources Management, Lake Forest, California, U.S.A.*

Kellina M. Craig-Henderson, Ph.D. / *Associate Professor, Social Psychology, Howard University, Washington, District of Columbia, U.S.A.*

Jon David / *The Fortress, New City, New York, U.S.A.*

Kevin J. Davidson, CISSP / *Senior Staff Systems Engineer, Lockheed Martin Mission Systems, Front Royal, Virginia, U.S.A.*

Jeffrey Davis, CISSP / *Senior Manager, Lucent Technologies, Morristown, New Jersey, U.S.A.*

Matthew J. Decker, CISSP, CISA, CISM, CBCP / *Principal, Agile Risk Management, Valrico, Florida, U.S.A.*

David Deckter, CISSP / *Manager, Deloitte & Touche Enterprise Risk Services, Chicago, Illinois, U.S.A.*

Harry B. DeMaio / *Cincinnati, Ohio, U.S.A.*

Gildas A. Deograt-Lumy, CISSP / *Information System Security Officer, Total E&P Headquarters, Idron, France*

John Dorf, ARM / *Actuarial Services Group, Ernst & Young LLP, U.S.A.*

Ken Doughty / *Manager of Disaster Recovery, Colonial, Cherry Brook, New South Wales, Australia*

Mark Edmead, CISSP, SSCP, TICSA / *President, MTE Software, Inc., Escondido, California, U.S.A.*

Adel Elmaghraby / *Department of Computer Engineering and Computer Science, University of Louisville, Louisville, Kentucky, U.S.A.*

Carl F. Endorf, CISSP / *Senior Security Analyst, Normal, Illinois, U.S.A.*

Scott Erkonen / *Hot skills Inc., Minneapolis, Minnesota, U.S.A.*

Vatcharaporn Esichaikul / *School of Advanced Technologies, Asian Institute of Technology, Pathumthani, Thailand*

Don Evans / *Government Systems Group, UNISYS, Houston, Texas, U.S.A.*

Eran Feigenbaum / *Technology Risk Services, PricewaterhouseCoopers, Los Angeles, California, U.S.A.*

Jeffrey H. Fenton, CBCP, CISSP / *Corporate IT Crisis Assurance/Mitigation Manager and Technical Lead for IT Risk Management, Corporate Information Security Office, Lockheed Martin Corporation, Sunnyvale, California, U.S.A.*

Bryan D. Fish, CISSP / *Security Consultant, Lucent Technologies, Dallas, Texas, U.S.A.*

Patricia A.P. Fisher / *President, Janus Associates Inc., Stamford, Connecticut, U.S.A.*

Todd Fitzgerald, CISSP, CISA, CISM / *Director of Systems Security and Systems Security Officer, United Government Services, LLC, Milwaukee, Wisconsin, U.S.A.*

Jeff Flynn / *Jeff Flynn & Associates, Irvine, California, U.S.A.*

Edward H. Freeman, JD, MCT / *Attorney and Educational Consultant, West Hartford, Connecticut, U.S.A.*

Louis B. Fried / *Vice-President, Information Technology, SRI International, Menlo Park, California, U.S.A.*

Stephen D. Fried, CISSP / *Vice President for Information Security and Privacy, Metavante Corporation, Pewaukee, Wisconsin, U.S.A.*

Robby Fussell, CISSP, NSA IAM, GSEC / *Information Security/Assurance Manager, AT&T, Riverview, Florida, U.S.A.*

Ed Gabrys, CISSP / *Senior Systems Engineer, Symantec Corporation, New Haven, Connecticut, U.S.A.*

Brian T. Geffert, CISSP, CISA / *Senior Manager, Deloitte & Touche Security Services Practice, San Francisco, California, U.S.A.*

Karen Gibbs / *Senior Data Warehouse Architect, Teradata, Dayton, Ohio, U.S.A.*

Alex Golod, CISSP / *Infrastructure Specialist, EDS, Troy, Michigan, U.S.A.*

Ronald A. Gove / *Vice President, Science Applications International Corp., McLean, Virginia, U.S.A.*

Geoffrey C. Grabow, CISSP / *beTRUSTed, Columbia, Maryland, U.S.A.*

Robert L. Gray, Ph.D. / *Chair, Quantitative Methods and Computer Information Systems Department, Western New England College, Devens, Massachusetts, U.S.A.*

Ray Haldo / *Total E&P Headquarters, Idron, France*

Frandinata Halim, CISSP, MCSE / *Senior Security Consultant, ITPro Citra Indonesia, Jakarta, Indonesia*

Nick Halvorson / *ISMS Program Manager, Merrill Corporation, Beresford, South Dakota, U.S.A.*

Sasan Hamidi, Ph.D. / *Chief Security Officer, Interval International, Inc., Orlando, Florida, U.S.A.*

Susan D. Hansche, CISSP-ISSEP / *Information System Security Awareness and Training, PEC Solutions, Fairfax, Virginia, U.S.A.*

William T. Harding, Ph.D. / *Dean, College of Business Administration, Texas A & M University, Corpus Christi, Texas, U.S.A.*

Chris Hare, CISSP, CISA, CISM / *Information Systems Auditor, Nortel, Dallas, Texas, U.S.A.*

Faith M. Heikkila, Ph.D., CISM, CIPP / *Regional Security Services Manager, Pivot Group, Kalamazoo, Michigan, U.S.A.*

Gilbert Held / *4-Degree Consulting, Macon, Georgia, U.S.A.*

Jonathan Held / *Software Design Engineer, Microsoft Corporation, Seattle, Washington, U.S.A.*

Foster J. Henderson, CISSP, MCSE, CRP, CAN / *Information Assurance Analyst, Analytic Services, Inc. (ANSER), Lorton, Virginia, U.S.A.*

Kevin Henry, CISA, CISSP / *Director, Program Development, (ISC)2 Institute, North Gower, Ontario, Canada*

Paul A. Henry, CISSP, CNE / *Senior Vice President, CyberGuard Corporation, Ocala, Florida, U.S.A.*

Rebecca Herold, CISM, CISA, CISSP, FLMI / *Information Privacy, Security and Compliance Consultant, Rebecca Herold and Associates LLC, Van Meter, Iowa, U.S.A.*

Debra S. Herrmann / *Technical Advisor for Information Security and Software Safety, Office of the Chief Scientist, Federal Aviation Administration (FAA), Washington, District of Columbia, U.S.A.*

Tyson Heyn / *Seagate Technology, Scotts Valley, California, U.S.A.*

Ralph Hoefelmeyer, CISSP / *Senior Engineer, WorldCom, Colorado Springs, Colorado, U.S.A.*

Joseph T. Hootman / *President, Computer Security Systems, Inc., Glendale, California, U.S.A.*

Daniel D. Houser, CISSP, MBA, e-Biz+ / *Senior Security Engineer, Nationwide Mutual Insurance Company, Westerville, Ohio, U.S.A.*

Joost Houwen, CISSP, CISA / *Network Computing Services, BC Hydro, Vancouver, British Columbia, Canada*

Patrick D. Howard, CISSP / *Senior Information Security Consultant, Titan Corporation, Havre de Grace, Maryland, U.S.A.*

Charles R. Hudson, Jr. / *Information Security Manager and Assistant Vice President, Wilmington Trust Company, Wilmington, Delaware, U.S.A.*

Javek Ikbal, CISSP / *Director, IT Security, Major Financial Services Company, Reading, Massachusetts, U.S.A.*

Lee Imrey, CISSP, CISA, CPP / *Information Security Specialist, U.S. Department of Justice, Washington, District of Columbia, U.S.A.*

Sureerut Inmor / *School of Advanced Technologies, Asian Institute of Technology, Pathumthani, Thailand*

Carl B. Jackson, CISSP, CBCP / *Business Continuity Program Director, Pacific Life Insurance, Lake Forest, California, U.S.A.*

Georges J. Jahchan / *Computer Associates, Naccache, Lebanon*

Stephen James / *Lincoln Names Associates Pte L, Singapore*

Leighton Johnson, III, CISSP, CISA, CISM, CSSLP, MBCI, CIFI / *Chief Operating Officer and Senior Consultant, Information Security and Forensics Management Team (ISFMT), Bath, South Carolina, U.S.A.*

Martin Johnson / *Information Systems Assurance and Advisory Services, Ernst & Young LLP, U.S.A.*

Sushil Jojodia / *George Mason University, Fairfax, Virginia, U.S.A.*

Andy Jones, Ph.D., MBE / *Research Group Leader, Security Research Centre, Chief Technology Office, BT Group, London, U.K.*

Leo Kahng / *Consulting Systems Engineer, Cisco Systems, Washington, District of Columbia, U.S.A.*

Ray Kaplan, CISSP, CISA, CISM / *Information Security Consultant, Ray Kaplan and Associates, Minneapolis, Minnesota, U.S.A.*

Deborah Keeling / *Department of Justice Administration, University of Louisville, Louisville, Kentucky, U.S.A.*

Christopher King, CISSP / *Security Consultant, Greenwich Technology Partners, Chelmsford, Massachusetts, U.S.A.*

Ralph L. Kliem, PMP / *Senior Project Manager, Practical Creative Solutions, Redmond, Washington, U.S.A.*

Kenneth J. Knapp, Ph.D. / *Assistant Professor of Management, U.S. Air Force Academy, Colorado Springs, Colorado, U.S.A.*

Walter S. Kobus, Jr., CISSP / *Vice President, Security Consulting Services, Total Enterprise Security Solutions, LLC, Raleigh, North Carolina, U.S.A.*

Bryan T. Koch, CISSP / *RxHub, St. Paul, Minnesota, U.S.A.*

Gerald L. Kovacich, Ph.D., CISSP, CFE, CPP / *Information Security Consultant, Coupeville, Washington, U.S.A.*

Joe Kovara, CTP / *Principal Consultant, Certified Security Solutions, Inc., Redmond, Washington, U.S.A.*

Micki Krause, CISSP / *Pacific Life Insurance Company, Newport Beach, California, U.S.A.*

David C. Krehnke, CISSP, CISM, IAM / *Principal Information Security Analyst, Northrop Grumman Information Technology, Raleigh, North Carolina, U.S.A.*

Mollie E. Krehnke, CISSP, CHS-II, IAM / *Senior Information Security Consultant, Insight Global, Inc., Raleigh, North Carolina, U.S.A.*

Kelly J. "KJ" Kuchta, CPP, CFE / *President, Forensics Consulting Solutions, Phoenix, Arizona, U.S.A.*

Stanley Kurzban / *Senior Instructor, System Research Education Center (Retired), IBM Corporation, Chappaqua, New York, U.S.A.*

Polly Perryman Kuver / *Systems Integration Consultant, Stoughton, Massachusetts, U.S.A.*

Paul Lambert / *Certicom, Hayward, California, U.S.A.*

Dennis Seymour Lee / *President, Digital Solutions and Video, Inc., New York, New York, U.S.A.*

Larry R. Leibrock, Ph.D. / *eForensics Inc., Austin, Texas, U.S.A.*

Ross A. Leo, CISSP / *Director of Information Systems and Chief Information Security Officer, University of Texas Medical Branch/Correctional Managed Care Division, Galveston, Texas, U.S.A.*

Sean C. Leshney / *Department of Computer and Information Science, Purdue University, West Lafayette, Indiana, U.S.A.*

Ian Lim, CISSP / *Global Security Consulting Practice, Accenture, Buena Park, California, U.S.A.*

Bill Lipiczky / *Tampa, Florida, U.S.A.*

David A. Litzau, CISSP / *San Diego, California, U.S.A.*

Andres Llana, Jr. / *Vermont Studies Group, West Dover, Vermont, U.S.A.*

Bruce A. Lobree, CISSP, CIPP, ITIL, CISM / *Senior Security Architect, Woodinville, Washington, U.S.A.*

Michael Losavio / *Department of Justice Administration, University of Louisville, Louisville, Kentucky, U.S.A.*

Jeffery J. Lowder, CISSP / *Chief of Network Security Element, United States Air Force Academy, Westlake Village, California, U.S.A.*

Perry G. Luzwick / *Director, Information Assurance Architectures, Northrop Grumman Information Technology, Reston, Virginia, U.S.A.*

David MacLeod, Ph.D., CISSP / *Chief Information Security Officer, The Regence Group, Portland, Oregon, U.S.A.*

Phillip Q. Maier / *Vice President, Information Security Emerging Technology & Network Group, Inovant, San Ramon, California, U.S.A.*

Franjo Majstor, CISSP, CCIE / *EMEA Senior Technical Director, CipherOptics Inc., Raleigh, North Carolina, U.S.A.*

Thomas E. Marshall, Ph.D., CPA / *Associate Professor of MIS, Department of Management, Auburn University, Auburn, Alabama, U.S.A.*

Bruce R. Matthews, CISSP / *Security Engineering Officer, Bureau of Diplomatic Security, U.S. Department of State, Washington, District of Columbia, U.S.A.*

George G. McBride, CISSP, CISM / *Senior Manager, Security and Privacy Services (SPS), Deloitte & Touche LLP, Princeton, New Jersey, U.S.A.*

Samuel C. McClintock / *Principal Security Consultant, Litton PRC, Raleigh, North Carolina, U.S.A.*

R. Scott McCoy, CPP, CISSP, CBCP / *Director, Enterprise Security, Xcel Energy, Scandia, Minnesota, U.S.A.*

Lowell Bruce McCulley, CISSP / *IT Security Professional, Troy, New Hampshire, U.S.A.*

Lynda L. McGhie, CISSP, CISM / *Information Security Officer (ISO)/Risk Manager, Private Client Services (PCS), Wells Fargo Bank, Cameron Park, California, U.S.A.*

David McPhee / *IT Security Professional, Racine, Wisconsin, U.S.A.*

Douglas C. Merrill / *Technology Risk Services, PricewaterhouseCoopers, Los Angeles, California, U.S.A.*

Jeff Misrahi, CISSP / *Information Security Manager, New York, New York, U.S.A.*

James S. Mitts, CISSP / *Principal Consultant, Vigilant Services Group, Orlando, Florida, U.S.A.*

Ron Moritz, CISSP / *Technology Office Director, Finjan Software, Ohio, U.S.A.*

R. Franklin Morris, Jr. / *IT Security Professional, Charleston, South Carolina, U.S.A.*

William Hugh Murray, CISSP / *Executive Consultant, TruSecure Corporation, New Canaan, Connecticut, U.S.A.*

Judith M. Myerson / *Systems Architect and Engineer and Freelance Writer, Philadelphia, Pennsylvania, U.S.A.*

K. Narayanaswamy, Ph.D. / *Chief Technology Officer and Co-Founder, Cs3, Inc., Los Angeles, California, U.S.A.*

Matt Nelson, CISSP, PMP / *Consultant, International Network Services, The Colony, Texas, U.S.A.*

Man Nguyen, CISSP / *Security Consultant, Microsoft Corporation, Bellevue, Washington, U.S.A.*

Felicia M. Nicastro, CISSP, CHSP / *Principal Consultant, International Network Services (INS), Morrison, Colorado, U.S.A.*

Matunda Nyanchama, Ph.D., CISSP / *National Leader, Security and Privacy Delivery, IBM Global Services, Oakville, Ontario, Canada*

David O'Berry / *Director of Information Technology Systems and Services, South Carolina Department of Probation, Parole and Pardon Services (SCDPPPS), Columbia, South Carolina, U.S.A.*

Jeffrey L. Ott / *Regional Director, METASeS, Atlanta, Georgia, U.S.A.*

Will Ozier / *President and Founder, Integrated Risk Management Group (OPA), Petaluma, California, U.S.A.*

Donn B. Parker / *(Retired), SRI International, Los Altos, California, U.S.A.*

Keith Pasley, CISSP / *PGP Security, Boonsboro, Maryland, U.S.A.*

Mano Paul / *SecuRisk Solutions, Pflugerville, Texas, U.S.A.*

Thomas R. Peltier, CISSP, CISM / *Peltier & Associates, Wyandotte, Michigan, U.S.A.*

Theresa E. Phillips, CISSP / *Senior Engineer, WorldCom, Colorado Springs, Colorado, U.S.A.*

Michael Pike, ITIL, CISSP / *Consultant, Barnsley, U.K.*

Bonnie A. Goins Pilewski, MSIS, CISSP, NSA IAM, ISS / *Senior Security Strategist, Isthmus Group, Inc., Aurora, Illinois, U.S.A.*

Christopher A. Pilewski, CCSA, CPA/E, FSWCE, FSLCE, MCP / *Senior Security Strategist, Isthmus Group, Inc., Aurora, Illinois, U.S.A.*

Ralph Spencer Poore, CFE, CISA, CISSP, CTM/CL / *Managing Partner, Pi R Squared Consulting, LLP, Arlington, Texas, U.S.A.*

Sean M. Price, CISSP / *Independent Information Security Consultant, Sentinel Consulting, Washington, District of Columbia, U.S.A.*

Satnam Purewal / *Independent Information Technology and Services Professional, Seattle, Washington, U.S.A.*

Anderson Ramos, CISSP / *Educational Coordinator, Modulo Security, Sao Paulo, Brazil*

Anita J. Reed, CPA / *Accounting Doctoral Student, University of South Florida, Tampa, Florida, U.S.A.*

David C. Rice, CISSP / *Adjunct Professor, Information Security Graduate Curriculum, James Madison University, Harrisonburg, Virginia, U.S.A.*

Donald R. Richards, CPP / *Former Director of Program Development, IriScan, Fairfax, Virginia, U.S.A.*

George Richards, CPP / *Assistant Professor of Criminal Justice, Edinboro University, Edinboro, Pennsylvania, U.S.A.*

Steve A. Rodgers, CISSP / *Co-Founder, Security Professional Services, Leawood, Kansas, U.S.A.*

Marcus Rogers, Ph.D., CISSP, CCCI / *Chair, Cyber Forensics Program, Department of Computer and Information Technology, Purdue University, West Lafayette, Indiana, U.S.A.*

Georgina R. Roselli / *College of Commerce and Finance, Villanova University, Villanova, Pennsylvania, U.S.A.*

Ben Rothke, CISSP, QSA / *International Network Services (INS), New York, New York, U.S.A.*

Ty R. Sagalow / *Executive Vice President and Chief Operating Officer, eBusiness Risk Solutions, American International Group, New York, New York, U.S.A.*

Ravi S. Sandhu / *Department of Math, George Mason University, Fairfax, Virginia, U.S.A.*

Don Saracco / *MLC & Associates, Inc., Costa Mesa, California, U.S.A.*

Sean Scanlon / *fcgDoghouse, Huntington Beach, California, U.S.A.*

Derek Schatz / *Lead Security Architect, Network Systems, Boeing Commercial Airplanes, Orange County, California, U.S.A.*

Craig A. Schiller, CISSP, ISSMP, ISSAP / *President, Hawkeye Security Training, LLC, Portland, Oregon, U.S.A.*

Thomas J. Schleppenbach / *Senior Information Security Advisor and Security Solutions and Product Manager, Inacom Information Systems, Madison, Wisconsin, U.S.A.*

Maria Schuett / *Information Security, Adminworks, Inc., Apple Valley, Minnesota, U.S.A.*

E. Eugene Schultz, Ph.D., CISSP / *Principal Engineer, Lawrence Berkeley National Laboratory, Livermore, California, U.S.A.*

Paul Serritella / *Security Architect, American International Group, New York, New York, U.S.A.*

Duane E. Sharp / *President, SharpTech Associates, Mississauga, Ontario, Canada*

Ken M. Shaurette, CISSP, CISA, CISM, IAM / *Engagement Manager, Technology Risk Manager Services, Jefferson Wells, Inc., Madison, Wisconsin, U.S.A.*

Sanford Sherizen, Ph.D., CISSP / *President, Data Security Systems, Inc., Natick, Massachusetts, U.S.A.*

Brian Shorten, CISSP, CISA / *Information Systems Risk Manager, Cancer Research, Kent, U.K.*

Carol A. Siegel, CISA / *Chief Security Officer, American International Group, New York, New York, U.S.A.*

Micah Silverman, CISSP / *President, M*Power Internet Services, Inc., Huntington Station, New York, U.S.A.*

Janice C. Sipior, Ph.D. / *College of Commerce and Finance, Villanova University, Villanova, Pennsylvania, U.S.A.*

Valene Skerpac, CISSP / *President, iBiometrics, Inc., Mohegan Lake, New York, U.S.A.*

Ed Skoudis, CISSP / *Senior Security Consultant, Intelguardians Network Intelligence, Howell, New Jersey, U.S.A.*

Eugene Spafford / *Operating Systems and Networks, Purdue University, West Lafayette, Indiana, U.S.A.*

Timothy R. Stacey, CISSP, CISA, CISM, CBCP, PMP / *Independent Senior Consultant, Houston, Texas, U.S.A.*

William Stackpole, CISSP / *Regional Engagement Manager, Trustworthy Computing Services, Microsoft Corporation, Burley, Washington, U.S.A.*

Stan Stahl, Ph.D. / *President, Citadel Information Group, Los Angeles, California, U.S.A.*

William Stallings / *Department of Computer Science and Engineering, Wright State University, Dayton, Ohio, U.S.A.*

Steve Stanek / *Writer, Chicago, Illinois, U.S.A.*

Christopher Steinke, CISSP / *Information Security Consulting Staff Member, Lucent World Wide Services, Dallas, Texas, U.S.A.*

Alan B. Sterneckert, CISA, CISSP, CFE, CCCI / *Owner and General Manager, Risk Management Associates, Salt Lake City, Utah, U.S.A.*

Carol Stucki / *Technical Producer, PurchasePro.com, Newport News, Virginia, U.S.A.*

Samantha Thomas, CISSP / *Chief Security Officer, Department of Financial Institutions (DFI), State of California, Sacramento, California, U.S.A.*

Per Thorsheim / *Senior Consultant, PricewaterhouseCoopers, Bergen, Norway*

James S. Tiller, CISM, CISA, CISSP / *Chief Security Officer and Managing Vice President of Security Services, International Network Services (INS), Raleigh, North Carolina, U.S.A.*

Peter S. Tippett / *Director, Computer Ethics Institute, Pacific Palisades, California, U.S.A.*

Harold F. Tipton, CISSP / *HFT Associates, Villa Park, California, U.S.A.*

William Tompkins, CISSP, CBCP / *System Analyst, Texas Parks and Wildlife Department, Austin, Texas, U.S.A.*

James Trulove / *Consultant, Austin, Texas, U.S.A.*

John R. Vacca / *TechWrite, Pomeroy, Ohio, U.S.A.*

Guy Vancollie / *MD EMEA, CipherOptics, Raleigh, North Carolina, U.S.A.*

Michael Vangelos, CISSP / *Information Security Officer, Federal Reserve Bank of Cleveland, Cleveland, Ohio, U.S.A.*

Adriaan Veldhuisen / *Senior Data Warehouse/Privacy Architect, Teradata, San Diego, California, U.S.A.*

George Wade / *Senior Manager, Lucent Technologies, Murray Hill, New Jersey, U.S.A.*

Burke T. Ward / *College of Commerce and Finance, Villanova University, Villanova, Pennsylvania, U.S.A.*

Thomas Welch, CISSP, CPP / *President and Chief Executive Officer, Bullzi Security, Inc., Altamonte Springs, Florida, U.S.A.*

Jaymes Williams, CISSP / *Security Analyst, PG&E National Energy Group, Portland, Oregon, U.S.A.*

Anna Wilson, CISSP, CISA / *Principal Consultant, Arqana Technologies, Inc., Toronto, Ontario, Canada*

Ron Woerner, CISSP / *Systems Security Analyst, HDR Inc., Omaha, Nebraska, U.S.A.*

James M. Wolfe, MSM / *Enterprise Virus Management Group, Lockheed Martin Corporation, Orlando, Florida, U.S.A.*

Leo A. Wrobel / *TelLAWCom Labs, Inc., Ovilla, Texas, U.S.A.*

John O. Wylder, CISSP / *Strategic Security Advisor, Microsoft Corporation, Bellevue, Washington, U.S.A.*

William A. Yarberry, Jr., CPA, CISA / *Principal, Southwest Telecom Consulting, Kingwood, Texas, U.S.A.*

Brett Regan Young, CISSP, CBCP, MCSE, CNE / *Director, Security and Business Continuity Services, Detek Computer Services, Inc., Houston, Texas, U.S.A.*

(Continued on inside back c

Volume IV (cont'd)

Volume IV (cont'd)

Contents

Volume I

Volume I (*cont'd.*)

Volume II

Volume II (*cont'd.*)

Volume III

Volume III (*cont'd.*)

Volume IV

Volume IV (*cont'd.*)

Volume IV (*cont'd.*)

Topical Table of Contents

Data Security

Data Security (*cont'd.*)

Digital Forensics

Enterprise Continuity

Incident Management

IT Systems Operations and Maintenance (*cont'd.*)

Network and Telecommunications Security

Access Control

Access Control Techniques

Architecture and Design

Communications and Network Security

E-Mail Security

Firewalls

Regulatory Standards Compliance

Health Insurance Portability and Accountability Act (HIPAA)

Information Law

Policies, Standards, Procedures and Guidelines

Security Risk Management

Strategic Security Management

Strategic Security Management (*cont'd.*)

System and Application Security

Application Issues

Systems Development Controls

Preface

As one can imagine, the creation of this encyclopedia was no easy task. Any attempt to provide a complete coverage of a domain as vast as information assurance is by definition a Herculean task. While not claiming to cover every possible topic area, this encyclopedia reached out to the community at large, and based on the input from a blue ribbon panel of experts from academia, government, and the private sector, we believe we have captured those conceptual areas that are the most critical. We also make no claims that information assurance is a static field. Given the dynamic nature of information assurance, this encyclopedia is considered a snapshot of the field today. As technology and issues evolve, updated versions of this encyclopedia will be published in order to reflect developments.

Along with the cream of the crop of experts serving on the editorial board, this encyclopedia brought together some of the leading authorities in the field of information assurance. These experts represent a cross section of the discipline and provide, in our opinion, a balanced examination of the topics. The impetus for this encyclopedia sprung out of the desire to capture in one place a body of work that defines the current and near-term issues in the field of information assurance. The coverage and depth of each of the topics and concepts covered have resulted in a set of reference materials that should be standard fare in any reference library and hopefully form a corpus of knowledge for years to come.

Acknowledgments

We would like to acknowledge the efforts of several people who have so greatly assisted with this project: JonAnn Gledhill, Tejashree Datar, and Claire Miller.

Aims and Scope

The *Encyclopedia of Information Assurance* provides overviews of core topics that shape the debate on information assurance. The encyclopedia is envisioned as being a much-needed resource for information and concepts related to the field of information security and assurance. The focus of the encyclopedia is holistic in nature and will examine this field from academic as well as practical and applied perspectives. The intended readership includes those from the government, the private sector (businesses and consultants), educational institutions, and academic researchers. The overall goal is to assemble authoritative and current information that is accessible to a wide range of readers: security professionals, privacy professionals, compliance professionals, students, journalists, business professionals, and interested members of the public.

About the Editors-in-Chief

Rebecca Herold, CIPP, CISSP, CISM, CISA, FLMI, is a widely recognized and respected information privacy, security, and compliance consultant, author, and instructor who has provided assistance, advice, services, tools, and products to organizations in a wide range of industries during the past two decades. A few of her awards and recognitions include the following:

- Rebecca has been named one of the "Best Privacy Advisers in the World" multiple times in recent years by *Computerworld* magazine.
- Rebecca was named one of the "Top 59 Influencers in IT Security" for 2007 by *IT Security* magazine.
- The information security program Rebecca created for Principal Financial Group received the 1998 CSI Information Security Program of the Year Award.
- Rebecca is a member of several advisory boards for a variety of journals as well as several business organizations, such as Alvenda, Wombat Security Technologies, and eGestalt.

Rebecca was one of the first practitioners to be responsible for both information security and privacy in a large organization, starting in 1992 in a multinational insurance and financial organization. In 2008, Rebecca coauthored the European ENISA "Obtaining support and funding from senior management" report, which used much of her *Managing and Information Security and Privacy Awareness and Training Program* book content. In June 2009, Rebecca was asked to lead the NIST Smart Grid privacy subgroup, where she also led the Privacy Impact Assessment (PIA) for the home-to-utility activity, the very first performed in the electric utilities industry. Rebecca launched the Compliance Helper service (http://www.ComplianceHelper.com) to help healthcare organizations and their business associates to meet HIPAA and HITECH compliance requirements. Rebecca has been an adjunct professor for the Norwich University Master of Science in Information Assurance (MSIA) program since 2004. Rebecca has written 15 books, over 200 published articles, and dozens of book chapters so far.

For more information, contact Rebecca at rebeccaherold@rebeccaherold.com, http://www.privacy guidance.com, or http://www.compliancehelper.com. TwitterID: PrivacyProf.

Marcus K. Rogers, PhD, CISSP, CCCI, DFCP, is the director of the Cyber Forensics Program in the Department of Computer and Information Technology at Purdue University. He is a professor, university faculty scholar, research faculty member, and fellow at the Center for Education and Research in Information Assurance and Security (CERIAS). Dr. Rogers is the international chair of the Law, Compliance and Investigation Domain of the Common Body of Knowledge (CBK) committee; chair of the Planning Committee for the Digital and Multimedia Sciences section of the American Academy of Forensic Sciences; and chair of the Certification and Test Committee—Digital Forensics Certification Board. He is a former police officer who worked in the area of fraud and computer crime investigations. Dr. Rogers is the editor-in-chief of the *Journal of Digital Forensic Practice* and sits on the editorial board for several other professional journals. He is also a member of other various national and international committees focusing on digital forensic science and digital evidence. Dr. Rogers has authored many books, book chapters, and journal publications in the field of digital forensics and applied psychological analysis. His research interests include applied cyber forensics, psychological digital crime scene analysis, and cyber terrorism.

Encyclopedia of Information Assurance
First Edition

Volume II
Data through Information Classification
Pages 767–1470

Data –
Denial

Digital –
E-Mail

Enclaves –
Enterprise

Espionage –
Firewalls

Forensics –
FTP

Global –
Health Insurance

Healthcare –
Identity

Incident –
Info Classification

Data Access Controls: Sensitive or Critical

Mollie E. Krehnke, CISSP, CHS-II, IAM
Senior Information Security Consultant, Insight Global, Inc., Raleigh, North Carolina, U.S.A.

David C. Krehnke, CISSP, CISM, IAM
*Principal Information Security Analyst, Northrop Grumman Information Technology, Raleigh,
North Carolina, U.S.A.*

Abstract
Corporations have incredible amounts of data that is created, acquired, modified, stored, and transmitted.
These data are the life blood of the corporation and must be protected like any other strategic asset. The
controls established to prevent unauthorized individuals from accessing a company's or a customer's data
will depend on the data itself and the laws and regulations that have been enacted to protect that data.
Appropriate access controls should be implemented to restrict access to all of these types of information.
The effectiveness of any control will depend on the environment in which it is implemented and how it is
implemented.

INTRODUCTION

Corporations have incredible amounts of data that is created, acquired, modified, stored, and transmitted. This data is the life blood of the corporation and must be protected like any other strategic asset. The controls established to prevent unauthorized individuals from accessing a company's or a customer's data will depend on the data itself and the laws and regulations that have been enacted to protect that data. A company also has proprietary information, including research, customer lists, bids, and proposals—information the company needs to survive and thrive. A company also has personal, medical, and financial information and security-related information such as passwords, physical access control and alarm documentation, firewall rules, security plans, security test and evaluation plans, risk assessments, disaster recovery plans, and audit reports. Suppliers and business partners may have shared their proprietary information to enable business processes and joint ventures. Appropriate access controls should be implemented to restrict access to all of these types of information. The effectiveness of any control will depend on the environment in which it is implemented and how it is implemented.

The need to protect individual, business, financial, and technology data in the United States has become paramount in the last 40 years because of the impact of unauthorized disclosure of such information. Key examples are the Privacy Act, the Health Insurance Portability and Accountability Act (HIPAA), the Sarbanes–Oxley Act (SOX), the Department of State International Traffic in Arms Regulations (ITAR), and the Department of Commerce Export Administration Regulations (EAR). The presence of this legislation regarding the protection of certain types of information has mandated the implementation of security controls in many sectors of the U.S. economy. Companies are required to show due diligence in the protection of such information, which is a worthwhile objective, given the impact on an individual, a company, or the nation if this information is disclosed.

Depending on the legislation, the ramifications associated with non-compliance may be minimal or very significant. The penalty for the unlawful export of items or information controlled under the ITAR is up to 10 years imprisonment or a fine of up to $1,000,000, or both, for criminal charges; civil charges have fines up to $500,000 per violation. The penalty for the unlawful export of items or information controlled under the EAR is a fine of up to $1,000,000 or five times the value of the exports, whichever is greater. For an individual, the fine is imprisonment up to 10 years or a fine of $10,000 to $120,000 per violation, or both. These are just the fines; not included are the costs of frequent reporting to the auditors for a designated time period regarding resolution of the data exposure and new corrective actions, damage to the brand of the company, or loss of current or prospective customers who will go elsewhere for their products and services. The cost of controls to protect such information is likely to be considerably less.

IDENTIFY THE ORGANIZATION'S DATA AND ITS CHARACTERISTICS

To identify the controls required to protect data, it is necessary to know what data the organization has. Some

Encyclopedia of Information Assurance DOI: 10.1081/E-EIA-120046280
Copyright © 2011 by Taylor & Francis. All rights reserved.

information may be more readily identified because human resources and finance departments and privacy offices have been identifying such data for a long time. But, to be complete in an analysis of corporate data, it is necessary to document all business processes and the associated data. What information is being created when the corporation builds a product, sells a product, or provides technical support on a product to a customer?

When the data has been identified, it is then necessary to determine its characteristics. Is it public data? Should access be restricted? Who can see and use the data? What persons cannot? Determining what information has to be protected will depend on the expertise of the data owners, account managers, program managers, business managers, research directors, and privacy and legal staff (and possibly others). In some instances, government legislation and regulations for certain types of data change over time, so a regular review of procedures and controls may be required to determine if the established controls are still appropriate. For the purposes of this entry, the terms "sensitive" or "restricted" data are used to represent data that must be protected from access by individuals not authorized to have that data. This entry is not addressing the protection of classified data, although many of the controls being described are used in protecting classified data.

Identify Data Owner and Data Custodians

After the company's data has been determined, an individual who is responsible for that data must be identified. The data owner is a key resource in the definition of the company's data, including the source, the type of data (personal, medical, financial), the business processes that use the data, the data form, the storage location of the data, and the means by which it is transmitted to others. This individual is also (ultimately) responsible for the integrity, confidentiality, and availability of the data under consideration. The data custodian is the person (or organization) entrusted with possession of and responsibility for the security of the specified data and must apply the rules established to protect the data. The cooperation of these individuals is vital to the determination of information sensitivity and criticality and the associated content-based data access controls.

Determine Information Sensitivity and Criticality

The two information designation categories are sensitivity and criticality, and each category may have multiple levels. The number of levels will depend not only on the varying types of information requiring protection but also on the protection measures available to protect a particular level of information. For example, if it is possible to implement only three levels of controls for a particular category because of resource restraints, then having five levels for that category will be more differentiation than can be implemented given those restraints. In instances where several levels have been identified, only the protection measures required for that specific level are applied to data associated with that level. The levels of sensitivity and criticality are usually determined by conducting a business impact assessment (BIA).

Sensitivity reflects the need to protect the confidentiality and integrity of the information. The minimum levels of sensitivity are sensitive and non-sensitive. Criticality reflects the need for continuous availability of the information. Here, the minimum levels are critical and non-critical. Sensitivity and criticality are independent designations. All corporate information should be evaluated to determine both its sensitivity and criticality. Information with any criticality level may have any level of sensitivity and vice versa.

Involve Key Resources in the Definition of Access Controls

When the data designations have been established for a given set of data, the controls to protect information with that sensitivity and criticality must then be defined. The information security organization will not be able to establish controls unilaterally and will require the cooperation and input of the human resources, legal, physical security, and information technology organizations—and, of course, senior management—to make this happen. These organizations will have to provide input regarding the mandated controls for protecting the data, identification of individuals or groups of individuals who are permitted to access the data, and what protective measures can be implemented and not adversely impact the conduct of business. Defining the required controls will also require knowledge of how the systems are configured, where the information is located, and who has access to those systems. This will require knowledge of the organization's enterprise information technology architecture and its security architecture in order to implement the appropriate physical and logical access controls. All types of restricted data can all be protected in the same way (system high), or the information can be grouped into different types by content and data-dependent access controls specified.

ESTABLISH PERSONNEL CONTROLS

Identify Job Functions Requiring Access Restricted Data

In many cases, the ability to access data is defined by the individual's job responsibilities; for example, human resources (HR) information is handled by HR specialists, medical information is handled by medical staff, and insurance information is handled by claims specialists. But, other company information will cross many organizational activities, including manufacturing, sales, and technical support for products sold. Identifying who is handling restricted information in an organization is not an easy process and requires an in-depth understanding of the company's business processes and data flows. The data access flows for a particular company depends on the demographics of the employees, characteristics of the data, business functions and associated processes, physical configuration of the business facilities, and information technology infrastructure characteristics and configuration.

Screen Personnel Prior to Granting Access

Personnel accessing restricted information as part of their job responsibilities should have a level of background screening that is based on the sensitivity and criticality of the information. Data that has a higher sensitivity or higher criticality should be accessed only by trustworthy individuals, and this may require a more extensive background screening process. Individuals providing support to applications, systems, or infrastructure—for the organization or for a customer—should also meet the established access requirements. This would include employees and consultants who are providing administrative or technical support to the company databases and servers. With off-shore technical support being provided for many commercial off-the-shelf (COTS) products and company services, there is a greater risk that unauthorized individuals may, inadvertently, have access to restricted information.

Badge Personnel

Each person should have a picture badge. [In the U.S. government, this badge is referred to as a personal identification verification (PIV) card.] The badge may contain a magnetic strip or smart chip that can be used to access areas where restricted data is used or stored. Those pictures can also be used in organizational charts for each business function to help employees understand who is authorized to access a given area. Permission to access areas containing restricted information can also be indicated on the badge by background color, borders, or symbols.

ESTABLISH PHYSICAL SECURITY CONTROLS

Legislation and federal regulations may mandate that an individual who does not have authorized access to information cannot be provided with an "opportunity" to access that information. Whether or not the individual would try to access the information has no bearing on this requirement—the possibility for exposure must not exist. What does this mean for the organization and its business processes?

Group Employees Working on Restricted Information

If possible, group individuals requiring access to a particular type of restricted information by floors or buildings. This reduces the opportunity for access by unauthorized individuals. If floors in a multiple-story building contain restricted information, badge readers can be installed to permit access to particular floors or corridors. Personnel granted access should not allow unauthorized persons to tailgate on their badges. Badge readers can also be installed in elevators that only permit access to certain floors by individuals with badges for those areas. Of course, persons exiting at a given floor must ensure that only authorized persons leave the elevator on that floor.

Define and Mark Restricted Areas

Persons who need to use restricted data as part of their job responsibilities should be physically separate from other employees and visitors in order to prevent inadvertent access to restricted data. Areas of restricted access should be defined based on employee job functions and marked with signs indicating that the area is a controlled access area, with a point of contact and telephone number for questions or assistance.

Implement badge readers

Each area containing restricted data should be controlled by a guard and hardcopy access control log or by a badge or biometric reader to grant and document access. The badge reader could be a contact reader or a proximity reader.

Provide secure storage for data

Employees using restricted data as part of their work responsibilities need to a have a secure location to store that information when it is not in use. This storage could be locked drawers and cabinets in the employee's work space or specifically created access-controlled filing areas.

Install alarms

Install physical alarms in restricted areas to alert guards regarding unauthorized physical access. Install electronic alarms on devices on the networks to alert security administrators to unauthorized access. Ensure that trained individuals are available to readily respond to such an alarm and reduce, if not resolve, the impact of the unauthorized access.

Mark hardcopy and label media

Restricted information, whether in electronic or non-electronic format, should be legibly and durably labeled as "RESTRICTED INFORMATION." This includes workstation screen displays, electronic media, and hard-copy output. The copy number and handling instructions should be included on hardcopy documents.

ESTABLISH MANAGEMENT CONTROLS

Develop Content-Dependent Access Control Policies and Procedures

Policies provide high-level direction and set management expectations, and procedures provide the step-by-step instructions for controlling access. It is human nature for users to perform tasks differently and inconsistently without proper direction. Inconsistent task performance increases the potential for unauthorized (accidental or intentional) access to take place. An acceptable and appropriate use policy sets management's expectations concerning the protection of sensitive and critical information and the work-related use of e-mail and the Internet, as well as browsing, modifying, or deleting information belonging to others.

Establish Visitor Controls

Visitors may be required to access individuals and information residing in a restricted area. Before the visitor can be granted access to the area, it is important to document the purpose of the visit, determine need-to-know and fulfillment of legislative requirements, and provide a trained escort for the visitor. Information about a visitor, such as the purpose of the visit, employer (or organization the visitor represents), proof of citizenship, need-to-know, length of visit, and point of contact at the company, should be reviewed, approved, documented, and maintained by a security organization. If proof of citizenship is necessary, the visitor should bring a passport, birth certificate, or notarized copy of either for a security officer to review and verify. If a birth certificate is used, the individual should also bring government proof of identity (e.g., driver's license).

A company should not allow individuals access to the company who have arrived at the last minute as part of a larger group from another organization. This is a common practice used by industrial espionage specialists, and it is quite effective because general courtesy would make it seem rude to exclude that person.

The escort for a visitor should be an individual who has an understanding of the information being requested, discussed, or presented and can make an accurate determination as to whether or not the visitor can receive, hear, or see the information. The escort should be prepared to remain with that individual throughout the visit or identify another appropriate employee who can assume the escort responsibilities as required.

Secure storage for a visitor's unauthorized personal items should be provided. Depending on the sensitivity of the visit and the information being discussed, visitors may not be permitted to bring cellular phones, camera phones, pagers, personal digital assistants (PDAs), laptop computers, or other data collection instruments into the restricted areas.

Secure visitor passage corridors should be established. A walk-through prior to the visit can be used to verify that restricted information is properly secured. Escorts assigned to visitors should ensure that the visitors are not exposed to information for which they are not authorized, such as on whiteboards in meeting rooms or employee cubicles, in conversations overheard in hallways or breakrooms, or in documents in employee cubicles. The escort should control tour groups to prevent one or more individuals from breaking away from the group to pursue unauthorized discussions or observations.

Prevent Information Leakage at External Gatherings

Presentations and presentation materials for trade shows, conferences, and symposiums should be approved in advance. Attendees should be instructed about what topics can and cannot be discussed. Employees should be trained on the risks of discussing business functions or products with family, friends, colleagues, and acquaintances.

Authorize Access

Each person's qualification for access should be verified based on job responsibilities (need to know), background screening, and any legislative requirements (e.g., U.S. citizen). This authorization should be documented in the individual's personnel file and electronic files such as Microsoft's Active Directory.® Several control models can be used to grant access to corporate information. Organizations implementing mandatory access controls assign security labels to each subject (user) and each data object; mandatory access control consists of the owner authorizing access based on need to know and the system allowing access based on the labeling. Discretionary access control allows data owners (representing organizational units) to specify the type of access (e.g., read, write, delete) others can have to their data; this decentralized approach is usually implemented through access control lists. Rule-based discretionary access control is based on specific rules linking subjects and objects. Administrator-based discretionary access control allows system administrators to control who has access to which objects. Role-based access control grants and revokes access based on a user's membership in a group; this method is used in most large organizations. For organizations with large data warehouses, data views are preapproved for various role-based groups. Content-based access control uses an arbiter program to determine whether a subject with discretionary access to a file can access specific records in the file. This model provides greater granularity than simple file access. Similar granularity is available using views for access to a database. Regardless of the access control model used, the design of access controls should be based on the principle of least privilege, and the continuing need for access should be revisited on an annual basis for each individual.

ESTABLISH ENTERPRISE SECURITY ARCHITECTURE

Require Approved Hardware and Software

To ensure the integrity of the computing infrastructure and the associated information, hardware and software should be standardized and controlled by an information technology governance committee or organization; that is, the hardware and software should be on the approved list and only acquired from approved sources. Personnel wishing to use hardware and software not on the list should first obtain approval from the information technology governance committee or organization.

Harden Computing Platforms

Hardening control standards should be implemented specific to each platform. These standards should be updated as new vulnerabilities are uncovered and updates are available. Platforms should not be deployed to a production environment prior to hardening. Unnecessary services and applications should be removed or disabled. Unnecessary default accounts and groups should be removed or disabled. Computers should be configured to deny log-in after a small number of failed attempts. Controls should be configured to limit privileged access, update and execute access to software, and write access to directories and files. Guidelines should be established regarding a user's password length and associated format complexity. Security mechanisms, such as tokens or certificates, can be configured to strengthen the system administrator authentication requirements.

Track Hardware and Software Vulnerabilities

Vulnerability advisories involving the software and hardware in use within the corporation should be tracked and corrective actions implemented as deemed appropriate. Vulnerabilities within a Web server might allow attackers to compromise the security of the servers and gain unauthorized access to resources elsewhere in the organization's network.

Implement Configuration and Change Management

Changes to hardware and software configurations should be managed to ensure that information resources are not inadvertently exposed to unnecessary risks and vulnerabilities. All changes should be appropriately tested, approved,

and documented. Inappropriate configuration or improper operation of a Web server may result in the disclosure of restricted corporate information, information about users or administrators of the Web server, including their passwords, or the configuration of the Web server or network that could be exploited in subsequent attacks.

Implement Software Security Features and Controls

Safeguards embedded in computer software should be activated to protect against compromise, subversion, or unauthorized manipulation. All features and files that have no demonstrable purpose should be disabled or removed. Default privileged log-on IDs, default passwords, and guest accounts should be disabled or removed. The use of administrative and root accounts for running production applications should be prohibited. Access to specific applications and files should be limited. Access to systems software utilities should be restricted to a small number of authorized users. Software that is unlicensed, borrowed, downloaded from online services, public domain shareware/freeware, or unapproved personal software should not be installed.

Sanitize Memory and Storage to Remove Data Residue

Allocated computer memory of shared devices should be sanitized before being made available for the next job (i.e., object reuse). Likewise, file storage space on shared devices should be sanitized before being reassigned.

Implement Virus Protection

Virus protection software should be installed and enabled. Centralization of automatic updates ensures that the latest versions of virus detection software and signature files are installed.

Implement Audit Logs

Audit logs should record significant operation-related activities and security-related events. Audit logs must be reviewed periodically for potential security incidents and security breaches. The use of an audit reduction tool increases the efficiency and accuracy of the log review.

Establish Separate Database Servers for Restricted Data

Corporate data is often stored in large databases or data warehouses that are accessible to all employees and contractors, but not all employees and contractors should have access to the data. The use of knowledge discovery in database (KDD) tools for data exploration (often called "data mining") in an iterative process can result in the discovery of "interesting" outcomes. It is possible that those outcomes can support the inference or actual discovery of restricted information, even with individual identification and authentication measures for data access in place. Information systems and databases containing restricted information should be separate from other servers, including Web and application servers, in order to ensure that unauthorized individuals cannot gain access to restricted information. Such database servers must also implement security controls appropriate for the level of sensitivity and criticality of the information they contain.

Control Web Bots

Web bots (also known as "agents" or "spiders") are software applications used to collect, analyze, and index Web content. An organization may not want its Web site appearing in search engines or have information disclosed that it would prefer to remain private or at least unadvertised (e.g., e-mail addresses, personal Internet accesses).

Implement File Integrity Checkers

A file integrity checker computes and stores a checksum for every guarded file. Where feasible, checksums should be computed, stored, and continually checked for unauthorized changes on restricted data.

Implement Secure Enclaves

Information designated as restricted may be placed in a secure enclave. Secure enclaves are network areas where special protections and access controls, such as firewalls and routers, are utilized to secure the information. Secure enclaves apply security rules consistently and protect multiple systems across application boundaries. Secure enclaves should employ protection for the highest level of information sensitivity in that enclave.

Protect the Perimeter

The perimeter between the corporate network and the Internet should be protected by implementing firewalls and demilitarized zones (DMZs). Firewalls should run on a dedicated computer with all non-essential firewall-related software, such as compilers, editors, and communications software, deleted. The firewall should be configured to deny all services not expressly permitted, audit and monitor all services including those not permitted, detect intrusions or misuse, notify the firewall administrator in near real time of any item that may require immediate attention, and stop passing packets if the logging function becomes disabled. Web servers and electronic commerce systems accessible to the public must reside within a DMZ with approved access control, such as a firewall or controlled interface. Sensitive and critical data should not reside within a DMZ. All inbound traffic to the intranet from the DMZ must be passed through a proxy-capable device.

Control Business Partner Connections

When establishing third-party connections, access controls and administrative procedures should be implemented to protect the confidentiality of corporate information and that of its business partners when such information is maintained in the corporate network.

IMPLEMENT OPERATIONAL CONTROLS

Authenticate Users

Authentication can be based on something the user knows (password, personal identification number (PIN), or pass phrases), something the user holds (token), or some user characteristic (biometric). The use of PINs should be restricted to applications with low risk. Passwords should be complex and at least eight characters in length. Personal passphrases are the preferred knowledge-based authenticator because they can be 15 or more characters in length; they can be made more complex by the use of upper- and lowercase alphabetic characters, numbers, and special characters; and they are easy to remember (i.e., they do not have to be written down). The number of unsuccessful authentication attempts should be limited, and the user should just be told that the access attempt failed, not why it failed.

Implement Remote Access Controls

Where remote access is required, remote access security should be implemented. Information resources requiring remote access should be capable of strong authentication. Remote access from a non-corporate site should require users or devices to authenticate at the perimeter or connect through a firewall. Personnel outside corporate firewalls should authenticate at the perimeter. In addition, personnel outside corporate firewalls should use an encrypted session, such as a virtual private network (VPN) or Secure Sockets Layer (SSL).

Implement Intrusion Detection and Intrusion Prevention Systems

Intrusion detection and prevention systems should be implemented to detect and shutdown unapproved access to information resources.

Encrypt Restricted Information

Restricted information transmitted over untrusted networks should be encrypted. Restricted information stored on portable devices and media (e.g., backups) that leave a secured area should be encrypted. Depending on the level of sensitivity, it may also be prudent to encrypt information in storage.

Implement Workstation Controls

Workstations should have an approved personal firewall installed. Other security controls may include, but are not limited to, positioning screen to restrict viewing from passersby, lockable keyboard, power lock, and desk-fastening hardware. Computer sessions should time out after a period of inactivity and require reauthentication to continue the session. The reauthentication can be a password, a token such as a fob or smart card, or a biometric. The location of the workstation and signal strength of the device must be considered for proximity fobs and smart cards to ensure that the session is not reactivated when the user and the user's device are in an adjacent hallway, breakroom, restroom, etc., because the signal may not be attenuated by interior wall and cubicles.

Implement Controls for Portable Devices

Portable devices must be protected against damage, unauthorized access, and theft. All personnel who use or have custody of portable devices, such as laptop computers, notebook computers, palm tops, handheld devices, wireless telephones, and removable storage media devices, are responsible for their safekeeping and the protection of any sensitive or critical information stored on them. Laptop and notebook computers should connect to the corporate intranet at least once a week to receive the latest software patches, antivirus pattern recognition files, and personal firewall patterns. In addition, sensitive information on portable devices must be protected (e.g., encrypted) when leaving a secure environment.

Release Information on Factory-Fresh or Degaussed Media

Before releasing information on electronic media outside the corporation, the information should be copied onto factory-fresh media (never used) or onto media appropriately degaussed to prevent the inadvertent release of restricted information.

Implement Precautions Prior to Maintenance

To prevent inadvertent disclosure of restricted information, all hardware and electronic media being released for maintenance outside of corporate facilities should, prior to release, undergo data eradication or the corporation should have in place a legally binding contract with the contractor or vendor regarding the secure handling and storage of the hardware and electronic media.

Eradicate Electronic Hardware and Media Prior to Disposal

To prevent inadvertent disclosure of restricted information, all electronic hardware and media must, prior to being disposed of, undergo data eradication. Unacceptable practices of erasure include a high-level file erase or high-level formatting that only removes the address location of the file. Acceptable methods of complete erasure include zero-bit formatting, degaussing, overwriting several times (the number depends on information sensitivity), and physical destruction.

Remove Access on Terminations and Transfers

Routine separation of personnel occurs when an individual receives reassignment or promotion, resigns, retires, or otherwise departs under honorable and friendly conditions. Unless adverse circumstances are known or suspected, such individuals should be permitted to complete their assigned duties and follow official employee departure procedures. When personnel leave under non-adverse circumstances, the individual's manager, supervisor, or contracting officer must ensure that all accountable items, including keys, access cards, laptop computers, and other computer-related equipment are returned; the individual's computer log-on ID and building access authorizations must be terminated coincident with the employee's or contractor's effective date of departure, unless needed in the new assignment; and all restricted information, in any format, in the custody of the terminating individual must be returned, destroyed, or transferred to the custody of another individual.

Removal or dismissal of personnel under involuntary or adverse conditions includes termination for cause, involuntary transfer, and departure with pending grievances. In addition to the routine separation procedures, termination under adverse conditions requires extra precautions to protect corporate information resources and property. The manager, supervisor, or contracting officer of an individual being terminated under adverse circumstances must ensure that the individual is escorted and supervised at all times while in any location that provides access to corporate information resources; immediately suspend and take steps to terminate the individual's computer log-on IDs, physical access to information systems, and building access authorizations; ensure prompt changing of all computer passwords, access codes, badge reader programming, and physical locks used by the individual being dismissed; and ensure the return of accountable items and correct disposition of "restricted information" as described under routine separation.

Train Users to Protect Restricted Data

Employees must be trained in the identification, marking, handling, and storage of restricted data. A company with a large number of employees that handle restricted information should consider creating an automated mechanism for training and tracking of training, so the security personnel are not bogged down. Security personnel should be available to answer questions, however. Materials and periodic opportunities should be created to remind employees of their responsibilities to protect information and provide annual refreshers.

Destroy Information No Longer Needed

Hardcopy containing restricted information no longer needed should be cross shredded on site or stored in a secure container for pickup by a service provider. Electronic removable media containing restricted information should be sanitized before reuse or destroyed.

MONITORING FOR COMPLIANCE

Inspect Restricted Data Areas

Physical reviews of areas containing restricted data should be conducted to ensure the data is being appropriately handled, marked, and stored. Other areas of the company should be reviewed to ensure that restricted data is not located in those spaces.

Review Electronic Data Access

System and applications logs should be reviewed for intrusion and unauthorized access to restricted information. Access authorizations should also be reviewed periodically to ensure that individual's who no longer require access have been removed.

Ramifications for Non-compliance

What will be the costs to a company for not implementing required information security controls? What fines would be imposed on its operations? Could the company be sued because exposure of an employee's personal information caused significant embarrassment or harm? Will the company's image be tarnished? What would the costs be in terms of loss of customers? It is hoped that the experiences of others can provide an incentive for action, although organizations must be prepared to address the "it can't happen here" attitude. They will have to depend on the expertise of the data owners, account managers, program managers, business managers, research directors, and privacy and legal staff (and possibly others) not only to determine what information has to be protected and how to protect it but also to help justify why it must be protected. The controls that may have to be put into place to protect the company's data may seem extensive, but the costs associated with not protecting the information can be enormous.

Data at Rest

Samuel W. Chun, CISSP
*Director of Information and Risk Assurance Services, TechTeam Global Government Solutions
Inc., Burke, Virginia, U.S.A.*

Leo Kahng
Consulting Systems Engineer, Cisco Systems, Washington, District of Columbia, U.S.A.

Abstract
Data at rest is one of the most challenging issues facing the information technology (IT) industry today. The volume and the rate at which data is accumulating has challenged the industry to secure the data not in active use (data at rest), which constitutes the vast majority of electronic data in the world today. The entry discussed the nature of data at rest, where it can reside, and the solutions and strategies that the industry is developing across many fronts to secure it. The entry concluded with a detailed case study of one alliance-based approach called secure information sharing architecture (SISA). No matter what the approach or technology the readers choose to implement for defending their data, the authors of this entry hope that the readers will have be benefited with an increased awareness of the need to protect data at rest.

INTRODUCTION

The ever-increasing volume and velocity in which electronic data is being accumulated has led to the rapid development of infrastructure technologies that allow for the quick storage and easy access of the stored information. In the past, the research and development efforts by technology vendors focused almost exclusively on addressing these two challenges: volume by ever-increasing storage capacities by advances in the media itself and velocity by innovating enabling technologies that allow for quicker access such as iSCSI and Fibrechannel. In those efforts, the technology vendors have been extremely successful, and storage infrastructure has been one of the most readily accessible and easy-to-deploy platforms in information technology (IT).

This success, however, does come with a cost, and it's not entirely financial. The data already accumulated and the increasing rate at which data is being transformed into "soft" form has lead to a new problem: the data "at rest." There is no single canonical definition of data at rest. However, the following statement identifies the key characteristics of data at rest:

> Data at rest is information stored on media that is not traversing a network or residing in memory.

This seemingly benign statement refers to almost all electronic content not actively in use by an organization. Vulnerabilities in the security infrastructure that protect data at rest can have enormous consequences to the organizational mission as almost everyone has some form of sensitive content that they need to protect against inappropriate access, theft, or inadvertent disclosure. Consequently, businesses, government agencies, and other organizations are becoming increasingly concerned about the threats against their data at rest. These threats are unfortunately real, and the following sections will describe some of the incidents that have occurred in the not-so-distant past.

DATA AT REST INCIDENTS

According to privacyrights.org, a site managed by the non-profit consumer protection organization Privacy Rights Clearinghouse, there is a data loss incident reported nationwide every 2 days with over 230 million private records lost since 2005 (the numbers are likely to be much higher because many incidents are not reported). These numbers are staggering, with a reported private record loss for almost every American. In the vast majority of these reported cases, data was lost at rest, as opposed to "on the wire" or "in active use." Consider the following sampling of incidents of loss of data at rest:

- The National Institutes of Health: A laptop containing private medical information on over 2000 patients in a clinical trial was lost in February 2008. The laptop contained 7 years of patient data including names, medical diagnoses, and patient cardiac images. None of the data was encrypted on the laptop, in clear violation of HIPAA privacy regulations.
- University of Minnesota Reproductive Medicine Center: A physician at the center lost a USB flash drive that contained unencrypted medical treatment information on over 3100 patients of the center.

Encyclopedia of Information Assurance DOI: 10.1081/E-EIA-120046766
Copyright © 2011 by Taylor & Francis. All rights reserved.

- Bank of America: Unencrypted backup tapes containing information from over 1.2 million federally issued credit cards were lost. The loss occurred during transit of tapes from one Bank of America facility to another. These missing tapes contained Social Security numbers and other financial information on over 900,000 federal workers including U.S. senators.
- Jefferson County Public Schools, Arvada, CO: A special education technician had a personal laptop and jump drive stolen during a home robbery. The jump drive may have contained data on more than 2900 special education students and their legal guardians.
- Idaho State University: A security breach was discovered in a server containing archival information about students, faculty, and staff. The breach of this archive server, which contained data almost exclusively at rest, contained names, Social Security numbers, birthdates, and grades of hundreds of individuals.

These incidents clearly demonstrate the breadth and scope of the dangers that organizations face with their data at rest. There are risks for organizations of all types—public/private, small/large, and regulated/non-real—and real breaches have occurred that have already violated the privacy rights of millions of individuals. With the rate of accumulation of sensitive data increasing, there is legitimate concern over how to secure this massive amount of data when not in active use. The concern is so real that currently both houses of Congress are evaluating amendments to Title 44, U.S. Code, to strengthen the requirements related to security breaches of data involving the disclosure of sensitive personal information. Senate Bill 1558 and House Resolution 2124 (which are identical), referred to as the "Federal Agency Data Breach Protection Act," were introduced in 2007 and specifically direct agency CIOs not only to enforce data breach policies, but also to develop an inventory of all personal computers, laptops, and other hardware that contain sensitive personal information.

WHERE DOES DATA AT REST RESIDE?

The data at rest incidents described in the previous section not only involve diverse organizations, but a wide array of technologies as well. Data at rest can be found everywhere, including places that are unexpected. As technologies mature, especially in the arena of solid state storage, data can reside in the smallest of spaces unimagined just a decade or so. For example, modern day mobile phones (i.e., smart phones) represent some of the most advanced *OS* and storage technologies available. Smart phones run operating systems little different than that of laptops or PCs (Windows® Mobile) and have the ability to store information on the phone itself as well as interfaces for micro flash drives for additional storage.

Identifying the potential places where data can rest in the enterprise is one of the first steps in improving the overall security posture of an organization. With the advances in technology in the past 10 years, especially in the areas of solid state miniaturization, data can now rest in the smallest and most difficult-to-control places.

The following sections discuss the seven categories of places where data typically rests in an organization.

Tokens

Tokens are the smallest, lightest, and most portable of storage devices. They are exclusively made of solid state technology, which makes them extremely fast and can carry enormous amounts of information (tens of Gb) at relatively low cost. The smallest of these available commercially is the microSD card, which is the size of a fingernail and can fit inside small handheld devices such as cell phones. Other examples of token-based storage include the ubiquitous thumb drives, flash cards, and smart cards.

Loss of tokens resulting in inappropriate release of sensitive information is far too common. USB thumb drives in particular represent so much risk to organizations that some IT environments disable the use of USB ports on their PCs, even resorting to injecting silicone into the ports. The main benefits of using token-based storage—high speed, ease of use, lots of space, cheap to buy, and easy to carry—make them extremely popular. However, these same benefits mean increased risk to organizations because they are easy to buy and use, regardless of policy, and also extremely easy to lose. Consequently, securing data at rest in tokens (or preventing the saving of data in tokens altogether) is becoming an increasingly important activity by IT departments.

Smart Handheld Devices

Advances in the miniaturization of technology have allowed handheld devices to become extremely powerful in a short period of time in processing power, storage, and memory. These devices were once designed, manufactured, and used as single purpose devices: phones, pagers, CD players, etc. However, advances in handheld hardware manufacturing and, just as importantly, handheld operating systems (e.g., Windows Mobile, Blackberry OS) allow them to be more general-purpose devices akin to desktops and PCs. Many even run the same applications (Java, Office, etc.).

The most prevalent of these in enterprise organizations are smart phones such as Blackberries that can create documents, send e-mail, surf the Web, view images, and take pictures. They all have on-board storage and, even worse, have built-in slots to support token storage devices such as SD cards. The standard practice of "pushing" or "pulling" content, especially e-mails/attachments, mean that organizations have data at rest in devices far outside of their physical (and oftentimes logical) span of control. The loss of a smart phone can mean dissemination of extremely sensitive data that resides on the handheld, and the security capabilities on these devices in general are not as mature as regular notebook-type PCs. However, some progress is being made. Some of the newest generation smart phones (Blackberries, in particular) allow the administrators to encrypt data as a policy on the mass storage devices that are inserted into the phone.

Endpoints

Data residing on unsecured desktops and laptops has been traditionally the biggest source of data loss in the industry. It has deservedly received the most amount of attention from the media. Some of the biggest IT security debacles in recent memory have been the loss of sensitive information (especially protected health information) from desktops and laptops stolen from cars and homes. It is surprising that these types of losses still occur on a regular basis across both private and public sectors.

The most unfortunate part of the continued loss of data at rest via endpoints is that technologies, both hardware and software, readily exist for desktops and laptops that allow for the protection of saved content. In many organizations, especially in the public sector, these technologies, which will be discussed later, are becoming mandated for the benefit of everyone.

Servers

Servers are one of the one most obvious places that data can rest. Access to data stored on servers is likely to be the most tightly controlled, and most environments do an extremely good job of implementing such control mechanisms as role-based access controls and file-level security. Some may even have implemented volume- or disk-based encryption that protects the data in the event of theft of the server itself. Traditionally, however, protecting data on servers has been focused on authentication. If a user authenticates appropriately to the available directory services, the user has access to files based on some group membership policy. Then these files can be used, e-mailed, saved on tokens, posted on portals, etc. What hasn't seen as much adoption is a digital rights policy on the files themselves that marks and protects the files after they have been saved or disseminated.

Enterprise Storage

Enterprise storage infrastructures are becoming a more common entity in IT organizations. They store massive amounts of data, most of which is not in active use. Enterprise storage infrastructures are the least likely to have protections for data at rest relying exclusively on the physical security policies, network operating systems, and directory services that interface with the users. The good news is that obvious physical loss of an enterprise

storage device is generally unlikely, although there are military environments that do require protections against physical loss. Securing data at rest on enterprise storage environments via encryption is likely to be lowest on the priority for organizations due to the obvious physical loss limitations of the infrastructure.

Backup Tapes

Backup tapes and the associated hardware and software components that go with them have been an ever-present aspect of IT from the very beginning. They serve an obvious and critical role for IT organizations, and until recently have not been viewed as a source of risk. However, recent events have shown that tapes can and will be lost during transit to off-site locations. This means that a copy of the entire IT infrastructure "at rest" can potentially be lost, literally falling off the "back of the truck." Consequently, there has been increasing effort by technology vendors to help protect tape-based data at rest, and exciting developments have been made recently on the hardware front to secure tapes and the data that resides on them.

Other Media

Similar to backup tapes and tokens, there are numerous other media types that can hold data. The most prevalent are CDs and DVDs, which can hold large amounts of data. They are easily transported, generally are not secured with any type of security, and due to their low cost are often disposed of without regard for the data they contain.

PROTECTING DATA AT REST

Unfortunately, there isn't a simple or monolithic answer to protect data at rest. There are so many different areas and devices that data can reside on that it requires a real earnest and comprehensive effort to identify the various places that data can reside and the risks to the data if it is lost or disclosed. Based on the location of the data at rest and the element of risk associated with inappropriate disclosure, IT security mechanisms can be implemented to protect that data. Although specific defense approaches in protecting inactive data exist, especially with encryption and digital rights management technologies, it is important to note that the initial defense mechanisms—physical security and end-user awareness—should already exist in most organizations.

PROTECTIVE COUNTERMEASURES FOR DATA AT REST

The intent of this section is not to present a "how to" on protecting all data at rest. Rather the emphasis is on presenting the strategies and technologies available for this daunting task. Some will be relatively intuitive and may exist in many organizations, others require careful evaluation of the appropriateness of the controls compared to the relative risk of losing the sensitive content. Although each of the discussed elements can play a vital role in an overall enterprise security policy for protecting data at rest, there are two strategies that bear mentioning first: 1) physical security and 2) end-user awareness and compliance.

- Physical security: Many of the losses of data in recent memory, arguably almost all of the most high-profile ones, involve theft of desktops, laptops, servers, or tokens. Good physical security, whether it's at the office or at home, may have prevented these losses. Simple and common sense actions performed by everyone in an enterprise, such as locking doors, securing laptops and handhelds at all times, and not letting strangers into buildings, should be the very first line of defense for protecting the organization from risk.
- End-user awareness and compliance: Many of the losses of data at rest are caused by lapses in judgment or lack of compliance to established policies by end users. Everyone knows someone who "just refuses to comply" with the security policies of an organization (not encrypting volumes, improper disclosure of passwords, etc.). Some of these users end up "losing" the data and violating the privacy rights of individuals. Security awareness programs that are relevant and engaging and policies that emphasize accountability for non-compliance should be the norm in organizations.

Technology-Based Countermeasures

- Network admission control: Tight controls that guard the entry to the network can help to defend data at rest from intruders and hackers. Too many organizations rely on network operating systems and directory services to control entry into the network. A more comprehensive network admission control mechanism that quarantines all network admission requests (e.g., into separate VLANs for posture check and correct) until properly authenticated and verified will help defend the data on the network.
- Standardization: The standardization of vendors and models of the IT infrastructure where data at rest resides can have enormous impact on the ability of IT departments to implement and manage countermeasures against potential threats. For example, there are vast differences between the offline vulnerabilities between Windows XP and Windows Vista (via BitLocker and TPM support). Standardizing on one will allow a single approach either to use a feature within an operating system (like BitLocker) or the

implementation of a third-party encryption product like PointSec.
- Virtualization: Virtualization is one of the most important trends occurring in the industry today. The ability to virtualize the entire IT infrastructure, including servers, switches, and desktops, offers enormous advantages in the securing of data at rest, because the data stores where the data will reside will likely be on a centralized storage infrastructure such as a SAN.
- Compartmentalization: The compartmentalization of data into functional areas within an organization can help to protect data at rest by preventing access by unauthorized users. The creation of virtual enclaves by user identity and role plays an important role in protecting data that should not be accessible based on functional role. For example, a user in a finance department can be isolated into a virtual compartment by being assigned a virtual desktop (with such technologies as VMware® Virtual Desktop infrastructure), virtual LAN (an 802.1q VLAN), virtual SAN compartment (with only data that the finance department should have access to), and virtual servers. Compartmentalization via a virtual path can be an effective and useful tool for protecting data at rest.

Encryption: The Line in the Sand

Ultimately, when all of the previously discussed countermeasures for protecting data at rest fail, the last line of defense is encryption. There are far too many encryption products and solutions to do a comprehensive review of each in this entry. Rather, it is more important to be able to classify them and identify some of the benefits of each in protecting data at rest. Also, these classes of encryption solutions can be layered into a defense-in-depth approach, which will be described later, along with the protective measures described earlier to maximize the protection scheme around an organization's data at rest.

The following list categorizes typical encryption technologies available in the market:

- Operating-system–based encryption: OS-based volume-level encryption is the most readily available, easy to deploy, cost-effective solution available to IT organizations on desktops, laptops, and servers (e.g., Windows EFS, BitLocker, Solaris Volume Manager). However, most smart handheld operation systems do not have native volume encryption capability; therefore, other approaches should be considered in encrypting data at rest on handhelds. In addition, OS-based volume-level encryption generally does not protect data being transferred to ports such as USB and media devices such as DVDs.
- Third-party software based encryption: Due to the limitation of OS-based encryption features, there is a large

market for protecting data at rest beyond the capabilities of typical operating systems. Technologies, such as Check Point Software's media protection, add encryption capabilities at a port level protecting media that are connected via ports (USB, DVD/CD). There are numerous software-based encryption based capabilities that also help protect data residing on smart handhelds. Open source software solutions, such as TrueCrypt®, that use FIPS-compliant algorithms, are available to virtually everyone, making software-based encryption an option for even the smallest of organizations.

- Hardware-based encryption: The main disadvantage of using any type of software-based encryption (including OS-based) is that it takes a performance toll on the operating system and hardware platform that the encryption software is residing on. Consequently, enterprise technology vendors have developed hardware-based solutions designed to encrypt data at the hardware level as the data traverses the storage infrastructure. For example, Cisco Systems' storage media encryption (SME) technology encrypts all data as it is saved both on the storage infrastructure and backup tapes with no impact on the server and backup performance. Additional features such as hardware-based key management, which is essential for large organizations, can be performed at the hardware, reducing complexity and cost to the administrators.

- Digital rights management: The most granular, controllable, and controversial encryption technology available for organizations is DRM. Each individual file or instance of content (both at rest and in flight) can be protected by encryption technology integrated with auditing, logging, and enterprise directories. Aside from the typical arguments regarding the application of DRM creative media (music, video, etc.), DRM can be an extremely powerful tool that can be used to share information with confidence as the protective schemes available from DRM providers allow data at rest to be persistent across organizations. DRM can also be applied on top of all of the other protection technologies for data at rest described previously, and the application of these technologies creates a fortress of concentric defenses around the content at rest, effectively separating data loss/theft with disclosure of content.

DEFENSE IN DEPTH: LESSONS FROM STALINGRAD

In the largest military battle in human history, the battle of Stalingrad in World War II, the German and Russian armies with soldiers counting in the millions used the strategy of defense in depth to counter offensives from the opposing armies to great effect. Both armies arranged

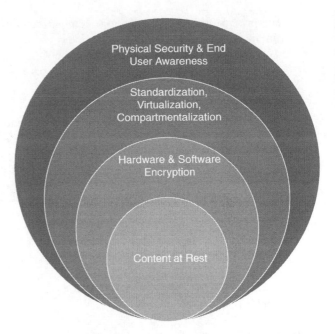

Fig. 1 Conceptual view of countermeasures and a potential defense-in-depth strategy.

their defenses in layers to reduce the momentum of the opposing armies at each layer. This approach of layering defenses has its roots in the battles of antiquity, and the strategy and the term has been borrowed to describe a similar tactic in information security. The layers of countermeasures that can be implemented to protect data at rest make it that much more difficult for an incident to occur. However, each layer adds to the overall cost of ownership of the information, and having a planned approach based on the balance of the sensitivity of the information and the costs associated with its defense is a vital element in an overall strategy toward defending data at rest.

Fig. 1 presents a conceptual view of the countermeasures that have been described and a potential defense-in-depth strategy that can be created with them. The following list describes actual in-depth strategies that can be implemented to protect the various places that data can rest. Although not explicitly listed, end-user awareness and physical security should always be included as the first layer of defense.

- Location of data at rest: Potential defense-in-depth layers
- Tokens: Standardization, DRM
- Smart phones: Standardization, DRM, third-party software encryption
- Endpoint: Standardization, virtualization, compartmentalization, DRM
- Servers: Standardization, virtualization, compartmentalization, OS-levelencryption, third-party software encryption

Data –
Denial

- Enterprise storage: Virtualization, compartmentalization, hardware-based encryption
- Backup tapes: Hardware-based encryption
- Other media: Standardization, DRM, third-party software encryption

The previous sections of this entry discussed the nature of data at rest and the countermeasures that are available to protect it in general and conceptual terms. However, no analysis of a topic is complete without a discussion of the application of concept to technologies. To that end, this entry will provide a case study of the Secure Information Sharing Architecture (SISA) and its approach toward protecting data at rest.

CASE STUDY: SECURE INFORMATION SHARING ARCHITECTURE

What Is SISA?

The Secure Information Sharing Architecture was publicly launched in July 2007, and is a secure, role-based, collaboration framework architected to support the sharing of sensitive information within and between communities of trust in a single security or classification level. SISA was born from an end-user requirement that was largely focused on the protection of information, both at rest and in transit. This end-user entity produced and distributed sensitive and often highly classified information in a tactical, multinational environment where the security and integrity of information was paramount.

SISA is also an industry alliance that was formed to meet the information security requirements of the

aforementioned end-user entity. The "customer" was heavily invested in technologies from the founding alliance partners, Cisco Systems,[1] EMC Corporation,[2] and Microsoft Corporation,[3] and approached these three technology vendors to architect cooperatively an information-sharing solution with commercial off-the-shelf (COTS) products that were generally available from each of the three companies. Additionally, three specialty technology partners were brought into the alliance to cover the baseline requirements of the reference architecture: Liquid Machines,[4] Titus Labs,[5] and Swan Island Networks.[6]

SISA History

As mentioned earlier, SISA was brought forth by an end-user entity requiring rapid deployment of resources to accommodate a multinational information-sharing environment where sensitive information needed to be distributed. The need to share information was the primary driver for the initiative. The quickest foreseeable path to implementation was via COTS products, but the question remained whether or not COTS products and solutions were mature enough to allow controlled information sharing in a multinational environment.

In its original implementation, SISA was designed around some key concepts surrounding data-at-rest security and the protection of information in flight to address the challenges faced by end-user entities as they adapt to meet the requirements of rapid and secure information sharing. The pre-SISA environment consisted of a network that resembled the notional topology shown in Fig. 2.

In a typical network deployment for the end users (Fig. 3), we see several server processes and applications

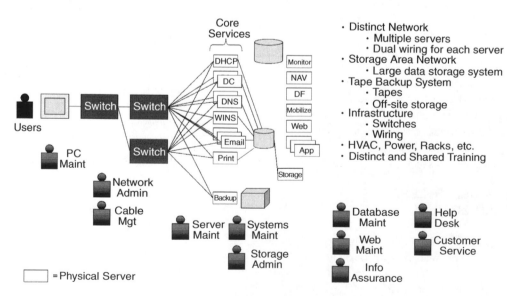

Fig. 2 Typical network and back office, single location.

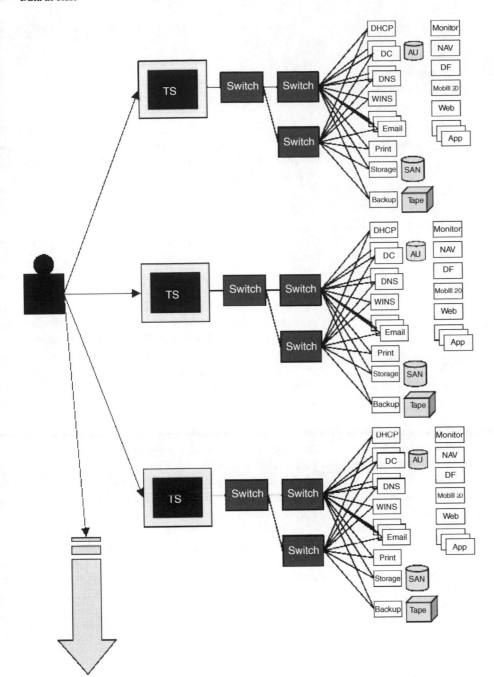

Fig. 3 Network and back office replication.

running in the back office, with nearly an equal number of dedicated personnel with skill sets tailored to specific servers or applications. However, the environment consisted of 11 of these networks within the same security level.

With this in mind, and taking into consideration the unique elements involved in a multinational environment, the complexity level of managing such an environment and maintaining the security of information was a daunting challenge. For instance, the organization maintained 11 different networks, each with unique configurations. Eleven different authentication sources were employed and, in many cases, end users had 11 sets of usernames and passwords just to gain access to network resources, applications, services, and storage.

In addition to cost concerns and the complexity of management, added security risks were involved when attempting to share information. Data needed to be created and duplicated many times over to share that information and place it on the various networks, depending on community-of-trust relationships. Having multiple copies of sensitive information residing on multiple networks introduced risk to the integrity of that information. This in and of itself made real-time collaboration and rapid distribution of sensitive materials very cumbersome tasks at best, and hardly immediate.

Data –
Denial

SISA Architecture

When SISA was being architected for this end-user entity, several key concepts were developed to provide a framework for successfully solving the identified problems:

- Sensitive and internal information had to be encrypted and protected upon creation and while remaining at rest or in flight.
- The protection of sensitive information would facilitate the ability to consolidate infrastructure to reduce the complexity of the topology greatly, which by its nature promotes rapid access to information that needs to be shared.
- Leveraging security mechanisms and ensuring the integrity of data at rest, coupled with the consolidation of infrastructure, allows interorganization information sharing and the ability to collaborate across trust boundaries.

In mapping these key concepts to technical requirements, Fig. 4 shows the major technical concepts surrounding the implementation:

- Role-based authentication and authorization: End users are mapped to roles, and these roles determine their level of access to resources and information in the environment.
- Virtual compartments: A consolidated physical infrastructure is compartmentalized so that end users can operate entirely within their own community of trust. This is also known as path isolation.
- Defense in depth: Where possible, multiple measures are employed to ensure that the environment cannot be breached from the outside and that communities of

trust remain isolated to preserve the integrity of information.

Technologies for Defense in Depth

Pursuing more detail, we further break SISA down into its security services, as shown in Fig. 5, where five key elements are identified to represent security best practices within SISA for data at rest and in flight.

Endpoint protection

In SISA, endpoint protection is focused primarily on protecting computers from viruses, malware, worms, spyware, the installation and launching of root kits, and day-zero attacks. It is recommended that antivirus, antispyware, updated operating system patches, and other related endpoint software applications be applied and maintained (up to date) to prevent these types of attacks.

Endpoint protection is also tightly coupled with the preservation of the integrity of information on endpoints, where localized encryption is employed to protect sensitive information, should the actual endpoint be stolen or lost. To protect end-points in such cases, encrypting the local file system can provide a necessary layer of security that leverages the role-based authentication and authorization practices that form the foundation of the SISA architecture to provide security of the local file system, transparent to the end user who applied the encryption, but linked to that individual and his or her role.

Additionally, the use of an endpoint security agent is prevalent in SISA to monitor for abnormal or unauthorized behavior on workstations and laptops. Endpoint security agents can deny such actions as copying sensitive information from one program or application to another, writing

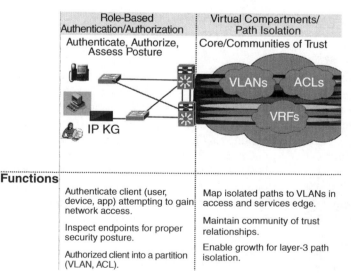

Fig. 4 SISA conceptual architecture goals.

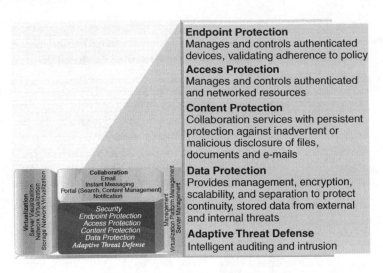

Endpoint Protection
Manages and controls authenticated
devices, validating adherence to policy

Access Protection
Manages and controls authenticated
and networked resources

Content Protection
Collaboration services with persistent
protection against inadvertent or
malicious disclosure of files,
documents and e-mails

Data Protection
Provides management, encryption,
scalability, and separation to protect
continuity, stored data from external
and internal threats

Adaptive Threat Defense
Intelligent auditing and intrusion

Fig. 5 SISA security services.

information from the endpoint to removable media such as a USB flash drive or writable CD, and attaching to shared network drives to transfer sensitive information off of the endpoint. Endpoint security agents operate between the kernel and operating system, thus monitoring operating system calls and enabling maximum application visibility with minimal impact to the stability and performance of the operating system. The agent applies rules-based intelligence to correlate these operating system calls and determines whether those actions are unacceptable or inappropriate, before blocking the requested actions and reporting the incident to the back office.

Endpoint protection also relies on access protection and content protection, as many elements of the SISA security services have dependencies on each other, which promotes defense in depth.

Access protection

In most cases, the first touch point to access resources is the physical network infrastructure, whether by on-site or remote methods. The primary access protection mechanism of SISA is network admission control coupled with authentication and authorization with the back-office infrastructure. Network admission control monitors access to the network at the port level, where network admission control appliances can monitor switch ports for authorized endpoints and allow or deny connectivity. At the same time, network admission control appliances can share end-user credentials with the back-office directory services (domain authorization), which provides the end user with a unified front for admission to the network. While credentials are being verified, endpoints are assessed for their security posture. For example, rules can be created to search specifically for the presence of certain operating system releases and patch level, the presence of antivirus software, up-to-date definitions, and the presence of an endpoint security agent, the agent's status, and its security

level settings. SISA best practices recommend that these posture checks occur in a quarantined environment where access to the authorized network segments can only be granted once the end user is authenticated, authorized, and the endpoint validated for the proper security posture and deemed "clean."

Access protection is also the mechanism by which SISA establishes network path isolation. Once the end user's authentication and authorization have been established, as well as that of the physical endpoint, the user is granted access to authorized network segments. Once this is established, the end user is now in the community of trust, which extends all the way to the back-office applications and storage environment.

Content protection

The primary goal of content protection is to prevent inadvertent or deliberate disclosure of sensitive information. Enterprise rights management plays a lead role in SISA for content protection by providing document marking and encryption directly linked to role-based authentication and authorization. In other words, content is encrypted and a role-based access policy is applied upon creation, leveraging the definition of end-user roles to allow or deny access to information based on community-of-trust participation.

Enterprise rights management also allows one to employ fine-grained controls such as:

- Allowing or preventing the removal or changing of security policies
- Controlling read, write, and print privileges
- Allowing or preventing copy/paste actions with respect to content
- Granular specification of individual access to secure documents

- The ability to expire a document and its access keys after a specified time from the endpoint to the back office

Data protection

Data protection in SISA is focused on data at rest in the storage environment. The obvious mechanism for this is data-at-rest encryption, which is a foundation technology still pervasive throughout SISA. Additionally, in a consolidated multiple-communities-of-trust environment, complexities arise, where advanced technologies such as device masking and zoning are employed to assign and mask access privileges to specific physical interfaces. The creation and management of virtual storage networking environments allows storage, in essence, to be partitioned into secure segments aligned to a specific community of trust.

Furthermore, access control is used to protect data further by leveraging role-based authentication and authorization within the isolated network path. For instance, device-level access controls are implemented to restrict access to hosts. Service-level access control is employed to authorize, authenticate, and audit service actions to prevent unauthorized actions.

Adaptive threat defense

Adaptive threat defense in SISA is primarily targeted at augmenting security information and event management by providing a means to apply a rules-based engine to aggregate critical events within a community of trust and provide correlation to isolate the source of intrusions and malicious activity. Applying this correlation capability allows for the identification of threats in the environment and provides notification of its impact on the network. The information can be used to monitor and assess actively the effectiveness of the security policy deployed in a particular environment.

Case Study Summary

Immediate benefits were realized once the end-user entity deployed SISA:

- Eleven networks were collapsed into one.
- Information is created and stored once.
- Security policy and encryption is applied once to documents/content.

- A single authentication source was used for the entire environment, which also leveraged single sign-on to keep the end-user experience as streamlined as possible.
- "Like-classification" data now traveled on a single wire, but community-of-trust information remained isolated, providing true network path isolation from the endpoint to the back office.

SISA's initial case study is one single example that speaks to the benefits of the architecture, but the key message from the initial exercise exposes technologies and best practices that pose significantly streamlined examples for realizing rapid and secure information sharing, while reducing the complexity of management and associated risks in many industry segments. As the SISA program evolves with the current and future security standards and policy management methods, new and unique use cases will further drive development within the program to present a truly adaptable architecture that is evolutionary in nature, with security at its core.

CONCLUSION

Data at rest is one of the most challenging issues facing the IT industry today. The volume and the rate at which data is accumulating has challenged the industry to secure the data not in active use (data at rest), which constitutes the vast majority of electronic data in the world today. The entry discussed the nature of data at rest, where it can reside, and the solutions and strategies that the industry is developing across many fronts to secure it. The entry concluded with a detailed case study of one alliance-based approach called SISA. No matter what the approach or technology the readers choose to implement for defending their data, the authors of this entry hope that the readers have benefited with an increased awareness of the need to protect data at rest.

REFERENCES

1. Cisco Systems, Inc., http://www.cisco.com.
2. EMC Corporation, http://www.emc.com.
3. Microsoft Corporation, http://www.microsoft.com.
4. Liquid Machines Corporation, http://www.liquidmachines.com.
5. Titus Labs, http://www.titus-labs.com.
6. Swan Island Networks, http://www.swanisland.net.

Data Centers: Security

John R. Vacca
TechWrite, Pomeroy, Ohio, U.S.A.

Abstract
This entry provides information technology (IT) managers with a set of data center management and intranet security software tools and methods. The information presented in this entry will enable IT management to better meet the challenges inherent in managing data center services, costs, and security as the use of distributed systems becomes evermore critical to the enterprise.

INTRODUCTION

Information technology (IT) is now used universally to support critical enterprise business decisions. It has evolved beyond basic applications such as billing and inventory, to the point where it directly supports customers and the manufacturing process. This sophisticated enterprise business information technology is entirely dependent on the diverse (and often incompatible) operating systems and hardware data center environments needed for their execution. All these systems must be managed and maintained if they are to continue to provide support for the ever-increasing applications on which the enterprise's data center depends. Information technology has a significant impact on the effectiveness of the intranet as a whole. Consequently, competitive performance of the enterprise is now directly affected by the management and control of data center computer resources. The measure of IT management's success or failure to support the enterprise is based on its ability to establish and meet required levels of performance, reliability, and availability—while staying within budgetary constraints.

The management and control of complex intranets and data centers are, however, daunting challenges to be met by IT professionals in the next decade. Some key areas that must be achieved are to

- establish and consistently meet service-level agreements with end users
- control costs to meet service levels at the lowest possible level of investment
- protect the wealth of enterprise information and key resources that often span multiple operating systems and hardware platforms

In addition, IT management must not only achieve and maintain all these goals, but it must do this while ensuring complete system integrity at all times. An increasingly large role in enterprise computing is being played by intranet and client/server configurations of midrange and desktop computing environments, and open systems such as UNIX®-based data center environments. Downsizing and decentralizing of processing resources is a result of the evolution toward a more global view—one that is replacing the traditional mainframe view of IT management.

In other words, IT management recognizes more and more that it needs both diverse and complementary information processing technologies if it is to meet the needs of the enterprise. Consequently, there has been substantial growth in complex heterogeneous systems that span multiple computing platforms. This leaves systems and data center intranet security management to contemplate some new concerns: it must now be recognized that midrange and desktop computing environments collectively represent a significant investment in information processing power. It must bring to each computing platform the standard systems management functionality that has been required on large mainframe systems: the need for the same level of automation, resource management, intranet security, and data integrity. Data center intranet security management is essential today for distributed systems, and this provides IT management with new challenges.

INTRANET SECURITY SOFTWARE AND SYSTEMS MANAGEMENT

In many ways, the challenges of distributed systems and data center intranet security management are the same as those of distributed applications. End-user applications, such as manufacturing and general ledger systems, are built on known database structures and application objectives. Distributed systems and data center intranet security management solutions, however, must address a very diverse and often perplexing variety of environments.

There are vast differences in the various operating systems of each platform, and management for distributed systems and data center intranet security must adjust

Encyclopedia of Information Assurance DOI: 10.1081/E-EIA-120046767
Copyright © 2011 by Taylor & Francis. All rights reserved.

Data –
Denial

accordingly. In order to present a unified whole, the goal is to insulate the administrator from the specific vagaries of each system.

Having the software solutions needed to provide comprehensive systems and data center intranet security management on each platform in the intranet is a significant part of mastering distributed systems and intranet security management. These solutions alone are only effective, however, if they can be tied together into a single point of management. Systems and intranet security administrators must be able to manage all or any desired part of the enterprise from any location within the intranet. Single point of management allows administrators to implement and enforce overall enterprise policies while continuing to provide the local controls necessary in a constantly changing environment to ensure responsiveness.

IT management must be able to provide the consistent, high service levels that are required by enterprises. Systems management and intranet security software should deliver integrated, total data center and intranet automation capabilities. At the same time, it should make possible the controlling of costs and ensuring protection of valuable data and resources. For example, enterprises provide distributed systems and intranet security management across multiple platforms. They also provide the ability to endorse and extend industry standards. This allows data center management software to be compliant with, fully support, and extend the capabilities of the Open Software Foundation's (OSF) initiatives for DCE (distributed computing environment) and DME (distributed management environment).

Systems and data center intranet security management software should provide a single point of management for complex heterogeneous systems. For example, data center management software should provide a single point of management through three strategic elements:

1. It meets the specific needs of the platform and exploits the special characteristics and benefits of each by providing robust solutions that are appropriate to each platform.
2. It has a flexible manager–agent architecture that enables each solution to work cooperatively with other solutions in the intranet; managing the flow of work; or performing work on behalf of other solutions in the intranet.
3. It provides a flexible user interface that enables each and every solution within the data center environment to be managed from a single location or multiple locations if desired.

This third element is known as the systems and data center intranet security management workstation, as shown in Fig. 1, it provides systems and data center intranet security management for a homogeneous or heterogeneous intranet.

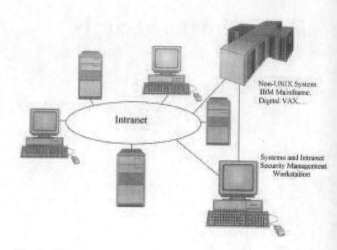

Fig. 1 The systems management and intranet security workstation.

INTRANET SECURITY AND SYSTEMS MANAGEMENT WORKSTATION

When managing all of the solutions in the data center environment, a systems and intranet security management workstation should provide the systems and intranet security administrator with a GUI (graphical user interface)-based user interface. Such a workstation could be used to administer a single UNIX system, a remote IBM mainframe, an OS/2 or Novell-based LAN, or even a heterogeneous intranet containing all of these components and others such as the IBM AS/400® and Digital VAX®/VMS®. The systems and intranet security management workstation should operate on a lower cost X-terminal.

For example, in an enterprise's systems management workstation, the modern interface reduces the complexity of systems and intranet security management. It also provides an intuitive and logical view of otherwise complex issues. The GUI adjusts for the particular aspects of each environment, where necessary. For example, the user interface is identical when managing a multi-node job scheduler for defining jobs within job sets; or, schedules and their relationships to one another. However, when opening up a job detail window for actually setting up individual jobs, the GUI would present a job from an IBM MVS™ system as a collection of JCL (Job Control Language) statements. A job on UNIX would display as a shell script, while a job on Digital VAX/VMS would contain Digital Control Language (DCL) in place of JCL or shell statements.

Control and flexibility of this type is essential for distributed systems and data center intranet security management. Being able to manage each platform from a common location with a common interface and preserving the concepts and terminology across the intranet are extremely useful—along with having the tools needed on each platform.

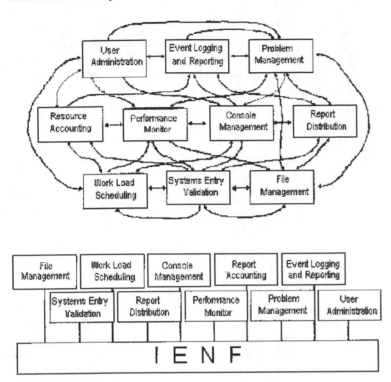

Fig. 2   An Integration Event Notification Facility (IENF).

Investments in the training of systems and data center intranet security administration personnel can be leveraged into new platforms by maintaining the model for each solution across the system. For example, users familiar with ACF2 or TOP SECRET security systems on IBM MVS would find the workload management and intranet security provided through UNIX familiar and easily understood.

CONNECTIVITY FACTOR

An enterprise's systems and intranet security management software should cover a broad range of interrelated functions required to manage and control data center and intranet activity. In addition, it should utilize service layers to interact with each other, adding value to the intranet's information technology systems as a whole.

Furthermore, an enterprise's blueprint for a software architecture and its underlying guiding principles should try to provide a comprehensive strategy for software development for the IT community. This approach, where all components work together across multiple platforms, is essential in maintaining sufficient responsiveness to the continually evolving priorities of enterprise-driven information processing requirements.

Automating each area of systems and data center intranet security management does not in itself result in a complete and successful approach to systems management. Each component of the systems and intranet security management solution must support and communicate with

every other component in order to achieve total data center and intranet automation. For example, intranet-wide information security cannot be ensured if each systems management solution uses its own security tables. Problem and change management cannot keep pace with the dynamic activities of large and complex data center environments if software that addresses functions such as scheduling, report distribution, storage management, and security cannot automatically open and update problem incidents. Clearly, global workload management is unattainable unless each platform provides workload scheduling and resource balancing capabilities that interface with all other platforms. Therefore, complete and effective integration requires both a design for integration and an architecture that support development and enhancement of the completely integrated solution. As shown in Fig. 2 for an Integration Event Notification Facility (IENF), an enterprise's services enable the integration of systems and data center intranet security management functions without an uncontrollable and unmanageable explosion of interfaces.

POWERFUL SOLUTIONS

The rule-based policies that govern data center procedures are particularly well-suited to automation and can be handled by systems and intranet security management software. This automation capability is essential in addressing the complex activities of multi-vendor and multi-operating system intranet environments where a variety of procedures are generally followed due to the variation in

Data –
Denial

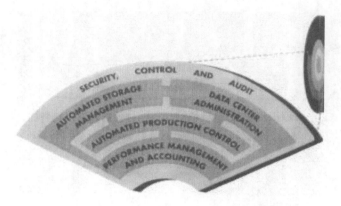

Fig. 3 Systems and intranet security management.

capabilities provided by the native platforms. An enterprise's systems management and intranet security software should simplify the management of these complex data center environments by extending native platform capabilities wherever necessary to ensure operational consistency, regardless of platform.

The otherwise numerous and complex procedures are significantly reduced, enabling operations staff to become familiar with all aspects of a streamlined, unified system. This dramatically reduces the training required of operational staff, particularly in complicated subsystem procedures, and eliminates the need for multiple subsystem specialists to closely monitor data center and intranet activities. An enterprise's systems management and intranet security software should provide a robust, fully integrated, distributed solution that covers the essential disciplines of automated production control, automated storage management (ASM), performance management and accounting, data center administration, and security, control, and audit (see Fig. 3).

To completely automate information technology systems and derive maximum benefit, all of these components must be present for all platforms. Vendors that offer only a part of this functionality and limit the functionality to specific platforms cannot effectively assist IT management in meeting its service-level objectives.

AUTOMATED PRODUCTION CONTROL SOLUTIONS

A data center should provide an integrated set of solutions for automated production control. These solutions cover all areas of functionality, including workload management; rerun, restart, and recovery; console management; report distribution; control language validation; report balancing; and production documentation.

Automated Workload Management

Workload management is concerned with complete automated management of production workloads, including

workload balancing, automatic submission and tracking of work based on user-defined scheduling criteria, priority, and system resource availability. This ensures that work is completed correctly and that critical deadlines are met.

Automated Rerun, Restart, and Recovery

Rerun, restart, and recovery automates the often complex, manual-intensive, and error-prone rerun and recovery process, thus enabling processing to restart at the optimum recovery point. In addition, it automatically handles the otherwise time-consuming manual procedures such as job setup, data set recovery, and backout.

Automated Console Management

Console management improves operating efficiency and reduces errors by automating the handling of console messages. It provides an advanced message/action capability that can alter, suppress, or reply to messages or initiate other actions, such as automatically issuing IPL/IMLs, alerts (through voice and pager notification capabilities), commands or invoking programs based on the content, and frequency and other characteristics of the message traffic. In addition, selective action based on specific console and terminal IDs allows the assignment of consoles to specialized applications, such as intranet monitoring, system monitoring, or tape mount processing. A simulation capability is also provided to assist in the development and verification of these event/action criteria.

When used in conjunction with a programmable workstation, this software provides a single focal point for all console operation activities in a multi-CPU, multi-operating system, and intranet environment. In addition, remote access to perform console management is available through remote dial-ups (PC, remote TSO, CICS, session) or through the telephone using the latest voice and touch-tone technology.

Automated Report Distribution Function

Report distribution provides extensive capabilities for the flexible and efficient production, tracking, and distribution of reports. This results in speeding the delivery time, increasing the accuracy, and improving the tracking of reports. Facilities are provided that automatically identify pages from existing reports, place them into bundles, and sort them by delivery location prior to actual printing.

These capabilities provide end users with the information they want, when and where they need it, while reducing or eliminating redundant information and the materials and efforts that are wasted in its distribution. Automated report distribution software also provides online viewing capabilities that can reduce the need for a hard copy of reports as well as the option to select all or parts of reports for printing. Report archiving capabilities enable the storing of reports offline for auditing purposes and for future viewing or reprinting.

A data center's report management software on intelligent workstations should extend report management capabilities by enabling end users to receive reports as files on their local computer. The ability to merge, annotate, or change reports using a familiar computer should be automated by the workstation-based software, and redistribution of these new reports should be provided through interaction with the software on the host system.

Advanced Control Language Validation

Virtually all systems in use today provide an interpretive control language for defining the execution of batch and online processing. Examples of these languages include IBM Job Control Language (JCL) and the UNIX Shell Script language. A data center's design for systems and intranet security management should include complete advanced control language validation capabilities that reduce or eliminate errors that can cause failures during production execution, and that aid the end user in diagnosing problems with control language programs. In addition, this software should enforce site-specific standards while providing the reports and cross-reference information that are needed for future maintenance.

Automated Report and File Balancing

Report balancing consists of extensive, automated report and file balancing capabilities that enable a quality level to be achieved that is unavailable through manual efforts. In addition to automatically ensuring the accuracy of reports after they are printed, this software can uniquely catch errors during the execution of production work cycles (both enabling fast and accurate resolution of problems), and prevent the completion of in-error production runs and the distribution of incorrect report output.

Production Control Documentation

Production documentation provides complete and consistent centralized online documentation system for the production control environment. Integration with other production control software enables documentation efforts to be automated and centralized, ensuring accessible and accurate information essential to data center operations, and particularly for contingency planning, disaster recovery, and future maintenance.

AUTOMATED STORAGE MANAGEMENT SOFTWARE

Automated storage management software significantly extends the native operating system's capabilities of storage and resource management. This software optimizes performance and access to information. It ensures availability, integrity, and reliability—regardless of the various media device types and differing configurations of mainframes, midrange computers, PCs, and LANs that define the IT processing environment.

Backup Management

Backup management provides the ability to back up files based on creation date and version, as well as supporting backups of multiple versions of the same file. It keeps track of which volume each file has been backed up to.

It also enables users, system, and intranet security administrators to view the media (tape vs. disk) and version of each backed-up file and easily initiate a restore, if needed. Backup management eliminates the problem of keeping track of where backed-up files are kept, and how to find them when a restore is needed.

Archive Management

Archive management makes sure that files have been removed from the online disk system and stored on other media that are based on storage management policies and are available when needed. It ensures that enough storage is always available on the file system to keep users working.

Archive Transparent Restore Processing

Through an ASM common file catalog, the archive management function can locate and initiate a restore of an archived file without user intervention. This function is known as automatic transparent restore, or IXR. With IXR processing, the user request, process, or program attempting to access an archived file is automatically suspended, the file is restored by ASM, and the process is allowed to continue without failure. IXR helps to ensure a successful file management plan by removing the greatest fear that users have of any storage management system—not having their data when they need it.

Threshold-Based Archiving

A specialized capability of an archive management function is threshold-based archiving. Regardless of how careful systems and intranet security administrators are in defining archive policies, inevitably there will come a time when a process unexpectedly demands more storage from the file system than was anticipated. Sudden and unexpected file shortages can be disastrous to planned work and the users of the system—as the file system becomes exhausted and work halts. Up until now, the only answer was to run another backup as quickly as possible, and try to guess which files could be deleted without causing too much other disruption. This process was slow, disruptive, and error-prone at best. Threshold-based archiving utilizes a common file catalog to determine which of the next set of files eligible for archive are currently backed up. The catalog is then updated to indicate that the files have been archived, and deletes it from the disk file system. No additional backups are taken, no best guesses are made, and no costly disruption of work in progress results. IXR, of course, stands ready to bring back any file needed.

MULTIMEDIA STORAGE MANAGEMENT

Multimedia management uses a rule-based, policy-oriented design to provide comprehensive storage resource functions for a wide variety of media, both permanently mounted file storage devices and removable tape, write-once, read many (WORM), and erasable optical technologies. These functions include space management, allocation control and management, I/O optimization, volume defragmentation, and mount management. Each of these capabilities is designed to provide the best possible utilization of the storage devices available, while maintaining the service levels defined by the enterprise's storage management policies.

Extended Data Storage Management

Extended data management enhances and fully automates all data management functions, regardless of platform. It includes reformatting, sorting, compression, and optimization of data seamlessly and independent of physical file organization and data format.

Performance and Error Management

Through data integrity and device failure recovery facilities, system throughput can be optimized and disruptions caused by failures can be minimized. In addition, high-cost, high-performance options of disk devices can be exploited to their full potential.

Finally, take a look at yet another useful data center intranet security method and tool: Xswatch.

WHAT IS XSWATCH?

Xswatch, like its predecessors, was built to watch log files for interesting information. Most log files that grow at a reasonably fast rate have a lot of data, but little useful information. There are several extant implementations that either scan an entire log file or use the equivalent of *tail -f* to monitor the file as new lines are added to it. They then cull log messages that are deemed important or interesting to the implementor. These implementations can be

as simple as *tail -f/grep pattern* to ones that are as complex as a full-blown C program complete with its own macro language.

All of these programs have the same basic structure: match a line of text against a pattern/action pair. If the pattern matches, execute the associated action. The application is up to the end user. For example, watching /var/adm/messages for *file system full*, then executing a job to remove all core files older than one day from the file system. Another example is monitoring for authentication failures. A third might be to send a page to an operator in case of an intranet fault.

Xswatch extends this idea by creating a very general architecture that allows the end user to execute almost any arbitrary pattern/action pair. It takes advantage of the PERL programming language's ability to create code on-the-fly instead of imposing a specialized syntax. The result is a workbench for monitoring almost anything that uses a log file.

What Is the Motivation for Writing It?

The motivation for writing (yet another) log watching program was something that did not have a limited subset of the functionality of the language the engine was written in Programming Extraction and Reporting Language (PERL). Something was also needed that would monitor multiple files simultaneously. Also, an application was needed that had at least the ability to scale. Xswatch's architecture depends on forwarding syslog entries to a central server. On a large intranet, the number of syslog datagrams could consume a significant amount of intranet bandwidth. It seems better to have Xswatch running on many machines, forward only the important data to a central server, and leave the uninteresting data on the local machine. Finally, writing Xswatch is an experiment in code reuse and software integration. A primary design goal was to avoid reinventing the wheel wherever possible. For Xswatch, there was at least partial success achieving these goals.

Xswatch Components

Xswatch has four main components: an engine, snippets, support libraries, and log files, as shown in Fig. 4. The engine is a small PERL program that essentially manages system resources for the user. The engine consists of four subparts: xtail, a signal handler, an event server, and a watcher function.

The Engine Itself

Xtail is a C program that tails off multiple log files at once. Xtail is the most operating system-dependent part of Xswatch. It tracks each file for conditions such as rollovers, truncations, even appearance and disappearance of files.

Data –
Denial

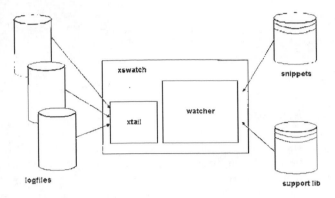

Fig. 4 Xswatch architecture.

The signal handler is mostly for managing Xswatch in the background. Sending a SIGHUP signal will tell Xswatch to kill the current xtail process, reset internal variables, and reload all of the snippets and resume operation. In this way, one can add or remove snippets without halting a running Xswatch process. Sending a SIGQUIT signal will tell Xswatch to write out configuration information to /tmp. This is useful for debugging snippets. Sending a SIGINT or SIGTERM will tell Xswatch to shut down gracefully.

The event server is a PERL module that handles the general housekeeping chores of managing system resources such as I/O, child processes, signals, and timers. The watcher function is a PERL function call (like any other PERL function), except that the function itself is created on-the-fly, based on snippets. Watcher provides the structure that holds the snippets together. Watcher will be called once by the event server for every line of input from xtail.

Snippets

Just what are snippets anyway? The Webster Dictionary definition of "snippet" is a small part, piece, or thing; specifically, a brief quotable passage. For Xswatch, a snippet is a small piece of PERL code that handles pattern/action pairs. They have a very simple structure. There is an initialization section that uses the standard PERL *BEGIN* block and then some code, the simplest of which can be:

```
/ ... some regular expression ... / && do {
... some action ...;
}
```

Snippets are catenated together and compiled into the watcher function. Watcher will be called each time there is a new line of input data written to a log file. The watcher function provides just two pieces of data: an input buffer in $_ , and the name of the log file where the data came from in $logfile. Anything else is up to the snippets.

The snippets are organized in a directory with file names that mimic the *System V rc.d* directories (*nn. Description,* where *nn* is a two-digit string ranging from 00 to 99). The

description can be anything (hopefully informative), with its length determined by the limits of the underlying operating system. This provides a simple way to order execution of the snippets without cutting and pasting. It is also an easy way to temporarily disable snippets. By changing the name from *10.Snippet to stop10.Snippet*, or anything that does not begin with *nn.*, Xswatch will not load the code and compile it into the watcher function. There are no restrictions as to what goes into a snippet. So, if a programmer wanted to put all his code in a single file, Xswatch would work just as well as with many smaller files.

The *BEGIN* block is where each snippet should register which log files it wants to monitor. This is done with the PERL *push* call:

```
BEGIN{
push @watchfiles, '/var/adm/messages';
}
```

Registering the same file more than once (i.e., in more than one snippet), is allowed. Xswatch will reduce the log files to a unique list. This is because so many people can add or subtract snippets from a common directory and not worry about interfering with other snippets. Notice in the following code that there are a lot of *BEGIN blocks*, and they are actually inside the function call definition of *watcher*. Not to worry though; when PERL compiles the function, the *BEGIN blocks* are executed immediately, once, and never again. When the watcher function is actually called by the event server, the *BEGIN blocks* are not touched.

Support Libraries

Since the snippets are simply PERL scripts, support libraries can be anything one needs or wants. For example, one can use the *Term::Cap* module for setting screen attributes, or one of the date and time parsers to convert the log file time stamp into seconds. Or one can include one's own modules to send a message to one's pager or e-mail.

Useful Features

Xswatch has a number of useful features. First, it is simple. Second, it uses no new grammars. Third, the use of snippets is widely accepted. Fourth, it can be extended using standard PERL libraries and contributed code. Finally, it is scalable.

A Simple Engine

The engine is simple. The main program is seven lines of code. It knows nothing about its inputs and does nothing with them except to pass them to the snippets in the form of the watcher function. This minimizes code maintenance:

```
$result = GetOptions(qw(help snippet-dir=s debug=i version));
usage("invalid parameters") unless $result;
usage("$0: v$version") if $opt_version;
parse_command_line;
init;
start_server;
exit(0);
```

No New Grammars

Instead of worrying about learning yet another macro language, parsing, and the accompanying errors, Xswatch uses PERL itself. As previously mentioned, PERL is well-suited for creating code on-the-fly. It also cuts down on training time. If one knows how to code in PERL, one can write snippets for Xswatch. One does not have to look around in the documentation for a syntax guide. Finally, PERL does a much better job at parsing and compiling code than one would ever want to write for a specialized tool like Xswatch.

Shortening the Development Cycle

Prototyping and testing are simplified because snippets are written in PERL. One can use *perl -cw* to check the syntax just like any other PERL script. If what one is looking for in a log file has a time domain component, one can do several things: save a time stamp in a variable and set an alarm, or create a new event using the event server. The source code shows a more elaborate sample that checks that the number of authentication failures from log-in does not exceed a certain threshold. This is to handle cases where a user dials in on a noisy phone line. The log-in program will record an authentication failure, but this is not really something to worry about. On the other hand, if Xswatch saw repeated login failures over a short period of time, one could guess that someone is trying to penetrate the intranet.

Finally, snippets are readable (well, as readable as PERL code gets). One can document snippets, put them under source code management, and essentially treat them like any other body of code:

```
BEGIN{
    push @watchfiles, '/var/log/authlog';
    require PagerTools;
}
if ($logfile eq '/var/log/authlog'){
TIMER_RESET:
    if (/INVALID|REPEATED|INCOMPLETE/){
    if (!defined $auth-trigger){
        $auth_trigger =
        register_timed_client([],600,sub
            ($hit-count=0});
    } else{
        cancel_registration($auth_trigger);
        if ($hit_count++ > 5){
            Pager::call_pager oncall, 'Authentication
                alert';
```

```
    }
        undef $auth_trigger;
        goto TIMER_RESET;
    }
    }
}
```

Scaling

As the number of systems to monitor increases, syslog packets flying back and forth might become a significant load on the intranet resources. By using Xswatch to filter out information at the local machine level, one could create an intranet of Xswatches that (using the standard PERL Sys::Syslog module) connects to a parent syslog daemon and forwards messages to a centralized server.

Distilling Data into Information

There are a number of applications for Xswatch, and one of the most important is distilling data into information. One of a system and intranet security administrator's key duties is to reduce, or at least maintain, entropy. Systems and intranets have a natural tendency toward increasing entropy. System and intranet security administrators are constantly bombarded with log files, e-mail messages, pages, even voice mail. Anyone who has ever had to plow through */var/log/syslog* looking for some clue as to what went wrong knows that it would be far better if, somehow, the system knew what was important and notified a human being in real-time. Xswatch allows an administrator, or even a group of administrators, to consolidate empirical knowledge (about log files) into a single directory. Snippets contain bits of experience learned over time about what to look for in a log file, and what to do about it. Another approach is discard the expected; everything else must be a fault or of some interest. In reference to firewalls, one really does not care when the system resists an attack, or someone tries to access a blocked port; the firewall has done its job. What one really wants to log is when something goes wrong.

Downsides of Xswatch

Xswatch has its flaws. During the development process, a few issues arose that should not come as a surprise—but did anyway. PERL-centrism is seductive. During the early development of Xswatch, and after several ineffective attempts, it was clear that although PERL may be portable, there are some things that really are better implemented in C or some other compiled 3GL. PERL is not cheap. A long-running PERL process will consume about 2 MB of virtual memory on a SPARCstation 5 running SunOS. The resident set size hovered around 1200 KB. Even so, the good news is that there need be only one of these processes running on any given machine. Also, if one considers that an xterm process consumes almost 500 KB, one Xswatch process does not hurt so much.

The holy grail of code reuse also has its problems. The most recent version of the EventServer module was incompatible with PERL. Contributed modules tend to lag behind releases of the main body of code, so it is important to track each revision carefully. There are also many PERL modules that, although useful and publicly available, would not work without some effort. Hopefully, as the body of available code matures, these library modules will become more stable.

Xswatch shows promise as an incremental refinement in the publicly available collection of log-watching programs. Note that there are now commercial products in the field that offer more integrated and scalable services. They might even be more affordable! Xswatch makes an effort to encourage code reuse and integration. The maintenance costs for tracking admittedly diverse software packages seem to be less than the cost of maintaining an equivalent amount of homegrown code. Xswatch was also an experiment in toolsmithing—to the extent that the main engine is seven lines of code long. It is modest in scope. The entire Xswatch program is six heavily commented pages of PERL code, including the 15 pages of online documentation. Using Xswatch is as simple as creating a few lines of PERL script with only two assumptions and installing the file into a directory. Finally, because xswatch does not have its own macro language, it is only limited by the functionality of PERL.

CONCLUSION

Distributed systems and intranet security management solutions must address a very diverse and often perplexing variety of data center environments, each with its own needs and challenges. Distributed systems and intranet security management must also adjust for the vast differences in the various operating systems of each platform, insulating the administrator from the specific vagaries of each system in order to present a unified whole. Through the single point of IT management, overall enterprise policies can be implemented and enforced while continuing to provide the local controls necessary to ensure responsiveness to the constantly changing data center environment.

Finally, Xswatch makes an effort to encourage code reuse and integration. Xswatch shows promise as an incremental refinement in the publicly available collection of log-watching programs.

Data Centers: Site Selection and Facility Design

Sandy Bacik
Information Security Professional, Fuquay Varina, North Carolina, U.S.A.

Abstract

Every enterprise must consider either building its own server room or data center, or outsourcing the facility to a supplier. This entry reviews items that need to be included when performing a facility audit, as well as items the enterprise needs to consider when reviewing a site and facility to host its enterprise assets. It also provides a guideline for determining which security essentials must be accomplished with the controls for site selection and facility design.

INTRODUCTION

Information technology (IT) has been complaining to Facilities about additional power and air requirements needed for the server room within the enterprise headquarters. IT has documented the current and future environmental requirements for production equipment. The business park, where headquarters is located, is having new construction being performed for other business expansions. While digging a new trench, the power company cuts the power to the entire business park. No problem; the generator kicks on and the server room equipment is continuing merrily on the production processing schedule. The power company gets the power back on, the generator senses the power and switches back to regular power. Oops, the building's uninterruptable power source (UPS) breaker trips and the server room does not have an additional UPS in place nor does it have a separate power source. As a result, all 200+ network devices and servers hard crash when the building breaker tripped and the generator did not come back on because it sensed the line power. IT needs 72 continuous hours to recover and bring all systems back online. Could this have been prevented? Were there simple items that should or could have been in place for business continuity and disaster recovery? Although the answer is yes, there may have been communication problems between IT and Facilities, or there might have been budget issues over who should have paid for the upgrades.

Every enterprise must consider either building its own server room or data center, or outsourcing the facility to a supplier. The enterprise might be outgrowing its existing internal facility or it may be reviewing plans to outsource the hosting. When an enterprise is looking for a site or a data center hosting facility, then the enterprise must look at where the site is going to be located and the facility design. This entry will review items that need to be included when performing a facility audit, as well as items the enterprise needs to consider when reviewing a site and facility to host

its enterprise assets. At a high level, the enterprise must determine the requirements for:

- Physical and material supplies: Number of components, terminals, desks, chairs, containers, tapes, disks, paper supplies, waste, cabling, wiring
- Facility: Building(s), room(s), work space, storage area(s)
- Physical environment: Air conditioning and flow, fire suppression, electricity, communication, water, power, backup power

In addition, to these three high-level requirements, the enterprise must review and determine which of the following security essentials must be accomplished with the controls for site selection and facility design:

- Demarcate by established, defined borders to create a defendable space.
- Control entry and exit through a limited number of portals.
- Deter unauthorized entities by ensuring the building appears strong and solid, and deny easy access to keys, information, badges, windows, and doors.
- Delay unauthorized entry by creating sound access controls.
- Monitor detection systems in case an intruder gets through the physical barriers.
- Communicate alarms immediately to an entity that is prepared to respond and react to an intrusion.

PHYSICAL AND MATERIAL SUPPLIES

What is the function of the facility? Is it just going to host networking and production computer equipment? What are the types and number of assets that will be hosted in a data center facility? Or is any staff going to reside

Encyclopedia of Information Assurance DOI: 10.1081/E-EIA-120046862
Copyright © 2011 by Taylor & Francis. All rights reserved.

within the facility? Assets can range from firewalls and other network devices to production servers containing the enterprise's most critical information assets. First and foremost, the enterprise must develop a list of assets that are going to be hosted and the environmental requirements of those assets. If staff are going to reside, even part time, within the facility, work areas and supplies will need to be included in the facility requirements. Depending upon the size of the facility, requirements for extra cabling, wiring, and hard drive space may be needed. Determining the square footage required for equipment and supplies will assist the enterprise in selecting the size of the facility.

FACILITY

Before getting into more detail, a site needs to be selected to host the equipment. When an enterprise does a site selection or decides to use an internal facility, the following items need to be taken into consideration when evaluating a site to limit the risk and threats to enterprise assets:

General Construction

- Can the structure withstand regional disasters? What natural disasters have occurred in the region? What man-made disasters have occurred in the region?
- How many controlled and uncontrolled ingresses and egresses exist?
- Is the structure new or has it been retrofitted?
- Does the construction company have an excellent reputation for service?
- Is there a gated entrance, and how is it controlled and monitored?
- Can exterior and interior doors be compromised easily? What are the alerts when this happens? What about the door frames?
- What utility grid does the site reside in? Are there redundant utilities for the site, such as power generators?
- How soundproof is the facility?
- Is there much glass on the exterior? Are there many windows in the facility susceptible to unauthorized access or for viewing activity from the outside?
- Does the facility have raised floors? What about a manhole or underground opening to access the facility?
- Does the facility contain signage (warnings, exits, emergency lights)?
- What are the hazards of the facility?
- What are the intrusion alerts, and how can they be set off?

Remember: just because a building is built to code does not mean it is a good design for the enterprise assets.

Site Vulnerabilities

- Is the site located in a high-crime area? Will staff feel safe when leaving after hours?
- Is the outside site area well lit or hazardous for staff leaving after sunset? Does the outside lighting illuminate critical areas (fire escapes, ground-level windows and doors, alleys)? Is there auxiliary power for the external lighting? Can the lighting be easily compromised?
- Is the facility internally well lit during the day, as well as at night? Is there auxiliary power for the internal lighting?
- How close are the emergency services (police, fire)?
- Does the site attract unwanted attention?
- Is the site marked as a hosting facility for random violence?
- If the enterprise places the assets on the site, who has access to the facility, and who monitors activities of staff?
- Can someone drive a truck through the wall of the site and damage internal assets?

Site Protections

- Where are the security cameras located, and how many are there? What are the closed-circuit television aspects of the facility? How are they being monitored?
- Are the security cameras tape or digital? What is the retention for the video footage? Does it meet the enterprise records-retention requirements?
- Are the rooms locked independently?
- Do guards regularly patrol the unsecured areas?
- Are there environmental controls (smoke detectors, fire detectors, fire suppression equipment, and heat and humidity sensors)?
- Will tampering with any of the environmental controls create alerts to appropriate personnel?
- What are the access controls? (Biometrics? Man-traps? Proximity cards?)
- If badges are used, is it easy to distinguish a visitor from a staff member?
- How are visitors and regular staff logged for entry to and exit from the facility?
- How is the enterprise alerted when there is a facility compromise?
- Can the site perform regular facility maintenance without affecting the enterprise operations?
- Does the facility have layered security controls: facility site, facility shell, data cages/rooms, work areas?
- When a facility staff member is terminated or resigns, what controls are in place to ensure access is removed and passwords have been modified?

Data –
Denial

- What is the screening method for facility staff members? Are the guards and staff rotated on a regular basis to ensure there are fresh eyes monitoring the environment?
- Are facility staff members provided special training for firearms, CPR, first aid, fire safety, etc.?

Adjacent or Nearby Buildings

- Are nearby buildings well maintained?
- Can someone compromise an adjacent building and acquire access to the enterprise facility?

These additional requirements will need to be considered if a server room is going to be used instead of a hosting facility:

- Does the room have full-height fireproof walls to close access through false ceiling tiles?
- Does the room have separate environmental controls from the enterprise building (power, air, fire suppression)?
- Who maintains and controls access to the room?

PHYSICAL ENVIRONMENT

After determining the physical and material supplies that will be housed in the facility, a list of the environmental requirements is needed.

- Does the facility meet the enterprise's current and future equipment power needs?
- Is the air flow and air conditioning sufficient for the current and future layout of the equipment?
- Is the power supply sufficient for the current and future layout of the equipment?
- Is the fire suppression equipment spread throughout the facility, and is it adequate to cover the enterprise's equipment? Or are there automatic sprinklers for fire suppression, and no protection for equipment when the sprinklers are activated?
- What type of communication lines are in place for the network devices and servers?
- What about voice communications for staff who may be working at the facility?
- What are the personal facilities and rest areas for staff working at the facility?
- Is there backup power and environmental controls? Are they tested on a regular basis?
- How does the facility respond to power spikes or brownouts?
- Are there any static controls for the equipment?

EFFECTIVE PHYSICAL SECURITY

This section lists things to consider and question about the facility design when building a facility/data center or server and even when using a hosting provider for the enterprise's data center.

Facility Auditing

Whether the enterprise has regulatory requirements for auditing computing facilities or not, the enterprise should implement regular processes to perform its own facility auditing. Following is a list of some facility auditing requirements:

- If the facility is hosted, can the enterprise obtain an annual risk assessment or SAS70 Type II audit from the hosting facility?
- Obtain and review a listing of authorized staff to the facility. Is it reviewed and approved on a regular basis? Who performs the authorization? Determine who is responsible for the enterprise staff access control and interview them to ensure they understand their responsibility.
- Obtain and review a list of application software, operating system version, and hardware with their function and owner that reside in the facility. Assess the equipment maintenance, change management, and configuration management processes for the facility. This may include interviews with the enterprise staff responsible for the equipment.
- Walk through the physical safeguards with the enterprise staff for accessing and maintaining the equipment in the facility. This would also include device and server console access and controls.
- Obtain and review the standard operating procedures for the facility as performed by enterprise staff.
- Obtain and review the business continuity and disaster recovery procedures for the enterprise staff operating the facility.
- Review the facility installation and maintenance of the environmental controls.
- Obtain and review the enterprise procedures for incident handling at the facility; also include the hosted facilities incident response procedures.
- Obtain procedures for routine testing of environmental facility controls.
- Determine via a facility walk-through whether access to the facility is easy as well as secure.
- Can enterprise staff perform their functions within the facility easily and securely?
- Remember the following for a basic checklist for a facility/data center/server room:

    — Dedicated and secured space
    — Reliable environment conditions
    — Clean work area

— Limited access
— Active monitoring
— Operational procedures
— Trained staff

TIA-942

For a generally accepted standard for facility wiring, please review TIA-942, a standard developed by the Telecommunications Industry Association to define guidelines for planning and building facilities. The TIA-942 specification references data center requirements for applications and procedures such as:

- Network architecture
- Electrical design

- File storage, backup, and archiving
- System redundancy
- Network access control and security
- Database management
- Web hosting
- Application hosting
- Content distribution
- Environmental control
- Protection against physical hazards (fire, flood, windstorm)
- Power management

The principal advantages of designing data centers in accordance with TIA-942 include standard nomenclature, failsafe operation, protection against natural or man-made disasters, and long-term expandability and scalability.

Data Sanitization: SQL Injection

Jonathan Held
Software Design Engineer, Microsoft Corporation, Seattle, Washington, U.S.A.

Abstract

Structured Query Language (SQL) injection is, by far, one of the most common security vulnerabilities of Web applications today, occurring almost as frequently as buffer overflows. While the effects of such vulnerabilities range from mild to severe, there are steps that both developers and testers can take to ensure that their applications are more secure. While security is never completely assured, these steps will, at the very least, help mitigate the effects of such attacks.

OVERVIEW

The Web, although extremely young, has in its short life invariably and permanently altered programming paradigms by changing the application programming domain. The change began in 1995 when Sun Microsystems introduced its Java® programming language. Java was unique in that it was the first technology that allowed users to dynamically download small applications from servers and run them locally in the context of a thin client (the browser). A plethora of applications were built around the technology but they were very limited in what they could do.

Meanwhile, the Web, although a novel innovation, remained, for the most part, uninterestingly static. The manner in which content was updated was cumbersome. It was done manually through the modification of existing HyperText Markup Language (HTML) pages, and then those pages were uploaded onto production servers. This was a time-consuming and tedious process; if the Web was going to come alive, something had to be done to solve this problem. Microsoft's Active Server Pages (ASP) quickly challenged Java by not only solving this problem, but also by changing the Web programming paradigm in another fundamental way. With ASP, applications were still accessible via the Web and thin clients; but rather than having the client download them, they were run on the server on which they resided. Consequently, there was no application code to download. Of course, it was not long before Sun came up with its own rendition of the technology, aptly calling it Java Server Pages (JSP).

However, both technologies had limitations that continued to frustrate developers; chief among them were browser incompatibility (as the browser war waged) and the cost of code maintenance. It was not until early 2001, with the introduction of Microsoft's .NET framework, that these issues were finally resolved. Meanwhile, the use of ASP and JSP prevailed, in large part due to their simplicity and because each technology came with its own model for accessing data [Microsoft's model is found in the ActiveX Data Objects (ADO) and Sun's resides in the Java Database Connectivity (JDBC) library]. Programmers now had the ability to easily create dynamic, data-aware applications. This capability, more than anything else the technologies offered, was what people wanted and leveraged and was fundamentally responsible for many of the Web-centric projects that followed. As such, these are the technologies that are prevalent today, in use in one form or another among almost every Web application.

Note: You can easily determine the technology associated with a Web application by simply identifying the suffix of a requested page. If the page name ends with "asp," it is using Microsoft's Active Server Pages technology. Similarly, pages ending in "jsp" are using Java Server Pages. Pages ending with "aspx" are using Microsoft's new .NET framework. Sun and Microsoft are not the only companies with technology offerings that allow one to integrate Web-based applications with back-end databases. There is also Macromedia's (formerly Allaire) ColdFusion,® with pages that end in "cfm."

With these new technologies, however, came severe security implications that, to this day, remain largely unrecognized by developers, often undetected by testers but frequently exploited by hackers. The dangers posed by Web applications are well understood but are oftentimes purposely understated or downplayed, resulting in a lack of design consideration during development and inadequate testing. The end result is that a system gets fielded that is inherent with flaws, and thus susceptible to a variety of security vulnerabilities. Often, these vulnerabilities are manifested only when the application is integrated with a database. However, this integration occurs almost every time the technologies are used.

The security of Web applications is a multifaceted problem, caused in part by a lack of a comprehensive testing security plan, by the application blindly accepting

Encyclopedia of Information Assurance DOI: 10.1081/E-EIA-120046721
Copyright © 2011 by Taylor & Francis. All rights reserved.

and attempting to work with user input without first filtering it, and by the semantics of the language used in querying databases (called Structured Query Language, or SQL). However, these problems have been around for quite some time. They are not new to developing software; it is just that in the rush to enter this new programming domain, developers and testers alike have put together Web applications without due regard for security-related issues.

The remainder of this entry demonstrates the nature of these security problems, how they work, how to programmatically preclude them from occurring, and provides techniques one can use in testing applications to identify potential SQL injection problems before one's Web site becomes tomorrow's front-page news.

SOURCE OF THE PROBLEM

Web application development brings with it a renewed need for security testing. It is a different application domain than that with which developers are accustomed to working, but the environment brings with it a set of concerns and considerations similar to traditional application development. In the examples provided, one sees that the problem is, in large part, due to input that the user provides. User input has always been a well-known source of potential errors in software—there are classes of characters in virtually all languages that are not only problematic, but require testing independent of all other tests performed against the software. The severity of the problems that can arise from user input varies: one can experience everything from minor, visual annoyances to the particularly troubling vulnerabilities where the end user cannot only gain access to all data, but can also arbitrarily modify or delete it, or potentially gain control of one's computing resources.

In many cases, the source of the problem quite simply stems from the failure of software developers to properly filter user input. It only takes one input provided by the user but not filtered by the developer to potentially destroy an entire application, the data it uses, or do even more harmful damage. Fortunately, with a little effort, the problem can be solved through data sanitization, a process whereby every character of input is carefully scrutinized. If there is something in the input that is not allowed, there is one of two possible ways to respond: 1) one can either alert the user to the input field that failed validation, or 2) one can arbitrarily but uniformly replace every problem character that occurs with whatever one defines as its replacement character. No matter what approach one decides to take, one must ensure that data sanitization always occurs on the server. With the validation code being performed on the server (commonly called server-side processing), one will

Fig. 1 Disabling active scripting in internet explorer.

never have to worry about what does or does not take place on the client.

A fairly common mistake many developers make is to assume that it is enough to place the validation code on the client, perhaps using a series of JavaScript functions to perform checks before the user's data is submitted. This client-side validation comes with absolutely no guarantees and is not foolproof, because the knowledgeable hacker will realize what one has done and either configure the browser to stop running all script code (as illustrated in Fig. 1) or save the page locally, modify it as needed, and then submit the contents of the modified page to the server for processing (absent this modified page are the JavaScript routines that validate user input).

The solution to precluding the user from bypassing validation code is to ensure that all validation algorithms are executed on the server. With traditional ASP pages, one does this using the <% %> ASP directives, between which are placed the necessary conditional statements that determine whether data is there to validate, how the data will be validated, and what will occur if the validation fails. It is, by far, much simpler to perform validation with ASP.NET, as this new programming paradigm contains four intrinsic, easy-to-use controls that help the developer with the task. Additionally, ASP.NET allows one to easily configure controls (including the validation controls) to run on the server by specifically setting the *runat* attribute of the control to "server" (see Table 1).

Data –
Denial

Table 1 ASP.NET validation controls.

Control	Description
RequiredFieldValidator	Makes an input control a mandatory field
CompareValidator	Compares the value entered by the user with the value in another control or a constant
RegularExpressionValidator	Ensures that a user's entry matches a specified pattern (defined by the regular expression syntax)
CustomValidator	Developer provides the code that determines whether the input is valid or fails validation

PERFORMING DATA SANITIZATION

Many approach the data sanitization process using a familiar methodology; they determine what characters are potentially problematic and then write routines to determine whether the input they are working with contains those characters. While this approach certainly works, it is a difficult process to know whether or not every invalid character is contained in that set—there may be other problematic characters that could very well have easily been overlooked. For this reason, the Computer Emergency Response Team (CERT) recommends working with a finite set of characters that can be well-defined, such as the set of valid characters (see http://www.cert.org). This solution, however, is more applicable to applications intended to work with only one character set, such as ASCII. When an application is intended for various international markets (such as Europe or Japan), the problem becomes inversely difficult (i.e., it is easier to specify the invalid characters than the valid ones). For this reason, whichever approach one decides to follow should be based on the intended audience.

To filter user input based on the recommendations of CERT, one might very well end up with a library function such as *FilterCharacters*, as shown in Table 2. This algorithm is extremely straightforward. Written in Visual Basic, it takes three string parameters: 1) the string to filter for invalid input, 2) the list of valid characters, and 3) the designated replacement string. This function iterates through the entire input string. If the character it is currently looking at is not found among the valid set of characters, it is replaced with the string value specified by the replacement character (which itself could be a single character or a string). While this may not be what one optimally wants to do with the input, it follows the recommendations provided by CERT and does not modify the original input string. One can, optionally and with a little modification, change this function to return a Boolean value if an invalid character is found.

Unfortunately, the problem with this algorithm is the hidden cost of its implementation. The *Instr* function it uses is a native Visual Basic function equivalent to a for/next loop. So, what one has is a loop nested within one's own, making the complexity of the algorithm $O(n^2)$ far from optimal. The more input that has to be filtered, the longer the algorithm will take to execute. Even if the algorithm is modified to exit as soon as the first invalid

character is found, the complexity would remain the same (the last character in any sequence could be the only one that is bad). With perhaps hundreds, if not thousands, of users hitting the Web application, the server would spend considerable time executing this function.

Because the performance cost is unacceptable, many software developers immediately opt to completely disregard filtering user input (surprisingly enough, this happens quite frequently). However, with careful thought and consideration, a developer could easily improve on this performance by using a cached hashtable, where the keys to the hashtable represent the bad characters that should be filtered from the input stream (the value of the key could represent the replacement character or string). Performance, now at $O(n)$, is much better, and developers no longer have an excuse as to why they cannot or will not implement some type of filtering system (see Table 3).

There are other solutions to performing data sanitization. One of the most frequently used tools is the regular expression. A regular expression is a pattern-matching syntax specification, which can be used to determine whether or not the pattern occurs in the input one is looking at. While around for quite awhile and now supported in script languages such as VBScript and JavaScript, as well as programming languages such as Visual Basic, C#, and Java, it was the Programming Extraction and Reporting Language (PERL) that popularized it. It is extremely powerful to use, but specifying the pattern can sometimes be a bit tricky.

As an example, consider how one would validate whether a number the user entered was a valid Social Security Number (SSN). The first problem is that the user could enter the number in one of two ways: with or without hyphens. So as not to be too restrictive in what the user can or cannot do, assume that the user can enter the number in either manner. If one is wondering how to perform this validation using regular expressions, consider the pattern:

$$\text{^\d\{ 3\} \ -\d\{ 2\} \ -\d\{ 4\} \$ | ^\d\{ 9\} \$}$$

Although this pattern is somewhat confusing to understand, referring to Table 4, which describes pattern syntax, should make it more intelligible. One sees that there are actually have two patterns, separated by the "|" character. The left-most pattern — ^\d{ 3} \ -\d{ 2} \ -\d{ 4} $ — starts at the beginning of the input and looks for three digits, followed by a hyphen, two digits, another hyphen, and then four digits.

Table 2 An algorithm for filtering user input—runs in $O(n^2)$.

```
`------------------------------------------------------------

`Function:      FilterCharacters
`Parameters:    sStringToFilter - string to filter for meta
               characters
`Purpose:       Filters the input string; returns a filtered
               string
`              (metacharacters are replaced by an underscore)
`Returns:       The filtered string
`------------------------------------------------------------

Public Function FilterCharacters (ByVal sStringToFilter
                                    As String, _
                                 ByVal sValidCharSet
                                    As String, _
                                 ByVal sReplacementChar
                                    As String) As String

   On Error Resume Next
   Dim sInput As String
   sInput = sStringToFilter
   Dim ix As Long, jx As Long
   jx = Len (sStringToFilter)
   For ix = 1 To jx
      If Not (InStr (sValidCharSet, Mid (sInput, ix, 1)) >= 1)
         Then
         If "" = sReplacementChar Then
            sInput = Replace (sInput, Mid (sInput, ix, 1), "")
            ix = ix - 1
         Else
            sInput = Replace (sInput, Mid (sInput, ix, 1),
               sReplacementChar)
         End If
         jx = Len (sInput)
      End If
   Next
   'Don't forget to escape the " ` "character
   FilterCharacters = Replace (sInput, " ` ", " ` ")
End Function
```

The "$" sign represents the end of input (i.e., the four digits should conclude the input being examined); if we omit this, a number such as 123-45-6789INVALID would erroneously be considered valid. Similarly, there is a second pattern — $^\backslash d\{ 9\} \$$ — that looks to match nine digits (the code for using this pattern is illustrated in Table 5).

Working with regular expressions takes some practice, but they are easy to test and provide a very powerful means for validating user input. If one is having problems developing the pattern needed for validation, visit http://www.regexlib.com/, which contains a library of useful patterns searchable by keyword.

Table 3 Executing the *FilterCharacters* function on user input.

```
Using

sValidCharSet=
    "ABCDEFGHIJKLMNOPQRSTUVWXYZabcdefghijklmnopqrstuvwxyz "
and sReplacementChar = "_"
Using FilterCharacters on the string "This string is $character$ filt@ered!" returns
This string is _character_ filt_ered_
```

Table 4   Regular expression pattern syntax.

Character	Description
\	Marks the next character as either a special character or a literal
^	Matches the beginning of input
$	Matches the end of input
*	Matches the preceding character zero or more times
+	Matches the preceding character one or more times
?	Matches the preceding character zero or one time
.	Matches any single character except a newline character
(pattern)	Matches *pattern* and remembers the match
x | y	Matches either *x* or *y*
{n}	*n* is a non-negative integer; matches exactly *n* times
{n,}	*n* is a non-negative integer; matches at least *n* times
{n,m}	*m* and *n* are non-negative integers; matches at least *n* and at most *m* times
[xyz]	A character set; matches any one of the enclosed characters
[^xyz]	A negative character set; matches any character not enclosed
[a-z]	A range of characters; matches any character in the specified range
[^m-z]	A negative range of characters; matches any character not in the specified range
\b	Matches a word boundary; that is, the position between a word and a space
\B	Matches a non-word boundary
\d	Matches a digit character
\D	Matches a non-digit character
\f	Matches a form-feed character
\n	Matches a newline character
\r	Matches a carriage return character
\s	Matches any white space, including space, tab, form-feed, etc.
\S	Matches any non-white space character
\t	Matches a tab character

SQL INJECTION

How is data sanitization related to the problem of SQL injection? The answer is found by looking at the semantics of SQL. For experienced SQL developers, it is well known that one of the common nuances in working with SQL is the problem encountered when user input consists of

Table 5   A regular expression that determines whether a number is a valid or invalid SSN.

```
Set re = New RegExp

re.Pattern = "^\d{3}\-\d{2}\-\d{4}$|^\d{9}$"
re.Global = true
Dim input
input = InputBox("Enter a SSN:")
if re.Test(input) then
   msgbox "You entered a valid SSN."
else
   msgbox "You entered an INVALID SSN."
end if
```

an apostrophe (or single quotation mark). When performing SQL queries, strings are always enclosed within a pair of apostrophes (the apostrophe is considered a special delimiter). So what happens if the input contains a single apostrophe? As far as what the SQL command ends up doing, any number of things can happen. As for SQL, when it comes to a single apostrophe that is part of the user input, it interprets that apostrophe as denoting the end of the string.

To get an idea of how problematic the single apostrophe character can be, consider a simple SQL insert statement such as the following:

```
"INSERT INTO USERS VALUES
(" ' " & username & " ' ","'" & ; password & " ' ")"
```

Assuming one has properly captured the input for username and password, this statement simply inserts those values into the database table USERS. The SQL statement will work correctly as long as the username and password do not contain an apostrophe. When the input contains this character, the intended insert operation will ultimately fail. If the developer has not properly handled the error, clients will see an error message in their browser similar to the one shown in Table 6. While too technical for most to understand, it is too much information. With this error revealed, a knowledgeable hacker will immediately know what mistake has been made and can easily use it to his advantage.

If one does not believe that this error is a potentially costly mistake, a simple example will certainly convince otherwise. Suppose that the client entered *Magician's* for the username and *Magic* for the password. The resultant SQL command that gets executed is:

```
INSERT INTO Users VALUES ('Magician's','Magic')
```

This statement will ultimately fail, but it is absolutely harmless and will most likely have no adverse effect on the application or its database. However, suppose instead that the client entered:

```
') use master exec xp_cmdshell 'dir * .exe' - - -
```

for the password and left the username blank. The resultant SQL statement then becomes:

```
INSERT INTO Users VALUES ('', '') use master
   exec xp_cmdshell 'dir * . exe' - - - ')
```

For clarity, the portion of the SQL clause that the user entered has been italicized and underlined. If one is familiar with SQL Server, this clause should immediately get one's attention. Inspection of the input reveals what the user did. The first apostrophe was added to immediately close off the value expected for the password. By including the left parenthesis, the user ended the SQL statement. Assuming that there are only two fields in the Users table, this statement is still valid and will execute without error.

What immediately follows the left parenthesis is the interesting part. There are two SQL directives: one that

Data –
Denial

Table 6 What the client sees if an SQL command failed and the developer has not properly handled the error condition.

```
Error Type:

Microsoft OLE DB Provider for SQL Server (0x80040E14)
Line 1: Incorrect syntax near 's'.
/createlogin.asp, line 44
```

indicates a change in the database (*use master*) and another that instructs SQL Server to execute a stored procedure (*xp_cmdshell*). Referring to the SQL Server documentation, *xp_cmdshell* executes the specified command (dir *.exe) as an operating system command shell and returns the output as a recordset. Here the user has been nice. The command could just as easily have been *xp_cmdshell* 'format d:'. Also notice the three hyphens at the end of the user input. These hyphens represent the SQL syntax for a comment and have been included on purpose to indicate that the closing apostrophe, which was included in the code, is ignored.

Of course, this is only one of many potential SQL commands that the user could have run without anyone's knowledge. Certainly just as possible are commands such as DROP DATABASE MASTER, *sp_addlogin* 'hacker', 'hacked' (this adds a user account to the SQL Server Logins), etc. This security vulnerability comes at the cost of failing to properly escape the apostrophe character, a problem that occurs more frequently with Web applications than one would initially think.

To circumvent the possibility of an SQL injection attack, testers should always consider the single apostrophe as a special type of input unto itself. Ultimately, there should be an apostrophe test case for every textbox and textarea where the user provides input. However, enumerating these particular cases is only the beginning. There are other HTML widgets, such as drop-down list boxes (select) and checkboxes that have corresponding values associated with them. Oftentimes, these values, like any others, are read by the Web application and saved to a database (the values associated with them are generally trusted by the application). One can therefore logically conclude that somebody could purposely alter these values and have one use them just as one would one's own values. Do not assume that someone will not go to the trouble of purposely looking for a way to break a Web application—someone will always try.

There are a number of ways one could potentially deal with the threat posed by the local alteration and submission of data to a Web application for processing. The first line of defense would be to identify the referrer of the request. Where no referrer exists, or the referrer is not within the domain where the Web application is hosted, one could determine in advance what action to take (such as sending the user to a predefined page, or reloading the page from the server). This approach, however, does have some problems: cross-domain applications that work in concert will likely fail, and it will preclude users from manually typing in a URL (no referrer exists in such a scenario). The second option one has is to validate that the data provided is a member of the set of data values expected. This option involves more work on part of the Web application developer, and it certainly has an impact on performance. Given the circumstances, however, and the fact that there are not too many other options from which to choose, this may be an appropriate course of action.

As for how to preclude problems inherent with the use of the apostrophe, take a look at the last line of code shown in Table 3. The line

```
FilterCharacters = Replace(sInput, "'", "''")
```

uses the Visual Basic routine *Replace* to substitute all occurrences of one apostrophe in a line of input with two apostrophes. Two apostrophes indicate that the single quotation mark is a literal value rather than a delimiter.

COMMON PROGRAMMATIC SQL MISTAKES

When the single quotation mark is not handled correctly, any number of problems can arise. However, a prevalent flaw that occurs today is that of authorization bypass. Many Web sites have gone to great lengths to implement their own custom authentication methods. Rather than opting to use tried-and-true authentication models, Web sites generally insist on using their own database that maintains a table of users and information about them. To determine whether or not a user has the right to access content on the site, the site will typically use a Web page to prompt the client to enter his username and password. The supplied credentials are then looked up in the database using an SQL command similar to the following:

```
"SELECT * from Users where username = '" + txtUserName + "'
    and password = '" + txtPassword + "'"
```

This simple query returns a recordset, which the programmer can then examine to determine whether or not access should be granted. Common among ASP application developers is the presumption that if the recordset is not empty, the user should be granted access. However, this is an erroneous assumption because by using an SQL injection attack, a hacker can access the site without having proper credentials.

The means by which authorization is granted generally requires only a few lines of code:

```
On Error Resume Next
Set RS = sqlConnection.Execute(sqlCommand)
If not RS.EOF then
    'Grant the user access
else
    'Deny access
    end if
```

Here, *sqlCommand* is the previous SQL SELECT statement and *RS* is the resulting recordset created by executing that statement. There is a subtle flaw in this logic, a flaw that many times goes unnoticed by even the experienced programmer. Assume that the quotation mark was not properly escaped (an SQL injection vulnerability exists) and that the client entered a username and password value of *'or '1 = 1*. Using that value in the SQL statement, the query becomes:

SELECT * from Users where username = *'' or '1=1'* and password = *'' or '1=1'*

This query is substantially different from what was intended. Here, the SELECT statement is asking for every record where the username is an empty string or 1=1. This latter condition is always true. The same condition is placed on the password. The end result of this query is that it will return every record in the database! Consequently, any user who provides input in this or a similar manner will be guaranteed access when the set of credentials he provided does not even exist.

To avoid this condition when an SQL injection attack is possible, the programmer should explicitly look at the contents of the recordset and ensure that they match the input the user entered. Additional conditions might check to ensure that the recordset count is 1, although it is a better practice to validate against the information that was provided.

In this case, SQL injection is only one potential way that a hacker can gain unauthorized access. Also probable, due to the way the conditional construct was developed, is the scenario in which the database is down. All too often, developers use the *On Error Resume Next* statement in their ASP code, but fail to check if error conditions are present. If the database is unavailable (due to network connectivity issues, machine failure, etc.) the recordset RS would be null. The subsequent statement that checks to see if one is at the end of the recordset or not would generate an error, but code execution would continue to the very next line where authorization is granted because the developer used the *On Error Resume Next* statement.

So, while SQL injection is one possible means by which unauthorized access can be granted, poor programming can do likewise.

CONCLUSION

Structured Query Language (SQL) injection is, by far, one of the most common security vulnerabilities of Web applications today, occurring almost as frequently as buffer overflows. While the effects of such vulnerabilities range from mild to severe, there are steps that both developers and testers can take to ensure that their applications are more secure. While security is never completely assured, these steps will, at the very least, help mitigate the effects of such attacks.

One of the primary means for precluding SQL injection attacks is *data sanitization*. Demonstrated in this entry were several methodologies for performing data sanitization. Whether one uses regular expressions or writes one's own algorithms, the methodology one chooses is entirely one's own choice, but the process of validating user input should never be avoided just because of the potential performance cost the application might incur (the cost that comes later could end up being far greater). Having written the sanitization routines, one will then want to spend an adequate amount of time testing them to ensure that they work as expected.

Other things one can do to test or prevent SQL injection vulnerabilities include:

- *Capture internal server errors (500).* These errors commonly provide enough technical details on the source of the error for hackers to use the information to their advantage. A 500 error is equivalent to an application crash, so no matter what error occurs, your Web application should gracefully handle it.
- *While performing tests on Web application, use a utility that can capture SQL commands.* After the test pass has concluded, one can then analyze the data to determine where the application might be susceptible to SQL injection attacks.
- *Ensure that access to Web application databases is done using a non-administrator user account.* Create a separate user account for each Web application and apply appropriate permission levels to the account for database access. This user account should ultimately have the minimum access rights required to get the job done. If this configuration is properly implemented, it will certainly limit the damage caused by an SQL injection attack. Moreover, developers and testers should spend adequate time and resources identifying, designing, and testing such an

implementation. Of all the configuration settings required by Web applications, this is fundamentally one of the most important and certainly one of the most abused.

While the apostrophe character is the leading problematic cause of SQL injection attacks, it is not the only means by which such an attack can occur. Frequently, Web applications encode and decode their input (using either Uniform Resource Locator (URL) or HTML character encoding). Care and consideration as to how input is encoded is yet another factor that needs to be examined when analyzing potential security vulnerabilities. Do your part in trying to break anything you develop; if you do not, someone else certainly will!

Data Warehouses: Datamarts and

Mollie E. Krehnke, CISSP, CHS-II, IAM
Senior Information Security Consultant, Insight Global, Inc., Raleigh, North Carolina, U.S.A.

D. K. Bradley
Insight Global, Inc., Raleigh, North Carolina, U.S.A.

Abstract

Maintaining adequate security is a crucial data warehouse and organizational concern. The value of the data warehouse (DW) is going to increase over time, and more users are going to have access to the information. Appropriate resources must be allocated to the protection of the data warehouse. The return on investment to the organization can be very significant if the information is adequately protected.

What do you think when you hear the term "data mart" or "data warehouse?" Convenience? Availability? Choices? Confusion from overwhelming options? Power? Success? Organizational information, such as marketing statistics or customer preferences, when analyzed, can mean power and success in today's and future markets. If it is more convenient for a customer to do business with a "remembering" organization—one that retains and uses customer information (e.g., products used, sales trends, goals) and does not have to ask for the information twice—then that organization is more likely to retain and grow that customer's base.[1] There are even organizations whose purpose is to train business staff to acquire competitor's information through legal, but espionage-like techniques, calling it "corporate intelligence."[2]

DATA WAREHOUSES AND DATA MARTS: WHAT ARE THEY?

Data warehouses and data marts are increasingly perceived as vital organizational resources and—given the effort and funding required for their creation and maintenance, and their potential value to someone inside (or outside) the organization—they need to be understood, effectively used, and protected. Several years ago, one data warehouse proponent suggested a data warehouse's justification that includes support for "merchandising, logistics, promotions, marketing and sales programs, asset management, cost containment, pricing, and product development," and equated the data warehouse with "corporate memory."[3]

The future looked (and still looks) bright for data warehouses, but there are significant implementation issues that need to be addressed, including scalability (size), data quality, and flexibility for use. These are the issues

highlighted today in numerous journals and books—as opposed to several years ago when the process for creating a data warehouse and its justification were the primary topics of interest.

Data Warehouse and Data Mart Differences

Key differences between a data warehouse and data mart are size, content, user groups, development time, and amount of resources required to implement. A data warehouse (DW) is generally considered to be organizational in scope, containing key information from all divisions within a company, including marketing, sales, engineering, human resources, and finance, for a designated period of time. The users, historically, have been primarily managers or analysts (a.k.a. power users) who are collecting and analyzing data for planning and strategy decisions. Because of the magnitude of information contained in a DW, the time required for identifying what information should be contained in the warehouse, and then collecting, categorizing, indexing, and normalizing the data, is a significant commitment of resources, generally taking several years to implement.

A data mart (DM) is considered to be a lesser-scale data warehouse, often addressing the data needs of a division or an enterprise or addressing a specific concern (e.g., customer preferences) of a company. Because the amount and type of data are less varied, and the number of users who have to achieve concurrence on the pertinent business goals is fewer, the amount of time required to initiate a DM is less. Some components of a DM can be available for use within nine months to a year of initiation, depending on the design and scope of the project. If carefully planned and executed, it is possible for DMs of an enterprise to actually function as components of a (future) DW for the entire company. These DMs are linked together to form a DW via a method of

Encyclopedia of Information Assurance DOI: 10.1081/E-EIA-120046722
Copyright © 2011 by Taylor & Francis. All rights reserved.

categorization and indexing (i.e., metadata) and a means for accessing, assembling, and moving the data about the company (i.e., middleware software). It is important to carefully plan the decision support architecture, however, or the combination of DMs will result in expensive redundancy of data, with little or no reconciliation of data across the DMs. Multiple DMs within an organization cannot replace a well-planned DW.[4]

Data Warehouse and Data Mart Similarities

Key similarities between a DW and DM include the decisions required regarding the data before the first byte is ever put into place:

- What is the strategic plan for the organization with regard to the DW architecture and environment?
- What is the design/development/implementation process to be followed?
- What data will be included?
- How will the data be organized?
- How and when will the data be updated?

Following an established process and plan for DW development will help ensure that key steps are performed—in a timely and accurate manner by the appropriate individuals. (Unless noted otherwise, the concepts for DWs also apply to DMs.) The process involves the typical development steps of requirements gathering, design, construction, testing, and implementation.

The DW or DM is not an operational database and, as such, does not contain the business rules that can be applied to data before it is presented to the user by the original business application. Merely dumping all the operational data into the DW is not going to be effective or useful. Some data will be summarized or transformed, and other data may not be included. All data will have to be "scrubbed" to ensure that quality data is loaded into the DW. Careful data-related decisions must be made regarding the following:[5]

- Business goals to be supported
- Data associated with the business goals
- Data characteristics (e.g., frequency, detail)
- Time when transformation of codes is performed (e.g., when stored, accessed)
- Schedule for data load, refresh, and update times
- Size and scalability of the warehouse or mart

Business goals identification

The identification of the business goals to be supported will involve the groups who will be using the system. Because DWs are generally considered to be non-operational decision support systems, they will contain select operational data. This data can be analyzed over time to identify pertinent trends or, as is the case with data mining, be used to identify some previously unknown relationship between elements that can be used to advance the organization's objectives. It is vital, however, that the DW be linked to, and supportive of, the strategic goals of the business.

Data associated with business goals

The data associated with the identified business goals may be quantitative (e.g., dollar amount of sales) or qualitative (i.e., descriptive) in nature. DWs are not infinite in nature, and decisions must be made regarding the value of collecting, transforming, storing, and updating certain data to keep it more readily accessible for analysis.

Data characteristics

Once the data has been identified, additional decisions regarding the number of years to be stored and the level of frequency to be stored have to be made. A related, tough decision is the level of detail. Are item sales needed: by customer, by sale, by season, by type of customer, or some other summary? Resources available are always going to be limited by some factor: funding, technology, or available support.

Data transformation and timing

Depending on the type of data and its format, additional decisions must be made regarding the type and timing of any transformations of the data for the warehouse. Business applications usually perform the transformations of data before they are viewed on the screen by the user or printed in a report, and the DW will not have an application to transform the data. As a result, users may not know that a certain code means engineering firm (for example) when they retrieve data about XYZ Company to perform an analysis. Therefore, the data must be transformed prior to its presentation, either before it is entered into the database for storage or before the user sees it.

Data reloading and updating

Depending on the type and quantity of data, the schedules for data reloading or data updating may require a significant amount of time. Decisions regarding the reload/update frequency will have to be made at the onset of the design because of the resources required for implementing and maintaining the process. A crucial decision to be made is: will data be reloaded en masse or will only changed data be loaded (updated)? A DW is non-operational, so the frequency for reload/update should be lower than that required for an operational database containing the same or

Data –
Denial

similar information. Longer reload and update times may impact users by limiting their access to the required information for key customer-related decisions and competition-beating actions. Data maintenance will be a substantial component of ongoing costs associated with the DW.

Size and scalability

Over time, the physical size of the DW increases because the amount of data contained increases. The size of the database may impact the data updating or retrieval processes, which may impact the usage rate; as well, an increase in the number of users will also impact the retrieval process. Size may have a strongly negative impact on the cost, performance, availability, risk, and management of the DW. The ability of a DW to grow in size and functionality and not affect other critical factors is called scalability, and this capability relies heavily on the architecture and technologies to be used, which were agreed upon at the time the DW was designed.

DATA QUALITY

The quality of data in a DW is significant because it contains summarized data, addresses different audiences and functions than originally intended, and depends on other systems for its data. The time-worn phrase "garbage in, garbage out" is frequently applied to the concept of DW data. Suggested ways to address data quality include incorporating metadata into the data warehouse structure, handling content errors at load time, and setting users' expectations about data quality. In addition, "it is mandatory to track the relationships among data entities and the calculations used over time to ensure that essential referential integrity of the historical data is maintained."[6]

Metadata Incorporation into DW Design

Metadata is considered to be the cornerstone of DW success and effective implementation. Metadata not only supports the user in the access and analysis of the data, but also supports the data quality of the data in the warehouse.

The creation of metadata regarding the DW helps the user define, access, and understand data needed for a particular analysis or exploration. It standardizes all organizational data elements (e.g., the customer number for marketing and finance organizations), and acts as a "blueprint" to guide the DW builders and users through the warehouse and to guide subsequent integration of later data sources.

Metadata for a DW generally includes the following:[7]

1. Organizational business models and rules
2. Data view definitions
3. Data usage model
4. Report dictionary
5. User profiles
6. Physical and logical data models
7. Source file data dictionaries
8. Data element descriptions
9. Data conversion rules

Standardization of Metadata Models

The importance of metadata to the usefulness of a DW is a concept mentioned by most of the authors reviewed. Metadata and its standardization are so significant that Microsoft has joined the Metadata Coalition (MDC) consortium. Microsoft turned its metadata model, the Open Information Model (OIM), over to the MDC for integration into the MDC Metadata Interchange Specification (MDIS). This standard will enable various vendors to exchange metadata among their tools and databases, and support proprietary metadata.[8] There are other vendors, however, that are reluctant to participate and are maintaining their own versions of metadata management.[9] But this present difference of opinions does not diminish the need for comprehensive metadata for a DW.

Setting User Expectations Regarding Data Quality

Metadata about the data transformations can indicate to the user the level of data quality that can be expected. Depending on the user, the availability of data may be more significant than the accuracy, and this may be the case for some DMs. But because the DW is intended to contain significant data that is maintained over the long term and can be used for trend analysis, data quality is vital to the organization's DW goals. In a "Report from the Trenches," Quinlan emphasizes the need to manage user expectations and identify potential hardships as well as benefits.[10] This consideration is frequently mentioned in discussions of requirements for a successful DW implementation.

Characteristics of data quality are:[11]

- *Accuracy:* degree of agreement between a set of data values and a corresponding set of correct values
- *Completeness:* degree to which values are present in the attributes that require them
- *Consistency:* agreement or logical coherence among data that frees them from variation or contradiction
- *Relatability:* agreement or logical coherence that permits rational correlation in comparison with other similar or like data
- *Timeliness:* data item or multiple items that are provided at the time required or specified
- *Uniqueness:* data values that are constrained to a set of distinct entries, each value being the only one of its kind
- *Validity:* conformance of data values that are edited for acceptability, reducing the probability of error

DW USE

The proposed use of a DW will define the initial contents, and the initial tools and analysis techniques. Over time, as users become trained in its use and there is proven applicability to organizational objectives, the content of a DW generally expands and the number of users increases. Therefore, developers and management need to realize that it is not possible to create the "perfect warehouse." Users cannot foresee every decision that they are going to need to make and define the information they need to do so. Change is inevitable. Users become more adept at using the DW and want data in more detail than they did initially; users think of questions they had not considered initially; and business environments change and new information is needed to respond to the current marketplace or new organizational objectives.[12] This is why it is important to plan strategically for the DW environment.

Types of Users

DWs are prevalent today in the retailing, banking, insurance, and communications sectors; and these industries tend to be leaders in the use of business intelligence/data warehouse (BI/DW) applications, particularly in financial and sales/marketing applications.[13] Most organizations have a customer base that they want to maintain and grow (i.e., providing additional products or services to the same customer over time). The use of DWs and various data exploration and analysis techniques (such as data mining) can provide organizations with an extensive amount of valuable information regarding their present or potential customer base. This valuable information includes cross-selling and up-selling, fraud detection and compliance, potential lifetime customer value, market demand forecasting, customer retention/vulnerability, product affinity analysis, price optimization, risk management, and target market segmentation.

Techniques of Use

The data characteristics of the DW are significantly different from those of a transactional or operational database, presenting large volumes of summary data that address an extensive time period, which is updated on a periodic (rather than daily) basis. The availability of such data, covering multiple areas of a business enterprise over a long period of time, has significant value in organizational strategic marketing and planning. The availability of metadata enables a user to identify useful information for further analysis. If the data quality is high, the user will have confidence in the results.

The type of analysis performed is determined, in part, by the capabilities of the user and the availability of software to support the analysis. The usefulness of the data can be related to the frequency of updates and the level of detail provided in the DW. There are three general forms of study that can be performed on DW data:[14]

1. *Analysis:* discovering new patterns and hypotheses for existing, unchanging data by running correlations, statistics, or a set of sorted reports
2. *Monitoring:* automatic detection of matches or violations of patterns to provide a timely response to the change
3. *Discovery:* interactive identification, a process of uncovering previously unknown relationships, patterns, and trends that would not necessarily be revealed by running correlations, statistics, or a set of sorted reports

The DW is more applicable for the "monitoring" and "discovery" techniques because the resources available are more fully utilized. It is possible that ad hoc analysis may be accepted in such a positive manner that scheduled reports are then performed as a result of that analysis, in which case the method changes from "discovery" to simply "analysis." However, the discovery of patterns (offline) can then be used to define a set of rules that will automatically identify the same patterns when compared with new, updated data online.

Data mining

Data mining is a prevalent DW data analysis technique. It can be costly and time-consuming, because the software is expensive and may require considerable time for the analyst to become proficient. The benefits, however, can be quite remarkable. Data mining can be applied to a known situation with a concrete, direct question to pursue (i.e., reactive analysis) or to an unknown situation with no established parameters. The user is "seeking to identify unknown patterns and practices, detect covert/unexplained practices, and have the capability to expose organized activity (i.e., proactive invigilation)."[14]

Data mining is an iterative process, and additional sources can be introduced at any time during the process. It is most useful in exploratory analysis scenarios with no predetermined expectations as to the outcome. Data mining is not a single-source (product/technology) solution, and must be applied, as any tool, with the appropriate methodological approach. When using data mining, the analyst must consider:

- organizational requirements
- available data sources
- corporate policies and procedures

There are questions that have to be answered to determine if the data mining effort is worthwhile, including:[15]

1. Are sufficient data sources available to make the effort worthwhile?

2. Is the data accurate, well coded, and properly maintained for the analyst to produce reasonable results?
3. Is permission granted to access all of the data needed to perform the analysis?
4. Are static extractors of data sufficient?
5. Is there an understanding of what things are of interest or importance to set the problem boundaries?
6. Have hypothetical examples been discussed beforehand with the user of the analysis?
7. Are the target audience and the intent known (e.g., internal review, informational purposes, formal presentation, or official publication)?

Activities associated with data mining are:[16]

- *Classification:* establishing a predefined set of labels for the records
- *Estimation:* filling in missing values in a particular field
- *Segmentation:* identification of subpopulations with similar behavior
- *Description:* spotting any anomalous or "interesting" information

Data mining goals may be:[17]

- *Predictive:* models (expressed as executable code) to perform some form of classification or estimation
- *Descriptive:* informational by uncovering patterns and relationships

Data to be mined may be:[17]

- *Structured:* fixed length, fixed format records with fields that contain numeric values, character codes, or short strings
- *Unstructured:* word or phrase queries, combining data across multiple, diverse domains to identify unknown relationships

The data mining techniques (and products) to be used will depend on the type of data being mined and the end objectives of the activity.

Data visualization

Data visualization is an effective data mining technique that enables the analyst and the recipients to discern relationships that may not be evident from a review of numerical data by abstracting the information from low-level detail into composite representations. Data visualization presents a "top-down view of the range of diversity represented in the data set on dimensions of interest."[18]

Data visualization results depend on the quality of data. "An ill-specified or preposterous model or a puny data set cannot be rescued by a graphic (or by calculation), no matter how clever or fancy. A silly theory means a silly graphic."[19] Data visualization tools can, however, support key principles of graphical excellence:[20]

- A well-designed presentation of interesting data through "substance, statistics, and design"
- Communication of complex ideas with "clarity, precision, and efficiency"
- Presentation of the "greatest number of ideas in the shortest time with the least ink in the smallest space"

Enterprise information portals

Extended use of the Internet and Web-based applications within an enterprise now supports a new form of access, data filtering, and data analysis: a personalized, corporate search engine—similar to the Internet personalized search engines (e.g., My Yahoo)—called a corporate portal, enterprise information portal, or business intelligence portal. This new tool provides multiple characteristics that would be beneficial to an individual seeking to acquire and analyze relevant information:[21]

- Ease of use through a Web browser
- Filtering out of irrelevant data
- Integration of numerical and textual data
- Capability of providing alerts when certain data events are triggered

Enterprise information portals (EIPs) can be built from existing data warehouses or from the ground up through the use of Extensible Markup Language (XML). XML supports the integration of unstructured data resources (e.g., text documents, reports, e-mails, graphics, images, audio, and video) with structured data resources in relational and legacy databases.[22] Business benefits associated with the EIP are projected to include:[23]

- Leverage of DW, Enterprise Resource Planning (ERP), and other IT systems
- Transforming E-commerce business into "true" E-business
- Easing reorganization, merger, and acquisition processes
- Providing improved navigation and access capabilities

But it is emphasized that all of the design and implementation processes and procedures, network infrastructures, and data quality required for successful DWs s must be applied to ensure an EIP's potential for supporting enterprise operations and business success.

Results

The results of data mining can be very beneficial to an organization, and can support numerous objectives: customer-focused planning and actions, business intelligence, or even fraud discovery. Examples of industries and associated data mining uses presented in *Data Mining Solutions, Methods and Tools for Real-World Problems*[18] include:

- *Pharmaceuticals:* research to fight disease and degenerative disorders by mapping the human genome
- *Telecommunications:* customer profiling to provide better service
- *Retail sales and marketing:* managing the market saturation of individual customers
- *Financial market analysis:* managing investments in an unstable Asian banking market
- *Banking and finance:* evaluation of customer credit policy and the reduction of delinquent and defaulted car loans
- *Law enforcement and special investigative units:* use of financial reporting regulations and data to identify money-laundering activities and other financial crimes in the United States by companies

Other examples are cited repeatedly throughout data management journals, such as *DM Review.* The uses of data mining continue to expand as users become more skilled, and as the tools and techniques increase in options and capabilities.

RETURNS ON DW INVESTMENT

Careful consideration and planning are required before initiating a DW development and implementation activity. The resources required are substantial, although the benefits can surpass the costs many times.

Costs

The DW design and implementation activity is very labor intensive, and requires the involvement of numerous business staff (in addition to Information Technology staff) over the entire life cycle of the DW, in order for the project to be successful by responding to organizational information needs. Although technology costs over time tend to drop, while providing even greater capabilities, there is a significant investment in hardware and software. Administration of the DWs is an ongoing expense. Because DWs are not static and will continue to grow in terms of the years of data and the types of data maintained, additional data collection and quality control are required to ensure continued viability and usefulness of the corporate information resource.

Costs are incurred throughout the entire DW life cycle; some costs are one-time costs, others are recurrent costs. One-time costs and a likely percentage of the total DW budget (shown in parentheses) include:[24]

- *Hardware:* disk storage (30%), processor costs (20%), network communication costs (10%)
- *Software:* database management software (10%); access/analysis tools (6%); systems management tools: activity monitor (2%), data monitor (2%); integration and transformation (15%); interface creation, metadata creation and population (5%)

Cost estimates (cited above) are based on the implementation of a centralized (rather than distributed) DW, with use of an automated code generator for the integration and transformation layer.

Recurrent costs include:[24]

- Refreshment of the data warehouse data from the operational environment (55%)
- Maintenance and update of the DW and metadata infrastructure (3%)
- End-user training (6%)
- Data warehouse administration—data verification of conformance to the enterprise data model (2%), monitoring (7%), archiving (1%), reorganization/restructuring (1%); servicing DW requests for data (21%); capacity planning (1%); usage analysis (2%); and *security administration* (1%) [emphasis added]

The recurrent costs are almost exclusively associated with the administrative work required to keep the DW operational and responsive to the organization's needs. Additional resources may be required, however, to upgrade the hardware (e.g., more storage) or for the network to handle an unexpected increase in the volume of requests for DW information over time. It is common for the DW budget to grow an order of magnitude per year for the first 2 years that the DW is being implemented. After the first few years, the rate of growth slows to 30% or 40% growth per year.[24]

The resources that should be expended for any item will depend on the strategic goals that the DW is intended to support. Factors affecting the actual budget values include:[24]

- Size of the organization
- Amount of history to be maintained
- Level of detail required
- Sophistication of the end user
- Competitive marketplace participant or not
- Speed with which DW will be constructed
- Construction of DW is manual or automated
- Amount of summary data to be maintained

Data –
Denial

- Creation of integration and transformation layer is manual or automated
- Maintenance of the integration and transformation layer is manual or automated

MEASURES OF SUCCESS

The costs for a DW can be extraordinary. Bill Inmon shows multiple DMs costing in the tens of millions in the graphics in his article on metadata and DMs.[4] Despite the costs, William McKnight indicates that that a recent survey of DW users has shown a range of return on investment (ROI) for a 3 year period between 1857% and 16,000%, with an average annual ROI of 401%.[25] However, Douglas Hackney cautions that the sample sets for some DW ROI surveys were self-selected and the methodology flawed. Hackney does say that there are other ROI measures that need to be considered: "pure financial ROI, opportunity cost, 'do nothing' cost and a 'functional ROI.' In the real world, your financial ROI may be 0%, but the overall return of all the measures can easily be over 100%."[26] So, the actual measures of success for the DW in an organization, and the quantitative or qualitative values obtained, will depend on the organization.

Internal customers and their focus should be considered when determining the objectives and performance measures for the DW ROI, including:[25]

- sales volume (sales and marketing)
- reduced expenses (operations)
- inventory management (operations)
- profits (executive management)
- market share (executive management)
- improved time to market (executive management)
- ability to identify new markets (executive management)

DWs respond to these objectives by bringing together, in a cohesive and manageable group, subject areas, data sources, user communities, business rules, and hardware architecture.

Expanding on the above metrics, other benefits that can significantly impact the organization's well-being and its success in the marketplace are:[25]

- Reduced losses due to fraud detection
- Reduced write-offs because of (previous) inadequate data to combat challenges from vendors and customers
- Reduced overproduction of goods and commensurate inventory holding costs
- Increased metrics on customer retention, targeted marketing and an increased customer base, promotion analysis programs with increased customer numbers and penetration, and lowering time to market

Mergers by companies in today's market provide an opportunity for cross-selling by identifying new, potential customers for the partners or by providing additional services that can be presented for consideration to existing customers. Responsiveness to customers' needs, such as speed (submitting offers to a customer prior to the customer making a decision) and precision (tailoring offerings to what is predicted the customer wants), can be facilitated with a well-designed and well-utilized DW. Associated actions can include the automatic initiation of marketing activity in response to known buying or attrition triggers, or tools that coordinate a "continuous customized communication's stream with customers." Data mining expands the potential beyond query-driven efforts by identifying previously unknown relationships that positively affect the customer base.[27]

MISTAKES TO AVOID

The Data Warehousing Institute conducted meetings with DW project managers and Information Systems executives in 1995 to identify the "ten mistakes to avoid for data warehousing managers" and created a booklet (Ten Mistakes Booklet) that is available from the institute.[28] Time has not changed the importance or the essence of the knowledge imparted through the experienced contributors. Although many authors have highlighted one or more topics in their writings, this source is very succinct and comprehensive. The "Ten Data Warehousing Mistakes to Avoid" and a very brief explanation are noted below.[29]

1. *Starting with the wrong sponsorship chain.* Supporters of the DW must include an executive sponsor with funding and an intense interest in the effective use of information, a project "driver" who keeps the project moving in the right direction with input from appropriate sources, and the DW manager.
2. *Setting expectations that one cannot meet and frustrating executives at the moment of truth.* DWs contain a select portion of organizational information, often at a summary level. If DWs are portrayed as "the answer" to all questions, then users are going to be disappointed. User expectations must be managed.
3. *Engaging in politically-naïve behavior.* DWs are a tool to support managers. To say that DWs will "help managers make better decisions" can alienate potential supporters (who may have been performing well *without* a DW).
4. *Loading the warehouse with information just because it was available.* Extraneous data makes it more difficult to locate the essential information and slows down the retrieval and analysis process. The data selected for inclusion in the DW must support organizational strategic goals.

5. *Believing that the data warehousing database design is the same as the transactional database design.* DWs are intended to maintain and provide access to selected information from operational (transactional) databases, generally covering long periods of time. The type of information contained in a DW will cross multiple divisions within the organization, and the source data may come from multiple databases and may be summarized or provided in detail. These characteristics (as well as the database objectives) are substantially different from those of operational or transactional databases.

6. *Choosing a data warehouse manager who is technology oriented rather than user oriented.* Data warehousing is a service business—not a storage business—and making clients angry is a near-perfect method of destroying a service business.

7. *Focusing on traditional internal record-oriented data and ignoring the potential value of external data and text, images, and—potentially—sound and video.* Expand the data warehouse beyond the usual data presentation options and include other vital presentation options. Users may ask: Where is the copy of the contract (image) that explains the information behind the data? Where is the ad (image) that ran in that magazine? Where is the tape (audio or video) of the key competitor at a recent conference talking about its business strategy? Where is the recent product launch (video)? Being able to provide the required reference data will enhance the analysis that the data warehouse designers and sponsors endeavor to support.

8. *Delivering data with overlapping and confusing definitions.* Consensus on data definitions is mandatory, and this is difficult to attain because multiple departments may have different meanings for the same term (e.g., sales). Otherwise, users may not have confidence in the data they are acquiring. Even worse, they may acquire the wrong information, embarrass themselves, and blame the data warehouse.

9. *Believing the vendor's performance, capacity, and scalability promises.* Planning to address the present and future DW capacity in terms of data storage, user access, and data transfer is mandatory. Budgeting must include unforeseen difficulties and costs associated with less than adequate performance by a product.

10. *Believing that once the data warehouse is up and running, one's problems are finished.* Once they become familiar with the data warehouse and the process for acquiring and analyzing data, users are going to want additional and different types of data than that already contained in the DW. The DW project team must be maintained after the initial design and implementation takes place for on-going DW support and enhancement.

11. *Focusing on ad hoc data mining and periodic reporting.* (Believing there are only ten mistakes to avoid is also a mistake.) Sometimes, ad hoc reports are converted into regularly scheduled reports, but the recipients may not read the reports. Alert systems can be a better approach and make a DW mission-critical, by monitoring data flowing into the warehouse and informing key people with a need-to-know as soon as a critical event takes place.

Responsiveness to key business goals—high-quality data, metadata, and scalable architecture—is emphasized repeatedly by many DW authors, as noted in the next section on suggestions for DW implementation.

DW IMPLEMENTATION

Although the actual implementation of a DW will depend on the business goals to be supported and the type and number of users, there are general implementation considerations and measures of success that are applicable to many circumstances.

General Considerations

As expected, implementation suggestions are (basically) the opposite of the mistakes to avoid. There is some overlap in the suggestions noted because there are multiple authors cited. Suggestions include:

1. Understand the basic requirements.
2. Design a highly scalable solution.
3. Deliver the first piece of the solution into users' hands quickly.[30]
4. Support a business function that is directly related to the company's strategy; begin with the end in mind.
5. Involve the business functions from the project inception throughout its lifecycle.
6. Ensure executive sponsorship understands the DW value, particularly with respect to revenue enhancement that focuses on the customer.
7. Maintain executive sponsorship and interest throughout the project.[31]
8. Develop standards for data transformation, replication, stewardship, and naming.
9. Determine a cost-justification methodology, and charge users for data they request.
10. Allow sufficient time to implement the DW properly, and conduct a phased implementation.
11. Designate the authority for determining data sources and populating the metadata and DW data to Data Administration.
12. Monitor data usage and archive data that is rarely or never accessed.[5]

13. Budget resources for metadata creation. Make metadata population a metric for the development team.

14. Budget resources for metadata maintenance. Any change in the data requires a change in the metadata.

15. Ensure ease of access. Find and deploy tools that seamlessly integrate metadata.[32]

16. Monitor DW storage growth and data activity to implement reasonable capacity planning.

17. Monitor user access and analysis techniques to ensure that they optimize usage of the DW resources.

18. Tune the DW for performance based on usage patterns (e.g., selectively index data, partition data, create summarization, and create aggregations).

19. Support both business metadata and technical metadata.

20. Plan for the future. Ensure that interface between applications and the DW is as automated as possible. Data granularity allows for continuous DW tuning and reorganization, as required to meet user needs and organization strategic goals.

21. Consider the creation of an "exploration warehouse" for the "out-of-the-box thinkers" who may want to submit lengthy resource-consuming queries—if they become a regular request.[33]

Qualitative Measures of DW Implementation Success

In 1994, Sears, Roebuck and Co. (a leading U.S. retailer of apparel, home, and automotive products that operates 3000 department and specialty stores) implemented a DW to address organizational objectives. The eight (qualitative) measures of success presented below are based on the experiences associated with the Sears DW implementation.

1. *Regular implementation of new releases.* The DW and applications are evolving to meet business needs, adding functionality through a phased implementation process.

2. *Users will wait for promised system upgrades.* When phases will deliver the functionality that is promised, at the expected quality level and data integrity level, planned implementation schedules (and possibly slippage) will be tolerated.

3. *New applications use the DW to serve their data requirements.* Increased reliance on the DW provides consistency company-wide and is cost effective.

4. *Users and support staff will continue to be involved in the DW.* Users become reliant on the DW and the part it plays in the performance of their work responsibilities. Therefore, there needs to be a permanent DW staff to support the constantly changing DW and business environment. When product timeliness is crucial to profitability, then designated staff (such as the Sears Business Support Team) and the DW staff

can provide additional, specialized support to meet user needs.

5. *The DW is used to identify new business opportunities.* As users become familiar with the DW, they will increasingly pursue new discovery opportunities.

6. *Special requests become the rule, not the exception.* The ability to handle special requests on a routine basis is an example of DW maturity and a positive leverage of DW resources.

7. *Ongoing user training.* New and advanced user training (e.g., trouble-shooting techniques, sophisticated functionality) and the provision of updated documentation (highlighting new features) facilitate and enhance DW use in support of business objectives.

8. *Retirement of legacy systems.* Use of legacy systems containing duplicate information will decline. Retirement of legacy systems should follow a planned process, including verification of data accuracy, completeness, and timely posting, with advance notification to identified users for a smooth transition to the DW applications.[34]

DW SECURITY IMPLICATIONS

The benefits of the well-implemented and well-managed DW can be very significant to a company. The data is integrated into a single data source. There is considerable ease of data access that can be used for decision-making support, including trends identification and analysis, and problem-solving. There is overall better data quality and uniformity, and different views of the same data are reconciled. Analysis techniques may even uncover useful competitive information. But with this valuable warehouse of information and power comes substantial risk if the information is unavailable, destroyed, improperly altered, or disclosed to or acquired by a competitor.

There may be additional risks associated with a specific DW, depending on the organization's functions, its environment, and the resources available for the DW design, implementation, and maintenance—which must be determined on an individual basis—that are not addressed here. Consider the perspective that the risks will change over time as the DW receives increased use by more sophisticated internal and external users; supports more functions; and becomes more critical to organizational operations.

DW Design Review

Insofar as the literature unanimously exhorts the need for upper-management support and applicability to critical business missions, the importance of the system is significant before it is even implemented. Issues associated with availability, integrity, and confidentiality should be addressed in the system design, and plans should include options for scalability and growth in the future. The DW must be available to users when they need the information; its integrity must be established and maintained; and only those with a need-to-know must access the data. Management must be made aware of the security implications and requirements, and security should be built into the DW design.

DW design is compliant with established corporate information security policy, standards, guidelines, and procedures

During the design phase, certain decisions are being made regarding expected management functions to be supported by the DW: user population (quantity, type, and expertise level); associated network connectivity required; information to be contained in the initial phase of the DW; data modeling processes and associated data formats; and resources (e.g., hardware, software, staff, data) necessary to implement the design. This phase also has significant security implications. The DW design must support and comply with corporate information security policies, including:

- Non-disclosure statements signed by employees when they are hired[35]
- Installation and configuration of new hardware and software, according to established corporate policies, guidelines, and procedures
- Documentation of acceptable use and associated organizational monitoring activities
- Consistency with overall security architecture
- Avoidance of liability for inadequately addressing security through "negligence, breach of fiduciary duty, failing to use the security measures found in other organizations in the same industry, failing to exercise due care expected from a computer professional, or failure to act after an 'actual notice' has taken place"[45]
- Protection from prosecution regarding inappropriate information access by defining appropriate information security behavior by authorized users[46]

DW data access rights are defined and modeled for the DW user population

When determining the access requirements for the DW, your initial users may be a small subset of employees in one division. Over time, it will expand to employees throughout the entire organization, and may include selected subsets of subcontractors, vendors, suppliers, or other groups who are partnering with the organization for a specific purpose. Users will not have access to all DW information, and appropriate access and monitoring

controls must be implemented. Areas of security concern and implementation regarding user access controls include:

- DW user roles' definition for access controls (e.g., role-based access controls)
- User access rights and responsibilities documentation
- Development of user agreements specifying security responsibilities and procedures[35]
- Definition of user groups and their authorized access to specific internal or external data
- User groups and their authorized levels of network connectivity and use definitions
- Definition of procedures for review of system logs and other records generated by the software packages[37]

DW data content and granularity is defined and appropriately implemented in the DW design

Initially, the DW content may be internal organizational numerical data, limited to a particular department or division. As time passes, the amount and type of data is going to increase, and may include internal organizational textual data, images, and videos, and external data of various forms as well. In addition, the required granularity of the data may change. Users initially may be comfortable with summary data; but as their familiarity with the DW and the analysis tools increases, they are going to want more detailed data, with a higher level of granularity than originally provided. Decisions that affect data content and its integrity throughout the DW life cycle include:

- Data granularity (e.g., summary, detail, instance, atomic) is defined.
- Data transformation rules are documented for use in maintaining data integrity.
- Process is defined for maintaining all data transformation rules for the life of the system.

Data sensitivity is defined and associated with appropriate access controls

Issues associated with data ownership, sensitivity, labeling, and need-to-know will need to be defined so that the data can be properly labeled, and access requirements (e.g., role-based access controls) can be assigned.

Establishment of role-based access controls "is viewed as effective and efficient for general enterprise security" and would allow the organization to expand the DW access over time, and successfully manage a large number of users.[38] Actions required that define and establish the data access controls include:

- Determination of user access control techniques, including the methods for user identification, authentication, and authorization
- Assignment of users to specific groups with associated authority, capabilities, and privileges[38] for role-based access controls
- Determination of database controls (e.g., table and data labeling, encryption)
- Establishment of a process for granting access and for the documentation of specified user roles and authorized data access, and a process for preventing the circumvention of the granting of access controls
- Establishment of a process for officially notifying the Database Administrator (or designated individual) when an individual's role changes and his or her access to data must be changed accordingly
- Establishment of a process for periodically reviewing access controls, including role-based access controls to ensure that only individuals with specified clearances and need-to-know have access to sensitive information

Data integrity and data inference requirements are defined and associated with appropriate access controls

Data integrity will be reviewed when the data is transformed for the DW, but should be monitored on a periodic basis throughout the life cycle of the DW, in cooperation with the DW database administration staff. Data inference and aggregation may enable an individual to acquire information for which he or she has no need-to-know, based on the capability to acquire other information. "An inference presents a security breach if higher-classified information can be inferred from lower-classified information."[39]

Circumstances in which this action might occur through data aggregation or data association in the DW need to be identified and addressed through appropriate data access controls. Data access controls to prevent or reduce unauthorized access to information obtained through a data inference process (i.e., data aggregation or data association) can include:[39]

- *Appropriate labeling of information:* unclassified information is reclassified (or labeled at a higher level) to prevent unauthorized inferences by data aggregation or data association.
- *Query restriction:* all queries are dominated by the level of the user, and inappropriate queries are aborted or modified to include only authorized data.
- *Polyinstantiation:* multiple versions of the same information item are created to exist at different classification levels.
- *Auditing:* a history of user queries is analyzed to determine if the response to a new query might suggest an inference violation.

- *Toleration of limited inferences:* inferred information violations do not pose a serious threat, and the prevention of certain inferences may be unfeasible.

Operating system, application, and communications security requirements are defined

Many DWs are using a Web-based interface, which provides easy accessibility and significant risk. Depending on the location of the system, multiple security mechanisms will be required. Actions required to define the security requirements should be based on a risk analysis and include:

- Determination of mechanisms to ensure operating system and application system availability and integrity (e.g., firewalls, intrusion detection systems)
- Determination of any secure communication requirements (e.g., Secure Socket Layer, encryption)

Plans for hardware configuration and backup must be included in the DW design

The creation of a DW as a separate, non-operational function will result in a duplication of hardware resources, because the operational hardware is maintained separately. In examples of mature DW utilizations, a second DW is often created for power users for "exploratory research" because the complexity of their analysis requests would take too much time and resources away from the other general users of the initial DW. This is then (possibly) a third set of hardware that must be purchased, configured, maintained, administered, and protected. The hardware investment keeps increasing. Documentation and updating of hardware and backup configurations should be performed as necessary.

Plans for software distribution, configuration, and use must be included in the DW design

The creation of one or multiple DWs also means additional operating system, application, middleware, and security software. In addition, as the number of users increases, the number of licensed software copies must also increase. Users may not be able to install the software themselves and so technical support may need to be provided. Distribution activities should ensure that:

- Users have authorized copies of all software.
- Technical support is provided for software installation, use, and troubleshooting to maintain licensing compliance and data integrity.

Plans for continuity of operations and disaster recovery must be included in the DW design

Capabilities for hardware and software backup, continuity of operations, and disaster recovery options will also have to be considered. The DW is used to implement strategic business goals, and downtime must be limited. As more users integrate the DW data into their routine work performance, more users will be negatively impacted by its unavailability. Activities in support of operations continuity and disaster recovery should include:

- Designations from the design team regarding the criticality of data and key functions
- Creation of an alternative hardware list
- Resource allocations for DW system backups and storage
- Resource allocations for business continuity and disaster recovery plans

Plans for routine evaluation of the impact of expanded network connectivity on organizational network performance must be included in the DW design

Over time, with the increased number of users and the increased amount and type of data being accessed in the DW and transmitted over the organizational network, network resources are going to be "stressed." Possible options for handling increased network loads will need to be discussed. Network upgrades may be required over the long term and this needs to be considered in the resource planning activities. Otherwise data availability and data integrity may be impacted at crucial management decision times—times when one wants the DW to stand out as the valuable resource it was intended to be. Changes in network configurations must be documented and comply with organizational security policies and procedures. Planning to address DW scalability and the ability of the network to respond favorably to growth should include:

- Evaluation of proposed network configurations and the expected service to be provided by a given configuration against DW requirements[40]
- Estimation of DW network requirements' impact on existing organizational network connectivity requirements and possible reduction in data availability or integrity
- Consideration of network connectivity options and the effects on the implementation of security

DW Security Implementation Review

A security review must be conducted to ensure that all the DW components supporting information security that were defined during the design phase are accurately and consistently installed and configured. Testing must be performed to ensure that the security mechanisms and database processes perform in a reliable manner and that the security mechanisms enforce established access controls. Availability of data must be consistent with defined requirements. The information security professional, the database administrator, and the network administrator should work together to ensure that data confidentiality, integrity, and availability are addressed.

Monitor the acquisition and installation of DW technology components in accordance with established corporate security policies

When acquired, the hardware and software DW components must be configured to support the corporate security policies and the data models defined during the design phase. During installation, the following actions should take place: 1) documentation of the hardware and software configurations; and 2) testing of the system before operational to ensure compliance with policies.

Review the creation/generation of database components for security concerns

A process should be established to ensure that data is properly labeled, access requirements are defined and configured, and all controls can be enforced. In cooperation with the design team, individuals responsible for security should perform a review of the database configurations for compliance with security policies and defined data access controls. Database processes must enforce the following data integrity principles:[39]

1. *Well-formed transactions*: Transactions support the properties of correct-state transformation, serialization, failure atomicity, progress (transaction completion), entity integrity, and referential integrity.
2. *Least privilege*: Programs and users are given the minimum access required to perform their jobs.
3. *Separation of duties*: Events that affect the balance of assets are divided into separate tasks performed by different individuals.
4. *Reconstruction of events*: User accountability for actions and determination of actions are performed through a well-defined audit trail.
5. *Delegation of authority*: Process for acquisition and distribution of privileges is well-defined and constrained.
6. *Reality checks*: Cross-checks with an external reality are performed.
7. *Continuity of operations*: System operations are maintained at an appropriate level.

Review the acquisition of DW source data

DW data is coming from other sources; ensure that all internal and external data sources are known and documented, and data use is authorized. If the data is external, ensure that appropriate compensation for the data (if applicable) has been made, and that access limitations (if applicable) are enforced.

Review testing

Configuration settings for the security mechanisms must be verified, documented, and protected from alteration. Testing to ensure that the security mechanisms are installed and functioning properly must be performed and documented prior to the DW becoming operational. A plan should also be established for the testing of security mechanisms throughout the life cycle of the DW, including the following situations:

- Routine testing of security mechanisms is done on a scheduled basis.
- Hardware or software configurations of the DW are changed.
- Circumstances indicate that an unauthorized alteration may have occurred.
- A security incident occurs or is suspected.
- A security mechanism is not functioning properly.

DW Operations

The DW is not a static database. Users and information are going to be periodically changing. The process of data acquisition, modeling, labeling, and insertion into the DW must follow the established procedures. Users must be trained in DW use and updated as processes or procedures change, depending on the data being made available to them. More users and more data mean additional demands will be placed on the organization's network, and performance must be monitored to ensure promised availability and data integrity. Security mechanisms must be monitored to ensure accurate and consistent performance. Backup and recovery procedures must also be implemented as defined to ensure data availability.

Participate as a co-instructor in DW user instruction/training

Training will be required for users to fully utilize the DW. This is also an opportunity to present (and reinforce) applicable information security requirements and the user's responsibility to protect enterprise information

and other areas of concern. Activities associated with this include:

- Promotion of users' understanding of their responsibilities regarding data privacy and protection
- Documentation of user responsibilities and non-disclosure agreements

Perform network monitoring for performance

Document network performance against established baselines to ensure that data availability is being implemented as planned.

Perform security monitoring for access control implementation

Review defined hardware and software configurations on a periodic basis to ensure no inappropriate changes have been made, particularly in a distributed DW environment. Security monitoring activities should include:

- Review of user accesses to verify established controls are in place and operational, and no unauthorized access is being granted (e.g., individual with role X is being granted to higher level data associated with role Y)
- Provision of the capability for the DW administrator to cancel a session or an ID, as might be needed to combat a possible attack[35]
- Review of operating system and application systems to ensure no unauthorized changes have been made to the configurations

Perform software application and security patches in a timely and accurate manner

All patches must be installed as soon as they are received and documented in the configuration information.

Perform data and software backups and archiving

As data and software are changed, backups must be performed as defined in the DW design. Maintaining backups of the current data and software configurations will support any required continuity of operations or disaster recovery activities. Backups must be stored offsite at a remote location so that they are not subject to the same threats. If any data is moved from the DW to remote storage because it is not currently used, then the data must be appropriately labeled, stored, and protected to ensure access in the event that the information is needed again.

Review DW data and metadata integrity

DW data will be reloaded or updated on a periodic basis. Changes to the DW data may also require changes to the metadata. The data should be reviewed to determine that the updates are being performed on the established schedule, are being performed correctly, and the integrity of the data is being maintained.

DW Maintenance

DW maintenance is a significant activity, because the DW is an ever-changing environment, with new data and new users being added on a routine basis. All security-relevant changes to the DW environment must be reviewed, approved, and documented prior to implementation.

Review and document the updating of DW hardware and software

Over time, changes will be made to the hardware and software, as technology improves or patches are required in support of functions or security. Associated activities include:

- Installation of all software patches in a timely manner and documentation of the software configuration
- Maintenance of software backups and creation of new backups after software changes
- Ensuring new users have authorized copies of the software
- Ensuring that system backup and recovery procedures reflect the current importance of the DW to organizational operations (If DW criticality has increased over time with use, has the ability to respond to this new level of importance been changed accordingly?)

Review the extraction/loading of data process and frequency to ensure timeliness and accuracy

The DW data that is to be updated will be extracted from a source system, transformed, and then loaded into the DW. The frequency with which this activity is performed will depend on the frequency with which the data changes, and the users' needs regarding accurate and complete data. The process required to *update* DW data takes significantly less time than that required to *reload* the entire DW database, but there has to be a mechanism for determining what data has been changed. This process needs to be reviewed, and adjusted as required, throughout the life cycle of the DW.

Scheduling/performing data updates

Ensure that data updates are performed as scheduled and the data integrity is maintained.

DW Optimization

Once the DW is established within an organization, it is likely that there will be situations in which individuals or organizations are working to make the DW better (e.g., new data content and types), cheaper (e.g., more automated, less labor intensive), and faster (e.g., new analysis tools, better network connectivity and throughput). Optimization will result in changes, and changes need to be reviewed in light of their impact on security. All changes should be approved before being implemented and carefully documented.

Participate in user refresher/upgrade training

Over time, additional data content areas are going to be added to the DW and new analysis tools may be added. Users will need to be trained in the new software and other DW changes. This training also presents an opportunity to present any new security requirements and procedures—and to review existing requirements and procedures associated with the DW.

Review and update the process for extraction/loading of data

As new data requirements evolve for the DW, new data may be acquired. Appropriate procedures must be followed regarding the access, labeling, and maintenance of new data to maintain the DW reputation regarding data integrity and availability.

Review the scheduling/performance of data updates

Over time, users may require more frequent updates of certain data. Ensure that data updates are performed as scheduled and that data integrity is maintained.

Perform network monitoring for performance

Document network performance against established baselines to ensure that data availability is being implemented as planned. An expanded number of users and increased demand for large volumes of data may require modifications to the network configuration or to the scheduling of data updates. Such modifications may reduce the network traffic load at certain times of the day, week, or month, and ensure that requirements for data availability and integrity are maintained.

Perform security monitoring for access

The DW information can have substantial operational value or exchange value to a competitor or a disloyal employee, as well as to the authorized users. With the use of corporate "portals" of entry, all of the data may be available through one common interface—making the means and opportunity for "acquisition" of information more easily achieved. Implementation of access controls needs to be continually monitored and evaluated throughout the DW life cycle. The unauthorized acquisition or dissemination of business-sensitive information (such as privacy data, trade secrets, planning information, or financial data) could result in lost revenue, company embarrassment, or legal problems. Monitoring access controls should be a continual security procedure for the DW.

Database analysis

Some existing DW data may not be used with the expected frequency and it may be moved to another storage location, creating space for data more in demand. Changes in DW data configurations and locations should be documented.

There may be additional risks associated with an actual DW, depending on the organization's functions, its environment, and the resources available for the DW design, implementation, and maintenance—which must be determined on an individual basis. But with careful planning and implementation, the DW will be a valuable resource for the organization and help the staff to meet its strategic goals—now and in the future.

CONCLUSION

The security section presented some of the security considerations that need to be addressed throughout the life cycle of the DW. One consideration not highlighted above is the amount of time and associated resources (including equipment and funding) necessary to implement DW security. Bill Inmon estimated Security Administration to be 1% of the total warehouse costs, with costs to double the first year and then grow 30% to 40% after that. Maintaining adequate security is a crucial DW and organizational concern. The value of the DW is going to increase over time, and more users are going to have access to the information. Appropriate resources must be allocated to the protection of the DW. The ROI to the organization can be very significant if the information is adequately protected. If the information is not protected, then someone else is getting the keys to the kingdom. Understanding the DW design and implementation process can enable security professionals to justify their involvement early on in the design process and throughout the DW life cycle, and empower them to make appropriate, timely security recommendations and accomplish their responsibilities successfully.

REFERENCES

1. Peppers, D.; Rogers, M. Mass customization: Listening to customers. DM Rev. **1999**, *9* (1), 16.
2. Denning, D.E. *Information Warfare and Security*; Addison-Wesley: Reading, MA, 1999, 148.
3. Saylor, M. Data warehouse on the web. DM Rev. **1996**, *6* (9), 22–26.
4. Inman, B. Meta Data for the Data Mart Environment. DM Rev. **1999**, *9* (4), 44.
5. Adelman, S. The Data Warehouse Database Explosion. DM Rev. **1996**, *6* (11), 41–43.
6. Imhoff, C.; Geiger, J. Data Quality in the Data Warehouse. DM Rev. **1996**, *6* (4), 55–58.
7. Griggin, J. Information Strategy. DM Rev. **1996**, *6* (11), 12, 18.
8. Mimmo, P.R. Building Your Data Warehouse Right the First Time, *Data Warehousing: What Works*, Vol. 9, November 1999, The Data Warehouse Institute Web site, http://www.dw-institute.com.
9. King, N. Metadata: Gold in the Hills, *Intelligent Enterprise*, **1999**, *2* (3), 12.
10. Quinlan, T. Report from the Trenches, *Database Programming & Design*, **1996**, *9* (12), 36–38, 40–42, 44–45.
11. Hufford, D. Data Warehouse Quality. DM Rev. **1996**, *6* (3), 31–34.
12. Rudin, K. The Fallacy of Perfecting the Warehouse. DM Rev. **1999**, *9* (4), 14.
13. Burwen, M.P. BI and DW: Crossing the Millennium. DM Rev. **1999**, *9* (4), 12.
14. Westphal, C.; Blaxton, T. *Data Mining Solutions, Methods and Tools for Solving Real-World Problems*; Wiley Computer Publishing: New York, 1998; 68–69.
15. Tufte, E.R. *The Visual Display of Quantitative Information*; Graphics Press: Cheshire, CT, 1983; 15, 51.
16. Osterfelt, S. Doorways to Data. DM Rev. April **1999**, *9* (4).
17. Finkelstein, C. Enterprise Portals and XML. DM Rev. **2000**, *10* (1), 21.
18. Schroeck, M. Enterprise Information Portals. DM Rev. **2000**, *10* (1), 22.
19. Inman, B. The Data Warehouse Budget. DM Rev. **1997**, *7* (1), 12–13.
20. McKnight, W. Data Warehouse Justification and ROI. DM Rev. *9* (10), 50–52, November 1999.
21. Hackney, D. How About 0% ROI?. DM Rev. **1999**, *9* (1), 88.
22. Suther, T. Customer Relationship Management. DM Rev. **1999**, *9* (1), 24.
23. The Data Warehousing Institute (TDWI), 849-J Quince Orchard Boulevard, Gaithersburg, MD 20878, (301) 947–3730, http://www.dw-institute.com.
24. The Data Warehousing Institute, Data Warehousing: What Works?, Gaithersburg, MD, Publication Number 295104, 1995.

25. Schroeck, M.J. Data Warehouse Best Practices. DM Rev. **1999**, *9* (1), 14.

26. Hackney, D. Metadata Maturity. DM Rev. **1996**, *6* (3), 22.

27. Inmon, B. Planning for a Healthy, Centralized Warehouse. *Teradata Review.* **1999**, *2* (1), 20–24.

28. Steerman, H. Measuring Data Warehouse Success: Eight Signs You're on the Right Track. *Teradata Review*, **1999**, *2* (1), 12–17.

29. Fites, P.; Kratz, M. *Information Systems Security: A Practitioner's Reference*; International Thomson Computer Press: Boston, MA, 10.

30. Wood, C.C. *Information Security Policies Made Easy*, Baseline Software: Sausalito, CA, 6, 5.

31. Murray, W. Enterprise Security Architecture. In *Information Security Management Handbook*, 4th Ed.; F.T. Harold, S.K. Micki, Eds., Auerbach: New York, 1999; chap. 13, 215–230.

32. Sandhu, R.S.; Jajodia, S. Data Base Security Controls. In *Handbook of Information Security Management*, Z.G. Ruthberg, H.F. Tipton, Eds.; Auerbach: Boston, MA, 1993, chap. II-3-2, 481–499.

33. Kern, H. *Managing the New Enterprise*, Prentice-Hall, Sun SoftPress: NJ, 1996, 120.

Data Warehouses: Security and Privacy

David Bonewell, CISSP, CISSP/EP, CISA
President, Accomac Consulting LLC, Cincinnati, Ohio, U.S.A.

Karen Gibbs
Senior Data Warehouse Architect, Teradata, Dayton, Ohio, U.S.A.

Adriaan Veldhuisen
Senior Data Warehouse/Privacy Architect, Teradata, San Diego, California, U.S.A.

Abstract

How will a company address security and privacy concerns with its customers in an ever-changing environment of increasing public concern for how personal information is collected, used, and distributed by commercial organizations? As consumers become accustomed to defining and deciding how their personal information should be used, they will likely expect their privacy preferences to be respected in *all* forms of interactions.

A growing portion of the concern about privacy invasion surrounds data mining and both its perceived and real threats to personal privacy. Recent events demonstrate how various representatives of the public worldwide are demanding protection against abuse of personal information by organizations using data mining techniques on their warehouse databases. The European Union (EU) has already passed legislation protecting personal privacy. Similar legislative and regulatory privacy protection considerations exist in other countries, including Australia, Canada, New Zealand, Hong Kong, and the Czech Republic, and more have already begun to follow. The U.S. government is encouraging American companies to follow voluntary compliance, reinforced by the Federal Communications Commission (FCC), Federal Trade Commission (FTC), and other regulatory bodies.

A strategy for addressing privacy concerns is to develop and execute sound practices and processes with the highest respect for individual privacy. To effect this, an organization must have the tools and infrastructure that will allow it to comply with regulatory constraints while continuing to gain business advantage with the information it needs to collect and use.

This entry first describes the business problem concerning privacy laws, rules, and regulations. Realistic business scenarios expose typical privacy-related business requirements from consumer, national, sector, and industry viewpoints that affect system architecture and technology decisions. Business requirements for enabling consumer privacy are illuminated during this discussion. The entry then illustrates the technical problem through various architectural function perspectives. In summary, this entry documents how security and privacy requirements impact both business and technical architectural systems across and within a data warehouse.

PROBLEM DESCRIPTION FOR ENABLING PRIVACY

Data warehousing is a strategic imperative for many companies. Unless adequate measures are taken to protect personal data today, there will be resistance to data mining as a technology in the future. Ignoring security and privacy in a data warehouse will, in particular, undermine an organization's data warehouse strategy if such resistance becomes widespread.

Furthermore, several regulatory activities are occurring worldwide. The EU Directives 95/46/EC[1] and 97/66/EC[2] are now in effect and require privacy legislation throughout the EU. The FCC interpretations of Section 222 of the Telecommunications Act places legal requirements on telecommunications companies regarding the use of Customer Proprietary Network Information (CPNI). Movement of citizen, employee, and consumer data between countries is also a significant privacy issue.

A company's response should be to take the necessary actions to be perceived as a leader in privacy protection by adding capabilities that help the company conform to the FTC, FCC, and EU directives, regulations, initiatives, and other emerging legislation.

Encyclopedia of Information Assurance DOI: 10.1081/E-EIA-120046723
Copyright © 2011 by Taylor & Francis. All rights reserved.

Privacy protection capabilities will help an organization:

- Determine which data is personally identifiable in a data warehouse
- Identify and modify personally identifiable data
- Utilize data mining techniques that respect consent choices (opt-in and opt-out) of consumers

Privacy: Opportunity or Threat to Business Drivers

Companies manage key business drivers through initiatives that are common to most industries in order to achieve their success. Two of these related business drivers are customer acquisition and customer retention, often accomplished by taking actions to maintain customer loyalty and improve customer service. Another of these business drivers is wallet share, usually achieved through endeavors to grow the customer's share of the market segment addressed. A fourth key driver is total cost of ownership (TCO), generally realized through measures to reduce expenses or improve efficiencies throughout the business' processes.

Table 1 captures some of the possible opportunities and potential threats across all industries that arise from privacy-related concerns and issues as they affect these key business drivers.

Enabling consumer privacy imposes both business and technical problems for many companies. Primary concentration on the business problem allows for clarification of key business issues prior to technology and development decisions; however, it is valuable to decompose each perspective of the privacy problem into its constituent parts for further examination. Separating the problem into business and technical discussions focuses attention on the key issues pertinent to each of these two areas and exposes hidden and false assumptions during analysis. Before proceeding to analyze the business and technical perspectives of the privacy problem, it is necessary to discern privacy from security and confidentiality, as well as to clearly understand the different sources for the rules that guide privacy policies. The next two subsections briefly explain these clarifications.

Clarification of Terms

It is important to understand the meaning of the terms "privacy," "security," and "confidentiality" in order to properly understand the business and technical perspectives of the privacy problem.

Privacy defines an individual's freedom from unauthorized intrusion (into matters considered by the individual to be personal).[3] This definition effectively addresses both the United States and European notions as well as legal histories, and applies well to data.

Security defines an attribute of information systems, and includes specific policy-based mechanisms and assurances for protecting the confidentiality and integrity of information, the availability of critical services, and indirectly, privacy.

Confidentiality defines an attribute of information. Confidential information is sensitive or secret information, or information whose unauthorized disclosure could be harmful or prejudicial. Because security is required to ensure privacy and confidentiality of personal information, it must be present throughout business processes in solutions that enable consumer privacy. Fig. 1 diagrams the flow of logic within a security system.

Fig. 1 is taken from Common Criteria ISO 15408 standard specifying the Privacy Class of Common Criteria.[4] It proposes that all security specifications and requirements should come from a general security context. This context states that "security is concerned with the protection of assets from threats, where threats are categorized as the potential for abuse of protected assets." The scope of threat prevention says that all threats should be considered; but in the domain of security, greater attention is given to those threats that are related to malicious or other human activities.

Table 1 Opportunities and threats as they affect business drivers.

	Opportunities	Threats
Use of personal information	Enhanced public trust through appropriate use	Public concern about misuse; potential for costs to an individual resulting from abuses
Legislation, regulation	Potential for customers' compliance useful as competitive weapon for improving company image and eliminating costs associated with litigation; help to stay focused on core business	Fines, suits, and a general inability to do business, potentially causing operational changes or new hardware/software purchases leading to decreased value for shareholders; reduced focus on core business
Economic impact	Data warehouse investments leading to increased value of collected data by removing useless or low-value data, decreasing marketing costs, and improving consumer satisfaction; increased value of information collection	Data warehouse investments in jeopardy, possibly leading to decreased value of collected information and increased costs associated with information removal

Data –
Denial

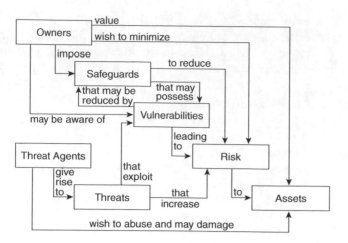

Fig. 1 Concepts and relationships (flow of logic) within a security system.

The Common Criteria framework follows a logical progression, wherein first a security environment is described, and then security objectives are determined based on the indicated security environment. More details dealing with security environment characteristics, security objectives, security services requirements and security functional requirements concerned with information protection are briefly discussed in Table 2.

The remainder of this entry assumes that a company has implemented security systems that assure privacy and confidentiality of personal information appropriate for the industry environments in which it does business. Other than identifying security as an ongoing requirement for privacy, no further detail will be explored. It can be further stated that one can have security in a data warehouse and not have privacy; but one cannot have privacy without security in this environment.

Clarification of Rules

Rules for guiding privacy policies are derived from a number of different sources, including national governmental authorities, corporations and market-sector organizations, and consumers.

Government rules are primarily defined and enforced by legislative and regulatory bodies and vary by government entities. An example is the European Directive passed by the European Union.[1,2]

Corporate and sector rules can be defined by businesses that constitute specific market segments or by government agencies covering these markets. An example is the Telecommunications Reform Act of 1995 governing customer proprietary network information.

Consumer rules are defined by private individuals. An example is the preference to receive marketing advertisements via hard-copy mail vs. telephone. Another example is the preference to have personal data not sold to third parties. Allowing individuals to specify personal privacy

preferences, or rules, maintains the integrity and credibility of the rules for each consumer.

THE BUSINESS PROBLEM

The privacy problem described in the previous sections can be summarized into the following, simple business problem statement:

Companies need to be able to market to their customers while respecting their customers' expectations as well as domestic and international laws regarding how personal information is collected and used.

This section examines the problem of enabling privacy from the business perspective by exploring a business scenario. Business requirements that are discovered during scenario exercises are captured and used to guide system architecture and technology decisions. Additional business requirements for privacy awareness and sensitivity derive from emerging and existing legislation and public pressures. Clarification of the ensuing privacy business requirements will assist in creating an architecture model illustrating the impacts of enabling consumer privacy.

Business Environment for Enabling Privacy

A business scenario includes a short description of the business environment, the actors involved in the scenario, and the business interactions between the actors. For companies, Fig. 2 illustrates the business environment for enabling consumer privacy.

The left side of Fig. 2 displays several choices for how and where a consumer may prefer to conduct interactions with a company. Examples shown include using hardcopy mail, by telephone, in person, through some special-purpose kiosk, or from a PC possibly via the Internet. Not explicitly shown are those interactions that may be conducted by third parties, such as automated applications performing automated decisions or intelligent agents. Interactions may or may not result in one or more transactions (actual exchanges for goods and services) instituting a relationship between a consumer and a company.

The right side of Fig. 2 introduces sources from which a company obtains the business rules that guide company privacy policies. Legislative requirements for ensuring consumer privacy differ among government jurisdictions. Industry sector and corporate rules for consumer privacy likewise differ for various regulated and non-regulated markets. Finally, consumer privacy preferences can be incorporated, depending on company policies.

Table 2   Security requirements (ISO 15408)/Common Evaluation Criteria (CEM).

Security Environment

- **Assumptions:** Descriptions of assumption elements are needed to specify the security aspects of the customer's environment. This should include information about intended usage of applications, potential asset value, possible limitations for use, as well as information about environment use such as physical, personnel, and connectivity aspects.
- **Threats:** These elements are characterized in terms of a threat agent, a presumed attack method, possible vulnerabilities, and protected asset identification.
- **Organizational Security Policies:** These elements are any and all laws, organization security policies, customs, and IT processes determined relevant to the defined environment.

If security objectives are derived from only threats and assumptions, then the description of the organization security polices can be omitted.

Security Objectives

The security objectives address the identified threats, the customer's organizational policies, and environmental assumptions. The intent of determining security objectives is to address all of the security concerns based on a process incorporating engineering judgment, security policy, economic factors, and risk acceptance decisions.

- **Legitimate Use:** Ensuring that information is not used by unauthorized persons or in unauthorized ways.
- **Confidentiality:** Ensuring that information is not disclosed or revealed to unauthorized persons.
- **Data Integrity:** Ensuring consistency, and preventing the unauthorized creation, alteration, and/or deletion of data.
- **Availability:** Ensuring that data and services are accessible when they are needed.

Security Services Requirements

Meeting security objectives requires a set of security services, or mechanisms. Security services fall into six categories:

1. **Authentication:** Services that assure that the user or system is who that person (or system entity) purports to be. Authentication services can be implemented using passwords, tokens, biometrics (e.g., fingerprint readers), and encryption.
2. **Access Control:** Services that assure that people, computer systems, and processes can use only those resources (e.g., files, directories, computers, networks) that they are authorized to use and only for the purposes for which they are authorized. Access control mechanisms can be identity based (e.g., UNIX protection bits, access control lists), label-based (also known as mandatory access controls), or role-based (implemented as a combination of the above, plus system privileges). Access control plays an important role in protecting against illegitimate use and in providing confidentiality and integrity protection.
3. **Confidentiality:** Services that protect sensitive and private information from unauthorized disclosure. Confidentiality services are generally implemented using encryption.
4. **Integrity:** Services that assure that data, computer programs, and system resources are as they are expected to be and that they cannot be modified by unauthorized people, software, or computer equipment. Mechanisms for implementing data integrity include cyclic redundancy checks and checksums, and encryption. Mechanisms for assuring system integrity include physical protection, virus-protection software, secure initialization mechanisms, and configuration control.
5. **Attribution:** Services that assure actions performed on a system are attributable to the entities performing them, and that neither individuals nor systems are able to repudiate their actions. Mechanisms providing attribution include audits, encryption, and digital signatures.
6. **Availability:** Services that assure that systems, applications, and data are available when they are needed. Considerable efforts must be made to safeguard data and critical system services, ensuring that correct and complete information and IT services to deliver and process that information are available to authorized individuals. A critical requirement of any privacy protection schema is to ensure that critical data and services are available at all times. Mechanisms for providing availability include fault-resilient computers, virus protection software, and RAID (Redundant Array of Inexpensive Disks) storage.

Security Functional Requirements

The Common Criteria v2.0 identifies four families of terms that are concerned with the protection against discovery and misuse of information.

1. **Anonymity** ensures that a user may use a resource or service without disclosing the user's identity. The requirements for anonymity provide protection of the user identity. Anonymity is not intended to protect the subject identity.
2. **Pseudonymity** ensures that a user may use a resource or service without disclosing its user identity, but can still be accountable for that use.
3. **Unlinkability** ensures that a user may make multiple uses of resources or services without others being able to link these uses together.
4. **Unobservability** ensures that a user may use a resource or service without others, especially third parties, being able to observe that the resource or service is being used.

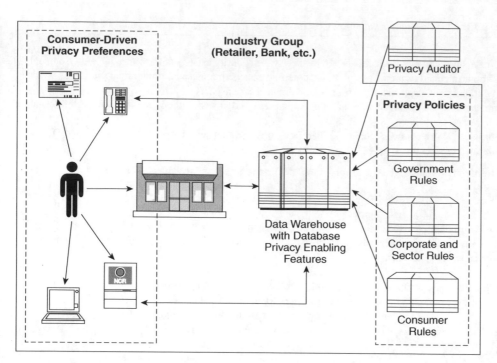

Fig. 2 Business environment for enabling consumer privacy.

The center of Fig. 2 focuses on the data warehouse as both the storage site for consumer personal data and the optimal position from which a company can ensure and enforce consumer privacy preferences.

Business Scenario for Enabling Privacy

Fig. 3 reveals a more thorough examination of the business interactions involved in this business scenario. The example assumes that privacy policies have been:

- Established by government, sector, and consumer rules
- Incorporated into database information structure, design, and metadata services
- Presented to the consumer at some point prior to the start of the interaction

Consumer Interactions

It is commonly accepted that an implied contract is established between a consumer and a transaction provider

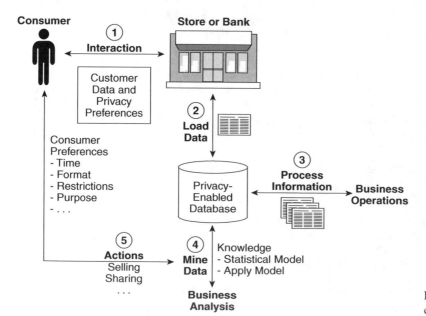

Fig. 3 Business interactions involved for enabling consumer privacy.

when that consumer voluntarily and knowingly engages in interactions that may ultimately result in transactions with that transaction provider. The contract implies agreement:

- By the consumer to supply personal data required for that transaction
- By the transaction provider to use, maintain, and store this data in some form, for some length of time, for the purpose of fulfilling the contract

Consumers are willing to share additional personal data (outside the required purpose) in relationships where the business is *trusted* and where there is an identified need or mutual benefit. The amount and type of data shared reflect explicit and implied consumer preferences, as well as business requirements.

Loading Data

Businesses need to examine the collection of consumer interactions and transactions in order to determine "what happened." This can be done from legal, business, monetary, fiscal, competitive, and other aspects that are necessary for legitimate business functions. Historically, typical storeowners and bankers "remembered" their customers' behaviors and preferences and modified ensuing interactions accordingly. Likewise, larger companies, aided by modern tools such as data warehouses, will be able to "remember" their customers' behaviors and preferences through the history of collected interactions and transactions that have been loaded into their databases.

Processing Information

Once businesses determine "what happened," the next logical step is to learn "why it happened." Numerous tools are available for businesses to use in processing interaction and transaction information. These tools help diagnose and visualize patterns in consumer behaviors and preferences that ultimately guide business operations toward greater efficiencies and optimize corporate behaviors to be consistent with company goals and objectives. Consumers are unlikely to object to such uses for their personal data as long as the insights gained for the business do not automatically lead to actions contrary to their privacy preferences.

Mining Data

After ascertaining "what happened" and "why it happened," businesses employ tools and techniques, such as data mining and analytical modeling, in attempts to predict "what will happen." Such analysis considers a business' memory of interactions and transactions, as well as possible additional information obtained from external sources. Businesses are responsible for ensuring that these external information sources are legal and accurate, and that they have the consent of affected consumers if personally identifiable data is involved. Resulting predictive models are applied to consumer records to forecast future behaviors, typically in the areas of consumer acquisition, retention, and growth. These models can also be used in determining business impact expectations affected by credibility, fraud, affluence, and other business conditions.

Taking Actions

The point at which businesses decide to take "actions" based on predictive modeling results is the final step in the business scenario for enabling consumer privacy. No actions should be taken that are in violation of the law or against the preferences of the consumer. Privacy considerations impact business behaviors and may provide either a threat of increased regulation leading to decreased ability to do business, or an opportunity to better understand and respond to consumer preferences, thereby strengthening the relationship.

In summary, it is crucial to examine the metamorphosis that data undergoes throughout business interactions, and where businesses control, store, and process consumer data. Ultimately, only companies decide how privacy will be executed within their businesses. No implementation will prevent businesses from taking actions contrary to the law or to consumer privacy preferences.

BUSINESS REQUIREMENTS FOR ENABLING PRIVACY

Legislative developments for protection of personal privacy range between rigorous government involvement and self-regulatory approaches. Voluntary guidelines establishing basic principles for data protection were adopted in 1980 by member nations of the Organization for Economic Cooperation and Development (OECD).[5] These guidelines encourage adoption of legislation and practices recognizing the rights of individual citizens with respect to personally identifiable data gathered about them, and defining parameters for what constitutes personally identifiable data.

A great deal of thought has already gone into consolidating privacy provisions specified in the OECD guidelines with the "key elements" of the Online Privacy Alliance[6] and the Articles of the EU Directive[1,2] in order to generate a comprehensive set of privacy requirements. This entry briefly summarizes six proposed privacy requirements and explicitly adds two more related

Data –
Denial

requirements, which, when applied to system architectures, help in determining the impacts of privacy interventions on each system.

1. *Notice*. Companies should be able to provide easily understood notice to their customers that personal data will be collected, which data will be collected, and how data will be used and disclosed. Notification should include the identities of the data collector and other intended recipients of the data, as well as information about "logic involved in automated processing."[1,2]

2. *Choice/Consent*. Companies should be able to provide their customers with suitable choices to opt-in or opt-out (Opt-in: choosing to participate. Opt-out: choosing not to participate.) of specific personal data items for collection, use, and disclosure, consistent with the jurisdictions and requirements the industry environment in which they do business.

3. *Access*. Companies should be able to provide assurance to their customers that the personal data they collect, use, and disclose is accurate and up to date. Accessibility includes the means for individuals to review and correct inaccurate or incomplete personal data, as well as the right to erase or "block" access to data not collected in accordance with the rules of local legislation.

4. *Security*. Companies should be able to provide assurance to their customers that the personal data they collect, use, and disclose is secure against loss, and against unauthorized access, destruction, alteration, use, or disclosure.

5. *Limitation*. Companies should be able to provide assurance to their customers that the collection and use of personal data will be limited to explicit, specified, and legitimate purposes, and that the data will be kept in identifiable form for no longer than necessary to accomplish original purposes.

6. *Accountability*. Companies should be able to establish procedures for their customers to seek resolution or redress for possible violations of stated privacy principles and practices. Accountability includes support for enforcement of existing legal and regulatory remedies (country specific) and notification to privacy authorities in each country of intent to collect personal data relating to their subjects.

7. *Traceability*. Companies should be able to provide assurance to regulators that all interactions and processing will be traceable and logged in such a way as to allow for internal assessments, as well as assessments by third parties, that demonstrate customer compliance with privacy policies. This is particularly important for those customers desiring compliance with Safe Harbor (U.S. Safe Harbor proposals are designed to balance the privacy concerns of EU

countries with the capabilities of U.S. companies to meet privacy requirements for doing business with citizens of EU countries.) proposals.

8. *Anonymity/Pseudonymity*. Companies should be able to provide assurance to their customers that personal data can be maintained in a state of either anonymity or pseudonymity, as elected by the individual, such that the data cannot be used later to target the individual.

Mapping Requirements to Architectural Components

The business environment and business scenario, explored previously in Figs. 2 and 3, depict the relationship between consumers and companies. When viewed architecturally, three components describe the primary areas impacted by enabling consumer privacy:

1. *Privacy presentation* serves as a "window" into consumer interactions and covers consumer, administrative, and operational devices as well as browsers.
2. *Business logic for enabling privacy* covers business interaction activities, transactions, translations, analysis, and management.
3. *Privacy data* covers query, look-up, and other data management activities for data warehouses, as well as for intermediate data stores, either within applications or stored in smaller databases.

The eight privacy business requirements discussed earlier impact these three architectural components as shown by the chart in Table 3. The Xs in the chart indicate which requirements for enabling consumer privacy must be met for each architectural component. For example, the requirement for notice must be implemented for both privacy presentation and business logic components, but not for the privacy data component. As stated previously,

Table 3 Mapping business requirements for enabling consumer privacy to architectural components.

	Privacy presentation	Business logic for enabling privacy	Privacy data
Notice	X	X	
Choice	X	X	X
Access	X	X	X
Security	X	X	X
Limitation		X	X
Accountability		X	
Traceability	X	X	X
Anonymity		X	X

security is required for any solution that enables consumer privacy; therefore, security considerations must be implemented for each architectural component.

Architecture Model for Enabling Consumer Privacy

Mapping business requirements to architectural components ensures that implementations are guided primarily by business considerations prior to evaluating technical options for those implementations. The architecture model in Fig. 4 illustrates this mapping graphically.

The model identifies several different types of users who can interact with a customer's business system, predictably with different types of interfaces, through the privacy presentation component. They include consumers, operators and administrators, and privacy auditors. Users can also be applications and agents operating on behalf of human beings. The model also indicates the various sources for privacy rules impacting the business logic component, that is, government, industry/sector, and consumer. It also illustrates how requirements for security envelop all business processes that are impacted for enabling consumer privacy.

The model shows that both privacy presentation and business logic components will need to contain sub-components that address requirements for notice, choice/consent (which involves data collection), and access (which may or may not involve data correction). It reveals that the requirements for time and use limitations, as well as anonymity/pseudonymity, will need to have sub-components contained in both business logic and privacy data components.

The model further represents that all three architectural components will need to contain sub-components dealing with requirements for traceability, which will likely be required to support requirements for accountability procedures defined by the business.

During interactions, and in addition to sending privacy policy notification, companies should be able to allow consumers to specify:

- Whether or not they can be tracked for purposes beyond the contracted business agreement
- What data they are willing to share beyond that which is required for the contracted business agreement
- Under what circumstances they will share data (loyalty programs) beyond that which is required for the contracted business agreement
- What data, if any, they are willing to have retained or sold

During business operations, companies should be able to allow:

- Consumers to examine their personal data
- Consumers to correct erroneous data
- Consumers to interact anonymously
- Regulators to examine company compliance with protecting personal data

During analysis, companies should be able to comply with:

- Regulations for retention periods
- Regulations for authorized use
- Anonymization rules
- Consumer rules for retaining or selling data

Popular thinking deems that the best place to control privacy is at the point of access; however, the authors maintain that the best place to control privacy is within the data warehouse where the rules for using personally identifiable information can be strictly enforced.

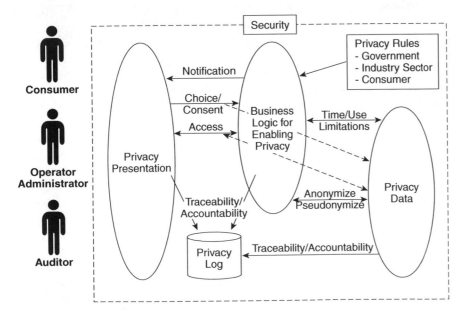

Fig. 4 Architecture model for enabling consumer privacy.

Additional details on the functions required for enabling consumer privacy, and how they map to the architecture model just described, is the focus of the next entry section.

THE TECHNICAL PROBLEM

The technical problem of enabling consumer privacy is complicated by customer investments in current technologies, rapid business environmental changes, emerging technologies, and evolving standards. The following technical problem statement captures these concerns:

Companies need technologies and services that sustain existing and emerging privacy requirements, and that offer flexibility for changes in privacy rules, scalability for growth, and acceptable changes in performance, reliability, availability, and manageability.

This section examines the problem of enabling privacy from various technical perspectives. The business requirements that were revealed during investigation of the business problem are further scrutinized to identify the functions, processes, and technologies necessary to meet the requirements. These business requirements, along with the business environment, influence technology decisions that help formulate the technical requirements impacting the architecture.

Functions Required for Enabling Privacy

Table 4 describes functions, along with the types of data, necessary to implement each business requirement for enabling privacy. Current and emerging technologies that apply to these functions are identified, and those that are advocated for this solution are underlined.

Technical Perspectives for Enabling Privacy

Technical perspectives depend on the focus of business objectives and other qualitative attributes, such as function or performance. Different attributes abstract specific details from the business environment with respect to different criteria, thus generating the different system perspectives. Each perspective can independently define the meanings for components, interrelationships, and guidelines, but resulting system perspectives are not independent.

Recognizing the fact that enabling consumer privacy requires changes to existing architectures and not entirely new architectures, each of the technical perspectives discussed below addresses only those specific aspects that must be considered when applying changes to a system's architecture that enable it for consumer privacy. The next four subsections examine functional, performance, availability/reliability, and OA&M (Operations, Administration, and Management) perspectives.

Functional perspective

The functional perspective exhibits architectural views of processes, data flows, communications, and presentation for each of the components identified in the architecture model. The functions exhibited within the architecture components comprise the architecture building blocks for enabling privacy.

Privacy presentation component

Fig. 5 captures the functions necessary within the privacy presentation component to support the business requirements for enabling consumer privacy. Five functional architecture building blocks are defined.

The left-most, vertically oriented building block within the privacy presentation component in Fig. 5 highlights the authentication and authorization functions necessary to fulfill the security requirements. The building block at the bottom of the figure highlights functions for tracking activities performed on, or with, personal data and privacy preferences that are necessary to fulfill the traceability and accountability requirements. The three remaining building blocks highlight the functions necessary to fulfill the privacy requirements for privacy policy notification, choice/consent, and access of personal data and privacy preferences.

The following describes the flow of data through the privacy presentation component. An initial communication occurs between some type of "user" (human, agent, or other application) and the appropriate "user" interface to an implementation of the privacy presentation component. The user may or may not have been previously notified regarding the privacy policy through various mechanisms, including hard-copy mail, brochure, electronic mail, HTTP, and others. Once the user is authenticated and authorized to operate within this component, all activities that "get," "move," or "use" personal data (including privacy preferences) are logged and monitored.

The privacy presentation component executes functions that send and receive personal data and privacy preferences between "users" and the component implementing business logic for enabling privacy. It also executes functions that allow these "users" to review and correct personal data and privacy preferences. Such review and correction may occur dynamically in the future; however, it is more likely that, for the present, these functions will be implemented through some type of paper-based, report-and-update mechanism.

For automated systems, privacy preferences can be specified periodically or maintained every time a consumer conducts business. For the latter case, programmable Web agents may be appropriate mechanisms to ease the overhead of specifying and maintaining privacy preferences. The recommended standards for communication among privacy presentation functions are HTTP and P3P

Table 4 Functions required for enabling privacy.

	Functions necessary	Types of data needed	Technologies
Notice	• Communicate privacy policy • Include explanations for any "automated processing" • Data usage tracing facility (to track the use of data within the IT system end-to-end)	• Company privacy policy	• Paper-based and Web-based devices and protocols • Specific devices, kiosks • Scripts • Metadata repository (documenting the use of privacyenabled data)
Choice/consent	• Identify specific data elements that must be displayed, which elements can be changed, and by whom • Present personal preference choice options/current settings • Make and change personal preference settings • Negotiate (option) personal preference settings • Commit/acknowledge personal preference setting changes	• Personal preference choice options • Personal preference current settings • Company privacy policy rules • Privacy metadata • Negotiation rules	• Paper-based and Web-based devices and protocols • Specific devices, kiosks • For interactions involving data warehouse (DW) then metadata standard for privacy is MDIS • For interactions not involving DW, then metadata standard for privacy is P3P • Data collection/update MUI (multimedia user interface) • Scripts • DB access

Access	• Identify specific data elements that must be displayed, which elements can be changed, and by whom
	• For user-initiated requests:
	  — Authenticate user
	  — Request access to view personal data
	  — Respond to access request
	• For business-initiated requests:
	  — Present current personal preference settings
	  — Request update to settings
	• Negotiate (option) or change personal preference settings
	• Delete all instances of specific and "allowable" elements
	• Commit and acknowledge personal preference setting changes
		• Personal preference current settings
		• Company privacy policy rules
		• Negotiation rules
			• Web-based devices, protocols, verification mechs (VeriSign)
			• Specific devices, kiosks
			• Call centers
			• Paper reports (OLAP/SQL)
			• For interactions involving DW, then metadata standard for privacy is MDIS
			• For interactions not involving DW, then metadata standard for privacy is P3P
			• Data collection/update MUI (multimedia user interface)
			• Scripts
			• DB access (create, delete, update, and delete)
			• Transaction integrity (to assure accuracy of database updates)

Limitation	• For "use" limitation (what company can do with personal data), enforce use preferences	• Company privacy policy rules	• Application logic assuring "legitimate purposes" are carried out

(Continued)

Table 4 Functions required for enabling privacy. (*Continued*)

	Functions necessary	Types of data needed	Technologies
	• For "retention" limitation (how long company can use personal data, may not be known), enforce retention preferences	• Personal preference current settings • Additional collected data	• Business processes handling manual and automated intervention for opting out of automated processing • For interactions involving DW, then "database views" control time/use limits • For interactions not involving DW, then stored procedures control time/use limits • One has potential to develop "privacy state information" to help enforce dynamic temporal changes • Possible application development technology that assures new applications adhere to rules • Possible application execution environment logic to assure legitimate use
Accountability	• For controller or processor of personal data (also requires traceability): — Interrogate systems and make corrections — Non-repudiation capability	• Company privacy policy rules • Personal preference current settings • Controller processor identification • Privacy log repository	• Business procedures • Security technologies (for non-repudiation and logging)
Traceability	• Architecture for managing traceability and verifying requirements • Log event occurrences, alarms, exceptions, etc. • UI to look at logs and reconcile between different data services • Generate reports • "Tracking facility" for privacy adherence/compliance • Enforce logging function and protect logged data • Establish logging of configuration controls	• Company privacy policy rules • Personal preference current settings • Privacy log repository	• Many, depending on chosen architecture for enabling traceability • Application execution environment logging (pre- and post-call logging)
Anonymity/ pseudonymity	• Anonymity (as it applies to usage, takes identifiers away; is NOT reversible) — Block, strip, or screen out personally identifiable data • Pseudonymity (assigns non-identifiable name to collection of data; is reversible) — Generate pseudonyms with appropriate controls	• Personal preference settings on usage • Personal preference settings on retention	• For interactions involving DW, then "database views" handle anonymity • For interactions not involving DW, then stored procedures handle anonymity • Pseudonym generators

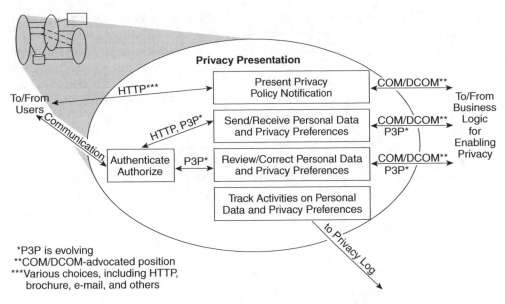

Fig. 5 Functions within privacy presentation component for enabling consumer privacy.

(Web-based client position for P3P, personal privacy protection, is the most evolved; however, the types and formats for defined privacy data elements can be extended to other operating environments).

An advocated position for communicating between privacy presentation functions and the functions for implementing business logic enabling privacy are Microsoft's messaging services (i.e., MSMQ), Microsoft's object request broker architecture (i.e., COM/DCOM), or Web-based services (i.e., HTTP, P3P). Industry-specific interfaces will apply on top of COM/DCOM (i.e., DNAfs) for financial.

Business logic for enabling privacy component

Fig. 6 captures the functions necessary within the business logic component to support the business requirements for enabling consumer privacy. Four functional architecture building blocks are defined. The first three building blocks within the business logic component in Fig. 6 highlight the functions necessary to fulfill the privacy requirements for privacy policy notification, choice/consent, and access of personal data and privacy preferences. Specifically, the functions maintain the privacy policy and enforce privacy rules for the business. The building block at the bottom of

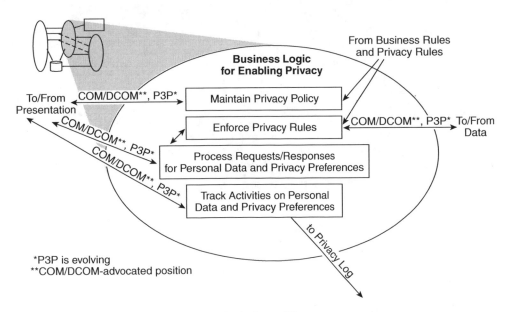

Fig. 6 Functions within business logic for enabling consumer privacy component.

Data –
Denial

the figure highlights functions for tracking activities performed on, or with, personal data and privacy preferences necessary to fulfill the traceability and accountability requirements.

The following describes the flow of data through the business logic component for enabling privacy. All activities that "get," "move," or "use" personal data (including privacy preferences) are logged and monitored.

The business logic component executes functions that process requests and responses regarding personal data and privacy preferences between the privacy presentation and privacy data components. As part of processing these requests and responses, the business logic component also executes functions that enforce privacy rules derived from the business rules and sources for government, industry/sector, and consumer privacy rules.

Where business logic functions are implemented within applications, there are no recommended standards for communication among these business logic functions. Business policies governing operational and analytical applications will likely dictate how information is communicated within these automated systems.

An *advocated* position for communicating between the functions for implementing business logic enabling privacy and privacy data functions are Microsoft's object request broker architecture (i.e., COM/DCOM) or Web-based services (i.e., P3P). The P3P session information passed across these component interfaces is different from that passed across for the privacy presentation component. Those customers with preexisting infrastructures (e.g., proprietary, CORBA, messaging, DB2) for data communication will likely maintain their infrastructures.

Privacy data component

Fig. 7 captures the functions necessary within the privacy data component to support the business requirements for enabling consumer privacy. Four functional architecture building blocks are defined.

The left-most, vertically oriented building block within the privacy data component in Fig. 7 highlights the data integrity protection and data access control functions necessary to fulfill security requirements. The building block at the bottom of the figure highlights functions for tracking activities performed on, or with, personal data and privacy preferences that are necessary to fulfill the traceability and accountability requirements. The two remaining building blocks highlight the functions necessary to fulfill privacy requirements for choice/consent and access of personal data and privacy preferences, time/use limitations, and anonymity/pseudonymity.

The following describes the flow of data through the privacy data component. All activities that "get," "move," or "use" personal data (including privacy preferences) are logged and monitored. The privacy data component executes functions that verify the integrity and access permissions for data requests received from the business logic component.

The privacy data component also executes functions that filter the data according to previously established privacy preferences prior to accessing personal data or responding back to the business logic component. Furthermore, the privacy data component executes functions providing privacy metadata services for personal data stored either in databases or within specific applications.

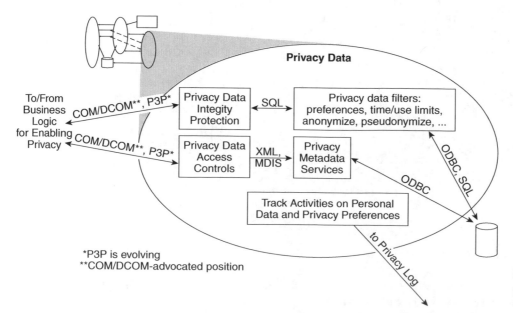

*P3P is evolving
**COM/DCOM-advocated position

Fig. 7 Functions within the privacy data component for enabling consumer privacy.

Where privacy data functions are implemented within non-database applications, there are no recommended standards for communication among these privacy data functions. Business policies governing operational and analytical applications will likely dictate how information is communicated within these automated systems. Where privacy data functions are implemented within database system applications, the recommended standards for communication among functions are SQL, XML, MDIS, and ODBC, as well as OLE/DB and OLE/DBO.

Performance perspective

The performance perspective addresses performance implications to the architecture as a result of enabling consumer privacy. As with any system, performance is balanced against features and functions. A trade-off is established between required features and functions, and acceptable performance.

Within the privacy presentation component depicted in Fig. 6, the functions most likely to affect performance are those implementing requirements for choice/consent and access (whether real-time or delayed), traceability (depending on the level of logging), and security. The functions implementing notice are expected to affect performance to a lesser degree.

Within the business logic component depicted in Fig. 7, the functions most likely to affect performance are those implementing requirements for choice/consent and access (related to enforcement of the privacy rules), and traceability. Functions implementing maintenance of the privacy rules are expected to affect performance to a lesser degree.

Within the privacy data component depicted in Fig. 7, the functions most likely to affect performance are those implementing requirements for access, time/use limitations, traceability, and security. Performance thus depends on where and how personal data is stored and maintained. For implementations using teradata data warehouses, performance is minimally affected because requirements for enabling consumer privacy are accommodated by the existing data warehouse design. Other data warehouses, intermediate data stores, and types of databases, as well as other types of applications maintaining personal data, will likely have performance degradations due to the additional functions imposed by privacy requirements.

There are also likely to be performance implications based on implementation choices for communications between the three main architectural components. The emerging World Wide Web Consortium (W3C) standard for P3P may have performance implications on server interactions; however, despite its current popularity and because this standard is evolving, these implications are unknown.

Availability/reliability perspective

The availability/reliability perspective is concerned with impacts to the availability and reliability of solutions based on the architecture resulting from enabling for consumer privacy. Availability focuses on the time between system failures. Reliability focuses on the frequency with which a system fails. As with any system, acceptable levels of availability and reliability are determined by the requirements for the industry's operating environment.

The question for each industry to ask itself is whether or not privacy is such an integral part of the system that the whole system is down when privacy-related elements, such as privacy log connections, are unavailable. Trade-offs will be made by each business' policies, based on the risk imposed by doing business when these privacy elements are unavailable. Given the current state of emerging personal privacy legislation worldwide, it is likely that most industries will need to specify high availability and reliability of all privacy-related elements. Obviously, the more complicated the rules are, the more complicated enforcement will be.

OA&M perspective

The OA&M perspective addresses impacts to the operation, administration, and management of solutions based on the architecture as a result of enabling for consumer privacy. As with any system, OA&M requirements are determined by the business' policies and operating environment. Only those aspects of OA&M systems impacted by privacy are of concern to the architecture.

OA&M systems are comprised of components implementing instrumentation, infrastructure, and management applications. Because management infrastructure exists wholly to support management functions, there are no expected impacts to this component arising from privacy requirements. Primary impact derives from any additional instrumentation required as a result of enabling privacy, as well as new management applications that may be created to handle the new instrumentation data.

Some of the events that can be instrumented for privacy include access to personal/sensitive data, frequency of access to personal/sensitive data elements, logging of critical events, backup and recovery of personal/sensitive data, and performance monitoring. Threshold values will need to be established for the number of hits on personal data items, the number of violations, and the number and types of alerts. Alerts can be instituted for attempts to access personal data, as well as for unexpected and unauthorized accesses.

For implementations using some form of database system to store and maintain personal data, existing data management system rules will need to be augmented with privacy-related utilities and management applications for monitoring privacy-related events. Authorized system and

Data –
Denial

database administrators must be aware of, and apply, legal issues and rules to the creation of additional rules and views required for enabling privacy. These authorized users must also have exclusive access to the privacy log for security reasons.

SUMMARY

This entry is intended as a guide as companies begin to launch activities that migrate their products and services toward including capabilities enabling consumer security and privacy within data warehouse environments. The expectation is that companies will examine their industry environments and leverage the content of this entry addressing security and privacy concerns as they evolve in the industry architectures. Recommendations to modify this entry are anticipated as a matter of course as better and more accurate information is gathered.

REFERENCES

1. Directive 95/46/EC of the European Parliament and of the Council, October 24, 1995.
2. Directive 97/66/EC of the European Parliament and of the Council, December 15, 1997.
3. Merriam Webster Collegiate Edition, 1998.
4. Privacy Class of Common Criteria v2.0 (CC2.0 part 2) Security Functional Requirements (ISO/IEC 15408).
5. OECD Guidelines on the Protection of Privacy and Transborder Flows of Personal Data, September 23, 1980, http://www.oecd.org/dsti/sti/secur/prod/PRIV-EN.htm.
6. FTC Releases Report on Consumers' Online Privacy, Report to Congress on Privacy Online, June 4, 1998, http://www.ftc.gov/opa/9806/privacy2.htm.

Database Integrity

William Hugh Murray, CISSP
Executive Consultant, TruSecure Corporation, New Canaan, Connecticut, U.S.A.

Abstract
This entry discusses the concept of database integrity. It contrasts this concept to those of data integrity and
database management system integrity. The purpose of the discussion is to arrive at a set of recommendations for the owners and operators of such databases on how to preserve that integrity.

CONCEPTS AND DESCRIPTIONS

This section sets forth some definitions and concepts that describe and bound the issue of database integrity.

Integrity

Integrity is the property of being whole, complete, and unimpaired; free from interference or contamination; unbroken; in agreement with requirements or expectations.

Data can be said to have integrity when it is internally consistent (e.g., the books are in balance) and when it describes what it intends (e.g., the books accurately reflect the performance and condition of the business). A system can be said to have integrity when it performs according to a complete specification most of the time, fails in a predictable manner, presents sufficient evidence of its failure to permit timely and effective corrective action, and permits orderly recovery.

Database

For purposes of this discussion, a database can be defined as a monolithic collection of related or interdependent data elements. Alternatively, it is a monolithic collection of information represented in coded data elements and specific relationships between those data elements. A database is usually intended to be shared across users, uses, or applications.

The abstraction of database is relatively novel, no older than the modern computer. Until the appearance of database management software for the microcomputer, perhaps a decade ago, it was esoteric. Analogous collections of data, such as the books of account for a business, existed before the computer. The term can properly be applied to most of the data that is usually recorded on such media as ledger cards or 3 × 5 cards. However, it is usually reserved for the most formal, rigorous, and systematic of such collections.

Information in a database can be explicitly represented in the form of coded data elements; employee name is a common example. However, there is other information in the database in the form of associations, both explicit and implicit, between the data elements.

Relationships are special kinds of associations between the data elements. For example, the various fields in an employee database record are related logically in much the same way as they are related on a piece of paper. The meaning and identity of each field is determined, in part, by this context. This information is at least as important as that in the data elements themselves.

The relationships can be expressed in the data itself (relational), in the arrangement or order of the elements within the database (structured), or in metadata, data about the data, that explicitly describes or encodes the relationships (e.g., indexed or object oriented). While databases can be characterized by how the relationships are primarily expressed, in practice, all databases use a combination of these mechanisms. For example, in those databases known as relational, some relationships are expressed in the structure (i.e., tables and views), some in the data (i.e., references to other tables), and some in metadata (the names of the columns).

Database Integrity

A database can be said to have integrity when it preserves the information in the data, that is, when both the data and the relationships are maintained. Database integrity is about the integrity of the records. The integrity of the database is separate from, and can be contrasted to, that of the data, on the one hand, and of the database management system on the other.

Database Management System

For our purposes, a database management system is a generalized, abstract, and automated mechanism for creating, maintaining, storing, preserving, and presenting a database to, and on behalf of, applications.

Encyclopedia of Information Assurance DOI: 10.1081/E-EIA-120046724
Copyright © 2011 by Taylor & Francis. All rights reserved.

Data –
Denial

Database managers are often characterized by the name of the mechanism on which they primarily rely to describe the relationships among the data elements. Thus, database managers in which the relationship between two data elements is normally implied in the data itself, for example, the content of a data element (two employee records have the same department number), or the ordering of the data (employee A precedes B in the sort order of the name field) can be called *relational database managers*. Those in which the relationship is implied by how the two elements are physically stored, (for example, all employees in the same department are stored together, or employee A is always stored before B) can be referred to as *structured database managers*.

Relational Integrity

Relational integrity is the aspect of database integrity that deals with the preservation of the special relationships between the data elements.

Referential integrity is an example and a special case of relational integrity. A reference is a relationship in which a value in one record points to another record, usually of another record type. For our purposes, it is an example and illustration of what it might mean to say that a database has integrity to the extent that relationships are preserved.

Consider the case of an employee record with a department number in it that refers to a department record. If the department number in the employee record is N, then referential integrity requires that there be a department record for department N. It would prohibit the creation of an employee record with a department number for which there was no corresponding department record, the deletion of department record N as long as any employee record pointed to it, and more than one department record N for the employee record to point to.

It should be noted that this kind of integrity is optional. That is, the condition could exist, coincidentally or accidentally, without any declaration, commitment, or enforcement. Likewise, it can be implemented and enforced either by using applications or the database management system. As a rule, it is preferable to have it implemented in the database management system so that the mechanism can be shared across applications and so that one application need not rely on another.

METHODS

This section discusses some of the methods for implementing database managers and preserving the integrity of the database.

Localization

By definition, a database is a monolith. That is, all of its elements and all of its relationships are essential to its identity. If any element or relationship is lost or broken, then the identity and the integrity are destroyed. Of course, this is separate from the physical database manager, which might contain two or more independent databases. However, all other things being equal, keeping the elements of the database together helps preserve its integrity. Therefore, most database managers strive to keep the database together.

Single Owning Process

An important form of localization is the single owning process. Because a database is a monolith, there must be a single process that can see all of it, manage it, and have responsibility for its integrity. This owning process is usually the database manager. An implication is that a database manager is usually a single process.

Redundancy

To make the database more reliable than the media and devices on which it is stored, most database managers apply some kind of redundant data. The data is recorded in more than the minimum number of bits otherwise required to express it.

Dynamic Error Detection and Correction

Often, redundancy takes the form of error detection and correction codes. The data is recorded in codes that make the alteration of a bit obvious and its timely and automatic correction possible. One such code is parity, in which an additional bit is added to each frame of 7 or 8 bits to make the frame conform to some arbitrary rule such as odd or even. A variance from the rule signals the alteration of a bit. Some codes are so powerful as to permit the automatic detection and correction of multiple bit errors. These codes can be implemented in both the storage device (i.e., below the line) or in the database manager (above the line between software and hardware-only mechanisms).

Duplication

Redundancy can be carried as far as one or more complete copies of the database or its elements. Such copies can be either inside or outside the database manager. Because relationships are usually best known to the database manager, they are best preserved using the duplication facilities that are provided by it.

Mirroring

One form of duplication is mirroring, in which two synchronized copies of the data are maintained. Mirroring is done internal to a mechanism; the copy is not visible from outside. For example, a file manager can mirror files. It will apply changes to both copies, satisfy requests from either, but conceal the existence of the second copy to processes outside itself. Mirroring can be done on the same device or on a different one. When done on a single device, mirroring protects against a media failure or a limited failure of the device (e.g., a bad track). When done across devices, it protects against a general device failure.

Backup

Backup copies of the database are made independent of the database manager. Among other losses, these copies are specifically intended to protect against damage that might occur to the data if the manager should fail or become corrupt.

Such copies can be prepared automatically by the database manager, or by using utilities or other program processes that are independent of the mechanism itself. Of course, although intended to protect against database manager failures, the use of an independent backup system may itself be a threat to the integrity of the database. It is difficult for an independent system to know and enforce the rules that the database manager itself enforces.

Checkpoints and Journals

A checkpoint is a special case of a backup copy. It is taken at a particular point in time. For example, the initial state of the database, even if empty, is a checkpoint. Checkpoints are used in conjunction with a journal or log of all update activity subsequent to the checkpoint to reconstruct the database. This mechanism preserves both integrity and currency.

Reconstruction

Such secondary copies can be employed to reconstruct the database, even from massive failures. However, this means that, at least under some circumstances, the integrity of the database will depend on the integrity of these copies.

Compartmentation

To compartmentalize is to place things into segregated compartments. The intent is to contain the effects of what happens in one compartment in such a way as to limit the impact on other compartments. For example, one might run multiple small database managers, in preference to a single large one, so as to limit the impact of a failure.

Segregation and Independence

Database management systems often implement segregation and independence of sub-processes to preserve integrity. For example, they may isolate the process that does an update from that which checks to see that it was done correctly and from the one that attempts corrective action. The purpose is to minimize the chances that the same fault will affect all three.

Encapsulation

The database manager can be viewed as a package, container, or capsule, one role of which is to protect the database from any outside interference or contamination. Encapsulation can be either physical or logical. For a database manager, physical encapsulation might be provided by placing it in a separate computer. Logical encapsulation might be provided by placing it in an isolated and protected process within an environment provided by a shared computer and its operating system. Logical encapsulation may also be provided, in part, and in static conditions, by the use of secret codes.

Most database management systems provide some encapsulation of the databases they contain. Object-oriented database management systems do so, by definition, explicitly and globally. Increasingly, one sees database managers themselves being encapsulated in their own hardware.

Hiding

Capsules hide or conceal their contents so that they cannot be seen or addressed from the outside. While this does not make the database safer from destruction, it does protect it from unauthorized disclosure and from malicious, but covert, change. Hiding can be implemented in many ways; the most common are by means of process-to-process isolation, data typing and type managers, and by the use of secret codes.

Binding

Binding is used to resolve and fix, for example, a data characteristic or reference, so as to resist later change. In computer science, one speaks of early and late binding. For example, in some programming, symbolic names are bound, that is, resolved so as to resist later change at compile time, while in others the same characteristic may not be bound until execution time.

Many structured database management systems can bind relationships in the database at programming time or at load time. This tends to improve both the integrity and performance at the expense of loss of flexibility and increased maintenance cost. Relational database managers also employ binding of table existence at creation time.

Binding applies only within the environment in which it takes place. If data or databases are removed from the database manager, then characteristics are no longer bound or reliable.

Atomic Update

Atomic update means that any change to the database takes place completely or not at all. There are no partial updates. This includes both data elements and relationships. Most database managers implement this by maintaining the

Data – Denial

ability to "roll back" any partial updates that they are unable to complete.

Locking

One potential threat to the integrity of a database results from concurrent use by two or more processes. For example, where two users make changes to a database, there is some potential that the second change will overwrite the first. Database management systems are expected to provide mechanisms, such as locking, that resist such problems.

Locking is a mechanism that database managers employ to ensure that partially updated elements and relationships are not used. It involves marking the element as "in use" or "asking for the lock" for all elements involved in an update. The mechanism will not permit a second use of an element that is in use and will not begin an update until it can obtain the locks for all elements involved. However, locking is ordinarily a logical, rather than physical, mechanism. It is usually just a bit or flag that is set by locking or unlocking.

Locking may come in several levels of transparency and granularity. Ideally, locking would be automatic and transparent to all users or using processes. However, this might have unnecessary performance impact. For example, for maximum transparency, a database management system might restrict access from application B to any data that A is looking at, on the assumption that A might elect to update it. Thus, B will see a performance penalty even if he does not care about potential updates.

Performance might also require that B's access be limited to only the smallest element that A might update. B should not be restricted from an entire table simply because A is interested in a single row of the table. Thus, maximum performance requires that both A and B declare their intent.

Access Control

Access control is a mechanism provided by the database management system to enable the owners and managers of the database to control which users or using processes can alter the database, its elements, or its relationships. These controls are most likely to be included in database management systems intended for use by multiple users. It is an integrity mechanism in that it reduces the size of the population that can alter the database to the intended population. It can also be used to enforce dual controls intended to resist errors and malice.

Privileged Controls

Most database management systems, particularly those that provide access controls, provide what can be referred to as privileged controls. These controls are intended for use by the managers of the system. They are intended for use to exercise ultimate control, particularly to remedy

unusual situations. Two unusual situations are of particular interest. The first is to override the access controls. This capability may be necessary to avoid a deadlock situation. The second is the use of such privilege to repair the database itself. In the early days of structured databases, such controls were frequently used to "repair broken chains."

It should be noted that such privilege includes the ability to contaminate or interfere with the database.

Reconciliation

Reconciliation refers to an act or process that brings the database into harmony or consistency; that is, the act or process of checking the database against expectation and correcting for variances. Normally, database management systems perform this kind of checking on a routine, automatic, frequent, and repetitive, if not quite continuous, basis. For example, after making a WRITE request to another process (e.g., the file system), the database manager can make an immediate inspection to satisfy itself that the request completed correctly. The routine and automatic nature of this activity, among other things, distinguishes it from recovery. Another is that it relies almost exclusively on internal resources.

Recovery

Recovery is the integrity mechanism of last resort, the one that is used when the database is broken beyond the ability of any other mechanism to repair it. It is usually externally invoked and relies on external resources such as backup copies of the data. While it must bring the database back to a state of integrity, it may do so at the expense of currency or even lost data.

CONCLUSIONS

Database integrity is essential. If one cannot rely on the data, it is useless. Integrity is easier to preserve than to recreate. No single tool or mechanism is sufficient unto itself. Database management systems will employ a variety of tools, and owners and managers will compensate for the inherent limitations of the database managers by employing tools that are completely external to it.

At least four things are necessary to preserve the integrity of a database:

1. One must preserve both the data elements and the relationships among them.
2. One must understand and exploit the mechanisms provided by the database management systems.
3. One must not compromise any of these mechanisms, either in the way one uses them or external to them.
4. One must understand the limitations of the database management system and compensate for them.

A simple copy of the data elements may not preserve the information contained in the relationships. For example, if a structured database contains information about the relationships in the physical location of the data within the device, then a copy of the data can preserve the relationships only if it is on an identical device.

Because all database management systems employ a combination of mechanisms to implement relationships and because most of these mechanisms are concealed, management or operational procedures that bypass the database management system are suspect. On the other hand, if there are no measures taken to preserve integrity that are independent of the database management system, then a failure of the mechanism can destroy the database.

It should be noted that the most robust database managers so encapsulate the database that they cannot be bypassed. Any attempt to do so will result, at best, in the distortion of the database, and, at worst, in the destruction of the database and the database management system. Most of these systems will also provide one or more built-in mechanisms for creating external representations of the database.

One final issue is that of scale. Most databases are relatively small when compared to the systems and devices on which they reside. However, many of the most important databases are very large and span tens or even hundreds of devices. In such databases, information about relationships can span many devices. The integrity of the database requires the preservation of the devices and their relationship to each other.

On the other hand, it is common in these databases to create external copies by backing up the devices rather than the database or even the files. Such backups are device and device-field dependent. While they provide adequate protection against the failure of one or two devices, recovery from the destruction of the entire environment might require the complete replication of the environment. Timeliness may require that this be done in days or even hours. Thus, in exactly the databases in which it may be most urgent to have device-independent backups, it may be least likely to have them.

RECOMMENDATIONS

This section sets forth recommendations for preserving the integrity of databases. These include some recommendations for using the database management system and some for compensating for its limitations.

1. Choose a database manager whose characteristics, features, and properties are sufficiently robust for the intended application and environment. Consider the size of the database and its importance to the enterprise.
2. Use the database management system according to directions. Note and respect all limitations.
3. Place the database and its manager in a robust environment.
4. Provide adequate resources (e.g., mirror files, devices, and control units) as indicated by the application and environment.
5. Prefer monolithic databases for integrity. Use distributed database managers only to the extent justified by major differences in performance.
6. For integrity, prefer a one-to-one relationship between a database, a database management system, and a processor. Share only to the extent indicated by major economies of scale. Keep in mind that today's computer systems can be more readily scaled to their applications. Large-scale sharing no longer offers the economies that it used to.
7. Prefer relational and object-oriented databases for integrity. Prefer structured databases for performance.
8. Applications and users should check those behaviors of the database manager that they rely on.
9. Limit access to the database and to elements within it to the minimum number of known users and processes consistent with the application.
10. Apply access controls in such a way as to involve multiple people in sensitive updates to the database.
11. Involve multiple people in the use of privileged or potent controls.
12. Keep multiple backup copies and generations of the data, including checkpoints and journals of update activity.
13. Prefer device-independent backups, particularly for databases that span multiple devices.
14. For device independence, prefer to make backups with services provided by the database manager. Use independent mechanisms for performance.
15. Prefer to make backups with services provided by the database manager for preservation of relationships. Prefer backups made by other means for independence and to protect against failure in the mechanism.
16. To protect external copies of the database, involve multiple people in their custody.
17. Check integrity after recovery and before use. Remember that even normal use of a corrupt database may spread the damage and that using bad data may result in serious damage to the enterprise.

Defense in Depth: Network, Systems, and Applications Controls

Jeffrey Davis, CISSP
Senior Manager, Lucent Technologies, Morristown, New Jersey, U.S.A.

Abstract

Diversity in information security is a practice that can greatly improve the security of an organization's information assets. Using different techniques and controls can multiply the effectiveness of security controls in an increasingly diverse risk environment. Using overlapping controls can also provide redundancy that is important if a control should fail. Information technology security controls and response processes address different areas within an environment. These include network controls, operating system controls, and application level controls, as well as monitoring and responses to security events. Attention must also be paid to the coverage of the different controls, as the failure to provide protection for one piece of the application or service may lead to compromise of other areas. Providing adequate protection for all the pieces of an application will ensure its proper functioning and reduce the risk of its being compromised. It is also possible for one control to provide overlapping protection for other areas. Maximizing the overlapping protection and providing diversity within each one of these controls and processes are important to minimizing the risk of a security failure with regard to the information or services being protected. In addition, response and monitoring processes must also be able to address incidents and provide solutions in a timely manner. These controls and processes can also take advantage of diversity to reduce the risk of a single point of failure. Together, these controls and processes work to provide confidentiality, integrity, and availability of the information or service being secured.

NETWORK CONTROL DIVERSITY

Controls can be classified into two basic types: preventive and detective. Preventive network controls prevent or block malicious network traffic, and detective network controls monitor the network for suspicious or malicious traffic that may require a response. One major function of preventive network controls is to allow only traffic necessary for the service to function. One way this can be accomplished is by using a firewall with access rules to control the network traffic. A way to provide diversity in this control is to implement the restriction not only via the firewall but also via access control lists on the routers that route the traffic within the network. This provides protection if the firewall is compromised or is bypassed maliciously. It can also provide a backup if a mistake is made in configuring the firewall. A drawback to this practice is that it does introduce an administrative burden and can make troubleshooting more difficult, and it is necessary to administer network access in more than one place.

Another method of providing diversity in network controls is to use multiple firewalls from different vendors. Various vendors may use different methods of implementing the control. This can prevent a weakness in one vendor's firewall from being exploited to bypass the network control it is implementing. If required, this can also be used to provide some separation of duties. This can be accomplished by having two different groups responsible for the administration of each firewall. If a change is required, it will require actions from both groups to be implemented.

Another security control used on a network is a network intrusion detection system. This is a detective type of control that is used to monitor the network for malicious traffic. The traffic is compared to signatures of known network attacks, and when a match is detected an alert is raised and some action may be taken. In some cases, an automated action may be taken to adjust an existing network control, like a firewall or router, to block any further traffic from getting to the target system. Another action may be to reset any resulting connection between the source of the traffic and the destination. If an automated action is not taken, then an appropriate incident response process should be in place to react to the alert and determine if any action is required. This control can complement other controls making their effectiveness visible. As a detective control, it can also be used to determine when another control has failed. This could be indicated by the presence of traffic that should not be there, such as an outbound connection attempt from a server in a protected network zone.

Network intrusion detection can also be implemented in a diversified fashion by using different types of vendors who employ various methods of detecting malicious traffic. In addition, most implementations use a list of traffic signatures that are known to be malicious. This signature

Encyclopedia of Information Assurance DOI: 10.1081/E-EIA-120046538
Copyright © 2011 by Taylor & Francis. All rights reserved.

list will vary in correctness and completeness. The correctness of the list is important in that, if a signature is not correct, it may result in generating false detection of the traffic or it may miss some malicious traffic completely. Utilizing multiple solutions will provide some protection against this. Some network intrusion detection prevention systems will also use heuristics or other methods to guess if particular network traffic may be malicious in nature. These implementations are vendor specific, and utilizing more than one vendor can also provide more assurance that the traffic that is identified as being malicious is a true indication of a problem.

Another type of network control is a network intrusion prevention device. This is a combination of a preventive control and a detective control. This type of control not only looks for known malicious network traffic but can also prevent it from reaching the system it is intended to attack. This is especially useful for single packet attacks or attacks that do not require a complete TCP (transmission control protocol) handshake. This control is usually implemented as an inline device in the network. This means that all network traffic will flow through the device, and it can be configured to discard any traffic it considers malicious. These devices are similar to network intrusion devices in that they utilize a list of signatures of malicious traffic that is compared to the traffic flowing across the link they are monitoring. As with the network intrusion devices, it can be helpful to utilize multiple vendors in order to ensure the correctness of the signature list and any method of heuristics. In addition, because the device is usually implemented inline, it is important to consider redundancy in order to reduce the risk of an outage due to a single point of failure.

One other network control is the use of a host-based firewall. This is a firewall that is implemented directly on the system providing the application or service. This firewall limits connectivity to services on the system and can provide that protection if other network controls fail. One disadvantage of a host-based firewall is that it depends on the host to actually implement and control the rule set. If the host is compromised, then the firewall rules can be modified to bypass the controls, as has been demonstrated by a number of viruses. When the virus has infected a system, it has disabled the firewall controls to provide further access to the infected host or to allow the continued spread of the virus. Timely management of these firewalls is also important for them to be successful at mitigating attacks. To be effective in an enterprise setting, these firewalls should be centrally controlled. If they are centrally controlled, then the enterprise can react more quickly to new threats by adjusting the network access rules on the hosts to block malicious traffic. A host-based firewall can augment network controls and provide redundant control of network traffic.

One other important process in securing a system is running periodic vulnerability scans using a network vulnerability scanner. These are used to identify vulnerabilities that could be used to compromise a host or application. If it is necessary to secure a large enterprise, running a network vulnerability scan is one of the most effective ways of ensuring that the system has been kept up to date with patches. One way to increase this effectiveness is to use more then one scanner. Vulnerability scanners test for the presence of a vulnerability in different ways. Some will attempt to actually exploit the vulnerability, and others will simply determines that a vulnerability may exist by checking the version level in the software. Still others may just indicate the possibility that a system is vulnerable and might require further investigation to see if a vulnerability actually exists. The scanners will have to be periodically updated to reflect any new vulnerabilities that have been discovered. This is also where utilizing more then one scanner will be of benefit as some vendors may keep there software more current than others.

Another important tool for securing networks is the use of encryption technologies. Encryption is used to provide protection against eavesdropping by third parties by encrypting the traffic using an encryption algorithm. Encryption along with hashing algorithms can also be used to authenticate the traffic between two network connections. Two types of encryption algorithms are utilized to encrypt network traffic: symmetric and asymmetric. Symmetric algorithms use a shared key that is known to both parties to encrypt the traffic. They are much faster and require fewer computing resources than asymmetric algorithms. Algorithms of this type include the Advanced Encryption Standard (AES) and Triple-DES (formed from the Data Encryption Standard). An important factor in the implementation of symmetric encryption is the size of the shared keys that are being used. The size of this key determines the key space or range of values that the key can have. The size of the key space is an important factor in determining the strength of the implementation of an encryption system. One type of attack, called a brute force attack, attempts to decrypt the encrypted data by trying every possible key value in the key space. Larger key sizes are used to provide more protection against these attacks. It is important that the key space be of sufficient size so the amount of time and resources required to attempt all of the keys in the key space is large enough to make it impractical to try.

The second type of encryption algorithms is asymmetric, also known as public/private key encryption. These types of algorithms use two related keys. One key is private and must be kept secret, and the second key is public and can be distributed freely. Any data encrypted with one of the keys can only be decrypted using the other related key. Examples of these types of algorithms include RSA (named for its developers, R. L. Rivest, A. Shimir, and L. Adleman), Diffie–Hellman, and ElGamal. Asymmetric algorithms generally are used to provide key exchange and authentication functions for protocols such as Internet Protocol Security (IPSec) and Secure Sockets Layer (SSL). When an asymmetric algorithm has been used to pass a

Data – Denial

shared or session key between the connecting parties, then a more efficient symmetric algorithm can be used to encrypt the traffic. In addition to encrypting the data being passed between two parties, encryption can also be used to provide authentication between them. This is important to prevent a man-in-the-middle attack. A man-in-the-middle attack occurs when a third party is able to intercept traffic between two parties and is able to read or modify the traffic without the knowledge of either communicating party. Protection against this attack requires the ability to verify the identity of the source of the traffic and the ability to verify that it has not been modified. This is done by using encryption in combination with hashing algorithms.

Some commonly used algorithms include Message Digest 5 (MD5) and Secure Hashing Algorithm Version 1 (SHA1). These hashing algorithms take data as an input and output a message digest that by design of the hashing algorithm is unique for that particular input. This output can then be encrypted using the private key of a public/private key algorithm to form a digital signature. This allows the verification of the source of the data and that it has not been modified while in transit. Encryption controls and hashing algorithms have been found to have a number of weaknesses. One problem that has occurred in the past is the discovery of a mathematical weakness in an algorithm that is being utilized. One example of this is the Message Digest 2 (MD2) hashing algorithm. This algorithm was shown to be vulnerable to mathematical attacks that could allow two different inputs to produce the same hash result. When this weakness was discovered, the hashing algorithm could no longer be considered a secure one. To protect against a possible mathematical weakness in a specific algorithm, various algorithms can be utilized in different parts of the network. Client-to-Web network communications using SSL can use one algorithm, and server-to-server IPSec traffic can use a different one. Another technique is to encrypt the traffic first using an encryption system employing one algorithm and then encrypt the encrypted traffic again using a different algorithm. This technique is referred to as super-encryption. One example of super-encryption is using SSL over an IPSec virtual private network (VPN). The network traffic is first encrypted by the SSL implementation and is then encrypted by the IPSec implementation, thereby double encrypting the data. Utilizing more then one encryption algorithm reduces the risk of a weakness in a flawed algorithm that could compromise the security of an application.

Another problem that can occur with the use of encryption is in the actual implementation of the algorithm within a protocol. Protocols such as SSL use a random function to create a session key to encrypt the data. If the method used to generate that random key is flawed, it may be possible to guess the key or to reduce it down to a range of keys that can then be subject to a brute force attack that could succeed in a practical amount of time. Again, using various

implementations that utilize different techniques will reduce the risk of a flawed implementation compromising an entire application. Another weakness in encryption systems can be in the mechanism used to protect the encryption keys. The most prevalent mechanism for protecting the key is to use a password scheme to encrypt the key and then storing it on the machine performing the encryption. In order to use the encryption key, the operator must supply the password to decrypt the key. A potential problem with this approach is that the password being used to protect the key may not be sufficiently complex. It could be subject to a guessing or dictionary attack, which uses lists of words to attempt to guess a password. It could also be intercepted and recorded by an attacker who has access to the machine on which it is used. To protect against this, complex passwords should be used, and every system should utilize a different password, so if one of the passwords is compromised then any potential damage will be limited only to that system.

Another mechanism for storing an encryption key is through the use of a smart card. This credit-card-sized card contains a chip that provides some protected storage and some simple encryption/decryption functions. It is also designed to be tamper resistant to protect against attempts to extract the information, even with physical access. When used to store encryption keys, a smart card can store the key and not allow it to be accessed unless a personal identification number (PIN) is supplied. This provides a much greater level of security as an attacker would have to have access to both the card and the PIN in order to compromise the encryption key. Using a combination of passwords and smart cards provides diversity in an encryption systems and lessens the risk of a failure in any part of the system leading to complete failure of the application.

These network controls can also complement other controls. Many major threats originate over the network, and good network controls can reduce the risk of the compromise of a system. If an operating system or application has a particular vulnerability to a network-based service, the network control can be adjusted to reduce or even eliminate the threat until an operating system or application can be patched or reconfigured. This is important, as the patching of these systems may take a long time and may require modification of the applications that are being run. Because the control is being implemented at the network, it can be implemented relatively quickly and provide protection against the threat. In addition, it is good security practice to allow only network traffic that is necessary to run the application or service to minimize the impact of new threats. Detective-type controls, such as network intrusion detection, can also help in determining the effectiveness of the other network controls by monitoring network traffic and assisting in determining if a network control has failed. Monitoring the log files of network controls is also important, as the logs produced by these controls can provide valuable information in determining when a machine has been compromised. Providing diversity within each network control and utilizing overlapping controls where possible can help in protecting and detecting network-based attacks and can lessen the risk of compromised applications.

HOST OPERATING SYSTEM CONTROLS

Another important set of controls that can be used to protect an application or service exists on the host operating system of the system running the application or service. These controls support the confidentiality, integrity, and availability of the applications or services running on the host. Some of these mechanisms are built into the operating systems, and others are implemented by loading additional software. If implemented properly and with diversity, these controls can complement network and application controls to provide better security and reduce the threat to an application or service.

A major control provided by a host is authenticating access. This control is used to verify the identity of users of the host. This identification can then be used by other controls to provide access controls. The authentication method used to verify the identity of the users is important, as that method controls the extent to which the identity can be trusted to be authentic. A variety of methods can provide authentication. The most prevalent method is through the use of a password that is known by the person who is authenticating. This is known as one-factor authentication and uses something that only that person knows. Another method is through the use of a password that is generated by a hardware token or a certificate on a smart card. This is commonly used in conjunction with a PIN. This approach is referred to as two-factor authentication, as it combines something that the user knows and something that the user physically has (the token or smart card). A third method of authentication is through the use of biometric information that is unique to the person. Examples of these include fingerprints, hand geometry, and iris/retina scans. When a person has established his or her identity through authentication, then the appropriate access controls can be used to restrict that person to the appropriate data and functions.

Utilizing diverse authentication methods can greatly reduce the threat of an identity being compromised. Network controls can also be used to limit the network locations from which a user can gain access. The implementation of an access control list on a firewall can prevent access to the system unless the request comes from an approved network. This can reduce the threat of attempts at unauthorized access by limiting the access to better controlled networks. In addition, if users are only expected to access the system from a specific network, then monitoring can reveal when access is attempted from other unauthorized networks. Action can then be taken to investigate why the access was attempted.

When a user has been properly authenticated, then the access controls of the operating system can be used to limit the data and functions that can be accessed. This is done by granting or revoking privileges within the operating system. Some examples of these include allowing specific users to log in from the network, specifying times that a user is allowed to access the system, and, when a user has logged into the system, what resources that user can access. Functional privileges are another type of privilege that control what a user is allowed to do, such as having the ability to shut down the system, access another user's files, start or stop services, and even grant privileges to other users. Some operating systems support very granular control and allow the individual granting of privileges, whereas others only support the granting of either all privileges or none at all. Only allowing users the minimum privileges to perform their jobs is an important part of reducing the risk if that user is compromised. One way that overlapping controls can be used is in the case of a user who apparently has logged on via the network and is attempting to access other functions or areas that are unauthorized. This can indicate that the user's ID may have been compromised and the matter should be investigated. If the access is via the network, then network controls can help to locate, isolate, and subsequently block any further access attempts from that network. This is an example of how host controls and network controls can work in conjunction to detect and respond to threats to a system.

One other way to provide host access control to data is through the use of file encryption. This can be employed as part of the host operating system or can be a separate add-on application and can be implemented on a file-by-file basis or on an entire volume. This can complement and provide diversity to existing access controls by restricting access to authorized users only and also requiring that the user provide the key to decrypt the data. In addition, using encryption algorithms different from those used in other areas of the system can reduce the risk that a compromise in one algorithm will compromise the entire system. Encryption also provides protection against physical attacks on the host that would allow direct access to the protected data. Even if the host controls were bypassed, the risk of the data being compromised would be less as the data would still be protected by the encryption as long as the key remained secret. Furthermore, if the encryption scheme is implemented separate from the host operating system, it can provide a separate independent control that will reduce the risk of the data being accessed by an unauthorized individual.

Another control that is important to mention is the use of a host intrusion detection system. This is a collection of processes that run on a system to monitor for activity that may indicate an intrusion is occurring or has occurred. It

Data –
Denial

can include various functions, such file integrity checking, monitoring of communications traffic, log file monitoring, and auditing of access rights. By performing these functions it can detect when an intrusion has occurred. When used in conjunction with other controls, such as network intrusion detection, it may be possible to pinpoint the source of the intrusion and take action to further investigate it or block any future intrusions. In addition, these controls can also provide important log information that may allow the organization to take legal action against the intruder.

One of the most important preventive host controls is provided by the addition of anti-virus software. Anti-virus software contains a number of features and functions that can help protect a system against compromise. One of the main functions of anti-virus software is the detection of malicious code in files. Most viruses will attempt to both install and run executable files or modify executable files that already exist on the system. These modifications can be used to provide unauthenticated access to the system or to spread the virus to other machines. Anti-virus software attempts to detect these infected files when they are accessed by the host system and prevent them from running. This is an important preventive control because it can provide protection against viruses and worms that use vulnerabilities that have not yet been patched on the host system. It may also be quicker to update the anti-virus signature files than to patch against the vulnerability used by the virus to spread.

Virus detection should also be used in other places to provide overlapping control. Although the most important place is on a host itself, another place that anti-virus software should be run is on e-mail servers. E-mail is one of the major methods or vectors used by viruses to spread from one system to another, so running anti-virus scanning software on the e-mail servers is an important control. It is important to implement diversity in this control, as well. Anti-virus implementations will use a variety of methods to detect viruses. Most implementations use signature files to identify the code used in a particular virus. This means that the virus signatures must be kept up to date in order to provide protection against the latest viruses. One way to provide extra protection through diversity is to utilize more then one anti-virus vendor solution. Anti-virus software companies can provide updates on different schedules. Some provide updates once a week, and others may provide them once a day. Also, anti-virus vendors will discover the virus and release their updates at different times. Utilizing multiple vendors allows an organization to take advantage of whichever vendor comes up with the detection and remediation first. When applied to e-mail solutions that use gateways and internal relays, this approach can be implemented by utilizing a different vendor's solution on the gateway than on the internal e-mail relays and, if possible,

a third solution on the hosts themselves to provide even further diversity.

APPLICATION CONTROLS

The next place where security controls can be implemented is in the application itself. Applications vary greatly in the amount of security controls that can be implemented. They can also be made up of diverse sets of systems such as browsers, Web servers, and databases. Each one of these pieces represents a place to attack the system as well as an opportunity to implement a control.

Applications rely on the system that is hosting the application in order to properly execute the application. If the underlying system that is hosting the application is compromised, then the application controls could be bypassed, making them ineffective. It is important to protect the system that is running the application. One way to reduce the risk of a system vulnerability being used to compromise an application is to use different types of systems to implement an application. If the application requires the use of multiple Web servers, possibly for load balancing, and can be run on more then one operating system, it is possible to take advantage of this and utilize two or more operating systems for those servers which can reduce the risk of a vulnerability in one operating system affecting the entire application. If a vulnerability is discovered, then the system that is vulnerable can be taken offline until it is patched or mitigated in some other manner, but the application can continue to function utilizing the other Web servers that use a different operating system. A drawback to this approach is that it greatly increases operating complexity by having to maintain and administer multiple operating systems; however, this complexity may be justified for critical applications that must be available all of the time.

Diversity should also apply to the clients used to access the applications. Particularly for Web-based applications, the application should support various browsers in order to prevent a flaw in any single browser from compromising the application or service. This can best be done by making sure the application does not depend on a specific feature of a specific browser to operate and uses standards that most browsers can support. This approach has some drawbacks in that the support of the application must be able to handle these multiple access platforms, and the application must be tested with them to ensure that it functions properly.

Applications may also provide their own authentication process that may be used either with the host authentication or as a totally separate authentication path. If the application authentication is done after a host authentication, then one way to reduce the threat of a compromise is to use a different method of authentication than that used by the host. This can prevent the compromise of the authentication method for the host from allowing access to the application.

Within applications, many access controls can be used to restrict access to functions and resources. For some enterprise applications, these can be very granular and can restrict access down to a particular transaction. Applications can also define roles or groups for its users that in turn define the type of access control, which can make it easier to administer these controls. These access controls can be used in the same manner as the host access controls to limit the functionality that is being accessed by users as well as combined with network controls to limit the sections of the network that can access a particular function within an application. An example of this combination control is not allowing high dollar transactions in a financial application to be initiated from the Internet. This can be done by limiting that functionality to an ID that can only be used to access the application from a controlled network. In addition, encryption can also be used to protect data within the application. Using encryption can prevent the disclosure of critical application data such as credit card numbers or other sensitive information that should be protected even from the administrators of the applications. Diverse access controls, including the use of encryption, can provide multiple layers of protection for the data that is contained within an application and reduce the risk of having the application data compromised.

Coordinating the use of network, host, and application controls can provide redundancy in protecting against compromises and detecting intrusions. This can be an administrative burden, as it requires the coordination of all the controls in order to provide appropriate access to authorized users, but combining all of these controls together can help in reducing the risk of a compromise due to a failure in any one of them.

DETECTION AND RESPONSE

Detection and response are integral parts of any security plan. Although most plans attempt to prevent incidents from occurring, it is also necessary to react to any detected problems. A system that involves a number of diverse security controls can make it challenging to deal with all of the events being generated. It is possible to use diversity in response to improve the likelihood that the response will be timely and allow administrators to resolve the problem with a minimum of impact to the applications.

One tool that can be used to help monitor diverse security controls is a security event correlation system. These systems can take events and logs from various sources such as firewalls, network intrusion detection systems, antivirus detection logs, host security logs, and many others type of logs and correlate them together. This then allows the events to be related together to determine if any action should be taken. An example of this is when a network intrusion detection system detects an attack against a system and the file integrity checker detects a change in a critical file. These events may be detected and responded to individually based only on the priority of that specific event occurring. If they are being processed by a security event correlation system, then it can recognize that these events may be related, and the priority of the events can be adjusted so they are addressed in a more timely manner. This can also help in managing the diversity of different events, as the security event correlation system can map the same type events from multiple sources to a common naming system or grouping of events. This is important, as multiple vendors may have different names for the same event, but this system allows events to be reacted to in the same fashion no matter what the source. This type of system is essential to an enterprise utilizing multiple diverse security controls and monitoring systems.

Another place where diversity can help is in the tools used in the alerting and response process. This can assist in ensuring that administrators will be able to respond to problems in a timely manner. Some alert processes rely on only one method of notification (usually e-mail to a pager). This can be a single point of failure, especially if the e-mail system or the network itself is the system that is affected by the problem. Utilizing other methods of notification, such as devices that will page directly from an event console, will increase the likelihood that the notification will occur in a timely manner. It is also important to protect the response tools and systems that run them as much as possible. These systems should be protected at the highest levels, as they are critical in assisting in containment, remediation, and recovery. Providing diversity for these tools is also a good idea. Being able to utilize tools that run on multiple operating systems is important, because the system that will be used to respond to the incident may be compromised by the same incident that is being responded to. It is also possible that the response system may not be accessible via the network because of the same incident. Having the ability to operate in many different environments will reduce an organization's dependency on any single system and increase the probability of being able to defend successfully against an attack.

Another place to practice diversity is in the actual tools required to respond. In some cases, a tool may not be able to function because the method it uses is blocked by a network control put in place to protect against the effects of an ongoing incident. An example of this was the Blaster worm. It used the Internet Control Messaging Protocol (ICMP) to locate other machines to infect. This resulted in massive amounts of ICMP traffic on networks with infected machines. A common practice was to block this protocol on those networks in order to allow the non-infected machines to communicate. A side effect of this was that it disabled a number of network tools, such as Ping and Tracert, that are commonly used to troubleshoot network issues. Other tools that did not use ICMP had to be utilized.

Another place where diversity is helpful is in the method of access that may be necessary to respond to an incident. For example, VPNs may be used to access the enterprise network from the Internet. If an incident has disabled that access, it will be necessary to have an alternative method available, such as dial-up or the ability to access the network directly by physically going to a location. This can also be useful if it is suspected that the normal method of access may be compromised or possibly is being monitored by an attacker.

CONCLUSION

The use of different security controls within an application environment can go a long way toward reducing the security risks of running the application. Utilizing diverse controls across the network, hosts, and applications, as well as the detection of and response to incidents, can provide multiple layers of protections. These layers can provide overlapping controls that will reinforce the security provided by each control. If one of the controls fails, then an overlapping control can still provide protection or detection. One drawback to using multiple overlapping controls is that administration of these controls requires more effort, which can be justified by the reduction of risk that these multiple controls can provide. Multiple controls can also provide some opportunities to separate critical duties in that different personnel can administer different controls, thereby not allowing any single person to compromise the entire application. Care must also be taken to implement the controls in an independent manner to reduce the risk that a failure in a single control will affect other controls. All in all, the implementation of multiple diverse controls that are layered throughout the network, host, and application can maximize the security of an organization's applications and minimize the risk of a compromise.

Denial-of-Service Attacks

K. Narayanaswamy, Ph.D.
Chief Technology Officer and Co-Founder, Cs3, Inc., Los Angeles, California, U.S.A.

Abstract
As with most things in life, there is good news and bad news in regard to distributed denial-of-service
(DDoS) attacks. The bad news is that there is no "silver bullet" in terms of technology that will make the
problem disappear. The good news, however, is that with a combination of common-sense processes and
practices with, in due course, appropriate technology, the impact of DDoS attacks can be greatly reduced.

A denial-of-service (DoS) attack is any malicious attempt
to deprive legitimate customers of their ability to access
services, such as a Web server. DoS attacks fall into two
broad categories:

1. *Server vulnerability DoS attacks:* attacks that exploit
   known bugs in operating systems and servers. These
   attacks typically will use the bugs to crash programs
   that users routinely rely upon, thereby depriving
   those users of their normal access to the services
   provided by those programs. Examples of vulnerable
   systems include all operating systems, such as
   Windows NT® or Linux®, and various Internet-
   based services, such as DNS, Microsoft's IIS
   Servers, Web servers, etc. All of these programs,
   which have important and useful purposes, also
   have bugs that hackers exploit to bring them down
   or hack into them. This kind of DoS attack usually
   comes from a single location and searches for a
   known vulnerability in one of the programs it is
   targeting. Once it finds such a program, the DoS
   attack will attempt to crash the program to deny
   service to other users. Such an attack does not require
   high bandwidth.
2. *Packet flooding DoS attacks:* attacks that exploit
   weaknesses in the Internet infrastructure and its protocols. Floods of seemingly normal packets are used
   to overwhelm the processing resources of programs,
   thereby denying users the ability to use those services. Unlike the previous category of DoS attacks,
   which exploit bugs, flood attacks require high bandwidth in order to succeed. Rather than use the attacker's own infrastructure to mount the attack (which
   might be easier to detect), the attacker is increasingly
   likely to carry out attacks through intermediary computers (called *zombies*) that the attacker has earlier
   broken into. Zombies are coordinated by the hacker
   at a later time to launch a *distributed* DoS (DDoS)
   attack on a victim. Such attacks are extremely difficult to trace and defend with the present-day Internet.

Most zombies come from home computers, universities, and other vulnerable infrastructures. Often, the
owners of the computers are not even aware that their
machines are being co-opted in such attacks. The
hacker community has invented numerous scripts to
make it convenient for those interested in mounting
such attacks to set up and orchestrate the zombies.
Many references are available on this topic.[1–4]

We will invariably use the term "DoS attacks" to mean all
denial-of-service attacks, and DDoS to mean flood attacks
as described above.

IMPORTANCE OF DDoS ATTACKS

Many wonder why network security and DDoS problems
in particular have seemingly increased suddenly in seriousness and importance. The main reason, ironically, is the
unanticipated growth and success of ISPs. The rapid
growth of affordable, high-bandwidth connection technologies (such as DSL, cable modem, etc.) offered by various
ISPs has brought in every imaginable type of customer to
the fast Internet access arena: corporations, community
colleges, small businesses, and the full gamut of home
users.

Unfortunately, people who upgrade their bandwidth do
not necessarily upgrade their knowledge of network security at the same time; all they see is what they can accomplish with speed. Few foresee the potential security dangers
until it is too late. As a result, the Internet has rapidly
become a high-speed network with depressingly low per-
site security expertise. Such a network is almost an ideal
platform to exploit in various ways, including the mounting of DoS attacks. Architecturally, ISPs are ideally situated to play a crucial role in containing the problem,
although they have traditionally not been proactive on
security matters.

A recent study by the University of San Diego estimates
that there are over 4000 DDoS attacks every week.[5]

Encyclopedia of Information Assurance DOI: 10.1081/E-EIA-120046523
Copyright © 2011 by Taylor & Francis. All rights reserved.

Data –
Denial

Financial damages from the infamous February 2000 attacks on Yahoo, CNN, and eBay were estimated to be around $1 billion.[6] Microsoft, Internet security watchdog CERT, the Department of Defense, and even the White House have been targeted by attackers. Of course, these are high-profile installations, with some options when it comes to responses. Stephen Gibson documents how helpless the average enterprise might be to ward off DDoS attacks (at http://www.scr.com). There is no doubt that DoS attacks are becoming more numerous and deadly.

WHY IS DDoS AN ISP PROBLEM?

When major corporations suffer the kind of financial losses just described and given the fanatically deterministic American psyche that requires a scapegoat (if not a reasonable explanation) for every calamity and the litigious culture that has resulted from it, rightly or wrongly, someone is eventually going to pay dearly. The day is not far off when, in the wake of a devastating DDoS attack, an enterprise will pursue litigation against the owner of the infrastructure that could (arguably) have prevented an attack with due diligence. A recent article explores this issue further from the legal perspective of an ISP.[7]

Our position is not so much that you need to handle DDoS problems proactively today; however, we do believe you would be negligent not to examine the issue immediately from a cost/benefit perspective. Even if you have already undertaken such an assessment, you may need to revisit the topic in light of new developments and the state of the computing world after September 11, 2001.

The Internet has a much-ballyhooed, beloved, open, chaotic, *laissez faire* philosophical foundation. This principle permeates the underlying Internet architecture, which is optimized for speed and ease of growth and which, in turn, has facilitated the spectacular explosion and evolution of this infrastructure. For example, thus far, the market has prioritized issues of privacy, speed, and cost over other considerations such as security. However, changes may be afoot and ISPs should pay attention.

Most security problems at various enterprise networks are beyond the reasonable scope of ISPs to fix. However, the DDoS problem is indeed technically different. Individual sites *cannot* effectively defend themselves against DDoS attacks without some help from their infrastructure providers. When under DDoS attack, the enterprise cannot block out the attack traffic or attempt to clear upstream congestion to allow some of its desirable traffic to get through. Thus, the very nature of the DDoS problem virtually compels the involvement of ISPs. The best possible outcome for ISPs is to jump in and shape the emerging DDoS solutions voluntarily with dignity and concern, rather than being perceived as having been dragged, kicking and screaming, into a dialogue they do not want.

Uncle Sam is weighing in heavily on DDoS as well. In December 2001, the U.S. Government held a DDoS technology conference in Arlington, Virginia, sponsored by the Defense Advanced Research Projects Agency (DARPA) and the Joint Task Force–Central Network Operations. Fourteen carefully screened companies were selected to present their specific DDoS solutions to the government. Newly designated Cyber-Security Czar Richard Clarke, who keynoted the conference, stressed the critical importance of DDoS and how the administration views this problem as a threat to the nation's infrastructure, and that protecting the Internet infrastructure is indeed part of the larger problem of homeland security. The current Republican administration, one might safely assume, is disposed toward deregulation and letting the market sort out the DDoS problem. In the reality of post-September 11 thinking, however, it is entirely conceivable that ISPs will eventually be forced to contend with government regulations mandating what they should provide by way of DDoS protection.

WHAT CAN ISPs DO ABOUT DDoS ATTACKS?

When it comes to DDoS attacks, security becomes a two-way street. Not only must the ISP focus on providing as much protection as possible against incoming DDoS attacks against its customers, but it must also do as much as possible to prevent outgoing DDoS attacks from being launched from its own infrastructure against others. All these measures are feasible and cost very little in today's ISP environment. Minimal measures such as these can significantly reduce the impact of DDoS attacks on the infrastructure, perhaps staving off more draconian measures mandated by the government.

An ISP today must have the ability to contend with the DDoS problem at different levels:

- Understand and implement best practices to defend against DDoS attacks.
- Understand and implement necessary procedures to help customers during DDoS attacks.
- Assess DDoS technologies to see if they can help.

We address each of these major areas below.

Defending against DDoS Attacks

In discussing what an ISP can do, it is important to distinguish the ISP's own infrastructure (its routers, hosts, servers, etc.), which it fully controls, from the infrastructure of the customers who lease its Internet connectivity, which the ISP cannot, and should not, control. Most of the measures we recommend for ISPs are also appropriate for their customers to carry out. The extent to which ISPs can encourage or enable their customers to follow these practices will be directly correlated to the number of DDoS attacks.

Step 1: Ensure the integrity of the infrastructure

An ISP plays a critical role in the Internet infrastructure. It is, therefore, very important for ISPs to ensure that their own routers and hosts are resistant to hacker compromise. This means following all the necessary best practices to protect these machines from break-ins and intrusions of any kind. Passwords for user and root accounts must be protected with extra care, and old accounts must be rendered null and void as soon as possible.

In addition, ISPs should ensure that their critical servers (DNS, Web, etc.) are always current on software patches, particularly if they are security related. These programs will typically have bugs that the vendor eliminates through new patches.

When providing services such as Telnet, FTP, etc., ISPs should consider the secure versions of these protocols such as SSH, SCP, etc. The latter versions use encryption to set up secure connections, making it more difficult for hackers using packet sniffing tools to acquire usernames and passwords, for example.

ISPs can do little to ensure that their users are as conscientious about these matters as they ought to be. However, providing users with the knowledge and tools necessary to follow good security practices themselves will be very helpful.

Step 2: Resist zombies in the infrastructure

Zombies are created by hackers who break into computers. Although by no means a panacea, tools such as intrusion detection systems (IDSs) provide some amount of help in detecting when parts of an infrastructure have become compromised. These tools vary widely in functionality, capability, and cost. They have a lot of utility in securing computing assets beyond DDoS protection. (A good source on this topic can be found in SANS Institute Resources.[8]) Certainly, larger customers of the ISP with significant computing assets should also consider such tools.

Where possible, the ISP should provide users (e.g., home users or small businesses) with the necessary software (e.g., downloadable firewalls) to help them. Many ISPs are already providing free firewalls, such as ZoneAlarm, with their access software. Such firewalls can be set up to maximize restrictions on the customers' computers (e.g., blocking services that typical home computers are never likely to provide). Simple measures like these can greatly improve the ability of these computers to resist hackers.

Most zombies can be now be discovered and removed from a computer by the traditional virus scanning software from McAffee, Symantec, and other vendors. It is important to scan not just programs but also any documents with executable content (such as macros). In other words, everything on a disk requires scanning. The only major problem with all virus scanning regimes is that they currently use databases that have signatures of known viruses, and these databases require frequent updates as new viruses are created.

As with firewalls, at least in cases where users clearly can use the help, the ISP could try bundling its access software, if any, with appropriate virus scanning software and make it something the user has to contend with before getting on the Internet.

Step 3: Implement appropriate router filters

Many DDoS attacks (e.g., Trinoo, Tribal Flood, etc.) rely on source address spoofing, an underlying vulnerability of the Internet protocols whereby the sender of a packet can conjure up a source address other than his actual address. In fact, the protocols allow packets to have completely fabricated, non-existent source addresses. Several attacks actually rely on this weakness in the Internet. This makes attacks much more difficult to trace because one cannot figure out the source just by examining the packet contents because the attacker controls that.

There is no legitimate reason why an ISP should forward outgoing packets that do not have source addresses from its known legitimate range of addresses. It is relatively easy, given present-day routers, to filter outgoing packets at the border of an ISP that do not have valid source addresses. This is called ingress filtering, described in more detail in RFC 2267.

Routers can also implement egress filtering at the point where traffic enters the ISP to ensure that source addresses are valid to the extent possible (e.g., source addresses cannot be from the ISP, packets from specific interfaces must match expected IP addresses, etc.). Note that such filters do not eliminate all DDoS attacks; however, they do force attackers to use methods that are more sophisticated and do not rely on ISPs forwarding packets with obviously forged source addresses.

Many ISPs also have blocks of IP addresses set aside that will never be the source or destination of Internet traffic (see RFC 1918). These are addresses for traffic that will never reach the Internet. The ISP should neither accept traffic with this destination, nor should it allow outbound traffic from those IP addresses set aside in this manner.

Step 4: Disable facilities you may not need

Every port that you open (albeit to provide a legitimate service) is a potential gate for hackers to exploit. Therefore, ISPs, like all enterprises, should ensure they block any and all services for which there is no need. Customer sites should certainly be provided with the same recommendations.

You should evaluate the following features to see if they are enabled and what positive value you get from their being enabled in your network:

- *Directed broadcast.* Some DDoS attacks rely on the ability to broadcast packets to many different addresses to amplify the impact of their handiwork. Directed broadcast is a feature that should not be needed for inbound traffic on border routers at the ISP.
- *Source routing.* This is a feature that enables the sender of a packet to specify an ISP address through which the packet must be routed. Unless there is a compelling reason not to, this feature should be disabled because compromised computers within the ISP infrastructure can exploit this feature to become more difficult to locate during attacks.

Step 5: Impose rate limits on ICMP and UDP traffic

Many DDoS attacks exploit the vulnerability of the Internet where the entire bandwidth can be filled with undesirable packets of different descriptions. ICMP (Internet Control Message Protocol, or ping) packets and User Datagram Protocol (UDP) are examples of this class of packets. You cannot completely eliminate these kinds of packets, but neither should you allow the entire bandwidth to be filled with such packets.

The solution is to use your routers to specify rate limits for such packets. Most routers come with simple mechanisms called class-based queuing (CBQ), which you can use to specify the bandwidth allocation for different classes of packets. You can use these facilities to limit the rates allocated for ICMP, UDP, and other kinds of packets that do not have legitimate reasons to hog all available bandwidth.

Assisting Customers during a DDoS Attack

It is never wise to test a fire hydrant during a deadly blaze. In a similar manner, every ISP will do well to think through its plans should one of its customers become the target of DDoS attacks. In particular, this will entail full understanding and training of the ISP's support personnel in as many (preferably all) of the following areas as possible:

- *Know which upstream providers forward traffic to the ISP.* ISP personnel need to be familiar with the various providers with whom the ISP has Internet connections and the specific service level agreements (SLAs) with each, if any. During a DDoS attack, bad traffic will typically flow from one or more of these upstream providers, and the options of an ISP to help its

customers will depend on the specifics of its agreements with its upstream providers.

- *Be able to identify and isolate traffic to a specific provider.* Once the customer calls during a DDoS directed at his infrastructure, the ISP should be able to determine the source of the bad traffic. All personnel should be trained in the necessary diagnostics to do so. Customers will typically call with the ISP addresses they see on the attack traffic. While this might not be the actual source of the attack, because of source spoofing, it should help the ISP in locating which provider is forwarding the bad traffic.
- *Be able to filter or limit the rate of traffic from a given provider.* Often, the ISP will be able to contact the upstream provider to either filter or limit the rate of attack traffic. If the SLA does not allow for this, the ISP can consider applying such a filter at its own router to block the attack traffic.
- *Have reliable points of contact with each provider.* The DDoS response by an ISP is only as good as its personnel and their knowledge of what to do and whom to contact from their upstream providers. Once again, such contacts cannot be cultivated after an attack has occurred. It is better to have these pieces of information in advance. Holding DDoS attack exercises to ensure that people can carry out their duties during such attacks is the best way to make sure that everyone knows what to do to help the customer.

Assessing DDoS Technologies

Technological solutions to the DDoS problem are intrinsically complex. DDoS attacks are a symptom of the vulnerabilities of the Internet, and a single site is impossible to protect without cooperation from upstream infrastructure. New products are indeed emerging in this field; however, if you are looking to eliminate the problem by buying an affordable rack-mountable panacea that keeps you in a safe cocoon, you are fresh out of luck.

Rather than give you a laundry list of all the vendors, I am going to categorize these products somewhat by the problems they solve, their features, and their functionality so that you can compare apples to apples. Still, the comparison can be a difficult one because various products do different things and more vendors are continually entering this emerging, niche market.

Protection against outgoing DDoS attacks

Unlike virus protection tools, which are very general in focus, these tools are geared just to find DoS worms and scripts. There are basically two kinds of products that you can find here.

Host-based DDoS protection. Such protection typically prevents hosts from being taken over as zombies in a DDoS attack. These tools work in one of two major ways: 1) signature analysis, which, like traditional virus scanners, stores a database of known scripts and patterns and scans for known attack programs; and 2) behavior analysis, which monitors key system parameters for the behavior underlying the attacks (rather than the specific attack programs) and aborts the programs and processes that induce the underlying bad behavior.

Established vendors of virus scanning products, such as McAffee, Symantec, and others, have extended their purview to include DoS attacks. Other vendors provide behavior-analytic DDoS protection that essentially detects and prevents DDoS behavior emanating from a host. The major problem with host-based DDoS protection, from an ISP's perspective, is that one cannot force the customers to use such tools or to scan their disks for zombies, etc.

Damage-control devices. A few recent products (such as Captus' *Captio* and Cs3, Inc.'s *Reverse Firewall* [9,10]) focus on containing the harm that DDoS attacks can do in the outgoing direction. They restrict the damage from DDoS to the smallest possible network. These devices can be quite useful in conjunction with host-based scanning tools. Note that the damage-control devices do not actually prevent an infrastructure from becoming compromised; however, they do provide notification that there is bad traffic from your network and provide its precise origin. Moreover, they give you time to act by throttling the attack at the perimeter of your network and sending you a notification. ISPs could consider using these devices as insurance to insulate themselves from the damage bad customers can do to them as infrastructure providers.

Protection against incoming attacks

As we have mentioned before, defending against incoming attacks at a particular site requires cooperation from the upstream infrastructure. This makes DDoS protection products quite complex. Moreover, various vendors have tended to realize the necessary cooperation in very different ways. A full treatment of all of these products is well beyond the scope of this entry. However, here are several issues you need to consider as an ISP when evaluating these products:

- *Are the devices inline or offline?* An inline device will add, however minimally, to the latency. Some of the devices are built using hardware in an effort to reduce latency. Offline devices, while they do not have that problem, do not have the full benefit of looking at all the traffic in real-time. This could affect their ability to defend effectively.
- *Do the devices require infrastructure changes and where do they reside?* Some of the devices either replace or deploy alongside existing routers and firewalls. Other technologies require replacement of the existing infrastructure. Some of the devices need to be close to the core routers of the network, while most require placement along upstream paths from the site being protected.
- *How do the devices detect DDoS attacks and what is the likelihood of false positives?* The degree of sophistication of the mechanism of detection and its effectiveness in indicating real attacks is all-important in any security technology. After all, a dog that barks the entire day does protect you from some burglars—but you just might stop listening to its warnings! Most of the techniques use comparisons of actual traffic to stored profiles of attacks, or "normal" traffic, etc. A variety of signature-based heuristics are applied to detect attacks. The jury is still out on how effective such techniques will be in the long run.
- *How do the devices know where the attack is coming from?* A major problem in dealing effectively with DDoS attacks is to know, with any degree of certainty, the source of the attacks. Because of source address spoofing on the Internet, packets do not necessarily have to originate where they say they do. All the technologies have to figure out is from where in the upstream infrastructure the attack traffic is flowing. It is the routers along the attack path that must cooperate to defend against the attack. Some of the approaches require that their devices communicate in real-time to form an aggregate picture of where the attack is originating.
- *What is the range of responses the devices will take and are you comfortable with them?* Any DDoS defense must minimally stop the attack from reaching the intended victim, thereby preventing the victim's computing resources from deteriorating or crashing. However, the real challenge of any DDoS defense is to find ways for legitimate customers to get through while penalizing only the attackers. This turns out to be *the* major technical challenge in this area. The most common response includes trying to install appropriate filters and rate limits to push the attack traffic to the outer edge of the realm of control of these devices. At the present time, all the devices that provide DDoS defense fall into this category. How effective they will be remains to be seen.

The products mentioned here are quite pricey even though the technologies are still being tested under fire. DDoS will have to be a very important threat in order for smaller ISPs to feel justified in investing their dollars in these devices. Finally, many of the approaches are proprietary in nature, so side-by-side technical comparisons are difficult to conduct. Some industry publications do seem to have tested some of these devices in various ways. A sampling of vendors and their offerings, applying the above yardsticks, is provided here:

Data –
Denial

- *Arbor Networks* (http://www.arbornetworks.com). Off-line devices, near core routers, anomaly-based detection; source is tracked by communication between devices, and defense is typically the positioning of a filter at a router where the bad traffic enters the network.
- *Asta Networks* (http://www.astanetworks.com). Offline devices that work alongside routers within a network and upstream, signature-based detection; source is tracked by upstream devices, and defense is to use filters at upstream routers.
- *Captus Networks* (http://www.captusnetworks.com). Inline device used to throttle incoming or outgoing attacks; uses windowing to detect non-TCP traffic and does not provide ways for customers to get in; works as a damage-control device for outgoing attacks.
- *Cs3, Inc.* (http://www.cs3-inc.com). Inline devices, modified routers, and firewalls; routers mark packets with path information to provide fair service, and firewalls throttle attacks; source of the attack provided by the path information, and upstream neighbors are used to limit attack traffic when requested; *Reverse Firewall* is a damage-control device for outgoing attacks.
- *Mazu Networks* (http://www.mazunetworks.com). Inline devices at key points in network; deviations from stored historical traffic profile indicate attack; the source of the attack is pinpointed by communication between devices, and defense is provided by using filters to block out the bad traffic.
- *Okena* (http://www.okena.com). Host-based system that has extended intrusion detection facilities to provide protection against zombies; it is a way to keep one's infrastructure clean but is not intended to protect against incoming attacks.

IMPORTANT RESOURCES

Finally, the world of DoS, as is indeed the world of Internet security, is dynamic. If your customers are important to you, you should have people that are on top of the latest threats and countermeasures. Excellent resources in the DoS security arena include:

- *Computer Emergency Response Team (CERT)* (http://www.cert.org). A vast repository of wisdom about all security-related problems with a growing section on DoS attacks; you should monitor this site regularly to find out what you need to know about this area. This site has a very independent and academic flavor. Funded by the Department of Defense, this organization is likely to play an even bigger role in putting out alerts and other information on DDoS.

- *System Administration, Networking and Security (SANS) Institute* (http://www.sans.org). A cooperative forum in which you can instantly access the expertise of over 90,000 professionals worldwide. It is an organization of industry professionals, unlike CERT. There is certainly a practical orientation to this organization. It offers courses, conferences, seminars, and White Papers on various topics that are well worth the investment. It also provides alerts and analyses on security incidents through incidents.org, a related facility.

REFERENCES

1. Houle, K.; Weaver, G. *Trends in Denial of Service Technology*, CERT Coordination Center, October 2001, http://www.cert.org/archive/pdf/DOS_trends.pdf.
2. Myers, M. *Securing Against Distributed Denial of Service Attacks*, Client/Server Connection, Ltd., http://www.cscl.com/techsupp/techdocs/ddossamp.html.
3. Paul, B. DDOS: Internet weapons of mass destruction, *Network Computing*, January 1, 2001, http://www.networkcomputing.com/1201/1201f1c2.html.
4. Harris, S. Denying denial of service, *Internet Security*, September 2001, http://www.infosecuritymag.com/articles/september01/cover.shtml.
5. Lemos, R. *DoS Attacks Underscore Net's Vulnerability*, CNETnews.com, June 1, 2001, http://news.cnet.com/news/0-1003-200-6158264.html?tag=mn_hd.
6. Yankee Group News Releases, February 10, 2000, http://www.yankeegroup.com/webfolder/yg21a.nsf/press/384D3C49772 576EF85256881007DC0EE?OpenDocument.
7. Radin, M.J. *Distributed Denial of Service Attacks: Who Pays?*, Mazu Networks, http://www.mazunetworks.com/radines.html.
8. SANS Institute Resources. Intrusion Detection FAQ, Version 1.52, http://www.sans.org/newlook/resources/IDFAQ/ID_FAQ.htm.
9. Savage, M. Reverse Firewall Stymies DDOS Attacks, *Computer Reseller News*, December 28, 2001, http://www.crn.com/sections/BreakingNews/breakingnews.asp?ArticleID=32305.
10. Desmond, P. *Cs3 Mounts Defense against DDOS Attacks*, eComSecurity.com, October 30, 2001, http://www.ecom-security.com/News_2001-10-30_DDos.cfm.

BIBLIOGRAPHY

1. Singer, A. *Eight Things that ISPs and Network Managers Can Do to Help Mitigate DDoS Attacks*; San Diego Supercomputer Center: San Diego, http://security.sdsc.edu/publications/ddos.shtml.

Digital Crime Scene Analysis (DCSA)

Marcus Rogers, Ph.D., CISSP, CCCI
*Chair, Cyber Forensics Program, Department of Computer and Information Technology,
Purdue University, West Lafayette, Indiana, U.S.A.*

Abstract

This entry discusses the background of criminalistics, general crime scene analysis, the theoretical frameworks surrounding digital investigations, and common concepts that can be used from the general model and implemented into digital crime scene analysis (DCSA). The author provides a working model of how the physical and digital crime scene analysis frameworks complement each other.

"One should always look for a possible alternative and provide against it. It is the first rule of criminal investigation."
—*Sherlock Holmes*
(*From "The Adventure of Black Peter," by Sir Arthur Conan Doyle*)

The world of criminalistics has changed in the last few years. Not only has there been a shift in how the popular media portray crime scene investigations (e.g., television shows such as *CSI*, *CSI Miami*, *NCIS*), but there has also been a change in demands placed on crime scene investigators. It has been estimated that, today, 80% of all cases have some form of digital evidence. As evidence quickly moves from being physical and document based to digital and electronic, the knowledge, skills, and abilities of those charged with identifying, collecting, and analyzing evidence must adapt to meet these new demands. Some, in the new emerging field of digital forensics, have suggested that, due to the unique nature of computers, networks, and digital evidence, traditional approaches to crime scene analysis must be abandoned in favor of new methods, techniques, and tools.[1]

The Department of Justice in the United States, the Royal Canadian Mounted Police (RCMP) in Canada, the Australian National Police, and Scotland Yard, to name just a few, are literally scrambling trying to develop new procedures and checklists to allow investigators to effectively deal with digital evidence and digital crimes scenes. Researchers such as Baryamureeba, Beebe, Carrier, and Mocas have developed various models to assist law enforcement and the judiciary in dealing with digital evidence. Despite these theoretical efforts, what is still lacking is an applied or practical approach to dealing with digital crime scenes and the digital evidence contained therein.

The thesis of this entry is that, although digital crime scenes and electronic evidence may introduce some unique requirements, these requirements will be at the higher strata of the process (e.g., specific tools). The lower, more conceptual layers of a crime scene, as discussed by Lee et al.,[2] Saferstein,[3] Nickell and Fischer,[4] will not be drastically different for physical and digital investigations; therefore, a common approach can be defined. This common approach will assist digital forensics in meeting the current and future requirements for being a forensic science and in satisfying the judicial criteria for admissibility as scientific evidence (e.g., Daubert).[5] The common ground also makes it possible to repurpose much of what we already know in criminalistics and physical crime scene analysis and provides a practical approach for examiners, analysts, and investigators.

This entry provides a brief background on criminalistics and general crime scene analysis. The reader is also introduced to some of theoretical frameworks that have been developed specifically for digital crime scenes and how common concepts can be reintroduced back into the general crime scene framework. A simplified process model is discussed that not only allows for a pragmatic approach to dealing with digital scenes but also is consistent with established protocols, thus increasing the probability that discovered evidence, either inculpatory or exculpatory, will be admissible in a court of law. Due to the unique characteristics of the practice of law and jurisprudence, the criteria for acceptance will be based on the U.S. common law standard. It has been said that "there is no new thing under the sun" (Ecclesiastes 1:9), and this entry is no exception. It merely examines what has already been done in the areas of physical crime scene analysis and digital investigative models and provides a pragmatic marrying of the two analogous disciplines.

BRIEF OVERVIEW OF CRIME SCENE ANALYSIS

Crime scene analysis can trace its roots back to the early 1900s when Edmund Locard published his now famous principle of exchange. The principle states: "When a

Encyclopedia of Information Assurance DOI: 10.1081/E-EIA-120046830
Copyright © 2011 by Taylor & Francis. All rights reserved.

Digital –
E-Mail

person commits a crime something is always left at the scene of the crime that was not present when the person arrived."[3] This relatively simple principle reshaped the manner in which the law enforcement community would forever more view the scene of a crime. The revelation suggested that not only could the crime scene provide clues as to what had transpired but it could also provide information on who might have been involved, either as a suspect or at the very least as a material witness.

Law enforcement investigators were now challenged to protect the scene and identify and collect potential evidence in a timely manner, as most scenes contained semipermanent evidence (e.g., bullet holes, broken glass) and transient or dynamic evidence (e.g., fingerprints, bodily fluids). The demands for identifying and collecting evidence had to be balanced with the concern over contamination (i.e., introducing items into the scene that were not originally there or destroying existing evidence). The various demands required that the law enforcement community develop protocols and standard operating procedures (SOPs). These SOPs eventually became universal and, having survived judicial scrutiny, became the framework for current-day crime scene analysis.[4]

Basic textbooks such as Henry Lee's *Crime Scene Handbook* present this framework as part of the foundations of criminalistics. The process encompasses five phases:[2,3]

- *Recognition*—Recognition involves knowing what to look for, what constitutes potential evidence, and, more importantly, what can be ignored. This phase also includes the collection of evidence.
- *Identification*—When evidence or potential evidence has been recognized, it must be identified. Identification consists of classification at the most basic level based on class characteristics (e.g., hair, blood, fingerprint). This acts as the foundation for the next phases.
- *Comparison*—The collected and identified evidence must be compared to some standard or control to determine that it came from a particular class (e.g., paint from a 1975 Ford Mustang).
- *Individualization*—The evidence is then further examined to determine any unique characteristics that would allow it to be differentiated from the larger category to a specific person or object based on its unique characteristics (e.g., paint from a 1975 ford Mustang owned by the primary suspect).
- *Reconstruction*—The last phase ties together the previous phases and allows the investigator to pull together the pieces of what has been to this point part of a jigsaw puzzle with no real picture to follow into a logical sequence of events consistent with established timelines.

Assumed within this model are the concepts of interpretation and reporting. Interpretation in this context refers to

assumptions and postulations based on evidence and the facts at hand. Obviously, the final output of the process is the production of a report that becomes discoverable and provides a chronology of what, when, why, where, and how the scene and identified evidence were handled or managed; this is critical when proving an unbroken chain of custody, which is one of the cornerstones of good crime scene and evidence management.[2,3,6]

The crime scene model is purposely high level and focuses on concepts as opposed to minute details. This allows the model to be used in various types of investigations (e.g., arson, homicide, sexual assault), while providing sufficient latitude for the analyst or investigator to be flexible and deal with the eccentricities and context of each particular scene/investigation.

CYBER CRIME SCENES

An interesting phenomenon has appeared within the field of digital investigations. For whatever reason, the forensic and law enforcement community has assumed that the introduction of technology has so drastically changed the nature of investigations and crime scenes that we must reinvent the wheel and develop new and different approaches to digital or computer crimes and their corresponding scenes. This opinion exists despite a lack of evidence to support it and actually runs contrary to what courts are demanding—adherence to a criteria for the admissibility of scientific and technical forensic evidence.[7] In the United States and Canada, the courts have decided on the *Daubert criteria* [*Daubert v. Merrell Dow Pharmaceuticals, Inc.*, 509 US 579, 1993. In a case involving the admissibility of scientific expert testimony, the U.S. Supreme Court held that: 1) such testimony was admissible only if relevant and reliable; 2) the Federal Rules of Evidence (FRE) assigned to the trial judge the task of ensuring that an expert's testimony rested on a reliable foundation and was relevant to the task at hand; and 3) some or all of certain specific factors—such as testing, peer review, error rates, and acceptability in the relevant scientific community—might possibly prove helpful in determining the reliability of a particular scientific theory or technique.] for determining whether evidence is scientific and thus given more weight. Briefly, the criteria state that the method or theory should be testable and generally agreed upon by the relevant scientific community, the error rate must be known or have the potential to be known, and the method used must have been peer reviewed and published.[8] The Daubert criteria and the subsequent Carmichael [In *Kumho Tire v. Carmichael*, the Daubert criteria were expanded to include testimony by engineers and other technical witnesses who are not scientists.] ruling, which extended the criteria to technical and engineering methods, place the judge in the position of "gatekeeper," whose role it is to decide what evidence becomes admissible and what will be heard by a jury. The criteria are designed to give assistance to judges, whom are not necessarily scientists, when determining true science from junk science.

As mentioned, the Department of Justice in the United States and its counterparts throughout the world have felt the pressure to develop standard operating procedures for dealing with digital-based evidence. The development of these SOPs is problematic given the fact that, although various *ad hoc* approaches exist, no international consensus has yet been reached on how to deal with the evidence. High-level concepts have been discussed by organizations such as the International Organization on Computer Evidence (IOCE) and the Scientific Working Group on Digital Evidence (SWGDE); however, apart from agreeing that evidence should not be altered and that everyone needs to be trained and adhere to the country's laws, nothing concrete has been accomplished. The lack of defined standards combined with the judicial scrutiny has placed the field of digital forensics in the precarious position of vacillating between a true scientific discipline and a pseudo science or art form. This is definitely not a comfortable position to be in for any protracted period of time.

To meet the criteria for scientific evidence, digital forensics must determine what actually constitutes a digital investigation.[9,10] This requires the identification of process models and investigative elements.[11] Although several theoretical digital crime scene process models have been developed, we will confine our discussions to the *integrated digital investigation process* (IDIP)[12] and the *hierarchical objectives-based framework* (HOBF).[13] These two models encompass earlier models, such as the incident response model, law enforcement process model, and the U.S. Air Force abstract process model.

DEFINITIONS

Before examining the digital crime scene process models, it is important that several key terms be agreed upon. Although the term *digital evidence* has found its way into the common vocabulary, it has never been sufficiently defined by the digital forensic community. Carrier and Spafford[12] defined digital evidence as "Digital data that establish that a crime has been committed, can provide a link between a crime and its victim, or can provide a link between a crime and the perpetrator." (p. 6)

This is a modification of the definition of physical evidence as presented by Saferstein.[3] Accordingly, the datum can exist in storage media, primary or secondary memory, and volatile memory or on the wire in transit between systems. This definition will suffice for the purposes of our discussion.

Given the definition of digital evidence, we can define a digital crime scene as the *electronic environment where digital evidence can potentially exist*. This is a slight modification of the Carrier and Spafford[12] definition. The terms "software" and "hardware" were dropped from the original definition, and the term "virtual" was replaced by "electronic." It was felt that the original terms introduced unnecessary constraints on the definition.

CURRENT PROCESS MODELS

Integrated Digital Investigation Process

The integrated digital investigation model (IDIP), one of the most well-known models of digital investigations, maps digital elements to physical investigative methods. Carrier and Spafford[12] examined earlier approaches from the areas of incident response, the military, and law enforcement. They concluded that any digital model must meet the following criteria:

- The model must be based on existing theory for physical crime scene investigations.
- The model must be practical and follow the same steps that an actual investigation would take.
- The model must be general with respect to technology and not be constrained to current products and procedures.
- The model must be specific enough that general technology requirements for each phase can be developed.
- The model must be abstract and apply to law enforcement investigation, corporate investigations, and incident response.

Based on these criteria, the IDIP has 17 phases combined into five groups:

- Readiness phase
- Deployment phase
- Physical crime scene investigation phase
- Digital crime scene investigation phase
- Review phase

Carrier and Spafford[12] break each of these five phases down into more basic elements and relate each back to physical investigations concepts and analogous requirements. The authors conclude that the IDIP provides a valid investigative model and argue that digital investigations encompass more than forensics, which they contend is primarily focused on issues related to comparison and identification, and is thus differentiated from digital forensics. They specifically point to the reconstruction of digital evidence as support for differentiating investigations from forensic analysis.[12]

Digital –
E-Mail

The IDIP has been criticized for being too theoretical and relegating the computer to being simply a "dead body" upon which a postmortem is to be conducted, as opposed to an actual crime scene analogous to the physical environment.[14] Given that the computer system, network, or storage media can be thought of as a distinct crime scene, a container for potential evidence inside a primary scene, and a victim upon which the incident has been perpetrated, the term *corpus delicti* is more fitting. *Corpus delicti* encompasses not only the notion of the body but also the sum total of the evidence that exists in the environment containing the body. Baryamureeba and Tushabe[14] further criticize the lack of specificity of the model and its vagueness in differentiating between multiple scenes such as the perpetrator's and the victim's computer systems.

Hierarchical Objectives-Based Framework

Beebe and Clark[13] leveraged the work of Carrier and Spafford[12] and defined an investigative framework based on concrete principles as opposed to single-tier, high-order principles. The goal was to use objectives-based subphases in order to make the framework more pragmatic.[13] The authors combined what they considered to be first-tier phases from previous approaches to construct their first-tier framework. This framework consists of

- Preparation
- Incident response
- Data collection
- Data analysis
- Presentation of findings
- Incident closure

A second tier framework was then added. The second tier was meant to cover all contingencies and types of digital evidence, as well as possible categories of crimes.[13] The authors further indicated that this layer was comprised of objectives-based subphases (OBSPs), which should be consistent across various contexts, and specific tasks and subtasks that were situational dependent. The remainder of the discussion was confined to illustrating the model focusing only on the analytical phase and defining the appropriate subphases such as survey, extract, and examine (data analytical approach).

Beebe and Clark[13] concluded that an objectives-based, multitiered approach had more utility than the first-tier-only models, as the multitiered model was more practical and at the same time more specific. They contended that a more detailed approach would assist researchers and tool developers; however, they cautioned against moving to a level of specificity that would produce standardized

checklists due to the quirks that can arise in real-world investigations.

As the authors point out, the model is incomplete and adds several layers of complexity.[13] The model also tries to be too all encompassing. The goal of being technology and operating system neutral is not practical given the reality of today's investigations. Certain technologies (e.g., cell phones, flash drives) and operating systems or file systems may have peculiarities that affect both the first tier and the objectives layer. This would lead to the necessity of defining additional subtiers within the model that would further increase the complexity and adversely affect its parsimony, thus limiting its real-world applicability. The model also attempts to be both generic and broad yet provide sufficient specificity to be practical—these two goals appear to be mutually exclusive in this context.

General Model Limitations

The most fundamental issue with the majority of the models to date is their reliance on incident response as both a framework and point of reference as opposed to being based on a solid criminalistics framework. While incident response seems like a logical foundation for the development of digital investigative models, it lacks some crucial components—namely, compliance with the rules of evidence, standard of proof, and chain of custody considerations.[15] Incident response procedures are predicated on computer science, networking, and information technology theory and standards. These disciplines look at the mechanical aspects of the devices, packets, and interconnections. This is crucial for troubleshooting and root-cause analysis at the mechanical level, but the models give little or no consideration to proper evidence handling or admissibility requirements.[15]

Current models also tend to reinforce the lack of stratification of various digital crime scene functions. In the traditional forensic disciplines, particular forensic disciplines have certain areas of specialty. Most larger law enforcement agencies, and increasingly smaller agencies as well, have crime scene technicians who are skilled in crime scene analysis. When a first responder arrives at a major crime scene, the scene is controlled and then the specialists are brought in to collect the appropriate evidence in a forensically sound manner. The evidence is then transported to other specialists whose function it is to deal with the evidence based on context or content (e.g., blood, hair and fiber, ballistics, DNA, fingerprints). The first responders will more than likely turn the case over to trained investigators (e.g., homicide, arson, robbery). Currently, digital investigations do not usually follow this same approach. It is not uncommon for the first responder to be expected to perform the role of a crime scene technician, investigative specialist, pathologist or coroner, and forensic scientist schooled in several different scientific disciplines. The mere fact that the scene is digital does not alter the reality that no one can live up to this unrealistic expectation of multiple domain expertise.

An additional limitation is that the investigative models are overly broad and do not lend themselves to a practical real-world approach for dealing with an entire investigation. This lack of pragmatism should come as no surprise, as no one model exists for all possible investigations based on evidence collected from a physical scene. Imagine trying to define an investigative model that covers every type of traditional crimes (e.g., homicide, rape, arson, break and enter) and every possible kind of physical evidence that can be collected from the scene (e.g., fingerprints, DNA, gun powder residue). When put into this context, it seems rather odd to define investigations solely based on the modality (i.e., physical vs. digital) of the scene that contained the evidence. It will be impossible to have a generic investigative approach to all digital cases. Models must deconstruct the investigative process into more logical, practical phases. These phases should be based on the demarcation between the crime scene, analysis, and reporting activities (see Fig. 1). Based on this framework, we need to concentrate our attention on the crime scene phase, as this forms the foundation upon which the analysis phase and reporting phases are built. This is also the primary target for activities related to the admissibility or suppression of evidence. If doubt is cast on the initial collection and management of evidence, output from the other phases is moot.

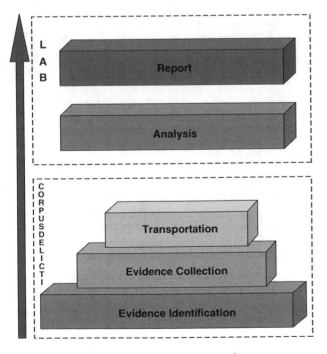

Fig. 1 Crime scene deconstruction.

Developing a practical general approach dealing with the higher level investigative phases (analysis and reporting) is problematic, as these phases are context and content dependent, as are their equivalents in the more traditional physical-based investigations.[11] Context relates to what type crime has been committed or assumed (e.g., hacking incident, internal fraud or malfeasance, child porn, intellectual property theft). Content relates to the type of operating system and corresponding file system (Windows 2000, OS X, Solaris, VMS), nature of the system (personal computer, workstation, server), and, in some cases, volume of potential evidence. Thus, confining the discussion to the lower layers makes more sense.

Practical Approach

The overriding principle behind the current approach is that computer crime scene analysis and computer forensics are not based on some tool, technology, or piece of software.[15] The exact tools, applications, etc., are irrelevant. What is important is adhering to the principles of being methodical and accurate, ensuring the authenticity and reproducibility of evidence, maintaining the chain of custody, and minimizing contamination of the original scene. Like a carpenter who uses various tools (e.g., hammer, saw, screwdriver), a forensic investigator uses various tools as needed; the tools do not define the discipline.

Although most of the current research has been directed toward all-encompassing generic models, a more realistic approach to assisting investigators—and at the same time appeasing the courts—is to develop investigative guidelines, or at the very least forensically sound tasks (FSTs) that are constrained to the actual crime scene or *corpus delicti* layer. By limiting the scope or domain of discussion in this fashion, several advantages arise. The first advantage stems from the fact that such an approach mirrors the real-world physical crime scene model, thus allowing for identification of analogous elements. A second advantage is that at the lower layer one can truly be generic and technology or platform neutral. The need for unique approaches based on context and content does not occur until the higher levels (e.g., analysis layer; see Fig. 1). As suggested by previous researchers and scholars, for digital crime scene analysis to be consistent with established forensic principles it must develop some basic formalisms. As already discussed, formalism will help to appease the courts' concerns and meet the criteria for scientific evidence.

Rather than reinvent the wheel, an approach is required that incorporates generally accepted practices and standards. Because so-called best practices do not really exist, the use of generally accepted practices is sufficient. This is not only consistent with physical crime scene practices but is also consistent with information technology approaches.[11,15,16] The information technology security field has struggled to identify best practices and has opted instead for generally accepted principles and practices (e.g., GAASP, GAISP, ISO 17799). These practices are based on higher order concepts dealing with confidentiality, integrity, and availability (the information security triad). Within the field of digital crime scene analysis and forensics, equivalent standards come from various governmental sources [e.g., the U.S. Department of Justice, National Institute of Justice, National White Collar Crime Center (NW3C), RCMP, Secret Service, Interpol, Scotland Yard, Department of Defense, GCHQ, G8], as well as the private sector (e.g., HTCIA, KPMG, Deloitte and Touche) and quasi-academia (e.g., IOCE, SWGDE). The current approach draws on work already conducted by these groups; the previous academic investigative models of Carrier and Spafford,[12] Beebe and Clark,[13] McKemmish,[15] and Mocas;[11] and the traditional crime scene approaches of Lee et al.[2] and Saferstein.[3]

As stated, the current approach is not new; it is based on the five phases or layers as proposed by Carrier and Spafford[12] but adds an additional hierarchy of *corpus delicti* (see Fig. 1) and lab. The *corpus delicti* layer encompasses what is traditionally thought of as the crime scene as well as a transportation phase. In this lower foundational phase, the computer can be part of a larger physical crime scene (secondary scene), its own primary scene, a material witness to events, or the corpse to be examined. The higher layers denoted as lab (analysis, examination, report) are not addressed, as they require unique approaches based on content and context. The term "lab" is used in the broadest sense to denote processes that usually occur in a controlled environment; the use of the term is not meant to indicate that these activities must be undertaken in some form of officially sanctioned or accredited laboratory [e.g., state ASCLD-Lab/ISO 17025-certified facility (American Academy of Crime Lab Directors (SCLD-Lab) is the current U.S. standard and is in the process of becoming compliant with the ISO 17025 lab certification standard.)].

The *corpus delicti* layer is further subdivided into the subphases of 1) identification and recognition, and 2) collection. Identification includes not only identifying what might constitute individual pieces of evidence but also identifying what devices or digital storage media could contain evidence. On the surface, this sounds rather sophomoric, but with the trend toward small-footprint storage devices (e.g., USB thumb drives, watches with USB connections, USB pens, music players such as the iPod) the process of recognition becomes very complicated. The advent of digital storage capacity and network capability in entertainment systems (e.g., Tivo, DVRs), game systems such the Xbox, and now even refrigerators further complicates the matter of identification for first responders or investigators. When the identification and recognition phase has been completed, the evidence must be collected in a forensically sound manner (we will discuss what this actually means in subsequent sections). The collection phase encompasses the traditional bagging and tagging of

computer systems and storage devices in some cases, as well as the acquiring of bitstream images from digital storage media in other cases.

For simplicity's sake, the forensically sound tasks are presented in a linear fashion; realistically, naturally occurring iterative relationships exist between various phases and tasks. Before proceeding further, an obligatory caveat is warranted: Never exceed your level of knowledge, skills, and abilities (KSA) or the abilities of the tools, applications, or techniques. Despite what vendors would have us believe, their tools have limitations (apologies to the vendor community who might actually read this).[15] This is without a doubt the best advice one can follow in any set of circumstances.

Properties and Rules

McKemmish[15] and Mocas[10] identified several fundamental properties or rules of computer forensics. These properties or rules are derived from the areas of information security and incident response, are sensitive to standards of proof, and are presumably compatible with private-sector functional requirements (e.g., getting back up and running in a reasonable amount of time). These properties consist of integrity, authenticity, reproducibility, maintaining the evidence chain (chain of custody), and minimalization. Integrity relates to the fact that the evidence was not changed from the time it was collected until it is presented in a court, hearing, etc. Integrity and authenticity are often interdependent. To be authentic, the courts need to be satisfied that the evidence is a true copy of the original or as true as is possible. An example is producing identical hash totals (MD5, SHA 256) of the original drive contents and the bitstream image. Reproducibility relates to the reliability of the methods or techniques used. Ideally, another individual following the exact same steps as the original technician should find the same results. The evidence chain of custody is sacrosanct, and proving an unbroken chain to the court is a minimum requirement for admissibility. Minimalization refers to contaminating crime scenes as little as possible; realistically, some minor contamination is introduced into all scenes. The fundamental properties have also been identified by the SWGDE and High-Tech Crime Investigators Association (HTCIA) and form the basis of their approach to training, in the case of the HTCIA, and policy and accreditation and certification standards, for the SWGDE. The properties or rules form the basis for a framework for the development of forensically sound tasks.

Forensically Sound Tasks

The focus of the tasks in Table 1 is on the application of crime scene techniques to the real world. The tasks are also technology neutral to the extent that they are conceptual based and purposely high level; the real world requires a

Table 1 Forensically sound tasks.

Task	Objective	Principle/ Rule
Control the scene.	Create the proper environment to conduct the evidence collection.	A, C, I, M, R
Survey the scene.	Determine the scope of the scene and the need for assistance in the next phases. Establish the context of the investigation.	M, R
Document the scene.	Allow investigators to describe the scene in detail and place activities conducted at the scene in context. Also, indicate the location of evidence, people, or evidence containers for possible use at the higher investigative levels	C, R
Identify potential evidence and containers of evidence.	Locate sources of potential evidence or objects that may contain evidence. If the search is conducted under a court order, determine that the order is valid or must be amended.	A, C, R
Determine the evidence modality (e.g., digital, physical, dynamic).	Begin categorizing the evidence or containers of evidence to determine the best process by which to handle the evidence or container.	A, I, M, R
Collect evidence based on modality.	Use techniques and tools appropriate to the modality of the evidence.	A, C, I, M, R
Collect any necessary standards.	Determine if any standards will be required for comparison at the higher levels and collect same if necessary.	A, I, R
Package for transport.	Ensure that no damage or contamination occurs and that all evidence is accounted for.	A, C, I, M, R
Turn over to lab or appropriate offsite facility.	Allow for detailed examination and analysis of evidence in a scientifically controlled environment and for the determination of long-term storage needs.	C, I, R

Note: A = authenticity, C = chain of custody, I = integrity, M = minimalization, R = reproducibility.

certain amount of flexibility albeit within some parameters. The parameters for our purposes are the rules of evidence, standard of proof, and chain of custody. The importance of proper documentation with all the tasks cannot be stressed enough. Although some might argue that too much documentation may provide fertile ground for others to criticize what was done or omitted, the inability to recall important steps or variations of technique usually results in the proverbial death sentence—full suppression of any and all evidence derived from the tasks.

Control the Scene

Controlling the scene is one of the most fundamental tasks. Failure to control a scene will negatively affect all of the other tasks and directly influences the five principles. The objective here is to create an adequate environment in which to carry out the subsequent tasks; however, unlike a pristine lab environment, the real world is not fully controllable. It is extremely rare to have absolutely no contamination, as an individual's mere presence at the scene has altered the original state to some extent, however minute.[17] Heisenberg's uncertainty principle would argue that merely viewing the scene causes changes at the quantum level; therefore, every scene is contaminated. Luckily, most courts have opted not to adopt such a literal interpretation of

contamination.[7,17] It is vital that detailed notes be taken describing all the actions taken. Also, it is important to:

- Quickly control the scene and all people and potential sources of evidence (e.g., isolating suspects, witnesses, systems from networks including the Internet). This may include disconnecting a system from any connections (wired and wireless networks, cable modems, dial-up modems) that may allow remote connections.
- Contain the scene, which is of the utmost importance in order to minimize the amount of contamination.

Survey the Scene

Understanding exactly what you are up against is necessary in order to determine what resources will be needed, both in terms of additional personnel, and equipment. The survey task should be conducted in a methodical, well-documented manner. This holds true whether the digital scene is primary, secondary, or the corpse. The ability to articulate the exact context of the scene and in some case reproduce the scene is an absolute necessity; this type of detail is often required when interpreting evidence in the analysis and examination phases, especially with event reconstruction. A survey will also assist in determining the approach that should be taken to the actual evidence identification and collection. It will also allow for determining strategies that minimize

Digital –
E-Mail

contamination and maximize the reproducibility of the actions taken. The investigator should:

- Step back and observe the scene from the perspective of a neutral third party. Obtain a mental picture of the environment, its contents, and their interactions and dependencies.
- Based on the observations, determine the approach that offers the greatest probability of obtaining the necessary evidence while at the same time producing the least amount of contamination.

Document the Scene

When a mental map of the scene has been processed, proceed to document the scene either diagrammatically or digitally (e.g., still camera, video). This task is the lynch pin for articulating the context and relationships of any evidence that is found. A picture or a video is really worth a thousand words when trying to describe to a forensic analyst, boss, tribunal, judge, jury, etc., what the scene looked like. This task is necessary even when the scene is confined to the actually computer itself (primary scene, corpse). One only has to think of trying to describe a small home network with four to five systems all interconnected or to remember what exact peripherals were attached to the suspect system. The chain of custody is dependent on effectively articulating the original location of evidence, thus the necessity for accurate documentation. In addition,

- Make detailed notes, sketches, and diagrams, and take pictures from various angles to ensure a sense of context for those reviewing the case details at some future time.
- If possible, take pictures of both the front and rear of all computer systems, devices. This will illustrate the state of connected peripherals and any unique cabling and connections.

Identification

Although it sounds odd to reiterate the need for identification, the fact that we are dealing with digital evidence that does not come in a one-size-fits-all mode requires this. Advances in technology have drastically altered what is considered storage media. As storage media is often the primary source of evidence, care must be taken not to overlook the obvious and now the unobvious. To counter claims of tunnel vision and neglect in conducting a thorough investigation, all evidence and potential containers of evidence (e.g., storage devices) must be identified. This accurate and complete identification is required to satisfy the principles of authenticity, reproducibility, and the evidence custody chain. The investigator should:

- Identify and recognize all possible storage media including both traditional devices (e.g., diskettes, hard drives, CDs, DVDs) and non-traditional devices (e.g., thumb drives, PDAs, cell phones, digital video recorders, Xboxes, USB devices).
- Do not ignore analog and document-based sources of potential evidence (e.g., printouts, log books, journals, diaries, manuals, drawings).

Evidence Modality and Collection

Determining the type of evidence (modality) allows the investigator to formulate a plan to effectively collect the evidence while minimizing the likelihood of contamination, maximizing authenticity and reproducibility, and maintaining the chain of custody. The modalities include physical, digital or electronic, and analog, as well as dynamic/transient (e.g., volatile memory, cache) and relatively stable (e.g., secondary memory storage, firmware, printouts). A thorough identification process greatly reduces the time required to carry out this task. Understanding the evidence modality and degree of transience also allows the investigator to prioritize the actual collection process. Dealing with both physical and digital or electronic evidence requires a diverse repertoire of tools, techniques, and processes. It is beyond the scope of this limited entry to discuss all possible contingencies. It suffices to say that if an investigator, technician, or first responder has correctly and diligently carried out the previous tasks, this task becomes more a matter of mechanics (i.e., the appropriate tool, technique, and process for the type of evidence). The same approach holds for the traditional crime scene analysis approach and is in fact the direct result of following a formal, methodical approach. The challenge becomes one of the collecting evidence without introducing any unnecessary contamination. The exact approach to this depends on the modality of the evidence, the degree of control over the scene (e.g., amount of isolation), and the overall context of the investigation:

- Determine priority by order of volatility (i.e., most transient first).
- Focus on digital or electronic evidence first, as it is usually more volatile than physical evidence.
- Further prioritize digital or electronic evidence based on its volatility.
- Use the correct tools, techniques, and processes.
- Document every step taken, and be prepared to discuss what was done and what may have been omitted from the task.

Collection Standards

The requirement for the comparison of any collected evidence to some standard is not just a concern for physical crime scenes and evidence. It may be the case that printouts, photographs, scans, etc. must be compared to electronic or digital versions of these same items discovered on a storage device or system. This goes to the authenticity of digital evidence and indirectly to the integrity. Successfully determining that the document in question and the file located on the suspect system are related is strong proof in the eyes of the court or jury that the digital evidence is trustworthy. It is therefore necessary to identify any potential standard. Again, the exact nature of what this constitutes is dependent on the context of the investigation and the environment being examined. Regardless, understanding that comparison and event reconstruction are important activities in the analysis and examination phases allows the individual collecting the evidence to be more observant:

- Do not overlook analog or document evidence such as printouts, pictures, photocopies, etc.
- Thoroughly document the relative position of any item seized as a potential standard for comparison.

Package for Transport

This task is probably the second most crucial event in crime scene analysis. More than a few investigations have crumbled because of a lack of attention to proper transportation or care in handling. It is only natural, with the "end of the tunnel" in sight, to rush this task and take short cuts. The potential negative impact on the evidence custody chain cannot be stressed enough. Evidence, for probably the first time since the scene was controlled, will leave the controlled "scientific" environment and enter the "no man's" land that lies between the scene and the lab. It is crucial to remember that the chain of evidence extends to all activities related to the life cycle of the evidence (this is often referred to as "from the birth to death of the evidence"). Any inability to account for the who, when, what, where, how, and why of the evidence greatly increases the chances of its being suppressed or at the very least having its authenticity and integrity questioned. This task also impacts on the potential for being held liable for damages directly or indirectly related to the negligent handling of evidence (e.g., loss of critical data, physical damage to computer systems or devices). Here, again, a thorough understanding of the sensitivity of various data or equipment is necessary (e.g., tolerable temperature and humidity ranges, sensitivity to vibrations and electromagnetic radiation, tolerance to long-term storage without electricity) . The investigator should:

- Use common sense and package evidence in appropriate containers (e.g., antistatic bags, bubble wrap).

- Understand the tolerance of various sources of evidence to electromagnetic sources (e.g., magnets, radio transmitters).
- Document all decisions made and be prepared to articulate the reasons for making decisions that could be considered outside of the norm (e.g., leaving computer systems exposed to extreme temperatures or particulates such as dust or transporting the components for prolonged periods without adequate protection from vibrations or external pressures).

Turn over to Lab

As already mentioned, the term "lab" is used in the loosest sense. The lab can be merely a controlled environment back at the office or police station, a private lab, or a governmental lab facility. Regardless of the actual facility, it must have procedures, standards, and processes in place to ensure that the integrity and chain of custody are maintained until the end of the evidence life cycle, which includes returning the system or device back to the owner, repurposing the system, returning the system or device or data back into the production environment, destroying it, storing it until appeal, etc. The lab environment is usually where the analysis, examination, and report phases and tasks take place. Depending on the exact circumstances of the investigation, the analysis and examination may take place on site (in situ). In these cases, the field examination is often just a cursory look to confirm the grounds for probable cause or the issuance of a court order or to assist in the field interview of any suspects. The investigator should:

- Document and have the person to whom the evidence has been turned over sign for the said evidence.
- Ensure that any facility has proper equipment, standards, and procedures in place to store digital or electronic evidence. Several organizations outline minimum standards for the storage and care of digital evidence (e.g., http://www.swgde.org, ASCLAD-LAB Standards, ISO 17025).
- Be sure that all persons in contact with the evidence have the prerequisite knowledge, skills, and abilities, as well as up-to-date training on how to deal with digital evidence.

CONCLUSIONS

Despite the introduction of technology to the crime scene, digital crime scenes are not all that different from the traditional physical crime scene, at least at the lower or more fundamental levels.[8,11,15] This similarity, while often overlooked in the development of all encompassing investigative models, allows digital crime scene analysis to be judged by the same scientific evidence criteria (i.e., Daubert) as the other more common forensic disciplines (e.g., DNA, fingerprint analysis). With the ever-increasing scrutiny and, in some regards, understanding of digital forensics, the judiciary is becoming more stringent in determining what evidence will be admissible.

On the criminal side, the field of computer forensics has historically relied on a lack of understanding and the fear of technology by judges, defense attorneys, and jurors. Times have changed. Judicial training programs are now incorporating workshops on digital evidence; bar associations are providing similar professional development training for both prosecutors and defense attorneys. Certificate, degree, and masters programs are popping up at colleges and 4-year degree granting institutions. The private sector has also jumped on the bandwagon with consulting services and training programs. Vendors and private for-profit groups are offering various certifications and "boot camps." This attention is placing a great demand on the discipline to mature rapidly and move from *ad hoc* approaches to some sort of formalized approach based on a strong theoretical foundation and pragmatic objectives.

Although it is not realistic to believe that the formalization will occur overnight, it is not unrealistic to demand that certain foundations be laid appropriately from a legal, scientific, or criminalistic and practical perspective. This entry was an attempt to nudge the field into a logical direction: the development of basic crime scene analysis processes analogous to what is currently being done and standardized with the traditional physical crime scenes. Rather than reinvent the wheel, following in the footsteps of Lee et al.[2] and adopting or repurposing a tried and tested approach only makes sense.

The theoretical work in the area of digital crime scene analysis and investigations provides a good launching point but is far from sufficient to meet the goal of developing a common approach. It is illogical to try to develop an approach that covers all contingencies and types of digital crime. Digital or computer crime is a vacuous term that is so all encompassing as to be of little utility when attempting to work at a granular level. We do not have one common investigative approach for all physical crimes, so why think digital would be any different? However, if we step back and deconstruct the digital investigation into its basic elements or phases, we find that, at certain levels, like in traditional investigations, generic or at least generalizable tasks across all cases can be identified (see Fig. 1). This also allows us to define overarching forensic principles or rules that act as constraints for gauging the degree of forensic "soundness." By focusing on these levels, forensically sound tasks can be identified and mapped to objectives and to the defined forensic principles.

The nine tasks as outlined in Table 1 are consistent with the methodology and tasks carried out with more traditional physical crime scenes. The tasks are high level, fairly generic, and consistent with the common principles of criminalistics and provide a necessary if not sufficient framework for conducting a digital crime scene analysis. The fact that the tasks may not be completely sufficient is understandable, as the approach is designed to be a minimum framework and not a maximum or checklist in the true sense. As Beebe and Clark[13] stated, a checklist can be a negative, as it tends to be restrictive and constrains the actual investigative process.

The approach described in this entry is not new. It is merely taking what has already been done in criminalistics, IT security, incident response, and theoretical digital forensics and combining the outputs into an approach that maps well to both the real world and the legal requirements that define a discipline as forensics. The objective was to provide some insight on crime scene analysis in general and on practical digital crime scene analysis in particular. More work is obviously necessary in order to mature digital forensics into a real forensic discipline that will assist government, law enforcement, and the private sector in dealing with the increasing amount of computer or cyber crime. What is ultimately required is a better marriage between traditional criminalistics and technological processes. This can only happen if the field becomes more future oriented and looks to the near- and long-term foreseeable challenges and issues, as opposed to the current approach of focusing on what has happened in the past. I believe that this entry is a step in that direction.

There is nothing more deceptive than an obvious fact.
—*Sherlock Holmes*
(*From "The Boscombe Valley Mystery," by Sir Arthur Conan Doyle*)

REFERENCES

1. Rogers, M.; Seigfried, K. The future of computer forensics: A needs analysis survey. Computers Security **2004**, *23* (1), 12–16.
2. Lee, H.; Palmbach, T.; Miller, M. *Henry Lee's Crime Scene Handbook*; Academic Press: San Diego, 2001.
3. Saferstein, R. Criminalistics: An Introduction to Forensic Science, 8th Ed.; Pearson Education: Upper Saddle River, NJ, 2004.
4. Nickell, J.; Fischer, J. Crime Science Methods of Forensic Detection; The University Press of Kentucky: Lexington, 1998.
5. Bates, J. Fundamentals of computer forensics. Int. J. Forensic Comput. Jan/Feb, **1997**.
6. Ahmad, A. The forensic chain-of-evidence model: Improving the process of evidence collection in incident handling procedures. In Proceedings of the 6th Pacific

Asia Conference on Information Systems, Tokyo, Japan, September 2–4, 2002, http://www.dis.unimelb.edu.au/staff/atif/AhmadPACIS.pdf.

7. Smith, F.; Bace, R. A Guide to Forensic Testimony: The Art and Practice of Presenting Testimony as an Expert Technical Witness. Addison-Wesley: Boston, 2003.

8. Meyers, M.; Rogers, M. Computer forensics: The need for standardization and certification within the U.S. court systems. Int. J. Digital Evidence **2004**, *3* (2).

9. Noblett, M.G.; Pollitt, M.M.; Presley, A.L. Recovering and examining computer forensic evidence. Forensic Sci. Commun. **2000**, *2* (4), http://www.fbi.gov/hq/lab/fsc/backissu/oct2000/computer.htm.

10. Reith, M.; Carr, C.; Gunsch, G. An examination of digital forensic models. Int. J. Digital Evidence **2002**, *1* (3).

11. Mocas, S. Building Theoretical Underpinnings for Digital Forensics Research, paper presented at the Digital Forensic Research Workshop (DFRWS), Cleveland, OH, August 2003.

12. Carrier, B.; Spafford, E. Getting physical with the digital investigation process. Int. J. Digital Evidence **2003**, *2* (2).

13. Beebe, N.; Clark, J. A Hierarchical, Objectives-Based Framework for the Digital Investigations Process, paper presented at the Digital Forensic Research Workshop (DFRWS), Baltimore, MD, June 2004.

14. Baryamureeba, V.; Tushabe, F. The Enhanced Digital Investigation Process Model, paper presented at the Digital Forensic Research Workshop (DFRWS), Baltimore, MD, June 2004.

15. McKemmish, R. What is forensic computing? *In Trends and Issues*, Vol. 118; Australian Institute of Criminology: Canberra, 1999.

16. Rogers, M. Computer forensics: Science or fad. Security Wire Dig. **2003**, *5* (55).

17. Farmer, D.; Venerna, V. *Forensic Discovery*; Addison-Wesley: Boston, 2004.

Digital Forensics and E-Discovery

Larry R. Leibrock, Ph.D.
eForensics Inc., Austin, Texas, U.S.A.

Abstract

This entry discusses the role of computer security officers (CSOs) as companies have evolved to rely on information systems. Because of their role, CSOs may be tasked to work with law enforcement agencies in collecting digital evidence. Because of this, the entry continues to discuss issues that a CSO or any other computer security professional would need to know. These issues focus mainly on collection, copying, examination, investigation, and reporting of digital evidence. A list of suggestions for dealing with e-discovery situations is also provided.

RELEVANCE

The profession of the systems security officer has become well defined as agencies and business entities have established and proactively manage information protection programs that involve the use of computers, networks, and digital devices supporting the flow of information, communications, business, and financial transactions. The role of a computer security officer (CSO) is increasingly involved with supporting the collection, safeguarding, and production of computer-based data which is needed for investigation and litigation of administrative, civil, and criminal matters. The CSO is sometimes tasked with providing both advice and assistance in collecting and producing digital information that has been requested by the investigating parties in these matters. As the utility of electronic discovery and digital forensics investigations becomes more apparent, the security professional should become more aware of these matters.

INTRODUCTION

Personal computers and the Internet have revolutionized communication, work, and leisure. Consider these facts:

- In 2004, an estimated 224 million personal computers were in use in the United States, 69 million in Japan, and 46 million in Germany.
- In 2001, over 60% of U.S. households owned at least one personal computer.
- E-mail and instant messaging are the dominant applications in personal computing.
- Some analysts estimate that our need to create, access, and store digital data increases about 50% to 100% each year.

- Both internal investigation and litigation frequently center on the discovery and legal review of documents that are in digital form.

INVESTIGATIVE AND LEGAL DISCOVERY

According to *Legal Definitions* on the Web, "discovery" is the process of gathering information in preparation for trial. This legal process is based on proper discovery of data, materials, and facts relevant to judicial disputes. Traditionally, the courts have used paper-based documentation to support or refute allegations. The legal investigation of digital information is a fairly new occurrence. Recently, many investigations have focused on electronic personal or business communications, such as e-mail and instant messaging. Examples that come to mind are the white-collar and improper stock-trading litigations dealing with both civil and criminal allegations. As our legal system becomes more aware of electronic discovery and the forensics processes of recovering data, we should expect more use of these types of investigations in a wide range of administrative, civil, and criminal issues. With the increasing range and capacities of digital devices, much evidence exists only in digital forms.

Many people believe that modern science founded electronic discovery and digital forensics, but the underlying scientific principle is historical. In 1910, Edmond Locard in Lyon, France, framed Locard's exchange principle, which states that when two objects (e.g., a person and a computer) come into contact, there is always transference of material from each object onto the other. The Locard exchange principle can be restated for our purposes as:

Each user's interaction with digital devices leaves *both user and usage* data on the particular computer device and certain remnants of data remain on the device.

Encyclopedia of Information Assurance DOI: 10.1081/E-EIA-120046831

Copyright © 2011 by Taylor & Francis. All rights reserved.

Electronic discovery is the practice of analyzing and developing opinions about data and information that once were stored in digital form and have been extracted, culled, sorted, and produced in paper or viewable formats. Typically, electronic discovery does not focus on binary data in the deleted, recycled, or unallocated form. In contrast to electronic discovery, digital forensics investigations focus on allocated, unallocated, and fragmentary data. As a working term, *digital forensics* is the legal and ethical practice of collecting, examining, investigating, reporting facts, and developing expert opinions about digital data in its native binary form. Procedures are based in science. Both electronic discovery and digital forensics investigations deal with these established processes: collection, examination, investigation, and reporting. The processes were developed to properly:

- Safeguard the original suspect data.
- Retrieve the suspect data, while not altering or potentially interfering with the original state of the suspect data.
- Investigate the suspect data for the presence of applications or contraband information and the matching of key search terms.
- Report opinions about findings in the suspect digital data. The opinions involve making expert characterizations of these items:

> Person (user account)
> Platform (the device, such as computer, cell phone, digital camera, or e-mail server)
> Application program
> Data and fragments of data
> Time and date tokens

These digital forensics tools perform the tasks listed above:

- *Collection*—Protect the data from any potential changes, chain of custody documentation, contemporized records with enumerated devices or media.
- *Copy*—Perform a sector-to-sector physical (not logical) copy, which serves to extract digital data and fragments contained on the media, and acquire suspect data. (Note that this is not an operating system copy or move, which alters certain data.) The sector-to-sector copy of the suspect media is typically completed with the use of a verification hash (SHA 1 or MD5) that serves to verify the integrity of the forensics copy.
- *Examination*—Use a forensics tool that serves to "undelete" digital data in the unallocated file space of the suspect platform; this serves to forensically recover the unallocated and data fragments in order to conduct further forensics investigations.
- *Investigation*—Conduct a series of key term searches of the extracted data for the presence of programs, graphic images, key words, or cryptographic tokens (known as string or term searching).
- *Reporting*—Prepare bench notes, investigator comments, specific screen captures, and a series of interim, final, and supplemental expert forensics reports that reflect the forensics examiner's opinions and the basis for these opinions.

EXAMINER FOCUS

The forensics examiner usually will focus on the following areas during the typical forensics examination of a computer system. This is the general step-by-step forensics examiner procedure:

- Sector-to-sector copy with hash integrity tools for verification
- File signature analysis
- Recycle bin review
- E-mail review
- Allocated files characterization
- Deleted files characterization
- Special operating files (SWAP, SLACK) review
- Browser history review
- Special or notable programs characterization
- Accounting and credit card data review
- Graphics and pictures review

TYPICAL DATA MORPHOLOGY FROM A FORENSICS PERSPECTIVE

Digital data contained in devices typically has distinct forms:

- *Archival*—Data stored on backup tapes or removable media (such as CDs or thumb drives)
- *Active*—Data that is in use by the operating system
- *Unallocated*—Data that is no longer in use by the operating system; the data is residual and the space it occupies subsequently may be used to store active data not now in use and available for future use

ALLOCATION AND DEALLOCATION OF DATA

Operating systems in most computer devices have constraints in efficiently controlling input/output storage needs and effectively conducting file management operations, such as:

- Creating data
- Writing data
- Accessing data
- Retiring unneeded data

All of these file management operations take place on the physical storage media, such as the magnetic disk, or removable storage device, such as a diskette or USB storage dongle. Most operating systems deallocate data from the operating system file table and write to the next available file space rather than overwriting the current data. This approach efficiently uses computational resources and saves system time. Reiterated, the allocation and deallocation of files efficiently balances computational resources and time. System users do not recognize that most environments do not delete data; rather, data is deallocated and subsequently overwritten by successive files, as the system performs file management operations.

SECURITY PROFESSIONALS IN ELECTRONIC DISCOVERY AND DIGITAL FORENSICS

Computer security professions should consider these suggestions:

- Information security managers or computer security officers should develop a close collaboration with the organization's legal office or corporate counsel. Communicate your roles and responsibilities to them and understand the different ways in which you can help in answering questions, developing responses to legal inquiries, managing requests for production of digital records needed in investigations, and aiding electronic discovery and digital forensics matters. Spend time understanding recent legislation (for example, Sarbanes–Oxley).
- Spend some time with your legal staff to develop an understanding of legal terms relevant to lawsuits and investigative processes. Typically, after a legal suit arises, the parties exchange requests to produce and exchange certain materials. Given some requirements for digital data, the opposing party may provide a written notice to preserve, which is sent to the counsel representing your agency or business. If your counsel receives this preservation notice and you are given a copy, carefully read the details and recognize the potential scope of the discovery requirements. Work with the IT staff to locate the potential storage points for the request, and notify the executive or legal team of any concerns you have about proper safeguarding and preservation.
- You may be asked to help map your networks and prepare lists of servers or client platforms that may contain data needed by the parties in this litigation. Be sure the mappings and reports are accurate and detailed. Make sure you communicate details about data archives, back-up locations, and potential repositories of digital data. These details should be recorded, and you should keep your own copy of these records.

- Do not undertake any forensics investigation unless you have:

   Been authorized by management to undertake the specific investigation
   Received competent forensics technical education
   Achieved the necessary skills with forensics protocols
   Current and practical experience in dealing with the forensics discovery and proper examination of specified types of computer devices (e.g., clients, servers, personal digital assistants, cell phones, digital cameras)
   A professional and personal disinterested relationship with the subjects of this investigative matter

- If you have received any administrative or legal notice to preserve digital devices or data, work with IT systems staff and management to immediately stop using any utility programs, archiving utilities, disk compaction tools, file managers, or virus programs that may potentially alter digital data in use on these devices. Prevent potential data destruction by immediately ceasing archival tape overwriting.
- Ensure that you have fully accounted for any subject equipment or digital devices by serial numbers, and make sure these devices are physically protected until they can be forensically examined as necessary in any discovery notice or court order for both inventory and evidentiary purposes.
- For digital devices that are specified for further forensics examinations, remember the following rule—If the digital device is on, let it stay on until a forensics sector-by-sector data extraction can be performed by a competent forensics specialist. If the device is off, keep it off until a forensic specialist is available to conduct the examination.
- Properly safeguard, in locked containers or restricted access rooms, backup media, archival data records, and disk storage replacements that are within the scope of the preservation notice. Access to the containers or room should be carefully controlled to maintain a chain of custody, which is necessary to properly preserve the data and records during the course of the litigation.
- Keep complete and correct records of your notices, preservation activities, and digital devices that are in the scope of your notice to preserve.
- Secure copies of the agency records retention policy, systems security policies, and agency or corporate acceptable use policy. These should be protected in your professional files and properly produced when requested by management or counsels.
- As the security professional in the security organization, provide all suitable technical aid and support for the forensics team in the scope of its investigation. Typically you will be asked to support certain activities

necessary for the collection and production of media, systems, or records.

- Understand that you may be deposed in adversary settings and your actions and your records will be subject to review and depositional questioning. As an information security professional, you must act to ensure that you have been diligent in performing your assigned duties to secure and protect digital data in these electronic discovery and forensics matters. Your record-keeping should be both correct and complete.

In recent litigation involving agencies and business entities, we have seen that frequently both the chief information officer (CIO) and the CSO are named parties and, therefore, the center of adversarial review in discovery matters. As named parties, these positions will have to respond to many requests for information, records, files, and materials for review by the opposing counsels. Also as named parties in a litigation matter, they should prepare and expect to undergo depositions for these electronic discovery matters. In the depositions, the records, agency or business policies, and actions and decisions of the CSO and CIO will undergo adversary scrutiny. Accordingly, the information security professional should build awareness and maintain high levels of currency in the skills necessary to meet these challenges of electronic discovery and digital forensics.

Directory Security

Ken Buszta, CISSP
Chief Information Security Officer, City of Cincinnati, Cincinnati, Ohio, U.S.A.

Abstract

Many organizations have invested in a wide variety of security technologies and appliances to protect their business assets. Some of these projects have taken their toll on the organization's information technology (IT) budget in the form of time, money, and the number of personnel required to implement and maintain them. Although each of these projects may be critical to an organization's overall security plan, IT managers and administrators continue to overlook one of the most fundamental and cost-effective security practices available—directory and file permission security. This entry addresses the dilemma created by this issue, the threats it poses, offers potential solutions, and then discusses several operating system utilities that can aid the practitioner in managing permissions.

UNDERSTANDING THE DILEMMA

Today, people desire products that are quick to build and even easier to use, and the information technology (IT) world is no different. The public's clamor for products that support such buzzwords as *user friendly* and *feature-enriched* has been heard by a majority of the vendors. We can press one button to power-on a computer, automate signing into an operating system, and have a wide variety of services automatically commence when we start up our computers. In the past, reviews referring to these as ease-of-use features have generally led to increased market share and revenues for these vendors. Although the resulting products have addressed the public's request, vendors have failed to address the business requirements for these products, including:

- *Vendors have failed to understand the growing business IT security model: protect the company's assets.* Vendors have created the operating systems with lax permissions on critical operating files and thereby placed the organization's assets at risk. By configuring the operating system permissions to conform to a stricter permission model, we could reduce the amount of time a practitioner spends in a reactive role and increase the time in proactive roles, such as performance management and implementing new technologies that continue to benefit the organization.
- *Vendors fail to warn consumers of the potential pitfalls created by using the default installation configuration.* Operating system file permissions are associated to user and group memberships and are among the largest pitfalls within the default installation. The default configuration permissions are usually excessive for the average user; and as a result, they increase the potential for unauthorized accesses to the system.
- *Vendors fail to address the average user's lack of computer knowledge.* Many engineers work very diligently to fully understand the operating system documentation that arrives with the software. Even with their academic backgrounds and experience, many struggle and are forced to invest in third-party documentation to understand the complex topics. How can vendors then expect the average user to decipher their documentation and configure their systems correctly?

THREATS AND CONSEQUENCES

For experienced security practitioners, we understand it is essential to identify all potential threats to an environment and their possible consequences. When we perform a business impact analysis on data, we must take into consideration two threats that arise from our file and directory permissions—user account privilege escalation and group membership privilege escalation.

User account privileges refer to the granting of permissions to an individual account. Group membership privileges refer to the granting of permissions to a group of individuals. Improperly granted permissions, whether they are overly restrictive or unnecessarily liberal, pose a threat to the organization. The security practitioner recognizes both of these threats as direct conflicts with the principle of least privilege.

The consequences of these threats can be broken into three areas:

1. *Loss of confidentiality.* Much of our data is obtained and maintained through sensitive channels (i.e., customer relationships, trade secrets, and proprietary methodologies). A disgruntled employee with unnecessarily elevated privileges could easily compromise the system's confidentiality. Such a breach could result in a loss of client data, trust, market share, and profits.

Encyclopedia of Information Assurance DOI: 10.1081/E-EIA-120046768
Copyright © 2011 by Taylor & Francis. All rights reserved.

2. *Loss of integrity.* Auditing records, whether they are related to the financial, IT, or production environments, are critical for an organization to prove to its shareholders and various government agencies that it is acting with the level of integrity bestowed upon it. Improper permissions could allow for accidental or deliberate data manipulation, including the deletion of critical files.

3. *Loss of availability.* If permissions are too restrictive, authorized users may not be able to access data and programs in a timely manner. However, if permissions are too lenient, a malicious user may manipulate the data or change the permissions of others, rendering the information unavailable to personnel.

ADDRESSING THE THREAT

Before we can address the threats associated with file and directory permissions, we must address our file system structure. In this context, we are referring to the method utilized in the creation of partitions. File allocation tables (FAT or FAT32), the Microsoft NT File System (NTFS), and Network File Systems (NFS) are examples of the more commonly used file systems. If practitioners are heavily concerned about protecting their electronic assets, they need to be aware of the capabilities of these file systems. Although we can set permissions in a FAT or FAT32 environment, these permissions can be easily bypassed. On the other hand, both NTFS and NFS allow us to establish the owners of files and directories. This ownership allows us to obtain a tighter control on the files and directories. Therefore, InfoSec best practices recommend establishing and maintaining all critical data on non-FAT partitions.

Once we have addressed our file systems, we can address the permission threat. Consider the following scenario. Your team has been charged with creating the administration scheme for all of KTB Corporation's users and the directory and file permissions. KTB has a centralized InfoSec department that provides support to 10,000 end users. Conservative trends have shown that 25 new end users are added daily, and 20 are removed or modified due to terminations or job transitions. The scheme should take into account heavier periods of activity and be managed accordingly. What would be the best way to approach this dilemma?

As stated earlier, operating systems associate files with users and group memberships. This creates two different paths for the practitioner to manage permissions—by users or by groups. After applying some thought to the requirements, part of your team has developed Plan A to administer the permissions strictly with user accounts. In this solution, the practitioner provides the most scrutiny over the permissions because he or she is delegating permissions on an individual case-by-case basis. The team's process includes determining the privileges needed, determining the resources needed, and then assigning permissions to the appropriate

users. The plan estimates that with proper documentation, adding users and assigning appropriate permissions will take approximately five minutes, and a deletion or modification will take ten minutes. The additional time for deletions and modifications can be attributed to the research required to ensure all of the user permissions have been removed or changed. Under this plan, our administrator will need a little over five and a half hours of time each day to complete this primary function. This would allow us to utilize the administrator in other proactive roles, such as implementation projects and metric collection.

Another part of your team has developed Plan B. Under this plan, the administrator will use a group membership approach. The team's process for this approach includes determining the privileges needed, determining the resources needed, examining the default groups to determine if they meet the needs, creating custom groups to address the unmet needs, assigning permissions to the appropriate groups, and then providing groups with the permissions required to perform their tasks. The team estimates that an administrator will spend approximately five minutes configuring each new user and only two minutes removing or modifying user permissions. The difference in the removal times is attributed to having only to remove the user from a group, as opposed to removing the user from each file or directory. Under Plan B, the administrator will need slightly over four hours to perform these primary duties.

Up until now, both plans could be considered acceptable by management. Remember: there was a statement in the scenario about "heavier periods of activity." What happens if the company goes through a growth spurt? How will this affect the availability of the administrator of each plan? On the other hand, what happens if the economy suffered a downturn and KTB was forced to lay off 10%, or 2000 members, of its workforce? What type of time would be required to fulfill all of the additional tasking? Under Plan A, the administrator would require over 330 tech hours (or over 8 weeks) to complete the tasking, while Plan B would require only 67 hours.

As one can see, individual user permissions might work well in a small environment, but not for a growing or large organization. As the number of users increase, the administration of the permissions becomes more labor intensive and sometimes unmanageable. It is easy for a practitioner to become overwhelmed in this scenario.

However, managing through group memberships has demonstrated several benefits. First, it is scalable. As the organization grows, the administrative tasking grows but remains manageable. The second benefit is ease of use. Once we have invested the time to identify our resources and the permissions required to access those resources, the process becomes templated. When someone is hired into the accounts payable department, we can create the new user and then place the user into the accounts payable group. Because the permissions are assigned to the group

Digital –
E-Mail

and not the individual, the user will inherit the permissions of the group throughout the system. Likewise, should we need to terminate an employee, we simply remove that person from the associated group. (Note: The author realizes there will be more account maintenance involved, but it is beyond the scope of this discussion.)

The key to remember in this method is for the practitioner to create groups that are based on either roles or rule sets. Users are then matched against these standards and then placed in the appropriate groups. This method requires some planning on the front end by the practitioner; but over time, it will create a more easily managed program than administering by user. When developing your group management plan, remember to adhere to the following procedure:

- Determine the privileges needed.
- Determine the resources needed.
- Examine the default groups to determine if they meet the needs.
- Create custom groups to address unmet needs.
- Assign users to the appropriate groups.
- Give groups the privileges and access necessary to perform their tasks.

Because each network's design is unique to the organization, careful consideration should be given to the use of custom groups. In 1998, Trusted Systems Services, Inc. (TSSI) addressed this very issue in its Windows NT Security Guidelines study for NSA Research. In this study, TSSI recommends alleviating most of the permissions applied to the public (everyone) group except for Read and Execute. TSSI then suggested the formation of the custom group called Installers that would take on all of these stripped permissions. The purpose of this group is to provide the necessary permissions for technicians who were responsible for the installation of new applications. Although this group would not enjoy the privileges of the administrator's group, it is still an excellent example of supporting the principle of least privilege through group memberships.

ESTABLISHING CORRECT PERMISSIONS

When establishing the correct permissions, it is important to understand not only the need to correctly identify the permissions at the beginning of the process but also that the process is an ongoing cycle. Regular audits on the permissions should be performed, including at least once a year by an independent party. This will help address any issues related to collusion and help ensure the integrity of the system.

Account maintenance is also a piece of the ongoing cycle. Whether an employee is transferred between departments or is terminated, it is essential for the practitioner to ensure that permissions are redefined for the affected user in a timely manner. Failure to act in such a manner could result in serious damage to the organization.

PERMISSIONS SETTINGS

For demonstration purposes of this entry, we examine the permission settings of two of the more popular operating systems—Microsoft and Linux. The practitioner will notice that these permissions apply to the server as well as the client workstations.

Windows-based permissions are divided into two categories—file and directory. The Window-based file permissions include Full Control, Modify, Read & Execute, Read, and Write. Each of these permissions consists of a logical group of special permissions. Table 1 lists each file

Table 1 Windows®-based file permissions.

Special permissions	Full control	Modify	Read & execute	Read	Write
Traverse Folder/Execute File	X	X	X		
List Folder/Read Data	X	X	X	X	
Read Attributes	X	X	X	X	
Read Extended Attributes	X	X	X	X	
Create Files/Write Data	X	X			X
Create Folders/Append Data	X	X			X
Write Attributes	X	X			X
Write Extended Attributes	X	X			X
Delete Subfolders and Files	X				
Delete	X	X			
Read Permissions	X	X	X	X	X
Change Permissions	X				
Take Ownership	X				
Synchronize	X	X	X	X	X

Table 2 Windows®-based folder permissions.

Special permissions	Full control	Modify	Read & execute	List folder contents	Read	Write
Traverse Folder/Execute File	X	X	X	X		
List Folder/Read Data	X	X	X	X	X	
Read Attributes	X	X	X	X	X	
Read Extended Attributes	X	X	X	X	X	
Create Files/Write Data	X	X				X
Create Folders/Append Data	X	X				X
Write Attributes	X	X				X
Write Extended Attributes	X	X				X
Delete Subfolders and Files	X					
Delete	X	X				
Read Permissions	X	X	X	X	X	X
Change Permissions	X					
Take Ownership	X					
Synchronize	X	X	X	X	X	X

permission and specifies which special permissions are associated with that permission. Note that groups or users granted Full Control on a folder can delete any files in that folder, regardless of the permissions protecting the file.

The Windows-based folder permissions include Full Control, Modify, Read & Execute, List Folder Contents, Read, and Write. Each of these permissions consists of a logical group of special permissions. Table 2 lists each folder permission and specifies which special permissions are associated with it. Although List Folder Contents and Read & Execute appear to have the same special permissions, these permissions are inherited differently. List Folder Contents is inherited by folders but not files, and it should only appear when you view folder permissions. Read & Execute is inherited by both files and folders and is always present when you view file or folder permissions.

For the Linux-based operating systems, the file permissions of Read, Write, and Execute are applicable to both the file and directory structures. However, these permissions may be set on three different levels: User ID, Group ID, or the sticky bit. The sticky bit is largely used on publicly writeable directories to ensure that users do not overwrite each other's files.

When the sticky bit is turned on for a directory, users can have read and/or write permissions for that directory; but they can only remove or rename files that they own. The sticky bit on a file tells the operating system that the file will be executed frequently. Only the administrator (root) is permitted to turn the sticky bit on or off. In addition, the sticky bit applies to anyone who accesses the file.

PERMISSION UTILITIES

To effectively manage permissions, the practitioner should understand the various tools made available to them by the vendors. Both vendors provide a graphical user interface (GUI) and a command line interface (CL). Although there are several high-profile third-party tools available, we will concentrate on the CL utilities provided by the operating system vendors. Table 3 lists the various CL tools within the Windows- and Linux-based operating systems. A brief discussion of each utility follows.

You can use *cacls* to display or modify access control lists (ACLs) of files or folders in a Windows-based environment. This includes granting, revoking, and modifying user access rights. If you already have permissions set for multiple users or groups on a folder or file, be careful using the different variables. An improper variable setting will remove all user permissions except for the user and permissions specified on the command line. It is recommended that the practitioner utilize the edit parameter (/e) whenever using this command line utility.

There are several parameters associated with the *calcs* command, and they can be viewed by simply entering *calcs* at the command prompt. The administrator can then view the permissions set for each of the files within the present directory.

The *chmod* command is used to change the permissions mode of a file or directory.

The *chown* command changes the owner of a file specified by the file parameter to the user specified in the owner parameter. The value of the owner parameter can

Table 3 Permission management utilities.

Utility	Operating environment
calcs	Windows
chmod	Linux/UNIX
chown	Linux/UNIX
usermod	Linux/UNIX

Digital –
E-Mail

be a user ID or a log-in name found in the password file. Optionally, a group can also be specified. Only the root user can change the owner of a file. You can change the group only if you are a root user or own the file. If you own the file but are not a root user, you can change the group only to a group of which you are a member.

Usermod is used to modify a user's log-in definition on the system. It changes the definition of the specified log-in and makes the appropriate log-in-related system file and file system changes.

The *groupmod* command modifies the definition of the specified group by modifying the appropriate entry in the /etc/ group file.

SPECIFIC DIRECTORY PERMISSIONS

As we consider directory permissions, there are three different types of directories—data directories, operating system directories, and application directories. Although the permission standards may differ among each of these directory types, there are two common permission threads shared among all of them—the system administrator group and the system will maintain inclusive permissions to each of them. (Note: The administrator's group does not refer to a particular operating system but to a resource level in general. We could easily substitute *root* for the administrator's title.) Because the administrator is responsible for the network, including the resources and data associated with the network, he must maintain the highest permission levels attainable through the permission structure. The *system* refers to the computer and its requirements for carrying out tasking entered by the user. Failure to provide this level of permission to the system could result in the unit crashing and a potential loss of data. Otherwise, unless explicitly stated, all other parties will maintain no permissions in the following discussions.

The data directories may be divided into home directories and shared directories. Home directories provide a place on the network for end users to store data they create or to perform their tasking. These directories should be configured to ensure adequate privacy and confidentiality from other network services. As such, the individual user assigned to the directory shall maintain full control of the directory. If the organization has defined a need for a dedicated user data manager resource, this individual should also have full control of the directory.

Share directories are placed on the network to allow a group of individuals access to a particular set of data. These directories should not be configured with individual permissions but with group permissions. For example, accounts payable data may be kept in a shared directory. A custom group could be created and assigned the appropriate permissions. The user permissions are slightly different from home directories. Instead of providing the appropriate user with full control, it has been recommended to provide the group with Read, Write, Execute, and Delete. This will only allow the group to manipulate the data within the file; they cannot delete the file itself. Additionally, these permissions should be limited to a single directory and not passed along to the subdirectories.

Security is often an after-thought in the actual application design, especially in the proprietary applications designed in-house. As unfortunate as this is, it is still a common practice; and we must be careful to check the directory permissions of any newly installed application—whether it is developed within the organization or purchased from a third party—because users are often given a full set of permissions in the directory structure. Generally, the application users will not need more than read permissions on these directories, unless a data directory has been created within the application directory structure. If this case exists, the data directory should be treated according to the shared data directory permissions previously discussed. Additionally, the installers group should have the ability to implement changes to the directory structure. This would allow them to apply service patches and upgrades to the application.

The third division is the operating system directories. It is critical for the practitioner to have the proper understanding of the operating system directory and file structure before beginning any installation. Failure to understand the potential vulnerabilities, whether they are in the directory structure or elsewhere, will result in a weak link and an opportunity for the e-criminal.

As stated earlier in the entry, vendors often create default installations to be user friendly. This provides for the most lenient permissions and the largest vulnerabilities to our systems. To minimize the vulnerability, establish read-only permissions for the average user. There will be situations in which these permissions are insufficient, and they should be dealt with on a case-by-case basis. Personnel who provide desktop and server support may fall into this category. In this case, create a custom group to support the specific activities and assign permissions equivalent to read and add. Additionally, all operating system directories should be owned by the administrator only. This will limit the amount of damage an e-criminal could cause to the system.

SENSITIVE FILE PERMISSIONS

Until now, we have only looked at the directory permissions. Although this approach addresses many concerns, it is only half of our battle. Several different file types within a directory require special consideration based on their roles. The particular file types are executable/binary compiled, print drivers, scripting files, and help files.

Executable/binary files are dangerous because they direct the system or application to perform certain actions.

Examples of these file extensions are DLL, EXE, BAT, and BIN. The average user should be restricted to read and execute permissions. They should not have the ability to modify these files.

Print drivers are often run with a full permission set. Manipulation of these files could allow the installation of a malicious program that runs at the elevated privilege. The average user should be limited to a read and execute permission set.

Improperly set permissions on scripting files, such as Java and ActiveX, could allow for two potential problems. By providing the elevated privileges on these files, the user has the ability to modify these files to place a call to run a malicious program or promote program masquerading. Program masquerading is the act of having one program run under the pretext that it is actually another program. For these reasons, these files should also have a read and execute permission set.

Help files often contain executable code. To prevent program masquerading and other spoofing opportunities, these files should not be writeable.

MONITORING AND ALERTS

After we have planned and implemented our permission infrastructure, we will need to establish a methodology to monitor and audit the infrastructure. This is key to ensuring that unauthorized changes are identified in a timely manner and to limit the potential damage that can be done to our networks. This process will also take careful planning and administration.

The practitioner could implement a strategy that would encompass all of the permissions, but such a strategy would become time-consuming and ineffective. The more effective approach would be to identify the directories and files that are critical to business operations. Particular attention should be given to sensitive information, executables that run critical business processes, and system-related tools.

While designing the monitoring process, practitioners should be keenly aware of how they will be notified in the event a monitoring alarm is activated and what type of actions will be taken. As a minimum, a log entry should be created for each triggered event. Additionally, a mechanism should be in place to notify the appropriate personnel of these events. The mechanism may be in the form of an e-mail, pager alert, or telephone call. Unfortunately, not all operating systems have these features built in; so the practitioner may need to invest in a third-party product. Depending on the nature of the organization's business, the practitioner may consider outsourcing this role to a managed services partner. These partnerships are designed to quickly identify a problem

area for the client and implement a response in a very short period.

Once a response has been mounted to an alert, it is also important for the team to review the events leading up to the alert and attempt to minimize the event's recurrence. One can take three definitive actions because of these reviews:

1. *Review the present standards and make changes accordingly.* If we remember that security is a business enabler and not a disabler, we understand that security must be flexible. Our ideal strategy may need slight modifications to support the business model. Such changes should be documented for all parties to review and approve and to provide a paper trail to help restore the system in the event of a catastrophic failure.
2. *Educate the affected parties.* Often, personnel may make changes to the system without notifying everyone. Of course, those who were not notified are the ones affected by the changes. The practitioner may avoid a repeat of the same event by educating the users on why a particular practice is in place.
3. *Escalate the issue.* Sometimes, neither educating users nor modifying standards is the correct solution. The network may be under siege either from an internal or external source, and it is the practitioner's duty to escalate these issues to upper management and possibly law enforcement officials. For further guidance on handling this type of scenario, one should contact one's legal department and conduct further research on the CERT and SANS Web sites.

AUDITING

Auditing will help ensure that file and directory systems are adhering to the organization's accepted standards. Although an organization may perform regular internal audits, it is recommended to have the file and directory structure audited by an external company annually. This process will help validate the internal results and limit any collusion that may be occurring within the organization.

CONCLUSION

While most businesses are addressing the markets' calls for user-friendly and ease-of-use operating systems, they are overlooking the security needs of most of the corporate infrastructure. This has led to unauthorized accesses to sensitive file structures and, as a result, is placing the organization in a major dilemma. Until we take the time to properly identify file and directory security permissions that best fit our organization's business charter, we cannot begin to feel confident with our overall network security strategy.

BIBLIOGRAPHY

1. Anonymous. *Maximum Linux Security*; Sams Publishing: Indianapolis, IN, 1999.

2. Jumes, J. G.; Cooper, N. F.; Chamoun, P.; Feirman, T. M. *Microsoft Windows NT 4.0 Security, Audit and Control*, Microsoft Press: Redmond, WA, 1999.

3. Internet Security Systems, Inc. *Microsoft Windows 2000 Security Technical Reference*; Microsoft Press: Redmond, WA, 2000.

4. Kabir, M. J. *Red Hat Linux Administrator's Handbook*, 2nd Ed.; M&T Books: Foster City, CA, 2001.

5. Schultz, E. E. *Windows NT/2000 Network Security*; Macmillan Technical Publishing: New York, 2000.

6. Sutton, S.; Cothrell, S. *Windows NT Security Guidelines*; Trusted Systems Services, Inc.: Urbana, IL, 1999.

Distributed Computing: Grid Environment

Sasan Hamidi, Ph.D.
Chief Security Officer, Interval International, Inc., Orlando, Florida, U.S.A.

Abstract

Regardless of how inexpensive hardware becomes, building a high-powered cluster computing environment is out of the reach of many organizations and individuals. Analyzing large chunks of data may require more CPU cycles and memory than an organization has in its arsenal. Enter grid computing: for a reasonable fee, and depending on the type and quantity of resources needed, a company can "rent" grid time from IBM and Sun Micro Systems. It is a beautiful concept: the power of a Big Blue for the price of a middle-tier server. The concept of grid computing has evolved in the past 30 years. In this short-time, the idea of utilizing unused processing cycles across a network for purposes other than what they were originally intended for has gone from a beautiful thought to reality. This entry discusses the evolution of grid computing, emphasizing security issues and standards that have risen as the direct result of its popularity. It reviews major developments in standardizing grid access and authentication, their strength and weaknesses, current vulnerabilities, and paths to the future.

INTRODUCTION

The idea of distributed computing has existed for a long time—since the days when man realized the limitations of processing cycles and memory. Even Gordon Moore's bold prediction 40 years ago has not reduced the need for more power and speed. In essence, distributed computing grew from the need to know more information faster. Its central idea is to use "parallel" processing instead of a first-in, first-out, single-processor scheme. From there, the concept grew from the "parallel" mode to the use of various computers across a network to accomplish a task. Grid computing is a form of distributed computing where computers across a vast network, and perhaps geographically dispersed, work together to form a "super computer." It was originally intended for the academic and research world, where obtaining fast computers was not economically feasible. Many universities started developing their own grids to support some very advanced research. Later on, as the concept began to take hold and many earlier issues were resolved, commercial uses of this environment became a reality. An example of an early grid is the Internet: a series of computers working together to allow millions of people to communicate and disseminate information through its many resources.

A BRIEF HISTORY OF SEARCH FOR EXTRATERRESTRIAL INTELLIGENCE

Any discussion of grid computing without mention of the SETI project would be incomplete. "SETI" stands for "Search for Extraterrestrial Intelligence." What are the possibilities that in amongst the billions of stars within our galaxy and billions of other galaxies there are life forms? What if these living entities have been searching for us as well? It seems that the most reasonable method of inter-galactic communication would be through some type of signal that can travel well beyond its source; signals such as microwave radio and optical waves could accomplish such a task.

In the early 1960s, astronomer Frank Drake conducted the very first search for microwave radio signals from our solar system by pointing an 85 foot antenna in the direction of two sun-like stars for a period of two months. Although Drake did not detect any signals of extraterrestrial origin, his research sparked the interest of many in the astronomical community, specifically Russian scientists. The Russians expanded Drake's search by utilizing multidirectional antennas. This search method allowed them to listen to a wider range of signals, and not just from nearby solar systems. The problem, however, was the enormous number of signals that they had to process. The resulting signal processing issues proved to be more than just merely backlogging work; chunks of data were being discarded to save time.

Interest in SETI gained momentum once again in the early 1970s; NASA's Ames Research Center in Mountain View, California began reviewing all the issues that were stumbling blocks to an effective search. A group of scientists put together a comprehensive report detailing existing issues and technologies, code-named *Cyclops*, which forms the foundation on which much of the future work by the SETI project would be based. One of the most important issues highlighted in Cyclops was the need for

Encyclopedia of Information Assurance DOI: 10.1081/E-EIA-120046769
Copyright © 2011 by Taylor & Francis. All rights reserved.

Digital –
E-Mail

"super computers" capable of processing billions of instructions per second, and parallel computing. Although much progress was made in advancing technologies required for this tremendous project, NASA lost its funding in 1992, and as of the publication of this entry, has not received funding to continue this research. Project Phoenix, spun from NASA's SETI project, fueled by private funding, promises to utilize the world's largest antennas and resources to answer perhaps one of the most profound questions ever raised.

May 17, 1999, marked the launch of the University of California at Berkley SETI@Home project, the very first open-grid computing system. SETI@Home takes advantage of millions of computers spread around the globe by allowing users to download a small program that acts similar to a screen saver. The concept is fairly simple: the program launches when the computer is idle and begins the task of searching signals collected from various sources. Once the analysis is complete, a connection to the Internet is established, the result of analysis is submitted and a new chunk of raw data is downloaded. The computing power harnessed by utilizing the cycles of individual PCs participating in the SETI@Home project comprises the biggest supercomputer in the world. This is a bold statement considering that the majority of this grid consists of home-based PCs with average CPU speed and memory.

INTRODUCTION TO GRID ARCHITECTURE

How are grids built? Is there an underlying architecture upon which they are designed? Are there any standards? These are questions that must be answered before any security discussion can take place.

There are three basic types of grids:

- *Cluster grids*: a group of computers clustered together in a network form a cluster grid. Normally, cluster grids are used by individual departments and designed for specific projects. For example, the Sun N1Grid consists of thousands of machines running Linux and Sun OS operating systems that are clustered together.
- *Enterprise grids*: a collection of cluster grids forms an enterprise grid. In many cases, as the need for more processing power arises, additional clusters can be added to an existing grid cluster. These additional resources allow multiple departments to share the computing cycles necessary to accomplish their projects.
- *Global grids*: when multiple enterprise grids are connected, they form a global grid. In this scheme, multiple organizations are sharing the resources of the grid and performing multiple tasks, each with their own policies and procedures.

BENEFITS OF GRID COMPUTING

A grid can often provide the following:

- *Cost-benefits*. It is much cheaper for an organization needing computing power to utilize a commercial grid instead of purchasing and building an in-house solution. In many cases, the time-to-market is shortened tremendously while hardware, software, and development costs are simultaneously reduced.
- *Scalability*. The grids' modular design allows for additions, integration and upgrades. These can expand as the needs of its users grow.
- *Flexibility*. As organizational needs change, so can the computing power of the grid. The power of the grid can adjust to consumption in almost real-time.

These following are some of the overall challenges of grid computing:

- Specialized middleware—the software glue that connects an application to the "plumbing" to make it run—is needed.
- This "glue" does not yet exist in a robust form.
- Mechanisms are needed for determining what computer and database resources are available.
- Methods for organizing them into a functioning system are needed.
- Perhaps the biggest challenge is security.

GRID SECURITY CONSIDERATIONS

In the beginning, the idea of assembling tremendous computing power was the single driving force behind the invention of the grid. There was not much talk of security because grid use was limited to academic and high-level research; neither of these environments was at that time concerned about possible compromise or loss of their data. However, as commercial use of these grids began to grow, designers realized that users demanded a much more secure environment. There was a definite need for standardizing security measures across all grids because that is the basic premise behind their existence: they are able to communicate with one another, seamlessly and unbeknownst to the user.

General Grid Security Issues

Grid security must:

- Allow access to trusted resources
- Trust in a dynamic environment (thousands of computers) that is hard to define

- Utilize commercial grid middleware, most of which are designed for "intra-grids" and not suitable for open grids
- Make use of virtual organization (VO). VOs are a set of individuals or institutions with some common purpose or interest that need to share their interests to further their goals; and one of the central issues with VOs is that they do not scale well

Specific Security Challenges

- Application protection: all applications on the grid must be protected from unauthorized access
- Authentication (X.509, proxy credentials): how, what, and where?
- Authorization (SAML)
- Access control (XACML)
- Accounting: auditing and monitoring
- Node-to-node communication: intercommunication amongst the grid computers
- Protection against malicious code, viruses, worms, etc.

One of the most widely used and implemented security standards was designed by the Globus Project in 1998. [Microsoft has since integrated Globus Security Infrastructure (GSI) into Passport.] The Globus Toolkit includes software for security, information infrastructure, resource management, data management, communication, fault detection, and portability. It is packaged as a set of components that can be used either independently or in concert to develop applications. Every organization has unique modes of operation, and collaboration between multiple organizations is hindered by incompatibility of such resources as data archives, computers, and networks. The Globus Toolkit was conceived to remove obstacles that prevent seamless collaboration. Its core services, interfaces and protocols allow users to access remote resources as if they were located within their own machine room while simultaneously preserving local control over who can use resources and when.

The GSI, part of the Globus Toolkit, addresses many security issues that stood in the way of utilizing grids in a commercial environment. The issues that prompted the design of GSI include:

- Users must be able to authenticate securely to the grid: authentication schemes, policies and procedures must be developed that implement standards across the grid.
- Elements within the grid must be able to communicate securely; hosts or clusters must be able to authenticate one another in a robust manner.
- Implementing security across organizational boundaries: in other words, there should not be a "centrally managed" security environment. Each organization could potentially apply its policies to the grid.

- A "single sign-on" solution must be in place for users so that they would not have to log in multiple times to various systems and applications.

The architecture of GSI is based on the freely available SSLeay security package. At the heart of the authentication scheme is the use of X.509 authentication certificates (based on PKI) which can be signed by multiple certificate authorities (CAs). A GSI certificate includes four primary pieces of information:

- A subject name, which identifies the person or object that the certificate represents.
- The public key belonging to the subject.
- The identity of a CA that has signed the certificate to certify that the public key and the identity both belong to the subject.
- The digital signature of the named CA.

One of the features of these certificates is the addition of an expiry date. These certificates are referred to as *proxy certificates*—a temporary binding of a new key pair to an existing user identity. The use of proxy certificates allows an entity to temporarily delegate its rights to remote processes or resources on the Internet. Each certificate has a time expiry allowing for additional security. Once a certificate has been authenticated, the holder will no longer be required to present these credentials again, thus allowing a "single sign-on" scheme.

If two parties have certificates, and if both parties trust the CAs that signed each other's certificates, then the two parties can prove to each other that they are who they say they are. The GSI uses the secure socket layer (SSL) for the mutual authentication protocol. Each party involved in this mutual authentication must have a copy of the other's trusted CA certificate, which contains the public key for that party.

Because the communication between parties includes public key information, it is not secured, meaning that there are no encryptions at this stage. However, GSI can be configured so that shared key information can be used. In this scheme, all authentications can be performed using encryption (today GSI supports many different encryption schemes, including AES).

One of the issues at the center of every key-based encryption is how to safeguard the private key. In the GSI scheme, the private key is stored on the local user's computer. As in other encryption algorithms, such as PGP, to use the GSI, the user must enter the passphrase for the private key. This is the "password" through which the key was originally encrypted. Without this passphrase, the user will not be able to authenticate within GSI's infrastructure to use the grid services.

A Bit About the Proxy Certificate

As mentioned earlier, the term *proxy certificate* is used to define a short-term restricted credential that can be created from a normal, long-term, X.509 credential.

One of the issues in using proxy certificate is how to restrict rights of a delegated proxy to a subset of those associated with the issuer. In other words, how can we ensure that only the issuer of the certificate is actually the one using the rights granted to it? The answer is through the use of a "restriction policy" embedded in the proxy certificate. The policy reduces the rights available to the proxy certificate to a subset of those held by the user. This, however, raises another concern, and that is the possibility of "policy language" wars. The GSI has been able to resolve this issue by including only the policy specification, without actually defining the language. The idea is that the language can evolve over time.

SUMMARY

Over the past decade, there has been tremendous progress in not only standardizing grid infrastructure, but as the use of commercial grids increases, so have security protections. Currently, Sun Microsystems, IBM, AT&T, and hundreds of other organizations offer grid services for commercial use. Many smaller organizations in need of computing power are taking advantage of these services. It is clear that many of the challenges that grid security architects face are those confronting normal computing environments.

BIBLIOGRAPHY

1. Foster, I.; Kesselman, C.; Tuecke, S. The anatomy of the grid. Int. J. High Perform. Comput. Appl. **2001**, *15*(3), 200–222.
2. Nagaratnam, N.; Janson, P.; Dayka, J.; Nadalin, A.; Siebenlist, F.; Welch, V.; Foster, I.; Tueck, S. The security architecture for open grid service, White Paper, Open Grid Service Architecture Security Working Group (OGSA-SEC-WC), July 2002, http://www.cs.virginia.edu/~humphrey/ogsa-sec-wg/OGSA-SecArch-v1-07192002.pdf (accessed October 2006).
3. Walker, D. W.; Li, M.; Rana, O.F.; Shields, M. S.; Huang, Y. The software architecture of a distributed problem-solving environment. Concurrency-Pract. Ex. **2000**, *12*(15), 1455–1480.
4. The Globus Project. Globus® Toolkit, http://www.globus.org (accessed October 2006).

Digital –
E-Mail

DoD Information Assurance Certification and Accreditation Process (DIACAP)

Robert B. Batie, Jr., CISSP-ISSAP, ISSEP, ISSMP, CAP
Cyber Defense Solutions, Network Centric Systems, Raytheon Company, Largo, Florida, U.S.A.

Abstract
All federal information technology (IT) systems must be certified and accredited in accordance with national policies, federal standards, and agency guidelines regardless of the sensitivity of the information processed on those information systems. These standards and guidelines define information assurance (IA) requirements and the certification and accreditation (C&A) process used to ensure the confidentiality, availability, integrity, and non-repudiation of the information processed on those systems.

INTRODUCTION

The Department of Defense Information Assurance Certification and Accreditation Process (DIACAP)[1] is the new process for the certification of all information systems. DIACAP includes 157 IA controls, grouped into eight categories. The level of controls required for a specific system depends on two factors: its mission assurance category (MAC) and its confidentiality level (CL).

The three mission assurance categories are information that is mission-vital, information that is important to the support of forces, and information that is used in the conduct of day-to-day business. There are also three CLs: classified, sensitive, and public, in descending order of the required controls. The nine combinations of MAC and CL establish nine baseline information assurance (IA) levels for the Global Information Grid (GIG). The MAC controls focus on integrity and availability, while the CL controls focus on confidentiality.

A confidentiality control, for example, would require that network access be gained only with an individual authenticator based on the Department of Defense (DoD) public key infrastructure (PKI). Integrity controls include accomplishment of identification and authentication using a DoD PKI class 3 or 4 certificate and a hardware security token. An availability control would require an annual IA review that evaluates existing policies and processes to ensure procedural consistency and uninterrupted operations.

While DIACAP was developed at the highest levels of DoD, once it was promulgated, it was up to individual DoD entities to develop policies and workflows for its implementation. Each department is implementing DIACAP in its own way. For example, the Air Force has issued a DIACAP workflow process called SISSU, which stands for security, interoperability, supportability, sustainability, and usability. The SISSU process includes four phases that are in sync with mandated DIACAP activities. As program managers (PM) and certification and accreditation (C&A) personnel go through the SISSU, they will be able to track the DIACAP activities throughout the five phases.

The Navy implemented instruction and two associated Web-based services—the DIACAP Knowledge Service (KS) and the Enterprise Mission Assurance Support Service (eMASS) Web portal. These services are designed to manage the C&A process from start to finish in a workflow format that allows the principal stakeholders access to the process flow for input, review, editing, and approval. It also provides access to all the IA controls, as well as best practices. Other services have implemented some variation of DIACAP that is consistent with the DoD policy.

The DIACAP KS provides process information as well as implementation guides, generic forms, and templates. KS also provides C&A News, updates to IA controls, and a central point for process data dissemination. eMASS aids in document production by automating the status reporting, workflows, and artifact creation. It also provides security control look-up and acts as a database for infrastructure documents. It tracks all enterprise systems and links the C&A efforts across organization.

DIACAP became effective immediately upon its release in November 2007, superseding DoD Information Technology Security Certification and Accreditation Process (DITSCAP) as the department's new process for the C&A of all information systems and determining when a system should be authorized to operate. DIACAP represents DoD's efforts to comply with the information security mandates required of all federal departments under the Federal Information Systems Management Act (FISMA). Its release triggered a process of transition from DITSCAP throughout all DoD components. But it is a true transition only in a limited sense. Newly built or newly acquired information systems must immediately comply with DIACAP, while systems that had been certified and accredited under DITSCAP (usually for a 3 year period) were allowed to run out the clock before

Encyclopedia of Information Assurance DOI: 10.1081/E-EIA-120045493
Copyright © 2011 by Taylor & Francis. All rights reserved.

Digital –
E-Mail

having to be recertified under DIACAP. This phased approach allowed the cost of transition to be spread over time. DIACAP establishes the DoD IA C&A process for authorizing the operation of DoD information systems, assigning, implementing, and validating DoDI 8500.2[2] standardized IA controls and managing IA posture across DoD information systems. It is consistent with DoD regulatory policy (IA 8500 series) and legislative policy (FISMA) and provides for availability of C&A status of DoD information systems across the GIG. DIACAP supports transition to GIG standards, e.g., from fixed system boundaries to a net-centric environment.

DIACAP PHASES

DIACAP is a five-phase process with subactivities in each phase as shown in Fig. 1. Within each phase there are activities that must be completed before moving to the next phase. These phases make up the DIACAP process, which begins with Initiate and Plan the IA C&A.

DIACAP Phase 1—Initiate and Plan the C&A activities begin by registering the systems with the certifying agency. Registering includes basic information about the system, its intended use, users, and MAC level. The DIACAP C&A team is made up of stakeholders in the program such as program management, subject matter experts, systems users, maintainers, and developers. IA

controls are assigned based on the MAC level and CL. The team develops a strategy as to how the C&A process will proceed. It outlines the type of accreditation that will be sought by the systems owners whether it be Platform IT, type accreditation, enclave, or outsource-based IT systems for example. Once these have been documented, finalized, and approved, the team is ready to begin implementation and validation in the next phase.

It is critical to identify those specific IA documents applicable to your program early and get an agreement with the key stakeholders involved in the systems development and C&A process. While the principal IA controls (requirements) documents are listed in NIST SP 800-53A, DoD 8500.2, and CNSS 1253, the C&A processes are DIACAP DoDIIS C&A Guideline, and other applicable documents. In other words, DIACAP is the process but the IA controls come from the NIST, DoD, and CNSS documents listed above. Implementing the IA C&A process is considered an art because of the management and coordination skills required and a science because of the technical implementations of the IA controls that must be accomplished.

DIACAP Phase 2—Implement and Validate the security controls for the system. The system will be configured according to security policies needed to satisfy the IA controls. When these tasks are complete, the system will be validated through testing to ensure it provides the necessary security countermeasures to protect the confidentiality, integrity, and availability of the information.

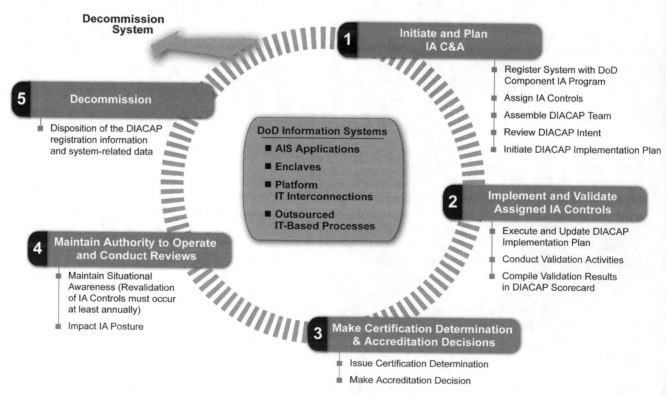

Fig. 1   DIACAP activities summaries.

After the validation activities are completed, the results are compiled and documented in the DIACAP Scorecard in preparation for the DAA to make the C&A decision in Phase 3.

DIACAP Phase 3—In DIACAP Phase 3, the results of all validation activities are analyzed to determine if the residual risk are at an acceptable level. The certifying official issues certification determination and makes the accreditation decision. This decision could be Interim Authority to Operate (IATO), Authority/Approval to Operate (ATO), or Denial of Authority to Operate (DATO). (Details of the accreditation decision are provided later in the section below.)

DIACAP Phase 4—Assuming the system received an IATO or ATO, it moves to Phase 4 where it maintains situation awareness, IA posture, and is monitored and periodically reviewed for continued compliance. The status of its security posture is reported according to security policy.

DIACAP Phase 5—At DIACAP Phase 5, the system is decommissioned. All activities related to the system, related data or objects, GIG supporting IA infrastructure, and core enterprise services are properly disposed of.

DIACAP GOVERNANCE

The DIACAP Enterprise Governance Structure is intended to synchronize and integrate DIACAP activities across all levels. The governance structure comprised of three major elements:

- Accreditation structure: aligned to GIG Mission Areas; it addresses cross-cutting issues.
- Configuration control and management (CCM) structure: the DIACAP Technical Advisory Group (TAG) supports KS content including IA controls.
- C&A process administration and certification structure: authority and responsibility for certification are vested in the DoD Component Senior IA Officials (SIAOs)—SIAOs serve as Certifying Authority (CA); CIO is responsible for administration of overall C&A process.

ACCREDITATION DECISIONS

The accreditation decision that may be made consists of the following four types:

1. ATO–Authority to Operate (no provisions)
2. IATO–Interim ATO [provisions set forth in Plan of Action and Milestone (POA&M) required]
3. IATT–Interim Authority to Test (inside given timeline only)
4. DATO–Denial of ATO (reassess the Implementation Plan)

When the decision is to grant an ATO, the system is fully accredited and authorized to operate. It is monitored for IA-Relevant Issues (vulnerabilities, exploits, policy changes, best practices, etc.), reviewed annually (at minimum), and reaccredited on a 3 year cycle unless significant changes are made. The system is decommissioned when no longer adequately supporting or performing its intended mission.

When the decision is an IATO, the Program of Actions and Milestones (POA&M) is imposed. The POA&M is a plan that identifies the systems deficiencies and what actions will be taken to resolve them. An IATO is granted for no longer than 180 days with the opportunity to be extended up to an additional 180 days if the system has shown significant progress during the initial period. If the system fails to adequately implement IA controls the decision to DATO may be imposed. In this case the developers must start the DIACAP process over.

IATT is issued for a short period of time to allow a system that is still under development to be testing in an operational environment. It may be connected to another accredited system but its intent and purpose is to validate if the system will perform as expected.

DIACAP C&A PACKAGE

The DIACAP C&A package is developed through DIACAP activities and maintained throughout a system's life cycle. These activities generate the C&A package components listed in the "Comprehensive Package," while the "Executive Package" contains a subset of the information contained in the "Comprehensive Package" necessary for an accreditation decision. The components that comprise the Comprehensive and Executive Packages are outlined in Table 1.

Comprehensive C&A Package

The Comprehensive C&A Package includes the full set of templates, diagram, and supporting documentation necessary to describe the system or site and its compliance with all required IACs. The Comprehensive Package includes the following components, along with their subcomponents:

- Systems Identification Profile (SIP)
- DIACAP Implementation Plan (DIP)
- Scorecard
- IT Security POA&M

Executive C&A Package

The Executive C&A Package is a subset of the Comprehensive C&A Package, and contains the key elements from the Comprehensive C&A Package required for

Table 1   DIACAP package content.

Item	Comprehensive DIACAP Package	Executive package
1	Systems Identification Profile	Systems Identification Profile
2	Implementation Plan • IA controls: inherited and implemented • Implementation status • Responsible entities • Resources • Estimated completion date for each IA control	
3	Supporting documentation for certification • Actual validation results • Artifacts associated with implementation of IA controls • Other	
4	DIACAP Scorecard • Certification determination • Accreditation determination	DIACAP Scorecard • Certification determination • Accreditation determination
5	POA&M (if required)	POA&M (if required)

an accreditation decision. The DAA may request the Comprehensive C&A Package vs. the Executive C&A Package when they determine that they need the additional elements contained in the Comprehensive C&A Package for their decision. The Executive C&A Package contains at a minimum the following components:

- SIP
- Scorecard
- IT Security POA&M

CONCLUSION

The DIACAP is a new process that is expected to streamline the C&A process and provide greater flexibility in implementing IA controls. It is a risk-based implementation rather than a policy-based implementation found in the DITSCAP. It covers five phases in order to align with the widely implemented systems development life cycle. DIACAP requirement to align with FISMA and eGovernment is being accomplished through the use of Web-based applications and portals such as eMASS and KS. These technical implementations make the process less cumbersome by providing stakeholders with electronic access to the comprehensive and executive packages instead of traditional means of paper and removable storage media.

The DIACAP is not perfect and like most of its C&A artifacts, it is a living document that will be updated, streamlined, and continuously improved over time. As the process matures, it will become more automated through technical implementations and the information systems certification process.

REFERENCES

1. DOD Information Assurance Certification and Accreditation Process (DIACAP) Handbook, Department of the United States Navy, Version 1.0. July 15, 2008.
2. DoDI, 8500.2. Information Assurance Implementation, February 6, 2003.

Domain Name Service (DNS) Attacks

Mark Bell
Independent Consultant, U.S.A.

Abstract
Although still a rare occurrence, DNS attacks are increasing. Data encryption makes DNS attacks pointless, and also protects many other services on the Internet.

INTRODUCTION

Of all the Internet services, the Domain Name Service (DNS) is the most used, and perhaps the most vulnerable. Without DNS, users would have to know the "dotted quad" address of every resource that they use on the Internet; humans have a poor memory for numbers, but can recall the names of Web sites without much difficulty. In many cases, a company's Web address can be derived by adding "www" and "com" to each side of the company name; for example, http://www.microsoft.com. All of this depends on DNS. Imagine having to enter 199.29.24.3 instead of http://www.crcpress.com into a browser, and having to somehow remember the address of all of the other Web sites in that way. If DNS is essential now, when Internet addresses are only 32 bits long (IPv4), imagine the problem when IPv6 is widely adopted and many addresses increase to 128 bits.

DNS was designed by Paul Mockapetris of USC in 1984, and was described in RFCs 882 and 883. At that time, little thought was given to security; the service was designed to be efficient and reliable so that it could be deployed and used with the minimum of effort. It fulfilled all expectations and has been in continuous use since its inception, with remarkably few problems. If the lack of concern for security seems surprising, it should be remembered that at that time, the Internet community was much smaller, and use of the Internet was restricted to universities, government departments, the military, etc.—and widespread use of the Internet was not envisaged. TCP/IP was supposed to be the "temporary" network, a stopgap suite of protocols that would be replaced in a few years by the OSI suite—what was the point of spending much time on something that would be obsolete in a few years? The fiction that OSI would replace TCP/IP continued until the late 1980s, and was responsible for many decisions that seem poor in retrospect.

How DNS Works

In order to understand the vulnerability of DNS, one needs to know how it functions—at least in enough detail to follow the flow of information. Nearly all TCP/IP applications and services are based on the client/server model; in UNIX®, telnet is the client and telnetd is the server. With telnet, a user enters "telnet service.crcpress.com," invoking the telnet client and passing the name of the host as a parameter. The client passes the parameter—in this case, service.crcpress.com—to a resolver routine compiled into the client code, and the resolver then attempts to resolve the name into a dotted quad address. The resolver first looks in a file on the host machine—"/etc/hosts" on UNIX—to see if there is an entry matching the destination host name. If there is no entry, the resolver then sends a query to the local name server, whose address must be known to the client host. (See Fig. 1.)

The name server will look in his cache to see if there is an entry for the host. There are several ways that the name may have been placed in the cache:

1. If the destination host is on the local network, the name and address will have been entered into a table by the DNS administrator. This table is kept on the hard disk, and is reloaded every time the name server boots up. These are the addresses for which this server is considered to be "authoritative." The name server is the "primary" server for these names.
2. The name server also has a list of servers entered into this same table, which are authoritative for other sites. When the name server boots, it will download the name/address table from each of these servers and add the contents to its own table. The name server is said to be "secondary" to these other servers.
3. The name server has resolved the same name for another client recently, and the entry is still valid.

If there is no entry in the cache, the name server will pass the query to one of the root servers or a parent server to see if the name exists in the cache on one of these machines. How does the name server know which root server to query? The last part of the name will be the domain in which the name resides, so the address "service.crcpress.com" is in the .com domain. The

Encyclopedia of Information Assurance DOI: 10.1081/E-EIA-120046520
Copyright © 2011 by Taylor & Francis. All rights reserved.

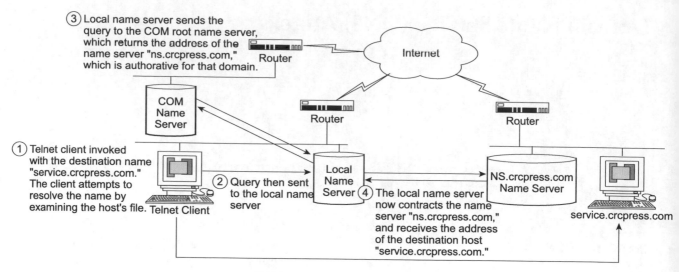

Fig. 1 Resolving a domain name.

domains are organized by function—a commercial, for-profit company is in the .com domain, government departments are in the .gov domain, and military installations are in the .mil domain, etc.

The com server has a table containing the address of all the name servers (at least "top level" servers) in the .com domain; every time a new company joins the .com domain, the address of its main name server is added to the table. The com server will return the address of a name server that can be queried for the address of the destination host, in this case ns.crcpress.com. The client's name server will then query ns.crcpress.com for the address associated with service.crcpress.com, and will be sent the dotted quad address, together with a time for which the name/address pair is guaranteed to be valid (TTL—Time to Live). This address will be added to the cache in the local name server, and kept there until the TTL has expired. In this way, the name server that resolves a query can control how long the query is to be considered valid by other name servers.

The client host can now open the telnet session with the destination host, but has had to trust the Domain Name Service completely—there is no real way of checking that the resolution is correct, and that the telnet session is being opened with the correct host. This is the problem with the DNS service—it relies on trust, which means that it is open to abuse.

Opportunities—Abusing the DNS Trust

The most obvious damage that can be inflicted on an Internet site is to corrupt the name server's table, or enter the names of invalid addresses with hosts, so that the users would not be able to initiate Internet services without knowing their dotted quad address; this would be relatively harmless, because the users would realize a problem existed, and would be able to flush the name server's cache. This is just mindless vandalism, quickly discovered and speedily resolved. There are other

possibilities, however, one of which will be explored in this entry.

Imagine a company (Careless Share Dealings, Inc.) carries out financial transactions with another company (Gullible Stocks PLC) via the Internet on a regular basis, and that another person or company (Hacker Information) could benefit if it could read these transactions in a timely manner—perhaps these transactions could be shared dealings between two brokers, with the transactions being automatically recorded every 30 minutes (see Fig. 2). If the company's name server could be persuaded that the address of the financial server at Gullible had changed, and the new address was relay.hacker.com, then all of the information would be sent to the new address. Now, all that the host at Hacker has to do is to copy the details of every packet to a file on the hard disk, and relay the packet on to its proper destination, Gullible Stocks. Assuming that the share dealing software used TCP, two sessions would be set up: one between Careless and Hacker and another between Hacker and Gullible. Note that the traffic from Gullible back to Careless would follow the same path; DNS is used by the original client (Careless) because Careless does not know the address of the server (Gullible). When the server receives a request to start a session, he gets the address of the client in the TCP/IP packet, so he has no need to use DNS. He is trusting that the client is who he says he is—in this case, a bad assumption. Even if the service between Careless and Gullible had passwords that changed every 30 seconds, this would not prevent the attack from taking place because Hacker does not need to know the password—he is passing on valid information from Careless.

Poisoning the Cache

The most obvious way to fool the Careless name server into believing that the address of the Gullible Finance server had changed would be to break into the name server at

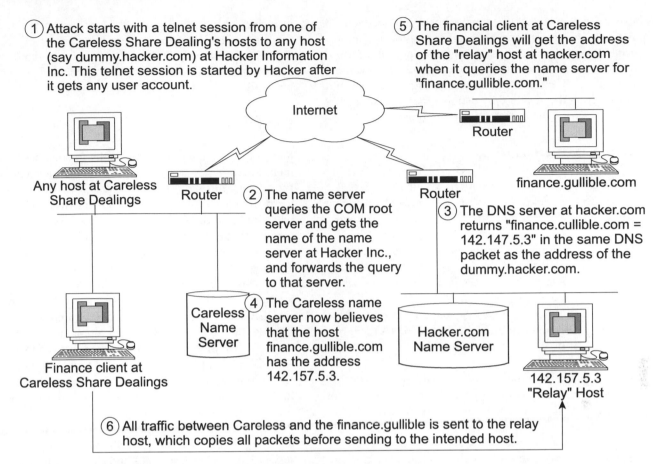

Fig. 2 Poisoning the DNS cache.

Digital –
E-Mail

Gullible and place the new address in the table. This would risk discovery, however, because all of the other hosts at Gullible would also get the incorrect address; if Gullible had a firewall, there would be logs showing that traffic between two hosts on the Gullible site is being diverted to another host on the Internet and relayed back, and the game would be over.

Another way that the attack can succeed for the longer term would be to penetrate the name server at Careless. Because the Careless name server does not have the name/address pair of the Gullible finance server in a permanent table, the Careless name server would have to serve as the primary server for the Gullible domain; this could be done without affecting the hosts at Gullible—they would still be sending their queries to the Gullible name server. However, the changes to the Careless name server would soon be noticed by the DNS administrator, and again the game would be over.

The best strategy is to use a name server somewhere else on the Internet and exploit the biggest weakness of name servers—the complete trust they must have in any other name servers in order to be efficient. When a name server sends a query, it not only accepts the answer to the original query, but will also accept answers to queries it has not made, and will cache those answers without attempting authentication. This allows a name server to send a list of recent updates any time that it answers a query, and helps to reduce the name resolution traffic on the Internet. Now, all that the attacker needs to do is to make a modification to the server at Hacker Information and then trigger a query to Hacker from Careless. This can be done in several ways; some examples follow:

1. Forge mail on the Careless mail server and address the mail to a user at Hacker Information. This would cause the mail server to query the name server at Careless for the Hacker mail server and, of course, the name server would eventually query the name server at Hacker after contacting the root name server.
2. Break into any machine on the Careless site, and telnet to any host on the Hacker site. This would trigger a DNS query, with the same results.
3. Alter a URL on a Web server at the Careless site or any Web server the users at Careless will visit. This will also trigger a name query.

This is almost a perfect "man-in-the-middle" attack, with very little chance of tracking down the attacker. Even if one could trace the machine running the relay software, it is probable that it belongs to an innocent third party who is unaware that his machine has been compromised. The hacker will be sending the captured information to an unused account on another innocent's machine, and will log in at leisure to collect it. The attacker could also improve the strategy by using someone else's DNS server to launch the initial poisoning attack.

Averting DNS Attacks

One of the popular misconceptions about DNS is that a "double reverse lookup" can be used to authenticate name resolution and prevent this attack. This works as follows:

1. The name is resolved in the usual manner (i.e., DNS).
2. When the client receives the answer, an inverse query is made, where the address is sent to a DNS server and a name is returned.
3. The client then compares the name returned with the name used in the original query, and aborts the transaction if the names do not coincide.

This sounds good, but in practice, this is unworkable for several reasons. What happens if the attacker has not only poisoned the cache with the name/address pair, but has also poisoned the inverse cache? The names would then coincide. If two servers were used—one to resolve the original query and one for the inverse check—there would be no guarantee that both servers had not been poisoned. The biggest problem with the double reverse lookup is that it can only be performed on the primary and secondary servers—the client would have to send the inverse query directly to the name server at Gullible. Name servers do not refer inverse queries they cannot resolve to other name servers; so, if the inverse query is sent to the Careless name server, it would be returned as unresolved.

The best way to prevent DNS attacks is to put the names and addresses of critical hosts in the host's file. The client resolver will look at this file before sending a query to DNS, and this will avert all DNS attacks using any of the host names in the host's file. The problem here is that this is labor intensive; the whole purpose of the DNS system is to prevent this kind of maintenance burden. In any case, this is only possible for relatively few hosts, although one could cut the amount of duplication by maintaining a central copy of the host's file, and distributing it to other hosts as needed.

Encryption

Many of the security problems on the Internet have a common cause—data is being transported in clear text or in other forms that can easily be read. The real answer to most of these problems is to encrypt all data in transit. What would be the point of the DNS attack, and copying the data from the resulting relay software on the Hacker host, if the data could not be read? The technology to encrypt data has been available for years. SNA has always been able to encrypt data so that it cannot be read in transit, and it is obvious (with hindsight) that this should have been part of the original IP specification. A secure channel can be imposed between Internet sites by the use of encryption routers that will scramble all of the data transmitted between specified sites. Custom applications should be written to encrypt all data in transit; the availability of encryption libraries from RSA and other vendors has simplified development of secure applications.

The real point here is that the choice has to be made between replacing DNS with a more secure service, or rendering DNS attacks pointless by data encryption. The first option only cures the problems with DNS—assuming that a truly secure version of DNS is possible. The second option will render DNS attacks pointless and also protect many other services on the Internet at the same time.

DNS attacks are still a rare occurrence on the Internet. Other attacks, such as the sniffer attack, can be launched more easily and require less knowledge. There are simpler and more direct ways of achieving the same ends—intercepting and copying data in transit—but as precautions are taken against these, simpler methods become more common, and life becomes more difficult for the hacker, one can expect to see an increase in the incidents of DNS attacks.

Downsizing: Maintaining Information Security

Thomas J. Bray, CISSP
Principal Security Consultant, SecureImpact, Atlanta, Georgia, U.S.A.

Abstract

Today, companies of every size are relying on Internet and other network connections to support their business. For each of those businesses, information, and network security have become increasingly important. Yet, achieving a security level that will adequately protect a business is a difficult task because information security is a multifaceted undertaking. A successful information security program is a continuous improvement project involving people, processes, and technology, all working in unison.

Companies are especially vulnerable to security breaches when significant changes occur, such as a reduction in workforce. Mischievous individuals and thieves thrive on chaos. Companies need even more diligence in their security effort when executing a reduction in workforce initiative. Security is an essential element of the downsizing effort.

EVEN IN GOOD TIMES

In good times, organizations quickly and easily supply new employees with access to the computer and network systems they need to perform their jobs. A new employee is a valuable asset that must be made productive as soon as possible. Computer and network administrators are under pressure to create accounts quickly for the new hires. In many instances, employees may have more access than they truly need. The justification for this, however misguided, is that "it speeds up the process."

When an employee leaves the company, especially when the departure occurs on good terms, server and network administrators tend to proceed more slowly. Unfortunately, the same lack of urgency exists when an employee departure is not on good terms or a reduction in the workforce occurs.

DISGRUNTLED EMPLOYEES

Preparing for the backlash of a disgruntled employee is vital during an employee layoff. Horror stories already exist, including one about an ex-employee who triggered computer viruses that resulted in the deletion of sales commission records. In another company, an ex-employee used his dial-up access to the company network to copy a propriety software program worth millions of dollars. An article in *Business Week* sounded an alarm of concern.[1]

The biggest threat to a company's information assets can be the trusted insiders. This is one of the first concepts learned by information security professionals, a concept substantiated on several occasions by surveys conducted by the Computer Security Institute (CSI) and the Federal Bureau of Investigation (FBI).

The market research firm Digital Research conducted a survey for security software developer Camelot and *eWeek* magazine. They found that, "Insiders pose the greatest computer security threat. Disgruntled insiders and accounts held by former employees are a greater computer security threat to U.S. companies than outside hackers." Out of 548 survey respondents, 43% indicated that security breaches were caused by user accounts being left open after employees had left the company.[2–4]

YEAH, RIGHT. WHAT ARE THE CASES?

In many cases of ex-employees doing harm to their former employers, the extent of the problem is difficult to quantify. Some companies do not initially detect many of the incidents, and others prefer to handle the incidents outside the legal system. A small percentage of incidents have gone through the legal system and, in some cases, the laws were upheld. Each time this occurs, it strengthens support for the implementation of information security best practices. Although many states have computer crime laws, there is still only a small percentage of case law.

Example Incident: *The Boston Globe*, by Stephanie Stoughton, Globe Staff, 6/19/2001[5]

Ex-tech worker gets jail term in hacking. A New Hampshire man who broke into his former employer's computer network, deleted hundreds of files, and shipped fake e-mails to clients was sentenced yesterday to six months in federal prison. U.S. District Judge Joseph DiClerico also ordered Patrick McKenna, 28, to pay $13,614.11 in restitution to Bricsnet's offices in Portsmouth, N.H.

Encyclopedia of Information Assurance DOI: 10.1081/E-EIA-120046566
Copyright © 2011 by Taylor & Francis. All rights reserved.

Digital –
E-Mail

Following McKenna's release from prison, he will be under supervision for 2 years.

HIGH-TECH MEASURES

E-Mail

E-mail is one of the most powerful business tools in use today. It can also be a source of communications abuse and information leakage during a downsizing effort. The retention or destruction of stored e-mail messages of ex-employees must also be considered.

Abuse

Do not allow former employees to keep e-mail or remote access privileges in an attempt to ease the pain of losing their jobs or help in their job searches. The exposure here is the possibility of misrepresentation and inappropriate or damaging messages being received by employees, clients, or business partners. If the company wants to provide e-mail as a courtesy service to exiting employees, the company should use a third party to provide these services. Using a third party will prevent employees from using existing group lists and addresses from their address books, thus limiting the number of recipients of their messages.

Employees who know they are to be terminated typically use e-mail to move documents outside the organization. The company's termination strategy should include a method for minimizing the impact of confidential information escaping via the e-mail system. E-mail content filters and file-size limitations can help mitigate the volume of knowledge and intellectual capital that leaves the organization via e-mail.

Leakage

E-mail groups are very effective when periodic communication to a specific team is needed. The management of the e-mail group lists is a job that requires diligence. If ex-employees remain on e-mail group lists, they will continue to receive company insider information. This is another reason the company should not let former employees keep company e-mail accounts active as a courtesy service.

Storage

E-mail messages of ex-employees are stored on the desktop system and the backup disk or tapes of the e-mail server. The disposal of these documents should follow the company's procedure for e-mail document retention. In the absence of an e-mail document retention policy, the downsizing team should develop a process for determining which e-mail messages and attachments will be retained and which will be destroyed.

LOW-TECH MEASURES

The fact that information security is largely a people issue is demonstrated during a reduction in force initiative. It is the business people working hand in hand with the people staffing the technical and physical security controls who will ensure that the company is less vulnerable to security breaches during this very disruptive time in the company.

Document Destruction

As people exit the company during a downsizing effort, mounds of paper will be thrown in the trash or placed in the recycling bin. Ensuring that confidential paper documents are properly disposed of is important in reducing information leaks to unwanted sources.

After one company's downsizing effort, I combed through their trash and recycling bins. During this exercise, I found in the trash several copies of the internal company memo from the CEO that explained the downsizing plan. The document was labeled *"Company Confidential—Not for Distribution Outside of the Company."* This document would have been valuable to the news media or a competitor.

All companies have documents that are confidential to the business; however, most companies do not have a document classification policy. Such a policy would define the classification designations, such as:

- Internal Use Only
- Confidential
- Customer Confidential
- Highly Restricted

Each of these classifications has corresponding handling instructions defining the care to be taken when storing or routing the documents. Such handling instructions would include destroying documents by shredding them when they are no longer needed.

Many organizations have also been entrusted with confidential documents of business partners and suppliers. The company has a custodial responsibility for these third-party documents. Sorting through paper documents that are confidential to the company or business partners and seeing that they are properly destroyed is essential to the information protection objective.

SECURITY AWARENESS

Security awareness is a training effort designed to raise the security consciousness of employees (see Table 1). The employees who remain with the organization after the downsizing effort must be persuaded to rally around the company's security goals and heightened security

Table 1   Checklist of security actions during reduction in workforce effort.

General

- Assemble a team to define the process for eliminating all computer and network access of downsized employees. The team should include representation from Human Resources, Legal, Audit, and Information Security.
- Ensure that the process requires managers to notify the employees responsible for Information Security and the Human Resources department at the same time.
- Educate remaining employees about Information Security company policy or best practices.
- Change passwords of all employees, especially employees with security administrative privileges.
- Check the computer and laptop inventory list and ensure that downsized employees return all computer equipment that was issued to them as employees.
- Be current with your software licenses—ex-employees have been known to report companies to the Software Piracy Association.

Senior Managers

- Explain the need for the downsizing.
- Persuade key personnel that they are vital to the business.
- Resist the temptation to allow downsized officers, senior managers, or any employees to keep e-mail and remote access privileges to ease the pain or help in their job search. If the company wants to provide courtesy services to exiting employees, the company should use a third party to provide these services, not the company's resources.

Server Administrators, Network Administrators, and Security Administrators

- Identify all instances of employee access:
  — Scan access control systems for IDs or accounts of downsized employees.
  — Scan remote access systems for IDs or accounts of downsized employees.
  — Call business partners and vendors for employee authorizations.
- Consult with departing employee management:
  — Determine who will take on the exiting employee's access.
  — Determine who will take control of exiting employee's files.

E-mail System Administrators

- Identify all instances of employee access:
  — Scan the e-mail systems for IDs or accounts of downsized employees.
- Forward inbound e-mail messages sent to an ex-employees' e-mail account to their manager.
- Create a professional process for responding to individuals who have sent e-mails to ex-employees, with special emphasis on the mail messages from customers requiring special care.
- Remove ex-employees from e-mail group lists.

Managers of Exiting Employees

- Determine who will take on the access for the exiting employees.
- Determine who will take control of exiting employee computer files.
- Sort through exiting employee paper files for documents that are confidential or sensitive to the business.

Prepare for the Worst

- Develop a list of likely worst-case scenarios.
- Develop actions that will be taken when worst-case scenarios occur.

posture. Providing the remaining team of employees with the knowledge required to protect the company's vital information assets is paramount. Employees should leave the security training with a mission to be security-aware as they perform their daily work. Some of the topics to be covered in the security awareness sessions include:

- Recognizing social engineering scenarios
- Speaking with the press
- Keeping computer and network access credentials, such as passwords, confidential

- Changing keys and combinations
- Encouraging system administrators and security administrators to be vigilant when reviewing system and security logs for suspicious activity
- Combining heightened computer and network security alertness with heightened physical security alertness

CONCLUSION

Information security involves people, processes, and technical controls. Information security requires attention to

Digital –
E-Mail

detail and vigilance because it is a continuous improvement project. This becomes especially important when companies embark on a downsizing project.

Companies should always be mindful that achieving 100% security is impossible. Mitigating risk to levels that are acceptable to the business is the most effective methodology for protecting the company's information assets and the network systems.

Businesses need to involve all employees in the security effort to have an effective security program. Security is most effective when it is integrated into the company culture. This is why security awareness training is so important.

Technology plays a crucial role in security once the policies and processes have been defined to ensure that people properly manage the technological controls being deployed. A poorly configured firewall provides a false sense of security. This is why proper management of security technologies provides for a better information protection program.

REFERENCES

1. http://www.businessweek.com/bwdaily/dnflash/jun2001/nf20010626_024.htm.
2. http://www.usatoday.com/life/cyber/tech/2001-06-20-insider-hacker-threat.htm.
3. http://www.zdnet.com/zdnn/stories/news/0,4586,2777325,00.html.
4. http://www.cnn.com/2001/TECH/Internet/06/20/security.reut/index.html.
5. http://www.boston.com/dailyglobe2/170/business/Ex_tech_worker_gets_jail_term_in_hacking+.shtml.

Due Care: Minimum Security Standards

Robert Braun
Partner, Corporate Department, Jeffer, Mangles, Butler & Marmaro, LLP, California, U.S.A.

Stan Stahl, Ph.D.
President, Citadel Information Group, Los Angeles, California, U.S.A.

Abstract

This entry discusses the need for privacy and safety with technology evolving constantly and explores the implications of contract and tort law on information security. The authors try to address two main questions: "What responsibility does an enterprise have for protecting the information in its computer systems, particularly information that belongs to others?" and "What responsibility does an enterprise have to keep its information systems from being used to harm others?" To answer these questions, the authors discuss the concept of an information security minimum standard of due care and present different laws and regulations that have been passed to help provide security in these modern times.

INTRODUCTION

The microcomputer revolution, and with it the rise of local area networks, wide area networks, and the Internet, is more than 20 years old. Interconnecting computers and networks has brought great gains in productivity and opened up exciting new realms of entertainment and information. And it has brought the world closer together. But these virtues are not without unintended, and sometimes undesired, consequences.

The Federal Trade Commission (FTC) estimates that approximately 3,000,000 Americans were the victims of identity theft in 2002, with the majority of these originating in thefts of information from computers or computer systems. At the same time, cyber-vandals write computer viruses that propagate from enterprise to enterprise at the speed with which untrained workers open attachments, causing significant economic loss while systems are being repaired. Electronic inboxes are clogged with spam. A Cyber-Mafia cruises the Internet, looking for easy prey from whom to steal money and other cyber data of value. Dangerous adults too easily hang around children and teenage chat rooms, seeking to prey on legitimate users, often with tragic consequences. And the Department of Homeland Security warns of terrorists taking over large numbers of unsuspecting computer systems to be used in coordination with a large-scale terrorist attack.

Computer crime is a serious challenge. And it is getting worse...exponentially worse. Every computer crime study over the past 5 years conclusively confirms this. Computer crime is growing exponentially. The speed with which computer viruses spread and the number of security weaknesses in our systems are growing exponentially. Consequently, the total cost to business, in lost productivity, theft, embezzlement, and a host of other categories, is growing exponentially.

Against this backdrop are two legal questions:

1. What responsibility does an enterprise have for protecting the information in its computer systems, particularly information that belongs to others?
2. What responsibility does an enterprise have to keep its information systems from being used to harm others?

As answers to these two questions emerge, we believe they will define an evolving *information security minimum standard of due care* that will serve to establish, at any point in time, an *adequacy baseline* below which an enterprise will have criminal or civil liability. The specific details of any *information security minimum standard of due care* are likely to vary among the patchwork quilt of federal and state laws, industry-specific developments, interpretations by different regulatory agencies, and how the judicial system addresses these issues.

There are three co-evolving forces that will serve to define any evolving information security minimum standard of due care.

1. The evolving legislative and regulatory landscape regarding the duty of information holders to protect non-public information about others in their computer systems
2. The evolving interpretation of contract and tort law as it pertains to securing information and information assets
3. The evolving recommended effective security practices of the professional information security community

Encyclopedia of Information Assurance DOI: 10.1081/E-EIA-120046832
Copyright © 2011 by Taylor & Francis. All rights reserved.

This entry begins with an exposition of the privacy and safety issues addressed by legislation and subsequent regulations. It then explores the implications of contract and tort law on information security. Subsequently, this entry explicates several current information security management practice models, which serve to define "effective security practices" in use by the information security profession. These are then brought together in the context of a *battle of the expert witnesses*, in which we identify what we believe is an *information security minimum standard of due care*. Finally, this entry discusses how this standard is likely to evolve over the next few years.

LAWS AND REGULATIONS AFFECTING PRIVACY IN COMPUTER TRANSACTIONS

Gramm–Leach–Bliley

It is the policy of the Congress that each financial institution has an affirmative and continuing obligation to respect the privacy of its customers and to protect the security and confidentiality of those customers' non-public personal information.

In furtherance of the policy ... each agency or authority ... shall establish appropriate standards for the financial institutions subject to their jurisdiction relating to administrative, technical, and physical safeguards

1. to insure the security and confidentiality of customer records and information;
2. to protect against any anticipated threats or hazards to the security or integrity of such records; and
3. to protect against unauthorized access to or use of such records or information which could result in substantial harm or inconvenience to any customer
   —*15 USC 6801, Gramm–Leach–Bliley Act*

With these words, Congress in 1999 passed the Gramm–Leach–Bliley Act (GLBA) (see also Table 1). The GLBA regulates the use and disclosure of non-public personal information about individuals who obtain financial products or services from financial institutions.

The GLBA, on its face, applies only to financial institutions. However, the broad definitions in the GLBA mean that it applies not only to banks and other traditional financial institutions but also to a wide variety of firms and individuals that assist in effecting financial transactions. These include not only banks, credit unions, broker dealers, registered investment advisors, and other "obvious" financial institutions, but also mortgage lenders, "pay day" lenders, finance companies, mortgage brokers, account servicers, check cashers, wire transferors, travel agencies operated in connection with financial services, collection agencies, credit counselors and other financial advisors, tax preparation firms, non-federally insured credit unions, and investment advisors. The Federal Trade Commission has even held that the GLBA applies to lawyers that provide tax and financial planning services (In a letter the American Bar Association, dated April 8, 2002, J. Howard Beales, Director of the Federal Trade Commission Bureau of Consumer Protection, states that attorneys are not exempt from the application of the GLBA privacy rule.), although that position has, predictably, been contested.

From the standpoint of maintaining the privacy of customer information, the GLBA generally prohibits a financial institution from disclosing non-personal public information to a non-affiliated third party, either directly or through an affiliate, unless the institution has disclosed to the customer in a clear and conspicuous manner, that the information may be disclosed to a third party; has given the consumer an opportunity to direct that the information not be disclosed; and described the manner in which the consumer can exercise the non-disclosure option.

Financial institutions must also prepare and make public *privacy statements* that describe the institution's policies with regard to disclosing non-public personal information to affiliates and non-affiliated third parties; disclosing non-public personal information of persons who have ceased to be customers of the institution; and the categories of non-public personal information the institution collects. The institution is required to disclose clearly and conspicuously those policies and practices at the time that it establishes a customer relationship and not less than annually during the continuation of the customer relationship. This has resulted in an avalanche of paper from banks, brokerage houses, accountants, and others who provide financial services.

In addition to regulating how financial institutions can intentionally share information, the GLBA also regulates what steps a business must take to prevent the unintentional sharing of non-public personal information in its computer systems. Each of the different federal and state agencies having GLBA jurisdiction has written separate information security safeguard regulations [66 FedReg 8616, 12 CFR 30 (Office of the Comptroller of the Currency); 12 CFR 208, 211, 225, 263, (Board of Governors of the Federal Reserve System); 12 CFR 308, 364 (Federal Deposit Insurance Corporation), 12 CFR 568, 570 (Office of Thrift Supervision), 16 CFR 314 (Federal Trade Commission); 17 CFR 248 (Securities and Exchange Commission).]. While no two are identical, all have a similar flavor:

- Executive management involvement
- Risk- and vulnerability-driven, based on regular assessments
- Written information security policies
- Employee training
- Control of third parties

Table 1 The Gramm–Leach–Bliley Act (16 CFR 314).

Federal Trade Commission

Standards for Safeguarding Customer Information

Sec. 314.3 Standards for safeguarding customer information.

(a) **Information security program.** You shall develop, implement, and maintain a comprehensive information security program that is written in one or more readily accessible parts and contains administrative, technical, and physical safeguards that are appropriate to your size and complexity, the nature and scope of your activities, and the sensitivity of any customer information at issue. Such safeguards shall include the elements set forth in Sec. 314.4 and shall be reasonably designed to achieve the objectives of this part, as set forth in paragraph (b) of this section.

(b) **Objectives.** The objectives of section 501(b) of the Act, and of this part, are to:

  (1) Insure the security and confidentiality of customer information;
  (2) Protect against any anticipated threats or hazards to the security or integrity of such information; and
  (3) Protect against unauthorized access to or use of such information that could result in substantial harm or inconvenience to any customer.

Sec. 314.4 Elements.

In order to develop, implement, and maintain your information security program, you shall:

(a) Designate an employee or employees to coordinate your information security program.

(b) Identify reasonably foreseeable internal and external risks to the security, confidentiality, and integrity of customer information that could result in the unauthorized disclosure, misuse, alteration, destruction or other compromise of such information, and assess the sufficiency of any safeguards in place to control these risks. At a minimum, such a risk assessment should include consideration of risks in each relevant area of your operations, including:

  (1) Employee training and management;
  (2) Information systems, including network and software design, as well as information processing, storage, transmission and disposal; and
  (3) Detecting, preventing and responding to attacks, intrusions, or other systems failures.

(c) Design and implement information safeguards to control the risks you identify through risk assessment, and regularly test or otherwise monitor the effectiveness of the safeguards' key controls, systems, and procedures.

(d) Oversee service providers, by:

  (1) Taking reasonable steps to select and retain service providers that are capable of maintaining appropriate safeguards for the customer information at issue; and
  (2) Requiring your service providers by contract to implement and maintain such safeguards.

(e) Evaluate and adjust your information security program in light of the results of the testing and monitoring required by paragraph (c) of this section; any material changes to your operations or business arrangements; or any other circumstances that you know or have reason to know may have a material impact on your information security program.

There has also been a spill-over effect from regulation under the GLBA. The key regulator under the GLBA is the Federal Trade Commission, and its experience has spurred it to explore areas not directly implicated under the GLBA (See discussion of FTC Safeguards Rule, below). Additionally, many industries that are directly impacted by the GLBA, such as the banking and insurance industries, are beginning to apply the standards imposed on them to their clients. For example, insurance companies are beginning to review privacy statements and policies of their insureds, and banks are beginning to consider these issues in their underwriting decisions.

Health Care and Insurance Portability and Accountability Act

One of the first significant attempts to adopt a standard of care for electronic transactions in the field of health care is the Health Care and Insurance Portability and Accountability Act of 1996 (HIPAA). While much of HIPAA addresses the rights of patients under the health-care insurance plans, HIPAA also includes key provisions relating to the privacy rights of patients in response to the concerns that this information was not being adequately protected. Insurance companies, doctors, hospitals, laboratories, and employers who

Digital – E-Mail

maintain employee health plans are subject to HIPAA provisions.

The Department of Health and Human Services (DHHS) has issued *privacy rule* regulations providing for the protection of the privacy of "individually identifiable health information" created, received, or otherwise in the possession of entities covered by HIPAA (45 CFR 160, 162, 164).

HIPAA information security regulations require covered entities to do the following to protect "individually identifiable health information" (45 CFR 162, Federal Register, Vol. 68, No. 34, 8377):

- Ensure the confidentiality, integrity, and availability of all electronic protected health information the covered entity creates, receives, maintains, or transmits.
- Protect against any reasonably anticipated threats or hazards to the security or integrity of such information.
- Protect against any reasonably anticipated uses or disclosures of such information that are not permitted or otherwise required.
- Ensure compliance by its workforce.

HIPAA is a broad-ranging act and has spawned significant regulation. Importantly, because it affects so many different entities, one can expect that the standards required by HIPAA will have a significant meaningful impact on non-health care-related industries.

Sarbanes–Oxley Act

The Sarbanes–Oxley (SOX) Act of 2002 has been called the most significant new securities law since the Securities and Exchange Commission was created in 1934. SOX places substantial additional responsibilities on officers and directors of public companies, and imposes very significant criminal penalties on CEOs, CFOs, and others who violate the various provisions of SOX.

While the corporate scandals at HealthSouth, Adelphia, Qwest, Tyco, and of course, Enron, the mother of SOX, made headline news, the new requirements under SOX promise to transform the way that all public companies are managed from top to bottom. Even corporations that are not public today, but hope to become publicly owned or to be sold to a public company in the future, need to be aware of the basic requirements for operating a company in compliance with certain requirements of SOX, particularly the requirements for establishing and following detailed internal controls and disclosure of these controls and procedures. These requirements will obligate all public companies to address their information security procedures and practices in a very public way.

Section 404 of Sarbanes–Oxley requires the management of a public company to assess the effectiveness of the company's internal control over financial reporting.

Section 404 also requires management to include in the company's annual report to shareholders, management's conclusion as a result of that assessment about whether the company's internal control is effective. While there are a variety of steps companies must take to comply with SOX, it is Section 404 that has the most relevance to information security with its requirement that management develop, document, test, and monitor its internal controls and its disclosure controls and procedures.

The most significant new responsibility faced by the CEO and CFO of every public company is the required personal certification of the company's annual and quarterly reports. The SEC has specified the exact form of personal certification that must be made, without modification, in every annual and quarterly report, including a certification that the CEO and CFO have evaluated the company's internal controls and disclosure controls within the past 90 days and disclosed to the audit committee and outside auditor any deficiencies in such controls. To meet the certification requirements regarding the internal controls and disclosure controls, the SEC recommends that every company establish a disclosure committee consisting of the CFO, controller, heads of divisions, and other persons having significant responsibility for the company's principal operating divisions. The disclosure committee should review the company's existing internal controls and disclosure controls and procedures, document them, evaluate their adequacy, correct any material weaknesses, and create monitoring and testing procedures that will be used every quarter to continuously evaluate the company's internal controls and disclosure controls and procedures.

It will be critical for every company to involve its auditors in the design and implementation of the internal controls and disclosure controls and procedures because, beginning in July 2003, the SEC requires a public company's outside auditor to audit and report on the company's internal controls and procedures. The big four accounting firms have issued public advice that they will not be able to audit a company's internal controls without some documentation of the design and procedures, including the monitoring and testing procedures used by the company. This means that a company will need to establish detailed records, as well as reporting, testing, and monitoring procedures that must be reviewed by the company's outside auditors. If a company's outside auditor finds that there are significant deficiencies or material weaknesses in the company's internal controls, the auditor will be required to disclose its findings in its audit report on the company's financial statements. The company will then be forced to correct the deficiencies, or its CEO and CFO will be unable to issue their personal certifications that the internal controls are adequate.

While SOX was adopted in response to perceived inadequacies and misconduct by corporate officers and directors, its focus on systems, and certification of the adequacy of reporting schemes, is likely to have a broad effect on the

Digital –
E-Mail

establishment of corporate controls and standards. A variety of consultants, including accounting firms, software developers, and others, have developed and are actively marketing automated systems to assist in establishing a reporting regimen for corporations, allowing certifying officers and boards of directors to establish compliance with the requirements imposed by SOX and ensuring that corporate controls are followed. These changes, moreover, do not exist in a vacuum; principles of corporate governance that first applied to public corporations have often been extended to private companies, sometimes through application of state laws and regulations applied to non-public companies, other times through market forces, such as auditors and insurance carriers who adopt similar standards for public and non-public companies. According to the American Society of Certified Public Accountants, "Many of the reforms could be viewed as best practices and result in new regulations by federal and state agencies [affecting non-public companies]."[1]

Children's Online Privacy Protection Act

The Children's Online Privacy Protection Act (COPPA) became effective April 21, 2000, and applies to any online operator who collects personal information from children under 13. The rules adopted under COPPA spell out what a Web site operator must include in a privacy policy, when and how to seek verifiable consent from a parent, and what responsibilities an operator has to protect the children's privacy and safety online. Unlike HIPAA and GLB, COPPA is designed to address a class of individuals—minors—and not a regulated business. It thus has a scope that is in many ways broader, although in some ways less inclusive, than prior existing laws. In addition to creating challenges for the design of Web sites—for example, many Web operators have redesigned their Web sites to make them less appealing to children under 13—COPPA and the rules adopted implementing COPPA impose requirements on privacy notices and create specific procedures that must be followed before an operator can obtain information from children. COPPA has caused many businesses (and should spur all businesses) to consider their privacy policies, both in form and substance, and develop practice guidelines.

FTC Safeguards Rule

As noted above, the Federal Trade Commission has been at the forefront of privacy regulations. In that role, the FTC has adopted a "safeguards rule" that requires each financial institution to:

> develop, implement, and maintain a comprehensive information security program that is written in one or more readily accessible parts and contains administrative, technical, and physical safeguards that are appropriate to

your size and complexity, the nature and scope of your activities, and the sensitivity of any customer information at issue. [16 CFR 314]

The FTC regulation is a step that is likely to take us beyond existing laws. Under its authority to protect consumers, the FTC is in a position to adopt regulations that cross the boundaries of all industries. Significantly, it also requires each business to make determinations that are consistent with the size and complexity of its business and activities, as well as a sensitivity of customer information at issue. It does not provide specific rules but does require that businesses regulate themselves. Companies are thus forced to analyze their operations, needs, and vulnerabilities in order to comply with the rule.

FTC Unfair and Deceptive Practice

One of the key tools used by the FTC to address privacy violations has been the application of the FTC's policy toward unfair and deceptive practices to online privacy practices. Under the FTC Act, the FTC is directed, among other things, to prevent unfair methods of competition, and unfair or deceptive acts or practices in or affecting commerce. The FTC has highlighted its intention to regulate online privacy as part of its privacy initiative:

> A key part of the Commission's privacy program is making sure companies keep the promises they make to consumers about privacy and, in particular, the precautions they take to secure consumers' personal information. To respond to consumers' concerns about privacy, many Web sites post privacy policies that describe how consumers' personal information is collected, used, shared, and secured. Indeed, almost all the top 100 commercial sites now post privacy policies. Using its authority under Section 5 of the FTC Act, which prohibits unfair or deceptive practices, the Commission has brought a number of cases to enforce the promises in privacy statements, including promises about the security of consumers' personal information.[2]

In enforcing this power, the FTC has brought and settled charges relating to online privacy with Eli Lilly and Company (relating to sensitive information collected on its Prozac Web site); Microsoft Corp. (regarding the privacy and security of personal information collected from consumers through its "Passport" Web services); and Guess, Incorporated (relating to potential disclosure of credit card and other information).

State Actions

California has been at the forefront of protecting the privacy of online and electronic information. California has attempted to address these matters through laws regarding identity theft, privacy obligations of online merchants, and remedies for disclosure. As with the FTC approach toward enforcement of the Safeguards Rule and claims of deceptive practices, these efforts are directed toward all businesses; in other words, all businesses are directly impacted by California developments because they typically impact any entity that does business in California.

California Civil Code 1798.84 (SB 1386)

California Senate Bill 1386 became effective July 1, 2003. It is designed to give prompt notice when personal information has been released, and impacts all businesses that do business in California, as well as governmental and non-profit agencies. Its application to a business does not require an office or significant presence in California; a single employee, a customer, or vendor located in California is enough to trigger the obligations under the law. The law requires these entities to notify their customers anytime they become aware of a breach of their security that involves the disclosure of unencrypted personal information.

The statute defines "personal information" as a person's first name or first initial and last name in combination with any one or more of the following elements, whether either the name or the elements are non-encrypted: 1) social security number; 2) driver's license or identification card number; or 3) account number, credit or debit card number, together with a code that permits access to a financial account. Thus, records with a name attached to any typical identifier can be considered personal information. It is important to know at the same time that the law does not define a financial account or access code, adding to the uncertainty of the law. Because of this, one cannot assume that the law applies to obvious targets, like credit cards and bank accounts. Electronic data interchange accounts, recordkeeping accounts (even if they do not provide for financial transactions), and other data bases are likely targets.

It should be noted that this law does not exist in a vacuum. The law is a reaction to the failure by the State of California's Teale Data Center to promptly notify an estimated 265,000 state employees whose personal data was exposed during a hacking incident in April 2002. The problem has not gone away: as recently as March 13, 2004, *The Los Angeles Times* reported that a malfunctioning Web site may have allowed the social security numbers, addresses, and other personal information of more than 2000 University of California applicants to be viewed by other students during the application process. The data displayed may have included names, phone numbers, birth dates, test scores, and e-mail addresses, in addition to social security numbers.

Senate Bill 27

In 2003, California adopted Senate Bill 27, which becomes operative on January 1, 2005. SB 27 allows consumers to

discover how companies disseminate personal information for direct marketing purposes. It obligates companies to designate a mailing address, an e-mail address, or toll-free number or facsimile number at which it will receive requests. It also requires companies to train agents and employees to implement a Web site privacy policy and make information readily available to customers. It opens the possibility that companies could avoid reporting by adopting an "opt-in" policy for third-party disclosures, at the price of restricting the company's ability to engage in cross-marketing and similar opportunities.

It should be noted that, like the other California laws discussed here, this is a broad-ranging law. It covers all businesses and makes specific disclosure requirements. It also incorporates the opt-in concept, which has become a prevalent means by which regulators and legislators seek to allow consumers to control access to their personal and financial information.

Assembly Bill 68: Online Privacy Protection Act

Effective July 1, 2004, all operators of Web sites and other online services are required to implement privacy policies with specific provisions. Each privacy policy must:

- Identify the categories of personally identifiable information that the operator collects and the categories of third parties with which the operator might share that information.
- Describe the process by which an individual consumer may review and request changes to his or her information.
- Describe the process by which the operator notifies consumers who use or visit its commercial Web site or online service of material changes to the operator's privacy policy.
- Identify the effective date of the policy.

The law includes specific requirements regarding the location and prominence of the privacy policy; and businesses should be aware that by adopting a privacy policy, as required by Assembly Bill 68, they are making themselves subject to FTC regulation on this very matter.

Other State Actions

There have been several cases in which a company victimized by cyber-criminals has faced liability under a state's consumer protection statues.

Victoria's Secret

On October 21, 2003, New York State Attorney General Eliot Spitzer announced an agreement with Victoria's Secret to protect the privacy of its customers.[3] The agreement follows the discovery that personal information of

Victoria's Secret customers was available through the company Web site, contrary to the company's published privacy policy.

Under the terms of the settlement, Victoria's Secret is to provide refunds or credits to all affected New York consumers, and is to pay $50,000 to the State of New York as costs and penalties. Also under the terms of the settlement, Victoria's Secret is required to

- Establish and maintain an information security program to protect personal information.
- Establish management oversight and employee training programs.
- Hire an external auditor to annually monitor compliance with the security program.

In announcing the agreement, Spitzer said: "A business that obtains consumers' personal information has a legal duty to ensure that the use and handling of that data complies in all respects with representations made about the company's information security and privacy practices."

Ziff-Davis Media, Inc.

In November 2001, Ziff-Davis, a New York-based multimedia content company, ran a promotion on its Web site, receiving approximately 12,000 orders for one of its magazines. According to legal briefs, inadequate security controls left these orders—including credit card numbers and other personal information—exposed to anyone surfing the Internet with the result that at least five consumers experienced credit card fraud.

Ziff-Davis, in its online security policy, made several representations concerning the privacy and security of information it collected from consumers, including the following:

> We use reasonable precautions to keep the personal information you disclose ... secure and to only release this information to third parties we believe share our commitment to privacy.

The Attorney Generals of California, New York, and Vermont brought suit against Ziff-Davis, arguing that, in light of the above experience, this representation constituted an unfair or deceptive act. In an agreement reached between the parties, Ziff-Davis agreed to

- Identify risks relating to the privacy, security, and integrity of consumer data.
- Address risks by means that include management oversight and training of personnel.
- Monitor computer systems.
- Establish procedures to prevent and respond to attack, intrusion, unauthorized access, and other system failures.[4]

CONTRACT AND TORT LAW

Specific Contractual Obligations Regarding Financial Transactions

The National Automated Clearing House Association (NACHA), along with both Visa and MasterCard, contractually impose information security requirements on their members.[5,6]

Visa's Cardholder Information Security Program (CISP) contractually imposes the following 12 basic security requirements with which all Visa payment system constituents must comply:

1. Install and maintain a working firewall to protect data.
2. Keep security patches up-to-date.
3. Protect stored data.
4. Encrypt data sent across public networks.
5. Use and regularly update anti-virus software.
6. Restrict access by "need to know."
7. Assign a unique ID to each person with computer access.
8. Do not use vendor-supplied defaults for passwords and security parameters.
9. Track all access to data by unique ID.
10. Regularly test security systems and processes.
11. Implement and maintain an information security policy.
12. Restrict physical access to data.

Breach of Contract

While there is, as yet, little case law in the area, it is possible, if not likely, that those harmed by a disclosure of sensitive information will seek redress through a breach of contract claim. An example would be a purchaser of technology or technology services, claiming an explicit or implicit warranty from security defects in the technology.

A second example concerns the unauthorized disclosure of information that could generate a contractual liability if it occurs contrary to a non-disclosure or confidentiality agreement.

Analogously, a statement in an organization's privacy policy could give rise to a contractual liability if it is not effectively enforced, as a potential plaintiff may seek to recast terms of use and privacy statements as a binding contract. As such, plaintiffs will analyze the sometimes "soft" statements made in privacy policies, and may bring breach of contract claims for failure to strictly follow the policy.

If a Web site operator, for example, states that it uses its "best efforts" to protect the identity of users, it may be brought to task for not taking every possible step to prevent disclosure, even if it uses reasonable efforts to do so.

Consequently, every privacy statement and terms of use must be analyzed carefully and tailored to its exact circumstances lest it inadvertently subject a business to a contractually higher standard of care than intended.

Tort Law

Numerous legal models are emerging arguing that tort law can be used to establish liability in information security situations. We investigate two of these:

1. Negligence claims
2. Shareholder actions

Negligence claims

Negligence is defined as the "failure to use such care as a reasonable prudent and careful person would use under similar circumstances."[7]

For a victim of a security breach to prevail in a negligence claim, the victim must establish four elements:

1. *Duty of care.* The defendant must have a legal duty of care to prevent security breaches.
2. *Breach of duty.* The defendant must have violated that duty by a failure to act "reasonably."
3. *Damage.* The plaintiff must have suffered actual harm.
4. *Proximate cause:* The breach of duty must be related to the harm closely enough to be either the direct cause of the harm or, if an indirect cause, then it must a) be a substantial causative factor in the harm and b) occur in an unbroken sequence linking to the harm.[7]

Beyond the obvious need to establish proximate cause, there are three challenges to a successful negligence claim: duty of care, economic loss doctrine, and shareholder actions.

Duty of care

At the present time, there is uncertainty over whether or not a legal duty exists in the case of an information security breach, except in those circumstances where a clear legal obligation or contractual relationship exists that requires the securing of information. Thus, financial institutions and health-care providers have a clear duty of care, as do businesses possessing non-public personal information about California residents. However, as more and more businesses adopt privacy policies or are required to do so (under federal or state law or FTC prodding), a more generalized duty of care may emerge. Thus, even in those circumstances where there is no statutory duty of care, analogous duty of care situations suggest a duty of care may also exist for the securing of information assets.

In the case of *Kline v. 1500 Massachusetts Avenue Apartment Corp.*, for example, the U.S. Court of Appeals for the District of Columbia Circuit ruled that a landlord has an obligation to take protective measures to ensure that his or her tenants are protected from foreseeable criminal acts in areas "peculiarly under the landlord's control." The plaintiff in this case had sought damages for injuries she sustained when an intruder attacked her in a common hallway of her apartment building. The court held that the landlord was in the best position to prevent crimes committed by third parties on his property. In remanding the case for a determination of damages, the court stated:

> "[I]n the fight against crime the police are not expected to do it all; every segment of society has obligation to aid in law enforcement and minimize the opportunities for crime."[8,9]

A similar argument would suggest that a business is in the best position to prevent cyber-crimes against its own computer systems, as these are "peculiarly under the business' control."

To the extent that the claim that business is in the best position to prevent cyber-crimes can be substantiated, it would raise the question of whether they legally "should" take the actions necessary to prevent such a crime. The issue is whether the cost of avoidance is small enough relative to the cost of an incident to warrant imposing a duty on the business to take steps to secure its information assets. This cost/benefit analysis follows from Judge Learned Hand's equation "B < PL" articulated in *United States v. Carroll Towing Co.*, in which Hand wrote that a party is negligent if the cost (B) of taking adequate measures to prevent harm is less than the monetary loss (L) multiplied by the probability (P) of its occurring [*United States v. Carroll Towing Co.*, 159 F.2d 169, 173–74 (2d Cir. 1947)]. As Moore's law continues to drive down the cost of basic protection and as cyber-crime statistics continue to show exponential growth, Hand's equation is certain to be valid: the cost of protection is often two or more orders of magnitude less than the expected loss.

Breach of duty

Equally uncertain, at the present time, is what constitutes "reasonable care." On the one hand, "reasonable care" is difficult to pin down precisely as the security needs and responsibilities of organizations differ widely.

On the other hand, two classic legal cases suggest that there is a standard of reasonable care applicable to the protection of information assets, even in circumstances where there is not yet a clear definition of exactly what that standard is. The first of these is the classic doctrine enunciated in *Texas & P.R v. Behymer* by Supreme Court Justice Holmes in 1903: "[w]hat usually is done may be evidence of what ought to be done, but what ought to be done is fixed by a standard of reasonable prudence,

Digital –
E-Mail

whether it usually is complied with or not" (*Texas & P.R. v. Behymer*, 189 U.S. 468, 470, 1903).

In the second case, *T. J. Hooper v. Northern Barge*, two barges towed by two tugboats sank in a storm. The barge owners sued the tugboat owners, claiming negligence noting that the tugboats did not have weather radios aboard. The tugboat owners countered by arguing that weather radios were not the industry norm. Judge Learned Hand found the tugboat owners liable for half the damages although the use of weather radios had not become standard industry practice, writing:

> Indeed in most cases reasonable prudence is in fact common prudence; but strictly it is never its measure; a whole calling may have unduly lagged in the adoption of new and available devices ... Courts must in the end say what is required; there are precautions so imperative that even their universal disregard will not excuse their omission. (*T.J. Hooper v. Northern Barge*, 60 F.2d 737 2d Cir., 1932)

Taken together, particularly in the context of the explosive growth in computer crime, these two statements can be interpreted to suggest that for a business to act "reasonably," it must take meaningful precautions to protect its critical information systems and the information contained in them.

Economic loss doctrine

Courts have traditionally denied plaintiffs recovery for damages if those damages are purely economic, as opposed to physical harm or damage to property. Because victims of information security breaches typically suffer only economic loss, the *economic loss doctrine* could present a challenge to a successful information security claim.

However, in recent decades, a number of courts have carved out exceptions to the economic loss doctrine. For example, the New Jersey Supreme Court in the case of *People Express Airlines v. Consolidated Rail Corp.* awarded damages to People Express after the airline suffered economic loss as a result of having to suspend operations due to a chemical spill at the defendant's rail yard. In awarding damages to People Express, the court wrote:

> A defendant who has breached his duty of care to avoid the risk of economic injury to particularly foreseeable plaintiffs may be held liable for actual economic losses that are proximately caused by its breach of duty.

> We hold therefore that a defendant owes a duty of care to take reasonable measures to avoid the risk of causing economic damages, aside from physical injury, to particular ... plaintiffs comprising an identifiable class with respect to whom defendant knows or has reason to know are likely to suffer such damages from its conduct.

[*People Express Airlines v. Consolidated Rail Corp.*, 495 A.2d. 107 (N.J. 1985)]

Shareholder actions

Shareholders damaged by a drop in the value of a company resulting from the cost of a security breach may seek to sue management for failing to take steps to protect information assets. The nexus of new and developing standards derived from so many new sources—new state laws, federal securities laws, the PATRIOT Act, requirements of auditors and insurers—will have an impact of allowing potential plaintiffs to establish claims based on failure to comply with accepted standards.

Consider, for example, a public company doing business in California that was the subject of a hacker who obtained sensitive personal and financial information regarding clients. Upon discovery, the corporation was obligated, under California law, to publicize the security breach, thus giving shareholders notice of potential wrongdoing. Not surprisingly, the company's stock price was adversely impacted by the disclosure and subsequent negative publicity about the company. Upon further investigation (or perhaps with little or no investigation), a shareholder engaged a class action lawyer to pursue a claim against the company. The attorney couched the claim on the basis that the company had failed to apply broadly accepted security standards, resulting in damage to the company's shareholders.

If the company had, in fact, followed industry standards, it might be able to assert a defense—that it had not been negligent, and that its actions were in full compliance not only with applicable law, but with the standards imposed by regulatory agencies, auditors, insurers and its industry in general. The existence of standards could prove not only to be a sword, but a shield.

EFFECTIVE INFORMATION SECURITY PRACTICES

At the same time as the legal risk associated with a failure to protect information assets is increasing, the professional information security community is developing a common body of Information Security Management Practice Models for use in effectively managing the security of information.

This section reviews three such models:

1. ISO 17799: Code of Practice for Information Security Management[10]
2. Generally Accepted Information Security Principles (GAISP), Version 3.0[11]
3. Information Security Governance: Guidance for Boards of Directors and Executive Management[12]

Digital –
E-Mail

Each of these three documents deal at an abstract level with the question of standards for the protection of information assets. Their points of view are quite different, as is their pedigree. ISO 17799 originated in Australia and Great Britain before being adopted by the International Standards Association. GAISP is being developed by an international consortium under the leadership of the Information Systems Security Association, with the majority of participants coming from the United States. Both of these practice models were developed by information security practitioners, whereas *Guidance for Boards of Directors and Executive Management* was developed by the Information Systems Audit and Control Association (ISACA).

Our objective in reviewing these three distinctly different practice models is to *triangulate* around a common set of activities that one could assert would be required for a business to demonstrate that it met a "reasonable" standard of care.

ISO 17799: Code of Practice for Information Security Management

ISO 17799 is an emerging international standard for managing information security. With roots in Australian information security standards and British Standard 7799, ISO 17799 is the first acknowledged worldwide standard to identify a "Code of Practice" for the management of information security.

ISO 17799 defines "information security" as encompassing the following three objectives:

1. *Confidentiality*: ensuring that information is accessible only to those authorized to have access
2. *Integrity*: safeguarding the accuracy and completeness of information and processing methods
3. *Availability*: ensuring that authorized users have access to information and associated assets when required

ISO 17799 identifies ten specific and vital Information Security Management Practices. An organization's information is secure only to the extent that these ten practices are being *systematically* managed. Weaknesses in any single practice can often negate the combined strength in the other nine. The ten Information Security Management Practices are:

1. Security policy
2. Organizational security
3. Asset classification and control
4. Personnel security
5. Physical and Environmental Security
6. Communications and operations management
7. Access control
8. Systems development and maintenance
9. Business continuity management
10. Compliance

Generally Accepted Information Security Principles, Version 3.0

The generally accepted information security principles (GAISP) is an ongoing project to collect and document information security principles that have been proven in practice and accepted by practitioners. The GAISP draws upon established security guidance and standards to create comprehensive, objective guidance for information security professionals, organizations, governments, and users. The use of existing, accepted documents and standards will ensure a high level of acceptance for the final GAISP product, and will enable a number of benefits to be achieved.

The GAISP:

* Promotes good information security practices at all levels of organizations
* Creates an increase in management confidence that information security is being assured in a consistent, measurable, and cost-efficient manner
* Is an authoritative source for opinions, practices, and principles for information owners, security practitioners, technology products, and IT systems
* Encourages broad awareness of information security requirements and precepts
* Enables organizations to seek improved cost structures and program management through use of proven practices and global principles rather than varied, local, or product-specific guidelines
* Is written hierarchically to allow application to any appropriate level of the organization or IT infrastructure, from the corporate board to the technical staff working "in the trenches"

The GAISP is organized around three levels of guiding principles that are applicable at varying levels of the organization:

1. *Pervasive principles*, which target organizational governance and executive management
2. *Broad functional principles*, guidelines to planning and execution of security tasks and to establishment of a solid security architecture
3. *Detailed principles*, written for information security professionals and which highlight specific activities to be addressed in day-to-day risk management

Pervasive principles

The *pervasive principles* outline high-level recommendations to help organizations solidify an effective information security strategy, and include conceptual goals relating to accountability, ethics, integration, and assessment.

- *Accountability principle.* Information security accountability and responsibility must be clearly defined and acknowledged.
- *Assessment principle.* The risks to information and information systems should be assessed periodically.
- *Awareness principle.* All parties, including but not limited to information owners and information security practitioners with a need to know, should have access to applied or available principles, standards, conventions, or mechanisms for the security of information and information systems, and should be informed of applicable threats to the security of information.
- *Equity principle.* Management shall respect the rights and dignity of individuals when setting policy and when selecting, implementing, and enforcing security measures.
- *Ethics principle.* Information should be used, and the administration of information security should be executed, in an ethical manner.
- *Integration principle.* Principles, standards, conventions, and mechanisms for the security of information should be coordinated and integrated with each other and with the organization's policies and procedures to create and maintain security throughout an information system.
- *Multidisciplinary principle.* Principles, standards, conventions, and mechanisms for the security of information and information systems should address the considerations and viewpoints of all interested parties.
- *Proportionality principle.* Information security controls should be proportionate to the risks of modification, denial of use, or disclosure of the information.
- *Timeliness principle.* All accountable parties should act in a timely, coordinated manner to prevent or respond to breaches of and threats to the security of information and information systems.

Broad functional principles

The second level of the GAISP consists of *broad functional principles*, designed to be the building blocks of the *pervasive principles* and which more precisely define recommended tactics from a management perspective. These *principles* are designed as guidelines to planning and execution of security tasks and to establishment of a solid security architecture.

- *Information security policy.* Management will ensure that policy and supporting standards, baselines, procedures, and guidelines are developed and maintained to address all aspects of information security. Such guidance must assign responsibility, the level of discretion, and how much risk each individual or organizational entity is authorized to assume.
- *Education and awareness.* Management will communicate information security policy to all personnel and ensure that all are appropriately aware. Education will

include standards, baselines, procedures, guidelines, responsibilities, related enforcement measures, and consequences of failure to comply.

- *Accountability.* Management will hold all parties accountable for their access to and use of information (e.g., additions, modifications, copying and deletions, and supporting information technology resources). It must be possible to affix the date, time, and responsibility, to the level of an individual, for all significant events.
- *Information asset management.* Management will routinely catalog and value information assets, and assign levels of sensitivity and criticality. Information, as an asset, must be uniquely identified and responsibility for it assigned.
- *Environmental management.* Management will consider and compensate for the risks inherent to the internal and external physical environment where information assets and supporting information technology resources and assets are stored, transmitted, or used.
- *Personnel qualifications.* Management will establish and verify the qualifications related to integrity, need-to-know, and technical competence of all parties provided access to information assets or supporting information technology resources.
- *Incident management.* Management will provide the capability to respond to and resolve information security incidents expeditiously and effectively in order to ensure that any business impact is minimized and that the likelihood of experiencing similar incidents is reduced.
- *Information systems life cycle.* Management will ensure that security is addressed at all stages of the system life cycle.
- *Access control.* Management will establish appropriate controls to balance access to information assets and supporting information technology resources against the risk.
- *Operational continuity and contingency planning.* Management will plan for and operate information technology in such a way as to preserve the continuity of organizational operations.
- *Information risk management.* Management will ensure that information security measures are appropriate to the value of the assets and the threats to which they are vulnerable.
- *Network and Internet security.* Management will consider the potential impact on the shared global infrastructure (e.g., the Internet, public switched networks, and other connected systems) when establishing network security measures.
- *Legal, regulatory, and contractual requirements of information security.* Management will take steps to be aware of and address all legal, regulatory, and contractual requirements pertaining to information assets.

Digital – E-Mail

Digital –
E-Mail

- *Ethical practices.* Management will respect the rights and dignity of individuals when setting policy and when selecting, implementing, and enforcing security measures.

Detailed principles

The third GAISP level consists of *detailed principles,* written for information security professionals and which highlight specific activities to be addressed in day-to-day risk management. The tactics in the *detailed principles* are step-by-step instructions necessary to achieve the appropriate tactical outcome from the *broad principles* and the conceptual goals of the *pervasive principles.*

Information Security Governance: Guidance for Boards of Directors and Executive Management

The Information Systems Audit and Control Association (ISACA) has developed a model for the overall "maturity" of an organization's security management. ISACA's model was built upon a software engineering management maturity framework that had been developed in the mid-to-late 1980s by the Software Engineering Institute, a national technology center at Carnegie Mellon University. The model "measures"—on a scale of 0 to 5—the extent to which information security is being formally and proactively managed throughout the organization.

The ISACA model provides an organization with a:

- Snapshot-in-time assessment tool, assisting the organization to identify the relative strengths of its information security management practices
- Tool for identifying an appropriate security management maturity level, to which the organization can evolve

- Method for identifying the gaps between its current security maturity level and its desired level
- Tool for planning and managing an organization-wide Information Security Management Improvement Program for systematically improving the organization's information security management capabilities
- Tool for planning and managing specific information security improvement projects

Note that each organization must determine what maturity level is appropriate for its specific circumstances.

Table 2 provides a brief overview of each of the six Information Security Management Maturity levels.

INFORMATION SECURITY MINIMUM STANDARDS OF DUE CARE: THE BATTLE OF THE EXPERT WITNESSES

Now consider what Einstein called a Gedanken experiment, a thought experiment. Imagine that company ABC suffers an information security incident resulting in damage to a third party, XYZ. Let us stipulate that ABC is not legally bound by the GLBA, has no printed privacy policy to which it must adhere, does not do business with California consumers, etc. and so has no *explicit duty of care* to protect. Let us also stipulate that XYZ's losses were not just economic. Finally, let us stipulate that ABC has at least 100 employees, 100 workstations, and several servers. Duty and reasonableness for a one-person home office would necessarily be different than for our hypothetical ABC. A software firewall, virus protection, regular patching, and the like may be all that a one-person home office need do.

Table 2 Information security management maturity levels.

Mgmt maturity	Description
Level 0	Security Management is Non-existent The organization does not manage the security of information assets
Level 1	Initial Ad-Hoc Security Management Security management is ad hoc and not organized; management responsibility is fragmented or non-existent
Level 2	Repeatable but Intuitive Security Management Basic security countermeasures and processes are implemented; management responsibility, authority, and accountability are assigned
Level 3	Defined Process Security management flows from organizational strategy and from an organizationwide risk management policy; employees receive regular training and education
Level 4	Managed and Measurable Security management is monitored and measured; regular feedback is used to assess and improve management effectiveness
Level 5	Security Management is Optimized Information security best practices are followed

In this situation, the case hinges on two points:

1. A point of law as to whether ABC has an *implicit* duty of care
2. A point of information security management as to whether the actions ABC took in protecting its information systems were *reasonable*

Let us now further stipulate that the plaintiff establishes that ABC has, indeed, a *duty of care*. The case now hinges on whether the actions ABC took in protecting its information systems were reasonable. Bring on the experts!

Hypothesis

The actions ABC took in protecting its information systems were reasonable if ABC can find an *unimpeachable* expert to testify that ABC's actions were reasonable. Correspondingly, XYZ will prevail if ABC's actions were so egregious that any attempt by ABC to present an expert testifying that ABC's actions were reasonable could be impeached by XYZ's attorneys.

In this context, an *unimpeachable* expert is someone with the following qualities:

- Experienced information security professional, respected by colleagues
- Either an information security certification, such as the *CISSP* designation, or some other credentials of expertise
- Active membership in an organization of information professionals, such as the Information Systems Security Association
- Expert in information security standards of practice, such as ISO 17799, the GAISP, and the ISACA guidelines
- Expert in the GLBA, HIPAA, and other information security standards

Imagine now that we have ABC's expert in the witness chair. She is an information security professional with all the qualities listed above. For this expert to testify that ABC's actions were reasonable, she would have to find evidence of the following six key information security management elements.

1. *Executive management responsibility.* Someone at the top has management responsibility for ABC's information security program, and this program is managed in accordance with its information security policies.
2. *Information security policies.* ABC has *documented* its management approach to security in a way that complies with its responsibilities and duties to protect information.

3. *User awareness training and education.* Users receive regular training and education in ABC's information security policies and their personal responsibilities for protecting information.
4. *Computer and network security.* ABC's IT staff is securely managing the technology infrastructure in a defined and documented manner that adheres to effective industry practices.
5. *Third-party information security assurance.* ABC shares information with third parties only when it is assured that the third party protects that information with at least the same standard of care as does ABC.
6. *Periodic independent assessment.* ABC has an independent assessment or review of its information security program, covering both technology and management, at least annually.

These six management elements form a common core, either explicitly or implicitly, of all three Information Security Management Practice Models examined, as well as the GLBA and HIPAA regulatory standards for protecting information. Therefore, we feel confident in asserting that if ABC's unimpeachable expert can testify that ABC is doing these six things, then ABC's actions are reasonable. We are correspondingly confident that, if the expert is truly an unimpeachable information security professional, then, in the absence of these six elements, she would not testify for ABC that its actions were reasonable. Indeed, we think that, in this case, she would line up to testify on behalf of XYZ.

It is these six key information security management elements, therefore, that we believe form a Minimum Information Security Standard of Due Care.

LOOKING TO THE FUTURE

As computer crime continues to rise, the legal and regulatory landscape will tilt toward more responsibility, not less.

The Corporate Governance Task Force of the National Cyber Security Partnership, a public–private partnership working with the Department of Homeland Security, has recently released a management framework and call to action to industry, non-profits, and educational institutions, challenging them to integrate effective information security governance (ISG) programs into their corporate governance processes.[13]

Among the recommendations of this task force are:

- Organizations should adopt the information security governance framework described in the report and embed cyber-security into their corporate governance process.
- Organizations should signal their commitment to information security governance by stating on their Web sites that they intend to use the tools developed by the Corporate Governance Task Force to assess their

Digital –
E-Mail

performance and report the results to their board of directors.

- All organizations represented on the Corporate Governance Task Force should signal their commitment to information security governance by voluntarily posting a statement on their Web sites. In addition, TechNet, the Business Software Alliance, the Information Technology Association of America, the Chamber of Commerce, and other leading trade associations and membership organizations should encourage their members to embrace information security governance and post statements on their Web sites.
- The Department of Homeland Security should endorse the information security governance framework and core set of principles outlined in this report, and encourage the private sector to make cyber-security part of its corporate governance efforts.
- The Committee of Sponsoring Organizations of the Treadway Commission (COSO) should revise the Internal Controls-Integrated Framework so that it explicitly addresses information security governance.

According to Art Coviello, president and CEO at RSA Security, and co-chair of the Corporate Governance Task Force, "It is the fiduciary responsibility of senior management in organizations to take reasonable steps to secure their information systems. Information security is not just a technology issue, it is also a corporate governance issue."

Bill Conner, chairman, president, and CEO of Entrust, Inc., who co-chaired the Task Force with Coviello, is quoted as saying "We cannot solve our cyber-security challenges by delegating them to government officials or CIOs. The best way to strengthen U.S. information security is to treat it as a corporate governance issue that requires the attention of boards and CEOs."[14]

Lest the private sector not step up to its responsibilities, the federal government is prepared to strengthen laws and regulations requiring the securing of information. As this is being written, Senator Dianne Feinstein (California) has introduced a bill extending California's "breach disclosure" law to all Americans. Congressman Adam Putnam (Florida), chairman of the House Technology, Information Policy, Intergovernmental Relations and the Census Subcommittee, has introduced legislation that would require every publicly held corporation in the United States to have an information security independent review and include a statement in the annual report that the review established compliance with SEC-mandated information security standards.

Also tilting the landscape toward a greater duty of reasonable care is that businesses, after taking their own security responsibilities seriously, are requiring the same of their trading partners. This will serve to accelerate the adoption of improved information security management that will then, in turn, accelerate the acceptance of the six key information security management elements as a Minimum Information Security Standard of Due Care.

As a result, it is safe to say that over the next few years, the Minimum Information Security Standard of Due Care will, if anything, get tougher—not easier. Thus, while one can expect technology to continue to aid in the battle for security, the need for management at the top, for policies, for training, and for the other key management elements will not go away.

REFERENCES

1. Hood & Strong, http://www.hoodstrong.com/InStep/2002/NFP%20YREND02%20Articles.html.
2. FTC, http://www.ftc.gov/privacy/privacyinitiatives/promises.html.
3. Office of New York State Attorney General Eliot Spitzer, Victoria's Secret Settles Privacy Case, October 21, 2003.
4. Assurance of Discontinuance between Ziff-Davis and the Attorney Generals of California, New York, and Vermont, August 28, 2002, http://www.oag.state.ny.us/press/2002/aug/aug28a_02_attach.pdf.
5. NACHA. Risk Management for the New Generation of ACH Payments 111, 2001.
6. Visa, Cardholder Information Security Program (CISP), 1999, http//www.usa.visa.com/business/merchants/cisp_index.html.
7. Black's Law Dictionary, 6th edition, 1032, 1225.
8. *Kline v. 1500 Massachusetts Avenue Apartment Corp.*, 439 F.2d 477, 482 (D.C. Cir. 1970).
9. *Morton v. Kirkland,* 558 A.2d 693, 694 (D.C. 1989).
10. Information Technology—Code of Practice for Information Security Management, International Standards Organization, ISO 17799, 2000.
11. The Information Systems Security Association. *Generally-Accepted Information Security Principles (GAISP), Version 3.0 (Draft)*; The Information Systems Security Association: Portland, OR, 2004.
12. Information Systems Audit and Control Foundation. *Information Security Governance: Guidance for Boards of Directors and Executive Management*, Information Systems Audit and Control Foundation; ISACA: Rolling Meadows, IL, 2001.
13. *Information Security Governance: A Call to Action*, Corporate Governance Task Force, National Cyber Security Partnership, April 2004.
14. Corporate Governance Task Force of the National Cyber Security Partnership Releases Industry Framework; NCSP: New York, NY, April 12, 2004.

Electronic Commerce: Auditing

Chris Hare, CISSP, CISA, CISM
Information Systems Auditor, Nortel, Dallas, Texas, U.S.A.

Abstract

The most significant challenge in the development and implementation of one's E-commerce environment will be gluing it all together. Success is dependent on a careful marriage of process, technology, and implementation to achieve the end result. Achieving the final goal depends on a comprehensive strategy, understanding legal and export issues, the processes in use, as well as the technology available to perform the work. Design the environment with confidentiality, integrity, and availability as priorities—not as after-thoughts.

With the proliferation of Internet access and the shift to performing some brick-and-mortar transactions online, the need for stability and reliability in the E-commerce arena is becoming increasingly apparent. E*Trade, one of the many successful E-commerce sites, depends completely on its online presence to stay in business. An outage, regardless of cause, can potentially cost millions of dollars. For example, consider the distributed denial-of-service (DDoS) attacks against Yahoo! and CNN. Once a way to stop the attack had been found, thousands of dollars were spent to facilitate the system cleanup, in addition to the lost revenue. This entry describes a methodology to assess the security and reliability of E-commerce. Based on this author's previous experiences with risk assessment, security, reliability, and Web "touch and feel – ease of use" can be identified as critical to the ongoing success of E-commerce. The approach described in this entry can assist any E-commerce Web site owner, manager, or auditor in identifying and securing some of these key risk areas.

STRATEGY

Do not get caught up in the waves of technology and methods of doing things. Technology is only one part of the entire puzzle. One uses technology to implement already-operational manual processes to reach a larger market. The operational aspect drives the technological requirements, which in turn affect the overall development of the required systems. The implementation of the project is often affected by changing business and legal needs rather than by changes in technology.

Strategy is the key to the development of an effective E-commerce implementation. The people within an organization must have a vision they can use to drive their planning and development activities. This vision determines the goals senior management has and lays the groundwork for how to measure success. Without a

strategy, it will be impossible for you, your employees, your shareholders, and customers to determine if you have achieved anything.

Strategy must also be based on the business decisions that an organization will make. The existing corporate policies must be reviewed and implemented to provide consistency in dealing with the public, regardless of the medium the customer uses to access one's services.

Technology Is Only the Method of Implementing Desire

One's team will use the strategy to establish goals they can translate into project plans and then into manageable activities to meet the strategy. When developing an E-commerce strategy, one must consider:

- What are you trying to achieve by moving to E-commerce?
- How closely is your electronic commerce strategy aligned with your existing corporate strategy?
- What existing corporate business processes must be integrated?
- Who is going to use the service? Is it business-to-business, business-to-consumer, or both?
- Who is going to use the services being offered?
- What do our customers want us to offer?

Armed with the answers to these questions, it becomes possible to start addressing the technology solutions that may provide the implementation. As illustrated in Fig. 1, the technology solution is complex and involves many components. Before choosing the individual components to achieve the technology implementation, one must understand how each component in the business process interacts with the others.

Encyclopedia of Information Assurance DOI: 10.1081/E-EIA-120046770
Copyright © 2011 by Taylor & Francis. All rights reserved.

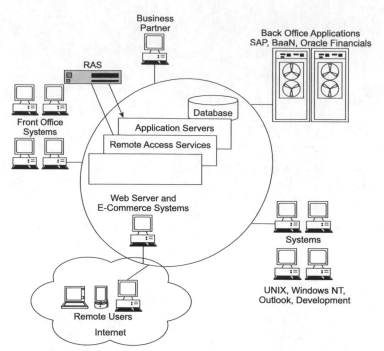

Fig. 1 E-commerce system infrastructure.

LEGAL

It is a challenge for most companies to ensure compliance with the legislation of the country where they are located or the countries in which they do business. There are local, state, national, and international laws. There are additional regulations, depending on the industry and whether you are a publicly traded company. However, doing business electronically poses new challenges.

PRIVACY

Consumers are concerned about the privacy of their information, while you are concerned about the privacy of information they provide to you or you share with them. Aside from legal requirements in various parts of the world regarding the privacy of information, it would not be good business not to provide privacy controls. If consumers are aware that you do not take this into consideration, they will not do business with you electronically.

The privacy issue can mean some real challenges for an organization. For example, during 1999, the European Union (EU) enacted standards surrounding privacy and the protections of information. The EU stated it might choose not to do business with companies or countries that do not implement similar privacy standards. Consequently, one should specifically state what the organization's privacy policy is. This demonstrates a commitment on the organization's part to the protection of its consumer's information.

Solving the privacy issue means that technical implementers will use words like encryption, digital signatures, and digital certificates. These are technologies used to provide the privacy components to help increase the protection of information sent and received while users interact with an electronic business site.

It is the privacy issue regarding consumer purchasing habit information that led to the development of Secure Electronic Transaction (SET) protocols by Mastercard and Visa, as illustrated in Fig. 2.

All transactions must be properly secured to prevent the loss, through transmission or unauthorized access, of important business information. This must be calculated into the strategy. Doing so will mitigate the risk of information loss and poor performance or reliability from improperly implemented processes or technology.

EXPORT CONTROLS

Export controls are established by governments to regulate export of materials to countries considered dangerous or

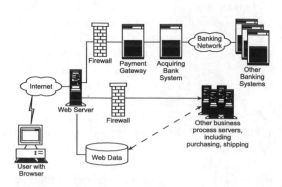

Fig. 2 Sample SET transaction environment.

not in support of the national interest. Most countries do this and in some situations, such as encryption technologies, there are countries that prevent the import of the material.

Compliance with relevant export control legislation is strongly advised. The punishments for non-compliance can be significant, depending on the country and the material exported. Recent years have seen changes in some export rules, again specifically surrounding encryption. Countries have been adopting changes in encryption import/export rules in an effort to allow their producers to compete in the global marketplace.

It is important to review import/export legislation when developing an E-commerce infrastructure. There may be information or technology affected by these rules and they may impact to whom one can deliver the service and resulting products.

LEGISLATION

Legislation is a major area for many companies. There is a variety of legislation controlling how privacy issues are handled and how business is conducted in general. Much of this legislation is not limited to electronic business. Internet laws and regulations pertain to everything from intellectual copyright to cyber squatting (registering URLs for profit).

The use of a qualified attorney is highly recommended due to the diverse issues and laws involved. With the assistance of an attorney, one should carefully consider the impact of law on the ability to get one's electronic business into full gear.

Considering the vast nature of the law, some areas of concern include, but certainly are not limited to:

- What national and international laws are applicable to E-commerce?
- How is legislative compliance ensured?
- What countries is the business prohibited from selling to through E-commerce?
- Are there distribution agreements and contracts that can be held in force electronically?
- Do the businesses support digital signatures, and are they considered legally binding within the business' jurisdiction?
- How are domestic and international disputes resolved?
- Is there technology or information requiring export permits before it can be available through the E-commerce infrastructure?

PROJECT MANAGEMENT

With the strategy defined, the team can proceed to define the manageable activities resulting in the actual development and implementation of the infrastructure. However, project management is geared more toward ensuring that everyone understands what work must be done, the timeline in which to do it, and how much to budget.

There are a lot of pitfalls in allowing the team to implement electronic commerce services without project management. It will be difficult to gauge where the project is, and even more difficult to determine when it is finished and how much it will cost.

Project management provides the needed controls to define the project, and ensure it meets the business requirements and is completed on time and within budget. A project management strategy is critical to define the tasks required to complete the project. The project plan defines who owns the project and related sub-projects, and how users will be involved in the definition, development, and testing of the E-commerce implementation.

The project manager defines the work breakdown structure and establishes the milestones to measure progress on the project. The project manager allocates responsibilities and manages cost and resource budgets.

Without effective project management, the E-commerce project can become an expensive, never-ending endeavor that fails to meet the business needs.

The ability to plan a project and then properly implement it allows for accurate cost control and planning decisions. Things to consider:

- Does the project plan accurately define the end objectives in a measurable fashion?
- Are there adequate people and other resources to deliver the project on time and without unplanned resource costs?
- Has a standard project management review been conducted?
- How are project costs captured?
- Is the project on track from both a work and a financial perspective?

RELIABILITY

The E-commerce infrastructure must be available whenever a customer wants to use it (availability), and it must operate as the customer expects it to (integrity). Most people do not realize it but reliability is a major component of security. Consumers want to have confidence that when they go shopping online, the merchant they want to deal with will have all of its systems operating so that they can browse the catalog, enter their order, have any payment transactions properly completed, and then see the order arrive in a reasonable timeframe.

But what happens when things go wrong? Customers need to have a method of contacting the merchant so they can advise that merchant of the problem and seek an

Digital –
E-Mail

acceptable resolution. However, reliability reaches beyond getting problems fixed. It includes the ability of an organization to know there may be a problem now or in the future. How will the performance of the system be measured? How does one resolve a problem for which one of the service providers is responsible?

Performance

The ability of the systems to provide a reliable, friendly, and valuable experience is essential. Users have high expectations about content, access to the services, and quickly finding what they are looking for. Performance, in the eye of the user, is measured by how long it takes to get the information displayed on their screen. A fancy Web site with numerous animations and pretty graphics may be eye-appealing once fully downloaded, but most users get frustrated and are not likely to revisit if the merchant's home page takes forever to load on their system. Develop for the smallest system, and it will work on all others that need to access it.

The customer's view of performance is affected by the capacity planning of the merchant's Internet access and the servers used to offer the customer services. Failure on the part of the merchant to contemplate the actual level of performance one wants people to have will impact that merchant in the end. Capacity planning surrounding the network and server performance must be tempered by how many users one expects to have access to the site.

Having a plan to quickly respond to performance issues regardless of their cause is essential to stay ahead of customer demand. This translates into having capacity planning expertise on the team. These experts monitor performance on a daily basis to maximize the number of customers who can use the site and ensure there is adequate capacity to handle the increased number of users tomorrow.

Architecture

The second component in addressing reliability has to do with the overall system and network architecture. What systems are involved in delivering the service to customers? It is important to understand how they interact with each other in providing the service. Just as capacity planners are important, E-commerce architects who understand the market are critical. Security professionals who understand security architectures to protect the overall corporation and how to implement them are also essential.

Measuring Performance

The collection of metrics for capacity planning, customer satisfaction, and usage is imperative. Operational statistics are collected as part of operating the business and include such items as technology outages and usage. These

Fig. 3 Operational statistics to indicators.

operational statistics are generally used to provide information regarding problems and assist in determining where efforts should be focused to correct operational problems. Help desks or customer service areas can be invaluable for recording these kind of metrics.

As all of the operational statistics are collected, they must be analyzed and collated into metrics to report the state of the operation. How is the E-commerce environment working? How many customers have used the site? How much was spent and what was bought? However, metrics must be combined from across the organization to establish the strategic indicators used by top management to determine how the organization is doing and what they should be concerned about. This relationship is illustrated in Fig. 3.

Some things to consider surrounding operational statistics and metrics include:

- What efforts are being made to collect, report, and validate the available metrics?
- What metrics are available from the internal and external service providers?
- Determine the reporting structure for these metrics.
- Determine how these metrics are used.
- What process is in place to use the metrics to create feedback to improve the system or correct problems?

Problem Resolution

The primary users of an E-commerce site are its customers. However, sometimes things go wrong, or customers have questions arise during their visit and would prefer to talk with someone regarding the issue. Consequently, they need to have a place to report these problems or ask their questions.

This requires the implementation of a customer call center where problem reports regarding the Web site can be taken and directed to the correct support groups for resolution, or product questions asked and answers provided. Effectively operating this customer call center requires the use of a call tracking system capable of tracking the customer's issue and a history of what was done to provide resolution.

If operating a global company—and face it, if you are running an E-commerce site, your consumer audience will be global—you will need to establish a method for people to reach you in real-time from anywhere in the world.

The customer call center must be able to respond quickly to customer needs and provide the information they are requesting in a timely fashion. Doing so establishes confidence in the mind of the consumer about your abilities and enhances their buying experience.

When considering the call center, the following questions should be considered:

- How do both you and the customer evaluate satisfaction level?
- How long does it take to solve a problem once reported? Is the customer satisfied with the resolution? Is follow-up necessary?
- What are the common problems reported and what has been done to rectify them?
- What problem tracking and resolution system is in use?
- Are problems recorded so that metrics can be obtained and trending reasonably retrieved?

Service Level Agreements

Service level agreements (SLAs) establish the terms of service, including expected operational performance and problem escalation and resolution. Both issues are important in E-commerce activities. The operational performance of the service provided is critical because poor performance means the E-commerce services will be unavailable to the customer. This in turn can negatively impact both the bottom line and the image of the company on the Internet.

Timely resolution of problems is also important for the same reasons. Customers expect service level timelines for issues to be met. What SLAs are there with service providers, and are there penalties if they do not meet their commitments?

SLAs are also used to assist in measuring the capabilities of your service providers and are useful to have when renewing contracts. Having collected and maintained good information regarding performance and issue resolutions, one will have more success negotiating changes in the contract and price due to good or bad performance in the service delivery.

Things to remember when reviewing the SLAs in place for an E-commerce environment include:

- Obtain SLAs from suppliers such as ISPs and network providers.
- What quality-of-service provisions are in the SLAs? Are the service providers meeting these agreements?
- Do the service providers and your own organization maintain records on their performance?

Maintaining the Business

The ability of the infrastructure to recover from a systems failure, connectivity loss, or other issue is essential. Order entry for product sales is a critical activity that must be maintained. How will the organization handle the partial or complete loss of its E-commerce infrastructure? Are appropriate plans in place to maintain the E-commerce business?

Business continuity and disaster recovery planning form important elements in any business, but are not centered solely on the E-commerce services being offered. Business continuity is centered on maintaining the business operations after a fatal systems failure. For example, can E-commerce operations be maintained if several systems suddenly fail?

These are important questions to ask support organizations. If the organization is heavily dependent on the ongoing operation of the E-commerce environment, then a failure for even a short period of several hours can have disastrous effects on the business. If operating an enterprise based more on "foot traffic," one may be able to afford the downtime.

However, in today's information age, when an online business is offline, everyone hears about it—very quickly.

Areas of concern surrounding business continuity include:

- Has a business impact analysis been conducted to determine how important E-commerce is to the survival of the organization?
- Are the Web servers and other systems involved in the E-commerce delivery part of a contingency plan?
- Are there backup procedures, dependable backups, and regular data and system recovery testing?
- Is the status of systems monitored to maintain integrity and operation?

DEVELOPMENT

As mentioned previously, customers will remember their experience with an E-commerce system based on how it worked for them. Consequently, the development of a consistent interface is required and can only be achieved through good development practices.

Standards and Practices

The key method of ensuring that consumers have a positive experience with an E-commerce site is to establish development standards and practices. These are independent of the "look and feel" established as their interactive experience.

The site developers use standards and practices to provide information and methods on how the applications will

Digital –
E-Mail

be developed. This includes things such as code standards, security, and how information submitted from the consumer will be validated and protected. Accordingly, security needs to be designed into the application from the start and not included as an after-thought.

Developers will make decisions regarding how they will develop and write their particular part of the system based on their previous experience or education. These differences make it difficult for ongoing maintenance and subsequent troubleshooting and issue resolution.

Change Control and Management

Change control is a critical part of the overall development/ production cycle. Proper change control reduces the risk of improperly tested application code being placed into production, causing problems with data integrity, confidentiality, or reliability. It is also used to identify the changes that are made from day to day to the application code and allows for proper issue resolution and developer education.

A major issue with the development of application code is the fact that it is often put into production systems and "debugged" while customers are using it. This type of activity not only impacts the development of the system, but also affects the user's perception of the E-commerce site and the online presence of your enterprise.

Proper change control ensures that development code is tested in a development environment and is able to process not only the accurate information that the consumer provides, but also handling errors in the input, made either deliberately or accidentally.

Proper processing of information that is collected on the Web site affects business operations. Failure to process it correctly may result in improper or incorrect charges to the consumer, or delivery errors resulting in lost merchandise and increased costs.

When assessing the configuration and change control environment, one must consider:

- Software release change and version control, including both the application code and operating system changes.
- Is it possible to maintain a stable operating environment in today's fast-paced world? Is it possible to automate the change process?
- Development, implementation, and migration standards.

CONNECTIVITY

Connectivity is specifically concerned with the technologies used to establish network connectivity to public and private networks, how available bandwidth is calculated, and how the network is designed. E-commerce is very dependent on a successful network design and adequate

capacity to ensure that consumers can get to a Web site, especially during the winter holiday season.

This means adequate Internet connectivity speed and capacity, and similar connectivity into your corporate network if applicable to your E-commerce design. Many network design people are leaders in their field, but adequate network capacity can be easily overlooked.

A network can also be overbuilt, having too much capacity and other resources built into it that ties up an enterprise's resources unnecessarily. It is necessary for the enterprise to have good technical management and network design staff to take the marketing and sales plans and build a network that will handle expected traffic and scale appropriately as demand increases.

The network staff must understand that an E-commerce site must be located in an appropriate place. This means that if one intends to operate on a global scale, one may want to consider having multiple locations to ensure the best connectivity and performance for the consumer. This can increase the complexity of one's environment in the process and in turn increase one's dependency on good planning.

Part of this planning includes redundancy, which in turn forms part of one's contingency and business continuity planning. If one component or location becomes unavailable for any reason, one is able to maintain presence and continue operation of E-commerce enterprises.

Consumers are looking for a positive, encouraging experience when interacting with an E-commerce environment. Failing to provide this experience reflects negatively on your online presence. This may result in a perception that the company is not prepared to handle E-commerce and consumers will be reluctant to conduct business with your site.

In reviewing network connectivity, remember to consider:

- Location(s) of E-commerce sites
- Network capacity
- Maintaining and monitoring of network availability
- Network topology
- Redundancy of the network
- Security
- How secure transmission links are
- Whether a switched network is used
- Whether any form of virtual private network (VPN) is used in E-commerce delivery

SECURITY

There are four major components that make up the security area:

1. Client or user side of the connection
2. Network transmission system

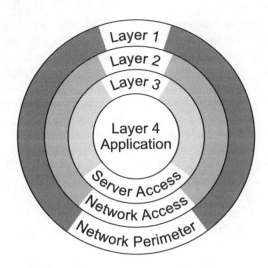

Fig. 4 Levels of protection.

3. Protection of the network information during transmission
4. User identification and authentication

Protection of the network security elements and the computer systems that reside in the E-commerce infrastructure is a major portion of protecting the data integrity and satisfying legal and best practices considerations. This level of protection is addressed through various means, all of which must be working cooperatively to establish defense-in-depth.

As seen in Fig. 4, the layering is visualized as a series of concentric circles, with the level of protection increasing to the center. Layer 1, or the network perimeter, guards against unauthorized access to the network itself. This includes firewalls, remote access servers, etc. Layer 2 is the network. Some information is handled on the network without any thought. As such, layer 2 addresses the protection of the data as it moves across the network. This technology includes link encryptors, VPN, and IPSec.

Layer 3 considers access to the server systems themselves. Many users do not need access to the server but to an application residing there. However, a user who has access to the server may have access to more information than is appropriate for that user. Consequently, layer 3 addresses access and controls on the server itself.

Finally, layer 4 considers application-level security. Many security problems exist due to inconsistencies in how each application handles or does not handle security. This includes access and authorization for specific functions within that application.

There are occasions where organizations implement good technology in bad ways, which results in a poor implementation. For example, the best firewall poorly configured by the user will not stop undesirable traffic to a site, or a database security system that has all of the data tables granted for "public" access does not protect the data they contain. This generally can lead to a false sense of security and lull the organization into complacency.

Consequently, by linking each layer (see Fig. 5), it becomes possible to provide security that the user does not see in some cases, and will have minimal interaction with to provide access to the desired services. Integration between each layer makes this possible.

The same is true when implementing security within the E-commerce environment. It must be considered at all layers: the client, the network, the perimeter, and the associated servers. The Web interface has four primary layers: the operating system, the CGI programs, the Web content, and the Web server. Each layer is dependent on the components of the other layers working correctly.

Client Side (User)

Clients interact with the E-commerce infrastructure through their Web browser. The users, however, have certain expectations about how the interaction will look, act, and perform at their computer. For the experience to be a positive one, certain programming considerations

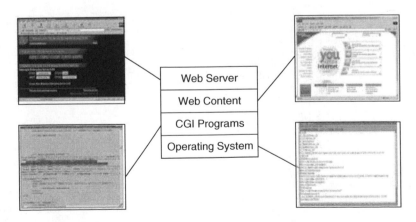

Fig. 5 Linking layers.

Digital –
E-Mail

must be addressed during design, development, and implementation.

The experience the user has will be different across the different browser implementations, and choosing to support browser extensions that are not supported by other browsers is not a good business decision. The HTML, dynamic, and graphic content must be compatible with the different Web browsers available. E-commerce applications must consider this requirement. Not all users will want to enable extended features in their browser, such as cookies, Java, and JavaScript. This greatly affects the functionality that can be offered in the design of the application.

The users and businesses that will use a service may not be connected directly to the Internet. They may be using a proxy server to provide security or cache network requests. They may also be using a slow-speed network link. These factors must be included in the design to maintain a positive experience.

When considering client-side issues:

- Examine what types of Web browsers and proxy servers are in use and in what operating environments.
- Determine how a customer registers for E-commerce access.
- Determine the ease of use of the E-commerce interface.
- Decide what applications will be used to develop the interface.

Firewalls

The firewall is an integral part of an E-business architecture. It is accepted that any computer directly on the Internet with no protection is a sacrificial host. One can expect it will be compromised at some point. Although it is not reasonable to hide everything behind the firewall, every system not needing to be directly visible to the Internet should be protected by a firewall. Additionally, no connections from any unprotected systems should pass directly through the firewall to the corporate network.

However, a firewall can be bolstered by the network design through the use of demilitarized zones (DMZs) and service networks (see Fig. 6). The DMZ protects its systems through filters and access control lists in the routers. The service network is a separate network connected to the firewall. Any system that does not need direct Internet connectivity and does not need to be on the corporate network is put in the service network.

The customer interacts with the systems in the DMZ. Additional services required to provide the customer with their experience are obtained by systems in the services network. Any additional information that must be retrieved from systems on the corporate network is retrieved by the intermediate servers. Although this seems to be an overly complex arrangement, there is a high degree of security inherent in the design. The systems outside the firewall have no ability to connect to the corporate network. The firewall is configured to only allow connections from the DMZ to the service network, and then only to specific IP addresses and network services. The systems in the service network are then authorized to connect with systems in the corporate network for the required information.

The use of intrusion detection systems and periodic evaluation using vulnerability assessment tools is also highly recommended as part of an E-commerce security architecture due to the nature of the service and likelihood of attack.

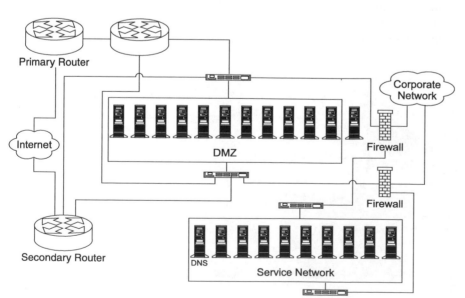

Fig. 6 Demilitarized zones (DMZ) and service networks.

When considering the firewall and network security implementation, examine:

- Vulnerability reports of all network elements using a network vulnerability tool such as Cybercop or ISS
- The DMZ systems to determine if they are "hardened" to reduce the potential attack points
- How the Web client and server negotiate SSL encryption and what encryption strengths are offered
- Non-HTTP ports opened through the firewall(s) for browsing and analyze security implications
- The firewall topology
- Firewall configuration files
- Access control lists of network devices
- Network communication protocols
- Configuration management on the network security elements

SECURING THE E-COMMERCE SERVER

The E-commerce server consists of a variety of components all connected together to provide the business service. Multiple systems are used to reduce the complexity of any single system in an effort to improve the chances of properly securing each system. These services include the HTTP or Web server itself, personalization systems, directory systems, e-mail gateways, and authentication systems.

Directory Services

Directory services provide a mechanism for maintaining an online repository of registered users and their related information. By using a central repository for this information, any of the systems requiring authentication data or information regarding the user can access it. Additionally, applications can query information regarding the user, including their mailing information when ordering or requesting hardcopy information or when products are shipped to them.

Several directory systems are available, but those based on X.500 and Lightweight Directory Access Protocol (LDAP) technology provide the highest level of integration and availability.

Because all of the information regarding the users is stored in a central repository, special care must be taken to protect the information on those systems and provide authenticated and secure transmission channels for the data. The repository must have high availability, as many systems will be dependent on its ability to provide the information when requested. As previously stated, the consolidation of the data makes it easier for the administrators to provide confidentiality and maintain integrity while the information is stored and during transmission across the network. One can argue that the consolidation of the data also makes the system a target for attack. However, the

centralization also provides network security personnel with the opportunity to protect the system.

When evaluating the directory services provided, consider:

- How much data will be stored
- How quickly must the directory provide the response
- How many queries can the directory handle at a single time
- What security functionality is integrated into the directory
- Does the directory support authenticated connections
- Does the customer understand that this data is being stored

Mail Server

Electronic mail is a key component in any E-commerce infrastructure. It allows for the delivery of information from the E-commerce infrastructure systems to a user or business. Customers depend on e-mail to request information and to interact with customer service or support people when questions or problems arise. It can also be used by customers to report things they like or dislike about the experience. E-mail, which is used for many things, should not be used as a transport method for information requiring special protection. Information sent via e-mail is as public as a postcard. Consequently, the distribution of credit card or purchase information, as well as user name and passwords, must not be distributed through e-mail. This can be made possible and secure through encryption technologies such as S/MIME.

The operation of the mail server is critical to the infrastructure. E-mail servers are also regularly used by hackers to access other systems or send unsolicited bulk e-mail, or spam, as they are often not considered to be a major security risk. Many of the available commercial mail servers have idiosyncrasies related to their configuration that both can protect and expose information. Consider the incorrectly configured mail server that allows external users to send e-mail as if they were employees of the company, or using the mail server to relay spam to other mail servers.

Such examples are written and documented on a daily basis in the security industry and are usually related to simple misconfigurations, the use of out-dated software implementations, or not remaining current with software patches.

When addressing e-mail security and availability, consider:

- Which mail transport agents and mail user agents are being used
- Access permissions for the mail transport agent's (MTA) configuration files

Digital –
E-Mail

- Periodic review of the mail server's delivery and error logs to determine the possibility of misuse
- Probing the MTA for common "exploits" to test vulnerabilities to various attacks
- Evaluating the use of virus protection technologies
- Content management and encryption technologies

Web Server

The Web server can be considered the most critical component in the E-commerce infrastructure. It is required to deliver Web-viewable content to the user, run programs to retrieve or send information to the user or other systems, and perform specific checks to determine the validity of requests. It is expected to be available all the time and to provide responses to the user within an acceptable time period. If users have to wait due to poor network or Web server performance, they will quickly leave your site. Once again they will form a negative perception of the business and not be likely to return.

There are a number of Web servers available, both as commercial and freeware software implementations. If one can afford it, buy a commercial implementation to have quick support when issues arise and gain vendor maintenance for the software. Although the initial expense for freeware implementations may be low, and they are quite robust, the post-installation maintenance and support expenses can be quite high. Consider company turnover and retention of experts to maintain the freeware implementation. It is likely to be much easier to find trained experts on commercial software than someone who is familiar with a tailored freeware implementation.

While configuring the Web server itself, development standards are needed for the design of applications and Web content. The Web server software must not execute on the system with any special or administrative permissions. This reduces the risk of an attacker gaining administrative privileges to compromise the server.

The operation of the server is also dependent on the availability of Common Gateway Interface (CGI) scripts to provide access to applications and forms. CGI programs require careful scrutiny during development and before final production to validate that there are no exposures to poorly written code resulting in security issues. Confidentiality and data integrity have been presented several times. The Web server should be capable of providing encrypted sessions through Secure Sockets Layer (SSL) or Transport Layer Security (TLS). Both SSL and TLS require no additional hardware and both use a server-side certificate. The issuance of a certificate for a site is beyond the scope of this entry. Several reputable firms can issue certificates for Web servers.

Using SSL or TLS, the organization and customer can be confident that the information being displayed or sent is protected while in transit across the network.

When reviewing the Web server, consider the following:

- Review the user ID and account permissions the Web server runs under (i.e., root, administrator).
- Determine which Web sites are public and which are controlled access.
- Analyze access permissions for HTML documents, ASP and CGI, directories and scripts.
- Examine Microsoft IIS or other Web server application configurations and log files.
- Determine how requests received by the Web server from the browser are verified.
- Determine how requests sent to a back-end processor are verified as completed.
- Examine Web-based applications and database connectivity, including Java, JavaScript, and XML.
- Check for the existence of well-known ASP and CGI scripts and utilities that pose a security risk.
- Examine Web and proxy server configuration files.
- Check the Web server configuration files and certificates to enable SSL communications.
- Analyze high-availability components in the E-commerce service.
- Evaluate operating system and Web software patch levels and configuration files on critical servers.
- Evaluate application patch levels and configuration files.
- Determine how external E-commerce systems authenticate to internal systems.
- Consider the certificate authority that issued the server certificate and if there is a method for the customer to validate the authenticity of the certificate.
- Evaluate the requirements of non-repudiation features.
- Evaluate CGI scripts and review the program code.
- Consider Web content management.

OPERATING SYSTEM SECURITY

All of the components previously described rely on the foundation services provided by the operating system. Although each of the individual application components can be made more secure, without a strong, secure foundation, other efforts are affected. Today, the vast majority of E-commerce systems run on either Windows NT or UNIX operating systems. Each of these environments has its own advantages and disadvantages and system vulnerabilities.

Windows NT™ Operating System

Windows NT is a popular operating system used to perform specific computing tasks in any infrastructure. Proper configuration of the operating system is essential. If not properly configured and security is

Digital –
E-Mail

not properly implemented, it can be trivial to compromise.

Windows NT relies heavily on the registry to provide both operating system and application configuration settings. Several key services in Windows NT operate at the same network service port. This can provide a remote user with the ability to probe the system and collect important registry information. With this information in hand, such as disk sharing information, user names, and system configuration details, a successful attack can be launched against the system.

When using Windows NT as an E-commerce operating system platform:

- Conduct a scan of all Windows NT systems providing E-commerce services using both host- and network-based vulnerability scanners. Analyze the results and attempt to exploit them on the operating system to gain unauthorized access.
- Review unnecessary services and ports.
- Review registry settings and operating system patch levels and configuration files on critical servers.
- Evaluate configuration and change management on the operating system components.
- Implement virus protection technologies.

UNIX® Operating System

The UNIX operating system provides a multi-user, multi-processing environment used for many different tasks. Like Windows NT, however, improper configuration of the security modules and operating system can make it trivial to compromise. UNIX is a much more popular E-commerce environment than Windows NT. Despite the relative maturity of the operating system, new problems with UNIX implementations are discovered on a weekly basis. The visibility of some of the new security issues even makes it to the news media due to the dependence in the computing world upon this operating system.

Like Windows NT, UNIX is not intended to be a secure operating environment. Any security expert can provide a multitude of ways to defeat the security systems on either operating system. Considerable effort is required to "harden" the operating system and reduce the vulnerabilities in the E-commerce environment. As a multi-user operating system, UNIX has a large number of network-based services providing major parts of the system's functionality. Many of these services and ports are not necessary in order to provide E-commerce functionality. These services are often exploited to initiate confidentiality, data integrity, or system availability attacks.

When using UNIX as an E-commerce operating system, be sure to:

- Conduct a scan of all UNIX systems providing E-commerce services using host- and network-based vulnerability scanners. Analyze the results and attempt to exploit them on the operating system to gain unauthorized access.
- Review unnecessary services and ports.
- Evaluate operating system patch levels and configuration files on critical servers.
- Evaluate configuration and change management on the operating system components.

BACK OFFICE APPLICATIONS

The E-commerce infrastructure has communications paths to various back office applications, including search engines, Oracle, BaaN, and SAP, to facilitate the ordering of products from the catalog. These systems are sufficiently protected, as well as the data sent across the network, to restrict protected information access. In addition, there are specific performance and security considerations for these applications.

Search Engine

The search engine is used to find specific documents or Web pages within the E-commerce environment. The quality of the search engine responses depends on how fast this "crawler" can traverse the Web links and pages to produce an index for the location of relevant material. Most search engines perform this work in two stages. First, the search engine "crawls" through the Web pages and collects information. Second, it builds a searchable index for use later when the user requests the search.

Different search engines offer different levels of performance in the collection of this information. This affects the validity of the search results when the user requests the search. If pages that exist cannot be found when the search is requested, the user will think the information does not exist. Consider the negative perception this can have on the user's experience at the Web site. If pages no longer exist or contain irrelevant information appear, the user will become frustrated.

For example, consider the graphs in Fig. 7. Both graphs illustrate basic system activity for two different search engines running on exactly the same hardware. The system on the top makes much better use of the system's resources during the crawling and indexing phases. This improved use of system resources suggests the engine is working effectively. The graph on the bottom shows much lower resource utilization, suggesting the engine may not be capable of handling the workload despite the hardware resources.

User interaction with the search engine is also critical. If the search engine itself has not been properly implemented,

Digital –
E-Mail

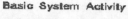

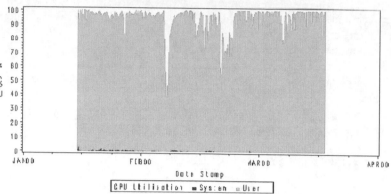

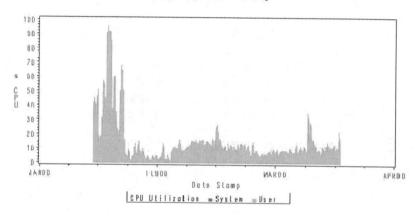

Fig. 7 Basic system activity for two different search engines.

it is possible for performance, including the search, to be slow, due either to the software or the hardware on which it is running. Some search engine implementations do not handle simultaneous searches well. Careful review of the product, combined with simulated load testing, is required prior to implementation.

When evaluating the search engine, review:

- How well the crawling and indexing features work
- The success rate and relevance of the returned documents
- The CPU and LAN utilization
- How quickly search responses returned to the user
- The vendor's reputation

The back office systems provide information to the E-commerce user over which the organization wants to maintain strict control. In general, these same systems will be used to provide the day-to-day operations for the rest of the company. Because they are generally within the protection of the corporate network, they can be considered protected. The "hard and crunchy" network perimeter is becoming less and less practical as more and more users and customers are demanding services and access technologies. However, the issues previously presented regarding development, application, and operating system configuration must all be applied here as well.

Communication to these systems from the external E-commerce system is controlled by the firewall. The firewall will only allow specific external systems to communicate with specific internal systems to minimize the risk of total compromise in the event of an attack.

Being successful in implementing connectivity and protecting these back office systems is dependent on a thorough understanding of how data is moved from one system to another, what protocols and transport methods are used, who creates the data, who processes it on the receiving computer, and the sensitivity of the information itself.

When evaluating and implementing connectivity to back office systems, one must:

- Evaluate protection of sensitive organizational data
- Evaluate configuration management on the back office components
- Evaluate the use of virus protection technologies
- Evaluate database configuration and administration practices

- Evaluate order transmission from the Web site to the order management system
- Evaluate the order fulfillment process

E-NOUGH!

This entry has discussed the components of E-commerce architecture and identified what the organization should focus on when developing its environment or preparing to perform an audit. This entry is by no means an all-encompassing examination of each of the technology areas, but is intended to show the reader the relationship and dependencies of various components that make up an E-commerce environment.

The implementation of an E-commerce environment allows any corporation to economically achieve global presence and enter the global marketplace successfully. In fact, some retailers have no or few storefront (bricks-and-mortar) premises due to E-commerce.

This is a challenging and fast-paced world where it is so important to be first, be visible, and be remembered. Do it fast, be quick, and do it right; if you do not, you blow it.

This is the nature of E-business. If one does not get it right the first time, one will not have enough time to fix it later. This is our E-dilemma!

ACKNOWLEDGMENTS

Very special thanks to my colleague and close friend, Mignona Cote. Her insight into many areas in technology, business, and risk areas have taught me many things. Without her assistance, this work would not have been completed.

E-Mail and Data Communications: Dial-In Hazards

Leo A. Wrobel
TelLAWCom Labs, Inc., Ovilla, Texas, U.S.A.

Abstract

As more workers use E-mail and data communications, the importance of security grows, and should be firmly established before the systems are used to generate revenue. Beginning with a sound telecommunications privacy policy, organizations should implement protective measures ranging from paging systems, dialback modems, and comprehensive after-market equipment to test firewalls, fully redundant configurations, and backup T1s.

PROBLEMS ADDRESSED

With the advent of nomadic and home office environments, remote access security is once again taking its place at the forefront of security planning activities. Everyone wants an Internet presence and Internet access. Telecommuting is gaining in popularity. Sales agents armed with laptops roam the countryside.

Opening up systems to casual access by nomadic and home office workers requires the implementation of security procedures before the systems become mission critical and revenue producing. This entry presents an overview of considerations to be addressed regarding dial-in and Internet access systems. Tips on how to ensure that standards for both physical equipment and privacy policies for today's mobile data world are also included. For information on protecting against dial-in hazards involving voice systems, see entry *Security Controls: Dial-Up*, p. 2598.

TELECOMMUNICATIONS PRIVACY POLICY

What happens if you read someone else's confidential E-mail? Can the company read yours? Does an employee have an absolute right to privacy? Many individuals and companies have no idea how to answer these questions.

For example, it is a violation of federal law to listen to a telephone conversation without the knowledge of the participants. We all know from television shows that there is a rigid process to secure a wire tap on a phone line. Do similar protections exist for E-mail?

Generally, a company's employee policy on E-mail privacy, usually in a telecommunications privacy document, sets the standard. Unfortunately, many organizations do not have such a document.

Every so often, a story in the paper underscores the vulnerability of E-mail far better than thousands of words by experts. The following is one example.

An office romance was blooming between two employees of a major service company. The company depended heavily on electronic mail in the conduct of daily business, and employees had every reason to believe this E-mail was secure. The young lady involved apparently thought it would be romantic to send a graphic E-mail letter, with an attached photograph, to her suitor. This would have been well and good if she had not clicked on the "All Users" button when sending the message. Suffice it to say this made for good office gossip and sent a clear message to everyone about the use of E-mail systems.

Notwithstanding such human errors, are E-mail systems really secure? Can an employer read E-mail? Do employees have a right to privacy? The entry *Security Controls: Dial-Up* discussed other forms of communication such as fax transmissions. Is a person breaking the law when he or she receives and reads a fax or E-mail intended for someone else? The answers may surprise you, and could call for a thorough review of security procedures for these systems.

A policy on telecommunications privacy should be broad enough in scope to cover not only E-mail, but voice mail and other mediums. Policies generally fit in between the following two ends of the spectrum:

- "Employees work for the company, and it owns the system. The company will listen to or monitor whatever we feel like monitoring or listening to," or
- "ABC Company is committed to absolute privacy of communications and each employee has the right to not have their communications monitored."

Which approach is right? That depends on your company. We usually opt for the latter, with a caveat, as follows:

- "ABC Company is committed to absolute privacy of communications, and each employee has the right to

Encyclopedia of Information Assurance DOI: 10.1081/E-EIA-120046361
Copyright © 2011 by Taylor & Francis. All rights reserved.

not have their communications monitored. However, if in the course of normal maintenance activity we inadvertently discover illegal activity, we reserve the right to report this activity to the responsible authorities."

Once again, it is wise to contact legal counsel when writing these policies. I was purposely casual in these illustrations to illustrate the range of options, but also because failure to contact legal counsel can leave organizations exposed to risk. An example of this is an employee who ran an illegal bookmaking operation out of a company system. He was fired but then reinstated because the company had no policy on privacy on which to base the dismissal. It is important to contact the corporate legal department, outside counsel, or an internal audit department for further details.

In addition to the establishment of the privacy policy, an evaluation of protective measures for dial-in lines should begin with an overview of their hazards. Any proposed solutions must address the types of intrusion discussed in the following sections if they are to ensure even a minimum level of protection.

HACKERS

Hackers are unauthorized users, often juveniles, who attempt to break into a system for kicks. They may or may not be lethal, but some rudimentary precautions can prevent these break-ins. Because these individuals often use demon dialers, which dial every number in a prefix to find modem lines (e.g., 555-0000, 555-0001, and so on), it is often not difficult for them to find numbers, especially if they are front ended with an identifying script. Therefore, security precautions must be evaluated to prevent this occurrence. These include:

- Modems that dial back the user.
- Modems that screen the CALLER ID of the calling party.
- Modems or equipment that answer initially with silence, rather than with a modem tone.
- Equipment that does not paint an initial screen, such as "Welcome to ABC Widget Company," which can serve to further encourage an unauthorized user.
- Equipment that logs and tracks unsuccessful log-in attempts.
- Equipment that requires a special hardware key to allow access.

Although none of these provides a definitive solution, several or all of these methods can provide a nearly impenetrable defense against unauthorized access.

SABOTEURS

The most unsettling types of attacks come from those who are knowledgeable of the environment. Disgruntled employees, for example, can cause more damage than anyone else, because they know exactly what attack can be the most damaging. Many organizations have a high level of employee trust, and have an established policy of allowing employees a high degree of system access. This is commendable, but care should be taken because even the most close-knit firms can never be sure when an employee will destroy a critical system because of a personal gripe.

Recommended minimum precautions include:

- A simple process for eliminating log in access when an employee leaves the company
- A mandatory process for eliminating log in access when any employee is terminated

TAILGATING

Tailgating is an old ploy used to gain access to a system. It goes like this:

1. A super user or system administrator dials into a remote system.
2. The hacker dials the number (obtained through a demon dialer) and gets a busy signal.
3. The hacker dials 0 and asks the local telephone operator to verify the line.
4. The operator interrupts the line, which usually drops the authorized super user.
5. The hacker is meanwhile dialing out at the same time on another line. If timed perfectly, the modem sees the drop of carrier as a temporary line hit and reestablishes the session with the hacker's modem.
6. The hacker is online with super user access; the super user in turn oftentimes does not even know he has been dropped and instead thinks the system has simply locked up.
7. Working quickly, the hacker grabs the password files and compromises the system for his next attempt later, before the super user realizes anything was amiss. When security logs are checked, only the super user is logged because his session was never terminated.

Sounds rather ingenious? Actually, compared with some of the other tricks, this one is elementary. It underscores that any additional security precautions implemented provide greater peace of mind and protection to organizational assets. Remember, security is a major concern when dozens or hundreds of employees are accessing mission-critical systems through the public telephone network. Careful planning can avoid major difficulties later.

Digital –
E-Mail

PREVENTIVE MEASURES

Inbound Call Accounting Systems

Each proposed solution should provide an accounting record of all call attempts to make a paper trail of dial-in access. Strength in screening, reporting, and presentation of this information must be a principal selection criterion in any protective system. A system showing 350 unsuccessful log-in attempts one night is sending a clear signal.

Paging Systems

Some systems that require a high degree of security provide automatic pager notification. When a user logs in, a system administrator's pager goes off. These can be combined with procedures for reporting mysterious login attempts that cannot otherwise be accounted for. They are not terribly expensive considering that a system administrator is instantly notified of anomalies.

Hardware Keys

Hardware devices such as hardware keys should be included in any security recommendations for mission-critical systems. Ease of use, such as plugging into a parallel port, and low cost should be both overriding criteria in the use of these devices.

The keys are a hardware device that usually plugs into a parallel port of a laptop computer. In conjunction with the attendant software, they provide a fairly bulletproof solution because an intruder would have to have both the encryption software, and the hardware key, to get even close to accessing a system.

Caller ID

Caller ID is available in many cities. Even in telephone wire centers where it is available, there are limitations. Caller ID is useful for more than just identification of annoying calls during dinnertime. Properly used, it can identify unauthorized users by their telephone number and often by name. Even nicer, caller ID is a built-in feature for many modems and ISDN (integrated services digital network) terminal adapters. The numbers can be logged on a call-by-call basis as part of the dial-in log described earlier.

Owing to the nonavailability of caller ID service in many areas, modems or other equipment that use this service as the sole underlying basis of a protective system may not be considered. Even if caller ID is available, there are still security concerns, namely:

- Caller ID data may not always be passed by interexchange carriers like AT&T, MCI, and Sprint. Your company would in a sense be vulnerable to long distance callers using carriers who do not pass this data. (This is rapidly changing as carriers comply with FCC regulations to pass caller ID data whenever possible.)
- Even if interexchange carriers were equipped to pass this data, the distant local central office might not be. A company would still be open to intrusion unless other methods were employed.
- Many local central offices in parts of the country are not caller ID capable for either local or long-distance calls.

Therefore, at least a few calls will still slip through with the "out of area" disclaimer on the modem or display device. Caller ID alternatives should be carefully considered as an exclusive security precaution until the service becomes more ubiquitous. Even after universal deployment, it is recommended that this service is used only to augment existing security measures and not as a solution. Even where caller ID is available, the user can in many cases dial the override code to block it. This demands another level of protection on a modem: rejection of users where the incoming data indicates that the caller ID information was deliberately blocked.

Dial-Back Modems

Many dial-back modems are available on the market today. These devices require that users login, and then hang up and call the incoming caller back at a predetermined number. These are fairly foolproof, but inconvenient. A nomadic user in a hotel will not have an authorized number and will not be able to dial into a call-back modem bank. Nonetheless, special modem banks and numbers can be set up for this purpose with special emphasis and screening for potential intruders.

Securing the Mainframe

Many users are stuck trying to protect legacy mainframe environments where security options for dial-in are marginal at best. While IBM has no graceful and simple solution for the mainframe, it can provide an additional level of security by front ending the protocol converter with a dial-in server. The IBM 8235 dial-in server is one candidate. It provides the necessary accounting, dial-back capability, and with an eight port maximum capacity, it seems sized correctly for any future growth. However, it is somewhat expensive.

More common are solutions where distributed devices are hung off the mainframe through the use of bridges and LAN (local area networks) switches. A PC-based system with appropriate protocol conversion software will often suffice in a pinch as a secure dial-in medium for the mainframe.

Software-Based Solutions

Because transparency for dial-in users is an issue (different departments often use a variety of software packages when dialing in), you may not want to consider a wholesale change of dial-in software emulation packages. This might prove disruptive to your present operating environment.

Software alternatives that augment or enhance the current hardware package in use are most preferable because the need for training on new packages is minimal.

After-Market Equipment

Often, the only way to provide acceptable security across a broad range of installed equipment and large cross-section of users is to adapt some sort of outboard solution. Naturally, the potential exists to black box a company to death by over-broadening the range of installed equipment. It pays to evaluate carefully. Following are several effective alternatives:

- A line of equipment distributed by CDI Incorporated of Clifton, NJ. This equipment seems to most adequately reflect pressing security concerns presented by most users. Although I have not had direct experience with this equipment, on paper it certainly seems to provide a most comprehensive solution to the dial-in security issue and should be carefully considered.
- Another cost-effective solution is brokered by LeeMah Data Comm Security Corp. of Hayward, CA. It also appears to meet criteria for transparency and accommodation of diverse remote users.

When evaluating these or another product, look for the following features:

1. The unit should serve as security device and modem manager. Anyone who has ever repeatedly hit a "ring-no-answer" when dialing a modem pool can appreciate this feature. Make sure the system can automatically busy these lines out, then alert you to the problem.
2. The unit should provide response time information by modem, by phone line, and by port. For example, it should interface to a personal computer for effective performance management. This makes a good source of information to a help desk for when users call in to report trouble connecting.
3. The product should offer effective upgradeability. For additional security, the product should offer token hardware devices that interfaces to a user's parallel port. Software token should also be available. DOS or Windows software both should be supported.
4. Software and hardware keys. Because transparency of equipment for users is usually an issue, try not to consider major changes in hardware used by remote users. This might prove too disruptive to the present operating environment. This may cost more later in maintenance and training.

An unbiased opinion makes LeeMah the favorite in terms of flexibility and cost-effectiveness. Some of the features offered provide effective evaluation criteria for whatever system you decide to acquire. These include:

- The unit is a multiple port challenge-response unit.
- It supports up to 32 modems (Traq-Net 2032).
- The unit installs between the phone line and modem, allowing for use of present modems.
- The product allows for use of (optional) proprietary LeeMah Security Modems for additional protection.
- The product employs either a hardware or software token at user request.
- It provides a full audit trail.
- The product meets DES security standard.
- The product operates transparently, allowing for use of all present emulation software.
- It offers reasonably priced software (Infodisk).
- The product supports, for example, Procomm, Qmodem, Crosstalk, PCAnywhere, and Smartcom.

LeeMah DataComm provides a standards-based, virtually impenetrable, flexible, and configurable, security solution for the protection of remote access to telecommunications and data communications network information and resources. LeeMah's remote access security solutions consist of three elements: access control systems, personal authentication devices, and security administration software.

The LeeMah system represents one of the most adaptable and feature-rich solutions to protect dial-in services over a wide variety of equipment types from mainframes to local area networks. However, it is still wise to evaluate several vendors and base a decision on each unique environment. An Internet search will probably uncover numerous other choices with similar capabilities.

INTERNET SECURITY RESPONSIBILITIES

No discussion of unauthorized data access is complete without mentioning the Internet. The Internet is a relatively new phenomenon for many companies, at least as a revenue generating system, and many companies have unresolved organizational issues about security responsibilities. Who maintains the equipment used for Internet access? Historically, these types of operations often have fallen under a special unit in the IS department, such as midrange computer services. However, today many companies have a separate group of technologists responsible for the actual operation of the Internet firewall and other components. There is not always a clear business unit responsible for Internet security.

Many clients have reported minor snafus (i.e., holes or vulnerabilities left temporarily exposed in the system) due to lack of a clear policy outlining who is responsible for which system and under what circumstances. Although this responsibility will ultimately gravitate to an IT security group (much like the LAN and mainframe services of today), vulnerabilities will continue in the immediate term, while the technology is in the "tweaking and tinkering" stage.

Another issue includes staffing and resource allocation. Many companies should consider a nominal increase in manpower to avoid creating too small a pool of specialists and provide better depth. When Internet access is established and any possible security breeches or holes are closed, organization changes may be readdressed. If a company has one person who is readily identified as the Internet guru, take note. These folks are in high demand and could leave you holding the bag if they accept other employment. Besides, outgunned and undermanned staffs have little time to probe for security violations.

Installation of Test Firewall

Many companies do not have firewall platform exclusively earmarked for testing and backup. For all intents and purposes, the present technology is single threaded in almost every way. This is not a major concern yet, but will be when the firewall goes into full operation, and the system becomes revenue producing.

Just as in mainframes and local area networks, it is important to establish a protocol and procedure that does not directly introduce new applications into a production environment. This lesson became apparent during 25 years of mainframe operations, and even the most renegade LAN managers have learned to adopt it as a gospel of prudent operation. Like many new technologies, these protocols have yet to catch up in the Internet arena for many firms.

A test firewall also can double as a backup in the event of a major equipment failure in the primary configuration. This will be important again when the system becomes fully revenue generating.

Because the Internet is a relatively new technology for many firms, staff should be encouraged to dabble. Although it is not prudent to experiment on a production platform, the backup firewall configuration can provide a practical option. The backup can be justified further by encouraging the staff to experiment, improve, and refine without jeopardizing operation of the enterprise. In summary, the extra expense of a backup firewall capability can be justified for the resiliency it provides the network and because it shortens

the educational curve when principal technologists are encouraged to try new processes.

Upgrading to a Fully Redundant Configuration

The issue of redundant physical componentry of the Internet firewall raises several items of concern. Again, these will not be major concerns until the Internet and firewalls go into full production and become revenue-generating systems, but they will demand increased attention in the future. The first is in the area of general fault tolerance on the physical components.

Many routers in use, such as the CISCO 4000 series, have no redundancy. The CISCO 5000 series has redundant power and a redundant CPU, which will be required later. Every other component in other systems generally has a redundant backplane, power supply, CPU, and other common logic. As usual in the world of technology, the newer systems play catch-up for a couple of years with regard to redundancy. CISCO appears to have responded commendably to user demands for such backup systems, as have other vendors. Organizations should explore these options and use them as soon as Internet access is about to become revenue generating or otherwise mission critical.

Backup T1s

Another issue to consider is that most large users install only one T1 to the Internet Service Provider (ISP), which creates a point of vulnerability. A wiser approach is to consider adding a second T1 along with "Round Robin DNS" for greater resiliency on the wide area network connectivity to the ISP. Many local telephone companies offer services designed to diversify T1 access as well. In Southwestern Bell territory, the service is called SecureNet™, which offers a completely diverse T1 circuit at a significantly reduced rate. Other components, such as CSUs and DSUs, are single threaded without redundancy. Spares should be kept or depot arrangements should be made with vendors to ensure that failed components can be replaced quickly, minimizing the impact on the business.

As the Internet becomes more and more of an integral part of a company's operations (as defined by impact on revenue or other valid measurement), storing of spare components, including hard drives, redundant controller cards, spare tape drives, and power supplies should be considered.

In summary, to ensure a system up to par with revenue-generating applications, companies should upgrade to series 5000 or 6000 routers (or equivalent), combined with dual connections to the ISP and "Round Robin DNS" at the same juncture. Depot arrangements should be established for spare parts, and services such as Southwestern Bell SecureNet and other methods for diversifying T1 access should be considered. Such precautions will provide cheap insurance for what will fast become a revenue-producing system.

RECOMMENDED COURSE OF ACTION

Although revenue-generating dial-in systems may seem to be far away for many companies, experience shows that systems like these have a way of catching on. Insurance companies love the idea of roving claims adjusters with dial-in laptop computers. Everyone wants to work at home. Commerce is blossoming on the Internet. Waiting until there is a revenue impact after a failure resigns an organization to be almost perpetually in the reactive mode of trying to keep up with the protection of a potentially business debilitating system. The alternative is to start now, while these systems are still relatively immature and design the protective systems in before the Internet becomes a fully functional business system.

E-Mail Retention Policy: Legal Requirements

Stephen D. Fried, CISSP
Vice President for Information Security and Privacy, Metavante Corporation, Pewaukee, Wisconsin, U.S.A.

Abstract

This entry discusses the security and privacy aspects concerning the use of electronic mail in the workplace, and is intended to inform the security professional of some of the various issues that need to be addressed when formulating an e-mail retention policy. The information presented in this entry, including potential policy suggestions, reflects the combined experiences of many organizations and does not reflect the security or legal policy of any one organization in particular. The security professional will need to apply the concepts presented in this entry to best suit the business, legal, and security needs of his or her own organization. In addition, the entry discusses legal matters pertaining to e-mail use, but should not be construed as giving legal advice. The security professional should consult with legal counsel skilled in these areas before determining an appropriate course of action. The views expressed are solely those of the author and not of any organization or entity to which the author belongs or by which he is employed.

SETTING THE SCENE

The scene, circa 1955:

> The young boy sees the old shoebox off to one side of the moldy attic. Unable to contain his curiosity, he picks up the dusty container, unties the loose string knot holding the lid on the box and cautiously peers inside. To his surprise, he sees a large bundle of letters wrapped tightly inside a red lace ribbon. Gently opening the frail envelopes yellowed with age, he reads the hand-written letters adorned with perfect penmanship. He is astonished to find the contents reveal a personal history of his greatgrandfather's fortune, as recounted through the exchange of letters between his great-grandfather and his soon-to-be great-grandmother as they courted over the distance. Some of the details are shocking, some loving, but much of it has never been recounted in the oral family history that has been passed down through the generations . . .

The scene, circa 2004:

> The young technician notes an interesting set of messages hidden deep in a directory tree. Unable to contain his curiosity, he browses to the disk where the files sit, opens the directory containing the messages, and cautiously peers at the contents. To his surprise, he sees a large archive of e-mail wrapped behind non-sensical subject headings and file names. Cautiously opening each message, he reads each piece of e-mail adorned with perfect grammatical clarity. He is astonished to find that the contents reveal a history of the company's rise to market dominance, as recounted through the exchange of e-mail messages between the CEO and the company's senior management as they plotted their rise over the years. Some of the details are shocking, some

> embarrassing, much of it never recounted in the official version of the company's past that had been told to the subcommittee just a few months ago . . .

It is not such a far-fetched idea, and it has happened countless times in the recent past. Companies are finding out that the e-mails exchanged between its employees, or between its employees and outsiders, are having an increasing impact on the way they do business and, more importantly, on how much the outside world knows about their internal activities. It is estimated that 31 billion e-mails were sent daily on the Internet in 2002, and that is expected to double by 2006 [International Data Corporation (IDC)]. In addition, more than 95% of business documents are now produced, managed, and stored solely in electronic format, never to be printed in physical form. As communication channels grow and expand to fit the way modern businesses interact with each other, it is a natural fit that much of this electronic information will find its way into the e-mail messages companies send and receive every day.

Unfortunately, this explosion of the use of e-mail for critical business communication has also had an unforeseen side effect. The communications medium that many see as a natural extension of verbal communications has, in fact, created a vast repository of critical, sensitive, and, in some cases, damaging evidence that organizations are seeking to limit and control. The production in discovery and use of company e-mail in legal proceedings has become a standard part of the legal process and has led to negative impacts on many legal cases for companies that failed to educate employees on the proper use and retention of internal e-mail.

Encyclopedia of Information Assurance DOI: 10.1081/E-EIA-120046567
Copyright © 2011 by Taylor & Francis. All rights reserved.

GOOD NEWS AND BAD NEWS

The explosive use of e-mail as a primary business communication medium over the past 10 years has been widely heralded as a boon to companies needing to communicate quickly and efficiently on a global scale. E-mail has many of the benefits of its analog predecessor, standard postal mail. It is fundamentally easy to use. It is a modern-day appliance application with a simplified user interface and an intuitive process:

1. Click "compose message."
2. Type message.
3. Enter the receiver's address (or point-and-click it from your "address book").
4. Click "Send."

Almost everyone, from a 5 year-old schoolchild to an 80 year-old grandmother, has the ability to easily send a message down the street or around the world. Also contributing to the rise of e-mail popularity has been its nearly universal acceptance in the social and economic fabric of everyday life. There is hardly a business on the planet today that does not have a World Wide Web URL or an e-mail address, and more and more individuals are joining the ranks of online communicators every day.

In a departure from its analog cousin, e-mail is relatively instantaneous. Instead of placing an envelope in a mailbox and waiting days or weeks for it to arrive at its destination, most e-mail messages arrive in seconds or minutes, and a reply can be on its way just as quickly. This immediacy in communications is rivaled only by the telephone, another ubiquitous communications device. Finally, e-mail has become a socially acceptable form of communication between individuals and businesses alike. Many people treat e-mail as another form of "live" communications and carry on lengthy conversations back and forth through the wire. Because people see e-mail as a more informal communications method than written documentation, they will often tend to say things in an e-mail that they would not say in person or in an official company document.

Ironically, despite the social informality associated with e-mail use, many organizations treat e-mail as formal business communication, using it for customer contact, internal approval processes, and command-and-control applications. In many business settings, a message sent by e-mail now has the same social and legal weight as the same message spoken or hand-written on paper. It is often used as documentation and confirmation of the sender's acts or intent. Setting aside the fact that the security of most modern e-mail systems is insufficient to protect against interception of, or tampering with, e-mail messages, e-mail now has the force of authority that was once reserved only for the hand-written word.

The economics of e-mail have also led to its universal acceptance as a communications medium for modern business. The cost of creating, processing, and delivering e-mail is a fraction of the cost of handling standard paper-based mail. There are no supplies to maintain (no envelopes or stamps, for example) and a user's management of dozens or hundreds of daily messages is simplistic compared to managing the same volume of physical letters each day. While it is true that the infrastructure required to manage e-mail (such as network connections, servers, and Internet connectivity) can have a substantial cost, most organizations establish and utilize these facilities as part of their general business information processing, with e-mail adding only incrementally to the cost of those facilities.

The cost to store e-mail has fallen dramatically over the past few years. The cost to store 13 million pages of hand-written letters would be prohibitive for all but the largest of corporations, and even then the use of microfiche or other information-miniaturizing technology would be required. However, the cost to store an equivalent amount of e-mail, approximately 40 gigabytes, is well below $100.00, well within reach of most consumers. With economics such as this, it is no wonder that many people choose to retain an archive of e-mail often stretching back several years.

And here begins the bad-news side of the e-mail explosion. The benefits of a simple, low-cost, ubiquitous communications medium cannot be without its detracting elements, and e-mail is no exception. One of the largest negative factors is the lack of standardized security mechanisms for protecting the confidentiality and integrity of e-mail content. While a detailed analysis of such issues is beyond the scope of this entry, they will be revisited briefly later in the discussion surrounding the uses of e-mail in legal proceedings. A second area brought on by the economics of widespread e-mail use is that of management of e-mail information. Because storage is so inexpensive, many users can afford to store their entire e-mail archives locally on their personal (albeit perhaps company-owned) computer. This may be a slight productivity gain for end users of e-mail systems, but it represents a huge loss of centralized control for the management of e-mail systems and the information these systems contain. When the need arises to uniformly search a company's e-mail archives for important information, whether for a disaster recovery exercise or for legal discovery purposes, it becomes difficult to efficiently or uniformly search the private archives of every single user. In a typical medium- to large-scale computing environment, policy and operational issues such as centralized information storage, records retention, and information destruction become much more complicated.

E-MAIL IS FOREVER

Many people think of e-mail messages in much the same ephemeral way as they regard personal conversations: once

Digital –
E-Mail

the exchange has been completed, the message has passed, never to be heard from again. Unfortunately, e-mail "conversations" are not nearly as ephemeral as their verbal counterparts. An examination of a typical e-mail session reveals just how long-lived an e-mail message can be.

1. The user opens an e-mail program and begins to type a message. If the session takes enough time, the e-mail program may store the message in a local cache or "Drafts" folder as a disaster-recovery method.
2. The user clicks "Send" to send the message. The message is stored on the local machine (typically in a "Sent Messages" folder), then transmitted to the local e-mail server.
3. The local server contacts the recipient's e-mail server and copies the message to that system.
4. The recipient opens an e-mail program and connects to their e-mail server. The message is then copied to the recipient's personal computer where it is read.

Just from this simple scenario, the e-mail message is copied to, and saved on, no fewer than four different systems. This scenario also assumes that the sender's and recipient's e-mail servers are directly connected, which is seldom the case in real life. If there are any intermediate e-mail servers or gateways between the sending and receiving servers, the message will additionally be stored on each of those servers on the way to its final destination. In addition, if the receiver forwards the mail to a PDA or another user, the mail will be copied yet again, perhaps multiple times. This method of transmission is known as *store-and-forward*, and leads to one of the biggest problems when it comes to e-mail retention and destruction: When a company wishes to find all instances of a mail message for use or destruction, or it wishes to find all the messages relating to a particular subject, the messages often reside in multiple locations, and some of those locations may be out of the administrative and security control of the organization. For an organization trying to recover the communications related to a specific event or produce electronic documents in connection with a legal proceeding, this represents a large logistical and legal problem.

E-MAIL RISKS ABOUND

Based on the description of the current e-mail landscape, and given its importance and widespread use, there are clearly risks associated with relying on e-mail as a primary communications method for business. Some of the more prevalent risks include:

- *Breach of confidentiality.* This is a frequent risk of e-mail communications, and can be realized in two ways. First, a malicious actor can deliberately send sensitive and proprietary information in an e-mail to a third party. Although many organizations have policies that allow them to monitor the content of e-mail sent from the organization, most do not have sufficient resources to routinely monitor all e-mail. Thus, it is highly likely that such a maliciously transmitted message will sneak out of the organization undetected. The second method for breaching confidentiality is through the inadvertent misdirection of mail to an unintended recipient. It is a simple matter to mistakenly put the wrong e-mail address in the "To:" section of the message, thus sending confidential information into the wrong hands. A popular reaction to this threat has been an increased use of disclaimers attached to the bottom of all e-mails emanating from an organization. The disclaimer typically identifies the sending organization of the message and requests that if the recipient has received the message in error, the sender should be notified and the recipient should destroy any and all copies of the message. While this may provide some legal protection, these types of disclaimers have been successfully challenged in some courts, so they are not foolproof.

- *Damage to reputation.* As e-mail messages have become recognized as statements of record, their potential to damage the financial stability or reputation of the sender has likewise grown. A poorly worded or offensive message falling into the wrong hands can have grave personal or economic consequences for the sender. A recent case in point comes from a woman in the United Kingdom whose boyfriend worked for Norton and Rose, a U.K. law firm. The woman sent an e-mail to her boyfriend discussing intimate details of their sex life. The message was somehow obtained by friends of the couple and forwarded multiple times to multiple people, eventually reaching millions on the Internet.

- *Legal liability.* As will be discussed in more detail, the widespread use of e-mail as a medium for business communications opens up an organization to legal risks. Many jurisdictions hold the organization, not the individual e-mail user, responsible for the use and content of e-mail messages sent from the organization's network. A 2003 joint study by the ePolicy Institute, the American Management Association, and Clearswift found that 14% had been ordered by a court or regulatory body to produce employee e-mail records. That figure is up from only 9% in 2001. In addition, 5% of companies have battled a workplace lawsuit triggered by e-mail.[1]

IT CAN HAPPEN TO YOU: CASE STUDIES AND LESSONS LEARNED

To understand the full impact of the business use for e-mail, and the ramifications involved in indefinite retention of e-mail messages, an examination of several real-life cases is in order. These cases show how e-mail messages left on corporate and personal systems have led to damaging evidence in trial court, and sometimes in the "court of public opinion."

One of the most widely publicized cases in recent memory was the U.S. Justice Department's antitrust case against Microsoft.[2] In that case, prosecution lawyers made use of numerous e-mail documents, some of them several years old, to make their case against the software giant. In one particularly damaging message, Microsoft Chairman Bill Gates allegedly describes how he tried to persuade Intuit against distributing Netscape's Internet browser with its financial software. In its defense, Microsoft claimed that the passages used as evidence in the case were taken out of context and were part of a much longer series of messages (commonly known as a *thread*), which altered the underlying meaning of the quote.

Many lessons come from the Microsoft case. The first exemplifies what has already been discussed: e-mail lives inside a company's network far longer than most people imagine. In the Microsoft case, many of the e-mail messages used as evidence were several years old by the time the case came to trial. The second major lesson emanates from the contextual argument used by Microsoft. Public figures whose comments have been quoted accurately yet inappropriately in the media have been subjected to this problem for many years. E-mail threads are often composed of small snippets of commentary sent back and forth by the participants in the communication. While this follows a more conversational style of communication between humans, rarely can a single paragraph or e-mail tell the whole story of the conversation. The lesson to be learned here is that e-mail users must be made aware that their comments, however incidental or incomplete, can come back to haunt them.

This last point is seen again in the case of *Linnen v. A.H. Robins Co.*[3] In that case, Robins was accused of not warning healthcare providers and consumers about the potential dangers of taking the combination of Pondimin (fenfluramine) and Ionamin (phentermine), which, when prescribed together, were commonly referred to as "fen/phen." The contentious legal battle took a significant turn when computer forensics experts were able to recover an e-mail from one company employee to another pertaining to the side effects of the fen/phen drug. The message read, in part, "Do I have to look forward to spending my waning years writing checks to fat people worried about a silly lung problem?" Partially as a result of that message, the case turned from heated litigation to settlement talks and led to American Home Products paying out billions of dollars in settlement claims. The lesson here is that the internal commentary of your employees, no matter how innocuous or off-the-cuff, can be hiding in your system and, if discovered, used against you.

Surprisingly, although it has received increased attention in the past several years, using e-mail as damaging evidence is nothing new to the legal arena. As far back as the 1980s, Colonel Oliver North tried to delete e-mail messages pertaining to the Iran-Contra affair from his computer system. His mistaken belief that the deletion was permanent, and his lack of understanding of how the White House e-mail system worked, led to damaging evidence against the administration of President Ronald Reagan.

E-MAIL USE AND THE (U.S.) LAW

In recent years, the use of e-mail as evidence in criminal and civil proceedings has become commonplace for prosecutors and defense attorneys alike. To be admissible in U.S. courts, evidence must meet certain threshold tests. The evidence must be authenticated; that is, it must be proven to be that which it purports to be (*Fed. R. Evid.*, 901, Authentication). Further, the evidence must be admissible under the rules of evidence. A common objection to documentary evidence is that it is "hearsay," but an equally common exception is that it meets the "business records" exception for the use of hearsay evidence. Most standard business records and communications formally kept and maintained as a normal part of a company's business processes fall under the hearsay exception (*Fed. R. Evid.*, Article VIII, Hearsay).

Federal Rules of Civil Procedure

The Federal Rules of Civil Procedure (Fed. R. Civ. P., or FRCP), together with such local practice rules as the district courts may implement, govern the conduct of civil cases in the U.S. federal district courts. While a full analysis of the rules governing any court is beyond the scope of this entry, some basic information is useful as background. These rules do not, by law, apply to suits brought in state courts, but the rules of many states have been closely modeled after those found in the FRCP. The two rules of the FRCP most germane to a discussion of e-mail as evidence are Rule 26(a) and Rule 34. Rule 26(a) specifically requires the disclosure of, or a description of, certain materials, including "data compilations" relevant to a party's claims or defenses. This rule, or some local rules (which may be more stringent than the federal rules), may require attorneys to locate all sources of such information that their clients might possess, including data stored on individual computers, hard disks, network servers, personal digital assistants, and removable media. Data in the possession of third parties, such as outsourcers, business partners, or Internet service providers may, under some circumstances, also be covered if it is under the party's control.

Digital –
E-Mail

Discovery

The practice of litigation in U.S. courts involves a process of *discovery* pursuant to which a party may obtain information that can be used at trial in proceedings in advance of the trial, thus reducing the potential for surprise. Because the use of e-mail records in court cases are a common occurrence, lawyers for both sides of cases can expect to receive a request for any and all e-mail records pertaining to a case as part of a discovery request, generally pursuant to FRCP Rule 34, which addresses, in part, the production of documents and things. While this sounds like a simple process, when it comes to the discovery of e-mail records the process of responding can be quite complicated. The organization served with a discovery request may need to locate material responsive to that request, which may be a very broad subject. For many organizations, simply identifying where all the information may be, and who had access to it, can be a daunting task.

If a company stores and processes all its mail in a central location, this can mean extracting relevant records from the central server. If, however, computer users in the company store mail locally on their PCs, the company must gather the relevant information from each of those individual PCs. E-mail records past a certain age can also be stored on backup tapes at alternate locations. To properly respond to a discovery motion, a company may be compelled to retrieve multiple sources of information looking for responsive data in those sources. This can amount to a substantial resource and financial drain on a company during a lengthy litigation.

Spoliation

When a claim is reasonably likely to be asserted, and certainly once asserted, a party must be careful to ensure that relevant information is preserved and not altered, damaged, or destroyed in any way. The result of not following established processes or mishandling information is called *spoliation* and can have serious legal consequences. One of the most prevalent mistakes resulting in spoliation is the failure to discontinue automatic document destruction policies when a company is served with a discovery request. Even if a company's policy states that all documents must be destroyed after 5 years (for example), once a company has reason to know it might be involved in litigation, arbitration, or investigation, all information relevant to the claim or issue must be retained until the final outcome (including all possible appeals) is decided. This holds true even if the litigation takes the information well past the 7 year retention cycle. Some complex cases or series of cases can take 10 years or more. A company that destroys relevant potential evidence while a case is still underway is risking large penalties, sanctions, or even criminal charges.

Another potential for a spoliation claim might arise from errors made in collection or imaging of electronic data. There are specific procedures for presenting a document in court to ensure its admissibility. If the gathering methodology alters the document such that it is no longer usable, the lost evidence may jeopardize a claim. Security professionals and legal teams are advised to seek out an experienced expert in forensic evidence gathering if they believe this might be an issue with their case.

Legal sanctions for allowing spoliation to occur can be severe. A court could bar evidence, render adverse rulings (for either the case or the specific issue in question), impose monetary sanctions, or instruct the jury that it may infer that the missing material was negative to the party that should have had the information (a so-called "adverse inference instruction"). There is even a risk of criminal prosecution for obstruction of justice through the destruction of evidence.

Authentication and Integrity

An issue that relates to both spoliation and a message's admissibility under the hearsay exception is the authentication of evidence and its integrity throughout the discovery process. To be admissible, evidence must be shown to be authentic and a true representation of the communication in question. At a practical level, this means that a party must show that the message came from an officially recognized source (i.e., the company's corporate e-mail system) and that it was handled in accordance with the company's accepted business practices for such information. This step is required even if the use of the hearsay exception for business records is not at issue.

A company must also prove the integrity of the communication and may need to prove that it has not been altered in any way from the moment it is identified as potential evidence until its production at trial. Altering relevant information (intentionally or inadvertently) can lead to a spoliation claim.

PLANNING AN E-MAIL RETENTION POLICY

Having worked through the issues surrounding the use, risks, and legal circumstances of e-mail use, it should be clear that this is an issue that is best served by a clear policy surrounding the retention of e-mail based information. By formulating a clear policy, disseminating that policy throughout the organization, and enforcing its application in an efficient and uniform manner, many of the issues previously addressed become easier to manage and the risks associated with e-mail use and retention can be reduced.

The basic principle behind an e-mail retention policy (as is the case with all such information retention policies) is that information should be uniformly and routinely destroyed after a predefined period of time unless exceptions are called for, most notably when the possibility of claims or litigation arise. While this may seem contradictory (calling it a retention policy when it, in fact, advocates the destruction of information), it is completely consistent with current business and legal leading practices. The reasoning behind defining a specific time period for retaining information comes from the need to shelter an organization from long-forgotten "surprise" evidence uncovered during a discovery procedure that could lead to an unfavorable ruling against the company. If an e-mail message is destroyed as a routine, established business practice (and assuming further that the company had no reason not to destroy it, such as a potential or pending claim) it cannot be produced as evidence (because it does not exist). At the same time, the practice protects the company from obstruction charges, because it followed an established procedure and did nothing special in relation to the message or messages in question. It should be noted again, as previously discussed, that such a process only protects a company if the information is destroyed prior to its identification as potential evidence. Once the potential need is known or the facts exist to suggest a potential claim, the information must be preserved despite any policies or procedures the company may have to the contrary.

On a strictly operational level, routine destruction of old information allows the organization to minimize long-term storage costs for outdated information and provides for a more efficient e-mail service for end users.

Management Guidance

As with all effective policies, an e-mail retention policy must start with the support and backing of the senior management of the organization. Management must be consulted to determine its concerns regarding e-mail retention and its tolerance for the varying levels of risk associated with retaining e-mail messages for longer or shorter periods of time. Once management has approved a strategy regarding e-mail retention, including a definition of acceptable risk, work can proceed on developing the company's e-mail retention policy.

Legal and Regulatory Guidance

An organization must take into account the legal and regulatory environment in which it operates when developing an e-mail retention policy. Most regulated industries have strict rules regarding the collection and maintenance of information pertaining to the operation of the business. These rules will include retention requirements and, in some cases, destruction requirements. In other industries, federal, state, or local laws may guide the retention of electronic information for certain periods of time. Additionally, if the company does business in multiple countries, the laws in those jurisdictions may need to be

taken into account as well. The organization must be mindful of these requirements so as not to violate any applicable laws or regulatory requirements.

The organization might consider establishing a cross-functional policy planning team. There are hundreds of federal and state record-keeping regulations that govern information retention, as well as many different technology products that attempt to help an organization manage some or all of the records management process. The best way to ensure success of the effort is to combine subject matter experts from the business' key functional areas, including the legal, IT, human resources, finance, and operations teams.

While it is most likely acceptable for an organization to retain records for a longer period of time than the law specifies, it is rarely, if ever, acceptable to destroy records before the time proscribed by law. An organization should always seek the advice of an attorney well versed in this area of the law before creating or amending any retention policy.

Distinguishing Corporate Use from Personal Use

Many organizations today allow the use of company e-mail facilities for limited personal use to send e-mail to friends and family or to conduct personal business during non-productive business time (before the workday begins or during a lunch break, for example). This may result in a commingling of personal and business e-mails on the user's PC and in the company's e-mail storage facilities. And, as has been previously discussed, those e-mails may be stored in multiple locations throughout the company's e-mail system. Should the company be served with a discovery motion for electronic business records, it may have the additional burden of wading through large amounts of personal mail in an effort to find relevant business messages. By the same token, if a company employee becomes involved in a legal dispute and the opposing counsel learns that the company allows use of its e-mail system for personal reasons, the company may be requested to search through its vast e-mail archive looking for any personal e-mails the employee sent that may be relevant to the case. An e-mail retention policy might need to address such a situation and specify an employee's ability to store personal e-mails on the company's computer system. This also raises many issues concerning employee privacy that are beyond the scope of this entry.

Records Management

The key to an effective e-mail retention policy is the establishment of clear policies and processes for records management. This affects all business records created and maintained by the company but should particularly stress compliance for e-mail communications.

A good place to start is by creating an inventory of current e-mail information in the organization. Close attention should be paid to historical records stored at off-site facilities, including magnetic tapes, disks, and microfiche. Once these information sources have been identified, they should be cataloged and categorized in as organized a manner as possible. These categories may include the source and destination of the message, the business unit or functional area affected by the message, and the sensitivity of the information contained in the message.

Based on the findings of the inventory, the organization can then begin to develop a strategy for how to deal with future e-mails sent to its employees. It may specify that different categories of e-mail messages must be handled in different ways, or that different categories of information have different retention requirements. Additionally, a policy might specify how employees are to archive mail they receive so as to make later discovery processes easier to manage. Whatever scheme is developed, the planners of the policy should strive to keep it as simple as possible for the average user to understand and implement. If the process is too complicated, users will resist its use.

Responding to Discovery Requests

Because the process of responding to a discovery motion is a complicated one, it should only be undertaken under the direct guidance and supervision of a qualified attorney. Mistakes made during the discovery phase of a trial can have grave consequences for the offending party. For this reason, an e-mail retention policy should clearly define who is responsible for responding to discovery motions and the authority that person or group has to obtain resources and information from other organizations inside the company.

A SAMPLE E-MAIL RETENTION POLICY

To assist organizations in the creation of their own e-mail retention policies, the following sample policy offers some guidance in the areas that should be considered when dealing with e-mail retention issues. This policy is for a fictional publishing company, HISM Enterprises, and contains many of the elements discussed thus far. As with any sample policy, the applicability to a particular organization will vary based on the structure and operating practices of that organization. The security professional can use this sample policy as the basis for establishing an organization's own policy, but should consult with the organization's business and legal representatives to determine the applicability of any particular aspect of the policy to the organization's goals.

Policy Number and Title

6.12: Retention and Destruction of Electronic Mail Records

Policy Background

Electronic mail ("e-mail") is an essential part of the tools that HISM uses to communicate with its customers, suppliers, and business partners. Because it is a primary method of communication, e-mail sent to and from HISM systems contains a great deal of sensitive information about HISM, its employees, and the third parties with which it deals. Unfortunately, some of that information may help HISM's competitors or prove damaging to HISM in the event of a legal dispute over its products, services, or conduct. For that reason, information contained in e-mails must be strictly controlled, processed, and destroyed according to applicable state and federal laws and consistent with internal HISM policies concerning destruction of company information.

Policy Statements

All information stored in HISM e-mail systems must be retained for a period of 5 years from the date of creation (in the case of e-mail originating from HISM) or the date of first receipt (in the case of e-mail originating from outside HISM).

Once the retention period has passed, the information must be destroyed and further use prevented. For information stored on electronic media (for example, tapes and disks), the information must be erased using a multi-pass overwriting system approved by the HISM Information Security organization. Once the magnetic information has been erased, the physical media must be destroyed. It cannot be reused for HISM information storage or recycled for use by other organizations.

All e-mail will be stored on centralized systems maintained by the HISM Information Technology (IT) organization. The operation of e-mail systems by groups other than IT is prohibited.

Sufficient storage must be made available to allow HISM users to keep e-mail from the past 90 days in online storage. E-mail older than 90 days must be archived to secondary media and stored in a secured location. The use of local e-mail storage (Personal Folders, for example) or the creation of directories on end-user systems for the purpose of creating an e-mail archive is strictly prohibited.

It is HISM policy to allow the limited judicious use of HISM computers and network resources (including e-mail) for personal reasons. A folder named "Personal" will be created in each user's electronic mailbox where users can place e-mail correspondence of a personal nature. This will allow HISM to respond more effectively to legal requests for corporate e-mail evidence without potentially infringing on the privacy rights of HISM employees.

HISM employees are not permitted to respond to court subpoenas or legal discovery requests without first consulting with the HISM Legal Department. All requests for access to e-mail information should be directed to the Legal Department.

In the event that HISM is a party in a legal proceeding that requires the extended retention of e-mail messages past the 5 year retention cycle, the HISM IT organization will provide sufficient facilities to store all affected e-mail messages until released from that responsibility by the HISM Legal Department.

Scope

This policy applies to all Company personnel who use HISM systems to create, read, store, or transmit electronic mail. It also pertains to non-employee workers, contractors, consultants, or other personnel performing work for HISM on a permanent or temporary basis.

This policy applies to all HISM business units and corporate functions. Where individual business units are required by law or by contractual obligation to follow e-mail retention policies other than those described in this policy, that business unit is required to seek a policy exception and approval from the Chief Information Officer, the Vice President for Information Security, and the Vice President for Legal Affairs.

Effective Dates, Grandfathering Provisions, and Sunset Provisions

This policy shall be effective immediately upon approval by the HISM Chief Information Officer.

This policy supersedes all previous policies pertaining to retention of e-mail information.

This policy shall continue to remain in effect unless superseded by a subsequent policy approved by the HISM Chief Information Officer.

Roles and Responsibilities

The HISM IT organization is responsible for establishing and maintaining e-mail resources for all HISM employees and associates. It is also responsible for adhering to this policy and developing appropriate procedures for implementing this policy in all HISM e-mail systems.

The Chief Information Officer, the Vice President of Information Security, and the Vice President for Legal Affairs must jointly evaluate and approve any exceptions to this policy. Exceptions will only be granted based on validated business need where compliance with this policy would place HISM in violation of applicable state or federal law.

All HISM sales teams and customer agents are responsible for ensuring that contracts with customers, suppliers, and other business partners do not place HISM in potential violation of this policy. Any potential violation issues should be immediately brought to the attention of the Vice President for Legal Affairs.

The HISM Information Security organization is responsible for specifying appropriate technology for destroying information stored on electronic media.

The HISM Legal Department is responsible for responding to legal inquiries for HISM e-mail information and managing the collection and analysis of that information.

Related Policies

- 5.24: Proper Disposal and Destruction of Sensitive Company Information
- 6.04: Use of Company Computing Resources for Non-Company Functions
- 6.05: Privacy of Personal Information on HISM Systems

CONCLUSION

Whether it is dusty old letters stuffed in an attic shoebox or obscure e-mail messages hidden in a long-forgotten directory, there will always be the opportunity to find hidden information among the remnants of long-past communications. Sometimes those remnants provide the catalyst to look back in amused nostalgia. But more and more often, those remnants are providing glimpses into a past best forgotten, information best not shared, or actions best not known. Unless proactive steps are taken to establish a formal e-mail retention policy, followed by an efficient e-mail retention and destruction process, a company is opening itself up to allowing investigators, litigators, and forensics experts to view its most closely held secrets.

REFERENCES

1. ePolicy Institute. Electronic Policies and Practices Survey, 2003, http://www.epolicyinstitute.com/survey/index.html.
2. *United States of America v. Microsoft Corporation*, Civil Action No. 98-1232, http://www.usdoj.gov/atr/cases/f4900/4909.htm.
3. *Linnen, v. A. H. Robins Co.*, 1999 WL 462015 (Mass Super June 16, 1999).

Digital – E-Mail

E-Mail: Pretty Good Privacy

William Stallings

Department of Computer Science and Engineering, Wright State University, Dayton, Ohio, U.S.A.

Abstract

Many users are unaware that their e-mail messages are completely public and can be monitored by someone else. This entry describes Pretty Good Privacy, an e-mail security package that allows users to send messages that are secure from eavesdropping and guaranteed to be authentic.

INTRODUCTION

Users who rely on electronic mail for business or personal communications should beware. Messages sent over a network are subject to eavesdropping. If the messages are stored in a file, they are subject to perusal months or even years later. There is also the threat of impersonation and that a message may not be from the party it claims to be from. Protection is available in the form of Pretty Good Privacy (PGP), an e-mail security package developed by Phil Zimmermann that combines confidentiality and digital signature capabilities to provide a powerful, virtually unbreakable, and easy-to-use package.

PGP DEFINED

The most notable features of this e-mail security program are that it:

- Enables people to send e-mail messages that are secure from eavesdropping. Only the intended recipient can read a Pretty Good Privacy message.
- Enables people to send e-mail messages that are guaranteed authentic. The recipient is ensured that the PGP message was created by the person who claims to have created it and that no one has altered the message since it was created.
- Is available as freeware on the Internet, many electronic bulletin boards, and most commercial services such as CompuServe.
- Is available in versions for Disk Operating System, Macintosh, UNIX, Amiga, OS/2, VMS, and other operating systems.
- Works with any e-mail package to create secure e-mail messages.

E-MAIL RISKS

PGP provides protection from the threat of eavesdropping. A message sent over the Internet can pass through a handful of mail forwarders and dozens of packet-switching nodes. A systems administrator or someone who has gained privileged access to any of these transfer points is in a position to read those messages.

Although e-mail users may feel they have nothing to hide, they may someday want to correspond with their lawyers or accountants using the Internet, or they may work for companies that want to send proprietary information over the Internet. Many people already use the Internet for sending highly personal or sensitive messages.

There is also a civil liberties issue to be concerned about. The police, intelligence, and other security forces of the government can easily monitor digital and computerized e-mail messages, looking for key words, names, and patterns of exchanges. Any user could be innocently caught up in such a net.

Authenticity of messages poses another potential risk. It is not difficult to spoof the network into sending a message with an incorrect return address, enabling impersonation. It is also relatively easy to trap a message along its path, alter the contents, and then send it on its way.

For example, if a user is on a shared system, such as a UNIX system, that hooks into the Internet, then the impersonator could be someone with "superuser" privileges on the system. Such a person could divert all incoming and outgoing traffic from an unsuspecting mailbox to a special file. The impersonator could also have access to a router, mail bridge, or other type of gateway through which all traffic between the user and a correspondent must pass. Such impersonators could use their privileged status on the gateway to intercept mail and to create and send mail with a fraudulent return address.

Encyclopedia of Information Assurance DOI: 10.1081/E-EIA-120046549

Copyright © 2011 by Taylor & Francis. All rights reserved.

PGP'S HISTORY: PRIVACY AT ISSUE

PGP is a legitimate tool that can be used for legitimate reasons by ordinary citizens, although some users consider it slightly suspect.

Phil Zimmerman began working on Pretty Good Privacy in the 1980s and released the first version in 1991. One of the key motivating factors for PGP's development was an effort by the FBI to secure passage of a law that would ban certain forms of security algorithms and force computer manufacturers to implement security features for e-mail that could be bypassed by government agencies. Zimmerman saw this as a threat to privacy and freedom. Thus, PGP was conceived as a package that could be used by the average person on a small system to provide e-mail privacy and authenticity. Zimmerman accomplished this by

- Selecting the best available security algorithms as building blocks.
- Integrating these algorithms into a general-purpose application that is independent of the operating system and processor and that is based on a small set of easy-to-use commands.
- Making the package and its documentation, including the source code, free and widely available.

Because PGP uses encryption algorithm, it was subject to export controls. An encryption algorithms lets users scramble a message in such a way that allows only the intended recipient to unscramble it.

Encryption algorithms are classified by the U.S. Government as armaments and fall under the International Trafficking in Armaments Regulations (ITAR). ITAR requires that users get an export license from the State Department to export armaments. In practice, the State Department will not grant any such license for strong encryption algorithms, and PGP uses two of the strongest.

This problem does not need to concern the average user because there is no law against using PGP in the United States. There is also no law outside the United States to prevent use of a product that was illegally exported from the United States. Furthermore, some of the more recent versions of PGP actually originated outside the United States, eliminating the problem altogether.

A second problem has to do with patents. One of the two encryption algorithms in PGP is known as Rivest-Shamir-Adleman (RSA). Anyone using PGP inside the US was, for a time, potentially subject to a lawsuit for Rivest-Shamir-Adleman patent infringement. A new release of PGP, known as version 2.6, which was developed at MIT with the supervision of Phil Zimmermann, has patent approval from the RSA patent holders. Like the original PGP, this version has also made its way onto bulletin boards and Internet sites outside the United States. In addition, a compatible non-US version 2.6 was created outside the United States. As long as a user chooses any of the flavors of version 2.6, there is no infringement on any patents.

CONVENTIONAL ENCRYPTION

PGP exploits two powerful security functions: conventional encryption and public-key encryption. Conventional encryption is the classic approach to secret codes that dates back to ancient Rome and even earlier. A conventional encryption scheme (see Fig. 1) includes the following five ingredients:

- *Plaintext.* This is the readable message or data that is fed into the algorithm as input.

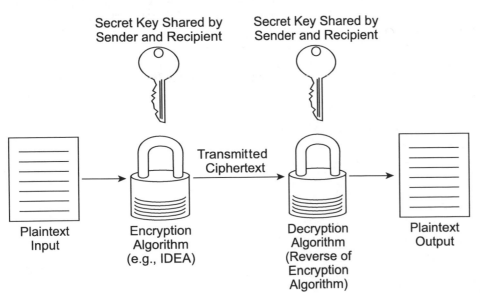

Fig. 1 Conventional encryption scheme.

Digital –
E-Mail

- *Encryption algorithm.* The encryption algorithm performs various substitutions and transformations on the plaintext.
- *Secret key.* The secret key is also input to the algorithm. The exact substitutions and transformations performed by the algorithm depend on the key.
- *Ciphertext.* This is the scrambled message produced as output. It depends on the plaintext and the secret key.
- *Decryption algorithm.* This is essentially the encryption algorithms run in reverse. It takes the ciphertext and the same secret key and produces the original plaintext.

CONVENTIONAL ENCRYPTION

The Caesar cipher, used by Julius Caesar, is a simple example of encryption. The Caesar cipher replaces each letter of the alphabet with the letter standing three places further down the alphabet, for example:

```
plain: meet me after the toga party
```

```
cipher: phhw ph diwhu wkh wrjd sduwb
```

The alphabet is wrapped around so that the letter following Z is A. The decryption algorithm simply takes the ciphertext and replaces each letter with the letter standing three places earlier on in the alphabet. A general Caesar cipher involves a shift of k letters, where k ranges from 1 through 25. In this case, k is the secret key to the algorithm.

The Caesar cipher is not very secure. Anyone who wanted to decipher the code could simply try every possible shift from 1 to 25. Pretty Good Privacy uses a much stronger algorithm known as the International Data Encryption Algorithm, or Interactive Data Extraction and Analysis.

International Data Encryption Algorithm

International Data Encryption Algorithm (IDEA) is a block-oriented conventional encryption algorithms developed in 1990 by Xuejia Lai and James Massey of the Swiss Federal Institute of Technology. The overall scheme for IDEA encryption is illustrated in Fig. 2. IDEA uses a 128-bit key to encrypt data in blocks of 64 bits.

OVERALL IDEA STRUCTURE

The IDEA algorithm consists of eight rounds, or iterations, followed by a final transformation function. The algorithm breaks the input into four 16-bit subblocks. Each of the iteration rounds takes four 16-bit subblocks as input and produces four 16-bit output blocks. The final transformation also produces four 16-bit blocks, which are concatenated to form the 64-bit ciphertext. Each of the iterations also uses six 16-bit subkeys, whereas the final transformation uses four subkeys, for a total of 52 subkeys. The right-hand portion of the figure indicates that these 52 subkeys are all generated from the original 128-bit key.

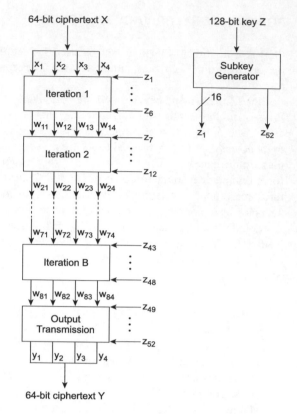

Fig. 2 IDEA encryption scheme.

Each iteration of IDEA uses three different mathematical operations. Each operation is performed on two 16-bit inputs to produce a single 16-bit output. The operations are:

- Bit-by-bit exclusive-OR, denoted as ∞.
- Addition of integers modulo 2^{16} (modulo 65536), with input and output treated as unsigned 16-bit integers. This operation is denoted as §.
- Multiplication of integers modulo $2^{16} + 1$ (modulo 65537), with input and output treated as unsigned 16-bit integers, except that a block of all zeros is treated as representing 2^{16}. This operation is denoted as [Theta].

For example,

$$0000000000000000 \text{ [Theta]} 1000000000000000 = 1000000000000001$$

because

$$2^{16} * 2^{15} \bmod (2^{16} + 1) = 2^{15} + 1$$

These three operations are incompatible because no pair of the three operations satisfies a distributive law. For example:

$$a§b\text{[Theta]}c \neq (a§b)\text{[Theta]}(a§c)$$

They are also incompatible because no pair of the three operations satisfies an associative law. For example:

$$a§(b\infty c) \neq (a§b)\infty c$$

Digital –
E-Mail

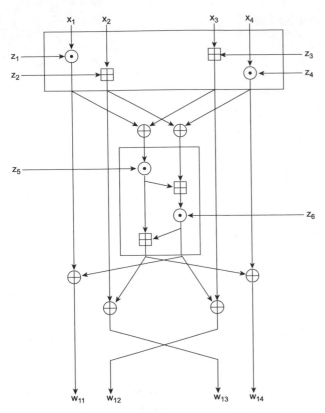

Fig. 3 Algorithm for a single iteration.

The use of these three separate operations in combination provides for a complex transformation of the input, making cryptanalysis very difficult.

Fig. 3 illustrates the algorithm for a single iteration. In fact, this figure shows the first iteration. Subsequent iterations have the same structure, but with different subkey and plaintext-derived input. The iteration begins with a transformation that combines the four input subblocks with four subkeys, using the addition and multiplication operations. This transformation is highlighted as the upper shaded rectangle. The four output blocks of this transformation are then combined using the XOR operation to form two 16-bit blocks that are input to the lower shaded rectangle, which also takes two subkeys as input and combines these inputs to produce two 16-bit outputs.

SINGLE ITERATION OF IDEA (FIRST ITERATION)

Finally, the four output blocks from the upper transformation are combined with the two output blocks of the MA structure using XOR to produce the four output blocks for this iteration. The two outputs that are partially generated by the second and third inputs (X_2 and X_3) are interchanged to produce the second and third outputs (W_{12} and W_{13}), thus increasing the mixing of the bits being processed and making the algorithm more resistant to cryptanalysis.

The ninth stage of the algorithm, labeled the output transformation stage in Fig. 2, has the same structure as the upper shaded portion of the preceding iterations (see Fig. 3). The only difference is that the second and third inputs are interchanged before being applied to the operational units. This has the effect of undoing the interchange at the end of the eighth iteration. This extra interchange is done so that decryption has the same structure as encryption. This ninth stage requires only four subkey inputs, compared to six subkey inputs for each of the first eight stages. The subkeys for each iteration are generated by a series of shifts on the original 128-bit key.

IDEA has advantages over older conventional encryption techniques. The key length of 128 bits makes it resistant to brute-force key search attacks. IDEA is also highly resistant to cryptanalysis and was designed to facilitate both software and hardware implementations.

PUBLIC-KEY ENCRYPTION

One essential characteristic of IDEA and all conventional encryption algorithm is the need for the two parties to share a secret key that is not known to anyone else. This is a tremendous limitation, especially for an e-mail application.

If Pretty Good Privacy depended solely on the use of IDEA, before a user could correspond with anyone, that user would somehow have to arrange to share a secret 128-bit number with the message recipient. If there is no way to communicate securely, it becomes difficult to send the key.

A new approach to encryption known as public-key encryption offers a solution to this problem. With this method, developed in 1976 by Whitfield Diffie, there is no need to convey a secret key. Instead, each person has a private key and a matching public key. Encryption is done with one of these two keys and decryption uses the other. The private key is kept secret, known only to its holder. The matching public key is just that—public. The private key holder can broadcast the matching public key.

Public-key encryption can be used to ensure privacy in much the same way as IDEA (see Fig. 4). Users put plaintext and the intended recipient's public key in the encryption algorithms. The algorithm uses the plaintext and the public key to produce ciphertext. At the receiving end, the decryption algorithm, which is the reverse of the encryption algorithms, is used. In this case, the input is the ciphertext and the receiver's private key. This message is secure from eavesdropping because only the receiver has the private key necessary for decryption. Anyone who has a copy of the recipient's public key can create a message that can be read only by this recipient.

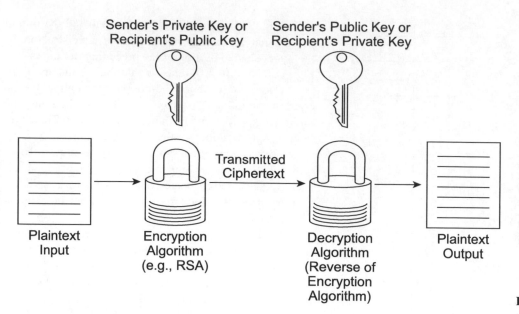

Fig. 4   Public-key encryption.

PUBLIC-KEY ENCRYPTION

Authentication can also be performed by putting plaintext and the sender's private key in the encryption algorithms. The algorithm uses the plaintext and the private key to produce ciphertext. At the receiving end, the decryption algorithm, which is the reverse of the encryption algorithms, is used. In this case, the input is the ciphertext and the sender's public key.

This message is guaranteed to be authentic because only the sender has the private key necessary for encryption. Anyone who has a copy of the sender's public key can read the message and verify that it must have come from the alleged sender. The public-key scheme used for PGP is the Rivest–Shamir–Adleman (RSA) algorithm. RSA takes variable-length keys. Typically, the key size for both the private and public keys is 512 bits.

RSA Algorithm

One of the first public-key schemes was developed in 1977 by Ron Rivest, Adi Shamir, and Len Adleman at MIT and first published in 1978. Named for its creators, the RSA scheme has since reigned as the only widely accepted and implemented approach to public-key encryption. RSA is a block cipher in which the plaintext and ciphertext are integers between 0 and $n - 1$ for some n. Encryption and decryption take the following form for some plaintext block M and ciphertext block C:

$C = M^e \bmod n$
$M = C^d \bmod n = (M^e)^d \bmod n = M^{ed} \bmod n$

Both sender and receiver must know the value of n. The sender knows the value of e, and only the receiver knows the value of d. Thus, this is a public-key encryption algorithms with a public key of KU = $\{e, n\}$ and a private key of

KR = $\{d, n\}$. For this algorithm to be satisfactory for public-key encryption, the following requirements must be met:

- It should be possible to find values of e, d, n such that M^{ed} = M mod n for all M < n.
- It should be relatively easy to calculate M^e and C^d for all values of M < n.
- It should be infeasible to determine d given e and n.

Fig. 5 summarizes the RSA algorithm. To understand the algorithm, users should begin by selecting two prime numbers, p and q, and calculating their product n, which is the modulus for encryption and decryption. Next, the quantity $\phi(n)$, which is referred to as the Euler totient of n, which is the number of positive integers less than n and relatively prime to n should be determined. Then an integer d, that is relatively prime to $f(n)$, (i.e., the greatest common divisor of d and $\phi(n)$ is 1), should be selected. Finally, e should be calculated as the multiplicative inverse of d, modulo $\phi(n)$. It can be shown that d and e have the desired properties.

The private key consists of $\{d, n\}$ and the public key consists of $\{e, n\}$. Suppose that user A has published its public key and that user B wishes to send the message M to A. Then, B calculates $C = M^e(\bmod n)$ and transmits C. On receipt of this ciphertext, user A decrypts by calculating $M = C^d(\bmod n)$.

An example is shown in Fig. 6. For this example, the keys are generated as follows:

- Two prime numbers, $p = 7$ and $q = 17$, are selected.
- Calculate $n = pq = 7 \times 17 = 119$.
- Calculate $f(n) = (p - 1)(q - 1) = 96$.
- Select e such that e is relatively prime to $f(n) = 96$ and less than $f(n)$; in this case, $e = 5$.

Digital –
E-Mail

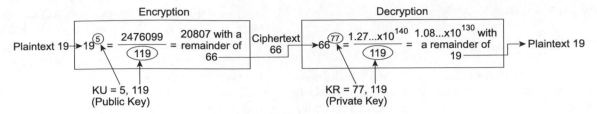

Fig. 5 RSA algorithm.

- Determine d such that $de = 1$ mod 96 and $d < 96$. The correct value is $d = 77$, because $77 \times 5 = 385 = 4 \times 96 + 1$.

The resulting keys are public key KU = {5, 119} and private key KR = {77, 119}. The example shows the use of these keys for a plaintext input of M = 19. For encryption, 19 is raised to the fifth power, yielding 2,476,099. Upon division by 119, the remainder is determined to be 66. Therefore, 195 [equiv]66 mod 119, and the ciphertext is 66. For decryption, it is determined that 66^{77} [equiv]19 mod 119.

How Hard Is It to Break the Code?

There are two possible approaches to defeating the RSA algorithm. The first is the brute-force approach: trying all possible private keys. Thus the larger the number of bits in e and d, the more secure the algorithm. However, because the calculations involved, both in key generation and in encryption/decryption, are complex, the larger the size of the key, the slower the system will run.

Most discussions of the cryptanalysis of RSA have focused on the task of factoring p into its two prime factors. Until recently, this was considered infeasible for numbers in the range of 100 decimal digits, which is about 300 or more bits. To demonstrate the strength of Rivest–Shamir–Adleman, its three developers, issued a challenge to decrypt a message that was encrypted using a 129-decimal-digit number as their public modulus. The authors predicted that it would take 40 quadrillion years with current technology to crack the code. Recently, the code was cracked by a worldwide team cooperating over the Internet and using more than 1600 computers after only eight months of work. This result does not invalidate the use of RSA; it simply means that larger key sizes must be used. Currently, a 1024-bit key size (about 300 decimal digits), is considered strong enough for virtually all applications.

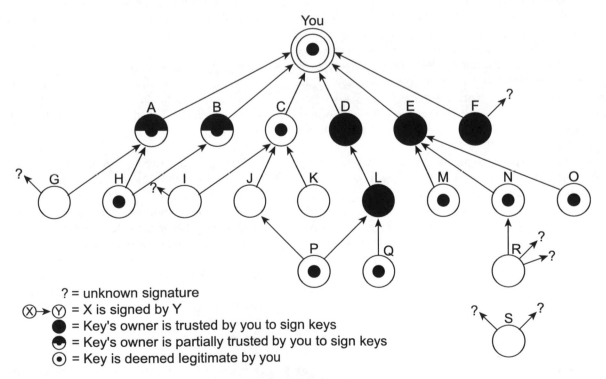

Fig. 6 RSA example.

Digital –
E-Mail

HOW PGP WORKS

Digital Signature

It may seem that Rivest–Shamir–Adleman is all that is needed for a secure e-mail facility. Everyone who wants to use Pretty Good Privacy (PGP) can create a matching pair of keys (PGP will do the necessary calculation) and then distribute the public key. To send a message, it must first be encrypted with the private key to guarantee its authenticity. Next, the result of step one must be encrypted with the recipient's public key to guarantee that no one else can read the message.

This scheme is technically valid but impractical. The problem is that RSA, and all other public-key schemes, are very slow. To double-encrypt messages of arbitrary length is far too time consuming. Users could experience delays of minutes or even hours waiting for their PCs to do the number-crunching.

Instead, PGP exploits the strengths of conventional and public-key encryption. When a message is sent, it goes through two security-related stages of processing: digital signature and encryption.

The digital signature is one of the most clever innovations to come out of the work on public-key encryption. To use digital signature, users take the message that they want to send and map it into a fixed-length code of 128 bits. The algorithm for doing this is called MD5 (message digest version 5). The 128-bit message digest is unique for this message. It would be virtually impossible for someone to alter this message or substitute another message and still come up with the same digest.

PGP then encrypts the digest using RSA and the sender's private key. The result is the digital signature, which is attached to the message. Anyone who gets this message can re-compute the message digest and then decrypt the signature using RSA and the sender's public key. If the message digest in the signature matches the message digest that was calculated, then the signature is valid. Because this operation only involves encrypting and decrypting a 128-bit block, it takes little time.

For the encryption stage, PGP randomly generates a 128-bit secret key and uses IDEA to encrypt the message plus the attached signature. The recipient can discover the secret key by using RSA. PGP takes the secret key as input to RSA, using the receiver's public key, and produces an encrypted secret key that is attached to the message. On the receiving end, PGP uses the receiver's private key to recover the secret key and then uses the secret key and IDEA to recover the plaintext message plus signature.

Getting Public Keys

Public-key encryption techniques make use of two keys for each user: a private key that is known only to one user, and a corresponding public key that is made known to all users. With these two keys, it is possible to create digital signatures that guarantee the authenticity of a message and to support the encryption of a message in such a way that only the intended recipient can read it.

There is, however, a common misconception that each user simply keeps his or her private key private and publishes the corresponding public key. Unfortunately, this is not a simple solution. An impostor can generate a public- and private-key pair and disseminate the public key as if it were someone else's. For example, suppose that user A wishes to send a secure message to user B. Meanwhile, user C has generated a public- and private-key pair, attached user B's name and an e-mail address that user C can access, and published this key widely. User A has picked this key up, uses the key to prepare her message for user B, and uses the attached e-mail address to send the message. Result: user C receives and can decrypt the message; user B either never receives the message or cannot read it without holding the required private key.

One way around this problem is to insist on the secure exchange of public keys. For example, if user B and user A know each other personally and live near each other, they could physically exchange keys on diskettes. But for PGP to be useful as a general-purpose e-mail security utility, it must be possible for people in widely distributed sites to exchange keys with others that they have never met and may not even know.

Public-Key Certificates and Distributed Security

The basic tool that permits widespread use of PGP is the public-key certificate. The essential elements of a public-key certificate are

- The public key itself
- A user ID consisting of the name and e-mail address of the owner of the key
- One or more digital signatures for the public key and user ID

The signer testifies that the user ID associated with this public key is valid. The digital signature is formed using the private key of the signer. Anyone in possession of the corresponding public key can verify that the signature is valid. If any change is made, either to the public key or the user ID, the signature will no longer compute as valid. Public-key certificates are used in several security applications that require public-key cryptography. In fact, it is the public-key certificate that makes distributed security applications using public keys practical.

One approach that might be taken to use public-key certificates is to create a central certifying authority. This is the approach recommended for use with the privacy-enhanced mail (PEM) scheme. Each user must register with the central authority and engage in a secure exchange that includes independent techniques for verifying user identity. Once the central authority is convinced of the identity of a key holder, it signs that key. If everyone who uses this scheme trusts the central authority, then a key signed by the authority is automatically accepted as valid.

There is nothing inherent in the PGP formats or protocols to prevent the use of a centralized certifying authority. However, PGP is intended as an e-mail security scheme for the masses. It can be used in a variety of informal and formal environments. Accordingly, Pretty Good Privacy is designed to support a so-called web of trust, in which individuals sign each other's keys and create an interconnected community of public-key users.

If user B has physically passed a public key to user A, then user A knows that this key belongs to user B and signs it. User A keeps a copy of the signed key and also returns a copy to user B. Later, user B wishes to communicate with user D and sends this person the public key, with user A's signature attached. User D is in possession of user A's public key and also trusts user A to certify the keys of others. User D verifies user A's signature on user B's key and accepts user B's key as valid.

COMPUTING TRUST

Although Pretty Good Privacy does not include any specification for establishing certifying authorities or for establishing trust, it does provide a convenient means of using trust, associating trust with public keys, and exploiting trust information.

Each user can collect a number of signed keys and store them in a PGP file known as a public-key ring. Associated with each entry is a key legitimacy field that indicates the extent to which PGP will trust that this is a valid public key for this user; the higher the level of trust, the stronger is the binding of this user ID to this key. This field is computed by Pretty Good Privacy. Also associated with the entry are zero or more signatures that the key ring owner has collected that sign this certificate. In turn, each signature has associated with it a signature trust field that indicates the degree to which this PGP user trusts the signer to certify public keys. The key legitimacy field is derived from the collection of signature trust fields in the entry. Finally, each entry defines a public key associated with a particular owner, and an owner trust field is included that indicates the degree to which this public key is trusted to sign other public-key certificates; this level of trust is assigned by the user. The signature trust fields can be thought of as cached copies of the owner trust field from another entry.

Trust Processing

If user A inserts a new public key on the public-key ring, PGP must assign a value to the trust flag that is associated with the owner of this public key. If the owner is in fact A, and this public key also appears in the private-key ring, then a value of ultimate trust is automatically assigned to the trust field. Otherwise, PGP asks user A for an assessment of the trust to be assigned to the owner of this key, and user A must enter the desired level. The user can specify that this owner is unknown, untrusted, marginally trusted, or completely trusted.

When the new public key is entered, one or more signatures may be attached to it. More signatures may be added later on. When a signature is inserted into the entry, PGP searches the public-key ring to see if the author of this signature is among the known public-key owners. If so, the OWNERTRUST value for this owner is assigned to the SIGTRUST field for this signature. If not, an unknown user value is assigned.

The value of the key legitimacy field is calculated on the basis of the signature trust fields present in this entry. If at least one signature has a signature trust value of ultimate, then the key legitimacy value is set to complete. Otherwise, PGP computes a weighted sum of the trust values. A weight of $1/X$ is given to signatures that are always trusted and $1/Y$ to signatures that are usually trusted, where X and Y are user-configurable parameters. When the total of weights of the introducers of a key/user ID combination reaches 1, the binding is considered to be trustworthy, and the key legitimacy value is set to complete. Thus, in the absence of ultimate trust, at least X signatures that are always trusted or Y signatures that are usually trusted or some combination, is needed.

Signature Trust and Key Legitimacy

Periodically, PGP processes the public-key ring to achieve consistency. In essence, this is a top-down process. For each OWNERTRUST field, PGP scans the ring for all signatures authored by that owner and updates the SIGTRUST field to equal the OWNERTRUST field. This process starts with keys for which there is ultimate trust. Then, all KEYLEGIT fields are computed on the basis of the attached signatures.

Fig. 7 provides an example of the way in which signature trust and key legitimacy are related. The figure shows the structure of a public-key ring. The user has acquired a number of public keys, some directly from their owners and some from a third party such as a key server.

PGP TRUST MODEL EXAMPLE

The node labeled "You" refers to the entry in the public-key ring corresponding to this user. This key is valid and the OWNERTRUST value is ultimate trust. Each other node in the key ring has an OWNERTRUST value of undefined unless some other value is assigned

Digital –
E-Mail

Key Generation

Select p, q	p and q both prime
Calculate n = p x q	
Calculate ø(n) = (p − 1) (q − 1)	
Select integer e	[ø(n), e] = 1; 1 < e < ø(n)
Calculate d	$d = e^{-1} \bmod ø(n)$
Public key	KU = (e, n)
Private key	KR = (d, n)

<ø should be replaced by a circle with a vertical line through it; could not find the symbol>

Encryption

Plaintext M < n

Ciphertext C = M * (mod n)

Decryption

Ciphertext C

Plaintext M = C^d (mod n)

Fig. 7 Structure of a public-key ring.

by the user. In this example, the user has specified that it always trusts users D, E, F, and L to sign other keys. This user also partially trusts users A and B to sign other keys.

The shading, or lack thereof, of the nodes in Fig. 7 indicates the level of trust assigned by this user. The tree structure indicates which keys have been signed by which other users. If a key is signed by a user whose key is also in this key ring, the arrow joins the signed key to the signer. If the key is signed by a user whose key is not present in this key ring, the arrow joins the signed key to a question mark, indicating that the signer is unknown to the user.

Fig. 7 illustrates that all keys whose owners are fully or partially trusted by the user have been signed by this user, with the exception of node L. Such a user signature is not always necessary, as the presence of node L indicates, but in practice most users are likely to sign the keys for most owners that they trust. So, for example, even though E's key is already signed by trusted introducer F, the user chose to sign E's key directly. It can be assumed that two partially trusted signatures are sufficient to certify a key. Hence, the key for user H is deemed valid by PGP because it is signed by A and B, both of whom are partially trusted.

A key may be determined to be valid because it is signed by one fully trusted or two partially trusted signers, but its user may not be trusted to sign other keys. For example, N's key is valid because it is signed by E, whom this user trusts, but N is not trusted to sign other keys because this user has not assigned N that trust value. Therefore,

although R's key is signed by N, PGP does not consider R's key valid. This situation makes perfect sense. If a user wants to send a secret message to an individual, it is not necessary that the user trust that individual in any respect. It is only necessary to ensure use of the correct public key for that individual.

Fig. 7 also shows a detached orphan node S, with two unknown signatures. Such a key may have been acquired from a key server. PGP cannot assume that this key is valid simply because it came from a reputable server. The user must declare the key valid by signing it or by telling PGP that it is willing to fully trust one of the key's signers. It is the PGP web of trust that makes it practical as a universal e-mail security utility. Any group, however informal and however dispersed, can build up the web of trust needed for secure communications.

CONCLUSION

PGP is already widely used. Pretty Good Privacy has become essential to those struggling for freedom in former Communist countries. Ordinary people throughout the world are active participants in the alt.security.PGP USENET newsgroup. Because PGP fills a widespread need, and because there is no reasonable alternative, its future is secure. One of the best lists of locations for obtaining PGP, with the file name getpgp.asc, is maintained at two File Transfer Protocol sites on the Internet: ftp.csn.net/mpj and ftp.netcom.com/pub/mp/mpj.

E-Mail: Security

Bruce A. Lobree, CISSP, CIPP, ITIL, CISM
Senior Security Architect, Woodinville, Washington, U.S.A.

Abstract

From the time that the first electronic message was sent to today's megabit communications systems, people have been trying to figure out new ways to copy, intercept, or just disrupt that messaging system. The value of getting one's data is proportionately equal to the value that data has if private, and is far greater if in the corporate world.

Our challenge in today's world of computer communications—voice, video, and audio communications—is to protect it: to make sure that when it is transmitted from one specific medium to another it is received in a fashion that the recipient will be able to hear it, read it, or see it. Both the author and the recipient are confident enough that the communications are secure and reliable enough that they do not have to worry about the message not getting to where it should.

When the first telegraph message was finally sent, the start of the electronic communications age was born. Then about 50 years ago, people working on a mainframe computer left messages or put a file in someone else's directory on a Direct Access Storage Device (DASD) drive, and so the first electronic messaging system was born. Although most believe that electronic mail, or e-mail as it is called today, was started with the ARPA net, that is not the case. Electronic communication has been around for a much longer period than that, and securing that information has always been and will always be a major issue for both government and commercial facilities as well as the individual user.

When Western Telegraph started telegraphing money from point to point, this represented the beginnings of electronic transfers of funds via a certified system. Banks later began connecting their mainframe computers with simple point-to-point connections via SNA networks to enhance communications and actual funds transfers. This enabled individual operators to communicate with each other across platforms and systems enabling expedited operations and greater efficiencies at reduced operating costs.

When computer systems started to "talk" to each other, there was an explosion of development in communications between computer users and their respective systems. The need for connectivity grew as fast as the interest in it was developed by the corporate world. The Internet, which was originally developed for military and university use, was quickly pulled into this communications systems with its redundant facilities and fail-safe design, and was a natural place for electronic mail to grow toward.

Today (see Fig. 1), e-mail, electronic chat rooms, and data transfers are happening at speeds that make even the most forward-thinking people wonder how far it will go.

Hooking up networks for multiple-protocol communications is mandatory for any business to be successful. Electronic mail must cross multiple platforms and travel through many networks for it to go from one point to another. Each time it moves between networks and connections, this represents another point where it can be intercepted, modified, copied, or in worst-case scenario stopped altogether.

Chat rooms on the Internet are really modified e-mail sites that allow multiple parties to read the mail simultaneously, similar to looking at a note stuck on a bulletin board. These services allow users to "post" a message to a board that allows several people to view it at once. This type of communication represents a whole new level of risk. There is controlling who has access to the site, where the site is hosted, how people gain access to the site, and many other issues that are created by any type of shared communications. The best example of a chat room is a conference call that has a publicly available phone number that can be looked up in any phone book. The difference is that when someone joins the conference, the phone usually has a tone indicating the arrival of a new individual or group. With many chat rooms, no such protocol exists and users may not know who is watching or listening to any particular session if there is no specific user authentication method in use.

Today, e-mail is a trusted form of corporate communications that just about every major government and corporation in the world are using. Internal networks move communications in cleartext with sometimes little to no authentication. These business-critical messages are moved across public phone lines that are utilized for internal communications. This traffic in most cases is never even questioned as to authenticity and data can be listened to and intercepted.

Encyclopedia of Information Assurance DOI: 10.1081/E-EIA-120046362
Copyright © 2011 by Taylor & Francis. All rights reserved.

Digital –
E-Mail

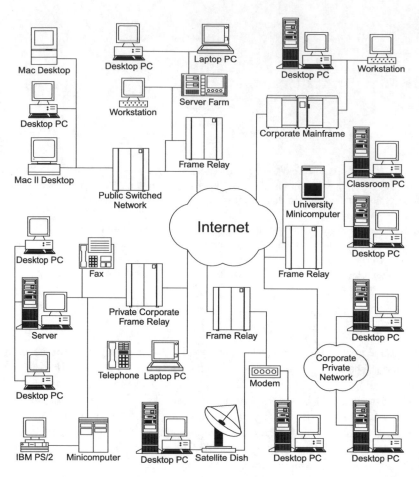

Fig. 1   Internet connectivity.

Messages are presumed to be from the original author although there is no certificate or signature verifying it. By today's standards, e-mail has become a de facto trusted type of communications that is considered legal and binding in many cases. Even today, for a document to be considered legal and binding, it must contain a third-party certificate of authenticity, or some form of binding notary. However, in the case of e-mail, people consider this a form of electronic signature although it is so easy to change the senders' names without much effort. It is possible for the most untrained person to quickly figure out how to change their identity in the message and the recipient quickly gets information that may cause major damage, both financially or reputationally.

What makes matters even worse is the sue-happy attitude that is prevalent in the United States and is quickly spreading around the globe. There have already been several cases that have tested these waters and proven fatal to the recipient of the message as well as the falsified sender. These cases have taken to task system administrators to prove where electronic information has come from and where it went. Questions like who actually sent it, when was it sent, and how can one prove it, became impossible to answer without auditing tools being in place that cover entire networks with long-term report or audit data retention.

Today, e-mail traffic is sharing communications lines with voice, video, audio, and just about anything else that can be moved through wire and fiber optics. Despite the best frame relay systems, tied to the cleanest wires with the best filters, there is still going to be bleed over of communications in most wired types of systems (note that the author has seen fiber-optic lines tapped). This is not as much an issue in fiber optic as it is in copper wire. System administrators must watch for capacity issues and failures. They must be able to determine how much traffic will flow and when are the time-critical paths for information. For example, as a system administrator, one cannot take down a mail server during regular business times. However, with a global network, what is business time, and when is traffic flow needed the most? These and many other questions must be asked before any mail system can be implemented, serviced, and relied upon by the specified user community.

Once the system administrator has answered all their questions about number of users, and the amount of disk space to be allocated to each user for the storage of e-mail, a system requirement can be put together. Now the administrative procedures can be completed and the configuration of the system can be put together. The administrator needs to figure out how to protect it without impacting the operational functionality of the system. The amount of security applied to any system will directly impact the operational functionality and speed at which the system can function.

Protection of the mail server becomes even more important as the data that moves through it becomes more and more mission critical. There is also the issue of protecting internal services from the mail server that may be handling traffic that contains viruses and Trojan horses. Viruses and Trojan horses as simple attachments to mail can be the cause for anything from simple annoyances or unwanted screen displays, all the way to complete destruction of computing facilities. Executives expect their mail to be "clean" of any type of malicious type of attachment. They expect the mail to always be delivered and always come from where the "FROM" in the message box states it came from.

The author notes that no virus can hurt any system until it is activated today. This may change as new programs are written in the future. This means that if a virus is going to do anything, the person receiving it via mail must open the mail message and then attempt to view or run the attachment. Simply receiving a message with an attached virus will not do anything to an individual's system. This hoax about a virus that will harm one's machine in this fashion is urban legend in this author's opinion.

Cookies or applets received over the Internet are a completely different subject matter that is not be discussed here. Users, however, must be aware of them and know how to deal with them. From a certain perspective, these can be considered a form of mail; however, by traditional definition, they are not.

TYPES OF MAIL SERVICES

Ever since that first message was sent across a wire using electricity, humanity has been coming up with better ways to communicate and faster ways to move that data in greater volume in smaller space. The first mainframe mail was based on simple SNA protocols and only used ASCII formatted text. The author contends that it was probably something as simple as a person leaving a note in another person's directory (like a Post-It on your computer monitor). Today, there is IP-based traffic that is moved through many types of networks using many different systems of communications and carries multiple fonts, graphics, and sound and other messages as attachments to the original message.

With all the different types of mail systems that exist on all the different types of operating systems, choosing which e-mail service to use is like picking a car. The only environment that utilizes one primary mail type is Mac OS. However, even in this environment, one can use Netscape or Eudora to read and create mail. With the advent of Internet mail, the possibility of integration of e-mail types has become enormous. Putting multiple mail servers of differing types on the same network is now a networking and security nightmare that must be overcome.

Sendmail™

Originally developed by Eric Allman in 1981, Sendmail is a standard product that is used across multiple systems. Regardless of what e-mail program is used to create e-mail, any mail that goes beyond the local site is generally routed via a mail transport agent. Given the number of "hops" any given Internet mail message takes to reach its destination, it is likely that every piece of Internet e-mail is handled by a Sendmail server somewhere along it's route.

The commercially available version of Sendmail began in 1997 when Eric Allman and Greg Olson formed Sendmail, Inc. The company still continues to enhance and release the product with source code and the right to modify and redistribute. The new commercial product line focuses on cost-effectiveness with Web-based administration and management tools, and automated binary installation.

Sendmail is used by most Internet service providers (ISPs) and shipped as the standard solution by all major UNIX vendors, including Sun, HP, IBM, DEC, SGI, SCO, and others. This makes the Sendmail application very important in today's Internet operations.

The Sendmail program was connected to the ARPAnet, and was home to the INGRES project. Another machine was home to the Berkeley UNIX project and had recently started using UUCP. Software existed to move mail within ARPAnet, INGRES, and BerkNet, but none existed to move mail between these networks. For this reason, Sendmail was created to connect the individual mail programs with a common protocol.

The first Sendmail program was shipped with version 4.1c of the Berkeley Software Distribution or BSD (the first version of Berkeley UNIX to include TCP/IP). From that first release to the present (with one long gap between 1982 and 1990), Sendmail was continuously improved by its authors. Today, version 8 is a major rewrite that includes many bug fixes and significant enhancements that take this application far beyond its original conception.

Other people and companies have worked on their versions of the Sendmail programs and injected a number of improvements, such as support for database management (dbm) files and separate rewriting of headers and envelopes. As time and usage of this application have continued, many of the original problems with the application and other related functions have been repaired or replaced with more efficient working utilities.

Today, there are major offshoots from many vendors that have modified Sendmail to suit their particular needs. Sun Microsystems has made many modifications and enhancements to Sendmail, including support for Network

Information Service (NIS) and NIS+ maps. Hewlett-Packard also contributed many fine enhancements, including 8BITMIME (multi-purpose Internet mail extensions that worked with 8-bit machines limited naming controls, which do not exist in the UNIX environment) support.

This explosion of Sendmail versions led to a great deal of confusion. Solutions to problems that work for one version of Sendmail fail miserably with others. Beyond this, configuration files are not portable, and some features cannot be shared. Misconfiguration occurs as administrators work with differing types of products, thus creating further problems with control and security.

Version 8.7 of Sendmail introduced multicharacter options and macro names, new interactive commands. Many of the new fixes resolved the problems and limitations of earlier releases. More importantly, V8.7 has officially adopted most of the good features from IDA, KJS, Sun, and HP's Sendmail, and kept abreast of the latest standards from the Internet Engineering Task Force (IETF). Sendmail is a much more developed and user-friendly tool that has an international following and complies with much needed e-mail standards.

From that basic architecture, there are many programs today that allow users to read mail—Eudora, MSmail, Lotus Notes, and Netscape Mail are some of the more common ones. The less familiar ones are BatiMail or Easymail for UNIX, and others. These products will take an electronically formatted message and display it on the screen after it has been written and sent from another location. This allows humans to read, write, and send electronic mail using linked computers systems.

Protecting E-mail

Protecting e-mail is no easy task and every administrator will have his own interpretation as to what constitutes strong protection of communication. The author contends that strong protection is only that protection needed to keep the information secured for as long as it has value. If the information will be forever critical to the organization's operation, then it will need to be protected at layer two (the data-link level) of the IP stack.

This will need to be done in a location that will not be accessible to outsiders, except by specific approval and with proper authentication.

The other side of that coin is when the information has a very short valued life. An example would be that the data becomes useless once is has been received. In this case, the information does not need to be protected any longer than it takes for it to be transmitted. The actual transmission time and speed at which this occurs may be enough to ensure security. The author assumes that this type of mail will not be sent on a regular basis or at predetermined times. Mail that is sent on a scheduled basis or very often is easier to identify and intercept than mail sent out at random times. Thieves have learned that credit card companies send out

their plastic on a specific date of every month and know when to look for it; this same logic can be applied to electronic mail as well.

Which ever side one's data is on, it is this author's conviction that all data should be protected to one level of effort or one layer of communication below what is determined to be needed to ensure sufficient security. This will ensure that should one's system ever be compromised, it will not be due to a flaw in one's mail service, and the source of the problem will be determined to have come from elsewhere. The assumption is that the hardware or tapes that hold the data will be physically accessible. Therefore, it is incumbent on the data to be able to protect itself to a level that will not allow the needed data to be compromised.

The lowest level of protection is the same as the highest level of weakness. If one protects the physical layer (layer 1 of the IP stack) within a facility, but does not encrypt communications, then when one's data crosses public phone lines, it is exposed to inspection or interception by outside sources.

When the time comes to actually develop the security model for a mail system, the security person will need to look at the entire system. This means that one must include all the communications that are under one's control, as well as that which is not. This will include public phone lines, third-party communications systems, and everything else that is not under one's physical and logical control.

IDENTIFYING THE MAILER

Marion just received an electronic message from her boss via e-mail. Marion knows this because in the "FROM" section is her boss' name. Marion absolutely knows this because who could possibly copy the boss' name into their own mailbox for the purpose of transmitting a false identity? The answer: anyone who goes into their preferences and changes the identity of the user and then restarts their specific mail application.

Whether talking about physical mail or electronic mail, the issue of authentication is an important subject. Authenticating the source of the communication and securing the information while in transit is critical to the overall security and reliability of the information being sent. In the physical world, a letter sent in a sealed, certified, bonded envelope with no openings is much safer and more reliable than a postcard with a mass mail stamp on it. So it goes with electronic mail as well.

Spoofing or faking an ID in mail is a fairly easy thing to do. Thankfully, not too many people know how to do it yet, and most will not consider it. To understand all the points of risk, one needs to understand how mail is actually sent. Not just what program has been implemented—but also the

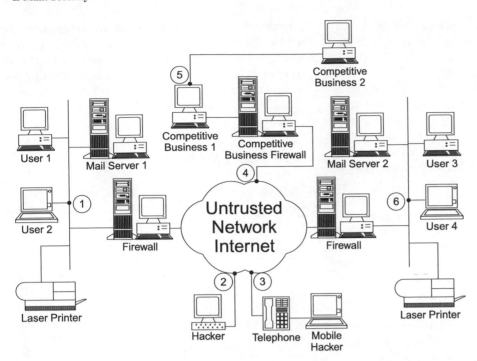

Fig. 2   Unsecured network.

physical architecture of what is happening when one sends it.

In Fig. 2, there are several points of intercept where a message can be infiltrated. Each point of contact represents another point of interception and risk. This includes the sender's PC which may store an original copy of the message in the sent box.

Network Architecture for Mail

User 1 wants to send an e-mail to User 4. If user 4 is connected to their network, then the mail will travel directly from User 1 to User 4 if all systems between the two users are functioning correctly. If User 4 is not connected, then the mail will be stored on User 4's mail server for later pickup. If any mail server in the path is not functioning correctly, the message may stop in transit until such time as it can be retransmitted, depending on the configuration of the particular mail servers.

For mail to go from one user to another, it will go through User 1's mail server. Then it will be routed out through the corporate firewall and off to User 4's firewall via the magic of IP addressing. For the purpose of this entry, one assumes that all of the routing protocols and configuration parameters have been properly configured to go from point User 1 to point User 4. As a user, it is presumed that one's mail is sent across a wire that is connected from one point to another with no intercepting points. The truth is that it is multiple wires with many connections and many points of intercept exist, even in the simplest of mail systems.

With the structure of our communications systems being what it is today, and the nature of the environment

and conditions under which people work, that assumption is dangerously wrong. With the use of electronic frame relay connections, multi-server connections, intelligent routers and bridges, a message crosses many places where it could be tapped into by intruders or fail in transmission all together.

Bad E-mail Scenario

One scenario that has played out many times and continues today looks like this (see Fig. 2):

1. User 1 writes and sends a message to User 4.
2. The message leaves User 1's mailbox and goes to the mail server, where it is recorded and readied for transmission by having the proper Internet packet information added to its header.
3. Then the mail server transmits the data out onto the Internet through the corporate firewall.
4. A hacker who is listening to the Internet traffic copies the data as it moves across a shared link using a sniffer (an NT workstation in promiscuous mode will do the same thing).
5. Your competition is actively monitoring the Internet with a sniffer and also sees your traffic and copies it onto their own network.
6. Unbeknownst to your competition, they have been hacked into and now share that data with a third party without even knowing about it.
7. The mail arrives at the recipient's firewall where it is inspected (recorded maybe) and sent onto the mail server.

8. The recipient goes out and gathers his mail and downloads it to his local machine without deleting the message from the mail server.

This message has now been shared with at least three people who can openly read it and has been copied onto at least two other points where it can be retrieved at a later date. There are well-known court cases where this model has been utilized to get old copies of mail traffic that have not been properly deleted and then became a focal point in the case.

As a security officer, it will be your job to determine the points of weakness and also the points of data gathering, potentially, even after the fact. How will one protect these areas; who has access to them; and how are they maintained are all questions that must be answered. To be able to do that, one needs to understand how e-mail works and what its intended use really was yesterday and how it is used today.

This form of communication was originally intended to just link users for the purpose of communicating simple items. It is the author's belief that the original creators of e-mail never initially intended for it to be used in so many different ways for so many different types of communications and information protocols.

Intercept point 1 in Fig. 2 represents the biggest and most common weakness. In 1998, the Federal Bureau of Investigation reported that most intercepted mail and computer problems were created internally to the company. This means that one's risk by internal employees is greater than outside forces. The author does not advocate paranoia internally, but common sense and good practice. Properly filtering traffic through routers and bridges and basic network protection and monitoring of systems should greatly reduce this problem.

Intercept points 2 through 4 all share the same risk—the Internet. Although this is considered by some to be a known form of communications, it is not a secure one. It is a well-known fact that communications can be listened in on and recorded by anyone with the most basic of tools. Data can be retransmitted, copied, or just stopped, depending on the intent of the hacker or intruder.

Intercept points 5 and 6 are tougher to spot and there may be no way to have knowledge of or about if they are compromised. This scenario has an intruder listening from an unknown point that one has no way of seeing. This is to say, one cannot monitor the network they are connected to or may not see their connection on one's monitoring systems. The recipient does not know about them and is as blind to their presence as you are. Although this may be one of the most unlikely problems, it will be the most difficult to resolve. The author contends that the worst-case scenario is when the recipients' mail is intercepted inside their own network, and they do not know about a problem.

It is now the job of the security officer to come up with a solution—not only to protect the mail, but to also be able to

determine if and when that system of communications is working properly. It is also the security officer's responsibility to be able to quickly identify when a system has been compromised and what it will take to return it to a protected state. This requires continuous monitoring and ongoing auditing of all related systems.

HOW E-MAIL WORKS

The basic principle behind e-mail and its functionality is to send an electronic piece of information from one place to another with as little interference as possible. Today's e-mail has to be implemented very carefully and utilize controls that are well-defined to meet the clients need and at the same time protect the communications efficiently.

Today, there are some general mail terms that one must understand when discussing e-mail. They are Multipurpose Internet Mail Extensions (MIME), which was standardized with RFC 822 that defines the mail header and type of mail content; and RFC 1521, which is designed to provide facilities to include multiple objects in a single message, to represent body text in character sets other than US-ASCII, to represent formatted multi-font text messages, to represent nontextual material such as images and audio fragments, and generally to facilitate later extensions defining new types of Internet mail for use by cooperating mail agents.

Then there is the Internet Message Access Protocol (IMAP) format of mail messages that is on the rise. This is a method of accessing electronic mail or bulletin board data. Finally, there is POP, which in some places means Point of Presence (when dealing with an Internet provider); but for the purpose of this book means Post Office Protocol.

IP Traffic Control

Before going any further with the explanation of e-mail and how to protect it, the reader needs to understand the TCP/IP protocol. Although to many this may seem like a simple concept, it may be new to others. In short, the TCP/IP protocol is broken into five layers (see Fig. 3). Each layer of the stack has a specific purpose and performs a specific function in the movement of data. The layers the author is concerned about are layers three and above (the network layer). Layers one and two require physical access to the connections and therefore become more difficult to compromise.

TCP/IP Five-Layer Stack

1. The e-mail program sends the e-mail document down the protocol stack to the transport layer.
2. The transport layer attaches its own header to the file and sends the document to the network layer.

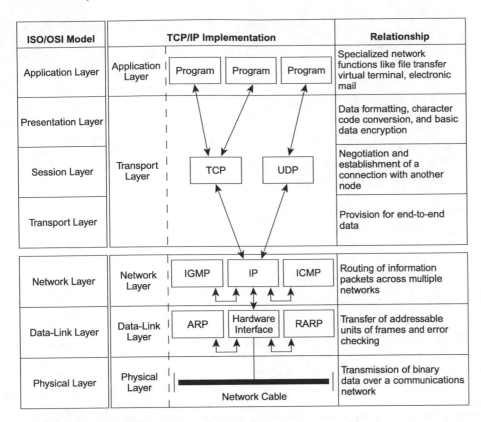

ISO/OSI Model	TCP/IP Implementation			Relationship
Application Layer	Application Layer	Program Program Program		Specialized network functions like file transfer virtual terminal, electronic mail
Presentation Layer	Transport Layer			Data formatting, character code conversion, and basic data encryption
Session Layer		TCP UDP		Negotiation and establishment of a connection with another node
Transport Layer				Provision for end-to-end data
Network Layer	Network Layer	IGMP IP ICMP		Routing of information packets across multiple networks
Data-Link Layer	Data-Link Layer	ARP Hardware Interface RARP		Transfer of addressable units of frames and error checking
Physical Layer	Physical Layer	Network Cable		Transmission of binary data over a communications network

Fig. 3 The five layers of the TCP/IP protocol.

Digital –
E-Mail

3. The network layer breaks the data frames into packets, attaches additional header information to the packet, and sends the packets down to the data-link layer.
4. The data-link layer sends the packets to the physical layer.
5. The physical layer transmits the file across the network as a series of electrical bursts.
6. The electrical bursts pass through computers, routers, repeaters, and other network equipment between the transmitting computer and the receiving computer. Each computer checks the packet address and sends the packet onward to its destination.
7. At the destination computer, the physical layer passes the packets back to the data-link layer.
8. The data-link layer passes the information back to the network layer.
9. The network layer puts the physical information back together into a packet, verifies the address within the packet header, and verifies that the computer is the packet's destination. If the computer is the packet's destination, the network layer passes the packet upward to the transport layer.
10. The transport layer, together with the network layer, puts together all the file's transmitted pieces and passes the information up to the application layer.
11. At the application layer, the e-mail program displays the data to the user.

The purpose of understanding how data is moved by the TCP/IP protocol is to understand all the different places

that one's data can be copied, corrupted, or modified by an outsider. Due to the complexity of this potential for intrusion, critical data needs to be encrypted and or digitally signed. This is done so that the recipient knows who sent, and can validate the authenticity of, a message that they receive.

Encryption and digital signatures need to authenticate the mail from layer two (the data-link layer) up, at a minimum in this author's opinion. Below that level will require physical access; if one's physical security is good, this should not be an area of issue or concern.

Multipurpose Internet Mail Extensions

Multipurpose Internet Mail Extensions (MIME) is usually one of the formats available for use with POP or e-mail clients (Pine, Eudora), Usenet News clients (WinVN, NewsWatcher), and WWW clients (Netscape, MS-IE). MIME extends the format of Internet mail.

STD 11, RFC 822, defines a message representation protocol specifying considerable detail about US-ASCII message headers, and leaves the message content, or message body, as flat US-ASCII text. This set of documents, collectively called the Multipurpose Internet Mail Extensions, or MIME, redefines the format of messages to allow:

- Textual message bodies in character sets other than US-ASCII
- An extensible set of different formats for nontextual message bodies

- Multi-part message bodies
- Textual header information in character sets other than US-ASCII

These documents are based on earlier work documented in RFC 934, STD 11, and RFC 1049; however, it extends and revises them to be more inclusive. Because RFC 822 said so little about message bodies, these documents are largely not a revision of RFC 822 but are new requirements that allow mail to contain a broader type of data and data format.

The initial document specifies the various headers used to describe the structure of MIME messages. The second document, RFC 2046, defines the general structure of the MIME media typing system and also defines an initial set of media types. The third document, RFC 2047, describes extensions to RFC 822 to allow non-US-ASCII text data in Internet mail header fields. The fourth document, RFC 2048, specifies various Internet Assigned Numbers Authority (IANA) registration procedures for MIME-related facilities. The fifth and final document, RFC 2049, describes the MIME conformance criteria as well as providing some illustrative examples of MIME message formats, acknowledgments, and the bibliography.

Since its publication in 1982, RFC 822 has defined the standard format of textual mail messages on the Internet. Its success has been such that the RFC 822 format has been adopted, wholly or partially, well beyond the confines of the Internet and the Internet SMTP transport defined by RFC 821. As the format has seen wider use, a number of limitations have been found to be increasingly restrictive for the user community.

RFC 822 was intended to specify a format for text messages. As such, nontextual messages, such as multimedia messages that might include audio or images, are simply not mentioned. Even in the case of text, however, RFC 822 is inadequate for the needs of mail users whose languages require the use of character sets with far greater size than US-ASCII. Because RFC 822 does not specify mechanisms for mail containing audio, video, Asian language text, or even text in most European and Middle Eastern languages, additional specifications were needed, thus forcing other RFCs to include the other types of data.

One of the notable limitations of RFC 821/822 based mail systems is the fact that they limit the contents of electronic mail messages to relatively short lines (i.e., 1000 characters or less) of 7-bit US-ASCII. This forces users to convert any nontextual data that they may wish to send into seven-bit bytes representable as printable US-ASCII characters before invoking a local mail user agent (UA). The UA is another name for the program with which people send and receive their individual mail.

The limitations of RFC 822 mail becomes even more apparent as gateways were being designed to allow for the exchange of mail messages between RFC 822 hosts and X.400 hosts. The X.400 requirement also specifies mechanisms for the inclusion of nontextual material within electronic mail messages. The current standards for the mapping of X.400 messages to RFC 822 messages specify either that X.400 nontextual material must be converted to (not encoded in) IA5Text format, or that they must be discarded from the mail message, notifying the RFC 822 user that discarding has occurred. This is clearly undesirable, as information that a user may wish to receive is then potentially lost if the original transmission is not recorded appropriately. Although a user agent may not have the capability of dealing with the nontextual material, the user might have some mechanism external to the UA that can extract useful information from the material after the message is received by the hosting computer.

There are several mechanisms that combine to solve some of these problems without introducing any serious incompatibilities with the existing world of RFC 822 mail, including:

- *A MIME-Version header field,* which uses a version number to declare a message to be in conformance with MIME. This field allows mail processing agents to distinguish between such messages and those generated by older or nonconforming software, which are presumed to lack such a field.
- *A Content-Type header field,* generalized from RFC 1049, which can be used to specify the media type and subtype of data in the body of a message and to fully specify the native representation (canonical form) of such data.
- *A Content-Transfer-Encoding header field,* which can be used to specify both the encoding transformations that were applied to the body and the domain of the result. Encoding transformations other than the identity transformation are usually applied to data to allow it to pass through mail transport mechanisms that may have data or character set limitations.
- Two additional header fields that can be used to further describe the data in a body include the *Content-ID* and *Content-Description header fields.*

All of the header fields defined are subject to the general syntactic rules for header fields specified in RFC 822. In particular, all these header fields except for Content-Disposition can include RFC 822 comments, which have no semantic contents and should be ignored during MIME processing.

Internet Message Access Protocol

Internet Message Access Protocol (IMAP) is the acronym for Internet Message Access Protocol. This is a method of accessing electronic mail or bulletin board messages that are kept on a (possibly shared) mail server. In other words, it permits a "client" e-mail program to access remote message stores as if they were local. For example, e-mail stored on an IMAP server can be manipulated from a desktop computer at home, a workstation at the office, and a notebook computer while traveling to different physical locations using different equipment. This is done without the need to transfer messages or files back and forth between these computers.

The ability of IMAP to access messages (both new and saved) from more than one computer has become extremely important as reliance on electronic messaging and use of multiple computers increase. However, this functionality should not be taken for granted and can be a real security risk if the IMAP server is not appropriately secured.

The IMAP includes operations for creating, deleting, and renaming mailboxes; checking for new messages; permanently removing messages; setting and clearing flags; server-based RFC-822 and MIME, and searching; and selective fetching of message attributes, texts, and portions thereof.

IMAP was originally developed in 1986 at Stanford University. However, it did not command the attention of mainstream e-mail vendors until a decade later. It is still not as well-known as earlier and less-capable alternatives such as using POP mail. This is rapidly changing, as articles in the trade press and the implementation of the IMAP are becoming more and more commonplace in the business world.

Post Office Protocol

The Post Office Protocol (POP), version 3 (POP-3) is used to pick up e-mail across a network. Not all computer systems that use e-mail are connected to the Internet 24 hours a day, 7 days a week. Some users dial into a service provider on an as-needed basis. Others may be connected to a LAN with a permanent connection but may not always be powered on (not logged into the network). Other systems may simply not have the available resources to run a full e-mail server. Mail servers may be shielded from direct connection to the Internet by a firewall security system, or it may be against organization policy to have mail delivered directly to user systems. In the case where e-mail must be directly mailed to users, the e-mail is sent to a central e-mail server where it is held for pickup when the user connects at a later time. POP-3 allows a user to logon to an e-mail post office system across the network and validates the user by ID and password. Then it will allow mail to be downloaded, and optionally allow the user to delete the mail from the server.

The widely used POP works best when one has only a single computer. POP e-mail was designed to support "offline" message access to increase network usability and efficiency. This means that messages can be down-loaded and then deleted from the mail server if so configured. This mode of access is not compatible with access from multiple computers because it tends to sprinkle messages across all of the computers used for mail access. Thus, unless all of those machines share a common file system, the offline mode of access that is using POP effectively ties the user to one computer for message storage and manipulation. POP further complicates access by placing user-specific information in several locations as the data is stored as well.

The pop3d command is a POP-3 server and supports the POP-3 remote mail access protocol. Also, it accepts commands on its standard input and responds on its standard output. One normally invokes the pop3d command with the inetd daemon with those descriptors attached to a remote client connection.

The pop3d command works with the existing mail infrastructure consisting of sendmail and bellmail.

```
Net::POP3 – Post Office Protocol 3 Client class
        (RFC1081)
```

IMAP is a server for the POP and IMAP mail protocols. POP allows a "post office" machine to collect mail for users and have that mail downloaded to the user's local machine for reading. IMAP provides the functionality of POP, and allows a user to read mail on a remote machine without moving it to the user's local mailbox.

The popd server implements POP, as described in RFC1081 and RFC1082. Basically, the server listens on the TCP port named pop for connections. When it receives a connection request from a client, it performs the following functions:

- Checks for client authentication by searching the POP password file in /usr/spool/pop
- Sends the client any mail messages it is holding for the client (the server holds the messages in /usr/spool/pop)
- For historical reasons, the MH POP defaults to using the port named pop (port 109) instead of its newly assigned port named pop3 (port 110)

To determine which port MH POP, check the value of the POPSERVICE configuration option. One can display the POPSERVICE configuration option by issuing any MH command with the -help option. To find the port number, look in the /etc/services file for the service port name assigned to the POPSERVICE configuration option. The port number appears beside the service port name.

The POP database contains the following entry for each POP subscriber:

```
name::primary_file:encrypted_passwd::
        user@<client_address>::::0
```

The fields represent the following:

- name — the POP subscriber's username
- primary_file — the mail drop for the POP subscriber (relative to the POP directory)
- encrypted_passwd — the POP subscriber's password generated by popwrd(8)

Digital –
E-Mail

- user@<client_address> — the remote user allowed to make remote POP (RPOP) connections

This database is an ASCII file and each field within each POP subscriber's entry is separated from the next by a colon. Each POP subscriber is separated from the next by a new line. If the password field is null, then no password is valid; therefore, always check to see that a password is required to further enhance the security of your mail services.

To add a new POP subscriber, edit the file by adding a line such as the following:

```
bruce:: bruce:::::::0i
```

Then, use popwrd to set the password for the POP subscriber. To allow POP subscribers to access their mail-drops without supplying a password (by using privileged ports), fill in the network address field, as in:

```
bruce:: bruce::: bruce@filteringisim.edu::::0
```

which permits "bruce@filteringisim.edu" to access the maildrop for the POP subscriber "bruce." Multiple network addresses can be specified by separating them with commas, as in:

```
bruce::bruce:9X5/m4yWHvhCc::bruce@
  filteringisim.edu,
bruce@rsch.isim.edu::::
```

To disable a POP subscriber from receiving mail, set the primary file name to the empty string. To prevent a POP subscriber from picking up mail, set the encrypted password to "*" and set the network address to the empty string. This file resides in home directory of the login "pop." Because of the encrypted passwords, it can and does have general read permission.

Encryption and Authentication

Having determined what your e-mail needs are, one will have to determine how and when one will need to protect the information being sent. The "when" part is fairly straightforward, as this is set by corporate policy. If the security officer does not have the proper documentation and description of the controls that will need to be in place for electronic data transfer, then now is the time to put it together, as later will be too late. Suffice it to say that this author presumes that all the proper detail exists already. This needs to be done so the security officer will be able to determine the classification of the information that he or she will be working with for traffic to move successfully.

Encryption is a process whereby the sender and the receiver will share an encryption and decryption key that will protect the data from someone reading the data while it is in transit. This will also protect the data when it is backed up on tape or when it is temporarily stored on a mail server.

This is not to say that encryption cannot be broken — it can, and has been done to several levels. What is being said is that the encryption used will protect the information long enough that the data is no longer of value to the person who intercepts it or has value to anyone else. This is important to remember, to ensure that too much encryption is not used while, at the same time, enough is used to sufficiently protect the data.

Authentication is meant to verify the sender to the recipient. When the sender sends the message to the other party, they electronically sign the document that verifies to the person receiving the document the authenticity of it. It also verifies what the person sent is what the person received. It does not however protect the data while in transit, which is a distinct difference from encryption and is often a misconception on the part of the general user community.

Encryption

There are many books outlining encryption methodology and the tools that are available for this function. Therefore, this entry does not go into great detail about the tools. However, the weaknesses as well as the strengths of such methods are discussed. All statements are those of the author and therefore are arguable; however, they are not conditional.

All mail can be seen at multiple points during its transmission. Whether it be from the sendmail server across the Internet, via a firewall to another corporation's firewall, or to their sendmail server, all mail will have multiple hops when it transits from sender to recipient. Every point in that transmission process is a point where the data can be intercepted, copied, modified, or deleted completely.

There are three basic types of encryption generally available today. They are private key (symmetric or single key) encryption, pretty good privacy (PGP) or public key encryption, and privacy enhanced mail (PEM). Each of these types of protection systems has strengths and flaws. However, fundamentally they all work the same way and if properly configured and used will sufficiently protect one's information (maybe).

Encryption takes the message that can be sent, turns it into unreadable text, and transmits it across a network where it is decrypted for the reader. This is a greatly simplified explanation of what occurs and does not contain nearly the detail needed to understand this functionality. Security professionals should understand the inner workings of encryption and how and when to best apply it to their environment. More importantly, they must understand the methods of encryption and decryption and the level at which encryption occurs.

Private key encryption is the least secure method of sending and receiving messages. This is due to a dependency on the preliminary setup that involves the sharing of keys between parties. It requires that these keys be transmitted either electronically or physically on a disk to the other party and that every person who communicates with this person potentially has a separate key. The person who supplies the encryption key must then manage them so that two different recipients of data do not share keys and data is not improperly encrypted before transmission. With each new mail recipient the user has, there could potentially be two more encryption keys to manage.

This being the problem that it is, today there is public key encryption available. This type of encryption is better known as pretty good privacy (or PGP). The basic model for this system is to maintain a public key on a server that everyone has access. User 1, on the other hand, protects his private key so that he is the only one who can decrypt the message that is encrypted with his public key. The reverse is also true in that if a person has User 1's public key, and User 1 encrypts using his private key, then only a person with User 1's public key will be able to decrypt the message. The flaw here is that potentially anyone could have User 1's public key and could decrypt his message if they manage to intercept it.

With this method, the user can use the second party's public key to encrypt the private (single or symmetric) key and thereby transmit the key to the person in a secured fashion. Now users are using both the PGP technology and the private key technology. This is still a complicated method. To make it easy, everyone should have a public key that they maintain in a public place for anyone to pick up. Then they encrypt the message to the recipient and only the recipient can decrypt the message. The original recipient then gets the original sender's public key and uses that to send the reply.

As a user, PGP is the easiest form of encryption to use. User 1 simply stores a public key on a public server. This server can be accessed by anyone and if the key is ever changed, User 1's decryption will not work and User 1 will know that something is amiss. For the system administrator, it is merely a matter of maintaining the public key server and keeping it properly secured.

There are several different algorithms that can be applied to this type of technology. If the reader would like to know more about how to build the keys or development of these systems, there are several books available that thoroughly describe them.

Digital Certificates

Like a written signature, the purpose of a digital signature is to guarantee that the individual sending the message really is who he or she claims to be. Digital signatures are especially important for electronic commerce and are a key component of most authentication schemes. A digital signature is an attachment to an electronic message used for security purposes. The most common use of a digital certificate is to verify that a user sending a message is who he or she claims to be, and to provide the receiver with the means to encode a reply.

The actual signature is a quantity associated with a message that only someone with knowledge of an entity's private key could have generated, but which can be verified through knowledge of that entity's public key. In plain terms, this means that an e-mail message will have a verifiable number generated and attached to it that can be authenticated by the recipient.

Digital signatures perform three very important functions:

1. *Integrity*: A digital signature allows the recipient of a given file or message to detect whether that file or message has been modified.
2. *Authentication*: A digital signature makes it possible to verify cryptographically the identity of the person who signed a given message.
3. *Non-repudiation*: A digital signature prevents the sender of a message from later claiming that they did not send the message.

The process of generating a digital signature for a particular document type involves two steps. First, the sender uses a one-way hash function to generate a message digest. This hash function can take a message of any length and return a fixed-length (e.g., 128 bits) number (the message digest). The characteristics that make this kind of function valuable are fairly obvious. With a given message, it is easy to compute the associated message digest. It is difficult to determine the message from the message digest, and it is difficult to find another message for which the function would produce the same message digest.

Second, the sender uses its private key to encrypt the message digest. Thus, to sign something, in this context, means to create a message digest and encrypt it with a private key.

The receiver of a message can verify that message via a comparable two-step process:

1. Apply the same one-way hash function that the sender used to the body of the received message. This will result in a message digest.
2. Use the sender's public key to decrypt the received message digest.

If the newly computed message digest matches the one that was transmitted, the message was not altered in transit, and the receiver can be certain that it came from the expected sender. If, on the other hand, the number does not match, then something is amiss and the recipient should be suspect of the message and its content.

The particular intent of a message digest, on the other hand, is to protect against human tampering by relying on functions that are computationally infeasible to spoof. A message digest should also be much longer than a simple checksum so that any given message may be assumed to result in a unique value. To be effective, digital signatures must be unforgeable; this means that the value cannot be easily replaced, modified, or copied.

A digital signature is formed by encrypting a message digest using the private key of a public key encryption pair. A later decryption using the corresponding public key guarantees that the signature could only have been generated by the holder of the private key. The message digest uniquely identifies the e-mail message that was signed. Support for digital signatures could be added to the Flexible Image Transport System, or FITS, by defining a FITS extension format to contain the digital signature certificates, or perhaps by simply embedding them in an appended FITS table extension.

There is a trade-off between the error detection capability of these algorithms and their speed. The overhead of a digital signature can be prohibitive for multi-megabyte files, but may be essential for certain purposes (e.g., archival storage) in the future. The checksum defined by this proposal provides a way to verify FITS data against likely random errors. On the other hand, a full digital signature may be required to protect the same data against systematic errors, especially human tampering.

An individual wishing to send a digitally signed message applies for a digital certificate from a certificate authority (CA). The CA issues an encrypted digital certificate containing the applicant's public key and a variety of other identification information. The CA makes its own public key readily available through print publicity or perhaps on the Internet.

The recipient of an encrypted digital certificate uses the CA's public key to decode the digital certificate attached to the message. Then they verify it as issued by the CA and obtain the sender's public key and identification information held within the certificate. With this information, the recipient can verify the owner of a public key.

A certificate authority is a trusted third-party organization or company that issues digital certificates used to verify the owner of a public key and create public-private key pairs. The role of the CA in this process is to guarantee that the individual granted the unique certificate is who he or she claims to be. Usually, this means that the CA has an arrangement with a financial institution, such as a credit card company, which provides it with information to confirm an individual's claimed identity. CAs are a critical component in data security and electronic commerce because they guarantee that the two parties exchanging information are really who they claim to be.

The most widely used standard for digital certificates is X.509. X.509 is actually an ITU Recommendation, which means that has not yet been officially defined or approved. As a result, companies have implemented the standard in different ways. For example, both Netscape and Microsoft use X.509 certificates to implement SSL in their Web servers and browsers. However, an X.509 certificate generated by Netscape may not be readable by Microsoft products, and vice versa.

Secure Sockets Layer

Secure Sockets Layer, SSL, is a protocol developed by Netscape for transmitting private documents via the Internet. SSL works using a private key to encrypt data that is transferred over the SSL connection. Both Netscape Navigator and Internet Explorer support SSL, and many Web sites use the protocol to obtain confidential user information, such as credit card numbers. By convention, Web pages that require an SSL connection start with https: instead of http:.

The other protocol for transmitting data securely over the World Wide Web (WWW) is Secure HTTP (S-HTTP). Whereas SSL creates a secure connection between a client and a server, over which any amount of data can be sent securely, S-HTTP is designed to securely transmit individual messages. SSL and S-HTTP, therefore, can be seen as complementary rather than competing technologies. Both protocols have been approved by the Internet Engineering Task Force (IETF) as a standard.

However, fully understanding what SSL is means that one must also understand HTTP (HyperText Transfer Protocol), the underlying protocol used by the World Wide Web (WWW). HTTP defines how messages are formatted and transmitted, and what actions Web servers and browsers should take in response to various commands. For example, when one enters a URL in the browser, this actually sends an HTTP command to the Web server directing it to fetch and transmit the requested Web page.

HTTP is called a stateless protocol because each command is executed independently, without any knowledge of the commands that came before it. This is the main reason why it is difficult to implement Web sites that react intelligently to user input. This shortcoming of HTTP is being addressed in a number of new technologies, including ActiveX, Java, JavaScript, and cookies.

S-HTTP is an extension to the HTTP protocol to support sending data securely over the World Wide Web. Not all Web browsers and servers support S-HTTP and, in the United States and other countries, there are laws controlling the exportation of encryption that can impact this functionality as well. Another technology for transmitting secure communications over the World Wide Web— Secure Sockets Layer—is more prevalent. However, SSL and S-HTTP have very different designs and goals, so it is possible to use the two protocols together. Whereas SSL is designed to establish a secure connection between two computers, S-HTTP is designed to send individual messages securely.

The other main standard that controls how the World Wide Web works is HTML, which covers how Web pages are formatted and displayed.

Good Mail Scenario

Combining everything discussed thus far and a few practical principles involved in networking, one now has the ability to put together a much more secure mail system. This will allow one to authenticate internal and external mail users. The internal requirements will only add one server and a router/filter outside the firewall, and the external requirements will require that there be a publicly available certificate authority (CA) for the world to access.

Now a system has been created that will allow users to segregate internally encrypted messages from externally. Each person will have two public keys to maintain:

- one that resides on the internally installed public key server
- one that resides on the external public key server

The private part of the public key pair will be a privately held key that the user will use to decrypt all incoming messages. Outside the firewall resides a server that will specifically handle all mail and will scan it for viruses and to be sure that all inbound mail is properly encrypted. If it is not, it will forward the message to a separate server that will authenticate the message to a specific user and will then scan and forward it after it has been properly accepted.

Now as we walk through the model of sending a message, no matter who intercepts it, or where it may be copied while in transit, the only place it can be understood will be at the final location of the keys. This method of PGP will not only secure the message, but it will act like a digital certificate in that the user will know limited information about the sender. If a digital signature is added to the model, then the recipient will know the source of the encryption session key. This will include the source of the digital signature and the senders' authentication information sufficiently enough to ensure that they are who they say they are.

There are many other components not discussed above that should be in place; these are outlined in the following steps. For more information, there are many books on router protocol and systems security that can be obtained at the local library.

Mail Sent Securely. The following steps break down the path with which a secure message can be sent (see Fig. 4). This is a recommended method of securing all one's internal and external mail.

1. Before sending or receiving any messages, the author of the message gets a private encryption key from his private network.
2. Then the author places two public keys out on the networks. One is placed on his internal key ring and the second is placed on a public key ring. The purpose of this is to keep his internal mail private and still be able to use public-private key encryption of messages. This will also allow the author to separate mail traffic relevant to its origin.
3. The author of an e-mail message logs on to his personal network and is also authenticated by the mail server via usage of a password to get ready to send electronic mail.
4. Then the author composes the message using his personal mail utility that has been preconfigured with the following settings:

   a. all messages will be sent with a digital signature,
   b. all messages will have receipt notice automatically sent,
   c. private key encryption will be automatically utilized.

5. The author signs and sends the document to a secure server. The message is encrypted and digitally signed before it leaves the author's machine.
6. The author's mail server is connected to the network with hardware-level encrypting routers that protect all internal communications. Note that the latency created by hardware-level encryption is nominal enough that most users will not notice a delay in transmission of data which is any different than already occurs.
7. The mail server determines whether the traffic is internal or external and forwards appropriately. This particular message is determined to be outbound and is therefore sent to the firewall and out to the Internet via an automated hardware encryption device.
8. In front of the firewall on the recipient's end is a hardware device that decrypts the traffic at layer three, but leaves it encrypted and signed as it was originally sent. Loss of this level of encryption is noted by the author. However, unless the outside recipient of this message has the proper hardware to decrypt the message, this level of protection will impede the communications and the recipient will not be able to read the message.
9. The message travels over the Internet. At this point, any interception that records the transmission will not assist another party in obtaining the information. To do so, they will have to

   a. be in the line of traffic at the proper time to intercept the message,
   b. have the decryption tools with which the message was encrypted,
   c. have a copy or method of recreating the digital certificate if they want to modify the message and retransmit it.

10. The message is then received by the recipient's firewall and allowed in based on the addressing of the message.

Digital –
E-Mail

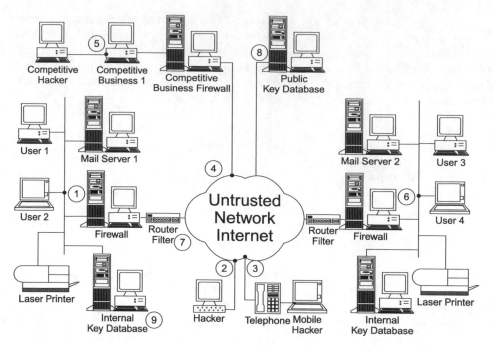

Fig. 4 Secured network.

11. The firewall forwards the message to a mail server that quickly scans the message for viruses (This will slow down mail traffic considerably in a high traffic environment). To determine if this level of security is needed, one must determine the damage a virus or Trojan horse can do to the individual or systems to which the individual is connected.

12. The message is stored on the mail server until the recipient logs on to the network and authenticates himself to that particular server. The mail server is password protected and all data contained there will also be encrypted.

13. The mail recipient goes out to the appropriate public key server (internal for internal users and off the public key for external users) and retrieves the sender's public key before trying to open the sender's message.

14. The mail server then forwards the message to the individual user, who then opens the message after it is decrypted and verifies the signature based matching message digests.

15. Notification of receipt is automatically created and transmitted back to the original author via a reverse process that will include the recipient's signature.

The author recognizes that in a perfect world, the level of encryption that is used would not be breakable by brute force or other type of attack. The certificate and signature that are used cannot be copied or recreated. However, this is not true; it is believed that with 128-bit encryption, with an attached digital signature, the message's information will be secure enough that it

will take longer to decrypt than the information would be viable or useful.

This methodology will slow down the communication of all e-mail. The return is the increased security that is placed on the message itself. There are several layers of protection and validation that show that the message is authentic. The sender and the recipient both know who the message is from and to whom it is being sent, and both parties have confirmation of receipt.

If senders are not concerned about protecting the content of their individual messages, then the encryption part could be skipped, thereby speeding up the process of delivery. It is this author's opinion that digital signatures should always be used to authenticate any business-related or personal message to another party.

CONCLUSION

From the beginning of time, people have tried to communicate over long distances—efficiently and effectively. The biggest concern then and today is that the message sent is the message received and that the enemy (e.g., corporate competition) does not intercept a message.

Our challenge in today's world of computer communications—voice, video, and audio communications—is to protect it: to make sure that when it is transmitted from one specific medium to another it is received in a fashion that the recipient will be able to hear it, read it, or see it. Both the author and the recipient are confident enough that the communications are secure and reliable enough that they do not have to worry about the message not getting to where it should.

Setting up a system of checks and balances to verify transmission, to authenticate users, to authenticate messages and protect them from prying eyes becomes the task at hand for the systems administrator and the security officer. Effective implementation of encryption, digital certificates, and configuration of mail servers placed in the proper areas of a network are all components of making this happen efficiently enough that users will not try to bypass the controls.

The security officer is responsible for the information in the corporation, and becomes a security consultant by default when the architecture of a mail system is to be built. The security officer will be asked how to, when to, and where to implement security, all the while keeping in mind that one must inflict as little impact on the user community as possible. The security officer will be asked to come up with solutions to control access to e-mail and for authentication methods.

To be able to do this, the security officer needs to understand the protocols that drive e-mail, as well as the corporate standards for classification and protecting information and the associated policies. If the policies do not exist, the security officer will need to write them. Then once they are written, one will need to get executive management to accept those polices and enforce them. The security officer will also need to make sure that all employees know and understand those standards and know how to follow them.

Most importantly, whenever something does not feel or look write, question it. Remember that even if something looks as if it is put together perfectly, one should verify it and test it. If everything tests out correctly and the messages are sent in a protected format, with a digital signature of some kind, and there is enough redundancy for high availability and disaster recovery, then all one has left to do is listen to the user community complain about the latency of the system and the complexity of successfully sending messages.

E-Mail: Spam

Al Bredenberg
Writer, Web Developer, and Internet Marketing Consultant, Orem, Utah, U.S.A.

Abstract
The cost of one unsolicited e-mail advertisement sent to an organization is negligible, but mass mailings consume significant resources as they pass across the Internet and reach enterprise systems. The organization pays a provider for its Internet access. As general Internet traffic increases, upstream providers are forced to upgrade equipment and increase bandwidth. These development costs must be passed on to customers. Unwanted e-mail traffic exacts a cost to the organization in increased Internet access fees.

COMMERCIAL INTERRUPTIONS

Mixed in with the great volume of e-mail business correspondence sent each day, many users receive messages similar to the following:

- An offer to find out about new "fountain of youth" scientific discoveries that minimize the effects of aging
- Offers to get in on great money-making schemes (usually multilevel marketing opportunities)
- An offer to save 40% on airfares
- An urgent message to stop the President from signing a certain piece of legislation
- An opportunity to participate in a pyramid scheme and make $5000 a month
- An offer to start a home-based business using a PC
- Three "newsletters" containing nothing but classified ads (mostly multilevel marketing and get-rich-quick opportunities)

This type of e-mail is called "spam," which refers to the sending of mass unsolicited messages—junk e-mail—over the Internet. Spamming includes posting promotional messages to large numbers of Usenet newsgroups. For many Internet users, unsolicited e-mail advertising is merely an annoyance, but because many companies and organizations connect to the Internet, e-mail spam also becomes a financial and productivity issue, especially as most bulk e-mailers sign users onto their lists without permission and make virtually no effort to target their lists. It is not uncommon for spam lists to reach into the hundreds of thousands or even millions of e-mail addresses.

PROBLEM WITH SPAM

The cost of one unsolicited e-mail advertisement sent to an organization is negligible, but mass mailings consume significant resources as they pass across the Internet and reach enterprise systems. The organization pays a provider for its Internet access. As general Internet traffic increases, upstream providers are forced to upgrade equipment and increase bandwidth. These development costs must be passed on to customers. Unwanted e-mail traffic exacts a cost to the organization in increased Internet access fees.

When it has found its way into the company's network, bulk e-mail consumes computing and network resources. Users within the company must spend time sorting out and deleting unwanted messages. Not only does this take time and increase the level of frustration of workers, but legitimate messages can also become confused with spam and be deleted accidentally. Many businesses institute anti-spam policies and procedures to counteract the costs and lost productivity resulting from unsolicited bulk e-mail.

It might be argued that some unsolicited e-mail contact may be necessary for companies marketing over the Internet. Some Internet advertisers have devised strategies of identifying closely targeted audiences and approaching users one at a time with brief, tactful commercial messages. Many users and companies tolerate this kind of e-mail advertising. The most vehement opposition arises when an advertiser goes to extremes and spews out a deluge of e-mail promotions to tens of thousands of users, practically none of whom has an interest in the message. Systems administrators may want to establish policies and procedures to fight this kind of network abuse, and no users should be placed on e-mail advertising lists without their permission. Bulk e-mailers who build their e-mail lists by signing users up without permission should and can be opposed by a firm strategy worked out within the enterprise.

HOW SPAMMERS OPERATE

Most of those who send out unsolicited bulk e-mail are not in the business of selling a product. They are in the business

Encyclopedia of Information Assurance DOI: 10.1081/E-EIA-120046363
Copyright © 2011 by Taylor & Francis. All rights reserved.

Table 1 Bulk e-mail advocates vs. opponents.

Spam Advocate Argues:	Spam Opponent Argues:
Bulk e-mail is no different from direct mail marketing.	The two are not comparable. The traditional direct mail marketer pays the entire cost of the advertising through postal fees, whereas the recipient pays about half the cost of e-mail. The advertising arrives "postage due."
Bulk e-mail is no different from telemarketing.	Again, the telemarketing advertiser pays for the call. With e-mail, the recipient incurs a cost. Suppose telemarketers were to call collect? Would this practice be tolerated? Because of its potential for abuse, legal restrictions have been placed on telemarketing.
Trying to stop bulk e-mail is a violation of the right to freedom of speech.	The content of the message is not the primary issue. The issue is the method of delivery. Because the recipient is forced to pay the cost of delivery of e-mail, the recipient (or the recipient's employer) has a right to try to prevent that delivery.
Direct e-mail is environmentally friendly, because it does not rely on turning trees into paper, as in print or mail advertising.	Electronic mail and other Internet services rely on highly intensive industrial efforts. Viewed from the environmental perspective, could it really be said that the information infrastructure and computer industry are nonpolluting and do not consume scarce resources?
Direct e-mail works as a marketing method, so practitioners should be allowed to develop it.	The effectiveness of unsolicited bulk e-mail has not been studied extensively and is still unproven. Even so, should an advertising method be judged only on the basis of whether it makes money or not? How about ethical concerns?

of selling a service: bulk e-mail. The direct marketers who manage their own lists and use them exclusively for the selling of their own products and services usually run smaller, targeted lists. The big-time spammers work very hard to build huge lists and then hire themselves out to advertisers on a contract basis. If a company wants to advertise healthcare products on the Internet, it might pay a spammer $500 for a one-time mailing of the ad to the spammer's entire database of 500,000 e-mail addresses. Or, for $50, the company could go in on a co-op mailing. In this case, the ad will be a shorter classified-type ad sent along with 20 or 30 others.

Professional spammers usually build their lists by vacuuming up e-mail addresses from public places. It is relatively simple to design a program that parses text for any continuous string of characters with an "@" sign in it. Such a program can be set up to strip e-mail addresses from newsgroup postings, World Wide Web sites, or membership directories for commercial online services (such as America Online and CompuServe). The addresses are then added to a database for the next big mailing. Some bulk e-mailers have gone into the business of selling do-it-yourself spamware programs which has resulted in a proliferation of small-time operators and "drive-by" spammers. One newsgroup posting or a one-time listing of an e-mail address on a Web site could potentially put that address on the lists of a dozen spammers.

On the surface, the practice of direct e-mail advertising looks like an effort to apply direct (postal) mail advertising to the Internet. Long-time Internet standards prohibit unsolicited advertising by e-mail, and this is still the policy of most access providers. Spam advocates argue that this is an outmoded antimarketing stand that inhibits businesses from realizing the marketing benefits of the Internet. It is argued that advertising cannot be successful unless the advertiser

can insert the message into the customer's view. To reach a few buyers, the advertiser must impose the advertising message on many Internet users. Table 1 lists some of the arguments frequently given in favor of unsolicited bulk e-mail and some possible rebuttals against them.

E-mail spamming is comparable to unsolicited fax advertising, a practice that is forbidden by law in the United States, unless the advertiser has a previous relationship with the recipient. This advertising method is proscribed because it costs the recipient in paper, toner, and equipment resources. Opponents of spam advertising often use technological retaliation to fight direct e-mailers; for example, they might send a "mail bomb" (a huge e-mail message) that can clog or even shut down a server.

Because of intense opposition to the practice of spamming, bulk e-mailers often take steps to protect themselves. Some mailers insulate themselves by "spoofing," or placing false e-mail addresses in the "From" headers of their messages. Some will move from one provider to another, setting up throw-away accounts as they go. They open an account, spam once, and then move to another account, knowing that the first provider will shut them down after receiving complaints from users and other providers. Most of the big spam businesses, however, own their own servers and full-time Internet connections, thus decreasing the likelihood that they will be shut down.

LEGITIMATE BULK E-MAIL

Many Internet-enabled businesses have devised nonabusive applications of bulk e-mail advertising. The list is built by voluntary sign-up. The user subscribes by e-mail or at a Web site. This produces a targeted list of users who have asked to receive the material. Such a list might take one of several forms:

Digital –
E-Mail

- Classified commercial list for advertising products in a certain category
- E-mail newsletter or "e-zine"
- Company "announcement list," to keep customers and prospects informed of company news, new products, and upgrades

Such lists might be a useful resource for users, keeping them informed and in touch with vendors and their products and services and providing other valuable commercial information.

REDUCING EXPOSURE TO SPAM

In all likelihood, Internet-abusive advertising will continue to increase. If e-mail spamming is a potential threat to an enterprise, it would be worthwhile for systems administrators to initiate implementing procedures that keep users off the spam lists. Most bulk e-mailers build their lists with programs that strip e-mail addresses from text. If the systems administrator can minimize the appearance of users' e-mail addresses in easily available locations, this may help keep them off the lists. Participation in newsgroups and other electronic forums may be essential to the work of some users. Likewise, if a company is using a commercial online service, there may be some benefit to keeping the users' e-mail addresses on the publicly available membership directory, but this kind of exposure ought to be examined anyway to ensure that users are not unnecessarily exposing themselves to e-mail harvesters.

Many users post their e-mail addresses on their company's World Wide Web site. The often-used "mail to:" HTML tag places an e-mail address in a prominent place on a publicly available Web page, which is in reality an easily parsed text document. True, it is desirable for Web visitors to be able to send e-mail to contacts within the company, but there is an easy work-around for this problem: Company e-mail addresses can be saved in an image file (e.g., .gif or .jpeg format) so only someone who actually visits the site personally can read the e-mail address. The image can be linked to an online form, where the visitor can send a message to the company contact. This is another strategy for minimizing spam exposure.

SPAM BATTLE PLANS

To control the effects of Internet-abusive advertising, an organization should institute definite procedures and educate all Internet-connected employees. Here are some possible measures to take against unsolicited bulk e-mail:

- *Just delete the offending message.* This is the solution most often recommended by advocates of bulk e-mail, as it does not interfere with their activities. If the mail system allows it, use e-mail filtering to delete messages from bulk e-mailers that can be identified.
- *Ask to be removed from the list.* Most senders will comply. Some use automated removal systems. In the view of many Internet users, though, this amounts to caving in to the spammer's Internet-abusive tactics.
- *Complain to the sender and advertisers.* Users should give them their opinion of this kind of advertising. They can boycott companies that advertise by e-mail spam. Some mailers will not care, but many individual advertisers have joined an e-mail scheme knowing little or nothing about the Internet and will respond positively to tactful complaints.
- *Complain to the postmaster (postmaster@domain. com) or administrator (admin@domain.com or root@ domain.com).* Some larger Internet providers have a special department that can be reached at abuse@ domain.com. The user should send along a complete copy of the message, including all header information. Sometimes this tactic yields results, and sometimes not. It could be that the spammer and postmaster are one and the same.
- *Try to reach the service providers who provide Internet access upstream by tracing the message in reverse order.* A "who is" search can divulge service provider contact information. Users can use the Web interface at http://rs.internic.net/cgi-bin/whois/. This kind of approach can put users in touch with people who have a stake in controlling e-mail spam—the Internet service providers.
- *Block Internet-abusive e-mail addresses and domains.* Depending on the nature of the Internet connection, the user or access provider should be able to set up the system to refuse and bounce back any e-mail from a certain address or domain. Sometimes spammer and provider are one and the same. Some providers profit from spammers' activities and intentionally harbor them, so some domains will not respond to complaints.

RETALIATING JUDICIOUSLY

Some who are opposed to e-mail spamming have resorted to technological retaliation—tying up advertisers' toll-free numbers, sending continuous faxes in the middle of the night, or sending mail bombs in an attempt to overload mailboxes and shut down systems. Mail bombs, however, are not necessary and qualify as harassment, which is illegal. If a spammer has been especially offensive, the offender will get enough single responses from individuals to achieve the same effect as a mail bomb. Likewise, the practice of "flaming" (i.e., sending abusive, insulting messages) will probably not accomplish much. Sometimes such a message will reach an innocent party or a clueless advertiser who has bought into a bulk e-mail scheme without really knowing what it is all about. Usually a firm but tactful complaint is the best approach.

Some companies have threatened legal action against spammers or have sent them invoices for the time and resources consumed by their unsolicited advertising. Whether there is any merit in such claims has yet to be determined. Some large providers have landed in court over the spam issue. For example, America Online has been in court several times in a dispute with bulk e-mailer Cyber Promotions.

It has been debated whether or not the government should try to regulate e-mail advertising, but many Internet users do not welcome government involvement in Internet issues. Also, the Internet is an international network. No one government can claim authority over activities that take place over the Internet, and the effect of any government's efforts is limited by national boundaries.

SPAMBUSTER RESOURCES

Table 2 offers a number of resources found on the Internet for dealing with unwanted e-mail advertising.

FUTURE OF SPAM?

Regardless of efforts to stop their activities or to prevent them from mailing into company and institutional networks, bulk e-mail advertisers are not going to give up easily because the cost of sending e-mail is so low and the Internet audience is growing so quickly. The promise of big profits will spur on the spammers. One encouraging development is the growth of legitimate bulk e-mail services. Although the spammers have been getting most of the attention, many business persons have been quietly building up voluntary e-mail lists of highly qualified buyers who have actually requested commercial material. This kind of bulk e-mailing is bound to increase and thrive in the future.

Those opposed to spam advertising are able to bring numerous forces to bear on the Internet abuser—complaints to the spammer's access provider, resulting in termination of the spammer's Internet account; mail bombing and other frontier justice sanctions; and even the threat of legal action. If it continues, the opposition to spammers' activities is bound to affect their strategies.

Already some bulk e-mailers are trying to develop "preference services" or "opt-out" lists of Internet users who do not want to receive e-mail advertising. Some bulk e-mailers even share their "do not mail" lists with each other in an effort to lessen the outcry against their methods.

If the tide of unsolicited e-mail continues to rise, users will increasingly demand commercial and technological solutions, such as better e-mail filtering, to help them get control over incoming e-mail. Many users guard their e-mail addresses carefully to keep them out of public places where they can be stripped and added to a database. Over time, more innovative solutions will be developed, possibly even a security service that specializes in protecting networks from invasion by unwanted messages. In the meantime, network administrators and support personnel can minimize the extra costs and lost productivity caused

Table 2   Resources for dealing with unwanted e-mail advertising.

Resource	Web Address	Description
Blacklist of Internet Advertisers	http://tinyurl.com/c7h2k	This site lists some of the most extreme Internet abusers, including some bulk e-mail senders. Also included are tips on dealing with unwanted commercial materials and suggestions for appropriate Internet advertising.
Fight Spam on the Internet!	http://spam.abuse.net	This site provides technical resources and instructions for filtering, blocking, and limiting spam.
Infinite Ink's Mail Filtering and Robots page	http://www.ii.com/internet/robots	This site includes strategies and resources for filtering and processing mail.
Net-Abuse Frequently Asked Questions (FAQ)	http://www.cybernothing.org/faqs/net-abuse-faq.html	This site includes questions and answers about spamming and other forms of Internet abuse, in addition to providing especially good instructions on how to identify spammers and lodge complaints with providers.
Newsgroups	http://www.killfile.org/~tskirvin/nana/	Newsgroups dealing with Internet abuse (news.admin.net-abuse.misc).
Responding to unsolicited commercial e-mail (panix.com)	http://www.panix.com/uce.html/panix.com	This site, sponsored by an ISP, furnishes guidelines for combating unwanted e-mail.

Digital –
E-Mail

by e-mail spamming by instituting company programs and policies. Some suggested elements of such a program might include:

- Determining what kind of e-mail advertising will be tolerated from outside and what will not be tolerated

- Devising procedures for users to follow when they receive spam e-mail
- Devising a system for identifying repeat spammers and the domains from which they operate
- Developing cooperative relationships with Internet providers and joining in with industry efforts to counteract the activities of e-mail spammers

Enclaves: Enterprise as Extranet

Bryan T. Koch, CISSP
RxHub, St. Paul, Minnesota, U.S.A.

Abstract

The time has come to apply the lessons learned in Internet and extranet environments to one's own organization. This entry proposes to apply Internet/extranet security architectural concepts to internal networks by creating protected *enclaves* within organizations. Access between enclaves and the enterprise is managed by *network guardians*. Within enclaves, the security objective is to apply traditional controls consistently and well. Outside of enclaves, current practice (i.e., security controls at variance with formal security policies) is tolerated (one has no choice). This restructuring can reduce some types of network security threats by orders of magnitude. Other threats remain and these must be addressed through traditional security analysis and controls, or accepted as part of normal risk/reward trade-offs.

Even in the most secure organizations, information security threats and vulnerabilities are increasing over time. Vulnerabilities are increasing with the complexity of internal infrastructures; complex structures have more single points of failure, and this in turn increases the risk of multiple simultaneous failures. Organizations are adopting new, untried, and partially tested products at ever-increasing rates. Vendors and internal developers alike are relearning the security lessons of the past—one at a time, painful lesson by painful lesson.

Given the rapid rate of change in organizations, minor or incremental improvements in security can be offset or undermined by "organizational entropy." The introduction of local area networks (LANs) and personal computers (PCs) years ago changed the security landscape, but many security organizations continued to function using centralized control models that have little relationship to the current organizational or technical infrastructures. The Internet has brought new threats to the traditional set of organizational security controls. The success of the Internet model has created a push for electronic commerce (E-commerce) and electronic business (E-business) initiatives involving both the Internet itself and the more widespread use of Internet Protocol (IP)-based extranets (private business-to-business networks).

Sophisticated, effective, and easy-to-use attack tools are widely available on the Internet. The Internet has implicitly linked competing organizations with each other, and linked these organizations to communities that are opposed to security controls of any kind. There is no reason to assume that attack tools developed in the Internet cannot or will not be used within an organization.

External threats are more easily perceived than internal threats, while surveys and studies continue to show that the majority of security problems are internal. With all of this as context, the need for a new security paradigm is clear.

SECURITY CONTEXT

Security policies, procedures, and technologies are supposed to combine to yield acceptable risk levels for enterprise systems. However, the nature of security threats, and the probability that they can be successfully deployed against enterprise systems, have changed. This is partly a result of the diffusion of computer technology and computer networking into enterprises, and partly a result of the Internet.

For larger and older organizations, security policies were developed to address security vulnerabilities and threats in legacy mainframe environments. Legacy policies have been supplemented to address newer threats such as computer viruses, remote access, and e-mail. In this author's experience, it is rare for current policy frameworks to effectively address network-based threats. LANs and PCs were the first steps in what has become a marathon of increasing complexity and inter-relatedness; intranet (internal networks and applications based on IP), extranet, and Internet initiatives are the most common examples of this.

The Internet has brought network technology to millions. It is an enabling infrastructure for emerging E-business and E-commerce environments. It has a darker side, however, because it also:

- Serves as a "proving ground" for tools and procedures that test for and exploit security vulnerabilities in systems
- Serves as a distribution medium for these tools and procedures

Encyclopedia of Information Assurance DOI: 10.1081/E-EIA-120046364
Copyright © 2011 by Taylor & Francis. All rights reserved.

- Links potential users of these tools with anonymously available repositories

Partly because it began as an "open" network, and partly due to the explosion of commercial use, the Internet has also been the proving ground for security architectures, tools, and procedures to protect information in the Internet's high-threat environment. Examples of the tools that have emerged from this environment include firewalls, virtual private networks, and layered physical architectures. These tools have been extended from the Internet into extranets.

In many sectors—most recently telecommunications, finance, and healthcare—organizations are growing primarily through mergers and acquisitions. Integration of many new organizations per year is challenging enough on its own. It is made more complicated by external network connectivity (dial-in for customers and employees, outbound Internet services, electronic commerce applications, and the like) within acquired organizations. It is further complicated by the need to integrate dissimilar infrastructure components [e-mail, calendaring, and scheduling; enterprise resource planning (ERP); and human resources (HR) tools]. The easiest solution—to wait for the dust to settle and perform long-term planning—is simply not possible in today's "at the speed of business" climate.

An alternative solution, the one discussed here, is to accept the realities of the business and technical contexts, and to create a "network security master plan" based on the new realities of the internal threat environment. One must begin to treat enterprise networks as if they are an extranet or the Internet and secure them accordingly.

ONE BIG NETWORK PARADIGM

Network architects today are being tasked with the creation of an integrated network environment. One network architect described this as a mandate to "connect everything to everything else, with complete transparency." The author refers to this as the One Big Network paradigm. In this author's experience, some network architects aim to keep security at arm's length—"we build it, you secure it, and we don't have to talk to each other." This is untenable in the current security context of rapid growth from mergers and acquisitions.

One Big Network is a seductive vision to network designers, network users, and business executives alike. One Big Network will—in theory—allow new and better business interactions with suppliers, with business customers, and with end-consumers. Everyone connected to One Big Network can—in theory—reap great benefits at minimal infrastructure cost. Electronic business-to-business

and electronic-commerce will be—in theory—ubiquitous.

However, one critical element has been left out of this brave new world: security. Despite more than a decade of networking and personal computers, many organizational security policies continue to target the legacy environment, not the network as a whole. These policies assume that it is possible to secure stand-alone "systems" or "applications" as if they have an existence independent of the rest of the enterprise. They assume that attackers will target applications rather than the network infrastructure that links the various parts of the distributed application together. Today's automated attack tools target the network as a whole to identify and attack weak applications and systems, and then use these systems for further attacks.

One Big Network changes another aspect of the enterprise risk/reward equation: it globalizes risks that had previously been local. In the past, a business unit could elect to enter into an outsource agreement for its applications, secure in the knowledge that the risks related to the agreement affected it alone. With One Big Network, the risk paradigm changes. It is difficult, indeed inappropriate, for business unit management to make decisions about risk/reward trade-offs when the risks are global while the benefits are local.

Finally, One Big Network assumes consistent controls and the loyalty of employees and others who are given access. Study after study, and survey after survey, confirm that neither assumption is viable.

NETWORK SECURITY AND THE ONE BIG NETWORK PARADIGM

It is possible that there was a time when One Big Network could be adequately secured. If it ever existed, that day is long past. Today's networks are dramatically bigger, much more diverse, run many more applications, connect more divergent organizations, all in a more hostile environment where the "bad guys" have better tools than ever before. The author believes that it is not possible to secure, to any reasonable level of confidence, any enterprise network for any large organization where the network is managed as a single "flat" network with "any-to-any" connectivity.

In an environment with no effective internal network security controls, each network node creates a threat against every other node. (In mathematical terms, where there are n network nodes, the number of threats is approximately n^2.) Where the organization is also on the Internet without a firewall, the effective number of threats becomes essentially infinite (see Fig. 1).

Effective enterprise security architecture must augment its traditional, applications-based toolkit with *network-based tools* aimed at addressing network-based threats.

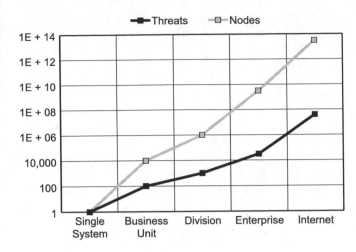

Fig. 1 Network threats (log scale).

INTERNET SECURITY ARCHITECTURE ELEMENTS

How does one design differently for Internet and extranet than one did for enterprises? What are Internet/ extranet security engineering principles?

- *Simplicity.* Complexity is the enemy of security. Complex systems have more components, more single points of failure, more points at which failures can cascade upon one another, and are more difficult to certify as "known good" (even when built from known good components, which is rare in and of itself).
- *Prioritization and valuation.* Internet security systems know what they aim to protect. The sensitivity and vulnerability of each element is understood, both on its own and in combination with other elements of the design.
- *Deny by default, allow by policy.* Internet security architectures begin with the premise that all traffic is to be denied. Only traffic that is explicitly required to perform the mission is enabled, and this through defined, documented, and analyzed pathways and mechanisms.
- *Defense in depth, layered protection.* Mistakes happen. New flaws are discovered. Flaws previously believed to be insignificant become important when exploits are published. The Internet security architecture must, to a reasonable degree of confidence, fail in ways that result in continued security of the overall system; the failure (or misconfiguration) of a single component should not result in security exposures for the entire site.
- *End-to-end, path-by-path analysis.* Internet security engineering looks at all components, both on the enterprise side and on the remote side of every transaction. Failure or compromise of any component can undermine the security of the entire system. Potential weak points must be understood and, if possible, managed.

Residual risks must be understood, both by the enterprise and by its business partners and customers.

- *Encryption.* In all Internet models, and most extranet models, the security of the underlying network is not assumed. As a result, some mechanism—encryption—is needed to preserve the confidentiality of data sent between the remote users and enterprise servers.
- *Conscious choice, not organic growth.* Internet security architectures are formally created through software and security engineering activities; they do not "just happen."

ENCLAVE APPROACH

This entry proposes to treat the enterprise as an extranet. The extranet model invokes an architecture that has security as its first objective. It means identifying what an enterprise genuinely cares about: what it lives or dies by. It identifies critical and securable components and isolates them into protected *enclaves*. Access between enclaves and the enterprise is managed by *network guardians*. Within enclaves, the security objective is to apply traditional controls consistently and well. Outside of enclaves, current practice (i.e., security controls at variance with formal security policies), while not encouraged, is acknowledged as reality. This restructuring can reduce some types of network security threats by orders of magnitude. Taken to the extreme, all business-unit-to-business-unit interactions pass through enclaves (see Fig. 2).

ENCLAVES

The enclaves proposed here are designed to contain high-value securable elements. Securable elements are systems for which security controls consistent with organizational security objectives can be successfully designed, deployed, operated, and maintained at any desired level of

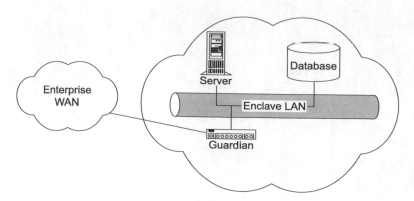

Fig. 2 Relationship of an enclave to the enterprise.

confidence. By contrast, nonsecurable elements might be semi-autonomous business units, new acquisitions, test labs, and desktops (as used by telecommuters, developers, and business partners)—elements for which the cost, time, or effort required to secure them exceeds their value to the enterprise.

Within a secure enclave, every system and network component will have security arrangements that comply with the enterprise security policy and industry standards of due care. At enclave boundaries, security assurance will be provided by network guardians whose rule sets and operational characteristics can be enforced and audited. In other words, there is some level of assurance that comes from being part of an enclave. This greatly simplifies the security requirements that are imposed on client/server architectures and their supporting applications programming interfaces (APIs). Between enclaves, security assurance will be provided by the application of cryptographic technology and protocols.

Enclave membership is earned, not inherited. Enclave networks may need to be created from the ground up, with existing systems shifted onto enclave networks when their security arrangements have been adequately examined.

Enclaves could potentially contain the elements listed below:

1. Mainframes
2. Application servers
3. Database servers
4. Network gateways
5. PKI certificate authority and registration authorities
6. Network infrastructure components (domain name and time servers)
7. Directories
8. Windows "domain controllers"
9. Approved intranet Web servers
10. Managed network components
11. Internet proxy servers

All these are shared and securable to a high degree of confidence.

NETWORK GUARDIANS

Network guardians mediate and control traffic flow into and out of enclaves. Network guardians can be implemented initially using network routers. The routers will isolate enclave local area network traffic from LANs used for other purposes (development systems, for example, and user desktops) within the same physical space. This restricts the ability of user desktops and other low-assurance systems to monitor traffic between remote enclave users and the enclave. (Users will still have the ability to intercept traffic on their own LAN segment, although the use of switching network hubs can reduce the opportunity for this exposure as well.)

The next step in the deployment of network guardians is the addition of access control lists (ACLs) to guardian routers. The purpose of the ACLs is similar to the functionality of "border routers" in Internet firewalls—screening incoming traffic for validity (antispoofing), screening the destination addresses of traffic within the enclave, and to the extent possible, restricting enclave services visible to the remainder of the enterprise to the set of intended services.

Decisions to implement higher levels of assurance for specific enclaves or specific enclave-to-enclave or enclave-to-user communications can be made based on later risk assessments. Today and for the near future, simple subnet isolation will suffice.

ENCLAVE BENEFITS

Adopting an enclave approach reduces network-based security risks by orders of magnitude. The basic reason is that in the modern enterprise, the number of nodes (n) is very large, growing, and highly volatile. The number of enclaves (e) will be a small, stable number. With enclaves, overall risk is on the order of $n \times e$, compared with $n \times n$ without enclaves. For large n, $n \times e$ is much smaller than $n \times n$.

Business units can operate with greater degrees of autonomy than they might otherwise be allowed, because the only data they will be placing at risk is their own data on their own networks. Enclaves allow the realignment of risk with reward. This gives business units greater internal design freedom.

Because they require documentation and formalization of network data flows, the presence of enclaves can lead to improved network efficiency and scalability. Enclaves enforce an organization's existing security policies, at a network level, so by their nature they tend to reduce questionable, dubious, and erroneous network traffic and provide better accounting for allowed traffic flows. This aids capacity planning and disaster planning functions.

By formalizing relationships between protected systems and the remainder of the enterprise, enclaves can allow faster connections to business partners. (One of the significant sources of delay this author has seen in setting up extranets to potential business partners is collecting information about the exact nature of network traffic, required to configure network routers and firewalls. The same delay is often seen in setting up connectivity to newly acquired business units.)

Finally, enclaves allow for easier allocation of scarce security resources where they can do the most good. It is far easier to improve the security of enclave-based systems by, say, 50% than it is to improve the overall security of all desktop systems in the enterprise by a similar amount, given a fixed resource allocation.

LIMITATIONS OF ENCLAVES

Enclaves protect only the systems in them; and by definition, they exclude the vast majority of the systems on the enterprise network and all external systems. Some other mechanism is needed to protect data in transit between low-assurance (desktops, external business partner) systems and the high-assurance systems within the enclaves. The solution is a set of confidentiality and authentication services provided by encryption. Providing an overall umbrella for encryption and authentication services is one role of public key infrastructures (PKIs).

From a practical perspective, management is difficult enough for externally focused network guardians (those protecting Internet and extranet connectivity). Products allowing support of an enterprisewide set of firewalls are just beginning to emerge. Recent publicity regarding Internet security events has increased executive awareness of security issues, without increasing the pool of trained network security professionals, so staffing for an enclave migration may be difficult.

Risks remain, and there are limitations. Many new applications are not "firewall friendly" (e.g., Java, CORBA, video, network management). Enclaves may not be compatible with legacy systems. Application security is just as important—perhaps more important than previously—because people connect to the application. Applications, therefore, should be designed

securely. Misuse by authorized individuals is still possible in this paradigm, but the enclave system controls the path they use. Enclave architecture is aimed at network-based attacks, and it can be strengthened by integrating virtual private networks (VPNs) and switching network hubs.

IMPLEMENTATION OF ENCLAVES

Enclaves represent a fundamental shift in enterprise network architecture. Stated differently, they re-apply the lessons of the Internet to the enterprise. Re-architecting cannot happen overnight. It cannot be done on a cookie-cutter, by-the-book basis. The author's often-stated belief is that "security architecture" is a verb; it describes a *process*, rather than a destination. How can an organization apply the enclave approach to its network security problems? In a word, planning. In a few more words, information gathering, planning, prototyping, deployment, and refinement. These stages are described more fully below.

INFORMATION GATHERING

Information is the core of any enclave implementation project. The outcome of the information-gathering phase is essentially an inventory of critical systems with a reasonably good idea of the sensitivity and criticality of these systems. Some readers will be fortunate enough to work for organizations that already have information systems inventories from the business continuity planning process, or from recent Year 2000 activities. A few will actually have accurate and complete information. The rest will have to continue on with their research activities.

The enterprise must identify candidate systems for enclave membership and the security objectives for candidates. A starting rule-of-thumb would be that no desktop systems, and no external systems, are candidates for enclave membership; all other systems are initially candidates. Systems containing business-critical, business-sensitive, legally protected, or highly visible information are candidates for enclave membership. Systems managed by demonstrably competent administration groups, to defined security standards, are candidates.

External connections and relationships, via dial-up, dedicated, or Internet paths, must be discovered, documented, and inventoried.

The existing enterprise network infrastructure is often poorly understood and even less well-documented. Part of the information-gathering process is to improve this situation and provide a firm foundation for realistic enclave planning.

Enclaves –
Enterprise

PLANNING

The planning process begins with the selection of an enclave planning group. Suggested membership includes senior staff from the following organizations: information security (with an emphasis on network security and business continuity specialists), network engineering, firewall management, mainframe network operations, distributed systems or client/server operations, E-commerce planning, and any outsource partners from these organizations. Supplementing this group would be technically well-informed representatives from enterprise business units.

The planning group's next objective is to determine the scope of its activity, answering a set of questions including at least:

- Is one enclave sufficient, or is more than one a better fit with the organization?
- Where will the enclaves be located?
- Who will manage them?
- What level of protection is needed within each enclave?

What is the simplest representative sample of an enclave that could be created within the current organization?

The purpose of these questions is to apply standard engineering practices to the challenge of carving out a secure enclave from the broader enterprise, and to use the outcome of these practices to make a case to enterprise management for the deployment of enclaves.

Depending on organizational readiness, the planning phase can last as little as a month or as long as a year, involving anywhere from days to years of effort.

PROTOTYPING

Enclaves are not new; they have been a feature of classified government environments since the beginning of computer technology (although typically within a single classification level or compartment). They are the basis of essentially all secure Internet electronic commerce work. However, the application of enclave architectures to network security needs of large organizations is, if not new, at least not widely discussed in the professional literature. Further, as seen in Internet and extranet environments generally, significant misunderstandings can often delay deployment efforts, and efforts to avoid these delays lead either to downward functionality adjustments, or acceptance of additional security risks, or both.

As a result, prudence dictates that any attempt to deploy enclaves within an enterprise be done in a stepwise fashion, compatible with the organization's current configuration and change control processes. The author recommends that organizations considering the deployment of the enclave architecture first evaluate this architecture in a prototype or laboratory environment. One option for doing this is an organizational test environment. Another option is the selection of a single business unit, district, or regional office.

Along with the selection of a locale and systems under evaluation, the enterprise must develop evaluation criteria: what does the organization expect to learn from the prototype environment, and how can the organization capture and capitalize on learning experiences?

DEPLOYMENT

After the successful completion of a prototype comes general deployment. The actual deployment architecture and schedule depends on factors too numerous to mention in any detail here. The list includes:

- *The number of enclaves.* (The author has worked in environments with as few as one and as many as a hundred potential enclaves.)
- *Organizational readiness.* Some parts of the enterprise will be more accepting of the enclave architecture than others. Early adopters exist in every enterprise, as do more conservative elements. The deployment plan should make use of early adopters and apply the lessons learned in these early deployments to sway or encourage the more change-resistant organizations.
- *Targets of opportunity.* The acquisition of new business units through mergers and acquisitions may well present targets of opportunity for early deployment of the enclave architecture.

REFINEMENT

The enclave architecture is a concept and a process. Both will change over time: partly through organizational experience and partly through the changing technical and organizational infrastructure within which they are deployed.

One major opportunity for refinement is the composition and nature of the network guardians. Initially, this author expects network guardians to consist simply of already-existing network routers, supplemented with network monitoring or intrusion detection systems. The router will initially be configured with a minimal set of controls, perhaps just anti-spoofing filtering and as much source and destination filtering as can be reasonably considered. The network monitoring system will allow the implementers to quickly learn about "typical" traffic patterns, which can then be configured into the router. The intrusion detection system looks for known attack patterns and alerts network administrators when they are found (see Fig. 3).

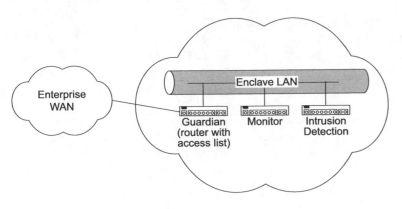

Fig. 3   Initial enclave guardian configuration.

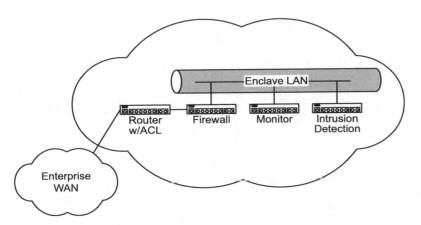

Fig. 4   Enclave with firewall guardian.

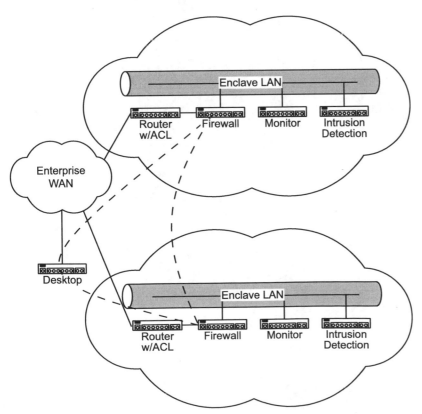

Fig. 5   Enclaves with encrypted paths (dashed lines).

In a later refinement, the router may well be supplemented with a firewall, with configuration rules derived from the network monitoring results, constrained by emerging organizational policies regarding authorized traffic (see Fig. 4).

Still later, where the organization has more than one enclave, encrypted tunnels might be established between enclaves, with selective encryption of traffic from other sources (desktops, for example, or selected business partners) into enclaves. This is illustrated in Fig. 5.

CONCLUSION

The enterprise-as-extranet methodology gives business units greater internal design freedom without a negative security impact on the rest of the corporation. It can allow greater network efficiency and better network disaster planning because it identifies critical elements and the pathways to them. It establishes security triage. The net results are global threat reduction by orders of magnitude and improved, effective real-world security.

Encryption Key Management

Franjo Majstor, CISSP, CCIE
EMEA Senior Technical Director, CipherOptics Inc., Raleigh, North Carolina, U.S.A.

Guy Vancollie
EMEA Managing Director, CipherOptics Inc., Raleigh, North Carolina, U.S.A.

Abstract

This entry discusses the importance of encryption key management, especially in relation to large-scale networks. After a brief background, the author discusses multiple large-scale network issues including performance, redundancy, load balancing, multicast, and multi-protocol label switching. Obviously, part of the security is to encrypt data, which is discussed in detail touching on three main encryption options: link-level, application-level, and network-level. The author also discusses the limitations of encryption, as well as the separation of the key management solution.

Enclaves – Enterprise

INTRODUCTION

All corporations need to protect their business transactions, customer data, and intellectual property. At a minimum, data loss or compromise can create public relations nightmares and even seriously hurt market reputation. In the long run, it can impact customer relationships or create serious financial damage from fraud, information theft, or public disclosure of intellectual properties. This problem has presented information technology with a technological challenge because the ideal network data protection solution should require no change to network infrastructure, should not impact network performance, must work over any network topology, and must secure any type of traffic. The challenge facing information security professionals is to secure data in motion as has never been possible before. It is obvious that encryption is the solution to addressing confidentiality and integrity of the data while it transits lines that we have no control over; however, its limitations have hampered its deployment, especially on large-scale networks. Standards are normally present when interoperability among different vendor solutions should take place, and multiple good ones have been used, for example, the Internet Protocol security (IPSec) standard framework. Although IPSec delivered a portion of the solution, it also introduced its own limitations and unnecessary overlay to an existing network infrastructure, making it even more difficult to manage, maintain, and operate.

LARGE-SCALE NETWORK ISSUES

Performance

Not so long ago data network infrastructures were used only for the bulk transfer of data over slow links of various, mostly unreliable, quality. The data carried over those network infrastructures was less important and, even if stolen, modified, or lost, there were always multiple paper copies and forms in existence to replace the data when needed. Nowadays a modern high-speed network infrastructure carries the most crucial pieces of information as well as multiple crucial applications that companies depend upon for their existence. Adding encryption to the communication paths, unless assisted with specialized hardware, typically slows down the overall communication speed and, therefore, impacts the usability of the high-speed communication paths.

Redundancy

High-speed, high-performance networks are required to stay up all the time, no matter what happens with individual communication components. Therefore, modern network design includes multiple redundant devices as well as multiple available paths built into the network itself. Redundancy built into the network keeps the availability of the communication paths between multiple points in the network; however, it often causes difficulty for security mechanisms.

Load Balancing

Multiple redundant paths do not necessarily have to work in a master–slave or active–standby mode, but could be active and used simultaneously to do load balancing and share the traffic load across the multiple links. This is the preferred way for efficient networks to use multiple available links, but it also has, unfortunately, some security implications. Security relationships are typically fixed between peers and are in trouble when they lose peer relationships that have to be dynamically established when network traffic chooses another path to the same destination.

Encyclopedia of Information Assurance DOI: 10.1081/E-EIA-120046726
Copyright © 2011 by Taylor & Francis. All rights reserved.

Enclaves –
Enterprise

Multicast

Any kind of group communication—multicast is just one of them—requires group security member relationships as well as group member control if any of the communication peers leaves or joins the group. That makes the encrypted group communication extremely difficult, with a heavy overlay of the peer-to-peer relationships that grows exponentially with the number of peers communicating. It is a known mathematical fact that for "n" number of peers it is required to have "$n \times (n-1)$" peer-to-peer relationships and that times 2 if each direction has to be secured separately.

Multi-Protocol Label Switching

Multi-Protocol Label Switching (MPLS) wide area networks provide most of the long-distance connectivity today and as such are replacing multiple older technologies such as Frame Relay, X.25, or leased lines. MPLS provides quite similar functionality compared to its predecessors through the creation of separate, isolated communication paths based on different labels. Traffic isolation, however, provides neither confidentiality nor authentication of the data traveling via the MPLS network and opens the data to multiple risks when traveling over a shared infrastructure, such as a possible data leakage due to configuration errors or even illegal tapping.

ENCRYPTION OPTIONS

It has been obvious throughout the history of communication protocols that protection of data while it travels over unsecured data channels could be achieved with encryption. However, encryption has proven to be a difficult task as it requires multiple other elements to be done correctly as well, so as not to impact modern data communication networks. As mentioned earlier, encryption impacts the performance, redundancy, and load balancing of modern-day networks, and also the requirement for any type of group communication makes the use of encryption problematic. Furthermore, there have been several options of where to implement encryption: on the link level, network level, or application level. Let us browse through them briefly to see the pros and cons of each.

Link-Level Encryption

Link-level encryption was one of the earliest types available and had no demand for standardization as there always

was a product of the same vendor on both sides of the link. Key management protocols were often also proprietary and built-in as part of the solution. Therefore, the price of such devices was high and when a device failed in a point-to-point topology both had to be replaced. The problems for link-level encryption came with new network media connectivity options, such as mesh topologies as well as multiple different paths through the same media. This led to the option of developing encryption on other levels, such as at the application or network level.

Application-Level Encryption

Application-level encryption is, from a security standpoint, the highest level—as the application that produces the data has the best visibility on how to protect it. It would be great if each and every application had the encryption possibility built-in; however, as security was in the past often not the issue, many legacy applications remained without it and have no option to turn it on. Newer applications mostly have the option to protect the data via encryption; however, each and every one of them has its own different way of how to do it, and that makes scalability as well as intra-application data protection transfer impossible or non-scalable.

Network-Level Encryption

Owing to the limitations and drawbacks of the other earlier mentioned options and levels to encrypt the data, the network layer has ended up as the most frequent choice. Network-level encryption provides for equal protection to legacy applications as well as new applications traversing the same network protocol and requires no other application changes. As Internet Protocol (IP) has become the most dominant network communication protocol today, we will narrow our discussion on the encryption features to within IP with its security protocol framework, IPSec. The IPSec protocol got standardized in the late 1990s and through numerous interoperable implementations, IPSec-based equipment has become much more affordable than link-level encryption devices used to be, but as usual it has its advantages as well as its limitations, which we will focus on going forward.

LIMITATIONS OF THE IPSEC ENCRYPTION

The IPSec set of request for comment (RFC) standards defined the authentication as well as the encryption of the

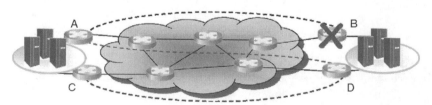

Fig. 1 Redundant network architecture.

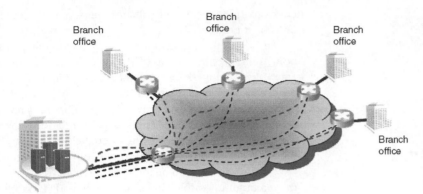

Central data center

Fig. 2 Group (multicast or broadcast) network architecture.

Enclaves –
Enterprise

IP packet. It also defined different modes of operation as well as the Internet key exchange (IKE) automated key-derivation protocol that helps with exchanging the keys based on a predefined time interval or amount of transferred data. Together, IKE and IPSec got wide implementation on routers, layer-three switches, and edge devices such as firewalls, as well as end nodes running on different operating systems. With wide implementation, however, IPSec and IKE have also introduced new limitations. IPSec and IKE are by definition a peer-to-peer protocol that impacts network communications if there are redundant paths or if load balancing is involved. Peer-to-peer trusted relationships also make encrypted group communication very difficult. This is illustrated in Figs. 1 and 2. Last but not least, if not implemented in hardware, certain encryption processes also impact the performance of the communication on any higher-speed network connections.

SEPARATION OF THE KEY MANAGEMENT SOLUTION

IPSec and IKE together represent three main functions most often implemented together in the very same, single running platform. These three functions are security policy definition, key exchange, and encryption. The most common implementation for all three functions as one IPSec/IKE

architecture is illustrated in Fig. 3. Implementation of all three of the main encryption components on the same physical platform seems to be an obvious choice; however, it brings with it its limitations of peer-to-peer relationships and, therefore, impacts modern network communications. To be able to achieve resilient and redundant network designs, the encryption security architecture should have its components designed the same way. The three main components in essence represent three individual roles: bulk encryption, which could be done on the policy enforcement point (PEP); key management, which a key authority point could take care of; and security policies, which could be done on a management and policy server. This distributed model represented by the three individual layers, management, distribution, and encryption, is illustrated in Fig. 4. Each of the main functional components could hence fulfill its job when implemented on individual platforms, thereby also bringing additional benefits such as scalability. Each of the layers in the three-tier model could be replicated up to the necessary service-scale level and support growth as required for large-scale network designs. The three-tier security architecture is illustrated in Fig. 5. The key distribution layer and policy distribution layer have to be designed with redundancy and failover mechanisms as well as incorporating hardware security modules for key generations. The key storage has to be a "hack-proof" system with no backdoor and no possible traffic-probing vulnerabilities. An additional problem to solve is

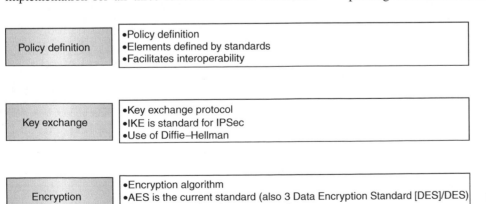

Fig. 3 IPSec/IKE common architecture.

Enclaves –
Enterprise

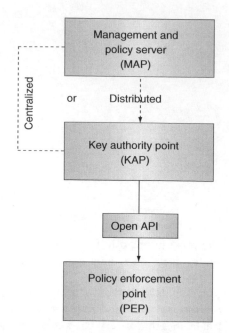

Fig. 4 Distributed policy and key management architecture.

security of the traffic between the layers. That could be resolved by utilizing either IKE or other secure but less heavy protocols, such as the Transport Layer Security protocol. Scaling in such a distributed model is built-in from the ground up by design. The three-layer architecture allows scalability of security policies never before possible using IPSec. Grouping networks and network device units together through group policy definitions dramatically simplifies policy generations. Therefore, the layered encryption security architecture can serve many thousands of end-node PEPs in the network and, as well, through the open application programming interface provide access to hundreds of thousands of multivendor devices, such as

desktops, notebooks, cell phones, personal digital assistants, and printers.

An additional element that helps break the point-to-point relationship is that PEPs responsible for the bulk encryption doing IPSec maintain the original IP address header, as is illustrated in Fig. 6.

With the original IP header preserved, there is no additional need to create any point-to-point relationships and, even more important, no need to create any overlay network on top of the existing infrastructure. That simplifies the encryption function on the existing modern networks to the maximum possible and as such only adds flexibility to enabling redundancy, load balancing, as well as group broadcast or multicast communication.

SUMMARY

The challenge in front of the information security professional is to secure data in motion like never before. Encryption is the obvious choice for the solution but the solution must work over any network topology and must secure any type of traffic. All of that is to be done preferably without requiring changes to the network infrastructure or impacting the network performance. The IPSec protocol provides part of the solution but is also part of the problem, with its point-to-point nature as well as the network overlay model. A layered encryption security architecture brings a solution to the requirements of modern data protection through the separation of the main roles and functions of encryption into three individual layers. Such a three-tier encryption security architecture brings inherited scalability and no longer requires a network overlay for the generation and distribution of policies and encryption keys. It provides data protection but does

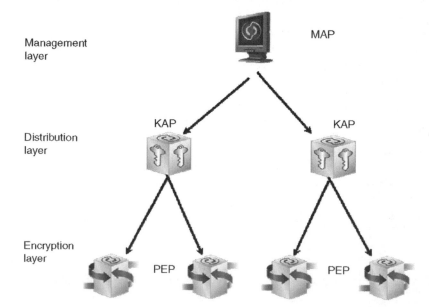

Fig. 5 Three-tier encryption security architecture.

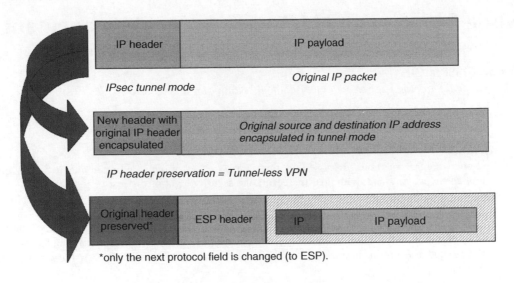

Fig. 6 IPSec tunnel-mode header preservation.

not require any changes to network infrastructure, does not impact network performance, and works over any network topology. It is a concept that should, once widely implemented, solve the problem of data protection through encryption in large-scale network deployments.

BIBLIOGRAPHY

1. Bauger, M.; Weis, B.; Hardjono, T.; Harney, H. *The Group Domain of Interpretation*; July 2003, RFC 3547.
2. Davis, C. R. *IPSec: Securing VPNs*; McGraw-Hill: Berkeley, CA, 2001.
3. Doraswamy, N.; Harkins, D. *IPSec: The New Security Standard for the Internet, Intranets and Virtual Private Networks*; Prentice-Hall PTR: Upper Saddle River, NJ, 1999.
4. Ferguson, N.; Schneier, B. *A Cryptographic Evaluation of IPSec*; April. 1999, http://www.counterpane.com/ipsec.html.
5. Frankel, S. *Demystifying the IPSec Puzzle*, Artech House Inc.: Boston, MA, 2001.
6. Harkins, D.; Carrel, D. *The Internet Key Exchange (IKE)*; November 1998, RFC 2409.
7. Kent, S.; Atkinson, R. *Security Architecture for the Internet Protocol*; November 1998, RFC 2401.
8. Kent, S.; Atkinson, R. *IP Authentication Header*; November 1998, RFC 2402.
9. Kent, S.; Atkinson, R. *IP Encapsulating Security Payload (ESP)*; November 1998, RFC 2406.
10. Kosiur, D. *Building and Managing Virtual Private Networks*; Wiley Computer Publishing: New York, 1998.
11. Maughan, D.; Schertler, M.; Schneider, M.; Turner, J. *Internet Security Association and Key Management Protocol (ISAKMP)*; November 1998, RFC 2408.
12. Perlman, R.; Kaufman, C. Key exchange in IPSec: Analysis of IKE. IEEE Internet Computing **2000**, *4*(6), 50–56.
13. Perlman, R.; Kaufman, C. *Analysis of the IPSec Key Exchange Standard*, In Proceedings of the IEEE 10th International Workshops on Enabling Technologies: Infrastructure for Collaborative Enterprises, MIT: Cambridge, MA, Jun 20–22, 2001, http://sec.femto.org/wetice-2001/papers/radia-paper.pdf.
14. Weis, B.; Gross, G.; Ignjatic, D. *Multicast Extensions to the Security Architecture for the Internet Protocol*; Nov 2008, RFC 5374, http://www.rfc-editor.org/rfc/rfc5374.txt.
15. Weis, B.; Hardjono, T.; Harney, H. *The Multicast Group Security Architecture*; July 2004, RFC 3740.

Enclaves – Enterprise

End Node Security and Network Access Management

Franjo Majstor, CISSP, CCIE
EMEA Senior Technical Director, CipherOptics Inc., Raleigh, North Carolina, U.S.A.

Abstract

End-node control methods discussed in this entry are performing end-node integrity and policy-compliance checking and, with that, increasing the security level of the rest of the network. Although agent-based solutions promise resolution to all issues, they also get stacked with scalability and deployment. Agentless solutions make an intermediate and fast cure for urgent problems, but do not necessarily automate and solve all necessary components. The problem remains on the shoulders of information security practitioners to closely watch and follow the developments and outcomes; armed with knowledge from this entry, they can better deploy the solutions that fit their immediate business demands.

Enclaves – Enterprise

INTRODUCTION

Acronym Jungle

As in almost any industry, the networking industry contains far too many technical acronyms. Security terminology is unfortunately not immune. Combining of security terms with networking terms has resulted in a baffling array of acronyms that will most probably not decrease in the near future. Therefore, an apology is given in advance to beginner readers with a recommendation to, when confronted with an unfamiliar acronym, refer to the end of the entry where all acronyms are defined.

Problem Definition

Acronyms are not the only problem. Currently, modern networks are responsible for employee productivity, product manufacturing, and receiving orders from customers and, as such, are business-critical systems. If these systems are not available or are under attack, the result is a denial of service, theft of sensitive information, or exposure to regulatory penalties. Traditional perimeter-focused security architectures are today powerless against the infected endpoints that connect to enterprise networks from various locations. Information security practitioners are dealing almost on a daily basis with situations such as the following: Sales persons, when traveling, frequently connect to an insecure hotel network or other public Internet service where their laptops could be exposed to a malware infection. Enterprise information technology departments have defined policies and equipped the salesperson's laptop with protections such as the latest antivirus software, personal firewalls, host intrusion prevention, operating system configurations, and patches to protect the system against compromise. Unfortunately, those protections can be turned off, uninstalled, or may simply have never been updated, leaving the salesperson's computer unprotected. Company guests and visitors would often use offered hospitality to connect via an internal enterprise wired or wireless network to the Internet. Their portable equipment could, if they are not up-to-date with the latest viral protection, already be compromised and, as such, could cause a compromise to the rest of the network resources they are connecting through.

These are just two examples out of many. The latest vulnerability statistics of the most popular computing equipment software platforms show us that, most of the time, an unintentional user or guest visitor caused an avalanche of problems to the rest of the network resources that are crucial for running the business.

Several initiatives from industry vendors have already addressed some problems of the individual endpoint security with applications like anti-virus agents and personal firewalls. Connectivity of the end node to the network infrastructure has already received the end node authentication via 802.lx protocol. However, all of those mechanisms individually have thus far proven to not be sufficient to stop problems of network resources under a threat. Hence, efforts from the leading market vendors as well as standardization organizations have resulted in several individual solutions to address the burning issue of both integrity and policy compliancy of the end node toward accepted rules of behavior from the network infrastructure. Information security practitioners exposed to an end node to an infrastructure interaction problem should be able to understand the essence of the issue and be capable of finding a proper end-node-to-infrastructure-interactivity security mechanism that would fit their business environment.

Encyclopedia of Information Assurance DOI: 10.1081/E-EIA-120046281
Copyright © 2011 by Taylor & Francis. All rights reserved.

END NODE SECURITY SOLUTIONS

Evolution

Initiatives to the problem of the end node causing availability, integrity, and confidentiality problems to the rest of the network were started by several combined vendor solutions. Networking vendor Cisco Systems, as well as operating system vendor Microsoft, developed unique proposals. Several other end node anti-viral software vendors joined the initiatives of both, while some others created their own solutions. Overall, it has created the panache of closed efforts locking the choice around a particular vendor's solution. To move out of the closed-group proposals, the Trusted Computing Group (TCG) organization of vendors released the Trusted Network Connect (TNC) specification that describes the problem and provides the framework for a vendor-interoperable solution. Even though it was later developed as an umbrella solution, it explains the detailed individual components of the system with their roles and functions. It is therefore the best starting point in explaining the concept of the future end-node security solutions.

Trusted Network Connect Specification

The TNC architecture and specifications were developed with the purpose of ensuring interoperability among the individual components for solutions provided by different vendors. The aim of the TNC architecture is to provide a framework within which consistent and useful specifications can be developed to achieve a multivendor network standard that provides the following four features:

1. Platform authentication: the verification of a network access requestor's proof of identity of their platform and the integrity-status of that platform.
2. Endpoint policy compliance (authorization): establishing a level of "trust" in the state of an endpoint, such as ensuring the presence, status, and upgrade level of mandated applications, revisions of signature libraries for antivirus and intrusion detection and prevention system applications, and the patch level of the endpoint's operating system and applications. Note that policy compliance can also be viewed as authorization, in which an endpoint compliance to a given policy set results in the endpoint being authorized to gain access to the network.

3. Access policy: ensuring that the endpoint machine and/or its user authenticates and establishes their level of trust before connecting to the network by leveraging a number of existing and emerging standards, products, or techniques.
4. Assessment, isolation, and remediation: ensuring that endpoint machines not meeting the security policy requirements for "trust" can be isolated or quarantined from the rest of the network and, if possible, an appropriate remedy applied, such as upgrading software or virus signature databases to enable the endpoint to comply with security policy and become eligible for connection to the rest of the network.

The basic TNC architecture is illustrated in Fig. 1.
The entities within the architecture are: access requestor (AR), policy enforcement point (PEP), and policy decision point (PDP):

1. Access requestor (AR): the AR is the entity seeking access to a protected network.
2. Policy decision point (PDP): the PDP is the entity performing the decision making regarding the AR's request, in light of the access policies.
3. Policy enforcement point (PEP): the PEP is the entity that enforces the decisions of the PDP regarding network access.

All entities and components in the architecture are logical ones, not physical ones. An entity or component may be a single software program, a hardware machine, or a redundant and replicated set of machines spread across a network, as appropriate for its function and for the deployment's needs. Entities of the TNC architecture are structured in layers. Layered TNC architecture levels (illustrated in Fig. 2) consist of the following:

1. The network access layer: components whose main function pertains to traditional network connectivity and security. Even though the name might imply so, this layer does not refer to the OSI network layer only, but may support a variety of modern networking access technologies such as switch ports or wireless, as well as virtual private networks (VPN) access or firewall access.
2. The integrity evaluation layer: the components in this layer are responsible for evaluating the overall integrity of the AR with respect to certain access policies.

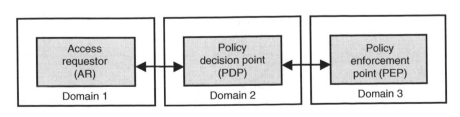

Fig. 1 Trusted network connect architecture.

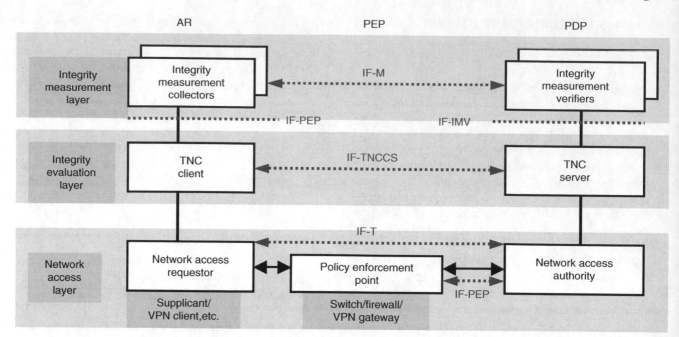

Fig. 2   Layered trusted network connect architecture.

3. The integrity measurement layer: this layer contains plug-in components that collect and verify integrity-related information for a variety of security applications on the AR.

The AR consists of the following components:

1. Integrity measurement collector (IMC): the IMC is a component of an AR that measures security aspects of the AR's integrity. Examples include the anti-virus parameters on the access requestor, personal firewall status, software versions, and others. The TNC Architecture accommodates implementation situations where multiple IMCs reside on a single AR, catering for corresponding different applications.
2. TNC client (TNCC): the TNCC is a component of an AR that aggregates integrity measurements from multiple IMCs and assists with the management of the integrity check handshake for the purpose of measurement and reporting of the AR integrity.
3. Network access requestor (NAR): the NAR is the component responsible for establishing network access. The NAR can be implemented as a software component that runs on an AR, negotiating its connection to a network. There may be several NARs on a single AR to handle connections to different types of networks. One example of a NAR is the supplicant in 802.lx, which is often implemented as software on a client system, or could also be VPN client software.

The policy decision point (PDP) consists of the following components:

1. Integrity measurement verifier (IMV): the IMV is a component that verifies a particular aspect of the AR's integrity, based on measurements received from IMCs and/or other data.
2. TNC server (TNCS): the TNCS is a component that manages the flow of messages between.
3. IMVs and IMCs: gathers IMV action recommendations from IMVs, and combines those recommendations (based on policy) into an overall TNCS action recommendation to the NAA.
4. Network access authority (NAA): the NAA is a component that decides whether an AR should be granted access. The NAA may consult a TNC server to determine whether the AR's integrity measurements comply with the NAA's security policy. In many cases, an NAA will be an AAA server such as a RADIUS server, but this is not required.

A third entity of the TNC architecture that sits in the middle of the AR and a PDP is the policy enforcement point (PEP) that consists of the following components:

- Policy enforcement point (PEP): The PEP is a typically the hardware component that controls access to a protected network. The PEP consults a PDP to determine whether this access should be granted. An example of the PEP is the authenticator in 802.lx, which is often implemented within the 802.11 wireless access point. It could also be an 802.lx-enabled switch port or a firewall as well as the VPN gateway.

Although not visibly evident within the TNC architecture, one important feature of the architecture is its extensibility

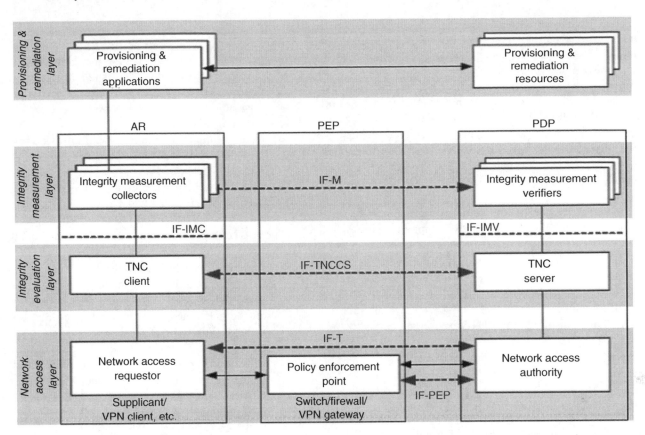

Fig. 3 TNC architecture with provisioning and remediation layer.

and support for the isolation and remediation of ARs, which do not succeed in obtaining network access permission due to failures in integrity verification. The TNC architecture with provisioning and remediation layer is illustrated in Fig. 3 and shows an additional layer addressing remediation and provisioning.

To understand the actions needed to remedy ARs that fail integrity verification, it is useful to view network connection requests in three basic phases from the perspective of integrity verification:

1. Assessment: in this phase, the IMVs perform the verification of the AR following the policies set by the network administrator and optionally deliver remediation instructions to the IMCs.
2. Isolation: if the AR has been authenticated and is recognized to be one that has some privileges on the network but has not passed the integrity verification by the IMV, the PDP may return instructions to the PEP to redirect the AR to an isolation environment where the AR can obtain integrity-related updates. Isolation environment mechanisms could be:

   a. VLAN containment: VLAN containment permits the AR to access the network in a limited

fashion, typically for the purpose of the limited access and to allow the AR to access online sources of remediation data (e.g., virus definition file updates, worm removal software, software patches).
   b. IP filters: In the case of IP filters, the PEP is configured with a set of filters which define network locations reachable by the isolated AR. Packets from the AR destined to other network locations are simply discarded by the PEP.

3. Remediation: Remediation is the process of the AR obtaining corrections to its current platform configuration and other policy-specific parameters to bring it inline with the PDP's requirements for network-access.

The remediation process requires remediation provisioning application and resources that can be implemented in several forms. An example would be the anti-virus application software that communicates with sources of anti-virus parameters (e.g., latest AV signature files) or could be an agent that updates the latest patches from the ftp server that contains the latest patches. Note that remediation is beyond the scope of the current TNC architecture document; it is treated briefly only for completeness.

Enclaves –
Enterprise

Although integrity measurement and reporting is core to the value proposition of the TNC philosophy and approach, the TNC architecture acknowledges other networking technologies as providing the infrastructure support surrounding the core elements of the TNC architecture. Note that the TNC specification is not standardizing specific protocol bindings for these technologies; it is rather defining only layer interfaces (as seen on the TNC architecture figure with an appendix IF-...) and is relying on already existing protocols, such as 802.1x, IPSec/IKE, PEAP, TLS for network access or RADIUS and DIAMETER for communication with and within PDP.

Although at this writing there is no commercially available nor widely deployed solution implementation based on TNC specification, TNC detailed architecture components description represent an open framework for vendor-neutral solutions where multiple vendors could provide individual modules of the complete end-node security solution. Several individual vendor or vendor alliances that have inspired the TNC specification work are described later.

NETWORK ADMISSION CONTROL

Network Admission Control Overview

Network admission control (NAC) architecture is an industry effort, led by Cisco Systems that initially started as an interoperable framework between a networking vendor and several anti-virus vendors with a goal to isolate the most urgent problem at the time: virus and worm infections from infected hosts at network connection points. NAC architecture achieves that by checking the end-node security compliancy before admitting it to connect to the network.

Security-policy compliance checks that NAC can perform include:

- Determining whether the device is running an authorized version of an operating system

- Checking to see if the OS has been properly patched, or has received the latest hotfix
- Determining if the device has anti-virus software installed, and whether it has the latest set of signature files
- Ensuring that anti-virus technology is enabled and has been recently run
- Determining if personal firewall, intrusion prevention, or other desktop security software is installed and properly configured
- Checking whether a corporate image of a device has been modified or tampered with

The NAC architecture components (illustrated in Fig. 4) are:

- Endpoint security software: NAC solution requires either a Cisco Trust Agent or a third party software agent that is capable of executing the integrity checks on the end node and communicating that during the network access request phase.
- Network access device: A network access device like a router, switch, VPN gateway, or firewall that can demand endpoint security "credentials" from the endpoint. This is in TNC terminology an analogy of a policy enforcement point.
- Policy/AAA server: This is a RADIUS server that evaluates endpoint security credentials relayed from the network access device and determines the appropriate access policy (permit, deny, quarantine, restrict) to be applied back to the network access device for the particular end node accessing the network.
- Anti-virus policy server: This is a third-party server that evaluates particular policy like anti-virus policy. As the NAC solution includes multiple vendors, third-party policy servers could be used to check the integrity of any application running on the end node system as well as hardware components compliancy. However, they need to interface with the policy/AAA server that is under control of Cisco Systems. Even though there is a plan to open and standardize it, this has not yet happened.

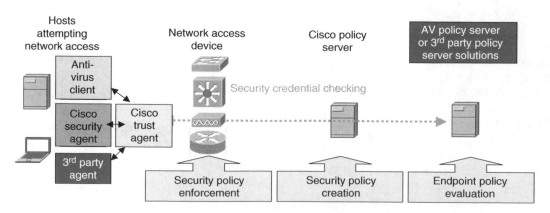

Fig. 4   Network admission control architecture components.

NAC Analysis

Even though the Endpoint Security Software of a NAC architecture uses standard communication protocols between the agent components and even though the interface software is provided free of charge by Cisco Systems, the exchange of "security credentials," as Cisco Systems refers to an end-node integrity state check, is still not standardized. Standards-based technologies that are used are EAP, 802.lx, and RADIUS. In some cases, these technologies may need to accommodate specific enhancements to support the NAC solution. Cisco Systems expects to drive adoption of these enhancements through appropriate standards bodies.

The Cisco trust agent (Endpoint Security Software) available from Cisco Systems collects security state information from the operating system and multiple security software clients, such as anti-virus and Cisco security agent software clients, and communicates this information to the connected network, where access control decisions are enforced. The Cisco trust agent that has the closest equivalent role of the TNCC in the TNC architecture has in the NAC architecture the following three main responsibilities:

- Network communications: respond to network requests for application and operating system information such as anti-virus and operating system patch details.
- Security model: authenticates the application or device requesting the host credentials and encrypts that information when it is communicated.
- Application broker: through an API, the application broker enables numerous applications to respond to state and credential requests.

The end-node protocol stack that is illustrated in Fig. 5 shows several layers of end-node agent security software.

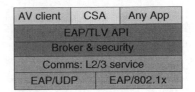

Fig. 5 NAC end-node protocol stack.

Cisco Systems decided to implement EAP over the user datagram protocol (UDP) protocol exchange first. EAP over UDP made the NAC solution immediately available to work on the layer 3. That helped nodes with an IP address that attempt to connect to the rest of the layer-3 network infrastructure to exchange EAP messages with the infrastructure and, based on the overall exchange, obtain access to the network resources. In essence, a router from Cisco Systems, as the very first implementation phase of NAC architecture solution, understands EAP over UDP control messages and performs EAP message exchanges with an Endpoint Security Software and policy server. Follow-up phases brought the EAP over layer 2 that allowed NAC communication to network devices, such as switches or wireless access points, where authentication and policy compliancy message exchanges could happen even before the IP address is obtained. NAC communication flow is illustrated in Fig. 6.

Policy enforcement actions are directly dependent on the communication method between the end-node software agent and the network node and were initially only permit, deny, or quarantine access via a simple layer-3 router access control list filter, while follow-up phases also introduced VLAN isolation.

Both layer-2 and layer-3 end nodes that demand network access, as well as network access devices themselves

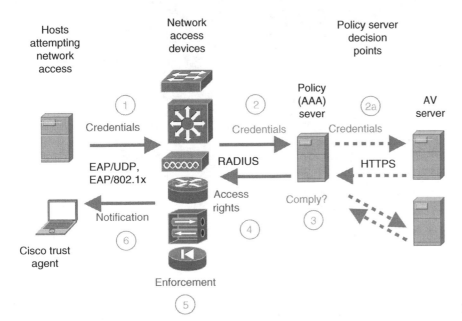

Fig. 6 NAC access control flow.

Enclaves – Enterprise

Enclaves – Enterprise

in the NAC solution, would need to be up to date with a compatible software release to be a valid member of the NAC solution. In the mean time, Cisco Systems also introduced the NAC appliances family of products, but its significance stays as one of the first integrity network access control implementers on the market. The NAC architecture brought an innovative breakthrough in the capability with which network access devices could police the state of the end node and make an intelligent decision before connecting it to the rest of the network. Consequently, Cisco Systems leveraged it as a crucial part of its self-defending network strategy.

NETWORK ACCESS PROTECTION

Network Access Protection Overview

The network-access protection (NAP) solution in Microsoft's next-generation Windows server with code name "Longhorn" provides policy enforcement components that help ensure that computers connecting to a network or communicating on a network meet administrator-defined requirements for system health. NAP uses a combination of policy validation and network isolation components to control network access or communication. It can also temporarily isolate computers that do not meet requirements to a restricted network. Depending on the configuration chosen, the restricted network might contain resources required to update the computers so that they then meet the health requirements for full network access or normal communication. When it will be available for deployment, NAP will be

able to create solutions for health policy validation, isolation, and ongoing health policy compliance.

NAP is currently defined with a core component of future Windows server and clients, a quarantine server that will be Microsoft Internet Authentication Services (IAS), and one or more policy servers. NAP will work by controlling network access via multiple connectivity mechanisms, as illustrated in Fig. 7.

In the initial release, NAP will require servers to run Windows Server "Longhorn" and clients to run Windows Vista, Windows Server "Longhorn," or Windows XP with Service Pack 2. Network isolation components in the NAP architecture will be provided for the following network technologies and connectivity methods:

* Dynamic host configuration protocol (DHCP)
* Virtual private networks (VPNs)
* 802.lx authenticated network connections
* Internet protocol security (IPSec) with x.509 certificates

DHCP quarantine consists of a DHCP quarantine enforcement server (QES) component and a DHCP quarantine enforcement client (QEC) component. Using DHCP quarantine, DHCP servers can enforce health policy requirements any time a computer attempts to lease or renew an IP version 4 (IPv4) address configuration on the network. DHCP quarantine is the easiest enforcement to deploy because all DHCP client computers must lease IP addresses. However, DHCP quarantine provides only weak network isolation.

VPN quarantine consists of a VPN QES component and a VPN QEC component. Using VPN quarantine, VPN

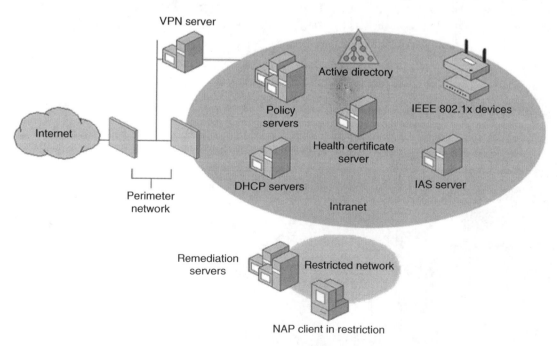

Fig. 7 Network access protection architecture.

Enclaves –
Enterprise

servers with the VPN QEC component could enforce health policy requirements any time a computer attempts to make a layer-2 tunneling protocol (L2TP) VPN connection to the network. VPN quarantine provides strong network isolation for all computers accessing the network through an L2TP VPN connection.

802.lx quarantine consists of an IAS server and an EAP host QEC component. Using 802.lx quarantine, an IAS server instructs an 802.lx access point (an ethernet switch or a wireless access point) to place a restricted access profile on the 802.lx client until it performs a set of remediation functions. A restricted access profile can consist of a set of IP packet filters or a virtual LAN identifier to confine the traffic of an 802.lx client. 802.lx quarantine provides strong network isolation for all computers accessing the network through an 802.lx connection.

IPSec quarantine comprises a health certificate server (HCS) and an IPSec QEC. The HCS issues x.509 certificates to quarantine clients when they are determined to be healthy. These certificates are then used to authenticate NAP clients when they initiate IPSec—secured communications with other NAP clients on an intranet. IPSec quarantine confines the communication on the network to those nodes that are considered healthy and because it is leveraging IPSec, it can define requirements for secure communications with healthy clients on a per-IP address or per-TCP/UDP port number basis. Unlike DHCP quarantine, VPN quarantine, and 802.lx quarantine, IPSec

quarantine confines communication to healthy clients after the clients have successfully connected and obtained a valid IP address configuration. IPSec quarantine is the strongest form of isolation in NAP architecture.

NAP quarantine methods could be used separately or together to isolate unhealthy computers and Microsoft IAS will act as a health policy server for all of these technologies as illustrated in Fig. 8.

There might be several system health agent (SHA) components that define a set of system health requirements such as SHA for anti-virus signatures, SHA for operating system updates, etc. A specific SHA might be matched to a remediation server. For example, an SHA for checking anti-virus signatures could be matched to the server that contains the latest anti-virus signature file. SHAs do not have to have a corresponding remediation server. For example, an SHA can just check local system settings to ensure that a host-based firewall is running or configured properly. To indicate the status of a specific element of system health, such as the state of the anti-virus software running on the computer or the last operating system update that was applied, SHAs create a statement of health (SoH) and pass their SoH to the quarantine agent (QA). Whenever an SHA updates its status, it creates a new SoH and passes it to the QA.

To draw a parallel with the TNC specification, QA can be seen as an equivalent role to TNC Client, whereas multiple SHAs are similar to IMVs and QECs playing the role of NARs, as will be described in more details.

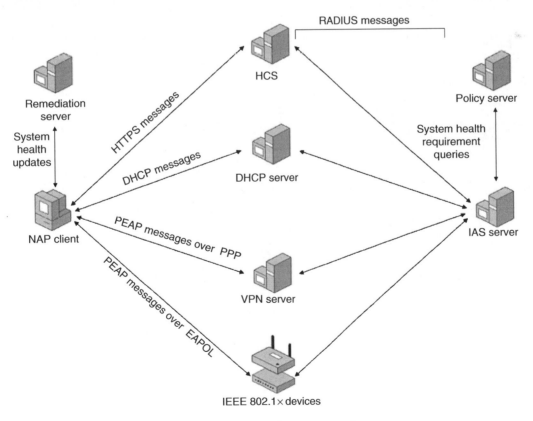

Fig. 8 Interaction between network access protection components.

Quarantine-enforcement clients

A quarantine-enforcement client (QEC) within a NAP client architecture is the one that requests, in some way, access to a network. During that phase, it will pass the end node's health status to a NAP server that is providing the network access, and indicate its status according to the information obtained from multiple SHAs, as illustrated in the NAP client architecture in Fig. 9.

The QECs for the NAP platform supplied in Windows Vista and Windows Server "Longhorn" will be the following:

- A DHCP QEC for DHCP-based IPv4 address configuration
- A VPN QEC for L2TP VPN based connections
- An EAP host QEC for 802.lx authenticated connections
- An IPSec QEC for x.509 certificate-based IPSec-based communications

DHCP QEC is a functionality in the DHCP client service that uses industry-standard DHCP messages to exchange system health messages and restricted network access information. The DHCP QEC obtains the list of SoHs from the QA. The DHCP client service fragments the list of SoHs, if required, and puts each fragment into a Microsoft vendor-specific DHCP option that is sent in DHCPDiscover, DHCPRequest or DHCPInform messages. DHCPDecline and DHCPRelease messages do not contain the list of SoHs.

VPN QEC is a functionality in the Microsoft Remote Access Connection Manager service that obtains the list of SoHs from the QA and sends the list of SoHs as a PEAP-type-length-value (TLV) message. Alternately, the VPN QEC can send a health certificate as a PEAP–TLV message.

EAP host QEC is a component that obtains the list of SoHs from the QA and sends the list of SoHs as a PEAP–TLV message for 802.lx connections. Alternately, the EAP host QEC can send a health certificate in a PEAP–TLV message.

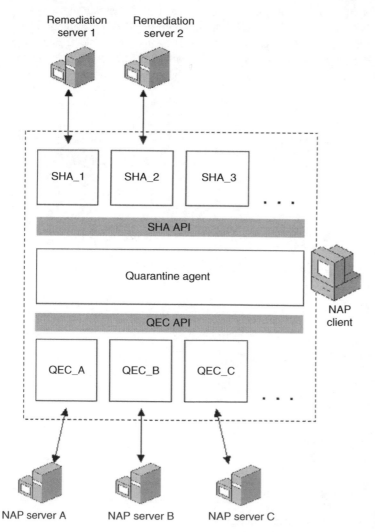

Fig. 9 NAP client architecture.

IPSec QEC is a component that obtains a health certificate from the HCS and interacts with the following:

- The certificate store to store the current health certificate
- The IPSec components of the TCP/IP protocol stack to ensure that IPSec-based communications use the current health certificate for IPSec authentication
- The host-based firewall (such as, Windows personal firewall) so that the IPSec-secured traffic is allowed by the firewall

Analysis of a NAP

Microsoft, with its proven track record of showing how complex things could be simplified to a level where they could be easily and widely deployed, certainly has a significant role in end-node integrity and policy-compliancy solution evolution. When it becomes available, NAP seems to be the lowest-cost solution that, for the client side, will require only Windows XP Service Pack 2. Considering the current Microsoft release policies, the server side of the NAP solution will most probably be offered as a free server component with next-generation server software. This means that the NAP solution could come after a regular Windows server update at no additional cost. It is also noteworthy that the NAP solution will not require any proprietary or new hardware because its strengths are all in software development and, in particular, in vendor-specific protocol extensions, such as with DHCP.

Sygate® Network Access Control

Sygate® network access control overview

Sygate is a vendor that developed its own end-node-to-network-infrastructure interactivity solution with the name *Sygate Network Access Control* (SNAC). In the mean time, Sygate has been acquired by Symantec, who initially kept the current Sygate solutions under the Sygate brand while expecting to re-brand the next version of the products and include additional functionality. However, this solution description will be narrowed only to an initial SNAC concept that allowed enforcement of end-node security in four ways:

1. Create SNAC policies: Using the Sygate Policy Manager for central managed and deployed network access control policies that include: templates for well-known anti-virus software, personal firewalls, anti-spyware, operating system configurations, and security patches.

2. Discover end-node integrity status: Sygate enforcers and agents discover new devices as they connect to the network and then perform baseline end-node integrity checks when they start up, at a configurable interval, and when they change network locations.
3. Enforce network access controls: At the time of network connection and for the duration of the network session, Sygate enforcers apply network access controls to endpoints attempting to connect to the enterprise network. If end nodes are in compliance with the policy, they are permitted on the network. If the end node is noncompliant, then it is either quarantined to a remediation network or blocked from network access.
4. Remediate non-compliant devices: When an end node fails one or more integrity checks, the agent will automatically perform a preconfigured operation to bring the end node into compliance without user intervention. Administrators can customize the user interaction that occurs during the remediation process and even give the user the option to delay non-critical remediation actions for a range of time. Once remediated, the agent will automatically start the SNAC process again and, because the end node is now in compliance, will obtain access to the corporate network.

The SNAC solution performs periodic host integrity checks when an end node starts up, at a configurable interval, and when it changes network locations, to discover its security state through the Sygate Enforcement Agent (SEA). That could be seen as the analogy of the AR in the TNC specification. Components of the SNAC solution are illustrated in Fig. 10.

Sygate also enhanced SNAC to a universal NAC system that combines SNAC with a solution for securing unmanaged devices, with several different enforcement mechanisms to extend SNAC protection to every type of network access (VPN, wireless, routers, DHCP, etc.), and on all endpoints, including laptops, desktops, servers, guest systems, and embedded devices.

The Sygate Universal NAC System's enforcement methods include:

1. Self-enforcement when computers leave the network
2. API-based integration with dialers and VPNs
3. Gateway enforcement for in-line enforcement on any network
4. On-demand agents for guests accessing the network
5. DHCP-based approach for LAN and wireless over any infrastructure
6. 802.Ix standards-based approach for LAN and wireless networks
7. Cisco NAC technology for Cisco routers

Enclaves – Enterprise

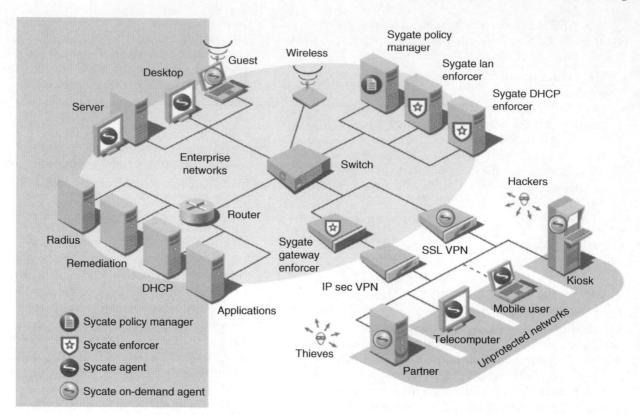

Fig. 10 SNAC solution overview.

SNAC analysis

The SNAC solution places great emphasis on the client agent software as the vital component of the solution. Even though Sygate is a member of Cisco Systems NAC initiative, it also has its own SNAC appliance, as well as backend policy servers that, as already mentioned, will most probably become part of the enhanced Symantec product portfolio. For an 802.1x access method, SNAC relies, like many other solutions, on third-party 802.1x clients, such as Funk Software (which has recently been acquired by Juniper Networks), Odyssey client, or Meetinghouse Aegis client. This, on top of the additional inline gateway device, represents extra costs in the overall SNAC solution deployment.

Automated Quarantine Engine

Automated quarantine engine overview

Alcatel was one of the first vendors to develop a solution that is complementary to those previously described. The main difference is that it does not require any agent-based software on the end-node device to be able to detect, block, or isolate the infected end node. Alcatel has devised a way to implement the concepts of automated end-node isolation by allowing an intrusion detector to pass information to their OmniVista central network management system.

OmniVista then works with an integrated automated quarantine engine (AQE) module to apply policies and place the infected system into a penalty VLAN where it can no longer infect the rest of the network. The AQE solution is illustrated in Fig. 11.

Based on the input from a detection sensor such as an intrusion detection/protection system (IDS/IPS) sensor and the Alcatel's home-grown layer-2 media access control (MAC) address trace-back mechanism, the AQE solution is capable of dynamically reconfiguring the access switch to allow or limit access of the particular end node to the rest of the network. This is accomplished via SNMPv3 commands communicated to a switch infrastructure to shut down the port or apply additional filtering mechanisms: either VLAN configuration or a simple access-list filter for the particular node accessing the network.

The important part of the AQE is that it transparently and dynamically applies policies to an individual switched port based on the device behavior accessing the port. The automatic reconfiguration reduces the response time to security threats and removes the need to have a network engineer create and apply an isolation policy (VLAN, ACL) to manage network access. This minimizes the need for manual configuration and application of network user policies. After the infected system is isolated, the network administrator is notified and given choices on how to handle the infected system.

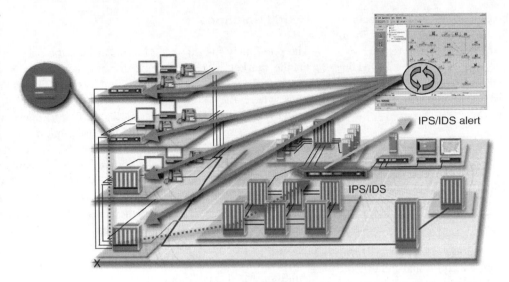

Fig. 11 Automated quarantine engine from Alcatel.

AQE analysis

The AQE solution is unique in the way that it works with IDS/IPS as an alerting mechanism to trigger the blocking, isolation, or protection configuration changes on the access switches' port level. Being an agentless solution makes it a quite powerful and complementary option to all other agent-based proposals on the market. As such, it is a very interesting alternative where end-node software is not possible or difficult to install due to legacy or not-supported end-node software. Alcatel also claims that from a switch network infrastructure viewpoint, their solution is fully interoperable with other vendor switches, which makes it an attractive and open solution for modern end-node access management. A missing part in the AQE solution is that is has only automated isolation, blocking, and quarantine parts, whereas end-node notification or remedy with a return of a cured node must be performed manually by the system operator.

TippingPoint™ Quarantine Protection

TippingPoint™ quarantine protection overview

Similar to the AQE solution, TippingPoint, now a division of 3Com, came out with an agentless solution based on their home-grown Intrusion Protection Systems (IPS). TippingPoint Quarantine Protection (TPQ) uses a network-based IPS mechanism to detect and stop the viral infection coming from the network attached infected end node. As an inline device to a traffic flow, IPS could stop the viral infection detected on the traffic flow coming from an infected end node and, if combined with a network infrastructure, could apply a blocking function based on the switch port, MAC address, or IP address on the edge switch or router. The quarantine function could be implemented via VLAN isolation and, being an inline-based solution, TPQ provides a possible remedy by performing an HTTP URL redirection. The TPQ solution is illustrated in Fig. 12.

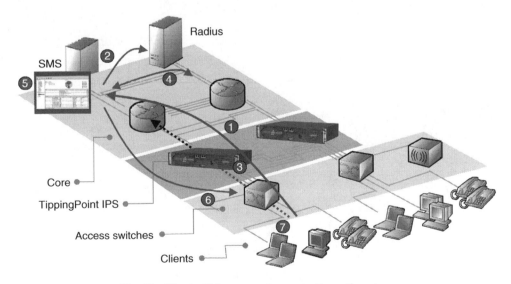

Fig. 12 TippingPoint quarantine protection action steps.

The flow of action goes through an end node connecting to a network and authenticating via the TippingPoint Security Management System (SMS) and RADIUS server, while the IPS engine detects the intrusion activity. Based on the configured policy action, SMS resolves the IP address to a MAC address and could instruct the blacklisting or policing of the access on the ingress access device.

TQP analysis

Technologically speaking, the IPS-based quarantine system is an in-line solution and, as such, avoids an end-node software installation issue. That makes TQP easier to scale for a large number of end nodes. Additionally, TPQ, like Alcatel AQE, is an end-node-operating-system-independent solution that gives an additional benefit of protecting non-user-based end nodes, such as printers, faxes, or IP phones. The biggest concern with both mentioned IPS-based solutions—TQP as well as AQE—is that the end node that is infecting the infrastructure could also infect the other nearby end nodes residing on the same segment before it could be blocked or isolated from the network. A solution to that issue is, however, also possible and is actually existing in the infrastructure functionality itself in the form of so-called private virtual local area networks (PVLANs). Operation of the PVLAN is illustrated in Fig. 13.

Even though not standardized, PVLAN functionality that exists in almost any switch vendor product is, if the application traffic flow permits, a very efficient mechanism to force the traffic from the network edge or access layer devices through the IPS systems. IPSs, which are typically hierarchically aggregated at a network distribution layer, then prevent the end nodes from infecting each other by isolating them before they access the rest of the network resources.

Hybrid Solutions

The previously mentioned solutions are not the only ones on the market. For instance, Enterasys has created both agent- and network-based Trusted End System (TES) solutions where they combine their switches with a policy server and end node agents from Check Point/Zone Labs or Sygate. Enterasys also provides the option to use vulnerability-patch assessment tools from Nessus to perform the end-node scan checks upon the network connections and then provide similar functions as NAC, NAP, or TNC. Foundry and Extreme also offer network-admission solutions with Sygate's client, whereas Vernier Networks, a startup originally focused on wireless security, recently announced its EdgeWall security appliances that also performs NAC. Intel, HP, and Nortel also announced their solutions for the end-node and network access management protection that are very similar or aligned with previously mentioned ones. This shows that the industry players are seriously considering solving the problem of the end-node-to-network-infrastructure interaction. At the same time, unfortunately, it also shows the panacea of solutions that are still mostly isolated from each other. This makes any strategic decision for information security practitioners that are dealing with virus infections a difficult one.

END-NODE SECURITY SOLUTIONS COMPARISON

Information security practitioners are already facing or will face in the near future a decision of which solution to use or deploy. Hence, comparison tables of currently available offers might help in comparing them to each other as well as provide a clear picture of the offered

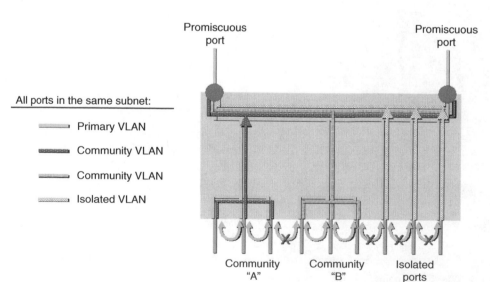

Fig. 13 Private VLAN (PVLAN) operation.

Table 1 End-node security solutions comparison.

	Features			
Solution	**Requires dedicated HW**	**Isolation**	**Access media supported**	**Remedy**
TNC	No	VLAN/ACL	Open	Out of Scope
NAC	Yes/No[a]	VLAN/ACL	802.1x, 802.1x/UDP, IPSec VPN	Third party
NAP	No	Subnet, VLAN, ACL	802.1x, L2TP VPN, IPSec VPN, DHCP	Third party
SNAC	Yes	VLAN, ACL	802.1x, 802.1x/UDP, L2TP VPN, IPSec VPN, DHCP	Yes
AQE	No[b]	Port block, MAC filter, VLAN, ACL	IP	Third party
TQP	No[b]	Port block, MAC filter, VLAN, ACL	IP	URL redirection to Third party
TES	Yes	Port block, MAC filter, VLAN, ACL	802.1x, IP	Yes

[a] NAC requires Cisco router or switch infrastructure; Cisco also released dedicated NAC appliance.
[b] No dedicated infrastructure HW needed, while both TQP and AQE require dedicated IDS/IPS fro malware activity detection.

features and functionalities. Such comparisons are provided in Table 1 and Table 2.

FUTURE DIRECTIONS

Although current proposals offer promising outcomes, looking a bit forward shows that there are still several open issues. Some of these issues are discussed here in no particular order of importance.

- Policy-server protocols are not standardized; they are closed into vendor-to-vendor API and the same goes for the remedy solutions that are out of the scope of the TNC specification.
- 802.1x protocol usage deployment is still very low.
- DHCP extensions are vendor-specific. This makes having a DHCP client and server from the same vendor a requirement. This leads to a locking

solution with a single vendor instead of an interoperable scalable solution where different components of the solution could be provided by different vendors.

- EAP methods used are still under development. PEAP, even though in the stable IETF draft at the point in time of writing this entry, is still not standardized. Hence, its implementations are not always interoperable, whereas new methods such as EAP FAST are already on the horizon.
- All layer-3 solutions are only IPv4-based and have no solution for the problem of forthcoming new protocols such as IPv6. Clients other than those that are Microsoft OS-based, such as mobile phones, pda's, or legacy OS systems are not covered in most agent-based solutions.
- Most solutions thus far are not focusing on the malicious user, but rather on the accidental problem. Although this might be sufficient for a beginning,

Table 2 End-node security solutions comparison.

	Features			
Solution	**Requires end node software**	**End node OS supported**	**Requires SW/HW upgrade**	**PVLAN recommended**
TNC	Yes	Open specification	Once implemented—Yes	No
NAC	Yes	Microsoft, Redhat	Yes	No
NAP	No[a]	Microsoft only	Yes	No
SNAC	Yes	Microsoft only	Yes	No
AQE	No	Any	No	Yes[b]
TQP	No	Any	No	Yes[b]
TES	Yes/No[c]	Microsoft/Any[c]	Yes/No[c]	No

[a] Bundled with Microsoft OS.
[b] PVLAN usage is not required, however is strongly recommended.
[c] Entersays TES has agent-based and network-based options.

follow-up developments for stopping malicious attacks either need to be specified or will again be driven into different proprietary extensions.

All of above are important points to be solved while the main issue going forward will be convincing the major players to commit to the development of interoperable, modular solutions, such as defined in the TNC specification. This is obviously not expected to happen overnight for obvious reasons: the once-lucrative network infrastructure business is now in danger of becoming a commodity, which encourages closed solutions and differentiations among vendors.

SUMMARY

Will an automated end-node protection mechanism be an ultimate solution for all sizes? Most probably not, but it will certainly add an additional level in the layered security architecture approach that information security practitioners could effectively use to mitigate security problems. However, every network admission solution today is proprietary, and puts information security practitioners into a trap of a single-vendor solution. The TNC specification gives hope to interoperability, but de facto standards will likely be driven by the major players in the networking infrastructure and desktop software market. In essence, it is important to understand that end-node control methods that were discussed in this entry are, by design, performing end-node integrity and policy-compliance checking and, with that, increasing the security level of the rest of the network. Information security practitioners should also be aware of what different options can and cannot be achieved. They should also be able to distinguish their potential benefits as well as be aware of their disadvantages and limitations.

A key dilemma remains: end node with agent, or agentless deployment. Although agent-based solutions promise resolution to all issues, they also get stacked with scalability and deployment. On the other hand, agentless solutions make an intermediate and fast cure for urgent problems; however, they do not necessarily automate and solve all necessary components. It is also important to look into future development and acceptance of 802.1x-based solutions vs. DHCP-extended solutions. In the 802.1x case, solutions are on solid ground with a standard-based access-control protocol. Even though well-defined for the authentication part, 802.1x still struggles with a variety of different EAP methods and hence is, with the possible exception of the wireless world, facing an issue of wider acceptance together with a scalability of deployment.

DHCP, as a protocol, has no built-in authentication; however, DHCP vendor extensions might fulfill the promise of easy and scalable deployment due to its simplicity and possibly faster and wider acceptance. Currently, there is no final conclusion of where to go, so the problem remains on the shoulders of information security practitioners to closely watch and follow the developments and outcomes, while where needed, armed with knowledge from this entry, deploy the solutions that fit their immediate business demands.

BIBLIOGRAPHY

1. AEQ. *Automated Quarantine Engine*, http://www.alcatel. com/enterprise/en/resources_library/pdf/wp/wp_enterprise_ security.pdf.
2. A Mirage Industry Report. *Getting the Knock of NAC: Understanding Network Access Control*, http://www. miragenetworks.com/products/white_papers.asp (accessed January 2006).
3. Cisco NAC vs Microsoft NAP, by Andrew Conry-Murray, 03/01/2005, IT Architect, http://www.itarchitect.com/ shared/article/showArticle.jhtml?articleId=60401143.
4. Durham, D.; Nagabhushan, G.; Sahita, R.; Savagaonka, U. *A Tamper-Resistant, Platform-Based, Bilateral Approach to Worm Containment.* , Ed.; Technology@Intel Magazine.
5. Enterasys Trusted End-System Solution, http://www. enterasys.com/solutions/secure-networks/trusted_end_system.
6. Introduction to Network Access Protection, Whitepaper, Microsoft Corporation, June 2004, Updated on July 2005.
7. Bryant, J. *Weblog: Network Access Protection (NAP) Architecture*, http://www.msmvps.com/secure/archive/2005/ 04/26/44630.aspx (accessed April 2005).
8. Network Access Protection Platform Architecture, Whitepaper, Microsoft Corporation, June 2004, Updated on July 2005.
9. NAC, Network Admission Control, http://www.cisco.com/ go/nac.
10. Grimes, Roger A. NAC vs NAP, Infoworld, http://www. infoworld.com/article/05/09/05/36FEbattlesecurity_1.html (accessed September 2005).
11. NAP, *Network Access Protection*, http://www.microsoft. com/technet/itsolutions/network/nap/default.mspx.
12. Nortel SNA, http://www2.nortel.com/go/solution_content. jsp?prod_id=55121.
13. SNAC, *Sygate Network Admission Control*, http://www.sygate. com/news/universal-network-access-control-snac_rls.htm.
14. TCG, *Trusted Computing Group*, http://www.trusted computinggroup.org/home.
15. TNC, *Trusted Network Connect*, http://www.trusted computinggroup.org/downloads/TNC.
16. Trusted Network Connect. *Can it connect?* Ellen Messmer, NetworkWorld.com, http://www.networkworld.com/weblogs/ security/008721.html (accessed May 2005).

Enterprise Information Assurance: Framework

Bonnie A. Goins Pilewski, MSIS, CISSP, NSA IAM, ISS
Senior Security Strategist, Isthmus Group, Inc., Aurora, Illinois, U.S.A.

Abstract

This entry focuses on enterprise assurance and the framework involved. In the entry, the author defines key terms and explains what level of confidence should be reached for enterprise assurance within a company. A framework is then described, which includes assurance components, assurance needs, claims, evidence, and the assumption zone. The author addresses each of these issues individually and then addresses the full picture. The author advises that every part of the enterprise must be examined before a judgment can be made about the state of security.

INTRODUCTION

Your company has made a commitment to security. It's good for your business, your customers, your staff, your data, and your systems. Senior management is fully on board; you have a budget and are encouraged to spend it. You have spent long days (and some nights) ensuring that your documentation is completed, your patches and configurations are up to date, and you have staff in sufficient number, with sufficient skill sets, to assist you in the effort. Ah, life is good. But, wait (there is always a catch)! Senior management and the Board want you to answer a question (your heart is pounding . . .): "How confident are you that our security needs have been met? Or, more simply put, how sure are you that everything you've done makes us secure? Can we have some assurance?" Gulp . . .

WHAT EXACTLY DOES "ASSURANCE" MEAN?

According to the Merriam–Webster dictionary, *assurance* is "something that inspires, or tends to inspire, confidence." In fact, *confidence* is given as a synonym for the word *assurance*. Merriam–Webster defines the word *confidence* as "the quality or state of being certain (i.e., certitude)." Okay, so now you have some idea of what the Board and senior management are asking. The question is, how does that relate to security? Douglas Landoll and Jeffrey Williams stated in their work, *An Enterprise Assurance Framework*,[1] that "there are many definitions of assurance used in security; however, the central theme in these definitions is that assurance is the degree of confidence that security needs are satisfied." To prove the point made earlier, the National Institute of Standards and Technology (NIST) has defined *assurance* as "grounds for confidence that a system design meets its requirements, or that its implementation satisfies specifications, or that some specific property is satisfied."

HOW MUCH "CONFIDENCE" IS ENOUGH?

Regardless of the rigor used in applying security to an environment, it is not possible to secure an environment completely. Restated, threats, and therefore risks, will always exist in an environment. That said, the people operating within that environment must come to understand that there will *always* be some doubt, and that some flaw or risk will *always* exist in the environment. This notion is sometimes a hard sell to senior management, due mainly to the fact that many of the security activities practiced within an environment are intangible, while the financial implications of implementing security are not.

A reasonable answer to this question of confidence aligns with the concept of risk. It is important for the security practitioner in the environment to determine, as quickly as possible, what tolerance for risk senior management demonstrates. Practitioners can assist themselves by educating senior management early that complete elimination of risk is not possible nor is complete elimination of doubt about the state of security within the environment. Talking candidly with the management chain can help practitioners determine what their level of "reasonable doubt" may be.

When this exercise is completed, you can begin the arduous task of translating this information into criteria to be evaluated as part of the determination of "how much assurance is enough?" You many consider the value of critical business functions, the current state of security and technology within the organization, the cost associated with proper controls, the value of your data, technical and physical assets, and costs associated with an appropriate level of security surrounding each of them.

Encyclopedia of Information Assurance DOI: 10.1081/E-EIA-120046771
Copyright © 2011 by Taylor & Francis. All rights reserved.

GIVING "CONFIDENCE" A FORM

It would seem that at least there is a place to start, but how do you inspire confidence in your enterprise solution? The first step is to recognize that assurance must, as a matter of course, take into account multiple factors within the organization. Is security only provided for information systems or network infrastructure? I would hope not, because, if so, the most serious threat to a secure environment has been neglected—the people within the organization. Also, don't most organizations provide security for their facilities? Before the advent of network intrusion detection, we had closed-circuit televisions and guard stations. Before we were duped by Trojans, worms, viruses, and logic bombs, we had mantraps, PINed, or proximity locks and electronic security methods. Physical security has been present for a very long time. The author is not aware of an organization (other than perhaps a virtual one or one so isolated that only the very strong can reach them) that does not employ physical security measures. So, facilities must also be considered. Assurance can be considered to be a global effort; that is, people, processes, technology, and facilities must all be addressed. In Landoll and Williams' work, they include the following areas for review: people, procedures, environment, and automated information systems (AISs).

AN ASSURANCE FRAMEWORK FOR THE ENTERPRISE

In *An Enterprise Assurance Framework*, Landoll and Williams[1] introduce a framework for assurance that is designed to be an aid to organizations looking to cut through the complexity of their enterprise security architectures and to produce a clean, clear framework that can answer the assurance questions asked previously in this entry.

Assurance Components

The authors point out five components that work together to structure what they call an *assurance argument*. As defined in their paper, an assurance argument is "a way of presenting evidence in a clear and convincing manner." Essentially, an assurance argument is a sensible representation of information and analysis (i.e., evidence) that is used to determine whether the organization's assurance expectations are met.

To see how this works we will use our original categories of people, process, facilities, and technology. To put them together in Landoll and Williams' framework, we will place facilities into the "environment" category and technology into "AIS." AIS can be broken down into deliverables (products); the organization's infrastructure, ranging from the network to end-user platforms; configurations for the architecture; development personnel; and the processes for each, as well as the development

environment itself. In constructing the AIS assurance argument, all of these aspects must be considered.

According to Landoll and Williams, the five elements that an organization can use to structure its assurance arguments are 1) assurance need, 2) claims, 3) evidence, 4) reasoning, and 5) an assumption zone. *Assurance need* represents the organization's confidence expectation. *Claims* represent statements that something has a particular property. *Evidence* is observable data that is used within the organization to make judgments or decisions. *Reasoning* represents statements that tie evidence together to establish a claim. The *assumption zone* represents the point at which claims made by the organization can no longer be supported by evidence.

Assurance needs

Assurance needs extend throughout the organization and are the expression of confidence in all the parts of the enterprise. These needs should be detailed enough to represent all of the things that the organization is concerned about (the breadth of the need). Activities that help focus an organization's concerns include business impact assessment (i.e., determination of assets), determination of business goals as aligned with the organization's strategic goals (its vision and mission), and risk, vulnerability, and security assessments of the organization's people, processes, data, facilities, and technology using both technical (tool-based) and non-technical (frameworks such as NIST SP 800:30) (risk) analyses, the National Security Agency Information Assurance Methodology, ISO 17799/BS7799, and the OCTAVE framework (security) means, in order to determine threats, vulnerabilities, and countermeasures. According to Landoll and Williams, assurance needs are typically characterized in an environment as policies. The assurance need also must reflect the level of confidence that the organization maintains in a particular countermeasure, as it relates to the ability of the countermeasure to protect against threat (the depth of the need). To determine the appropriate depth, the organization must prioritize its risks and establish what level of validation will be required to measure the success of the countermeasure.

Claims

To properly analyze assurance, we must look to appropriate security properties. Examples of security properties, as provided in *An Enterprise Assurance Framework*, include:

- Properties that are capable of being validated, such as structure, complexity, and modularity. This is the property of being *analyzable*. An example could include a software package (i.e., complexity, modularity).
- Properties possessing desired or required skills. This is the property of being *capable*. An example could include a sufficiently skilled human resource within the enterprise.

- Properties that are without defect, based on a particular higher level specification. This is the property of being *correct*. An example could include validated data input.
- Properties that can be utilized, implemented, managed, and maintained easily. This is the property of being *easy to use*. An example could include an appropriately designed human interface for intrusion detection or other security tools.
- Properties that create a minimum of waste. This is the property of being *efficient*. An example could include a streamlined process within the enterprise.
- Properties that demonstrate a task or activity that has been repeated. This is the property of being *experienced*. An example could include a highly experienced, long-term human resource within the enterprise.
- Properties that possess essential information. This is the property of being *knowledgeable*. See the example for the experienced property.
- Properties that can be reproduced. This is the *repeatable* property. An example of this could include an appropriate calculation, conducted millions of times, by an AIS.
- Properties that can be defended, that are difficult to break or are resistant to attacks. This is the property of being *strong*. An example of this could include a properly secured enterprise architecture.
- Properties of confidence that promote the character (truth) of a person. This is the *trustworthy* property. An example could include an ethical professional or a lifelong friend.

Evidence

Evidence can be defined as anything that can assist in validating a claim. Examples of evidence include deliverables or documentation, assessment reports (such as risk or vulnerability assessments, SAS 70s), corroborated interviews, and so on. Evidence can be aggregated if doing so makes its digestion easier (as long as the aggregation can still be validated). Evidence, like claims, has properties, including *correctness*, *analyzability*, and *completeness*. In fact, as Landoll and Williams point out, claims about evidence can be supported by collection and presentation of additional evidence. This evidence is called *circumstantial* and can contribute to the believability of a claim, even though it is not directly related to other evidence for the claim. It is important to note that the relationship between claims and evidence is not one to one. A single piece of evidence may have many properties and support many claims. A good example of this is an assessment or audit deliverable, such as a SAS 70, risk assessment, or vulnerability analysis. A large amount of evidence does not necessarily validate claims. In order to do so, the evidence must be compelling. This is also true of complex systems or environments, where many pieces of evidence must be placed together to create a

validation of the entire system or environment. This is fourth category of assurance, known as *reasoning*.

Assumption zone

Remember what was stated earlier in this entry—that there is no such thing as perfect security? Remember also that a discussion ensued that stated that senior management could report the point at which they felt comfortable they could accept this "doubt." The "Assumption Zone" is that threshold where the assurance claims are presented, with evidence minimal or absent, with the outcome being that the claims are still accepted by the organization. Examples include elements that do not have direct or significant impact on the security of the organization. This could include documentation surrounding non-critical functions or personnel.

ENTERPRISE ASSURANCE THROUGH SECURITY PRACTITIONER'S EYES

Now that we have reviewed the assurance components, we must now translate them into security terms. Imagine that we represent a healthcare provider that has determined it has the following security needs:

- Critical business functions must be available 24/7, 365 days per year.
- Electronic protected health information (ePHI) must carry the maximum protection to achieve compliance and prevent unauthorized disclosure.
- Data assets must be catalogued and reviewed periodically to ensure data integrity.
- All compliance objectives within the Health Insurance Portability and Accountability Act (HIPAA) security rule must be met with at least the minimum necessary protection.

As stated, these security needs could be detailed in a corporate or compliance security policy, along with the requisite procedures. It is important that these deliverables also include measurable expectations (i.e., depth).

According to Landoll and Williams, the properties most relevant to security include analyzability, correctness, completeness, and strength. These four properties translate to the enterprise as follows:

- The property of *analyzability* indicates that complexity is properly managed within the enterprise.
- The property of *correctness* indicates that all functions within the enterprise perform correctly as advertised.
- The property of *completeness* attests to the enterprise completing its due diligence by identifying all known threats (i.e., those that can be found) and ensuring that policies and procedures are created, implemented,

maintained, monitored, and enforced for the expressed purpose of mitigating, transferring, or accepting risk.

- The property of *strength* indicates the enterprise's ability to stave off, or minimize the impact from, an attack.

Now, it is essential for the enterprise to gather and present its evidence to support its assurance claims. Evidence that applies to the entire enterprise is preferred to evidence that relates only to a subset of the enterprise. Appropriate evidence can include the following:

- Information security documentation, such as a corporate security program, business continuity plan, security incident response plan, or corporate security policies and procedures
- Corporate strategic documentation, such as the business plan or information technology or security strategy documents
- Risk, vulnerability, or security assessments
- Audits
- Interview results
- Satisfaction surveys
- Metrics (such as service levels)
- Contractual agreements

In our example of the healthcare provider, collected evidence could include:

- Business associate agreements
- Information about service levels, both internal and external
- Mandatory HIPAA risk assessment (with appropriate findings generalized to the entire organization)
- Vulnerability scanning results
- Penetration testing results
- Patching and configuration management plans
- Security incident response plan, including the tracking of occurrences and their reporting
- Business continuity plan
- HIPAA policies and procedures, utilized throughout the organization
- Staff security awareness training results
- Compliance walkthroughs
- Internal audits

The provision of supporting, or *circumstantial*, evidence can also support assurance claims made by the organization. Such claims can include the property of trustworthiness or effectiveness. For example, trustworthy and effective people may have a lesser chance of creating security issues for the enterprise. Processes that include intrusion detection, access control activities, logging and monitoring, appropriate media handling, protection against malware, and others augment enterprise protection, lessening the exposure of the environment to vulnerability, particularly if the processes are easy to use and correct. Strong

environments can protect the enterprise from many vulnerabilities, including unauthorized access, terrorism, or a catastrophic event that threatens business continuance, such as a weather emergency. The strong environments do so through appropriately designed facilities (blueprints), physical access controls, and biometric devices, among others. Analyzable, complete, correct, strong, and easy-to-use systems can reduce inadvertent errors that introduce risk or can thwart an attack from a malicious outsider.

When the enterprise has collated its evidence, the hard work begins of evaluating whether the security mechanisms in place meet the stated enterprise assurance needs. To perform this reasoning, claims, evidence, and supporting (circumstantial) evidence are tied together and linked to the appropriate assurance argument. This process should be repeated for all identified assurance needs.

To revisit the question of "How much is enough?" we will now apply it to the evidence we have gathered. No security analog for rating the amount of evidence collected exists, but a legal analog does. This analog was used by Landoll and Williams in the construction of their enterprise framework. These standards include:

- *Evidence beyond a reasonable doubt*—In this standard, evidence cannot be rejected by a reasonable person.
- *Clear and convincing evidence*—In this standard, evidence is presented that a reasonable person could believe.
- *Preponderance of evidence*—In this standard, more evidence exists for than against.
- *Substantial evidence*—In this standard, a significant amount of evidence exists and is available for review.

It is apparent that the issue with these standards is that no terms have been defined, so it leaves them open to interpretation; that is, what is reasonable and what is significant? As metrics in the area of assurance mature, it is likely that more quantifiable standards will be introduced.

CONCLUSION

It takes a great deal of effort and diligence for an organization to come to an assurance judgment. Inspecting security implementations in a vacuum, piece by piece, will not guarantee that an enterprise is appropriately secured. Every part of the enterprise must be examined before a judgment can be made about the state of security. After proper evaluation and measurement, and with a little luck, you can go back to the senior management and the Board and emphatically state, "I am confident that we are on the right track!"

REFERENCE

1. Landoll, D.J.; Williams, J.R. *An Enterprise Assurance Framework*; Arca Systems: Vienna, VA, 1998.

BIBLIOGRAPHY

1. Carnegie Mellon University, Software Engineering Institute, *SSE-CMM*, http://www.sei.cmu.edu/publications.

2. Ferraiolo, K.; Gallagher, L.; Thompson, V. *Building a Case for Assurance from Process*; Arca Systems: Vienna, VA, 1998.
3. Landoll, D.J.; Williams, J.R. *A Framework for Reasoning About Assurance*. National Institute of Standards and Technology: Washington, D.C., 1995, http://www.nist.gov.
4. National Security Agency Information Assurance Methodology (NSA IAM), http://www.nsa.gov.
5. Perrone, P. J. *Practical Enterprise Assurance*; Assured Technologies: Crozet, VA, 2000.
6. Zehetner, A. *Creating Enterprise Assurance*; Electronic Warfare Associates: Mawson Lakes, South Australia, 2003.

Enclaves –
Enterprise

Enterprise Information Assurance: Key Components

Duane E. Sharp
President, SharpTech Associates, Mississauga, Ontario, Canada

Abstract

The major stages of an information technology (IT) security implementation—audit, requirements analysis, framework construction, project planning, and implementation—have been described in this entry, with a focus on some of the approaches that can be used to implement a security framework, as well as some of the key issues to consider.

The value of information to an organization cannot be overemphasized, particularly in today's knowledge-based economy. Information is probably *the* most valuable single asset of many organizations.

Corporate data assets are more distributed than in the past, both from a management and geographic location perspective. As well, the number of internal users requiring access to corporate data has increased and the traditionally solid information technology (IT) perimeter has become much more easily accessed.

One objective of IT management is to provide high-value information services to its end users—its customers—in a timely fashion. Information is valuable in proportion to its timely availability and, in most cases, to its *secure* availability.

With a dizzying array of products and technologies available to provide secure information in various forms and in complex IT environments, the best solution is to develop a comprehensive security framework. This framework will integrate security in a cost-effective manner, subject to the needs of the entire enterprise.

Among the topics to be discussed in this entry are the following:

- The need for security
- The requirements for implementing security
- Characteristics of an optimal security framework
- Key technology solutions to meet security requirements
- Building an effective security framework that matches technologies with requirements

NEED FOR SECURITY: ACCESSING CORPORATE DATA

In a number of geographic sectors of the globe, underground networks of hackers have developed and shared publicly some very sophisticated tools for intercepting and modifying data being transmitted over the Internet. These tools have even enabled successful interception of data behind the relative safety of the walls of corporate office buildings.

Some of the tools used for sniffing, hijacking, and spoofing are freely available on the Internet, a vast, loosely interconnected (and unsecured) network. Initially created as an open, accessible medium for the free exchange of information, it offers numerous opportunities to access data flowing through its global network. For example, a single e-mail message from one individual to a co-worker, buyer, vendor, client, doctor, patient, friend, or relative at a remote location may "hop" through several intermediate "nodes" before arriving at its final destination. At any point along the way, the contents of that e-mail could be visible to any number of people, including competitors, their agents, or individuals who would access the data for fraudulent purposes.

Over the past several years, the threat to organizations from hackers on the Internet has received wide publicity, as several major hacking incidents have interrupted the operations of both business and government. The fact is that although earlier surveys indicated that more than 50% of all intrusions occurred from *within* an organization, this trend seems to be reversing according to more recent analyses of hacking incidents. These studies indicate that the majority of attacks are coming from *outside* the organization. It is not uncommon for such attacks to go unnoticed or unreported, so the statistics probably understate the seriousness of the threat.

In one recent analysis of 2213 Web sites of widely differing content, conducted by the Computer Security Institute, it was found that 28% of some commonly used sites were "highly vulnerable" to attack, 30% were somewhat vulnerable, and only 42% were considered safe. The sites surveyed were grouped into six categories: banks, credit unions, U.S. federal sites, newspapers, adult sites, and a miscellaneous group.

In another more recent study, companies reported annual increases of more than 35% in data or network sabotage incidents from 1997 to 1999. In this same survey,

Encyclopedia of Information Assurance DOI: 10.1081/E-EIA-120046568
Copyright © 2011 by Taylor & Francis. All rights reserved.

organizations reported annual increases of more than 25% in financial fraud perpetrated online. Insider abuse of network access increased by over 20%, resulting in losses of more than $8 million.

These studies point to the seriousness of the threat to organizations from financial fraud, through unauthorized access and use of corporate data flowing through the Internet and internal networks, and underline the requirement to provide a secure network environment.

INFORMATION SECURITY REQUIREMENTS

While security is a requirement at several levels in the handling of information, many security implementations focus on addressing a particular problem, as opposed to considering *all* levels. For example, most implementations have attempted to address problems such as authentication (ensuring that the users are who they say they are) or on protecting a specific resource such as the customer database. Taken by themselves, these solutions are often quite good at the job they do.

However, as with any assembly of unintegrated point products, these solutions will most likely be less than perfect, as well as being expensive to use and maintain due to their dissimilar user and administrative interfaces.

So, what should an information manager do to reduce the likelihood of significant loss from one of the enterprise's most valuable assets, without disrupting users, delaying current deliverables, and breaking the budget? The simple answer is: implement a comprehensive information security framework for the enterprise, one that stresses seamless integration with the existing IT environment; and implement it incrementally where it is most needed first.

Some of the specifics of a security framework are described later in this entry. First, this entry examines some of the requirements of an effective security framework and provides an overview of some of the techniques used to meet these requirements.

PRIMARY SECURITY FUNCTIONS

The five primary functions of a good security framework include:

1. *Authentication*: to verify with confidence the identities of the users
2. *Access control*: to enable only authorized users to access appropriate resources
3. *Privacy*: to ensure confidentiality of communication among authorized parties and of data in the system
4. *Data integrity*: to ensure that communications, files, and programs are not tampered with

5. *Non-repudiation*: to provide undeniable proof that a certain user sent a certain message and to prevent the receiver from claiming that a different message was received

Functions such as virus protection are not specifically addressed because these are often combined with integrity, access control, and authentication functions.

Authentication

Authentication, the process of verifying the identity of a party or parties to an electronic communication, forces the party to produce proof of identity: something they know, something they have, or something they are. In situations where an individual is physically present to provide identification, these attributes can be provided through biometrics, a physical characteristic of the individual; for example, a fingerprint, voice print, or retinal scan. The first two categories are most commonly used because they are relatively inexpensive to implement.

In other situations where electronic communications are occurring without the facility to acquire a biometric form of identification, the easiest mechanism to implement is a simple password scheme. This mechanism forces the user to provide a known password in order to authenticate. To be effective, password authentication requires the use of a secure channel through the network to transmit the encrypted password; otherwise, the password might be compromised by electronic eavesdroppers.

Passwords by themselves are not very secure. They are usually short and often easy to guess or observe, and they have been proven to be the weakest link in any system where a user participates in some form of digital commerce. Moreover, because users are increasingly being required to set numerous passwords for various systems, the tendency is to use a single password for all access requirements. They invariably either select from a very short list of known passwords or simply write down all passwords on a piece of paper near their computers. In either case, it is possible for someone to compromise several systems at once.

A cost-effective authentication scheme is to combine a password (something one knows) with an inexpensive smart-card token (something one has). A common example of this is the ATM (automatic teller machine) card. The ATM card is something an individual carries on their person, and the PIN (personal identification number) is something the individual knows. The combination provides improved protection (two-factor authentication) over just one or the other.

An important aspect of authentication is whether it is unilateral (sender authenticates to a server) or bilateral (user and server authenticate to each other). For example, using an ATM at a bank branch assumes that the ATM is legitimate. But can one be as confident when using an

ATM sitting alone in a parking lot? There have been well-documented cases of thieves constructing extremely convincing but fraudulent ATMs in parking lots. Dozens of ATM card numbers and PINs, as well as cash, have been taken from unsuspecting customers. While these cases are admittedly rare, they do demonstrate the importance of *bilateral* authentication.

In an electronic environment, public key cryptography systems (usually referred to as PKI, for public key infrastructure), combined with digital certificates, provide a straightforward, secure mechanism for bilateral authentication. The success of public/private key systems and the trustworthiness of digital certificates lie in keeping the private key secret. If an individual's private key is stolen or accessed by an unauthorized party, then all communications to or from that person are compromised. The storage of private keys on PCs throughout an organization becomes a serious security risk. Because the private key is held on an individual's PC, the user must be authenticated on that PC to achieve security. The strongest security systems will store this information on a smart card and will require a PIN for access.

Access Control

Access control (or authorization), as the name implies, deals with ensuring that users only have access to appropriate resources (systems, directories, databases, even records) as determined by the security policy administrator. Technologies commonly used to enforce access control include trusted operating systems through the use of access control lists (ACLs), single sign-on products, and firewalls. Single sign-on products enable a user to authenticate to the environment once per session. The user will thus be authorized to access any of the appropriate resources without the need for additional authentication during that session.

Privacy

Privacy is the cornerstone of any security environment. Although the definition of privacy can vary significantly between users and owners, privacy issues are important for data with financial, personnel, or research value. Even on a corporate intranet, the privacy issue is important. However, extranet sites often face the greatest challenge in handling data because individuals and corporate data must be protected while multiple corporate entities are provided with some level of access to the data.

Depending on its sensitivity, information must be rendered indecipherable to unauthorized people, whether stored on disk or communicated over a network. Privacy can be implemented through physical isolation. In today's computing environments, however, this is generally too inefficient for most users. The ideal solution for most enterprises is to implement a decentralized cryptographic environment enabling users to maintain and exchange encrypted information.

The entire set of trust requirements for E-security (security of electronic data) builds on the foundation of encryption. There are numerous cryptographic systems available, both asymmetric and symmetric. However, asymmetric coding procedures typically have a severe disadvantage: they are computationally very expensive in comparison with symmetric procedures.

To minimize this problem, fast symmetric coding systems are usually combined with slower asymmetric ones, and a combination of public and private keys is used to decode and decrypt the message. In a secure environment, each user is assigned a user name, together with a public and private key. The public key is published, that is, made available to all interested parties, together with the user name; the private key is only known to its key holder.

There are also efficient procedures to protect the integrity of information, by generating and verifying electronic signatures, combining asymmetric encoding with checksum algorithms, which are efficiently and easily implemented.

An interested partner can now authenticate the key holder through the capability of adding an electronic signature to data elements. However, this only ensures that the partner corresponds to that key; authentication of the partner by name requires a mechanism to guarantee that names and public keys belong together. The problem is comparable to that of a personal identity card, in that a match between the partner and the photo on the identity card does not mean that the partner's name is actually that shown on the identity card.

The idea of the identity card can be carried over to an electronic form. The corresponding "identity cards" are called certificates, which attest to the public key-name pair. It is also possible to distribute pairs of names and keys to the partners via secure channels and store them with write protection. If there are few subscribers, the names and public keys of all possible communication partners can be stored in a table in the electronic message handling system. To avoid a man-in-the-middle attack, it is necessary to ensure that the names and public keys actually belong together. In practice, this means that the pairs of names and keys must be distributed via secure channels and stored in the systems with write protection.

Data Integrity

Integrity involves the protection of data from corruption, destruction, or unauthorized changes. This requirement also extends to the configurations and basic integrity of services, applications, and networks that must be protected. Maintaining the integrity of information is critical. When information is communicated between two parties, the parties must have confidence that it has not been tampered with. Conceptually similar to checksum information, most cryptographic systems provide an efficient means for ensuring integrity.

Non-repudiation

This requirement is important for legal reasons. As more and more business, both internal and external, is conducted electronically, it becomes necessary to ensure that electronic transactions provide some form of legal proof of sender and message received when they are completed. This requirement goes hand-in-hand with the need to verify identity and control access.

IT REQUIREMENTS

A good security framework must implement the functions discussed in the preceding entry section, while at the same time supporting the following requirements:

- The varying security robustness requirements throughout the enterprise
- Integration with point security products such as security gateways and firewalls already in place in the IT infrastructure
- The heterogeneous platforms, applications, networks, networking equipment, and tools found in all IT departments
- The availability and performance requirements of the users and system administrators
- Cross-departmental, cross-geographical, and potentially inter-enterprise interaction
- The ease-of-use requirements of the users
- Flexible and cost-effective implementation under the control of the IT organization
- Stepwise implementation and deployment throughout the enterprise

The best security is transparent to the user community. When a dignitary makes a public visit, the security agents one actually sees are generally only a small fraction of the security forces deployed for that person's protection. Information security should also be largely invisible to the user community and most of the security framework should be behind the scenes.

In the open system environments commonly found in IT departments, transparency can be problematic. Consuming technology from multiple vendors enhances the value of a solution by enabling selection of best-of-breed technology and by creating competition. It is important, however, that technologies from multiple vendors fit together seamlessly, based on open standards, or this benefit is lost in the integration effort.

Ultimately, the IT organization "owns the problem." Rather than buying a number of unintegrated security "point" products such as firewalls and smart cards, it is better to implement an integrated security framework. Framework components would be designed to interoperate seamlessly, using standard programming interfaces, with each other and with the existing IT application base. The products may still come from multiple sources, but they should plug into a framework that represents the requirements of the entire enterprise.

In today's electronic economy, organizations need to communicate transparently with other organizations, a factor that has contributed to the commercial explosion of the Internet. The world's networking environment is now laced with intranets and extranets, many of which are interwoven with the Internet, that enhance the capabilities of organizations to communicate with each other. Throughout all of these networking environments, the security of data must be maintained.

The following components form the essential framework of an integrated, comprehensive, security system, designed to protect corporate data from unauthorized access and misuse.

ENCRYPTION: THE KEY TO SECURITY

Encryption refers to the process of transforming messages and documents from cleartext to ciphertext using a secret code known only to the sender and the intended recipient. Decryption is the inverse process—restoring the cleartext from the ciphertext. There are a number of methods available for document encryption. These generally fall into the categories of symmetric and asymmetric cryptography.

Symmetric key structures, such as the Data Encryption Standard (DES), use a single key shared between sender and receiver. This key, when applied to the cleartext, yields the ciphertext and, when applied to the ciphertext, yields the cleartext. With symmetric keys, both the sender and receiver must share the same key. Symmetric keys tend to perform well, but the sharing protocol may not scale well in a large environment as more and more users need to communicate encrypted information to one another.

Asymmetric key structures use a public and private key-pair, a different key to encrypt and decrypt. The significance of public key encryption technology is that only the user has access to his private key; that user gives out his public key to others. Other people encrypt documents with the public key for communication to the user, and the user encrypts the documents with his private key.

There is a strict inverse mathematical relationship between public and private keys that ensures that only the user with his private key can decrypt messages encrypted with his public key. As well, with that private key, the user with his private key could have encrypted messages, while other people can decrypt with his public key. This characteristic enables the use of keys to "sign" documents digitally.

Strong Encryption: A Necessary Requirement

One security technology in widespread use today, so much so that it has become a *de facto* standard, is the RSA strong public/private key-pairs with digital certificates. Strong encryption refers to the use of encryption technology that is nearly impossible to break within an amount of time that would enable the information to be of any value. The distinction is made between strong and weak encryption, due in part to the running debate over restrictions the U.S. Government has placed on the exportability of message encryption technologies.

The technology of providing strong encryption is considered a munition and its export from the United States is, for the most part, prohibited. The export of weaker encryption is permitted with certain restrictions.

Cleartext e-mail messages and other documents sent over the Internet can be intercepted by hackers, as experience shows. If encryption is the solution, then what prevents a hacker from guessing someone's key and being able to decrypt that person's encrypted messages? In most cases, nothing more than time.

One method used by hackers is to take a sample of cleartext and corresponding encrypted text and repeatedly try random bit sequences by brute force to reconstruct the key used to encrypt the text. Therefore, all the hacker needs is a fast computer or network of computers working together and samples of the clear and encrypted texts. To protect against these brute-force attacks, cryptographic keys must be "strong."

Assessing the Strength of an Encryption System

In a strong encryption scenario, the hacker's strategy will be to use high-powered computing resources to try to crack the encryption key. The solution to this hacking process is to generate sufficiently large keys such that it will take the hacker too long to break them. It is important to remember that computing speeds are doubling roughly every 18 months. The size of a key must be large enough to prevent hacking now and in the future. Also, one does not want to have to change one's key very often.

How large should a key be? Strong encryption means encryption based on key sizes large enough to deter a brute-force attack. Thus, hackers using even a large number of powerful computers should not be able to break the key within a useful amount of time; that is, on the order of many, many years. Key sizes of 56 bits or less are considered weak. Key sizes in excess of 128 bits are considered very strong. One rule of thumb for key sizes is that keys used to protect data today should be at least 75 bits long. To protect information adequately for the next 20 years in the face of expected advances in computing power, keys in newly deployed systems should be at least 90 bits long.

Key Management

Managing keys securely is extremely important and there are a number of products from the security industry that address this issue. Most attacks by hackers will involve an attempt to compromise the key management vs the keys themselves, because a brute-force attack would require a long time to break a key with 128 or more bits.

There are several key management considerations for users. They must be able to:

- Create or obtain their own keys in a highly secure and efficient manner.
- Distribute their keys to others.
- Obtain other people's keys with confidence in the identity of the other party.

Without secure key management, a hacker could tamper with keys or impersonate a user. With public/private key-pairs, a form of "certification" is used, called digital certificates, to provide confidence in the authenticity of a user's public key.

Using Keys and Digital Certificates

Digital certificates must be secure components in the security framework. That is, it must not be possible to forge a certificate or obtain one in an unsecured fashion. Nor should it be possible to use legitimate certificates for illegitimate purposes. A secure infrastructure is necessary to protect certificates, which in turn attest to the authenticity of public keys.

One of the important functions of the certificate infrastructure is the revocation of certificates. If someone's private key is lost or stolen, people communicating with that individual must be informed. They must no longer use the public key for that individual nor accept digitally signed documents from that individual with the invalid private key. This is analogous to what happens when one loses, or someone steals, a credit card.

When keys are generated, they receive an expiration date. Keys need to expire at some point or they can be compromised due to attrition. The expiration date must be chosen carefully, however, as part of the set of security policies in force in the environment. Because other users must be made aware of the expiration, having keys expire too frequently could overload the certificate and key management infrastructure.

Digital signatures and certification

Encryption works to ensure the privacy of communication; but how is authentication handled? That is, how can a person, as the receiver of a document, be sure that the sender of that document really is who he says he is? And vice versa? The authentication of both parties is

Enclaves –
Enterprise

accomplished by a combination of a digital signature and certification mechanism.

A digital certificate from a mutually trusted third party verifies the authenticity of the individual's public key. This party is the Certificate Authority (CA), and operates in a similar manner to a notary public in the non-electronic world. The certificate contains some standard information about the individual and holds that individual's public key. The CA digitally "signs" the individual's certificate, verifying his or her digital identity and the validity of his or her public key.

Digital signatures have legal significance for parties to an electronic transaction. Encrypting creates the signature using the private key of the signatory, information that is verifiable by both parties. The signature provides proof of the individual's identity: only the owner of the private key could have encrypted something that could be decrypted with his or her public key.

In the case of the CA signing a digital certificate, the CA uses its private key to encrypt select information stored in the digital certificate—information such as the person's name, the name of the issuing CA, the serial number and valid dates of the certificate, etc. This information is called the message authentication code (MAC). Both the sender and the receiver of the transmission have access to the certificate; thus, the MAC information is verifiable by both parties.

Anyone can verify a digital certificate by fetching the public key of the CA that signed it. When sending an encrypted document, one exchanges certificates with the other party as a separate step from the actual document exchange, to establish trust and verification.

As an example, consider a two-party exchange of private messages between Jane and Sam, and the mutual verification process. If Jane wants to send an encrypted document to Sam, she first gets Sam's digital certificate, which includes his public key signed by his CA. Jane also gets the CA's public key to verify the CA's signature, and now has confidence that the public key she has does indeed belong to Sam, because the CA's private key was used to sign it. Sam invokes a similar procedure when he receives Jane's certificate.

Of course, most of the work in this process is software controlled, transparent to the user, and, given current technology, performs with nearly imperceptible delay.

Certification Infrastructure

The previous description of a transaction between two parties describes the public key cryptography and certification process. This is a simplified example because even within the same enterprise, security policy might dictate segregating certificate management along departmental or geographic lines to provide a finegrained level of security control and accountability.

One solution to this problem is to have a single master CA issue all certificates throughout the world. This business model has been attempted; however, the CA quickly becomes a bottleneck for organizations needing fast access to hundreds or thousands of certificates. An important fundamental in the security foundation is the capability to control one's own resources. A critical responsibility such as managing certificates should not be left to third parties.

One solution that some organizations have adopted is to establish a hierarchical certification infrastructure. A single "Top CA" within the organization is identified to certify the lower level user or departmental CAs (UCAs). The Top CA maintains certificate revocation lists (CRLs) for the organization, but would otherwise not be involved in day-to-day certificate management. The UCAs handle this stage in the certification process. Outside the organization, a top-level CA is appointed, the Policy Certificate Authority (PCA), who certifies all Top CAs and manages inter-organization CRLs to provide trust between enterprises. Finally, all PCAs in the world are certified by an Internet PCA Registration Authority, ensuring trust between certification infrastructures.

IMPLEMENTING ENTERPRISE SECURITY FRAMEWORK

Implementing an enterprise information security environment is a major, complex task, one that will be different within each enterprise. The implementation should be done in stages, with the first stage being to establish a set of security regulations and a design for the framework, both of which need to be structured to meet both current and future needs as well as budgetary considerations. Consideration must also be given to the inter-enterprise requirements: who are the vendors, partners, and customers involved in the exchange of electronic data? In what order of priority does one wish to secure these communications?

The following entry sections provide a reasonably comprehensive description of the tasks generally involved in implementing a secure IT environment for the enterprise.

Security Audit

The security implementation should begin with a security audit by a qualified firm. The roles of the audit are to

- Map out the current IT environment.
- Understand all aspects of the security mechanisms currently in place—physical security as well as software and hardware solutions.
- Obtain a detailed and confidential analysis of security breaches that have or may have already occurred.

- Provide an assessment of the current security mechanisms with specific emphasis on deficiencies as compared with other organizations.
- Provide an independent assessment as to the root causes of previous incidents.
- Provide recommendations for improvements to the security infrastructure.

Business Analysis and Development of Security Policy

The next step is to conduct an in-depth security analysis along with a business analysis based on the audit findings. Then a set of security policies to meet the needs of the enterprise can be developed. The security framework will be adapted to adhere to these policies. This process encompasses the following multi-stage process:

1. *Establish the organizational relationship between security personnel and the IT organization.* Is there a separate security organization; and if so, how are its policies implemented in the IT organization? What is the security budget, and how are resources shared?
2. *Define the security and IT distribution models.* Does the headquarters organization set policy and implement at all sites, or do remote sites have authority and accountability for their own IT environments?
3. *Understand the security goals at a business level.* Determine the key resources requiring protection and from whom. Who are the typical users of these resources, and what do they do with them? What auditing mechanisms are in place, and what are the physical isolation vs. hardware/software considerations?
4. *Assess the IT-vendor business issues*: dealing with a single vendor vs. several, buying product and service from different vendors, experience with training and support, etc.
5. *List the applications, data files, and server and client systems* that need to be enhanced with security.
6. *Plan the current, near-term, and longer-term IT environment*: addressing issues such as major data flows between business components, platform, hardware, network topology, third-party electronic interaction requirements, space planning, and physical security.
7. *Propose a high-level security paradigm* for defining and controlling access to corporate data, for example, access control server with firewall, smart-card tokens vs. single-factor authentication, centralized vs. peer-to-peer certification, etc.
8. *Develop a high-level set of security policies for the enterprise,* including site security personnel, access

control, certification, and the interaction of the security infrastructure with other enterprise resources.
9. *Analyze and document key dependencies* within the security framework and between the framework and the applications.

Project Planning

Once high-level security policies and a framework have been established, the project plan will have a basic structure. The next stage is to break down the framework into tasks that can be sized, cost-justified, and scheduled for delivery and deployment.

There is no single, definable approach to the planning phase—it will consume resources from potentially many different groups. There are various trade-offs that can be made in terms of an implementation model, such as cost based or complexity based. A project manager should be identified at this stage. This individual should have a broad technical background in IT development projects and a fairly deep knowledge of security implementations.

Selecting an implementation model

It is difficult to advise on the selection of an implementation model because so much depends on other work going on in the IT organization. For example, if the organization is about to embark on a major software program, implementing a thorough security program would be a prudent approach because all systems may be open for modification and enhancement with security components. Conversely, if resources are already over-allocated, few large security-related programs can be implemented.

A recommended guideline for rolling out a security implementation is to proceed in stages from a localized client/server (group) level, to a site-wide deployment, to the full enterprise, and finally to an inter-enterprise configuration. At each stage, the issues can be tackled in a similar manner. For example, it might be best to start by installing a basic authentication and access control implementation that provides basic security for individual devices and the network perimeter.

The next stage would be an enhanced level of authentication and access control with centralized services at the network level, as well as a cryptographic environment for privacy and integrity. Finally, truly robust security can be provided at the network perimeter and inside the network with access control, strong cryptography, certification, token management, and non-repudiation.

It is good design practice to start the design form with legacy systems because:

- These systems tend to transcend the many organizational changes common to business today.
- They are often at the core of the business.

- Modifying these applications may be sufficiently onerous that it is considered a better strategy to "surround" the system with security vs. adding it in.

There are two basic approaches to the development of a security framework. One approach is to begin with the servers and work outward. This approach has the advantage of integrating security into the enterprise at the primary data source. However, for a decentralized IT organization, a better approach might be to build up the levels of security from the clients inward.

One technique that can be used for the client-inward approach is to incorporate smart-card readers into all client PCs up front and require local authentication via the smart card. This functionality could later be expanded to provide single-sign-on access to the network and other features. The disadvantage of this approach is that the client side is difficult to measure, in terms of numbers, because it is usually a changing number, as clients may be added, removed, or receive software upgrades fairly frequently in some organizations. This approach may not catch strategically important server data, which needs protection.

Skills Assessment

Once the implementation model is chosen, a skills inventory needs to be developed. This inventory of skills will be used to determine the appropriate staff resources available and the training requirements. The use of open, standards-based security tools is essential in minimizing the need for extensive training in a proprietary environment.

It is advisable to prepare a high-level workflow diagram to identify the affected organizations requiring representation on the project teams. All affected organizations should be identified and staffing resources within each organization nominated. If physical equipment isolation requiring space planning is required, for example, building operations may need to become involved.

At this stage, project teams can be formed with representation from IT and other organizations. To ensure that all departments have input to the security framework design, end-user departments should have representatives on project teams.

Sizing and Resource Planning

The next major stage in the design process is to prepare project sizing estimates and a resource plan. This is the point at which the security framework project should dovetail with any other planned IT projects. A complete IT budget and staffing plan review may be necessary. In some cases, project priorities will need to be adjusted. The security implementation sub-tasks should be prioritized in groups, where dependencies were identified in the framework, to ensure that the priorities are consistent.

As for any major IT project, price/performance tradeoffs within a sub-task need to be analyzed. In the analysis of business requirements and the development of security policy performed previously, the determination might have been made that the enterprise had numerous physically isolated resources, relative to the threat of attack. In this situation, a hardware/software technology solution might better optimize resources across the enterprise, while still providing more than adequate security.

Local authentication processes can range from simply verifying the user's network address to sophisticated biometrics with varying degrees of robustness and cost.

It is also important to evaluate price-performance tradeoffs for hardware/software combinations. It might, for example, be more cost-effective to implement a Windows NT®-based firewall and accept somewhat less performance scaling than to use a more powerful UNIX product. These decisions will be influenced by the technical skill sets available within the IT organization.

SELECTING TECHNOLOGY VENDOR

Once high-level security policies and the project plan have been established, it is time to approach the security product vendor community to assess product offerings. A system integrator may also be required to supplement the local IT resources and ensure the proper interface of all components. Request for Proposals and Request for Informations for security products can be quite extensive and should include the following criteria, which are the most important characteristics required from a security product vendor:

- *Performance, scalability.* How much delay is incurred in implementing security, and how does the solution scale as users and resources are added to the system?
- *Robustness.* How secure is the solution against a complex attack?
- *Completeness.* How broad and deep is the solution, and for what type of environment is the solution best suited?
- *Interoperability.* How well does the solution integrate into the proposed environment?
- *Support, availability.* How available is the solution, and what are the support and maintenance characteristics?

In support of these five basic and fundamental characteristics, the following set of extensive questions on vendor products should form part of the vendor evaluation process, along with any other concerns involving a specific IT environment.

Enclaves – Enterprise

1. Which of the five primary security functions—access control, authentication, privacy, integrity, and non-repudiation—are provided by the products, and how do they work?
2. Describe the types of attacks the products are designed to thwart.
3. What is the level of network granularity (client only, local client/server, site-wide, full enterprise, interenterprise) for which the products are best suited?
4. What type, if any, of encryption do the products use?
5. Does the encryption technology ship from the United States? If so, when messages travel between countries, is encryption "weakened," and down to what level?
6. Do the products use certification and signing? Describe the architecture.
7. Who conducted the security audit? Present the results.
8. To what standards do the products conform, and where have proprietary extensions been added?
9. With which third-party security offerings do the products inter-operate "out of the box"?
10. How precisely do the products interface with one's existing security products, such as security gateways and network managers? Where are modifications required?
11. On which of the proposed platforms, applications, and tools will the products work without modification?
12. Does the product function identically on all supported platforms, or will separate support and training be required?
13. What are the availability levels of the products (e.g., routine maintenance required, periodic maintenance required (7x24)?
14. How are the products managed, and can they be easily integrated with the rest of the proposed system and network management infrastructure?
15. Is the product support provided by the vendor, or is it outsourced? Will the vendor support mission-critical environments around the clock?
16. Do the products support cross-departmental, cross-geographical, and potentially inter-enterprise interaction? How exactly? Does the vendor have reference sites available with this functionality running? How easy are the products to use based on references?
17. Does one need to deploy the products all at once, or can they be phased in? That is, do the products run in a hybrid environment, enabling communication, for example, between secure and unsecured users?
18. Provide quantitative information on the scalability of the solution as users and secured resources are added.

Implementation and Testing

The project implementation will always reveal issues not identified in the planning stages. For this reason, it is important to develop a well-thought-out framework for the implementation, and to choose manageable, well-defined tasks for the project plan. As the implementation progresses from design to development, testing, and eventually deployment, it is important that new requirements not be introduced into the process, potentially resulting in major delays. New requirements should be collected for a revision to the project that would go through the same methodology.

When the project has exited the testing phase, to ensure a smooth transition, a localized pilot test that does not interfere with mission-critical systems should be performed. The pilot should match as closely as possible the live configuration in a controlled environment and should last as long as necessary to prove the technology, as well as the processes and practices used in developing the security framework.

CONCLUSION

This entry on enterprise security provided an overview of the security requirements needed to protect corporate information from unwarranted access, and a detailed process for designing and implementing an enterprisewide security framework. Some of the solutions available to implement this security framework were described, along with recommendations for the appropriate processes and guidelines to follow for a successful, effective implementation.

The security of information in the enterprise must be viewed from five perspectives:

1. Authentication
2. Access control
3. Privacy
4. Integrity
5. Non-repudiation

An effective enterprise security framework will integrate these functions with the existing IT environment, and the final system will have the following characteristics:

- Flexible enough to provide IT management with the capability to control the level of security
- Minimal disruption to users
- Cost-effective to implement
- Usable in evolving enterprise network topologies, spanning organizational and geographic boundaries; the security framework must also provide interoperability with organizations outside the enterprise

Enterprise Information Security: Architectural Design and Deployment

Mollie E. Krehnke, CISSP, CHS-II, IAM
Senior Information Security Consultant, Insight Global, Inc., Raleigh, North Carolina, U.S.A.

David C. Krehnke, CISSP, CISM, IAM
Principal Information Security Analyst, Northrop Grumman Information Technology, Raleigh, North Carolina, U.S.A.

Abstract

The enterprise information security architecture is a complex model that incorporates business functions, technology, security policy, physical security, configuration management, risk management, contingency planning, users, and business partners and vendors. Generally speaking, all of these concepts will have to be applied to every business function or application, and the justification for the associated resources will have to be presented to senior management. Business functions have to be linked to security functions, and then added value has to be presented in a way that makes sense to senior management and positively affects the business bottom line.

INTRODUCTION

Ours is a connected world, and a dependent world. The condition and livelihood of any organization is dependent on the integrity, availability, and confidentiality of information obtained from or protected from other sources. Today, organizations are at greater risk and their security stance against malicious actors, in the form of individuals, criminal cartels, terrorists, or nation-states, will affect the well-being of many persons, other companies, and perhaps the nation. These organizations often depend upon cyberspace—hundreds of millions of interconnected computers, servers, routers, switches, and fiber-optic cables that allow our critical infrastructures to work.[1]

Threat Opportunities Abound

Individuals and organizations with malicious intent will use any means to disrupt business processes; obtain the data the information systems create, maintain, and transmit; and acquire the power that the information systems and associated networks possess for other unauthorized acts. Malicious actors have the intent (political, economic, national security), the tools (widely available), and the targets (many and well-known vulnerabilities). Malicious actors also have the time and the financial resources necessary to implement attacks. These attacks can have serious consequences, such as disruption of critical operations, causing loss of revenue and intellectual property, or loss of life. Such attacks could use any available cyber resources, including computers located in homes or small businesses to initiate attacks on critical infrastructure organizations—exploiting weaknesses, disrupting communications, hindering defensive or offensive responses, or delaying emergency responders.

Vulnerabilities result from weaknesses in technology and improper implementation and oversight of technological products.[1] The majority of vulnerabilities can be mitigated through good security practices, although such practices must go beyond mere installation, and include proper training, operation, regular patching, and virus updates. The vulnerabilities within an organization can be used to mount an attack against that organization or against other organizations.

Responding to an Increasing Threat

The cyberspace vulnerabilities must be addressed at an individual level and an organizational level. "Each American who depends on cyberspace must secure the part that they own or for which they are responsible."[1] Likewise, each organization must establish and maintain an effective enterprise information security architecture that contributes to its own security, its employees, customers, business partners—and that of the nation.

The effective deployment of security for an enterprise is dependent on the business functions of the enterprise. To gain business commitment, the security functions determined to be necessary must support the business functions of the organization and provide "added value." The provision of added value in the form of enterprise information security is dependent upon many factors: accurate identification of business functions; configuration and management of the existing and planned resources (e.g., networks and technologies); business and security infrastructures; enterprise business processes; people (employees, business

Encyclopedia of Information Assurance DOI: 10.1081/E-EIA-120046772
Copyright © 2011 by Taylor & Francis. All rights reserved.

Enclaves –
Enterprise

partners, and vendors); physical security of facilities, equipment, and remote sites; and associated security or security-supporting policies and processes. The mere presence of certain security mechanisms will not guarantee an acceptable level of risk for the enterprise. Therefore, an enterprise information security architecture must be defined, installed, monitored, assessed, and upgraded on a periodic basis to ensure that the security architecture is appropriate for the enterprise. The major key to successful implementation of security is the commitment of upper management.

ARCHITECTURAL DESIGN CONCEPTS

Association of Business Functions to Security Services

To add value to an organization's business functions, those functions must be understood. A business will have documentation that presents an overview of those functions. Certain individuals will be good resources as well, and should be delighted to discuss security from an added-value standpoint. Business unit managers who oversee specific lines of business (business domains) and subject

matter experts can support the documentation of business functions and provide the business perspective to the sequencing of automated and non-automated processes to address the business mission. The business functions to be addressed also have to be viewed in light of capital planning, enterprise engineering, and program management.

Fig. 1 presents an approach for enterprise architecture development. If such an architecture exists for the enterprise, then the creation of a security architecture has a firm foundation. Business functions and associated business processes, data and data flows, applications and associated functionality, present technology architecture, business locations, business partners and vendors, and strategic goals to support the business mission may already exist—in some form.

The 3 to 5 year target enterprise architecture is a good resource for determining future goals of the organization that will have to be addressed from a security standpoint. Any goals beyond that timeframe will not be as useful for the establishment of an effective information security architecture—technology, customer focus, and external requirements are key drivers in this architecture and they are not easily defined beyond that time with any accuracy.

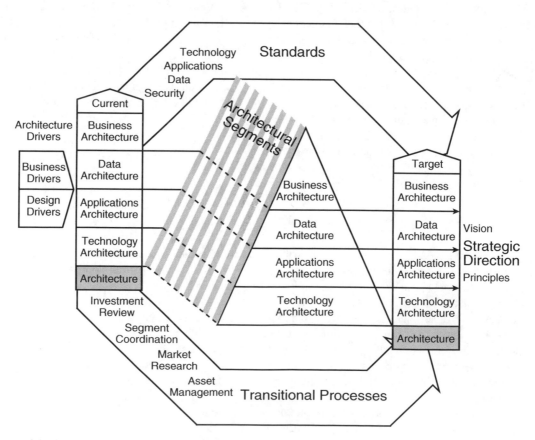

Fig. 1 Structure of the federal enterprise architecture framework.
Source: From A Practical Guide to Federal Enterprise Architecture, Chief Information Officer Council, Version 1.0, February 2001, Fig. 6, Structure of the FEAF Components.[7]

Association of Enterprise Architecture to Information Security Architecture

The target enterprise architecture can provide answers to the following questions that will be invaluable to the enterprise security architecture initiative:

- What are the strategic business objectives of the organization?
- What information is needed to support the business?
- What applications are needed to provide information?
- What technology is needed to support the applications?
- What is the needed level of interoperability between the data sources and the users of the data?
- What information technology is needed to support the enterprise's technical objective?
- What systems are going to be replaced in the near term? In the long term? What systems are going to be migrated to the new enterprise architecture?
- What risks are associated with the current sequencing plan?
- What alternatives are currently available if funding or resources are delayed?
- What are the budgetary and territorial concerns?

The enterprise architecture can be managed as "a program that facilitates systematic agency [business] change by continuously aligning technology investments and projects with agency mission needs."[2] There are going to be areas in which the enterprise architecture information, such as data information and flows, can move directly into an enterprise information security architecture as factors in establishing processes and functionality. There will be others, such as the identification of the business areas or information needs with the greatest potential payoff for the enterprise, which will have to be tempered with other security considerations. Although an organization certainly wants to address these high payoff areas in terms of information availability, integrity, and confidentiality, there may be other less "visible" areas that have higher areas of risk that will also have to be appropriately addressed in order to ensure the security of all business functions.

General Enterprise Architecture Principles

Federal agencies are now required to establish an enterprise architecture that will be used to streamline the collection, storage, and analysis of information, and the provision of applicable information to the general public. The process for the identification and documentation of information required to establish a federal enterprise architecture has aspects that can be applied to private industry as well.

Excerpts from the Chief Information Officer (CIO) Council guide[2] provide principles that help in the establishment of a enterprise architecture and, for our purposes, the establishment of an enterprise information security architecture:

- Architectures must be appropriately scoped, planned, and defined based on the intended use of the architecture.
- Architectures must be compliant with the law.
- Architectures facilitate change.
- Architectures must reflect the organization's strategic plan.
- Architectures continuously change and require transition toward the target architecture.
- Target architectures should project no more than 3 to 5 years into the future.
- Architectures provide standard business processes and common operating environments.
- The quality of the associated architecture documentation is dependent upon the information obtained from subject matter experts and business owners.
- Architectures minimize the burden of data collection, streamline data storage, and enhance data access.
- Target architectures should be used to control the growth of technical diversity.[3]

Although the CIO architecture model mentions security as a concept[2] that "overlies" the enterprise life cycle, and the Interoperability Clearinghouse, a non-profit organization that develops architectures,[4] includes security as a domain architecture, the impact that security should have in the establishment of the architecture is not fully presented. The implementation of an enterprise information security architecture requires the establishment of strong, far-reaching business practices that ensure system compliance with the security architecture and needs continuous assessment to enforce compliance (with the full support of senior management). Otherwise, there is no way to assure that the enterprise information security architecture meets the established business needs and functions at an acceptable level of risk.

General Enterprise Information Security Architecture Principles

Objectives of an enterprise information security architecture, in support of the business mission, must include the following:

- Not impede the flow of authorized information or adversely affect user productivity
- Protect information at the point of entry into the enterprise
- Protect the information throughout its useful life
- Enforce common processes and practices throughout the enterprise
- Be modular to allow new technologies to replace existing ones with as little impact as possible

Enclaves – Enterprise

- Be virtually transparent to the user
- Accommodate the existing infrastructure[5]

Inputs to the Security Architecture

Fig. 2 depicts the inputs to the initial process in formulating an enterprise information security architecture. The process should, at a minimum, consider the following inputs:

- Business-related inputs:

  — Business goals and objectives for protecting the organization's business interests, assets, personnel, and the public; and the future direction of the business and supporting information systems
  — Business operational considerations of how the business will operate day to day (e.g., centralized or decentralized approach to security administration)
  — Current business directions and initiatives for the installed information systems and those under development
  — Business information system requirements (e.g., access requirements, availability requirements, business partner connectivity)

  — Business policies and processes defining what is acceptable and what is not acceptable business behavior
  — Business assets to be protected by the architecture
  — Existing infrastructure including a characterization of the current technical environment and what may help or negatively affect information security
  — Business risk tolerance for information disclosure, unauthorized modification and loss, unavailability, downtime due to hackers and viruses, and defaced Web pages
  — Legal and regulatory requirements including laws and regulations such as privacy, basic due care and due diligence, and sentencing guidelines
  — Threats to the existing infrastructure or business operations
  — Vulnerabilities associated with the existing infrastructure or computing operations

- Security-related inputs:

  — Security goals and objectives (e.g., safeguard information assets from unauthorized and inappropriate use, loss, or destruction; protect sensitive information from unauthorized disclosure and

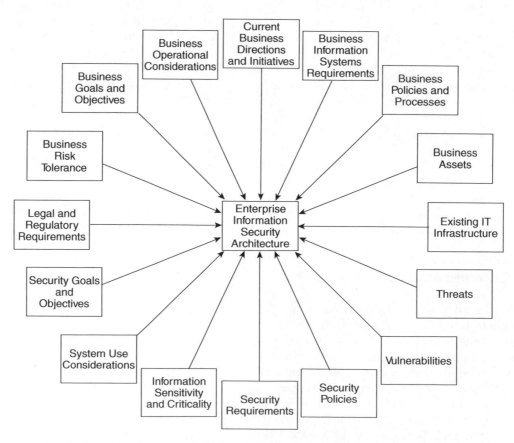

Fig. 2   Considerations for formulating an enterprise information security architecture.

Enclaves –
Enterprise

manipulation; and protect the availability of critical information)

— System use considerations including who will use the information systems (employees, contractors), what level of background screening, when (time of day, days of the week), where (office, home, travel), why (inquiries, file updating, research), etc.

— Sensitivity and criticality of the information to be protected, including the impact due to unavailability or loss

— Security requirements to protect information, applications, platforms, and networks based on the sensitivity and criticality of the information (e.g., label sensitive media, back up information, store backups off site, encrypt information stored in non-secure locations or transmitted over untrusted networks)

• Security policies on what is and what is not acceptable security behavior

MOVING FROM DESIGN TO DEPLOYMENT

Building a Secure Computing Environment

As depicted in Fig. 3, a well-defined enterprise information security architecture provides the foundation for a secure infrastructure and a secure computing environment. The building blocks of a secure computing environment include:

• Well-defined enterprise information security architecture, with accountability, deployment strategies, technology, and security services.
• Effective information security processes, procedures, and standards, derived from policies, but dealing with specific components and technologies and providing detailed specifications that can be audited.
• Effective information security training, including new-hire training; job-related operational training for executives, managers, supervisors, privileged users, and general users; and periodic awareness training.

• Effective information security administration and management, including configuration management, information resources management (IRM), hardened platforms with the latest security patches and virus signature files, virus scanning, vulnerability scans, intrusion detection, penetration testing, logging, alarms, and reviews of common vulnerabilities and exposures (CVEs).
• Aggressive information security assurance, including certification, accreditation, self-assessments, inspections, audits, and independent verification and validation (IV&V).
• Secure infrastructure, including DMZ, routers, filters, firewalls, gateways, air gaps, protected distribution systems (PDSs), virtual private networks (VPNs), secure enclaves, and separate test environments.
• Secure applications, including well-designed, structured, and documented modules; software quality assurance; code review; file integrity checking or change detection software, including products such as Tripwire and Advanced Intrusion Detection Environment (AIDE); and access based on the principles of clearance, need-to-know, and least privilege.
• Secure information, including encryption, backups, and integrity checking software.

Information Security Life Cycle

Fig. 4 indicates how the information security life cycle interacts with the foundation and core components of an information security program. As the outer ring illustrates, organizations should continuously perform the following functions during the information security life cycle:

• Assess business security needs and the risks to the organization
• Design security solutions to appropriately address the assessed risks
• Acquire or develop security solutions

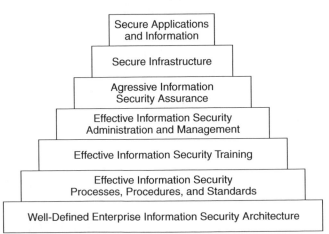

Fig. 3 Building blocks of a secure computing environment.

Enclaves – Enterprise

Enclaves – Enterprise

Fig. 4 Information security life cycle and the information security program.

- Integrate and test security solutions
- Deploy security solutions
- Operate and manage security solutions
- Evaluate and assess security solutions to assure their effectiveness

The organization can perform these functions directly or outsource them, and ensure they are implemented effectively. These functions should be performed continuously because security is an ongoing process, not a one-time destination. Business, technology, risk, and organization structure are not static.

The inner ring illustrates the foundation or essential ingredients of an information security program:

- *Goals and objectives*: Confidentiality and possession, integrity and authenticity, availability and utility, accountability, non-repudiation, and assurance
- *Organization*: Full-time and *ad hoc* personnel identified to implement the information security programs
- *Policies*: High-level management instructions that support an enterprisewide information security program that incorporates prudent practices from industry and government

- *Processes*: Methodologies that support the information security policies and cost effectively implement information security in the enterprise
- *Procedures and standards*: Detail components, technologies, and step-by-step actions that support the policies and processes
- *Guidelines*: Recommended activities to provide a more secure environment

The inner elements are the functional core components of an information security program:

- *Information classification*: The process and consulting support by which the sensitivity of each application is determined.
- *Business impact assessment*: The process and consulting support by which the criticality of each application is determined.
- *Risk management*: The process and consulting support for the identification and assessment of assets, threats, vulnerabilities, and the resulting risks and their successful mitigation, transfer, or acceptance.
- *Security requirements determination*: The process and consulting support for identifying the information

security requirements given the sensitivity, criticality, and risks.

- *Safeguards determination*: The process and consulting support for identifying information security safeguards or controls that will satisfy the security requirements.
- *Access control*: The process of identification and authentication of users, maintaining audit records of their access, and enforcing individual accountability that prevents unauthorized access to information systems.
- *Configuration management*: The rigorous management of the change process that provides hardware and software integrity, and change and version control.
- *Business continuity planning*: The process and consulting support that implements effective planning for continued business operations under all conditions and situations.
- *Security training*: The operational and awareness guidance that ensures all employees are trained in the security aspects of their jobs and their associated security responsibilities, and the secure, appropriate use of information systems and data.
- *Information security assurance (also known as certification and accreditation)*: The formal security evaluation and management approval process that ensures the information system is protected at a level appropriate to its sensitivity and criticality classifications; identifies the controls that satisfy the security requirements, and are documented in a security plan. Determines the residual risk before the information system is put into production as it is, and periodically reviewed over the life of the information system. Periodically tests and evaluates the effectiveness of protection mechanisms, based on current threats and vulnerabilities.
- *Incident management*: The process and consulting support that ensures appropriate actions for detecting, reporting, and responding to information security incidents. Receives and tracks information security incident reports through resolution, escalates serious incidents, and incorporates "lessons learned" into ongoing security awareness and operational training programs.
- *Monitoring*: The monitoring of logs and activities to verify the security stance, ensure appropriate resource use, and defend resources from attack.
- *Technology assessment*: The review, evaluation, and recommendation of advanced security technologies. Evaluates infrastructure and commercial-off-the-shelf (COTS) products for common vulnerabilities and exposures (CVEs).
- *Hardware and software security*: The procurement, configuration, installation, operation, and maintenance of hardware and software in a manner that ensures information security. Includes platform hardening and software integrity checking.

- *Network and communications security*: Perimeter protection, intrusion detection, vulnerability scans, penetration testing, remote access management, and control of modems. Determines the criteria for the evaluation of firewalls, recommends encryption solutions, determines when secure enclaves are required, and provides consulting support for the review of network connectivity requests.
- *Personnel security*: Identifies sensitive positions and ensures individuals assigned to those positions have an appropriate clearance. Includes information security in job descriptions, and through performance appraisals holds individuals accountable for carrying out their information security responsibilities and for their actions.
- *Physical and environmental security*: Protects hardware, software, and information through physical and environmental controls.
- *Compliance*: Administrative inspections, reviews, evaluations, audits, and investigations for the purpose of maintaining effective information security. Consulting support on best practices from industry and government on remedial action to address any significant deficiencies. Confiscation and removal of unauthorized hardware and software, and hardware, software, and data required for use as evidence of wrongdoing.
- *Information security architecture*: The framework for information security and the road map for implementation to ensure the confidentiality, integrity, and availability of applications and information.

Defense-in-Depth for a Secure Computing Environment

Fig. 5 depicts the requirements for a secure computing environment. The lack of security in any one of these components is going to negatively impact the security of the computing environment. If there is no policy, there can be no uniform management direction on how to protect the business, its operations, its people, and its information. If there are no processes and procedures with associated standards, implementation of policy will be based on an individual's interpretation of policy—which is likely to vary from person to person. If there is no physical security, then logical and administrative controls can be easily circumvented without being discovered. The lack of environmental controls can bring down the enterprise and cause more destruction than a malicious agent. If there is inadequate personnel security, the likelihood of insider threat increases dramatically and the impact may not be detected for a significant period of time. The need for communications and network security is obvious; we live in a connected world. However, the unapproved use and unknown presence of a modem or wireless network access points will circumvent firewall protection. Hardware controls must be in line with the equipment functionality—e.g.,

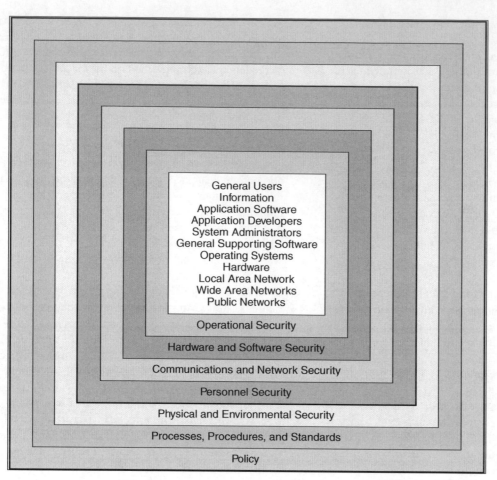

General Users
Information
Application Software
Application Developers
System Administrators
General Supporting Software
Operating Systems
Hardware
Local Area Network
Wide Area Networks
Public Networks

Operational Security

Hardware and Software Security

Communications and Network Security

Personnel Security

Physical and Environmental Security

Processes, Procedures, and Standards

Policy

Fig. 5 Defense-in-depth.

servers must be hardened before deployment if it is going to be effective. Software and its associated controls must be up to date, including patches and updated virus signature files. Employees, contractors, vendors, and visitors must know what is expected of them to support enterprise information security. Public networks, although vital to many business operations, must be viewed as untrusted components of the enterprise architecture and handled appropriately. Wide area networks (WANs) and local area networks (LANs) have certain operational requirements that must be implemented to ensure information confidentiality, integrity, and availability. Hardware must be assessed on its ability to perform the required functions, and must be protected so it cannot be reconfigured to perform unauthorized functions. Software must be licensed, purchased from a trusted source, and assessed to ensure it does not contain malicious code even if it is shrink-wrapped. System administration and application developers must be trusted personnel with the appropriate clearances who have been trained to perform their job responsibilities accurately and effectively. Application software must be accurately designed, developed, and implemented to protect information and the business environment. Information is the lifeblood of the organization and must be protected from unauthorized disclosure, while

being made available when required in an accurate, usable, and complete format. General users represent a significant threat to the secure computing environment, accidentally or with malicious intent. The actions of users must be controlled, and users must be trained in secure operations and use of information and computing and communications resources. The user is the weakest component of the secure computing environment, and carelessness or social engineering can result in established controls being circumvented. Therefore, defense-in-depth must also include checks and balances, with multiple security functions and associated components to address the security requirements. The standardization of security components is represented in this entry as information security services.

DEFINING ENTERPRISE INFORMATION SECURITY ARCHITECTURE

Information Security Services

Information security services provide the enterprise information security architecture with standard methods to support the integration and implementation of information security across the organization infrastructure. These services must be standardized, shareable, and reusable. Information security services include people and technology services.

- *Accountability*: Associates each unique identifier (e. g., user account or log-on ID) with one and only one user or process to enable tracking of all actions of that user or process.
- *Assurance*: Provides a formal information security evaluation and management approval process to ensure information applications and the supporting infrastructure are protected at a level appropriate to their sensitivity and criticality.
- *Authentication*: Verifies the claimed identity of an individual, workstation, or process.
- *Authorization*: Determines whether and to what extent access should be granted to specific information, applications, and information systems.
- *Availability*: Ensures information, applications, and information systems will be accessible by authorized personnel or other information resources when required.
- *Confidentiality*: Ensures that information is not made available or disclosed to unauthorized individuals, entities, or processes.
- *Identification*: Associates a user with a unique identifier by which that user or process is held accountable for the actions and events initiated by that identifier.
- *Integrity*: Ensures the correct operation of applications and information systems, consistency of data structures, and accuracy of the stored information.

Information Security Functions

Each information security service consists of one or more security functions that further identify and define the security action or process needed to secure the information and information systems. Examples of such information security functions include, but are not limited to, authorization, identification, authentication, accountability, risk assessment, confidentiality, encryption, physical access control, logical access control, digital signatures, integrity, intrusion protection, virus protection, non-repudiation, availability, security administration, audit logging and reviews, information security assurance, incident handling, monitoring, and compliance.

Enterprise Information Security Services Matrix

Table 1 summarizes information security services and their related security functions. The table is organized as follows:

- *Information Security Service*: Names the information security service that addresses one or more specific security needs or requirements identified to secure information and information systems and comply with applicable laws, statutes, regulations, policies, and best industry practices. Securing information and information systems may require the use of one or more information security services.
- *Security Function*: Lists the security functions that comprise an information security service.
- *Security Function Description*: Provides a brief description of the security function.
- *Vehicle*: Enumerates the mechanisms, processes, controls, and technologies that support, contribute, and implement the named information security service. Each information security service may be implemented through multiple processes and technologies.

ASSESSING ENTERPRISE INFORMATION SECURITY ARCHITECTURE

Controlling the Growth of Technical Diversity

The priorities established for the enterprise architecture will have to address all enterprise information security considerations. On the flip side, security projects, like business projects, will have to be reviewed in light of several considerations:

- *Business alignment*: Does the project support established strategic plans, goals, and objectives?
- *Business case solution*: What is the impact on the organization's information technology and business environments?
- *Sequencing plan*: Is the proposed investment consistent with the sequence (plan) and priorities established to reach the target architecture?
- *Technical plan compliance*: Does the proposed project comply with the enterprise standards and the architecture levels?

Ensuring Continued Support by Addressing Design Principles

The establishment of an enterprise security architecture is a significant undertaking. The perceived (or actual) complexity of the product could entice the viewer to assume that the architecture can successfully support the design, development, operation, and retirement of an information system. Periodically throughout the implementation of the architecture, it is good to look at the model in light of a system that supports a business function and see if it complies with security principles that support the system throughout its life cycle: initiation, development or acquisition, implementation, operation and maintenance, and

Table 1 Enterprise information security services.

Information security service	Security function	Security function description	Vehicle
Accountability	Non-repudiation	Assures the sender cannot deny he sent the message and recipient cannot claim that he received a different message	Digital signature and certificates
	User deterrence	Places restraint on deviant activities by increasing the likelihood of identification and prosecution of personnel conducting such activities	Security awareness training Operational security training Policy, processes, and procedures
Assurance	Data designation	Determines the sensitivity and criticality of information and information systems	Data element assessment
	Monitoring	Provides surveillance of the activity being performed within the information systems as well as at its boundaries; the surveillance service is carried out on networks and on servers/hosts: network monitoring and host/server-based monitoring	Intrusion detection systems (IDS) Host-based IDS
	Intrusion detection	Detects attempts at system break-ins, behavior patterns, and anomalies with respect to activities at the boundaries of the information system (e.g., network, mainframe, or other device)	IDS
	Malicious code protection	Security code review provides assurance that the information system does and will only execute authorized operations that ensure, preserve, and maintain the integrity of the system and all the information systems accessed	Security code review
		Virus protection monitors, analyzes, and protects the information resource from possible virus attacks	Virus scanning Pattern distribution
	Security administration	Implements management constraints, operational procedures, and supplemental controls established to provide adequate protection of an information system	Configuration management Information resource life cycle Database administration
	Acceptable use monitoring	Ensures information resources will be used in an approved, ethical, and lawful manner to avoid loss or damage to operations, image, or financial interests	Audit logging Monitoring Content filtering
	Compliance	Reviews and examines the records, procedures, and activities to assess the information system security posture and ensure adherence with established criteria	Audit logging Monitoring Content filtering Inspection Independent assessment Penetration testing
	Audit	Provides the information systems with reviews as well as examination of records and activities to test for adequacy of the security controls, compliance with established policies, and operational procedures, and possibly recommends changes to policies and procedures	Audit logging Inspection Independent assessment
	Assessment of business impact	Determines the level of sensitivity, criticality, recovery time objective (RTO); the potential consequences due to information and information system unavailability or loss; and the identification of security requirements	Business impact assessment
	Assessment of risk	Identifies vulnerabilities, threats, likelihood of occurrence, potential loss or impact, expected effectiveness of security measures, and residual risk for an information resource	Risk assessment COTS vulnerability assessment
	Security testing and evaluation	Provides support for testing to determine if all the required security controls and countermeasures described in the security plan are in place and functioning correctly	Security test and evaluation plan

(Continued)

Enclaves – Enterprise

Table 1 Enterprise information security services. *(Continued)*

Information security service	Security function	Security function description	Vehicle
	Certification	Establishes the extent to which the information system meets a specified set of security requirements	C&A process
	Accreditation	Provides support to management in their formal acceptance of the residual risk for operating the information system and approval to deploy	C&A process
	Enclaving	Allows for configuration of special network areas that provide additional protections and access controls to secure information resources	Enclaving process Firewalls IDS Vulnerability scans
	Network connectivity	Protects network and communications infrastructure by managing network connectivity	Network connectivity process
	Penetration testing and vulnerability scans	Checks the robustness and effectiveness of the boundary countermeasures implemented for a given information resource	Vulnerabilities test plan
	Physical security	Identifies specific physical weaknesses, vulnerabilities, and threats for a facility, network, enclave, and information system and implements countermeasures	Site security review System security plan Locks, mantraps, locking turnstiles Guards Fences Lighting CCTV Motion detectors
	Environmental security	Identifies specific environmental weaknesses, vulnerabilities, and threats to a facility, network, enclave, and information system and implements countermeasures	Redundant power UPS Backup diesel generators Redundant telecommunications Backup HVAC
	Personnel security	Identifies sensitive positions and provides the structure to ensure personnel are cleared and their information security responsibilities are defined and included in their performance evaluation	Personnel clearances Job descriptions Performance appraisals Sanctions Conditions of continued employment Job rotation
	Incident management	Provides security incident handling and analysis	Incident reporting process
Authentication	Authentication	Verifies the claimed identity of an individual, workstation, or originator	Passwords and PINs Biometrics Smart cards Tokens Digital certificates
Authorization	Authorization	Determines whether and to what extent personnel should have access to specific information and information systems	User registration and authorization management
Availability	Fault isolation	Hardware: Allows the detection of hardware malfunction and the identification of the component that caused it	System alerts Network management systems/protocols
		Software: Allows the detection of software malfunction and the identification of the component that caused it	Audit logging Network management systems/protocols

(Continued)

Table 1 Enterprise information security services. *(Continued)*

Information security service	Security function	Security function description	Vehicle
	Contingency planning	Provides contingency planning for information and information systems, personnel, and the facilities that house them	Emergency plan Contingency plan Facility recovery plan Personnel evacuation plan
Confidentiality	Confidentiality	Ensures information is not disclosed to unauthorized individuals, entities, or processes; confidentiality applies to hardcopy and electronic media in storage, during processing, and while in transit	Eradicate media Encryption Secure storage Key management Information classification Screen savers Physical access controls Physical access controls Public key infrastructure Logical access controls Separation of duties
Identification	Trusted identification	Associates a user with a unique identifier (e.g., user account or log-on ID) by which that user is held accountable for the actions and events initiated by that identifier	Unique user identifier
Integrity	Data integrity	Ensures the consistency of data structures and accuracy of transmitted or stored information	Hashing Checksum Digital signature
	Information system integrity	Ensures the correct operation of information system	System development methodology Independent security testing and evaluation Configuration management Session management Screen savers Test environment restrictions Server hardening

Enclaves – Enterprise

disposal. Have the following design principles been addressed?

- Establish a sound security policy as the "foundation" for design.
- Treat security as an integral part of the overall system design.
- Clearly delineate the physical and logical security boundaries governed by associated security policies.
- Reduce risk to an acceptable level.
- Assume that external systems are insecure.
- Identify potential trade-offs between reducing risks and increased costs and decreases in other aspects of operational effectiveness.
- Implement layered security (ensure no single point of vulnerability).
- Implement tailored system security measures to meet organizational security goals.
- Strive for simplicity.

- Design and operate an information technology system to limit vulnerability and to be resilient in response.
- Minimize the system elements to be trusted.
- Implement security through a combination of measures distributed physically and logically.
- Provide assurance that the system is, and continues to be, resilient in the face of expected threats.
- Limit or contain vulnerabilities.
- Formulate security measures to address multiple overlapping information domains.
- Isolate public access systems from mission-critical resources (e.g., data, processes).
- Use boundary mechanisms to separate computing systems and network infrastructures.
- Where possible, base security on open standards for portability and interoperability.
- Use common language in developing security requirements.
- Design and implement audit mechanisms to detect unauthorized users and to support incident investigations.

- Design security to allow for regular adoption of new technology, including a secure and logical technology upgrade process.
- Authenticate users and processes to ensure appropriate access control decisions both within and across domains.
- Use unique identities to ensure accountability.
- Implement least privilege.
- Do not implement unnecessary security mechanisms.
- Protect information while it is being processed, in transit, and in storage.
- Strive for operational ease of use.
- Develop and exercise contingency or disaster recovery procedures to ensure appropriate availability.
- Consider custom products to achieve adequate security.
- Ensure proper security in the shutdown or disposal of a system.
- Protect against all likely classes of "attacks."
- Identify and prevent common errors and vulnerabilities.
- Ensure that developers are trained in how to develop secure software.[6]

CONCLUSION

Benefits of Architectures

The profit margin for most businesses is small, and the reduction of costs is vital to the success of the business. The enterprise security architecture can "reduce the response time for impact assessment, trade-off analysis, strategic plan redirection, and tactical action" with regard to security.

Some additional benefits are:

- Support for capital planning and investment management.
- Capturing a "snapshot in time" of business and technology assets.
- Provision of a strategy for systems and business migration.
- Help to mitigate risk factors in enterprise modernization.
- Identification of possible sites for innovative technology deployment.
- Support for key management decision making throughout the organization.[7]

Some direct cost-saving benefits include:

- Discounts on new products through bulk purchasing.
- Capital planning assistance from department CIO offices to ease the paperwork burden on division CIOs.
- Better career opportunities for information technology and security workers because their skill sets can be used on any of the standard systems that will be deployed throughout the department (enterprise).
- Increased ability to provide standardized training with a higher return on investment, because the number of people being trained by the same curriculum is greater

for all levels of training, including users, technical support, and administrators.
- Ability to allocate human resources to areas other than their usual assignments to address key security concerns or incidents.

Helpful Hints from a Security Architecture Practitioner

The security architect is becoming a key function in many organizations, and functions as "the 'corporate clutch,' providing an interface between the security policy-makers and those tasked with providing information systems solutions to businesses." Concepts supporting a successful deployment and utilization of an enterprise security architecture include:

- Available architectural frameworks will have to be modified to adequately address security at the enterprise level.
- Avoid product focus (and resulting product wars) in the establishment of the security architecture.
- Deviations from initial security requirements must be managed to ensure compensating controls are used to minimize risk.
- Architectural documentation must be current and complete, or decisions will be made on obsolete information and ultimately require reworking.
- Documentation is a key deliverable of the architecture team; the lack of it can be costly—more so than the personnel costs associated with creating and maintaining the documentation.
- Project management supports the timely completion of tasking and deliverables.
- Publish all the information that can be provided to all members of the architectural team to facilitate their understanding of the security target architecture.
- Risk assessments are a valuable tool for any security architecture initiative and help to support a responsive architecture that avoids obsolescence and addresses business needs.
- Use business cases as a forum to assign costs to risks, focus the team on providing cost-effective solutions, and to contrast the costs of alternative (less desirable) solutions.
- Make presentation of architectural concepts and associated requests to senior management.
- Architecture supports policy and serves as a policy advocate, working to shape security requirements into practical solutions.[7]

BOTTOM LINE

The enterprise information security architecture is a complex model that incorporates business functions, technology,

Enclaves –
Enterprise

security policy, physical security, configuration management, risk management, contingency planning, users, and business partners and vendors. Generally speaking, all of these concepts will have to be applied to every business function or application, and the justification for the associated resources will have to be presented to senior management. Business functions have to be linked to security functions, and then added value has to be presented in a way that makes sense to senior management and positively affects the business bottom line.

REFERENCES

1. The National Strategy to Secure Cyberspace. Department of Homeland Security; February 2003; vii, xi, 11.
2. A Practical Guide to Federal Enterprise Architecture. Chief Information Officer Council, Version 1.0; February 2001; 40, 8.
3. A Practical Guide to Federal Enterprise Architecture. Chief Information Officer Council, Version 1.0; February 2001; Appendix E, Sample Architectural Principles.
4. ICHnet.org Enterprise Architecture Reference Model. Achieving Business-Aligned and Performance-Based Enterprise Architectures: An Interoperability Clearinghouse White Paper on Enterprise Architecture Frameworks and Methods, Interoperability Clearinghouse; May 22, 2002; 4, http://www.ICHnet.org.
5. Hare, C. Firewalls. Ten percent of the solution: A security architecture primer: In *Information Security Management*, 6th Ed. (CD-ROM); Tipton, H. F., Krause, M., Eds.; CRC Press: Boca Raton, FL, 2007.
6. Zyskowski, J. Building for the Future: Enterprise Architecture Emerges as a Blueprint for Better IT Management. *Federal Computer Week*; January 2, 2002.
7. Scammell, T. Security Architecture: One Practitioner's View. Inform. Syst. Control J., **2003**, *1*, 24–28.

Enterprise Security Capability: Common Models

Matthew J. Decker, CISSP, CISA, CISM, CBCP
Principal, Agile Risk Management, Valrico, Florida, U.S.A.

Abstract
Enterprise security architecture (ESA) comprises all aspects of a security program, including corporate leadership, strategy, organizational structure, policies, procedures, standards, and technical components. The purpose of this entry is to present a road map for achieving an effective ESA, via implementation of common security models, standards, and practices.

SYSTEM SECURITY MODELS

The three system security models[1] briefed in this section are well known, and have formed the basis for the development of secure systems, pursuant to the needs of the entities that employed them. Each offers a different definition for a secure system. This drives home the point, at a most fundamental level, that an organization must clearly define security in terms of what makes sense for them. The models are presented in the order that they were published, from earliest to most recent.

Bell and LaPadula Model

The Bell and LaPadula (BLP) Model[1] is most commonly associated with the classification policy used by the military, which is more concerned with the confidentiality of data at higher levels of sensitivity than the ability of users to modify that data, intentionally or not. The BLP is a finite-state machine model that employs the following logic: if a machine starts in a secure state and all possible transitions between states within the machine result in secure states, then the machine is secure.

There are four components to the BLP Model, as follows:

1. *Subjects* are the users and system executable processes.
2. *Objects* are the data elements.
3. *Modes of access* include read, write, execute, and combinations thereof.
4. *Security levels* are essentially security classification levels.

These four components are used to establish three security principles to formulate the basis for the BLP Model. The three principles are as follows:

1. *Simple security property*, which states that the level of the subject must be at least the level of the object if the mode of access allows the level to be read.

2. *Confinement property* (a.k.a. *"star" property*, or **-property*), which states that the level of the object must be at least the level of the subject if the mode of access allows the subject to write.
3. *Tranquility principle*, which states that the operation may not change the classification level of the object.

Confidentiality of data is protected, but the fact that users with lower privileges are permitted to write data to objects with a higher sensitivity level does not sit well in many environments. Biba developed a model to address this integrity issue.

Biba Model

The Biba Integrity Model[2] was published at Mitre after Biba noticed that the BLP Model did not address data integrity. The problem was that lower-level security users could overwrite classified documents that they did not have the authority to read. Although the Biba Model has not been widely implemented, it is well known. The Biba Model is based on a hierarchy of integrity levels. Integrity levels (a hierarchy of security classifications) are assigned to subjects (e.g., users and programs) and objects (data elements), and are based on axioms (rules) that define the integrity policy to follow.

The Biba Model supports five different integrity policies, including:

1. *Low Water Mark Policy* permits the integrity level of a subject to change. The new integrity level is set to the lower of the integrity levels for the object, or for the subject that last performed an operation on the object.
2. *Low Water Mark Policy for Objects* adds permission to permit the integrity level of an object to change.
3. *Low Water Mark Integrity Audit Policy* adds axioms to measure the possible corruption of data.
4. *Ring Policy* enforces a static integrity level for the life of both subjects and objects. Subjects cannot write to objects with higher integrity levels, or read

Encyclopedia of Information Assurance DOI: 10.1081/E-EIA-120046773
Copyright © 2011 by Taylor & Francis. All rights reserved.

Enclaves –
Enterprise

objects with lower integrity levels. Further, subjects cannot invoke other subjects with higher integrity levels or write to objects with a higher integrity level, but can read objects at a higher integrity level.

5. *Strict Integrity Policy* adds to the Ring Policy the axiom that a subject cannot read objects with a higher integrity level.

The BLP Model works well for military environments, although it is not well suited to commercial entities because it does not address data integrity. The Biba Model addresses this integrity issue but is still not sufficient in commercial environments to prevent a single individual with a high level of authority from manipulating critical data, unchecked. The Clark–Wilson Model,[3] discussed next, addresses both of these issues.

Clark–Wilson Model

The Clark–Wilson Model is most commonly used in a commercial environment because it protects the integrity of financial and accounting data, and reduces the likelihood of fraud. This model defines three goals of integrity, as follows:

1. Unauthorized subjects cannot make any changes.
2. Authorized subjects cannot make any unauthorized changes.
3. Internal and external consistency is maintained.

In a commercial environment, these goals are well suited to ensuring the integrity of corporate financial and accounting data. Not only are unauthorized individuals prohibited access to protected data, but even individuals authorized to access this data are prohibited from making changes that might result in the loss or corruption of financial data and records.

Clark–Wilson introduced an integrity model employing two mechanisms to realize the stated integrity goals, as follows:

1. *Well-formed transactions*, which introduces the concept of duality for each transaction. Each transaction is recorded in at least two places such that a duplicate record exists for each transaction. This is not necessarily a copy of the transaction, but a separate record that is used to validate the accuracy and validity of the original transaction.
2. *Separation of duty*, which prohibits one person from having access to both sides of a well-formed transaction, and also prohibits one individual from having access to all steps of a complete transaction process. This reduces the likelihood of fraud by forcing collusion between multiple users if the fraud is to go undetected.

This integrity model does not apply classification levels to data, or users. Instead, it places strict controls on what programs have permission to manipulate certain data, and what users have access to these various programs.

COMMON STANDARDS AND PRACTICES

Common security standards and practices are tools used in conjunction with modeling techniques and should be adopted by organizations as a matter of policy. In fact, although they are called "standards," they are actually guidelines until they are adopted by an organization as its standard. Publications addressed in this section include ISO 17799, COBIT, Common Criteria (ISO 15408),[4] and NIST's Generally Accepted Principles and Practices for Securing Information Technology Systems. The first three are internationally accepted standards, whereas the fourth one is exactly what it states to be, which is a statement of generally accepted principles and practices. Each of these shares a number of common characteristics, including:

- They are all reasonable and practical.
- Where they overlap, they are generally consistent with one another.
- They are applicable for use in any organization, or any industry.
- Tuning to the organization and culture by adopting only those focus areas relevant to the business or mission is expected for an effective implementation.
- They can be employed in parallel; thus, selection of one does not preclude use of the others.

Of course, for these statements to be true, it is clear that all aspects of these common standards and practices are not utilized by every organization. Every organization, especially from different lines of business, should select its own standard(s), and then the components of the standard(s) with which it intends to comply. Each of the standards presented in this section is well known, and has been thoroughly implemented in practice.

BS 7799 and ISO 17799

BS 7799 Parts 1 and 2 and ISO 17799 are addressed together in this entry because they are so closely related. BS 7799 Part 1 has essentially been adopted as ISO 17799, and thus warrants no further discussion for our immediate purposes. We discuss ISO 17799 shortly; thus, providing highlights of BS 7799 Part 1 would prove redundant. So why mention BS 7799 in this entry at all? There are two reasons for this. The first objective is to make clear the origins of the ISO standard. The second and more significant point is that BS 7799 Part 2 establishes the concept of an Information Security Management System (ISMS), which is not addressed in the ISO standard and is not likely to be adopted by ISO any time in the near future.

BS 7799 Part 2 (BS 7799-2:2002) was published on September 5, 2002. It provides the framework for an ISMS establishing monitoring and control of security systems, thereby providing a framework to minimize business risk. The concept of an ISMS may be of greater importance than the original Code of Practice (Part 1) because it enables a security program to continue to fulfill corporate, customer, and legal requirements.

BS 7799-2:2002 provides for the following:

- Guidance on creating an ISMS
- A Plan-Do-Check-Act (PDCA) Model for creating and maintaining an effective ISMS
- Critical success factors to successfully implement information security
- Ability to continually improve the security management process
- Ability to continually assess security procedures in the light of changing business requirements and technology threats

ISO 17799 (ISO/IEC 17799:2000) is essentially BS 7799 Part 1, with minor revisions.[5] The purpose of the standard is to establish a Code of Practice for Information Security Management. This standard establishes a hierarchy of 127 controls, within 36 control objectives, within 10 security domains.

The ten security domains that form the framework of the standard are as follows:

1. Security Policy
2. Organizational Security
3. Asset Classification and Control
4. Personnel Security
5. Physical & Environmental Security
6. Communications and Operations Management
7. Access Control
8. Systems Development and Maintenance
9. Business Continuity Management
10. Compliance

Within these ten domains lies the set of 36 control objectives, which are further broken down to reveal 127 more detailed controls. An organization should select those controls that are important to achieving their security goals, and set aside the others. Organizations choosing to adopt this standard need not attempt to comply with every aspect of the standard. Like every other standard, it should be applied in accordance with the needs of the organization.

ISO 17799 maintains a focus on IT security. It is specific in terms of what constitutes sound security practices, yet does not recommend technology specific guidelines. Certification to the standard can be made an organizational

goal but most organizations simply use the standard to benchmark their security capability against sound practices.

BS 7799-2:2002 and ISO/IEC 17799:2000 are available online (http://www.iso-standards-international.com/bs-7799.htm) or via CD-ROM for a nominal fee.

COBIT®

COBIT (Control Objectives for Information and related Technology) was developed jointly by the IT Governance Institute and the Information Systems Audit and Control Association (ISACA) as a generally applicable standard for sound information technology (IT) security and control practices, and is now in its third edition.[6] This widely accepted standard provides a reference framework for management, users, auditors, and security practitioners.

COBIT is a mature standard that continues to be updated and improved. The COBIT IT processes, business requirements, and detailed control objectives define what needs to be done to implement an effective control structure. The IT control practices provide the more detailed how and why needed by management, service providers, end users, and control professionals to implement highly specific controls based on an analysis of operational and IT risks.

COBIT provides an IT governance and objectives framework, stated in business terms. Broader than just security, this is a six-volume work containing an IT governance guideline, and an entire volume of management guidelines that provide management tools to use for evaluating the status and effectiveness of the enterprise. This standard establishes a hierarchy of 318 detailed control objectives within 34 high-level control objectives (IT processes), and are organized within 4 domains.

The framework for these four domains, and the number of IT processes addressed within each, is as follows:

- Planning and Organization (PO) contains 11 high-level control objectives.
- Acquisition and Implementation (AI) contains six high-level control objectives.
- Delivery and Support (DS) contains 13 high-level control objectives.
- Monitoring (M) contains four high-level control objectives.

It is beyond the scope of this entry to delve into the details of the detailed control objectives; however, it is worthwhile to tie in how this standard can be used to assist with establishing an overall enterprise security architecture (ESA). A breakout of one of the 34 high-level control objectives is used to emphasize this point. The sample below is taken from the COBIT Framework document, Planning and Organization domain, Objective 8 (PO8),

Enclaves – Enterprise

ensuring compliance with external requirements. COBIT structures this high-level control objective as follows:

Control over the IT process of
ensuring compliance with external requirements

that satisfies the business requirement
to meet legal, regulatory, and contractual obligations

is enabled by
identifying and analyzing external requirements for their IT impact, and taking appropriate measures to comply with them

and takes into consideration

- Laws, regulations and contracts
- Monitoring legal and regulatory developments
- Regular monitoring for compliance
- Safety and ergonomics
- Privacy
- Intellectual property

This sample illustrates several points related to establishing an overall ESA:

- *That IT controls are driven by external factors, not within the control of the organization.* Other high-level control objectives address internal factors as well.
- *That controls placed into operations are there to satisfy a specific business requirement.* All of the high-level control objectives identify the business requirement for the stated control.
- *A clear indication that a legal representative should play a key role in the overall security program and architecture.* Other high-level control objectives bring out the need for involvement of additional non-security, non-IT functions, each of which should have a say in the overall security scheme.

The majority of COBIT 3rd edition is available for complimentary download, as an open standard, from http://www.isaca.org/cobit.htm. The entire COBIT 3rd edition print and CD-ROM, six-volume set can be purchased for a nominal fee, and is discounted to ISACA members.[6]

Common Criteria (ISO 15408)

Version 2.1 of the Common Criteria for Information Technology Security Evaluation (Common Criteria) is a revision that aligns it with International Standard ISO/IEC 15408:1999.[5] This standard largely supersedes the Trusted Computer System Evaluation Criteria (5200.28-STD—Orange Book, also known as TCSEC), dated December 26, 1985. TCSEC is one of the best-known documents comprising the rainbow series, which is a library of documents that

addressed specific areas of computer security. Each of the documents is a different color, which is how they became to be referred to as the Rainbow Series. If the reader is interested in further information about the Rainbow Series, most of the documents can be found online at http://www.radium.ncsc.mil/tpep/library/rainbow/.

The objective of the Common Criteria is to provide a standard approach to addressing IT security during the processes of development, evaluation, and operation of targeted systems. Common Criteria can thus be adopted as a standard for use within an organization's system development life cycle (SDLC). It is sound practice to reduce the risk of project failure by adopting an SDLC to guide developers throughout development projects. Common SDLC methodologies generally fall into either "Heavy" or "Agile" camps, and there are literally dozens of widely known and accepted methodologies within each camp. Some common examples include Waterfall Methodology, Rapid Application Development (RAD), Spiral/Cyclic Methodology, Microsoft Solutions Framework (MSF), Scrum, and Extreme Programming (XP). One of the critical success factors met by the Common Criteria is the fact that it does not mandate any specific development methodology or life-cycle model; thus, it can be used by developers without forcing them into a methodology not suitable to their approach to system development.

Security specifications written using Common Criteria, and IT products or systems shown to be compliant with such specifications, are considered ISO/IEC 15408:1999 compliant, although certification of compliance can only be achieved through accredited evaluation facilities known as Common Criteria Testing Laboratories (CCTLs). It is important to note that Common Criteria is not applied as a whole to any particular system, or target of evaluation (TOE), as the standard is very large and complex. A security target (ST) is created using elements of the Common Criteria in an effort to provide the basis for evaluation and certification against the standard. Protection profiles (PPs) are developed and used to provide implementation-independent statements of security requirements that are shown to address threats that exist in specified environments.

PPs are needed when setting the standard for a particular product type, or to create specifications for systems or services as the basis for procurement. Numerous validated protection profiles have been created and approved, and are available online at http://niap.nist.gov/cc-scheme/. This site also contains information regarding validated products, accredited CCTLs, and other useful information.

NIST SP 800-14

NIST (National Institute of Standards and Technology) is a U.S. government organization whose mission is to develop and promote measurement, standards, and technology to enhance productivity, facilitate trade, and improve the quality of life. NIST has a Computer Security Division (CSD) that is dedicated to improving information systems security by:

- Raising awareness of IT risks, vulnerabilities, and protection requirements
- Researching, studying, and advising agencies of IT vulnerabilities
- Devising techniques for the cost-effective security and privacy of sensitive federal systems
- Developing standards, metrics, tests, and validation programs
- Developing guidance to increase secure IT planning, implementation, management, and operation

NIST Special Publication (SP) 800-14, *Generally Accepted Principles and Practices for Securing Information Technology Systems*, is an excellent resource for providing a baseline that organizations can use to establish and review their IT security programs.[7] The document gives a foundation that organizations can reference when conducting multi-organizational business as well as internal business. The intended audience for the guideline includes management, internal auditors, users, system developers, and security practitioners. The following 14 common IT security practices are addressed in this publication:

1. Policy
2. Program management
3. Risk management
4. Life-cycle planning
5. Personnel/user issues
6. Preparing for contingencies and disasters
7. Computer security incident handling
8. Awareness and training
9. Security considerations in computer support and operations
10. Physical and environmental security
11. Identification and authentication
12. Logical access control
13. Audit trails
14. Cryptography

The entire 800 series of NIST documents provides a wealth of information to the security practitioner. Some of the documents are tuned to securing federal systems, but most are largely applicable to both the public and private sectors. These documents are freely available online at http://csrc.nist.gov/publications/nistpubs/.

SECURITY GOVERNANCE MODEL

The purpose of the Security Governance Model is to assist in marrying existing corporate organizational structures and cultures with new security program development activities, which are usually brought about by changing business needs. This is accomplished by identifying and classifying the existing organizational structure as a specific security governance type, and determining if the business needs of the organization can be met by achieving a security capability within this type. Dramatic changes to organizational structures can have a negative impact on a business, and most business leaders will find it preferable to interject security into the existing corporate culture, rather than change the corporate culture to achieve a specific security capability.

The Security Governance Model addresses the way information security is mandated, implemented, and managed across the enterprise. Governance is generally categorized as being either centralized or decentralized, but these labels are oversimplified for practical modeling purposes. This is because many entities must apply both attributes to achieve their security goals in a cost-effective manner; thus, they are often both centralized and decentralized at the same time. We can model this by first recognizing that security governance has two primary components—control and administration—each of which can be centralized or decentralized. The following definitions for control, administration, centralized, and decentralized are used for this model:

- *Control* refers to the authority to mandate how security will be managed for an organization. Primary objectives are to develop policy and provision budget for security initiatives.
- *Administration* refers to the authority to apply, manage, and enforce security, as directed. Primary objectives include the plan, design, implementation, and operation of security in accordance with policy, and within the confines of budget.
- *Centralized* indicates a single authority, which can be a person, committee, or other unified body.
- *Decentralized* indicates multiple entities with a common level of authority.

Combining the above definitions provides the standard terminology used for this model. The terms "centralized" and "decentralized" no longer stand by themselves, but are coupled with the two primary components of security governance. This yields the following four terms, which form the basis for the Security Governance Model:

1. *Centralized control* (CC) is indicative of an organization where the authority for policy and budget decisions is granted to a representative person or assembly, and is applicable throughout the organization.
2. *Decentralized control* (DC) is indicative of an organization where no one person or body has been authorized to formulate security policy and develop budget for security initiatives.

Enclaves –
Enterprise

3. *Centralized administration* (CA) grants authority to apply and manage security policy to security or system administrative personnel who share a common reporting chain.

4. *Decentralized administration* (DA) grants authority to apply and manage security policy to security or system administrative personnel who have multiple reporting chains.

Given an understanding of the terminology, the reader is now in a position to pair each of these control and administration components to formulate the four basic types of security governance:

1. *Centralized control/centralized administration (CC/CA)*: one central body is responsible for developing policies that apply across the entire organization, and all administration is performed by personnel within a single chain of command.

2. *Centralized control/decentralized administration (CC/DA)*: one central body is responsible for developing policies that apply across the entire organization, yet administration is performed by personnel within multiple chains of command.

3. *Decentralized control/centralized administration (C/CA)*: several entities are responsible for developing policies that apply within their areas of responsibility, yet all administration is performed by personnel working within a single chain of command.

4. *Decentralized control/decentralized administration (C/DA)*: several entities are responsible for developing

policies that apply within their areas of responsibility, and administration is performed by personnel within multiple chains of command.

To utilize this model (Fig. 1), an organization first defines the security needs of the business or mission, and classifies the type of security governance currently in place. A security strategy for the organization is then developed, taking into account the governance type and business needs. Once a strategy is realized that can be effectively accomplished within the governance type, it is reasonable to proceed with further development of the ESA within the existing organizational structure. If the strategy cannot be realized within the governance type, then one is forced to change something. Assuming the main drivers have been properly identified as the business needs, there remain four areas of focus. The easiest approach is to revisit the security strategy. If the strategy can be revised such that an effective security capability can be achieved within the existing governance type, then the process is greatly simplified. If not, then the organizational structure must be modified to achieve the best cost/benefit security governance type for the organization.

This model does not mandate a specific organizational structure. Rather, the model associates aspects of the organizational structure to align business needs with the security capability desired by the organization by identifying the governance type that will best achieve the security strategy for the organization.

To assist with clarifying the four types of governance, organizational structure examples are provided for each

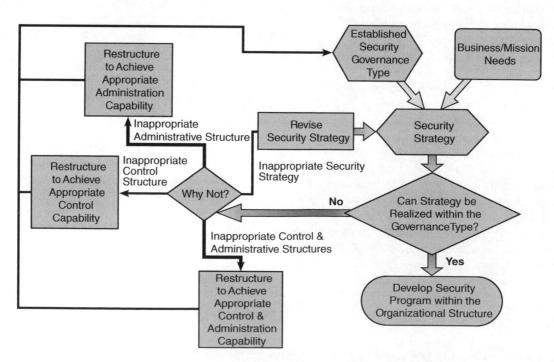

Fig. 1 Security governance model.

type. The following should be noted when reviewing the samples provided:

- All of the examples with a CIO (Chief Information Officer) or CSO (Chief Security Officer) show them reporting to a COO (Chief Operating Officer). This is for example purposes only and is not intended as a recommended reporting structure. The CIO and CSO might report to any number of executives, including directly to the CEO (Chief Executive Officer).
- The CIO and CSO are intentionally identified as peers. If a CSO exists in the organization, then the CIO and CSO should report to the same executive officer, primarily to resolve their inherent conflicts of interest and to ensure unbiased appropriation of budgets.
- There are almost as many different organizational charts as there are organizations. The examples provided herein are intended to help clarify why an organizational structure fits a particular security governance type.

Centralized Control/Centralized Administration (CC/CA)

CC/CA identifies a truly centralized security capability (Fig. 2). One central body is responsible for developing policies that apply across the entire organization, and personnel within a single chain of command perform all administration. Representatives for each department are assigned to a steering committee that ensures that each has appropriate influence over the policy-making process. This influence is depicted by the arrows in Fig. 2, vs. traditional organizational structure reporting.

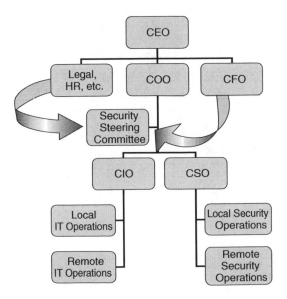

Fig. 2 Centralized control/centralized administration.

In this case, the CEO has designated that the COO is responsible for a security program. The COO has delegated this responsibility by creating a CSO position. The steering committee exists to ensure that each department is given appropriate input to the policy-making process, because each department has security issues that must be addressed. Legal and regulatory issues such as the PATRIOT Act, Gramm–Leach–Bliley, Sarbanes–Oxley, HIPAA, and Safe Harbor, just to name a few, must also be addressed. The CSO typically chairs the security steering committee. Although the CSO must maintain proper control and administration over security, it is a function that impacts the entire organization.

Security operations and IT operations have been completely separated. The CSO is responsible for all things security, while the CIO is responsible for IT operations. There is no overlapping of responsibility, although both groups will have responsibilities on the same devices. Firewalls provide a good example. IT operations must be able to reboot, or restore a firewall if a failure occurs, but need not be authorized to make changes to the rule set. Authority to make changes to the rule set falls to the security operations group, but this group must not be permitted to interrupt traffic or adversely affect operations except during scheduled maintenance periods. These groups work together to support organizational needs, but do not share operational tasks.

Centralized Control/Decentralized Administration

Centralized control/decentralized administration (CC/DA) (Fig. 3) is the most commonly implemented governance model type for mid- to large-sized organizations. One central body is responsible for developing policies that apply across the entire organization, yet personnel within multiple chains of command perform administration.

As in the prior example, the CEO has designated that the COO is responsible for a security program, the COO has delegated this responsibility by creating a CSO position, and the steering committee exists to ensure that each department is given appropriate input to the policy-making process. Again, the influence of each department over the security development process is depicted in Fig. 3 by arrows. The aspects of centralized control have not changed.

The relationship between security operations and IT operations has changed dramatically. This organizational structure passes greater responsibility to IT managers located at remote facilities by permitting each to manage security and IT operations, inclusively. The CSO may have dotted-line control over security personnel at some remote facilities, as noted in the diagram, but there is not one central point of control for all security operations.

Enclaves – Enterprise

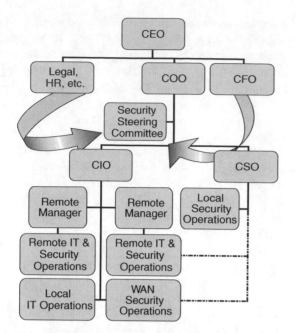

Fig. 3 Centralized control/decentralized administration.

Decentralized Control/Centralized Administration

Decentralized control/centralized administration (DC/CA) (Fig. 4) is appropriate for some small organizations that do not have the resources to justify a steering committee. Several entities are responsible for developing policies that apply within their areas of responsibility, and these policies are pushed to operations managers for implementation and enforcement. This influence is depicted in the Fig. 4 by arrows, vs. traditional organizational structure reporting. Personnel within a single chain of command, in this case the COO, perform all administration.

Note that remote location IT managers might include co-location arrangements, where IT operations are outsourced to a third party, while ownership and some measure of control of the IT assets are maintained by the organization.

Decentralized Control/Decentralized Administration

Decentralized control/decentralized administration (DC/DA) (Fig. 5) identifies a truly decentralized security capability. This structure is appropriate for some small organizations that neither have the resources to justify a steering committee nor keep their critical IT operations in-house. In this example, the CFO manages a contract for outsourcing company financials, HR manages the contract for outsourcing human resources, and IT operations has little or nothing to do with either. The outsourced companies are responsible for the policies and procedures that apply to the systems within their control, and the customer either accepts these policies, or takes its business elsewhere.

The administration portion of the above example, under the COO, is indicative of a CA structure, yet the organization is classified as DA because the COO has no control over security administration for the outsourced IT capabilities. In this case, the responsibility for ensuring adequate controls over the security of company financial data is relegated to the outsourcing provider.

The advantages and disadvantages of each governance type will differ from organization to organization. One that is more expensive to implement in one organization may prove cheaper to implement in another. The fundamental objective is to achieve organizational security goals as effectively and painlessly as possible.

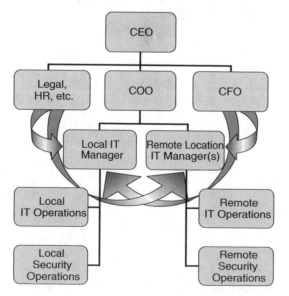

Fig. 4 Decentralized control/centralized administration.

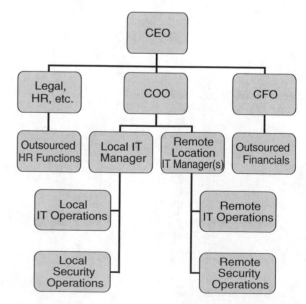

Fig. 5 Decentralized control/decentralized administration.

Enclaves –
Enterprise

ENTERPRISE SECURITY ARCHITECTURE MODEL

Enterprise security architecture incorporates all aspects of security for an organization, including leadership, strategy, organizational structure, planning, design, implementation, and operations. It encompasses the people, processes, and technology aspects of security. Numerous models have been developed, and those that communicate sound security practices share a common approach to enterprise security. The ESA Model shown in Fig. 6 is an open source model that this author has developed to communicate this approach.

Executive Sponsorship

Organizations should elicit executive sponsorship for developing a corporate security program; otherwise, the program leader will lack buy-in from other departments and will not have the ability to enforce compliance with the program. A brief policy statement, typically issued in the form of a formal corporate memo, should be presented from the highest corporate level in order to authorize the existence of a corporatewide security program. This directive will justify development of the security program, thus establishing the requirement to develop a security program charter.

The security program charter authorizes development of a formal security program, and delegates an authority appropriate for the organization [e.g., the Chief Operating Officer (COO)]. This executive would then typically delegate this responsibility by creating a CSO or equivalent position. Note that without executive sponsorship, the CSO will likely have difficulty applying and enforcing security directives that impact other departments.

Security Program Strategy

The CSO then formulates a formal policy statement in response to the corporate directive. This broad policy document will define the goals of the security program, as well as the organizational structure. These must generally be approved by the corporate Board of Directors. In this example, the CEO has designated that the COO is responsible for the security program, and the COO has delegated this responsibility to a CSO. Many organizations have appropriately created a CSO position that reports directly to the Board of Directors, which is preferable for organizations that face significant risks to their business from security breaches.

A security program strategy is drafted to meet the business or mission needs of the organization. The CSO drafts the overall security program strategy by aligning the organizational approach to security with sound industry practices, and by leveraging common standards and practices such as the ISO 17799, COBIT, Common Criteria (ISO 15408), and NIST publications mentioned previously in this entry. Application of the Security Governance Model can be applied in this layer to assist in marrying an effective strategy with an appropriate organizational structure.

In many organizations, sound practices suggest that the CSO formulate a security steering group, or

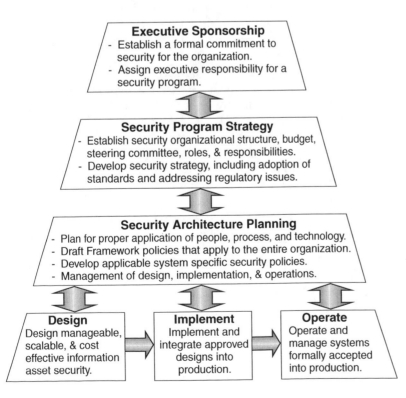

Fig. 6 Enterprise security architecture.

intra-organizational policy board, comprising representatives from each functional business area. Customer Operations, Engineering, Finance, Internal Communications, HR, IT, Legal, Marketing, and Sales are examples of departments that might be represented in this group. This steering group will oversee most security policy development for the company in order to establish the organization's overall approach to computer security.

Security Architecture Planning

Planning the architecture refers to planning that takes place within an established security organization. Planning to execute security initiatives is an exercise in futility if executive sponsorship and security program strategy have *not* been established. Planning encompasses the people, processes, and technology aspects of security, and thus addresses policy, procedure, and technical implementation. Having established executive sponsorship and security program strategy for the organization, one can continue to develop the ESA.

If COBIT has been determined to be the standard to be used by the organization, then guidance offered within the Planning and Organization domain falls primarily within this layer of the model, and the other three COBIT domains will each be spread across the design, implementation, and operations components of the lowest layer of this model. The model is scalable such that existing standards can and should be used, yet sufficiently flexible that no one standard must be used. Developing security policies is a critical component of this layer of the ESA Model. Again, selection of one standard does not preclude the use of other well-known and accepted publications. A sample approach to developing security policies in accordance with the guidance from NIST SP 800-14 follows.

Program-framework policies can now be drafted to establish the organization's overall approach to computer security. This is a set of corporatewide policy statements that establish a framework for the security program. Board-level direction is recommended for establishing most program policy statements because these policies provide organizationwide direction on broad areas of program implementation. This board-level direction is the fundamental function of the steering group, because representatives of the board are included in this committee. Policy statements at this level reflect high-level decisions about priorities given to the protection of corporate data. Board-level direction is recommended for acceptable use, remote access, information protection (a.k.a. data management), data retention, special access (root level), network connection, system acquisition and implementation, and other policies, as required. Program policy is usually broad enough that it does not require much modification over time. Additional policies will need to be developed, and are categorized as issue specific and system specific.

Board-level direction is also recommended for development of *issue-specific policies*, which address specific issues of concern to the organization. Whereas program-framework policy is intended to address the broad, organizationwide computer security program, issue-specific policies are developed to focus on areas of current relevance, concern, and possible controversy to an organization. Issue-specific policies are likely to require frequent revision as changes in technology and related factors take place. An example of an issue-specific policy is one that addresses peer-to-peer file sharing via programs such as Kazaa and Morpheus.

System owners, vs. board-level representatives, are responsible for systems under their control, and as such should establish *system-specific policies* for these systems. System-specific policies focus on decisions taken by management to protect a particular system. Program policy and issue-specific policy both address policies from a broad level, usually encompassing the entire organization. However, they do not provide sufficient information or the direction, for example, to be used in establishing an access control list or in training users on what actions are permitted. A system-specific policy fills this need. It is much more focused because it addresses only one system.

In general, for issue-specific and system-specific policies, the issuer is a senior official. The more global, controversial, or resource intensive the policy statement, the more senior the policy issuer should be.

Many security policy decisions will apply only at the system level and will vary from system to system within the same organization. While these decisions might appear to be too detailed to be policy, they can be extremely important, with significant impacts on system usage and security. A management official should make these types of decisions, as opposed to a technical system administrator. Technical system administrators, however, often analyze the impacts of these decisions.

Once a policy structure is in place, the overall planning and management of the security life cycle is maintained at this layer of the ESA Model.

Security Architecture Design, Implementation, and Operations

Security architecture planning establishes how an organization will realize its security strategy. Security architecture design, implementation, and operations are where the "rubber meets the road." Planned activities are realized and executed, usually in phases and with interim planning steps conducted throughout the cycle.

Support, prevention, and recovery occur in a continuous cycle at the foundation of this model. These activities can be effective when they occur as part of a well-structured security program. As an example, a qualitative risk assessment for the organization is among the activities to be executed. This includes identifying major functional areas of information, and then performing a risk assessment on those assets. The output of this process includes tables detailing the criticality of corporate systems and data in terms of confidentiality, integrity, and availability. Additional services or capabilities that are likely addressed include, but are certainly not limited to, the following:

- Firewall architecture
- Wireless architecture
- Router and switch security
- Network segmentation and compartmentalization
- Intrusion detection systems
- Business continuity
- Anti spam and malicious code protection
- Incident response and digital forensics
- Vulnerability assessments and penetration testing
- Patch management

Additional models can be employed to address the technical security services associated with the design, implementation, and operations components comprising this foundational layer of the ESA Model. The model presented to address this issue is the Security Services Model.

SECURITY SERVICES MODEL

One model that should be considered in the design, implementation, and operations of technical security capabilities is detailed in NIST SP 800-33, *Underlying Technical Models for Information Technology Security.*[8]

This publication defines a specific security goal, which can be met through achievement of five security objectives. The stated goal for IT security is to:

Enable an organization to meet all of its mission/business objectives by implementing systems with due care consideration of IT-related risks to the organization, its partners and customers.

The five security objectives are generally well understood by security professionals, and are as follows:

1. Availability (of systems and data for intended use only)
2. Integrity (of system and data)
3. Confidentiality (of data and system information)
4. Accountability (to the individual level)
5. Assurance (that the other four objectives have been adequately met)

This model next identifies and classifies 14 primary services that can be implemented to satisfy these security objectives. The 14 services are classified according to three primary purposes: support, prevent, and recover.

Definitions of each of the primary purposes, as well as the 14 primary services classified within each, are as follows:

- *Support.* These services are generic and underlie most information technology security capabilities.

  — Identification (and naming)
  — Cryptographic key management
  — Security administration
  — System protections

- *Prevent.* These services focus on preventing a security breach from occurring.

  — Protected communications
  — Authentication
  — Authorization
  — Access control enforcement
  — Non-repudiation
  — Transaction privacy

- *Recover.* The services in this category focus on the detection and recovery from a security breach.

  — Audit
  — Intrusion detection and containment
  — Proof of wholeness
  — Restore "secure" state

The underlying technical Security Services Model is depicted in Fig. 7. This shows the primary services and supporting elements used in implementing an information technology security capability, along with their primary relationships.

Remember that we endeavor to meet a specific security goal by achieving five security objectives. It stands to reason that the above model must be broken out five different ways—one for each objective—in order to allow us to effectively implement a comprehensive technical security capability. The NIST publication does this, and it can be found at http://csrc.nist.gov/publications/nistpubs/800-33/sp800-33.pdf, if the reader is interested in delving into the further details of this model.

CONCLUSION

This entry presented a number of security models that were brought together to form a road map to achieving an effective ESA. The ESA Model provides this road map at a high level, and additional models have been introduced that can be applied within the layers of this model. System Security Models have been presented; these help to form the basis for the development of secure systems. Common standards and practices were presented that assist in the development

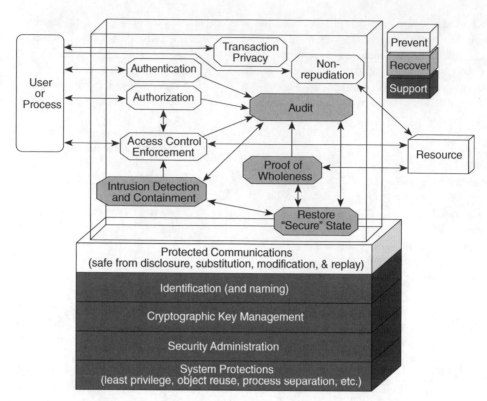

Fig. 7 Security services model.
Source: From *Underlying technical models for information technology security.*[8]

and realization of the security strategy. The Security Governance Model assists with categorizing and developing an organizational structure for the security program, and the Security Services Model details the primary services and supporting elements used in implementing an information technology security capability.

The models, standards, and practices presented in this entry neither constitute a complete collection, nor is it the intent of this entry to suggest that this is the only approach to an ESA. Numerous additional models and suggested standards exist, and can likely be substituted for those presented herein.

REFERENCES

1. Bell, D.E.; LaPadula, L.J. *Secure Computer System: Unified Exposition and Multics Interpretation*; MITRE Corp.: Bedford, MA, March 1976; MTR-2997. Available as NTIS ADA 023 588.
2. Biba, K.J. *Integrity Considerations for Secure Computer Systems*; USAF Electronic Systems Division, 1977.
3. Clark, D.D.; Wilson, D.R. A comparison of commercial and military computer security policies. IEEE Symposium on Security and Privacy: Oakland, CA, 1987; 184–194.
4. *Common Criteria for Information Technology Security Evaluation (CC),* Version 2.1, August 1999.
5. ISO/IEC. *ISO/IEC 17799.* ISO/IEC, Geneva, 2000.
6. Information Systems Audit and Control Association. COBIT 3rd Ed. ISACA: Rolling Meadows, IL, 2000.
7. NIST Special Publication 800-14. *Generally Accepted Principles and Practices for Securing Information Technology Systems* Marianne Swanson and Barbara Guttman, September 1996.
8. NIST Special Publication 800-33. *Underlying Technical Models for Information Technology Security*; Gary Stoneburner, December 2001.

BIBLIOGRAPHY

1. COSO: Committee of Sponsoring Organisations of the Treadway Commission. *Internal Control—Integrated Framework.* 2 Volumes. American Institute of Certified Accountants: Jessey City, NJ, 1994.
2. Fisch, E.; White, G. *Secure Computers and Networks: Analysis, Design, and Implementation*, CRC Press: Boca Raton, FL, 2000.
3. OECD Guidelines: Organisation for Economic Co-operation and Development. *Guidelines for the Security of Information.* Paris, 1992.

Enclaves – Enterprise

Enterprise Security Information

Matunda Nyanchama, Ph.D., CISSP
National Leader, Security and Privacy Delivery, IBM Global Services, Oakville, Ontario, Canada

Anna Wilson, CISSP, CISA
Principal Consultant, Arqana Technologies, Inc., Toronto, Ontario, Canada

Abstract

This entry discusses the sources of information that are useful for security management and the nature of the information they produce. Among technologies discussed are intrusion detection systems (IDSs), firewalls, routers, switches, and operating systems. Also explored are their primary function in security management, the manner in which they collect information, and how this information can be analyzed, collectively, to offer an enterprise-wide security view. Ways of collecting this information and how it informs the security management process are also discussed.

Today's business and computing environments have blurred traditional boundaries between what is considered trusted and untrusted. As a result, organizations are taking measures to protect their information assets. Information from various sources in an organization's network is key to managing security. Such information comes from a number of security devices (intrusion detection systems and firewalls), operating systems, and network devices such as switches and routers.

In general, each of these devices performs a function that contributes to the overall enterprise needs and hence its security posture. Moreover, each of these technologies has a responsibility in the overall security management of the computing environment. Collectively, these devices produce a large amount of information.

The challenge before us is to make sense of all this information and to mange it in a way that is useful in protecting the computing environment, and in a manner that will benefit the entire enterprise. To achieve this, one must first understand the technology one is dealing with, how it collects and interprets information, and at what point one needs to intervene in the overall process. Having this understanding will allow one to set out the best strategy in one's approach to the management of enterprise security information.

This entry discusses issues pertaining to challenges of managing security information for purposes of improving an organization's security posture through aggregation, analysis, and correlation.

This entry discusses the sources of information that are useful for security management and the nature of the information they produce. Among technologies discussed are intrusion detection systems (IDSs), firewalls, routers, switches, and operating systems. Also explored are their primary function in security management, the manner in which they collect information, and how this information can be analyzed, collectively, to offer an enterprisewide security view. Ways of collecting this information and how it informs the security management process are also discussed.

Having this appreciation, one can look into the various strategies available in the overall management of this security information. In addition, there is a quick overview of the issues of security management and the challenges for managing this information in a manner that raises security effectiveness. This knowledge is intended to empower security information security practitioners in planning the most effective way in which to blend technology and man, ongoing efforts to keep business environments secure.

The material in this entry should be read in conjunction with suggested references. In discussing various network and security technologies, the authors do so with a view to understanding the nature of information they produce and how this information can be used to ensure enterprise security. Specific technologies are not discussed in sufficient detail to make this entry a stand-alone technical reference with respect to the said technologies. However, the entry does include discussions of the following:

- The need for and sources of enterprise security information, including:

  — IDSs
  — Firewalls
  — System logs
  — Switches and routers

Some strategies for enterprise security management are discussed; these include approaches to collection and analysis strategies. The section also touches on the challenges

Encyclopedia of Information Assurance DOI: 10.1081/E-EIA-120046569
Copyright © 2011 by Taylor & Francis. All rights reserved.

of associating vulnerability data to business risk. The final section offers a summary and pointers to future challenges for managing security information.

SOURCES OF ENTERPRISE SECURITY INFORMATION

This entry section focuses on the need for security information, sources of such information, and how this information helps with the management of enterprise security. Understanding the need to collect security information is important because it is this need that determines the nature of desirable information, the means of collection, and the necessary manipulation that helps in security management.

Need for Security Information

The past decade has seen tremendous growth of issues of information security, including technology, skilled professionals, and security-related information. This growth, spurred by the central role computers and networking continue to play in all aspects of daily endeavors and commerce, has resulted in reaches beyond physical boundaries. Networking has extended this reach into areas outside organizations' and individuals' immediate control. Further, it has contributed to the development of today's commercially available security technologies, in an effort to assert control over one's "territory."

On the other hand, networking has resulted in complex systems composed of differing network devices. The ensuing systems produce information used in the ongoing management of the networks and computing resources. This information must be analyzed to better understand the environment in which it is produced.

On the whole, security information forms a component of the total information produced in entire systems within organizations. Such security information is important for making security-related decisions, without which the situation would be tantamount to getting behind the steering wheel of a car, blindfolded, and hoping for the best. The value of information from security systems and devices is useful for making informed, cost-effective choices about how best to protect and manage computing environments.

Be it an audit log, firewall log, or intrusion information, such information is useful in many different ways. It can be used for performing system audits to determine the nature of activity in the system. It can also be used for the diagnosis required from time to time, especially in cases of a security incident; and is also useful for forensic analysis, which forms a core component of incident resolution. In general, security information is useful to determine an enterprise's security.

Sources of Security Information

To be effective, information security management requires varied pieces of information across an enterprise. This information that originates from various sources contributes to an enterprise's information security jigsaw puzzle. Each piece of information is useful for what it reveals. Aggregation of these information pieces contributes to a better understanding of the overall security posture.

Perhaps the most familiar source of security information is operating system logs. Operating system logs have been a common feature of computers for a long time, even before security administration became entrenched as it is today. During this time, system administrators have used system logs to manage computing environments, specifically pertaining to determining who was doing what, where, and when, in a fairly detailed manner.

With the growth of inter-networking, the need to connect internal networks to other external networks has continued to grow. Invariably, connecting to untrusted networks creates a need to control communication between internal and external networks. This is the role filled by the use of firewalls as they act as gateways between internal and external networks. Firewalls are a common feature in today's networking. And just as operating systems produce logs pertaining to system activity, firewalls track activity at the gateway.

With operating system logs recording activity on systems and the firewalls controlling and logging activity through the gateway, one might assume that a network would be secure against external attacks. Right? Not exactly! This is because those who venture on the dark side are also pretty clever. They have a knack of getting around established defenses and backdoors, exploiting weaknesses in communication protocols, applications, and operating systems.

This creates a need for intrusion monitoring to supplement the firewalls defenses. IDSs provide information about flagged events on systems and networks. IDSs track suspicious network activity, which may indicate attack attempts, probing, or successful intrusion. Information provided by an IDS may reveal missed or unforeseen weaknesses or holes in internal systems and the gateway. This affords the opportunity to harden or close the exposures caused by the security weakness and holes.

Systems, firewalls, and IDSs play different but complementary roles in enforcing security. Each of these is responsible for a specified role in the computing infrastructure. In practice, however, their boundaries may not be as distinct as may be suggested here. And given the different roles they play, there exist differences in the type of information they produce, the way it is collected, and how it is analyzed and interpreted.

Security information also comes from routers and switches in a network. Routers and switches play a critical role in networking and are critical to the availability of infrastructure segments.

When combined, this information from diverse sources provides a holistic picture of enterprise security. The resulting aggregation benefits from the power of correlation and may yield useful patterns and trends in a manner that informs the security management process. For example, such information can improve the management of security incidents and ensure that lessons learned will help improve future management of similar incidents, helping shift the management of incidents from a reactive to proactive mode.

Security information, if used and managed appropriately, can offer the prescription for the total security "health" (We deliberately use the term "health" because an organization's security posture can be seen in terms of health.) of our computing environments.

INTRUSION DETECTION SYSTEMS

This entry section focuses on IDSs, what they are, and their role in the management of enterprise security. IDSs can be seen as devices that monitor the pulse of the enterprise health. They depend on anomalies and known attacks to raise alarms about potential attacks and intrusions. They are limited to the extent that they can recognize anomalies or associate an activity to a known attack based on activity signature.

Introduction

IDSs play an important role in the monitoring and enforcement of security in an enterprise. They are usually deployed at vantage points where they detect activity and take action as desired, including logging the associated activity, raising an alarm or a pager, or sending an e-mail message to specified users for attention.

IDSs detect flagged activity that is deemed suspicious for which they generate specified action. Whether monitoring traffic on a network or watching for suspicious changes on a specific host, IDSs form part of the "active security" components in an organization.

IDSs continue to evolve as they face ever-growing security challenges. These challenges include keeping up with hacker exploits that evade IDS detection. IDSs must also contend with denial-of-service attacks intended to bring them down.

In general, intrusion detection technology is relatively young. Although there are minor differences among security professionals as to what constitutes an IDS, there is substantial agreement on the role that IDSs play in enterprise security management. Further, there is concurrence on the need for analysis of IDS information as an aid to security management. In general, IDSs are a major source of information which, when analyzed and acted upon, helps improve enterprise security.

An ideal IDS has several automated components that define its functionality, including:

- Providing information about events on a computer system or network
- Analyzing the information in a manner that aids the security process
- Logging and storing security-sensitive event information for future use, specifically for making improvements
- Acting on that information in a manner that improves security
- Performing all of the above in a flawless and timely manner

The above list is an ultimate IDS dream for all security professionals. Whether such a system exists is a matter for another discussion.

There are two key approaches to IDS monitoring. These include knowledge-based and anomaly detection IDSs. Moreover, there are two key strategies for IDS deployment; that is, on the network or on a host. These are discussed individually, along with an overview of incident response, given the close relationship between IDS and incident response.

Knowledge-Based Intrusion Detection Systems

Misuse detection-based IDSs, also called knowledge based IDSs, are the most widely used today. Such IDSs contain accumulated knowledge about known attacks and vulnerabilities based on signatures. Using this knowledge base of attack signatures of exploits, the IDS matches patterns of events to the attack signatures. When an attack attempt is detected, the IDS may trigger an alarm, log the event, raise a pager, or send an e-mail message.

Knowledge-based IDSs are easy to implement and manage due to their simplicity. They are very effective at quickly and reliably detecting attacks. With continued tuning and update of signatures, it is possible to lower the false alarm rate. In the process, this enables security professionals to respond to incidents very effectively, regardless of their level of expertise.

There is a downside to misusing detection-based IDSs; they are most effective when the information in their knowledge base remains current. The predefined rules or attack signatures must be continuously updated. Moreover, there is usually a time lag between the time an exploit is publicized and when an associated attack signature is available. This leaves a window of opportunity for a new, undetectable attack. Such IDSs can be seen to be blind to potentially many attacks that they do not "know" about, especially where there is a substantial time lag in the update of the IDS' knowledge base.

Anomaly Detection (Behavior-Based IDS)

Anomaly detection, or behavior-based, IDSs operate on the premise of identifying abnormal or unusual behavior.

Anomalies on a host or network stand apart from what is considered normal or legitimate activity. These differences are used to identify what could be an attack.

To determine what an anomaly is, systems develop profiles representing normal user activity on hosts or networks over a period of time. The system collects event data and uses various metrics to determine if an activity being monitored is a deviation from what is considered "normal behavior."

To determine such normal behavior, some, all, or a combination of the following techniques are used:

- Rules
- Statistical measurements
- Thresholds

However, these systems are subject to false alarms because patterns of activity considered to be normal behavior can change and vary dramatically.

The key advantage of behavior-based IDSs is that they are able to detect new attack forms without previous specific knowledge of the attacks. Further, there is the possibility of using the information produced by anomaly detection to define attack patterns for use in knowledge-based IDSs.

Host-Based Intrusion Detection Systems

Host-based IDSs are installed on specific hosts on which they perform monitoring. A host-based IDS can be seen as system specific. It uses the system's audit, system, and application logs for IDS information. Using the system's various logs lends to the quality of the information available to the IDS. Given that it is dealing with a specific operating system, the accuracy of the associated information will be substantially high because the operating system retains a good sense of activity on the host on which it is installed.

A host-based IDS responds when flagged events happen on the host. These events could pertain to file changes, privilege escalation, or any such activity deemed security sensitive. This makes a host-based IDS very effective in detecting integrity attacks. Using an operating system's audit trails, a detected inconsistency in a process could be an indication of a Trojan horse or some other similar attack.

Additional advantages of a host-based system include the ability to detect attacks that go undetected by network-based systems. Depending on where information sources are generated, host-based systems can operate in environments in which network traffic is encrypted. Where switching technology is utilized on a network, host-based systems remain unaffected.

Host-based IDSs suffer some drawbacks. Given that they are usually designed for specific systems and applications, host-based systems may not be very portable. Moreover, an IDS that supports one platform may not support another. In a complex environment in which there are varied systems and applications, there may be a temptation to install a different host-based IDS on each of the systems. This would result in a complex environment with many different IDSs, which, in turn, presents a challenge in the monitoring and management of all the resulting information from the diverse systems.

Despite these disadvantages, a host-based IDS remains an important tool, as the resources on those hosts are the targets for many attackers—which leads to yet another disadvantage. Suppose a specific host on a network running an IDS is under attack. What will be the first target on that host?

Network-Based Intrusion Detection Systems

A network-based IDS monitors network traffic in the network segment on which it is installed. It functions by analyzing every packet to detect any anomalies or performing pattern matching against captured packets based on known attack signatures. Based on the information in the packet, the IDS attempts to identify anything that may be considered hostile or patterns that match what may have been defined as hostile activity.

Packet analysis presents a challenge in that the information may no longer be as revealing as in the host-based system. Indeed, a substantial degree of inference is required to determine whether observed patterns or detected signatures constitute hostile activity. This is because one can determine the physical source of a packet but one may not know who is behind it.

Network-based IDSs have some key advantages, including their non-intrusive stealth nature. As well, unlike host-based IDSs that may impact hosts on which they reside, network-based IDS performance does not impact systems. As well, network-based IDS packet analysis is beneficial over the host-based system when under some type of fragmentation attack.

One major disadvantage of network-based IDSs is the inability to scale well with respect to network traffic. The ability to inspect every packet under high traffic conditions offers a challenge to IDSs. The result is packet loss. Where such packet loss is substantial, there may be less IDS information to manage but that information may be critical to the desired security.

After examining the pros and cons of the various IDS technologies, one can clearly see that the most effective use of an IDS would be to use some combination of all.

IDS Selection and Deployment

The selection and deployment of an IDS must take a number of factors into consideration, including the:

- Purpose for which it is intended: host- or network-based intrusion detection
- Ability to scale up to high volumes of traffic if it is a network-based IDS

Enclaves –
Enterprise

- Scope of attack signatures, where it is knowledge-based, or the ability to perform accurate anomaly detection

Other factors that determine deployment include the volume of information being analyzed, the degree of analysis desired, and the significance of the intrusions or attacks one wants to monitor.

The physical location of an IDS is determined by the type of activity intended to be monitored. Placing a network-based IDS outside the security perimeter (e.g., outside the firewall) will monitor for attacks targeted from outside, as well as attacks launched from inside but targeted outside the perimeter. On the other hand, placing an IDS inside the security perimeter will monitor for successful intrusions. Placing the IDS on either side of the firewall will effectively monitor the firewall rules (policy), because it will offer the difference between activity outside the firewalls and successful intrusions.

In deploying an IDS, one must select the mode of operation, which can be either real-time (in which IDS information is passed in real-time for analysis) or interval-based (also known as batch) mode (in which information is sent in intervals for offline analysis). Real-time analysis implies immediate action from the IDS due to the constant flow of information from its various sources. Interval-based or offline analysis refers to the storage of intrusion-related information for future analysis.

The choice of one of these methods over the other depends on the need for the IDS information. Where immediate action is desirable, real-time mode is used; where analysis can wait, batch-mode collection of information would be advantageous.

Incidence Response

IDSs are useful for detecting suspicious activity. As discussed in the previous entry section, IDSs log and transmit intrusion-related information. Security management requires that this information be transformed into suitable format for storage and analysis. Potentially, anything identified by an IDS—whether it is an attack, intrusion, or even a false alarm—represents an incident requiring analysis and action. The materiality of the incident depends on the threat posed by the incident.

In cases where an intrusion is thought to have occurred, the security organization must respond quickly and act urgently to contain the intrusion, limit the damage caused by the intrusion, repair any damage, and restore the system to full function.

Once things have calmed down, it is important to perform a root cause analysis to determine the nature of the attack and then use this information to improve defenses against future attack. Without applying the "lessons learned" into the process of security enforcement, an organization risks future attack and exploitation.

In general, the incident response process should take a system approach based on detection, response, repair, and prevent. The IDS performs detection, raising the alert to an incident. Human intervention must respond to the incident, perform the repair, and ensure that the lessons learned help improve security.

IDSs can be configured to help manage incidents better based on how they are configured to respond to attacks and intrusions. These responses can be passive (e.g., logging) or active (e.g., generating a page to the security administrator).

Active responses involve automated actions based on the type of intrusion detected. In some cases, IDSs can be configured to attempt to stop an attack, for example, through actively killing the offensive packets. It can also involve terminating the attacker's connection by reconfiguring routers and firewalls to block ports, services, or protocols being utilized by the attacker. Further, network traffic can also be blocked based on the source or destination address and, if necessary, all connections through a particular interface.

The least offensive approach for an active response is to raise the attention of a security administrator, who will then review the logged information about the attack. The analysis will show the nature of the attack and the associated response necessary. Based on the outcome of this analysis, the sensitivity of the IDS can be adjusted to reflect the need for response.

This can be accomplished by increasing the sensitivity of the system to collect a broader scope of information, assisting in the diagnosis of whether an attack actually occurred. Collection of this information will also support further investigation into an attack and provide evidence for legal purposes, if necessary.

There are other approaches to responding to perceived attacks, including fighting back. This involves actively attempting to gain information about the attacker or launching an attack against them. Despite being appealing to some, this type of approach should be used only to the extent of gathering information about the attacker. Actively launching an attack against a perceived attack has a number of potential perils. For example, suppose the source IP has been spoofed, and the last hop of the attack has been just a launch pad rather than originating the attack. Moreover, this has legal implications. As such, professionals should be very clear about their legal boundaries and take care not to cross them.

Most of today's commercially available IDSs depend on the passive responses by logging attack information and raising alarms. Invariably, this requires human intervention to respond to the information provided by the IDS. These come in the form of alarms, notifications, and simple network management protocol (SNMP) traps. An alarm or notification is triggered when an attack is detected and can take the form of a pop-up window or an on-screen alert, e-mail notification, or an alert sent to a cellular phone or pager.

Enclaves –
Enterprise

To some degree, some commercial IDSs give users the options to do "active kills" of suspicious traffic.

To send alarm information across the network, many systems use SNMP traps and messages to send alarms to a network management system. One is beginning to see security-focused management systems coming onto the market that consolidate security events and manage them through a single console. The benefit of such a system is its holistic nature, allowing the entire network infrastructure to play a role in the response to an attack. Many of the recognized network management systems have incorporated security-specific modules into their systems to meet this demand.

Is IDS Technology Sufficient for Security?

Given an understanding of the role of the IDS and the role of incidence response in security management, IDS technology can only go so far; that is, cause alerts, log security-sensitive events, and to a limited degree, perform active kills of offensive traffic. The information generated by IDSs across an enterprise must then be used to make informed decisions intended for security improvements.

Even if we have a state-of-the-art IDS deployed, the analysis of incidents by experts provides critical data for the enhancement of the response and management process. Once an alerted incident has been identified and determined to be, in fact, a critical incident, the response team will react quickly to ensure the event is contained and the network and systems are protected from any further possible damage. At this point, the role of forensics comes into play. The forensics experts will conduct a detailed analysis to establish the cause and effect of the incident, and the resulting data from this forensic analysis will provide the information necessary to find a solution. Taking this information and organizing it into various categories such as hostile attacks, denial-of-service, or misuse of IT resources, to name a few, allows for statistical reporting to improve the handling and response of future incidents.

Finally, one needs to use this information to address any weaknesses that may have been identified during the analysis. These can range from technical vulnerabilities or limitations on the systems and network, to administrative controls such as policies and procedures. One must effectively inoculate against possible future incidents to prevent them from occurring again. Case in point: How many security professionals repeatedly have to deal with the effects of the same virus being released as a variant, simply because the lessons from a previous infection were not learned? These post-mortem activities will serve to improve one's security posture, contribute to lessons learned, and heighten security awareness.

Other IDS management issues include ensuring that the IDSs are updated and constantly tuned to catch the most recent attacks and also filter false alarms. Like all systems, IDSs require constant maintenance to ensure the usefulness of the information they collect.

FIREWALLS: TYPES AND ROLE IN SECURITY ENFORCEMENT

This entry section reviews firewalls and their role in protecting information, including the different firewall types and advantages and limitations in security management.

Introduction

A firewall is a device that provides protection between different network zones by regulating access between the zones. Typically, a firewall filters specific services or applications based on specified rules, and provides protection based on this controlled access between network segments. Firewalls have major advantages, including:

- The ability to consolidate security via a common access point; where there is no firewall, security is solely the function of the specific hosts or network devices. This consolidation allows for centralized access management to protected segments.
- Being a single access point, the firewall provides a point for logging network traffic. Firewall logs are useful in many ways as log reviews can offer major insights into the nature of traffic transiting at the firewall. Such traffic could be intrusion related, and its analysis helps to understand the nature of associated security threats.
- The capability to hide the nature of the internal network behind the firewall, which is a major boon to privacy.
- The ability to offer services behind a firewall without the threat of external exploitation. (This is true for a single access point network. This claim is questionable for networks with multiple access points that blur the concept of what is in and what is out.)

While providing a core security function, a firewall cannot guarantee security for the organization. Effective firewall security depends on how it is administered, including associated processes and procedures for its management. Further, there must be trained personnel to ensure proper configuration and administration of the firewall.

Although overall, firewalls help to enhance organization security, they have some disadvantages. These include hampered network access for some services and hosts, and being a potential single point of failure. Most vendors offer high-availability solutions. This, however, is additional cost to network infrastructure. As well, load balancing is a challenge for many firewall vendors.

There are two major approaches to firewall configuration, namely:

1. Permit all (e.g., packets or services) except those specified as denied
2. Deny all (packets or services) except those specified as allowed

The "permit all" policy negates the desired restrictive need for controlled access. Typically, most firewalls implement the policy of "deny all except those specified as allowed."

Firewall Types

Packet filters

Packet filtering firewalls function at the IP layer and examine packet types, letting through only those packets allowed by the security policy while dropping everything else. Packet filtering can be filtering based on packet type, source and destination IP address, or source and destination TCP/UDP ports. Typically, packet filtering is implemented with routers.

The major advantage of packet filters is that they provide security at a relatively inexpensive price as well as high-level performance. As well, their use remains transparent to users.

Packet filters have disadvantages, however. These include:

- They are more difficult to configure, and it is more difficult to verify configurations. The high potential for misconfiguration increases the risk of security holes.
- They neither support user-level authentication nor access based on the time of day.
- They have only limited auditing capability and have no ability to hide the private network from the outside world.
- They are susceptible to attacks targeted at protocols higher than the network layer.

Application gateways

Application gateways function at the application layer and examine traffic in more detail than packet filters. They allow through only those services for which there is a specified proxy. In turn, proxy services are configured to ensure that only trusted services are allowed through the firewall. New services must have their proxies defined before being allowed through.

In general, application gateways are more secure than packet filtering firewalls.

The key advantages of firewalls based on application gateways are

- They provide effective information hiding because the internal network is not "visible" from the outside. In

effect, application gateways have the ability to hide the internal network architecture.
- They allow authentication, logging, and can help centralize internal mail delivery.
- Their auditing capability allows tracking of information such as source and destination addresses, size of information transferred, start and end times, as well as user identification.
- It is also possible to refine the filtering on some commands within a service. For example, the FTP application gateway has the ability to filter **put** and **get** commands.

The downside of application gateways is that the client/server connection is a two-stage process. Their functioning is not transparent to the user. Moreover, because of the extent of traffic inspection employed, application gateways are usually slower than packet filters.

Firewall Management Issues

Good security practices require that firewall activity be logged. If all traffic into and out of the secured network passes through the firewall, log information can offer substantial insight into the nature of traffic, usage patterns, and sources and destinations for different types of network traffic. Analysis of log information can provide valuable statistics—not only for security planning, but also with respect to network usage.

Where desirable, a firewall can provide a degree of intrusion detection functionality. When properly configured with appropriate alarms, the firewall can be a good source of information about whether the firewall and network are being probed or attacked. This plays a complementary role when used in conjunction with an IDS.

Network usage statistics and evidence of probing can be used for several purposes. Of primary importance is the analysis of whether or not the firewall can withstand external attacks, and determining whether or not the controls on the firewall offer robust protection. Network usage statistics are a key input into network requirements studies and risk analysis activities.

More recent techniques for study of attacks and intrusions use "honey pots" for studying traffic patterns, potential attacks, and the nature of these attacks on enterprise. Here, a honey pot with known vulnerabilities is deployed to capture intrusion attempts, their nature, their success, and the source of the attacks. Further analysis of the honey pot traffic can help determine the attackers motives and the rate of success of specific types of attacks. The Honeynet Project (http://www.honeynet.org) has taken this concept further by creating typical environments for attack and using forensic methodologies to study attacks, their sources, and the motives of attackers.

Enclaves – Enterprise

Is Firewall Security Sufficient?

There are many organizations that install a firewall, configure it, and move on, feeling confident that their information is secure. In real life, a firewall is like that giant front door through which most intruders are likely to come should they find holes they can exploit. In reality, there are many ways an intruder can evade or exploit the firewall to gain access to the internal network. This includes exploitation of protocol or application-specific weaknesses or circumventing the firewall where there are alternate routes for traffic into and out of the internal network. This is the case where users have dialup access to the Internet while logged on to the internal network.

In reality, the issues that guarantee maximum security pertain to processes, people, and technology. The technology must be right, there must be trained people to manage the technology, and processes must be in place for managing the security and the people enforcing security.

Key processes include:

- Applying updates or upgrades of the software
- Acquiring and applying the patches
- Properly configuring the firewall to include collection of logs and log information
- Reviewing log information for security-sensitive issues
- Correlating the log information with information from other security devices in the network
- Determining the findings from the security information and acting on the findings
- Repeating the cycle

OPERATING SYSTEM LOGS

This section reviews system logs, what they are, and why they are required; different means of collecting log information; strategies for managing system logs; and the challenges of managing log information and its impact on system security.

Introduction

Operating system logs are an important and very useful tool in the gathering and analysis of information about systems. They serve to provide valuable detailed information regarding system activity. Logs are divided into several categories responsible for recording information about specific activities, including user, security, and system, and application related events. They can support ongoing operations and provide a trail of the activity on a system, which can then be used to determine if the system has been compromised and, in the event of criminal activity, provide important evidence in a court of law.

Types of Logs, Their Uses, and Their Benefits

The auditing of operating systems logs information about system activity, application activity, and user activity. They may function under different names depending on the operating system but each is responsible for recording activity in its category. A system can log activity in two ways: event oriented or recording every keystroke on the system (keystroke monitoring).

The event-oriented log contains information related to activities of the system, an application, or user, telling us about the event, when it occurred, the user ID associated with the event, what program was used to initiate it, and the end result.

Keystroke monitoring is viewed as a special type of system logging, and there can be legal issues surrounding it that must be understood prior to its use. Using this form of auditing, a user's keystrokes are recorded as they are entered, and sometimes the computer's response to those keystrokes are also recorded. This type of system logging can be very useful for system administrators for the repair of damage that may have been caused by an intruder.

System log information is used for monitoring system performance. Activities such as drivers loading, processes and services starting, and throughput can provide valuable information to the system administrator for fine-tuning the system. In addition, these logs can capture information about access to the system and what programs were invoked.

Events related to user activity establish individual accountability and will record both successful and unsuccessful authentication attempts. These logs will also contain information about commands invoked by a user and what resources, such as files, were accessed. If additional granularity is required, the detailed activity within an application can be recorded, such as what files were read or modified. The application logs can also be used to determine if there are any defects within the application and whether any application-specific security rules were violated.

The benefits of these audit logs are numerous. By recording user-related events, not only does one establish individual accountability but, in addition, users may be less likely to venture into forbidden areas if they are aware their activities are being recorded. The system logs can also work with other security mechanisms such as an access control mechanism or an intrusion detection system to further analyze events. In the event operations cease, the logs are very useful in determining activity leading up to the event and perhaps even revealing the root cause.

Of course, for these logs to be useful, they must be accurate and available, reinforcing the need for appropriate controls to be placed on them. Protection of the integrity of log records is critical to its usefulness, and the disclosure of this information could have a negative impact if vulnerabilities or flaws recorded in the logs are disclosed to the wrong parties. In many situations, the audit or operating system logs may be a target of attack by intruders or insiders.

Challenges in Management and Impact

Without a doubt, the operating system logs are a very important aspect of our systems, but the amount information being collected can be very difficult to manage effectively. The information contained in the logs is virtually useless unless it is reviewed on a regular basis for anomalous activities. This can be an arduous task for a group of individuals, let alone one person. The reviewers must know what they are looking for to appropriately interpret the information and take action. They must be able to spot trends, patterns, and variances that might indicate unusual behavior among the recorded events. When one considers the amount of information recorded in logs each day, and adds the responsibility of managing it in an effective manner to an already busy security professional, the challenge becomes all too apparent. This could easily become a full-time job for one person or a group of individuals.

If the management of this vast amount of information can cause a security professional to reach for pain relief, imagine the impact on a system during collection of this information—not to mention the additional overhead for storage and processing.

Fortunately, there are analysis tools designed to assist in the ongoing management of all this information. Audit reduction tools will reduce the amount of data by removing events that have little consequence on security, such as activities related to normal operations, making the remaining information more meaningful. Trends/variance detection and attack-signature detection tools similar to the functionality associated with intrusion detection systems will extract useful information from all the available raw data.

Conclusion

Operating system logs can provide a wealth of useful information in the ongoing security management of an organization's systems and resources, but not without a price. Managing this information in a meaningful way requires a commitment of time, computing resources, and perseverance, making it an ongoing challenge.

OTHER: ROUTERS AND SWITCHES

Routers and switches play a critical role in enterprise networks. Routers connect different network segments and mediate in routing traffic from one segment to another. They can be considered as "sitting" at critical points of the network.

Routers are the glue that connects the pieces of a network. Even in the simplest networks, this is not a simple task.

Like routers, switches are critical components in networks. Switches sort out traffic intended for one network, while allowing separation of network segments.

Switches and routers continue to evolve into fairly complex devices with substantial computing power. Further, given their criticality in the network function, their impact on security is critical. Routers have evolved into highly specialized computing platforms, with extremely flexible but complex capabilities. Such complexity lends itself to vulnerabilities and attacks.

Issues pertaining to routers and switches deal with:

- *Access*: who has what access to the device
- *Configuration*: what kind of configuration ensures security of the device
- *Performance*: once deployed, how well it performs to meet intended requirements

It is of interest to track information on the above to ensure the "health" of the network devices and their performance. Ensuring device health means that the device is kept functioning based on its intended purposes. Not only must one keep track of changes and performance of the device, but one must also determine whether the changes are authorized and the impact on the security of the device.

Issues of managing routers and switches are similar to those pertaining to network devices such as firewalls and IDSs. Like firewalls and IDSs, switches and routers require due care; that is, logging suspicious activity, generating alarms where necessary, and constant reviewing of logged activity for purposes of improving their protection.

Similar to using firewalls and IDSs, users must ensure that routers and switches are not deployed with default configurations and that there exist processes for updating and patching the devices.

Typically, switches and routers are used in an internal network. For many, this may suggest a lower level of protection than that required for devices on the perimeter. Indeed, there are some who may feel that once the perimeter is secured, the degree of protection on the inside must be lower. This would be a false sense of security, considering that most attacks arise from sources in the internal network. Moreover, in the case of a successful attack, the intruder will have a free reign where there is insufficient protection on internal network devices.

There is more. The distinction between the inside and outside of a network continues to blur. Typically, an enterprise network is composed of intranets, extranets, the internal network, as well as the Internet. It takes the weakest link to break the security chain. And this could be the switch or router through which one links the business partner. As such, as much attention must be paid to managing these devices securely as is required for devices on the perimeter.

Enclaves –
Enterprise

Security information from routers and switches should be part of total enterprise security information. This will help define a holistic picture of the enterprise security posture.

STRATEGIES FOR MANAGING ENTERPRISE INFORMATION

Managing security information presents a number of challenges to enterprise security and risk managers. The challenges include the potentially overwhelming amounts of information generated by a diverse number of network devices, analyzing the information, correlating security events, and relating technical risks to business risk. Moreover, security and risk managers must continuously perform these security-related activities to be aware of the organization's security posture while finding ways to improve this posture.

To have meaningful insight into an enterprise's security posture, information from diverse sources must be aggregated and correlated in a meaningful manner. Subsequent analysis would show underlying patterns, trends, and metrics associated with the information.

Patterns can be indicators of profiles of system usage. These profiles, in turn, may be due to the nature of the project and maintenance process for security in the enterprise. Trends, on the other hand, indicate variation in various security aspects over time. They may be indicators of improvements realized; they may also indicate problem areas that need improvements. Metrics and patterns are also useful for root cause analysis and problem resolution.

The most challenging tasks for security and risk managers include analyzing information collected across an enterprise from diverse network devices—devices that are used for different but complementary security functions. For example, information coming from firewalls, intrusion systems, and syslogs is complementary in nature with respect to security. Defining a suitable association for information from these diverse sources remains a key test.

Aside from dealing with the volumes of data collected, specific analysis techniques are required to ease the analysis process. These techniques can be based on anomalies, correlation, association with known exposures, trends, and user profiles. These techniques act as filters and aggregators for security information, converting massive data elements to useful information for decision-making.

In general, the range of issues is technical, process, people, and business related. They must be viewed with this totality for the information to be meaningful for improving security posture.

The remainder of this entry section offers an overview of security information management issues and approaches to meeting the challenges of the complexity of managing the security information. While many practices identified in this entry section are useful in improving an organization's security predisposition, their total application is key to improved enterprise security bearing. Practitioners of information security realize that security is both social and technical. As such, practices and norms in an organization, especially those pertaining to self-improvement, are core to improving the organization's security.

Security Data Collection and Log Management Issues

Collection, storage, and analysis of security-related information across an enterprise are crucial to understanding an organization's security predisposition. Managers must determine ways of managing the potentially huge amounts of information in a manner that makes business sense. Specifically, how does one translate technical vulnerability data to business risk?

There is a potential danger of being overwhelmed by the amount of information generated if proper filtering is not applied to ensure that only critical security-related information gets collected. The choice of filters for security-related information is borne out of experience and depends on the nature of the environment to which the information pertains.

There remains the challenge of collecting information in a manner that retains security-sensitive information and yet eliminates the amount of "noise" in the information collected. As an example, most intrusion detection systems raise a lot of false positives based on the configuration of the IDS sensors. In practice, a lot of information they generate can be classified as "white noise" and is of little value to security management. Security managers are faced with the challenge of designing appropriate filters to enable the filtering of white noise and thus lessen the burden of managing the collected information.

There are other fundamental issues pertaining to collecting security information. These include ensuring sufficient storage space for log information and periodic transmittal of collected information to a central log collection host. In many cases, projects are executed without sufficient planning for collection of log data, a fact that makes it extremely difficult to do root cause analysis when incidents occur.

Other log management issues pertain to the process in place for reviewing log information. In many organizations, information is logged but hardly examined to discern whether any serious security breach might have taken place. Given that security is more than technology, the process of managing security is as important as the technology used and the qualification of the people charged with managing that security. Technically proficient people managing security not only will understand the technology they are managing, but also appreciate security-related issues pertaining to their technology, including the role of the technology in ensuring security in the organization.

Issues of log management and associated technical personnel to execute them must be part of an organization's security management plan arising from an enterprise's security policy.

Data Interchange and Storage

The lack of an industry standard for exchange of security information presents a major problem for management of security information. Although the XML standard promises to close this gap, it has yet to be adopted as widely in industry as desirable. Thus, while users wait for vendors to adopt a standard for exchanging information, they must live with managing security from diverse sources in the different formats presented by vendors.

A security information exchange standard such as XML is one step, however. A long-term challenge is to find a common classification of security information from different products in the same security space. For example, IDSs would classify data the same way so that a security event generated by one IDS would be treated the same way as a similar event generated by an IDS from a different vendor.

Although there is no industry standard for data interchange yet, most products have the ability to store security-related information in a database. Being Open Database Connectivity (ODBC) compliant allows for data interchange between different programs and databases.

Storage issues include the determination of the amount of data collected and the format of storage. Typically, a database schema must be designed that makes sense with respect to the information collected. The schema will determine the nature of the breakdown of security events and their storage.

In designing storage requirements, security managers must incorporate such known concepts as backup and restoration properties. Others include high availability and remote access provision.

Correlation and Analysis

To get an enterprisewide security view, security information must be aggregated across the enterprise. This includes information from a diverse range of devices (intrusion detection systems, firewalls, system hosts, applications, routers, switches, and more) in the enterprise network. The above information, along with vulnerability data, can help discern an organization's security posture.

Log Data Analysis

Ultimately, the analysis of security information is intended to better understand the associated technical risk. Better still, the information would be useful for managing business risk. Few organizations have been successful in showing the link between technical vulnerability/risk data and associated business risk.

The information aggregation principle is based on the fact that the sum of the information from individual parts is less than the information obtained from the whole composed of the parts. Given the number of potential security-related events generated in an enterprise, there is a big challenge to associate, in a meaningful manner, related security-sensitive information or events.

A security event detected by an IDS can be related to a similar event recorded by the firewall or a Web server in an enterprise's DMZ. Indeed, such an event can be associated with specific activity in back-end systems behind the DMZ.

Event correlation has the power to give insight into the nature of a security-related event. One can play out different scenarios of how an event manifests itself once it hits an organization's network.

Take an event that has been detected by an IDS sitting on the DMZ. Now suppose that it was not detected by the firewall. This may be due to the failure to configure the firewall appropriately; and if the event is detected and blocked by the firewall, it is well and good. However, if it is not detected, it may require investigation. And if picked up by the Web server at the DMZ, then there is cause for concern. Correlation also allows for incorporation of the desirable response based on the criticality of the device under attack. Event correlation is dealt with in greater detail in Nyanchama and Sop (2001).[?]

It makes sense to associate security events seen at the firewall with those seen by the firewall and (if necessary) those happening in the DMZ and even the backend applications behind the DMZ. The collective picture gained is powerful and offers a more holistic view of security-related events in an organization.

Event correlation requires an enterprisewide strategy to become meaningful. Fig. 1 depicts one possible way to organize collection and correlation of information. In this example, there are collections agents that can be configured in peer-to-peer or master-slave modes. Peer-to-peer agents have similar control in the communication. The master-slave relationship retains control within the matter.

To be effective and offer a totality of an organization's security posture, the agents must be capable of handling information from a diverse range of sources, including event logs, syslogs, intrusion systems, firewalls, routers, and switches. Special agents can also be deployed for specific network devices (e.g., firewalls) to offer a view of the security configuration of firewalls. There are products on the market that claim to perform event correlation across different network devices. As of writing this entry (March 2001), there is no a single product with convincing performance to warrant such a claim.

The above example shows a possible scenario in which collection agents are deployed across the enterprise but organized along the way the enterprise is organized. This ensures that business units can collect their information

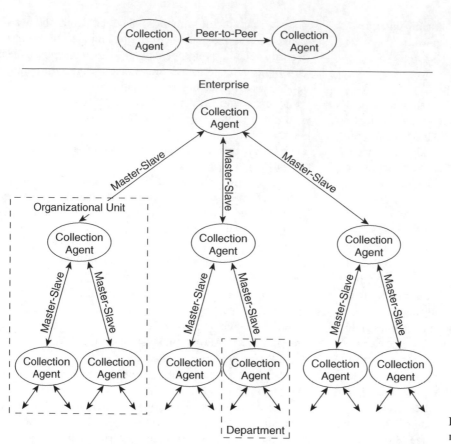

Enclaves –
Enterprise

Fig. 1 Collection and correlation of information.

and pass up the chain only specific flagged information, in the form of aggregates, that contributes to the overall picture of enterprise security posture.

There may be other models along which information is organized. For example, collection agents can be deployed as peer-to-peer, master-slave, or a mix of both. Organizations must determine which model best suits them.

Vulnerability Data

Log data analysis and correlation alone is not sufficient to ensure enterprise security posture, although it is important as a component of the "active security" of an organization. Typically, further analysis will include vulnerability data from network assessments.

Vulnerability data usually pertains to scans targeted at discovering such things as the number of ports open, the types of services running, the kind of exposures to which said services are vulnerable, and the potential severity of these exposures.

There are few guidelines on the market indicating how vulnerability data should be manipulated. However, creating data mining can give indications on such aspects as the following:

- Risk profiles (e.g., per network, department, etc.) based on the number of vulnerabilities in that network segment

- Metrics about proportions of vulnerabilities regarded as high risk vs. those with high risk
- Indication of trends of vulnerability data based on scans taken at different periods of time; interpolation and extrapolation of such trends will offer insight into any improvements in the security posture and whether or not there are improvements

Specific risk profiles will be useful in root cause analysis. It may be that certain vulnerability risk profiles indicate specific weaknesses pertaining to a number of factors such as the process of security planning, design and implementation, as well as the strength of the security process.

For security practitioners, the challenge is to determine the best way to present vulnerability data so as to help improve the way security is managed; specifically, lessons learned from correlation, trends in vulnerability data, and the metrics in performance as well as root cause analysis. And while these insights can be useful in managing security, the ultimate goal would be to associate technical vulnerability information to business risk. The data is not in yet but it is possible that certain vulnerability data profiles suggest specific types of likely business risks. Others, such as Donn Parker,[1] argue that such an approach is not suitable. Instead, Parker advocates the concept of due care based on the fact that one cannot quantify the cost of avoiding potential security failure.

SUMMARY AND CONCLUSIONS

In an enterprise, there are diverse sources of security information that comes from devices that perform various network functions. Technologies such as firewalls and IDSs play a key role in enforcing security, while information from routers, switches, and system logs helps in providing a view of an organization's security posture.

Security managers face the challenge of collecting, storing, and analyzing the information in an effective manner that informs and improves the security management process. It must be understood that while security depends a lot on technology, it remains an issue pertaining to people and processes around managing security.

Strategies for the collection of information include the application of filters at strategic locations, complete with filters that pass only that information which must be passed on. This may use intelligent agents that correlate and aggregate information in useful ways to help minimize the amount of information collected centrally.

Security management is also faced with the challenge of creating measures for various aspects of enterprise security. These include metrics such as the percentage of network devices facing particular risks. This requires comparative criteria for measuring technical risk. Further, the said metrics can be used for root cause analysis to both identify and solve problems in a computing environment. Future challenges include being able to associate technical and business risk measures.

There is more. Taking technical risk numbers over time can be used to obtain trends. Such trends would indicate whether there are improvements to the organization's security posture over time.

Security and risk managers, apart from understanding the function of network technologies, face other major challenges. Coming to grips with the reality of the complexity of security management is one step. Defining clear processes and means of managing the information is a step ahead. Yet, using information in a manner that informs the security process and contributes to improvement of the security posture would be a major achievement. Finally, defining metrics

and trends useful for managing business risk will be a critical test in the future.

REFERENCES

1. Parker, D. Risk reduction out, enablement and due care in. Comput. Secur. J. *16* (4), 37–41.
2. Nyanchama, M.; Sop, P. Enterprise Security Management: Managing Complexity. Inform. Syst. Secur. January/February **2001**.

BIBLIOGRAPHY

1. Zwicky, E.D.; Cooper, S.; Chapman, D.B. *Building Internet Firewalls*, 2nd Ed, O'Reilly, 2000, http://csrc.nist.gov/publications/nistpubs/800-7/node155.html.
2. Wack, J.; Carnhan, L. Keeping Your Site Comfortably Secure: An Introduction to Internet Firewalls. NIST Special Publication 800-10. U.S. Department of Commerce. National Institute of Standards and Technology, February 1995, http://csrc.nist.gov/publications/nistpubs/800-10/main.html.
3. Ballew, S.M. *Managing IP Networks with Cisco Routers*, 1st Ed, O'Reilly, 1997.
4. Goncalves, M. *Firewalls Complete*, McGraw-Hill: New York, 1998.
5. Syslog the UNIX System Logger, http://www.scrambler.net/syslog.htm.
6. http://njlug.rutgers.edu/projects/syslog/.
7. Explanation and FAQ for RME Syslog Analyzer, http://www.cisco.com/warp/public/477/RME/rme_syslog.html.
8. Marshall, V.H. Intrusion Detection in Computers. Summary of the Trusted Information Systems (TIS) Report on Intrusion Detection Systems, January 1991.
9. Carson, M.; Zink, M. NIST Switch: A Platform for Research on Quality of Service Routing 1998, http://www.antd.nist.gov/itg/nistswitch/qos.spie.ps.
10. Parker, D. Risk Reduction Out, Enablement and Due Care In CSI comput. Secur. J. **2000**, *16* (4), 37–41.
11. Base, R.; Mell, P. NIST Special Publication on Intrusion Detection Systems.
12. Security Portal; The Joys of the Incident Handling Response Process.
13. Ranum, M. Intrusion Detection Ideals, Expectations and Realities.
14. NIST Special Publication, 800-12, Introduction to Computer Security. *The NIST Handbook*.

Espionage: Counter-Economic

Craig A. Schiller, CISSP, ISSMP, ISSAP
President, Hawkeye Security Training, LLC, Portland, Oregon, U.S.A.

Abstract

The Attorney General of the United States defined economic espionage as "the unlawful or clandestine targeting or acquisition of sensitive financial, trade, or economic policy information; proprietary economic information; or critical technologies." Note that this definition excludes the collection of open and legally available information that makes up the majority of economic collection. This means that aggressive intelligence collection that is entirely open and legal may harm U.S. companies but is not considered espionage, economic or otherwise. The FBI has extended this definition to include the unlawful or clandestine targeting or influencing of sensitive economic policy decisions.

Intelligence consists of two broad categories—open source and espionage. Open-source intelligence collection is the name given to legal intelligence activities. Espionage is divided into the categories of economic and military/political/governmental; the distinction is the targets involved. A common term, *industrial espionage* was used (and is still used to some degree) to indicate espionage between two competitors. As global competitors began to conduct these activities with possible assistance from their governments, the competitor-vs.-competitor nature of industrial espionage became less of a discriminator. As the activities expanded to include sabotage and interference with commerce and proposal competitions, the term *economic espionage* was coined for the broader scope.

Today's economic competition is global. The conquest of markets and technologies has replaced former territorial and colonial conquests. We are living in a state of world economic war, and this is not just a military metaphor—the companies are training the armies, and the unemployed are the casualties.

—Bernard Esambert,
President of the French Pasteur Institute,
at a Paris Conference on Economic Espionage

The Attorney General of the United States defined economic espionage as "the unlawful or clandestine targeting or acquisition of sensitive financial, trade, or economic policy information; proprietary economic information; or critical technologies." Note that this definition excludes the collection of open and legally available information that makes up the majority of economic collection. This means that aggressive intelligence collection that is entirely open and legal may harm U.S. companies but is not considered espionage, economic or otherwise. The FBI has extended this definition to include the unlawful or clandestine targeting or influencing of sensitive economic policy decisions.

Intelligence consists of two broad categories—open source and espionage. Open-source intelligence collection is the name given to legal intelligence activities. Espionage is divided into the categories of economic and military/political/governmental; the distinction is the targets involved. A common term, *industrial espionage* was used (and is still used to some degree) to indicate espionage between two competitors. As global competitors began to conduct these activities with possible assistance from their governments, the competitor-vs.-competitor nature of industrial espionage became less of a discriminator. As the activities expanded to include sabotage and interference with commerce and proposal competitions, the term *economic espionage* was coined for the broader scope.

While the examples and cases discussed in this entry focus mainly on the United States, the issues are universal. The recommendations and types of information gathered can and should be translated for any country.

BRIEF HISTORY

The prosperity and success of this country are due in no small measure to economic espionage committed by Francis Cabot Lowell during the Industrial Revolution. Britain replaced costly, skilled hand labor with water-driven looms that were simple and reliable. The looms were so simple that they could be operated by a few unskilled women and children. The British government passed strict patent laws and prohibited the export of technology related to the making of cotton. A law was passed

Encyclopedia of Information Assurance DOI: 10.1081/E-EIA-120046282
Copyright © 2011 by Taylor & Francis. All rights reserved.

Espionage –
Firewalls

making it illegal to hire skilled textile workers for work abroad. Those workers who went abroad had their property confiscated. It was against the law to make and export drawings of the mills.

So Lowell memorized and stole the plans to a Cartwright loom, a water-driven weaving machine. It is believed that Lowell perfected the art of *spying by driving around*. Working from Edinburgh, he and his wife traveled daily throughout the countryside, including Lancashire and Derbyshire, the hearts of the Industrial Revolution. Returning home, he built a scale model of the loom. His company built its first loom in Waltham. Soon, his factories were capable of producing up to 30 miles of cloth a day.[1] This marked America's entry into the Industrial Revolution.

By the early twentieth century, we had become "civilized" to the point that Henry L. Stimson, our Secretary of State, said for the record that "Gentlemen do not read other gentlemen's mail" while refusing to endorse a code-breaking operation. For a short time the U.S. Government was the only government that believed this fantasy. At the beginning of World War II, the United States found itself almost completely blind to activities inside Germany and totally dependent on other countries' intelligence services for information. In 1941, the United States recognized that espionage was necessary to reduce its losses and efficiently engage Germany. To meet this need, first the COI and then the OSS were created under the leadership of General "Wild Bill" Donovan.

It would take tremendous forces to broaden this awakening to include economic espionage.

WATERSHED: END OF COLD WAR, BEGINNING OF INFORMATION AGE

In the late 1990s, two events occurred that radically changed information security for many companies. The end of the Cold War—marked by the collapse of the former Soviet Union—created a pool of highly trained intelligence officers without targets. In Russia, some continued to work for the government, some began to work in the newly created private sector, and some provided their services for the criminal element. Some did all three. The world's intelligence agencies began to focus their attention on economic targets and information war, just in time for watershed event number-two—the beginning of the information age.

John Lienhard, M.D. Anderson Professor of Mechanical Engineering and History at the University of Houston, is the voice and driving force behind the "Engines of Our Ingenuity," a syndicated program for public radio. He has said that the change of our world into an information society is not like the Industrial Revolution. No; this change is more like the change from a hunter-gatherer society to an agrarian society. A change of this magnitude happened only once or twice in all of history. Those who

were powerful in the previous society may have no power in the new society. In the hunter-gatherer society, the strongest man and best hunter rules. But where is he in an agrarian society? There, the best hunter holds little or no power. During the transition to an information society, those with power in the old ways will not give it up easily. Now couple the turmoil caused by this shift with the timing of the "end" of the Cold War.

The currency of the new age is information. The power struggle in the new age is the struggle to gather, use, and control information. It is at the beginning of this struggle that the Cold War ended, making available a host of highly trained information gatherers to countries and companies trying cope with the new economy. Official U.S. acknowledgment of the threat of economic espionage came in 1996 with the passage of the Economic Espionage Act.

For the information security professional, the world has fundamentally changed. Until 1990, a common practice had been to make the cost of an attack prohibitively expensive. How do you make an attack prohibitively expensive when your adversaries have the resources of governments behind them?

Most information security professionals have not been trained and are not equipped to handle professional intelligence agents with deep pockets. Today, most business managers are incapable of fathoming that such a threat exists.

ROLE OF INFORMATION TECHNOLOGY IN ECONOMIC ESPIONAGE

In the 1930s, the German secret police divided the world of espionage into five roles.[2] Table 1 illustrates some of the ways that information technology today performs these five divisions of espionage functionality.

In addition to these roles, information technology may be exploited as a target, used as a tool, used for storage (for good or bad), used as protection for critical assets as a weapon, used as a transport mechanism, or used as an agent to carry out tasks when activated.

- *Target.* Information and information technology can be the target of interest. The goal of the exploitation may be to discover new information assets (breach of confidentiality), deprive one of exclusive ownership, acquire a form of the asset that would permit or facilitate reverse-engineering, corrupt the integrity of the asset—either to diminish the reputation of the asset or to make the asset become an agent—or to deny the availability of the asset to those who rely on it (denial of service).
- *Tool.* Information technology can be the tool to monitor and detect traces of espionage or to recover information assets. These tools include intrusion detection systems, log analysis programs, content monitoring programs, etc. For the bad guys, these tools would

Table 1 Five divisions of Espionage functionality.

Role	WWII description	IT equivalent
Collectors	Located and gathered desired information	People or IT (hardware or software) agents, designer viruses that transmit data to the Internet
Transmitters	Forwarded the data to Germany, by coded mail or shortwave radio	E-mail, browsers with convenient 128-bit encryption, FTP, applications with built-in collection and transmission capabilities (e.g., comet cursors, Real Player, Media Player, or other spyware), covert channel applications
Couriers	Worked on steamship lines and transatlantic clippers, and carried special messages to and from Germany	Visiting country delegations, partners/suppliers, temporary workers, and employees that rotate in and out of companies with CD-R/CD-RW, Zip disks, tapes, drawings, digital camera images, etc.
Drops	Innocent-seeming addresses of businesses or private individuals, usually in South American or neutral European ports; reports were sent to these addresses for forwarding to Germany	E-mail relays, e-mail anonymizers, Web anonymizers, specially designed software that spreads information to multiple sites (the reverse of distributed DoS) to avoid detection
Specialists	Expert saboteurs	Viruses, worms, DDoS, Trojan horses, chain e-mail, hoaxes, using e-mail to spread dissension, public posting of sensitive information about salaries, logic bombs, insiders sabotaging products, benchmarks, etc.

include probes, enumeration programs, viruses that search for PGP keys, etc.

- *Storage.* Information technology can store stolen or illegal information. IT can store sleeper agents for later activation.
- *Protection.* Information technology may have the responsibility to protect the information assets. The protection may be in the form of applications such as firewalls, intrusion detection systems, encryption tools, etc., or elements of the operating system such as file permissions, network configurations, etc.
- *Transport.* Information technology can be the means by which stolen or critical information is moved, whether burned to CDs, e-mailed, FTP-ed, hidden in a legitimate http stream, or encoded in images or music files.
- *Agent.* Information technology can be used as an agent of the adversary, planted to extract significant sensitive information, to launch an attack when given the appropriate signal, or to receive or initiate a covert channel through a firewall.

IMPLICATIONS FOR INFORMATION SECURITY

Implication 1

A major tenet of our profession has been that, because we cannot always afford to prevent information system-related losses, we should make it prohibitively expensive to compromise those systems. How does one do that when the adversary has the resources of a government behind him? Frankly, this tenet only worked on adversaries who

were limited by time, money, or patience. Hackers with unlimited time on their hands—and a bevy of unpaid researchers who consider a difficult system to be a trophy waiting to be collected—turn this tenet into Swiss cheese.

This reality has placed emphasis on the onion model of information security. In the onion model you assume that all other layers will fail. You build prevention measures but you also include detection measures that will tell you that those measures have failed. You plan for the recovery of critical information, assuming that your prevention and detection measures will miss some events.

Implication 2

Information security professionals must now be able to determine if their industry or their company is a target for economic espionage. If their company/industry is a target, then the information security professionals should adjust their perceptions of their potential adversaries and their limits. One of the best-known quotes from the *Art of War* by Sun Tsu says, "Know your enemy." Become familiar with the list of countries actively engaging in economic espionage against your country or within your industry. Determine if any of your vendors, contractors, partners, suppliers, or customers come from these countries. In today's global economy, it may not be easy to determine the country of origin. Many companies move their global headquarters to the United States and keep only their main R&D offices in the country of origin. Research the company and its founders. Learn where and how they gained their expertise. Research any publicized accounts regarding economic espionage/intellectual property theft attributed to the company, the country, or other companies from the country. Pay particular attention to the methods used and the nature of the known targets. Contact the FBI or its equivalent and see if they can provide additional information. Do not forget to check your own organization's history with each company. With this information you can work with your business leaders to determine what may be a target within your company and what measures (if any) may be prudent.

> He who protects everything, protects nothing.
> —*Napoleon*

Applying the wisdom of Napoleon implies that, within the semipermeable external boundary, we should determine which information assets truly need protection, to what degree, and from what threats. Sun Tsu speaks to this need as well. It is not enough to only know your enemy.

> Therefore I say, "Know the enemy and know yourself; in a hundred battles you will never be in peril."
> When you are ignorant of the enemy but know yourself, your chances of winning or losing are equal.
> If ignorant both of your enemy and yourself, you are certain in every battle to be in peril.
> —*Sun Tzu (The Art of War (III.31–33))*

A company can "know itself" using a variation from the business continuity concept of a business impact assessment (BIA). The information security professional can use the information valuation data collected during the BIA and extend it to produce information protection guides for sensitive and critical information assets. The information protection guides tell users which information should be protected, from what threats, and what to do if an asset is found unprotected. They should tell the technical staff about threats to each information asset and about any required and recommended safeguards.

A side benefit gained from gathering the information valuation data is that, in order to gather the value information, the business leaders must internalize questions of how the data is valuable and the degrees of loss that would occur in various scenarios. This is the most effective security awareness that money can buy.

After the information protection guides have been prepared, you should meet with senior management again to discuss the overall posture the company wants to take regarding information security and counter-economic espionage. Note that it is significant that you wait until after the information valuation exercise is complete before addressing the security posture. If management has not accepted the need for security, the question about desired posture will yield damaging results.

Here are some potential postures that you can describe to management:

- *Prevent all.* In this posture, only a few protocols are permitted to cross your external boundary.

- *City wall.* A layered approach, prevention, detection, mitigation, and recovery strategies are all, in effect, similar to the walled city in the Middle Ages. Traffic is examined, but more is permitted in and out. Because more is permitted, detection, mitigation, and recovery strategies are needed internally because the risk of something bad getting through is greater.
- *Aggressive.* A layered approach, but embracing new technology, is given a higher priority than protecting the company. New technology is selected, and then security is asked how they will deal with it.
- *Edge racer.* Only general protections are provided. The company banks on running faster than the competition. "We'll be on the next technology before they catch up with our current release." This is a common position before any awareness has been effective.

Implication 3

Another aspect of knowing your enemy is required. As security professionals we are not taught about spycraft. It is not necessary that we become trained as spies. However, the FBI, in its annual report to congress on economic espionage, gives a summary about techniques observed in cases involving economic espionage.

Much can be learned about modern techniques in three books written about the Mossad—*Gideon's Spies* by Gordon Thomas, and *By Way of Deception,* and *The Other Side of Deception*, both by Victor Ostrovsky and Claire Hoy. These describe the Mossad as an early adopter of technology as a tool in espionage, including their use of Trojan code in software sold commercially. The books describe software known as Promis that was sold to intelligence agencies to assist in tracking terrorists; and the authors allege that the software had a Trojan that permitted the Mossad to gather information about the terrorists tracked by its customers. *By Way of Deception* describes the training process as seen by Ostrovsky.

Implication 4

Think globally, act locally

The Chinese government recently announced that the United States had placed numerous bugging devices on a plane for President Jiang Zemin. During the customization by a U.S. company of the interior of the plane for its use as the Chinese equivalent of Air Force One, bugs were allegedly placed in the upholstery of the president's chair, in his bedroom, and even in the toilet.

When the United States built a new embassy in Moscow, the then-extant Soviet Union insisted it be built using Russian workers. The United States called a halt to its construction in 1985 when it discovered it was too heavily bugged for diplomatic purposes. The building remained unoccupied for a decade following the discovery.

The *1998 Annual Report to Congress on Foreign Economic Collection and Industrial Espionage* concluded with the following statement:

> ... foreign software manufacturers solicited products to cleared U.S. companies that had been embedded with spawned processes and multithreaded tasks.

This means that foreign software companies sold products with Trojans and backdoors to targeted U.S. companies.

In response to fears about the Echelon project, in 2001 the European Union announced recommendations that member nations use open-source software to ensure that Echelon software agents are not present.

Security teams would benefit by using open-source software tools if they could be staffed sufficiently to maintain and continually improve the products. Failing that, security in companies in targeted industries should consider the origins of the security products they use. If your company knows it is a target for economic espionage, it would be wise to avoid using security products from countries actively engaged in economic espionage against your country. If unable to follow this strategy, the security team should include tools in the architecture (from other countries) that could detect extraneous traffic or anomalous behavior of the other security tools.

In this strategy you should follow the effort all the way through implementation. In one company, the corporate standard for firewall was a product of one of the most active countries engaging in economic espionage. Management was unwilling to depart from the standard. Security proposed the use of an intrusion detection system (IDS) to guard against the possibility of the firewall being used to permit undetected, unfiltered, and unreported access. The IDS was approved; but when procurement received the order, they discovered that the firewall vendor sold a special, optimized version of the same product and—without informing the security team—ordered the IDS from the vendor that the team was trying to guard against.

Implication 5

The system of rating computers for levels of security protection is incapable of providing useful information regarding products that might have malicious code that is included intentionally. In fact, companies that have intentions of producing code with these Trojans are able to use the system of ratings to gain credibility without merit.

It appears that the first real discovery by one of the ratings systems caused the demise of the ratings system and a cover-up of the findings. I refer to the Multilevel Information System Security Initiative (MISSI) ratings system's discovery of a potential backdoor in Checkpoint Firewall-1 in 1997. After this discovery, the unclassified

X31 report[3] for this product and all previous reports were pulled from availability. The Internet site that provided them was shut down, and requestors were told that the report had been classified. The federal government had begun pulling Checkpoint Firewall-1 from military installations and replacing it with other companies' products. While publicly denying that these actions were happening, Checkpoint began correspondence with the NSA, owners of the MISSI process, to answer the findings of that study. The NSA provided a list of findings and preferred corrective actions to resolve the issue. In Checkpoint's response to the NSA, they denied that the code in question, which involved simple network management protocol (SNMP) and which referenced files containing IP addresses in Israel, was a backdoor (Letter of reply from David Steinberg, Director, Federal Checkpoint Software, Inc. to Louis F. Giles, Deputy Chief Commercial Solutions & Enabling Technology; 9800 Savage Road Suite 6740, Ft. Meade, MD, dated September 10, 1998). According to the NSA, two files with IP addresses in Israel "could provide access to the firewall via SNMPv2 mechanisms." Checkpoint's reply indicated that the code was dead code from Carnegie Mellon University and that the files were QA testing data that was left in the final released configuration files.

The X31 report, which I obtained through an Freedom of Information Act (FOIA) request, contains no mention of the incident and no indication that any censorship had occurred. This fact is particularly disturbing because a report of this nature should publish all issues and their resolutions to ensure that there is no complicity between testers and the test subjects.

However, the letter also reveals two other vulnerabilities that I regard as backdoors, although the report classes them as software errors to be corrected. The Checkpoint response to some of these "errors" is to defend aspects of them as desirable. One specific reference claims that most of Checkpoint's customers prefer maximum connectivity to maximum security, a curious claim that I have not seen in their marketing material. This referred to the lack of an ability to change the implicit rules in light of the vulnerability of stateful inspection's handling of Domain Name Service (DNS) using User Datagram Protocol (UDP), which existed in Version 3 and earlier.

Checkpoint agreed to most of the changes requested by the NSA; however, the exception is notable in that it would have required Checkpoint to use digital signatures to sign the software and data electronically to prevent someone from altering the product in a way that would go undetected. These changes would have provided licensees of the software with the ability to know that, at least initially, the software they were running was indeed the software and data that had been tested during the security review.

It is interesting to note that Checkpoint had released an internal memo nine months prior to the letter responding to the NSA claims in which they claimed nothing had ever happened (e-mail from Craig Johnson dated June 3, 1998, containing memo dated Jan 19, 1998, to all U.S. Sales of Checkpoint).

Both the Information Technology Security Evaluation Criteria (ITSEC) and Common Criteria security rating systems are fatally flawed when it comes to protection against software with intentional malicious code. Security companies are able to submit the software for rating and claim the rating even when the entire system has not been submitted. For example, a company can submit the assurance processes and documentation for a targeted rating. When it achieves the rating on just that portion, it can advertise the rating although the full software functionality has not been tested. For marketing types, they gain the benefit of claiming the rating without the expense of full testing. Even if the rating has an asterisk, the damage is done because many that authorize the purchase of these products only look for the rating. When security reports back to management that the rating only included a portion of the software functionality, it is portrayed as sour grapes by those who negotiated the "great deal" they were going to get. The fact is that there is no commercial push to require critical software such as operating systems and security software to include exhaustive code reviews, covert channel analysis, and to only award a rating when it is fully earned.

To make matters worse, if it appears that a company is going to get a poor rating from a test facility, the vendor can stop the process and start over at a different facility, perhaps in another country, with no penalty and no carry-over.

WHAT ARE THE TARGETS?

The U.S. Government publishes a list of military critical technologies (MCTs). A summary of the list is published annually by the FBI (see Table 2).

There is no equivalent list for non-military critical technologies. However, the government has added "targeting

Table 2 Military critical technologies (MCTs).

Information systems
Sensors and lasers
Electronics
Aeronautics systems technology
Armaments and energetic materials
Marine systems
Guidance, navigation, and vehicle signature control
Space systems
Materials
Manufacturing and fabrication
Information warfare
Nuclear systems technology
Power systems
Chemical/biological systems
Weapons effects and countermeasures
Ground systems
Directed and kinetic energy systems

Table 3 National security threat list issues.

Terrorism
Espionage
Proliferation
Economic espionage
Targeting the national information infrastructure
Targeting the U.S. Government
Perception management
Foreign intelligence activities

the national information infrastructure" to the National Security Threat List (NSTL). Targeting the national information infrastructure speaks primarily to the infrastructure as an object of potential disruption, whereas the MCT list contains technologies that foreign governments may want to acquire illegally. The NSTL consists of two tables. One is a list of issues (see Table 3); the other is a classified list of countries engaged in collection activities against the United States. This is not the same list captured in Table 4. Table 4 contains the names of countries engaged in economic espionage and, as such, contains the names of countries that are otherwise friendly trading partners. You will note that the entire subject of economic espionage is listed as one of the threat list issues.

According to the FBI, the collection of information by foreign agencies continues to focus on U.S. trade secrets and science and technology products, particularly dual-use technologies and technologies that provide high profitability.

Examining the cases that have been made public, you can find intellectual property theft, theft of proposal information (bid amounts, key concepts), and requiring companies to participate in joint ventures to gain access to new country markets—then either stealing the IP or awarding the contract to an internal company with an identical proposal. Recently, a case involving HP found a planted employee sabotaging key bench marking tests to HP's detriment. The message from the HP case is that economic espionage also includes efforts beyond the collection of information, such as sabotage of the production line to cause the company to miss key delivery dates, deliver faulty parts, fail key tests, etc.

You should consider yourself a target if your company works in any of the technology areas on the MCT list, is a part of the national information infrastructure, or works in a highly competitive international business.

Table 4 Most active collectors of economic intelligence.

China
Japan
Israel
France
Korea
Taiwan
India

WHO ARE THE PLAYERS?

Countries

This section is written from the published perspective of the U.S. Government. Readers from other countries should attempt to locate a similar list from their government's perspective. It is likely that two lists will exist: a "real" list and a "diplomatically correct" edition.

For the first time since its original publication in 1998, the *Annual Report to Congress on Foreign Economic Collection and Industrial Espionage 2000* lists the most active collectors of economic intelligence. The delay in providing this list publicly is due to the nature of economic espionage. To have economic espionage you must have trade. Our biggest trading partners are our best friends in the world. Therefore, a list of those engaged in economic espionage will include countries that are otherwise friends and allies. Thus the poignancy of Bernard Esambert's quote used to open this entry.

Companies

Stories of companies affected by economic espionage are hard to come by. Public companies fear the effect on stock prices. Invoking the economic espionage law has proven very expensive—a high risk for a favorable outcome—and even the favorable outcomes have been inadequate considering the time, money, and commitment of company resources beyond their primary business. The most visible companies are those that have been prosecuted under the Economic Espionage Act, but there have only been 20 of those, including:

- Four Pillars Company, Taiwan, stole intellectual property and trade secrets from Avery Dennison.
- Laser Devices, Inc., attempted to illegally ship laser gun sights to Taiwan without Department of Commerce authorization.
- Gilbert & Jones, Inc., New Britain, Connecticut, exported potassium cyanide to Taiwan without the required licenses.
- Yuen Foong Paper Manufacturing Company, Taiwan, attempted to steal the formula for Taxol, a cancer drug patented and licensed by the Bristol-Myers Squibb (BMS) Company.
- Steven Louis Davis attempted to disclose trade secrets of the Gillette Company to competitors Warner-Lambert Co., Bic, and American Safety Razor Co. The disclosures were made by fax and e-mail. Davis worked for Wright Industries, a subcontractor of the Gillette Company.
- Duplo Manufacturing Corporation, Japan, used a disgruntled former employee of Standard Duplicating Machines Corporation to gain unauthorized access into a voicemail system. The data was used to compete against Standard. Standard learned of the issue through an unsolicited phone call from a customer.

- Harold Worden attempted to sell Kodak trade secrets and proprietary information to Kodak rivals, including corporations in the People's Republic of China. He had formerly worked for Kodak. He established his own consulting firm upon retirement and subsequently hired many former Kodak employees. He was convicted on one felony count of violating the Interstate Transportation of Stolen Property law.
- In 1977, Mitsubishi Electric bought one of Fusion Systems Corporation's microwave lamps, took it apart, then filed 257 patent actions on its components. Fusion Systems had submitted the lamp for a patent in Japan 2 years earlier. After 25 years of wrangling with Mitsubishi, the Japanese patent system, Congress, and the press, Fusion's board fired the company's president (who had spearheaded the fight) and settled the patent dispute with Mitsubishi a year later.
- The French are known to have targeted IBM, Corning Glass, Boeing, Bell Helicopter, Northrup, and Texas Instruments (TI). In 1991, a guard in Houston noticed two well-dressed men taking garbage bags from the home of an executive of a large defense contractor. The guard ran the license number of the van and found it belonged to the French Consul General in Houston, Bernard Guillet. Two years earlier, the FBI had helped TI remove a French sleeper agent. According to *Cyber Wars*[4] by Jean Guisnel, the French intelligence agency (the DGSE) had begun to plant young French engineers in various French subsidiaries of well-known American firms. Over the years they became integral members of the companies they had entered, some achieving positions of power in the corporate hierarchy. Guillet claims that the primary beneficiary of these efforts was the French giant electronics firm, Bull.

WHAT HAS BEEN DONE?
REAL-WORLD EXAMPLES

Partnering with a Company and then Hacking the Systems Internally

In one case, very senior management took a bold step. In the spirit of the global community, they committed the company to use international partners for major aspects of a new product. Unfortunately, in selecting the partners, they chose companies from three countries listed as actively conducting economic espionage against their country. In the course of developing new products, the employees of one company were caught hacking sensitive systems. Security measures were increased but the employees hacked through them as well. The company of the offending partners was confronted. Its senior management claimed that the employees had acted alone and that their actions were not sanctioned. Procurement, now satisfied that their fragile quilt of partners was okay, awarded the accused partner company a lucrative new product partnership. Additionally, they erased all database entries regarding the issues and chastised internal employees who continued to voice suspicions. No formal investigation was launched. Security had no record of the incident. There was no information security function at the time of the incident.

When the information security function was established, it stumbled upon rumors that these events had occurred. In investigating, they found an internal employee who had witnessed the stolen information in use at the suspect partner's home site. They also determined that the offending partner had a history of economic espionage, perhaps the most widely known in the world. Despite the corroboration of the partner's complicity, line management and procurement did nothing. Procurement knew that the repercussions within their own senior management and line management would be severe because they had pressured the damaged business unit to accept the suspected partner's earlier explanation. Additionally, it would have underscored the poor choice of partners that had occurred under their care and the fatal flaw in the partnering concept of very senior management. It was impossible to extricate the company from this relationship without causing the company to collapse. IT line management would not embrace this issue because they had dealt with it before and had been stung, although they were right all along.

Using Language to Hide in Plain Sight

Israeli Air Force officers assigned to the Recon/Optical Company passed on technical information beyond the state-of-the-art optics to a competing Israeli company, El Op Electro-Optics Industries Ltd. Information was written in Hebrew and faxed. The officers tried to carry 14 boxes out of the plant when the contract was terminated. The officers were punished upon return to Israel—for getting caught (Fialka 1997, pp. 181–184).[1]

In today's multinational partnerships, language can be a significant issue for information security and for technical support. Imagine the difficulty in monitoring and supporting computers for five partners, each in a different language.

The *Annual Report to Congress 2000*[5] reveals that the techniques used to steal trade secrets and intellectual property are limitless. The insider threat, briefcase and laptop computer thefts, and searching hotel rooms have all been used in recent cases. The information collectors are using a wide range of redundant and complementary approaches to gather their target data. At border crossings, foreign officials have conducted excessive attempts at elicitation. Many U.S. citizens unwittingly serve as third-party brokers to arrange visits or circumvent official visitation procedures. Some foreign collectors have invited U.S. experts to present papers overseas to gain access to their expertise

in export-controlled technologies. There have been recent solicitations to security professionals asking for research proposals for security ideas as a competition for awarding grants to conduct studies on security topics. The solicitation came from one of the most active countries engaging in economic espionage. Traditional clandestine espionage methods (such as agent recruitment, U.S. volunteers, and co-optees) are still employed. Other techniques include:

- Breaking away from tour groups
- Attempting access after normal working hours
- Swapping out personnel at the last minute
- Customs holding laptops for an extended period of time
- Requests for technical information
- Elicitation attempts at social gatherings, conferences, trade shows, and symposia
- Dumpster diving (searching a company's trash for corporate proprietary data)
- Using unencrypted Internet messages

To these I would add holding out the prospect of lucrative sales or contracts, but requiring the surrender or sharing of intellectual property as a condition of partnering or participation.

WHAT CAN WE, AS INFORMATION SECURITY PROFESSIONALS, DO?

We must add new skills and improve our proficiency in others to meet the challenge of government funded/supported espionage. Our investigative and forensic skills need improvement over the level required for non-espionage cases. We need to be aware of the techniques that have been and may be used against us. We need to add the ability to elicit information without raising suspicion. We need to recognize when elicitation is attempted and be able to teach our sales, marketing, contracting, and executive personnel to recognize such attempts. We need sources that tell us where elicitation is likely to occur. For example, at this time, the Paris Air Show is considered the number-one economic espionage event in the world.

We need to be able to raise the awareness of our companies regarding the perceived threat and real examples from industry that support those perceptions. Ensure that you brief the procurement department. Establish preferences for products from countries not active in economic espionage. When you must use a product from a country active in economic espionage, attempt to negotiate an indemnification against loss. Have procurement add requirements that partners/suppliers provide proof of background investigations, particularly if individuals will be on site.

Management and procurement should be advised that those partners with intent to commit economic espionage are likely to complain to management that the controls are too restrictive, that they cannot do their jobs, or that their contract requires extraordinary access. You should counter these objectives before they occur by fully informing management and procurement about awareness, concerns, and measures to be taken. The measures should be applied to all suppliers/partners. Ensure that these complaints and issues will be handed over to you for an official response. Treat each one individually and ask for specifics rather than generalities.

If procurement has negotiated a contract that commits the company to extraordinary access, your challenge is greater. Procurement may insist that you honor their contract. At this time you will discover where security stands in the company's pecking order. A stance you can take is, "Your negotiated contract does not and cannot relieve me of my obligation to protect the information assets of this corporation." It may mean that the company has to pay penalties or go back to the negotiating table. You should not have to sacrifice the security of the company's information assets to save procurement some embarrassment.

We need to develop sources to follow developments in economic espionage in industries and businesses similar to ours. Because we are unlikely to have access to definitive sources about this kind of information, we need to develop methods to vet the information we find in open sources. The FBI provides advanced warning to security professionals through ANSIR (Awareness of National Security Issues and Responses) systems. Interested security professionals for U.S. corporations should provide their e-mail addresses, positions, company names and addresses, and telephone and fax numbers to ansir@leo.gov. A representative of the nearest field division office will contact you. The FBI has also created InfraGard (http://www.infragard. net/fieldoffice.htm) chapters for law enforcement and corporate security professionals to share experiences and advice.[6]

InfraGard is dedicated to increasing the security of the critical infrastructures of the United States. All InfraGard participants are committed to the proposition that a robust exchange of information about threats to and actual attacks on these infrastructures is an essential element in successful infrastructure protection efforts. The goal of InfraGard is to enable information flow so that the owners and operators of infrastructures can better protect themselves and so that the U.S. Government can better discharge its law enforcement and national security responsibilities.

BARRIERS ENCOUNTERED IN ATTEMPTS TO ADDRESS ECONOMIC ESPIONAGE

A country is made up of many opposing and cooperating forces. Related to economic espionage, for information security, there are two significant forces. One force champions the businesses of that country. Another force champions the relationships of that country to other countries. Your efforts to protect your company may be hindered by the effect of the opposition of those two forces. This was evident in the first few reports to Congress by the FBI on economic espionage. The FBI was prohibited from listing even the countries that were most active in conducting economic espionage. There is no place in the U.S. government that you can call to determine if a partner you are considering has a history of economic espionage, or if a software developer has been caught with backdoors, placing Trojans, etc.

You may find that, in many cases, the FBI interprets the phrase *information sharing* to mean that you share information with them. In one instance, a corporate investigator gave an internal e-mail that was written in Chinese to the FBI, asking that they translate it. This was done to keep the number of individuals involved in the case to a minimum. Unless you know the translator and his background well, you run the risk of asking someone that might have ties to the Chinese to perform the translation. Once the translation was performed, the FBI classified the document as secret and would not give the investigator the translated version until the investigator reasoned with them that he would have to translate the document with an outside source unless the FBI relented.

Part of the problem facing the FBI is that there is no equivalent to a DoD or DoE security clearance for corporate information security personnel. There are significant issues that complicate any attempt to create such a clearance. A typical security clearance background check looks at criminal records. Background investigations may go a step further and check references, interview old neighbors, schoolmates, colleagues, etc. The most rigorous clearance checks include viewing bank records, credit records, and other signs of fiscal responsibility. They may include a psychological evaluation. They are not permitted to include issues of national origin or religion unless the United States is at war with a particular country. In those cases, the DoD has granted the clearance but placed the individuals in positions that would not create a conflict of interest. In practice, this becomes impossible. Do you share information about all countries and religious groups engaging in economic espionage, except for those to which the security officer may have ties? Companies today cannot ask those questions of its employees. Unfortunately, unless a system of clearances is devised, the FBI will always be reluctant to share information, and rightfully so.

Another aspect of the problem facing the FBI today is the multinational nature of corporations today. What exactly is a U.S. corporation? Many companies today were conceived in foreign countries but established their corporate headquarters in the United States, ostensibly to improve their competitiveness in the huge U.S. marketplace. What of U.S. corporations that are wholly owned by foreign corporations? Should they be entitled to assistance, to limited assistance, or to no assistance? If limited assistance, how are the limits determined?

Within your corporation there are also opposing and cooperating forces. One of the most obvious is the conflict between marketing/sales and information security. In many companies, sales and marketing personnel are the most highly paid and influential people in the company. They are, in most cases, paid largely by commission. This means that if they do not make the sale, they do not get paid. They are sometimes tempted to give the potential customer anything they want, in-depth tours of the plant, details on the manufacturing process, etc., in order to make the sale. Unless you have a well-established and accepted information protection guide that clearly states what can and cannot be shared with these potential customers, you will have little support when you try to protect the company.

The marketing department may have such influence that they cause your procurement personnel to abandon reason and logic in the selection of critical systems and services. A Canadian company went through a lengthy procurement process for a massive wide area network contract. A Request for Proposal (RFP) was released. Companies responded. A selection committee met and identified those companies that did not meet the RFP requirements. Only those companies that met the RFP requirements were carried over into the final phase of the selection process. At this point, marketing intervened and required that procurement re-add two companies to the final selection process—companies that had not met the requirements of the RFP. These two companies purchased high product volumes from this plant. Miracle of miracles: one of the two unqualified companies won the contract.

It is one thing for the marketing department to request that existing customers be given some preference from the list of qualified finalists. It is quite another to require that unqualified respondents be given any consideration.

A product was developed in a country that conducts economic espionage operations against U.S. companies in your industry sector. This product was widely used throughout your company, leaving you potentially vulnerable to exploitation or exposed to a major liability. When the issue was raised, management asked if this particular product had a Trojan or evidence of malicious code. The security officer responded, "No, but due to the nature of this product, if it did contain a Trojan or other malicious code, it could be devastating to our company. Because there are many companies that make this kind of product in countries that do not conduct economic espionage in our industry sector, we should choose one of those to replace this one and thus avoid the risk."

Management's response was surprising: "Thank you very much, but we are going to stay with this product and spread it throughout the corporation—but do let us know if you find evidence of current backdoors and the like." One day the security team learned that, just as feared, there

had indeed been a backdoor; in fact, several. The news was reported to management. Their response was unbelievable. "Well, have they fixed it?" The vendor claimed to have fixed it, but that was not the point. The point was that they had placed the code in the software to begin with, and there was no way to tell if they had replaced the backdoor with another. Management responded, "If they have fixed the problem, we are going to stay with the product, and that is the end of it. Do not bring this subject up again." In security you must raise every security concern that occurs with a product, even after management has made up its mind. To fail to do so would set the company up for charges of negligence should a loss occur that relates to that product. "Doesn't matter; do not raise this subject again."

So why would management make a decision like this? One possible answer has to do with pressure from marketing and potential sales to that country. Another has to do with embarrassment. Some vice president or director somewhere made a decision to use the product to begin with. They may even have had to fall on a sword or two to get the product they wanted. Perhaps it is because a more powerful director had already chosen this product for his site. This director may have forced the product's selection as the corporate standard so that staff would not be impacted. One rumor has it that the product was selected as a corporate standard because the individual choosing the standard was being paid a kickback by a relative working for a third-party vendor of the product. If your IT department raises the issue, it runs the risk of embarrassing one or more of these senior managers and incurring their wrath. Your director may feel intimidated enough that he will not even raise the issue.

Even closer to home is the fact that the issue was raised to your management in time to prevent the spread of the questionable product throughout the corporation. Now if the flag is raised, someone may question why it was not raised earlier. That blame would fall squarely on your director's shoulders.

Does it matter that both the vice president and the director have fiduciary responsibility for losses related to these decisions should they occur? Does it matter that their decisions would not pass the prudent man test and thus place them one step closer to being found negligent? No, it does not. The director is accepting the risk—not the risk to the corporation, but the risk that damage might occur during his watch. The vice president probably does not know about the issue or the risks involved but could still be implicated via the concept of respondent superior. The director may think he is protecting the vice president by keeping him out of the loop—the concept of plausible deniability—but the courts have already tackled that one. Senior management is responsible for the actions of those below them, regardless of whether they know about the actions.

Neither of these cases exists if the information security officer reports to the CEO. There is only a small opportunity for it to exist if the information security officer reports to the

CIO. As the position sinks in the management structure, the opportunity for this type of situation increases.

The first time you raise the specter of economic espionage, you may encounter resistance from employees and management: "Our company isn't like that. We don't do anything important. No one I know has ever heard of anything like that happening here. People in this community trust one another."

Some of those who have been given evidence that such a threat does exist have preferred to ignore the threat, for to acknowledge it would require them to divert resources (people, equipment, or money) from their own initiatives and goals. They would prefer to "bet the company" that it would not occur while they are there. After they are gone it no longer matters to them.

When you raise these issues as the information security officer, you are threatening the careers of many people—from the people who went along with it because they felt powerless to do anything, to the senior management who proposed it, to the people in between who protected the concept and decisions of upper management in good faith to the company. Without a communication path to the CEO and other officers representing the stockholders, you do not have a chance of fulfilling your fiduciary liability to them.

The spy of the future is less likely to resemble James Bond, whose chief assets were his fists, than the Line X engineer who lives quietly down the street and never does anything more violent than turn a page of a manual or flick on his computer.

—*Alvin Toffler,*
(Power Shift: Knowledge, Wealth and Violence at the
Edge of the 21st Century)

REFERENCES

1. Fialka, John J. *War by Other Means*; W.W. Norton Company: New York and London, 1997, 181–184.
2. Sayers, M.; Kahn, Albert E. *Sabotage! The Secret War Against America*; Harper & Brothers: New York, 1942, 25.
3. NSA X3 Technical Report X3-TR001–97 Checkpoint Firewall-1 Version 3.0a, Analysis and Penetration Test Report.
4. Guisnel, Jean, *Cyber Wars*; Perseus Books: New York, 1997.
5. *Annual Report to Congress on Foreign Economic Collection and Industrial Espionage—2000.* Prepared by the National Counterintelligence Center.
6. Infragard National By-Laws, undated, http://www.infragard.net/applic_requirements/natl_bylaws.htm.

Ethics

Peter S. Tippett
Director, Computer Ethics Institute, Pacific Palisades, California, U.S.A.

Abstract
The computer security professional needs both to understand and to influence the behavior of everyday computer users. Traditionally, security managers have concentrated on building security into the system hardware and software, on developing procedures, and on educating end users about procedures and acceptable behavior. Now, the computer professional must also help develop the meaning of ethical computing and help influence computer end users to adopt notions of ethical computing into their everyday behavior.

FUNDAMENTAL CHANGES TO SOCIETY

Computer technology has changed the practical meaning of many important, even fundamental, human and societal concepts. Although most computer professionals would agree that computers change nothing about human ethics, computer and information technologies have caused and will pose many new problems. Indeed, computers have changed the nature and scope of accessing and manipulating information and communications. As a result, computers and computer communications will significantly change the nature and scope of many of the concepts most basic to society. The changes will be as pervasive and all encompassing as the changes accompanying earlier shifts from a society dependent on hunters and gatherers to one that was more agrarian to an industrial society.

Charlie Chaplin once observed, "The progress of science is far ahead of man's ethical behavior." The rapid changes that computing technology and the digital revolution have brought and will bring are at least as profound as the changes prompted by the industrial revolution. This time, however, the transformation will be compressed into a much shorter time frame.

It will not be known for several generations whether the societal changes that follow from the digital revolution will be as fundamental as those caused by the combination of easy transportation, pervasive and near-instantaneous news, and inexpensive worldwide communication brought on by the industrial and radio revolutions. However, there is little doubt that the digital age is already causing significant changes in ways that are not yet fully appreciated.

Some of those changes are bad. For example, combining the known costs of the apparent unethical and illegal uses of computer and information technology—factors such as telephone and PBX fraud, computer viruses, and digital piracy—amounts to several billion dollars annually. When these obvious problems are combined with the kinds of computing behavior that society does not yet fully comprehend as unethical and that society has not yet labeled illegal or antisocial, it is clear that a great computer ethics void exists.

No Sandbox Training

By the time children are 6 years old, they learn that eating grasshoppers and worms is socially unacceptable. Of course, 6 year-olds would not say it quite that way. To express society's wishes, children say something more like: "Eeewwww! Yich! Johnny, you are not going to eat that worm, are you?"

As it turns out, medical science shows that there is nothing physically dangerous or wrong with eating worms or grasshoppers. Eating them would not normally make people sick or otherwise cause physical harm. But children quickly learn at the gut level to abhor this kind of behavior—along with a whole raft of other behavior. What is more, no obvious rule exists that leads to this gut-feeling behavior. No laws, church doctrine, school curriculum, or parental guides specifically address the issue of eating worms and grasshoppers. Yet, even without structured rules or codes, society clearly gives a consistent message about this. Adults take the concept as being so fundamental that it is called common sense.

By the time children reach the age of ten, they have a pretty clear idea of what is right and wrong, and what is acceptable and unacceptable. These distinctions are learned from parents, siblings, extended families, neighbors, acquaintances, and schools, as well as from rituals like holiday celebrations and from radio, television, music, magazines, and many other influences.

Unfortunately, the same cannot be said for being taught what kind of computing behavior is repugnant. Parents, teachers, neighbors, acquaintances, rituals, and other parts of society simply have not been able to provide influence or insight based on generations of experience. Information technology is so new that these people and institutions simply

Encyclopedia of Information Assurance DOI: 10.1081/E-EIA-120046570
Copyright © 2011 by Taylor & Francis. All rights reserved.

Espionage – Firewalls

Espionage –
Firewalls

have no experience to draw on. The would-be teachers are as much in the dark as those who need to be taught.

A whole generation of computer and information system users exists. This generation is more than one hundred million strong and growing. Soon information system users will include nearly every literate individual on earth. Members of this new generation have not yet had their sandbox training. Computer and information users, computer security professionals included, are simply winging it.

Computer users are less likely to know the full consequences of many of their actions than they would be if they could lean on the collective family, group, and societal experiences for guidance. Since society has not yet established much of what will become common sense for computing, individuals must actively think about what makes sense and what does not. To decide whether a given action makes sense, users must take into account whether the action would be right not only for themselves personally but also for their peers, businesses, families, extended families, communities, and society as a whole. Computer users must also consider short-term, mid-term, and long-term ramifications of each of the potential actions as they apply to each of these groups. Since no individual can conceivably take all of this into consideration before performing a given action, human beings need to rely on guides such as habit, rules, ritual, and peer pressure. People need to understand without thinking about it, and for that, someone needs to develop and disseminate ethics for the computer generation.

Computer security professionals must lead the way in educating the digital society about policies and procedures and behavior that clearly can be discerned as right or wrong. The education process involves defining those issues that will become gut feelings, common sense, and acceptable etiquette of the whole society of end users. Computer professionals need to help develop and disseminate the rituals, celebrations, habits, and beliefs for users.

In other words, they are the pivotal people responsible for both defining computer ethics and disseminating their understanding to the computer-using public.

COMMON FALLACIES OF
THE COMPUTER GENERATION

The lack of early, computer-oriented, childhood rearing and conditioning has led to several pervasive fallacies that generally (and loosely) apply to nearly all computer and digital information users. The generation of computer users includes those from 7 to 70 years old who use computing and other information technologies. Like all fallacies, some people are heavily influenced by them, and some are less so. There are clearly more fallacies than those described here, but these are probably the most important. Most ethical problems that surface in discussions show roots in one or more of these fallacies.

Computer Game Fallacy

Computer games like Solitaire and game computers like those made by Nintendo and Sega do not generally let the user cheat. So it is hardly surprising for computer users to think, at least subliminally, that computers in general will prevent them from cheating and, by extension, from otherwise doing wrong.

This fallacy also probably has roots in the very binary nature of computers. Programmers in particular are used to the precise nature that all instructions must have before a program will work. An error in syntax, a misplaced comma, improper capitalization, and transposed characters in a program will almost certainly prevent it from compiling or running correctly once compiled. Even non-programming computer users are introduced to the powerful message that everything about computers is exact and that the computer will not allow even the tiniest transgression. DOS commands, batch file commands, configuration parameters, macro commands, spreadsheet formulas, and even file names used for word processing must have precisely the right format and syntax, or they will not work.

To most users, computers seem entirely black and white—sometimes frustratingly so. By extension, what people do with computers seems to take on a black-and-white quality. But what users often misunderstand while using computers is that although the computer operates with a very strict set of inviolable rules, most of what people do with computers is just as gray as all other human interactions.

It is a common defense for malicious hackers to say something like "If they didn't want people to break into their computer at the [defense contractor], they should have used better security." Eric Corley, the publisher of the hacker's *2600 Magazine*, testified at hearings for the House Telecommunications and Finance Subcommittee (June 1993) that he and others like him were providing a service to computer and telecommunication system operators when they explored computer systems, found faults and weaknesses in the security systems, and then published how to break these systems in his magazine. He even had the audacity while testifying before Congress to use his handle, Emanuel Goldstein (a character from the book *1984*), never mentioning that his real name was Eric Corley.

He, and others like him, were effectively saying "If you don't want me to break in, make it impossible to do so. If there is a way to get around your security, then I should get around it in order to expose the problem."

These malicious hackers would never consider jumping over the four-foot fence into their neighbor's backyard, entering the kitchen through an open kitchen window, sitting in the living room, reading the mail, making a few phone calls, watching television, and leaving. They would not brag or publish that their neighbor's home was not secure enough, that they found a problem or loophole, or that it was permissible to go in because it was possible to do so. However, using a computer to perform analogous activities makes perfect sense to them.

The computer game fallacy also affects the rest of the members of the computer-user generation in ways that are a good deal more subtle. The computer provides a powerful one-way mirror behind which people can hide. Computer users can be voyeurs without being caught. And if what is being done is not permissible, the thinking is that the system would somehow prevent them from doing it.

Law-Abiding Citizen Fallacy

Recognizing that computers can't prevent everything that would be wrong, many users understand that laws will provide some guidance. But many (perhaps most) users sometimes confuse what is legal, which defines the minimum standard about which all can be justly judged, with what is reasonable behavior, which clearly calls for individual judgment. Sarah Gordon, one of the leaders of the worldwide hobbyist network FidoNet said, "In most places, it is legal to pluck the feathers off of a live bird, but that doesn't make it right to do it."

Similarly, people confuse things that they have a right to do with things that are right to do. Computer virus writers do this all the time. They say: "The First Amendment gives me the constitutional right to write anything I want, including computer viruses. Since computer viruses are an expression, and a form of writing, the constitution also protects the distribution of them, the talking about them, and the promotion of them as free speech."

Some people clearly take their First Amendment rights too far. Mark Ludwig has written two how-to books on creating computer viruses. He also writes a quarterly newsletter on the finer details of computer virus authors and runs a computer virus exchange bulletin board with thousands of computer viruses for the user's downloading pleasure. The bulletin board includes source code, source analysis, and tool kits to create nasty features like stealthing, encryption, and polymorphism. He even distributes a computer virus CD with thousands of computer viruses, a source code, and some commentary.

Nearly anyone living in the United States would agree that in most of the western world, people have the right to write almost anything they want. However, they also have the responsibility to consider the ramifications of their actions and to behave accordingly. Some speech, of course, is not protected by the constitution—like yelling "fire" in a crowded theater or telling someone with a gun to shoot a person. One would hope that writing viruses will become non-protected speech in the future. But for now, society has not decided whether virus writing, distribution, and promotion should be violently abhorred or tolerated as one of the costs of other freedoms.

Shatterproof Fallacy

How many times have computer novices been told "Don't worry, the worst you can do with your computer is accidentally erase or mess up a file—and even if you do that, you can probably get it back. You can't really hurt anything."

Although computers are tools, they are tools that can harm. Yet most users are totally oblivious to the fact that they have actually hurt someone else through actions on their computer. Using electronic-mail on the Internet to denigrate someone constitutes malicious chastisement of someone in public. In the non-digital world, people can be sued for libel for these kinds of actions; but on the Internet, users find it convenient to not be held responsible for their words.

Forwarding e-mail without at least the implied permission of all of its authors often leads to harm or embarrassment of participants who thought they were conferring privately. Using e-mail to stalk someone, to send unwanted mail or junk mail, and to send sexual innuendoes or other material that is not appreciated by the recipient all constitute harmful use of computers.

Software piracy is another way in which computer users can hurt people. Those people are not only programmers and struggling software companies but also end users who must pay artificially high prices for the software and systems they buy and the stockholders and owners of successful companies who deserve a fair return on their investment.

It is astonishing that a computer user would defend the writing of computer viruses. Typically, the user says, "My virus is not a malicious one. It does not cause any harm. It is a benign virus. The only reason I wrote it was to satisfy my intellectual curiosity and to see how it would spread." Such users truly miss out on the ramifications of their actions. Viruses, by definition, travel from computer to computer without the knowledge or permission of the computer's owner or operator.

Viruses are just like other kinds of contaminants (e.g., contaminants in a lake) except that they grow (replicate) much like a cancer. Computer users cannot know they have a virus unless they specifically test their computers or diskettes for it. If the neighbor of a user discovers a virus, then the user is obliged to test his or her system and diskettes for it and so are the thousand or so other neighbors that the user and the user's neighbors have collectively.

The hidden costs of computer viruses are enormous. Even if an experienced person with the right tools needs only 10 minutes to get rid of a virus—and even if the virus infects only 4 or 5 computers and only 10 or 20 floppy disks in a site (these are about the right numbers for a computer virus incident in a site of 1000 computers), then the people at the site are obliged to check all 1000 computers and an average of 35,000 diskettes (35 active diskettes per computer) to find out just which five computers are infected.

As of early 1995, there were demonstrably more than a thousand people actively writing, creating, or intentionally

Espionage – Firewalls

Espionage –
Firewalls

modifying the more than 6000 computer viruses that currently exist—and at least as many people knowingly participated in spreading them. Most of these people were ignorant of the precise consequences of their actions.

In 1993, there was a minor scandal in the IRS when clerical IRS employees were discovered pulling computerized tax returns of movie stars, politicians, and their neighbors—just for the fun of it. What is the harm? The harm is to the privacy of taxpayers and to the trust in the system, which is immeasurably damaged in the minds of U.S. citizens. More than 350 IRS employees were directly implicated in this scandal. When such large numbers of people do not understand the ethical problem, then the problem is not an isolated one. It is emblematic of a broad ethical problem that is rooted in widely held fallacies.

The shatterproof fallacy is the pervasive feeling that what a person does with a computer could hurt at most a few files on the machine. It stems from the computer generation's frequent inability to consider the ramifications of the things we do with computers before we do them.

Candy-from-a-Baby Fallacy

Guns and poison make killing easy (i.e., it can be done from a distance with no strength or fight) but not necessarily right. Poisoning the water supply is quite easy, but it is beyond the gut-level acceptability of even the most bizarre schizophrenic.

Software piracy and plagiarism are incredibly easy using a computer. Computers excel at copying things, and nearly every computer user is guilty of software piracy. But just because it is easy does not mean that it is right.

Studies by the Software Publisher's Association (SPA) and Business Software Alliance (BSA) show that software piracy is a multibillion dollar problem in the world today—clearly a huge problem.

By law and by any semblance of intellectual property held both in Western societies and most of the rest of the world, copying a program for use without paying for it is theft. It is no different than shoplifting or being a stowaway on an airliner, and an average user would never consider stealing a box of software from a computer store's display case or stowing away on a flight because the plane had empty seats.

Hacker's Fallacy

The single most widely held piece of the hacker's ethic is "As long as the motivation for doing something is to learn and not to otherwise gain or make a profit, then doing it is acceptable." This is actually quite a strong, respected, and widely held ethos among people who call themselves non-malicious hackers.

To be a hacker, a person's primary goal must be to learn for the sake of learning—just to find out what happens if one does a certain thing at a particular time under a specific condition.[1] Consider the hack on Tonya Harding (the Olympic ice skater who allegedly arranged to have her archrival, Nancy Kerrigan, beaten with a bat). During the Lillehammer Olympics, three U.S. newspaper reporters, with the *Detroit Free Press, San Jose Mercury News,* and *The New York Times,* discovered that the athletes' E-mail user IDs were, in fact, the same as the ID numbers on the backs of their backstage passes. The reporters also discovered that the default passwords for the Olympic Internet mail system were simple derivatives of the athlete's birthdays. Reporters used this information to gain access to Tonya Harding's e-mail account and discovered that she had 68 messages. They claim not to have read any of them. They claim that no harm was done, nothing was published, no privacy was exploited. As it happens, these journalists were widely criticized for their actions. But the fact is, a group of savvy, intelligent people thought that information technology changed the ground rules.

Free Information Fallacy

There is a common notion that information wants to be free, as though it had a mind of its own. The fallacy probably stems from the fact that once created in digital form, information is very easy to copy and tends to get distributed widely. The fallacy totally misses the point that the wide distribution is at the whim of people who copy and disseminate data and people who allow this to happen.

ACTION PLAN

The following procedures can help security managers encourage ethical use of the computer within their organizations:

- Developing a corporate guide to computer ethics for the organization.
- Developing a computer ethics policy to supplement the computer security policy.
- Adding information about computer ethics to the employee handbook.
- Finding out whether the organization has a business ethics policy, and expanding it to include computer ethics.
- Learning more about computer ethics and spreading what is learned.
- Helping to foster awareness of computer ethics by participating in the computer ethics campaign.
- Making sure the organization has an E-mail privacy policy.
- Making sure employees know what the E-mail policy is.

Table 1 through 6 contain sample codes of ethics for end users that can help security managers develop ethics policies and procedures.

Table 1 The Ten Commandments of computer ethics.

In 1991 the Computer Ethics Institute held its first National Computer Ethics Conference in Washington, D.C. The conference theme was "In Pursuit of a 'Ten Commandments' of Computer Ethics." These commandments were drafted by Dr. Ramon C. Barquin, founder and president of the Institute, as a working document for that conference. Since then, they have been among the most visible guidelines for computer ethics. The following are the ten commandments:

1. Thou shalt not use a computer to harm other people.
2. Thou shalt not interfere with other people's computer work.
3. Thou shalt not snoop around in other people's computer files.
4. Thou shalt not use a computer to steal.
5. Thou shalt not use a computer to bear false witness.
6. Thou shalt not copy or use proprietary software for which you have not paid.
7. Thou shalt not use other people's computer resources without authorization or proper compensation.
8. Thou shalt not appropriate other people's intellectual output.
9. Thou shalt think about the social consequences of the program you are writing or the system you are designing.
10. Thou shalt use a computer in ways that ensure consideration and respect for your fellow humans.

Table 2 The end user's basic tenets of responsible computing.

In an effort to define responsible computing behavior in terms that are easy to grasp, the Working Group on Computer Ethics created the End User's Basic Tenets of Responsible Computing. These tenets are not intended as a panacea for the myriad of complex information ethics dilemmas; rather, they are intended to address many of the day-to-day problems faced by individual end users.

Responsible and ethical computing is not a black and white issue. However, many problems can be avoided by abiding by the following basic tenets:

1. I understand that just because something is legal it isn't necessarily moral or right.
2. I understand that people are always the ones ultimately harmed when computers are used unethically. The fact that computers, software, or a communications medium exists between me and those harmed does not in any way change my moral responsibility toward my fellow humans.
3. I will respect the rights of authors, including authors and publishers of software as well as authors and owners of information. I understand that just because copying programs and data is easy, it is not necessarily right.
4. I will not break into or use other people's computers or read or use their information without their consent.
5. I will not write or knowingly acquire, distribute, or allow intentional distribution of harmful software like bombs, worms, and computer viruses.

Table 3 Four primary values.

The National Conference on Computing and Values proposed four primary values for computing. These were originally intended to serve as the ethical foundation and guidance for computer security. However, they seem to provide value guidance for all individuals who create, sell, support, use, or depend upon computers. That is, they suggest the values that will tend to improve and stabilize the computer and information world and to make these technologies and systems work more productively and appropriately for society.

The four primary values state that we should strive to:

1. Preserve the public trust and confidence in computers.
2. Enforce fair information practices.
3. Protect the legitimate interests of the constituents of the system.
4. Resist fraud, waste, and abuse.

Table 4 Unacceptable internet activities.

In January 1989, the Internet Activities Board (IAB) published a document called Ethics and the Internet (RFC 1087). It proposes that access to and use of the Internet is a privilege and should be treated as such by all users of this system. The IAB "strongly endorses the view of the Division Advisory Panel of the National Science Foundation Division of Network, Communications Research and Infrastructure." That view is paraphrased here. Any activity is characterized as unethical and unacceptable that purposely:

- Seeks to gain unauthorized access to the resources of the Internet.
- Disrupts the intended use of the Internet.
- Wastes resources (people, capacity, computer) through such actions.
- Destroys the integrity of computer-based information.
- Compromises the privacy of users.
- Involves negligence in the conduct of Internetwide experiments.

Table 5 Considerations for conduct.

Donn Parker, who is with SRI International and is the author of "Ethical Conflicts in Information and Computer Science, Technology and Business" (QED Information Sciences, Inc.), defined several principles for resolving ethical conflicts. The following summarizes this work:

You are probably aware of the obvious unethical information activities you should avoid, such as violating others' privacy by accessing their computers and causing others losses by giving away copies of the software others own or sell. But how do you deal with the really tough problems of deciding the best action in complex or unclear situations where a decision may be okay in one respect but not in another? These are the more difficult decisions to make. The following principles of ethical information conduct and examples may help you as a periodic review to make fairer decisions when needed or as a checklist for a methodical approach to solve a problem and reach a decision. You may not remember all of these principles on every occasion, but reading them now and every once in a while or having them handy when making a decision can help you through a difficult process.

(Continued)

Espionage – Firewalls

Table 5 Considerations for conduct. *(Continued)*

1. Try to make sure that those people affected are aware of your planned actions and that they don't disagree with your intentions even if you have rights to do these things (informed consent).

2. Think carefully about your possible alternative actions and select the most beneficial necessary one that would cause the least or no harm under the worst circumstances (higher ethic in the worst case).

3. Consider that an action you take on a small scale or by you alone might result in significant harm if carried out on a larger scale or by many others (change of scale).

4. As a person who owns or is responsible for information, always make sure that the information is reasonably protected and that ownership of it and rights to it are clear to all users (owners' conservation of ownership).

5. As a person who uses information, always assume it is owned by others and their interests must be protected unless you explicitly know it is public or you are free to use it in the way you wish (users' conservation of ownership).

Table 6 The code of fair information practices.

In 1973 the Secretary's Advisory Committee on Automated Personal Data Systems for the U.S. Department of Health, Education & Welfare recommended the adoption of a "Code of Fair Information Practices" to secure the privacy and rights of citizens. The Code is based on four principles:

1. There must be no personal data record-keeping systems whose very existence is secret.

2. There must be a way for a person to find out what information about the person is in a record and now it is used.

3. There must be a way for a person to prevent information about the person that was obtained for one purpose from being used or made available for other purposes without the person's consent.

4. Any organization creating, maintaining, using, or disseminating records of identifiable personal data must assure the reliability of the data for their intended use and must take precautions to prevent misuses of the data.

RESOURCES

The following resources are useful for developing computer-related ethics codes and policies.

Computer Ethics Institute

The Computer Ethics Institute is a non-profit organization concerned with advancing the development of computers and information technologies within ethical frameworks. Its constituency includes people in business, the religious communities, education, public policy, and computer professions. Its purpose includes the following:

- The dissemination of computer ethics information.
- Policy analysis and critique.
- The recognition and critical examination of ethics in the use of computer technology.
- The promotion of identifying and applying ethical principles for the development and use of computer technologies.

To meet these purposes, the Computer Ethics Institute conducts seminars, convocations, and the annual National Computer Ethics Conference. The Institute also supports the publication of proceedings and the development and publication of other research. In addition, the Institute participates in projects with other groups with similar interests. The following are ways to contact the institute:

Dr. Patrick F. Sullivan
Executive Director
Computer Ethics Institute
P.O. Box 42672
Washington, D.C. 20015
Voice and Fax: 301-469-0615
psullivan@brook.edu

Internet Listserve:cei-1@listserv.american.edu

This is a listserv on the Internet hosted by American University in Washington, D.C., on behalf of the Computer Ethics Institute. Electronic mail sent to this address is automatically forwarded to others interested in computer ethics and in activities surrounding the Computer Ethics Institute. To join the list, a person should send e-mail to:

listserv@american.edu

The subject field should be left blank. The message itself should say:

subscribe cei-1 <yourname>

The sender will receive postings to the list by e-mail (using the return address from the e-mail site used to send the request).

National Computer Ethics and Responsibilities Campaign

The National Computer Ethics and Responsibilities Campaign (NCERC) is a campaign jointly run by the Computer Ethics Institute and the National Computer Security Association. Its goal is to foster computer ethics awareness and education. The campaign does this by making tools and other resources available for people who want to hold events, campaigns, awareness programs, seminars, and conferences or to write or communicate about computer ethics.

The NCERC itself does not subscribe to or support a particular set of guidelines or a particular viewpoint on

Espionage – Firewalls

computer ethics. Rather, the Campaign is a non-partisan initiative intended to foster increased understanding of the ethical and moral issues peculiar to the use and abuse of information technologies.

The initial phase of the NCERC was sponsored by a diverse group of organizations, including (alphabetically) The Atterbury Foundation, The Boston Computer Society, The Business Software Alliance, CompuServe, The Computer Ethics Institute, Computer Professionals for Social Responsibility, Merrill Lynch, Monsanto, The National Computer Security Association, Software Creations BBS, The Software Publisher's Association, Symantec Corporation, and Ziff-Davis Publishing. The principal sponsor of the NCERC is the Computer Ethics Institute.

Other information about the campaign is available on CompuServe (GO CETHICS), where a repository of computer privacy, ethics and similar tools, codes, texts, and other materials are kept.

Computer Ethics Resource Guide

The Resource Guide to Computer Ethics is available for $12. (Send check or credit card number and signature to: NCERC, 10 S. Courthouse Ave., Carlisle, PA, 17013, or call 717-240-0430 and leave credit card information as a voice message.) The guide is meant as a resource for those who wish to do something to increase the awareness of and discussion about computer ethics in their workplaces, schools, universities, user groups, bulletin boards, and other areas.

National Computer Security Association

The National Computer Security Association (NCSA) provides information and services involving security, reliability, and ethics. NCSA offers information on the following security-related areas: training, testing, research, product certification, underground reconnaissance, help desk, and consulting services. This information is delivered through publications, conferences, forums, and seminars—in both traditional and electronic formats. NCSA manages a CompuServe forum (CIS: GO NCSA) that hosts private online training and seminars in addition to public forums and libraries addressing hundreds of issues concerning information and communications security, computer ethics, and privacy.

The information about computer ethics that is not well suited to electronic distribution can generally be obtained through NCSA's InfoSecurity Resource Catalog, which provides one-stop-shopping for a wide variety of books, guides, training, and tools. (NCSA: 10 S. Courthouse Ave., Carlisle, PA, 17013, 717-258-1816).

SUMMARY

Computer and information technologies have created many new ethical problems. Compounding these problems is the fact that computer users often do not know the full consequences of their behavior.

Several common fallacies cloud the meaning of ethical computing. For example, many computer users confuse behavior that they have a right to perform with behavior that is right to perform and fail to consider the ramifications of their actions. Another fallacy that is widely held by hackers is that as long as the motivation is to learn and not otherwise profit, any action using a computer is acceptable.

It is up to the system managers to destroy these fallacies and to lead the way in educating end users about policies and procedures and behavior that can clearly be discerned as right or wrong.

REFERENCE

1. Goldstein, E. Q & A. 2600: The Hacker Quarterly, Spring **1994**, *11* (1).

Espionage – Firewalls

Ethics: Internet

Micki Krause, CISSP
Pacific Life Insurance Company, Newport Beach, California, U.S.A.

Abstract

Technology is a double-edged sword, consistently presenting us with benefits and disadvantages. The Internet is no different. The Net is a powerful tool, providing the ability for global communications in a heartbeat; sharing information without boundaries; a platform for illicit and unethical shenanigans.

This entry has explored the types of behavior demonstrated in cyberspace, antisocial behavior, which has led to many discussions about whether or not this activity can be inhibited by self-regulation or the introduction of tougher laws. Although we do not know how the controversy will end, we know it will be an interesting future in cyberspace.

The research for this entry was done entirely on the Internet. The Net is a powerful tool. This author dearly hopes that the value of its offerings is not obviated by those who would treat the medium in an inappropriate and unethical manner.

Ethics: Social values; a code of right and wrong

INTRODUCTION

The ethical nature of the Internet has been likened to "a restroom in a downtown bus station," where the lowest of the low congregate and nothing good ever happens. This manifestation of antisocial behavior can be attributed to one or more of the following:

- The relative anonymity of those who use the Net
- The lack of regulation in cyberspace
- The fact that one can masquerade as another on the Internet
- The fact that one can fulfill a fantasy or assume a different persona on the net, thereby eliminating the social obligation to be accountable for one's own actions

Whatever the reason, the Internet, also known as the "Wild West" or the "untamed frontier," is absent of law and therefore is a natural playground for illicit, illegal, and unethical behavior.

In the ensuing pages, we will explore the types of behavior demonstrated in cyberspace, discuss how regulation is being introduced and by whom, and illustrate the practices that businesses have adopted in order to minimize their liability and encourage their employees to use the Net in an appropriate manner.

GROWTH OF THE INTERNET

When the Internet was born approximately 30 years ago it was a medium used by the government and assorted academicians, primarily to perform and share research. The user community was small and mostly self-regulated. Thus, although a useful tool, the Internet was not considered "mission-critical," as it is today. Moreover, the requirements for availability and reliability were not as much a consideration then as they are now, because Internet usage has grown exponentially since the late 1980s.

The increasing opportunities for productivity, efficiency and world-wide communications brought additional users in droves. Thus, it was headline news when a computer worm, introduced into the Internet by Robert Morris, Jr., in 1988, infected thousands of Net-connected computers and brought the Internet to its knees.

In the early 1990s, with the advent of commercial applications and the World Wide Web (WWW), a graphical user interface for Internet information, the number of Internet users soared. Sources such as the *Industry Standard*, "The Newsmagazine of the Internet Economy," published the latest Nielsen Media Research Commerce Net study in late 1998, which reported the United States Internet population at 70.5 million (out of a total population of 196.5 million).

Today, the Internet is a utility, analogous to the electric company, and "dotcom" is a household expression. The spectrum of Internet users extends from the kindergarten classroom to senior citizenry, although the Gen-X generation, users in their 20s, are the fastest adopters of Net technology (see Table 1).

Because of its popularity, the reliability and availability of the Internet are critical operational considerations, and activities that threaten these attributes, e.g., spamming, spoofing, hacking and the like, have grave impacts on its user community.

Encyclopedia of Information Assurance DOI: 10.1081/E-EIA-120046571
Copyright © 2011 by Taylor & Francis. All rights reserved.

Table 1   GenX internet use.

A Higher Percentage of Gen-Xers Use the Web ...	
	Used the Web in the past 6 months
Generation X	61%
Total U.S. Adults	49%
... More Regularly...	
	Use the Web regularly
Generation X	82%
Baby Boomers	52%
... Because it's the Most Important Medium	
	Most Important Media
Internet	55%
Television	39%

Source: From *The Industry Standard.*

UNETHICAL ACTIVITY DEFINED

Spamming, in electronic terminology, means electronic garbage. Sending unsolicited junk electronic mail, for example, such as an advertisement, to one user or many users via a distribution list, is considered spamming.

One of the most publicized spamming incidents occurred in 1994, when two attorneys (Laurence Carter and Martha Siegel) from Arizona, flooded the cyber waves, especially the Usenet newsgroups (Usenet newsgroups are limited communities of Net users who congregate online to discuss specific topics.), with solicitations to the immigrant communities of the United States to assist them in the green card lottery process to gain citizenship. Carter and Siegel saw the spamming as "an ideal, low-cost and perfectly legitimate way to target people likely to be potential clients" (*Washington Post*, 1994). Many Usenet newsgroup users, however, saw things differently. The lawyers' actions resulted in quite an uproar among the Internet communities primarily because the Internet has had a long tradition of non-commercialism since its founding. The attorneys had already been ousted from the American Immigration Lawyers' Association for past sins, and eventually they lost their licenses to practice law.

There have been several other spams since the green card lottery, some claiming "MAKE MONEY FAST," others claiming "THE END OF THE WORLD IS NEAR." There have also been hundreds, if not thousands, of electronic chain letters making the Internet rounds. The power of the Internet is the ease with which users can forward data, including chain letters. More information about spamming occurrences can be found on the Net in the Usenet newsgroup (alt.folklore.urban).

Unsolicited Internet e-mail has become so widespread that lawmakers have begun to propose sending it a misdemeanor. Texas is one of 18 states considering legislation that would make spamming illegal. In February 1999, Virginia became the fourth state to pass an antispamming law. The Virginia law makes it a misdemeanor for a spammer to use a false online identity to send mass mailings, as many do. The maximum penalty would be a $500 fine. However, if the spam is deemed malicious and results in damages to the victim in excess of $2500 (e.g., if the spam causes unavailability of computer service), the crime would be a felony, punishable by up to 5 years in prison. As with the Virginia law, California law allows for the jailing of spammers. Laws in Washington and Nevada impose civil fines.

This legislation has not been popular with everyone, however, and has led organizations such as the American Civil Liberties Union (ACLU), to complain about its unconstitutionality and threat to free speech and the First Amendment.

Like spamming, threatening electronic mail messages have become pervasive in the Internet space. Many of these messages are not taken as seriously as the one that was sent by a high school student from New Jersey, who made a death threat against President Clinton in an electronic mail message in early 1999. Using a school computer that provided an option to communicate with a contingent of the U.S. government, the student rapidly became the subject of a Secret Service investigation.

Similarly, in late 1998, a former investment banker was convicted on eight counts of aggravated harassment when he masqueraded as another employee and sent allegedly false and misleading Internet e-mail messages to top executives of his former firm.

Increasingly, businesses are establishing policy to inhibit employees from using company resources to perform unethical behavior on the Internet. In an early 1999 case, a California firm agreed to pay a former employee over $100,000 after she received harassing messages on the firm's electronic bulletin board, even though the company reported the incident to authorities and launched an internal investigation. The case is a not-so-subtle reminder that businesses are accountable for the actions of their employees, even actions performed on electronic networks.

Businesses have taken a stern position on employees surfing the Web, sending inappropriate messages, and downloading pornographic materials from the Internet. This is due to a negative impact on productivity, as well as the legal view that companies are liable for the actions of their employees. Many companies have established policies for appropriate use and monitoring of computers and computing resources, as well as etiquette on the Internet, or "Netiquette."

These policies are enhancements to the Internet Advisory Board's RFC (Request for Comment) 1087, "Internet Ethics," January 1989, which proposed that access to and use of the Internet is a privilege and should be treated as such by all users of the system. The IAB strongly endorsed the view of the Division Advisory Panel of the National Science Foundation Division of Network Communications Research and Infrastructure. That view is paraphrased below.

Espionage – Firewalls

Espionage –
Firewalls

Any activity is characterized as unethical and unacceptable that purposely:

- Seeks to gain unauthorized access to the resources of the Internet
- Disrupts the intended use of the Internet
- Wastes resources (people, capacity, computers) through such actions
- Destroys the integrity of computer-based information
- Compromises the privacy of users
- Involves negligence in the conduct of Internet-wide experiments

—RFC 1087, "Ethics and the Internet," Internet Advisory Board, January 1989

A sample "Appropriate Use of the Internet" policy is attached as Appendix A. Appendix B contains the partial contents of RFC 1855, "Netiquette Guidelines," a product of the Responsible Use of the Network (RUN) Working Group of the Internet Engineering Task Force (IETF).

In another twist on Internet electronic mail activity, in April 1999, Intel Corporation sued a former employee for doing a mass e-mailing to its 30,000 employees, criticizing the company over workers' compensation benefits. Intel claims the e-mail was an assault and form of trespass, as well as an improper use of its internal computer resources. The former employee contends that his e-mail messages are protected by the First Amendment. "Neither Intel nor I can claim any part of the Internet as our own private system as long as we are hooked up to this international network of computers," said Ken Hamidi in an e-mail to *Los Angeles Times* reporters. The case was not settled as of this writing (*Los Angeles Times*, 1999).

Using electronic media to stalk another person is known as "cyber stalking." This activity is becoming more prevalent, and the law has seen fit to intercede by adding computers and electronic devices to existing stalking legislation. In the first case of cyber stalking in California, a Los Angeles resident, accused of using his computer to harass a woman who rejected his romantic advances, is the first to be charged under a new cyber stalking law that went into effect in 1998. The man was accused of forging postings on the Internet, on America Online (AOL), and other Internet services, so that the messages appeared to come from the victim. The message provided the woman's address and other identifying information, which resulted in at least six men visiting her home uninvited. The man was charged with one count of stalking, three counts of solicitation to commit sexual assault, and one count of unauthorized access to computers.

In another instance where electronic activity has been added to existing law, the legislation for gambling has been updated to include Internet gambling. According to recent estimates, Internet-based gambling and gaming has grown from about a $500 million-a-year industry in the late 1990s, to what some estimate could become a $10 billion-a-year enterprise by 2000. Currently, all 50 states regulate in-person gambling in some manner. Many conjecture that the impetus for the regulation of electronic gambling is financial, not ethical or legal.

PRIVACY ON THE INTERNET

For many years, American citizens have expressed fears of invasion of privacy, ever since they realized that their personal information is being stored on computer databases by government agencies and commercial entities. However, it is just of late that Americans are realizing that logging on to the Internet and using the World Wide Web threatens their privacy as well. Last year, the Center for Democracy and Technology (CDT), a Washington, D.C. advocacy group, reported that only one third of federal agencies tell visitors to their Web sites what information is being collected about them.

AT&T Labs conducted a study early last year, in which they discovered that Americans are willing to surrender their e-mail address online, but not much more than that. The study said that users are reluctant to provide other personal information, such as a phone number or credit card number.

The utilization of technology offers the opportunity for companies to collect specific items of information. For example, Microsoft Corporation inserts tracking numbers into its Word program documents. Microsoft's Internet Explorer informs Web sites when a user bookmarks them by choosing the "Favorites" option in the browser. In 1998, the Social Security Administration came very close to putting a site on line that would let anyone find out another person's earnings and other personal information. This flies in the face of the 1974 Privacy Act, which states that every agency must record "only such information about an individual as is relevant and necessary to accomplish a purpose of the agency required to be accomplished by statute or by executive order of the President."

There is a battle raging between privacy advocates and private industry aligned with the U.S. government. Privacy advocates relate the serious concern for the hands-off approach and lack of privacy legislation, claiming that citizens are being violated. Conversely, the federal government and private businesses, such as American Online, defend current attempts to rely on self-regulation and other less government-intrusive means of regulating privacy, for example, the adoption of privacy policies. These policies, which state intent for the protection of consumer privacy, are deployed to raise consumer confidence and increase digital trust. The CDT has urged the federal government to post privacy policies on each site's home page, such as is shown in Table 2 from the Health and Human Services Web site from the National Institute of Health (http://www.nih.gov).

Table 2 Information collected when e-mail is sent.

Information Collected when You Send Us an E-mail Message.
When inquiries are e-mailed to us, we again store the text of your message and e-mail address information, so that we can answer the question that was sent in, and send the answer back to the e-mail address provided. If enough questions or comments come in that are the same, the question may be added to our Question and Answer section, or the suggestions are used to guide the design of our Web site.

We do not retain the messages with identifiable information or the e-mail addresses for more than 10 days after responding unless your communication requires further inquiry. If you send us an e-mail message in which you ask us to do something that requires further inquiry on our part, there are a few things you should know.

The material you submit may be seen by various people in our Department, who may use it to look into the matter you have inquired about. If we do retain it, it is protected by the Privacy Act of 1974, which restricts our use of it, but permits certain disclosures.

Also, e-mail is not necessarily secure against interception. If your communication is very sensitive, or includes personal information, you might want to send it by postal mail instead.

Source: From National Institute of Health. http://www.nih.gov.

HHS WEB PRIVACY NOTICE

(as of April 13, 1999)

Thank you for visiting the Department of Health and Human Services Web site and reviewing our Privacy Policy. Our Privacy Policy for visits to http://www.hhs.gov is clear:

We will collect no personal information about you when you visit our Web site unless you choose to provide that information to us.
Here is how we handle information about your visit to our Web site.

Information Collected and Stored Automatically

If you do nothing during your visit but browse through the website, read pages, or download information, we will gather and store certain information about your visit automatically. This information does not identify you personally. We automatically collect and store only the following information about your visit:

- The Internet domain (for example, "xcompany.com" if you use a private Internet access account, or "yourschool.edu" if you connect from a university's domain), and IP address (an IP address is a number that is automatically assigned to your computer whenever you are surfing the Web) from which you access our Web site
- The type of browser and operating system used to access our site
- The date and time you access our site
- The pages you visit

- If you linked to our Web site from another Web site, the address of that Web site

We use this information to help us make our site more useful to visitors—to learn about the number of visitors to our site and the types of technology our visitors use. We do not track or record information about individuals and their visits.

Links to Other Sites

Our Web site has links to other federal agencies and to private organizations. Once you link to another site, it is that site's privacy policy that controls what it collects about you.

ANONYMITY ON THE INTERNET

Besides a lack of privacy, the Internet promulgates a lack of identity. Users of the Internet are virtual, meaning that they are not speaking with, interacting with, or responding to others, at least not face to face. They sit behind their computer terminals in the comfort of their own home, office, or school. This anonymity makes it easy to masquerade as another, since there is no way of proving or disproving who you are or who you say you are.

Moreover, this anonymity lends itself to the venue of Internet chat rooms. Chat rooms are places on the Net where people congregate and discuss topics common to the group, such as sports, recreation, or sexuality. Many chat rooms provide support to persons looking for answers to questions on health, bereavement, or disease and, in this manner, can be very beneficial to society.

Conversely, chat rooms can be likened to sleazy bars, where malcontents go seeking prey. There have been too many occurrences of too-good-to-be-true investments that have turned out to be fraudulent. Too many representatives of the dregs of society lurk on the net, targeting the elderly or the innocent, or those who, for some unknown reason, make easy marks.

A recent *New Yorker* magazine ran a cartoon showing a dog sitting at a computer desk, the caption reading "On the Internet, no one knows if you're a dog." Although the cartoon is humorous, the instances where child molesters have accosted their victims by way of the Internet are very serious. Too many times, miscreants have struck up electronic conversations with innocent victims, masquerading as innocents themselves, only to lead them to meet in person with dire results. Unfortunately, electronic behavior mimics conduct that has always occurred over phone lines, through the postal service, and in person. The Internet only provides an additional locale for intentionally malicious and anti-social behavior. We can only hope that advanced technology, as with telephonic caller ID, will assist law enforcement in tracking anonymous Internet "bad guys."

Attempts at self-regulation have not been as successful as advertised, and many question whether the industry can

Espionage –
Firewalls

police itself. Meanwhile, there are those within the legal and judicial systems that feel more laws are the only true answer to limiting unethical and illegal activities on the Internet. How it will all play out is far from known at this point in time. The right to freedom of speech and expression has often been at odds with censorship. It is ironic, for example, that debates abound on the massive amounts of pornography available on the Internet, and yet, in early 1999, the entire transcript of the President Clinton impeachment hearings was published on the Net, complete with sordid details of the Monica Lewinsky affair.

INTERNET AND THE LAW

The Communications Decency Act of 1996 was signed into law by President Clinton in early 1996 and has been challenged by civil libertarian organizations ever since. In 1997, the United States Supreme Court declared the law's ban on indecent Internet speech unconstitutional.

The Childrens' Internet Protect Act (S.97, January 1999), introduced before a recent Congress, requires "the installation and use by schools and libraries of a technology for filtering or blocking material on the Internet on computers with Internet access to be eligible to receive or retain universal service assistance."

MONITORING THE WEB

Additionally, many commercial businesses have seen the opportunity to manufacture software products that will provide parents the ability to control their home computers. Products such as Crayon Crawler, Family-Connect, and KidsGate are available to provide parents with control over what Internet sites their children can access, although products like WebSense, SurfControl and Webroot are being implemented by companies that choose to limit the sites their employees can access.

APPENDIX A: "APPROPRIATE USE AND MONITORING OF COMPUTING RESOURCES"

Policy

The Company telecommunications systems, computer networks, and electronic mail systems are to be used only for business purposes and only by authorized personnel. All data generated with or on the Company's business resources are the property of the Company; and may be used by the Company without limitation; and may not be copyrighted, patented, leased, or sold by individuals or otherwise used for personal gain.

Electronic mail and voice mail, including pagers and cellular telephones, are not to be used to create any

offensive or disruptive messages. The Company does not tolerate discrimination, harassment, or other offensive messages and images relating to, among other things, gender, race, color, religion, national origin, age, sexual orientation, or disability.

The Company reserves the right and will exercise the right to review, monitor, intercept, access, and disclose any business or personal messages sent or received on Company systems. This may happen at any time, with or without notice.

It is the Company's goal to respect individual privacy, while at the same time maintaining a safe and secure workplace. However, employees should have no expectation of privacy with respect to any Company computer or communication resources. Materials that appear on computer, electronic mail, voice mail, facsimile and the like, belong to the Company. Periodically, your use of the Company's systems may be monitored.

The use of passwords is intended to safeguard Company information, and does not guarantee personal confidentiality.

Violations of company policies detected through such monitoring can lead to corrective action, up to and including discharge.

APPENDIX B: NETIQUETTE

RFC 1855
Netiquette Guidelines

Status of This Memo

This memo provides information for the Internet community. This memo does not specify an Internet standard of any kind. Distribution of this memo is unlimited.

Abstract

This document provides a minimum set of guidelines for Network Etiquette (Netiquette) which organizations may take and adapt for their own use. As such, it is deliberately written in a bulleted format to make adaptation easier and to make any particular item easy (or easier) to find. It also functions as a minimum set of guidelines for individuals, both users and administrators. This memo is the product of the Responsible Use of the Network (RUN) Working Group of the IETF.

Introduction

In the past, the population of people using the Internet had "grown up" with the Internet, were technically minded, and understood the nature of the transport and the protocols. Today, the community of Internet users includes people who are new to the environment. These "newbies" are unfamiliar with the culture and do not need to know about transport and protocols. To bring these new users into the Internet culture quickly, this Guide offers a minimum set of behaviors which organizations and individuals may take and adapt for their own use. Individuals should be aware that no matter who supplies their Internet access, be it an Internet Service Provider through a private account, or a student account at a University, or an account through a corporation, that those organizations have regulations about ownership of mail and files, about what is proper to post or send, and how to present yourself. Be sure to check with the local authority for specific guidelines.

We have organized this material into three sections: One-to-one communication, which includes mail and talk; One-to-many communications, which includes mailing lists and NetNews; and Information Services, which includes ftp, WWW, Wais, Gopher, MUDs and MOOs. Finally, we have a Bibliography, which may be used for reference.

One-to-One Communication (Electronic Mail, Talk)

We define one-to-one communications as those in which a person is communicating with another person as if face-to-face: a dialog. In general, rules of common courtesy for interaction with people should be in force for any situation and on the Internet it is doubly important where, for example, body language and tone of voice must be inferred. [For more information on Netiquette for communicating via electronic mail and talk, check references 1, 23, 25 and 27 in the bibliography.]

User Guidelines

For mail:

- Unless you have your own Internet access through an Internet provider, be sure to check with your employer about ownership of electronic mail. Laws about the ownership of electronic mail vary from place to place.
- Unless you are using an encryption device (hardware or software), you should assume that mail on the Internet is not secure. Never put in a mail message anything you would not put on a postcard.
- Respect the copyright on material that you reproduce. Almost every country has copyright laws.
- If you are forwarding or reposting a message you have received, do not change the wording. If the message was a personal message to you and you are reposting to a group, you should ask permission first. You may shorten the message and quote only relevant parts, but be sure you give proper attribution.
- Never send chain letters via electronic mail. Chain letters are forbidden on the Internet. Your network

privileges will be revoked. Notify your local system administrator if your ever receive one.

- A good rule of thumb: Be conservative in what you send and liberal in what you receive. You should not send heated messages (we call these "flames") even if you are provoked. On the other hand, you should not be surprised if you get flamed and it is prudent not to respond to flames.
- In general, it is a good idea to at least check all your mail subjects before responding to a message. Sometimes a person who asks you for help (or clarification) will send another message which effectively says "Never Mind." Also make sure that any message you respond to was directed to you. You might be cc:ed rather than the primary recipient.
- Make things easy for the recipient. Many mailers strip header information which includes your return address. To ensure that people know who you are, be sure to include a line or two at the end of your message with contact information. You can create this file ahead of time and add it to the end of your messages. (Some mailers do this automatically.) In Internet parlance, this is known as a ".sig" or "signature" file. Your .sig file takes the place of your business card. (And you can have more than one to apply in different circumstances.)
- Be careful when addressing mail. There are addresses which may go to a group but the address looks like it is just one person. Know to whom you are sending.
- Watch "CCs" when replying. Do not continue to include people if the messages have become a two-way conversation.
- In general, most people who use the Internet do not have time to answer general questions about the Internet and its workings. Do not send unsolicited mail asking for information to people whose names you might have seen in RFCs or on mailing lists.
- Remember that people with whom you communicate are located across the globe. If you send a message to which you want an immediate response, the person receiving it might be at home asleep when it arrives. Give them a chance to wake up, come to work, and log in before assuming the mail didn't arrive or that they do not care.
- Verify all addresses before initiating long or personal discourse. It is also a good practice to include the word "long" in the subject header so the recipient knows the message will take time to read and respond to. Over 100 lines is considered "long."
- Know whom to contact for help. Usually you will have resources close at hand. Check locally for people who can help you with software and system problems. Also, know whom to go to if you receive anything questionable or illegal. Most sites also have "Postmaster" aliased to a knowledgeable user, so you can send mail to this address to get help with mail.
- Remember that the recipient is a human being whose culture, language, and humor have different

Espionage – Firewalls

Espionage –
Firewalls

points of reference from your own. Remember that date formats, measurements, and idioms may not travel well. Be especially careful with sarcasm.

- Use mixed case. UPPER CASE LOOKS AS IF YOU ARE SHOUTING.
- Use symbols for emphasis. That *is* what I meant. Use underscores for underlining. _War and Peace_ is my favorite book.
- Use smileys to indicate tone of voice, but use them sparingly. :-) is an example of a smiley (Look sideways). Do not assume that the inclusion of a smiley will make the recipient happy with what you say or wipe out an otherwise insulting comment.
- Wait overnight to send emotional responses to messages. If you have really strong feelings about a subject, indicate it via FLAME ON/OFF enclosures. For example:

FLAME ON

This type of argument is not worth the bandwidth it takes to send it. It is illogical and poorly reasoned. The rest of the world agrees with me.
FLAME OFF

- Do not include control characters or non-ASCII attachments in messages unless they are MIME attachments or unless your mailer encodes these. If you send encoded messages make sure the recipient can decode them.
- Be brief without being overly terse. When replying to a message, include enough original material to be understood but no more. It is extremely bad form to simply reply to a message by including all the previous message: edit out all the irrelevant material.
- Limit line length to fewer than 65 characters and end a line with a carriage return.
- Mail should have a subject heading which reflects the content of the message.
- If you include a signature keep it short. Rule of thumb is no longer than four lines. Remember that many people pay for connectivity by the minute, and the longer your message is, the more they pay.
- Just as mail (today) may not be private, mail (and news) are (today) subject to forgery and spoofing of various degrees of detectability. Apply common sense "reality checks" before assuming a message is valid.
- If you think the importance of a message justifies it, immediately reply briefly to an e-mail message to let the sender know you got it, even if you will send a longer reply later.
- "Reasonable" expectations for conduct via e-mail depend on your relationship to a person and the context of the communication. Norms learned in a particular e-mail environment may not apply in general to your e-mail communication with people across the Internet. Be careful with slang or local acronyms.
- The cost of delivering an e-mail message is, on the average, paid about equally by the sender and the recipient (or their organizations). This is unlike other media such as physical mail, telephone, TV, or radio.

Sending someone mail may also cost them in other specific ways like network bandwidth, disk space or CPU usage. This is a fundamental economic reason why unsolicited e-mail advertising is unwelcome (and is forbidden in many contexts).

- Know how large a message you are sending. Including large files such as Postscript files or programs may make your message so large that it cannot be delivered or at least consumes excessive resources. A good rule of thumb would be not to send a file larger than 50 kb. Consider file transfer as an alternative, or cutting the file into smaller chunks and sending each as a separate message.
- Do not send large amounts of unsolicited information to people.
- If your mail system allows you to forward mail, beware the dreaded forwarding loop. Be sure you have not set up forwarding on several hosts so that a message sent to you gets into an endless loop from one computer to the next to the next.

BIBLIOGRAPHY

This bibliography was used to gather most of the information in the sections above as well as for general reference. Items not specifically found in these works were gathered from the IETF-RUN Working Group's experience.

1. Angell, D.; Heslop, B. *The Elements of E-mail Style*; Addison-Wesley: New York, 1994.
2. Answers to Frequently Asked Questions about Usenet, Original Author: jerry@eagle. UUCP (Jerry Schwarz) Maintained by: netannounce@deshaw.com (Mark Moraes) Archive-name: usenet-faq/part1.
3. Cerf, V. Guidelines for Conduct on and Use of Internet, http://www.isoc.org/policy/conduct/conduct.html.
4. Dern, D. *The Internet Guide for New Users*; McGraw-Hill: New York, 1994.
5. Emily Postnews Answers Your Questions on Netiquette, Original Author: brad@looking.on.ca (Brad Templeton) Maintained by: netannounce@deshaw.com (Mark Moraes) Archive-name: emily-postnews/part1.
6. Gaffin, A. *Everybody's Guide to the Internet*; MIT Press: Cambridge, MA, 1994.
7. Guidelines for Responsible Use of the Internet from the US House of Representatives gopher, gopher://gopher.house.gov:70/OF-1%3a208%3aInternet%20Etiquette.
8. How to find the right place to post (FAQ) by buglady@bronze.lcs.mit.edu (Aliza R. Panitz) Archive-name: finding-groups/general.
9. Hambridge, S.; Sedayao, J. Horses and Barn Doors: Evolution of Corporate Guidelines for Internet Usage, LISA VII, Usenix, November 1–5, 1993, 9–16, ftp://ftp.intel.com/pub/papers/horses.ps or horses.ascii.
10. Heslop, B.; Angell, D. *The Instant Internet Guide: Hands-on Global Networking*; Addison-Wesley: Reading, MA, 1994.
11. Miller, G. Ruling is due on Mass E-mail campaign against Intel. Los Angeles Times, Apr 19, 1999.

12. Horwitz, S. Internet Etiquette Tips, ftp://ftp.temple.edu/pub/info/help-net/netiquette.infohn.

13. Internet Activities Board, Ethics and the Internet, RFC 1087, IAB, January 1989. ftp://ds.internic.net/rfc/rfc1087.txt.

14. Kehoe, B. *Zen and the Art of the Internet: A Beginner's Guide*; Prentice-Hall: Englewood Cliffs, NJ, 1994; Netiquette information is spread through the chapters of this work. 3rd Ed.

15. Kochmer, J. *Internet Passport: NorthWestNet's Guide to Our World Online,* 4th Ed.; North-WestNet, Northwest Academic Computing Consortium: Bellevue, WA, 1993.

16. Krol, Ed. *The Whole Internet: User's Guide and Catalog*; O'Reilly & Associates: Sebastopol, CA, 1992.

17. Lane, E.; Summerhill, C. *Internet Primer for Information Professionals: A Basic Guide to Internet Networking Technology*; Meckler: Westport, CT, 1993.

18. LaQuey, T.; Ryer, J. The Internet companion, Chapter 3. *Communicating with People*; Addison-Wesley: Reading, MA, 1993; 41–74.

19. Mandel, T. Surfing the Wild Internet, SRI International Business Intelligence Program, Scan No. 2109. March, 1993. gopher://gopher.well.sf.ca.us:70/00/Communications/surf-wild.

20. Martin, J. There's Gold in them thar Networks! or Searching for Treasure in all the Wrong Places, FYI 10, RFC 1402, January 1993. ftp://ds.internic.net/rfc/rfcl402.txt.

21. Pioch, N. A Short IRC Primer, Text conversion by Owe Rasmussen. Edition 1.1b, February 28, 1993, http://www.kei.com/irc/IRCprimer1.1.txt.

22. Polly, J. Surfing the Internet: An Introduction, Version 2.0.3. Revised May 15, 1993, ftp://ftp.nyser-net.org/pub/resources/guides/surfing.2.0.3.txt.

23. A Primer on How to Work With the Usenet Community Original Author: chuq@apple.com (Chuq Von Rospach) Maintained by: netannounce@deshaw.com (Mark Moraes) Archive-name: usenet-primer/part1.

24. Rinaldi, A. The Net: User Guidelines and Netiquette, September 3, 1992, http://www.fau.edu/rinaldi/net/index.htm.

25. Rules for posting to Usenet, Original Author: spaf@cs.purdue.edu (Gene Spafford) Maintained by: netannounce@deshaw.com (Mark Moraes) Archive-name: posting-rules/part1.

26. Shea, V. *Netiquette*, Albion Books: San Francisco, 1994.

27. Strangelove, M.; Bosley, A. How to Advertise on the Internet, ISSN 1201-0758.

28. Tenant, R. Internet Basics, ERIC Clearinghouse of Information Resources, EDO-IR-92-7. September, 1992, gopher://nic.merit.edu:7043/00/introducing.the.Internet/Internet.basics.eric-digest gopher://vega.lib.ncsu.edu:70/00/library/reference/guides/tennet.

29. Wiggins, R. *The Internet for Everyone: A Guide for Users and Providers*; McGraw-Hill: New York, 1995.

Event Management

Glenn Cater, CISSP
Director, IT Risk Consulting, Aon Consulting, Inc., Freehold, New Jersey, U.S.A.

Abstract

In many organizations, security policies or business regulations require that security events are monitored and that security logs are reviewed to identify security issues. Information captured in security logs is often critical for reconstructing the sequence of events during investigation of a security incident, and monitoring security logs may identify issues that would be missed otherwise. The problem is that the amount of information generated by security devices and systems can be vast and manual review is typically not practical. Security event management (SEM) or security information management (SIM) aims to solve this problem by automatically analyzing all that information to provide actionable alerts. In a nutshell, security event management deals with the collection, transmission, storage, monitoring and analysis of security events.

In addition to traditional security devices such as firewalls and intrusion detection systems, most systems on a typical network are capable of generating security events. Examples of security events include authentication events, audit events, intrusion events, and anti-virus events, and these events are usually stored in operating system logs, security logs or database tables.

INTRODUCTION

When implemented correctly, a security event management (SEM) solution can benefit a security operations team responsible for monitoring infrastructure security. Implementing SEM can relieve much of the need for hands-on monitoring of security systems such as intrusion detection systems, which typically entails staring at a consoles or logs for lengthy periods. This allows the security monitoring team to spend less time monitoring consoles, and more time on other tasks, such as improving incident response capabilities.

This improvement is achieved by implementing rules in the SEM system that mimic the know-how or methods used by the security practitioner when reviewing security events on a console or in a log. The SEM system can even go beyond this and look for patterns in the data that would not be detected by human analysis, such as "low and slow" (deliberately stealthy) attacks. Building this intelligence into the system is not a trivial task however and it can take many months to start realizing the benefits from implementing a SEM system.

When planning a security event management solution, the following issues should be considered:

- Which systems should be monitored for security events
- Which events are important and what information should be collected from logs

- Time synchronization, time zone offsets, and daylight savings
- Where, how, and for how long the logs should be stored
- Security and integrity of the logs during collection and transmission
- Using the SEM system as a system of record
- How to process security events to generate meaningful alerts or metrics
- Tuning the system to improve effectiveness and reduce false positives
- Monitoring procedures
- Requirements for choosing a commercial security event management solution

The remainder of this entry discusses the factors associated with planning and implementing a security event management system, and factors to consider when purchasing a commercial SEM solution.

SELECTING SYSTEMS AND DEVICES FOR MONITORING

Systems or devices to be monitored will typically fall into one of three categories:

- Security systems: includes systems and devices that perform some security function on your network. For example, authentication systems, firewalls, network intrusion detection and prevention systems (IDS/IPS), virtual private network devices (VPNs), host-based intrusion detection systems (HIDS), wireless security devices, and anti-malware systems
- Business critical systems: includes those systems that are important for running the network. For example,

Encyclopedia of Information Assurance DOI: 10.1081/E-EIA-120046833
Copyright © 2011 by Taylor & Francis. All rights reserved.

mail servers, DNS servers, web servers, authentication servers. When establishing which infrastructure systems are most critical, try to determine what the business impact would be if the system was unavailable. This category of system also includes more traditional network devices such as routers, switches, and wireless network devices.

- Critical infrastructure systems: includes those systems that are important for running the network. For example, mail servers, DNS servers, Web servers, authentication servers. When establishing which infrastructure systems are most critical, try to determine what the business impact would be if the system was unavailable. This category of system also includes more traditional network devices such as routers, switches, and wireless network devices.

Because budgets, time, and resources are not unlimited, you will have to do some up-front work to define the set of systems that should be monitored by the SEM system. It is a good idea to start with a risk assessment to determine which systems are most important to your business. Each of the categories (security, business, and infrastructure) above should be taken into account during the assessment. If regulatory requirements are a driving factor, then those requirements will help to define which systems should be monitored.

When prioritizing the order in which monitoring should be implemented, take into account the following:

- The criticality of the system to the business. Critical systems that process high value data will have a higher priority.
- Risk of inappropriate access. Internet facing systems or systems that process information from untrusted networks should have a higher priority.
- The "security value" of the available events. If a security system generates events that provide more value than another system, it makes sense to prioritize those first. For example, an IDS system typically generates more valuable information than a firewall.

DETERMINING WHICH SECURITY EVENTS ARE IMPORTANT

Security logs allow administrators or security personnel to proactively identify security issues or to backtrack through the timeline of events to investigate a security incident after it has occurred. Normally, a company's security policy will outline which security events need to be logged and what the requirements are for storage and review of those events, so it is likely that some or all systems are already configured to log security events.

It is important to perform a review for each type of device that will feed into the SEM system to identify which security events are important. Administrator's manuals should provide details on the logging capabilities of a device, although manual review of log samples is recommended to determine which events should be logged.

During this review you will probably find that many of the events being logged do not provide that much value. For example, perimeter firewalls are always dropping packets on their external interfaces due to Internet "noise." Although this information might be useful in rare cases, it is much more useful to know which connections made it through your firewall, or if a connection was allowed somewhere it was not supposed to be allowed. When planning an SEM system, unimportant events like these can be filtered or suppressed so that only more important events are collected and analyzed. This has the advantage of reducing the processing and storage needs of the SEM system.

Use the following checklist when reviewing the logging capabilities for each type of device:

- Review the manual that describes the logging capabilities.
- Obtain samples of logs from the device.
- Ensure that events which must be logged because of security, regulatory, or business requirements are included in the log configuration.
- For other types of events, assess the value of including that type of event in the log configuration. Some events do not provide much value and can probably be ignored.

The overall value of the SEM system is affected by the value of the data it processes and stores, so ensure that valuable data is not missed because of an incorrect logging configuration.

After the review is completed, standard logging configurations can be created for each type of device. Standardization is important to ensure that devices are logging common information. The standard logging configurations can be included with the organization's security requirements, and can be rolled out across all devices during implementation of the SEM system.

TIME SYNCHRONIZATION, TIME ZONES, AND DAYLIGHT SAVINGS

In addition to a defining a standard logging configuration, it is also important to ensure that all monitored devices and systems, and especially the SEM servers, are synchronized with a reliable and accurate time source. For smaller organizations, public Network Time Protocol (NTP) servers could be used for this purpose. There are lists of public NTP servers available on the Internet which can be used for time synchronization. It is good etiquette to limit usage of public servers and to notify the hosting organization before

Espionage – Firewalls

Espionage –
Firewalls

using their time servers. Larger organizations can set up local NTP servers that are synchronized with public NTP servers. To avoid having to change server names across many devices if authoritative NTP servers change, standard DNS aliases (such as time1.organization.com and time2.organization.com) should be created for the time servers to be used in lieu of the real server names.

For systems that are geographically dispersed across time zones, time zone offsets become an issue. Even if the systems are all located in the same time zone, it is important to be aware of the time zone so that there is no confusion when presenting logs to third parties such as law enforcement. Ideally, timestamps on all logs should be converted to Universal Time (UTC), as this eliminates the possibility of confusion. Alternatively, the time zone offset can be stored with the logs; for example, –0500 for Eastern Standard Time (meaning 5 hours behind UTC). Time offset changes due to daylight savings time is something to be aware of as well and there are a couple of ways to deal with this issue. For monitored systems where having local time is important, the time zone and time zone offset can be set as normal on the system; then when logs are collected, the collection agent can note the time zone and include it with the logs. Another way to deal with this situation is to create a database on the logging servers that contains the time zone information for each system. The time zone information can then be used during conversions or preprocessing of the data.

Possibly the easiest way to deal with the time zone problem is to set the time zone on monitored systems to UTC, then as long as administrators know that the time zone is UTC it becomes a non-issue. This might not be feasible for all systems, but it might work for certain devices, such as routers or intrusion detection systems, that are managed by network operations or security operations teams. Something to note is that although the data is stored with UTC timestamps, it can be shown in reports or on screen as local time with a simple conversion. This is beneficial if personnel are also spread out geographically because timestamps are shown to them in their local time.

CENTRALIZED LOGGING ARCHITECTURE

Commercial SEM systems all have their own solutions for collection, processing, and storage of security events. However, generally the approach is to centralize these functions so that security events are forwarded to centrally managed, dedicated SEM servers. There are many advantages to this approach such as centralized backups, searching, and analysis capabilities. For scalability, the SEM servers can be organized in a hierarchical manner, with local SEM servers situated near to the monitored systems. The function of local SEM servers is to collect, process, and queue events for transmission to the next tier. Fig. 1 depicts a hierarchical system with local SEM servers and a master SEM server.

The primary requirement of the master SEM server is plenty of local storage (hard disk, optical disk, tape). If searches, analysis, or other processing is performed on this server, it also needs fast CPUs, RAM, and disk. Local SEM servers will have leaner specifications because they do not need to store or process as much information. In more

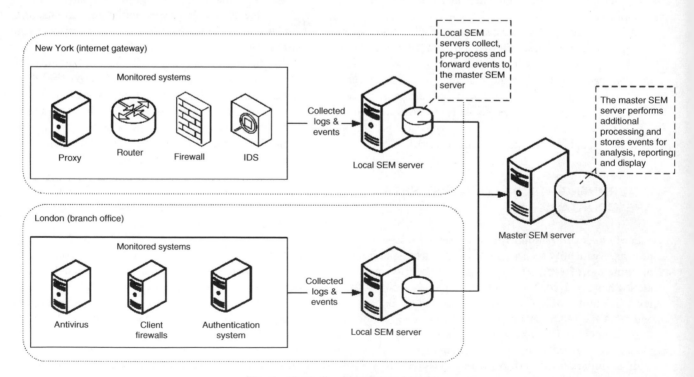

Fig. 1 Centralized logging architecture.

complex environments, a relational database (RDBMS) is typically used to store security events. Relational databases organize and index security logs, alerts, and other information for rapid searches and report generation. Commercial SEM systems use databases to organize and store security events for analysis, reporting, and display.

After security events reach the central SEM server, they will be stored on disk for some period of time. How long the logs are on disk depends on the size of the logs, budget, security requirements, and business requirements. Typically, logs will be stored on disk ("online") for a few weeks or months, and this is mostly dependent on how much disk space is available. It is advantageous to keep logs on disk because this allows for convenient access to the data, and all operations such as searching will be quicker. There might be a security requirement to store logs in a read-only form, in which case a write-once, read-many (WORM) form of media such as an optical disk will be necessary. Encryption may also be a requirement, in which case encryption software or a hardware encryption solution will also be necessary. Online storage is usually at a premium, so periodically the logs will need to be archived to cheaper offline storage such as tape and removed from disk to make space for newer logs.

To save disk or tape space in long term storage, compression techniques such as GZip or Zip will maximize the amount of data that can be stored. Short term "online" storage should remain uncompressed to improve searching or processing of the data. For example, there may be one month of "online" uncompressed data on disk, another five months of compressed data on disk for quick access, then up to 7 years of compressed data archived onto tape. These periods are only an example, and should be dependent upon business and security policies, and the amount of available disk space. Batch jobs can be set up to periodically compress, archive and remove old data from storage.

An organization's data retention policies should dictate how long information such as logs must be stored, and what requirements there are for storage and disposal of the information. If there is no data retention policy, then this needs to be defined so that information is kept for as long as it is needed, but for no longer than is necessary. There may be local legal or regulatory requirements which dictate a minimum term for which information needs to be stored (usually a maximum of 7 years, depending on the type of information).

The security of the SEM servers is very important. These servers need to be hardened and locked down to expose only the minimum services to the outside. It is a good idea to firewall these servers from the rest of the network, or to utilize the built-in firewall capability of the operating system to limit access to the servers. When building an SEM server, the following steps should be performed:

- Implement standard operating system security hardening techniques.

- Limit services exposed and listening on the network.
- Limit access to the server only to the administrators or security personnel that require access.
- Perform periodic network and host-based vulnerability scans on the SEM servers.
- Use external or built-in firewalls to limit connectivity to and from known hosts only.
- Ensure that the server is synchronized to a reliable and accurate time source (such as a public NTP server).

To avoid having to change server names across many devices if logging servers change, standard DNS aliases (such as log1.organization.com and log2.organization.com) should be created for the SEM servers to be used in lieu of the real server names.

INTEGRATING SYSTEMS AND COLLECTING SECURITY EVENTS

Commercial SEM systems typically provide "agents" or other mechanisms to securely gather security events or logs from systems, but it is possible that the SEM system does not have an agent or mechanism for every type of system in a network. It is also possible to entirely roll your own SEM system, so some techniques are presented here for gathering and transmitting security logs in a secure manner. Because it is important to maintain the integrity of the security logs, care must be taken in choosing methods for collection and transmission, and methods used must meet the organization's security requirements.

There are three general methods for collection of logs or events. Commercial SEM systems typically use all three approaches, depending on the type of system or device that is being monitored:

- Direct transmission of events to the SEM servers, for example via RADIUS accounting or SNMPv3 traps. Direct transmission is a good method if the device supports it and the mechanism is appropriately secure.
- Agent-based collection and transmission of logs or events. A software agent runs continuously or periodically on the monitored system and sends new security events over to the SEM servers.
- Server-based collection of logs from monitored systems. A SEM server will periodically poll the monitored systems for new security events. This requires that the SEM system has an appropriate level of permission on the target system.

The method chosen will depend on the capability of the target system and security requirements. For example, hosts located within a DMZ (de-militarized zone), usually have strict security policies applied to them and outbound data connections to the internal network might not be allowed. In this situation, a server-based polling mechanism is probably the best approach if the SEM server is not located within the DMZ.

Generally, encrypted and/or authenticated connections should be used to transmit events between devices and the SEM servers to maintain integrity of the logs; however, this is not always possible. Following are various options for gathering events (see Fig. 2).

- SSL (Secure Sockets Layer) or TLS (Transport Layer Security). For example, Web servers can be used to "serve" logs to trusted hosts via an SSL connection.
- SCP (Secure Copy) or SFTP (Security File Transfer Protocol). SCP or SFTP are simple protocols that can be scripted into batch jobs.
- IPSec connections or tunnels between systems. IPSec can be used to secure specific connections or all traffic for a host.

- VPN (Virtual private network) tunnels. VPN tunnels can be used if the target system and SEM server are far apart, or if the target system does not support any other method of transmission.
- RADIUS (Remote Authentication Dial In User Service) accounting. RADIUS accounting is a good option that is supported by many network devices.
- SNMP (Simple Network Management Protocol) v3 traps, which are common with network devices. SNMPv1 is not encrypted so its use is not recommended.
- Encrypted file transfer over FTP [using PGP (Pretty Good Privacy) or another file encryption tool]. This is another option that can be scripted for use in batch jobs.
- Secured database connections can be used to read events directly from logs stored in databases.
- Syslog-ng combined with s-tunnel. Standard syslog uses cleartext UDP packets so security and integrity

Espionage –
Firewalls

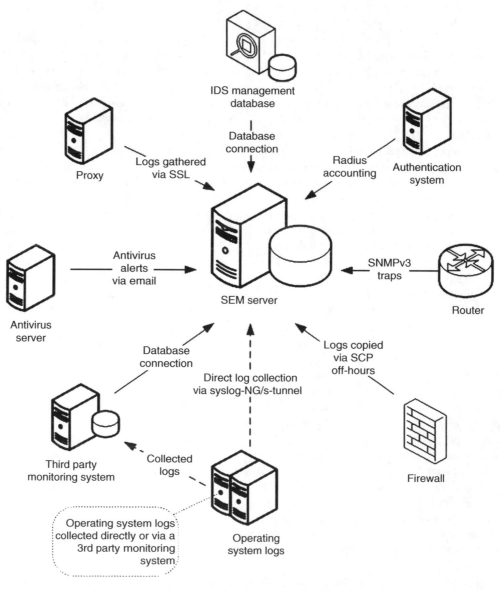

Fig. 2 Secure transmission of data.

is difficult to maintain. Syslog-ng can use TCP and can be combined with s-tunnel to transmit logs securely.

- Native authenticated file sharing mechanisms, such as CIFS (Windows) with appropriate security applied. NFS could be used if secured appropriately. This can be a simple solution if the target system supports it.
- E-mail alerts sent directly to the SEM server. Often antivirus, IDS or other systems have the ability to send alerts via e-mail. The SEM server can be configured to receive and process e-mail alerts via SMTP. Although not the most secure method it can be convenient.
- Third-party monitoring solutions, typically used to monitor and manage the network, have the ability to gather logs from systems. These systems can be configured to send logs to a SEM system for analysis.

Encryption keys used with SSL, SCP, or other connections should be stored securely and in accordance with security policies. Because security log collection is almost always automated, the agents or batch jobs that perform collection and transmission need to have access to the encryption keys. Possibly the cleanest way to do this is to run the agents with a non-privileged account with just enough permission to read the logs and to access the encryption keys. If security requirements do not prohibit it, the encryption keys can be stored without passwords but with file-level security so that only the agent is allowed to access them. Each system (including the SEM servers) should have a unique key pair so that compromise of one system does not compromise the whole SEM infrastructure. There are other ways to provide automated access to encryption keys that may be more secure but will also be more difficult to automate and maintain.

Because log files tend to be large, it is beneficial to use compression techniques such as GZip or Zip before encryption or transmission. Text files will usually compress to a fraction of their original size, which saves disk space and network bandwidth. Processes can compress data before encryption and transmission, and uncompress data on the other side after it has been received and decrypted. Compression should always be done before encryption because the random nature of encrypted data makes compression ineffective.

Whatever collection and transmission mechanisms are used, they should have fault tolerance built in to detect and recover from failures such as system outages, network outages, or insufficient disk space. This is important to ensure integrity and completeness of the collected events.

USING THE SEM SYSTEM AS A SYSTEM OF RECORD

Because a SEM system collects and stores security logs from many devices across the network, it can be implemented as the "system of record" for security logs. This means the SEM system will be considered the definitive and authoritative

source for security logs for the organization. This distinction places additional requirements on the system because it becomes important to ensure the integrity and timeliness of data feeds, so that the SEM system has complete, accurate, and up-to-date logs. Access to the information should be strictly controlled via approved mechanisms, and updates to the information should be logged so that the integrity of the data can be audited. Cryptographic checks such as hashes or digital signatures can help to ensure the integrity of the data from collection through to storage.

EVENTS, ALERTS, AND THE RULE SYSTEM

As discussed, "events" are the individual log messages gathered from systems and devices, such as firewalls, intrusion detection systems, hosts, routers, etc. For example, a single "login" event will contain a hostname, a username, and a timestamp. After events are gathered by the SEM system, they pass through a series of "rules" for processing events called the "rule system." The rule system will generate "alerts" based on characteristics of events being processed. Alerts indicate that a significant event or series of events has happened that needs attention. Alerts are typically intended for review by a security analyst, and will normally be displayed on the SEM console and stored in the database for tracking and reporting purposes.

TECHNIQUES FOR PROCESSING SECURITY EVENTS

The goal of the SEM rule system is to reduce the data volume from an unmanageable number of events down to a small number of actionable alerts that can be reviewed by security analysts. Security events are collected by the system, and pass through categorization, prioritization, filtering, and other stages in which alerts are generated. The end result is that a smaller number of actionable alerts are generated for security analysts to review. Commercial systems generally operate in a similar way with several processing stages. Fig. 3 depicts how processing stages affect event volume.

Following is a discussion of some techniques used to process security events in the SEM rule system. Commercial SEM systems provide pre-built rules to perform many functions and normally allow customized rules to be created to meet customer needs. For this reason, SEM systems need to be very flexible and are usually scriptable or programmable to allow advanced customization. Flexibility and programmability are key features of any SEM system.

Event Parsing

Event parsing is usually the first stage in a SEM system. The goal of this stage is to extract useful information from the security events so that they can be further processed by

Espionage –
Firewalls

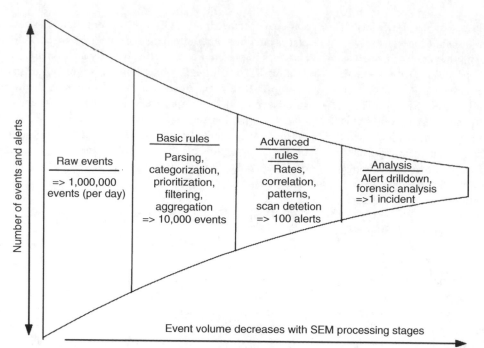

Fig. 3 Effect of processing on event volume.

later stages. Security events are extracted into "fields" of information such as timestamp, event source, event type, username, hostname, source IP address, target IP address, source port, target port, message, etc. Because each device generates events in a different format, specific parsers need to be created for each type of device. The parsing stage needs to be very flexible to handle many event formats. Vendors of commercial SEM systems usually provide a list of devices that they directly support, but the SEM system is usually flexible enough to allow customized parsing rules to be built for unsupported devices. The output from this stage is a parsed event, with fields separated out so that they are available to the rest of the rule system. Parsed security events may be stored as rows in a database table with fields populated with information from the event. The overall value of the SEM system is affected by the value of the data it processes and stores, so ensure that all valuable fields are parsed and stored properly. Fig. 4 depicts a sample "failed authentication" event, and shows how it is parsed into fields for storage in the SEM database. This example also shows why an extensible database schema is useful for capturing important fields from differing message formats.

Event Categorization

After events are parsed usually the next step is to assign categories, and subcategories, to the events. For example, an event category of "virus" and a sub category of "quarantined," meaning that the event was caused by a virus that was detected and quarantined. Categorization aids in display and analysis, reporting, and further processing of events.

Event Prioritization

After events are categorized, the next step is to assign a priority to the event. Priorities could be on a numeric scale, for example 0–100, with "0" meaning that the event has no relevance and "100" meaning that the event is a critical issue that needs to be investigated. The priority can be used to filter events of little significance to reduce the volume for later processing stages.

Event Aggregation or Summarization

Event aggregation or summarization functions look for many events that are similar. The events do not necessarily need to arrive at the same time, so the function will store state. Events are summarized into one "aggregated" event that is passed to the next stage with an aggregate count that indicates how many events comprise the aggregated event. For certain types of devices, such as firewalls, this can significantly reduce the volume of data. For example, if a firewall logs 50 connection (SYN) attempts to a particular port, it could be summarized to one event with a count of 50. The aggregated count may then cause another rule to fire because of a high volume of SYN packets, for example. The problem with summarization is that information is lost as part of the summarization operation, so only fields that are included in the summarization operation will be available to the next stage. The more fields that are included, the less effective the summarization becomes. Therefore, with the firewall event example, it is possible that the only fields included in the summarization operations are the

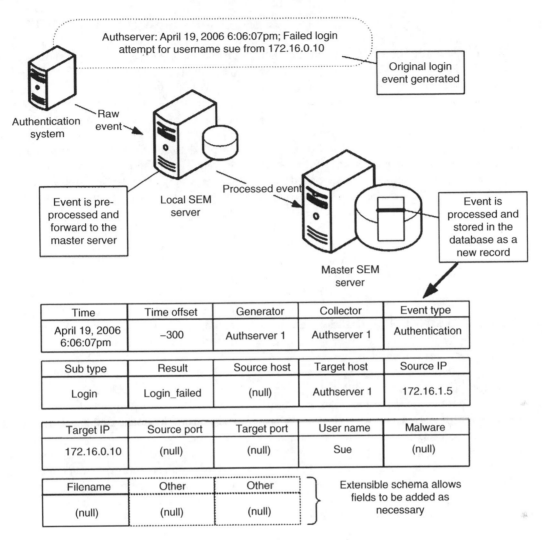

Time	Time offset	Generator	Collector	Event type
April 19, 2006 6:06:07pm	–300	Authserver 1	Authserver 1	Authentication

Sub type	Result	Source host	Target host	Source IP
Login	Login_failed	(null)	Authserver 1	172.16.1.5

Target IP	Source port	Target port	User name	Malware
172.16.0.10	(null)	(null)	Sue	(null)

Filename	Other	Other
(null)	(null)	(null)

Extensible schema allows fields to be added as necessary

Fig. 4 Example of message parsing.

event type (SYN) and the port number; all other fields would be discarded.

Pattern Matching

Pattern matching is a simple technique that looks for patterns in the event fields. Exact matches, substring matches, or regular expressions are used to extract important events from the stream. Typically, the pattern-matched events will then become alerts for display and review. For example, a pattern matching rule could look for the words "buffer overflow" in an IDS event, which could result in that event being promoted to an alert for display.

Scan Detection

Scan detection refers to port scans, vulnerability scans, ping sweeps, and other scanning activities and works best with firewall or IDS events. Scanning is usually a prelude to an attack of some sort, so it is a useful rule. Network worms use this technique to locate systems to infect, so this rule can be useful to identify infected hosts on a network. The scan detection rule looks for a large number of events from a source host with many target hosts, ports, or event types. The scan detection rule may also look for a large number of different types of events against a host, which can indicate a vulnerability scan. Because state can be kept for a long time, scan detection rules can also be tuned to look for "low and slow" or stealthy scanning techniques that would not normally be discovered by human review.

Event Counts and Rate Thresholds

Event counts are simply counts of a certain type of event, such as virus detections. After this count reaches a predefined threshold, the rule will fire and generate an alert for display. Rate thresholds work by calculating the rate of a certain type of event; for example, 20 failed login messages within a minute is indicative of a password-guessing attack.

Espionage –
Firewalls

Event Correlation

Correlation refers to the ability of a SEM system to take multiple events or pieces of information from various sources and to infer that some activity is happening. For example, if vulnerability scan data is available to a SEM system, it can determine whether an attempted attack on a system is likely to succeed because it can correlate IDS "attack" events with known system vulnerabilities. The priority can then be raised to indicate a successful attack. In another example, host information has been loaded into the SEM system, and a UNIX-specific attack is detected against a Windows host. Because this attack could not succeed, the SEM system can lower the priority and discard the event. Other possibilities exist when correlating events across sources because patterns indicative of malicious behavior can be detected and alerted upon.

TUNING AND CUSTOMIZING THE RULE SYSTEM

After event sources have been integrated into the security event management system and events start to flow, the system will initially generate too many alerts, or a lot of false positive (erroneous) alerts. Like intrusion detection systems, security event management systems need to be tuned to be effective because the default rules are built in a generic way and need to be customized for local conditions. To get the best results, tuning requires expert knowledge of the SEM system, the network, and many of the devices being monitored. Depending on the size of the network, this may require input from many people.

If too many false positives or insignificant alerts are being generated, begin at the event sources generating those alerts (systems or devices) and determine methods to limit the events being collected so that only the more significant events are allowed through. Often the monitored system can be configured to filter out insignificant events. For example, IDS systems can be tuned to filter out low priority "informational" events. Be careful not to tune out events that could adversely affect the value of the SEM system.

Another way to reduce the volume of alerts is to filter out lower priority events after the event prioritization step (see the section on event prioritization above). Care should be taken with this type of "blanket" approach so that significant alerts triggered by low priority events are not affected.

To continue tuning, follow the event flow through the rule system to locate points where alerts are generated and determine if the alerting criteria, such as a thresholds or counts, are valid. Because alerts are getting through that are not significant, there should be ways to reduce or eliminate them entirely without affecting legitimate alerts. If not, then a compromise will be necessary to reduce false positives or insignificant alerts in favor of important alerts.

MONITORING THE SEM SYSTEM

Alerts generated by the rule system are usually stored in a relational database (RDBMS) along with the original security events for fast querying capability. Alerts are also normally presented on a console for review by an analyst. Documented procedures should be developed for analysts describing how to monitor the system and respond to alerts. During audits, auditors will look for evidence that these procedures are being followed. SEM systems may provide workflow type features or integrate with ticketing systems to track incidents and document actions taken by analysts and incident managers. This documentation will provide evidence that procedures are being followed.

SEM systems normally offer the ability to "drill down" into alerts to perform "forensic analysis." Typically, the analyst will be able to select the alert and perform various queries to determine what caused the alert to fire. For example, if "vulnerability scan" alert was detected against a system, the console should allow the operator to query the event store to pull up more details about which events comprised the alert. The analyst can then make an informed decision about the criticality of the alert, and whether to escalate it into an incident. Analysts typically need strong technical and analytical skills to perform this function.

A lot of data is collected by a security event management systems and this data can contain valuable nuggets of information. Data mining tools exist to perform deep analysis of the data to extract information that is not immediately apparent. These tools tend to be CPU and resource intensive, so they need to be used carefully. For larger organizations with numerous security events, it might make sense to take periodic samples of data for analysis, or run analysis in a batch mode at off-peak times. Security event management systems also include the ability to generate pre-canned and custom reports. Reports can be useful to provide metrics to upper management showing trends and graphs of activity over time.

CRITERIA FOR CHOOSING A COMMERCIAL SECURITY EVENT MANAGEMENT SYSTEM

It is important to evaluate and compare different solutions when choosing a commercial security event management system. Following are some of the more important factors, other than cost, to take into account during the evaluation:

- Types of devices supported: Ensure that all devices, software, and operating systems that need to be monitored are supported by the SEM system.
- Event collection mechanisms: Ensure that methods used to collect events (such as agent based collection)

will work within the environment and meet security or architectural requirements.

- Usability of rule system: Review the rule system to ensure that it is understandable and that alerting criteria are clear. Also review how locally customized rules can be distinguished from built-in system rules.
- Storage flexibility and completeness: Ensure that the SEM database (or store) is flexible enough to store all information fields valuable to your organization. This is an important factor because if data is not stored in the database it won't be available to the SEM system for reporting, analysis or display which reduces the value of the whole system.
- Upgrade path: Review the upgrade policy and the process of applying upgrades to the SEM system to ensure that upgrades do not interfere with local customizations.
- Handling of time zones and daylight savings time: If the monitored systems are spread over multiple time zones, ensure that the SEM system can readily handle time zone offsets and daylight savings time.
- Scalability and performance: Ensure that the SEM system is capable of processing the maximum expected rate of security events generated from all devices. Also ensure that there is enough capacity to meet future needs.
- Security: Ensure that the SEM system meets the organization's security requirements. This includes the security of the whole event collection mechanism, SEM servers and applications, databases, and user interfaces. Also ensure that the system keeps adequate audit logs. Review the requirement to separate functions by role such as system administrator, security analyst, and incident manager, and ensure that the SEM system can accommodate role separation.
- Usability and functionality of the user interfaces: Probably the most important function is the act of monitoring the SEM system. The analyst's console needs to present all information in an understandable and intuitive way. Review the ability to perform analyst functions such as alert inspection, drill down, canned and custom queries, work flow, and escalation features. Also review the reporting system to ensure that canned reports are usable and meet requirements and that custom reports can be created in cases where canned reports are not adequate.

- Ability to integrate with external databases: If there is a need to integrate with other databases such as Configuration Management Databases (CMDB), ticketing systems, or company directories, then this capability should be reviewed.
- Programming interface: To allow advanced customizations, programmability is a key feature of a SEM system. The usability and flexibility of the programming interface should be reviewed.

CONCLUSION

A correctly implemented security event management solution will improve the effectiveness of security monitoring and incident response functions. Analysts will spend less time monitoring consoles and reviewing security logs because this function is automated by the SEM system. Senior analysts can build expert know-how into the rule system to improve the quality of alerts for all analysts, and reduce cases of false positives.

Having all security events collected into one central database is a key benefit of a SEM system. This information is very valuable for security analysts, incident response teams, and other IT teams. Reports and security metrics can be generated for managers and data mining tools can uncover interesting information from the data.

The benefits do come at a cost, however, and it will take several months to start realizing the benefit of implementing an SEM system. In addition to the cost of purchasing a commercial solution, perhaps two of the most resource intensive efforts are integrating security event sources into the system and performing tuning of the rule system. Vendors offer professional assistance, but it is beneficial for analysts to be involved in the implementation process to understand the workings of the whole system. Analysts will also need training in the use and administrator of the system.

Perhaps one of the most important factors when implementing a SEM system is to ensure that all data of importance is collected and available within the database. If the data is not available, then it cannot be queried or displayed and it is frustrating to run a query or report only to find that a needed field is not available because it has not been collected. The value of the SEM system then is only as good as the information it contains.

Espionage – Firewalls

External Networks: Secured Connections

Steven F. Blanding, CIA, CISA, CSP, CFE, CQA
Former Regional Director of Technology, Arthur Andersen, Houston, Texas, U.S.A.

Abstract

This entry identifies areas of security that should be considered with connections to external networks. Security policies must be developed for user identification and authorization, software import controls, encryption, and system architecture, which include the use of Internet firewall security capabilities. Entry sections discuss security policy statements that address connections to external networks including the Internet. Each section contains multiple sample policies for use at the different risk profiles. Some areas provide multiple examples at the same risk level to show the different presentation methods that might be used to get the message across.

A private network that carries sensitive data between local computers requires proper security measures to protect the privacy and integrity of the traffic. When such a network is connected to other networks, or when telephone access is allowed into that network, the remote terminals, phone lines, and other connections become extensions of that private network and must be secured accordingly. In addition, the private network must be secured from outside attacks that could cause loss of information, breakdowns in network integrity, or breaches in security.

Many organizations have connected or want to connect their private local area networks (LANs) to the Internet so that their users can have convenient access to Internet services. Because the Internet as a whole is not trustworthy, their private systems are vulnerable to misuse and attack. Firewalls are typically used as a safeguard to control access between a trusted network and a less trusted network. A firewall is not a single component; it is a strategy for protecting an organization's resources from the Internet. A firewall serves as the gatekeeper between the untrusted Internet and the more trusted internal networks. Some organizations are also in the process of connecting their private networks to other organizations' private networks. Firewall security capabilities should also be used to provide protection for these types of connections.

RISKS AND ASSUMPTIONS

An understanding of the risks and assumptions is required before defining security policies for external connections. It is beyond the scope of this entry to quantify the probability of the risks; however, the risks should cover a broad, comprehensive area. The following are the risks and assumptions:

- The data being protected, while not classified, is highly sensitive and would do damage to the organization and its mission if disclosed or captured.
- The integrity of the internal network directly affects the ability of the organization to accomplish its mission.
- The internal network is physically secure; the people using the internal network are trustworthy.
- PCs on the internal network are considered to be unsecured. Reliance is placed on the physical security of the location to protect them.
- Whenever possible, employees who are connected from remote sites should be treated as members of the internal network and have access to as many services as possible without compromising internal security.
- The Internet is assumed to be unsecured; the people using the Internet are assumed to be untrustworthy.
- Employees are targets for spying; information they carry or communicate is vulnerable to capture.
- Passwords transmitted over outside connections are vulnerable to capture.
- Any data transmitted over outside connections are vulnerable to capture.
- There is no control over e-mail once it leaves the internal network; e-mail can be read, tampered with, and spoofed.
- Any direct connection between a PC on the internal network and one on the outside can possibly be compromised and used for intrusion.
- Software bugs exist and may provide intrusion points from the outside into the internal network.
- Password protection on PCs directly reachable from the outside can be compromised and used for intrusion.

Encyclopedia of Information Assurance DOI: 10.1081/E-EIA-120046365
Copyright © 2011 by Taylor & Francis. All rights reserved.

Espionage – Firewalls

- Security through obscurity is counter-productive. Easy-to-understand measures are more likely to be sound, and are easier to administer.

SECURITY POLICIES

Security policies fall into two broad categories: technical policies to be carried out by hardware or software, and administrative policy to be carried out by people using and managing the system. The final section of this entry discusses Internet firewall security policies in more detail.

Identification and Authentication

Identification and authentication are the processes of recognizing and verifying valid users or processes. Identification and authentication information is generally then used to determine what system resources a user or process will be allowed to access. The determination of who can access what should coincide with a data categorization effort.

The assumption is that there is connectivity to internal systems from external networks or the Internet. If there is no connectivity, there is no need for identification and authentication controls. Many organizations separate Internet-accessible systems from internal systems through the use of firewalls and routers.

Authentication over the Internet presents several problems. It is relatively easy to capture identification and authentication data (or any data) and replay it in order to impersonate a user. As with other remote identification and authorization controls, and often with internal authorization systems, there can be a high level of user dissatisfaction and uncertainty, which can make this data obtainable via social engineering. Having additional authorization controls for use of the Internet may also contribute to authorization data proliferation, which is difficult for users to manage. Another problem is the ability to hijack a user session after identification and authorization have been performed.

There are three major types of authentication available: static, robust, and continuous. Static authentication includes passwords and other techniques that can be compromised through replay attacks. They are often called reusable passwords. Robust authentication involves the use of cryptography or other techniques to create one-time passwords that are used to create sessions. These can be compromised by session hijacking. Continuous authentication prevents session hijacking.

Static authentication

Static authentication only provides protection against attacks in which an impostor cannot see, insert, or alter the information passed between the claimant and the verifier during an authentication exchange and subsequent session. In these cases, an impostor can only attempt to assume a claimant's identity by initiating an access control session as any valid user might do and trying to guess a legitimate user's authentication data. Traditional password schemes provide this level of protection, and the strength of the authentication process is highly dependent on the difficulty of guessing password values and how well they are protected.

Robust authentication

This class of authentication mechanism relies on dynamic authentication data that changes with each authenticated session between a claimant and verifier. An impostor who can see information passed between the claimant and verifier may attempt to record this information, initiate a separate access control session with the verifier, and replay the recorded authentication data in an attempt to assume the claimant's identity. This type of authentication protects against such attacks, because authentication data recorded during a previous session will not be valid for any subsequent sessions.

However, robust authentication does not provide protection against active attacks in which the impostor is able to alter the content or flow of information between the claimant and verifier after they have established a legitimate session. Since the verifier binds the claimant's identity to the logical communications channel for the duration of the session, the verifier believes that the claimant is the source of all data received through this channel.

Traditional fixed passwords would fail to provide robust authentication because the password of a valid user could be viewed and used to assume that user's identity later. However, one-time passwords and digital signatures can provide this level of protection.

Continuous authentication

This type of authentication provides protection against impostors who can see, alter, and insert information passed between the claimant and verifier even after the claimant/verifier authentication is complete. These are typically referred to as active attacks, since they assume that the impostor can actively influence the connection between claimant and verifier. One way to provide this form of authentication is to apply a digital signature algorithm to every bit of data that is sent from the claimant to the verifier. There are other combinations of cryptography that can provide this form of authentication, but current strategies rely on applying some type of cryptography to every bit of data sent. Otherwise, any unprotected bit would be suspect.

Espionage – Firewalls

Applying identification and authorization policies

Although passwords are easily compromised, an organization may find that a threat is not likely, would be fairly easy to recover from, or would not affect critical systems (which may have separate protection mechanisms). In low-risk connections, only static authentication may be required for access to corporate systems from external networks or the Internet.

In medium-risk connections, Internet access to information and processing (low impact if modified, unavailable, or disclosed) would require a password, and access to all other resources would require robust authentication. Telnet access to corporate resources from the Internet would also require the use of robust authentication.

Internet access to all systems behind the firewall would require robust authentication. Access to information and processing (high impact if modified, unavailable, or disclosed) would require continuous authentication.

PASSWORD MANAGEMENT POLICIES

The following are general password policies applicable for Internet use—these are considered to be the minimum standards for security control:

- Passwords and user log-on IDs will be unique to each authorized user.
- Passwords will consist of a minimum of 6 alphanumeric characters (no common names or phrases). There should be computer-controlled lists of proscribed password rules and periodic testing (e.g., letter and number sequences, character repetition, initials, common words, and standard names) to identify any password weaknesses.
- Passwords will be kept private—i.e., not shared, coded into programs, or written down.
- Passwords will be changed every 90 days (or less). Most operating systems can enforce password change with an automatic expiration and prevent repeated or reused passwords.
- User accounts will be frozen after 3 failed log-on attempts. All erroneous password entries will be recorded in an audit log for later inspection and action, as necessary.
- Sessions will be suspended after 15 minutes (or other specified period) of inactivity and require the password to be reentered.
- Successful log-ons should display the date and time of the last log-on and log-off.
- Log-on IDs and passwords should be suspended after a specified period of non-use.
- For high-risk systems, after excessive violations, the system should generate an alarm and be able to simulate a continuing session (with dummy data, etc.) for the failed user (to keep this user connected while personnel attempt to investigate the incoming connection).

Robust authentication policy

The decision to use robust authentication requires an understanding of the risks, the security gained, and the cost of user acceptance and administration. User acceptance will be dramatically improved if users are appropriately trained in robust authentication and how it is used.

There are many technologies available that provide robust authentication including dynamic password generators, cryptography-based challenge/response tokens and software, and digital signatures and certificates. If digital signatures and certificates are used, another policy area is opened up: the security requirements for the certificates.

Users of robust authentication must receive training prior to use of the authentication mechanism. Employees are responsible for safe handling and storage of all company authentication devices. Authentication tokens should not be stored with a computer that will be used to access corporate systems. If an authentication device is lost or stolen, the loss must be immediately reported to security so that the device can be disabled.

Digital signatures and certificates

If identification and authorization makes use of digital signatures, then certificates are required. They can be issued by the organization or by a trusted third party. Commercial public key infrastructures (PKI) are emerging within the Internet community. Users can obtain certificates with various levels of assurance. For example, level 1 certificates verify electronic mail addresses. This is done through the use of a personal information number that a user would supply when asked to register. This level of certificate may also provide a name as well as an electronic mail address; however, it may or may not be a genuine name (i.e., it could be an alias). Level 2 certificates verify a user's name, address, social security number, and other information against a credit bureau database. Level 3 certificates are available to companies. This level of certificate provides photo identification (e.g., for their employees) to accompany the other items of information provided by a Level 2 certificate.

Once obtained, digital certificate information may be loaded into an electronic mail application or a web browser application to be activated and provided whenever a web site or another user requests it for the purposes of verifying the identity of the person with whom they are communicating. Trusted certificate authorities are required to administer such systems with strict controls, otherwise fraudulent certificates could easily be issued.

Many of the latest web servers and web browsers incorporate the use of digital certificates. Secure Socket Layer (SSL) is the technology used in most Web-based applications. SSL version 2.0 supports strong authentication of the Web server, while SSL 3.0 adds client-side authentication. Once both sides are authenticated, the session is encrypted, providing protection against both eavesdropping and session hijacking. The digital certificates used are based on the X.509 standard and describe who issued the certificate, the validity period, and other information.

Oddly enough, passwords still play an important role even when using digital certificates. Since digital certificates are stored on a computer, they can only be used to authenticate the computer, rather than the user, unless the user provides some other form of authentication to the computer. Passwords or "passphrases" are generally used; smart cards and other hardware tokens will be used in the future.

Any company's systems making limited distribution data available over the Internet should use digital certificates to validate the identity of both the user and the server. Only company-approved certificate authorities should issue certificates. Certificates at the user end should be used in conjunction with standard technologies such as Secure Sockets Layer to provide continuous authentication to eliminate the risk of session hijacking. Access to digital certificates stored on personal computers should be protected by passwords or passphrases. All policies for password management must be followed and enforced.

SOFTWARE IMPORT CONTROL

Data on computers is rarely static. Mail arrives and is read. New applications are loaded from floppy, CD-ROM, or across a network. Web-based interactive software downloads executables that run on a computer. Each modification runs the risk of introducing viruses, damaging the configuration of the computer, or violating software-licensing agreements. Organizations need to protect themselves with different levels of control depending on the vulnerability to these risks. Software Import Control provides an organization with several different security challenges:

- Virus and Trojan horse prevention, detection, and removal
- Controlling Interactive Software (Java, ActiveX)
- Software licensing

Each challenge can be categorized according to the following criteria:

- Control: who initiates the activity, and how easily can it be determined that software has been imported

- Threat type: executable program, macro, applet, violation of licensing agreement
- Cleansing action: scanning, refusal of service, control of permissions, auditing, deletion

When importing software onto a computer, one runs the risk of getting additional or different functionality than one bargained for. The importation may occur as a direct action, or as a hidden side effect, which is not readily visible. Examples of direct action include:

- File transfer — utilizing FTP to transfer a file to a computer.
- Reading e-mail — causing a message which has been transferred to a computer to be read, or using a tool (e.g., Microsoft Word) to read an attachment.
- Downloading software from a floppy disk or over the network can spawn indirect action. Some examples include 1) reading a Web page which downloads a Java applet to your computer and 2) executing an application such as Microsoft Word and opening a file infected with a Word Macro Virus.

Virus prevention, detection, and removal

A virus is a self-replicating program spread from executables, boot records, and macros. Executable viruses modify a program to do something other than the original intent. After replicating itself into other programs, the virus may do little more than print an annoying message, or it could do something as damaging as deleting all of the data on a disk. There are different levels of sophistication in how hard a virus may be to detect.

The most common "carrier" of viruses has been the floppy disk, since "sneaker net" was the most common means of transferring software between computers. As telephone-based bulletin boards became popular, viruses travelled more frequently via modem. The Internet provides yet another channel for virus infections, one that can often bypass traditional virus controls.

For organizations that allow downloading of software over the Internet (which can be via Internet e-mail attachments) virus scanning at the firewall can be an appropriate choice—but it does not eliminate the need for client and server based virus scanning, as well. For several years to come, viruses imported on floppy disks or infected vendor media will continue to be a major threat.

Simple viruses can be easily recognized by scanning for a signature of byte strings near the entry point of a program, once the virus has been identified. Polymorphic viruses modify themselves as they propagate. Therefore, they have no signature and can only be found (safely) by executing the program in a virtual processor environment. Boot record viruses modify the boot record such that the virus is executed when the system is booted.

Applications that support macros are at risk for macro viruses. Macro viruses are commands that are embedded in data. Vendor applications, such as Microsoft Word, Microsoft Excel, or printing standards such as Postscript are common targets. When the application opens the data file the infected macro virus is instantiated.

The security service policy for viruses has three aspects:

- Prevention—policies which prevent the introduction of viruses into a computing environment
- Detection—determination that an executable, boot record, or data file is contaminated with a virus
- Removal—deletion of the virus from the infected computing system may require reinstallation of the operating system from the ground up, deleting files, or deleting the virus from an infected file

There are various factors that are important in determining the level of security concern for virus infection of a computer. Viruses are most prevalent on DOS, Windows (3.x, 95), and NT operating systems. However some UNIX viruses have been identified.

The frequency that new applications or files are loaded on to the computer is proportional to the susceptibility of that computer to viruses. Configuration changes resulting from exposure to the Internet, exposure to mail, or receipt of files from external sources are more at risk for contamination.

The greater the value of the computer or data on the computer, the greater the concern should be for ensuring that virus policy as well as implementation procedures are in place. The cost of removal of the virus from the computing environment must be considered within your organization as well as from customers you may have infected. Cost may not always be identified as monetary; company reputation and other considerations are just as important.

It is important to note that viruses are normally introduced into a system by a voluntary act of a user (e.g., installation of an application, executing a file, etc.). Prevention policies can therefore focus on limiting the introduction of potentially infected software and files to a system. In a high-risk environment, virus-scanning efforts should be focused on when new software or files are introduced to maximize protection.

Controlling interactive software

A programming environment evolving as a result of Internet technology is Interactive Software, as exemplified by Java and ActiveX. In an Interactive Software environment, a user accesses a server across a network. The server downloads an application (applet) onto the user's computer that is then executed. There have been various claims that when utilizing languages such as Java, it is impossible to

introduce a virus because of restrictions within the scripting language for file system access and process control. However, security risks using Java and ActiveX have been documented.

Therefore, there are several assumptions of trust that a user must make before employing this technology:

- The server can be trusted to download trustworthy applets.
- The applet will execute in a limited environment restricting disk reads and writes to functions that do not have security.
- The applet can be scanned to determine if it is safe.
- Scripts are interpreted, not precompiled.

FIREWALL POLICY

Firewalls are critical to the success of secured connections to external networks as well as the Internet. The main function of a firewall is to centralize access control. If outsiders or remote users can access the internal networks without going through the firewall, its effectiveness is diluted. For example, if a traveling manager has a modem connected to his office PC that he or she can dial into while traveling, and that PC is also on the protected internal network, an attacker who can dial into that PC has circumvented the controls imposed by the firewall. If a user has a dial-up Internet account with a commercial Internet Service Provider (ISP), and sometimes connects to the Internet from his office PC via modem, he is opening an unsecured connection to the Internet that circumvents the firewall.

Firewalls can also be used to secure segments of an organization's intranet, but this document will concentrate on the Internet aspects of firewall policy.

Firewalls provide several types of protection, to include:

- They can block unwanted traffic.
- They can direct incoming traffic to more trustworthy internal systems.
- They hide vulnerable systems, which can't easily be secured from the Internet.
- They can log traffic to and from the private network.
- They can hide information like system names, network topology, network device types, and internal user IDs from the Internet.
- They can provide more robust authentication than standard applications might be able to do.

Each of these functions is described in more detail in this section.

As with any safeguard, there are trade-offs between convenience and security. Transparency is the visibility of the firewall to both inside users and outsiders going

Espionage –
Firewalls

through a firewall. A firewall is transparent to users if they do not notice or stop at the firewall in order to access a network. Firewalls are typically configured to be transparent to internal network users (while going outside the firewall); on the other hand, firewalls are configured to be non-transparent for outside network coming through the firewall. This generally provides the highest level of security without placing an undue burden on internal users.

Firewall Authentication

Router-based firewalls don't provide user authentication. Host-based firewalls can provide various kinds of authentication. *Username/password authentication* is the least secure, because the information can be sniffed or shoulder-surfed. *One-time passwords* use software or hardware tokens and generate a new password for each session. This means that old passwords cannot be reused if they are sniffed or otherwise borrowed or stolen. Finally, *Digital Certificates* use a certificate generated using public key encryption.

Routing vs. Forwarding

A clearly defined policy should be written as to whether or not the firewall will act as a router or a forwarder of Internet packets. This is trivial in the case of a router that acts as a packet filtering gateway because the firewall (router in this case) has no option but to route packets. Applications gateway firewalls should generally not be configured to route any traffic between the external interface and the internal network interface, since this could bypass security controls. All external to internal connections should go through the application proxies.

Source routing

Source routing is a routing mechanism whereby the path to a target machine is determined by the source, rather than by intermediate routers. Source routing is mostly used for debugging network problems but could also be used to attack a host. If an attacker has knowledge of some trust relationship between your hosts, source routing can be used to make it appear that the malicious packets are coming from a trusted host. Because of this security threat, a packet filtering router can easily be configured to reject packets containing source route option.

IP spoofing

IP spoofing is when an attacker masquerades his machine as a host on the target's network (i.e., fooling a target machine that packets are coming from a trusted machine on the target's internal network). Policies regarding packet routing need to be clearly written so that they will be handled accordingly if there is a security problem. It is necessary that authentication based on source address be combined with other security schemes to protect against IP spoofing attacks.

Types of Firewalls

There are different implementations of firewalls, which can be arranged in different ways. These include packet filtering gateways, application gateways, and hybrid or complex gateways.

Packet filtering gateways

Packet filtering firewalls use routers with packet filtering rules to grant or deny access based on source address, destination address, and port. They offer minimum security but at a very low cost, and can be an appropriate choice for a low-risk environment. They are fast, flexible, and transparent. Filtering rules are not often easily maintained on a router, but there are tools available to simplify the tasks of creating and maintaining the rules.

Filtering gateways do have inherent risks, including:

- The source and destination addresses and ports contained in the IP packet header are the only information that is available to the router in making a decision whether or not to permit traffic access to an internal network.
- They don't protect against IP or DNS address spoofing.
- An attacker will have a direct access to any host on the internal network once access has been granted by the firewall.
- Strong user authentication isn't supported with packet filtering gateways.
- They provide little or no useful logging.

Application gateways

An application gateway uses server programs called proxies that run on the firewall. These proxies take external requests, examine them, and forward legitimate requests to the internal host that provides the appropriate service. Application gateways can support functions such as user authentication and logging.

Because an application gateway is considered the most secure type of firewall, this configuration provides a number of advantages to the medium-high risk site:

- The firewall can be configured as the only host address that is visible to the outside network, requiring all connections to and from the internal network to go through the firewall.
- The use of proxies for different services prevents direct access to services on the internal network, protecting the enterprise against insecure or misconfigured internal hosts.

- Strong user authentication can be enforced with application gateways.
- Proxies can provide detailed logging at the application level. Application level firewalls shall be configured such that outbound network traffic appears as if the traffic had originated from the firewall (i.e., only the firewall is visible to outside networks). In this manner, direct access to network services on the internal network is not allowed. All incoming requests for different network services such as Telnet, FTP, HTTP, RLOGIN, etc., regardless of which host on the internal network will be the final destination, must go through the appropriate proxy on the firewall.

Applications gateways require a proxy for each service, such as FTP, HTTP, etc., to be supported through the firewall. When a service is required that is not supported by a proxy, an organization has three choices:

1. Deny the service until the firewall vendor has developed a secure proxy. This is the preferred approach, as many newly introduced Internet services have unacceptable vulnerabilities.
2. Develop a custom proxy. This is a fairly difficult task and should be undertaken only by very sophisticated technical organizations.
3. Pass the service through the firewall. Using what are typically called "plugs," most application gateway firewalls allow services to be passed directly through the firewall with only a minimum of packet filtering. This can limit some of the vulnerability but can result in compromising the security of systems behind the firewall.

Hybrid or complex gateways

Hybrid gateways combine two or more of the above firewall types and implement them in series rather than in parallel. If they are connected in series, then the overall security is enhanced; on the other hand, if they are connected in parallel, then the network security perimeter will be only as secure as the least secure of all methods used. In medium- to high-risk environments, a hybrid gateway may be the ideal firewall implementation.

Suggested ratings are identified in Table 1 for various firewall types.

Firewall Architectures

Firewalls can be configured in a number of different architectures, providing various levels of security at different costs of installation and operation. Organizations should match their risk profile to the type of firewall architecture selected. The following describes typical firewall architectures and sample policy statements.

Multi-homed host

A multi-homed host is a host (a firewall in this case) that has more than one network interface, with each interface connected to logically and physically separate network segments. A dual-homed host (host with two interfaces) is the most common instance of a multihomed host.

A dual-homed firewall is a firewall with two network interface cards (NICs) with each interface connected to different networks. For instance, one network interface is typically connected to the external or untrusted network, while the other interface is connected to the internal or trusted network. In this configuration, a key security tenet is not to allow traffic coming in from the untrusted network to be directly routed to the trusted network, that is, the firewall must always act as an intermediary. Routing by the firewall shall be disabled for a dual-homed firewall so that IP packets from one network are not directly routed from one network to the other.

Screened host

A screened host firewall architecture uses a host (called a bastion host) to which all outside hosts connect, rather than allow direct connection to other, less secure internal hosts. To achieve this, a filtering router is configured so that all connections to the internal network from the outside network are directed toward the bastion host. If a packet filtering gateway is to be deployed, then a bastion host should be set up so that all connections from the outside network go through the bastion host to prevent direct Internet connection between the internal network and the outside world.

Screened subnet

The screened subnet architecture is essentially the same as the screened host architecture, but adds an extra stratum of

Espionage –
Firewalls

Table 1 Firewall security risk.

Firewall Architecture	High-Risk Environment (e.g., hospital)	Medium-Risk Environment (e.g., university)	Low-Risk Environment (e.g., florist shop)
Packet filtering	Unacceptable	Minimal security	Recommended
Application gateways	Effective option	Recommended	Acceptable
Hybrid gateways	Recommended	Effective option	Acceptable

security by creating a network at which the bastion host resides (often call perimeter network) which is separated from the internal network. A screened subnet is deployed by adding a perimeter network in order to separate the internal network from the external. This assures that if there is a successful attack on the bastion host, the attacker is restricted to the perimeter network by the screening router that is connected between the internal and perimeter network.

Intranet

Although firewalls are usually placed between a network and the outside untrusted network, in large companies or organizations, firewalls are often used to create different subnets of the network, often called an intranet. Intranet firewalls are intended to isolate a particular subnet from the overall corporate network. The reason for the isolation of a network segment might be that certain employees can access subnets guarded by these firewalls only on a need-to-know basis. An example could be a firewall for the payroll or accounting department of an organization.

The decision to use an intranet firewall is generally based on the need to make certain information available to some but not all internal users, or to provide a high degree of accountability for the access and use of confidential or sensitive information.

For any systems hosting internal critical applications, or providing access to sensitive or confidential information, internal firewalls or filtering routers should be used to provide strong access control and support for auditing and logging. These controls should be used to segment the internal network to support the access policies developed by the designated owners of information.

Firewall Administration

A firewall, like any other network device, has to be managed by someone. Security policy should state who is responsible for managing the firewall.

Two firewall administrators (one primary and one secondary) shall be designated by the Chief Information Security Officer (or other manager) and shall be responsible for the upkeep of the firewall. The primary administrator shall make changes to the firewall, and the secondary shall only do so in the absence of the former so that there is no simultaneous or contradictory access to the firewall. Each firewall administrator shall provide their home phone number, pager number, cellular phone number, and other numbers or codes in which they can be contacted when support is required.

Qualification of the firewall administrator

Two experienced people are generally recommended for the day-to-day administration of the firewall. In this manner availability of the firewall administrative function is largely ensured. It should be required that on-call information about each firewall administrator be written down so that one may be contacted in the event of a problem.

Security of a site is crucial to the day-to-day business activity of an organization. It is therefore required that the administrator of the firewall have a sound understanding of network concepts and implementation. For instance, since most firewalls are TCP/IP based, a thorough understanding of this protocol is compulsory. An individual that is assigned the task of firewall administration must have good hands-on experience with networking concepts, design, and implementation so that the firewall is configured correctly and administered properly. Firewall administrators should receive periodic training on the firewalls in use and in network security principles and practices.

Remote firewall administration

Firewalls are the first line of defense visible to an attacker. By design, firewalls are generally difficult to attack directly, causing attackers to often target the administrative accounts on a firewall. The username/password of administrative accounts must be strongly protected.

The most secure method of protecting against this form of attack is to have strong physical security around the firewall host and to only allow firewall administration from an attached terminal. However, operational concerns often dictate that some form of remote access for firewall administration be supported. In no case should remote access to the firewall be supported over untrusted networks without some form of strong authentication. In addition, to prevent eavesdropping, session encryption should be used for remote firewall connections.

User accounts

Firewalls should never be used as general purpose servers. The only user accounts on the firewall should be those of the firewall administrator and any backup administrators. In addition, only these administrators should have privileges for updating system executables or other system software. Only the firewall administrator and backup administrators will be given user accounts on the COMPANY firewall. Any modification of the firewall system software must be done by the firewall administrator or backup administrator and requires approval of the cognizant manager.

Firewall Backup. To support recovery after failure or natural disaster, a firewall, like any other network host, has to have some policy defining system backup. Data files as well as system configuration files need to be components of a backup and recovery plan in case of firewall failure.

The firewall (system software, configuration data, database files, etc.) must be backed up daily, weekly and monthly so that in case of system failure, data and configuration files can be recovered. Backup files should be stored securely on read-only media so that data in storage is not over-written inadvertently, and locked up so that the media is only accessible to the appropriate personnel.

Another backup alternative would be to have another firewall configured as one already deployed and kept safely in case there is a failure of the current one. This backup firewall would simply be turned on and used as the firewall while the previous one is undergoing a repair. At least one firewall should be configured and reserved (not-in-use) so that in case of a firewall failure, this backup firewall can be switched in to protect the network.

OTHER FIREWALL POLICY CONSIDERATIONS

Firewall technology has only been around for the last 5 years. In the past 2 years, however, firewall products have diversified considerably and now offer a variety of technical security controls that can be used in ever more complex network connections.

This section discusses some of the firewall policy considerations in the areas of network trust relationships, virtual private networks, DNS and mail resolution, system integrity, documentation, physical firewall security, firewall incident handling, service restoration, upgrades, and audit trail logging.

Network Trust Relationships

Business networks frequently require connections to other business networks. Such connections can occur over leased lines, proprietary Wide area networks, value added networks (VANs), or public networks such as the Internet. For instance, many local governments use leased lines or dedicated circuits to connect regional offices across the state. Many businesses use commercial VANs to connect business units across the country or the world.

The various network segments involved may be under control of different organizations and may operate under a variety of security policies. By their very nature, when networks are connected the security of the resulting overall network drops to the level of the weakest network. When decisions are made for connecting networks, trust relationships must be defined to avoid reducing the effective security of all networks involved.

Trusted networks are defined as networks that share the same security policy or implement security controls and procedures that provide an agreed upon set of common security services. Untrusted networks are those that do not implement such a common set of security controls, or where the level of security is unknown or unpredictable. The most secure policy is to only allow connection to trusted networks, as defined by an appropriate level of management. However, business needs may force

temporary connections with business partners or remote sites that involve the use of untrusted networks.

Virtual Private Networks (VPN)

Virtual private networks allow a trusted network to communicate with another trusted network over untrusted networks such as the Internet. Because some firewalls provide VPN capability, it is necessary to define policy for establishing VPNs. The following are recommended policy statements:

- Any connection between firewalls over public networks shall use encrypted virtual private networks to ensure the privacy and integrity of the data passing over the public network.
- All VPN connections must be approved and managed by the Network Services Manager.
- Appropriate means for distributing and maintaining encryption keys must be established prior to operational use of VPNs.

DNS and Mail Resolution

On the Internet, the Domain Name Service (DNS) provides the mapping and translation of domain names to IP addresses, such as "mapping server1. acme.com to 123.45.67.8". Some firewalls can be configured to run as a primary, secondary, or caching DNS server.

Deciding how to manage DNS services is generally not a security decision. Many organizations use a third party, such as an Internet Service Provider, to manage their DNS. In this case, the firewall can be used as a DNS caching server, improving performance but not requiring your organization to maintain its own DNS database.

If the organization decides to manage its own DNS database, the firewall can (but doesn't have to) act as the DNS server. If the firewall is to be configured as a DNS server (primary, secondary, or caching), it is necessary that other security precautions be in place. One advantage of implementing the firewall as a DNS server is that it can be configured to hide the internal host information of a site. In other words, with the firewall acting as a DNS server, internal hosts get an unrestricted view of both internal and external DNS data. External hosts, on the other hand, do not have access to information about internal host machines. To the outside world all connections to any host in the internal network will appear to have originated from the firewall. With the host information hidden from the outside, an attacker will not know the host names and addresses of internal hosts that offer service to the Internet. A security policy for DNS hiding might state: If the firewall is to run as a DNS server, then the firewall must be configured to hide information about the network so that internal host data is not advertised to the outside world.

Espionage –
Firewalls

System Integrity

To prevent unauthorized modifications of the firewall configuration, some form of integrity assurance process should be used. Typically, checksums, cyclic redundancy checks, or cryptographic hashes are made from the run-time image and saved on protected media. Each time the firewall configuration has been modified by an authorized individual (usually the firewall administrator), it is necessary that the system integrity online database be updated and saved onto a file system on the network or removable media. If the system integrity check shows that the firewall configuration files have been modified, it will be known that the system has been compromised.

The firewall's system integrity database shall be updated each time the firewall's configuration is modified. System integrity files must be stored on read only media or off-line storage. System integrity shall be checked on a regular basis on the firewall in order for the administrator to generate a listing of all files that may have been modified, replaced, or deleted.

Documentation

It is important that the operational procedures for a firewall and its configurable parameters be well documented, updated, and kept in a safe and secure place. This assures that if a firewall administrator resigns or is otherwise unavailable, an experienced individual can read the documentation and rapidly pick up the administration of the firewall. In the event of a break-in such documentation also supports trying to recreate the events that caused the security incident.

Physical Firewall Security

Physical access to the firewall must be tightly controlled to preclude any authorized changes to the firewall configuration or operational status, and to eliminate any potential for monitoring firewall activity. In addition, precautions should be taken to assure that proper environment alarms and backup systems are available to assure the firewall remains online.

The firewall should be located in a controlled environment, with access limited to the Network Services Manager, the firewall administrator, and the backup firewall administrator. The room in which the firewall is to be physically located must be equipped with heat, air-conditioner, and smoke alarms to assure the proper working order of the room. The placement and recharge status of the fire extinguishers shall be checked on a regular basis. If uninterruptible power service is available to any Internet-connected systems, such service should be provided to the firewall as well.

Firewall Incident Handling

Incident reporting is the process whereby certain anomalies are reported or logged on the firewall. A policy is required to determine what type of report to log and what to do with the generated log report. This should be consistent with Incident Handling policies detailed previously. The following policies are appropriate to all risk environments:

- The firewall shall be configured to log all reports on daily, weekly, and monthly bases so that the network activity can be analyzed when needed.
- Firewall logs should be examined on a weekly basis to determine if attacks have been detected.
- The firewall administrator shall be notified at anytime of any security alarm by e-mail, pager, or other means so that he may immediately respond to such alarm.
- The firewall shall reject any kind of probing or scanning tool that is directed to it so that information being protected is not leaked out by the firewall. In a similar fashion, the firewall shall block all software types that are known to present security threats to a network (such as ActiveX and Java) to better tighten the security of the network.

Restoration of Services

Once an incident has been detected, the firewall may need to be brought down and reconfigured. If it is necessary to bring down the firewall, Internet service should be disabled or a secondary firewall should be made operational. Internal systems should not be connected to the Internet without a firewall. After being reconfigured, the firewall must be brought back into an operational and reliable state. Policies for restoring the firewall to a working state when a break-in occurs are needed.

In case of a firewall break-in, the firewall administrator(s) are responsible for reconfiguring the firewall to address any vulnerabilities that were exploited. The firewall shall be restored to the state it was before the break-in so that the network is not left wide open. While the restoration is going on, the backup firewall shall be deployed.

Upgrading the Firewall

It is often necessary that the firewall software and hardware components be upgraded with the necessary modules to assure optimal firewall performance. The firewall administrator should be aware of any hardware and software bugs, as well as firewall software upgrades that may be issued by the vendor. If an upgrade of any sort is necessary, certain precautions must be taken to continue to maintain a high level of operational security. Sample policies that should be written for upgrades may include the following:

- To optimize the performance of the firewall, all vendor recommendations for processor and memory capacities shall be followed.
- The firewall administrator must evaluate each new release of the firewall software to determine if an upgrade is required. All security patches recommended by the firewall vendor should be implemented in a timely manner.
- Hardware and software components shall be obtained from a list of vendor-recommended sources. Any firewall specific upgrades shall be obtained from the vendor. NFS shall not be used as a means of obtaining software components. The use of virus checked CD-ROM or FTP to a vendor's site is an appropriate method.
- The firewall administrator(s) shall monitor the vendor's firewall mailing list or maintain some other form of contact with the vendor to be aware of all required upgrades. Before an upgrade of any of the firewall components, the firewall administrator must verify with the vendor that an upgrade is required. After any upgrade the firewall shall be tested to verify proper operation prior to going operational.

Given the rapid introduction of new technologies and the tendency for organizations to continually introduce new services, firewall security policies should be reviewed on a regular basis. As network requirements change, so should security policy.

Logs and Audit Trails (Audit/Event Reporting and Summaries)

Most firewalls provide a wide range of capabilities for logging traffic and network events. Some security-relevant events that should be recorded on the firewall's audit trail logs are: hardware and disk media errors, login/logout activity, connect time, use of system administrator privileges, inbound and outbound e-mail traffic, TCP network connect attempts, inbound and outbound proxy traffic type.

SUMMARY

Connections to external networks and to the Internet are rapidly becoming commonplace in today's business community. These connections must be effectively secured to protect internal trusted networks from misuse and attack. The security policies outlined above should provide an effective guideline for implementing the appropriate level of controls to protect internal networks from outside attack.

Extranet Access Control

Christopher King, CISSP
Security Consultant, Greenwich Technology Partners, Chelmsford, Massachusetts, U.S.A.

Abstract

Many businesses are discovering the value of networked applications with business partners and customers. Extranets allow trading partners to exchange information electronically by extending their intranets. The security architecture necessary to allow this type of communication must provide adequate protection of corporate data and the proper separation of data among users (e.g., confidential partner information). The information security technologies must minimize the risk to the intranet while keeping the extranet configuration flexible. Corporations are acting as service providers, providing a common network and resources to be shared among the user base. The Web server is evolving into a universal conduit to corporate resources. Without adequate security controls, extranet security will become unmanageable.

INTRODUCTION

Most extranets are used for business-to-business (B2B) and electronic commerce applications between trading partners and external customers. Historically, these applications used value-added networks (VAN) with electronic data exchange (EDI) transactions. The VANs provided a private point-to-point connection between the enterprises, and EDI's security was inherent in the format of the data and the manual process after transmission. VANs, by design, were outsourced to VAN providers (e.g., Sterling, IBM, GEIS, and Harbinger). With the advent of virtual private network (VPN) technology, providing a private channel over a public network (i.e., the Internet), VAN-based EDI growth is currently at a standstill. A new data interchange format based on Extensible Markup Language (XML) is rivaling EDI for Internet-enabled applications.

Companies can use an extranet to:

- Supplement and possibly replace existing VANs using EDI
- Project management and control for companies that are part of a common work project
- Provide a value-added service to their customers that are difficult to replace
- Share product catalogs exclusively with wholesalers or those "in the trade"
- Collaborate with other companies on joint development efforts

There are two distinct types of extranets: a one-to-many and a many-to-many. A one-to-many is more common, linking many companies to a single resource (e.g., home banking). A many-to-many extranet is viewed as the intersection of a number of different company intranets (e.g., the Automotive Network Exchange). Extranets are soaring because they facilitate a seamless flow of information and commerce among employees, suppliers, and customers and because they sharply reduce communication costs. Extranet connectivity can be used for short- and long-term business relationships. This entry concentrates on the access control mechanism and the administration aspects of extending one's intranet. The access control enforcement mechanisms generally fall into the following categories: **network**—VPN, firewall, intrusion detection; **authentication**—certificate, token, password; **platform**—intrusion detection, compliance management, Web-to-Web server, Web agent, monitoring, and auditing.

For an extranet to be successful it must be contained within a secure environment and add value to the existing line of business. Organizations that are currently implementing intranets should consider a security infrastructure that allows them to securely extend the intranet to form an extranet. This will allow them to leverage information sharing between trading partners.

WHO IS ON THE WIRE?

Intranet, extranet, and the Internet are all networks of networks. The major difference between the three classes of networks is the aspect of network traffic control (i.e., who are the participants in the network). Intranets are owned by individual organizations (i.e., intra-enterprise systems). Some organizations operate their own network, and some outsource that function to network operations groups (e.g., EDS, AT&T Data Solutions, etc.). A key characteristic of intranet implementation is that protected applications are not visible to the Internet at large. Intranet access control relies heavily on the physical access point to the corporate LAN. Once physical access is gained into a corporate site, application access controls are the only constraint on access

Encyclopedia of Information Assurance DOI: 10.1081/E-EIA-120046366
Copyright © 2011 by Taylor & Francis. All rights reserved.

Espionage – Firewalls

to corporate resources. Secure intranets are separated from the Internet by means of a firewall system. Inbound Internet traffic is NOT allowed into the corporate security perimeter except for e-mail. Outbound network traffic destined to the Internet from the intranet is not usually filtered. Some corporations constrain outbound traffic to allow only Web-based protocols (e.g., HTTP, FTP, and IIOP).

The rise in remote access usage is making the reliance on physical proximity to the corporate LAN a moot point. With a growing number of access points in today's corporate intranets, network and application security has to become more stringent to provide adequate protection for corporate resources. The lines between the intranet and other classes of networks are becoming blurred.

A one-to-many (e.g., provider-centric) extranet is a *secure* extension of an enterprise intranet. A many-to-many (e.g., user-centric) extranet is a secure extension of two or more enterprise intranets. This secure extension allows well-defined interactions between the participating organizations. This private network uses the Internet protocols and possibly the public network as a transport mechanism. "Private" means that this network is not publicly accessible. Only the extranet providers' suppliers, vendors, partners, and customers are allowed onto this network. Once access is gained to the network, fine-grained application and platform controls must exist (i.e., a combination of network and application security must be in place) to further restrict access to data and resources. The technology for building an extranet is essentially the same as that for intranets (e.g., Web-based). This does not mean that access to extranet resources will allow an extranet user to communicate with the provider's intranet directly. There must be a secure partition between the extranet and the provider's intranet. Extranet security must be tight so corporations can develop stronger business relationships and forge closer ties with individuals who need differing levels of access to information or resources on their network. The challenge is to develop a proper security architecture that allows semi-trusted users to *share* a network with other individual organizations. These organizations could be competitors, so access control is of the utmost importance.

Internet applications that employ application-level security do not constitute an extranet. There must be a *clear separation* between the extranet resources (e.g., database, application logic or platforms) and the Internet and intranet. An extranet requires a higher level of security and privacy than traditional intranets. Most corporations have strong perimeter security and lenient security controls once inside the intranet (i.e., hard and crunchy outside and soft and chewy middle). The extranet also has to be designed with industry-standard development techniques (e.g., IP, SQL, LDAP, S/MIME, RADIUS, and especially Web).

The Internet is a global network of networks providing ubiquitous access to an increasing user base. Enterprises use the Internet and its technologies to save money and to generate revenue. The Internet technology (e.g., Web) has influenced the other classes of networks. Web development tools are plentiful and come at a relatively low cost with a short development cycle. The problems with the current state of the Internet are security and reliability. Enterprises should not rely too heavily on the Internet for time-sensitive or critical applications.

Some of the differences between an intranet and the Internet are the quality of service (QoS) or lack of service level agreements (SLAs) which describe availability, bandwidth, latency, and response time. Most Internet service providers (ISPs) and networking device vendors are developing an Internet level of service capability. This will allow for classes of services with a price differential (see Table 1).

EXTRANET SECURITY POLICY

The goal of an extranet security policy is to act as the foundation upon which all information-security related activities are based. In order for this security policy to be effective, it must receive approval and support from all the extranet participants (i.e., senior management). The security policy must keep up with the technological pace of the information systems technology. In other words, as access to corporate resources changes with the technology, the security must be updated. The security policy must balance the organization's operational requirements with the state-of-the-art in security solutions. Because both of these are under constant change, the policy must stay current. Some of the high-level statements in an extranet policy follow.

The extranet security architecture supports the following statements:

- The extranet must be securely partitioned from the corporate intranet.
- Secure network connectivity must be provided using a dedicated line or using a VPN.
- Extranet users must be uniquely identified using adequate authentication techniques.
- Authorization must adhere to the least-privilege principle.
- Extranet managers will receive monthly access reports to verify the proper use of the network.
- The extranet must NOT provide a routable path to the participant networks (i.e., the extranet provider's network should not allow packets to flow between partner networks).
- A real-time monitoring, auditing, and alerting facility must be employed to detect fraud and abuse.

Before the extranet can be connected to the outside world, the extranet provider must understand its network and the application vulnerabilities of extranet users and internal intranet users. This usually involves a detailed risk assessment by a certified third party. It also includes a formal review of the baseline security policy and security

Table 1 Security enforcement categories for each network classification.

Enforcement	Intranet	Extranet	Internet
Security policy enforcement	The enterprisewide security policy is enforced by the intranet security architecture.	The majority is provided by the network facilitator and agreed upon by the extranet user base.	The Internet is under no auspices for security policy enforcement.
Physical/ platform access enforcement	Highly controlled—only data center personnel have physical access to application server and network equipment.	Highly controlled—only the enterprise hosting the data center personnel has physical access to application server and network equipment. If a business partner owns a piece of equipment, it is shared between both organizations.	No physical access is provided to external users.
Network access enforcement	Private—only corporate personnel have access to this network via WAN and remote access methods. All network protocols are allowed.	Semi-private—only extranet users (e.g., business partners) have access to this network. Network protocols must be filtered to protect the intranet.	Public—all external users have ubiquitous access to an organization's public information. No network protocols other than e-mail and Web are allowed.
Application access enforcement	Semi-private—application provides some level of access control. In most cases it is a very lax security environment.	Private—users must be authenticated and authorized to perform operations depending on their rights (i.e., least privilege).	None—Web-based applications are used to disseminate static information. There are some instances of protected access pages using basic authentication.
Quality-of-service guarantee	High—with the proper networking equipment (e.g., smart switches and advanced routing protocols).	Depends on the extranet provider network and participating client network provider.	None—SLA between ISPs does not exist, yet. It is in the works.

architecture that it meets. The assessments should be periodic, exhaustive, and include all of the member organizations of the extranet.

Secure extranet applications provide a well-defined set of data and resources to a well-defined set of authenticated individuals. To properly design authorization into an application, some basic security concepts must be employed, such as separation of duties, least privilege, and individual accountability. Separation of duties is the practice of dividing the steps in a critical function [e.g., direct database management system (DBMS) access, Java applet updates] among different individuals. The least-privilege principle is the practice of restricting a user's access (DMBS updates or remote administration), or type of access (read, write, execute, delete) to the minimum necessary to perform the job. Individual accountability consists of holding someone responsible for his actions. Accountability is normally accomplished by identifying and authenticating users of the system and subsequently tracing actions on the system to the user who initiated them.

NETWORK PARTITIONING

To enforce the proper separation of networks, a commercial suite of network access control devices must be used. Separating the networks from each other offers one level of security necessary for a secure extranet solution. The proper network topology must exist to further protect the

networks. A combination of firewalls and real-time intrusion detection configured to be as stringent as possible should adequately control network traffic flow. Fig. 1 depicts such a topology.

Each network is protected using a commercial firewall product (e.g., Checkpoint Firewall-1, Cisco PIX). There is no direct connection from the Internet to the intranet. The firewall closest to the Internet (FWA) only allows encrypted traffic into the VPN gateway. Most commercial

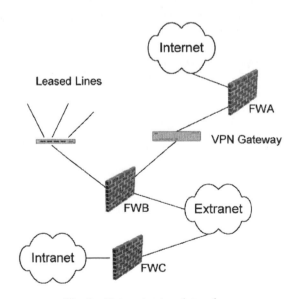

Fig. 1 Extranet network topology.

Espionage – Firewalls

Espionage –
Firewalls

firewalls have been around since 1994; VPN devices started appearing in early 1998. Because VPN devices are latecomers to the Internet, it is better to protect them with a firewall than to leave them unprotected from current and future Internet threats. Because the data is decrypted after the VPN gateway, it should be filtered before entering the extranet (FWB). The provider's intranet is protected from any extranet threats using an additional firewall (FWC).

Extranet users gain access to the extranet by traditional means (e.g., leased lines) or by using VPNs. In a one-to-many extranet, clients must not be able to communicate directly with each other via the extranet. The network routing rules must enforce a non-loopback policy (i.e., a network route between two clients).

EXTRANET AUTHENTICATION

User accountability is the ability to bind critical data functions to a single user. It holds users responsible for their actions. The extranet security architecture must enforce user accountability. At the network level, user accountability is impossible because of proxy servers, application gateway firewalls, and address translation. All the users from an organization will have the same IP address. Authentication must be performed at the application layer.

Extranet authentication is not a trivial task due to its political nature, not due to its technology. Most users already have too many passwords to remember to access their own system. Because user administration is typically distributed to the partnering organization, once users have authenticated themselves to their own organization, they should not have to authenticate themselves again to the extranet. The extranet application should leverage the authentication information and status from the user's originating organization using a proxy authentication mechanism. This allows users to gain access to the extranet resources once they have authenticated themselves to their local domain.

Device authentication includes VPN gateways and public key infrastructure (PKI)-aware servers (e.g., Web

and directory servers using Secure Socket Layer, SSL). VPN gateways optionally can use a shared secret instead of certificates, but this technique is unmanageable if the device count is too high.

Specific examples of proxy authentication techniques are NT domain authentication, cross certification with digital certificates, RADIUS, and a shared directory server.

EXTRANET AUTHORIZATION

Once network access is granted, it is up to the application (most likely Web-based with a database back end) to provide further authentication and authorization. Most Web server access control is provided using basic authentication. The user's rights (i.e., Web files and directories they have access to) and authentication information combined is called a user's profile. This information is stored and enforced locally on the Web server. Local Web access controls are not a scalable solution, if the user base is large, then this type of solution is unmanageable. Access to Web files and directories is sufficient for static content security. New Web development tools ease the access into database, mainframe, and BackOffice systems. Web applications are starting to look more and more like traditional client/server applications of a few years ago. The Web server is becoming a universal conduit to corporate resources.

There are many access control enforcement points between the Web server and the data being accessed, such as the browser, the firewall, the application server, or the DBMS.

Fig. 2 depicts how third-party Web access control (WAC) products such as Encommerce getAccess, Netegrity Siteminder, and Axent Webdefender provide Web login, authentication, authorization, personal navigation, and automated administration. Due to the Web's stateless nature, cookies are used to keep state between the browsers and the server. To prevent modification of the cookie by the end user, it is encrypted. The Web server must be modified to include a Web agent. The Web agent uses the Web server API (e.g., NSAPI for Netscape Enterprise Server and ISAPI for Microsoft's Internet Information

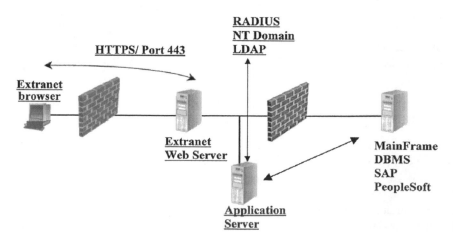

Fig. 2 Web access control architecture.

Server). Access control information is controlled from a single point. Once a change is made in the security rulebase, it is replicated to all of the protected Web servers.

EXTRANET ADMINISTRATION

Extranet system administration is performed by the organization providing the service. However, user administration remains a touchy subject. The user administration of the extranet is dictated by the relationships between the participating organizations. Extranet managers are the points-of-contact at each organization and are legally responsible for their users. For example, is user authentication centrally administered by the extranet provider, or is it distributed among the participants, leveraging it off their existing authentication database? It would be difficult to manage 1000 business partners with 1000 users each.

Corporate users are already inundated with username/password pairs. If extranet access were provided over the corporate network, another authentication scheme would only complicate the issue. Several questions that need to be addressed come to mind: 1) How can we integrate with an external business partner's security infrastructures? 2) How do we leverage the participants' existing security infrastructure?

Authentication is only a piece of the pie; what about authorization? Do we provide authorization at the user level, or use the concept of roles, grouping users into functions, for example, business managers, accountants, user administrators, clerks, etc.?

The way users get access to sensitive resources (i.e., items you wish to protect) is by a role-resource and user-role relationship. The extranet authorization model consists of the totality of all the user-role and role-resource relationships. This information is usually stored within a relational DBMS or a directory server. The extranet's system administrator, with input from the resource owners, is responsible for creating and maintaining this model.

The principle of least privilege will be used when an administrator assigns users to the system. Least privilege requires that an administrator grant only the most restrictive set of privileges necessary to perform authorized tasks. In other words, users will access their necessary resources to perform their job function with a minimum amount of system privileges.

EXTRANET CONNECTION AGREEMENTS

Allowing access to private data from external business partners could pose some liability issues. One of the major problems is that the legal systems lag significantly behind the advances in technology. From an insurance coverage standpoint, the problem that underwriters have is the inability to calculate the security exposure for a given

information system. The best defense is a proper security architecture derived from a detailed security policy. This solves the enterprise security problem, but in most cases the corporate security policy cannot be extended outside the enterprise. A separate extranet data connection agreement must be developed and adhered to by all participants. This agreement would specify the basic terms and conditions for doing business together in a secure fashion.

The following lists some considerations for data connection agreements:

- A description of the applications and information that will be accessible by the external partner
- A point of contact(s) for each participating organization, to be contacted in the event of a security incident
- The legal document (e.g., non-disclosure, and security procedures) signed by partners and the external customer's authorized representative
- The term or length (days), and start and end dates, of the service
- A protection of information statement that details the safeguard requirements (e.g., copying, transmitting to third parties, precautions, destruction) of the data transmitted
- The sharing of responsibilities by both parties; this includes the necessary access for a physical security audit and a logical security audit (e.g., network penetration tools) at each facility
- An indemnification statement that each party agrees to compensate the other party for any loss or damages incurred as a result of unauthorized access to the data facilities and misuse of information
- A termination statement that is executed if either party fails to adhere to the data connection agreement provisions
- Security awareness training for users at external or partner sites

EXTRANET MONITORING

Extranet monitoring is important for security and business reasons. Frequent analysis of audit data is useful in case questions arise about improper systems access and to generate marketing report data (i.e., how many times were my resources accessed and by whom).

Security monitoring usually occurs wherever access control decisions are being made, for example, the firewall, authentication server, and the application itself. The problem with monitoring is that there is no real-time analysis of the data, just log entries in some file or database. Data reduction from raw data logs is not a trivial task. No standards exist for data storage or formats, and users must compile diverse logs of information and produce their own reports from the application, firewall, or network operating system. The audit trail entries must contain a specific user

ID, timestamp, function, and requested data. Using a scripting language such as PERL, a security manager will have to write a set of scripts to generate reports of log-in times, data accessed, and services used. In more security-intensive applications, the enterprise should install some real-time analysis tools (e.g., Internet Security Systems' RealSecure or Cisco's Net Ranger) to generate additional data and monitor for anomalous behavior.

EXTRANET SECURITY INFRASTRUCTURE

The extranet security infrastructure consists of all the supporting security services that are required to field a security architecture. Such an architecture would include a directory server, a certificate server, an authentication server, and Web security servers. These require firewall server management, the issuance and use of digital certificates or similar means of user authentication, encryption of messages; and the use of virtual private networks (VPNs) that tunnel through the public network.

VPN TECHNOLOGY

Virtual private network technology allows external partners to securely participate in the extranet using public networks as a transport (i.e., Internet). VPNs rely on tunneling and encapsulation techniques, which allow the Internet Protocol (IP) to carry a wide range of popular non-IP traffic (e.g., IPX, NetBEUI). VPN technology provides encryption and authentication features within an ancillary network device to firewalls and routers called a VPN gateway. Performance enhancements in the Internet backbone and access equipment now provide the throughput needed to compete with private networks. All of these enabling technologies are based on standards that yield end-to-end interoperability. Finally, preparing Points of Presence (POPs) for VPNs is relatively simple and inexpensive. Low costs with high margin VPNs are good business.

Because VPN technology uses encryption as the basis for its security, interoperability among vendors is a major issue. The Internet Engineering Task Force (IETF) IP Security (IPSec) specification was chosen to alleviate this problem. The IETF developed IPSec as a security protocol for the next generation IPv6. IPSec is an optional extension for the implementation of the current version, IPv4. IPv4 is widespread on the Internet and in corporate networks, but its design does not include any security provisions. IPSec provides confidentiality and integrity to information transferred over IP networks through network layer encryption and authentication. IPSec protects networks from IP network attacks, including denial of service, man-in-the-middle, and spoofing. Refer to Requests for Comment (RFC) 2401 through 2412 for full details.

Before VPN devices can communicate, they must negotiate a mutually agreeable way of securing their data. As part of this negotiation, each node has to verify that the other node is actually the node it claims to be. VPN authentication schemes use digital certificate or a shared secret between communicating devices. A shared secret is a password agreed upon by the two device administrators in advance. When the administrators try to communicate, each must supply the agreed-upon password. Authentication based on certificates is more secure than password-based authentication because of distribution and formation. Passwords have to be difficult to guess and shared in a secure fashion. Because certificates are based on public key technology, they are immune to this problem.

With all of this said, using VPNs has the following drawbacks:

Drawback	Description
Not fault tolerant	VPN devices are not fault tolerant. The IPSec protocol does not currently support failover. This should be addressed and implemented before the end of 2000.
Performance	There are many implementation choices for VPNs (e.g., software, black box, and outboard cryptographic processors). Software solutions tend to be used for clients. Because VPN gateways are aggregating many simultaneous connections, a software-only gateway cannot keep up. Outboard cryptographic processors are used to assist in the intense cryptographic function by host-based devices (e.g., PCI slot). None of these solutions can compete with a dedicated hardware device (e.g., black box).
Reliable transport	The Internet service providers are not yet capable of providing adequate, peak or scalable bandwidth at a reasonable cost. Cisco and some of the large ISP are testing a technology called MultiProtocol Label Switching (MPLS). MPLS allows the ISPs to offer different levels of service to their customer base.
Network placement	Most enterprises manage their own or outsource control over their Internet firewall. Where should the VPN gateway be placed? In front of, behind, parallel with, or on the firewall? These are questions with many trade-offs.
Addressing	Networks are not generally additive. Special care has to be taken in terms of addressing before joining two or more disparate networks. If two or more of the networks are using private address space (e.g., 10.x.x.x) with any overlap, routing can be tricky.
Key management (PKI)	VPN formation requires cryptographic information. Shared secrets between points are not scalable. The only solution is certificates. The problem that exists is that this technology is about six to nine months behind the VPN technology, which was finalized in November 1998.
Interoperability	IPSec compliance is a term that is overused by VPN vendors. The only real compliance is an interoperability report among heterogeneous vendors. As of this writing there are only six vendors who can fully interoperate.

Espionage – Firewalls

RESIDUAL RISKS/LIABILITY

There is no such thing as complete security. There is an associated cost with providing an adequate level of security; the adequacy is measured against the best business practices in the industry. The addition of more security safeguards comes at a high cost and only offers a minor increase in the overall security level. Extranet security has the additional burden of providing even more security and privacy from participants who are competitors. Unauthorized access to repositories of information and applications could, in the wrong hands, prove detrimental to their participants. The resolution is to manage the risk and to weigh the benefits against the resultant risk. As a supplement to all of the security mechanisms, a lawyer should be involved in the extranet data agreement. The lawyer can draw up necessary warnings to deter casual intruders as well as agreements to protect your company in the event of misuse of the data. An alternative might be to outsource the extranet to a service provider.

EXTRANET OUTSOURCING

Many ISPs and telcos are offering extranet services that provide a managed network with controlled access. Extranet service providers have a strong technical knowledge of networking and security. They also have invested in the infrastructure required to manage an extranet, for example, a PKI with an X.500 directory service. Another advantage is that the service provider can offer better network reliability and bandwidth (e.g., service level agreements). If all the extranet participants utilize this existing service provider, an SLA can be negotiated. See Fig. 3 for an example architecture of an outsourced extranet.

AUTOMOTIVE NETWORK EXCHANGE

The Automotive Network eXchange (ANX) is a many-to-many extranet between Chrysler Corp., General Motors Corp., and Ford Motor Company and their suppliers. This extranet utilizes VPN technology. ANX will be used to electronically route product shipment schedules, order information, engineering and drawing files for product designs, purchase orders, and other financial information. ANX replaces 50 to 100 direct-dial connections to the automakers, reducing telecommunication costs up to 70%, but the real payoffs are in the speed and ease of communications between suppliers and manufacturers. The real benefit is monetary savings estimated in the billions from the traditional supply-chain costs and the speed of new automotive designs to less than a 3 year design cycle. The improved exchange of information should result in new business practices between vendors and manufacturers.

SUMMARY

Extranets have indeed arrived and may well mean changes to how business relationships are viewed. The key to maximizing participation is to make the extranet as accessible to as many partners as possible, regardless of their technical adeptness. The more participants there are, the greater the rates of return from the system. Major enterprise resource planning (ERP) systems (e.g., Baan and SAP) are providing hooks to allow external business partners to connect with automated back-office systems.

The network boundaries (extra, intra, and Inter) continue to erode so one will have to depend on application layer security. The problem is providing a common, or standard, protection scheme for applications. This is another emerging field of security, probably with a two- or more-year development and integration cycle.

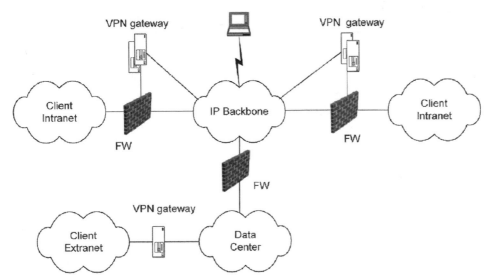

Fig. 3 Outsourced extranet architecture.

The desire to provide an enhanced layer of security, reliability, and quality of service on top of the Internet will be the primary driver of VPNs as a subset of electronic commerce extranet deployment. These features are not offered by most ISPs. Next-generation Internet and Internet2 research and development projects are testing very high-speed (gigabit) networks. Large telephone companies are laying the foundation for the networks into which the Internet may eventually evolve, as well as the support equipment (routers, switches, hubs, and network interface cards) needed to drive networks at such high speeds. Network security and virtual private network technologies will be improved, which will facilitate future extranets.

Espionage –
Firewalls

Fax Machines

Ben Rothke, CISSP, QSA
International Network Services (INS), New York, New York, U.S.A.

Abstract

Most companies do not lack for information security products. Their data centers are likely full of firewalls, virtual private networks, security appliances, and much more. Yet there is a device, hundreds of them perhaps, in many organizations, that lacks any sort of security. This is the lowly fax machine.

The fax machine poses serious potential security issues and risks to every company that uses it. The good news is that most of these risks can easily be mitigated. The issue is that most companies are oblivious to these threats and do not take the appropriate countermeasures.

GROUP 3 FAX PROTOCOLS

An introduction to basic fax operations is in order. The reason faxing is so seamless is that all modern fax machines operate using the same protocol, namely the Group 3 Facsimile Protocol (G3). The G3 was first published in 1980 by the ITU (International Telecommunications Union: http://www.itu.int).

The G3 standard for facsimile communications over analog telephone lines was originally approved by the Consultative Committee for International Telegraphy and Telephony (CCITT) in its T.4 and T.30 recommendations in 1980. This standard is supported by nearly every fax machine in use today and continues to be updated.

G3 is specified in two standards:

- T.4—image-transfer protocol
- T.30—session-management procedures that support the establishment of a fax transmission

T.30 allows the two endpoints to agree on such things as transmission speed and page size. Because G3 is specified for switched analog networks, and it is an all-digital procedure, it must use modems or a fax relay. They are also specified in ITU standards:

- V.21 (300 bps) for the T.30 procedures and for image transfer
- V.27 ter (2400/4800 bps)
- V.29 (7.2 k, 9.6 k)
- V.17 (7.2 k, 9.6 k, 12 k, 14.4 k)
- Real-time Internet Protocol fax transport is specified in T.38 and replaces modems

There is a G4 standard, but this is for digital telephone networks and was approved in 1984 and updated in 1988.

This standard has found greater acceptance in Europe and Japan than in the United States and is predominately used for fixed point-to-point high-volume communications.

The T.30 specification divides a call into five phases:

- Phase A—call setup
- Phase B—premessage procedures
- Phase C—image transfer
- Phase D—postmessage procedures including multipage and end of procedure signals
- Phase E—call release

These five phases are detailed in the following Fig. 1:[1]

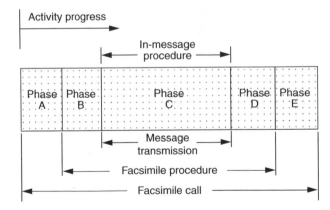

Fig. 1 Five phases of a fax transmission.
Source: From http://www.commetrex.com/whitepapers/FaxTech. html.[1]

SECURE FAXING

One of the important works on fax security was *Guidelines on Facsimile Transmission Security,* issued by the

Encyclopedia of Information Assurance DOI: 10.1081/E-EIA-120046283
Copyright © 2011 by Taylor & Francis. All rights reserved.

Information and Privacy Commissioner of Ontario, Canada, back in 1989. This document was one of the first to bring to light the need to deal with fax security. The document was updated in 2003,[2] and it sets out guidelines for government organizations to consider when developing systems and procedures to maintain the confidentiality and integrity of information transmitted by fax. Although the entry was written for government organizations, most of the issues and guidelines are relevant for non-government organizations also.

According to Ontario, Canada-based Natural Data, Inc., there are over 100 million fax machines in use worldwide today. Almost all of these fax machines are unable to connect to the Internet and as a result can send and receive faxes using only the unsecured public fax line services.

FAX ADVANTAGES AND SECURITY ISSUES

The fax machine, like all technologies, has security risks. The most notable fax issues are that the faxed document will sometimes not reach its intended destination. This is due to both human error (wrong number dialed) and technical issues (poor communication lines, incompatible equipment, and more).

Although there are fax security issues, one of the main benefits of a fax is that unlike an e-mail attachment, a fax document is an image file and, therefore, is inherently not an editable file. That means that no one can alter the original itself to embed another program within it, meaning a fax can never cause a computer virus or worm to invade one's network.

SECURE FAX DESIGNATION

It is important to note that in a perfect world, every fax machine will be deployed with the highest levels of security. In the real world, such an approach is not practical.

Creating a Secure Fax Infrastructure

Computer security is simply attention to detail and good design, and effective information security is built on risk management, good business practices, and project management. Creating a secure fax infrastructure is no different.

The initial step in this infrastructure is to establish policies around the use of fax machines. See Table 1 for some useful tips. The ultimate level of fax security is built on this foundation of effective policies and procedures that govern their use. At the end of this entry is a set of core policies around fax security that can be used.

Although the basic use of a fax machine is often intuitive, the secure use of a fax machine is often not so intuitive. By creating a set of standard operating procedures (SOPs) around the use of secure faxes, you can mitigate most of the threats involved.

Some of the basic procedures around fax security include ensuring that the number of pages received for the fax is the same as that being sent, reassembling the received document, distributing it appropriately, confirming receipt, and more.

Cover Sheets

As part of the SOPs, all faxes sent should have a standardized cover sheet containing the name, title, and company name of both the sender and the recipient and the total number of pages faxed.

Some organizations request that the recipient confirm successful receipt of the fax, but such a request should be used with caution, as such a request can be onerous to the receiving party.

Many companies include disclaimers on their fax cover sheets stating that the information in the fax is confidential and that the information should not be distributed, copied, or disclosed to any unauthorized persons without prior approval of the sender.

Receiving Misdirected Faxes

Just as your users will eventually and invariably send a fax to the wrong number, you will also invariably be on the receiving end of an errant fax. Your SOPs should deal with such scenarios and detail to employees what they should do when an errant fax is received.

The first thing to do is to notify the sender that a fax was received in error. It is assumed that the sender followed guidelines and used a cover sheet.

Your users should be instructed that incorrectly sent faxes should never be forwarded to the recipient. They should either be returned to the sender or shredded.

Number Confirmation

Many organizations have master lists of fax numbers. The challenge with such master lists is that fax numbers are often changed. If such lists are used, they should be audited regularly to ensure that the numbers are indeed current and accurate.

Secure Fax Locations

A key point to realize about security is that nearly every operating system, from UNIX to Linux, NetWare, Windows, and more, places the foundation of its security architecture at the physical server level. Unfortunately, physical security is often an afterthought when deciding where to place a fax machine. Such consequences can leave fax machines open to a security breach.

To create a secure fax infrastructure, fax machines must be isolated in a secure area. This area must be restricted to only authorized employees. These secure fax machines should be placed in locations that are not accessible to the general populace. Given that faxes can come in at any

Table 1 Fax machine use policies.

Title	Policy	Commentary
Machine repair staff confidentiality agreements	Prior to beginning their work, all external office equipment repair staff must have signed a Company X confidentiality agreement.	This policy prevents industrial or military espionage. Recent models of ordinary office equipment such as copiers and fax machines now have up to 5 MB of recent information stored in them. If repairpersons were to swap the chip that contains this information, they could walk away with significant intellectual property without detection. If there is a paper jam, some sensitive information may have been printed on that paper but it may not have been removed from the machine.

The policy is written with a broad scope, and general-purpose computers, including handhelds, would be included within its purview. Some organizations refer to confidentiality agreements as non-disclosure agreements. |
| Maintaining classification labels | Workers in possession of any information containing a Company X data classification sensitivity label must maintain, propagate, and if need be, reestablish this same label whenever the information changes form, format, or handling technology. | This policy tells users that they must be diligent when they change the form, format, or technology used to handle sensitive information.

For example, assume that information labeled as "confidential" was sent by fax to a remote location. The recipient could then extract certain details from the fax and include these details in an e-mail message. This policy would require that the "confidential" label be included in the e-mail message. Because users are in control of many of the changes in form, format, and handling technology that occur, they must be the ones to ensure that a label continues to be attached to sensitive information. This policy could be expanded to include labels and restrictions provided by third parties, such as copyright notices.

The words "any information containing a Company X data classification sensitivity label" may be too stringent for some organizations; they may prefer to use the words "any information with a secret classification label" (and thus save some money). |
| Equipment in secret information areas | Printers, copiers, and fax machines must not be located in the physically isolated zones within Company X offices that contain secret information. | This policy prevents people from making paper copies, from printing computer-resident information, and from otherwise removing hard-copy versions of secret information. If the devices to perform this process are not provided within a secured area no one will be able to make unauthorized copies of the information contained therein. All other avenues through which secret information could flow must also be blocked. For example, an isolated local area network could be used to prevent users from sending the secret information out over the Internet as part of an e-mail message. The very high security approach reflected in this policy works best if the movement of paper-resident secret information is strictly controlled, perhaps with sensors that detect that it has been removed from an isolated area.

This policy also creates a paperless office that, when deployed in high security areas, has the potential to be more secure than any paper-based office could ever be. Diskless workstations could be employed in such an environment to increase the level of security. |

(Continued)

Table 1 Fax machine use policies. (*Continued*)

Title	Policy	Commentary
Fax logs	Logs reflecting the involved phone numbers and the number of pages for all inbound and outbound fax transmissions must be retained for 1 year.	This policy provides a legal record of the faxes that were sent and received. This is important in business environments where contracts, purchase orders, invoices, and other legally binding promises are handled by fax. The maintenance and retention of a fax log can help resolve day-to-day operational problems. Such fax logs may additionally be useful for the preparation of expense reports and internal charge-back system reports.

Many new personal computer software packages that support faxing come with their own logs, which, according to this policy, should be turned on. Fax servers also support extensive logging. Modern versions of more expensive fax machines also keep their own logs. This policy can be carried out automatically by the involved equipment as well as manually by the involved operators. |
| Faxing sensitive information—notification | If secret information is to be sent by fax, the recipient must have been notified of the time when it will be transmitted and also have agreed that an authorized person will be present at the destination machine when the material is sent. An exception to this policy is permitted when the destination fax machine is physically or logically restricted such that persons who are not authorized to see the material being faxed may not enter the immediate area or otherwise gain access to faxes received. | One scenario for inadvertent disclosure involves sensitive materials that have been sent by fax but not yet picked up by the intended recipient. This policy ensures that no unauthorized person examines sensitive faxed materials sitting in a fax machine. If the recipient knows a fax is coming, he or she will also be concerned if it does not arrive when expected. The policy presumes the existence of another policy that defines the term "secret." This term may be readily replaced with the comparable label used within the organization in question. Note that the policy recognizes the reality of modern fax servers that can restrict access to faxes received using recipient passwords. |
| Faxing sensitive information—human presence | Sensitive materials must not be faxed unless the sender has immediately beforehand confirmed that an authorized staff member is on hand to handle the materials at the receiving machine properly.

When the transmission is complete, the staff member at the receiving end must confirm to the sender that a certain number of pages were received. An exception is allowed if the receiving machine is in a locked room accessible only to authorized personnel or if a password-protected fax mailbox is used to restrict unauthorized release of faxed materials. | One common scenario for inadvertent disclosure of faxed materials involves faxes that have been sent but not yet picked up by the intended recipient. This policy requires an authorized staff member to be present throughout the entire faxing process and to confirm that the faxing process was completed successfully. In addition to the exception noted in the third sentence of the policy, another exception may be permitted in those situations in which two fax machines support encryption.

A higher security approach would be to prohibit the faxing of any sensitive information unless both the sending and the receiving machines employ encryption. Only with encryption can the sender and recipient be reasonably assured that a fax was not intercepted in transit. This policy assumes that the word "sensitive" has been defined elsewhere. |
| Faxing sensitive information—intermediaries | Sensitive Company X information must not be faxed through untrusted intermediaries including, but not limited to, hotel staff, airport office services staff, and rented mailbox store staff. | Workers may be traveling for business, pressed for time, and not thinking about the people who may be exposed to sensitive information. The policy could be expanded to include preferred methods for sending the information, for example, by bonded courier.

The use of encryption is irrelevant here because the issue is whether intermediaries can examine the information in hard-copy form. The policy requires senders to do the faxing personally to help assure that unauthorized parties are not exposed to the information in question. The word "sensitive" should have been defined in another policy. |

(Continued)

Policy	Policy Statement	Commentary
Faxing sensitive information—cover sheet	When sensitive information must be faxed, a cover sheet must be sent and acknowledged by the recipient, after which the sensitive information may be sent through a second call.	This policy ensures that sensitive information is being faxed to the correct fax machine and that the sender is using the correct phone number. The policy prevents unauthorized call forwarding from interfering with the intended fax communication path. With so many fax machines in use these days, the chance that a wrong number would make connection with another fax machine is quite high. This policy prevents that type of error from causing unauthorized disclosure of the material on the involved fax. Another intention of this policy is to ensure that an authorized party is on hand and actually watching the destination fax machine. This prevents unauthorized parties from viewing the sensitive faxed material. Confirming that an authorized recipient is on hand is also desirable in case the second call is unsuccessful. Thus the recipient would call the sender and ask for a retransmission if some of the pages were missing, if there was a paper jam, etc. This policy could be augmented with another sentence requiring the recipient to confirm receipt of the second transmission. The policy does not specify how the destination party acknowledges receipt. This would most often occur on a separate voice line or by other means such as a pager or instant messaging.
Faxing sensitive information—unencrypted	Sensitive information may be faxed over unencrypted lines only when time is of the essence, no alternative or higher-security transmission methods are available, and voice contact with the receiving party is established immediately prior to transmission.	This policy notifies staff that sensitive information should not be faxed over unencrypted lines on a regular basis. If there is a need for regular transmission of sensitive information, then workers should request encrypting fax machines. Some international export restrictions may apply to encryption technology so check with legal counsel if establishing encrypting fax machines for international transmissions. The policy shown here may also include words requiring confirmation of receipt of a fax that includes sensitive information. Transmission to an attended stand-alone fax machine may be preferable to transmission to a fax server, if that server does not have adequate access controls and if it may be readily accessed by a number of people. This distinction may be stated explicitly in the policy. The word "sensitive" should have been defined in another policy.
Faxing sensitive information—physical security	Secret or confidential information must not be sent to an unattended fax machine unless the destination machine is in a locked room for which the keys are possessed only by people authorized to receive the information.	This policy ensures that no unauthorized person examines sensitive faxed materials. By physically restricting access, unauthorized persons are prevented from seeing secret or confidential faxes. This policy says nothing about notification of the recipient. The policy can be implemented by placing a special fax machine in a locked closet. Some organizations may wish to eliminate the reference to physical keys because there are other technologies that might be used, such as magnetic card access control systems. The policy presumes the existence of another policy that defines the terms "secret" and "confidential."
Faxing secret information—encryption	Secret information must not be sent by fax unless the transmission is encrypted using methods approved by the Company X Information Security Department.	Encryption prevents sensitive information from being revealed to wiretappers and others who may have access to it as it travels by common carriers. At the destination, the information can be decrypted, or recovered by reversing the encryption process. Even though the transmission is encrypted, the information coming out of a destination fax machine will be readable to any person who happens to be present when the fax is received. To prevent this, other controls such as a password to print a fax will be required. This policy thwarts fax transmission wiretapping. It is relatively easy to place a wiretap, record an unencrypted fax transmission, and later play it back into another fax machine to generate readable hardcopy. If this were done, neither the sender nor the recipient would ordinarily be aware that a wiretap has taken place. This comment is equally true of the new faxing services that use the Internet rather than dial-up lines. They too can be tapped unless the transmission is encrypted. The policy presumes the existence of a policy that defines the term "secret."

Espionage –
Firewalls

Table 1 Fax machine use policies. (*Continued*)

Title	Policy	Commentary
Faxing confidential information—speed dial	When confidential information is sent by fax, the operator must not use preset destination telephone numbers, but must instead manually enter the destination number.	This policy prevents the misdirection of faxes because of a mistaken entry of a speed-dial number. These types of errors can result in embarrassing situations in which, for example, one important customer sees that another important customer has a different price for the same product they bought yesterday. A high-visibility case involved the misdirection of a confidential merger contract to a business newspaper. If fax operators manually key in the phone number, they may make an error, but the error is likely to be a single digit. This will often cause the fax not to go through because a voice line or a modem line will be reached instead of another fax line. There is, however, no such automatic safety net when preset fax numbers are employed. This policy also helps to prevent the scenario in which some unauthorized person with access to the sending machine changes a previously selected speed-dial fax number, such that a sensitive fax is misdirected to an unauthorized recipient.
Faxing secret information—passwords	Secret information must not be sent by fax unless the receiving machine, prior to the initiation of a transmission, successfully receives a correct password from an authorized person at the receiving end of the transmission.	This policy helps to ensure that the correct fax machine has been reached. Only when a correct password is entered is this connection confirmed. There have been many reported cases in which sensitive faxes were sent to the wrong machine, and this policy helps to prevent additional problems of this nature. Two compatible machines, each supporting passwords, are likely to be required for this policy to work. This will reduce the number of machines to which secret faxes can be sent. This may also require that certain fax machines throughout an organization, machines that were manufactured by various vendors, be replaced with fax machines from a single vendor. Other passwords for printing faxes also may be required. The policy presumes the existence of a policy that defines the term "secret." The restriction of the scope of this policy to secret information means that normal (less sensitive) faxes need not bother with this process.
Fax cover sheet notice	All outgoing Company X faxes must include a cover sheet that includes wording approved by the legal department.	This policy is intended to be responsive to the significant number of faxes that are mistakenly sent to the wrong number. Not only can this involve entering the wrong telephone number on the fax machine, it may also involve telephone system malfunctions, internal mail systems that incorrectly deliver faxes to the wrong person, or monitoring of transmissions by telephone company technicians. A standard cover sheet will ensure that certain legal words precede all outbound faxes. Typically such a cover sheet includes a notice that the transmission is for use only by the intended individual or entity. This notice may also state that if the reader of the fax is not the intended recipient, then the reader must not use, disseminate, distribute, or copy the information. The notice may request that the sender be notified if the fax has been sent someplace other than the intended destination. The notice can be supplemented with words requesting the destruction of a misdirected fax and that no action be taken relying on the information contained in the fax itself. The policy discussed gives the greatest flexibility in that the words on the cover can be changed without the need to change the policy itself. Changes in the words on the cover will be necessary as the legal and business status of faxes evolves over time.

time, 24/7/365, this level of segregation ensures that confidential information sent during off-hours is not compromised.

Confirmation Page

Even with the advent of e-mail, one significant advantage the fax has over other forms of data exchange is that the sender immediately knows if the transmission was successful. When it comes to e-mail, it can often take hours or days for the information to actually appear on the recipient's desktop.

With that, all fax machines have the capability to print a fax confirmation sheet after each fax sent. This sheet confirms if the fax has been successfully transmitted, the destination fax number, and the number of pages transmitted. The sender of each fax should confirm the success of a transmission by checking this log after each secure fax message is sent.

Similarly, recipients should be trained to match the number of pages received against the transmitted fax cover sheet. In the event that pages are missing, the recipient should contact the sender and request a retransmission.

Secure Fax Hardware

To use fax encryption technology, both senders and recipients must have the same type of fax encrypting hardware. Most secure fax machines are identical in appearance to a typical fax machine, built on a standard commercial-based platform of product sold for general use. For secure fax machines, most of the functionality is transparent to the end user.

There are various standards for secure fax machines, including:

- MIL-STD-188-161D
- NATO STANAG 5000
- NSA NSTISSAM 1-92 TEMPEST Level 1
- NATO AMSG720B

TEMPEST models are internally shielded to prevent electromagnetic emissions from escaping, preventing interception of transmitted data signals. This is needed as anyone with the proper equipment can monitor, intercept, and reconstruct those signals, possibly while parked outside a corporate headquarters or military base. The downside is that TEMPEST capabilities can increase the price of a standard fax machine to well over $2000.

When communicating in a secure mode, a fax uses an RS-232C connection to cryptographic equipment, such as an STE (secure terminal equipment), a device that looks much like a telephone and utilizes digital signaling.

CONCLUSION

Creating a secure fax infrastructure does not take a lot. The function of this entry was to raise the issue and be a starting point for companies in creating their secure fax plan.

EXHIBIT A: SECURE FAX HARDWARE AND SOFTWARE

The following is a starters list of secure fax vendors. A Google search on secure fax will provide a much more definitive list of the various vendors.

Ricoh SecureFax
http://www.ricoh-usa.com/products/category_main.asp?pCategoryId=17&pCatName= SecureFax
Cryptek Secure Fax
http://www.cryptek.com/fax/default.asp
Gateway Fax Systems
http://www.gwfs.com/JITCCertification/JITCcert.html
Venali
http://www.venali.com/solutions/index.php
Business Security AB SecuriFax
http://www.bsecurity.se
TCC CSD 3700
http://www.tccsecure.com/products/voice-fax-data-encryption/CSD3700-summary.html

EXHIBIT B: POLICY

Policy is critical to the effective deployment of a secure fax infrastructure. A comprehensive security policy is required to map abstract security concepts to the real world implementation of security products. It is the policy that defines the aims and goals of the business. It comes down to the fact that if you have no policies, you have no information security.

After policy comes the need for SOPs. Organizations that take the time and effort to create formal information security SOPs demonstrate their commitment to security. By creating SOPs, they drastically lower their costs [greater return on investment (ROI)] and drastically increase their level of security.

The following policies are from *Information Security Policies Made Easy*, version 10,[3] which is the definitive information security policy resource. (Used with permission from Information Shield, Inc.)

REFERENCES

1. http://www.commetrex.com/whitepapers/FaxTech.html.
2. http://www.ipc.on.ca/index.asp?navid=46&fid1=413.
3. https://www.informationshield.com/ispmemain.htm.

Espionage – Firewalls

Firewall Architectures

Paul A. Henry, CISSP, CNE
Senior Vice President, CyberGuard Corporation, Ocala, Florida, U.S.A.

Abstract

Just a year or so ago, URL filtering was considered a nice thing to have but not a necessity; it now finds itself as a first line of defense in phishing. Two-factor authentication in the form of tokens were long considered a luxury and are now effectively being mandated by regulatory agencies for Internet banking and I expect will find their way in to environments that are entrusted to secure any personal information such as that which could potentially be used in identity theft and perhaps even medical records.

PERSPECTIVE

2005 can be described as a tough year for network security or, perhaps better yet, as a tough year for those who did not take network security seriously. ID theft was a hot topic for the year with breach after breach exposing the personal data of so many individuals. There is unfortunately no hard data that details specifically just how many of the data exposures actually resulted in cases of ID theft. The potential credit nightmares that the individuals will potentially face should not be taken lightly. Cleaning up your credit as a result of ID theft is time consuming, can be expensive, and even after it is cleaned up can still haunt the victim for many years. In looking at data found on the Internet in Table 1 for the first six months of 2005 alone, nearly 50 million individuals had their personal information exposed:

Organizations were warned that unless they got serious about security, government regulations would be imposed. With the high-profile breeches continuing to rise and setting new heights in 2005, our government took action and legislation was passed at the state level to address the issue as detailed in Table 2.

The Internet remains in flux. As organizations take measures to plug a known security hole, hackers simply first move on to easier targets, and then as the target environment dwindles they alter their tactics to enable them to continue to wreak their havoc against a new target-rich environment. This was clearly demonstrated by the decline in the number of broad-based protocol-level attacks we have witnessed as the hacking community seemed to shift its focus to the application layer. The majority of protective mechanisms in place today only offer protection by filtering on IP addresses and port (serviced) numbers; it is no wonder that application layer attacks have gained in popularity. More recently, social engineering has risen dramatically in the form of phishing, again demonstrating the flexibility and or adaptability of the hacking community.

The data from the 2005 CSI/FBI crime report paints a grim picture of the state of network security:

- The damage from virus attacks continues to be the highest overall cost to organizations.
- Unauthorized access had a dramatic increase in cost and has now replaced denial of service (DoS) attacks as the new second-most significant contributor to losses from computer crime
- Although the overall losses are perhaps lower, there has been a measurable increase in the losses associated with unauthorized access to information and the theft of proprietary information.
- Website defacements/incidents have increased sharply.
- The number of organizations reporting computer crime incidents to law enforcement continues to decline. The primary reason cited is the fear of negative publicity.

In the past, many organizations have cited competitive pressure as their primary reason for choosing popularity over security in consideration of how they go about securing their networks. Time and again I have heard that although an architecture or product is inarguably more secure, a company would be giving their competitor an advantage if the company offered its customers less transparency or convenience in connecting to its network.

In light of current legislation and the resulting first wave of civil penalties now being assessed, there may finally be sufficient motivation for a decisive change in how network security is viewed. Simply put, an organization's ability to mitigate the risk of the aforementioned civil penalties effectively moves network security from the deficit column to the asset column of the organization's balance sheet.

In closing, I recall a quote from October of 2000 from a friend and world renowned security expert Marcus Ranum, which I believe is still highly relevant today: "Firewall customers once had a vote, and voted in favor of

Encyclopedia of Information Assurance DOI: 10.1081/E-EIA-120046863

Copyright © 2011 by Taylor & Francis. All rights reserved.

Table 1 Loss or theft of personal identification information in Q1–Q2 2005.

Date made public	Name	Type of breach	Number of exposed people
2/15/2005	ChoicePoint	ID thieves accessed	145,000
2/25/2005	Bank of America	Lost backup tape	1,200,000
2/25/2005	PayMaxx	Exposed online	25,000
3/8/2005	DSW/Retail	Ventures Hacking	100,000
3/10/2005	LexisNexis	Passwords compromised	32,000
3/11/2005	Univ. of CA, Berkeley	Stolen laptop	98,400
3/11/2005	Boston College	Hacking	120,000
3/12/2005	NV Dept. of Motor Vehicles	Stolen computer	8900
3/20/2005	Northwestern Univ.	Hacking	21,000
3/20/2005	Univ. of Nevada, Las Vegas	Hacking	5000
3/22/2005	Calif. State Univ., Chico	Hacking	59,000
3/23/2005	Univ. of CA, San Francisco	Hacking	7000
4/1/2005	Georgia DMV	Dishonest insider	"Hundreds of thousands"
4/5/2005	MCI	Stolen laptop	16,500
4/8/2005	San Jose Med. Group	Stolen computer	185,000
4/11/2005	Tufts University	Hacking	106,000
4/12/2005	LexisNexis	Passwords compromised	Additional 280,000
4/14/2005	Polo Ralph Lauren/HSBC	Hacking	180,000
4/14/2005	California FasTrack	Dishonest insider	4500
4/15/2005	California Dept. of Health Services	Stolen laptop	21,600
4/18/2005	DSW/Retail Ventures	Hacking Additional	1,300,000
4/20/2005	Ameritrade	Lost backup tape	200,000
4/21/2005	Carnegie Mellon Univ.	Hacking	19,000
4/26/2005	Michigan State Univ.'s Wharton Center	Hacking	40,000
4/26/2005	Christus St. Joseph's	Hospital stolen computer	19,000
4/28/2005	Georgia Southern Univ.	Hacking	"Tens of thousands"
4/28/2005	Wachovia, Bank of America, PNC Financial Services Group and Commerce Bancorp	Dishonest insiders	676,000
4/29/2005	Oklahoma State Univ.	Missing laptop	37,000
5/2/2005	Time Warner	Lost backup tapes	600,000
5/4/2005	Colorado Health Dept.	Stolen laptop	1,600 (families)
5/5/2005	Purdue Univ.	Hacker	11,360
5/7/2005	Dept. of Justice	Stolen laptop	80,000
5/11/2005	Stanford Univ.	Hacker	9900
5/12/2005	Hinsdale Central High School	Hacker	2400
5/16/2005	Westborough Bank	Dishonest insider	750
5/18/2005	Jackson Comm. College, Michigan	Hacker	8000
5/19/2005	Valdosta State Univ., GA	Hacker	40,000
5/20/2005	Purdue Univ.	Hacker	11,000
5/26/2005	Duke Univ.	Hacker	5500
5/27/2005	Cleveland State Univ.	Stolen laptop	44,420
5/28/2005	Merlin Data Services	Bogus acct. set up	9000
5/30/2005	Motorola	Computers stolen	Unknown
6/6/2005	Citifinancial	Lost backup tapes	3,900,000

(Continued)

Espionage –
Firewalls

Table 1 Loss or theft of personal identification information in Q1–Q2 2005. *(Continued)*

Date made public	Name	Type of breach	Number of exposed people
6/10/2005	Federal Deposit Insurance Corp. (FDIC)	Not disclosed	6000
6/16/2005	Cardsystems	Hacker	40,000,000
6/18/2005	Univ. of Hawaii	Dishonest insider	150,000
6/25/2005	Univ. of Connecticut	Hacker	72,000
Total			49,857,830

transparency, performance and convenience instead of security; nobody should be surprised by the results."[1]

FIREWALL FUNDAMENTALS: A REVIEW

The level of protection that *any* firewall is able to provide in securing a private network when connected to the public Internet is directly related to the architecture(s) chosen for the firewall by the respective vendor. Generally, most commercially available firewalls utilize one or more of the following firewall architectures:

- Static packet filter
- Dynamic (stateful) packet filter
- Circuit-level gateway

Table 2 State laws regarding security breech notification.

State	Law	Effective date
Arkansas	SB 1167	6/1/2005
California	SB 1386	7/1/2003
Connecticut	SB 650	1/1/2006
Delaware	HB 116	6/28/2005
Florida	HB 481	7/1/2005
Georgia	SB 230	5/5/2005
Illinois	HB 1633	1/1/2006
Indiana	SB 503	7/1/2006
Louisiana	SB 205	1/1/2006
Maine	LD 1671	1/31/2006
Minnesota	HF 2121	1/1/2006
Montana	HB 732	3/1/2006
Nevada	SB 347	10/1/2005
New Jersey	A4001	1/1/2006
New York	SB 5827	12/7/2005
North Carolina	HB 1048	2/17/2006
North Dakota	SB 2251	6/1/2005
Ohio	HB 104	2/17/2006
Pennsylvania	SB 721	7/1/2006
Rhode Island	HB 6191	7/10/2005
Tennessee	HB 2170	7/1/2005
Texas	SB 122	9/1/2005
Washington	SB 6403	7/24/2005

- Application-level gateway (proxy)
- Stateful inspection
- Cutoff proxy
- Air gap
- Intrusion prevention
- Deep packet inspection
- Total stream protection
- Unified threat management (UTM)

Network Security: A Matter of Balance

Network security is simply the proper balance of trust and performance. All firewalls rely on the inspection of information generated by protocols that function at various layers of the OSI model as shown in Fig. 1. Knowing the OSI layer at which a firewall operates is one of the keys to understanding the different types of firewall architectures. Generally speaking, firewalls follow two known rules:

- The higher the OSI layer the architecture goes to examine the information within the packet, the more processor cycles the architecture consumes.
- The higher in the OSI layer at which an architecture examines packets, the greater the level of protection the architecture provides because more information is available upon which to base decisions.

Historically, there had always been a recognized trade-off in firewalls between the level of trust afforded and speed (throughput). Faster processors and the performance advantages of symmetric multiprocessing (SMP) have narrowed the performance gap between the traditional fast packet filters and high-overhead-consuming proxy firewalls.

One of the most important factors in any successful firewall deployment is "who" makes the trustperformance decisions: 1) the firewall vendor, by limiting the administrator's choices of architectures, or 2) the administrator, in a robust firewall product that provides for multiple firewall architectures.

In examining firewall architectures, the most important fields, as shown in Fig. 2, within the IP packet are:

- IP header as detailed in Fig. 3
- TCP header as detailed in Fig. 4
- Application level header
- Data-payload header

Espionage– Firewalls

OSI model   TCP/IP model

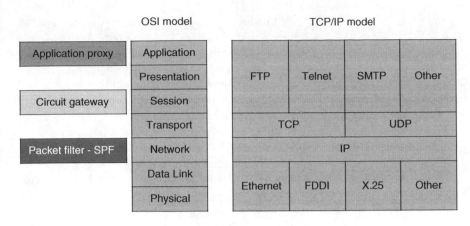

Fig. 1 OSI and TCP/IP models.

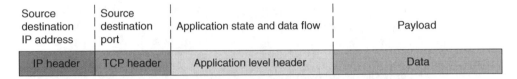

Fig. 2 The most important fields within the IP packet.

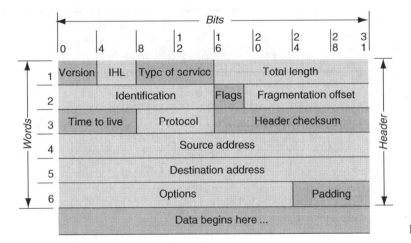

Fig. 3 The IP header.

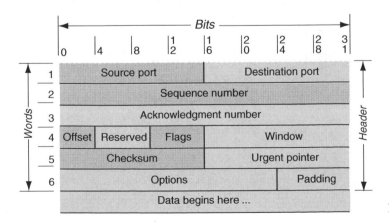

Fig. 4 The TCP header.

Static Packet Filter

The packet-filtering firewall is one of the oldest firewall architectures. A static packet filter as shown in Fig. 5 operates at the network layer, or OSI layer 3.

The decision to accept or deny a packet is based upon an examination of specific fields as shown in Fig. 6 within the packet's IP and protocol headers:

- Source address
- Destination address
- Application or protocol
- Source port number
- Destination port number

Before forwarding a packet, the firewall compares the IP header and TCP header against a user-defined table—rule base—which contains the rules that dictate whether the firewall should deny or permit packets to pass. The rules are scanned in sequential order until the packet filter finds a specific rule that matches the criteria specified in the packet-filtering rule. If the packet filter does not find a rule that matches the packet, then it imposes a default rule. The default rule explicitly defined in the firewall's table typically instructs the firewall to drop a packet that meets none of the other rules.

There are two schools of thought on the default rule used with the packet filter: 1) ease of use, and 2) security first. "Ease of use" proponents prefer a default "allow all" rule that permits all traffic unless it is explicitly denied by a prior rule. "Security first" proponents prefer a default "deny all" rule that denies all traffic unless explicitly allowed by a prior rule.

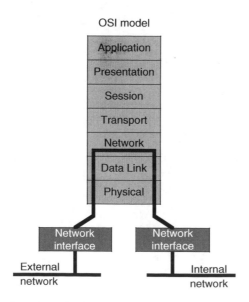

Fig. 5 A static packet filter operates at the network layer (OCI layer 3).

Within the static packet filter rules database, the administrator can define rules that determine which packets are accepted and which packets are denied. The IP header information allows the administrator to write rules that can deny or permit packets to and from a specific IP address or range of IP addresses. The TCP header information allows the administrator to write service-specific rules (i.e., allow or deny packets to or from ports) related to specific services.

The administrator can write rules that allow certain services such as HTTP from any IP address to view the Web pages on the protected Web server. The administrator can also write rules that block certain IP address or entire ranges of addresses from using the HTTP service and viewing the Web pages on the protected server. In the same respect, the administrator can write rules that allow certain services such as SMTP from a trusted IP address or range of IP addresses to access files on the protected mail server. The administrator could also write rules that block access for certain IP addresses or entire ranges of addresses to access the protected FTP server.

The configuration of packet filter rules can be difficult because the rules are examined in sequential order. Great care must be taken in establishing the order in which packet-filtering rules are entered into the rule base. Even if the administrator manages to create effective rules in the proper order of precedence, a packet filter has one inherent limitation: a packet filter only examines data in the IP header and TCP header; it cannot know the difference between a real and a forged address. If an address is present and meets the packet filter rules along with the other rule criteria, the packet will be allowed to pass.

Suppose the administrator took the precaution to create a rule that instructed the packet filter to drop any incoming packets with unknown source addresses. This packet-filtering rule would make it more difficult, but not impossible, for a hacker to access at least some trusted servers with IP addresses. The hacker could simply substitute the actual source address on a malicious packet with the source address of a known trusted client. This common form of attack is called *IP address spoofing*. This form of attack is very effective against a packet filter. The CERT Coordination Center has received numerous reports of IP spoofing attacks, many of which resulted in successful network intrusions. Although the performance of a packet filter can be attractive, this architecture alone is generally not secure enough to deter hackers determined to gain access to the protected network.

Equally important is what the static packet filter does not examine. Remember that in the static packet filter only specific protocol headers are examined: 1) source-destination IP address and 2) sourcedestination port numbers (services). Hence, a hacker can hide malicious commands or data in unexamined headers. Furthermore, because the static packet filter does not inspect the packet payload, the hacker has the opportunity to hide malicious

Espionage – Firewalls

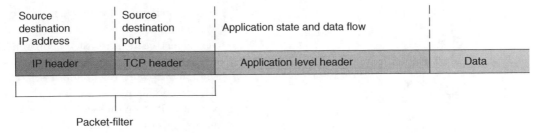

Fig. 6 The decision to accept or deny a packet is based upon an examination of specific fields within a packet's IP and protocol headers.

commands or data within the packet's payload. This attack methodology is often referred to as a *covert channel attack* and is becoming more popular.

Lastly, the static packet filter is not state aware. The administrator must configure rules for both sides of the conversation to a protected server. To allow access to a protected Web server, the administrator must create a rule that allows both the inbound request from the remote client as well as the outbound response from the protected Web server. Of further consideration is that many services such as FTP and e-mail servers in operation today require the use of dynamically allocated ports for responses; therefore, an administrator of a static packet-filtering firewall has little choice but to open up an entire range of ports with static packet-filtering rules.

Both the pros and the cons of static packet filter considerations are detailed in Table 3.

Dynamic (Stateful) Packet Filter

The dynamic (stateful) packet filter is the next step in the evolution of the static packet filter. As such it shares many of the inherent limitations of the static packet filter with one important difference: state awareness.

The typical dynamic packet filter, as shown in Fig. 7, like the static packet filter, operates at the network layer (OSI layer 3). An advanced dynamic packet filter may operate up into the transport layer—OSI layer 4—to collect additional state information.

Most often, the decision to accept or deny a packet is based upon examination of the packet's IP and protocol headers as shown in Fig. 8:

- Source address
- Destination address
- Application or protocol
- Source port number
- Destination port number

In simplest terms, the typical dynamic packet filter is "aware" of the difference between a new and an established connection. After a connection is established, it is entered into a table that typically resides in RAM. Subsequent packets are compared to this table in RAM, most often by software running at the operating system (OS) kernel level. When the packet is found to be an existing connection, it is allowed to pass without any further inspection. By avoiding having to parse the packet filter rule base for each and every packet that enters the firewall and by performing this test at the kernel level in RAM for an already-established connection, the dynamic packet filter enables a measurable performance increase over a static packet filter.

There are two primary differences in dynamic packet filters found among firewall vendors:

- Support of SMP
- Connection establishment

In writing the firewall application to fully support SMP, the firewall vendor is afforded up to a 30% increase in dynamic packet filter performance for each additional processor in operation. Unfortunately, many implementations of dynamic packet filters in current firewall offerings operate as a single-threaded process, which simply cannot take advantage of the benefits of SMP. To overcome the

Table 3 Static packet filter considerations.

Pros	Cons
Low impact on network performance	Operates only at network layer, therefore it only examines IP and TCP headers
Low cost—now included with many operating systems	Unaware of packet payload—offers low level of security
	Lacks state awareness—may require numerous ports be left open to facilitate services that use dynamically allocated ports
	Susceptible to IP spoofing
	Difficult to create rules (order of precedence)
	Only provides for a low level of protection

Espionage –
Firewalls

Espionage –
Firewalls

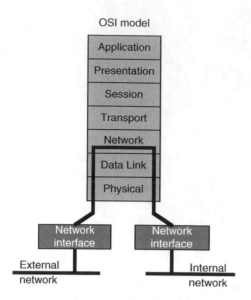

OSI model

| Application |
| Presentation |
| Session |
| Transport |
| Network |
| Data Link |
| Physical |

Network interface   Network interface

External network   Internal network

Fig. 7 The typical dynamic packet filter, like the static packet filter, operates at the network layer (OSI layer 3).

performance limitation of their single-threaded process, these vendors usually require powerful and expensive RISC-processor-based servers to attain acceptable levels of performance. As available processor power has increased and multiprocessor servers have become widely utilized, this single-threaded limitation has become more visible. For example, vendor A running an expensive RISC-based server offers only 150 Mbps dynamic packet filter throughput, while vendor B running on an inexpensive off-the-shelf Intel multiprocessor server can attain dynamic packet filtering throughputs of above 600 Mbps.

Almost every vendor has their own proprietary methodology for building the connection table, but beyond the issues discussed above, the basic operation of the dynamic packet filter for the most part is essentially the same.

In an effort to overcome the performance limitations imposed by their single-threaded process-based dynamic packet filters, some vendors have taken dangerous short-cuts when establishing connections at the firewall. RFC guidelines recommend following the three-way handshake to establish a connection at the firewall. One popular vendor will open a new connection upon receipt of a single SYN packet, totally ignoring RFC recommendations. In effect, this exposes the servers behind the firewall to single-packet attacks from spoofed IP addresses.

Hackers gain great advantage from anonymity. A hacker can be much more aggressive in mounting attacks if he can remain hidden. Similar to the example in the examination of a static packet filter, suppose the administrator took the precaution to create a rule that instructed the packet filter to drop any incoming packets with unknown source addresses. This packet-filtering rule would make it more difficult, but again not impossible, for a hacker to access at least some trusted servers with IP addresses. The hacker could simply substitute the actual source address on a malicious packet with the source address of a known trusted client. In this attack methodology, the hacker assumes the IP address of the trusted host and must communicate through the three-way handshake to establish the connection before mounting an assault. This provides additional traffic that can be used to trace back to the hacker.

When the firewall vendor fails to follow RFC recommendations in the establishment of the connection and opens a connection without the three-way handshake, the hacker can simply spoof the trusted host address and fire any of the many well-known single-packet attacks at the firewall or servers protected by the firewall while maintaining his complete anonymity. One presumes that administrators are unaware that their popular firewall products operate in this manner; otherwise, it would be surprising that so many have found this practice acceptable following the many historical well-known single-packet attacks like LAND, "ping of death," and "tear drop" that have plagued administrators in the past.

Both the pros and the cons of dynamic packet filter considerations are shown in Table 4.

Circuit-Level Gateway

The circuit-level gateway operates at the session layer (OSI layer 5) as shown in Fig. 9. In many respects, a circuit-level gateway is simply an extension of a packet filter in that it typically performs basic packet filter operations and then adds verification of proper handshaking and the legitimacy of the sequence numbers used in establishing the connection.

The circuit-level gateway examines and validates TCP and user datagram protocol (UDP) sessions before opening a connection, or circuit, through the firewall. Hence the circuit-level gateway has more data to act upon than a standard static or dynamic packet filter.

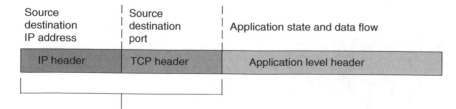

Source destination IP address   Source destination port   Application state and data flow

| IP header | TCP header | Application level header |

Fig. 8 The decision to accept or deny a packet is based upon examination of the packet's IP and protocol headers.

Table 4 Dynamic packet filter considerations.

Pros	Cons
Lowest impact of all examined architectures on network performance when designed to be fully symmetric multiprocessing (SMP)-compliant	Operates only at network layer, therefore, it only examines IP and TCP headers
Low cost—now included with some operating systems	Unaware of packet payload—offers low level of security
State awareness provides measurable performance benefit	Susceptible to IP spoofing
	Difficult to create rules (order of precedence)
	Can introduce additional risk if connections can be established without following the RFC-recommended three-way handshake
	Only provides for a low level of protection

Most often, the decision to accept or deny a packet is based upon examining the packet's IP header and TCP header as detailed in Fig. 10:

- Source address
- Destination address
- Application or protocol
- Source port number
- Destination port number
- Handshaking and sequence numbers

Similar to a packet filter, before forwarding the packet, a circuit-level gateway compares the IP header and TCP header against a user-defined table containing the rules that dictate whether the firewall should deny or permit packets to pass. The circuit-level gateway then determines that a requested session is legitimate only if the SYN flags, ACK flags and sequence numbers involved in the TCP handshaking between the trusted client and the untrusted host are logical.

If the session is legitimate, the packet filter rules are scanned until it finds one that agrees with the information in a packet's full association. If the packet filter does not find a rule that applies to the packet, then it imposes a default rule. The default rule explicitly defined in the firewall's table "typically" instructs the firewall to drop a packet that meets none of the other rules.

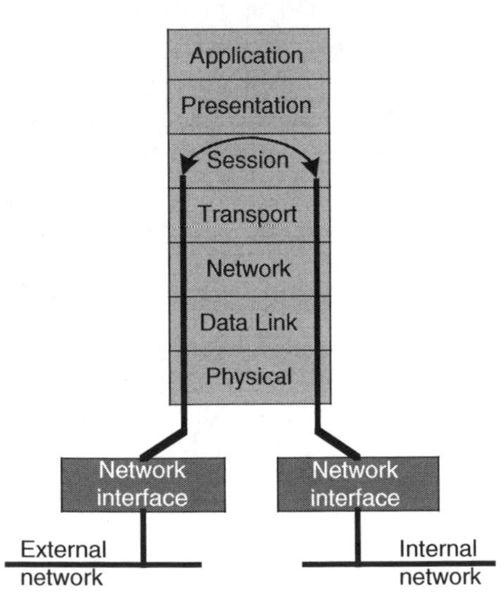

The circuit-level gateway is literally a step up from a packet filter in the level of security it provides. Further, like a packet filter operating at a low level in the OSI model, it has little impact on network performance. However, once a circuit-level gateway establishes a connection, any application can run across that connection because a circuit-level gateway filters packets only at the session and network layers of the OSI model. In other words, a circuit-level gateway cannot examine the data content of the packets it relays between a trusted network and an untrusted network. The potential exists to slip harmful packets through a circuit-level gateway to a server behind the firewall.

Both the pros and the cons of circuit-level gateway considerations are shown in Table 5.

Application-Level Gateway

Like a circuit-level gateway, an application-level gateway intercepts incoming and outgoing packets, runs proxies that copy and forward information across the gateway, and functions as a proxy server, preventing any direct connection between a trusted server or client and an untrusted host. The proxies that an application-level gateway runs often differ in two important ways from the circuitlevel gateway:

- The proxies are application specific.
- The proxies examine the entire packet and can filter packets at the application layer of the OSI model as shown in Fig. 11.

Unlike the circuit gateway, the application-level gateway accepts only packets generated by services they are designed to copy, forward, and filter. For example, only an HTTP proxy can copy, forward, and filter HTTP traffic. If a network relies only on an application-level gateway,

OSI model

Fig. 9 The circuit-level gateway operates at the session layer (OSI layer 5).

Espionage – Firewalls

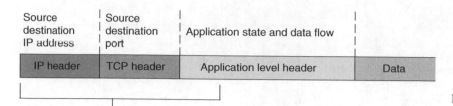

Circuit-level gateway

Fig. 10 The decision to accept or deny a packet is based upon examining the packet's IP header and TCP header.

Espionage –
Firewalls

incoming and outgoing packets cannot access services for which there is no proxy. If an application-level gateway ran FTP and HTTP proxies, only packets generated by these services could pass through the firewall. All other services would be blocked.

The application-level gateway runs proxies that examine and filter individual packets, rather than simply copying them and recklessly forwarding them across the gateway. Application-specific proxies check each packet that passes through the gateway, verifying the contents of the packet up through the application layer (layer 7) of the OSI model. These proxies can filter on particular information or specific individual commands in the application protocols the proxies are designed to copy, forward, and filter. As an example, an FTP application-level gateway can filter dozens of commands to allow a high degree of granularity on the permissions of specific users of the protected FTP service.

Current technology application-level gateways are often referred to *as strong application proxies*. A strong application proxy extends the level of security afforded by the application-level gateway. Instead of copying the entire datagram on behalf of the user, a strong application proxy actually creates a new empty datagram inside the firewall. Only those commands and data found acceptable to the strong application proxy are copied from the original datagram outside the firewall to the new datagram inside the firewall. Then, and only then, is this new datagram forwarded to the protected server behind the firewall. By employing this methodology, the strong application proxy can mitigate the risk of an entire class of covert channel attacks.

An application-level gateway filters information at a higher OSI layer than the common static or dynamic packet filter, and most automatically create any necessary packet filtering rules, usually making them easier to configure than traditional packet filters.

By facilitating the inspection of the complete packet, the application-level gateway is one of the most secure firewall architectures available; however, some vendors (usually those that market stateful inspection firewalls) and users have made claims that the security offered by an application-level gateway had an inherent drawback: a lack of transparency.

In moving software from older 16-bit code to current technology's 32-bit environment and with the advent of SMP, many of today's application-level gateways are just as transparent as they are secure. Users on the public or trusted network, in most cases, do not notice that they are accessing Internet services through a firewall.

Both the pros and cons in the consideration of the application level gateway are shown in Table 6.

Stateful Inspection

Stateful inspection combines the many aspects of dynamic packet filtering, circuit-level and applicationlevel gateways as shown in Fig. 12. Although stateful inspection has the inherent ability to examine all seven layers of the OSI model, in the majority of applications observed by the author, stateful inspection was operated only at the network layer of the OSI model and used only as a dynamic packet filter for filtering all incoming and outgoing packets based on source and destination IP addresses and port numbers. Although the vendor claims this is the fault of the administrator's configuration, many administrators claim that the operating overhead associated with the stateful inspection process prohibits its full utilization.

As indicated, stateful inspection can also function as a circuit-level gateway, determining whether the packets in a session are appropriate. For example, stateful inspection can verify that inbound SYN and ACK flags and sequence numbers are logical. However, in most implementations,

Table 5 Circuit-level gateway considerations.

Pros	Cons
Low to moderate impact on network performance	Shares many of the same negative issues associated with packet filters
Breaks direct connection to server behind firewall	Allows any data to simply pass through the connection
Higher level of security than a static or dynamic (stateful) packet filter	Only provides for a low to moderate level of security

OSI model

Proxy application

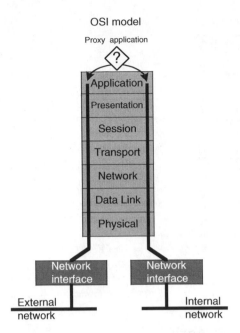

Fig. 11 The proxies examine the entire packet and can filter packets at the application layer of the OSI model.

the stateful-inspection–based firewall operates only as a dynamic packet filter and, dangerously, allows new connections to be established with a single SYN packet. A unique limitation of one popular stateful inspection implementation is that it does not provide the ability to inspect sequence numbers on outbound packets from users behind the firewall. This leads to a flaw whereby internal users can easily spoof IP address of other internal users to open holes through the associated firewall for inbound connections.

Finally, stateful inspection can mimic an application-level gateway. Stateful inspection can evaluate the contents of each packet up through the application layer and ensure that these contents match the rules in the administrator's network security policy.

Better performance, but what about security?

Like an application-level gateway, stateful inspection can be configured to drop packets that contain specific commands within the application header. For example, the administrator could configure a stateful inspection firewall to drop HTTP packets containing a "Put" command. However, historically, the performance impact of application-level filtering by the single-threaded process of stateful inspection has caused many administrators to abandon their use and to simply opt for dynamic packet filtering to allow the firewall to keep up with their network load requirements. In fact, the default configuration of a popular stateful inspection firewall utilizes dynamic packet filtering and not stateful inspection of the most popular protocol on today's Internet—HTTP traffic.

Do current stateful inspection implementations expose the user to additional risks?

Unlike an application-level gateway, stateful inspection does not break the client-server model to analyze application-layer data. An application-level gateway creates two connections: 1) one between the trusted client and the gateway and 2) another between the gateway and the untrusted host. The gateway then copies information between these two connections. This is the core of the well-known proxy vs. stateful inspection debate. Some administrators insist that this configuration ensures the highest degree of security; other administrators argue that this configuration slows performance unnecessarily. In an effort to provide a secure connection, a stateful-inspection–based firewall has the ability to intercept and examine each packet up through the application layer of the OSI model. Unfortunately, because of the associated performance impact of the single-threaded stateful inspection process, this configuration is not the one typically deployed.

Looking beyond marketing hype and engineering theory, stateful inspection relies on algorithms within an

Espionage – Firewalls

Table 6 Application-level gateway considerations.

Pros	Cons
Application gateway with symmetric multiprocessing (SMP) affords a moderate impact on network performance	Poor implementation can have a high impact on network performance
Breaks direct connection to server behind firewall eliminating the risk of an entire class of covert channel attacks	Must be written securely. Historically some vendors have introduced buffer overruns within the application gateway itself
Strong application proxy that inspects protocol header lengths can eliminate an entire class of buffer overrun attacks	Vendors must keep up with new protocols. A common complaint of application-level gateway users is lack of timely vendor support for new protocols
Highest level of security	A poor implementation that relies on the underlying operating system (OS) Inetd daemon will suffer from a severe limitation to the number of allowed connections in today's demanding high simultaneous session environment

Espionage –
Firewalls

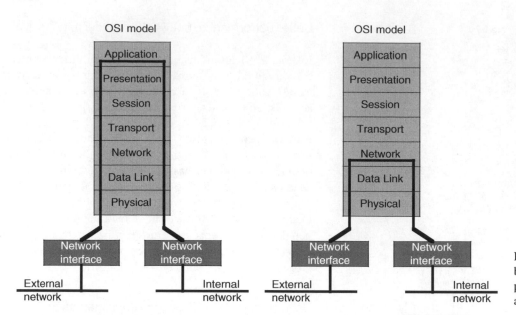

Fig. 12 Stateful inspection combines the many aspects of dynamic packet filtering, circuit-level and application-level gateways.

inspect engine to recognize and process application-layer data. These algorithms compare packets against known bit patterns of authorized packets. Respective vendors have claimed that theoretically they are able to filter packets more efficiently than application-specific proxies. However, most stateful inspection engines represent a single-threaded process. With current technology SMPbased application-level gateways operating on multiprocessor servers, the gap has dramatically narrowed. As an example, one vendor's SMP-capable multi-architecture firewall that does not use stateful inspection outperforms a popular stateful inspection based firewall up to 4:1 on throughput and up to 12:1 on simultaneous sessions. Further, due to limitations in the inspect language used in stateful inspection engines, application gateways are now commonly being used to fill in the gaps.

Both the pros and the cons of stateful inspection considerations are shown in Table 7.

Cutoff Proxy

The cutoff proxy is a hybrid combination of a dynamic (stateful) packet filter and a circuit-level proxy. In simplest terms, the cutoff proxy first acts as a circuit-level proxy in verifying the RFC-recommended three-way handshake and any required authenticating actions, then switches over to a dynamic packet filtering mode of operation. Hence, it initially works at the session layer (OSI layer 5) then switches to a dynamic packet filter working at the network layer (OSI Layer 3) after the connection-authentication process is completed as shown in Fig. 13.

It was pointed out what the cutoff proxy does; now, more importantly, we need to discuss what it does *not* do. The cutoff proxy is not a traditional circuit-level proxy that breaks the client/server model for the duration of the connection. There is a direct connection established between

Table 7 Stateful inspection considerations.

Pros	Cons
Offers the ability to inspect all seven layers of the OSI model and is user configurable to customize specific filter constructs	The single-threaded process of the stateful inspection engine has a dramatic impact on performance, so many users operate the stateful inspection based firewall as nothing more than a dynamic packet filter
Does not break the client/server model	Many believe the failure to break the client/server model creates an unacceptable security risk as the hacker has a direct connection to the protected server
Provides an integral dynamic (stateful) packet filter	A poor implementation that relies on the underlying operating system (OS) Inetd demon will suffer from a severe limitation to the number of allowed connections in today's demanding high simultaneous session environment
Fast when operated as dynamic packet filter, however many symmetric multiprocessing (SMP)-compliant dynamic packet filters are actually faster	Low level of security. No stateful inspection-based firewall has achieved higher than a Common Criteria EAL 2. Per the Common Criteria EAL 2 certification documents, EAL 2 products are not intended for use in protecting private networks when connecting to the public Internet

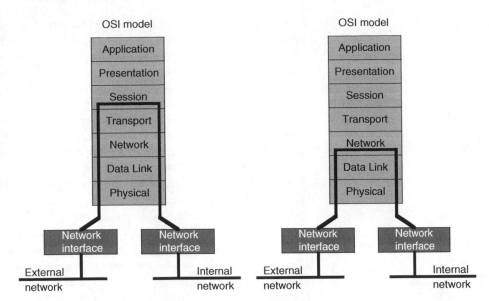

Fig. 13 The cutoff proxy initially works at the session layer (OSI layer 5) then switches to a dynamic packet filter working at the network layer (OSI layer 3) after the connection–authentication process is completed.

the remote client and the protected server behind the firewall. This is not to say that a cutoff proxy does not provide a useful balance between security and performance. At issue with respect to the cutoff proxy are vendors who exaggerate by claiming that their cutoff proxy offers a level of security equivalent to a traditional circuitlevel gateway with the added benefit of the performance of a dynamic packet filter.

In clarification, the author believes that all firewall architectures have their place in Internet security. If your security policy requires authentication of basic services, examination of the three-way handshake, and does not require breaking of the client/server model, the cutoff proxy is a good fit. However, administrators must be fully aware and understand that a cutoff proxy clearly is not equivalent to a circuit-level proxy as the client/server model is not broken for the duration of the connection.

Both the pros and the cons of cut off proxy considerations are shown in Table 8.

Air Gap

At the time of this writing, the security community has essentially dismissed the merits of air-gap technology as little more than a marketing spin. With air-gap technology, the external client connection causes the connection data to be written to a SCSI e-disk. The internal connection then reads this data from the SCSI e-disk. By breaking the direct connection between the client to the server and independently writing to and reading from the SCSI e-disk, the respective vendors believe they have provided a higher level of security and a resulting "air gap." However, when considering the level of inspection, the air-gap technology offers little more protection then an application-level gateway as shown in Fig. 14.

Air-gap vendors claim that although the operation of air gap technology resembles that of the application-level gateway, an important difference is the separation of the content inspection from the "front-end" by the isolation provided by the air gap. This may very well be true for those firewall vendors who implement their firewall on top of a standard commercial OS, but with the current technology firewall operating on a kernel-hardened OS, there is little distinction. Simply put, vendors who chose to implement kernel-level hardening of the underlying OS utilizing multilevel security (MLS) or containerization methodologies provide no less security than current air-gap technologies.

Table 8 Cutoff proxy considerations.

Pros	Cons
Lower impact on network performance than a traditional circuit gateway	It is not a circuit gateway
IP spoofing issue is minimized as the three-way connection is verified	Still has many of the remaining issues of a dynamic packet filter
	Unaware of packet payload—offers low level of security
	Difficult to create rules (order of precedence)
	Can offer a false sense of security as vendors incorrectly claim it is equivalent to a traditional circuit gateway

Espionage – Firewalls

Espionage –
Firewalls

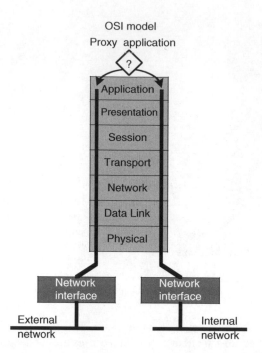

OSI model

Proxy application

Fig. 14 When considering the level of inspection, the air-gap technology offers little more protection then an application-level gateway.

Any measurable benefit of air-gap technology has yet to be verified by any recognized third-party testing authority. Further, current performance of most air-gap-like products falls well behind that obtainable by traditional application-level-gateway-based products. Without a verifiable benefit to the level of security provided, the necessary performance costs are prohibitive for many system administrators.

Both the pros and cons of air gap considerations are shown in Table 9.

Application-Specific Integrated Circuit-Based Firewalls

Looking at current application-specific integrated circuit (ASIC)-based firewall offerings, the author finds that virtually all are still nothing more than VPN/firewall hybrids. These hybrids take advantage of the fast encryption and decryption capabilities of the ASIC, but provide no more

than a dynamic packet filter for most Internet protocols. Although some ASIC-based firewall vendors claim to offer full layer-7 awareness and stateful inspection capabilities, a quick look at the respective vendor's GUI shows that there is no user-configurable functionality above layer 4. Although the technology might be "capable" of layer-7 inspection, the product (as delivered) provides no real administrator-configurable security options above layer 4.

The term *ASIC-based firewall* can be misleading. In fact, for most ASIC-based firewall vendors, only a small subset of firewall operations actually occurs in the ASIC. The majority of firewall functions are really accomplished in software operating on a typical microprocessor. Although there has been a lot of discussion about adding additional depth of inspection at the application layer in ASIC-based firewalls, to date no vendor has been able to successfully commercialize an ASIC-based firewall that provides the true application awareness and configurable granularity of current technology application proxybased firewalls.

Application-specific integrated circuit technology is now finding its way into intrusion detection system (IDS) and intrusion prevention system (IPS) products. The fast string comparison capability of the ASIC can provide added performance to string or signature-based IDS/IPS products. There has been a substantial amount of marketing spin about the eventual marriage of a firewall and IPS embedded within an ASIC, but no vendor has successfully fulfilled on the promise. Furthermore, relying on a system that depends on knowing the signature of every possible vulnerability is a losing battle when more than one hundred new vulnerabilities are released each month.

One of the newer and more interesting ASIC-based firewall products includes an ASIC-based embedded antivirus. By design, an ASIC lends itself well to fast string comparison, which makes the ASIC a natural fit for applications such as anti-virus. But do we really need faster antivirus? Typically, anti-virus is limited to e-mail and a few extra seconds in the delivery of an e-mail is not necessarily a problem for most users. Therefore, one might question the trade-off in flexibility one has to accept when selecting an ASIC-based product measured against real-world performance.

Internet security standards are in a constant state of flux. Hence, ASIC designs must be left programmable or "soft"

Table 9 Air gap considerations.

Pros	Cons
Breaks direct connection to server behind firewall eliminating the risk of an entire class of covert channel attacks	Can have a high negative impact on network performance
Strong application proxy that inspects protocol header lengths can eliminate an entire class of buffer overrun attacks	Vendors must keep up with new protocols; a common complaint of application-level gateway users is the lack of timely response from a vendor to provide application-level gateway support for a new protocol
As with an application-level gateway an air gap can potentially offer a high level of security	Currently not verified by any recognized third-party testing authority

enough that the full speed of an ASIC cannot actually be unleashed. Application-specific integrated circuit technology has clearly delivered the best performing VPN products in today's security marketplace. By design, IPsec encryption and decryption algorithms perform better in hardware than in software. Some of these ASIC or purpose-built IPsec accelerators are finding their way into firewall products that offer more than layer-4 packet filtering. Administrators get the best of worlds: the blazing speed of IPsec VPN and the added security of a real application-proxy firewall.

Both the pros and cons of ASIC-based firewall considerations are shown in Table 10.

Intrusion Prevention Systems

The past 3 years has seen a rush of products to the market that claimed to offer new and exciting "intrusion prevention" capabilities. Intrusion-prevention-product vendors' claims are many and include

1. Interpreting the intent of data contained in the application payload
2. Providing application level analysis and verification
3. Understanding enough of the protocol to make informed decisions without the overhead of implementing a client/server model as is done with application proxies
4. Utilizing pattern matching, heuristics, statistics and behavioral patterns to detect attacks and thereby offer maximum attack prevention capability

Unfortunately many intrusion prevention systems are still at best "born-again" intrusion detection systems with the ability to drop, block, or reset a connection when it senses something malicious. Nearly all IPS systems depend on a library of signatures of malicious activity or known vulnerabilities to compare to packets as they cross the wire. The real value of the IPS is the accuracy and timeliness of the signature database of known vulnerabilities. With BugTraq, Xforce, and others currently posting well over 100 new vulnerabilities each month in commercial and opensource applications and operating systems, the chances of something being missed by the IPS vendor are quite high. The IPS methodology places the administrator in the middle of an arms race between the malicious hacker community (developing exploits) and the IPS vendor's technical staff (developing signatures).

The author is still of the opinion that signature-based IPS systems that rely explicitly on the knowledge of all possible vulnerabilities expose the user to unnecessary risk. Using a modern application layer firewall with a well thought-out security policy and patching all servers that are publicly accessible from the Internet could ultimately afford better protection.

Alternate IPS approaches, especially host-based approaches that rely upon heuristics, statistics, and behavioral patterns, still show promise but need to develop more of a track record for success before they should be relied upon as a primary security device. Therefore, at this point in time, the author considers IPS to be a technology to complement an existing conventional network security infrastructure, not replace it.

Both the pros and cons of IPS considerations are shown in Table 11.

Deep Packet Inspection

Deep-packet-inspection-based firewalls are still, in 2006, doing little more than comparing old outdated vulnerability signatures against traffic flow. Similar to the early days of anti-virus products, someone must get hacked before the vulnerability shows up on radar. The user or administrator then must wait for the vendor to research and define a signature so they can download it to begin to have some degree of risk mitigation from the threat.

Table 10 Application-specific integrated circuit (ASIC)-based firewall considerations.

Pros	Cons
ASIC provides a dramatic improvement in IPSec encryption and decryption speeds	SSL VPN is gaining popularity quickly and current ASIC-based vendors do not support SSL encryption and decryption; current technology ASIC-based devices will become obsolete and will need to be replaced with next generation products
ASIC fast string comparison capability dramatically speeds up packet inspection against known signatures	While this works well up through layer 4 it has not been shown to offer a benefit above layer 4 where the majority of attacks are currently targeted
ASIC-based firewalls offer the ability to inspect packets at all 7 layers of the OSI model	No current ASIC-based product offers administrator configurable security options above layer 4 within the respective product's GUI
ASIC firewalls are beginning to expand inspection up from basic protocol anomaly detection at layer 4 to the application layer to afford a higher level of security	Current ASIC-based firewall inspection methodologies are signature-based and try to block everything that can possibly be wrong in a given packet; more than 100 new vulnerabilities appear on the Internet every month making this a difficult task at best

Table 11 Intrusion Prevention System (IPS) considerations.

Pros	Cons
Provide application level analysis and verification	Current IPS product inspection methodologies are primarily signature-based and try to block everything that can possibly be wrong in a given packet. More than 100 new vulnerabilities appear on the Internet every month making this a difficult task
IPS is leading edge and can include heuristics, statistics and behavioral patterns in making determinations regarding decisions to block or allow specific traffic	Network security is a place for leading edge, not bleeding edge solutions. The use of heuristics, statistics and behavioral patterns are great ideas but lack the track record to be field proven as a reliable decision point to defend a network
	It is not rocket science. As the list of known signatures grows, IPS performance slows. The rate of newly discovered known bad things on the Internet is ever accelerating and, over time, could render the use of signature-based IPS unusable

The best description I have heard of deep packet inspection is standing in front of a fire house running at full blast while trying to grab cups of water that are known to be bad before the stream of oncoming water has a chance to pass by you.

Although I believe this signature-based model can afford a faster response from a vendor to support a new protocol or afford fast support of additional granularity in the application controls as applications mature, I also feel that a signature-based-only model is dangerous from a security perspective. This methodology carries all of the legacy issues seen in the flawed anti-virus signature-based approach: Because white space is tolerated by most applications, a little white space in the data before or after a command could logically cause the signature to fail to match the data. The hacker would then get to execute a command that the deep packet inspection firewall was supposed to prevent.

With Secunia reporting up to 100 new vulnerabilities a week as shown in Fig. 15 and vendors trying to keep up with developing new signatures to match the reported vulnerabilities, managing updates for the firewall signature database could become a daunting task.

Signature-based deep packet inspection effectively puts you in an arms race against an enemy with tens of thousands of more experienced people than you have within your organization.

Last, scalability must be considered. How long will it take to exhaust the processor resources of today's deep packet inspection firewall? In analyzing the literature for one popular deep packet inspection firewall, it states that the initial product release will provide for 250 signatures and the total firewall signature capacity is stated at only 600 signatures. At the current rate of new vulnerabilities reported by Gartner, you could effectively be out of room for new signatures in a matter of weeks. Furthermore, the

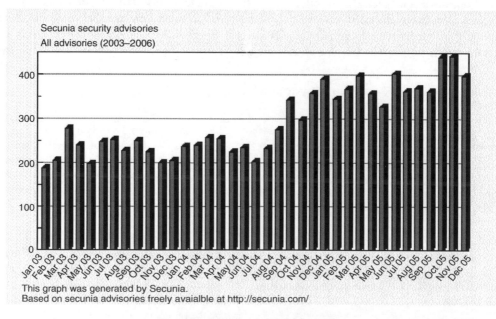

Fig. 15 Secunia security advisories.

popular open-source IDS, Snort, today has nearly 4000 signatures for malicious packets. Today's deep packet inspection firewalls ship with a signature database of only 250 signatures. What about the other 3750 signatures known to define malicious packets? Current deep packet inspection firewalls effectively allow a third party with no vested interest in your organization to determine or prioritize which attacks to protect you from and which attacks to not impede.

The signature-based model used by the majority of deep packet inspection offerings is simply the wrong approach. Best practices permit only those packets you define within your policy to enter or exit your network. This is a time-proven methodology and the bottom line is that it is a good common-sense approach to network security.

The lack of protocol anomaly detection is the Achilles' heel of deep packet inspection. A vendor's approach to protocol anomaly detection reveals a great deal about their basic design philosophy and the capabilities of their network security products as shown in Fig. 16. The tried-and-true practice with strong application-proxy firewalls is to allow only the packets that are known to be "good" and to deny everything else. Because most protocols used on the Internet are standards-based, the best approach is to design the application proxy to be fully protocol-aware, and to use the standards as the basis for deciding whether to admit or deny a packet. Only packets that demonstrably conform to the standard are admitted; all others are denied.

Deep packet inspection firewalls, like most stateful inspection firewalls and many IDS and intrusion detection and prevention (IDP) products, take the opposite approach. Rather than focusing on recognizing and accepting only good packets, they try to find—and then deny—only the "bad" packets. Such devices are vulnerable because they require updates whenever a new and more creative form of "bad" is unleashed on the Internet. Sometimes, especially with ASIC vendors who implement these packet rules in silicon, it is impossible to make these changes at all without replacing the ASIC itself.

Another problem with the "find and deny the bad" methodology is its intrinsic inefficiency. The list of potentially "bad" things to test for will always be much greater than the pre-defined and standardized list of "good" things.

One can, of course, argue that the "find and deny the bad" approach provides additional information about the nature of the attack, and the opportunity to trigger a specific rule and associated alert. However, it is unclear how this really benefits the network administrator. If the attack is denied because it falls outside the realm of "the good," does the administrator really care which attack methodology was being employed? As many have seen with IDS, an

Espionage –
Firewalls

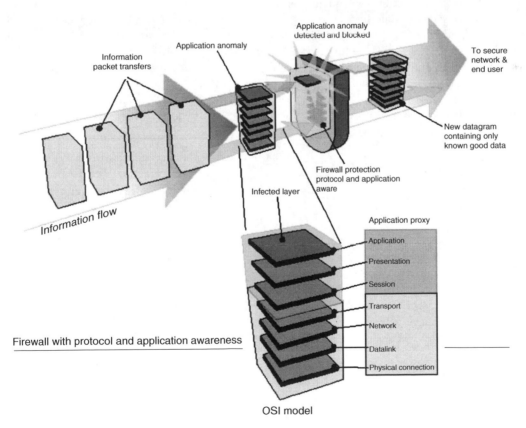

Fig. 16 Vendor's approach to protocol anomaly detection reveals a great deal about their basic design philosophy and the capabilities of their network security products.

administrator in a busy network may be distracted or over-whelmed by useless noise generated by failed attacks.

The simplified path of a packet traversing a strong application proxy is as follows:

1. The new packet arrives at the external interface.

    Layer-4 data is tested to validate that the IP source and destination, as well as service ports, are accep-table to the security policy of the firewall. Up to this point, the operation of the application proxy is similar to that of stateful packet filtering. For the most part, the similarities end here.

    The RFC-mandated TCP three-way-handshake (http://www.faqs.org/rfcs/rfc793.html) is fully vali-dated for each and every connection as shown in Fig. 17.

    If the three-way handshake is not properly com-pleted, the connection is immediately closed before any attempt is made to establish a connection to the protected server. Among other benefits, this approach effectively eliminates any possibility of SYN flooding a protected server.

    This is where vital differences become apparent. Many stateful inspection firewalls do not validate the three-way handshake to achieve higher performance and packet throughput. In the author's opinion, this approach is dangerous and ill-conceived because it could allow malicious packets with a forged IP address to sneak past the stateful firewall.

    More troubling is the "fast path" mode of operation employed by some stateful inspection firewall ven-dors. When "fast path" is engaged, the firewall inspects only those packets in which the SYN flag is set. This is extremely dangerous. Given the avail-ability of sophisticated and easy-to-use hacking tools

online, any 13-year-old with a modem and a little spare time can exploit this weakness and penetrate the fast-path-mode firewall simply by avoiding the use of SYN-flagged packets. The result: malicious packets pass directly through the firewall without ever being inspected. An informed network adminis-trator is unlikely to open this gaping hole in his or her security infrastructure to gain the marginal increase in throughput provided by fast path.

2. For each "good" packet, a new empty datagram is created on the internal side of the firewall.

    Creating a brand new datagram completely elim-inates the possibility that an attacker could hide mal-icious data in any unused protocol headers or, for that matter, in any unused flags or other datagram fields. This methodology—part of the core application proxy functionality found within strong application proxy firewalls—effectively eliminates an entire class of covert channel attacks.

    Unfortunately, this capability is not available in any stateful inspection firewall. Instead, stateful inspection firewalls allow attackers to make a direct connection to the server, which is supposedly being protected behind the firewall.

3. Protocol anomaly testing is performed on the packet to validate that all protocol headers are within clearly defined protocol specifications.

    This is not rocket science, although there is some elegant engineering needed to do this quickly and efficiently. Because Internet protocols are based on published standards, the application proxy uses these as the basis for defining what is acceptable and denies the rest.

    Stateful inspection firewall vendors have tried to address this requirement by adding limited filtering

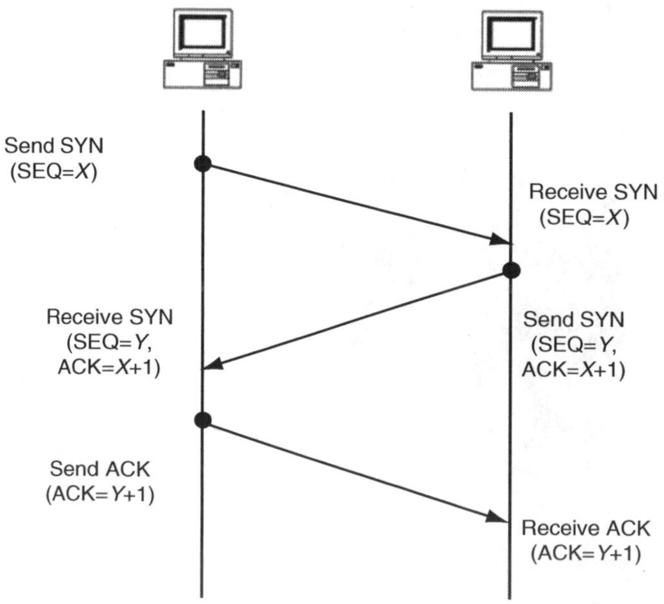

Fig. 17 The RFC-mandated TCP three-way-handshake is fully validated for each and every connection.

capabilities intended to identify attack-related protocol anomalies and then deny these "bad" packets. Unfortunately, this approach is inherently flawed.

Most stateful inspection firewalls employ a keyword-like filtering methodology. Rather than using the RFC-defined standards to validate and accept good packets (our "virtue is its own reward" approach), stateful inspection firewalls typically filter for "bad" keywords in the application payload. By now, the problem with this approach should be evident. There will always be new "bad" things created by malicious users. Detecting and accepting only those packets that adhere to RFC standards is a more efficient and—in this writer's opinion—a far more elegant solution.

Consider the SMTP protocol as an example. A strong application proxy applies the RFC 821 standard for the format of ARPA Internet text messages (http://www.faqs.org/rfcs/rfc821.html) and RFC 822 simple mail transfer protocol (http://www.faqs.org/rfcs/rfc822.html) standards to validate protocol adherence. It also lets you define "goodness" using another dozen or so protocol- and application-related data points within the SMTP packet exchange. This enables an administrator to minimize or eliminate the risk of many security issues that commonly plague SMTP applications on the Internet today, such as:

- Worms and virus attacks
- Mail relay attacks
- Mime attacks
- SPAM attacks
- Buffer overflow attacks
- Address spoofing attacks
- Covert channel attacks

In contrast, a stateful inspection firewall must compare each packet to the pre-defined signatures of hundreds of known SMTP exploits—a list that is constantly growing and changing. This places the security professional in a virtual "arms race" with the entire hacker community. You will never be able completely filter your way to a secure network; it is an insurmountable task.

Another element of risk with filter-based approaches is vulnerability. Attackers frequently "fool" the filter simply by adding white space between the malicious commands. Not recognizing the command, the firewall passes the packet to the "protected" application, which will then disregard the white spaces and process the commands. As with any filter, if the signature does not explicitly match the packet, the packet will be allowed. No network administrator can confidently rely on such a vulnerable technology.

With the strong application proxy approach, virtually all SMTP-related attacks could be mitigated more effectively and efficiently than is possible with the filtering approach used by stateful inspection vendors.

4. The application proxy applies the (very granular) command-level controls and validates these against the permission level of the user.

The application proxy approach provides the ultimate level of application awareness and control. Administrators have the granularity of control needed to determine exactly what kind of access is available to each user. This capability is nonexistent in the implementation of most stateful inspection firewalls.

It is difficult or impossible to validate claims made by many stateful inspection firewall vendors that they provide meaningful application-level security. As we have seen, the "find and deny the bad" filter-based approaches are inefficient and vulnerable. They simply do not provide the same level of security as a strong application proxy firewall.

5. After the packet has been recognized as protocol-compliant and the application-level commands validated against the security policy for that user, the permitted content is copied to the new datagram on the internal side of the firewall.

The application proxy breaks the client/server connection, effectively removing any direct link between the attacker and the protected server. By copying and forwarding only "good" contents, the application proxy firewall can eliminate virtually all protocol level and covert channel attacks.

Stateful inspection firewalls do not break the client/server connection; hence, the attacker can establish a direct connection to the protected server if an attack is successful. Because all protection requires the administrator to update the list of "bad" keywords and signatures, there is no integral protection to new protocol level attacks. At best, protection is only afforded to known attacks through inefficient filtering techniques.

A strong application proxy elevates the art of protocol and application awareness to the highest possible level as shown in Fig. 18.

Unified Threat Management

One of the latest developments in firewalling is the Unified Threat Management (UTM) appliance.

IDC defines universal threat management security appliances as products that unify and integrate multiple security features integrated onto a single hardware platform. Qualification for inclusion within this category requires network firewall capabilities, network IDP, and

Espionage –
Firewalls

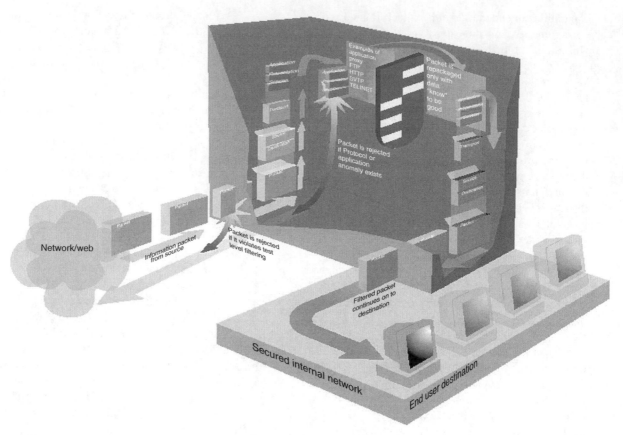

Fig. 18   A strong application proxy elevates the art of protocol and application awareness to the highest possible level.

gateway anti-virus (AV) functionality. All of these security features do not need to be utilized concurrently, but need to exist in the product.

The UTM segment of the firewall market is currently the fastest growing segment and has resulted in a large number of entries in to the market that can, at best, be called "premature" entries.

The author regards a UTM product offering as one that also brings together best-of-breed technologies. Unfortunately for the consumer, for a vast number of product entries in to this market, vendors are falling far short of utilizing best-of-breed technologies. Many vendors, to both enter the market quickly and to increase product margins, have chosen to build basic UTM functionality themselves or to use rudimentary open-source solutions (see Table 12).

When it comes to UTM appliances, caveat emptor certainly applies. I will offer six simple questions to help you in your analysis of any UTM product:

1. Is the OS hardened to the kernel level utilizing type enforcement or MLS?
2. Does the vendor have a record of zero vulnerabilities in the product and the underlying OS?
3. Is the on box anti-virus solution a best-of-breed solution from a recognized leader?

4. Is the on the box anti-spam solution a best-of-breed solution from a recognized leader?
5. Is the on the box URL filter solution a best-of-breed solution from a recognized leader?
6. Is the on the box IPS based on the known good security model?

A "NO" answer to any of the above questions should immediately raise a red flag about the vendor's offering. Let me elaborate on why these six questions are so important.

1. To reduce costs, many vendors are simply utilizing an off-the-shelf commercial OS or a patched open-source OS, either of which comes with inherent risks. Why hack the firewall when you can simply hack the underlying OS and create a policy that allows you do whatever you wish?
2. Would you buy a new car if you knew in advance that the product had been the subject of a few dozen safety recalls in the past year or so? It is just as important to look at the record of vulnerabilities from security product vendors at reporting websites such as CERT.
3. To reduce costs and to get to the market quickly, some vendors are utilizing sub-standard homegrown anti-virus solutions or inadequate signature-based-only open-source solutions.

Table 12   Disparity in Unified Threat Management (UTM) Products.

	Vendor A	Vendor B
Operating system (OS)	Kernel-hardened OS with a strict compartmentalization approach to eliminate vulnerabilities	Patched *nix like OS. Vendor has a long history of OS vulnerabilities
Anti-virus	Best of breed market leading product with ability to block over 100,000 viruses	Vendors own antivirus solution containing only 66 virus signatures
Anti-spam	Best of breed full featured integrated anti-spam solution	Single anti spam signature available as an option
URL filtering	Integrated award winning web content filtering	No on the box URL filtering
Intrusion detection and prevention (IDP) capability	Full complement of layer-7 application defenses including protocol anomaly detection and controls. Real time user configurable alerts and user definable actions	Layer 7 filtering through signatures available as an option

4. To reduce costs and to get to the market quickly, some vendors are utilizing sub-standard antispam solutions that can be little more then a handful of signatures that produce more false positives then they tend to catch real spam. Furthermore, some vendors claim to offer anti-spam capabilities, but it is an off-the-box option that requires additional hardware and licensing expenses.

5. URL filtering is quickly becoming a first line of defense in the battle against the zero-hour threat. Many UTM vendors are offering what ranges from giving the user the ability to write their own URL list for those that the administrator desires to block, to a static list of old outdated URL's from a substandard URL filtering product. Relatively few UTM appliances use best-of-breed URL filtering capabilities on-box.

6. Spam has grown from a simple menace to a complicated threat in a very short time. It is imperative to reduce risk by reducing spam with a comprehensive best-of-breed anti-spam capability onboard the UTM appliance. Again, many UTM product offerings fall short in handling anti-spam by the reliance on inadequate signatures or moving the anti-spam duties off-board and requiring additional hardware and software licensing.

The author believes that the high growth rate of the UTM firewall segment will continue for the foreseeable future. The UTM firewall fills a long-empty void in the marketplace, specifically for the small to medium enterprise that needs the ease of use and lower total cost of ownership that can be afforded by a properly architected UTM appliance.

ACKNOWLEDGMENT

This, the fourth edition of the firewall architectures text, is based on a number of related white papers I have recently written as well as numerous books, white papers, presentations, vendor literature and several Usenet news group discussions I have read or participated in throughout my career. Any failure to cite any individual for anything that in any way resembles a previous work is unintentional.

REFERENCE

1. Marcus J. Ranum. The Grandfather of Firewalls. Firewall Wizard Mailing List, October 2000.

**Espionage –
Firewalls**

Firewall Architectures: Other Issues

Paul A. Henry, CISSP, CNE
Senior Vice President, CyberGuard Corporation, Ocala, Florida, U.S.A.

Abstract

Unfortunately for the Internet community at large, many administrators today design their security policy for their organization around the limited capabilities of a specific vendor's product. The author firmly believes all firewall architectures have their respective place or role in network security. Selection of any specific firewall architecture should be a function of the organization's security policy and should not be based solely on the limitation of the vendor's proposed solution. When connecting to the public Internet, the only viable methodology in securing a private network is the proper application of multiple firewall architectures to support the organization's security policy and provide the acceptable balance of trust and performance.

REMOTE ACCESS SECURITY

Telecommuting offers the enterprise a cost benefit while in many cases also improving the work environment and perhaps even the quality of life for the telecommuter. Unfortunately for many organizations, the rush to telecommuting has not been accompanied with the necessary security mechanisms to mitigate the increased risks that come with remote employee network access.

The first step in implementing telecommuting is to establish a security policy for remote workers. The remote access policy should augment your current enterprise security policy and should provide a periodic re-evaluation of access requirements. At a minimum, the policy should clearly address the following issues:

- Encryption of All data that traverses public networks
- Security of the remote endpoint

    — Firewall

        ○ Compromised remote laptop or PC can provide complete unimpeded access for a hacker behind the enterprise firewall using the provided VPN tunnel.

    — Anti-virus

        ○ Out-of-date anti-virus signatures—an anti-virus product with signatures that are 30 days or older is as bad as no anti-virus at all.

- Authentication

    — Internal authentication—password
    — External authentication—token

- Personal use of the PC or laptop by the employee
- Actions of a disgruntled employee
- Security management

Encryption of All Data That Traverses Public Networks

The most common solution to encryption for remote telecommuters is client-to-server VPN. Several enterprise firewalls provide IPsec VPN capabilities that can work seamlessly with edge devices at the employee's connection to the Internet. Managing the VPN connection in a small enterprise can be daunting, but it is achievable. However, in the large enterprise with perhaps hundreds or thousands of remote telecommuters, managing VPNs can be overwhelming. The maturity of IPsec VPN technology has caused the primary consideration to move from technology to manageability in selecting VPN solutions.

Security of the Remote Endpoint: Firewalls

In too many organizations, telecommuter security mechanisms are nothing more than a software firewall and anti-virus package on the remote PC or laptop with a VPN client connecting the mobile user to the corporate LAN at a point behind the gateway firewall. Although at first glance this may seem to be a secure solution, there are several risks that need to be considered.

Security of the Remote Endpoint: Anti-Virus Updates

Several firewall vendors now provide validation of anti-virus signatures on remote devices. They quarantine the user and do not allow access to any resources on the LAN

Encyclopedia of Information Assurance DOI: 10.1081/E-EIA-120046864
Copyright © 2011 by Taylor & Francis. All rights reserved.

while still providing access to the Internet to allow automatic updating of the anti-virus signatures.

Authentication

Authentication within the corporate network has its risks, but they pale in comparison to the risk of authentication across the public Internet. The tools available to the black-hat community, such as Rainbow Crack, have effectively rendered passwords obsolete. The IT manager is able to exercise additional controls within the LAN to mitigate at least some of the risks associated with internal authentication, but for the most part those controls cannot be enforced on the Internet. Although passwords may be acceptable within the LAN (at least for now), any authentication across the Internet has to be fully encrypted and should provide for a token to be used at the endpoint.

Personal Use of the PC or Laptop by the Employee

To minimize the risk of a remote employee laptop or PC being compromised and subsequently impacting the corporate LAN, Internet access for the remote laptop or PC must be controlled. The best solution is to configure the remote laptop or PC to use the enterprise gateway as the user's Internet gateway. This prohibits the user from surfing the Internet without complete policy enforcement by the enterprise gateway. The IT manager gets the benefit of the security mechanisms afforded by the enterprise gateway in providing a degree of control over where the user can surf with URL filtering and a second layer of anti-virus protection provided by the gateway for any files downloaded by the remote user.

Actions of a Disgruntled Employee

The actions of a disgruntled employee can be contained, but that depends on the connection point for remote users to the corporate network. Most organizations simply punch a hole through the corporate gateway and terminate VPN tunnels on a VPN server behind the firewall. This effectively bypasses policy enforcement by the gateway firewall. To facilitate complete policy enforcement, VPN tunnels should terminate at the gateway firewall. In the worst case, the VPN server should be located on a separate network segment and the gateway firewall should provide full policy enforcement for any LAN access.

Security Management

Security policy must be managed from the core of the enterprise to the edge. Relying on an unmanaged end point is a recipe for disaster. The end user should not be able to make any changes to the security policy of the remote firewall. The clearest methodology is to utilize a firewall that operates independently of the laptop or PC.

This can be facilitated with a standalone device or with an embedded device that operates independently of the laptop or PC (firewall PCI card). By keeping the firewall independent of the end user you solve the respective management issue. You also minimize the impact of vulnerabilities in the software or OS being taken advantage of by a hacker on the remote device.

PRIVACY ISSUES

Simply put, organizations were not meeting expectations and privacy concerns have reached the point where legislation was needed to ensure that personal privacy is protected. In the United States as well as in many other countries, nearly all Internet-related legislation enacted over the past few years has included some form of privacy protection. Privacy protection is much more than simply encrypting your employees' or customers' personal information. It begins by properly securing your Internet gateway and must include properly protecting your complete enterprise network. Rather than repeating it again here, please review the regulatory concerns section of this entry.

Apart from regulatory issues, the IT manager must consider threats to privacy from adware and spyware on internal employees. Current adware and spyware have become significantly more malicious and go well beyond installing cookies and reporting back where your internal users are spending time on the Internet. Recent adware and spyware packages have included payloads that set up key-loggers to capture user personal data and credentials, as well as Trojans that open back channels from the infected host to the hacker. Today, the IT manager must consider adware and spyware as top security threats and deal with them with the urgency and high priority required to mitigate broadening associated risks.

Most adware and spyware today rely upon application-layer vulnerabilities to infect hosts. The first step in mitigating the risk is to prevent adware and spyware from entering the LAN at the gateway. It is crucial that addressing application-layer security be part of your gateway firewall topology.

INSIDER THREATS

The insider threat to the corporate LAN has been declining since 2000 when it represented nearly 70% of attacks to well under 50% today. However, the hacking tools available for today's malicious users within the LAN have become both much more sophisticated in their capabilities and much easier to use. Although we have seen a decrease in frequency, it is not hard to imagine that with today's tools insider attacks are much more effective.

The first step in mitigating insider threats begins with security policy/procedures. The most important policy

Espionage –
Firewalls

area for mitigating the insider threat is how the organization handles employee terminations. Many organizations let respective managers' personal feelings and emotions determine how to handle security decisions when an employee is about to leave the company. Far too many organizations let the employee go about business for the two weeks many employees give as notice rather than risk offending the employees by terminating network access.

There are several schools of thought on how terminations should be handled, but the most effective method is to simply terminate all network access immediately upon learning of the termination.

When an employee is about to leave a company, chances are they have been looking for a job for some time prior to giving notice. The risk of the employee taking the opportunity to send customer lists and other intellectual property belonging to the enterprise directly to a new employer or perhaps home for later use is more common than many imagine. Using content filtering on all outbound access such as e-mail and FTP can help to mitigate the risk and give the HR and legal departments an opportunity to address the issue more effectively.

With any monitoring of employee communications, due care must be taken to properly inform employees that their communication is being monitored by the organization and that all communications using corporate-provided facilities are not private, are the property of the company, and are not intended for the personal use of employees. It is important to have your legal department weigh in on regulatory issues prior to implementing any monitoring or content-filtering programs.

The second-most important policy area is in defining zones of trust for business units within the organization. The zones of trust can then be enforced by either the gateway firewall or with internal firewalls. There should be a clear understanding that the current threat vector is at the application layer. Simply providing access control internally at layer 4 to enforce zones of trust falls short of addressing today's threats.

VLANs are incorporated into most firewalls available for both the gateway and internal use in the LAN. Many organizations today rely on VLAN technology as their primary means of security in separating zones of trust. While VLAN technology has matured and it has been some time since a notable vulnerability surfaced, my preference is to use physical interfaces to separate zones of trust and to use VLAN technology to afford additional segmentation within a specific zone of trust.

Beyond separating zones of trust, there are several other methodologies to support greater risk mitigation for insider threats, i.e., explicit application level access controls, encryption within the LAN, desktop firewalls, anomaly detection, and LAN-segment-based IDS. But it is important to note that the insider threat is a "people" issue, not a technology issue. Just like the Internet threat, you will not solve the insider threat by simply applying technology.

Priority should be first placed on policy, procedures, and awareness, then on technology.

INFRASTRUCTURE

With respect to firewalls, most infrastructure issues for IT managers can be avoided by simply not using equipment that affords only proprietary technologies. In most cases when I have been contacted about a particular client's infrastructure issue, the root cause was the previous installation of a proprietary product that now limited the client's future decisions.

- Selecting a proprietary VPN capability within a firewall in many cases limits your selection of clients and additional VPN servers to a specific vendor.

  — Care should be taken to use only IPsec-compliant VPN offerings and to validate the range of compliance with a third party such as the Virtual Private Network Consortium (http://www.vpnc.org).

- Selecting a proprietary authentication mechanism within a firewall in many cases limits your ability to expand the use of additional firewalls to that specific vendor.

  — Authentication methodologies such as RADIUS, Kerberos, and Open LDAP are becoming much more common non-vendor-specific alternates to proprietary authentication schemes.

- Selecting a firewall that affords a proprietary methodology to interact with other security products also limits the expansion of your security infrastructure to a limited set of partner vendors.

  — Open-source alternatives such as ICAP offer a viable alternative to vendor-specific communication schemes to third-party products across many different firewall vendor platforms.

There are several other infrastructure issues that are created by poor planning of network architecture. One common example is the failure to plan IP address space properly, thereby limiting addresses for future expansion. Several vendors recognized the need for a niche product to meet this need and a transparent firewall was offered to facilitate the lack of an available IP address. From a security perspective, a transparent firewall acts like a network address translation (NAT) device and also moves the filtering from layer 4, where the IP address is found, to layer 2, where decisions are made based on routing information. After looking carefully at several transparent firewall offerings, most cannot provide the necessary level of inspection to combat today's current threats. One has to wonder whether most infrastructure issues should not be solved by correcting the infrastructure instead of using a band-aid approach and seeking out a niche solution that avoids solving the problem and actually sacrifices security.

The balance of infrastructure considerations such as speed, protocol support, and features such as VLAN support and bandwidth management have been addressed by most mainstream firewall vendors.

APPLICATION SECURITY

With virtually every stateful firewall vendor jumping on the application security bandwagon, the job of the IT manager to select or manage a specific application security solution has become much more difficult.

A firewall vendor's approach to application security reveals a great deal about their basic design philosophy and the resulting capabilities of their network security products. The tried and true practice with strong application proxy firewalls is to allow only the packets that are known to be "good" and to deny everything else. Because most protocols used on the Internet are standards-based, the best approach is to design the application proxy to be fully protocol-aware, and to use the standards as the basis for deciding whether to admit or deny a packet. Only packets that demonstrably conform to the standard are admitted; all others are denied.

Most stateful inspection firewalls—as well as many IDS and IDP products—take the opposite approach. Rather than focusing on recognizing and accepting only good packets, they try to find—and then deny—only the "bad" packets. Such devices are vulnerable because they require updates whenever a new and more creative form of "bad" is unleashed on the Internet. Sometimes, especially with ASIC vendors that implement these packet rules in silicon, it is impossible to make these changes at all without replacing the ASIC itself.

Another problem with the "find and deny the bad" methodology is its intrinsic inefficiency. The list of potentially "bad" things to test for will always be much greater than the pre-defined and standardized list of "good" things. It's a lot like getting into heaven. Virtue should be its own reward.

One can argue that the "find and deny the bad" approach provides additional information about the nature of the attack, and the opportunity to trigger a specific rule and associated alert. However, it is unclear how this really benefits the network administrator. If the attack is denied because it falls outside the realm of "the good," does the administrator really care which attack methodology was being employed? As many have seen with IDS, an administrator in a busy network may be distracted or overwhelmed by useless noise generated by failed attacks.

WIRELESS SECURITY

Before we discuss the IT manager's firewall considerations with respect to wireless security, to put it into perspective we need to examine some (but clearly not all) of the more prevalent insecurity issues of wireless networks.

Wireless security has had its share of vulnerabilities. Just 3 years ago I would have never used the word "secure" in the same sentence as the words "wireless network." But many of the more serious security issues have been addressed and the ease of use and cost savings provided by properly configured wireless networks, for the most part, outweigh current security concerns.

To date the biggest issue with wireless security focused on the weakness of wireless equivalent protocol (WEP), the encryption methodology that was professed to afford an equal level of security as that which would be found in a hard-wired network. A poor implementation of the key scheduling algorithm of RC4 allowed publicly available hacking/cracking tools like AirSnort and WEPcrack to actually calculate the encryption key after passively collecting and analyzing a sufficient number of packets. Having tested AirSnort against my own home 802.11b wireless network, I found that by using a ping flood against the IP address of my access point, I was able to collect enough data to successfully crack the encryption key.

Many chose to implement VPN tunnels over 802.11b to overcome the issues of WEP, but managing VPN tunnels was a labor intensive issue and did not correct the underlying problem. The 802.11i standard seems to be on track for solving many of the insecurities of previous wireless standards. Other solutions to the WEP issue included technology solutions such as LEAP, which reduced the threat imposed by WEP by providing frequent encryption key changes. LEAP was a workable solution but had numerous compatibility issues with the installed base of existing wireless network products and it has simply not become a dominant product in wireless security.

WEP2 was developed as a secure replacement for WEP1 but was found to not be a panacea for the problems that plagued WEP1.

One of the most important developments in securing wireless networks has been WiFi protected access (WPA) as a replacement for WEP. WiFi protected access solves the encryption key issue by periodically generating a unique encryption key for each client. Other enhancements include extensible authentication protocol (EAP) that provides mutual authentication for further security enhancement. Although WPA has solved the WEP problem, it has created a separate issue in that it is a simple matter to run a DoS attack against a WPA-enabled device. A malicious hacker simply has to send two packets per second using the wrong key to bring down the wireless network.

For the IT manager considering firewalls with respect to wireless networks, the most important issue is the placement of the wireless access point. In the past, the most

Espionage –
Firewalls

common practice in introducing a wireless network for a corporate LAN was to plug the device in behind the firewall, enable WEP, and perhaps enable MAC address filtering. Quickly, IT managers learned that WEP could be cracked and MAC addresses could be forged, completely bypassing all wireless network security and putting the attacker behind the firewall with full unrestricted access to the enterprise LAN.

Regardless of any promise of security from any new wireless security technology, it is unthinkable to place an access point without firewalling the connection to the LAN.

Although WPA and EAP appear to have solved the encryption and perhaps the authentication issues, it is still prudent to carefully control access to the LAN. Should an attacker compromise a wireless-enabled device, it is conceivable they will use the wireless network to attack the LAN necessitating the use of a firewall. Further, with the most prevalent attacks today taking place at the application layer, it is suggested that the firewall be an application-layer firewall.

PATCH MANAGEMENT

Although many firewall vendors would like you to believe otherwise, patch management is a critical necessity, even for many firewalls. A quick check on the Internet's vulnerability reporting sites offers an eye-opening view of many firewall issues that required immediate patches to protect the private network connected to the Internet from possible compromise or DoS attack.

Beyond recognizing that firewalls are not beyond having vulnerabilities themselves, the next consideration for the IT manager should be handling patch management centrally for all firewalls within the enterprise. Many enterprises today utilize numerous firewalls within their security topology to secure and protect access to and from the LAN. Having to physically touch each and every firewall within the LAN to apply security patches or feature release patches creates a nightmare that most IT managers do not consider until they are in a situation where the task needs to be completed immediately to protect the network.

The best predictor of how to expect the frequency and urgency of firewall vendor patch releases is to examine the respective vendor's legacy of vulnerabilities by researching third-party reporting Web sites.

From a patch management perspective, the firewall vendor's centralized management software should be capable of

- Automatically periodically checking for available patches
- Downloading and validating the MD5 Hash of the respective patch
- Alerting the administrator to both the availability of the downloaded patch and urgency of the patch

- Allowing the IT manager to schedule/select which firewalls to apply the patch to and when
- Validating the patch has been installed correctly on those firewalls the patch was deployed upon
- Providing periodic "reminder" alerts as to the firewalls the IT manager chose not to apply patches to

LOOKING TOWARD THE FUTURE

Few vendors other then those that had always afforded real application-layer security were able to offer meaningful threat mitigation in 2005 to meet the shift to application-layer attacks. Although a flurry of new products or existing product retrofits appeared that tried to apply some form of application filtering at the application layer, most were only reactive in nature and were barely successful at blocking historical attacks.

Three new trends are upon us from the hacker community today:

- Zero-hour threats
- Socially engineering blended threats
- P2P (peer-to-peer) threats—Skype

Zero-Hour Threats

Historically, we had months to respond to new vulnerabilities before they manifested themselves into a viable threat. Simply put, over time the bad guys became better and the time between when a new vulnerability was discovered and when it became a viable threat quickly shrank from months to weeks and then to days. A new term called "zero-day" threat was used to describe these new threats that went from discovered vulnerability to viable threat in as little as 24 hours zero-day threat was unfortunately a short-lived term. By the end of 2005, hackers were developing and releasing exploits that automatically altered their signatures as they infected each and every new machine. Every new compromised machine went on to compromise the next after altering the malicious code in a manner that made it impossible to detect if a signature developed on the current machine were used to detect an attack on the second machine.

The current environment reminds the author of the early days of signature-only anti-virus products. As the threat evolved to the point that it was impossible for vendors to create signatures fast enough to keep up, new methodologies such as heuristics were added to anti-virus products to give them a fighting chance.

Fortunately for the security community at large, application-layer firewalls that work within the construct of the "known good security model" already have an inherent heuristic capability. Those vendors that rely upon signatures only and use the "known bad security model" unfortunately will not be able to afford meaningful protection against the current zero-hour threats we are faced with and will be forced to evolve or perish.

Socially Engineered Blended Threats

The best example of a socially engineered blended threat would be phishing. The hacker uses a socially engineered e-mail to entice a victim to a fake Web site where his credentials are stolen with some form of a "man in the middle" (MITM) attack. The threat requires a combination of methodologies to mitigate the risk:

- Anti-spam
- URL filtering
- Application-layer protection
- Strong two-factor authentication

P2P-Skype: Both a Technical Marvel and Perhaps a Pandora's Box

- Technical marvel—free high-quality VOIP for the masses.

  — Voice quality is reasonable to very good and you cannot beat the cost—it is free when calling from any Skype-enabled PC to another Skype-enabled PC. Furthermore, the available feature to call a landline phone from a Skype-enabled PC is reasonably priced, even when looking at international calls. Clearly, the quality and price of calls made with Skype (and other VOIP alternatives) will change telephone communications as we (and the telephone companies) know it today.

- Opening Pandora's box. There are several inherent security risks to permitting the use of Skype or similar P2P/VOIP applications within an enterprise environment:

  — Skype includes the ability to send and receive files similar to other peer to peer programs/services.
  — Because the file transfers are over an encrypted channel (HTTPS), the inbound file transfers can effectively bypass the enterprise gateway security mechanisms.

- Confidential corporate data from within the enterprise could potentially be sent out over the Skype encrypted channel, effectively bypassing any enterprise SOX control mechanisms

  — Skype offers a "chat" capability that also utilizes the encrypted channel that potentially can hide the chat communications from many current chat control mechanisms that have been deployed to attain Sarbanes–Oxley compliance.
  — Lastly, the lack of centralized telephone call records could potentially be another SOX issue.

Because many administrators simply allow internal users to initiate HTTPS sessions to the public Internet, virtually all of the activities taking place when Skype is used will remain hidden to the enterprise security mechanisms.

Version 1.4 of Skype offers the ability to set a registry key to disable file transfers, but a knowledgeable user can simply change the key, restart Skype, and turn the feature back on.

Beyond simply blocking all outbound HTTPS for your users or perhaps using an application-layer defense that is able to participate in the HTTPS handshake and detect a known anomaly unique to Skype, the only other effective methodology to control Skype today is to utilize SSL scanning technologies that effectively facilitate a man-in-the-middle attack on the Skype communication channel. In the simplest of terms, the Skype connection is intercepted by the SSL scanner and is decrypted using a local certificate enabling full content inspection and policy enforcement. If the data is compliant with the enterprise security policy, the connection is then encrypted using the remote certificate and is forwarded across the public Internet to the end point.

ACKNOWLEDGMENT

This, the fourth edition of the firewall architectures text, is based on a number of related white papers I have recently written as well as numerous books, white papers, presentations, vendor literature and several Usenet news group discussions I have read or participated in throughout my career. Any failure to cite any individual for anything that in any way resembles a previous work is unintentional.

Firewall Architectures: Platforms

Paul A. Henry, CISSP, CNE
Senior Vice President, CyberGuard Corporation, Ocala, Florida, U.S.A.

Abstract

In spite of claims by respective vendors, no single firewall architecture is the "Holy Grail" in network security. It has been said many times, in many ways by network security experts, "If you believe any one technology is going to solve the Internet security problem, you don't understand the technology and you don't understand the problem." Unfortunately for the Internet community at large, many administrators today design their security policy for their organization around the limited capabilities of a specific vendor's product. The author firmly believes all firewall architectures have their respective place or role in network security. Selection of any specific firewall architecture should be a function of the organization's security policy and should not be based solely on the limitation of the vendor's proposed solution. When connecting to the public Internet, the only viable methodology in securing a private network is the proper application of multiple firewall architectures to support the organization's security policy and provide the acceptable balance of trust and performance.

FIREWALL PLATFORMS

OS Hardening

One of the most misunderstood terms in network security with respect to firewalls today is "OS hardening" or "hardened OS." Many vendors claim their network security products are provided with a "hardened OS." What you will find in virtually all cases is that the vendor simply turned off or removed unnecessary services and patched the OS for known vulnerabilities. Clearly, this is not a "hardened OS" but really a "patched OS."

What is a "real," hardened OS? A hardened OS is one in which the vendor has modified the kernel source code to provide for a mechanism that clearly provides a security perimeter between the non-secure application software, the secure application software, and the network stack. One common method of establishing a security perimeter is to write a label embedded within each packet as it enters the firewall. The label determines specifically what permissions the packet has and which applications can act upon the packet. If the packet's label does not afford the necessary permissions, then the packet is dropped as shown in Fig. 1. Although this methodology provides tight control over which packets can be acted upon by both secure and non-secure applications, it also affords a security perimeter in that external packets can be rejected if they attempt to act upon the secure OS kernel, secure network, and underlying hardware. This effectively eliminates the risk of the exploitation of a service running on the hardened OS that could otherwise provide root level privilege to the hacker.

The security perimeter is typically established using one of two popular methodologies:

1. Multilevel security: establishes a perimeter using labels assigned to each packet and applies rules for the acceptance of said packets at various levels of the OS and services.
2. Compartmentalization: not to be confused with a mere CHROOT jail, compartmentalization goes well beyond that of just a traditional sandbox approach—strong CHROOT jail whereby effectively an application runs in a dedicated kernel space with no path to another object within the kernel. Compartmentalization includes a full mandatory access control implementation and several other kernel-level hardening features:

- Network stack separation
- Triggers for intrusion detection
- Control of "super user" privileges
- Principle of least privilege

In contrast, a patched OS is typically a commercial OS from which the administrator turns off or removes all unnecessary services and installs the latest security patches from the OS vendor. A patched OS has had no modifications made to the kernel source code to enhance security.

Is a patched OS as secure as a hardened OS? No. A patched OS is only secure until the next vulnerability in the underlying OS or allowed services is discovered. An administrator may argue that when he has completed installing his patches and turning off services, his OS is secure. The bottom-line question is: with more than 100 new vulnerabilities being posted to Bug Traq each month, how long will it *remain* secure?

Encyclopedia of Information Assurance DOI: 10.1081/E-EIA-120046865

Copyright © 2011 by Taylor & Francis. All rights reserved.

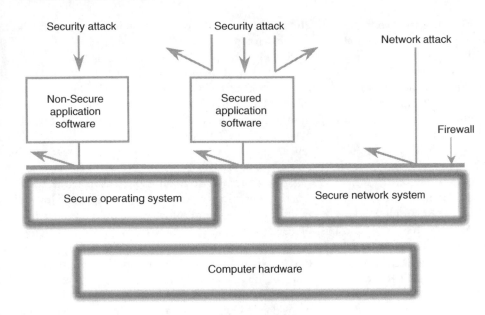

Fig. 1 The label determines specifically what permissions the packet has and which applications can act upon the packet. If the packet's label does not afford the necessary permissions, then the packet is dropped.

How do you determine if a product is provided with a hardened OS? If the product was supplied with a commercial OS, you can rest assured that it is not a hardened OS. The principal element here is that to harden an OS, you must own the source code to the OS so you can make the necessary kernel modifications to harden the OS. If you really want to be sure, ask the vendor to provide third-party validation that the OS is, in fact, hardened at the kernel level, i.e., http://www.radium.ncsc.mil/tpep/epl/historical.html.

Why is OS hardening such an important issue? Too many in the security industry have been lulled into a false sense of security. Decisions on security products are based primarily on popularity and price with little regard to the actual security the product can provide. With firewalls moving further up the OSI model, more firewall vendors are providing application proxies that operate in kernel space. These proxies, if written insecurely, could provide a hacker with root access on the firewall itself. This is not a "what if?" proposition; it just recently happened with a popular firewall product. A flaw in their HTTP security mechanism potentially allows a hacker to gain root access to the firewall, which runs on a commercial "patched" OS.

Where can I find additional information about OS vulnerabilities?

- http://www.securiteam.com
- http://www.xforce.iss.net
- http://www.rootshell.com
- http://www.packetstorm.securify.com
- http://www.insecure.org/sploits.html

Where can I find additional information about patching an OS? More than 40 experts in the SANS community worked together for more than a year to create two elegant and effective scripts:

- For Solaris: http://yassp.parc.xerox.com/
- For Red Hat Linux: http://www.sans.org/newlook/projects/bastille_linux.htm

Lance Spitzner has written a number of great technical documents (http://www.enteract.com/~lspitz/pubs.html):

- "Armoring Linux"
- "Armoring Solaris"
- "Armoring NT"

Stanford University has also released a number of excellent technical documents (http://www.stanford.edu/group/itss-ccs/security/Bestuse/Systems/):

- Redhat Linux
- Solaris
- SunOS
- AIX 4.x
- HPUX
- NT

Hardware-Based Firewalls

The marketing term hardware-based firewall is still a point of confusion in today's firewall market. For clarification, there is simply no such thing as a purely hardware-based firewall that does not utilize a microprocessor, firmware, and software (just like any other firewall) on the market today. Some firewall vendors eliminate the hard disk, install a flash disk, and deem their product a hardware-based firewall appliance. Some may go as far as to use an ASIC to complement the microprocessor, but they still rely upon underlying firmware, software, and, of course, a microprocessor to accomplish the tasks that make it a firewall.

Ironically, those vendors that eliminated the "spinning media" hard disk in an effort to improve environmental considerations such as vibration and temperature are now seeing next-generation hard drives that can exceed some of the environmental conditions of the flash or electronic media that was developed to replace them. In high-temperature environments, a traditional firewall with a hard disk might very well offer better physical performance characteristics than a supposed "hardware-based" firewall that uses a form of flash memory.

Another consideration in the hardware-based firewall approach is a either severely limited or complete lack of an historical log and local alert archiving. Although at first glance a hardware-based appliance looks like a simple approach, you may very well have to add the complexity of a remote log server to have a useable system with at least some form of minimal forensic capability in the event of an intrusion.

Other Considerations

Firewall topologies

The use of a multilayer dual-firewall topology is relatively new in network security, but it is rapidly gaining in popularity. In many respects, a dual-firewall topology is similar to that of an industrial process control system's one-out-of-two (1oo2) protection schemes (Fig. 2). This 1oo2 protection scheme has been used

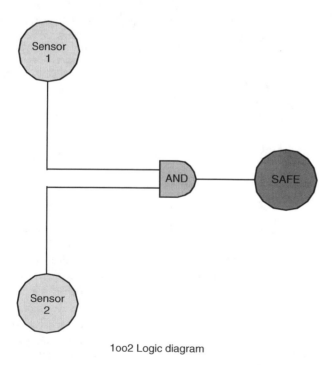

1oo2 Logic diagram

Fig. 2 A dual-firewall topology is similar to that of an industrial process control system's on-out-of-two (1oo2) protection schemes.

effectively to mitigate risk in industrial process control systems for many years.

Network security can benefit from the lessons learned in the evolution of process control systems. In an industrial process control system, it was recognized long ago that the failure of a single critical input from a sensor that signals an unsafe condition could have catastrophic results. In an effort to mitigate this risk, industrial process control system designers devised a scheme whereby instead of relying on a single sensor measuring a process variable, two separate sensors were used and each sensor had a "vote" on whether conditions were safe or not. The voting logic of the industrial process control system would consider the vote of each sensor and, if both sensors did not agree that conditions were safe, the system would initiate a safe shutdown process to prevent a catastrophic failure. Hence, to continue normal operations, both of the two sensors must agree conditions are safe.

A dual-firewall topology is similar to an industrial process-control system 1oo2 voting scheme in that both firewalls must agree that a received packet does not pose a security risk (conditions are safe) or the packet is denied and not permitted to be passed to the protected network as shown in Fig. 1. Hence, to continue normal operations (allowing packets to pass through the firewall), both of the two firewalls (sensors) must agree conditions are safe as shown in Fig. 3.

I have seen a clear increase in the use of dual-firewall topology in the enterprise network security environment. Unfortunately, many of the deployments I have seen include a critical error that eliminates most, if not all, of the risk mitigation capability normally found in a properly designed topology. Although they have indeed used two firewalls in series, the system designer has made the error of using a packet-filtering firewall in front of an application-proxy firewall in the mistaken assumption that this dual-firewall topology will increase risk mitigation. The bottom line in this topology is that all that has been accomplished is a decrease in reliability and manageability with no increase in risk mitigation.

Let me explain why I believe this topology is incorrect and why many are now living unknowingly with a false sense of security derived from relying on the dual-firewall topology described above. Clearly, hackers have exhausted the available "protocol level" attacks up through layer 4. Today, the majority of attacks launched against private enterprise networks via the Internet are application-level attacks. In a dual-firewall topology where a packet-filtering firewall is in front of an application-proxy firewall, an application-level attack simply passes through the first firewall completely unchecked and your only defense is the second firewall. There is no increased risk mitigation when the first firewall never inspects the payload of the packet and you are relying completely on the second firewall as your defense as shown in Fig. 4.

Espionage –
Firewalls

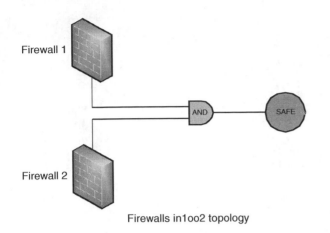

Firewalls in1oo2 topology

Fig. 3 To continue normal operations, both of the two firewalls (sensors) must agree conditions are safe.

Some might argue that in the topology above there is an increase in security because the attacker has to break through the first firewall and is then confronted by a second layer of defense provided by the application-level firewall. The logic in this argument fails because, in fact, the attacker does not have to "break" through the first firewall to pass his application-level attack. The attack simply passes through the open packet-filtered ports of the first firewall without detecting the application-level attack. It is as if the application-level attack did not exist. The only potential for risk mitigation is in the second firewall's application proxy. As far as the attacker is concerned, during an application-level attack in this topology, the first firewall does not exist.

The only possible benefit to the enterprise in the topology described above would be that, by screening packets, the first firewall may enhance the performance of the second firewall. If you only allow those services supported by the application proxy firewall (second in line) to be passed by the packet-filtering firewall (first in line) you eliminate the CPU load of having to screen all of the

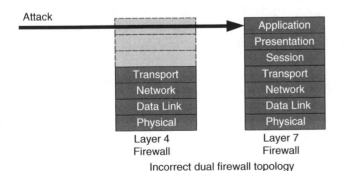

Incorrect dual firewall topology

Fig. 4 There is no increased risk mitigation when the first firewall never inspects the payload of the packet and you are relying completely on the second firewall as your defense.

packets on the second firewall. Personally, I believe your money would be better spent purchasing a faster hardware platform for the application-level firewall than spending money on a packet-filtering firewall to reduce the load on the application-level firewall.

Reliability is also a consideration in a dual-firewall topology. With two firewalls in series, you are reducing overall reliability. A failure of either firewall, whether it is a failure of the firewall hardware or failure due to an attack directed against a vulnerability in the firewall software or underlying OS, can shut down your Internet connectivity. A firewall is not necessarily the "holy grail." Firewalls themselves are not immune to vulnerabilities. A search at CERT, CIAC, X-Force, or CVE will reveal numerous vulnerabilities in many popular firewalls.

The risk increases when running a firewall on top of a commercial OS because of the associated vulnerabilities observed in these respective operating systems. Vulnerability statistics for any commercially available or open source operating systems can be found at http://www.secunia.com.

Multiple firewalls in a 1oo2 topology: getting it right

Increased risk mitigation is clearly attainable in a 1oo2 topology through the use of a multiple-firewall topology between the public Internet and private networks. However, to attain this higher risk mitigation there are three simple rules that must be followed:

1. Both firewalls must inspect all seven layers of the OSI model.

    Using a packet-filter firewall that inspects packets only up to layer 4 of the OSI model as your first firewall and a firewall that inspects all seven layers of the OSI model as your second firewall effectively eliminates any risk mitigation. At the same time, it decreases overall reliability and manageability when compared to using a single standalone firewall.

2. The inspection methodologies must use disparate technology.

    Using two firewalls that inspect all seven layers of the OSI model but rely on the same software and inspection methodology provides little, if any, risk mitigation; at the same time, it decreases overall reliability when compared to using a standalone firewall.

3. The firewalls must operate on top of disparate operating systems.

    Using the same OS on both firewalls reduces risk mitigation because a single exploit of the OS can take out both firewalls.

With current technology, industrial process-control system designers have actually gone further in increasing

Espionage – Firewalls

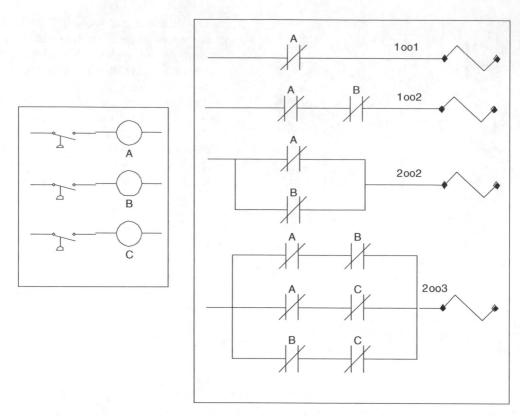

Fig. 5   Current process control system topologies.

Espionage –
Firewalls

risk mitigation and have effectively solved the reduced reliability issues in a one out of two (1oo2) voting scheme by developing two-out-of-three (2oo3) voting schemes that afford redundancy in the voting logic as shown in Fig. 5. Inherently, 2oo3 voting schemes offer measurably higher risk mitigation while increasing overall reliability through redundancy of key failure points in the system.

In network security, a 2oo3 firewall topology is likely to be too complex and expensive to deploy and manage. At a minimum, however, we can learn from the designers of the industrial 2oo3 scheme and obtain a cost-effective increase in reliability, at least with respect to the firewall hardware, through the use of redundancy in 1oo2 multiple firewall topologies as shown in Fig. 6.

By using pairs of redundant firewalls in a 1oo2 voting scheme, you can mitigate a majority of the reliability issues related to firewall hardware while providing higher risk mitigation as shown in Fig. 7.

The ability to easily manage your 1oo2 firewall topology is critical to its long-term success. You need to be able to manage both firewalls together as if they were one to minimize configuration issues and errors. Using a centralized management scheme on the 1oo2 firewall topology, the administrator only has to deal with learning a single GUI and managing a single security policy. If a change is made on the central manager to the "single policy," it is automatically published to both firewalls in their respective proper data formats.

To meet the requirements for disparity of the filtering methodology and disparity of the underlying OS, network security system designers have typically had to source firewalls from separate firewall vendors. Managing firewalls from different vendors can be problematic because most commercial product vendors are not willing to share their intellectual property with competing application-level firewall vendors. Historically this has resulted in the inability of most application-firewall vendors to offer a centralized management product that was capable of managing products from multiple vendors. However, this is now beginning to change. Industry consolidation and the development of nextgeneration firewall technologies have led some vendors to develop management capabilities that could handle their existing products and their next-generation products as well as products acquired through consolidation. These vendors are now able to offer 1oo2 firewall topology solutions that meet the guidelines for disparity in the firewall technology and disparity in the OS along with comprehensive centralized management.

Using two firewalls in a multilayer dual-firewall topology (1oo2) can afford a beneficial increase in risk mitigation without negatively impacting reliability and manageability. However, unless done properly, there will be no appreciable increase in risk mitigation and, furthermore, it will cause a decrease in reliability and manageability.

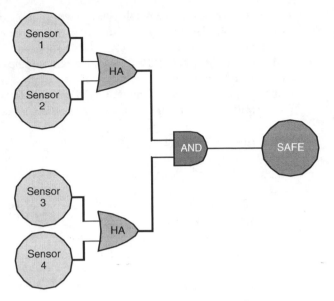

Fig. 6 Hybrid 1oo2 logic diagram.

Due to consolidation in the firewall industry as well as development of next-generation firewalls, it is possible today for the network security designer to acquire a bundled multilayer dual-firewall topology (1oo2) system from a single vendor that will meet all of the requirements of a properly configured topology, including redundancy, while providing a single management interface to reduce the management burden.

Firewall Considerations for the Security Manager

Regulatory compliance

The information provided is not to be considered an all encompassing guideline to achieving regulatory compliance as its intent is only to provide some of the firewall considerations for a subset of requirements for specific regulations. In

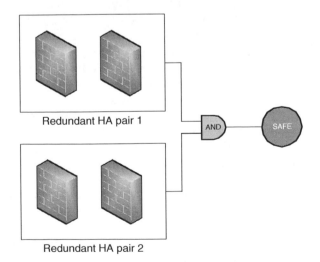

Fig. 7 Using HA pairs in 1oo2 topology.

the post-Enron era, IT managers are dealing with several regulatory requirements that were developed to help restore confidence in public corporations and, more specifically, the financial services industry. These regulatory requirements mandate corporate responsibility for financial as well as personal data. Although not an all-inclusive list, the major regulatory issues facing IT managers today are:

- Sarbanes–Oxley Act (SOX)
- California Senate Bill 1386
- Gramm–Leach–Bliley Act (GLBA)
- EU Data Protection Directive
- Basel II Accord
- USA Patriot Act
- Health Insurance Portability and Accountability Act (HIPAA)

Sarbanes–Oxley Act. Since the Securities Exchange Act of 1934, we have not seen any legislation other then perhaps the Foreign Corrupt Practices Act of 1977 that has so widely affected publicly traded companies. In the simplest of terms, Sarbanes–Oxley holds the officers of publicly traded companies personally responsible for the accurate reporting of financial information to investors and the general public. Private companies also need to comply with Sarbanes–Oxley requirements if they anticipate either becoming a public company in the future or being acquired by a public company.

With the requirement of personal responsibility upon them, executives are looking to the IT manager for the security controls that afford the required integrity of financial information.

Sarbanes–Oxley, in part, contains three rules that affect the management of electronic records. The first rule deals with destruction, alteration or falsification of records:

Sec. 802(a) "Whoever knowingly alters, destroys, mutilates, conceals, covers up, falsifies, or makes a false entry in any record, document, or tangible object with the intent to impede, obstruct, or influence the investigation or proper administration of any matter within the jurisdiction of any department or agency of the United States or any case filed under title 11, or in relation to or contemplation of any such matter or case, shall be fined under this title, imprisoned not more than 20 years, or both." (http://www.sox-online.com/act_section_802.html.)

The second rule, while very broad, defines the retention period for records storage:

Sec. 802(a)(1) "Any accountant who conducts an audit of an issuer of securities to which section 10A(a) of the Securities Exchange Act of 1934 (15 U.S.C 78j-1(a)) applies, shall maintain all audit or review work-papers for a period of 5 years from the end of the fiscal period in which the audit or review was concluded." (http://www.sox-online.com/act_section_802.html.)

A third rule, while again very broad, defines the type of business records that need to be stored. The rule covers all business records and communications, including electronic communications:

> Sec. 802(a)(2) "The Securities and Exchange Commission shall promulgate, within 180 days, such rules and regulations, as are reasonably necessary, relating to the retention of relevant records such as work papers, documents that form the basis of an audit or review, memoranda, correspondence, communications, other documents, and records (including electronic records) which are created, sent, or received in connection with an audit or review and contain conclusions, opinions, analyses, or financial data relating to such an audit or review." (http://www.sox-online.com/act_section_ 802.html.)

In meeting the intent of the first rule, the integrity of the business records and the respective communicating of them are a primary concern to the IT manager with respect to firewalls.

- With respect to integrity, access controls are important, but simply utilizing stateful packet filtering firewalls (layer-4-based technologies) to secure the business records in today's environment of application layer (layer 7)-based attacks is not a viable solution. It has been estimated that up to 70% of the installed base of firewalls is operating as stateful packet filters offering little or no defense from today's application layer attack.
- With respect to the communication of business records, a VPN is necessary to maintain confidentiality. Caution must be urged, as many have mistakenly assumed that a VPN also provides some level of data integrity protection. A VPN only protects the integrity of data in transit. The endpoints of the VPN tunnel must also be secured (firewall) to achieve data integrity. Because most firewalls today also provide VPN capability, this requirement can be reasonably met with a wide variety of products. However, care should be taken in selecting the firewall architecture. If no Internet access is afforded to protected servers storing financial data records behind the VPN/firewall, a layer-4 firewall may be adequate. But, if the VPN/firewall is also protecting access to private servers storing financial data records accessible to the Internet, then a layer-7 firewall is needed for data integrity.

In meeting the intent of the second rule, records must be maintained for a period of 5 years. Financial record storage must provide for the integrity of the data while stored and the confidentially of the data while in transit to and from storage. To protect data integrity, access controls are important but simply utilizing stateful packet-filtering

firewalls (layer-4-based technologies) to secure the stored business records in today's environment of application layer (layer 7)-based attacks is not a viable solution.

In meeting the intent of the third rule regarding the type of records to be retained, the requirement encompasses all business records and communications. The consideration of a firewall to support this requirement should include:

- Filtering and logging mail traffic. While it is a simple matter to store e-mail archives from the mail server, corporate e-mail is only part of the issue.

  — If the organization permits the use of Web mail from services such as Yahoo, AOL, or MSN in business-related communications, then that e-mail could also be included as part of business records and must also be logged. A firewall that can recognize and specifically log Web-based e-mail offers a centralized logging mechanism for permitted chat traffic.
  — If the organization wishes to block Web-based e-mail, then a firewall capable of filtering Web-based e-mail from within the HTTP data stream is required and the firewall logs should be able to reflect the blocked traffic.

- Consideration should also be given to the firewall's ability to provide a change control mechanism to provide proof of ongoing organizational compliance after an audit has concluded that the configuration meets SOX requirements.

California Senate Bill 1386. This California law effective July 1, 2003, is also referred to as the Security Breach Information Act. The law requires that all companies that do any business in California or that have any customers in the state notify those customers promptly whenever specific personal information may have been exposed to unauthorized parties in unencrypted form (http://info.sen.ca.gov/ pub/01-02/bill/sen/sb_1351-1400/sb_1386_bill_20020926_ chaptered.html).

Other than establishing that encryption is necessary to mitigate the requirement to notify, this law does not specify other "security controls" required for compliance. In an effort to meet the law's requirements, many organizations have implemented encryption to avoid the embarrassment and expense of notification.

Encryption by and of itself may be insufficient to assure compliance. There have been numerous organizations that were compromised prior to the law taking effect that lacked the necessary firewall log data to answer the basic question: "Was the confidential information stored on our servers exposed?"

Well before California Senate Bill 1386, I can recall one specific public company that was punished severely by Wall Street with a dramatic decrease in share value because weeks after they were attacked and the hackers bragged publicly about capturing their customers' credit card information from their database, they could not definitively state whether the data had, in fact, been exposed or not.

The IT manager's firewall considerations with respect to California Senate Bill 1386 should go well beyond implementing data encryption on stored customer records and should also include properly securing the Internet gateway with a firewall to first mitigate an attack and also to provide granular logging of a failed attack attempt to prove that data was not exposed. The firewall consideration should go beyond the popular trend of using a stateful packet filter limited to only defending against protocol level attacks at layer 4 and should provide for application layer attack mitigation to meet today's current Internet attack threats.

To provide data integrity, access controls are important but simply utilizing stateful packet-filtering firewalls (layer-4-based technologies) to secure the stored business records in today's environment of application layer (layer 7)-based attacks is not a viable solution.

Consideration should also be given to the firewall's ability to provide a change control mechanism to provide proof of ongoing organizational compliance after an audit has concluded that the configuration meets the requirements of California Senate Bill 1386.

Gramm–Leach–Bliley Act. The GLBA mandates privacy and protection of customer records maintained by financial institutions (http://www.ftc.gov/privacy/glbact/):

- Section 501(b) requires that financial services companies establish "administrative, technical, and physical safeguards." A set of guidelines is typically provided by respective regulatory bodies that offer a general but comprehensive closed-loop framework to provide regulatory compliance. Compliance with the Gramm–Leach–Bililey Act requires that financial institutions provide for the confidentiality and integrity of customer records including stored records and records being transmitted electronically.
- With respect to integrity, access controls are important but simply utilizing stateful packetfiltering firewalls (layer-4-based technologies) to secure the business records in today's environment of application layer (layer 7)-based attacks is not a viable solution. It has been estimated that up to 70% of the installed firewall base is operating as a stateful packet filter offering little or no defense from a current-day application-layer attack.
- With respect to communicating business records, a VPN is necessary to maintain confidentiality. Caution must be urged as many have mistakenly assumed that a VPN also provides some level of data integrity protection.

— A VPN only protects the integrity of data in transit and the endpoints of the VPN tunnel must also be secured (firewall) to achieve data integrity. Because most firewalls today also provide VPN capability, this requirement can be reasonably met with a wide variety of products. However, care should be taken in selecting the firewall architecture. If no Internet access is afforded to protected servers storing financial data records behind the VPN/firewall, a layer-4 firewall may be adequate, but, if the VPN/firewall is also protecting access to private servers storing financial data records accessible to the Internet, then a layer-7 firewall is needed for data integrity.

- Consideration should also be given to the firewall's ability to provide a change control mechanism to provide proof of ongoing organizational compliance after an audit has concluded that the configuration meets the requirements of the GLBA.

EU Data Protection Directive. This European Union Directive required that each of the 15 member nations of the European Union pass legislation requiring protection of the integrity and confidentiality of networks, systems, and data containing personal information. Any U.S. organization doing business with or having employees in the European Union could be impacted by the laws in the European Union that were enacted by this directive. For the most part, current regulations in the United States have only explicitly addressed the integrity and confidentially of customer records, but this directive clearly includes employee personal records as well (http://www.dataprivacy.ie/6aii.htm):

- With respect to the integrity of personal records, access controls are important but simply utilizing stateful packet-filtering firewalls (layer-4-based technologies) to secure the business records in today's environment of application layer (layer 7)-based attacks is not a viable solution. It has been estimated that up to 70% of the installed firewall base operates as a stateful packet filter offering little or no defense from a current day application layer attack.
- With respect to communicating personal records, a VPN is necessary to maintain confidentiality. Caution must be urged as many have mistakenly assumed that a VPN also provides some level of data integrity protection.

— A VPN only protects the integrity of data in transit and the endpoints of the VPN tunnel must also be secured (firewall) to achieve data integrity. Because most firewalls today also provide VPN capability, this requirement can be reasonably met with a wide variety of products.

- Consideration should also be given to the firewall's ability to provide a change control mechanism to provide proof of ongoing organizational compliance after an audit has concluded that the configuration meets the legal requirements passed by the European Union Directive.

Basel II Accord. Developed by the Bank of International Settlements, it was anticipated that the Basel II Accord would be finalized by the fourth quarter of 2003, with implementation to take effect in member countries by yearend 2006. The accord was enacted to regulate banks that operate internationally and it provides broad guidance for calculating operational risk to banks. Risk calculation includes identifying, assessing and managing risks the banking organization is facing. Based on the calculation, the bank is required to set aside a reserve to offset the risk. The higher the calculated risk, the higher the reserve requirements, a factor that could effectively lower the working capital available for the respective international bank (http://www.bis.org/publ/bcbsca.htm).

For the time being, the Basel II Accord is limited to banks operating internationally. Most U.S. securities firms are not obliged to comply. However, under rules proposed in late 2003, several large independent U.S. securities houses will also be subject to Basel II under the SEC Consolidated Supervised Entities (CSE).

Although the accord does not specifically address network security issues in any detail, international banks that offer Internet banking or are connecting their private networks to the public Internet would clearly face additional operational risks that would impact the their risk calculation.

- From a network security perspective, calculating risk for banks affected by the Basel II Accord should include the potential for loss of data confidentiality and integrity for financial records and customer personal information. Unprotected, the international bank would face dramatically higher reserves to offset this risk. Hence, a properly implemented network security program to protect the financial and customer records of the bank could have a significant impact on the bottom line though lowering reserve requirements.

  — With respect to Web sites operated for Internet banking, due consideration must also be given to protecting the confidentiality of data transmitted between the client and the bank's Web server. Further, data integrity for any data stored on the Web server, the Web server itself and any back end supporting systems that may be rendered accessible or compromised from an Internet-based attack must also be considered.

  — Risks associated with the losses at international banks from the current dramatic increase in phishing e-mail scams will undoubtedly come into consideration and will further increase the reserves required for banks offering account access for clients over the public Internet.

- With respect to the integrity of financial records and personal information, access controls are important but simply utilizing stateful packet filtering firewalls (layer-4-based technologies) to secure the business records in today's environment of application layer (layer 7)-based attacks is not a viable solution. It has been estimated that up to 70% of the installed firewall base are operating as stateful packet filters affording little or no defense from a current day application layer attack.

- Transmitting data via SSL to facilitate confidentiality while traversing the public Internet in Internet banking requires special consideration. There is a growing trend toward decrypting SSL on the firewall or just prior to the firewall to afford policy enforcement to mitigate the risk of malicious code reaching the Internet bank's Web server. After enforcing policy, the data stream can be encrypted again using a separate digital certificate to facilitate confidentiality while the data is routed within the bank's intranet.

- With respect to communicating financial records and personal information other than communication specifically between a client Web browser and the bank's Web server, a VPN is necessary to maintain confidentiality. Caution must be urged as many have mistakenly assumed that a VPN also provides some level of data integrity protection.

  — A VPN only protects the integrity of data in transit and the endpoints of the VPN tunnel also must be secured (firewall) to achieve data integrity. Since most firewalls today also provide VPN capability, this requirement can be reasonably met with a wide variety of products. However care should be taken in selecting the firewall architecture. If no Internet access is afforded to protected servers storing financial data records behind the VPN/firewall, a layer-4 firewall may be adequate; but if the VPN/firewall is also protecting access to private servers storing financial data records accessible to the Internet then a layer-7 firewall is needed for data integrity.

- Consideration should also be given to the firewall's ability to provide a change control mechanism to provide proof of ongoing organizational compliance after an audit has concluded that the configuration meets the requirements of the Basel II Accord.

USA Patriot Act. Enacted nearly 3 years ago, the Patriot Act did not really introduce any new legal instruments or actions because virtually all components covered within the Patriot Act were already present in existing law. The impact of the Patriot Act, for the most part, was to reduce requirements for judicial oversight on searches and seizures. It permits searches and seizures of electronic information by law enforcement without requiring notification of the person subject to the search or seizure for a reasonable time. Further, investigations can require a complete information blackout, forbidding IT managers or their staff from informing subjects that they are, in fact, under investigation (http:// www.epic.org/privacy/terrorism/ hr3162.html).

Under the Patriot Act, law enforcement has the authority to require you to take actions that may have a negative impact on business. This could include shutting down critical business servers causing business disruption or perhaps requiring that you not take any action and thereby allow a disruptive attack to continue while it is being investigated further. In the process of their investigation, they need have little regard for the consequences to your network and the resultant impact on your business.

For the IT manager it is not simply the actions of your employees or customers that you need be concerned with in an effort to keep your organization from being caught up in a Patriot Act investigation. The compromise of one of your network servers by an Internet-based attacker that is then used in an attack against a third party could very well land you in the middle of a Patriot Act investigation.

It is imperative that the IT manager have a security policy and incident handling procedure in place to effectively address the issues of being involved in a Patriot Act investigation.

The IT manager's primary consideration of firewalls with respect to the Patriot Act should address preventing both attacks which originate with malicious persons inside the corporate network and Internet-based attacks that compromise one of your servers which is then used in an attack against a third party.

To prevent malicious persons within the corporate network from involvement in an attack against an external network care should be taken to allow only the minimal outbound services necessary to meet organizational business objectives.

- For those services that are explicitly permitted an application layer firewall (layer 7) should be used to restrict the use of specific protocol and application commands to those deemed acceptable to the organization's security policy and procedures.

  — A stateful packet-filtering firewall (layer 4) does not inspect the payload in an allowed protocol and therefore provides little if any risk mitigation in an attack from within your network to another Internet-connected organization.

To prevent malicious persons outside the corporate network from compromising a publicly accessible server within your network and using that server in an attack against a third party, care should be taken to allow only the minimal inbound services necessary to meet organizational business objectives.

- For services that are explicitly permitted, an application-layer firewall (layer 7) should be used to restrict the use of specific protocol and application commands to those deemed acceptable to the organization's security policy and procedures.
- Each publicly accessible sever should be isolated on a single subnet to facilitate granular access control rules which could prevent the attacker from using the compromised server to attack other servers.

  — Access controls should only allow access to the publicly accessible server to be initiated from an individual on the public Internet.
  — No connections should be permitted either outbound to the public Internet or inbound to the corporate intranet from the publicly accessible server.

Consideration should also be given to the firewall's ability to provide a change control mechanism to provide proof of ongoing organizational compliance after an audit has concluded that the configuration meets the requirements of the Patriot Act.

Health Insurance Portability and Accountability Act. The HIPAA was enacted in 1996 to ensure the portability, privacy, and security of personal medical information. The act impacts any healthcare organization that maintains any electronic health information. Furthermore, it also impacts the healthcare organization's respective vendors or business partners. The act requires that these covered organizations must effectively implement administrative, technical and physical safeguards to protect the confidentiality and availability of electronic health information for their customers (http://www.cms.hhs.gov/hipaa/).

There are three primary rules under the HIPAA:

1. The privacy standard, which establishes privacy requirements for all of a customer's individually identifiable health information, including specific definitions of both authorized and unauthorized disclosures.
2. The transactions and code sets standard, which mandates that healthcare payers, providers and clearinghouses across the United States use predefined transaction standards and code sets for communications and transactions. This specific rule required compliance by October 2003.

3. The security standard, which specifically mandates securing the confidentiality, integrity and availability of customer's individually identifiable health information. Furthermore, the standard provides for patients' access to their specific records online upon request. This specific rule requires compliance by April 2005.

The IT manager's firewall considerations with respect to HIPAA should include:

- Properly securing the Internet gateway with a firewall to mitigate an attack against a network that contains personal medical records
- Providing granular access control for the server that contains the personal medical records
- Implementing data encryption on stored customer records
- Providing encryption of all data in transit across both public and private networks
- Providing granular logging of all external and internal network access to all secured records

The firewall considerations for the IT manager should go beyond the popular trend of using a stateful packet filter limited to only defending against protocol-level attacks at layer 4 and should provide application-layer attack mitigation to meets today's current Internet attack threats.

To provide data integrity access controls are important, but any access to database servers within private networks that are accessible from the public Internet should require the use an "application specific" strong application proxy for maximum risk mitigation.

Health Insurance Portability and Accountability Act requires proactive security measures including regular network testing and auditing to secure electronic information. Therefore, consideration should also be given to the firewall's ability to provide a change control mechanism to provide proof of ongoing organizational compliance after an audit has concluded that the configuration meets the requirements.

Lastly, in closing this section on regulatory compliance, several states have recently enacted new legislation as detailed in Table 1 for security breach notification. The author expects yet further changes before this current entry is published and urges IT managers to research the changes in state regulations that his organization is doing business in on a regular and ongoing basis.

Manageability. With respect to firewall manageability the ability to easily manage your firewall topology is critical to its long term success.

You can have the best firewalls available protecting your organization and yet still fail if you cannot properly, quickly, and, just as importantly, easily manage them.

Table 1 State laws regarding security breach notification.

State	Law	Effective date
Arkansas	SB 1167	6/1/2005
California	SB 1386	7/1/2003
Connecticut	SB 650	1/1/2006
Deleware	HB 116	6/28/2005
Florida	HB 481	7/1/2005
Georgia	SB 230	5/5/2005
Illinois	HB 1633	1/1/2006
Indiana	SB 503	7/1/2006
Louisiana	SB 205	1/1/2006
Maine	LD 1671	1/31/2006
Minnesota	HF 2121	1/1/2006
Montana	HB 732	3/1/2006
Nevada	SB 347	10/1/2005
New Jersey	A4001	1/1/2006
New York	SB 5827	12/7/2005
North Carolina	HB 1048	2/17/2006
North Dakota	SB 2251	6/1/2005
Ohio	HB 104	2/17/2006
Pennsylvania	SB 721	7/1/2006
Rhode Island	HB 6191	7/10/2005
Tennessee	HB 2170	7/1/2005
Texas	SB 122	9/1/2005
Washington	SB 6403	7/24/2005

To minimize configuration issues and errors, you must be able to manage all firewalls from core to edge across the organization and, indeed, the global enterprise together as a group as if they were one.

In using a centralized management scheme on the organization's firewall topology, the administrative team only has to deal with learning a single GUI and, effectively, managing a single security policy. A change made on the central manager to the "single policy" is automatically published to all firewalls in their respective proper data formats.

- Define and distribute firewall rules to one firewall or hundreds simultaneously
- Share configuration data between firewalls
- Support entities with multiple policies
- Configure firewall and VPN connectivity, including both VPN star and mesh topology
- Monitor and control firewall activity
- Simplify routine administrative tasks
- Manage ongoing changes to their security policies
- Manage other network devices (such as routers)

Object-based central management can allow administrators to define an object, such as a firewall, group of firewalls, network, or interfaces once and then reuse those objects wherever they are needed. When security policies change, an administrator can modify the objects and propagate the changes instantly throughout the enterprise.

Managing firewalls from different vendors can be problematic because most commercial firewall product vendors are not willing to share their intellectual property with competing firewall vendors. Historically, this has resulted in the inability of most application firewall vendors to offer a centralized management product that was capable of managing products from multiple vendors. However, this is now beginning to change. Industry consolidation and the development of next-generation firewall technologies have led some vendors to develop management capabilities that could handle their existing products and their next generation products as well as products acquired through consolidation. These vendors are now able to offer comprehensive central management across multiple firewall platforms.

ACKNOWLEDGMENT

This, the fourth edition of the firewall architectures text, is based on a number of related white papers I have recently written as well as numerous books, white papers, presentations, vendor literature and several Usenet news group discussions I have read or participated in throughout my career. Any failure to cite any individual for anything that in any way resembles a previous work is unintentional.

Espionage –
Firewalls

Firewall Architectures: Viruses and Worms

Paul A. Henry, CISSP, CNE
Senior Vice President, CyberGuard Corporation, Ocala, Florida, U.S.A.

Abstract

Although worms have evolved from both technological and social engineering perspectives, there has been little change in the basic method of propagation—the initial scanning phase in which the worm looks for the vulnerable hosts. Future worms will take advantage of new fast scanning routines that will dramatically accelerate the initial propagation phase and even use prescanning data to virtually eliminate that first slow phase of scanning for vulnerable hosts.

MITIGATION OF VIRUSES AND WORMS

AntiVirus Considerations

Times have changed. Virus authors used to write their malicious code to get their 15 minutes of fame. Today, virus writers are using malicious code to create armies of zombie computers referred to as *botnets*. These botnets are sold to spammers as e-mail relays and traded as currency that can be used to launch distributed denial-of-service (DDoS) attacks within the malicious hacker community.

Viruses have become more malicious, not only deleting files but including payloads of Trojans and keyloggers. At the same time, they have become more efficient, some even install their own miniature mail server to help speed distribution. Simply put, viruses and worms are hitting us with more malicious payloads, are spreading faster and, just as importantly, are mutating faster, clearly putting a strain on many antivirus vendors' abilities to effectively respond to the threat.

Regardless of the personal perspective you draw from the historical data found on the Internet, we can all agree that we have gone from single instances of viruses and worms that took perhaps weeks or maybe months to inflict measurable damage to viruses that spread in hours or perhaps minutes and quickly evolve into hundreds of variants, each more malicious then the last.

As we look toward the future, the pressure on antivirus vendors will not let up. New variants of each virus have grown from dozens to hundreds and virus creators are now using code that can actually alter the code within the viruses with new infection, making it much more difficult to identify the virus.

Most antivirus vendors would have customers believe that it is as simple as keeping your antivirus software up-to-date and you will be safe. However, looking at historical data the time that is required for vendors to respond can vary dramatically and leaves a considerable amount of time for exposure.

The time between a virus first being sighted and the release of an antivirus vendor's update that identifies the virus is commonly referred to as the *window of opportunity* for the given threat. Reviewing available data on the Internet still shows that while a handful of vendors are able to detect malicious programs and code without dependence on the explicit identification of the threat in a product update, some current-day antivirus vendors are still struggling to keep up with product updates in the face of ever faster and more malicious threats leaving users exposed to a window of opportunity that is simply unacceptable.

Different approaches by antivirus vendors include:

- Signature-based antivirus

  - Signature-based antivirus is probably the oldest type of antivirus. It is an exact science and produces very definitive results—either the virus matches the known signature or it does not. One of the big advantages to signature based antivirus is speed; it does not take a huge number of CPU cycles to compare malicious code to known signatures. Although it is a somewhat dated technology, it is gaining in popularity again as some security product vendors are now adding antivirus capabilities to their all-in-one security solutions and are trying to minimize the performance impact of the added capability.

  - Of further consideration is that signature-based antivirus offers good protection from only known threats, it is not effective against additional unknown variants of known threats and offers no protection from new unknown threats. This renders signature-based antivirus fully dependent upon the vendor's ability to react quickly and

Encyclopedia of Information Assurance DOI: 10.1081/E-EIA-120046866
Copyright © 2011 by Taylor & Francis. All rights reserved.

develop new signatures for new threats and release them to their users.

- Advanced signature-based antivirus

  — By reducing the signature size of a known vulnerability to a smaller segment of malicious code, antivirus vendors have been able to improve upon traditional signature-based antivirus in protecting against variants of known threats. However, this methodology really only provides a probability of a threat and is prone to false positives. Lastly, it suffers from the same issues of new vulnerabilities not having any known signature; it therefore has no real protection from new unknown threats

  — To reduce the maximum window of opportunity, a clever approach in both traditionalsignature- and advanced-signature-based antivirus deployment is the use of multiple antivirus products effectively connected in a series. The potentially infected code is inspected by each product one after the other and if any one of the vendors finds a match to their respective signatures, the code is flagged as malicious and appropriate action is taken. This methodology reduces the risk that the one vendor you chose to use has the worst response time for a given event by spreading the risk across multiple vendor's products— you take advantage of hopefully one of them perhaps being faster than the rest.

- Sandboxing-based antivirus

  — Rather then relying upon signatures, sandboxing actually provides a mechanism for the running of the potentially malicious code in an isolated environment in some form of a virtual machine. Sandboxing is more effective then signature-based antivirus but can still be fooled by a smart malicious code programmer that does a sufficient job of hiding the code's malicious intent, i.e., encrypting portions of the program that contain the malicious actions within the code's data section and only later decrypting the malicious code and applying it against the host.

  — There is a serious trade-off in performance vs. protection as the software for a sandbox methodology can consume significantly more processor cycles and will use considerably more of the host's physical memory than a signature-based antivirus methodology.

- Passive heuristics-based antivirus

  — In a passive heuristic antivirus methodology, you are doing little more than an advanced signature-based

antivirus. The vendor has established a library of code segments that are highly probable of being malicious and then searches through the potentially malicious code for the respective code segments. If found within the code, the subject is considered malicious and appropriate action is taken.

  — Although faster then sandboxing and perhaps more effective than traditional signature based antivirus, passive heuristic-based antivirus can still be easily fooled by a knowledgeable malicious code programmer using encryption, run-time packagers, or polymorphism. Lastly, passive heuristics, when used as the exclusive protective mechanism, has been known to produce high false-positive rates that, in and of itself, is a troublesome issue.

- Advanced heuristics-based antivirus

  — Advanced heuristics antivirus methodologies can vary dramatically by vendor but share, in part, some common functionality:

    ○ Signature-based antivirus
    ○ Advanced-signature-based antivirus
    ○ Traditional or advanced sandboxing

  — The advanced heuristic-based antivirus typically first employs the "reasoning" of known past events in the form of signature scanning. Then, by executing some portions of the potentially malicious code in an isolated environment, a virtual machine affords the protection of a traditional sandbox approach. Lastly, current-technology antivirus provides for what is referred to as *theoretical reasoning* that is based upon algorithmic analysis of the potentially malicious code, thereby eliminating the need to actually run the potentially malicious code.

  — Although this methodology "can" afford good protection from both known and unknown (day zero) code and offers a more acceptable false-positive rate, it is slower than a traditional pure signature approach, but it can, in fact, afford better performance than a traditional sandbox approach. Keep in mind that the advanced heuristic antivirus methodology does still require regular updates to stay in front of evolving threats.

- Prescanning-based antivirus

  — Another novel approach is a combination of methodologies called *prescanning*. The idea builds on the development of sandboxing and uses a three-way approach that verifies digital signatures and, in so doing, blocks any untrusted program code, screens and blocks any suspicious code based on its potential behavior, and finally filters out any potentially harmful code that tries to exploit any vulnerabilities on the client, i.e.:

— Examines any ActiveX controls and Java applets for digital signatures and verifies that the signed data has not been altered since the signature had been applied or if an untrusted authority has signed them

— A heuristic analysis is performed looking for certain instructions or commands within a program that are not found in typical application programs. Potential function calls are iterated regardless of the actual program flow and known functions are classified based on a given set of rules. Further, in a process akin to fingerprint analysis, digital signatures are linked to a library of previously examined, safe Active X controls for comparison.

— In the third and final step, any "remaining suspects"—scripts that try to exploit vulnerabilities on the client—are scanned and filtered out. It may be that the scripts themselves are not malicious. However, they are potential enablers to inject or execute further malicious code. Detecting and filtering such scripts interrupts any malicious payload being distributed to the clients.

What AntiVirus Solution is Right for You?

The correct antivirus solution depends on your application. In most enterprise environments today, while facing both internal and external threats, antivirus is being applied in a multilayer architecture. The Internet threat is being countered by operating at the gateway or perhaps on a server near the gateway, while the internal threat is being countered at the desktop.

As in any multilayer approach, best practice normally dictates using disparate technologies from disparate vendors to reduce the risk of a single point of failure of one layer from being carried through the other layer. Others, however, would argue that because you are really talking about countering two independent threats, then perhaps the best solution would be to use the best available technology on both the gateway and on the desktop.

One of the ironic measures of security is always performance—any security professional knows that despite vendor claims, there will always be a trade-off in security and performance. To say you can have the best performance and the best security in any one methodology is perhaps stretching things a bit. I have seen some vendors avoid the

performance argument completely by removing the word "performance" from their claims and introducing the term "efficient" in describing its operation. This is an interesting marketing concept—we may not be as fast as product X, but we are more "efficient."

Future of AntiVirus Technologies

As with any product in network security today, every architecture or methodology has its place. However, the increased overall protection as well as the reduced dependence on the timeliness of antivirus vendor updates offered in the current hybrid antivirus technologies is simply too hard to dismiss.

The arms race between malicious code writers in the blackhat community and the teams working in the antivirus vendor's labs will simply continue. Occasionally, vendors will catch up and the windows of exposure will be reduced. Things will be quiet on the Internet for a period of time and then, suddenly, the bad guys, thinking out of the box, will find new methodologies that deploy their code faster and perhaps in more stealthy manners to allow them to do more damage to a wider user base in a shorter period of time and antivirus vendors will again scramble to catch up. As this cycle continues, more and more antivirus users will abandon signature-only-based solutions and will eventually move to more current technologies, such as advanced heuristics and at least somewhat limit their complete dependence on a given vendor's ability to respond to new threats.

With respect to antivirus use that is embedded within the currently trendy all-in-one security product offerings: in some respects, antivirus is only a checkbox item in many of the all-in-one type security products today. Many of these security product vendors use traditional signature-based antivirus for its low cost, high performance, and simplicity. This will eventually create issues for the security product vendors using them, as next-generation malicious threats take advantage of the inherent limitations of signature-based antivirus. As the market for all-in-one appliances gains traction and begins to stabilize, I would expect that perhaps individual vendors will begin to differentiate themselves from their competitors by offering higher levels of available antivirus technology embedded within their products.

Before we end this section on antivirus considerations, we need to address one more important point: gateway-located antivirus offers no protection from an internal user plugging in a USB drive with an infected file or a mobile user connecting an infected laptop to the network behind the gateway.

Deploying antivirus on the desktop can mitigate the risk of an internal user infecting the network by installing an infected file from a floppy or USB device. Some now offer the ability to isolate the user if his antivirus signatures are not current, thereby helping to mitigate the threat of a

Espionage –
Firewalls

mobile user connecting to and infecting the network. However, relying on desktop deployment can have a significant impact on network traffic because infected e-mails are forwarded by the e-mail server to internal users.

The combined approach of gateway- and desktop-based antivirus deployment is best and can be further enhanced by choosing products that utilize both signature and heuristic approaches. Last, to minimize the risk of one vendor being slower to provide signature updates than another, one suggestion would be to use products from disparate vendors—one vendor on the gateway and a different vendor for the desktop.

In closing, I look at antivirus technology in a similar way to that of current firewall technology offerings in the market today: whether it is a signature-based antivirus product or a signature-based firewall offering, the ability to keep up with signatures for known vulnerabilities puts the vendor in an arms race with the hacking community. Although that, in and of itself, is daunting enough, in the long run signature-based methodologies will simply be overrun by the shear number of known signatures for malicious code or packets that the product needs be able to identify in an effort to afford any reasonable level of protection.

Worm Considerations

The SQL Slammer worm struck January 25, 2003, and entire sections of the Internet began to go down almost immediately:

- Within minutes, Level 3's transcontinental chain of routers began to fail, overwhelmed with traffic.
- Three hundred thousand cable modems in Portugal went dark.
- South Korea fell right off the map and 27 million people were without cell phone or Internet service.
- Unconfirmed reports said that 5 of the Internet's 13 root-name servers—all hardened systems—succumbed to the storm of packets.
- Corporate e-mail systems jammed.
- Web sites stopped responding.
- Emergency 911 dispatchers in suburban Seattle resorted to paper.
- Unable to process tickets, Continental Airlines canceled flights from its Newark hub. Most of the company's 75,000 servers were affected within the first 10 minutes (http://www.csoonline.com/whitepapers/050504_cyberguard/EvolutionoftheKillerWorms.pdf).

SQL Slammer took advantage of a known vulnerability in Microsoft SQL Server software, a limit to the actual number of servers compromised. Using the now-familiar random-address-scanning technique to search for vulnerable hosts, SQL Slammer included elements that enabled it to propagate rapidly:

- By using the inherently faster UDP communications protocol in lieu of TCP as a communications protocol, SQL Slammer eliminated the overhead of a connection-oriented protocol.
- At only 367 bytes, SQL Slammer was one of the smallest worms on record.

A variation of SQL Slammer was reported to have been responsible for a disruption at a nuclear power plant in Ohio on June 20, 2003 (http://www.inel.gov/nationalsecurity/features/powerplay.pdf).

Some reports suggest that a SQL Slammer variant may have played a role in the August 14, 2003, power failure that blacked out cities from Ohio to New York. Damage estimates for SQL Slammer were $1.2 billion (http://www.somix.com/files/SMS-SQL-Slammer-Article.pdf).

Future Worm Considerations

Although worms have evolved from both technological and social engineering perspectives, there has been little change in the basic method of propagation—the initial scanning phase in which the worm looks for the vulnerable hosts. After a worm reaches an installation base of 10,000 or more hosts, propagation becomes exponentially faster. In virtually all cases to date, worms have been slow to find the initial 10,000 or so exploitable hosts. During this scanning phase, worms produce quite a bit of "noise" as they scan random address ranges across the Internet looking for targets. This causes firewalls and IDS systems to generate alerts and serves as an early warning that a new worm is winding its malicious way across the Internet.

All of this is about to change. Future worms will take advantage of new fast scanning routines that will dramatically accelerate the initial propagation phase and even use prescanning data to virtually eliminate that first slow phase of scanning for vulnerable hosts.

This new strain of worms is referred to as a "fast scanning" worm, sometimes called a Warhol worm. An excellent paper that discusses the Warhol worm concept was written by Nicholas C. Weaver at the University of Berkeley in 2001: "A Warhol worm: an Internet plague in 15 min!" (http://www.cs.berkeley.edu/~nweaver/warhol.old.html). This entry is recommended reading for all network administrators.

Even with 14 hours of advance warning, networks and systems were completely overwhelmed with the speed of Code Red. There was no chance to defend against SQL Slammer as it circled the globe in about an hour. What will the devastation be when a worm eliminates the initial scanning phase of hunting for 10,000 vulnerable hosts? Estimates indicate that it would take an average of about six minutes for this new type of worm to completely saturate the Internet. It is no longer a matter of how this can be accomplished, it is simply a matter of when.

Espionage – Firewalls

The technology is here to facilitate this new worm. All that is lacking is the attacker with the will and malicious intent.

Here are the top 12 things you can do to harden your enterprise against Worm attacks.

1. Patch all of your systems (both servers and desktops) and remove or disable all unnecessary services.
2. Review your security policy and re-evaluate the business need for services you allow access to on the Internet. Eliminate all but those services that are essential to operating your business.
3. Use application proxies with complete packet inspection on all traffic inbound to your publicly accessible servers.
4. Isolate all publicly accessible servers, each on their own physical network segment. Servers should be grouped by trust, not by convenience.
5. Create granular access controls that prevent your publicly accessible servers from originating connections either to the public Internet or to your intranet.
6. Create access controls to limit outbound access for internal users to only services that are necessary.
7. Strip all potentially malicious e-mail attachments within your SMTP application proxy firewall.
8. Use an antivirus server on an isolated network segment to eradicate virus and worms from permitted e-mail attachments before allowing e-mail through your firewall.
9. Deploy antivirus software on all desktops throughout your business.
10. Use ingress anti-spoofing filters on your border router to prevent spoofed packets that are common to worm propagation from entering your network. (Refer to http://www.zvon.org/tmRFC/RFC2827/Output/chapter3.html for a good explanation of ingress filtering.)
11. Use egress anti-spoofing on your border router to prevent a worm or potentially malicious internal user from launching spoofed IP address-related attacks across the Internet from inside your network. (Refer to http://www.sans.org/y2k/egress.htm for a good explanation of egress filtering.)
12. Create an incident response plan that includes an out-of-band communications method to your bandwidth provider so you can head off attacks and shun IP addresses on the provider's border routers, minimizing any impact within your pipe.

ACKNOWLEDGMENT

This, the fourth edition of the firewall architectures text, is based on a number of related white papers I have recently written as well as numerous books, white papers, presentations, vendor literature and several Usenet news group discussions I have read or participated in throughout my career. Any failure to cite any individual for anything that in any way resembles a previous work is unintentional.

Firewall Technologies: Comparison

Per Thorsheim
Senior Consultant, PricewaterhouseCoopers, Bergen, Norway

Abstract
A firewall should be configured to protect itself, in addition to the various networks and systems that it moves data to and from. In fact, a firewall should also "protect" the Internet, meaning that it should prevent internal "hackers" from attacking other parties connected to the Internet, wherever and whoever they are. Surrounding network equipment such as routers, switches, and servers should also be configured to protect the firewall environment in addition to the system itself.

In early January 2001, a new Web page was launched. It was named Netscan,[1] and the creators had done quite a bit of work prior to launching their Web site. Actually, the work was quite simple, but time-consuming. They had pinged the entire routed IPv4 address space; or to be more exact, they pinged every IP address ending with .0 or .255. For each PING sent, they expected one PING REPLY in return. And for each network that replied with more than one packet, they counted the number of replies and put the data into a database. All networks that did reply with more than one packet for each packet sent were considered to be an amplifier network. After pinging the entire Internet (more or less), they published on their Web site a list of the 1024 worst networks, including the e-mail address for the person responsible for the IP address and its associated network. The worst networks were those networks that gave them the highest number of replies to a single PING, or the best amplification effect.

The security problem here is that it is rather easy to send a PING request to a network, using a spoofed source IP address. And when the recipient network replies, all those replies will be sent to the source address as given in the initial PING. As shown in Fig. 1, the attacker can flood the Internet connection of the final recipient by repeating this procedure continuously.

In fact, the attacker can use an ISDN connection to create enough traffic to jam a T3 (45-Mbit) connection, using several SMURF amplifier networks to launch the attack. And as long as there are networks that allow such amplification, a network can be the target of the attack even if the network does not have the amplification problem itself, and there is not much security systems such as firewalls can do to prevent the attack.

This type of attack has been used over and over again to attack some of the biggest sites on the Internet, including the February 2000 attacks against Yahoo, CNN, Ebay, and Amazon.

Today, there are several Web sites that search for SMURF amplifier networks and publish their results publicly. In a presentation given in March 2001, this author pointed out the fact that the number of networks not protected from being used as such amplifiers had increased more than 1000% since January 2001.

One of the interesting findings from these attacks was that routers got blamed for the problems—not firewalls. And they were correct; badly configured Internet routers were a major part of the problem in these cases. Even worse is the fact that the only requirement for blocking this specific PING-based attack was to set one parameter in all routers connecting networks to the Internet. This has now become the recommended default in RFC 2644/BCP 34, "Changing the Default for Directed Broadcast in Routers." Security professionals should also read RFC 2827/BCP 0038, "Network Ingress Filtering: Defeating Denial-of-Service Attacks Which Employ IP Source Address Spoofing," to further understand spoofing attacks.

Another interesting observation after these attacks was President Clinton's announcement of a National Plan for Information Systems Protection, with valuable help from some of the top security experts in the United States. In this author's opinion, this serves as the perfect example of who should be at the top and responsible for security—the board of directors and the CEO of a company.

Finally, Web sites such as CNN, Yahoo, and Amazon all had firewalls in place, yet that did not prevent these attacks. Thus, a discussion of firewall technologies and what kind of security they can actually provide is in order.

FIREWALL TECHNOLOGIES EXPLAINED

The Internet Firewalls FAQ (Marcus J. Ranum and Matt Curtin)[2] defines two basic types of firewalls: network-layer firewalls and application-layer firewalls (also

Encyclopedia of Information Assurance DOI: 10.1081/E-EIA-120046367
Copyright © 2011 by Taylor & Francis. All rights reserved.

Espionage – Firewalls

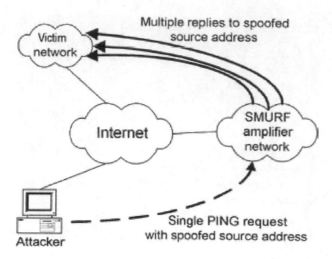

Fig. 1 Attacker using spoofed PING packets to flood a network by using a vulnerable intermediary network.

Espionage –
Firewalls

referred to as application proxy firewalls, or just proxies). For this entry, stateful inspection firewalls are defined as a mix of the first two firewall types, in order to make it easier to understand the similarities and differences between them.

The reader may already be familiar with the OSI layer model, in which the network layer is layer 3 and the application layer is at layer 7, as shown in Fig. 2.

A firewall can simply be illustrated as a router that transmits packets back and forth between two or more networks, with some kind of security filtering applied on top.

Network-Level Firewalls: Packet Filters

Packet filter firewalls are very often just a router with access lists. In its most basic form, a packet filter firewall controls traffic based on the source and destination IP address of each IP packet and the destination port. Many packet filter firewalls also allow checking the packets based on the incoming interface (is it coming from the Internet, or the internal network?). They may also allow control of the IP packet based on the source port, day and time, protocol type (TCP, UDP, or ICMP), and other IP options as well, depending on the product.

Application
Presentation
Session
Transport
Network
Data link
Physical

Fig. 2 The OSI seven-layer model.

The first thing to remember about packet filter firewalls is that they inspect every IP packet by itself; they do not see IP packets as part of a session. The second thing to remember about packet filter firewalls is that many of them, by default, have a fail-open configuration, meaning that, by default, they will let packets through unless specifically instructed not to. And finally, packet filters only check the HEADER of a packet, and not the DATA part of the packet. This means that techniques such as tunneling a service within another service will easily bypass a packet filter (e.g., running Telnet on port 80 through a firewall where the standard Telnet port 23 is blocked, but HTTP port 80 is open. Because the packet filter only sees source/destination and port number, it will allow it to pass).

Why use packet filter firewalls?

Some security managers may not be aware of it, but most probably there are lots of devices already in their network that can do packet filtering. The best examples are various routers. Most (if not all) routers today can be equipped with access lists, controlling IP traffic flowing through the router with various degrees of security. In many networks, it will just be a matter of properly configuring them for the purpose of acting as a packet filter firewall. In fact, the author usually recommends that all routers be equipped with at least a minimum of access lists, in order to maintain security for the router itself and its surroundings at a minimal level. Using packet filtering usually has little or no impact on throughput, which is another plus over the other technologies. Finally, packet filter firewalls support most (if not all) TCP/IP-based services.

Why not use packet filter firewalls?

Well, they only work at OSI layer 3, or the network layer as it is usually called. Packet filter firewalls only check single IP packets; they do not care whether or not the packet is part of a session. Furthermore, they do not do any checking of the actual contents of the packet, as long as the basic header information is okay (such as source and destination IP address). It can be frustrating and difficult to create rules for packet filter firewalls, and maintaining consistent rules among many different packet filter firewalls is usually considered very difficult. As previously mentioned, the typical fail-open defaults should be considered dangerous in most cases.

Stateful Inspection Firewalls

Basically, stateful inspection firewalls are the same thing as packet filter firewalls, but with the ability to keep track of the state of connections in addition to the packet filtering abilities. By dynamically keeping track of whether a session is being initiated, currently transmitting data (in either direction), or being closed, the firewall can apply stronger security to the transmission of data. In addition, stateful inspection firewalls have various ways of handling popular services such as HTTP, FTP, and SMTP. These last options (of which there are many variants of from product to product) enable the firewall to actually check whether or not it is HTTP traffic going to TCP port 80 on a host in a network by "analyzing" the traffic. A packet filter will only assume that it is HTTP traffic because it is going to TCP port 80 on a host system; it has no way of actually checking the DATA part of the packet, while stateful inspection can partially do this.

A stateful inspection firewall is capable of understanding the opening, communication, and closing of sessions. Stateful inspection firewalls usually have a fail-close default configuration, meaning that they will not allow a packet to pass if they do not know how to handle the packet. In addition to this, they can also provide an extra level of security by "understanding" the actual contents (the data itself) within packets and sessions, compared to packet filters. This last part only applies to specific services, which may be different from product to product.

Why use stateful inspection firewalls?

Stateful inspection firewalls give high performance and provide more security features than packet filtering. Such features can provide extra control of common and popular services. Stateful inspection firewalls support most (if not all) services transparently, just like packet filters, and there is no need to modify client configurations or add any extra software for them to work.

Why not use stateful inspection firewalls?

Stateful inspection firewalls may not provide the same level of security as application-level firewalls. They let the server and the client talk "directly" to each other, just like packet filters. This may be a security risk if the firewall does not know how to interpret the DATA contents of the packets flowing through the firewall. Even more disturbing is the fact that many people consider stateful inspection firewalls to be easier to configure wrongly, compared to application-level firewalls. This is due to the fact that packet filters and stateful inspection firewalls support most, if not all, services transparently, while application-level firewalls usually support only a very limited number of services and require modification to client software in order to work with non-supported services.

In a white paper from Network Associates, (Network Associates, "Adaptive Proxy Firewalls—The Next Generation Firewall Architecture.") the Computer Security Institute (CSI) was quoted as saying, "It is quite possible, in fact trivial, to configure stateful inspection firewalls to permit dangerous services through the firewall.... Application proxy firewalls, by design, make it far more difficult to make mistakes during configuration."

Of course, it should be unnecessary to say that no system is secure if it is not configured correctly.

And human faults and errors are the number one, two, and three reasons for security problems, right?

Application-Level Firewalls

Application-level firewalls (or just proxies) work as a "man-in-the-middle," where the client asks the proxy to perform a task on behalf of the client. This could include tasks such as fetching Web pages, sending mail, retrieving files using FTP, etc. Proxies are application specific, meaning that they need to support the specific application (or, more exactly, the application-level protocol) that will be used. There are also standards for generic proxy functionality, with the most popular being SOCKS. SOCKS was originally authored by David Koblas and further developed by NEC. Applications that support SOCKS will be able to communicate through firewalls that also support the SOCKS standard. Note that there are two major versions of SOCKS: SOCKS V4 and SOCKS V5. Version 4 does not support authentication or UDP proxying, while version 5 does.

Similar to a stateful inspection firewall, the usual default of an application-level firewall is fail-close, meaning that it will block packets/sessions that it does not understand how to handle.

Why use application-level firewalls?

First of all, they provide a high level of security, primarily based on the simple fact that they only support a very limited number of services; however, they do support most, if not all, of the usual services that are needed on a day-to-day basis. They understand the protocols at the application layer and, as such, they may block parts of a protocol (allow receiving files using FTP, but denying sending files using FTP as an example). They can also detect and block vulnerabilities, depending on the firewall vendor and version.

Furthermore, there is no direct contact being made between the client and the server; the firewall will handle all requests and responses for the client and the server. With a proxy server, it is also easy to perform user authentication, and many security practitioners will

Espionage – Firewalls

appreciate the extensive level of logging available in application-level firewalls.

For performance reasons, many application-level firewalls can also cache data, providing faster response times and higher throughput for access to commonly accessed Web pages, for example. The author usually does not recommend that a firewall do this because a firewall should handle the inspection of traffic and provide a high level of security. Instead, security practitioners should consider using a stand-alone caching proxy server for increasing performance while accessing common Web sites. Such a stand-alone caching proxy server may, of course, also be equipped with additional content security, thus controlling access to Web sites based on content and other issues.

Why not use application-level firewalls?

By design, application-level firewalls only support a limited number of services. If support for other applications/services/protocols is desired, applications may have to be changed in order to work through an application-level firewall. Given the high level of security such a firewall may provide (depending on its configuration, of course), it may have a very negative impact on performance compared to packet filtering and stateful inspection firewalls.

What the Market Wants vs. What the Market Really Needs

Many firewalls today seem to mix these technologies together into a simple and easy-to-use product. Firewalls try to be a "turnkey" or "all-in-one" solution. Security in a firewall that can be configured by more or less plugging it in and turning it on is something in which this author has little faith. And, the all-in-one solution that integrates VPN, antivirus, content security/filtering, traffic shaping, and similar functionality is also something in which this author has little trust. In fact, firewalls seem to get increasingly complex in order to make them easier to configure, use, and understand for the end users. This seems a little bit wrong; by increasing the amount of code in a product, the chances of security vulnerabilities in the product increase, and most probably exponentially.

In the author's opinion, a firewall is a "black box" in a network, which most regular users will not see or notice. Users should not even know that it is there.

The market decides what it wants, and the vendors provide exactly that. But does the market always know what is good for it? This is a problem that security professionals should always give priority to—teaching security understanding and security awareness.

Firewall Technologies: Quick Summary

As a rule of thumb, packet filters provide the lowest level of security, but the highest throughput. They have limited security options and features and can be difficult to administrate, especially if there is a large number of them in a network.

Stateful inspection firewalls provide a higher level of security, but may not give the same throughput as packet filters. The leading firewalls on the market today are stateful inspection firewalls, often considered the best mix of security, manageability, throughput, and transparent integration into most environments.

Application-level firewalls are considered by many to give the highest level of security, but will usually give less throughput compared to the two other firewall technologies.

In any case, security professionals should never trust a firewall by itself to provide good security. And no matter what firewall a company deploys, it will not provide much security if it is not configured correctly. And that usually requires quite a lot of work.

PERIMETER DEFENSE AND HOW FIREWALLS FIT IN

Many people seem to believe that all the bad hackers are "out there" on the Internet, while none of their colleagues in a firm would ever even think of doing anything illegal, internally or externally. Sadly, however, there are statistics showing that internal employees carry out maybe 50% of all computer-related crime.

This is why it is necessary to explain that security in a firewall and its surrounding environment works two ways. Hackers on the Internet are not allowed access to the internal network, and people (or hostile code such as viruses and Trojans) on the internal network should be prevented from sending sensitive data to the external network. The former is much easier to configure than the latter. As a practical example of this, here is what happened during an Internet penetration test performed by the author some time ago.

Practical Example of Missing Egress (Outbound) Filtering

The client was an industrial client with a rather simple firewall environment connecting them to the Internet. They wanted a high level of security and had used external resources to help configure their Internet router act as a packet filter firewall, in addition to a stateful inspection firewall on the inside of the Internet router, with a connection to the internal network. They had configured their

Espionage – Firewalls

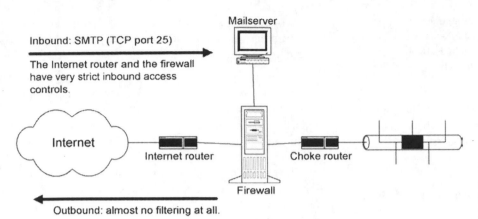

Inbound: SMTP (TCP port 25)

The Internet router and the firewall
have very strict inbound access
controls.

Outbound: almost no filtering at all.

Fig. 3 Missing egress filtering in the router and the firewall may disclose useful information to unauthorized people.

Espionage – Firewalls

router and firewall to only allow e-mail (SMTP, TCP port 25) back and forth between the Internet and their antivirus (AV) e-mail gateway placed in a demilitarized zone (DMZ) on the stateful inspection firewall. The antivirus e-mail gateway would check all in- and outgoing e-mail before sending it to the final recipient, be it on the internal network or on the Internet. The router was incredibly well configured; inbound access lists were extremely strict, only allowing inbound SMTP to TCP port 25. The same thing was the case for the stateful inspection firewall.

While testing the anti-virus e-mail gateway for SMTP vulnerabilities, the author suddenly noticed that each time he connected to the SMTP connector of the anti-virus e-mail gateway, it also sent a Windows NetBIOS request in return, in addition to the SMTP login banner.

This simple fact reveals a lot of information to an unauthorized person (see Fig. 3). First of all, there is an obvious lack of egress (outbound) filtering in both the Internet router and the firewall. This tells us that internal systems (at least this one in the DMZ) can probably do NetBIOS communication over TCP/IP with external systems. This is highly dangerous for many reasons. Second, the antivirus e-mail gateway in the DMZ is installed with NetBIOS, which may indicate that recommended good practices have not been followed for installing a Windows server in a high-security environment. Third, it may be possible to use this system to access other systems in the DMZ or on other networks (including the internal network) because NetBIOS is being used for communication among windows computers in a workgroup or domain. At least this is the author's usual experience when doing Internet penetration testing. Of course, an unauthorized person must break into the server in the DMZ first, but that also proves to be easier than most people want to believe.

How can one prevent such information leakage?

Security managers should check that all firewalls and routers connecting them to external networks have been properly configured to block services that are considered "dangerous," as well as all services that are never supposed to be used against hosts on external networks, especially the Internet.

As a general rule, security managers should never allow servers and systems that are not being used at the local console to access the Internet in any way whatsoever. This will greatly enhance security, in such a way that hostile code such as viruses and Trojans will not be able to directly establish contact with and turn over control of the system to unauthorized persons on any external network.

This also applies to systems placed in a firewall DMZ, where there are systems that can be accessed by external people, even without any kind of user authentication. The important thing to remember here is: who makes the initial request to connect to a system?

If it is an external system making a connection to a mail server in a DMZ on TCP port 25 (SMTP), it is okay because it is (probably) incoming e-mail. If the mail server in the DMZ makes a connection to an external system on TCP port 25, that is also okay because it does this to send outgoing e-mail. However, if the only purpose of the mail server is to send and receive mail to and from the Internet, the firewalls and even the routers should be configured in accordance with this.

For the sake of easy administration, many people choose to update their servers directly from the Internet; some even have a tendency to sit directly on production servers and surf the World Wide Web without any restrictions or boundaries whatsoever. This poses a high security risk for the server, and also the rest of the surrounding environment, given the fact that 1) Trojans may get into the system, and 2) servers tend to have the same usernames and passwords even if they do not have anything in common except for being in the same physical/logical network.

To quote Anthony C. Zboralski Gaius (quoted with permission)[3] and his article "Things to Do in Cisco Land when You're Dead" in *Phrack Magazine*[4]:

It's been a long time since I stopped believing in security. The core of the security problem is really because we are trusting trust (read Ken Thomson's article, Reflections on Trusting Trust). If I did believe in security then I wouldn't be selling penetration tests.

It can never be said that there is a logical link between high security and easy administration, nor will there ever be. Security is difficult, and it will always be difficult.

Common Mistakes that Lead to System and Network Compromises

Many security professionals say that "networks are hard on the outside, and soft on the inside," a phrase this author fully agrees with. The listing that follows shows some of the common weaknesses encountered over and over again.

- Remote access servers (RAS) are connected to the internal network, allowing intruders access to the network just like internal users, as soon as they have a username and password.
- Access lists and other security measures are not implemented in WAN routers and networks. Because small regional offices usually have a lower level of physical security, it may be easier to get access to the office, representing a serious risk to the entire network.
- Many services have default installations, making them vulnerable. They have known weaknesses, such as standard installation paths; default file and directory permissions that give all uses full control of the system, etc.
- Employees do not follow written password policies, and password policies are usually written with users (real people) in mind, and not generic system accounts.
- Many unnecessary services are running on various systems without being used. Many of these services can easily be used for denial-of-service (DoS) attacks against the system and across the network.
- Service applications run with administrator privileges, and their passwords are rarely changed from the default value. As an example, there are backup programs in which the program's username and password are the same as the name of the program, and the account has administrative privileges by default. Take a look at some of the default usernames/passwords lists that exist on the Internet; they list hundreds of default usernames and passwords for many, many different systems.[5]
- Companies have trust in authentication mechanisms and use them as their only defense against unauthorized people trying to get access to the various systems in the network. Many companies and people do not seem to understand that hackers do not need a username or password to get access to different systems; there are many vulnerabilities that give them full control within seconds.

Most, if not all, security professionals will recognize many of these as problems that will never go away. At the same time, it is very important to understand these problems, and professionals should work continuously to reduce or remove these problems.

When performing penetration testing, common questions and comments include: "How are you going to break into our firewall?" and "You are not allowed to do this and this and that." First of all, penetration testing does not involve breaking into firewalls, just trying to bypass them. Breaking into a firewall by itself may show good technical skills, but it does not really do much harm to the company that owns it. Second, hackers do not have to follow any rules, either given by the company they attack or the laws of the country. (Or the laws of the many countries they are passing through in order to do the attack over the Internet, which opens up lots more problems for tracking down and punishing the hackers, a problem that many security professionals are trying to deal with already.)

What about security at the management workstations?

Many companies are deploying extremely tight security into their Internet connection environment and their internal servers. What many of them do wrong is that they forget to secure the workstations that are being used to administrate those highly secured systems. During a recent security audit of an Internet bank, the author was given an impressive presentation with firewalls, intrusion detection systems, proxies, and lots of other stuff thrown in. When checking a bit deeper, it was discovered that all the high-security systems were managed from specific workstations located on their internal network. All those workstations ("owned" by network administrators) were running various operating systems (network administrators tend to do this...) with more or less default configurations, including default usernames and passwords, SNMP[6] (Simple Network Management Protocol), one of the author's favorite ways of mapping large networks fast and easy—also mentioned as number 10 on the SANS' Institute "Top Ten Vulnerabilities" list—and various services. All those workstations were in a network mixed with normal users; there were no access restrictions deployed except username/password to get access to those management stations. They even used a naming convention for their internal computers that immediately revealed which ones were being used for "critical system administration." By breaking into those workstations first

(Trojans, physical access, other methods), it did not take long to get access to the critical systems.

Intrusion Detection Systems and Firewalls

Lately, more and more companies have been deploying intrusion detection systems (IDSs) in their networks. Here is another area in which it is easy to make mistakes. First of all, an IDS does not really help a company improve its security against hackers. An IDS will help a company to better detect and document an attack, but in most cases it will not be able to stop the attack. It is tempting to say that an IDS is just a new term for extensive logging and automated/manual analysis, which have been around for quite some time now.

Some time ago, someone came up with the bright idea of creating an IDS that could automatically block various attacks, or reconfigure other systems like firewalls to block the attacks. By doing a spoofing attack (very easy these days), hackers could create a false attack that originated from a trusted source (third party), making the IDS block all communications between the company and the trusted source. And suddenly everybody understood that the idea of such automated systems was probably a bad idea.

Some IDSs are signature based, while others are anomaly based. Some IDSs have both options, and maybe host and network based agents as well. And, of course, there are central consoles for logging and administrating the IDS agents deployed in the network. (How good is the security at those central consoles?)

- *Problem 1.* Signature-based detection more or less depends on specific data patterns to detect an attack. Circumventing this is becoming easier every day as hackers learn how to circumvent the patterns known by the IDS, while still making patterns that work against the target systems.
- *Problem 2.* Most IDSs do not understand how the receiving system reacts to the data sent to it, meaning that the IDSs can see an attack, but it does not know whether or not the attack was successful. So, how should the IDS classify the attack and assess the probability of the attack being successful?
- *Problem 3.* IDSs tend to create incredible amounts of false alerts, so who will check them all to see if they are legitimate or not? Some companies receive so many alerts that they just "tune" the system so that it does not create that many alerts. Sometimes this means that they do not check properly to see if there is something misconfigured in their network, but instead just turn off some of the detection signatures, thus crippling the IDS of its functions.
- *Problem 4.* Anomaly-based detection relies on a pattern of "normal" traffic and then generates alerts based on unusual activity that does not match the "normal" pattern. What is a "normal" pattern? The author has seen IDS deployments in which an IDS was placed into a network that was configured with all sorts of protocols, unnecessary services, and clear-text authentication flying over the wire. The "normal" template became a template for which almost everything was allowed, more or less disabling the anomaly detection capability of the IDS. (This is also very typical for "personal firewalls," which people are installing on their home systems these days.)

An IDS can be a very effective addition to a firewall because it is usually better at logging the contents of the attack compared to a firewall, which only logs information such as source/destination, date/time, and other information from the various IP/TCP/UDP headers. Using an IDS, it is also easier to create statistics over longer periods of time of hacker activity compared to just having a firewall and its logs. Such statistics may also aid in showing management what the reality is when it comes to hacking attempts and illegal access against the company's systems, as well as raising general security awareness among its users.

On the other hand, an IDS requires even more human attention than a firewall, and a company should have very clearly defined goals with such a system before buying and deploying it. Just for keeping hackers out of your network is not a good enough reason.

GENERAL RECOMMENDATIONS AND CONCLUSIONS

Security professionals should consider using user authentication before allowing access to the Internet. This will, in many situations, block viruses and Trojans from establishing contact with hosts on the Internet using protocols such as HTTP, FTP, and Telnet, for example.

It may be unnecessary to say, but personal use of the Internet from a company network should, in general, be forbidden. Of course, the level of control here can be discussed, but the point is to prevent users from downloading dangerous content (viruses, Trojans) and sending out files from the internal network using protocols such as POP3, SMTP, FTP, HTTP, and other protocols that allow sending files in ASCII or binary formats.

Finally, other tools should be deployed as well to bring the security to a level that actually matches the level required (or wanted) in the company security policy. In the author's experience, probably less than 50% of all firewall installations are doing extensive logging, and less than 5% of the firewall owners are actually doing anything that even resembles useful log analysis, reporting, and statistics. To some, it seems like the attitude is "we've got a firewall, so we're safe." Such an attitude is both stupid and wrong.

Firewalls and firewall technologies by themselves cannot be trusted, at least not in our present Internet age of communications with hackers hiding in every corner. Hackers tunneling data through allowed protocols and ports can easily bypass today's firewalls, using encryption schemes to hide their tracks. Security professionals should, nonetheless, understand that a firewall, as part of a consistent overall security architecture, is still an important part of the network security in a company.

The best security tool available is still the human brain. Use it wisely and security will improve.

REFERENCES

1. http://www.netscan.org.
2. http://www.interhack.net/pubs/fwfaq/.
3. http://www.hert.org.
4. http://www.phrack.com.
5. http://packetstorm.securify.com/.
6. http://www.sans.org/topten.htm.

Firewalls: Checkpoint Security Review

Ben Rothke, CISSP, QSA
International Network Services (INS), New York City, New York, U.S.A.

Abstract

This entry focuses on performing a firewall review for a Checkpoint Firewall-1. Most of the information is sufficiently generic to be germane to any firewall, including Cisco PIX, NAI Gauntlet, Axent Raptor, etc. One caveat: it is important to note that a firewall review is not a penetration test. The function of a firewall review is not to find exploits and gain access into the firewall; rather, it is to identify risks that are inadvertently opened by the firewall.

Finally, it must be understood that a firewall review is also not a certification or guarantee that the firewall operating system or underlying network operating system is completely secure.

Altered States was not just a science fiction movie about a research scientist who experimented with altered states of human consciousness; it is also a metaphor for many firewalls in corporate enterprises.

In general, when a firewall is initially installed, it is tightly coupled to an organization's security requirements. After use in a corporate environment, the firewall rule base, configuration, and underlying operating system often gets transformed into a radically different arrangement. This altered firewall state is what necessitates a firewall review.

A firewall is only effective to the degree that it is properly configured. And in today's corporate environments, it is easy for a firewall to become misconfigured. By reviewing the firewall setup, management can ensure that its firewall is enforcing what it expects, and in a secure manner.

NEED FOR A FIREWALL REVIEW

Firewalls, like people, need to be reviewed. In the workplace, this is called a performance review. In the medical arena, it is called a physical. The need for periodic firewall reviews is crucial, as a misconfigured firewall is often worse than no firewall. When organizations lack a firewall, they understand the risks involved and are cognizant of the fact that they lack a fundamental security mechanism. However, a misconfigured firewall gives an organization a false sense of security.

In addition, because the firewall is often the primary information security mechanism deployed, any mistake or misconfiguration on the firewall trickles into the entire enterprise. If a firewall is never reviewed, any of these mistakes will be left unchecked.

REVIEW, AUDIT, ASSESSMENT

Firewall reviews are often called audits. An audit is defined as "a methodical examination and review." As well, the terms "review," "assessment," and "audit" are often synonymous. It is interesting to note that when security groups from the Big Five (PricewaterhouseCoopers, Ernst & Young, Deloitte & Touche, Arthur Andersen, KPMG) accounting firms perform a security review, they are specifically prohibited from using the term "audit." This is due to the fact that the American Institute of Certified Public Accounts (http://www.aicpa.org), which oversees the Big Five, prohibits the use of the term "audit" because there is no set of official information security standards in which to audit the designated environment.

On the other hand, financial audits are performed against the Generally Accepted Accounting Principles (GAAP). While not a fixed set of rules, GAAP is a widely accepted set of conventions, standards, and procedures for reporting financial information. The Financial Accounting Standards Board (http://www.fasb.org) established GAAP in 1973. The mission of the Financial Accounting Standards Board is to establish and improve standards of financial accounting and reporting for the guidance and education of the public, including issuers, auditors, and users of financial information.

As of January 2001, the Generally Accepted System Security Principles (GASSP) Committee was in the early stages of drafting a business plan that reflects their plans for establishing and funding the International Information Security Foundation (IISF).[1] While there is currently no set of geerally accepted security principles (in which a firewall could truly be *audited* against), work is underway to create such a standard. Working groups for the GASSP are in place. Work is currently being done to research and complete the authoritative foundation and develop and

Encyclopedia of Information Assurance DOI: 10.1081/E-EIA-120046357
Copyright © 2011 by Taylor & Francis. All rights reserved.

Espionage – Firewalls

approve the framework for GASSP. The committee has developed a detailed plan for completing the GASSP Detailed Principles and plans to implement that plan upon securing IISF funding.

The lack of a GASSP means that there is no authoritative reference on which to maintain a protected infrastructure. If there were a GAAP, there would be a way to enforce a level of compliance and provide a vehicle for the authoritative approval of reasonably founded exceptions or departures from GASSP.

Similar in theory to GASSP is the Common Criteria Project (http://csrc.nist.gov/cc). The Common Criteria is an international effort that is being developed as a way to evaluate the security properties of information technology (IT) products and systems. By establishing such a common criteria base, the results of an IT security evaluation will be meaningful to a wider audience.

The Common Criteria will permit comparability between the results of independent security evaluations. It facilitates this by providing a common set of requirements for the security functions of IT products and systems and for assurance measures applied to them during a security evaluation. The evaluation process establishes a level of confidence that the security functions of such products and systems, and the assurance measures applied to them, meet these requirements. The evaluation results help determine whether the information technology product or system is secure enough for its intended application and whether the security risks implicit in its use are tolerable.

STEPS IN REVIEWING A FIREWALL

A comprehensive review of the firewall architecture, security plans, and processes should include:

- Procedures governing infrastructure access for employees and business partners accessing the infrastructure
- Physical and logical architecture of the infrastructure
- Hardware and software versions of the infrastructure and underlying network operating systems
- Infrastructure controls over access control information
- Review of log event selection and notification criteria
- All access paths, including those provided for maintenance and administration
- Security policies and administrative procedures (i.e., addition or deletion of users and services, review of device and system audit logs, system backup and retention of media, etc.)
- Access controls over the network operating system, including user accounts, file system permissions, attributes of executable files, privileged programs, and network software
- Emergency Response Plans for the infrastructure in the event of an intrusion, denial-of-service attack, etc.

- Access to and utilization of published security alert bulletins

There are many methodologies with which to perform a firewall review. Most center around the following six steps:

1. Analyze the infrastructure and architecture.
2. Review corporate firewall policy.
3. Run hosts and network assessment scans.
4. Review Firewall-1 configuration.
5. Review Firewall-1 Rule Base.
6. Put it all together in a report.

The following discussion expands on each step.

Step 1: Analyze the Infrastructure and Architecture

An understanding of the network infrastructure is necessary to ensure that the firewall is adequately protecting the network. Items to review include:

- Internet access requirements
- Understanding the business justifications for Internet/extranet access
- Validating inbound and outbound services that are allowed
- Reviewing firewall design (i.e., dual-homed, multi-homed, proxy)
- Analyzing connectivity to internal/external networks:

  — Perimeter network and external connections
  — Electronic commerce gateways
  — Inter- or intra-company LAN-WAN connectivity
  — Overall corporate security architecture
  — The entire computing installation at a given site or location

- Interviewing network and firewall administrators

If there is a fault in the information security architecture that does not reflect what is corporate policy, then the firewall can in no way substitute for that deficiency.

From a firewall perspective, to achieve a scalable and distributable firewall system, Checkpoint has divided the functionality of its Firewall-1 product into two components: a Firewall Module and a Management Module. The interaction of these components makes up the whole of the standard Checkpoint Firewall architecture.

The management module is a centralized controller for the other firewall modules and is where the objects and rules that define firewall functionality exist. The rules and objects can be applied to one or all of the firewall modules.

All logs and alerts generated by other firewall modules are sent to this management system for storage, querying, and review.

The firewall module itself is the actual gateway system in which all traffic between separate zones must pass. The firewall module is the system that inspects packets, applies the rules, and generates logs and alerts. It relies on one or more management modules for its rule base and log storage, but may continue to function independently with its current rule base if the management module is not functioning.

An excellent reference to use in the design of firewall architectures.[2,3]

Step 2: Review Corporate Information System Security Polices

Policy is a critical element of the effective and successful operation of a firewall. A firewall cannot be effective unless deployed in the context of working policies that govern use and administration.

Marcus Ranum[4] defines a firewall as "the implementation of your Internet security policy. If you haven't got a security policy, you haven't got a firewall. Instead, you've got a thing that's sort of doing something, but you don't know what it's trying to do because no one has told you what it should do." Given that, if an organization expects to have a meaningful firewall review in the absence of a set of firewall policies, the organization is in for a rude awakening.

Some policy-based questions to ask during the firewall review include:

- Is there a published firewall policy for the organization?
- Has top management reviewed and approved policies that are relevant to the firewall infrastructure?
- Who has responsibility for controlling the organization's information security?
- Are there procedures to change the firewall policies? If so, what is the process?
- How are these policies communicated throughout the organization?

As to the management of the firewall, some of the issues that must be addressed include:

- Who owns the firewalls, and is this defined?
- Who is responsible for implementing the stated policies for each of the firewalls?
- Who is responsible for the day-to-day management of the firewall?
- Who monitors the firewall for compliance with stated policies?
- How are security-related incidents reported to the appropriate information security staff?

- Are CERT, CIAC, vendor-specific, and similar advisories for the existence of new vulnerabilities monitored?
- Are there written procedures that specify how to react to different events, including containment and reporting procedures?

Change control is critically important for a firewall. Some change controls issues are:

- Ensure that change control procedures documents exist.
- Ensure that test plans are reviewed.
- Review procedures for updating fixes.
- Review the management approval process.
- Process should ensure that changes to the following components are documented:

  — Any upgrades or patches require notification and scheduling of downtime
  — Electronic copies of all changes
  — Hard-copy form filled out for any changes

Finally, backup and contingency planning is crucial when disasters occur. Some issues are:

- *Maintain a golden copy of Firewall-1.* A golden copy is full backup made before the host is connected to the network. This copy can be used for recovery and also as a reference in case the firewall is somehow compromised.
- *Review backup procedures and documentation.* Part of the backup procedures must also include restoration procedures. A backup should only be considered complete if one is able to recover from the backups made. Also, the backups must be stored in a secure location. Should the firewall need to be rebuilt or replaced, there are several files that will need to be restored (see Table 1). These files can be backed up via a complete system backup, utilizing an external device such as a tape drive or other large storage device. The most critical files for firewall functionality should be able to fit on a floppy disk.
- *Review backup schedule.*
- *Determine if procedures are in place to recover the firewall system should a disruption of service occur.*
- *Review contingency plan.*
- *Contingency plan documentation.*

It should be noted that while many safes will physically protect backup media, they will not protect this media against the heat from a fire. The safe must be specifically designed for data storage of media such as tapes, floppies, and hard drives.

Espionage – Firewalls

Espionage –
Firewalls

Table 1 Critical Firewall-1 configuration files to backup.

Management Module

$FWDIR/conf/fw.license
$FWDIR/conf/objects.C
$FWDIR/conf/*.W
$FWDIR/conf/rulebases.fws
$FWDIR/conf/fwauth.NDB*
$FWDIR/conf/fwmusers
$FWDIR/conf/gui-clients
$FWDIR/conf/product.conf
$FWDIR/conf/fwauth.keys
$FWDIR/conf/serverkeys.*

Firewall Module

$FWDIR/conf/fw.license
$FWDIR/conf/product.conf
$FWDIR/conf/masters
$FWDIR/conf/fwauth.keys
$FWDIR/conf/product.conf
$FWDIR/conf/smtp.conf
$FWDIR/conf/fwauthd.conf
$FWDIR/conf/fwopsec.conf
$FWDIR/conf/product.conf
$FWDIR/conf/serverkeys.*

* See http://www.phoneboy.com/fw1/faq/0196.html.

Information Security Policies and Procedures (Thomas Peltier, Auerbach Publications) is a good place to start a policy roll-out. While not a panacea for the lack of a comprehensive set of policies, *Information Security Policies and Procedures* enables an organization to quickly roll-out policies without getting bogged down in its composition.

It must be noted that all of this analysis and investigation should be done in the context of the business goals of the organization. While information systems security is about risk management, if it is not implemented within the framework of the corporate strategy, security is bound to fail.

Step 3: Perform Hosts Software Assessment Scan

A firewall misconfiguration can allow unauthorized parties, outsiders, to break into the network despite the firewall's presence. By performing software scans against the individual firewall hosts, specific vulnerabilities can be detected. These scanning tools can identify security holes, detail system weaknesses, validate policies, and enforce corporate security strategies. Such tools are essential for checking system vulnerabilities.

Some of the myriad checks that scanners can identify include:

- Operating system misconfiguration
- Inappropriate security and password settings
- Buffer overflow
- Detection of SANS Top 10 Internet Security Threats
- Segmentation fault affecting FreeBSD

- Detection of unpassworded NT guest and administrator accounts

Some popular scanning tools[5] include:

- NAI Cybercop, http://www.pgp.com/products/cybercop-scanner
- ISS Internet Scanner, http://www.iss.net/internet_scanner/index.php
- SAINT, http://www.wwdsi.com/saint
- Symantec (formerly Axent) NetRecon, http://enterprise security.symantec.com/products
- Netcat, http://www.l0pht.com/~weld/netcat/
- nmap, http://www.insecure.org/nmap/index.html

It must be noted that running a host software assessment scan on a firewall is just one aspect of a firewall review. Tools such as Cybercop are extremely easy to run; as such, there is no need to bring in a professional services firm to run the tools. The value added by security professional service firms is in the areas of comprehensive architecture design, analysis, and fault amelioration. Any firm that would run these tools and simply hand the client the output is doing the client a serious injustice.

This only serves to reiterate the point that a security infrastructure must be architected from the onset. This architecture must take into consideration items such as security, capacity, redundancy, and management. Without a good architecture, system redesign will be a constant endeavor.

Step 4: Review Firewall-1 Configuration

While Firewall-1 affords significant security, that security can be compromised if Firewall-1 is misconfigured. Some of the more crucial items to review are listed below (not in any specific order).

IP forwarding

Set to *Control IP Forwarding*. IP Forwarding should be disabled in the operating system kernel. This ensures that IP Forwarding will be never be enabled unless Firewall-1 is operating.

Firewall administrators

Ensure that the number of Firewall-1 administrators is limited only to those who truly need it. The purpose of every account on the firewall (both for the operating system and the firewall operating system) must be justified. Fig. 1 provides a list of firewall administrators and their permissions.

Screen shots in this entry are from Firewall-1 v4.1 for Windows NT, but are germane for all platforms and

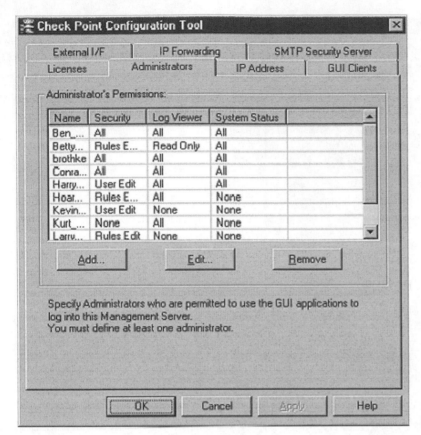

Fig. 1   Firewall administrators and their permissions.

versions. See C/fw1/docs/4.0-summary.html for the new features and up-grades in Firewall-1 version 4.x.

Trained staff

A firewall cannot be effective unless the staff managing the firewall infrastructure is experienced with security and trained in Firewall-1 operations. If a person is made responsible for a firewall simply because he or she has experience with networking, the firewall should be expected to be filled with misconfigurations, which in turn will make it much easier for adversaries to compromise the firewall.

Synchronize (SYN) flood protection

Denial-of-service (DoS) attacks enable an attacker to consume resources on a remote host to the degree it cannot function properly. SYN flood attacks are one of the most common types of DoS attacks.

Ensure that SYN flood protection is activated at the appropriate level: None, SYN Gateway, or Passive SYN Gateway (see Fig. 2).

Operating system version control

For both the Checkpoint software and network operating system, ensure that the firewall is running a current and supported version of Firewall-1. While the latest version does not specifically have to be loaded, ensure that current patches are installed.

Physical security

The firewall must be physically secured. It should be noted that all network operating systems base their security models on a secure physical infrastructure. A firewall must be located in areas where access is restricted only to authorized personnel; specifically:

- The local console must be secure.
- The management console should not be open to the external network.
- The firewall configuration should be fully protected and tamper-proof (except from an authorized management station).
- Full authentication should be required for the administrator for local administration.
- Full authentication and an encrypted link are required for remote administration.

Remove unneeded system components

Software such as compilers, debuggers, security tools, etc. should be removed from the firewall.

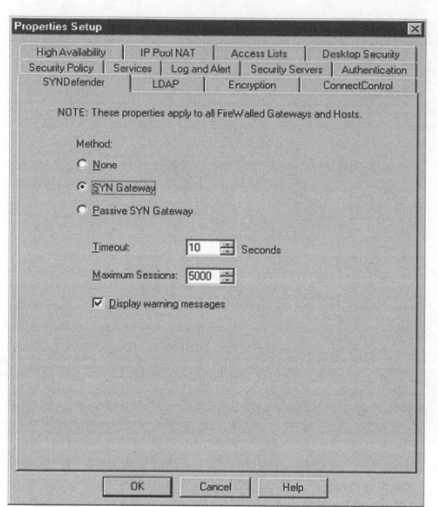

Espionage –
Firewalls

Fig. 2 Setting the SYN flood protection.

Adequate backup power supplies

If the firewall lacks a UPS, security will not be completely enforced in the event of a power disruption.

Log review

The logs of both the firewall and network operating system need to be reviewed and analyzed. All events can be traced to the logs, which can be used for debugging and forensic analysis.

Ideally, logs should be written to a remote log host or separate disk partition. In the event of an attack, logs can provide critical documentation for tracking several aspects of the incident. This information can be used to uncover exploited holes, discover the extent of the attack, provide documented proof of an attack, and even trace the attack's origin. The first thing an attacker will do is cover his or her tracks by modifying or destroying the log files. In the event that these log files are destroyed, backups will be required to track the incident. Thus, frequent backups are mandatory.

Time synchronization

Time synchronization serves two purposes: to ensure that time-sensitive events are executed at the correct time and that different log files can be correlated. Logs that reference an incorrect time can potentially be excluded as evidence in court and this might thwart any effort to prosecute an attacker.

The Network Time Protocol (NTP) RFC 1305 is commonly used to synchronize hosts. For environments requiring a higher grade and auditable method of time synchronization, the time synchronization offerings from Certified Time (http://www.certifiedtime.com) should be investigated.

Integrity checking

Integrity checking is a method to notify a system administrator when something on the file system has changed to a critical file. The most widely known and deployed integrity checking application is Tripwire (http://www.tripwire.com).

Limit the amount of services and protocols

A firewall should have nothing installed or running that is not absolutely required by the firewall. Unnecessary protocols open needless communication links. A port scan can be used to see what services are open. Too many services can hinder the efficacy of the firewall, but each service should be authorized; if not, it should be disabled.

Dangerous components and services include:

- X or GUI related packages
- NIS/NFS/RPC related software
- Compilers, Perl, TCL
- Web server, administration software
- Desktop applications software (i.e., Microsoft Office, Lotus Notes, browsers, etc.)

On an NT firewall, only the following services and protocols should be enabled:

- TCP/IP
- Firewall-1
- Protected Storage
- UPS
- RPC
- Scheduler
- Event log
- Plug-and-Play
- NTLM Security Support provider

If other functionality is needed, add them only on an as-needed basis.

Harden the operating system

Any weakness or misconfiguration in the underlying network operating system will trickle down to Firewall-1. The firewall must be protected as a bastion host to be the security stronghold. A firewall should never be treated as a general-purpose computing device.

The following are excellent documents on how to harden an operating system:

- *Armoring Solaris*, http://www.enteract.com/~lspitz/armoring.html
- *Armoring Linux*, http://www.enteract.com/~lspitz/linux.html
- *Armoring NT*, http://www.enteract.com/~lspitz/nt.html

Those needing a pre-hardened device should consider the Nokia firewall appliance (http://www.nokia.com/securitysolutions/network/firewall.html). The Nokia firewall is a hardware solution bundled with Firewall-1. It runs on the IPSO operating system that has been hardened and optimized for firewall functionality.

Firewall-1 properties

Fig. 3 shows the Security Policies tab. One should uncheck the Accept boxes that are not necessary:

- *ICMP*. In general, one can disable this property, although one will need to leave it enabled to take advantage of Checkpoint's Stateful Inspection for ICMP in 4.0.
- *Zone transfer*. Most sites do not allow users to perform DNS downloads. The same is true for RIP and DNS lookup options.

Firewall-1 network objects

A central aspect of a Firewall-1 review includes the analysis of all of the defined network objects. Firewall-1 network objects are logical entities that are grouped together as part of the security policy. For example, a group of Web servers could be a simple network object to which a rule is applied. Every network object has a set of attributes, such as network address, subnet mask, etc. Examples of entities that can be part of a network object include:

- Networks and sub-networks
- Servers
- Routers
- Switches
- Hosts and gateway
- Internet domains
- Groups of the above

Firewall-1 allows for the creation of network objects within the source and destination fields. These network objects can contain and referenceanywhere from a single device to entire networks containing thousands of devices. The latter creates a significant obstacle when attempting to evaluate the security configuration and security level of a Firewall-1 firewall. The critical issue is how to determine the underlying security of the network object when it contains numerous objects.

This object-oriented approach to managing devices on Firewall-1 allows the firewall administrator to define routers or any other device as network objects, and then to use those objects within the rules of the firewall security policy. The main uses of network objects are for efficiency in referencing a large amount of network devices. This obviates the need to remember such things as the host name, IP address, location, etc. While network objects provide a significant level of ease of use and time-saving by utilizing such objects, an organization needs to determine if it inherently trusts all of the devices contained within the object. Fig. 4 shows the Network Objects box that shows some of the existing objects. Fig. 5 shows an example of a Network Object with a number of workstations in the group.

Espionage –
Firewalls

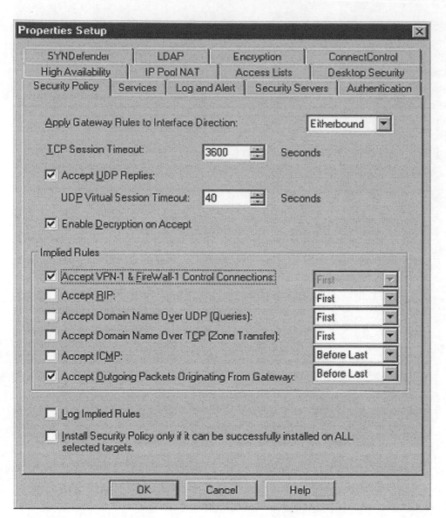

Fig. 3 The Security Policy tab.

As stated, such use of network objects is time-saving from an administrative perspective; but from a security perspective, there is a problem in that any built-in trust that is associated with the network object is automatically created for every entity within that network object. This is due to the fact that in large networks, it is time-consuming to inspect every individual entity defined in the network object. The difficulty posed by such a configuration means that in order to inspect with precision and accuracy the protection that the firewall rule offers, it is essential to inspect every device within the network object.

Step 5: Review Firewall-1 Rule Base

The purpose of a rule base review is to actually see what services and data the firewall permits. An analysis of the rule base is also meant to identify any unneeded, repetitive, or unauthorized rules. The rule base should be made as simple as possible. One way to reduce the number of rules is by combining rules, because sometimes repetitive rules can be merged.

The function of a rule base review is to ensure that the firewall is enforcing what it is expected to. Security expert

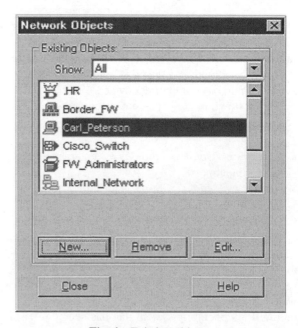

Fig. 4 Existing objects.

Espionage –
Firewalls

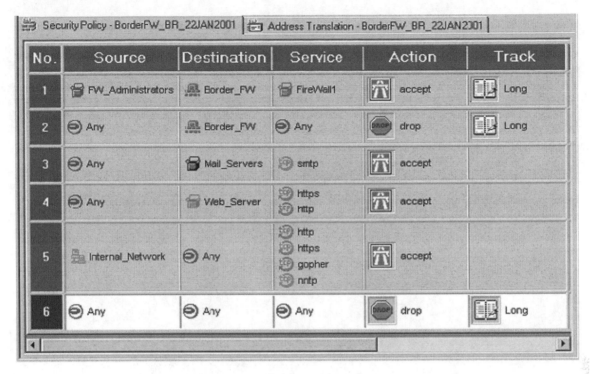

Fig. 5 A network object with a number of workstations in the group.

Espionage – Firewalls

Lance Spitzner writes in *Building Your Firewall Rule Base*[6] that "building a solid rule base is a critical, if not the most critical, step in implementing a successful and secure firewall. Security administrators and experts all often argue what platforms and applications make the best firewalls. However, all of this is meaningless if the firewall rule base is misconfigured."

The rule base is the heart and soul of a Checkpoint firewall. A rule base is a file stored on the firewall that contains an ordered set of rules that defines a distinct security policy for each particular firewall. Access to the rule base file is restricted to those that are either physically at the firewall or a member of the GUI client list specified in the configuration settings.

A rule describes a communication in terms of its source, destination, and service. The rule also specifies whether the communication should be accepted or rejected and whether a log entry is created.

The Firewall-1 inspection engine is a "first-fit" as opposed to a "best-fit" device. This means that if one has a rule base containing 20 rules, and the incoming packet matches rule #4, the inspection engine stops immediately (because rules are examined sequentially for each packet) and does not go through the remainder of the rule base.

As for the rule base review, Spitzer recommends that the goal is to have no more than 30 rules. Once there are more then 30 rules, things exponentially grow in complexity and mistakes then happen.

Each rule base has a separate name. It is useful to standardize on a common naming convention. A suggested format is: firewall-name_administrators-initials_date-of-change; for example, fw1_am_071298.

The result of this naming convention is that the firewall administrator knows exactly which firewall the rule base belongs to; when the rule base was last changed; and who last modified the current configuration. For the rule base review, each and every rule must be examined.

An example of a simple rule base with six rules is as shown in Fig. 6:

- **Rules 1 and 2** enforce the concept of the stealth rule, in that nothing should be able to connect directly to the firewall, other than administrators that are GUI authorized. Rule 1 tells Firewall-1 to drop any packet unless it is from a member of the FW_Administrators group. The Firewall-1 service is predefined and defines all the Firewall-1 administrative ports. For the stealth rule, one specifically wants to drop the packet, as opposed to rejecting it. A rejected packet tells the sender that there is something on the remote side, while a dropped packet does not necessarily indicate a remote host. In addition, this rule is logged; thus, detailed information can be gleaned about who is attempting to make direct connections to the firewall.
- **Rule 3** allows any host e-mail connectivity to the internal mail servers.

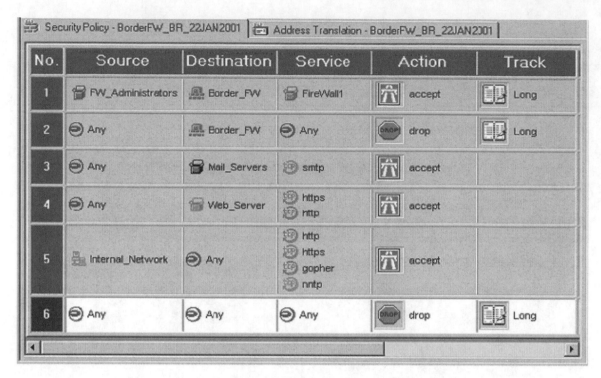

Fig. 6 A simple rule base.

- **Rule 4** allows any host HTTP and HTTPS connectivity to internal Web servers.
- **Rule 5** allows internal host connectivity to the Internet for the four specified protocols.
- **Rule 6** is the cleanup rule. Any packet not handled by the firewall at this point will be dropped and logged. The truth is that any packet not handled by the firewall at that point would be dropped anyway. The advantage to this cleanup rule is that these packets will be logged. In this way, one can see which packets are not being handled by the firewall. This can be of assistance in designing a more scalable firewall architecture.

The above rule base example had only six rules and was rather simple. Most corporate rule bases are more detailed and complex. Going through a rule base containing 50 rules and thousands of network objects could take a while to complete.

Fig. 7 displays a rule base that is a little more involved:

- **Rule 1** enforces the stealth rule.
- **Rules 2–4** allow mail traffic between the mail servers and clients.
- **Rule 5** allows any host HTTP connectivity to internal Web servers.
- **Rule 6** stops traffic between the DMZ and an intranet.
- **Rules 7–8** stop incoming and outgoing traffic between the DMZ and an intranet.

- **Rule 9** drop protocols that cause a lot of traffic—in this case, nbdatagram, nbname, and nbsession.
- **Rule 10** is the cleanup rule.

When performing a review and there is doubt that a specific rule is needed, it can be disabled. As a general rule, if a rule is disabled and no one complains, then the rule can be deleted. Fig. 8 shows an example of a disabled rule.

Implied pseudo-rules

Implied pseudo-rules are rules that do not appear in the normal rule base, but are automatically created by Firewall-1 based on settings in the Properties Setup of the Security Policy.[7] These rules can be viewed along with the rule base in the Security Policy GUI application. Fig. 9 displays an example of the implied pseudo-rules from a rule base with a single rule.

Although the single and only rule implicitly drops all traffic, there is a lot of traffic that can still pass through the firewall. As seen from these implied pseudo-rules, most of the connectivity deals with the internal operations of the firewall.

Step 6: Put It All Together in a Report

After all the work has been completed, the firewall review needs to be documented. The value in a post-review report

Espionage –
Firewalls

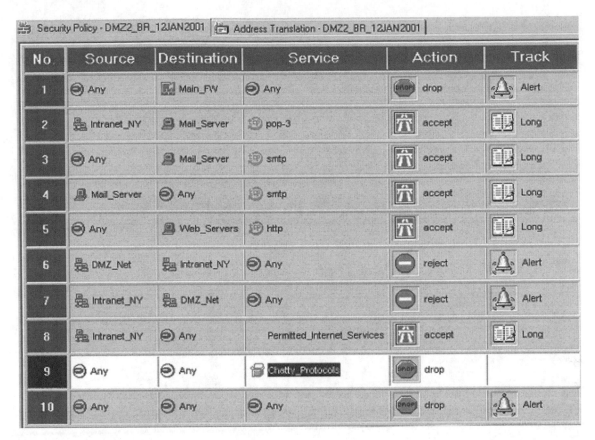

No.	Source	Destination	Service	Action	Track
1	Any	Main_FW	Any	drop	Alert
2	Intranet_NY	Mail_Server	pop-3	accept	Long
3	Any	Mail_Server	smtp	accept	Long
4	Mail_Server	Any	smtp	accept	Long
5	Any	Web_Servers	http	accept	Long
6	DMZ_Net	Intranet_NY	Any	reject	Alert
7	Intranet_NY	DMZ_Net	Any	reject	Alert
8	Intranet_NY	Any	Permitted_Internet_Services	accept	Long
9	Any	Any	Chatty_Protocols	drop	
10	Any	Any	Any	drop	Alert

Fig. 7 Complex rule base.

is that it can be used as a resource to correct the anomalies found.

As previously stated, the ease of use afforded by scanning tools makes the creation of a huge report effortless. But for a firewall review to have value for a client, it should:

- Contain current security state: detail the baseline of the current networking environment and current security posture; this must reference the corporate risk assessment to ensure synchronization with the overall security goals of the organization.
- Identify all security vulnerabilities.
- Recommend corrections, solutions, and implementation priorities; a detailed implementation plan must be provided, showing how all of the solutions and fixes will coalesce.

- Provide detailed analysis of security trade-offs, relating the risks to cost, ease of use, business requirements, and acceptable levels of risk.
- Provide baseline data for future reference and comparison to ensure that systems are rolled out in a secure manner.

CONCLUSION

A firewall is effective to the degree that it is properly implemented. And in today's corporate environments, it is easy for a firewall to become misconfigured. By reviewing the firewall setup, firewall administrators can ensure that their firewall is enforcing what they expect it to, in a secure manner. This makes for good sense and good security.

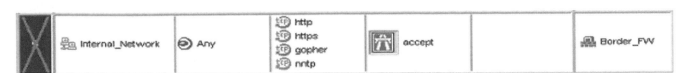

	Internal_Network	Any	http https gopher nntp	accept		Border_FW

Fig. 8 Disabled rule.

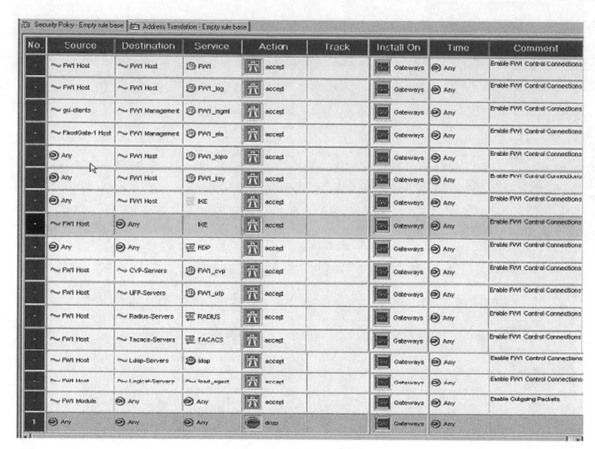

Fig. 9 Implied pseudo-rules.

REFERENCES

1. http://web.mit.edu/security/www/gassp1.html.
2. Zwicky, E.D.; Cooper, S.; Chapman, D.B. *Building Internet Firewalls*; O'Reilly & Associates, Inc.: Sebastopol, CA, 2000, ISBN: 1565928717.
3. Rothke, B. Choosing the Right Firewall Architecture Environment, ESJ, http://www.esj.com/library/1998/June/0698028.htm, June 1998.
4. Ranum, M. Publications, Rants, Presentations, & Codes, http://www.net/pub/mjr/pubs/index.shtml.
5. http://www.hackingexposed.com/tools/tools.html.
6. http://www.enteract.com/~lspitz.
7. http://www.phoneboy.com/fw1/faq/0345.html.

BIBLIOGRAPHY

1. Checkpoint Knowledge Base, http://support.checkpoint.com/public/.
2. Checkpoint resource library, http://cgi.us.checkpoint.com/rl/resourcelib.asp.
3. Phoneboy, excellent Firewall-1 resource with large amounts of technical information, http://www.phoneboy.com.
4. Spitzner, Auditing Your Firewall Setup, http://www.enteract.com/~lspitz/audit.html; http://www.csiannual.com/pdf/f7f8.pdf.
5. Spitzner, Building Your Firewall Rule Base, http://www.enteract.com/~lspitz.
6. Firewall-1 discussion threads, http://msgs.securepoint.com/fw1/.
7. SecurityPortal, latest and greatest firewall products and security news, http://www.itsecurityportal.com.
8. Pragmatic security information, http://www.ranum.com/security/computer_security/editorials/index.html.
9. Internet Firewalls Frequently Asked Questions, http://www.interhack.net/pubs/fwfaq/.
10. SecurityFocus.com, http://www.securityfocus.com.
11. ICSA Firewall-1 Lab Report, http://www.icsa.net/html/communities/firewalls/certification/vendors/checkpoint/firewall1/nt/30a_report.shtml.
12. WebTrends Firewall Suite, http://www.webtrends.com/products/firewall/default.htm.
13. Intrusion Detection for FW-1, http://www.enteract.com/~lspitz.
14. Cheswick, W.; Bellovin, S. *Firewalls and Internet Security*; Addison Wesley: Upper Saddle River, NJ, 2001; ISBN: 020163466X.
15. Garfinkel, S.; Spafford, G. *Practical UNIX and Internet Security*; O'Reilly & Associates: Sebastopol, CA, 1996, ISBN: 1-56592-148-8.
16. Norberg, S.; *Securing Windows NT/2000 Server*, O'Reilly & Associates: Sebastopol, CA, 2001, ISBN 1-56592-768-0.

Espionage –
Firewalls

17. Scambray, J.; McClure, S.; Kurtz, G. *Hacking Exposed: Network Security Secrets and Solutions*; McGraw-Hill, 2000, ISBN: 0072127481

18. CERT/CC Advisories, http://www.cert.org/contact_cert/certmaillist.html.

19. @stake, http://www.atstake.com/research/advisories/index.html.

20. CIAC, http://ciac.llnl.gov/.

21. Firewall-1 mailing list, http://www.checkpoint.com/services/mailing.html.

22. Firewalls mailing list, http://lists.gnac.net/firewalls/.

23. Firewall Wizards list, http://www.nfr.com/forum/firewall-wizards.html.

24. CERIAS, http://www.cerias.purdue.edu/.

25. Bugtraq, Bugtraq-request@fc.net.

26. NTBugtraq, Ntbugtraq-request@fc.net.

27. ISS X-Force Advisories, http://www.iss.net/mailinglist.php.

28. Sun, http://www.sun.com/security/siteindex.html.

29. Microsoft, http://www.microsoft.com/security.

30. SANS, http://www.sans.org.

Espionage – Firewalls

Firewalls: Internet Security

E. Eugene Schultz, Ph.D., CISSP
Principal Engineer, Lawrence Berkeley National Laboratory, Livermore, California, U.S.A.

Abstract

The Internet has presented a new, complex set of challenges that even the most sophisticated technical experts have not been able to solve adequately. Achieving adequate security is one of the foremost of these challenges. The major security threats that the Internet community faces are described in this entry. It also explains how firewalls—potentially one of the most effective solutions for Internet security—can address these threats, and it presents some practical advice for obtaining the maximum advantages of using firewalls.

INTERNET SECURITY THREATS

The vastness and openness that characterizes the Internet presents an extremely challenging problem—security. Although many claims about the number and cost of Internet-related intrusions are available, valid, credible statistics about the magnitude of this problem will not be available until scientific research is conducted. Exacerbating this dilemma is that most corporations that experience intrusions from the Internet and other sources do not want to make these incidents known for fear of public relations damage and, worse yet, many organizations fail to even detect most intrusions. Sources, such as Carnegie Mellon University's Computer Emergency Response Team, however, suggest that the number of Internet-related intrusions each year is very high and that the number of intrusions reported to CERT (which is one of dozens of incident response teams) is only the tip of the iceberg. No credible statistics concerning the total amount of financial loss resulting from security-related intrusions are available; but judging from the amount of money corporations and government agencies are spending to implement Internet and other security controls, the cost must be extremely high.

Many types of Internet security threats exist. One of the most serious methods is IP spoofing. In this type of attack, a perpetrator fabricates packets that bear the address of origination of a client host and sends these packets to the server for this client. The server acknowledges receiving these packets by returning packets with a certain sequence number. If the attacker can guess this packet sequence number and incorporate it into another set of fabricated packets that is then sent back to the server, the server can be tricked into setting up a connection with a fraudulent client. The intruder can subsequently use attack methods, such as use of trusted host relationships, to intrude into the server machine.

A similar threat is domain name service (DNS) spoofing. In this type of attack, an intruder subverts a host within a network and sets up this machine to function as an apparently legitimate name server. The host then provides bogus data about host identities and certain network services, enabling the intruder to break into other hosts within the network.

Session hijacking is another Internet security threat. The major tasks for the attacker who wants to hijack an ongoing session between remote hosts are locating an existing connection between two hosts and fabricating packets that bear the address of the host from which the connection has originated. By sending these packets to the destination host, the originating host's connection is dropped, and the attacker picks up the connection.

Another Internet security threat is network snooping, in which attackers install programs that copy packets traversing network segments. The attackers periodically inspect files that contain the data from the captured packets to discover critical log-on information, particularly user IDs and passwords for remote systems. Attackers subsequently connect to the systems for which they possess the correct log-on information and log on with no trouble. Attackers targeting networks operated by Internet service providers (ISPs) have made this problem especially serious, because so much information travels these networks. These attacks demonstrate just how vulnerable network infrastructures are; successfully attacking networks at key points, where router, firewalls, and server machines are located, is generally the most efficient way to gain information allowing unauthorized access to multitudes of host machines within a network.

A significant proportion of attacks exploit security exposures in programs that provide important network services. Examples of these programs include sendmail, Network File System (NFS), and Network Information Service (NIS). These exposures allow intruders to gain access to remote hosts and to manipulate services supported by these hosts or even to obtain superuser access. Of increasing concern is the susceptibility of World Wide Web services and the hosts that house these services to successful attack. The ability of intruders to exploit

Encyclopedia of Information Assurance DOI: 10.1081/E-EIA-120046368
Copyright © 2011 by Taylor & Francis. All rights reserved.

vulnerabilities in the HTTP and in Java, a programming language used to write WWW applications, seems to be growing at an alarming rate.

Until a short time ago, most intruders attempted to cover up indications of their activity, often by installing programs that selectively eliminated data from system logs. These also avoided causing system crashes or causing massive slowdowns or disruption. However, a significant proportion of the perpetrator community has apparently shifted its strategy by increasingly perpetrating denial-of-service attacks. For example, many types of hosts crash or perform a core dump when they are sent a packet internet groper or ping packet that exceeds a specified size limit or when they are flooded with synchronize (SYN) packets that initiate host-to-host connections. (Packet internet groper, or ping, is a service used to determine whether a host on a network is up and running.) These denial-of-service attacks make up an increasing proportion of observed Internet attacks. They represent a particularly serious threat because many organizations require continuity of computing and networking operations to maintain their business operations.

Not to be overlooked is another type of security threat called social engineering. Social engineering is fabricating a story to trick users, system administrators, or help desk personnel into providing information required to access systems. Intruders usually solicit passwords for user accounts, but information about the network infrastructure and the identity of individual hosts can also be the target of social engineering attacks.

INTERNET SECURITY CONTROLS

As previously mentioned, Internet security threats pose a challenge because of their diversity and severity. An added complication is an abundance of potential solutions.

Encryption

Encryption is a process of using an algorithm to transform cleartext information into text that cannot be read without the proper key. Encryption protects information stored in host machines and transmitted over networks. It is also useful in authenticating users to hosts or networks. Although encryption is an effective solution, its usefulness is limited by the difficulty in managing encryption keys (i.e., of assigning keys to users and recovering keys if they are lost or forgotten), laws limiting the export and use of encryption, and the lack of adherence to encryption standards by many vendors.

One-Time Passwords

Using one-time passwords is another way in which to challenge security threats. One-time passwords captured

while in transit over networks become worthless because each password can only be used once. A captured password has already been used by the legitimate user who has initiated a remote log-on session by the time the captured password can be employed. Nevertheless, one-time passwords address only a relatively small proportion of the total range of Internet security threats. They do not, for example, protect against IP spoofing or exploitation of vulnerabilities in programs.

Installing fixes for vulnerabilities in all hosts within an Internet-capable network does not provide an entirely suitable solution because of the cost of labor, and, over the last few years, vulnerabilities have surfaced at a rate far faster than that at which fixes have become available.

Firewalls

Although no single Internet security control measure is perfect, the firewall has, in many respects, proved more useful overall than most other controls. Simply, a firewall is a security barrier between two networks that screens traffic coming in and out of the gate of one network to accept or reject connections and service requests according to a set of rules. If configured properly, it addresses a large number of threats that originate from outside a network without introducing any significant security liabilities. Because most organizations are unable to install every patch that CERT advisories describe, these organizations can nevertheless protect hosts within their networks against external attacks that exploit vulnerabilities by installing a firewall that prevents users from outside the network from reaching the vulnerable programs in the first place. A more sophisticated firewall also controls how any connection between a host external to a network and an internal host occurs. Moreover, an effective firewall hides information, such as names and addresses of hosts within the network, as well as the topology of the network which it is employed to protect.

Firewalls can defend against attacks on hosts (including spoofing attacks), application protocols, and applications. In addition, firewalls provide a central method for administering security on a network and for logging incoming and outgoing traffic to allow for accountability of user actions and for triggering incident response activity if unauthorized activity occurs.

Firewalls are typically placed at gateways to networks to create a security perimeter, as shown in Fig. 1, primarily to protect an internal network from threats originating from an external one (particularly from the Internet). This scheme is successful to the degree that the security perimeter is not accessible through unprotected avenues of access. The firewall acts as a choke component for security purposes. Fig. 1 displays routers that are located in front and in back of the firewall. The first router (shown above the firewall) is an external one used initially to route incoming traffic, to direct outgoing traffic to external

Espionage –
Firewalls

Espionage –
Firewalls

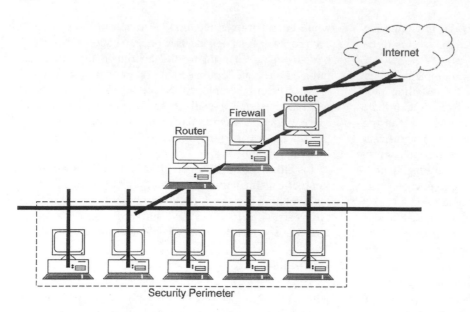

Fig. 1 A typical gate-based firewall architecture.

networks, and to broadcast information that enables other network routers (as well as the router on the other side of the firewall) to know how to reach the host network. The other internal router (shown below the firewall) sends incoming packets to their destination within the internal network, directs outgoing packets to the external router, and broadcasts information on how to reach the internal network and the external router. This belt-and-suspenders configuration further boosts security by preventing the broadcast of information about the internal network outside the network the firewall protects. An attacker finding this information can learn IP addresses, subnets, servers, and other information that is useful in perpetrating attacks against the network. Hiding information about the internal network is much more difficult if the gate has only one router.

Another way in which firewalls are deployed (although less frequently) is within an internal network—at the entrance to a subnet within a network—rather than at the gateway to the entire network. The purpose of this configuration (shown in Fig. 2) is to segregate a subnetwork (a screened subnet) from the internal network at large, a wise strategy if the subnet has tighter security requirements than the rest of the security perimeter. This type of deployment more carefully controls access to data and services within a subnet than is otherwise allowed within the network. The gate-based firewall, for example, may allow File Transfer Protocol (FTP) access to an internal network from external sources. However, if a subnet contains hosts that store information, such as lease bid data or salary data, then allowing FTP access to this subnet is less advisable. Setting up the subnet as a screened subnet may provide suitable security control; that is, the internal firewall that provides security screening for the subnet is configured to deny all FTP access, regardless of whether the access requests originated from outside or inside the network.

Simply having a firewall, no matter how it is designed and implemented, does not necessarily protect against externally originated security threats. The benefits of firewalls depend to a large degree on the type used and how it is deployed and maintained.

USING FIREWALLS EFFECTIVELY

To ensure that firewalls perform their intended function, it is important to choose the appropriate firewall and to implement it correctly. Establishing a firewall policy is also a critical step in securing a system, as is regular maintenance of the entire security structure.

Choosing the Right Firewall

Each type of firewall offers its own set of advantages and disadvantages. Combined with the vast array of vendor firewall products and the possibility of custom-building a firewall, this task can be potentially over-whelming. Establishing a set of criteria for selecting an appropriate firewall is an effective aid in narrowing down the choices.

One of the most important considerations is the amount and type of security needed. For some organizations with low to moderate security needs, installing a packet-filtering firewall that blocks only the most dangerous incoming service requests often provides the most satisfactory solution because the cost and effort are not likely to be great. For other organizations, such as banks and insurance corporations, packet-filtering firewalls do not generally provide the granularity and control against unauthorized actions usually needed for connecting customers to services that reside within a financial or insurance corporation's network.

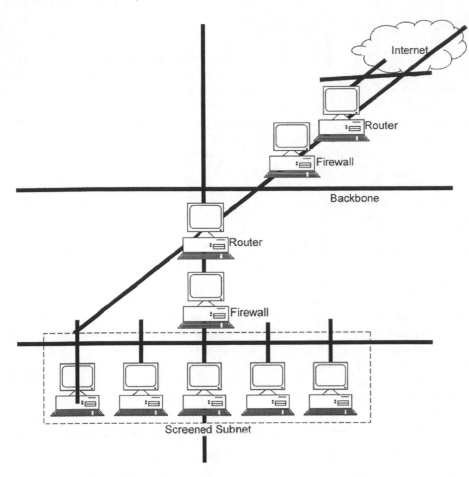

Fig. 2   A screened subnet.

Espionage –
Firewalls

Additional factors, such as the reputation of the vendor, the arrangements for vendor support, the verifiability of the firewall's code (i.e., to confirm that the firewall does what the vendor claims it does), the support for strong authentication, the ease of administration, the ability of the firewall to withstand direct attacks, and the quality and extent of logging and alarming capabilities, should also be strong considerations in choosing a firewall.

Importance of a Firewall Policy

The discussion to this point has focused on high-level technical considerations. Although these considerations are extremely important, too often security professionals overlook other considerations that, if neglected, can render firewalls ineffective. The most important consideration in effectively using firewalls is developing a firewall policy.

A firewall policy is a statement of how a firewall should work—the rules by which incoming and outgoing traffic should be allowed or rejected. A firewall policy, therefore, is a type of security requirements document for a firewall. As security needs change, firewall policies must change accordingly. Failing to create and update a firewall policy for each firewall almost inevitably results in gaps between expectations and the actual function of the firewall,

resulting in uncontrolled security exposures in firewall functionality. For example, security administrators may think that all incoming HTTP requests are blocked, but the firewall may actually allow HTTP requests from certain IP addresses, leaving an unrecognized avenue of attack.

An effective firewall policy should provide the basis for firewall implementation and configuration; needed changes in the way the firewall works should always be preceded by changes in the firewall policy. An accurate, up-to-date firewall policy should also serve as the basis for evaluating and testing a firewall.

Security Maintenance

Many organizations that employ firewalls feel a false sense of security once the firewalls are in place. Properly designing and implementing firewalls can be difficult, costly, and time consuming. It is critical to remember, however, that firewall design and implementation are simply the beginning points of having a firewall. Firewalls that are improperly maintained soon lose their value as security control tools.

One of the most important facets of firewall maintenance is updating the security policy and rules by which each firewall operates. Firewall functionality invariably must change as new services and applications are introduced in (or sometimes removed from) a network. Undertaking the task of daily inspections of firewall logs to discover attempted and possibly successful attacks on both the firewall and the internal network that it protects should be an extremely high priority. Evaluating and testing the adequacy of firewalls for unexpected access avenues to the security perimeter and vulnerabilities that lead to unauthorized access to the firewall should also be a frequent, high-priority activity.

Firewall products have improved considerably over the past several years and are likely to continue to improve. Several vendor products, for example, are not network addressable, which makes breaking into these platforms by someone who does not have physical access to them virtually impossible. At the same time, however, recognizing the limitations of firewalls and ensuring that other appropriate Internet security controls are in place is becoming increasingly important because of such problems as third-party connections to organizations' networks that bypass gate-based security mechanisms altogether. Therefore, an Internet security strategy that includes firewalls in addition to host-based security mechanisms is invariably the most appropriate direction for achieving suitable levels of Internet security.

CONCLUSION

Internet connectivity can be extremely valuable to an organization, but it involves many security risks. A firewall is a key tool in an appropriate set of security control measures to protect Internet-capable networks. Firewalls can be placed at the gateway to a network to form a security perimeter around the networks that they protect or at the entrance to subnets to screen the subnets from the rest of the internal network.

Developing an accurate and complete firewall policy is the most important step in using firewalls effectively. This policy should be modified and updated as new applications are added within the internal network protected by the firewall and as new security threats emerge. Maintaining firewalls properly and regularly examining the log data that they provide are almost certainly the most neglected aspects of using firewalls. Yet, these activities are among the most important in ensuring that the defenses are adequate and that incidents are quickly detected and handled. Performing regular security evaluations and testing the firewall to identify any exploitable vulnerabilities or misconfigurations are also essential activities. Establishing a regular security procedure minimizes the possibility of system penetration by an attacker.

Forensics

Kelly J. "KJ" Kuchta, CPP, CFE
President, Forensics Consulting Solutions, Phoenix, Arizona, U.S.A.

Abstract

This entry discusses breaches in security as analogous to a crime scene. The focus of the entry is on employees, especially those who have been fired. The author gives a brief description of possible scenarios and then helps the reader understand what they can do to help prevent evidence tainting when these breaches take place. Some of the techniques described include ensuring data is not tainted by holding onto an ex-employees hard drive for a minimum of 60–90 days; having strict personnel regulations in place such as hiring practices and "acceptable use" policies; and developing a process to secure evidence through proper collection and storage.

Envision coming across the dead bodies and the related carnage of a crime scene at night. It is a place of chaos and confusion, smoke, shadows, and debris. Victims wander around dazed and stumble into each other; bystanders and the curious mill around in anxious speculation and anticipation. No one really knows what happened, or even when. They just know that it has happened. The authorities are supposedly on the way. Then suddenly, someone runs up to you and puts you in charge. Why? Because you know the neighborhood.

This sounds like a nightmare and in reality, it is—especially when the crime scene is somewhere in your network and involves your information systems.

I use the crime scene analogy because forensics issues involving information systems are like a crime scene. From decades of watching TV cop shows (or the O.J. trial), most people know that you do not trample over evidence because valuable information and clues about the crime could be inadvertently destroyed or tainted. At the crime scene, we know to check to see whether there is anyone who needs medical assistance and then just pick up the phone and dial 911—thereby letting those who have the requisite training, background, and expertise analyze the crime scene and work it.

What do you do when you find out later that something bad has happened in your network and you need information about an event in the past? If someone in your organization has the appropriate skills, that person will appreciate early notice about the incident and your efforts to leave the crime scene intact.

As emergency personnel will often tell you, the initial decisions made following an incident have the greatest impact on the outcome. Today's information systems usually do not leave many outward signs that something is terribly wrong. Actually, it is the people that using the system who will provide insight into incidents.

With increasing frequency, we are seeing theft of confidential data and other misuse of computers. The best advice I can give people and corporations in handling future incidents is to develop a "behavioral pattern matrix" (see Table 1) of personnel security-related events that need closer scrutiny (more on this later) and when in doubt preserve the evidence by removing the hard drive of the victimized computer. Hard drives are inexpensive, and the amount of downtime from pulling a hard drive and installing a new hard drive with your organizations' standard loadset is minimal. The effort to do this can save the organization money and headaches.

Consider the employee who resigns after working in a sensitive area of your business. If anything illegal or unethical has taken place, you will probably not find out about it until 30 to 60 days after the employee has left, if ever. I suggest saving the hard drives from laptops or desktops of resigned and terminated employees for a minimum of 60 to 90 days and longer if possible. At the end of this period of time, cleanse the disk and put it back into production. Why? Because once the hard drive and the residing data is reformatted and placed back into circulation, the chances of recovering any usable information from that hard drive for forensic analysis will be next to impossible and limited by the amount of time and money you have to spend.

In most instances when evidence is tainted, it is through ignorance, not through intentional acts of deception. I have witnessed corporations and individuals who attempt to use their investigative skills after an incident by having the system administrator look for clues or evidence. In one case, they were able to find incriminating data; however, after finding the information, they opened the file and copied it to a floppy disk. This action modified the key dates and contaminated the electronic evidence, preventing its use in a court of law.

Encyclopedia of Information Assurance DOI: 10.1081/E-EIA-120046834
Copyright © 2011 by Taylor & Francis. All rights reserved.

Table 1 Sample of behavioral matrix.

Employee	Risk Score Yes = 1 No = 0	Weight 100 (%)	Weighted Score (%)
Did the employee work with sensitive information?	1	5	0.05
Was the separation hostile?	0	20	0
Did the employee go to work for a competitor?	1	20	0.2
Could the employee have been involved in any unexplained events?	0	5	0
Was the separation unexpected?	0	10	0
Is there a chance that the employee's actions might be involved in litigation?	0	25	0
Has the entity been the target of intelligence gathering?	1	15	0.15
Evidence preservation score			40

Guidelines for evidence preservation

0% to 24% no apparent need to preserve evidence

25% to 49% good reason to preserve evidence

>49% strong reason to preserve evidence

This is a sample behavioral matrix you can customize to your needs.

Computer forensic professionals view the system dates as vital pieces of information. Created, last written, and last access dates are used to establish a chain of events that give important insight into what happened in the past. Computer forensics methodology dictates that computer forensics professionals must not change any piece of evidence, including the dates. When reviewing the data on a suspected system, great lengths are taken to prevent the operating system from writing to the hard drive. Even if you are not a computer forensics professional, you owe your organization the opportunity to fight back by preserving the original evidence.

When a computer is started, right away the operating system changes or modifies a large number of file dates on the system. The actual number of files may vary depending on what type of system, anti-virus applications, or network protocols the organization is using. A typical Windows 98 machine will have over 12,000 files loaded on it. During the start-up process, hundreds of these files may be changed during the POST (power on self test) process. If the anti-virus application is set to inoculate any viruses found, having the malicious code removed will modify the file. This process will change the last access and last written dates.

To keep as many options available as possible, consider setting the hard drives aside for a reasonable amount of time. If you think that putting each hard drive in a probationary period will not work because of the potential expense, consider doing it on a limited basis. Earlier, I mentioned developing a behavioral pattern matrix for exiting employees who might give you reason to preserve their hard drives. The objective is to find predictors that would indicate the future need to review the hard drive of the computer.

My experience has shown that human behavior is a key predictor that must be considered at a digital crime scene.

Each organization will experience different behaviors that constitute a warning. Each organization will need to develop its own behavior pattern that fits its culture. In this case, past events can be good indicators of future events. The sources of information to consider should come from human resources, corporate investigations, information security, as well as the legal department and the business units themselves.

Some factors that might weigh into your behavioral pattern matrix are as follows: Did the employee work with sensitive data? Was the resignation a surprise? Is the termination likely to result in legal proceedings? Is the employee going to work for a competitor? Have there been any events that are of concern to the organization in which the employee might have been involved? Was the employee vague about why he or she was leaving? The answer "yes" to any of these questions should trigger at least considering saving the hard drive for a reasonable period of time.

I often hear, "I knew there was something suspicious about the person!" when working on employee or former employee issues. There are other signs that are frequently overlooked, but by considering all the facts, organizations realize in retrospect that they missed the warning signs. The warnings are generally spread out over multiple areas, such as human resources, corporate investigations, business units, and information security.

Human resources and the business units hold the keys about the behavior of the individual and the possible reason for the departure of the employee. Corporate investigations might be able to provide insight on external events and intelligence information. This could include events under investigation but not publicly known, attempts by

Forensics – FTP

competitors to gain proprietary information, and other possible related matters. Information security might have some information about suspicious behavior the individual demonstrated recently. Examples of suspicious behavior could be linked to attempting access to restricted information, copying large amount of data, allegations of technology misuse, or browsing suspicious Internet sites.

The best process I have witnessed was to have the human resources personnel in charge of the employee exit process give notice to the three groups listed previously. They should give each group a reasonable amount of time to respond that they would like the hard drive held for the proscribed period of time or want immediate analysis relating to a specific event. Of course, Human Resources personnel might make this request themselves based on their information.

Do not forget the importance of having an "acceptable use" policy to guide new employees. As existing employees are getting ready to turn in their PCs, they should be instructed on what they can or cannot do. Depending on business needs and culture, you might establish a policy that restricts the employee's ability to use wipe utilities (especially non-standard products) or other products that could sabotage forensics results. Although this is a difficult subject to deal with in corporate America, it is vitally important. On more than one occasion, I have seen cases in which a mildly disgruntled employee deliberately erased valuable client information and used a wipe utility to make the information unrecoverable. You should make a conscious decision about this issue, even if it is to have no policy on this issue!

To develop a process that is customized to your organization, consider getting input from the above-named individuals and your legal counsel. If the employee is part of a unionized labor force, special rules may apply. There may also be special considerations based on state law or if the organization fulfills government contracts. The preserved evidence is probably discoverable with a subpoena. Your legal counsel can help you determine what legal requirements you need to adhere to.

Assume that you have adopted a process similar to the one outlined. The organization has made the decision to preserve a hard drive. How do you go about it? The major concerns are establishing a chain of custody, documenting specific details, and securing the hard drive. Each of these areas is vitally important if there is a chance that the electronic evidence you have preserved will be presented in a court of law.

You must establish a chain of custody to prove authentication and refute allegations of evidence tampering. Many defense attorneys have successfully argued that if you cannot prove that the evidence has been under your control, you cannot prove that it has not been changed or modified to construct the incriminating evidence. To establish the chain of custody, you must document possession from the point of acquiring it until the matter is resolved. This includes an appeals process through the court system.

Part of the documentation process will be to identify as many details about the original PC that the evidence came from as possible. This is important because an analysis completed later will go much smoother if a few key pieces of information are known. You should document the following:

- What types of operating system are on the hard drive?
- What are other systems specifications (RAM, SCSI, or IDE; processor type)?
- Are any partitions likely to be found?
- What applications are known to be on the hard drive?
- What, if any, encryption was used?
- Is there a list of any known passwords, keys, or certificates?
- To what systems did the owner of the hard drive have access?
- What type of system did the hard drive come from (manufacturer, model)?
- Is there a history of hardware problems, including any maintenance logs?

Having the answers to these questions will make the forensics analysis a much faster and efficient process.

A master log should accompany the evidence from the time it is acquired. It should include date and time, a detailed description of the evidence, and who seized the evidence. The log should also include a transfer-of custody section, which should include reason for transfer, method (hand-delivered or courier), released by and date (signature and date of person transferring custody), and received by and date (signature and date of person taking custody). People listed as having custody of the evidence will need to demonstrate that the evidence was under their control and secured to prevent tampering.

A secured location is a lockable container that has limited access. It can be a file cabinet with locks, a safe, an evidence locker, or even a room with a lock. The best possible scenario is to have only one person with access to the evidence. If that is not possible, the evidence must be stored in a limited area and everyone with access to the area should be documented. The more persons with access to evidence will mean more people testifying that they did not modify the evidence. It is easier to provide a lockable container with single access than one with multiple access. If you will be securing evidence on a regular basis, consider purchasing an evidence locker. Your evidence locker should also include a master log of evidence it holds. When evidence is stored, it should be logged in. Each time it is removed, custody should be transferred out to the individual removing it. The design of the log outlined above can also be utilized here. The purpose of this log is to document each and every time the evidence locker is

Forensics –
FTP

accessed as well as to provide supporting documentation about particular evidence.

If it is necessary to send evidence to another location, I recommend using a courier service that can provide documentation of its custody. This should include tracking forms and numbers. Most of the traditional delivery services provide this service. The senders should seal the package themselves and the recipients observe that the package has not been breached. For additional protection, it is suggested that the evidence is sealed in a container so that the recipient can attest that the document has not been tampered with. Reasonable steps should be taken to protect the evidence during shipping. The evidence will do little good if it has been damaged.

Taking these steps will increase the odds of determining what happened in the past. Understanding history to change the future is the ultimate goal. To understand the history we must have good information. To preserve information, you do not need to be a computer forensics professional—just understand the process and why it is important. Also, practice techniques that will work for your company and be prepared to have good information on "what happened."

Forensics and Legal Proceedings

Thomas Welch, CISSP, CPP
President and Chief Executive Officer, Bullzi Security, Inc., Altamonte Springs, Florida, U.S.A.

Abstract
Computer forensics is the study of computer technology as it relates to the law. The objective of the forensic process is to learn as much about the suspect system as possible. This generally means analyzing the system using a variety of forensic tools and processes. Bear in mind that the examination of the suspect system may lead to other victims and other suspects. The actual forensic process will be different for each system analyzed, but the following guidelines should help the investigator/analyst conduct the forensic analysis.

COMPUTER FORENSICS

There are many tools available to the forensic analyst to assist in the collection, preservation and analysis of computer-based evidence. The makeup of a forensic system will vary from lab to lab, but at a minimum, each forensic system must have the ability to:

- Conduct a Disk Image Backup of the Suspect System
- Authenticate the File System
- Conduct Forensic Analysis in a Controlled Environment
- Validate Software and Procedures

Before analyzing any system it is extremely important to protect the systems and disk drives from static electricity. The analyst should always use an anti-static or static-dissapative wristband and mat before conducting any forensic analysis.

Conduct a Disk Image Backup of the Suspect System

A disk image backup is different from a file system backup in that it conducts a bit level copy of the disk, sector-by-sector, rather then merely copying the system files. This process provides the capability to back up deleted files, unallocated clusters and slackspace. The backup process can be accomplished by using either disk imaging hardware, such as the Image-Master 1000, or through a variety of software programs. Most of these programs run under DOS or Windows and will back up most any type of hard disk or floppy disk, regardless of the operating system. The image backup process is conducted as depicted in Table 1.

Authenticate the File System

File system authentication helps to ensure the integrity of the seized data and the forensic process. Before actually analyzing the suspect disk, a message digest is generated for all system directories, files and disk sectors. A message digest is a signature that uniquely identifies the content of a file or disk sector. It is created using a one-way hashing algorithm. In the past a 32-bit CRC32 algorithm was used, but due to the advancements in cryptographic research and along with more powerful machines, two more advanced, one-way hashing algorithms are now being used. MD5 is a 128-bit hash, while SHA is a 160-bit hash. These strong cryptographic hashing algorithms virtually guarantee the integrity of the processed data. Doing this now will help refute any argument by the defense, that the evidence was tampered with.

The concept of a one-way hash, using MD5 for example, is that a file is read into memory. The file is then processed, bit by bit, until it reaches the end of the file. The hashing process creates a 128-bit signature for the file that is based upon the file content. Even the change of a single bit will change the signature produced by the hashing algorithm. The significance of the one-way hash is that it only works one way. Knowledge of the hash value can not produce the file content itself.

The only problem with executing the authentication process is that it will change the file's last access time. The mere process of reading the file, to produce the hash value will change this time. That is why a separate backup is used for the authentication process.

Conduct Forensic Analysis in a Controlled Environment

After restoring at least one of the backup tapes to a disk, of equal capacity to the original disk (identical disk, if possible), the restored data should be analyzed. This should be done in a controlled environment on a forensic system. Everything on the system must be checked, starting with the file system and directory structure. The analyst should create an

Encyclopedia of Information Assurance DOI: 10.1081/E-EIA-120046867
Copyright © 2011 by Taylor & Francis. All rights reserved.

Forensics –
FTP

Table 1 Image backup process.

Step	Disk image backup procedure
1	Remove the internal hard disk(s) from suspect machine and label (if not already done). Make a note of which logical disk you are removing. Follow the ribbon cables from the disk to the I/O board to accomplish this task. It is a good idea to photograph the inside of the system including the connections to the I/O boards and disk drives.
2	Identify the type of disk (i.e., IDE or SCSI). Identify the make and model
3	Identify the disk capacity. Make a note of cylinders, heads and sectors.
4	Place each disk, one at a time, in a clean forensic examination machine as the next available drive. Beware that the suspect disk may have a virus (keep only the minimal amount of software on the forensic examination machine). Note, if you are using a hardware-based disk duplication method (i.e., ImageMaster 1000), then this step is not necessary.
5	Backup (Disk Image) the suspect disk(s) to tape—Make at least 4 copies of each suspect disk
6	Check the disk image backup logs to make sure that there were no errors during the backup process.
7	Place the original suspect disk(s), along withone of the backup tapes, and backup logs in the appropriate container. Seal, mark and log into evidence.
8	Return a copy of the original disk to the victim (if applicable)
9	Use the last two copies for the forensic analysis (one is used for the authentication)

Forensics –
FTP

organizational chart of the disk file system and then inventory all files on the disk. There are a number of commercially available utilities that allow the analyst to quickly create a directory tree, list system files, identify hidden files, and to conduct keyword searches. The analyst should make notes during each step in the process, especially when restoring hidden or deleted files, or modifying the suspect system (i.e., repairing a corrupted disk sector w/Norton Utilities). The analyst should also note that what may have happened on the system may have resulted from error or incompetence rather from than a malicious user. It is a good idea to check for viruses at this point to, first, note their existence, and secondly, to avoid potential contamination.

Since forensic analysis can be a laborious and time-consuming process, it is sometimes better to distribute the workload to, both, other analyst and case agents. Since it would be too costly to have multiple forensic systems and to have to replicate the suspect data on multiple hard drives, it may be more effective to make CD copies of the hard disk contents that can be distributed and analyzed by different individuals. This is certainly more cost effective and may possibly accelerate the analysis process.

When using CD-R or WORM (Write Once Read Many) technology, the data should be structured in way that will enhance the forensic process. One method of data organization that works quite well is to create a logical directory structure that will store and organize all data from the target disk. This should include all files and directories from the original file structure, deleted files, hidden files, data in slack space, data in unallocated space, compressed data, encrypted data and data generated from search results.

To initiate this process, the analyst should copy (file copy) the complete file structure, starting from the root directory, from the image copy to a newly created hard disk partition. This type of copy will not pick up deleted files, data in slack space, or data in unallocated space, therefor the analyst must manually copy this data from the target

system to the new disk partition. Before copying this data, individual sub-directories must be created for each data type: DELETED, SLACK, UNALLOC. The file copy process will copy the swap file, but it may be best to move the file to a SWAP sub-directory. The next step in the process is to review the information in the original file system, looking for files with hidden file attributes, compressed files, encrypted files and files that meet the criteria of key-word searches. These, too, should be copied to specific directories, so that later it is understood where the data came from. The following directories should be created to store and organize this data: HIDDEN, COMPRESS, ENCRYPT, and SEARCH.

The final process is to use a disk editor utility to look for "BAD" clusters that have data in them and to run key-word searches at the disk editor level (below the operating system). Any data found during this analysis should be copied to the newly created file system. A BAD sub-directory can be created under the HIDDEN sub-directory and an EDITOR sub-directory can be created under the SEARCH sub-directory. Once the new file system is populated with all the data, the information can be burnt into a CD-R or WORM drive. This information can then be made available to other forensic analysts or case agents. If damaging evidence is discovered upon review of the data stored on the CD-R or WORM drive, the original information can easily be recovered from the original image copy.

A quick background on file times should be given before continuing on. Most computer systems, including Windows 95, NT and UNIX store three values for file times: creation time, update time, last access time. Any or all of these file times may have an impact on the investigation. The access time is the one most susceptible to modification because any read to access to the file changes this time. The image backup will not change this time, but the file authentication process will! The creation time is the time the file was originally created. It is not accessible from the file manager or the DIR command. The update time is the time the file was last modified (written to). This is the time the file manager displays. The last access time is recorded whenever any other program or command, including read, copy, etc touches the file. This time is also not accessible from the file manager but can be seen in the under file properties.

When searching through files and directories, the first things to look for are file names or document content that have case-relevant names. For example, if the case you are working is an espionage or theft of trade secrets case, then look for file names with the word (or partial word) of the trade secret item itself. If trade secret was related to the release of a new, database software product, called SplitDB, then look for files with the name "split.xls," "db.doc," or "database.ppt." Another search may find the word "split," "db," or "database" in the body of a word processing document (i.e., a hidden file named sys.dll with the following phase, "For this database structure to work effectively...."). Another indicator that something is afoul, is when the file extension doesn't match the file signature. All files have a signature, which identify the type of file, somewhere in the first 50 characters of the file. This file signature normally correlates to a particular file extension. For example, a bitmap graphic file normally has a file extension of .bmp and a file signature of BM as the first two bytes of the file. If these two items do not match up, then it may mean that someone modified the file extension to hide the presence of the file. A pedophile can use this technique to hide a bitmap image containing child pornography in the c:\windows\system directory as system.dll. A cursory review of the system may miss this file completely, thinking that it is a Windows system file, when in fact it is damaging evidence.

Search tools

There are many search tools that can assist the forensic analyst in his endeavor to locate damaging evidence. Most of these tools are commercial off-the-shelf (COTS) applications that were created for some other reason, other than forensics. It just so happens that these applications work well in a forensic environment. Norton Utilities, although not the end all, is a must for all forensic investigators. Norton provides file searching utilities, disk editor functions, data recovery, etc. Some other tools are listed below:

- Quick View Plus
- Expert Witness
- Computer Forensics Laboratory
- Drag and View
- Rescue Professional
- Super Sleuth
- Outside/In

Searching for obscure data

Once the basic analysis is complete, the next step is to conduct a more detail analysis of more obscure data. It may be necessary to use forensic data recovery techniques to locate and recover:

- Hidden files

    — Hidden by attributes
    — Hidden through steganography
    — Hidden in slack space
    — Hidden in good clusters marked as BAD

- Modifying the size of the file in the directory entry
- Hidden directories
- Erased or deleted files
- Reformatted media
- Encrypted data
- Overwritten (wiped) files

The fact that a file is hidden is a good indicator of its evidentiary value. If someone took the time to hide the file, it was probably hidden for a reason. The simplest way to hide a file is to alter the file attribute to Hidden, System, or Volume Label. Files with these attributes do not normally appear in a DIR listing or even in the Windows file manager. Simply changing the attribute back will make the file accessible. Files with the Hidden attribute set are usually further hidden in a hidden directory. An example of hidden directory would be the .directory in UNIX or creating a directory with the ALT 255 character in a Windows or DOS system. Many times these hidden directories are deeply nested to avoid discovery. The "chkdsk" utility will display the number of hidden files on the DOS system, while Norton Utilities will display a listing of the hidden file and its location.

A file can also be hidden in slack space. Slack space is the area left over in a cluster that is not utilized by a file. For example, if a 2K file is stored in a 32K cluster, then there is 30K of slack space, which may contain data from a previous file. This area can also be used to hide data. A cluster, which is the basic allocation unit, is the smallest unit of space that DOS uses for a file. The amount of slack space for a given file varies based upon the file size and cluster size. The cluster size usually expands as hard disk capacity increases.

Another, more elaborate way to hide data is to first, write data to a file in the normal way. When this is complete, the suspect can use a disk editor to ascertain the sector and cluster of the newly created file, go to that cluster and mark the cluster as BAD. When the operating system sees a BAD cluster, it simply ignores the area. The data is still present on the disk even though it can not be accessed. The analyst will need to locate the cluster by using a sector searching utility, then go to the specific cluster and remove the BAD label.

Files and directories can also be deleted. But when DOS or Windows deletes a file, it only changes the first character of the file name to 0xE5, which merely makes the file space available. The file is not actually removed. The data in the cluster previously allocated by the file is still available until overwritten by a new file. On DOS and Windows systems, the analyst can use the un-erase utility to recover deleted files. These utilities only recover the first cluster that the file occupied. If the file occupied multiple clusters, this data may be lost, as the cluster chain is no longer available. Cluster chains can be re-built although not reliably.

If the disk is formatted, the analyst can attempt to use the "un-format" command in the DOS or Windows environment. If the disk has been wiped, which is also known as shredding, the data is not easily recoverable. The cost of recovery is usually exorbitant, far exceeding the initial loss.

Steganography

Steganography is the art of hiding communications. Unlike encryption, which utilizes an algorithm and a seed value to scramble or encode a message in order to make it unreadable, steganography makes the communication invisible. This takes concealment to the next level—that is, to deny that the message even exists. If a forensic analyst were to look at an encrypted file, it would be obvious that some type of cypher process has been used. It is even possible to determine what type of encryption process was used to encrypt the file, based upon a unique signature. However, steganography hides data and messages in a variety of picture files, sound files and even slack space on floppy diskettes. Even the most trained security specialist or forensic analyst may miss this type of concealment during a forensic review.

Steganography simply takes one piece of information and hides it within another. Computer files, such as images, sound recordings, and slack space contain unused or insignificant areas of data. For example, the least significant bits of a 24-bit bitmap image can be used to hide messages, usually without any material change in the original file. Only through a direct, visual comparison of the original and processed image can the analyst detect the possible use of steganography. Since many times the suspect system only stores the processed image, the analyst has nothing to use as a comparison and generally has no way to tell that the image in question contains hidden data. There is research underway that will help in the forensic process when dealing with steganography. New tools are being developed that will look at the file contents to determine if there is a steganographic signature within the file. But with over 25 different types of steganography being used today, this new research may take some time.

Review communications programs

A good source of contact and associate information can many times be found on-line. Since many technically competent individuals use technology for the same reasons businesses do, electronic Rolodexes, databases of contacts, and communication programs should be searched. Applications like Microsoft Outlook, ACT and others can be tremendously beneficial during an investigation to link your suspect to other individuals or businesses. Some computers store Caller ID files, while others may contain war dialer (or demon dialer) logs. Review communications programs, such as Procomm, to ascertain if any numbers are stored in the application.

Microprocessor output

One final note, before moving on to the next step in the forensic process, is to understand that not all microprocessors are created equal. If a forensic analyst is forced to dump the contents of a file in binary or hexadecimal format, he must not only understand how to read these hieroglyphic notations, but must know the type of microprocessor that produced the output. For example, the Intel 30286 is a 16-bit, little endian processor. A 16-bit microprocessor is capable of working with binary numbers of up to 16 places or bits. That translates to the decimal number 65,536. The Intel 30486 and newer Pentium processors are 32-bit computers, capable of handling binary numbers of up to 32 bits or up to the decimal number 4,294,967,296. The little endian attribute of the Intel chip signifies the byte, not bit, ordering sequence. In this case the bytes are reversed, where the high order byte(s) is stored low order byte location. A big endian processor does not reverse the byte order. It is important to understand that the same value dumped out on two different systems may produce different results.

Reassemble and Boot Suspect System (with Clean Operating System)

The next step in the process is to reassemble the suspect system, using one of the copies of the suspect disk. Place a clean copy of the forensic operating system (usually DOS or Windows) into the floppy drive. Start the boot process and enter the CMOS setup. Check the CMOS to make sure that the boot sequence looks to the floppy drive first, then the hard disk second. This will allow the investigator to boot from the clean operating system diskette. Also, if the system is password protected at the CMOS level, remove and reinstall or short out the CMOS battery. Continue with the boot process and pay particular attention to the Boot-up process, looking for a modified BIOS or EPROM.

It is very important to boot from a clean operating system, as the target system utilities may contain a Trojan Horse or Logic Bomb that will do other than what's intended. (e.g., Modified command.com—conducting a Delete with the Dir command). The first thing to do once the system is booted is to check the system time. This time, even if not accurate, will give the analyst or investigator a reference for all file times. After the system time is obtained, run a complete Systems Analysis Report. This report should, at a minimum, provide the following:

- System Summary—contains basic system configuration
- Disk Summary
- Memory Usage w/Task List
- Display Summary
- Printer Summary
- TSR Summary
- DOS Driver Summary
- System Interrupts
- CMOS Summary
- Listing of all environment variables as set by Autoexec.bat, config.sys, win.ini, system.ini, etc.

Audit trails can be viewed any time subsequent to the image backup, but before a through analysis can be completed, the analyst will need a time reference, which is obtained from booting the suspect system. Check the audit logs for system and account activity. Check with the victim organization to ascertain if the Audit logs are used in the normal course of business. The following questions must be asked:

- Is there a corporate security policy on how the logs are to be used? If so, has the policy been followed?
- What steps have been taken to ensure the integrity of the audit trail?
- Has the audit trail been tampered with? If so, when?

Boot Suspect System (with Original Operating System)

The next step in the forensic process is to boot the target system using the original, target system operating system. This is done to see if any rouge programs were left on the system. The analyst should let the system install all background programs (set by autoexec.bat and config.sys). Once this has been done, the analyst should check what programs (including TSR's) are running and what system interrupts have been set. The goal is to learn if there are any Trojan horses or other rouge programs, such as keystroke monitors, activated. Execute some of the basic operating system commands to see if the command.com file had been altered.

Searching Backup Media

Remember that if the data is not on the hard disk, it may be on backup tapes or some other form of backup media. Even if the data was recently deleted from the hard disk, there may be a backup that has all of the original data. Many times a "snapshot" of the system is taken on a weekly or monthly basis and saved in the long term archives for disaster contingency purposes. Search for PCMCIA flash disks, floppy diskettes, optical disks, Ditto tapes, Zip and Jazz cartridges, Kangaroo drives, or any other form of backup media. Restore and review all data. Many organizations store backups off-site, and although a warrant may be required to obtain the media, don't forget to ascertain if this practice is being done. Before analyzing floppy diskettes, always write-protect the media.

Searching Access Controlled Systems and Encrypted Files

During a search the investigator may be confronted with a system which is secured physically and/or logically. Some physical security devices, such as CPU key locks, prevent only a minor obstacle, whereas other types of physical access control systems may be harder to break.

Logical access control systems may pose a more challenging problem. The analyst may be confronted with a software security program that requires a unique user-name and password. Some of these systems can be simply bypassed by entering a control-c or some other interrupt command. The analyst must be cautious that any of these commands may invoke a Trojan horse routine that may destroy the contents of the disk. A set of "password cracker" programs should be part of the forensic tool-kit. The analyst can always try to contact the publisher of the software program in an effort to gain access. Most security program publishers leave a back door into their systems.

The investigator should look around the suspects work area for documents that may provide him with a clue to the proper user-name/password combination. Check desk drawers, the suspect's Rolodex, acquaintances, friends, etc. It may be possible to compel a suspect to provide access information. It is a good idea to first ask the suspect for his password, before going through the process of compelling him to do so. The following cases set precedence for ordering a suspect, whose computer is in the possession of law enforcement, to divulge password or decryption key:

- *Fisher v. US* (1976), 425 US 391, 48 LED2 39
- *US v. Doe* (1983), 465 US 605, 79 LED2d 552
- *Doe v. US* (1988), 487 US 201, 101 LED2d 184
- *People v. Sanchez* (1994) 24 CA4 1012

The caveat is that the suspect might use this opportunity to command the destruction of potential evidence. The last resort may be that the system needs to be hacked. This can be done as follows:

- Search for passwords written down (It may be part of the evidence collected)

- Try words, names or numbers that are related to the suspect
- Call the software vendor and request their assistance (Some charge for this)
- Try to use password cracking programs which are readily available on the net
- Try a brute force or dictionary attack

LEGAL PROCEEDINGS

A brief description of the legal proceedings that occur subsequent to the investigation are necessary so the victim and the investigative team understand the full impact of their decision to prosecute. The post-incident legal proceedings generally result in additional cost to the victim, until the outcome of the case, at which time they may be reimbursed.

Discovery and Protective Orders

Discovery is the process whereby the prosecution provides all investigative reports, information on evidence, list of potential witnesses, any criminal history of witnesses, and any other information except how their going to present the case to the defense. Any property or data recovered by law enforcement will be subject to discovery if a person is charged with a crime. However, a protective order can limit who has access, who can copy, and the disposition of the certain protected documents. These protective orders allow the victim to protect proprietary or trade secret documents related to a case.

Grand Jury and Preliminary Hearings

If the defendant is held to answer in a preliminary hearing or the grand jury returns an indictment, a trial will be scheduled. If the case goes to trail, interviews with witnesses will be necessary. The victim company may have to assign someone to work as the law enforcement liaison.

Trial

The trail may not be scheduled for some time based upon the backlog of the court that has jurisdiction in the case. Additionally, the civil trial and criminal trial will occur at different times, although much of the investigation can be run in parallel. The following items provide tips on courtroom testimony:

- The prosecutor does not know what the defense attorney will ask.
- Listen to the questions carefully to get the full meaning and to determine that this is not a multiple part or contradictory question.

- Do not answer quickly; Give the prosecutor time to object to the defense questions that are inappropriate, confusing, contradictory or vague.
- If you do not understand the question, ask the defense attorney for an explanation, or answer the question by stating "I understand your question to be..."
- You can not give hearsay answers. This generally means that you can not testify to what someone has told you.
- Do not lose your temper and get angry as this may affect your credibility.
- You may need to utilize expert witnesses.

Recovery of Damages

To recover the costs of damages, such as reconstructing data, re-installing an uncontaminated system, repairing a system, or investigating a breach, you can file a civil law suit against the suspect in either Superior Court or Small Claims Court.

Post Mortem Review

The purpose of the Post Mortem review is to analyze the attack and close the security holes that led to the initial breach. In doing so, it may also be necessary to update the corporate security policy. All organizations should take the necessary security measures to limit their exposure and potential liability. The security policy should include an:

- Incident Response Plan
- Information Dissemination Policy
- Incident Reporting Policy
- Electronic Monitoring Statement
- Audit Trail Policy
- Inclusion of a Warning Banner—This should:

  — Prohibit unauthorized access; and
  — Give notice that all electronic communications will be monitored.

One final note is that many internal attacks can be avoided by conducting background checks on potential employees and consultants.

SUMMARY

As you probably gleaned from this entry, computer crime investigation is more an art than a science. It is a rapidly changing field that requires knowledge in many disciplines. But although it may seem esoteric, most investigations are based on traditional investigative procedures. Planning is integral to a successful investigation. For the internal investigator, an Incident Response Plan should be formulated prior to an attack. The Incident Response Plan will help set the objective of the investigation and will identify each of the steps in the investigative process. For the external investigator, investigative planning may have to happen post incident. It is also important to realize that no one person will have all the answers and that teamwork is essential. The use of a Corporate CERT Team is invaluable, but when no team is available, the investigator may have the added responsibility of building a team of specialists.

The investigator's main responsibility is to determine the nature and extent of the system attack. From there, with knowledge of the law and forensics, the investigative team may be able to piece together who committed the crime, how and why the crime was committed, and maybe more importantly, what can be done to minimize the potential for any future attacks. For the near term, convictions will probably be few, but as the law matures and as investigations become more thorough, civil and criminal convictions will increase. In the mean time, it is extremely important that investigations be conducted so as to better understand the seriousness of the attack and the overall impact to business operations.

Finally, to be successful, the computer crime investigator must, at a minimum, have a thorough understanding of the law, the rules of evidence as they relate to computer crime, and computer forensics. With this knowledge, the investigator should be able to adapt to any number of situations involving computer abuse.

Forensics: Computer Crime Investigation

Thomas Welch, CISSP, CPP
President and Chief Executive Officer, Bullzi Security, Inc., Altamonte Springs, Florida, U.S.A.

Abstract
The computer crime investigation should start immediately following the report of any alleged criminal activity. Many processes ranging from reporting and containment to analysis and eradication need to be accomplished as soon as possible after the attack. An Incident Response Plan should be formulated and a Computer Emergency Response Team (CERT) should be organized prior to the attack. The Incident Response Plan will help set the objective of the investigation and will identify each of the steps in the investigative process.

COMPUTER CRIME INVESTIGATION

The use of a corporate Computer Emergency Response Team (CERT) is invaluable. Due to the numerous complexities of any computer-related crime, it is extremely advantageous to have a single group that is acutely familiar with the Incident Response Plan to call upon. The CERT team should be a technically astute group, that is knowledgeable in the area of legal investigations, the Corporate Security Policy (especially the Incident Response Plan), the severity levels of various attacks, and the company position on information dissemination and disclosure.

The Incident Response Plan should be part of the overall Corporate Computer Security Policy. The plan should identify reporting requirements, severity levels, guidelines to protect the crime scene and preserve evidence, etc. The priorities of the investigation will vary from organization to organization but the issues of containment and eradication are reasonably standard, that is to minimize any additional loss and resume business as quickly as possible. The following sections describe the investigative process starting with the initial detection.

Detection and Containment

Although intrusion detection is covered elsewhere in this manual, it must be mentioned that before any investigation can take place, the system intrusion or abusive conduct must first be detected. The closer the detection is to the actual intrusion event will not only help to minimize system damage, but will also assist in the identification of potential suspects.

To date, most computer crimes have either been detected by accident or through the laborious review of lengthy audit trails. While audit trails can assist in providing user accountability, their detection value is somewhat diminished because of the amount of information that must be reviewed and because these reviews are always post-incident. Accidental detection is usually made through observation of increased resource utilization or inspection of suspicious activity, but again, is not effective due to the sporadic nature of this type of detection.

These types of reactive or passive detection schemes are no longer acceptable. Proactive and automated detection techniques need to be instituted in order to minimize the amount of system damage in the wake of an attack. Real-time intrusion monitoring can help in the identification and apprehension of potential suspects and automated filtering techniques can be used to make audit data more useful.

Once an incident is detected it is essential to minimize the risk of any further loss. This may mean shutting down the system and reloading clean copies of the operating system and application programs. It should be noted, that failure to contain a known situation (i.e., system penetration) might result in increased liability for the victim organization. For example, if a company's system has been compromised by an external attacker and the company failed to shut down the intruder, hoping to trace him, the company may be held liable for any additional harm caused by the attacker.

Report to Management

All incidents should be reported to management as soon as possible. Prompt internal reporting is imperative in order to collect and preserve potential evidence. It is important that information about the investigation be limited to as few people as possible. This should be done on a need-to-know basis. This limits the possibility of the investigation being leaked. Additionally, all communications related to the incident should be made via an out-of-band method to ensure the intruder does not intercept any incident-related information. In other words, do not use e-mail to discuss the investigation

Encyclopedia of Information Assurance DOI: 10.1081/E-EIA-120046868
Copyright © 2011 by Taylor & Francis. All rights reserved.

on a compromised system. Based on the type of crime and type of organization it may be necessary to notify:

- Executive Management
- Information Security Department
- Physical Security Department
- Internal Audit Department
- Legal Department

Preliminary Investigation

A preliminary internal investigation is necessary for all intrusions or attempted intrusions. At a minimum, the investigator must ascertain if a crime has occurred; and if so, he must identify the nature and extent of the abuse. It is important for the investigator to remember that the alleged attack or intrusion may not be a crime at all. Even if it appears to be some form of criminal conduct, it could merely be an honest mistake. Most internal losses occur from errors, not from overt criminal acts. There is no quicker way to initiate a lawsuit than to mistakenly accuse an innocent person of criminal activity.

The preliminary investigation usually involves a review of the initial complaint, inspection of the alleged damage or abuse, witness interviews, and, finally, examination of the system logs. If during the preliminary investigation, it is determined that some alleged criminal activity has occurred, the investigator must address the basic elements of the crime to ascertain the chances of successfully prosecuting a suspect either civilly or criminally. Additionally, the investigator must identify the requirements of the investigation (dollars and resources). If it is believed that a crime has been committed, neither the investigator nor any other company personnel should confront or talk with the suspect. Doing so would only give the suspect the opportunity to hide or destroy evidence.

Determine if Disclosure is Required

It must be determined if a disclosure is required or warranted, due to laws or regulations. Disclosure may be required by law or regulation or may be required if the loss affects a corporation's financial statement. Even if disclosure is not required, it is sometimes better to disclose the attack to possibly deter future attacks. This is especially true if the victim organization prosecutes criminally and/or civilly. Some of the following attacks would probably result in disclosure:

- Large Financial Loss of a Public Company
- Bank Fraud
- Public Safety Systems (i.e., Air Traffic Control)

The Federal Sentencing Guidelines also require organizations to report criminal conduct. The stated goals of the Commission were to "provide just punishment, adequate deterrence, and incentives for organizations to maintain internal mechanisms for preventing, detecting, and reporting criminal conduct." The Guidelines also state that organizations have a responsibility to "maintain internal mechanism for preventing, detecting, and reporting criminal conduct." The Federal Sentencing Guidelines do not prevent an organization from conducting preliminary investigations to ascertain if, in fact, a crime has been committed. One final note of the Federal Sentencing Guidelines, is that they were designed to punish computer criminals for acts of recidivism and using their technical skills and talents to engage in criminal activity.

If the decision is made to disclose an alleged incident or intrusion, be sure to be especially careful when dealing with the media. The media has a history of sensationalizing these types of events and can easily distort the facts that could portray the victim organization as the "Goliath," using the "David vs. Goliath" analogy. Make sure that you have all the facts and provide the media with the "slant" that best serves your purposes. Do not lie to the media! A "No Comment" is better then lying.

Investigation Considerations

Once the preliminary investigation is complete and the victim organization has made a decision related to disclosure, the organization must decide on the next course of action. The victim organization may decide to do nothing or they may attempt to eliminate the problem and just move on. Deciding to do nothing is not a very good course of action as the organization may be held to be culpably negligent should another attack or intrusion occur. The victim organization should at least attempt to eliminate the security hole that allowed the breach, even if they do not plan to bring the case to court. If the attack is internal, the organization may wish to conduct an investigation that might only result in the dismissal of the subject. If they decide to further investigate the incident, they must also determine if they are going to prosecute criminally or civilly, or are they merely conducting the investigation for insurance purposes. If an insurance claim is to be submitted, a police report is usually necessary.

When making the decision to prosecute a case, the victim must clearly understand the overall objective. If the victim is looking to make a point by punishing the attacker, then a criminal action is warranted. This is one of the ways to deter potential future attacks. If the victim were seeking financial restitution or injunctive relief, then a civil action would be appropriate. Keep in mind that a civil trial and criminal trial can happen in parallel. Information obtained during the criminal trial can be used as part of the civil trial. The key is to know what you want to do at the outset, so all activity can be coordinated.

The evidence or lack thereof, may also hinder the decision to prosecute. Evidence is a significant problem in any legal proceeding, but the problems are compounded when computers are involved. Special knowledge is needed to locate and collect the evidence while special care is required to preserve the evidence.

There are many factors to consider when deciding upon whether or not to further investigate an alleged computer crime. For many organizations, the primary consideration will be the cost associated with an investigation. The next consideration will probably be the impact to operations or the impact to business reputation. The organization must answer the following questions:

- Will productivity be stifled by inquiry process?
- Will the subject system have to be shut down to conduct an examination of the evidence or crime scene?
- Will any of the system components be held as evidence?
- Will proprietary data be subject to disclosure?
- Will there be any increased exposure for failing to meet a "standard of due care"?
- Will there be any adverse publicity related to the loss?
- Will a disclosure invite other perpetrators to commit similar acts or will an investigation and subsequent prosecution deter future attacks?

The answers to these questions may have an impact on how the investigation is handled and who is called in to conduct the investigation. Furthermore, these issues must be addressed early on, so that the proper authorities can be notified if required. Prosecuting an alleged criminal offense is a very time consuming task. Law enforcement and the prosecutor will expect a commitment of time and resources for the following:

- Interviews to prepare crime reports and search warrant affidavits.
- Engineers or computer programmers to accompany law enforcement on search warrants.
- Assistance of the victim company to identify and describe documents, source code, and other found evidence.
- A company expert who may be needed for explanations and assistance during the trial.
- Discovery—Documents may need to be provided to the defendant's attorney for discovery. They may ask for more than you want to provide. Your attorney will have to argue against broad ranging discovery. Defendants are entitled to seek evidence they need for their defense.
- You and other company employees who will be subpoenaed to testify.

Who Should Conduct the Investigation?

Based upon the type of investigation (i.e., civil, criminal, insurance, or administrative) and extent of the abuse, the victim must decide who is to conduct the investigation. This used to be a fairly straightforward decision, but high-technology crime has altered the decision making process. Inadequate and untested laws combined with the lack of technical training and technical understanding, has severely hampered the effectiveness of our criminal justice system when dealing with computer-related crimes.

In the past, society would adapt to change, usually at the same rate of that change. Today, this is no longer true. The information age has ushered in dramatic technological changes and achievements, which continue to evolve at exponential rates. The creation, the computer itself, is being used to create new technologies or advance existing ones. This cycle means that changes in technology will continue to occur at an ever-increasing pace. What does this mean to the system of law? It means we have to take a look at how we establish new laws. We must adapt the process to account for the excessive rate of change. Unfortunately, this is going to take time! In the mean time, if they are to launch an investigation, the victim must choose from the following options:

- Conduct an internal investigation
- Bring in external private consultants/investigations
- Bring in local/state/federal law enforcement

Table 1 identifies each of the tradeoffs.

Law enforcement officers have greater search and investigative capabilities than private individuals, but they also have more restrictions than private citizens. For law enforcement to conduct a search, a warrant must first be issued. No warrant is needed if the victim or owner of compromised system gives permission to conduct the search. Issuance of the search warrant is based upon probable cause (reason to believe the something is true). Once probable cause has been identified, law enforcement officers have the ability to execute search warrants, subpoenas and wire taps. The warrant process was formed in order to protect the rights of the people. The Fourth Amendment to the Constitution of the United States established the following:

> The right of the people to be secure in their persons, houses, papers, and effects, against unreasonable searches and seizures, shall not be violated, and no Warrants shall issue, but upon probable cause, supported by oath or affirmation, and particularly describing the place to be searched, and the persons or things to be seized.

There are certain exceptions to this. The "exigent circumstances" doctrine allows for a warrantless seizure, by law enforcement, when the destruction of evidence is impending. In *United States v. David*, the court held that "When destruction of evidence is imminent, a warrantless seizure of that evidence is justified if there is probable cause to believe that the item seized constitutes evidence of criminal activity."

Table 1 Tradeoffs for three options compensating for rate of change.

Group	Cost	Legal issues	Information dissemination	Investigative control
Internal Investigators	Time/People Resources	Privacy Issues Limited Knowledge of Law and Forensics	Controlled	Complete
Private Consultants	Direct Expenditure	Privacy Issues	Controlled	Complete
Law Enforcement Officers	Time/People Resources	Fourth Amendment Issues Jurisdiction Miranda Privacy Issues	Uncontrolled Public Information (FOIA)	None

Internal investigators (non-government) or private investigators, acting as private citizens, have much more latitude in conducting a warrantless search, due to a ruling by the Supreme Court, in *Burdeau v. McDowell*. In this case, the Supreme Court held that evidence obtained in a warrantless search, could be presented to a grand jury by a government prosecutor, because there was no unconstitutional government search and hence no violation of the fourth amendment.

Normally, a private (party) citizen is not subject to the rules and laws governing search and seizure, but a private citizen becomes a police agent, and the Fourth Amendment applies, when

- the private party performs a search which the government would need a search warrant to conduct;
- the private party performs that search to assist the government, as opposed to furthering its own interest; and
- the government is aware of that party's conduct and does not object to it.

The purpose of this doctrine is to eliminate the opportunity for government to circumvent the warrant process by eliciting the help of a private citizen. If a situation required law enforcement to obtain a warrant, due to the subject's expectations of privacy, and the government knowingly allowed a private party to conduct a search in order to disclose evidence, the court would probably rule that the private citizen acted as a police agent. A victim acting to protect its property by assisting police to prevent or detect a crime does not become a police agent.

Law enforcement personnel are not alone in their ability to obtain a warrant. A private party can also obtain a warrant, albeit a civil one, to search and seize specifically identified property which they make claim to. This civil warrant, also known as a Writ of Possession, allows the plaintiff to seize property that is rightfully theirs. In order to obtain such a court order, the plaintiff much prove to a judge or magistrate that the property in question is theirs and that an immediate seizure is essential to minimizing any collateral monetary loss. Additionally, the plaintiff must also post a bond, double the value of the property in question. This places an enormous burden on the plaintiff, should they be unsuccessful in their endeavor, but it also protects individuals and businesses against frivolous requests made to the court.

The biggest issues affecting the decision on who to bring in (in order of priority) are information dissemination, investigative control, cost, and the associated legal issues. Once an incident is reported to law enforcement, information dissemination becomes uncontrolled. The same holds true for investigative control. Law enforcement controls the entire investigation, from beginning to end. This is not always bad, but the victim organization may have a different set of priorities. Cost is always a concern and the investigation costs only add to the loss initially sustained by the attack or abuse. Even law enforcement agencies, which are normally considered "free," add to the costs because of the technical assistance they require during the investigation.

Another area that affects law enforcement is jurisdiction. Jurisdiction is the geographic area where the crime had been committed and any portion of the surrounding area over, or through which the suspect passed, is enroute to, or going away from, the actual scene of the crime. Any portion of this area adjacent to the actual scene over which the suspect, or the victim, might have passed, and where evidence might be found, is considered part of the crime scene. When a system is attacked remotely, where did the crime occur? Most courts submit that the crime scene is the victim's location. But what about "enroute to?" Does this suggest that a crime scene may also encompass the telecommunications path used by the attacker? If so, and a theft occurred, is this interstate transport of stolen goods? There seem to be more questions than answers but only through cases being presented in court can precedence be set. It will take time for the answers to shake out.

There are advantages and disadvantages to each of the groups identified above. Internal investigators will know your systems the best, but may lack some of the legal and forensic training. Private investigators, who specialize in high-technology crime, also have a number of advantages, but usually result in higher costs. Private security practitioners and private investigators are also private businesses and may be more sensitive to business resumption than law enforcement. If you elect to retain the services of a private investigator or computer consultant, it is best if your corporate counsel retains them. This protects the victim organization from unwarranted or untimely disclosure. All communications are treated as privileged communications, under the Attorney–Client Privilege. Additionally, all work product is protected by the same privilege and is protected from disclosure. This includes details of the investigation, witness interviews, forensic analysis, etc. It also includes any past criminal activity, by the victim organization, which may be uncovered during the investigation.

Should you decide to contact your local police department, call the detective unit directly. Chances are you will get someone who is more experienced and knowledgeable and someone who can be more discrete. If you call 911, a uniformed officer will arrive on your doorstep and possibly alert the attacker. Furthermore, the officer must create a report of the incident that will become part of a public log. Now the chances for a discretionary dissemination of information and a covert investigation are gone.

Ask the detective to meet with you in plain clothes. When they arrive at your business have them announce themselves as consultants. If you decide that you would like Federal authorities to be present, do so, but you should inform the local law enforcement authorities. Be aware that your local law enforcement agency may not be well equipped to handle hightech crime. The majority of law enforcement agencies have limited budgets and, as such, place an emphasis on problems related to violent crime and drugs. Also, with technology changing so rapidly, most law enforcement officers lack the technical training to adequately investigate an alleged intrusion.

The same problems hold true for the prosecution and the judiciary. To successfully prosecute a case, both the prosecutor and the judge must have a reasonable understanding of high-tech laws and the crime in question. This is not always the case. Additionally, many of the current laws are woefully inadequate. Even though an action may be morally and ethically wrong, it is still possible that no law is violated (i.e., LaMacchia case). Even when there is a law that has been violated, many of these laws remain untested and lack precedence. Because of this many prosecutors are reluctant to prosecute high-tech crime cases.

Many recent judicial decisions have indicated that judges are lenient toward techno-criminal just as with other white-collar criminals. Furthermore, the lack of technology expertise may cause "doubt," thus rendering "not guilty" decisions. Since many of the laws concerning computer crime are new and untested, many judges have a concern with setting precedence, which may later be overturned in an appeal. Some of the defenses that have been used, and accepted by the judiciary, are

- If you have no system security or lax system security, then you are implying that there is no company concern. Thus, there should be no court concern.
- If a person is not informed that access is unauthorized, then it can be used as a defense.

- If an employee is not briefed and does not acknowledge understanding of policy and procedures, then they can use it as a defense.

Investigative Process

As with any type of criminal investigation the goal of the investigation is to know who, what, when, where, why, and how. It is important that the investigator logs all activity and account for all time spent on the investigation. The amount of time spent on the investigation has a direct impact on the total dollar loss for the incident. This may result in greater criminal charges and, possibly, stiffer sentencing. Finally, the money spent on investigative resources can be reimbursed as compensatory damages in a successful civil action.

Once the decision is made to further investigate the incident, the next course of action for the investigative team is to establish a detailed investigative plan, including the search and seizure plan. The plan should consists of an informal strategy that will be employed throughout the investigation, including the search and seizure:

- Identify any potential suspects
- Identify potential witnesses
- Identify what type of system is to be seized
- Identify the search and seizure team members
- Obtain a search warrant (if required)
- Determine if there is risk of the suspect destroying evidence or causing greater losses

Identify any potential suspects

The type of crime and the type of attacker will set the stage for the overall investigation. Serious attacks against government sites, military installations, financial centers, or a telecommunications infrastructure must be met with the same fervor as that of a physical terrorist attack. Costs will not be the issue. On the other hand, when an organization plans to conduct an investigation pertaining to unauthorized access or a violation of company policy all the factors should considered. This includes the anticipated cost and the chances of success. In either case, there will always be the usual suspects: insiders and outsiders.

Insiders are usually trusted users who abuse their level of authorized access to the system. They are normally the greatest source of loss. They know the value of your assets! They are usually motivated by greed, need (e.g., drug habit, gambling problem, divorce, etc.), or perceived grievance. Most importantly that have the access and the opportunity. Outsiders, as the name implies, attack your systems and networks from the outside. They attack systems for a variety of reasons, with attacks increasing at alarming rates because of advancements such as the Internet. Some examples of outsiders are as follows:

- Hackers and crackers
- Organized crime
- Terrorists
- Pedophiles
- Industrial/corporate spies

While, individually, each of these groups continue to be a problem, it is especially disturbing to realize the potential for collaboration between any two or more of the groups. When organized crime groups or terrorist factions gain access to the technical expertise provided by hackers and crackers, the potential for widespread harm and exorbitant financial losses is intensified. Albert Einstein said it best when he said, "Technological progress is like an axe in the hands of a pathological criminal."

When commencing with the investigation, it is important to understand how and why a system is being attacked. The how will provide you with information pertaining to technical expertise required to conduct the attack. The why will potentially indicate motive. The how and why together, along with the when and the where, may provide the who.

Identify potential witnesses

It is important to identify potential witnesses early on in the investigation. It is just as important not to alert the suspect to the investigation, therefore selecting whom will be interviewed and when may have an impact on the investigation. The key to obtaining good witness statements is to ascertain the facts in the case, not opinions. Also, it is wise not to ask leading questions. Sources of information may be staff members, expert witnesses, associates, etc. Interviews are not the same as interrogations and great care should go into not confusing the two. If a hostile witness does not want to be interviewed, then the process should cease immediately. If a witness or potential witness is detained against their will, there may be criminal and/or civil liability to the individuals and business responsible for the investigation. Never intimidate,coerce, or harass a potential witness.

Technically competent personnel should conduct interviews of technical witnesses or suspects. A potential suspect, who is technically competent, will have a field day if interviewed by a non-technical investigator. Many times these individuals are arrogant to start with. If they feel that they have the upper hand, because of their "esoteric knowledge," they may be less inclined to provide a truthful statement. Also, it is sometimes better to interview a technical suspect (e.g., programmer) first, before seizing his system. If you advise the suspect that you will be seizing his systems if he does not cooperate, he may assist in the investigation.

One final note on conducting interviews. It is always a good idea to have the witness write out and sign their statement, in their own handwriting. This statement can then be types for better readability, but you can always point to the original. This helps to counter statements made by the witness in court, that that is not what they meant.

Identify the type of system that is to be seized

It is imperative to learn as much as possible about the target computer system(s). If possible, obtain the configuration of the system, including the network environment (if any), hardware, and software. The following data should be acquired prior to the seizure:

- Identify system experts. Make them part of the team.
- Is a security system in place on the system, If so, what kind? Are passwords used? Can a root password be obtained?
- Where is the system located? Will simultaneous raids be required?
- Obtain the required media supplies in advance of the operation
- What law has been violated? Discuss the elements of proof. These should be the focus of the search and seizure.
- What is your probable cause? Obtain a warrant if necessary.
- Determine if the analysis of the computer system will be conducted on site or back in the office or forensics lab.

Identify the search and seizure team members

There are different rules for search and seizure based upon who's conducting the search. Under the Fourth Amendment, law enforcement must obtain a warrant, which must be based on probable cause. Regardless of who's conducting the search and seizure, a team should be identified and should consist of the following members:

- Lead investigator
- Information security department
- Legal department
- Technical assistance—system administrator, as long as he is not a suspect

If a corporate CERT is already organized, then this process is already complete. A chain of command needs to be established and it must be determined who is to be in charge. This person is responsible for delegating assignments to each of the team members. A media liaison should be identified if the attack is to be disclosed. This will control the flow of information to the media.

Obtaining and serving search warrants

If it is believed that the suspect has crucial evidence at his home or office, then a search warrant will be required to seize the evidence. If a search warrant is going to be

Forensics – FTP

needed, then it should be done as quickly as possible before the intruder can do further damage. The investigator must establish that a crime has been committed and that the suspect is somehow involved in the criminal activity. He must also show why a search of the suspect's home or office is required. The victim may be asked to accompany law enforcement when serving the warrant to identify property or programs.

If you must take along documents with you when serving the search warrant, consider coping them onto a colored paper to prevent the defense from inferring that what you might have found was left by you.

Is the system at risk?

Prior to the execution of the plan, the investigative team should ascertain if the suspect, if known, is currently working on the system. If so, the team must be prepared to move swiftly, so that evidence is not destroyed. The investigator should determine if the computer is protected by any physical or logical access control systems and be prepared to respond to such systems. It should also be decided early on, what will be done if the computer is on at the commencement of the seizure. The goal of this planning is to minimize any risk of evidence contamination or destruction.

Executing the Plan

The first step in executing the plan is to secure and control the scene. This includes securing the power, network servers, and telecommunications links. If the suspect is near the system, it may be necessary to physically remove him. It may be best to execute the search and seizure after normal business hours to avoid any physical confrontation. Keep in mind, that even if a search is conducted after hours, the suspect may still have remote access to the system via a LAN-based modem connection, PC-based modem connection, wireless modem connection, or Internet connection. Many times it is required to seize a disk from the suspects computer, mirror image a copy of the disk and then replace the original with a copy of the disk, all without the suspect knowing what is happening. This allows the investigative team to protect the evidence and continue with the investigation, while retaining secrecy of the investigation.

Enter the area slowly so as not to disturb or destroy evidence. Evaluate the entire situation. In no other type of investigation, can evidence be destroyed more quickly. Do not touch the keyboard as this may invoke a Trojan horse or some other rogue or malicious program. Do not turn off the computer unless it appears to be active (i.e., formatting the disk, deleting files, initiating some I/O process, etc.). Look for the disk activity light and listen for disk usage. If you must turn off the computer, pull the plug from the wall, rather than using the on/off switch. Look for notes, documentation, passwords, encryption codes, etc. The

following questions must be answered in order to effectively control the scene:

- Is the subject system turned on?
- Is there a modem attached? If so,

  — Check for internal and wireless modems
  — Check for telephone lines connected to the computer

- Is the system connected to a LAN?

The investigator may wish to videotape the entire evidence collection process. There are two schools of thought on this. The first is that if you videotape the search and seizure, any mistakes can nullify the whole operation. The second school of thought is that if you videotape the evidence collection process, many of the claims by the defense can be silenced. In either case, be careful what you say if the audio is turned on!

Sketch and photograph the crime scene before touching anything. Sketches should be drawn to scale. Take still photographs of critical pieces of evidence. At a minimum, the following should be captured:

- The layout of desks and computers (Include dimensions and measurements)
- The configuration of the all computers on the network
- The configuration of the suspect computer, including network connections, peripheral connections, internal and external components, and system backplane
- The suspect computer display

A drawing package, such a Visio—Technical Edition, is excellent for these types of drawings. Visio allows the investigator to sketch the scene using a drag and drop graphical user interface (GUI). Most computer and network graphics, desk and furniture graphics, etc., are included with the application. The output is a professional product that is made part of the report and can be used later to recreate the environment or to present the case in court.

If the computer is on, the investigator should capture what is on the monitor. This can be accomplished by video taping what is on the screen. The best way to do this, without getting the "scrolling effect" caused by the video refresh, is to use a National Television Standards Committee (NTSC) adapter. Every monitor has a specific refresh rate (i.e., horizontal: 30–66 kHz, vertical: 50–90 Hz), which identifies how frequently the screen's image is redrawn. It is this redrawing process that causes the videotaped image to appear as if the vertical hold is not properly adjusted. The NTSC adapter is connected between the monitor and the monitor cable, and directs the incoming signal into the camcorder directly. The adapter converts the computer's analog signal (VGA) to a NTSC format. Still photos are a good idea too. Do not use a flash, because it can "white out" the image. Even if the computer is off, check the monitor for burnt-in images. This does not happen as much with the new monitors, but it may still help in the discovery of evidence.

Once you have reviewed and captured what's on the screen, pull the plug on the system. This is for PC-based systems only. Mini-systems or mainframes must be logically power-downed. It is best to conduct a forensic analysis (technical system review with a legal basis focused on evidence gathering) on a forensic system, in a controlled environment. If necessary, a forensic analysis can be conducted on site, but never using the suspect system's operating system or system utilities. See the section on forensic analysis for the process that should be followed.

Once the computer is turned off, remove the cover and photograph and sketch the inside of the computer. The analyst or investigator should use a static-dissipative grounding kit when working inside of the computer. You should note any peculiarities, such as booby traps. Identify each drive and its logical ID (e.g., C: drive) by tracing the ribbon cables to the I/O board. Also identify any external drives. Once this has been completed, remove, label and pack all drives. Check the floppy drives for any media. If a disk is in the drive, remove the disk, and mark on the evidence label where it was found. Next, place a blank diskette into the floppy drive(s). Place evidence tape over the floppy drives and the on/off switch, once it is placed in the off position.

Identify, mark and pack all evidence according to the collection process under the Rules of Evidence. Identify and label all computer systems, cables, documents, disks, etc. The investigator should also seize all diskettes, backup tapes, PCMCIA disks, magnetic cartridges, optical disks, and printouts. All diskettes should be write protected. Make an entry for each in the evidence log. Check the printer. If it uses ribbons, make sure it (or at least the ribbon) is taken as evidence. Keep in mind that many of the peripheral devices may contain crucial evidence in their memory and/or buffers. Some items to consider are LAN servers, routers, printers, etc. You must check with the manufacturer on how to output the memory buffers for each device. Also, keep in mind that most buffers are stored in volatile memory. Once the power is cut, the information may be lost.

Additionally, check all drawers, closets and even the garbage for any forms of magnetic media (e.g., hard drives, floppy diskettes, tape cartridges, optical disks, etc.) or documentation. It seems that many computer literate individuals conduct most of their correspondence and work product on a computer. This is an excellent form of leads, but take care to avoid an invasion of privacy. Even media that appears to be destroyed can turn out to be quite useful. One case involved an American serviceman who contracted to have his wife killed and wrote the letter on his computer. In an attempt to destroy all the evidence, he cut up the floppy disk containing the letter into 17 pieces. The Air Force

Office of Special Investigations (AFOSI) was able to reconstruct the diskette and read almost all the information.

Don't overlook the obvious, especially hacker tools and any ill-gotten gains (e.g., password or credit card lists). This will help your case when trying to show motive and opportunity. The State of California has equated hacker tools to burglary tools; the mere possession constitutes a crime. Possession of a Red Box, or any other telecommunications instrument that has been modified with the intent to defraud, is also prohibited under U.S.C. Section 1029. Some of the hacker tools that you should be aware of are

- Password crackers
- Network sniffers
- Automated probing tools (e.g., SATAN)
- Anonymous remailers
- War dialers
- Encryption and steganography tools

Finally, phones, answering machines, desk calendars, day-timers, fax machines, pocket organizers, electronic watches, etc., are all sources of potential evidence. If the case warrants, seize and analyze all sources of data, both, electronic and manual. Document all activity in an activity log and if necessary secure the crime scene.

Surveillance

There are two forms of surveillance used in computer crime investigations. They are physical surveillance and computer surveillance. The physical surveillance can be generated at the time of the abuse, via CCTV security camera, or after the fact. When done after the fact, physical surveillance is usually performed undercover. It can be used in an investigation to determine a subject's personal habits, family life, spending habits, or associates.

Computer surveillance is achieved in a number of ways. It is done passively through audit logs or actively by way of electronic monitoring. Electronic monitoring can be accomplished via keyboard monitoring, network sniffing, or line monitoring. In any case, it generally requires a warning notice and/or explicit statement in the security policy, indicating that the company can and will electronically monitor any and all system or network traffic. Without such a policy or warning notice, a warrant is normally required.

Before you conduct electronic monitoring, make sure you review Chapters 2500 & 2700 of the Electronic Communications Privacy Act, Title 18 of the U.S. Code as it relates to keystroke monitoring or system administrators looking into someone's account. If you do not have a banner or if the account holder has not been properly notified, the system administrator and the company can be guilty of a crime and liable for, both, civil and criminal penalties. Failure to obtain a warrant could result in the evidence being suppressed or worse yet, litigation by the suspect for invasion of privacy or violation of the ECPA.

One other method of computer surveillance that is used are "sting operations." These operations are established so as to continue to track the attacker, on-line. By baiting a trap or setting up "honey pots," the victim organization lures the attacker to a secured area of the system. This is what was done in the Cuckoo's Egg. The system attackers were enticed into accessing selected files. Once these files or their contents are downloaded to another system, their mere presence can be used as evidence against the suspect. This enticement is not the same as entrapment as the intruder is already predisposed to commit the crime. Entrapment only occurs when a law enforcement officer induces a person to commit a crime that the person had not previously contemplated.

It is very difficult to track and identify a hacker or remote intruder, unless there is a way to trace the call (e.g., Caller ID, wire tap, etc.). Even with these resources, many hackers meander through communication networks, hopping from one site to the next, via a multitude of telecommunications gateways and hubs, such as the Internet! Bill Cheswick, author of Firewalls and Internet Security, refers to this a "connection laundering." Additionally, the organization can not take the chance of allowing the hacker to have continued access to their system and potentially cause any additional harm.

Telephone traps require the equivalent of a search warrant. Additionally, the victim will be required to file a criminal report with law enforcement and must show probable cause. If sufficient probable cause is shown, a warrant will be issued and all incoming calls can be traced. Once a trace is made, a pen register is normally placed on the suspects phone to log all calls placed by the suspect. These entries can be tied to the system intrusions based upon the time of the call and the time the system was accessed.

Investigative and Forensic Tools

Table 2, although not exhaustive, identifies some of the investigative and forensic tools that are commercially available. The first table identifies the hardware and software tools that should be part of the investigator's toolkit,

Table 2 Investigative and forensic tools.

Investigative Tools	
Investigation and Forensic Toolkit Carrying Case	Static Charge Meter
Cellular Phone	EMF/ELF Meter (Mangetometer)
Laptop Computer	Gender Changer (9 Pin and 25 Pin)
Camcorder w/NTSC adapter	Line Monitor
35mm Camera (2)	RS232 Smart Cable
Wide Angle & Telephoto Lens	Nitrile Anti-static Gloves
Night Vision Adapter for Camera and Camcorder	Alcohol Cleaning Kit
Polaroid Camera	CMOS Battery
Tape Recorder (VOX)	Extension Cords
Scientific Calculator	Power Strip
Label Maker	Keyboard Key Puller
Crime Seene/Security Barrier Tape	Cable Tester
PC Keys	Breakout Box
IC Removal Kit	Transparent Static Shielding Bags (100 Bags)
Compass	Anti-Static Scaling Tape
Diamond Tip Engraving Pen Extra Diamond Tips	Serial Port Adapters (9 Pin 25 Pin & 25 Pin 9 Pin)
Felt Tip Pens	Foam-Filled Carrying Case
Evidence Seals (250 Seals/Roll)	Static-Dissipative Grounding Kit w/Wrist Strap
Plastic Evidence Bags (100 Bags)	Foam-Filled Disk Transport Box
Evidence Labels (100 Labels)	Computer Dusting System (Air Spray)
Evidence Tape—2″ X 165′	Small Computer Vacuum
Tool Kit containing:	Printer and Ribbon Cables
Screwdriver Set (inc. Precision Set)	9 Pin Serial Cable
Torx Screwdriver Set	25 Pin Serial Cable
25′ Tape Measure	Null Modem Cable

(Continued)

Table 2 Investigative and forensic tools. *(Continued)*

Investigative Tools

Razor Knife	Centronics Parallel Cable
Nut Driver	50 Pin Ribbon Cable
Pliers Set	LapLink Parallel Cable
LAN Template	Telephone Cable for Modem
Probe Set	
Neodymium Telescoping Magnetic Pickup	
Allen Key Set	
Alligator Clips	
Wire Cutters	
Small Pry Bar	
Hammer	
Tongs and/or Tweezers	
Cordless Driver w/Rechargeable Batteries (2)	Batteries for Camcorder, Camera, Tape Recorder, etc. (AAA, AA, 9-volt)
Pen Light Flashlight	
Magnifying Glass 3 1/4″	
Inspection Mirror	

Computer supplices	Software tools
Diskettes:	Sterile O/S Diskettes
3 1/2″ Diskettes (Double & High Density Format)	
5 1/4″ Diskettes (Double & High Density Format)	
Diskette Labels	Virus Detection Software
5 1/2″ Floppy Diskette Sleeves	SPA Audit Software
3 1/2″ Floppy Diskette Container	Little-Big Endian Type Application
CD-ROM Container	Password Cracking Utilities
Writer Protect labels for 5 1/4″ Floppies	Disk Imaging Software
Tape and Cartridge Media	Auditing Tools
1/4″ Cartridges	Test Data Method
4mm & 8mm DAT	Integrated Test Facility (ITF)
Travan	Parallel Simulation
9-Track/1600/6250	Snapshot
QIC	Mapping
Zip Drives	Code Comparison
Jazz Drives	Checksum
Hard Disks	File Utilities (DOS, Windows, 95, NT, Unix)
IDE	
SCSI	
Paper	Zip/Unzip Utilities
8 1/2 x 11 Laser Paper	
80 Column Formfeed	
132 Column Formfeed	

Miscellaneous supplies	Miscellaueous supplies
Paper Clips	MC60 Microcassette Tapes
Scissors	Camcorder Tapes
Rubber Bands	33mm Film (Various Speeds)
Stapler and Staples	Polaroid Film
Masking Tape	Graph Paper
Duct Tape	Sketch Pad
Investigative Folders	Evidence Checklist
Cable Ties/Labels	Blank Forms–Schematics
Numbered and Colored Stick-on Labels	Label Maker Labels

while the second table identifies forensic software and utilities.

Other Investigative Information Sources

When conducting an internal investigation it is important to remember that the witness statements and computer-related evidence are not the only sources of information useful to the investigation. Personnel files provide a wealth of information related to an employee's employment history. It may show past infractions by the employee or disciplinary action by the company. Telephone and fax logs can possibly identify any accomplices or associates of subject. At a minimum they will identify the suspects most recent contacts. Finally, security logs, time cards, and check-in sheets will determine when a suspected insider had physical access to a particular system.

Investigative Reporting

The goal of the investigation is to identify all available facts related to the case. The investigative report should provide a detailed account of the incident, highlighting any discrepancies in witness statements. The report should be a well organized document that contains a description of the incident, all witness statements, references to all evidentiary articles, pictures of the crime scene, drawings and schematics of the computer and the computer network (if applicable), and finally, a written description of the forensic analysis. The report should state final conclusions, based solely on the facts. It should not include the investigator's opinions, unless he is an expert. Keep in mind that all documentation related to the investigation is subject to discovery by the defense, so be careful about what is written down!

Forensics: Non-Liturgical Examinations

Carol Stucki
Technical Producer, PurchasePro.com, Newport News, Virginia, U.S.A.

Abstract

This entry discusses the non-liturgical forensic examination used for investigations. The author encourages the readers conduct the investigation as if the material would be presented in court, although several times non-liturgical examinations do not go to trial. The process discussed in this entry covers isolation of equipment, isolation of files, tracking web sites visited, cookies, bookmarks, history buffers, caches, temporary internet files, tracking log-on time and duration, recent document lists, and tracking non-approved software installation and use.

When you have obtained the go-ahead from management to begin an investigation, you will find the steps and procedures for many types of investigations in this entry. The most common and main type of investigation that this entry discusses is the non-liturgical examination. The non-liturgical investigation is one that is not foreseen to be taken to trial or involve litigation; however, you should always conduct the investigation using the same procedures as if you are going to trial. By conducting an investigation in this manner, you will have all the evidence you need in the necessary format to present to company management or in a courtroom.

One of the first things to consider is whether or not you need to isolate equipment or files. If it is necessary to do so, you will need to move quickly on this in order to preserve any possible evidence. What you preserve and find on the equipment, most likely a PC, will be the basis of your forensic examination. This entry reviews such topics as the isolation of equipment, isolation of files, tracking Web sites visited, tracking log-on duration and times, tracking illicit software installation and use, and how to correlate the evidence found.

ISOLATION OF EQUIPMENT

Should you need to isolate or quarantine equipment as a part of your investigation, you need to take a few steps to 1) ensure protection of the equipment, 2) isolate and protect data from tampering, and 3) secure the investigation scene. First, you need to make sure that you have the authority to take the equipment. If you are taking any equipment, you should first get authorization from management, and if you take working equipment arrangements will have to be made to replace it while you conduct your investigation.

The first thing to do is to be sure that the PC you are about to take as part of your investigation is the correct unit, the one actually used in the illegal activity by the employee under investigation. This can be done by checking the asset records, or the records that are kept in some corporations by the operations department. If you need to take an employee's PC, you must have a witness and have the employee sign a form stating that you took the PC. Record the serial number, make, and model; when you took it; and the reason for taking it. If you do not have such a form, still somehow record what action was taken, obtain the employee's signature, and secure the suspect equipment. Any time it becomes necessary to take an employee's PC, you must move quickly to ensure that the evidence is preserved intact and not tainted, altered, or even destroyed.

When you have the PC in your possession, you need to preserve the "chain of evidence." You can preserve the chain of evidence by making sure that neither you nor anyone else is left alone with the equipment. You should always record your actions with the equipment. A good way to record all the actions and whereabouts of equipment or any other piece of evidence under investigation is to keep a log. This log should show 1) who has access to the equipment, 2) who retains control over the log, and 3) where the log is stored. Additionally, you should record the when (dates and times), where, and why of your every action, so every minute you have the equipment or data in your possession is accountable. Even if you put the PC in a locked cabinet or secured area, this action must be recorded in the log.

One of the first things you should do with the PC is to "ghost" it by backing up everything on the PC. In this way, you can make sure that you will not lose any data when you are conducting your investigation. Ghosting the data preserves the original data that might be disturbed during the investigation. For the backup of any data under investigation it is very important to make sure that the programs used to perform this backup are independent and have

Encyclopedia of Information Assurance DOI: 10.1081/E-EIA-120046835
Copyright © 2011 by Taylor & Francis. All rights reserved.

integrity; that is, the programs should not be under the influence or control of any person or other program or system that is outside the investigation team. The integrity of the data and equipment has to be ensured by the use of programs that will not alter the original data in any way, either intentionally or accidentally. A number of programs are used to perform such backups that are independent and have integrity. One such program is SafeBack, freeware that is available on the Web.

ISOLATION OF FILES

Not all the data required for an investigation will reside on a user's PC; therefore, you will need to gain access to the same files and directories that the user has access to. The first thing to do is to disable the user's ID. Be sure that the administrator verifies how the user's profile and accounts might be affected if the user's ID is disabled. Only after verifying that no data will be lost, altered, or destroyed by disabling the ID should the administrator proceed to disable the user's ID. Security personnel or someone with administrative authority should disable the users' ID. Operations personnel or a systems/data security office can do this. The easiest way to disable the user's ID is to change the password, but this is not the best approach, as the user could regain access if he or she is able to guess the new password. Be sure that the administrator disables the ID but does not delete it. In some security setups, deleting a user ID will cause data and files to be deleted as well. Because this is not what you want to happen, only disable the ID. When the ID is disabled, the next and most important step is to copy all the files to which the user had access. This provides a backup for your investigation, as the data cannot be quarantined. The confiscated data, however, cannot be used by the business for as long as it takes to conduct your investigation.

Operations or security personnel should have paper files with access requests, and they can run a report that shows what the user had access to on the system. Make sure the list or report they give you contains the group access and public access files for the user. You need to investigate all of the places a user could have copied or hidden data. For the investigation, you might be able to ignore those files with read-only access, but it is always best to be sure and get it all. Now that you know what the user had access to, request that operations personnel copy the files into a secure location that only you and your team have access to. Copy the file structure as well—all directories and subdirectories. Make two copies of the data: one as a backup and one for you to use in the investigation. This is similar to taking a picture of the crime scene before you start moving things around. Now that you have a copy of the data to use, refer to the following sections in this entry which provide various examples of potential investigative areas and demonstrate how you can use the data collected as part of your investigation.

TRACKING WEB SITES VISITED

If your investigation requires that you track what Web sites have been visited by an employee, you should begin by reviewing the following items:

- Cookies
- Bookmarks
- History buffer
- Cache
- Temporary Internet files

Here we briefly define each of these items, where to find them, how to capture the findings, and how to evaluate what you have found.

Cookies

Cookies are messages given to a Web browser by a Web server. The browser stores the message in a text file called *cookie.txt*. The message is then sent back to the server each time the browser requests a page from the server. The main purposes of cookies are to identify users and possibly prepare customized Web pages for them. When you enter a Web site that uses cookies, you may be asked to fill out a form providing such information as your name and interests. This information is packaged into a cookie file and sent to your Web browser, which stores it for later use. The next time you go to the same Web site, your browser will send the cookie to the Web server. The server can use this information to present you with custom Web pages. Thus, for example, instead of seeing just a generic welcome page, you might see a welcome page with your name on it.

The name *cookie* evolved from UNIX objects called *magic cookies*. These are tokens that are attached to a user's ID or program and change depending on the areas entered by the user's ID or program. Cookies are also sometimes called *persistent cookies* because they typically stay in the browser for long periods of time. You will find cookies on the hard drive of the PC, usually the C: drive. Cookies is a subdirectory under the Windows directory. The best way to access the Cookies subdirectory and subsequent files stored there is via MS Windows Explorer (see Fig. 1). When you open this directory using Windows Explorer, you will find a listing of the Cookies for those Web sites that you have visited. If there are no files under this directory, they have been deleted. If there are files under this directory, you can view the dates and times they were last accessed. You will also see the ID that was used to access these sites on this PC.

Cookies can be deleted in several ways. One way is manually. The user can access the cookies folder and delete all information from the folder. If the deletion was done manually, one place to look for cookies is in the Recycle Bin. There is a Disk Cleanup program that comes with Windows 98 and higher that deletes the information in the following folders: Cookies, Temporary Internet,

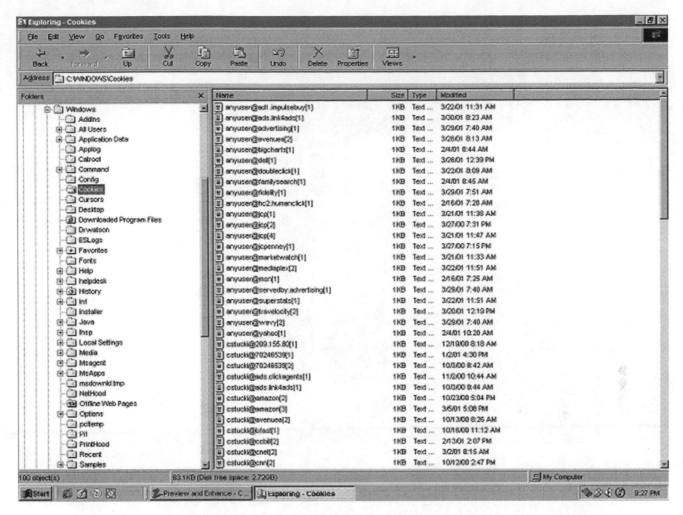

Fig. 1 Cookies subdirectory file contents.

Downloadable Program Files, Recycle Bin, Old ScanDisk Files, and Temporary Files. See Fig. 2 for a look at the Disk Cleanup program. The Disk Cleanup program does not leave any place to look for deleted files. There are also Cookie Manager programs that will automatically delete old or expired cookies from the cookie folders. These programs allow users to set their own expiration and archive dates. For example, the user can set the Cookie Manager to delete or archive all cookies more than 5 days old. Some of these manager programs put the deleted cookies into the Recycle Bin, and some put them in a temporary archive folder. To find these archive folders, it is necessary to research the program.

For your investigation, you need to determine where each cookie takes you, keeping in mind that cookies can be named many things (see Fig. 1). By seeing where each cookie takes you, you can determine what the user has been doing on the Web sites where the cookies came from. Note the date and time of each cookie; these indicate when the cookies were created or accessed by the user for the first time for a particular site. However, some cookies are generated without the user actually visiting a particular

site. These magic cookies, which are generated without a user having to actually access a particular site, are often marketing gimmicks or ploys to get the user to go to their Web site. To determine where a user actually visited, you need to compare the cookies files to the history files. History files are described later in this entry.

Bookmarks

A bookmark is a marker or address that identifies a document or a specific place in a document. Bookmarks are Internet shortcuts that users can save on the Web browser so they do not have to remember or write down the URL or location of Web sites they might like to revisit in the future. Nearly all Web browsers support a bookmarking feature that lets users save the address (URL) of a Web page so they can easily revisit the page at a later time. Bookmarks or favorites are stored in two places. One is in the Web browser under Favorites (see Fig. 3). Another is on the C: (or hard) drive under the Windows folder, in a subfolder called Favorites (see Fig. 4).

Forensics – FTP

**Forensics –
FTP**

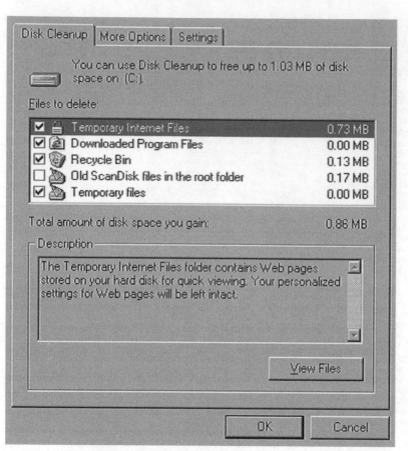

Fig. 2   Disk clean-up program from Windows 98.™

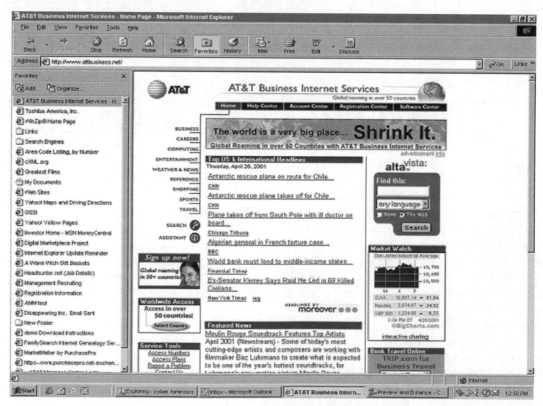

Fig. 3   Favorites from a Web browser (Explorer™).

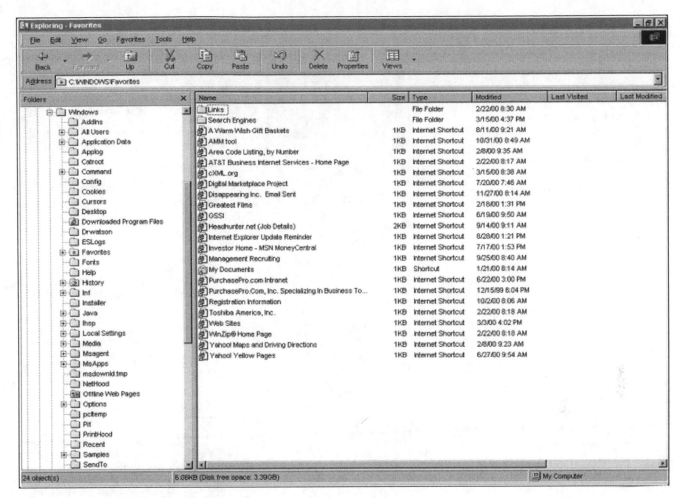

Fig. 4 Bookmarks from hard-drive view.

The bookmarks or favorites are stored under the user's desired names. By clicking on each of the bookmarks, you can visit the same Web sites the user has. Because bookmark names can be changed by the user, be sure to examine each one carefully. Avoid casually skipping over an apparently irrelevant bookmark simply because it does not look like it would be pointing to an unauthorized Web site (e.g., PrettyFlowers@Home). There is no real way to hide a bookmark, but users can bury a bookmark in a folder they create in the bookmark area, so be sure to open any folders you see in the Bookmarks listing. An advantage of viewing the favorites listing in the C: drive view is that you can see the dates and times when the bookmarks were created or modified; however, this does not provide you with a listing of the times and dates when the sites were actually visited or indicate how frequently they have been visited.

History Buffer

A buffer is a temporary storage area, usually in RAM. The purpose of most buffers is to act as a holding area

that allows the CPU to manipulate data before transferring it to a device (e.g., a printer or other external device). Because the process of reading and writing data to a disk is relatively slow, many programs keep track of data changes in a buffer and then copy the buffer to a disk; for example, word processors employ a buffer to keep track of changes to files. When the user actively saves the file, the word processor updates the disk file with the contents of the buffer. This is much more efficient than accessing the file on the disk each time a change is made to the file. Note that because changes are initially stored in a buffer, not on the disk, all changes will be lost if the computer fails during an editing session. For this reason, it is a good idea to save files periodically. Most word processors automatically save files at regular intervals.

A history buffer is a Web browser storage area of URL sites. The Web browser's history buffer shows you a list of what URLs or sites have been visited and what screens have been opened under each URL (see Fig. 5). To get to the history buffer, go to the Web browser. On the tool bar you will find an icon or button called History (see Fig. 5). The history buffer can be cleared out by the user simply by

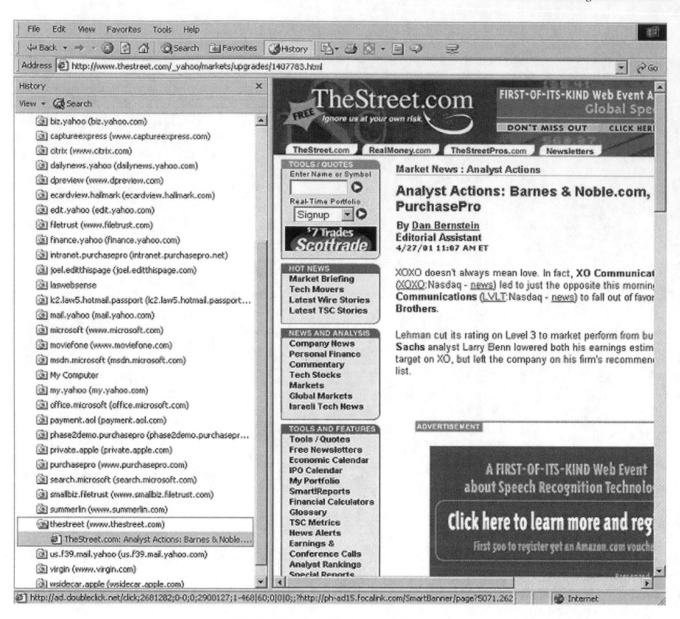

Fig. 5   History buffer from web browser.

highlighting and deleting the items on the list. The deleted contents from this list are not stored anywhere else in the Web browser, but they can still be found in the hard-drive history buffer. Viewing the hard-drive history buffer is done in a little different way (see Fig. 6). This history buffer can be viewed via the path Windows → History. This history buffer will show you the days of the week that the user actually accessed the Web. By opening one of the days of the week subfolders, you can see the actual listings of the URLs visited by the user and the time and dates the sites were last visited. By combining each day's lists, you can identify a pattern of visitation (and browser utilization) for each Web site.

Such information may document or prove that an employee (or at least the individual who sat at the particular PC under review) was accessing the Web: 1) in violation of company policy; 2) during working hours instead of only during predetermined allowable times (i.e., lunch breaks); 3) on weekends or during other off-schedule, non-normal times when employees or other personnel should not be in the building; or 4) to visit unapproved or unauthorized sites.

Cache

Cache can be either a reserved section of main memory or an independent high-speed storage device. Two types of caching are commonly used in personal computers: memory caching and disk caching. A memory

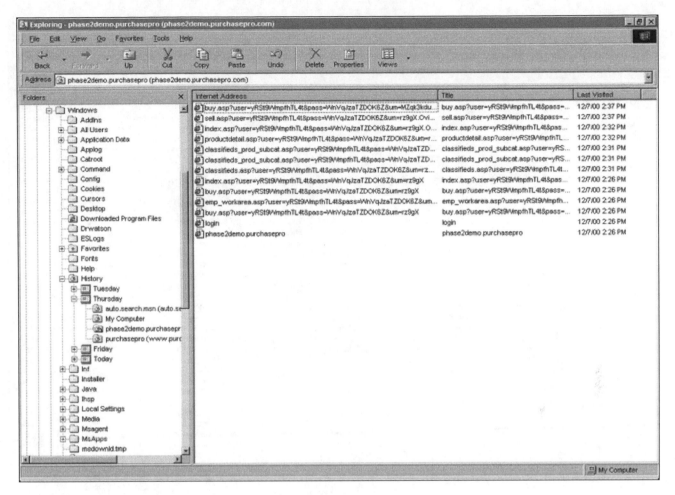

Fig. 6 History buffer from hard-drive view.

cache, sometimes called a cache store or RAM cache, is a portion of memory made of highspeed static RAM (SRAM) instead of the slower and less expensive dynamic RAM (DRAM) used for main memory. Memory caching is effective because most programs access the same data or instructions over and over. By keeping as much of this information as possible in SRAM, the computer avoids accessing the slower DRAM. Some memory caches are built into the architecture of microprocessors. The Intel 80486 microprocessor, for example, contains an 8K memory cache, and the Pentium has a 16K cache. Such internal caches are often called Level 1 (L1) caches. Most modern PCs also come with external cache memory, referred to as Level 2 (L2) caches. These caches sit between the CPU and the DRAM. Like L1 caches, L2 caches are composed of SRAM but are much larger.

Disk caching works under the same principle as memory caching, but, instead of using high-speed SRAM, a disk cache uses conventional main memory. The most recently accessed data from the disk (as well as adjacent sectors) is stored in a memory buffer. When a program needs to access data from the disk, it first checks the disk cache to see if the data is there. Disk caching can dramatically improve the performance of applications because accessing a byte of data in RAM can be thousands of times faster than accessing the same byte on a hard disk. When data is found in the cache, it is called a *cache hit*, and the effectiveness of a cache is judged by its hit rate. Many cache systems use a technique known as smart caching, in which the system can recognize certain types of frequently used data.

Why is this cache important to computer forensics? The last set of instructions or data that was saved in the cache might provide the evidence you need for your investigation. Unfortunately, capturing the cache information is tricky and can only be done with special programs.

Temporary Internet Files

Temporary Internet files are "image captures" of each screen or site that you visit when you access the Internet or an intranet (see Fig. 7). Temporary Internet Files is a

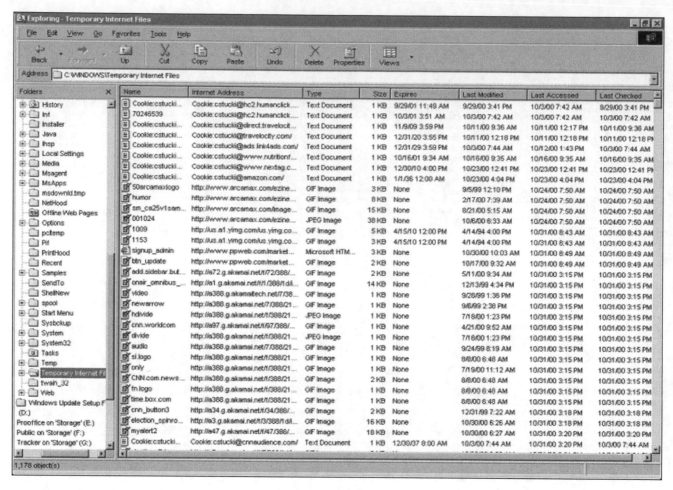

Fig. 7 Temporary internet files.

subfolder under the Windows folder on the C: drive (or hard drive) of the PC. The advantage of looking at the temporary Internet files compared to any other files is that they show you the address of the site visited and when it was last modified, last accessed, and last checked. This can be very useful when gathering evidence regarding too much Internet access or inappropriate Internet access. These files can also be useful in proving a pattern of log-on and duration times.

TRACKING LOG-ON DURATION AND TIMES

If you need to review log-on duration and times for a given user, you should contact the organization's network operations group (or similarly named or empowered department). This group can provide reports on any given IP address, user ID, and the times that the IP address and ID were logged into the network. Some of these reports can actually tell what addresses the user accessed and when. The most basic report should be able to tell when the ID was logged into the system and when it logged off. With some of the current system architecture, the reports track

and log all user activity down to the keystroke; however, this kind of detailed logging can drag down the performance of servers, so logging is not always done to this level of detail. You must ask your network operations personnel what type of reporting and subsequent information is available.

Ask for the entire detail report and see what they record; do not just ask for the basics. You might save time and effort if you ask for everything up front. You should ask for not only the activity report but also server monitor reports that pertain to the user, traffic monitoring reports, and site click-through reports. You want every report that exists that might show what a given user was doing at any moment. You might be surprised at just how much information is available and how eager operations staff personnel are to apply their expertise. Some of the evidence you can gather to help determine log-on and duration times can be derived from the Temporary Internet Files and Recent Documents lists. These files can help establish and support patterns of use. Although a smart user might clean up these files frequently by using the Disk Cleanup utilities that Windows provides, it is always a good idea to check to see what information is still

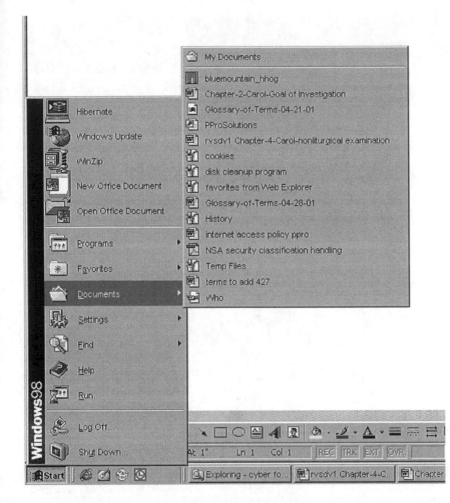

Fig. 8 Recent document list from Start menu.

available. The cleanup utilities can be accessed by Start Menu → Programs → Accessories → Disk Cleanup. These utilities erase the Internet files, temporary files, and most cookies. See prior sections of this entry on how to find and access temporary files.

RECENT DOCUMENTS LIST

The Recent Documents list can show you the latest documents that a user has accessed. There are two ways to see this list of documents, but only one shows you when the items on the list were accessed. First, you can see the documents from the Start menu, under the Documents "tab"/selection. You can click on any one of the documents listed to bring the document is up on the screen (see Fig. 8). You can also access the same list, via the Recent subfolder under the Windows folder (see Fig. 9). This view will give you the name of the document and when each was last modified. Windows 95 does not have this directory; only Windows 98 and more recent copies of Windows have a Recent directory.

TRACKING ILLICIT SOFTWARE INSTALLATION AND USE

If you are investigating a user who may be loading illegal, illicit, or non-work-related software on his or her PC, there are a number of places to check within the user's PC to prove or disprove these unauthorized (and maybe even illegal) actions. Some of these key places include the System Registry and System Information, or the contents of the hard drive can be viewed. Before you begin this part of an investigation, you must first get a listing of all approved software that can reside on a given PC. This list most probably contains things such as Word, Excel, Microsoft Office, and other work-related software. There should be a master list (i.e., database) of what software resides on every PC that operations maintains; however, due to some site license agreements, software appearing on a master checklist that operations personnel use to set up new PCs might not be on every PC.

The company policies and procedures should have an outline of the software that is not permitted to be loaded on a company-owned PC. The most recognizable programs

Forensics –
FTP

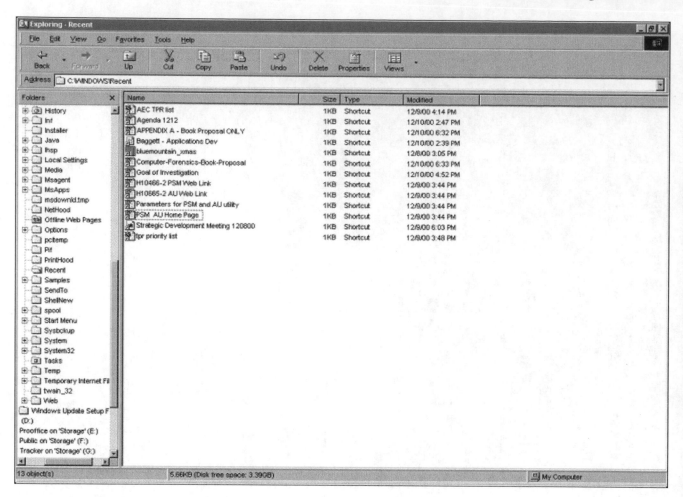

Fig. 9   Recent documents list from hard-drive view.

that are usually not work related are games. When looking for these types of programs, look carefully at the names of the files; users often change the names to avoid detection. To double-check the legitimacy of a program, launch all .exe files to reveal what is actually behind a file name and what resides on the PC. Remember that this procedure should be carried out on the mirror-imaged, working copy data, not on the original PC. This prevents corrupting seized data as well as disrupting networked services or other legitimate data that may reside on the PC in question.

As you are checking the software list, you should also note all the serial numbers and registration numbers of all software that resides on the PC. These numbers should be compared to the software licenses held by the company to ensure that the loaded software is both legal and authorized. For example, a user might have MS Access on his or her PC, but the company might not have authorized or actually loaded this software on that user's PC. The user might have obtained certain software packages in some manner not complying with company procedures and thus it has been illegally installed on the PC. This is the

most common incidence of illegally installed software on company equipment today. Such software installations are risky to a company because software license infringement can be expensive if it is discovered and not corrected.

So, how do you actually begin to search for this evidence? First, you need your lists of what can be on any given PC and what is registered to be on the specific PC you are investigating. You are also looking for a list of all information that pertains to the PC under review—specifically, information such as verification of assignment of the PC to a specific employee and, if available, all software licensed for the given PC. You should then check and compare the information on these lists against the master list maintained by operations personnel. Next, you should list all the programs that currently reside on the PC. One way to do so is to use the System Registry files, referred to as a system review. Another method is to review all files via the PC directories (i.e., Explorer), referred to as a manual review. Both methods are discussed briefly in the following sections.

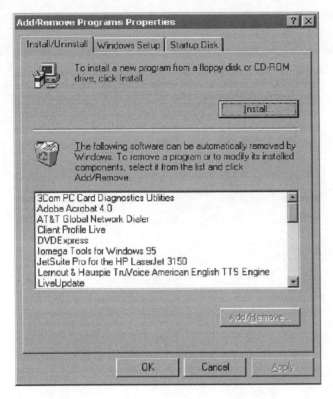

Fig. 10 Add/remove programs software listing.

System Review

The system review can be conducted using some automated methods. One of these methods is to use the System Registry files. There are several system registries. We will discuss the two primary Microsoft registry files: 1) a list of all software loaded on the PC and 2) a more comprehensive list of what is loaded, when it was loaded, and how it is configured. Both can be used to verify that illegal or non-work-related software was loaded onto a given PC or hardware added. A simple list of what has been loaded can be viewed by accessing the path from the Control Panel to the Add/Remove Programs icon (see Fig. 10). A more comprehensive list of software and hardware that have been loaded onto a PC can be obtained via the Microsoft System Information panels. The following path can access these: Start → Programs → Accessories → System Tools → System Information (see Fig. 11). This screen shows basic system information for the PC being investigated. The most useful information about a PC can be found under the Components directory. This is where you will find some history—when things were loaded and last modified (see Fig. 12). Three levels of information are shown on this screen: Basic, Advanced, and History. All three can

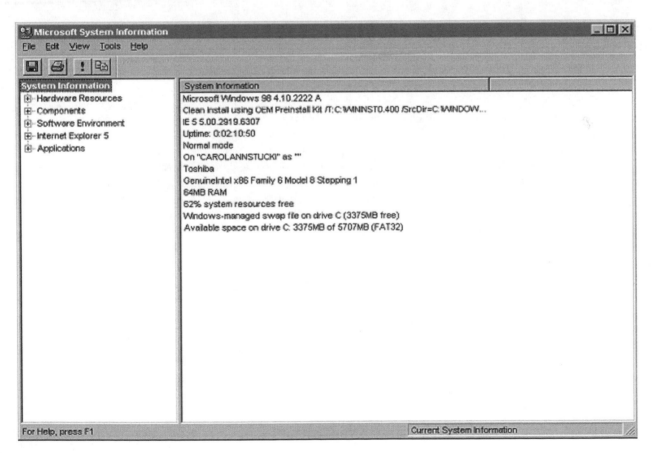

Fig. 11 System information base screen.

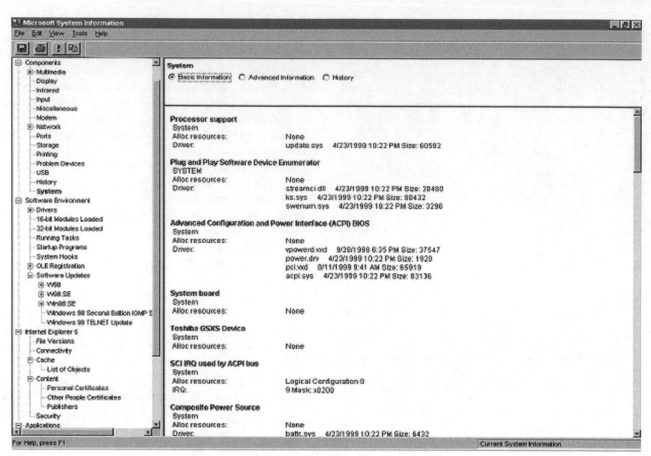

Fig. 12   System components/System/Basic information.

Forensics –
FTP

provide needed information in an investigation, depending on what you are looking to prove.

The Components/System/Basic information can help determine if illegal or non-work-related software was loaded onto a PC (see Fig. 12). To determine if there is illegal software or non-work-related software on the PC, first you need a list of all legal software that should be on the machine, along with any serial or license numbers for the software. This list should be available from operations personnel who distribute and fix the PCs. Next, take this list and verify what software is on the machine; be sure to check the serial numbers. The components/system/basic information list tells you what software is on the machine and when it was loaded, but the serial numbers will be in the "About" information or start-up screen for the software. If the software is not work related, it will not be on your list from the operations department.

Another view to see if software has been loaded onto the PC from the Web is available via Windows Explorer, in the Windows Directory under the Download Program subfolder (see Fig. 13). The Components/System/History

information can show when a component (piece of hardware or firmware) was loaded and when it was last modified (see Fig. 14); however, many components are modified when the user reboots or turns on the computer. The "red herring" items to look for in this history would be things that were not issued with the computer and the user added himself. These might include graphics cards, emulators, or sound cards. The Component/History files are not much different in the information that they provide (see Fig. 14). Fig. 15 shows what has been updated in the last 7 days. The Complete History file shows when items were loaded or when they were modified since last being loaded.

Manual Review

One of the reasons for conducting a manual review in addition to a system review is to be sure that you have covered all of the bases. What the manual review will tell you that the system review will not is what actual applications reside on the PC. The first step in the manual review is to locate all executable programs and applications on the

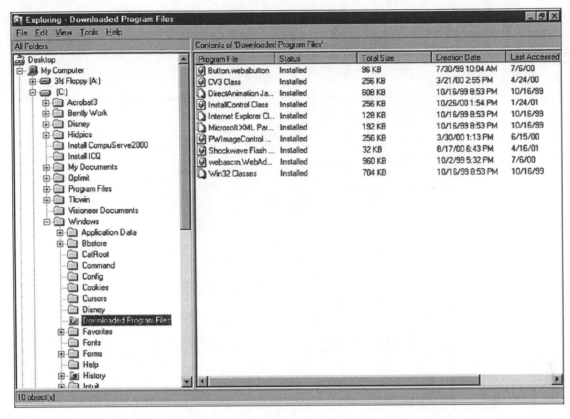

Fig. 13 Downloaded programs viewed from windows explorer.

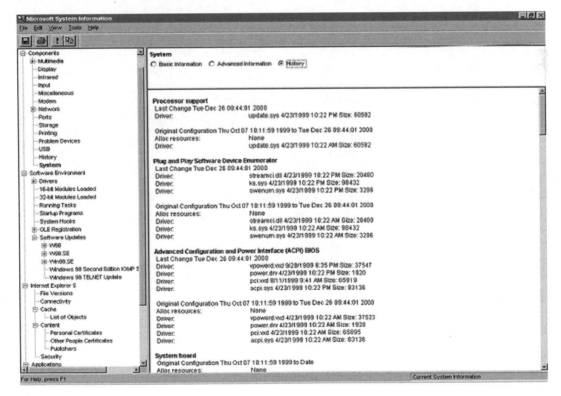

Fig. 14 System information/Components/System/History.

Forensics –
FTP

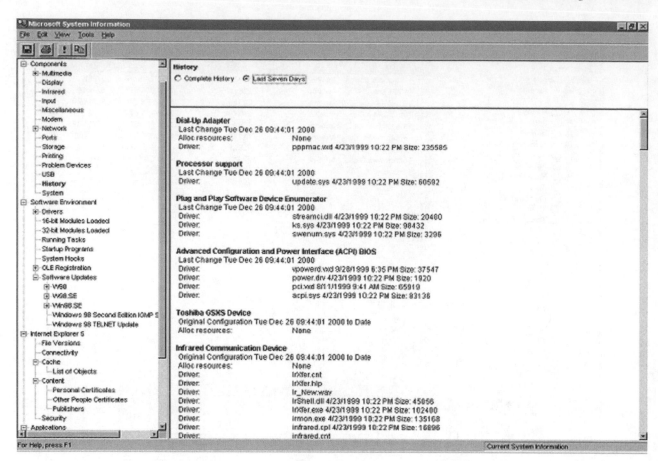

Fig. 15   System information/Components/History for the last 7 days.

Forensics –
FTP

PC. Start Explorer—not the Web browser Internet Explorer, but Microsoft Explorer. From the top menu select Tools → Find → Files and Folders. This will give you a pop-up box where you can identify what you want to search for. In this case, we use a wild card query to find all files ending with .exe, or all executable files. Set the "Look in" field to the drive you are investigating, which is usually the C: drive. Select the option to look at all of the C: drive. See Fig. 16 for an example of the results of this search. This can be quite an extensive list; however, you should check each of these references to ensure that they do belong to authorized programs. Most unauthorized programs are put under the Programs directory, but do not assume anything; check them all. You can check them by actually launching them. You can do this by clicking on the file from the Find screen. To record your findings, it might be best to print this screen and manually check off each item on the list as you verify it. A quick review of the items in the list might narrow your investigation. If you see icons on the far left that represent something suspicious, you might investigate these first. Suspicious items might include game or playing card icons. See Fig. 17 for an example of an excerpt of the full list. Fig. 17 shows an item on the list with a playing card icon—see the freeplus item? This is actually a game,

and for most companies and systems may be a violation and it should not be installed on the PC. Another thing to watch out for on your listing of files are Hidden files (see discussion below). You need to check the system standards and settings to determine if the File Manager allows you to see these or not before assuming that your file list is complete.

HIDDEN FILES

A hidden file is a file with a special hidden attribute turned on so the file is not normally visible to users. Hidden files are not listed when you execute the DOS DIR command, but most file management utilities allow you to view hidden files. DOS hides some files, such as MSDOS.SYS and IO.SYS so you cannot accidentally corrupt them. You can also turn on the hidden attribute for normal files, thereby making them invisible to casual snoopers. On a Macintosh, you can hide files with the ResEdit utility. Why are hidden files important to your investigation? If the Folder Options is not set to allow you to view hidden files, you might miss evidence. To review the settings on the PC you are investigating to verify that you are seeing hidden files, you need to launch Explorer. From the top menu within Explorer,

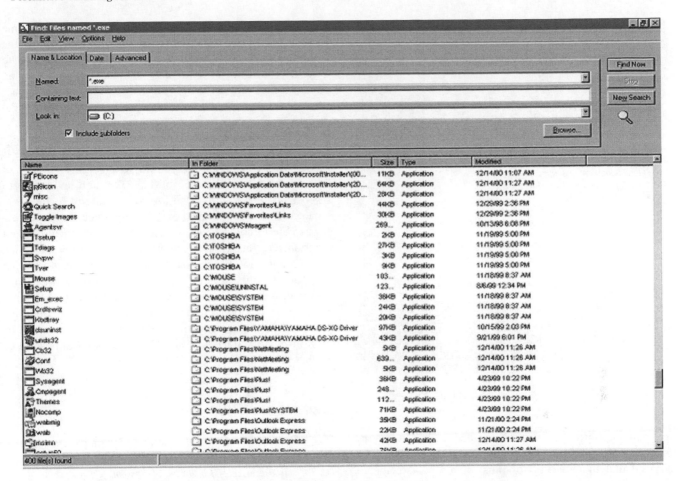

Fig. 16 Find files named *.exe.

select View → Folder Options → View tab on the pop-up box (see Fig. 18). If the radio buttons are marked so the hidden files are not to be shown, you will not see all the files. You should reset these so you can see the hidden files and know that you have a complete list.

HOW TO CORRELATE THE EVIDENCE

Now that you have captured the file evidence and the data, you can graph an access pattern or list the illegal software and when it was loaded. Next, you need to check the access and download dates and times against the timesheets, surveillance, and other witness accounts to ensure that the suspect under investigation actually had the opportunity to engage in unauthorized acts using the PC in question. In other words, you need to ensure that the employee under investigation actually had access to the equipment on the dates and times listed in the evidence. For example, if the employee had a desktop PC and did not come to work on the date that illegal software was downloaded on his PC, then you might need to look

Name	In Folder	Size	Type
Network Diagram Wizard	C:\Program Files\Visio\Solutions\Network Diagram	837...	Application
Network Database Wizard	C:\Program Files\Visio\Solutions\Network Diagram	1,0...	Application
Network Equipment Information	C:\Program Files\Visio\Solutions\Network Diagram	69KB	Application
Unwise	C:\Program Files\freeplus	70KB	Application
freeplus	C:\Program Files\freeplus	121...	Application
Imgstart	C:\Program Files\Iomega\Tools	19KB	Application
Iowatch	C:\Program Files\Iomega\Tools	21KB	Application

Fig. 17 Results of search to find files named *exe (excerpt of list).

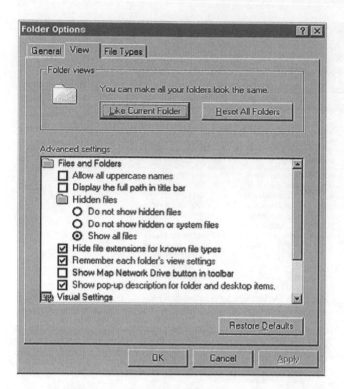

Fig. 18 Folder options to see hidden files.

for other supporting evidence (e.g., access logs indicating potential access from an external/remote location). Be advised that the investigator must obtain solid evidence that the employee under investigation actually had an opportunity and was actually using the PC at the time that the unauthorized action took place. Failing to link the employee to the PC and to corroborate and substantiate the evidence, in an irrefutable manner, will result in an inability to hold the employee accountable for his or her actions and prosecute the employee via the existing legal system.

When reviewing the evidence you have gathered, you need to follow and show the facts—and only the facts. If you have to make leaps in your logic to get from point A to point B, then you do not have enough evidence to substantiate a claim. Also, you need to ensure that you can adequately explain how the employee under review was able to commit the offense, illegal act, unauthorized action, etc. and must also be able to present evidence regarding how it was done. This proof should be simple to follow so there is no doubt that the offense was committed. Someone's career, in addition to his or her legal freedoms, could be on the line as a result of your findings, as well as the organization's liability (for a wrongful or unsubstantiated accusation). Thus, you want to be sure of what you have found.

BIBLIOGRAPHY

1. Webopedia, (computer terms and definitions Web site). http://www.webopedia.com.
2. Tinnirello, P., *Handbook of Systems Development 1999*; Auerbach: Boca Raton, FL, 1999.

Forensics –
FTP

Forensics: Operational

Michael J. Corby, CISSP
Director, META Group Consulting, Leichester, Massachusetts, U.S.A.

Abstract

This entry discusses operational forensics and how it may impact businesses. Since companies are mostly computer based now, it can be detrimental to shut everything down when something goes wrong. Operational forensics can help prevent that by using a two-part process: properly collect the data, and check the systems which will then allow the system to be recovered. The entry also discusses policies, guidelines, procedures, planning, and the investigation that constitute operational forensics.

The increased complexities of computer systems today make it difficult to determine what has happened when a malfunction occurs or a system crashes. Sometimes, it is difficult to even make the basic identification of whether the cause was accidental or intentional. If the cause was intentional, legal action may be in order; if the cause was operational, the reason must be identified and corrected. Both require a planned and measured response.

Unfortunately, with today's emphasis on immediate recovery in the networked environment, and with the obligation to get back online as quickly as possible, determining the cause may be impossible. The tendency to restart, or reboot, may remove information that could be valuable in ascertaining cause or providing evidence of criminal wrongdoing.

Operational forensics is a two-phased approach to resolving this problem. The first phase is the proper collection of operational information such as data logs, system monitoring, and evidence-tracking methods. The appropriate attention to this phase makes it much easier to identify the problem in the second phase, the recovery.

At recovery time, the information at hand can be used to decide whether a formal intrusion investigation needs to be initiated and evidence collected needs to be preserved. By responding in prescribed ways, which can include repair/replacment of the equipment, correction of a software weakness, or identification of human caused error(s) that resulted in the disruption, the system can be returned to operation with a much reduced probability of the same event occurring in the future.

RELATED BUSINESS REQUIREMENTS

Technology has been more than an efficiency enhancement to the organization. It has become the lifeblood of the successful enterprise and the sole product of the networked application service provider. As such, the maximum availability of this essential resource is critical. When a failure occurs or the system is not operating at expected levels, proper procedures should be used to accurately identify and correct the situation. Failing to do so will result in unpredictable operations, inefficiencies and possibly lost revenue, tarnished image, and failure to thrive. The business case for investing in the time, procedures, and the relatively small cost of computer hardware or software components seems clear.

Why then, do companies not have operational forensics (or the same functions by other names) programs in place? Well, for two reasons: First, people have started with the assumption that computers are perfectly reliable and therefore will only fail under rare circumstances if programs are well-written—why waste resources in pointing the finger at something that should never occur? Second, the topic of methodical, procedural investigations is new to other than law enforcement, and only recently has come into the foreground with the advent of computer crimes, cyber terrorism, and the relationship of vengeance and violence linked to some computer "chat rooms," e-mail, and personal private data intrusions.

The good news is that operational forensics is not an expensive option. There is some additional cost needed to properly equip the systems and the process for secure log creation; but unless the need is determined for a full-scale criminal investigation and trial preparation, the process is almost transparent to most operations.

The business objectives of implementing an operational forensics program are threefold:

1. Maintain maximum system availability (99.999% or five-nines "uptime").
2. Quickly restore system operations without losing information related to the interruption.
3. Preserve all information that may be needed as evidence, in an acceptable legal form, should court action be warranted.

The acceptable legal form is what calls for the operational forensics process to be rigorously controlled through

Encyclopedia of Information Assurance DOI: 10.1081/E-EIA-120046836
Copyright © 2011 by Taylor & Francis. All rights reserved.

standard methods and a coordinated effort by areas outside the traditional IT organization.

JUSTIFICATION OPTIONS

The frequent reaction to a request to start an operational forensics program is one of financial concerns. Many stories abound of how forensic investigations of computer crimes have required hundreds or thousands of hours of highly paid investigators pouring over disk drives with a fine-tooth comb—all of this while the business operation is at a stand-still. These stories probably have indeed occurred, but the reason they were so disruptive, took so long, or cost so much, was because the operational data or evidence had to be reconstructed. Often, this reconstruction process is difficult and may be effectively challenged in a legal case if not prepared perfectly.

Operational forensics programs can be justified using the age-old 80-20 rule: an investigation cost is 80% comprised of recreating lost data and 20% actually investigating. An effective operational forensics program nearly eliminates the 80% data recreation cost.

A second way in which operational forensics programs have been justified is as a positive closed-loop feedback system for making sure that the investment in IT is effectively utilized. It is wise investment planning and prudent loss reduction. For example, an operational forensics program can quickly and easily determine that the cause of a server crashing frequently is due to an unstable power source, not an improperly configured operating system. A power problem can be resolved for a few hundred dollars, whereas the reinstallation of a new operating system with all options can take several days of expensive staff time, and actually solve nothing.

No matter how the program is justified, organizations are beginning to think about the investment in technology and the huge emphasis on continuous availability, and a finding ways to convince management that a plan for identifying and investigating causes of system problems is a worthwhile endeavor.

BASICS OF OPERATIONAL FORENSICS

Operational forensics includes developing procedures and communicating methods of response so that all flexibility to recover more data or make legal or strategic decisions is preserved. Briefly stated, all the procedures in the world and all the smart investigators that can be found cannot reverse the course of events once they have been put into action. If the Ctrl-Alt-Delete sequence has been started, data lost in that action is difficult and expensive, if not impossible to recover. Operational forensics, therefore, starts with a state of mind. That state of mind prescribes a "think before reacting" mentality. The following are the basic components of the preparation process that accompany that mentality.

For all situations:

- Definition of the process to prioritize the three key actions when an event occurs:

  — Evidence retention
  — System recovery
  — Cause identification

- Guidelines that provide assistance in identifying whether an intrusion has occurred and if it was intentional
- Methods for developing cost-effective investigative methods and recovery solutions
- Maintenance of a secure, provable evidentiary chain of custody

For situations where legal action is warranted:

- Identification or development of professionally trained forensic specialists and interviewers/interrogators, as needed
- Procedures for coordination and referral of unauthorized intrusions and activity to law enforcement and prosecution, as necessary
- Guidelines to assist in ongoing communication with legal representatives, prosecutors, and law enforcement, as necessary
- Instructions for providing testimony, as needed

Notice that the evidence is collected and maintained in a form suitable for use in cases where legal action is possible, even if the event is purely an operational failure. That way, if after the research begins, it is determined that what was thought initially to be operational, turns out to warrant legal action, all the evidence is available.

Consider the following scenario. A Web server has stopped functioning, and upon initial determination, evidence shows that the building had a power outage and when the server rebooted upon restoration, a diskette was left in the drive from a previous software installation. Initial actions in response include purchasing a new UPS (uninterruptable power supply) capable of keeping the server functioning for a longer time, and changing the boot sequence so that a diskette in the drive will not prevent system recovery. All set? Everybody thinks so, until a few days after the recovery, someone has discovered that new operating parameters have taken effect, allowing an intruder to install a "trap door" into the operating system. That change would take effect only after the system rebooted. Is the data still available to identify how the trap door was installed, whether it posed problems prior to this event, and who is responsible for this act of vandalism?

An operational forensics program is designed to identify the risk of changes to the system operation when it is rebooted and conduct baseline quality control, but also to

Forensics –
FTP

preserve the evidence in a suitable place and manner so that a future investigation can begin if new facts are uncovered.

BUILDING THE OPERATIONAL FORENSICS PROGRAM

Policy

To start building an operational forensics program, the first key element, as in many other technical programs, includes defining a policy. Success in developing this process must be established at the top levels of the organization. Therefore, a policy endorsed by senior management must be written and distributed to the entire organization. This policy both informs and guides.

This policy informs everyone that the organization has corporate endorsement to use appropriate methods to ensure long-term operational stability, and thus ensure that the means to accurately identify and correct problems will be used. It should also inform the organization that methods will be used to take legal action against those who attempt to corrupt, invade, or misuse the technology put in place to accomplish the organization's mission. There is a subtle hint here meant to discourage employees who may be tempted to use the system for questionable purposes (harassing, threatening, or illegal correspondence and actions), that the organization has the means and intent to prosecute violators.

The policy guides in that it describes what to do, under what circumstances, and how to evaluate the results. With this policy, the staff responsible for operating the system components, including mainframes, servers, and even workstations, as well as all other peripherals, will have a definition of the process to prioritize the three key actions when an event occurs:

1. Evidence retention
2. System recovery
3. Cause identification

In general, this policy defines a priority used for establishing irrefutable data that identifies the cause of an interruption. That priority is to first ensure that the evidence is retained; then recover the system operation; and, finally, as time and talent permit, identify the cause.

Guidelines

As a supplement to these policies, guidelines can be developed that provide assistance in identifying whether an intrusion has occurred and if it was intentional. As with all guidelines, this is not a specific set of definitive rules, but rather a checklist of things to consider when conducting an initial response. More detailed guidelines are also provided in the form of a reminder checklist of the process used to secure a site for proper evidence retention. The

suggested method for publishing this guideline is to post it on the wall near a server, firewall, or other critical component. Items on this reminder checklist can be constructed to fit the specific installation, but typical entries can include:

Before rebooting this server:

1. Take a photograph of the screen (call Ext xxxx for camera).
2. Verify that the keyboard/monitor switches are set correctly.
3. Record the condition of any lights/indicators.
4. Use the procedure entitled *Disabling the disk mirror.*
5. …
6. …
7. etc.

Accompanying these posted instructions are a series of checklists designed to help record and control the information that can be collected throughout the data collection process.

Log Procedures

Policies and guidelines can help provide people with the motivation and method to act thoughtfully and properly when responding to an event, but they are insufficient by themselves to provide all that is needed. Most operating system components and access software (modem drivers, LAN traffic, Internet access software, etc.) provide for log files to be created when the connection is used, changed, or when errors occur. The catch is that usually these logs are not enabled when the component is installed. Furthermore, the log file may be configured to reside on a system device that gets reset when the system restarts. To properly enable these logs, they must be

- Activated when the service is installed
- Maintained on a safe device, protected from unauthorized viewing or alteration
- Set to record continuously despite system reboots

Additional third-party access management and control logs can and should be implemented to completely record and report system use in a manner acceptable for use as legal evidence. This includes data that can be independently corroborated, non-repudiated, and chain-of-custody maintained.

Configuration Planning

The operational forensics program also includes defining methods for maximizing the data/evidence collection abilities while providing for fast and effective system recovery. That often can be accomplished by planning for operational forensics when system components are configured. One technique often used is to provide a form of disk mirroring on all devices where log files are stored. The intent is to capture data as it exists as close as possible to the event. By maintaining mirrored disks, the "mirror" can be disabled and removed for evidence preservation while the system is restarted. This accomplishes the preservation of evidence and quick recovery required in a critical system.

The process for maintaining and preserving this data is then to create a minimum of three copies of the mirrored data:

1. One copy to be signed and sealed in an evidence locker pending legal action (if warranted)
2. One copy to be used as a control copy for evidence/ data testing and analysis
3. One copy to be provided to opposing attorney in the discovery phase, if a criminal investigation proceeds

LINKING OPERATIONAL FORENSICS TO CRIMINAL INVESTIGATION

The value of a well-designed operational forensics program is in its ability to have all the evidence necessary to effectively develop a criminal investigation. By far, the most intensive activity in preparing for a legal opportunity is in the preparation of data that is validated and provable in legal proceedings. Three concepts are important to understanding this capacity:

1. Evidence corroboration
2. Non-repudiation
3. Preservation of the chain of custody

Evidence Corroboration

If one is at all familiar with any type of legal proceeding, from the high profile trials of the 1990s to the courtroom-based movies, television programs, or pseudo-legal entertainment of judicial civil cases, evidence that is not validated through some independent means may by inadmissible. Therefore, to provide the maximum potential for critical evidence to be admitted into the record, it should be corroborated through some other means. Therefore, based on the potential for legal action, several log creation utilities can be employed to record the same type of information. When two sources are compared, the accuracy of the data being reported can be assured. For example, access to a system from the outside reported only by a modem log may be questioned that the data was erroneous. However, if the same information is validated by access to the system from system login attempt, or from an application use log, the data is more likely to be admitted as accurate.

Non-repudiation

A second crucial element necessary for a smooth legal process is establishing evidence in a way that actions cannot be denied by the suspect. This is called "non-repudiation." In many recent cases of attempted system intrusion, a likely suspect has been exonerated by testifying that it could not have been his actions that caused the violation. Perhaps someone masqueraded as him, or perhaps his password was compromised, etc. There is no way to definitely make all transactions pass the non-repudiation test; but in establishing the secure procedures for authenticating all who access the system, non-repudiation should be included as a high-priority requirement.

Preservation of the Chain of Custody

Finally, the last and perhaps most important legal objective of operational forensics is to preserve the chain of custody. In simple terms, this means that the data/evidence was always under the control of an independent source and that it could not have been altered to support one side of the case. This is perhaps the most easily established legal criterion, but the least frequently followed. To establish a proper chain of custody, all data must be properly signed-in and signed-out using approved procedures, and any chance of its alteration must be eliminated—to a legal certainty. Technology has come to the rescue with devices such as read-only CDs, but there are also some low-technology solutions like evidence lockers, instant photography, and voice recorders to track activity related to obtaining, storing, and preserving data.

For all legal issues, it is wise and highly recommended that the organization's legal counsel be included on the forensic team, and if possible, a representative from the local law enforcement agency's (Attorney General, Prosecutor or FBI/state/local police unit) high-tech crime unit. In the case of properly collecting evidence when and if a situation arises, prior planning and preparation is always a good investment.

LINKING OPERATIONAL FORENSICS TO BUSINESS CONTINUITY PLANNING

What makes operational forensics an entity unto itself is the ability to use the time and effort spent in planning for benefits other than prosecuting criminals. The key benefit is in an organization's ability to learn something from every operational miscue. Countless times, systems stop running because intruders who only partially succeed at gaining access have corrupted the network connections. In most instances, all the information that could have been used to close access vulnerabilities goes away with the Ctrl-Alt-Delete keys. Systems do not crash without cause.

If each cause were evaluated, many of them could be eliminated or their probability of reoccurring significantly reduced.

In the current age of continuous availability, maximum network uptime is directly linked to profit or effectiveness. Implementing an operational forensics program can help establish an effective link to business continuity planning risk reduction and can raise the bar of attainable service levels.

Although evidence collected for improving availability does not need to pass all legal hurdles, an effective method of cause identification can help focus the cost of prevention on *real* vulnerabilities, not on the whole universe of possibilities, no matter how remote. Cost justification of new availability features is more readily available, and IT can begin to function more like a well-defined business function than a "black art."

SUMMARY AND CONCLUSION

When a system interruption occurs, operational forensics is a key component of the recovery process and should be utilized to identify the nature and cause of the interruption as well as collecting, preserving, and evaluating the evidence. This special investigation function is essential because it is often difficult to conclusively determine the nature, source, and responsibility for the system interruption. As such, to improve the likelihood of successfully recovering from a system interruption, certain related integral services, such as establishing the data/activity logs, monitoring system, evidence collection mechanisms, intrusion management, and investigative management should be established prior to a system interruptions occurrence. This is the primary benefit of operational forensics. One will see much more of this in the near future.

Forensics – FTP

Forensics: Rules of Evidence

Thomas Welch, CISSP, CPP
President and Chief Executive Officer, Bullzi Security, Inc., Altamonte Springs, Florida, U.S.A.

Abstract
This entry covers computer crime and the rules of evidence, to prepare to respond to both internal and external attacks.

Incidents of computer-related crime and telecommunications fraud have increased dramatically over the past decade, but due to the esoteric nature of this crime there have been very few prosecutions and even fewer convictions. The same technology that has allowed for the advancement and automation of many business processes has also opened to the door to many new forms of computer abuse. While some of these system attacks merely use contemporary methods to commit older, more familiar types of crime, others involve the use of completely new forms of criminal activity that have evolved along with the technology.

Computer crime investigation and computer forensics are also evolving sciences which are affected by many external factors: continued advancements in technology, societal issues, legal issues, etc. There are many gray areas that need to be sorted out and tested through the courts. Until then, the system attackers will have a clear advantage and computer abuse will continue to increase. We, as computer security practitioners, must be aware of the myriad of technological and legal issues that affect our systems and its users, including issues dealing with investigations and enforcement.

COMPUTER CRIME

According to the American Heritage Dictionary, a "crime" is any act committed or omitted in violation of the law. This definition causes a perplexing problem for law enforcement when dealing with computer-related crime, since much of today's computer-related crime is without violation of any formal law. This may seem be a contradictory statement, but traditional criminal statutes, in most states, have only been modified throughout the years to reflect the theories of modern criminal justice. These laws generally envision applications to situations involving traditional types of criminal activity, such as burglary, larceny, fraud, etc. Unfortunately, the modern criminal has kept pace with the vast advancements in technology and he has found ways to apply such innovations as the computer to his criminal ventures. Unknowingly and probably unintentionally, he has also revealed the difficulties in applying

older traditional laws to situations involving "computer related crimes."

In 1979 the United States Department of Justice established a definition for "computer crime," stating that "a computer crime is any illegal act for which knowledge of computer technology is essential for its perpetration, investigation, or prosecution." This definition was too broad and has since been further refined by new or modified, state and federal criminal statutes.

Criminal Law

Criminal law identifies a crime as being a wrong against society. Even if an individual is victimized, under the law, society is the victim. A conviction under criminal law normally results in a jail term or probation for the defendant. It could also result in a financial award to the victim as restitution for the crime. The main purpose for prosecuting under criminal law is punishment for the offender. This punishment is also meant to serve as a deterrent against future crime. The deterrent aspect of punishment only works if the punishment is severe enough to discourage further criminal activity. This is certainly not the case in the United States, where very few computer criminals ever go to jail. In other areas of the world there are very strong deterrents. For example, in China in 1995, a computer hacker was executed after being found guilty of embezzling $200,000 from a national bank. This certainly will have a dissuading value for other hackers in China!

To be found guilty of a criminal offense under criminal law, the jury must believe, beyond a reasonable doubt, that the offender is guilty of the offense. The lack of technical expertise, combined with the many confusing questions posed by the defense attorney, may cause doubt for many jury members, thus rendering a "not guilty" decision. The only short-term solution to this problem, is to provide simple testimony in layman terms and to use demonstrative evidence whenever possible. Even with this, it will be difficult for many juries to return a guilty verdict.

Criminal conduct is broken down into two classifications depending on severity. A felony is the more serious of

Encyclopedia of Information Assurance DOI: 10.1081/E-EIA-120046869

Copyright © 2011 by Taylor & Francis. All rights reserved.

the two, normally resulting in a jail term of more than 1 year. Misdemeanors are normally punishable by a fine or a jail sentence of less than a year. It is important to understand that if we wish to deter future attacks, we must push for the stricter sentencing, which only occurs under the felonious classification. The type of attack and/or the total dollar loss has a direct relationship to the crime classification. As we cover investigation procedures, we will see why it is so important to account for all time and money spent on the investigation.

Criminal law falls under two main jurisdictions: Federal and State. Although there is a plethora of federal and state statutes which may be used against traditional criminal offenses, and even though many of these same statutes may apply to computer related crimes with some measure of success, it is clear that many cases fail to reach prosecution or fail to result in conviction because of the gaps which exists in the Federal Criminal Code and the individual state criminal statutes.

Because of this, every state in the United States, with the exception of one, along with the Federal government, have adopted new laws specific to computer related abuses. These new laws, which have been redefined over the years to keep abreast of the constant changes in the technological forum, have been subjected to an ample amount of scrutiny due to many social issues, which have been impacted by the proliferation of computers in society. Some of these issues, such as privacy, copyright infringement, and software ownership are yet to be resolved, thus we can expect many more changes to the current collection of laws. Some of the computer related crimes, which are addressed by the new state and federal laws, are

- Unauthorized access
- Exceed authorized access
- Intellectual property theft or misuse of information
- Child pornography
- Theft of services
- Forgery
- Property theft (e.g., computer hardware, chips, etc.)
- Invasion of privacy
- Denial of services
- Computer fraud
- Viruses
- Sabotage (data alteration or malicious destruction)
- Extortion
- Embezzlement
- Espionage
- Terrorism

All but one state, Vermont, have created or amended laws specifically to deal with computer-related crime. Twenty-five of the states have enacted specific computer crime statutes, while the other 24 states have merely amended their traditional criminal statutes to confront computer crime issues. Vermont has announced legislation under Bill H.0555, which deals with theft of computer services. The elements of proof, which define the basis of the criminal activity, vary from state to state. Security practitioners should be fully cognizant of their own state laws, specifically the elements of proof. Additionally, traditional criminal statutes, such as theft, fraud, extortion and embezzlement, can still be used to prosecute computer crime.

Just as there has been numerous new legislation at the State level, there have also been many new federal policies, such as the:

- Electronic Communications Privacy Act
- Electronic Espionage Act of 1996
- Child Pornography Prevention Act of 1996
- Computer Fraud and Abuse Act of 1986, 18 U.S.C. 1001

These laws and policies have been established, precisely to deal with computer and telecommunications abuses at the Federal level. Additionally, many modifications and updates have been made to the Federal Criminal Code, Sections 1029 and 1030, to deal with a variety of computer related abuses. Even though these new laws have been adopted for use in the prosecution of a computer-related offense, some of the older, proven federal laws, identified below, offer a "simpler" case to present to judges and juries:

- Wire fraud
- Mail fraud
- Interstate transportation of stolen property
- Racketeer influenced & corrupt organizations (RICO)

The Electronic Communications Privacy Act (ECPA) is being tested more today than ever before. The ECPA prohibits all monitoring of wire, oral, and electronic communications unless specific statutory exceptions apply. This includes monitoring of e-mail, network traffic, keystrokes, or telephone systems. The ECPA was not meant to prohibit network providers from monitoring and maintaining their networks and connections, thus the ECPA provides an exception for monitoring network traffic for legitimate businesses purposes. Additionally, the ECPA also allows monitoring when the network users are notified of the monitoring process.

The two new Acts enacted in 1996, the Child Pornography Prevention Act (CPPA) and the Electronic Espionage Act (EEA) have proved that the legislative process is working, albeit a bit slower than one would like. The CPPA is especially impressive in that it eradicates many of the loopholes afforded by newer technology. The CPPA was enacted specifically to combat the use of computer technology to produce pornography that conveys the impression that children were used in the photographs or images, even if the participants are actually adults. The

Court held that any child pornography, including simulated or morphed images, stimulate the sexual appetites of pedophiles and that the images themselves may persuade a child to engage in sexual activity by viewing other children. The CPPA was contested by the Freedom of Speech Coalition (FSC), but was upheld by the Court in *FSC v. Reno*.

The EEA hopefully will curtail some of the industrial espionage that is going on today, but it will also have an impact on how business is conducted in the United States, especially intelligence gathering. According to the EEA, it is a criminal offense to take, download, receive, or possess trade secret information obtained without the owner's authorization. Penalties can reach $10 million in fines, up to 15 years in prison, and forfeiture of property used in the commission of the crime. This could have tremendous, far-reaching consequences for businesses should an employee improperly use information gained from any previous employment.

Civil Law

Civil law (or tort law) identifies a tort as a wrong against an individual or business, which normally results in damage or loss to that individual or business. The major differences between criminal and civil law, are the type of punishment and the level of proof required to obtain a guilty verdict. There is no jail sentence under the civil law system. A victim may receive financial or injunctive relief as restitution for their loss. An injunction against the offender will attempt to thwart any further loss to the victim. Additionally, a violation of the injunction may result in a Contempt of Court order, which would place the offender in jeopardy of going to jail. The main purpose for seeking civil remedy is for financial restitution, which can be awarded as follows:

- Compensatory damages
- Punitive damages
- Statutory damages

In a civil action, if there is no culpability on the part of the victim, the victim may be entitled to compensatory (restitution), statutory, and punitive damages. Compensatory damages are actual damages to the victim and include attorney fees, lost profits, investigation costs, etc. Punitive damages are just that—damages set by the jury, with the intent to punish the offender. Even if the victim is partially culpable, an award may be made on the victim's behalf, but may be lessened due to the victim's culpable negligence. Statutory damages are damages determined by law. Mere violation of the law entitles the victim to a statutory award.

Civil cases are much easier to convict under because the burden of proof required for a conviction is much less. To be found guilty of a civil wrong, the jury must believe, based only upon the preponderance of the evidence, that the offender is guilty of the offense. It is much easier to show that the majority (51%) of the evidence is pointing to the defendant's guilt.

Finally, just as a search warrant is used by law enforcement as a tool in the criminal investigation, the court can issue an inpoundment order or writ of possession, which is a court order to take back the property in question. The investigator should also keep in mind that the criminal and civil case could take place simultaneously, thus allowing items seized during the execution of the search warrant to be used in the civil case.

Insurance

An insurance policy is generally part of an organization's overall risk mitigation/management plan. The policy offsets the risk of loss to the insurance company in return for an acceptable level of loss (the insurance premium). Since many computer-related assets (software and hardware) account for the majority of an organization's net worth, they must be protected by insurance. If there is a loss to any of these assets, the insurance company is usually required to pay out on the policy. One important factor to bear in mind, is the principle of culpable negligence. This places part of the liability on the victim if the victim fails to follow a "standard of due care" in the protection of identified assets. If a victim organization is held to be culpably negligent, the insurance company may be required to pay only a portion of the loss. Also, an insurance company can attempt to deny coverage, arguing that an employee's "dishonest" acts caused the damage.

Two important insurance issues related to the investigation are prompt notification of the loss and understanding that the insurance company has a duty to defend. Regarding prompt notification, insurance companies may deny coverage by arguing that the claim was received too late. Some states even allow insurance companies to void its insurance obligations if the notice or claim is proven to be late.

RULES OF EVIDENCE

Before delving into the investigative process and computer forensics, it is essential that the investigator have a thorough understanding of the Rules of Evidence. The submission of evidence in any type of legal proceeding generally amounts to a significant challenge, but when computers are involved, the problems are intensified. Special knowledge is needed to locate and collect evidence and special care is required to preserve and transport the evidence. Evidence in a computer crime case may differ from traditional forms of evidence inasmuch as most computer-related evidence is intangible—in the form of an electronic pulse or magnetic charge.

Before evidence can be presented in a case, it must be competent, relevant and material to the issue and it must be presented in compliance with the rules of evidence. Anything which tends to prove directly or indirectly, that a person may be responsible for the commission of a criminal offense may be legally presented against him. Proof may include the oral testimony of witnesses or the introduction of physical or documentary evidence.

By definition, **evidence** is any species of proof or probative matter, legally presented at the trial of an issue, by the act of the parties and through the medium of witnesses, records, documents, objects, etc., for the purpose of inducing belief in the minds of the court and jurors as to their contention. In short, **evidence** is anything offered in court to prove the truth or falsity of a fact at issue. This section will cover each of the Rules of Evidence as they relate to computer crime investigations.

Types of Evidence

There are many types of evidence that can be offered in court to prove the truth or falsity of a given fact. The most common forms of evidence are direct, real, documentary and demonstrative. Direct evidence is oral testimony, whereby the knowledge is obtained from any of the witness's five senses and is, in itself, proof or disproof of a fact in issue. Direct evidence is called to prove a specific act (i.e., eye witness statement). Real evidence, also known as associative or physical evidence, is made up of tangible objects that prove or disprove guilt. Physical evidence includes such things as tools used in the crime, fruits of the crime, perishable evidence capable of reproduction, etc. The purpose of the physical evidence is to link the suspect to the scene of the crime. It is this evidence which has material existence and can be presented to the view of the court and jury for consideration. Documentary evidence is evidence presented to the court in the form of business records, manuals, printouts, etc. Much of the evidence submitted in a computer crime case is documentary evidence. Finally, demonstrative evidence is evidence used to aid the jury. It may be in the form of a model, experiment, chart, or an illustration offered as proof.

It should be noted that in order to aid the court and the jury in their quest to understand the facts at issue, demonstrative evidence is being used more often, especially in the form of simulation and animation. It is very important to understand the difference between these two types of evidence because the standard of admissibility is affected. A computer simulation is a prediction or calculation about what will happen in the future given known facts. A traffic reconstruction program is a perfect example of computer simulation. There are many mathematical algorithms used in this type of program, that must be either stipulated to, or proven to the court to be completely accurate. It is generally more difficult to admit a simulation as evidence, because of the substantive nature of the process.

Computer animation, on the other hand, is simply a computer-generated sequence, illustrating an expert's opinion. Animation does not predict future events. It merely supports the testimony of an expert witness through the use of demonstrations. An animation of a hard disk spinning, while the read/write heads are reading data, can help the court or jury understand how a disk drive works. There are no mathematical algorithms that must be proven. The animation solely aids the court and jury through visualization. The key to having animation admitted as evidence is in the strength of the expert witness. Under Rule 702, the expert used to explain evidence must be qualified to do so through skill, training or education.

When seizing evidence from a computer-related crime, the investigator should collect any and all physical evidence, such as the computer, peripherals, notepads, documentation, etc., in addition to computer-generated evidence. There are four types of computer-generated evidence. They are

- Visual output on the monitor
- Printed evidence on a printer
- Printed evidence on a plotter
- Film recorder (Includes magnetic representation on disk, tape or cartridge, and optical representation on CD)

Best Evidence Rule

The Best Evidence Rule, which had been established to deter any alteration of evidence, either intentionally or unintentionally, states that the court prefers the original evidence at the trial, rather than a copy, but they will accept a duplicate under the following conditions:

- Original lost or destroyed by fire, flood or other acts of God. This has included such things as careless employees or cleaning staff.
- Original destroyed in the normal course of business.
- Original in possession of a third party who is beyond the court's subpoena power.

This rule has been relaxed to now allow duplicates unless there is a genuine question as to the original's authenticity, or admission of the duplicate would under the circumstances be unfair.

Exclusionary Rule

Evidence must be gathered by law enforcement in accordance with court guidelines governing search and seizure or it will be excluded (Fourth Amendment). Any evidence collected in violation of the Fourth Amendment is considered to be "Fruit of the Poisonous Tree," and will not be admissible. Furthermore, any evidence identified and gathered as a result of the initial inadmissible evidence will also be held to be inadmissible. Evidence may also be excluded for other reasons, such as violations of the Electronic Communications Privacy Act (ECPA) or violations related to provisions of Chapters 2500 and 2700 of Title 18 of the United States Penal Code.

Private citizens are not subject to the Fourth Amendment's guidelines on search and seizure, but are exposed to potential exclusions for violations of the ECPA or Privacy Act. Therefore, internal investigators, private investigators, and Computer Emergency Response Team (CERT) team members should take caution when conducting any internal search, even on company computers. For example, if there were no policy in place explicitly stating the company's right to electronically monitor network traffic on company systems, then internal investigators would be well advised not to set up a sniffer on the network to monitor such traffic. To do so may be a violation of the ECPA.

Hearsay Rule

A legal factor of computer-generated evidence is that it is considered hearsay. Hearsay is second-hand evidence; evidence which is not gathered from the personal knowledge of the witness but from another source. Its value depends on the veracity and competence of the source. The magnetic charge of the disk or the electronic bit value in memory, which represents the data, is the actual, original evidence. The computer-generated evidence is merely a representation of the original evidence.

Under the US Federal Rules of Evidence, all business records, including computer records, are considered "hearsay" because there is no firsthand proof that they are accurate, reliable, and trustworthy. In general, hearsay evidence is not admissible in court. However, there are some well-established exceptions (Rule 803) to the hearsay rule for business records. In *Rosenberg v. Collins*, the court held that if the computer output is used in the regular course of business, then the evidence shall be admitted.

Business Record Exemption to the Hearsay Rule

US Federal Rule of Evidence 803(6) allows a court to admit a report or other business document made at or near the time by, or from information transmitted by, a person with knowledge, if kept in the course of regularly conducted business activity, and if it was the regular practice of that business activity to make the [report or document], all as shown by testimony of the custodian or other qualified witness, unless the source of information or the method or circumstances of preparation indicate lack of trustworthiness.

To meet Rule 803(6), the witness must:

- Have custody of the records in question on a regular basis
- Rely on those records in the regular course of business
- Know that they were prepared in the regular course of business

Audit trails would meet the criteria if they were produced in the normal course of business. The process to produce the output will have to be proven to be reliable. If computer-generated evidence is used and admissible, the court may order disclosure of the details of the computer, logs, maintenance records, etc. in respect to the system generating the printout, and then the defense may use that material to attack the reliability of the evidence. If the audit trails are not used or reviewed (at least the exceptions—e.g., failed log-on attempts) in the regular course of business, then they may not meet the criteria for admissibility.

US Federal Rule of Evidence 1001(3) provides another exception to the Hearsay Rule. This rule allows a memory or disk dump to be admitted as evidence, even though it is not done in the regular course of business. This dump merely acts as statement of fact. System dumps (in binary or hexidecimal) would not be hearsay because it is not being offered to prove the truth of the contents, but only the state of the computer.

Chain of Evidence (Custody)

Once evidence is seized, the next step is to provide for its accountability and protection. The Chain of Evidence, which provides a means of accountability, must be adhered to by law enforcement when conducting any type of criminal investigation, including a computer crime investigation. It helps to minimize the instances of tampering. The Chain of Evidence must account for all persons who handled or who had access to the evidence in question.

The Chain of Evidence shows:

- Who obtained the evidence
- Where and when the evidence was obtained
- Who secured the evidence
- Who had control or possession of the evidence

It may be necessary to have anyone associated with the evidence testify at trial. Private citizens are not required to maintain the same level of control of the evidence as law enforcement although they would be well advised to do so. Should an internal investigation result in the discovery and collection of computer-related evidence, the investigation team should follow the same, detailed chain of evidence as required by law enforcement. This will help to dispel any objection by the defense, that the evidence is unreliable, should the case go to court.

Admissibility of Evidence

The admissibility of computer-generated evidence is, at best, a moving target. Computer-generated evidence is always suspect because of the ease with which it can be tampered—usually without a trace! Precautionary measures must be taken in order to ensure that computer-generated evidence has not been tampered with, erased, or added to. In order to ensure that only relevant and reliable evidence is entered into the proceedings, the judicial system has adopted the concept of admissibility.

- *Relevancy of Evidence*—Evidence tending to prove or disprove a material fact. All evidence in court must be relevant and material to the case.
- *Reliability of Evidence*—The evidence and the process to produce the evidence must be proven to be reliable. This is one of the most critical aspects of computer-generated evidence.

Once computer-generated evidence meets the Business Record Exemption to the hearsay rule, is not excluded for some technicality or violation, follows the Chain of Custody, and is found to be both relevant and reliable, then it is held to be admissible. The defense will attack both the relevancy and reliability of the evidence, so great care should be taken to protect both.

Evidence Life Cycle

The Evidence Life Cycle starts with the discovery and collection of the evidence. It progresses through the following series of states until it is finally returned to the victim or owner:

- Collection and identification
- Analysis
- Storage, preservation and transportation
- Presented in court
- Returned to victim (owner)

Collection and identification

As the evidence is obtained or collected, it must be properly marked so that it can be identified as being the particular piece of evidence gathered at the scene. The collection must be recorded in a logbook identifying the particular piece of evidence, the person who discovered it, and the date, time and location discovered. The location should be specific enough for later recollection in court. All other types of identifying marks, such as make, model or serial number, should also be logged. It is of paramount

importance to list any type of damage to the particular piece of evidence. This is not only for identification purposes, but it will also limit any potential liability should a claim be made later on that you damaged the evidence. When marking evidence, the following guidelines should be followed:

- Mark the actual piece of evidence if it will not damage the evidence, by writing or scribing your initials, the date and the case number if known. Seal this evidence in the appropriate container and again, mark the container by writing or scribing your initials, the date and the case number, if known.
- If the actual piece of evidence cannot be marked, then seal the evidence in an appropriate container, then mark the container by writing or scribing your initials, the date and the case number, if known.
- The container should be sealed with evidence tape and your marking should write over the tape, so that if the seal is broken it can be noticed.
- Be extremely careful not to damage the evidence while engraving or marking the piece.

When marking glass or metal, a diamond scriber should be used. For all other objects, a felt tip pen with indelible ink is recommended. Dependent on the nature of the crime, the investigator may wish to preserve latent fingerprints. If so, static free gloves should be used if working with computer components, instead of standard latex gloves.

Try to always mark evidence the same way, because you will be asked to testify to the fact that you are the person identified by the evidence markings. Keep in mind, that the defense is going to try to discredit you as a witness or try some way to keep the evidence out of court, so something as simple as quick, positive identification of your mark is largely beneficial to the your case.

Storage, preservation, and transportation

All evidence must packed and preserved to prevent contamination. It should be protected against heat, extreme cold, humidity, water, magnetic fields, and vibration. The evidence must be protected for future use in court and for return to the original owner. It the evidence is not properly protected, the person or agency responsible for the collection and storage of the evidence may be held liable for damages. Therefore, the proper packing materials should be used whenever possible. Documents and disks (hard, floppy, optical, tapes, etc.) should be seized and stored in appropriate containers to prevent their destruction. For example, hard disks should be packed in a sealed, staticfree bag, within a cardboard box with a foam container. The box should be sealed with evidence tape and an electromagnetic field (EMF) warning label should be affixed to the box. It may be wise to defer to the system administrator or a technical advisor on how to best protect a particular type of system, especially mini-systems or mainframes.

Finally, evidence should be transported to a location where it can be stored and locked. Sometimes the systems are too large to transport, thus the forensic examination of the system may need to take place on site.

Presented in court

Each piece of evidence that is used to prove or disprove a material fact needs to be presented in court. After the initial seizure, the evidence is stored until needed for trial. Each time the evidence is transported to and from the courthouse for the trial, it needs to be handled with the same care as with the original seizure. Additionally, the chain of custody must continue to be followed. This process will continue until all testimony related to the evidence is completed. Once the trail is over, the evidence can be returned to the victim (owner).

Returned to victim (owner)

The final destination of most types of evidence is back with its original owner. Some types of evidence, such as drugs or paraphernalia (i.e., contraband) are destroyed after the trial. Any evidence gathered during a search, even though maintained by law enforcement, is legally under the control of the courts. Even though a seized item may be yours and may even have your name on it, it may not be returned to you unless the suspect signs a release or after a hearing by the court. Unfortunately, many victims don't want to go to trial. They just want to get their property back.

Many investigations merely need the information on a disk to prove or disprove a fact in question, thus there is no need to seize the entire system. Once a schematic of the system is drawn or photographed, the hard disk can be removed and then transported to a forensic lab for copying. Mirror copies of the suspect disk are obtained using forensic software and then one of those copies can be returned to the victim so that business operations can resume.

Format String Vulnerabilities

Mano Paul
SecuRisk Solutions, Pflugerville, Texas, U.S.A.

Abstract

Today, with the advent and evolution of programming languages, format string vulnerabilities are not as prevalent as they used to be. Nevertheless, it is critical to know and understand what a format string vulnerability is and how it can be exploited because the impact of successful exploitation can be catastrophic.

INTRODUCTION

Format string vulnerabilities were first discovered in the early 1990s when C shell (csh) was being fuzz tested for defects. But it was not until 2000, when a publication on a format string exploit of the Washington University File Transfer Protocol daemon (WU-FTPD) was made, that the Bugtraq mailing list exposed what was primarily restricted to certain "hacking" groups.

Although initially deemed to be innocuous, this newly discovered class of vulnerability, called "format string vulnerability," soon proved to be extremely potent, with successful exploitation leading to serious consequences, including information leakage, execution of arbitrary code, or crashing programs.

In 2004, the famous Unreal game engine made by Epic Games software (http://www.epicgames.com) was found susceptible to format string attacks in which gamers could crash the servers by inserting a "%n" character into ingress packets. That same year, the Windows® FTP server was found vulnerable to format string vulnerabilities, with a more serious impact because the server just did not crash but allowed a user to execute arbitrary code remotely when %n and %s characters were input.

FORMAT STRING VULNERABILITIES

To understand format string vulnerabilities, one must first understand what a format string is. Format string vulnerability is not specific to operating system (OS) and affects any OS that has a C compiler (which is pretty much every OS known today).

Some functions in the C/C++ `printf` family of functions do not have a fixed number of arguments. Determining the number of variable arguments (va_args) is usually done by passing the number as one of the arguments. But this is optional because the ANSI C standard has a mechanism to access the arguments, passed on to the stack, irrespective of the number of arguments actually passed. In case of the `printf` family of functions, the number of variable arguments can be calculated by the format string passed to it. The `printf` function creates and outputs strings at runtime. These functions allow programmers to create a string based on the format specified along with the variable list of arguments.

Table 1 lists the most common `printf` family of functions and their descriptions in the standard C library. Although, the `printf` family of functions is primarily implemented in the C/C++ programming languages, they can also be implemented in other languages, such as Perl.

Format string vulnerability is best demonstrated by the following example. The first concept of programming that one probably learns when introduced to the C programming language is the well-known "Hello World" program that outputs to the console the string "Hello World" using the C `printf` function as shown in Fig. 1. One graduates from there to learning variations of the `printf` function, handling user input arguments and displaying (printing) them as output. Fig. 2 illustrates a simple program that takes in user-supplied arguments and outputs the first argument as a string.

The first part of the `printf` statement, denoted as "%s," is a format string and the second part, denoted by argv[l], is the argument list referencing the first argument in the array list of variables supplied by the user. The format string, also known as the "format token" or "format specifier," is what tells the function the format in which to output the argument (in this case, a string). Table 2 lists common format tokens used in everyday programming.

This function is dependent on the user to supply the variable corresponding to the format token as its second argument. In the Intel® architecture, arguments are pushed on to the stack [a data structure in memory, that uses a last in, first out (LIFO) mechanism for data access] prior to its creation, and when functions reference their arguments on this platform, they reference the data that is on the stack. If a variable corresponding to the format token is not supplied

Encyclopedia of Information Assurance DOI: 10.1081/E-EIA-120046572
Copyright © 2011 by Taylor & Francis. All rights reserved.

Table 1 `printf` family of functions.

Function	Description
printf	Print formatted data to standard output (stdout)
fprintf	Write formatted output to stream
sprintf	Write formatted data to string
vfprintf	Write formatted variable argument list to stream
vprintf	Print formatted variable argument list to standard output (stdout)
vsprintf	Print formatted variable argument list to string

by the user, the program does not fail to compile; however, there is no valid address for the omitted variable on the stack, and at runtime, the function will read and output whatever data occupies the memory address at the top of the stack. This is the crux of what makes a format string attack possible. Additionally, not only is it possible to read data from protected memory space or an invalid address on the stack, but it is possible to write data on the stack as well. Because one can read and write data on the stack, this class of format string vulnerabilities should be deemed extremely dangerous. An attacker can specify any pointer, using the %n format token, control memory addresses of choice, and cause instructions at that pointer to be executed, which could be malicious shell code. If the pointer specified is valid, then arbitrary code where the pointer points to can be executed; if it is not valid, the program will crash, causing a denial of service.

IMPACT ON CONFIDENTIALITY, INTEGRITY, AND AVAILABILITY

Exploiting format string vulnerabilities by specifying format tokens without their corresponding variables can lead to any or all of the following: information leakage (disclosure), overwriting data on stack and memory addresses (alteration), or crashing programs and services (destruction).

Confidentiality Impact

When a program is run, execution instructions, dynamic variables, and some global variables are stored on the heap [a data structure in memory that uses a first in, first out (FIFO) mechanism for instructions or data access].

```
printf("Hello World");
```

Fig. 1 Hello world program using `printf` function.

```
#include <stdio.h>
int main (int argc, char *argv[])
{
    printf("%s", argv[1]);
    return 0;
}
```

Fig. 2 User supplied argument output using `printf` function.

Function calls, local variables, and information that need not be persisted are stored on the stack. If the program has any sensitive information (such as cryptographic keys, license keys, passwords, and other data that would be deemed intellectual property), these would be loaded onto the stack. If the program is susceptible to format string vulnerabilities, this information can be read (leaked) when an attacker exploits the vulnerability. Even code from dynamically linked libraries that is loaded on the stack can be disclosed. Stack protection mechanisms have been proven not to be successful in addressing format string vulnerabilities. It is also important to be aware that format string attacks are not exclusive to affecting the stack, and although it may be a little challenging, overwriting null terminators with non-null data can convert a format string vulnerability on the stack to overflow the heap.

Integrity Impact

Because one can read and write to memory using format tokens without corresponding variables in the argument list, an attacker can overwrite a function pointer or return address in memory and get to run arbitrary code. An attacker could also overwrite global offset tables (GOT) that handle non-static relocations for functions and destructors (DTORS), which is the code run before a program exits. The ability to write and make unauthorized modifications in memory is what gives rise to serious integrity threats.

Table 2 Common format tokens.

Token	Output
%s	String format
%i	Singed integer string
%d	Signed decimal string
%f	Signed decimal string of the form (xx:yy)
%u	Unsigned decimal string
%x	Unsigned hexadecimal string
%c	Character format
%p	Formats a pointer to as address
%n	Number of bytes written so far (nothing is visible)
%%	Just inserts %

Availability Impact

Integrity violations by format string attacks also have a potential bearing on availability. Writing changes to memory can lead to crashing programs and segmentation violations (SEGV) when address pointers are overwritten (using the %n format token) to point to invalid addresses, causing a denial of service.

CONTROL/MITIGATION MEASURES

Format string vulnerabilities are possible for two reasons. One may assert that one reason for format string attacks to be possible is indolence on part of the programmer for not ensuring that all format tokens have corresponding variables on the stack. This kind of programming inefficiency can be mitigated by simple secure-coding measures. The other reason is more fundamental and has to do with how the C/C++ programming languages handle arguments in the family of functions that output formatted strings, for which there are no real mitigation measures.

Format string vulnerabilities exist due to the fact that an untrusted user is given the ability to change the format strings of the output statements in the `printf` family of functions. This can be controlled and addressed by secure-coding mechanisms, such as ensuring that all arguments are specified when format routines are called, and by ensuring that all user data supplied is validated. However, as previously mentioned, the inherent reason that format string attacks are possible in the first place, for which there is no real mitigation measure, is due to the accommodative (or one could say lax) nature in which output functions (`printf` family of functions) in the C programming languages handle functions with variable arguments, combined with stack overflows in C/C++ on Intel x86 processors. Still, this is not a problem with the implementation of the C language, but instead is the ANSI C89 standard way of dealing with functions with a variable number of arguments.

Because the problem seems to be intrinsic to the ANSI C89 standard, it may seem like there is really no good control or risk control measure for format string vulnerabilities. There are, however, certain management and technical control measures that can be taken to address format string vulnerabilities.

MANAGEMENT CONTROLS

The first and foremost thing to do is to find out if your production systems have applications written in C/C++, the programming languages in which format string vulnerabilities are possible. Most legacy applications may fall into this category. If your applications are written in

C/C++, management should consider requesting a source code audit of deployed code in production, with minimal disruptions to business operations. When the audit is performed, it is recommended that other application vulnerabilities besides format string vulnerabilities are checked for and addressed as well.

Additionally, developing a policy or standard to mitigate application security risks with specific procedural instructions for handling format string vulnerabilities should be considered.

TECHNICAL CONTROLS

Technically, the programmer must ensure that any time the `printf` family of functions are called, a format token is always specified and a corresponding value (variable) of argument for the format token exists. The code shown in Fig. 3 shows a `printf` function with format tokens and corresponding arguments, both specified. Table 3 demonstrates the improper and proper usage of some of the most common `printf` family of functions.

Source code checks for format string vulnerabilities are relatively easy. One can use a GREP (global regular expression parser) to look at functions and make sure that the number of variable arguments (va_args) corresponds with the format tokens specified. This is possible when source code is available. In cases where the source code is not available, the format string vulnerabilities can be checked by using fuzzing, a form of software testing in which the tester provides random data (called fuzz) as inputs to the program and defects are detected and identified, based on how the program responds to the inputs.

Use of static code analyzers can assist in the automation of these checks. SPlint, Flawfinder, and FormatGuard are some freely available static code checkers, and commercial static code checkers may be worth your investment if your organization deals extensively with C/C++ technologies.

Another effective countermeasure against format string attacks is dynamically maintaining a whitelist (allowable) of address ranges that allows printing functions to write-to and is checked prior to writing (using the %n format token) in to those address ranges. Any valid address locations that are written-to are dynamically added to the whitelist for improved performance in subsequent calls. Finally, upon completion of the printing functions, the programmer should safely free up or "unregister" the memory address location.

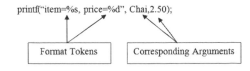

Fig. 3 Format tokens with matching arguments specified.

Forensics – FTP

Table 3 Improper and proper use of `printf` family of functions.

Function	Improper use	Proper use
`printf`	`printf` ("Some String");	`printf` ("%s," "Some String");
`fprintf`	`fprintf` (pFile, name);	`fprintf` (pFile, "Name : %s\n," name);
`sprintf`	`sprintf` (buffer, a+b);	`sprintf` (buffer, "The sum is %d," a+b);
`vfprintf`	`vfprintf` (stream, args);	`vfprintf` (stream, format, args);
`vprintf`	`vprintf` (args);	`vprintf` (format, args);
`vsprintf`	`vsprintf` (buffer, args);	`vsprintf` (buffer, format, args);

There are other mitigation measures, such as hardened libraries, runtime detection of illegal memory writes, type-safe implementation of C, code rewriting, and fault isolation, that have been proven effective with certain limitations. Some of these limitations are missing wrappers that call the `printf` family of functions or restricting format tokens, especially the %n format token that can be used for overwriting memory.

FORMAT STRING VULNERABILITY AND BUFFER OVERFLOW

Both format string vulnerabilities and buffer overflows may lead to information leakage, execution of arbitrary code by overwriting function pointers in memory, or crashing programs, and so have been mistakenly classified in the past under the same category. However, there is a fundamental difference between format string vulnerabilities and buffer overflows, and this has to do with the location where memory is overwritten and its control by the attacker.

Buffer overflows are primarily data boundary errors in which unsafe C string copy functions such as strcpy() are used to copy data larger than the size of the buffer, causing it to overflow, with no control by the attacker as to where memory is overwritten. Input validation is a good countermeasure against buffer overflow attacks.

Format string vulnerabilities, as we have seen, are due to the fact that externally supplied user data is interpreted as part of the format string arguments and a format string attacker can choose where memory is overwritten.

CONCLUSION

In summary, format string vulnerabilities happen when data inputted by a user is outputted in the format as specified by the format string (format token) of the `printf` family of functions. When an attacker supplies format tokens without a corresponding variable in the argument list on the stack, data values, including memory addresses, are used in the variable's place. This could have a serious impact on confidentiality by information disclosure, on integrity by overwriting data on stack or memory locations, and on availability by crashing programs and services, besides affording the possibility to run arbitrary code by an attacker. Although format string vulnerabilities are growing rarer with the evolution of programming languages, it is imperative to address and mitigate format string vulnerabilities without fail. It is important that a defense-in-depth strategy should be implemented, with layered countermeasures implemented and used in conjunction with one another as a measure of maximum security against format string attacks.

Forensics –
FTP

Fraud: Employee Identification

Rebecca Herold, CISM, CISA, CISSP, FLMI
Information Privacy, Security and Compliance Consultant, Rebecca Herold and Associates
LLC, Van Meter, Iowa, U.S.A.

Abstract

Information security and privacy training and awareness are challenges in every organization. Most people do not like to participate in training; however, ensuring that employees understand their responsibilities for protecting information is vital to an organization's success and is required by law for many industries and jurisdictions. Helping employees understand how to identify and report fraud is especially important in today's business climate. A fraud awareness and training program must support an organization's business environment, be integrated within the information security program and policies, and meet applicable regulatory requirements. Personnel must be motivated to learn how to identify and report fraud by tangible and specific rewards and penalties to support an organization's fraud prevention efforts. Fraud prevention training must become part of the job appraisal process to build a truly effective fraud prevention education program. Corporate leaders must not only ensure compliance with regulatory issues but also effectively communicate fraud prevention policy and regulatory issues to the organization. Organizations cannot have a successful awareness and training program if personnel do not understand the impacts and consequences of non-compliance.

FRAUD LANDSCAPE

On February 1, 2005, the Federal Trade Commission (FTC) released its annual fraud report[1] detailing consumer complaints and listing the top ten fraud complaint categories reported by consumers in 2004. Identity theft was the number one complaint for the fifth consecutive year. Consumers filed over 635,000 complaints to the FTC in 2004, which was up from 542,378 in 2003. Of the complaints received in 2004, 61% were complaints about fraud and 39% were identity theft reports. The top eight categories of consumer fraud complaints within the FTC 2004 fraud report included the following:

- Internet auctions—16%
- Shop-at-home/catalog sales—8%
- Internet services and computer complaints—6%
- Foreign money offers—6%
- Prizes, sweepstakes, and lotteries—5%
- Advance fee loans and credit protection—3%
- Telephone services—2%
- Business opportunities and work-at-home plans—2%

The increase of fraud is indeed a concern and caught the attention of the Executive Branch. President Bush's fiscal year 2006 budget[2] allotted $212 million for the FTC, an $8 million increase over the appropriation for fiscal year 2005. The higher budget provided the FTC with more resources to handle anti-fraud and privacy legislation, such as the Controlling the Assault of Non-Solicitated Pornography and Marketing (CAN-SPAM) Act and the Fair and Accurate Credit Transactions (FACT) Act, which establish identity theft and consumer credit protection responsibilities with the FTC.

Fraud concerns are not just at the federal level. Many states are also taking legislative moves in an effort to turn the tide of fraud activity levels. The following are just a few examples of proposed bills covering just identity theft:

- *Texas*—H.B. 1527 would require companies to alert their customers if a breach of security puts them at risk of identity theft.
- *New York*—A.4254 and S.2161 would require businesses and state agencies to notify consumers of any security breach of their data. Two other bills, A.5487 and S.3000, would only cover "business entities," not state agencies.
- *Washington*—S.B. 6043 would require companies that own and license computerized data containing personal information to inform Washington consumers of any breach of data security.
- *Minnesota*—H.F. 1410 and S.F. 1307 would require systems that own or license computerized data that includes personal information to notify Minnesota residents if there is reason to believe that the information was taken by an unauthorized person.
- *Georgia*—S.B. 251 would require certain businesses to give notice to consumers of security breaches.

Encyclopedia of Information Assurance DOI: 10.1081/E-EIA-120046573
Copyright © 2011 by Taylor & Francis. All rights reserved.

- *Illinois*—Governor Rod Blagojevich (D-Il1.) proposed legislation in February that would require consumer notification in Illinois in cases where corporate security systems have been breached and consumer information has been compromised.
- *Rhode Island*—2005-S-0880 would require any business experiencing a security breach to immediately notify all Rhode Island residents in an affected database that their identities or financial documents may have been compromised.
- *Florida*—An amendment was proposed to pending legislation (S.B. 284 and H.B. 129 CS) that would require immediate disclosure any time an individual's private personal financial information or Social Security number is stolen from a data-collection agency.
- *California*—S.B. 852 would require organizations to notify individuals for breach of personal information in any format, not just electronic.

Government leaders recognize the importance of businesses in fraud prevention efforts. In some instances, they legally require businesses to take active anti-fraud steps and to implement ongoing fraud prevention awareness and training programs. This trend is likely to continue. It is important that corporate leaders know and understand their obligations not only for anti-fraud activities but also for the anti-fraud training and awareness requirements for management, personnel, business partners, and customers.

REGULATORY AND LEGAL REQUIREMENTS FOR TRAINING

Why Is Regulatory Education Important?

Privacy and security awareness and training are important activities and key components of an effective fraud prevention and security program. In fact, many regulations require awareness and training as part of compliance, a few specifically for fraud prevention but many for information security, which encompasses fraud prevention activities. The most commonly discussed right now are the Health Insurance Portability and Accountability Act (HIPAA), the Sarbanes–Oxley (SOX) Act, and the Gramm–Leach–Bliley (GLB) Act. However, personnel education has been a requirement under other guidelines and regulations for several years. An increasing number of laws and regulations require some form of training and awareness activities to occur within the organizations over which they have jurisdiction. For example, the Federal Sentencing Guidelines,[3] enacted in 1991, updated to create more corporate management responsibility in 2004, and often used to determine fines and restitution for convictions, have seven requirements, one of which is for executive

management to educate and effectively communicate to their employees the proper business practices with which personnel must comply. Issues that impact the severity of the judgments include consideration of the following:

- How frequently and how well does the organization communicate its policies to personnel?
- Are personnel effectively getting trained and receiving awareness?
- What methods does the organization use for such communications?
- Does the organization verify the desired results from training that has occurred?
- Does the organization update the education program to improve communications and to get the appropriate message out to personnel?
- Does the training cover ethical work practices?
- Is there ongoing compliance and ethics dialog between staff and management?
- Is management getting the same educational messages as the staff?

Implementing an effective, ongoing awareness, and training program will:

- Establish accountability.
- Comply with regulatory requirements for education.
- Help ensure compliance with published policies.
- Demonstrate due diligence.

Sentences under the guidelines can be as high as $290 million plus jail time, or even higher in some circumstances, but are these guidelines really ever applied? The U.S. Sentencing Commission documents that, in 1995,[4] 111 organizational defendants were sentenced according to the guidelines, with 83 cases receiving associated fines. By 2001,[5] the number of organizational defendants sentenced rose to 238, with 137 getting fines and 49 getting both fines and restitution. The average fine was $2.2 million, and the average amount of restitution awarded was $3.3 million. Of those sentenced, 90 had no compliance program, which was a documented culpability factor in the sentencing. Having a poor compliance program was also a documented factor in other decisions.

It is likely that the numbers of fines and penalties will increase with implementation of the updated guidelines.[6] Recent amendments include establishing an effective compliance program and exercising due diligence in the prevention and detection of criminal conduct. Any organizations with some type of compliance requirements or plans (basically all public entities, given the Sarbanes–Oxley Act of 2002) are directly impacted by the new guidelines. One way such due diligence is demonstrated is through an effective, executive-supported information security, and privacy awareness program.

Forensics – FTP

The organizational sentencing guidelines motivate organizations to create a program to reduce and, ultimately, eliminate criminal conduct by implementing an effective ethics and compliance program that includes compliance with all applicable laws. The updates to the sentencing criteria incorporate leading practices that have been referenced and identified in such regulations as the Sarbanes–Oxley Act, HIPAA, GLBA, and other internationally recognized standards. The 2004 updates are contained within new guidelines at § 8B2.1 and elaborate upon the need for organizations to more rigorously demonstrate responsibility and demonstrate executive leadership.

To have a program that is effectively described by the guidelines, an organization must demonstrate that it exercises due diligence in meeting compliance requirements and also promotes "an organizational culture that encourages ethical conduct and a commitment to compliance with the law." It is important to note that the guidelines describe functional requirements, and it does not matter if an organization calls the program a compliance program, ethics program, or some other description. The actions and activities will be what are reviewed if a due diligence and sentencing situation arises. At a high level, the following are the organizational requirements described in the updated guidelines:

- Develop and implement standards and procedures designed to prevent and detect criminal conduct.
- Assign responsibility at all levels and provide adequate resources and authority for the compliance or ethics program.
- Perform personnel screening as applicable (in accordance with laws, regulations, and labor union requirements) and as related to program goals and the responsibilities of the staff involved.
- Provide adequate and effective awareness and training throughout all levels of the organization.
- Ensure that auditing, monitoring, and evaluating activities occur to verify program effectiveness.
- Implement internal reporting systems that eliminate retaliatory reactions.
- Provide incentives and enforce discipline to promote compliance.
- Consistently take reasonable steps to respond to violations and prevent similar violations from occurring.

According to wide discussion, the motivation behind these updated guidelines seems to be to ensure that, if an organization is convicted of a federal offense, the leader will face stiff sentences and civil penalties unless they have proof of having a stringent, well-communicated compliance program. This should drive organizations to make ongoing, continuously communicated, compliance programs, including awareness and training components, a priority. The new 2004 U.S. Federal Sentencing Guidelines[7] state:

§8B2.1. Effective Compliance and Ethics Program

a. To have an effective compliance and ethics program, for purposes of subsection (f) of §8C2.5 (Culpability Score) and subsection (c)(1) of §8D1.4 (Recommended Conditions of Probation—Organizations), an organization shall

1. exercise due diligence to prevent and detect criminal conduct; and
2. otherwise promote an organizational culture that encourages ethical conduct and a commitment to compliance with the law.

Such compliance and ethics program shall be reasonably designed, implemented, and enforced so that the program is generally effective in preventing and detecting criminal conduct. The failure to prevent or detect the instant offense does not necessarily mean that the program is not generally effective in preventing and detecting criminal conduct.

b. Due diligence and the promotion of an organizational culture that encourages ethical conduct and a commitment to compliance with the law within the meaning of subsection (a) minimally require the following:

1. The organization shall establish standards and procedures to prevent and detect criminal conduct.
2. i. The organization's governing authority shall be knowledgeable about the content and operation of the compliance and ethics program and shall exercise reasonable oversight with respect to the implementation and effectiveness of the compliance and ethics program.
    ii. High-level personnel of the organization shall ensure that the organization has an effective compliance and ethics program, as described in this guideline. Specific individual(s) within high-level personnel shall be assigned overall responsibility for the compliance and ethics program.
    iii. Specific individual(s) within the organization shall be delegated day-to-day operational responsibility for the compliance and ethics program. Individual(s) with operational responsibility shall report periodically to high-level personnel and, as appropriate, to the governing authority, or an appropriate subgroup of the governing authority, on the effectiveness of the compliance and ethics program. To carry out such operational responsibility, such individual(s) shall be given adequate resources,

Forensics – FTP

Forensics –
FTP

appropriate authority, and direct access to the governing authority or an appropriate subgroup of the governing authority.

3. The organization shall use reasonable efforts not to include within the substantial authority personnel of the organization any individual whom the organization knew, or should have known through the exercise of due diligence, has engaged in illegal activities or other conduct inconsistent with an effective compliance and ethics program.

4. i. The organization shall take reasonable steps to communicate periodically and in a practical manner its standards and procedures, and other aspects of the compliance and ethics program, to the individuals referred to in subdivision (B) by conducting effective training programs and otherwise disseminating information appropriate to such individuals' respective roles and responsibilities.

   ii. The individuals referred to in subdivision (A) are the members of the governing authority, high-level personnel, substantial authority personnel, the organization's employees, and, as appropriate, the organization's agents.

5. The organization shall take reasonable steps

   i. to ensure that the organization's compliance and ethics program is followed, including monitoring and auditing to detect criminal conduct;

   ii. to evaluate periodically the effectiveness of the organization's compliance and ethics program; and

   iii. to have and publicize a system, which may include mechanisms that allow for anonymity or confidentiality, whereby the organization's employees and agents may report or seek guidance regarding potential or actual criminal conduct without fear of retaliation.

6. The organization's compliance and ethics program shall be promoted and enforced consistently throughout the organization through

   i. appropriate incentives to perform in accordance with the compliance and ethics program; and

   ii. appropriate disciplinary measures for engaging in criminal conduct and for failing to take reasonable steps to prevent or detect criminal conduct.

7. After criminal conduct has been detected, the organization shall take reasonable steps to respond appropriately to the criminal conduct and to prevent further similar criminal conduct, including making any necessary modifications to the organization's compliance and ethics program.

c. In implementing subsection (b), the organization shall periodically assess the risk of criminal conduct and shall take appropriate steps to design, implement, or modify each requirement set forth in subsection (b) to reduce the risk of criminal conduct identified through this process.

It is no longer enough simply to write and publish information security and privacy policies and procedures. Organizational leaders must now have a good understanding of the program, support the program, and provide oversight of the program as reasonable for the organization. This reflects a significant shift in the responsibilities of compliance and ethics programs from positions such as the compliance officer or committee to the highest levels of management. The guidelines require that executive leaders support and participate in implementing the program. To accomplish this, an effective ongoing information privacy, security, and compliance education program must be in place.

Every compliance plan, including information security and privacy, must include continuing involvement of the highest level of organizational management in its design and implementation. Compliance will then, as a result, become part of upper management daily responsibilities. Requirements for effective training and awareness now extend not only to personnel and business partners and associates but also to the highest levels of management and must be ongoing.

When considering due diligence, it follows that a standard of due care must be observed. Quite simply, this means that organizational leaders have a duty to ensure the implementation of information security and privacy even if they are not aware of the specific legal requirements. If leaders do not ensure actions are taken to reasonably secure information and ensure privacy, and as a result others experience damages, it is possible that both the organization and the leaders could face legal action for negligence. This certainly should motivate leaders to invest time, resources, and personnel in establishing an ongoing, effective, well-documented information security and privacy awareness and training program.

LAWS AND REGULATIONS REQUIRING EDUCATION

Many existing laws and regulations include requirements for information security training and making personnel, management, or customers aware of certain aspects of the laws, such as the need to identify and prevent potentially fraudulent activities. Table 1 provides excerpts from the actual regulatory text that are applicable to information security awareness and training activities for just a few of the existing U.S. laws and regulations. Organizations should review this list and discuss it with their legal departments to determine which ones apply to their particular businesses. This list does not include state laws and regulatory requirements, many of which also contain personnel training and awareness requirements. Be sure to research the state and local regulations and laws that are applicable to the organization's facilities and customer locations.

TRAINING MOTIVATORS

Information security and fraud prevention must be integrated with job performance and the appraisal process. Personnel become motivated to actively support anti-fraud initiatives when they know that their job advancement, compensation, and benefits will be impacted. Studies about employee motivation in general have been demonstrating this since the 1920 (Mayo, Roethlisberger and Dixon, and Landsberger, to name a few). When personnel do not have this motivation, then an organization is destined to ultimately depend only on technology for information security assurance and fraud prevention. Organizations must understand the importance of implementing these motivators to validate due diligence and to be in compliance with laws and regulations such as those previously discussed. Much research has been done about job motivators, and many theories abound. Good managers want to know how to be more effective with their business efforts, and the human resources department is usually willing to try a motivator if it is well presented and explained. Legal compliance, revenue support, and due diligence are enhanced by training and implementing motivation for training.

Organizational motives for information security and fraud prevention must support primary business objectives and meet regulatory compliance; they cannot be an afterthought or superfluous. For example, fraud prevention and information security activities are necessary to

- Comply with applicable laws and regulations.
- Demonstrate due diligence.
- Help prevent loss and thus increase profit.
- Protect the organization from liabilities related to security negligence.
- Enhance and/or support customer and public reputation.

So, what are personnel information security and fraud prevention activity motivators? The details will vary from organization to organization; however, high-level personnel motivators include at least the following, in no particular order:

- Complying with laws and regulations
- Getting a good report following a regulator's compliance review
- Meeting security requirements during internal compliance reviews
- Getting the respect and admiration of coworkers
- Having good relationships and interactions with coworkers
- Doing work that is interesting and fulfilling
- Following personal, ethical, and social principles
- Reducing information security risks
- Personally experiencing a security incident or loss
- Learning the loss experiences of others
- Showing dedication and faithfulness to the employer
- Making the boss happy
- Protecting personal and employer reputation
- Competing to succeed beyond peers
- Doing something that is fun and interesting
- Creating good working conditions
- Feeling achievement and satisfaction from a job well done
- Obtaining power and affiliation with others in power
- Getting good press for the employer for demonstrated effective security and anti-fraud practices
- Avoiding bad press for the employer because security was ineffective or a fraud was instigated
- Preventing a fraud or security incident from happening again after experiencing one
- Implementing automated security and anti-fraud mechanisms that are transparent to the end user and do not degrade systems performance or slow business processing
- Making security more convenient than alternative (non-secure) methods
- Creating an anticipation for receipt of rewards for security and fraud prevention activities relative to corresponding job responsibilities
- Creating fear and reminding of experiences of penalties for inadequate security and fraud prevention activities relative to corresponding job responsibilities

The last two items on this list are the most powerful motivators to individuals. They relate directly to the human need for safety and security as demonstrated in such models as Maslow's Hierarchy of Needs.[8] They are also the two items from this long list that organizations can most effectively control. Rewards and penalties are not new ideas; they have been traditional job performance motivators in business since business began and should be used for motivating personnel to be secure and help to prevent fraud as well. Rewards for participating in training and taking anti-fraud

Forensics – FTP

Table 1 Laws and regulations.

The following lists some of the U.S. laws and regulations that have requirements for information security, sometimes specifically indicating fraud prevention, awareness, and training within various organizations and industries. This is not an exhaustive list but will serve as a good starting point for researching an organization's regulatory training and awareness requirements. The actual regulatory text that applies specifically to awareness or training is indicated in italics. Read the full regulation or law to learn all the requirements for meeting compliance.

Health Insurance Portability and Accountability Act (HIPAA)[a]

Privacy Rule—Sec. 164.530(b)(1)[b] Standard:

Training. A covered entity must train all members of its workforce on the policies and procedures with respect to protected health information required by this subpart, as necessary and appropriate for the members of the workforce to carry out their function within the covered entity.

Security Rule—Sec. 164.308(a)(5)(i)[c] Standard:

Security awareness and training. Implement a security awareness and training program for all members of its workforce (including management).

21 CFR Part 11: Electronic Records; Electronic Signatures

Sec. 11.10(i).[d] Controls for Closed Systems:

Determination that persons who develop, maintain, or use electronic record/electronic signature systems have the education, training, and experience to perform their assigned tasks.

Computer Security Act of 1987

Sec. 5. Federal Computer System Security Training:[e]

a.   IN GENERAL. Each Federal agency shall provide for the mandatory periodic training in computer security awareness and accepted computer security practice of all employees who are involved with the management, use, or oration of each Federal computer system within or under the supervision of that agency. Such training shall be

   1.   provided in accordance with the guidelines developed pursuant to section 20(a)(5) of the National Bureau of Standards Act (as added by section 3 of this Act), and in accordance with the regulations issued under subsection (c) of this section for Federal civilian employees; or
   2.   provided by an alternative training program approved by the head of that agency on the basis of a determination that the alternative training program is at least as effective in accomplishing the objectives of such guidelines and regulations.

b.   TRAINING OBJECTIVES. Training under this section shall be started within 60 days after the issuance of the regulations described in subsection (c). Such training shall be designed

   1.   to enhance employees' awareness of the threats to and vulnerability of computer systems;
   2.   to encourage the use of improved computer security practices; and
   3.   *to include emphasis on protecting sensitive information in federal databases and federal computer sites that are accessible through public networks.*

c.   REGULATIONS. Within six months after the date of enactment of this Act, the Director of the Office of Personnel Management shall issue regulations prescribing the procedures and scope of the training to be provided Federal civilian employees under subsection (a) and the manner in which such training is to be carried out.

Computer Security Enhancement Act[f]

10/13/1998—Senate preparation for floor; status—placed on Senate Legislative Calendar under General Orders (Calendar No. 718):

Section 9. Federal computer system security training

This section amends section 5(b) of the Computer Security Act of 1987 by adding an emphasis on protecting sensitive information in Federal databases and Federal computer sites that are accessible through public networks.

Computer Fraud and Abuse Act (CFAA)[g]

Sec. 1030. Fraud and related activity in connection with computers:

One court has interpreted the CFAA as providing an additional cause of action in favor of employers who may suffer the loss of trade secret information, or other negative impact, at the hands of disloyal employees.[h] It has been widely discussed and debated that, to enforce, employees must have communicated related policies.

(Continued)

Forensics – FTP

Table 1 Laws and regulations. *(Continued)*

Privacy Act[i] (Applies to U.S. Government Agencies)

5 U.S.C. Sec. 552a(01/16/96)(e). Agency requirements:

Each agency that maintains a system of records shall

(9) establish rules of conduct for persons involved in the design, development, operation, or maintenance of any system of records, or in maintaining any record, and instruct each such person with respect to such rules and the requirements of this section, including any other rules and procedures adopted pursuant to this section and the penalties for non-compliance

Freedom of Information Act (FOIA)[J]

5 U.S.C. Sec. 552:

(a)(4)(A)(i) In order to carry out the provisions of this section, each agency shall promulgate regulations, pursuant to notice and receipt of public comment, specifying the schedule of fees applicable to the processing of requests under this section and establishing procedures and guidelines for determining when such fees should be waived or reduced. Such schedule shall conform to the guidelines which shall be promulgated, pursuant to notice and receipt of public comment, by the Director of the Office of Management and Budget and which shall provide for a uniform schedule of fees for all agencies.

(a)(6)(B)(iv) Each agency may promulgate regulations, pursuant to notice and receipt of public comment, providing for the aggregation of certain requests by the same requestor, or by a group of requestors acting in concert, if the agency reasonably believes that such requests actually constitute a single request, which would otherwise satisfy the unusual circumstances specified in this subparagraph, and the requests involve clearly related matters. Multiple requests involving unrelated matters shall not be aggregated.

(a)(6)(D)(i) Each agency may promulgate regulations, pursuant to notice and receipt of public comment, providing for multitrack processing of requests for records based on the amount of work or time (or both) involved in processing requests.

(a)(6)(E)(i) Each agency shall promulgate regulations, pursuant to notice and receipt of public comment, providing for expedited processing of requests for records

Federal Information Security Management Act (FISMA)[k]

Sec. 3544. Federal Agency Responsibilities:

a. IN GENERAL. The head of each agency shall

(4) ensure that the agency has trained personnel sufficient to assist the agency in complying with the requirements of this subchapter and related policies, procedures, standards, and guidelines.

b. AGENCY PROGRAM. Each agency shall develop, document, and implement an agency wide information security program, approved by the Director under section 3543(a)(5), to provide information security for the information and information systems that support the operations and assets of the agency, including those provided or managed by another agency, contractor, or other source, that includes

(4) security awareness training to inform personnel, including contractors and other users of information systems that support the operations and assets of the agency, of

i. information security risks associated with their activities; and

ii. their responsibilities in complying with agency policies and procedures designed to reduce these risks.

Digital Millennium Copyright Act (DMCA)[l]

Sec. 512(h). Conditions for Eligibility:

1. Accommodation of Technology. The limitations on liability established by this section shall apply only if the service provider

A. has adopted and reasonably implemented, and informs subscribers of the service of, a policy for the termination of subscribers of the service who are repeat infringers

Gramm–Leach–Bliley (GLB) Act

Sec. 314.4. Safeguards Rule:[m]

b. Identify reasonably foreseeable internal and external risks to the security, confidentiality, and integrity of customer information that could result in the unauthorized disclosure, misuse, alteration, destruction or other compromise of such information, and assess the sufficiency of any safeguards in place to control these risks. At a minimum, such a risk assessment should include consideration of risks in each relevant area of your operations, including

(Continued)

Table 1 Laws and regulations. *(Continued)*

1. employee training and management;
2. information systems, including network and software design, as well as information processing, storage, transmission and disposal; and
3. detecting, preventing and responding to attacks, intrusions, or other systems failures.

Sarbanes–Oxley (SOX) Act[n]

Title III Sec. 302 (a) (4):

4. the signing officers

   i. are responsible for establishing and maintaining internal controls;
   ii. have designed such internal controls to ensure that material information relating to the issuer and its consolidated subsidiaries is made known to such officers by others within those entities, particularly during the period in which the periodic reports are being prepared.

SEC Guidance That Emphasizes Training and Awareness[o]

III. Components of Objectives-Oriented Standard Setting

  I. Behavioral Changes. i. Exercise of Professional Judgment

   Second, there is the long-run consequence. Since the application of an objectives-oriented regime relies on preparers and auditors' ability to identify the objectives of the standard (as well as the specific guidance) and match that to the underlying transaction or event, there is a need to train preparers and auditors in understanding the substance of the class of transactions. Additionally, it appears likely that in moving to a more objectives-oriented regime, the FASB will issue more standards that rely on fair value as the measurement attribute. If so, it would be imperative that accounting professionals be trained in valuation theory and techniques.

IV. Implementation Issues

  I. Transition Costs

   We believe that the transition costs would be relatively small, as the transition to an objectives-oriented approach already is underway, at least in part, and should continue on a gradual basis. We believe that the accounting profession itself would incur only *de minimis* transitional costs in the immediate term, since we expect the FASB to continue to implement these recommendations on a gradual basis through its continuing standard-setting efforts. Going forward, however, as objectives-oriented accounting standards are adopted, to the extent that a different type of professional judgment is called for on the part of practitioners, accounting firms will find that they may have to further strengthen their training, quality control and oversight mechanisms for all accounting personnel within the firm. Moreover, there may be additional efforts needed internally on training and education to accommodate the heightened professional and intellectual demands that will be placed on practitioners. On the other hand, this extra cost may be offset by the reduction in training associated with the elimination of excessively detailed standards associated with a rules-based approach.

Bank Protection Act (12 CFR Chapter V, Sec. 568)[p]

Sec. 568.3. Security Program:

a. Contents of security program. The security program shall
   (3) provide for initial and periodic training of officers and employees in their responsibilities under the security program and in proper employee conduct during and after a burglary, robbery, or larceny.

Sec. 568.4. Report:

  The security officer for each savings association shall report at least annually to the association's board of directors on the implementation, administration, and effectiveness of the security program.

U.S. Patriot Act[q]

Sec. 352. Anti-Money Laundering Programs:

  (a) IN GENERAL. Section 5318(h) of Title 31, U.S.C., is amended to read as follows:
  (h) ANTI-MONEY LAUNDERING PROGRAMS.

(Continued)

Table 1 Laws and regulations. *(Continued)*

1. IN GENERAL. In order to guard against money laundering through financial institutions, each financial institution shall establish anti-money laundering programs, including, at a minimum

   A. the development of internal policies, procedures, and controls;
   B. the designation of a compliance officer;
   C. an ongoing employee training program.

Sec. 908. Training of Government Officials Regarding Identification and Use of Foreign Intelligence:

   a. PROGRAM REQUIRED. The Attorney General shall, in consultation with the Director of Central Intelligence, carry out a program to provide appropriate training to officials described in subsection (b) in order to assist such officials in

      1. identifying foreign intelligence information in the course of their duties; and
      2. utilizing foreign intelligence information in the course of their duties, to the extent that the utilization of such information is appropriate for such duties.

Sec. 1005. First Responders Assistance Act:

   (c) ANTITERRORISM TRAINING GRANTS. Antiterrorism training grants under this subsection may be used for programs, projects, and other activities to address

      1. intelligence gathering and analysis techniques;
      2. community engagement and outreach;
      3. critical incident management for all forms of terrorist attack;
      4. threat assessment capabilities;
      5. conducting follow up investigations; and
      6. stabilizing a community after a terrorist incident.

FFEIC Customer Identification Program[r]

Customer Identification Programs for Banks, Savings Associations, and Credit Unions:[s]

A. Regulations Implementing Sec. 326:
Under the proposed regulation, the CIP must be incorporated into the bank's anti-money laundering (BSA) program. A bank's BSA program must include 1) internal policies, procedures, and controls to ensure ongoing compliance; 2) designation of a compliance officer; 3) an ongoing employee training program; and 4) an independent audit function to test programs. Each of these requirements also applies to a bank's CIP.

---

[a] http://www.hhs.gov/ocr/combinedregtext.pdf.

[b] http://www.hhs.gov/ocr/combinedregtext.pdf (p. 38).

[c] http://www.hhs.gov/ocr/combinedregtext.pdf (p. 14).

[d] http://www.fda.gov/ora/compliance_ref/part11/FRs/background/pt11finr.pdf (p. 13465).

[e] http://thomas.loc.gov/cgi-bin/cpquery/?&dbname=cpl05&maxdocs=100&report=sr412.105&sel=TOC_35315&.

[f] http://csrc.nist.gov/secplcy/csa_87.txt.

[g] http://www.usdoj.gov/criminal/cybercrime/1030_new.html.

[h] http://www.southeasttechwire.com/ (Millen, P. M., The Computer Fraud and Abuse Act: A New Tool for Protection of Trade Secrets, September 16, 2003).

[i] http://foia.state.gov/privacy.asp.

[j] http://foia.state.gov/foia.asp.

[k] The Federal Information Security Management Act of 2002 (Title III—Information Security, Electronic Government Act, Public Law (P.L.) 107–137.

[l] http://thomas.loc.gov/cgi-bin/query/D?cl05:2:./temp/~cl05MmcQjh::.

[m] http://www.ftc.gov/os/2002/05/67fr36585.pdf (p. 36494).

[n] http://frwebgate.access.gpo.gov/cgi-bin/getdoc.cgi?dbname=107_cong_bills&docid=f:h3763enr.txt.pdf.

[o] http://www.sec.gov/news/studies/principlesbasedstand.htm.

[p] http://www.ffiec.gov/ffiecinfobase/resources/info_sec/ots-12_cfr_568_security_proced_bank_protection_act.pdf (66 FR 8639, February 1, 2001).

[q] http://frwebgate.access.gpo.gov/cgi-bin/getdoc.cgi?dbname=107_cong_public_laws&docid=f:publ056.107.pdf.

[r] http://www.fdic.gov/news/news/financial/2002/FIL0292.html.

[s] http://www.fdic.gov/regulations/laws/federal/02joint723.html.

Forensics – FTP

precautions and actions can include one or more of the following, in addition to other rewards not listed:

- Job promotion and advancement
- New privileges and benefits
- Additional vacation
- Gifts, prizes, and awards
- Praise and recognition
- Financial rewards, such as bonuses or raises

Penalties for not engaging in anti-fraud activities, on the other hand, can include one or more of the following, in addition to other penalties not listed:

- Loss of employment
- Demotion
- Loss of benefits, privileges, or perks
- Salary reduction
- Unpaid leave
- Legal action
- Internal publication of non-compliant personnel

Some of the above may work very well in some environments but may be completely unacceptable, or possibly illegal, in other organizational environments. Always discuss any of the motivators, prizes, penalties, and sanctions with the human resources and legal departments prior to implementation. It is important to ensure that the plans are in compliance with existing laws, contracts, and policies and to ensure that the information security and fraud prevention departments have the support of the legal and human resources areas.

IMPLEMENTING INFORMATION SECURITY MOTIVATION

Donn Parker covers the previously described topics of motivation factors, in addition to creating a framework to integrate security into job responsibilities, in his book *Fighting Computer Crime: A New Framework for Protecting Information.*[9] The following is the essence of his sage advice as it applies to building a fraud prevention education program.

- *Make demonstrated due diligence the objective of security and fraud prevention activities.* Risk reduction and fraud prevention are the ultimate desired outcomes, but they really have little inherent motivational value. Personnel demonstrate due diligence by being in compliance with security standards (such as ISO 17799 or NIST), laws and regulations (such as HIPAA or GLBA), organizational policies, and accepted industry best practices and by taking proactive anti-fraud actions.
- *Update organizational policies and standards to include documentation of rewards, motivation, and penalties.* An organization's information security policy must be current, be accepted and supported by stakeholders (such as executive management and business unit leaders), and be practical to achieve. It should also document motivators for personnel compliance.
- *Include fraud prevention and information security as specific objectives in job descriptions.* Work with management to develop the objectives in each area of the organization. Do what applicable labor unions and laws allow. Job descriptions should include specific security and fraud prevention assignments that will comply with regulations and policies and provide accountability for the organization's assets.
- *Require all personnel to regularly sign an information security agreement.* State in the contract that the individual will support organizational information security and fraud prevention policies and standards, will actively work to prevent fraudulent activities, and will promptly report fraudulent activities and security incidents. Require employees to sign the agreement upon initial employment and on an annual basis. This ensures that personnel have reviewed the policies and provides accountability for compliance.
- *Establish fraud prevention and reporting activities as a specific objective in performance appraisals.* It is important to have the support of management and unions. This motivator is particularly effective for employees whose job descriptions explicitly state anti-fraud activities.
- *Engage top management to explicitly review the information security performance of all managers.* Managers with poor security and anti-fraud practices also have direct reports with poor security and anti-fraud practices. Managers who model good security practices have direct reports with good security practices. Top-down motivation of managers is necessary to achieve security and anti-fraud support through all levels of an organization.
- *Implement rewards and penalties that are supported and carried out consistently by management.* When penalties and rewards are documented, they must be consistently applied to make them effective motivators. When establishing rewards and penalties, do not require more security and anti-fraud activities than are necessary for the organization's business circumstances. When an organization tries to "overdo" security with no justification behind the requirements it will not get support from management; the security and anti-fraud efforts will be negatively impacted and possibly fail.

Motivators are effective when they are consistently applied. Do a little research and observe. Determine the motivators that will work best for the organization and environment. These answers will not come neatly packaged from anywhere else other than from understanding the organization's personnel and organization.

ANTI-FRAUD AWARENESS AND TRAINING INFORMATION

Employees can perform many different activities that will help to identify potential fraudulent activities. It is the responsibility of the organization's board of directors to support a written security program and training designed to help employees identify potential fraud and report potentially fraudulent activities to appropriate management. Personnel must be made aware of actions they need to take to help prevent fraud and what to do when they suspect or identify fraudulent activities. The following anti-fraud information and activities should be incorporated into the organization's fraud prevention awareness materials and training curriculum as is applicable and appropriate for the particular business and organization:

- Regularly communicate, via awareness messages and through formal training, the organization's security procedures to discourage robberies, burglaries, larcenies, and fraudulent activities. This will help employees to assist in the identification and prosecution of persons who commit such acts.
- Train personnel on the appropriate administrative, technical, and physical safeguards to protect the security, confidentiality, and integrity of customer information.
- Designate a security officer with the authority to develop and administer a written security and prevention program for each business unit and office. Communicate to personnel who the officer is, the responsibilities of the officer, and when the officer should be contacted.
- Establish procedures for opening and closing business facilities and for safekeeping all currency, negotiable securities, and similar valuables at all times. Communicate these procedures to all personnel.
- Establish procedures to assist in identifying persons committing crimes against the organization. These procedures should preserve evidence that may aid in their identification and prosecution. Appropriate personnel need to be made aware of the procedures. Such procedures and actions to consider include, but are not limited to, the following:

  — Use a hidden or closed circuit camera to record all office activities.
  — Use identification devices, such as prerecorded serial-numbered bills or chemical and electronic devices.
  — Retain a record of all robberies, burglaries, larcenies, and frauds committed against the organization.

- Provide initial and regularly scheduled ongoing officer and employee training and awareness that explains personnel and management responsibilities under the security program and proper employee conduct during and after a burglary, robbery, larceny, or fraudulent activity.

- Train appropriate personnel with related job responsibilities in how to select, test, operate, and maintain security, fraud prevention, and fraud detection devices. Such devices may include the following:

  — Mechanisms to protect cash and other liquid assets, such as a vault, safe, or other secure spaces A lighting system for illuminating the area around the vault, if the vault is visible from outside the facilities
  — Tamper-resistant locks on publicly accessible doors and windows
  — Alarm systems or devices to immediately notify the nearest law enforcement officers of an attempted or perpetrated robbery or burglary
  — Automated network tools to detection discrepancies within data that indicate potential fraudulent transactions
  — Other devices as appropriate, taking into consideration:

    o The incidence of crimes against financial institutions in the area
    o The amount of currency and other valuables exposed to robbery, burglary, or larceny
    o The distance of the facilities from the nearest law enforcement office
    o The cost of the security devices
    o Other security measures used within the facilities
    o The physical characteristics of facility structures and surrounding environment

- Train personnel who service customers how to verify the identity of each person seeking to open an account following the organization's approved identity verification procedures.
- Train personnel how to determine if individuals appear on any lists of known or suspected terrorists or terrorist organizations provided to the financial institution by any government agency.
- Communicate regularly to personnel the organization's beliefs and values that fraud is unacceptable and will not be tolerated. This applies social pressure on fraudsters not to attempt the crime in the first place and on others to report suspicion of fraud.
- Communicate to personnel the organization's sanctions for committing or assisting with fraud. Let personnel know that the organization regularly reviews activities and systems to detect fraud and that it is the responsibility of personnel to assist with fraud prevention.
- Communicate information security policies and procedures to personnel. Fraud prevention begins with good security.

Forensics –
FTP

- Teach personnel the appropriate procedures to report fraud as quickly as they suspect or detect such activities. Be sure to include examples of suspicious activities and case studies to be most effective.
- Establish ways to confirm that suspected fraud is a fraud and not a "false positive." Be sure appropriate personnel understand how to appropriately gather evidence related to such crimes.
- Implement appropriate sanctions for fraudulent activities. Such sanctions can include disciplinary, civil, and criminal actions. Combinations of sanctions can often occur simultaneously, such as dismissing an employee and pressing charges.
- When fraud has been proven, make every effort to recover the losses. Make employees aware of the efforts that must be made.
- Establish fraud activity "red flags" and communicate them to employees.
- Instruct employees to conduct checks for identity theft before issuing loans or other forms of credit to individuals.
- Instruct employees how to obtain sufficient information to verify a customer's identity to reduce the risk that the organization will be used as a conduit for money laundering and terrorist financing.
- Teach employees the procedures for responding to circumstances when they cannot confirm the true identity of a customer.

Credit card fraud prevention activities for employees should include the following:

- Teach employees to ask to see the customer's credit card for all in-person purchases.
- For credit card purchases, teach employees to swipe the card for electronic data. If the card will not swipe, an imprint should be secured and the embossed information examined.
- Teach employees to always compare the account number on the receipt with the number on both the front and back of the card.
- Teach employees to always compare the name on the store receipt with the name on the front of the card. If the card is not signed, consider implementing a procedure to have the employee ask the customer to sign the card, ask for another form of identification, and compare the signatures. If the customer refuses, the transaction should not be completed, and the employee should advise the customer to contact the credit card company at the number on the back of the card.
- Teach employees to always get a signature on the printed receipt for all face-to-face transactions. The employee should not complete the transaction if the signature on the receipt does not match the name on the front of the card and the signature on the back of the card.

- Teach employees not to accept a fax or photocopy of a credit card to complete a transaction.
- Establish procedures to ensure that personnel and the credit card processor are submitting all the magnetic stripe information required by the credit card companies. Be sure to train appropriate personnel to follow these procedures.
- Instruct employees to obtain the expiration date for all methods (electronic, keyed, or manual) of credit card authorization requests.
- Instruct employees to follow steps similar to the following when processing credit cards manually or when the magnetic stripes on credit cards are unreadable:

  — If your business authorizes payment electronically and the magnetic stripe is unreadable, instruct employees to key the transaction and expiration date into the terminal for authorization approval. When processing charge requests manually, always get a voice authorization from the applicable credit card company.
  — Obtain an imprint of the credit card on a paper sales draft that conforms with the applicable credit card company requirements.
  — Require the customer to sign the paper receipt and compare the signature.

TRAINING AND AWARENESS METHODS

Much has been written about the need for security and privacy education through effective awareness and training activities. A regulatory and fraud prevention education program should address the organization's interpretation of applicable privacy and security laws and regulations as well as support activities of the organization to mitigate fraud risk. It is vital for organizations to evaluate, and continue to reevaluate, the effectiveness of these education programs. Too many organizations spend considerable time and money to launch awareness and training programs only to let them then wane, wither, and die on the vine because they did nothing beyond the big implementation; they failed to put forth the effort and activities necessary to evaluate, update, and modify their programs as necessary to be truly effective.

Evaluation Areas

The methods you use for evaluation and measurements are diverse. The following objects of evaluation identified by Verduin and Clark[10] are useful. Tailor them to facilitate an evaluation of the organization's fraud prevention education programs by considering the questions listed with each object:

- *Access.* What groups are you reaching? Are any groups missing? Is everyone in the target group participating?

Are you providing appropriate delivery methods for your target audiences? Can all of your target audience access your training and awareness materials and participate in your delivery methods?

- *Relevancy.* Is your fraud prevention education program relevant to your organization's business goals and expectations? Are your training and awareness messages and information relevant to job responsibilities? Will your education program have a noticeable impact on business practices? Was your training content appropriate for your target participants? Did your training cover regulatory and policy requirements?
- *Quality.* Is the quality of your awareness materials adequate to get attention and effectively deliver the intended message? Does the quality of your training materials contribute to your students' success? Do your trainers and teachers deliver quality education? Do they know how to interactively adjust to the abilities and experiences of their students? Were the conditions right for learning and for each learner's subjective satisfaction?
- *Learning outcomes.* Is the amount of time allowed for learning appropriate for successfully understanding the message? What do your participants say about the usefulness and effectiveness of your training and awareness activities? Do you tell the participants the expected outcomes of your education activities? What did the participants actually learn? Did your participants indicate they had a satisfactory learning experience?
- *Impact.* What is the impact of your education program on your organization as a whole? Were activities and habits changed appropriately following training and awareness activities? What are the long-term impacts? Did the training methods promote the desired skills? Did job performance improve? What is the pattern of student outcomes following each training session? Did you assist managers with determining their own workforce performance? Did you create return on investment statistics to support training and awareness funds?
- *Cost effectiveness.* What time requirements are involved? What are the costs for the materials? How many people are in your targeted groups? How is training being delivered? Are you using inside or outside training and awareness resources? What is the value of the method of awareness activity or training session you used compared to other awareness and training options?
- *Knowledge generation.* Do you understand what is important for your personnel and managers to know? Do you understand what works and what does not work in your education program? Are you utilizing your evaluation results? Did you assist employees in determining their own performance success? Did you compile trend data to assist instructors in improving both learning and teaching?
- *General to specific.* Do your instructors give students enough information to allow them to self-evaluate their own success in implementing what they learn? Are students told overall goals and the specific actions necessary to achieve them? Are goals and actions realistic and relevant? What is the necessary, prerequisite general and specific knowledge?

Evaluation Methods

Consider using a combination of the following methods for determining the effectiveness of fraud prevention education within the organization, but be sure to discuss the methods with the legal department prior to implementation to make sure the program is not violating any applicable laws, labor union requirements, or employee policies:

- Videotape your training sessions. Review and critique to identify where it might be necessary to improve delivery, content, organization, and so on.
- Give quizzes immediately following training to measure comprehension.
- Distribute a fraud-prevention awareness survey to some or all personnel. Do this prior to training to establish a baseline then after training to help determine training effectiveness.
- Send follow-up questionnaires to people who have attended formal training approximately four to six months after the training to determine how well they have retained the information presented.
- Monitor the number of compliance infractions for each issue for which training is provided. Is this number decreasing or increasing?
- Measure fraud prevention knowledge as part of yearly job performance appraisals.
- Place feedback and suggestion forms on an appropriate intranet Web site, preferably one devoted to fraud prevention information.
- Track the number and type of fraud and security incidents that occur before and after the training and awareness activities.
- Conduct spot checks of personnel behavior; for example, walk through work areas and note if workstations are logged in while unattended or if negotiable check stock or customer information printouts are not adequately protected.
- Record user IDs and completion status for Web- and network-based training. Send a targeted questionnaire to those who have completed the online training.
- Ask training participants to fill out evaluation forms at the end of the class.
- Identify the percentage of the target groups that participate in training.
- Determine if the number of instructors is adequate and if they have the necessary level of expertise for the corresponding training topics.

Forensics – FTP

- Determine if the training materials address all the organization's goals and objectives. Identify the gaps and make a plan to fill them.
- Review training logs to see trends in attendance.
- Tape or film participants performing their work after training to determine if they are utilizing the skills taught.
- Administer occasional tests to personnel. Use multiple choice, short answer, essay tests, or a combination. Avoid using true or false tests.
- Perform interviews with past training participants as well as personnel who have not yet been trained. Use structured and unstructured interview sessions.

TRAINING DESIGN AND DEVELOPMENT

Design the training curriculum based on the learning objectives for the associated target groups. The training delivery method should be based on the best way to achieve the organization's objectives. In choosing a delivery method, select the best method for the learning objectives, the number of students, and the organization's ability to efficiently deliver the material.

Training Materials

A curriculum must be created for the following if it does not already exist:

- Computer-based training (CBT)
- Briefings
- Web-based training
- Videos
- Telephone conferences
- Quarterly meetings
- Classroom

Design and Development

During the design and development phase, keep these things in mind:

- Outline the class content.
- Divide the training into instructional units or lessons.
- Determine time requirements for each unit and lesson.
- Create content based on what personnel need to know to perform their job responsibilities.
- Include interactive activities that can be taken back to their jobs and used right away.
- Be clear about the behaviors, actions, and activities expected of the students when performing their jobs.
- Describe how personnel would demonstrate successfully meeting the objectives being taught.
- Build upon existing capabilities and experiences within the group.

- Sequence topics to build new or complex skills onto existing ones and to encourage and enhance the student's motivation for learning the material.
- Use multiple learning methods.

When determining the best instructional method for your target groups, keep the following in mind:

- *Consider the people within the target group audience.* Consider the audience size and location. Consider experience levels. Consider time constraints. If the audience is large and geographically dispersed, a technology-based solution, such as Web-based, CD, or satellite learning, may work best.
- *Consider the business needs.* If the budget is limited, then a technology-based delivery or bringing in an outside instructor with already prepared materials may be appropriate.
- *Consider the course content.* Some topics are better suited for instructor-led, video, Web-based, or CBT delivery. There are many opinions about what type of method is best. Much depends on the organization. It will be helpful to get the advice of training professionals who can assess materials and make recommendations.
- *Consider what kind of student–teacher interaction is necessary.* Is the course content best presented as self-paced individual instruction or as group instruction? Some topics are best covered with face-to-face and group interaction, and other topics are best suited for individualized instruction. For example, if the goal is just to communicate policies and procedures, a technology-based solution may be most appropriate; however, if students need to perform problem-solving activities in a group to reinforce understanding or demonstrate appropriate actions, then a classroom setting would be better.
- *Consider the type of presentations and activities necessary.* If the course content requires students to fill out forms, to use a specialized software program, or to participate in role playing, a classroom setting would be best.
- *Consider the stability of the class content.* The stability of content is a cost issue. If content will change frequently (e.g., procedures are expected to change as a result of mergers, acquisitions, or divestitures) or if new software systems are planned, the expense of changing the materials needs to be estimated by considering difficulty, time, and money. Some instructional methods can be changed more easily and cost-efficiently than others.
- *Consider the technology available for training delivery.* This is a critical factor in deciding the instructional strategy. Will all students have access to the technologies required? For Web-based training, will all students have access to the intranet or Internet? Do students have the necessary bandwidth for certain types of multimedia?

Forensics – FTP

The content for each target group should be based on the organization's information security policy, fraud prevention guidelines, and appropriate business unit practices and guidelines. Additionally, content must support applicable security and privacy laws, regulations, and accepted standards. Following is a list of the content topics generally common to all target groups (core content) and the content that will have to be specialized for each target group (targeted content):

- *Core content*

  — Background fraud information
  — Corporate fraud prevention policy
  — Business impact of fraudulent activities
  — Fraud-related terms and definitions
  — Legal requirements for fraud prevention and reporting
  — The organization's fraud prevention procedures

- *Targeted content*

  — The fraud and risk implications for the targeted group based on their business responsibilities
  — Actions for the target group related to their job responsibilities, interactions with customers, interactions with third-party business partners, and so on
  — The organization's fraud prevention fundamentals, rules, policies, standards, procedures, and guidelines applicable to the target group
  — Case studies designed specifically for the target group
  — Review of key points
  — Tools and checklists specific to the target group to meet fraud prevention goals
  — Resources
  — Summary
  — Questions

Content Based on Fraud Prevention Goals

Fraud prevention and detection training content must include information that supports the organization's security and fraud prevention goals and principles. When creating training curriculum, the following can be used to guide content development. These are the methods of training delivery most commonly used, and indicated with each method are the benefits and drawbacks for the corresponding method.

Instructor-led classroom training

Instructor-led classroom training is recommended for target groups that have the most decision-making responsibilities and procedures.

- *Benefits*

  — Is typically the most high-quality and interactive method.
  — Is comparatively easy to update and can most easily be tailored to the audience compared to other methods.
  — Allows for the most interaction compared to other methods.
  — Gets participants away from distracting environments.
  — Can gauge and measure participant understanding.

- *Disadvantages*

  — May be costly with regard to time and resources necessary.
  — Can train only a relatively small number of participants at a time.
  — Often requires a large time investment for participants.
  — Takes participants away from their work area.

Computer-based training or CD-ROM training

This type of training is recommended for general audiences and training remote participants.

- *Benefits*

  — Allows participants to remain in their work areas.
  — Costs less overall than most other methods.
  — Can be taken in modules.
  — Allows participants to be widely dispersed geographically.
  — Allows a large number of participants to undergo training in a short amount of time.

- *Disadvantages*

  — Does not allow instructor interaction.
  — Is a type of static training that may quickly become outdated.
  — Is difficult to gauge participant understanding.

Web-based live training ("Webinars," net meetings)

- *Benefits*

  — Can reach a large number of participants in a short amount of time.
  — Accommodates participants in many different locations.

Forensics –
FTP

— Can be recorded and subsequently viewed any-
where, anytime, anyplace.
— Offers the option of on-line support.
— Is cost effective.

- *Disadvantages*

— Could require a large amount of network
resources.
— Provides for only limited interaction.

Videos

- *Benefits*

— Can be shown anywhere, anytime, anyplace.
— Typically does not require any instructor–student
interaction.
— Can be viewed by a large number of participants
in a short period of time.

- *Disadvantages*

— Is not interactive.
— May be expensive.

Satellite presentations

- *Benefits*

— Allows for live interactions.
— Is more timely and up-to-date than videos and
computer-based training.
— Is interactive.
— Reaches a large number of participants.

- *Disadvantages*

— May be costly to establish if infrastructure is not
already in place.
— Can be difficult to coordinating times to accommodate wide range of geographic locations.

Many instructional elements will be consistent from
course to course, regardless of the instructional methods
used. Most courses will involve delivery with voice, text,
and graphics. To make instruction more effective, consider
incorporating pictures or graphics, video, demonstrations,
role playing, simulations, case studies, and interactive
exercises. Several of these presentation methods will be
used in most courses. Remember that it is generally
considered most effective for student understanding to
deliver the same message or information multiple times
using multiple methods. The students (employees and
other applicable personnel) all have their own unique
learning styles, and what works well for one person will
not necessarily be effective for others. Develop instructional methods based on instructional objectives, course
content, delivery options, implementation options, technological capabilities, and available resources. Web-based
training is often a good alternative for large audiences
and can provide an overview of the topic and communicate
policies and facts; however, this type of instruction method
is often not appropriate for audiences that are learning
procedures or how to act in specific types of situations in
which role playing is necessary.

REFERENCES

1. http://www.consumer.gov/sentinel/pubs/Top10Fraud2004.pdf.
2. http://a255.g.akamaitech.net/7/255/2422/07feb20051415/
www.gpoaccess.gov/usbudget/fy06/pdf/budget/other.pdf.
3. http://www.ussc.gov/2003guid/2003guid.pdf.
4. http://www.ussc.gov/ANNRPT/1995/ANNUAL95.htm.
5. http://www.ussc.gov/ANNRPT/2001/SBtoc01.htm.
6. http://www.ussc.gov/2004guid/gl2004.pdf.
7. U.S. Sentencing Commission. Sentencing Guidelines for
United States Courts, http://www.ussc.gov/FEDREG/
05_04_notice.pdf.
8. http://web.utk.edu/~gwynne/maslow.HTM.
9. Parker, D. *Fighting Computer Crime: A New Framework
for Protecting Information*; John Wiley & Sons: New York,
1998; 462–473.
10. Verduin, Jr. J.R., Clark, T.A. *Distance Learning*; Jossey-
Bass: San Francisco, CA, 1991.

FTP: Secured Data Transfers

Chris Hare, CISSP, CISA, CISM
Information Systems Auditor, Nortel, Dallas, Texas, U.S.A.

Abstract

This discussion has shown how one can control access to an FTP server and allow controlled access for downloads or uploads to permit the safe exchange of information for interactive and automated FTP sessions. The extended functionality offered by the wu-ftpd FTP server provides extensive access, and preventative and detective controls to limit who can access the FTP server, what they can do when they can connect, and the recording of their actions.

Several scenarios exist that must be considered when looking for a solution:

- The user with a log-in account who requires FTP access to upload or download reports generated by an application. The user does not have access to a shell; rather, his default connection to the box will connect him directly to an application. He requires access to only his home directory to retrieve and delete files.
- The user who uses an application as his shell but does not require FTP access to the system.
- An application that automatically transfers data to a remote system for processing by a second application.

It is necessary to find an elegant solution to each of these problems before that solution can be considered viable by an organization.

SCENARIO A

A user named Bob accesses a UNIX® system through an application that is a replacement for his normal UNIX log-in shell. Bob has no need for, and does not have, direct UNIX command-line access. While using the application, Bob creates reports or other output that he must upload or download for analysis or processing. The application saves this data in either Bob's home directory or a common directory for all application users.

Bob may or may not require the ability to put files onto the application server. The requirements break down as follows:

- Bob requires FTP access to the target server.
- Bob requires access to a restricted number of directories, possibly one or two.
- Bob may or may not require the ability to upload files to the server.

SCENARIO B

Other application users in the environment illustrated in Scenario A require no FTP access whatsoever. Therefore, it is necessary to prevent them from connecting to the application server using FTP.

SCENARIO C

The same application used by the users in Scenarios A and B regularly dumps data to move to another system. The use of hard-coded passwords in scripts is not advisable because the scripts must be readable for them to be executed properly. This may expose the passwords to unauthorized users and allow them to access the target system. Additionally, the use of hard-coded passwords makes it difficult to change the password on a regular basis because all scripts using this password must be changed.

A further requirement is to protect the data once stored on the remote system to limit the possibility of unauthorized access, retrieval, and modification of the data.

While there are a large number of options and directives for the /etc/ ftpaccess file, the focus here is on those that provide secured access to meet the requirements in the scenarios described.

CONTROLLING FTP ACCESS

Advanced FTP servers such as wu-ftpd provide extensive controls for controlling FTP access to the target system. This access does not extend to the IP layer, as the typical FTP client does not offer encryption of the data stream. Rather, FTP relies on the properties inherent in the IP (Internet Protocol) to recover from malformed or lost packets in the data stream. This means one still has no control over the network component of the data transfer. This may allow for the exposure of the data if the network is

Encyclopedia of Information Assurance DOI: 10.1081/E-EIA-120046284
Copyright © 2011 by Taylor & Francis. All rights reserved.

compromised. However, that is outside the scope of the immediate discussion.

wu-ftpd uses two control files: /etc/ftpusers and /etc/ftpaccess. The /etc/ftpusers file is used to list the users who do **not** have FTP access rights on the remote system. For example, if the /etc/ftpusers file is empty, then all users, including root, have FTP rights on the system. This is not the desired operation typically, because access to system accounts such as root are to be controlled. Typically, the /etc/ftpusers file contains the following entries:

- root
- bin
- daemon
- adm
- lp
- sync
- shutdown
- halt
- mail
- news
- uucp
- operator
- games
- nobody

When users in this list, root for example, attempt to access the remote system using FTP, they are denied access because their account is listed in the /etc/ftpusers file. This is illustrated in Table 1.

By adding additional users to this list, one can control who has FTP access to this server. This does, however, create an additional step in the creation of a user account, but it is a related process and could be added as a step in the script used to create a user. Should a user with FTP privileges no longer require this access, the user's name can be added to the /etc/ftpusers list at any time. Similarly, if a denied user requires this access in the future, that user can be removed from the list and FTP access restored.

Recall the requirements of Scenario B: the user has a log-in on the system to access his application but does not have FTP privileges. This scenario has been addressed through the use of /etc/ftpusers. The user can still have UNIX shell access or access to a UNIX-based application through

Table 1 Denying FTP access.

```
C:\WINDOWS>ftp 192.168.0.2
Connected to 192.168.0.2.
220 poweredge.home.com FTP server (Version wu-
   2.6.1(1) Wed Aug 9 05:54:50 EDT 20
00) ready.
User (192.168.0.2:(none)): root
331 Password required for root.
Password:
530 Login incorrect.
Login failed.
ftp>
```

the normal UNIX log-in process. However, using /etc/ftpusers prevents access to the FTP server and eliminates the problem of unauthorized data movement to or from the FTP server. Most current FTP server implementations offer the /etc/ftpusers feature.

EXTENDING CONTROL

Scenarios A and C require additional configuration because reliance on the extended features of the wu-ftpd server is required. These control extensions are provided in the file /etc/ftpaccess. A sample /etc/ftpaccess file is shown in Table 2. This is the default /etc/ftpaccess file distributed with wu-ftpd. Before one can proceed to the problem at hand, one must examine the statements in the /etc/ftpaccess file. Additional explanation for other statements not found in this example, but required for the completion of our scenarios, are also presented later in the entry.

The class statement in /etc/ftpaccess defines a class of users, in the sample file a user class named all, with members of the class being real, guest, and anonymous. The syntax for the class definition is:

```
class <class> <typelist> <addrglob>[<addrglob> ...]
```

Typelist is one of real, guest, or anonymous. The real keyword matches users to their real user accounts. Anonymous matches users who are using anonymous FTP access, while guest matches guest account access. Each of these classes can be further defined using other options in this file. Finally, the class statement can also identify the list of allowable addresses, hosts, or domains that connections will be accepted from. There can

Table 2 Sample /etc/ftpaccess file.

```
class all real,guest,anonymous *
email root@localhost
loginfails 5
readme      README*      login
readme      README*      cwd=*
message /var/ftp/welcome.msg  login
message .message              cwd=*
compressyesall
taryesall
chmodnoguest,anonymous
deletenoguest,anonymous
overwritenoguest,anonymous
renamenoguest,anonymous
log transfers anonymous,real inbound,outbound
shutdown /etc/shutmsg
passwd-check rfc822 warn
```

be multiple `class` statements in the file; the first one matching the connection will be used.

Defining the hosts requires additional explanation. The host definition is a domain name, a numeric address, or the name of a file, beginning with a slash ("/") that specifies additional address definitions. Additionally, the address specification may also contain IP `address:netmask` or IP address/CIDR definition. (CIDR, or Classless Internet Domain Routing, uses a value after the IP address to indicate the number of bits used for the network. A Class C address would be written as 192.168.0/24, indicating 24 bits are used for the network.)

It is also possible to exclude users from a particular class using a "!" to negate the test. Care should be taken in using this feature. The results of each of the `class` statements are OR'd together with the others, so it is possible to exclude an allowed user in this manner. However, there are other mechanisms available to deny connections from specific hosts or domains. The primary purpose of the `class` statement is to assign connections from specific domains or types of users to a class. With this in mind, one can interpret the `class` statement in Table 2, shown here as:

```
class all real,guest,anonymous *
```

This statement defines a `class` named `all`, which includes user types `real`, `anonymous`, and `guest`. Connections from any host are applicable to this class.

The `email` clause specifies the e-mail address of the FTP archive maintainer. It is printed at various times by the FTP server.

The `message` clause defines a file to be displayed when the user logs in or when they change to a directory. The statement

```
message /var/ftp/welcome.msg login
```

causes wu-ftpd to display the contents of the file `/var/ftp/welcome.msg` when a user logs in to the FTP server. It is important for this file be somewhere accessible to the FTP server so that anonymous users will also be greeted by the message.

NOTE: Some FTP clients have problems with multiline responses, which is how the file is displayed.

When accessing the test FTP server constructed for this entry, the message file contains:

```
***** WARNING *****
This is a private FTP server. If you do not have an
  account, you are not welcome here.
*******************
It is currently %T local time in Ottawa, Canada.
You are %U@%R accessing %L.
for help, contact %E.
```

The `%<char>` strings are converted to the actual text when the message is displayed by the server. The result is:

```
331 Password required for chare.
Password:
230-***** WARNING *****
230-This is a private FTP server. If you do
  not have an account,
230-you are not welcome here.
230-*******************
230-It is currently Sun Jan 28 18:28:01 2001
  local time in Ottawa, Canada.
230-You are chare@chris accessing
  poweredge.home.com.
230-for help, contact root@localhost.
230-
230-
230 User chare logged in.
ftp>
```

The `%<char>` tags available for inclusion in the message file are listed in Table 3.

It is allowable to define a class and attach a specific message to that class of users. For example:

```
classrealreal*
classanonanonymous*
message/var/ftp/welcome.msgloginreal
```

Table 3   %char definitions.

Tag	Description
%T	Local time (form Thu Nov 15 17:12:42 1990)
%F	Free space in partition of CWD (kbytes)
%C	Current working directory
%E	The maintainer's e-mail address as defined in ftpaccess
%R	Remote host name
%L	Local host name
%u	Username as determined via RFC931 authentication
%U	Username given at log-in time
%M	Maximum allowed number of users in this class
%N	Current number of users in this class
%B	Absolute limit on disk blocks allocated
%b	Preferred limit on disk blocks
%Q	Current block count
%I	Maximum number of allocated inodes (+1)
%i	Preferred inode limit
%q	Current number of allocated inodes
%H	Time limit for excessive disk use
%h	Time limit for excessive files
%xu	Uploaded bytes
%xd	Downloaded bytes
%xR	Upload/download ratio (1:n)
%xc	Credit bytes
%xT	Time limit (minutes)
%xE	Elapsed time since log-in (minutes)
%xL	Time left
%xU	Upload limit
%xD	Download limit

Forensics – FTP

Table 4 Directory-specific messages.

```
User (192.168.0.2:(none)): anonymous
331 Guest login ok, send your complete
    e-mail address as password.
Password:
230 Guest login ok, access restrictions
    apply.
ftp> cd etc
250-***** WARNING *****
250-There is no data of any interest in the
    /etc directory.
250-
250 CWD command successful.
ftp>
```

Now, the message is only displayed when a real user logs in. It is not displayed for either anonymous or guest users. Through this definition, one can provide additional information using other tags listed in Table 3. The ability to display `class`-specific message files can be extended on a user-by-user basis by creating a `class` for each user. This is important because individual limits can be defined for each user.

The message command can also be used to display information when a user enters a directory. For example, using the statement

```
message /var/ftp/etc/.message CWD=*
```

causes the FTP server to display the specified file when the user enters the directory. This is illustrated in Table 4 for the anonymous user. The message itself is displayed only once to prevent annoying the user.

The `noretrieve` directive establishes specific files no user is permitted to retrieve through the FTP server. If the path specification for the file begins with a "/", then only those files are marked as non-retrievable. If the file specification does not include the leading "/", then any file with that name cannot be retrieved.

For example, there is a great deal of sensitivity with the password file on most UNIX systems, particularly if that system does not make use of a shadow file. Aside from the password file, there is a long list of other files that should not be retrievable from the system, even if their use is discouraged. The files that should be marked for non-retrieval are files containing the names:

- passwd
- shadow
- .profile
- .netrc
- .rhosts
- .cshrc
- profile
- core
- .htaccess
- /etc

- /bin
- /sbin

This is not a complete list, as the applications running on the system will likely contain other files that should be specifically identified.

Using the `noretrieve` directive follows the syntax:

```
noretrieve[absolute|relative]
    [class=<classname>] ...
[-] <file- name> <filename> ...
```

For example,

```
noretrieve passwd
```

prevents any user from downloading any file on the system named passwd.

When specifying files, it is also possible to name a directory. In this situation, all files in that directory are marked as non-retrievable. The option `absolute` or `relative` keywords identify if the file or directory is an absolute or relative path from the current environment. The default operation is to consider any file starting with a "/" as an absolute path. Using the optional `class` keyword on the `noretrieve` directive allows this restriction to apply to only certain users. If the `class` keyword is not used, the restriction is placed against all users on the FTP server.

Denying Connections

Connections can be denied based on the IP address or domain of the remote system. Connections can also be denied based on how the user enters his password at log-in.

NOTE: This password check applies only to anonymous FTP users. It has no effect on real users because they authenticate with their standard UNIX password.

The password-check directive informs the FTP server to conduct checks against the password entered. The syntax for the password-check directive is

```
passwd-check <none|trivial|rfc822> (<enforce|warn>)
```

It is not recommended to use `password-check` with the `none` argument because this disables analysis of the entered password and allows meaningless information to be entered. The `trivial` argument performs only checking to see if there is an "@" in the password. Using the argument is the recommended action and ensures the password is compliant with the RFC822 e-mail address standard.

If the password is not compliant with the `trivial` or `rfc822` options, the FTP server can take two actions. The `warn` argument instructs the server to warn the user that his password is not compliant but still allows access. If the `enforce` argument is used, the user is warned and the connection terminated if a non-complaint password is entered.

Use of the `deny` clause is an effective method of preventing access from specific systems or domains. When a

Forensics – FTP

user attempts to connect from the specified system or domain, the message contained in the specified file is displayed. The syntax for the `deny` clause is:

```
deny <addrglob> <message_file>
```

The file location must begin with a slash ("/"). The same rules described in the class section apply to the `addrglob` definition for the `deny` command. In addition, the use of the keyword `!nameservd` is allowed to deny connections from sites without a working nameserver.

Consider adding a deny clause to this file; for example, adding `deny!nameservd /var/ftp/.deny` to `/etc/ftpaccess`. When testing the `deny` clause, the denied connection receives the message contained in the file. Using the `!nameservd` definition means that any host not found in a reverse DNS query to get a host name from an IP address is denied access.

```
Connected to 192.168.0.2.
220 poweredge.home.com FTP server
  (Version wu-2.6.1(1)
  Wed Aug 9 05:54:50 EDT 20
00) ready.
User (192.168.0.2:(none)): anonymous
331 Guest login ok, send your complete
  e-mail address as password.
Password:
530-**** ACCESS DENIED ****
530-
530-Access to this FTP server from your
  domain has been denied by the
  administrator.
530-
530 Login incorrect.
Login failed.
ftp>
```

The denial of the connection is based on where the connection is coming from, not the user who authenticated to the server.

Connection Management

With specific connections denied, this discussion must focus on how to control the connection when it is permitted. A number of options for the server allow this and establish restrictions from throughput to access to specific files or directories.

Preventing anonymous access to the FTP server is best accomplished by removing the `ftp` user from the `/etc/passwd` file. This instructs the FTP server to deny all anonymous connection requests.

The `guestgroup` and `guestuser` commands work in a similar fashion. In both cases, the session is set up exactly as with anonymous FTP. In other words, a `chroot()` is done and the user is no longer permitted to issue the `USER` and `PASS` commands. If using

`guestgroup`, the `groupname` must be defined in the `/etc/group` file; or in the case of `guestuser`, a valid entry in `/etc/passwd`.

```
guestgroup <groupname>[<groupname> ...]
guestuser <username>[<username> ...]
realgroup <groupname>[<groupname> ...]
realuser <username>[<username> ...]
```

In both cases, the user's home directory must be correctly set up. This is accomplished by splitting the home directory entry into two components separated by the characters "/./". The first component is the base directory for the FTP server and the second component is the directory the user is to be placed in. The user can enter the base FTP directory but cannot see any files above this in the file system because the FTP server establishes a restricted environment.

Consider the `/etc/passwd` entry:

```
systemx:<passwd>:503:503:FTP Only
  Access from
systemx:/var/ftp/./systemx:/etc/ftponly
```

When `systemx` successfully logs in, the FTP server will `chroot("/var/ftp")` and then `chdir("/systemx")`. The guest user will only be able to access the directory structure under `/var/ftp` (which will look and act as `/` to systemx), just as an anonymous FTP user would.

Either an actual name or numeric ID specifies the group name. To use a numeric group ID, place a "%" before the number. Ranges may be given and the use of an asterisk means all groups. `guestuser` works like `guestgroup` except uses the username (or numeric ID).

`realuser` and `realgroup` have the same syntax but reverse the effect of `guestuser` and `guestgroup`. They allow real user access when the remote user would otherwise be determined a guest. For example:

```
guestuser *
realuser chare
```

causes all non-anonymous users to be treated as `guest`, with the sole exception of user chare, who is permitted real user access. Bear in mind, however, that the use of `/etc/ftpusers` overrides this directive. If the user is listed in `/etc/ftpusers`, he is denied access to the FTP server.

It is also advisable to set timeouts for the FTP server to control the connection and terminate it appropriately. The timeout directives are listed in Table 5. The `accept` timeout establishes how long the FTP server will wait for an incoming connection. The default is 120 seconds. The `connect` value establishes how long the FTP server will wait to establish an outgoing connection. The FTP server generally makes several attempts and will give up after the defined period if a successful connection cannot be established.

The data timeout determines how long the FTP server will wait for some activity on the data connection. This should be kept relatively long because the remote client may have a low-speed link and there may be a lot of data

Table 5 Timeout directives.

Timeout value	Default	Recommended
Timeout accept <seconds>	120	120
Timeout connect <seconds>	120	120
Timeout data <seconds>	1200	1200
Timeout idle <seconds>	900	900
Timeout maxidle <seconds>	7200	1200
Timeout RFC931 <seconds>	10	10

queued for transmission. The idle timer establishes how long the server will wait for the next command from the client. This can be overridden with the $-a$ option to the server. Using the access clause overrides both the command-line parameter if used and the default.

The user can also use the SITE IDLE command to establish a higher value for the idle timeout. The maxidle value establishes the maximum value that can be established by the FTP client. The default is 7200 seconds. Like the idle timeout, the default can be overridden using the $-A$ command-line option to the FTP server. Defining this parameter overrides the default and the command line. The last timeout value allows the maximum time for the RFC931 ident/AUTH conversation to occur. The information recorded from the RFC931 conversation is recorded in the system logs and used for any authentication requests.

Controlling File Permissions

File permissions in the UNIX environment are generally the only method available to control who has access to a specific file and what they are permitted to do with that file. It may be a requirement of a specific implementation to restrict the file permissions on the system to match the requirements for a specific class of users.

The defumask directive allows the administrator to define the umask, or default permissions, on a per-class or systemwide basis. Using the defumask command as

defumask 077

causes the server to remove all permissions except for the owner of the file. If running a general access FTP server, the use of a 077 umask may be extreme. However, umask should be at least 022 to prevent modification of the files by other than the owner.

By specifying a class of user following the umask, as in

defumask 077 real

all permissions are removed. Using these parameters prevents world writable files from being transferred to your FTP server. If required, it is possible to set additional controls to allow or disallow the use of other commands on the FTP server to change file permissions or affect the files. By default, users are allowed to change file permissions and delete, rename, and overwrite files. They are also allowed to change the umask applied to files they upload. These commands allow or restrict users from performing these activities.

```
chmod <yes|no> <typelist>
delete <yes|no> <typelist>
overwrite <yes|no> <typelist>
rename <yes|no> <typelist>
umask <yes|no> <typelist>
```

To restrict all users from using these commands, apply the directives as:

```
chmod no all
delete no all
overwrite no all
rename no all
umask no all
```

Setting these directives means no one can execute commands on the FTP server that require these privileges. This means the FTP server and the files therein are under the full control of the administrator.

ADDITIONAL SECURITY FEATURES

There are a wealth of additional security features that should be considered when configuring the server. These control how much information users are shown when they log in about the server, and print banner messages among other capabilities.

The greeting directive informs the FTP server to change the level of information printed when the user logs in. The default is full, which prints all information about the server. A full message is:

```
220 poweredge.home.com FTP server (Version wu-2.6.1(1)
Wed Aug 9 05:54:50 EDT 2000) ready.
```

A brief message on connection prints the server name as:

```
220 poweredge.home.com FTP server ready.
```

Finally, the terse message, which is the preferred choice, prints only:

```
220 FTP server ready.
```

The full greeting is the default unless the greeting directive is defined. This provides the most information about the FTP server. The terse greeting is the preferred choice because it provides no information about the server to allow an attacker to use that information for identifying potential attacks against the server.

The greeting is controlled with the directive:

```
greeting <full|brief|terse>
```

An additional safeguard is the banner directive using the format:

`banner <path>`

This causes the text contained in the named file to be presented when the users connect to the server prior to entering their username and password. The path of the file is relative from the real root directory, not from the anonymous FTP directory. If one has a corporate log-in banner that is displayed when connecting to a system using Telnet, it would also be available to use here to indicate that the FTP server is for authorized users only.

NOTE: Use of this command can completely prevent non-compliant FTP clients from establishing a connection. This is because not all clients can correctly handle multi-line responses, which is how the banner is displayed.

```
Connected to 192.168.0.2.
220-
220-* *
220-*                       * W A R N I N G**
220-* *
220-* ACCESS TO THIS FTP SERVER IS FOR
  AUTHORIZED USERS ONLY.*
220-* ALL ACCESS IS LOGGED AND MONITORED.
  IF YOU ARE NOT AN*
220-* AUTHORIZED USER, OR DO NOT AGREE TO
  OUR MONITORING POLICY,*
220-* DISCONNECT NOW.*
220-* *
220-* NO ABUSE OR UNAUTHORIZED ACCESS
  IS TOLERATED.*
220-* *
220-
220-
220 FTP server ready.
User (192.168.0.2:(none)):
```

At this point, one has controlled how the remote user gains access to the FTP server, and restricted the commands they can execute and the permissions assigned to their files. Additionally, certain steps have been taken to ensure they are aware that access to this FTP server is for authorized use only. However, one must also take steps to record the connections and transfers made by users to fully establish what is being done on the FTP server.

LOGGING CAPABILITIES

Recording information in the system logs is a requirement for proper monitoring of transfers and activities conducted on the FTP server. There are a number of commands that affect logging, and each is presented in this section. Normally, only connections to the FTP server are logged. However, using the `log commands` directive, each command executed by the user can be captured. This may create a high level of output on a busy FTP server and

may not be required. However, it may be advisable to capture traffic for anonymous and guest users specifically. The directive syntax is:

`log commands <typelist>`

As with other directives, it is known that `typelist` is a combination of `real`, `anonymous`, and `guest`. If the `real` keyword is used, logging is done for users accessing FTP using their real accounts. `Anonymous` logs all commands performed by anonymous users, while `guest` matches users identified using the `guestgroup` or `guestuser` directives.

Consider the line

`log commands guest, anonymous`

which results in all commands performed by anonymous and guest users being logged. This can be useful for later analysis to see if automated jobs are being properly performed and what files are uploaded or downloaded.

Like the `log commands` directive, `log transfers` performs a similar function, except that it records all file transfers for a given class of users. The directive is stated as:

`log transfers <typelist> <directions>`

The `directions` argument is `inbound` or `outbound`. Both arguments can be used to specify logging of transfers in both directions. For clarity, `inbound` are files transferred to the server, or uploads, and `outbound` are transfers from the server, or downloads. The `typelist` argument again consists of `real`, `anonymous`, and `guest`.

It is not only essential to log all of the authorized functions, but also to record the various command and requests made by the user that are denied due to security requirements. For example, if there are restrictions placed on retrieving the `password` file, it is desirable to record the security events. This is accomplished for `real`, `anonymous`, and `guest` users using the `log security` directive, as in:

`log security <typelist>`

If `rename` is a restricted command on the FTP server, the `log security` directive results in the following entries

```
Feb 11 20:44:02 poweredge ftpd[23516] : RNFR dayo.wav
Feb 11 20:44:02 poweredge ftpd[23516] : RNTO day-o.wav
Feb 11 20:44:02 poweredge ftpd[23516] : systemx of
  localhost.home.com[127.0.0.1]
tried to rename /var/ftp/systemx/dayo.wav to /var/
  ftp/systemx/day-o.wav
```

This identifies the user who tried to rename the file, the host that the user connected from, and the original and desired filenames. With this information, the system administrator or systems security personnel can investigate the situation.

Downloading information from the FTP server is controlled with the `noretrieve` clause in the `/etc/ftpaccess` file. It is also possible to limit uploads to specific directories. This may not be required, depending

Forensics – FTP

on the system configuration. A separate entry for each directory one wishes to allow uploads to is highly recommended. The syntax is:

```
upload[absolute|relative] [class=<classname>] ...[-]
   <root-dir>
<dirglob> <yes|no> <owner> <group>
   <mode>["dirs"|"nodirs"] [<d_mode>]
```

This looks overly complicated, but it is in fact relatively simple. Define a directory called `<dirglob>` that permits or denies uploads. Consider the following entry:

```
upload /var/ftp /incoming yes ftpadmin
ftpadmin 0440 nodirs
```

This means that for a user with the home directory of `/var/ftp`, allow uploads to the incoming directory. Change the owner and group to be `ftpadmin` and change the permissions to `readonly`. Finally, do not allow the creation of directories. In this manner, users can be restricted to the directories to which they can upload files. Directory creation is allowed by default, so one must disable it if required.

For example, if one has a user on the system with the following password file entry:

```
chare:x:500:500:Chris Hare:/home/chare:/
   bin/bash
```

and one wants to prevent the person with this `userid` from being able to upload files to his home directory, simply add the line:

```
upload /home/chare no
```

to the `/etc/ftpaccess` file. This prevents the user `chare` from being able to upload files to his home directory. However, bear in mind that this has little effect if this is a real user, because real users will be able to upload files to any directory they have write permission to. The `upload` clause is best used with anonymous and guest users.

NOTE: The wu-ftpd server denies anonymous uploads by default.

To see the full effect of the upload clause, one must combine its use with a guest account, as illustrated with the systemx account shown here:

```
systemx:x:503:503:FTP access from System X:/home/
systemx/./:/bin/false
```

Note in this password file entry the home directory path. This entry cannot be made when the user account is created. The `'/./'` is used by wu-ftpd to establish the `chroot` environment. In this case, the user is placed into his home directory, `/home/systemx`, which is then used as the base for his `chroot` file system. At this point, the guest user can see nothing on the system other than what is in his home directory.

Using the upload clause of

```
upload /home/chare yes
```

means the user can upload files to this home directory. When coupled with the `noretrieve` clause discussed earlier, it is possible to put a high degree of control around the user.

COMPLETE `/etc/ftpaccess` FILE

The discussion thus far has focused on a number of control directives available in the wu-ftpd FTP server. It is not necessary that these directives appear in any particular order. However, to further demonstrate the directives and relationships between those directives, the `/etc/ftpaccess` file is illustrated in Table 6.

REVISITING THE SCENARIOS

Recall the scenarios from the beginning of this entry. This section reviews each scenario and defines an example configuration to achieve it.

Scenario A

A user named Bob accesses a UNIX system through an application that is a replacement for his normal UNIX

Table 6 The `/etc/ftpaccess` file.

```
#
# Define the user classes
#
class  all         real,guest *
class  anonymous   anonymous  *
class  real        real       *
#
# Deny connections from systems with no reverse DNS
# deny !nameservd /var/ftp/.deny
#
# What is the email address of the server
  administrator. Make sure
# someone reads this from time to time.
email root@localhost
#
# How many login attempts can be made before logging
  an error message and
# terminating the connection?
#
loginfails 5
greeting terse

readme   README*   login
readme   README*   cwd=*
#
# Display the following message at login
#
message /var/ftp/welcome.msg login
banner /var/ftp/warning.msg
```

(Continued)

Forensics –
FTP

Table 6 The /etc/ftpaccess file. (*Continued*)

```
#
# display the following message when entering the
  directory
#
message .message          cwd=*

#
# ACCESS CONTROLS
#
# What is the default umask to apply if no other
  matching directive exists
#
defumask 022
chmod      no          guest,anonymous
delete     no          guest,anonymous
overwriteno            guest,anonymous
rename     no          guest,anonymous
# remove all permissions except for the owner if
  the user is a member of the
# real class
#
defumask 077real
guestuser   systemx
realuser    chare
#
#establish timeouts
#
timeout  accept   120
timeout  connect  120
timeout  data  1200
timeout  idle  900
timeout  maxidel 1200

#
# establish non-retrieval
#
# noretrieve  passwd
# noretrieve  shadow
# noretrieve  .profile
# noretrieve  .netrc
# noretrieve  .rhosts
# noretrieve  .cshrc
# noretrieve  profile
# noretrieve  core
# noretrieve  .htaccess
# noretrieve  /etc
# noretrieve  /bin
# noretrieve  /sbin
noretrieve  /
allow-retrieve  /tmp

upload /home/systemx / no

#
# Logging
#
log commands anonymous,guest,real
log transfers anonymous,guest,real inbound,outbound
log security anonymous,real,guest

compress yes      all
tar yes           all

shutdown /etc/shutmsg

passwd-check rfc822 warn
```

log-in shell. Bob has no need for, and does not have, direct UNIX command-line access. While using the application, Bob creates reports or other output that he must retrieve for analysis. The application saves this data in either Bob's home directory or a common directory for all application users.

Bob may or may not require the ability to put files onto the application server. The requirements break down as follows:

- Bob requires FTP access to the target server.
- Bob requires access to a restricted number of directories, possibly one or two.
- Bob may or may not require the ability to upload files to the server.

Bob requires the ability to log into the FTP and access several directories to retrieve files. The easiest way to do this is to deny retrieval for the entire system by adding a line to /etc/ftpaccess as

```
noretrieve /
```

This marks every file and directory as non-retrievable. To allow Bob to get the files he needs, one must set those files or directories as such. This is done using the allow-retrieve directive. It has exactly the same syntax as the noretrieve directive, except that the file or directory is now retrievable. Assume that Bob needs to retrieve files from the /tmp directory. Allow this using the directive

```
allow-retrieve /tmp
```

When Bob connects to the FTP server and authenticates himself, he cannot get files from his home directory.

```
ftp> pwd
257 "/home/bob" is current directory.
ftp> get .xauth xauth
200 PORT command successful.
550 /home/chare/.xauth is marked
unretrievable
```

However, Bob can retrieve files from the /tmp directory.

```
ftp> cd /tmp
250 CWD command successful.
ftp> pwd
257 "/tmp" is current directory.
ftp> get .X0-lock X0lock
200 PORT command successful.
150 Opening ASCII mode data connection for
  .X0-lock (11 bytes).
226 Transfer complete.
ftp: 12 bytes received in 0.00Seconds
12000.00Kbytes/sec.
ftp>
```

If Bob must be able to retrieve files from his home directory, an additional allow-retrieve directive is required:

```
class real real *
allow-retrieve /home/bob class=real
```

When Bob tries to retrieve a file from anywhere other than /tmp or his home directory, access is denied.

Additionally, it may be necessary to limit Bob's ability to upload files. If a user requires the ability to upload files, no additional configuration is required, as the default action for the FTP server is to allow uploads for real users. If one wants to prohibit uploads to Bob's home directory, use the upload directive:

```
upload /home/bob / no
```

This command allows uploads to the FTP server.

The objective of Scenario A has been achieved.

Scenario B

Other application users in the environment illustrated in Scenario A require no FTP access whatsoever. Therefore, it is necessary to prevent them from connecting to the application server using FTP.

This is done by adding those users to the /etc/ftpaccess file. Recall that this file lists a single user per line, which is checked. Additionally, it may be advisable to deny anonymous FTP access.

Scenario C

The same application used by the users in Scenarios A and B regularly dumps data to move to another system. The use of hard-coded passwords in scripts is not advisable because the scripts must be readable for them to be executed properly. This may expose the passwords to unauthorized users and allow them to access the target system. Additionally, the use of hard-coded passwords makes it difficult to change the password on a regular basis because all scripts using this password must be changed.

A further requirement is to protect the data once stored on the remote system to limit the possibility of unauthorized access, retrieval, and modification of the data.

Accomplishing this requires the creation of a guest user account on the system. This account will not support a log-in and will be restricted in its FTP abilities. For example, create a UNIX account on the FTP server using the source hostname, such as systemx. The password is established as a complex string but with the other compensating controls, the protection on the password itself does not need to be as stringent. Recall from an earlier discussion that the account resembles

```
systemx:x:503:503:FTP access from System X:/home/
systemx/./:/bin/false
```
Also recall that the home directory establishes the real user home directory, and the ftp chroot directory. Using the upload command

```
upload /home/systemx / no
```

means that the systemx user cannot upload files to the home directory. However, this is not the desired function in this case. In this scenario, one wants to allow the remote system to transfer files to the FTP server. However, one does not want to allow for downloads from the FTP server. To do this, the command

```
noretrieve /
upload /home/systemx / yes
```

prevents downloads and allows uploads to the FTP server.

One can further restrict access by controlling the ability to rename, overwite, change permissions, and delete a file using the appropriate directives in the /etc/ftpaccess file:

```
chmodnoguest,anonymous
deletenoguest,anonymous
overwritenoguest,anonymous
renamenoguest,anonymous
```

Because the user account has no interactive privileges on the system and has restricted privileges on the FTP server, there is little risk involved with using a hard-coded password. While using a hard-coded password is not considered advisable, there are sufficient controls in place to compensate for this. Consider the following controls protecting the access:

> The user cannot retrieve files from the system.
> The user can upload files.
> The user cannot see what files are on the system and thus cannot determine the names of the files to block the system from putting the correct data on the server.
> The user cannot change file permissions.
> The user cannot delete files.
> The user cannot overwrite existing files.
> The user cannot rename files.
> The user cannot establish an interactive session.
> FTP access is logged.

With these compensating controls to address the final possibility of access to the system and the data using a password attack or by guessing the password, it will be sufficiently difficult to compromise the integrity of the data.

The requirements defined in the scenario have been fulfilled.

SUMMARY

This discussion has shown how one can control access to an FTP server and allow controlled access for downloads or uploads to permit the safe exchange of information for interactive and automated FTP sessions. The extended functionality offered by the wu-ftpd FTP server provides extensive access, and preventative and detective controls to limit who can access the FTP server, what they can do when they can connect, and the recording of their actions.

Global Transmissions: Jurisdictional Issues

Ralph Spencer Poore, CFE, CISA, CISSP, CTM/CL
Managing Partner, Pi R Squared Consulting, LLP, Arlington, Texas, U.S.A.

Abstract

In the information age, where teleconferences replace in-person meetings, where telecommuting replaces going to the office, and where international networks facilitate global transmissions with the apparent ease of calling your next-door neighbor, valuable assets change ownership at the speed of light. Louis Jionet, Secretary-General of the French Commission on Data Processing and Liberties, stated that "Information is power and economic information is economic power." Customs officials and border patrols cannot control the movement of these assets. But does this mean companies can transmit the data, which either represents or is the valuable asset, without regard to the legal jurisdictions through which they pass? To adequately address this question, this entry discusses both the legal issues and practical issues involved in transnational border data flows.

LEGAL ISSUES

All legally incorporated enterprises have *official books of record*. Whether in manual or automated form, these are the records governmental authorities turn to when determining the status of an enterprise. The ability to enforce a subpoena or court order for these records reflects the effective sovereignty of the nation in which the enterprise operates. Most countries require enterprises incorporated, created, or registered in their jurisdiction to maintain official books of record physically within their borders. For example, a company relying on a service bureau in another country for information processing services may cause the official records to exist only in that other country. This could occur if the printouts or downloads to management PCs reflect only an historic position of the company, perhaps month-end conditions, where the current position of the company—the position on which management relies—exists only through online access to the company's executive information system. From a nation's perspective, two issues of sovereignty arise:

1. That other country might exercise its rights and take custody of the company's records—possibly forcing it out of business—for actions alleged against the company that the company's "home" nation considers legal.
2. The company's "home" nation may be unable to enforce its access rights.

Another, usually overriding, factor is a nation's ability to enforce its tax laws. Many nations have valueadded taxes (VATs) or taxes on "publications," "computer software," and "services." Your organization's data may qualify as a "publication" or as "computer software" or

even as "services" in some jurisdictions. Thus, many nations have an interest in the data that flows across their borders because it may qualify for taxation. The Internet has certainly added to this debate over what, if anything, should be taxable. In some cases, the tax is a tariff intended to discourage the importation of "computer software" or "publications" in order to protect the nation's own emerging businesses. More so than when the tax is solely for revenue generation, protective tariffs may carry heavy fines and be more difficult to negotiate around.

National security interests may include controlling the import and export of information. State secrecy laws exist for almost all nations. The United States, for example, restricts government-classified data (e.g., Confidential, Secret, Top Secret) but also restricts some information even if it is not classified (e.g., technical data about nuclear munitions, some biological research, some advanced computer technology, and cryptography). The USA PATRIOT Act, for example, included provisions for interception of telecommunications to help combat terrorism.

Among those nations concerned with an individual's privacy rights, the laws vary greatly. Laws such as the United States Privacy Act of 1974 (5 USC 552a) have limited applicability (generally applying only to government agencies and their contractors). More recent privacy regulations stemming from the Gramm–Leach–Bliley Act (15 USC 6801 et seq.) and the Health Insurance Portability and Accountability Act (HIPAA) (45 CFR Part 164 §§ C&E) provide industry-specific privacy and security strictures. The United Kingdom's Data Protection Act of 1984 [1984 c 35 (*Halsbury's Statutes, 4th edition*, Butterworths, London, 1992, Vol. 6, pp. 899–949)], however, applies to the commercial sector as does the 1981 Council of Europe's Convention for the Protection of Individuals with Regard to Automatic Processing of Personal Data

Encyclopedia of Information Assurance DOI: 10.1081/E-EIA-120046837
Copyright © 2011 by Taylor & Francis. All rights reserved.

(an excellent discussion of this can be found in Anne W. Brandscomb's *Toward a Law of Global Communications Networks*, The Science and Technology section of the American Bar Association, Longman, New York, 1986). Privacy laws generally have at least the following three characteristics:

1. They provide notice to the subject of the existence of a database containing the subject's personal data (usually by requiring registration of the database or mailing of a formal notice).
2. They provide a process for the subject to inspect and to correct the personal data.
3. They provide a requirement for maintaining an audit trail of accessors to the private data.

The granularity of privacy law requirements also varies greatly. Some laws [e.g., the U.S. Fair Credit Reporting Act of 1970 (see 15 USC 1681 et seq.)] require only the name of the company that requested the information. Other laws require accountability to a specific office or individual. Because the granularity of accountability may differ from jurisdiction to jurisdiction, organizations may need to develop their applications to meet the most stringent requirements, that is, individual accountability. In this author's experience, few electronic data interchange (EDI) systems support this level of accountability (*UNCID Uniform Rules of Conduct for Interchange of Trade Data by Teletransmission,* ICC Publishing Corporation, New York, 1988. All protective measures and audit measures are described as options, with granularity left to the discretion of the parties).

To further complicate data transfer issues, patent, copyright, and trade secrets laws are not uniform. Although international conventions exist [e.g., General Agreement on Tariffs and Trade (GATT)], not all nations subscribe to these conventions; and the conventions often allow for substantial differences among signatories. Rights one might have and can enforce in one jurisdiction may not exist (or may not be enforceable) in another. In some cases, the rights one has in one jurisdiction constitute an infringement in another jurisdiction. For example, one might hold a United States registered trademark on a product. A trademark is a design (often a stylized name or monogram) showing the origin or ownership of merchandise and reserved to the owner's exclusive use. The Trade-Mark Act of 1946 (see 15 USC 1124) provides that no article shall be imported which copies or simulates a trademark registered under U.S. laws. A similar law protecting, for example, trademarks registered in India might prevent one from using the trademark in India if a similar or identical trademark is already registered there.

Disclosure of information not in accordance with the laws of the jurisdictions involved may subject the parties to criminal penalties. For example, the United Kingdom's Official Secrets Act of 1989 clearly defines areas wherein disclosure of the government's secrets is a criminal offense. Most nations have similar laws (of varying specificity), making the disclosure of state secrets a crime. However, technical information considered public in one jurisdiction may be considered a state secret in another. Similarly, biographical information on a national leader may be mere background information for a news story in one country but be viewed as espionage by another. These areas are particularly difficult because most governments will not advise you in advance what constitutes a state secret (as this might compromise the secret). Unless the organization has a presence in each jurisdiction sensitive to these political and legal issues to whom it can turn for guidance, one should seek competent legal advice before transmitting text or textual database materials containing information about individuals or organizations.

From a business perspective, civil law rather than criminal law may take center stage. Although the United States probably has the dubious distinction as the nation in which it is easiest to initiate litigation, lawsuits are possible in almost all jurisdictions. No company wants to become entangled in litigation, especially in foreign jurisdictions. However, when information is transmitted from one nation to another, the rules may change significantly. For example, what are the implied warranties in the receiving jurisdiction?[1] What constitutes profanity, defamation, libel, or similar actionable content? What contract terms are unenforceable (e.g., can you enforce a non-disclosure agreement of 10 years' duration?)?

In some jurisdictions, ecclesiastical courts may have jurisdiction for offenses against a state-supported religion. Circumstances viewed in one jurisdiction as standard business practices (e.g., "gifts") might be viewed in another as unethical or illegal. Whether an organization has standing (i.e., may be represented in court) varies among nations. An organization's rights to defend itself, for example, vary from excellent to nil in jurisdictions ranging from Canada to Iran.

Fortunately, companies can generally choose the jurisdictions in which they will hold assets. Most countries enforce their laws (and the actions of their courts) against corporations by threat of asset seizure. A company with no seizable assets (and no desire to conduct future business) in a country is effectively judgment proof in that country's jurisdiction (although treaty arrangements among jurisdictions may give them recourse through other countries). The reverse can also be true; that is, a company may be unable to enforce a contract (or legal judgment) because the other party has no assets within a jurisdiction willing to enforce the contract or judgment. When contracting with a company to develop software, for example, and that company exists solely in a foreign country, your organization should research the enforceability of any contract and, if you have any doubt, require that a bond be posted in your jurisdiction to ensure at least bond forfeiture as recourse.

Global –
Health Insurance

TECHNICAL ISSUES

Any nation wishing to enforce its laws with regard to data transmitted within or across its borders must have the ability to 1) monitor/intercept the data and 2) interpret/understand the data. Almost all nations can intercept wire (i.e., telephone or telegraph) communications. Most can intercept radio, microwave, and satellite transmissions. Unless an organization uses exotic technologies (e.g., point-to-point laser, extremely low frequency [ELF], or super high frequency), interception will remain likely.

The second requirement, however, is another matter. Even simple messages encoded in accordance with international standards may have meaning only in a specific context or template not inherent in the message itself. For example, "412667456043052" could be a phone number (e.g., 412-667-4560 x43052), a social security number and birthday (e.g., 412-66-7456 04/30/52), dollar amounts ($41,266.74 $560,430.52), inventory counts by part number (PN) (e.g., PN 412667 45, PN 604305 2), or zip codes (e.g., 41266, 74560, 43052). Almost limitless possibilities exist even without using codes or ciphers. And this example used human-readable digits. Many transmissions may be graphic images, object code, or compressed text files completely unintelligible to a human "reading" the data on a datascope.

From the preceding, one might conclude that interception and interpretation by even a technologically advanced nation is too great a challenge. This is, however, far from true. Every "kind" of data has a signature or set of attributes that, when known, permits its detection and identification. This includes encrypted data where the fact of encryption is determinable. Where transmitting or receiving encrypted messages is a crime, a company using encryption risks detection. Once the "kind" of data is determined, applying the correct application is often a trivial exercise. Some examples of such strong typing of data include:

- Rich-text format (RTF) documents and most word processing documents
- SQL transactions
- Spreadsheets (e.g., Lotus 1-2-3, Microsoft Excel)
- Most executables
- Standardized EDI messages
- Internet traffic

If this were not the case, sending data from one computer to another would require extensive advanced planning at the receiving computer—severely impacting data portability and interoperability, two attributes widely sought in business transactions.

Countries with sufficient technology to intercept and interpret an organization's data may pose an additional problem beyond their law enforcement: government-sponsored industrial espionage. Many countries have engaged in espionage with the specific objective of obtaining technical or financial information of benefit to the countries' businesses. A search of news accounts of industrial espionage resulted in a list including the following countries: Argentina, Peoples Republic of China, Iran, India, Pakistan, Russia, Germany, France, Israel, Japan, South Korea, and North Korea. Most of these countries have public policies against such espionage, and countries like the United States find it awkward to accuse allies of such activities (both because the technical means of catching them at it may be a state secret and because what one nation views as counter-espionage another nation might view as espionage).

PROTECTIVE TECHNOLOGIES

For most businesses, the integrity of transmitted data is more important than its privacy. Cryptographic techniques a business might otherwise be unable to use because of import or export restrictions associated with the cryptographic process or the use of a privacy-protected message can be used in some applications for data integrity. For example, symmetric key algorithms such as Triple DES, Rijndael (AES), and The International Data Encryption Algorithm (IDEA), when used for message authentication [e.g., in accordance with the American National Standard X9.19 for the protection of retail financial transactions or similar implementations supporting a message authentication code (MAC)], may be approved by the U.S. Department of the Treasury without having to meet the requirements of the International Trade in Arms Regulations (ITAR). Triple DES is based on a multiple-key implementation of DES. For more information, see ANS X9.52 Triple Data Encryption Algorithm Modes of Operation. The Advanced Encryption Standard (AES) is documented in FIPS 197, available through the National Institute of Standards and Technology (NIST).[2] Xuejia Lai and James Massey developed IDEA in Zurich, Switzerland. Ascom Systec Ltd. is the owner of the encryption algorithm IDEA.

Integrity measures generally address one or both of the following problems:

- Unauthorized (including accidental) modification or substitution of the message
- Falsification of identity or repudiation of the message

The techniques used to address the first problem are generally called Message Authentication techniques. Those addressing the second class of problems are generally called Digital Signature techniques.

Message authentication works by applying a cryptographic algorithm to a message in such a way as to produce a resulting message authentication code (MAC) that has a

Table 1 Sample codebook.

Code	Meaning
Red Sun	Highest authorized bid is
Blue Moon	Stall, we aren't ready
White Flower	Kill the deal; we aren't interested
June	1.00
April	2.00
July	3.00
December	4.00
August	5.00
January	6.00
March	7.00
September	8.00
November	9.00
May	0.00

very high probability of being affected by a change to any bit or bits in the message. The receiving party recalculates the MAC and compares it to the transmitted MAC. If they match, the message is considered authentic (i.e., received as sent); otherwise, the message is rejected.

Because international standards include standards for message authentication (e.g., ISO 9797), an enterprise wanting to protect the integrity of its messages can find suitable algorithms that should be (and historically have been) acceptable to most jurisdictions worldwide. For digital signatures this may also be true, although several excellent implementations (both public key and secret key) rely on algorithms with import/export restrictions. The data protected by a digital signature or message authentication, however, is not the problem as both message authentication and digital signature leave the message in plaintext. Objections to their use center primarily on access to the cryptographic security hardware or software needed to support these services. If the cryptographic hardware or software can be obtained legally within a given jurisdiction without violating export restrictions, then using these services rarely poses any problems.

Digital signature techniques exist for both public key and secret key algorithm systems (also known as asymmetric and symmetric key systems, respectively). The purpose of digital signature is to authenticate the sender's identity and to prevent repudiation (where an alleged sender claims not to have sent the message). The digital signature implementation may or may not also authenticate the contents of the signed message. Note that symmetric techniques for "digital signatures" require an additional step called "notarization" to prevent the receiving party from forging the sending party's message using the shared symmetric key. This technique predates the advent of public key cryptography, which has almost universally displaced it.

Privacy measures address the concern for unauthorized disclosure of a message in transit. Cipher systems (e.g., AES)

transform data into what appears to be random streams of bits. Some ciphers (e.g., a Vernam cipher with a key stream equal to or longer than the message stream) provide almost unbreakable privacy. As such, the better cipher systems almost always run afoul of export or import restrictions.

In some cases, the use of codes is practical and less likely to run into restrictions. As long as the "codebook" containing the interpretations of the codes (see Table 1) is kept secret, an organization could send very sensitive messages without risk of disclosure if intercepted en route. For example, an oil company preparing its bid for an offshore property might arrange a set of codes as follows. The message "RED SUN NOVEMBER MAY MAY" would make little sense to an eavesdropper, but would tell your representative the maximum authorized bid is 900 (the units would be prearranged, so this could mean $900,000).

Other privacy techniques that do not rely on secret codes or ciphers include:

1. Continuous stream messages (the good message is hidden in a continuous stream of otherwise meaningless text). For example: "THVSTOPREAXZTRECEEBNKLLWSYAINNTHELAUNCHGBMEAZY" contains the message "STOP THE LAUNCH." When short messages are sent as part of a continuous, binary stream, this technique (one of a class known as steganography) can be effective. This technique is often combined with cipher techniques where very high levels of message security are needed.

2. Split knowledge routing (a bit pattern is sent along a route independent of another route on which a second bit pattern is sent; the two bit streams are exclusive-ORed together by the receiving party to form the original message). For example, if the bit pattern of the message you want to send is 0011 1001 1101 0110, a random pattern of equal length would be exclusive-ORed with the message (e.g., 1001 1110 0101 0010) to make a new message 1010 0111 1000 0100. The random pattern would be sent along one telecommunication path and the new message would be sent along another, independent telecommunication path. The recipient would exclusively OR the two messages back together, resulting in the original message. Because no cryptographic key management is required and because the exclusive-OR operation is very fast, this is an attractive technique where the requirement of independent routing can be met. Wayner describes a particularly clever variation on this using bit images in his book entitled *Disappearing Cryptography*.[3]

3. The use of templates (which must remain secret) that permit the receiver to retrieve the important values and ignore others in the same message. For example, our string used above:

"THVSTOPREAXZTRECEEBNKLLWSYAINN THELAUNCHGBMEAZY"

Global –
Health Insurance

used with the following template reveals a different message:

"XXXXXXXNNXXXNNNXXXXXXXXXXXXNXXXN
XXXXXXXXXXXXXXX"

where only the letters at the places marked with "N" are used: RETREAT.

The first technique may also be effective against traffic analysis. The second technique requires the ability to ensure independent telecommunication routes (often infeasible). The third technique has roughly the same distribution problems that codebook systems have; that is, the templates must be delivered to the receiver in advance of the transmission and in a secure manner. These techniques do, however, avoid the import and export problems associated with cryptographic systems. These problems are avoided for two reasons: 1) cryptographic transmissions appear to approach statistical randomness (which these techniques do not) and 2) these techniques do not require the export or import of any special technology. Although no system of "secret writing" will work for citizens of nations that prohibit coded messages, unfortunately, such jurisdictions can claim that any message—even a plaintext message—is a "coded" message.

In addition to cryptographic systems, most industrialized nations restrict the export of specific technologies, including those with a direct military use (or police use) and those advanced technologies easily misused by other nations to suppress human rights, improve intelligence gathering, or counter security measures. Thus, an efficient relational database product might be restricted from export because oppressive third-world nations might use it to maintain data on their citizens (e.g., "subversive activities lists"). Finding a nation in which the desired product is sold legally without the export restriction can sometimes avert restrictions on software export. (Note: check with your legal counsel in your enterprise's official jurisdiction as this workaround may be illegal—some countries claim extraterritorial jurisdiction or claim that their laws take precedence for legal entities residing within their borders). For example, the Foreign Corrupt Practices Act (see 15 USC 78) of the United States prohibits giving gifts (i.e., paying graft or bribes) by U.S. corporations even if such practice is legal and traditional in a country within which you are doing business. Similarly, if the Peoples Republic of China produces clones of hardware and software that violate intellectual property laws of other countries but which are not viewed by China as a punishable offense, using such a product to permit processing between the United States and China would doubtlessly be viewed by U.S. authorities as unacceptable.

LONG VIEW

New technologies may make networks increasingly intelligent, capable of enforcing complex compliance rules, and allowing each enterprise to carefully craft the jurisdictions from which, through which, and into which its data will flow. North America, the European Community, Japan, and similar "informationage" countries will probably see these technologies in the near term but many nations will not have these capabilities for decades.

Most jurisdictions will acquire the ability to detect cryptographic messages and to process clear text messages even before they acquire the networking technologies that would honor an enterprise's routing requests. The result may be a long period of risk for those organizations determined to send and to receive whatever data they deem necessary through whatever jurisdictions happen to provide the most expeditious routing.

SUMMARY

Data daily flows from jurisdiction to jurisdiction, with most organizations unaware of the obligations they may incur. As nations become more sophisticated in detecting data traffic transiting their borders, organizations will face more effective enforcement of laws, treaties, and regulations ranging from privacy to state secrets, and from tax law to intellectual property rights. The risk of state-sponsored industrial espionage will also increase. Because organizations value the information transferred electronically, more and more organizations will turn to cryptography to protect their information. Cryptography, however, has both import and export implications in many jurisdictions worldwide. The technology required to intelligently control the routing of communications is increasingly available but will not solve the problems in the short term. Companies will need to exercise care when placing their data on open networks, the routings of which they cannot control.

REFERENCES

1. Wright, B. *Business Law and Computer Security: Achieving Enterprise Objectives through Data Control*; SANS Press: Bethesda, MD, 2003.
2. National Institute of Standards and Technology (NIST), http://csrc.nist.gov/publications/fips/fips197/fips-197.pdf.
3. Peter, W. *Disappearing Cryptography: Being and Nothingness on the Net*; AP Professional: Chestnut Hill, MA, 1996.

Global –
Health Insurance

Hackers: Attacks and Defenses

Ed Skoudis, CISSP
Senior Security Consultant, Intelguardians Network Intelligence, Howell, New Jersey, U.S.A.

Abstract

Computer attackers continue to hone their techniques, getting ever better at undermining our systems and networks. As the computer technologies we use advance, these attackers find new and nastier ways to achieve their goals—unauthorized system access, theft of sensitive data, and alteration of information. This entry explores some of the recent trends in computer attacks and presents tips for securing your systems. To create effective defenses, we need to understand the latest tools and techniques our adversaries are throwing at our networks. With that in mind, we will analyze four areas of computer attack that have received significant attention in the past year or so: wireless LAN attacks, active and passive operating system fingerprinting, worms, and sniffing backdoors.

WIRELESS LAN ATTACKS (WAR DRIVING)

In the past year, a very large number of companies have deployed wireless LANs, using technology based on the IEEE 802.11b protocol, informally known as *Wi-Fi*. Wireless LANs offer tremendous benefits from a usability and productivity perspective: a user can access the network from a conference room, while sitting in an associate's cubicle, or while wandering the halls. Unfortunately, wireless LANs are often one of the least secure methods of accessing an organization's network. The technology is becoming very inexpensive, with a decent access point costing less than $200 and wireless cards for a laptop or PC costing below $100. In addition to affordability, setting up an access point is remarkably simple (if security is ignored, that is). Most access points can be plugged into the corporate network and configured in a minute by a completely inexperienced user. Because of their low cost and ease of (insecure) use, wireless LANs are in rapid deployment in most networks today, whether upper management or even IT personnel realize or admit it. These wireless LANs are usually completely unsecure because the inexperienced employees setting them up have no idea of or interest in activating security features of their wireless LANs.

In our consulting services, we often meet with CIOs or Information Security Officers to discuss issues associated with information security. Given the widespread use of wireless LANs, we usually ask these upper-level managers what their organization is doing to secure its wireless infrastructure. We are often given the answer, "We don't have to worry about it because we haven't yet deployed a wireless infrastructure." After hearing that stock answer, we conduct a simple wireless LAN assessment (with the CIO's permission, of course). We walk down a hall with a wireless card, laptop, and wireless LAN detection software. Almost always we find renegade, completely unsecure wireless networks in use that were set up by employees outside of formal IT roles. The situation is similar to what we saw with Internet technology a decade ago. Back then, we would ask corporate officers what their organizations were doing to secure their Internet gateways. They would say that they did not have one, but we would quickly discover that the organization was laced with homegrown Internet connectivity without regard to security.

Network Stumbling, War Driving, and War Walking

Attackers have taken to the streets in their search for convenient ways to gain access to organizations' wireless networks. By getting within a few hundred yards of a wireless access point, an attacker can detect its presence and, if the access point has not been properly secured, possibly gain access to the target network. The process of searching for wireless access points is known in some circles as *network stumbling*. Alternatively, using an automobile to drive around town looking for wireless access points is known as *war driving*. As you might guess, the phrases *war walking* and even *war biking* have been coined to describe the search for wireless access points using other modes of transportation. I suppose it is only a matter of time before someone attempts *war hanggliding*.

When network stumbling, attackers set up a rig consisting of a laptop PC, wireless card, and antenna for discovering wireless access points. Additionally, a global positioning system (GPS) unit can help record the geographic location of discovered access points for later attack. Numerous software tools are available for this task as well. One of the most popular is NetStumbler (available at http://www.netstumbler.com), an easy-to-use GUI-based tool written by Marius Milner. NetStumbler

Encyclopedia of Information Assurance DOI: 10.1081/E-EIA-120046285
Copyright © 2011 by Taylor & Francis. All rights reserved.

runs on Windows systems, including Win95, 98, and 2000, and a PocketPC version called *Mini-Stumbler* has been released. For UNIX, several war-driving scripts have been released, with Wi-scan (available at http://www.dis.org/wl/) among the most popular.

This wireless LAN discovery process works because most access points respond, indicating their presence and their services set identifier (SSID) to a broadcast request from a wireless card. The SSID acts like a name for the wireless access point so that users can differentiate between different wireless LANs in close proximity. However, the SSID provides no real security. Some users think that a difficult-to-guess SSID will get them extra security. They are wrong. Even if the access point is configured not to respond to a broadcast request for an SSID, the SSIDs are sent in cleartext and can be intercepted.

In a recent war-driving trip in a taxi in Manhattan, an attacker discovered 455 access points in 1 hour. Some of these access points had their SSIDs set to the name of the company using the access point, gaining the attention of attackers focusing on juicy targets.

After discovering target networks, many attackers will attempt to get an IP address on the network, using the Dynamic Host Configuration Protocol (DHCP). Most wireless LANs freely give out addresses to anyone asking for them. After getting an address via DHCP, the attacker will attempt to access the LAN itself. Some LANs use the Wired Equivalent Privacy (WEP) protocol to provide cryptographic authentication and confidentiality. While WEP greatly improves the security of a wireless LAN, it has some significant vulnerabilities that could allow an attacker to determine an access point's keys. An attacker can crack WEP keys by gathering a significant amount of traffic (usually over 500 MB) using a tool such as Airsnort (available at airsnort.shmoo.com/).

Defending against Wireless LAN Attacks

So, how do you defend against wireless LAN attacks in your environment? There are several levels of security that you could implement for your wireless LAN, ranging from totally unsecure to a strong level of protection. Techniques for securing your wireless LAN include:

- *Set the SSID to an obscure value.* As described above, SSIDs are not a security feature and should not be treated as such. Setting the SSID to an obscure value adds very little from a security perspective. However, some access points can be configured to prohibit responses to SSID broadcast requests. If your access point offers that capability, you should activate it.
- *Use MAC address filtering.* Each wireless card has a unique hardware-level address called the media access control (MAC) address. A wireless access point can be configured so that it will allow traffic only from specific MAC addresses. While this MAC filtering does improve

security a bit, it is important to note that an attacker can spoof wireless card MAC addresses.

- *Use WEP, with periodic rekeying.* While WEP keys can be broken using Airsnort, the technology significantly improves the security of a wireless LAN. Some vendors even support periodic generation of new WEP keys after a given timeout. If an attacker does crack a WEP key, it is likely that they break the old key, while a newer key is in use on the network. If your access points support dynamic rotating of WEP keys, such as Cisco's Aironet security solution, activate this feature.
- *Use a virtual private network (VPN).* Because SSID, MAC, and even WEP solutions have various vulnerabilities as highlighted above, the best method for securing wireless LANs is to use a VPN. VPNs provide end-to-end security without regard to the unsecured wireless network used for transporting the communication. The VPN client encrypts all data sent from the PC before it gets sent into the air. The wireless access point simply collects encrypted streams of bits and forwards them to a VPN gateway before they can get access to the internal network. In this way, the VPN ensures that all data is strongly encrypted and authenticated before entering the internal network.

Of course, before implementing these technical solutions, you should establish specific policies for the use of wireless LANs in your environment. The particular wireless LAN security policies followed by an organization depend heavily on the need for security in that organization. The following list, which I wrote with John Burgess of Predictive Systems, contains recommended security policies that could apply in many organizations. This list can be used as a starting point, and pared down or built up to meet specific needs.

- All wireless access points/base stations connected to the corporate network must be registered and approved by the organization's computer security team. These access points/base stations are subject to periodic penetration tests and audits. Unregistered access points/base stations on the corporate network are strictly forbidden.
- All wireless network interface cards (i.e., PC cards) used in corporate laptop or desktop computers must be registered with the corporate security team.
- All wireless LAN access must use corporate-approved vendor products and security configurations.
- All computers with wireless LAN devices must utilize a corporate-approved virtual private network (VPN) for communication across the wireless link. The VPN will authenticate users and encrypt all network traffic.
- Wireless access points/base stations must be deployed so that all wireless traffic is directed through a VPN device before entering the corporate network. The VPN device should be configured to drop all unauthenticated and unencrypted traffic.

While the policies listed above fit the majority of organizations, the policies listed below may or may not fit, depending on the technical level of employees and how detailed an organizations' security policy and guidelines are:

- The wireless SSID provides no security and should not be used as a password. Furthermore, wireless card MAC addresses can be easily gathered and spoofed by an attacker. Therefore, security schemes should not be based solely on filtering wireless MAC addresses because they do not provide adequate protection for most uses.
- WEP keys can be broken. WEP may be used to identify users, but only together with a VPN solution.
- The transmit power for access points/base stations near a building's perimeter (such as near exterior walls or top floors) should be turned down. Alternatively, wireless systems in these areas could use directional antennas to control signal bleed out of the building.

With these types of policies in place and a suitable VPN solution securing all traffic, the security of an organization's wireless infrastructure can be vastly increased.

ACTIVE AND PASSIVE OPERATING SYSTEM FINGERPRINTING

Once access is gained to a network (through network stumbling, a renegade unsecured modem, or a weakness in an application or firewall), attackers usually attempt to learn about the target environment so they can hone their attacks. In particular, attackers often focus on discovering the operating system (OS) type of their targets. Armed with the OS type, attackers can search for specific vulnerabilities of those operating systems to maximize the effectiveness of their attacks.

To determine OS types across a network, attackers use two techniques: 1) the familiar, time-tested approach called active OS fingerprinting, and 2) a technique with new-found popularity, passive OS fingerprinting. We will explore each technique in more detail.

Active OS Fingerprinting

The Internet Engineering Task Force (IETF) defines how TCP/IP and related protocols should work. In an ever-growing list of Requests for Comment (RFCs), this group specifies how systems should respond when specific types of packets are sent to them. For example, if someone sends a TCP SYN packet to a listening port, the IETF says that a SYN ACK packet should be sent in response. While the IETF has done an amazing job of defining how the protocols we use every day should work, it has not thoroughly defined every case of how the protocols should fail. In

other words, the RFCs defining TCP/IP do not handle all of the meaningless or perverse cases of packets that can be sent in TCP/IP. For example, what should a system do if it receives a TCP packet with the code bits SYN-FIN-URG-PUSH all set? I presume such a packet means to SYNchronize a new connection, FINish the connection, do this URGently, and PUSH it quickly through the TCP stack. That is nonsense, and a standard response to such a packet has not been devised.

Because there is no standard response to this and other malformed packets, different vendors have built their OSs to respond differently to such bizarre cases. For example, a Cisco router will likely send a different response than a Windows NT server for some of these unexpected packets. By sending a variety of malformed packets to a target system and carefully analyzing the responses, an attacker can determine which OS it is running.

An active OS fingerprinting capability has been built into the Nmap port scanner (available at http://www.insecure.org/nmap). If the OS detection capability is activated, Nmap will send a barrage of unusual packets to the target to see how it responds. Based on this response, Nmap checks a user-customizable database of known signatures to determine the target OS type. Currently, this database houses over 500 known system types.

A more recent addition to the active OS fingerprinting realm is the Xprobe tool by Fyodor Yarochkin and Ofir Arkin. Rather than manipulating the TCP code bit options like Nmap, Xprobe focuses exclusively on the Internet Control Message Protocol (ICMP). ICMP is used to send information associated with an IP-based network, such as ping requests and responses, port unreachable messages, and instructions to quench the rate of packets sent. Xprobe sends between one and four specially crafted ICMP messages to the target system. Based on a very carefully constructed logic tree on the sending side, Xprobe can determine the OS type. Xprobe is stealthier than the Nmap active OS fingerprinting capability because it sends far fewer packets.

Passive OS Fingerprinting

While active OS fingerprinting involves sending packets to a target and analyzing the response, passive OS fingerprinting does not send any traffic while determining a target's OS type. Instead, passive OS fingerprinting tools include a sniffer to gather data from a network. Then, by analyzing the particular packet settings captured from the network and consulting a local database, the tool can determine what OS type sent that traffic. This technique is far stealthier than active OS fingerprinting because the attacker sends no data to the target machine. However, the attacker must be in a position to analyze traffic sent from the target system, such as on the same LAN or on a network where the target frequently sends packets.

Global – Health Insurance

One of the best passive OS fingerprinting tools is p0f (available at http://www.stearns.org/p0f/), originally written by Michal Zalewski and now maintained by William Stearns. P0f determines the OS type by analyzing several fields sent in TCP and IP traffic, including the rounded-up initial time-to-live (TTL), window size, maximum segment size, don't fragment flag, window scaling option, and initial packet size. Because different OSs set these initial values to varying levels, p0f can differentiate between 149 different system types.

Defending against Operating System Fingerprinting

To minimize the impact an attacker can have using knowledge of your OS types, you should have a defined program for notification, testing, and implementation of system patches. If you keep your systems patched with the latest security fixes, an attacker will be far less likely to compromise your machines even if they know which OS you are running. One or more people in your organization should have assigned tasks of monitoring vendor bulletins and security lists to determine when new patches are released. Furthermore, once patches are identified, they should be thoroughly but quickly tested in a quality assurance environment. After the full functionality of the tested system is verified, the patches should be rolled into production.

While a solid patching process is a must for defending your systems, you may also want to analyze some of the work in progress to defeat active OS fingerprinting. Gaël Roualland and Jean-Marc Saffroy wrote the IP personality patch for Linux systems, available at ippersonality. sourceforge.net/. This tool allows a system administrator to configure a Linux system running kernel version 2.4 so that it will have any response of the administrator's choosing for Nmap OS detection. Using this patch, you could make your Linux machine look like a Solaris system, a Macintosh, or even an old Windows machine during an Nmap scan. Although you may not want to put such a patch onto your production systems due to potential interference with critical processes, the technique is certainly worth investigating.

To foil passive OS fingerprinting, you may want to consider the use of a proxy-style firewall. Proxy firewalls do not route packets, so all information about the OS type transmitted in the packet headers is destroyed by the proxy. Proxy firewalls accept a connection from a client, and then start a new connection to the server on behalf of that client. All packets on the outside of the firewall will have the OS fingerprints of the firewall itself. Therefore, the OS type of all systems inside the firewall will be masked. Note that this technique does not work for most packet filter firewalls because packet filters route packets and, therefore, transmit the fingerprint information stored in the packet headers.

RECENT WORM ADVANCES

A computer worm is a self-replicating computer attack tool that propagates across a network, spreading from vulnerable system to vulnerable system. Because they use one set of victim machines to scan for and exploit new victims, worms spread on an exponential basis. In recent times, we have seen a veritable zoo of computer worms with names like Ramen, L10n, Cheese, Code Red, and Nimda. New worms are being released at a dizzying rate, with a new generation of worm hitting the Internet every two to six months. Worm developers are learning lessons from the successes of each generation of worms and expanding upon them in subsequent attacks. With this evolutionary loop, we are rapidly approaching an era of super-worms. Based on recent advances in worm functions and predictions for the future, we will analyze the characteristics of the coming super-worms we will likely see in the next six months.

Rapidly Spreading Worms

Many of the worms released in the past decade have spread fairly quickly throughout the Internet. In July 2001, Code Red was estimated to have spread to 250,000 systems in about 6 hours. Fortunately, recent worms have had rather inefficient targeting mechanisms, a weakness that actually impeded their speeds. By randomly generating addresses and not taking into account the accurate distribution of systems in the Internet address space, these worms often wasted time looking for non-existent systems or scanning machines that were already conquered.

After Code Red, several articles appeared on the Internet describing more efficient techniques for rapid worm distribution. These entries, by Nicholas C. Weaver and the team of Stuart Staniford, Gary Grim, and Roelof Jonkman, described the hypothetical Warhol and Flash worms, which theoretically could take over all vulnerable systems on the Internet in 15 minutes or even less. Warhol and Flash, which are only mathematical models and not actual worms (yet), are based on the idea of fast-forwarding through an exponential spread. Looking at a graph of infected victims over time for a conventional worm, a hockey-stick pattern appears. Things start out slowly as the initial victims succumb to the worm. Only after a critical mass of victims succumbs to the attack does the worm rapidly spread. Warhol and Flash jump past this initial slow spread by prescanning the Internet for vulnerable systems. Through automated scanning techniques from static machines, an attacker can find 100,000 or more vulnerable systems before ever releasing the worm. The attacker then loads these known vulnerable addresses into the worm. As the worm spreads, the addresses of these prescanned vulnerable systems would be split up among the segments of the worm propagating across the network. By using this initial set of vulnerable systems, an attacker could easily infect 99% of vulnerable systems on the Internet in less than an hour. Such a worm could conquer the Internet before most people have even heard of the problem.

MultiPlatform Worms

The vast majority of worms we have seen to date focused on a single platform, often Windows or Linux. For example, Nimda simply ripped apart as many Microsoft products as it could, exploiting Internet Explorer, the IIS Web server, Outlook, and Windows file sharing. While it certainly was challenging, Nimda's Windows-centric approach actually limited its spread. The security community implemented defenses by focusing on repairing Windows systems.

While single-platform worms can cause trouble, be on the lookout for worms that are far less discriminating from a platform perspective. New worms will contain exploits for Windows, Solaris, Linux, BSD, HP-UX, AIX, and other operating systems, all built into a single worm. Such worms are even more difficult to eradicate because security personnel and system administrators will have to apply patches in a coordinated fashion to many types of machines. The defense job will be more complex and require more time, allowing the worm to cause more damage.

Morphing and Disguised Worms

Recent worms have been relatively easy to detect. Once spotted, the computer security community has been able to quickly determine their functionalities. Once a worm has been isolated in the lab, some brilliant folks have been able to rapidly reverse-engineer each worm's operation to determine how best to defend against it.

In the very near future, we will face new worms that are far stealthier and more difficult to analyze. We will see polymorphic worms, which change their patterns every time they run and spread to a new system. Detection becomes more difficult because the worm essentially recodes itself each time it runs. Additionally, these new worms will encrypt or otherwise obscure much of their own payloads, hiding their functionalities until a later time. Reverse-engineering to determine the worm's true functions and purpose will become more difficult because investigators will have to extract the crypto keys or overcome the obfuscation mechanisms before they can really figure out what the worm can do. This time lag for the analysis will allow the worm to conquer more systems before adequate defenses are devised.

Zero-Day Exploit Worms

The vast majority of worms encountered so far are based on old, off-the-shelf exploits to attack systems. Because they have used old attacks, a patch has been readily available for administrators to fix their machines quickly after infection or to prevent infection in the first place. Using our familiar example, Code Red exploited systems using a flaw in Microsoft's IIS Web server that had been known for over a month and for which a patch had already been published.

In the near future, we are likely going to see a worm that uses brand-new exploits for which no patch exists. Because they are brand new, such attacks are sometimes referred to as *zero-day exploits*. New vulnerabilities are discovered practically every day. Oftentimes, these problems are communicated to a vendor, who releases a patch. Unfortunately, these vulnerabilities are all—too easy to discover, and it is only a matter of time before a worm writer discovers a major hole and first devises a worm that exploits it. Only after the worm has propagated across the Internet will the computer security community be capable of analyzing how it spreads so that a patch can be developed.

More Damaging Attacks

So far, worms have caused damage by consuming resources and creating nuisances. The worms we have seen to date have not really had a malicious payload. Once they take over hundreds of thousands of systems, they simply continue to spread without actually doing something nasty. Do not get me wrong; fighting Code Red and Nimda consumed much time and many resources. However, these attacks did not really do anything *beyond* simply consuming resources.

Soon, we may see worms that carry out some plan once they have spread. Such a malicious worm may be released in conjunction with a terrorist attack or other plot. Consider a worm that rapidly spreads using a zero-day exploit and then deletes the hard drives of ten million victim machines. Or, perhaps worse, a worm could spread and then transfer the financial records of millions of victims to a country's adversaries. Such scenarios are not very far-fetched, and even nastier ones could be easily devised.

Worm Defenses

All of the pieces are available for a moderately skilled attacker to create a truly devastating worm. We may soon see rapidly spreading, multi-platform, morphing worms using zero-day exploits to conduct very damaging attacks. So, what can you do to get ready? You need to establish both reactive and proactive defenses.

Incident response preparation

From a reactive perspective, your organization must establish a capability for determining when new vulnerabilities are discovered, as well as rapidly testing patches and moving them into production. As described above, your security team

Global – Health Insurance

should subscribe to various security mailing lists, such as Bugtraq (available at http://www.securityfocus.com), to help alert you to such vulnerabilities and the release of patches. Furthermore, you must create an incident response team with the skills and resources necessary to discover and contain a worm attack.

Vigorously patch and harden your systems

From the proactive side, your organization must carefully harden your systems to prevent attacks. For each platform type, your organization should have documentation describing to system administrators how to build the machine to prevent attacks. Furthermore, you should periodically test your systems to ensure they are secure.

Block unnecessary outbound connections

Once a worm takes over a system, it attempts to spread by making outgoing connections to scan for other potential victims. You should help stop worms in their tracks by severely limiting all outgoing connections on your publicly available systems (such as your Web, DNS, e-mail, and FTP servers). You should use a border router or external firewall to block all outgoing connections from such servers, unless there is a specific business need for outgoing connections. If you do need some outgoing connections, allow them only to those IP addresses that are absolutely critical. For example, your Web server needs to send responses to users requesting Web pages, of course. But does your Web server ever need to *initiate* connections to the Internet? Likely, the answer is no. So, do yourself and the rest of the Internet a favor by blocking such outgoing connections from your Internet servers.

Non-executable system stack can help stop some worms

In addition to overall system hardening, one particular step can help stop many worms. A large number of worms utilize buffer overflow exploits to compromise their victims. By sending more data than the program developer allocated space for, a buffer overflow attack allows an attacker to get code entered as user input to run on the target system. Most operating systems can be inoculated against simple stack-based buffer overflow exploits by being configured with non-executable system stacks. Keep in mind that non-executable stacks can break some programs (so test these fixes before implementing them), and they do not provide a bulletproof shield against all buffer overflow attacks. Still, preventing the execution of code from the stack will stop a huge number of both known and as-yet-undiscovered vulnerabilities in their tracks. Up to 90% of buffer overflows can be prevented using this technique. To create a non-executable stack on a Linux system, you can use the free kernel patch at http://www.openwall.com/linux.

On a Solaris machine, you can configure the system to stop execution of code from the stack by adding the following lines to the/etc/system file:

```
set noexec_user_stack = 1
set noexec_user_stack_log = 1
```

On a Windows NT/2000 machine, you can achieve the same goal by deploying the commercial program SecureStack, available at http://www.securewave.com

SNIFFING BACKDOORS

Once attackers compromise a system, they usually install a backdoor tool to allow them to access the machine repeatedly. A backdoor is a program that lets attackers access the machine on their own terms. Normal users are required to type in a password or use a cryptographic token; attackers use a backdoor to bypass these normal security controls. Traditionally, backdoors have listened on a TCP or UDP port, silently waiting in the background for a connection from the attacker. The attacker uses a client tool to connect to these backdoor servers on the proper TCP or UDP port to issue commands.

These traditional backdoors can be discovered by looking at the listening ports on a system. From the command prompt of a UNIX or Windows NT/2000/XP machine, a user can type "netstat-na" to see which TCP and UDP ports on the local machine have programs listening on them. Of course, normal usage of a machine will cause some TCP and UDP ports to be listening, such as TCP port 80 for Web servers, TCP port 25 for mail servers, and UDP port 53 for DNS servers. Beyond these expected ports based on specific server types, a suspicious port turned up by the netstat command could indicate a backdoor listener. Alternatively, a system or security administrator could remotely scan the ports of the system, using a port-scanning tool such as Nmap (available at http://www.insecure.org/nmap). If Nmap's output indicates an unexpected listening port, an attacker may have installed a backdoor.

Because attackers know that we are looking for their illicit backdoors listening on ports, a major trend in the attacker community is to avoid listening ports altogether for backdoors. You may ask, "How can they communicate with their backdoors if they aren't listening on a port?" To accomplish this, attackers are integrating sniffing technology into their backdoors to create sniffing backdoors. Rather than configuring a process to listen on a port, a sniffing backdoor uses a sniffer to grab traffic from the network. The sniffer then analyzes the traffic to determine which packets are supposed to go to the backdoor. Instead of listening on a port, the sniffer employs pattern matching on the network traffic to determine what to scoop up and pass to the backdoor. The backdoor then executes the commands and sends responses to the attacker. An excellent example of a sniffing backdoor is the Cd00r program

Global – Health Insurance

written by FX. Cd00r is available at http://www.phenoelit.de/stuff/cd00r.c.

There are two general ways of running a sniffing backdoor, based on the mode used by the sniffer program to gather traffic: the so-called non-promiscuous and promiscuous modes. A sniffer that puts an Ethernet interface in promiscuous mode gathers all data from the LAN without regard to the actual destination address of the traffic. If the traffic passes by the interface, the Ethernet card in promiscuous mode will suck in the traffic and pass it to the backdoor. Alternatively, a non-promiscuous sniffer gathers traffic destined only for the machine on which the sniffer runs. Because these differences in sniffer types have significant implications on how attackers can use sniffing backdoors, we will explore non-promiscuous and promiscuous backdoors separately below.

Non-promiscuous Sniffing Backdoors

As their name implies, non-promiscuous sniffing backdoors do not put the Ethernet interface into promiscuous mode. The sniffer sees only traffic going to and from the single machine where the sniffing backdoor is installed. When attackers use a non-promiscuous sniffing backdoor, they do not have to worry about a system administrator detecting the interface in promiscuous mode.

In operation, the non-promiscuous backdoor scours the traffic going to the victim machine looking for specific ports or other fields (such as a cryptographically derived value) included in the traffic. When the special traffic is detected, the backdoor wakes up and interacts with the attacker.

Promiscuous Sniffing Backdoors

By putting the Ethernet interface into promiscuous mode to gather all traffic from the LAN, promiscuous sniffing backdoors can make an investigation even more difficult. To understand why, consider the scenario shown in Fig. 1. This network uses a tri-homed firewall to separate the DMZ and internal network from the Internet. Suppose an attacker takes over the Domain Name System (DNS) server on the DMZ and installs a promiscuous sniffing backdoor. Because this backdoor uses a sniffer in promiscuous mode, it can gather all traffic from the LAN. The attacker configures the sniffing backdoor to listen in on all traffic with a destination address of the Web server (not the DNS server) to retrieve commands from the attacker to execute. In our scenario, the attacker does not install a backdoor or any other software on the Web server. Only the DNS server is compromised.

Now the attacker formulates packets with commands for the backdoor. These packets are all sent with a destination address of the Web server (*not* the DNS server). The Web server does not know what to do with these commands, so it will either discard them or send a RESET or related message to the attacker. However, the DNS server with the sniffing backdoor will see the commands on the LAN. The sniffer will gather these commands and forward them to the backdoor where they will be executed. To further obfuscate the situation, the attacker can send all responses from the backdoor using the spoofed source address of the Web server.

Given this scenario, consider the dilemma faced by the investigator. The system administrator or an intrusion detection system complains that there is suspicious traffic going to and from the Web server. The investigator conducts a detailed and thorough analysis of the Web server. After a painstaking process to verify the integrity of the applications, operating system programs, and kernel on the Web server machine, the investigator determines that this system is intact. Yet backdoor commands continue to be sent to this machine. The investigator would only discover what is really going on by analyzing other systems connected to the LAN, such as the DNS server. The investigative process is significantly slowed down by the promiscuous sniffing backdoor.

Defending against Sniffing Backdoor Attacks

It is important to note that the use of a switch on the DMZ network between the Web server and DNS server does not eliminate this dilemma. Attackers can use active sniffers to conduct ARP cache poisoning attacks and successfully sniff a switched environment. An active sniffer such as Dsniff (available at http://www.monkey.org/~dugsong/dsniff/) married to a

Global –
Health Insurance

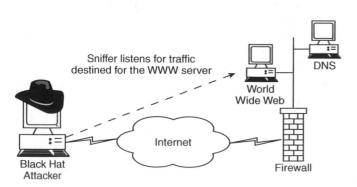

Fig. 1 A promiscuous sniffing backdoor.

sniffing backdoor can implement this type of attack in a switched environment.

So if a switch does not eliminate this problem, how can you defend against this kind of attack? First, as with most backdoors, system and security administrators must know what is supposed to be running on their systems, especially processes running with root or system-level privileges. Keeping up with this information is not a trivial task, but it is especially important for all publicly available servers such as systems on a DMZ. If a security or system administrator notices a new process running with escalated privileges, the process should be investigated immediately. Tools such as lsof for UNIX (available at ftp://vic.cc.purdue.edu/pub/tools/unix/lsof/) or Inzider for Windows NT/2000 (available at http://ntsecurity.nu/toolbox/inzider/) can help to indicate the files and ports used by any process. Keep in mind that most attackers will not name their backdoors "cd00r" or "backdoor," but instead will use less obvious names to camouflage their activities. In my experience, attackers like to name their backdoors "SCSI" or "UPS" to prevent a curious system administrator from questioning or shutting off the attackers' processes.

Also, while switches do not eliminate attacks with sniffers, a switched environment can help to limit an attacker's options, especially if it is carefully configured. For your DMZs and other critical networks, you should use a switch and hard-code all ARP entries in each host on the LAN. Each system on your LAN has an ARP cache holding information about the IP and MAC addresses of other machines on the LAN. By hard-coding all ARP entries on your sensitive LANs so that they are static, you minimize the possibility of ARP cached poisoning. Additionally, implement port-level security on your switch so that only specific Ethernet MAC addresses can communicate with the switch.

CONCLUSIONS

The computer underground and information security research fields remain highly active in refining existing methods and defining completely new ways to attack and compromise computer systems. Advances in our networking infrastructures, especially wireless LANs, are not only giving attackers new avenues into our systems, but they are also often riddled with security vulnerabilities. With this dynamic environment, defending against attacks is certainly a challenge. However, these constantly evolving attacks can be frustrating and exciting at the same time, while certainly providing job security to solid information security practitioners. While we need to work diligently in securing our systems, our reward is a significant intellectual challenge and decent employment in a challenging economy.

Global – Health Insurance

Hackers: Hiring Ex-Criminal

Ed Skoudis, CISSP
Senior Security Consultant, Intelguardians Network Intelligence, Howell, New Jersey, U.S.A.

Abstract

This entry analyzes the issues associated with hiring ex-criminal hackers so you can think through your own organization's approach to this issue. The entry looks at both sides of the problem, and then the author states his opinion on the matter, for what it is worth. While the author attempts to evenhandedly argue both sides of this topic, keep in mind that the author does not necessarily agree with all of these arguments. Instead, the concepts raised are those most often advanced by proponents on either side of this divide.

Making their way, the only way they know how.
That's just a little bit more than the law will allow.
—*Waylon Jennings, "Good Ol' Boys"*
Theme song from Dukes of Hazzard

Suppose someone applies for a system administrator job, or, better yet, an open slot on your computer security team. The applicant is eminently qualified for the position, having wizard-like skills on the exact operating systems deployed throughout your organization. You need his skills, big time. However, the candidate poses a bit of a problem. This otherwise-stellar applicant has a bit of a spotty record with the criminal justice system. By spotty, I mean that your potential hire was found guilty of hacking a Fortune 500 company and stealing some sensitive data. He did the crime, but he has also done the time.

Should you still consider such a person for a position on your security team? Or, should you let bygones be bygones and just move forward? Some companies shy away from such individuals immediately. Others take a "Don't ask...Don't tell" stance. Still others actively embrace such people for their great skills. If your organization hires an ex-criminal hacker, would you be legally responsible if he damages a customer or supplier's computer systems? You could be found guilty of negligent hiring, whereby an employer is liable for taking a hiring risk and exposing customers, suppliers, and other employees to it.

This entry analyzes the issues associated with hiring ex-criminal hackers so you can think through your own organization's approach to this issue. The entry looks at both sides of the problem, and then the author states his opinion on the matter, for what it is worth. While the author attempts to evenhandedly argue both sides of this topic, keep in mind that the author does not necessarily agree with all of these arguments. Instead, the concepts raised are those most often advanced by proponents on either side of this divide.

The discussion in this entry does *not* refer to non-criminal hackers. Remember, as used in the computer underground, the term "hacker" does not by itself imply that the person has done wrong. People who have hacking skills may have acquired them completely lawfully, by studying computer security or conducting legitimate penetration testing against consenting targets, such as their employers or customers. There are many of these "white-hat" hackers in the information technology business. The author himself falls into this white-hat category, as do many others, and would like to think we are very hirable without concerns.

This entry analyzes the question of whether to hire hackers who have an actual prior criminal conviction, or are known to have been involved in criminal activity but may have not been prosecuted (yet). We refer to them as ex-criminal hackers because they were either busted and did some time in jail or are known to have committed crimes. In other words, we are talking about actual former black hats or deeply gray hats.

WHY THIS MATTERS

One might wonder if this analysis really matters that much. Actually, it really does (of course I think that...I would not be writing about it if I didn't). But, think about it. Information technology (IT) carries and stores the life-blood of most organizations today: information. The people who run this technology have tremendous access to the most sensitive information an organization has: personnel employment and health records, sensitive customer data, legal and regulatory compliance information, comprehensive financial results, and perhaps even launch codes. Just to keep the organization running, the IT department often acts as a high-tech priesthood given wide-open access to the very soul of the business.

Encyclopedia of Information Assurance DOI: 10.1081/E-EIA-120046574
Copyright © 2011 by Taylor & Francis. All rights reserved.

Global –
Health Insurance

If IT has a bad egg as an employee, the damage that can be done to an organization's finances, reputation, and very existence might be devastating. Inside personnel know how to hit an organization where it hurts, undermining technology and processes to maximize not only their own personal gain but also the damage inflicted on their target. Looking at statistics regarding computer crime compiled annually by the Computer Security Institute and the FBI, the number of attacks from insiders and outsiders is virtually the same.[1] However, the cost of damages from computer attacks commonly perpetrated by insiders (insider net abuse, financial fraud, and theft of proprietary information) significantly outweighs the cost of attacks by outsiders. That is because insiders know how to cause trouble for their organizations.

The 2002 CSI/FBI survey also indicated that 65% of organizations would not consider hiring reformed hackers as consultants; 17% of others would consider it; while the remaining just do not know. In this author's experience, even the 65% of those who say they would rule out hiring ex-criminal hackers do not have explicit policies regarding this decision or even very detailed background checks to enforce it. Therefore, even among those whose guts tell them not to hire ex-criminal hackers, many unwittingly hire them without understanding their background. Is this wise? Let us explore the case for and against hiring ex-criminal hackers in more detail.

CASE FOR HIRING EX-CRIMINAL HACKERS

Yes, I am a criminal. My crime is that of curiosity. My crime is that of judging people by what they say and think, not by what they look like. My crime is that of outsmarting you, something that you will never forgive me for. I am a hacker, and this is my manifesto. You may stop this individual, but you can't stop us all ...

—From the Hacker Manifesto, *written by "The Mentor" in the mid-1980s*

This creed by "The Mentor" is still very relevant today, as it highlights many of the issues associated with hackers and the computer underground, including whether organizations should employ ex-criminal hackers. We analyze some of the issues brought up in the *Hacker Manifesto*, as well as related topics. The arguments for hiring ex-criminal hackers fall into three general categories: questions associated with who is really to blame, doubt about how dangerous computer attackers really are, and society's need for exceptional technical talent.

It's Not Really Their Fault ...

I went to the lost and found department at my local shopping mall. I told the kid behind the counter that I'd

lost my youthful exuberance. He said they'd call me if it turned up.

—*William J. Basile, my college roommate*

One of the primary arguments for hiring ex-criminal attackers involves looking at whether we can really assign blame; and, if we do, who is really at fault. First, consider the focus of our criminal justice system—reform. By definition, a penitentiary is where someone repents for past crimes, and is reformed to become a contributing member of society. After their release, they have done their time, and should be able to contribute fully to society. Harshly turning down such people from employment may doom them to perpetuate their life of crime. For crime in general, the recidivism rate is far lower when someone returns to society as a productive member of the workforce, especially for young people.[2] Turning the other cheek, as it were, may help them have a positive impact on society. They have paid for their past sins, and it is time for forgiveness. Who is a potential employer to judge when the criminal justice system has already not only judged, but punished?

Furthermore, young people commit many computer crimes in their high-school or college years. Such perpetrators are not hardened criminals; they are merely satisfying their youthful wanderlust by exploring computer systems. As with many young people, they are merely pushing the boundaries of their environment to understand how the world works. If they do not really cause much damage, can we really damn them for simply discovering vulnerabilities and pushing the boundaries of human knowledge? Is that not what being young is all about? This line of argument fills the pages of the always interesting and often-provocative *2600* magazine.[3] This self-titled, "Hacker Quarterly" magazine is published every three months and can be found in most major bookstores' magazine rack. In addition to some technical content describing attacks, the magazine also actively promotes the culture of disaffected youth exploring computers for fun and learning. According to this mind-set, these noble adventurers are not setting out to do damage, and are simply misunderstood by a society either too evil or too stupid to understand the subtleties of the computer underground.

Also, our overall society seems to encourage adventuresome computer hacking. Consider recent movies like *The Matrix* from 1999, or its 2003 sequels. In those movies, a corrupt culture tries to stifle an innocent computer hacker who may expose its ultimate lie. In another classic hacker movie, 1983's *WarGames*, a hacker is the ultimate hero, saving the world from a nuclear holocaust (which, of course, he accidentally triggered in the first place). In these and many other examples, the hackers are the good guys, trying to save the world from corruption. Does it make sense to limit job opportunities to such people simply

Global – Health Insurance

because they have followed the lead given by our mass entertainment culture?

Are They Really That Dangerous, or Do They Help?

> Want to play a game?
> —WOPR, the computer from the movie WarGames

A second and related argument associated with hiring ex-criminal computer attackers involves a consideration of the real damage done in a large number of computer attacks. According to this argument, a computer attack involves minimal real-world damage, with an attacker just exploring a network and copying some files. No lives are in jeopardy, and usually, minimal real-world losses are incurred. However, the attacker may find himself in jail simply because his case was novel and his target especially juicy. For cases with little or no real-world damage, computer attackers should be given another chance at using their skills for good.

Also, numerous people in the computer security industry have gotten started by youthful exploration of computer systems with little harm to society as a whole. Some of the most skilled computer security personnel today cut their teeth by surreptitiously breaking into other people's computers. Sure, goes this argument, now that we are all grown up, we recognize the errors of our youth. If we put everyone in jail who learned computer security by breaking into systems, we just may decimate the computer security industry. Furthermore, some of the folks who encourage tough penalties for computer crime are, in fact, hypocrites, given their own shady pasts. While such people may criticize those who were unlucky enough to get caught, they themselves were just as guilty of computer attacks when they were youngsters.

This argument is bolstered by the wonderful contributions of some high-profile individuals who have bent or even broken the law in computer and related attacks in the past. For example, consider Steve Jobs, the celebrated founder and current CEO of Apple Computer, Inc. Back in college, Jobs entered the hardware business not by selling candy-colored, easy-to-use computer systems. Instead, he made money the old-fashioned way (at least for the 1970s): he sold blue-box hardware that generated specific tones allowing users to explore or defraud the public telephone system. Although Jobs was never charged with a computer-related crime, clearly his exploits were not in the best interests of the telephone company. Yet, looking at the sum total of his activities in the computer field, Jobs has greatly improved the computer industry, helping to introduce the personal computer and then the graphical user interface to the masses, birthing Apple Computer, and then saving Apple from near extinction.

Another example involves Kevin Poulsen, one of the best journalists in the computer security industry today. Poulsen once served significant jail time for some elaborate attacks against a large California-based telephone company.[4] But that is his past; he is now helping advance the cause of computer security as the chief editor of the online security news and editorial section of SecurityFocus.com. Poulsen's past is checkered; his current stuff is extremely helpful in understanding how to and why we should secure our systems.

This argument extends to numerous other individuals. Much of the computer and Internet industries was built by people who push the limits of both technology and the law. These concerns point to the often-blurred line between computer professionals and computer attackers, the indistinct separation of white hats and black hats into a gray goo. Let's face it, if Jobs, Poulsen, and others built their technical and business savvy, as well as our overall networked world, by illegally tapping into computers and helping others to do so, today's computer attackers may be tomorrow's computer security professionals, professors, CEOs, or even presidents. I can just picture the bumper stickers now—Kevin for President. Kevin Mitnick, noted computer attacker of the 1980s and early 1990s, served a lengthy jail sentence. During his incarceration, a significant movement sprung up trying to get Mitnick released. Spearheaded by 2600 magazine, this movement is recognized for its widespread distribution of "Free Kevin" bumper stickers. For more information, see The Fugitive Game[5] and Shimomura and John Markoff.[6]

But We Need Them . . .

Another area for consideration on the issue of hiring ex-criminal attackers involves our society's need for technically sophisticated personnel. Although a recent recession has furloughed many IT professionals, people with very strong security skills remain in high demand. Looking at the vast numbers of gaping holes in corporate networks and major software packages, it is clear that businesses just cannot get enough good security people to shore up their networks against attack. Putting our best and brightest in prison and never hiring them after they have been reformed is a waste of some very valuable human capital. Given the great contribution these folks can make, as compared with the costs of keeping someone on public assistance or in prison, society as a whole benefits from having ex-criminal hackers gainfully employed.

Focusing on the computer security industry, ex-criminal hackers understand computer attacks far better than anyone else does. They truly know the hacker mind-set. While they may or may not have the best skills in conducting overall computer security architecture, such people are among the best in doing detailed penetration tests. For such testing, one needs to think like an attacker and employ the skills and mind-set associated with deep, focused analysis on ripping apart networks, operating systems, and applications. The best penetration tests are done by those who not only

Global – Health Insurance

consider today's known vulnerabilities, but also look deeper for new holes and exploits. Sometimes, ex-criminal hackers are the absolute best at doing this.

In fact, many of the major vulnerabilities discovered today are found by those labeled "gray hats," people who may be in trouble with the law but continue to do computer research. If one looks beyond some of their bravado and unusual culture, these people may actually be helping the information security industry do research, understand problems, and fix vulnerabilities before the serious bad guys do. Our underlying technology is so severely feeble from a security perspective that finding and pointing out these vulnerabilities is really valuable. On a daily basis, major vulnerabilities are discovered in systems of all types: desktops, servers, personal digital assistants, routers ... you name it. If it has software in it, chances are that someone has found security flaws in it, and quite often that person is a reformed, ex-criminal hacker.

Gobbles, a group of security researchers, found some major security vulnerabilities, including a significant flaw allowing complete remote compromise of Apache Web servers in mid-2002. Their brash style, together with their penchant for full disclosure including the release of easy-to-use exploitation code, have rubbed many in the computer security industry the wrong way. However, would you rather have Gobbles discover and publish such findings, or a major terrorist group or foreign country's cyber-warfare troops exploit such holes in a massive attack against the world's infrastructure? Clearly, full disclosure from Gobbles is the better (although perhaps not the best) alternative, as it allows us to fix our problems. Despite Gobbles' strong gray-hat status, they have helped improve Apache's security.

Similarly, Adrian Lamo has broken into and explored the sensitive inner networks of *The New York Times*, Yahoo, and WorldCom. Although he has publicly admitted that such adventures may run afoul of the law, Lamo points out how he has helped these companies secure themselves. Lamo's "victims" have expressed gratitude for his open attitude of sharing information about his exploits with these companies before going public. By discovering flaws in our systems, Lamo, Gobbles, and many others run up against the law and in some cases explicitly violate it. However, in doing so, they ultimately improve the state of computer security by making us focus on computer problems.

Consider a biological analogy that sheds some light on this whole issue. According to recent research, if children are not exposed to any common colds while they are under age ten, their immune systems are in fact weaker as they grow up. As youngsters, they have not built up strength and immunities. In a similar way, computer attackers represent colds periodically impacting the computer industry. Just like colds, they build our defenses by making us harden our systems and deploy patches. That way, we will be much better off when a really serious computer attack occurs. For example, when the Code Red worm spread rapidly in July 2001, it was not only a nuisance. In fact, it made many of us patch our systems and revisit our computer incident handling capabilities. In a counter-intuitive way, some computer attackers help improve computer security by actually attacking our systems in violation of the law.

On top of that argument, we also have to consider what happens if we do not employ the ex-criminal attackers in helping improve computer security. We may very well miss some big vulnerabilities. If ex-criminal hackers cannot use their skills for good, they will use them for evil. By hiring such individuals, the computer industry can keep some of our best and brightest people focused on improving computer security, rather than unraveling the network and systems from underneath us. If these people are gainfully employed in the computer business when they discover vulnerabilities, they will be more likely to share their findings in a responsible way, disclosing it to the appropriate vendors and helping to seek a positive solution for the problem.

One analogy for this situation involves the dilemma over Russian nuclear scientists. After the end of the Cold War, these brilliant researchers were no longer needed to design and build bombs for the now-defunct Soviet Union. Many people fear that, with hard economic times in Russia and a skill set that cannot be readily applied to other jobs, these scientists may help rogue states or terrorists fulfill their nuclear attack fantasies. Because of this concern, the international community has set up programs to employ such scientists in managing and even safely destroying nuclear stockpiles. In a similar way, if we do not utilize our ex-criminal hackers, the criminal underground may hire them to conduct seriously nasty attacks. A computer attacker who has served jail time may have made contact with non-computer criminals while in prison. If the ex-criminal hackers cannot find a means to support themselves using their computer skills because they are blackballed from employment, they may turn to their "friends" from prison for funding. Nastier computer attacks result. By hiring such individuals and directing them toward good, we help to alleviate this sort of problem.

CASE AGAINST HIRING EX-CRIMINAL HACKERS

As one might guess, not everyone agrees with the line of arguments above (now, there is an understatement!). So, how do critics respond? Let us take a look at their critiques, lining them up in the same order as the arguments presented above.

But It Really Is Their Fault

Ex-criminal hackers have already demonstrated that they cannot be trusted with access to computer systems. Many of them have been judged in a criminal justice system with safeguards to protect the innocent. "Sure," goes the argument from many organizations, "we believe in reforming criminals and forgiveness in general, but it's not *our* organization's job to spread forgiveness and improve the world by putting ourselves at risk." Most organizations are in business to either make a profit or deliver services to a constituency. Management and employees of these organizations have a fiduciary responsibility to protect customers, employees, and shareholders from unnecessary risks. Hiring ex-criminals into an information technology department and giving them access to a network with sensitive data to help make the world a better place is not a palatable trade-off for most organizations.

Not hiring ex-criminal hackers can also have a deterring effect. Especially in cases of computer crime involving young people, strong penalties will discourage them from turning to a life of crime. Indeed, right now, some elements of the computer underground perversely joke that if they do ever get busted, they will do their time in jail and become highly paid security consultants after they get out. As a society, it is just not right to reward malfeasance with the promise of six-figure salaries after a year or so in prison. By reversing this logic and making sure that committing computer crime means that you seriously damage your career in technology, we can dampen young people's interest in computer crime. Instead, they may turn their skills to responsible and beneficial computer research, rather than breaking into systems.

Additionally, the idea that it is really not a criminal's fault because *The Matrix* and *WarGames* glorify hacking just shifts blame from the legitimate perpetrator. There are numerous movies that glorify lewd behavior or even mass murder, but we do not decriminalize these activities. Even Robin Hood preached stealing from the rich and giving to the poor, yet we still criminalize theft. We simply do not rely on Hollywood to define our hiring practices, let alone our criminal justice penalties.

They Really Can Be Dangerous!

Let's play Global Thermonuclear War.

—David Lightman,
Matthew Broderick's character
in the movie WarGames

Although it may be true that some computer security personnel and other technology industry luminaries skirted the law over the past three decades, this fact does not exonerate the current generation of computer criminals. In the 1970s, 1980s, and early 1990s, computers in general and the Internet in particular were far less important to the functioning of our society. The Robert Tappan Morris, Jr. Worm took down major components of the early Internet in November 1988. Yes, this story did make the evening news

back then, but it resulted in little real damage. Today, with information technology permeating our financial, healthcare, and government systems, even a less virulent attack could cause many orders of magnitude more damage, disabling the Internet, causing vital systems to crash, and possibly damaging life and limb. Self-replicating worms, distributed denial-of-service, and highly automated computer attack tools can be very dangerous. With such technologies, the criminally minded hacker could wreak havoc purposely or even accidentally.

Sadly, the playful hacking of yesteryear is truly obsolete, now that our world is incredibly dependent on computers. It is not cute anymore. It is time for people to act responsibly with computer technology.

But We Do Not Need Them That Badly!

Let us now turn our attention to the argument about hiring ex-criminals because we really need their technical skills. True, our society really needs people with strong computer skills. However, we need employees with the *proper* skill set and attitude. For the vast majority of IT occupations, the skills needed to break into a computer system are not the same skills needed to defend a system from attack. Consider a system administrator, whose job it is to provide care and feeding to dozens of workstation and server systems. This job title is probably one of the most common roles in your IT organization that has daily access to very sensitive data. A good system administrator needs the following skills:

- Knowledge of how to keep machines up and running
- Insight into how the operating system functions at a fairly detailed level, including networking, a variety of services, and user-level applications
- Problem-solving proficiency to troubleshoot difficulties
- The ability to document and follow detailed processes, such as system configuration guides and backup/restoration procedures
- Talent for writing simple scripts to automate tasks needed to keep the system running
- Understanding of how to configure systems securely, hardening them against attacks
- The ability to apply and test patches distributed by a vendor
- An aptitude for recognizing suspicious activities and reporting them to an incident handling team

Many ex-criminal hackers do not really have these basic system administration skills. As a general rule, in both the real world and information technology, it is much easier to break things than to build them up and maintain them. Some attackers can construct elaborate methods for absolutely ripping apart a system without breaking a sweat, but have not mastered the most basic ideas of how to keep the

Global –
Health Insurance

system running. Sure, some attackers may be able to write the code for a mutating kernel module to stealthily conquer a machine, but can they troubleshoot a flaky network connection while keeping hundreds of users happy? For many of these people, the answer is an emphatic, "No!" because their skills and attitudes do not match the job requirements.

I received strong confirmation of this point at the DefCon conference in August 2002. This annual hacker fest, held in Las Vegas, Nevada, includes a highly competitive Capture the Flag competition. In this game, teams of hackers, enthusiasts, and computer professionals are pitted against each other to vie for the highest score in a 28 hour hackathon. You get points by hacking into the other team's system, but lose points if they hack into your machine. Therefore, in the Capture the Flag contest, both offense and defense are critical. The contest starts your adrenaline pumping and remains very intense, as dozens of top-notch hackers from around the world are hammering your system simultaneously. During the contest this year, a friend of mine reflected the intensity of the sport by shouting expletives. "I know how to hack into these @#$%^ machines," he exclaimed, "but darned if I can stop someone else from getting into my own box!" He had attack skills, but his defense was not up to snuff.

Now, some ex-criminal hackers really do have the skills needed to be superb system administrators, but they also carry a lot of excess and damaging baggage with them. Although employers want these skills, they emphatically do not want system administrators who know how to rip apart systems. Most organizations do not want to hire system administrators, no matter how good they are, who can code elaborate hacks if they have demonstrated in the past that they have used their skills illegally. These organizations would rather have someone who may be less gifted technically, but can do a solid job without jeopardizing the organization.

Beyond system administrators, there are some jobs that really do require computer attack skills, in particular, ethical hacking. Ethical hackers penetrate systems on behalf of the systems' owner to find holes before malicious attackers do. With knowledge of the vulnerabilities, the organizations can deploy defenses based on what the ethical hackers discover. As organizations get more serious about measuring their true security stance, the ethical hacking business continues to grow, employing thousands of very talented security personnel throughout the world. To be effective, these people need skills for breaking into computers. However, the very nature of ethical hacking jobs, with their deep access into very sensitive computer systems, necessitates very careful hiring practices for these roles. Ex-criminal hackers in such positions could be extremely dangerous. They have already demonstrated the illegal use of their skills and could use a role as an "ethical" hacker to simply commit more crimes.

Let us look at the argument that criminal attackers actually make us more secure by pointing out our

weaknesses before serious bad guys do major harm. Ethical hackers can serve this same function, provided that organizations actually establish an ethical hacking function. As the computer industry sorts out the liability issues associated with unsecure software and computer attacks, ethical hacking very well may become even more commonplace than it is today. Increasingly, with companies striving to limit their liability and manage risk, ethical hacking will help to measure and enforce a standard minimal set of security practices.

SORTING IT ALL OUT

So, both sides of this argument are emphatic about the logic of their respective positions. What should we make of these arguments, and should your company consider hiring ex-criminal hackers? In this author's opinion, most organizations today should avoid hiring ex-criminal attackers. Because most IT positions do involve some level of very sensitive access, you should carefully screen your potential hires to understand any computer crime activities in their past.

However, there are a small number of job roles where computer attack skills actually come in handy: vulnerability research and reporting. Vulnerability researchers do not attack particular companies' computer systems. Instead, they look for holes in computer systems in a laboratory environment, without sensitive real-world data. Their job involves finding security problems so that vendors can fix their systems, and ethical hackers can test for these holes. Universities, software vendors, governments, security consultants, and more hard-core technical publications employ such people to find vulnerabilities and figure out fixes to the problems they discover. Here is one area where ex-criminal hackers can actually make some significant contributions. Using the analogy of the out-of-work Russian nuclear scientists who get employment helping secure or destroy warhead stockpiles, our society can actually use ex-criminal hackers for vulnerability research and reporting.

However, such employment does bring risks. These ex-criminal hackers who are now doing research have to be carefully monitored to make sure their skills are being used for good. You certainly do not want to pay people to find vulnerabilities, and have them share them with criminals, foreign adversaries, or terrorists, all the while hiding the results of their research from their employer. A careful mentor program, as described below, can really help to make sure the ex-criminal hacker's skills are being used for good purposes.

BEWARE! RECRUITING LEGAL ISSUES NEED HR SUPPORT

Before finalizing the decision of whether you would want to hire ex-criminal hackers, let us discuss some important

Global – Health Insurance

limitations you may face in finding out where your job applicants fit on the black-hat/white-hat spectrum. When interviewing and making hiring decisions, you must keep in mind any restrictions imposed by your own Human Resources organization, as well as employment laws and regulations. The U.S. Equal Employment Opportunity Commission (EEOC) does not have any explicit restrictions regarding whether or not to hire ex-convicts. However, the EEOC has determined that a blanket exclusion of employees with criminal convictions could be discriminatory, in that it may have a disparate impact on minorities.[7] Therefore, such issues are generally handled on a case-by-case basis and depend heavily on the risk and sensitivity of the particular job position. As discussed above, many IT jobs and especially information security jobs are highly sensitive, but that does not mean that you can do whatever you want on this issue. Make sure you label job requisitions for IT personnel, and especially security personnel, as being very sensitive, requiring a clean background check.

This ambiguity in laws can be a major problem in establishing your own policies. Based on the lack of clear regulations on this point, many companies prohibit interviewers from asking job applicants about criminal background activities, unless a clean slate is an explicit, *bona fide* job requirement. Additionally, in many companies, you can only ask about actual criminal convictions, and not mere indictments or arrests. So, you may be allowed to find out that a job applicant was convicted of unsuccessfully trying to hack into a system and steal one million dollars. However, you may *not* be able to find out about another job applicant who successfully stole ten times that amount, but was acquitted on a technicality. Because the former case resulted in conviction but the latter was dismissed, you may only get the useful information about the first.

Your best bet here is to check with your Human Resources organization. After all, these folks get paid to know about the laws in your area regarding recruitment and to interpret those laws within your organization. Get a copy of any restrictions on interview questions or hiring limitations in writing from your HR organization before moving forward.

BACKGROUND CHECKS THAT REALLY MEAN SOMETHING

One of the most important things you can do to ensure the trustworthiness of your employee base is good old-fashioned background checks of potential hires. Start with investigating the references included in the candidate's resume. Some organizations just assume that the recruiter or headhunter who identified the candidate double-checked all references. Unfortunately, in the vast majority of cases, that is just not true. To conduct a thorough interview process, call each reference and verify the candidate's background and skills. Any discrepancies could indicate a big problem that you can nip in the bud in the interview process.

Beyond calling references, you may want to consider checking with the National Fraud Center (http://www.nationalfraud.com) or other background checking services to see if they have any records indicating fraudulent activity by the interviewee. These services are available for a nominal fee and can provide significant value to an organization. A record with the National Fraud Center is a significant red flag in the hiring process.

Although it has less value, you also may want to check the credit history of the potential employee. Credit histories have less value in the employment process simply because a large debt load and even a history of failure to pay debts may simply indicate that person really just needs a job. Credit problems do not necessarily indicate the risk factor of a potential hire. Carefully consider your policy on credit checks, and document in writing how you will use this information in your hiring decisions. What would you do if someone has bad credit? Would you not hire them? You may determine that credit checks do not really provide you the information you need to make hiring decisions.

Many companies also perform drug testing before any new employees can start a job. While some people consider these tests invasive, they are becoming quite commonplace. (I personally do not think such tests are very persuasive in determining someone's criminal background with respect to computer attacks.)

Reference checks, fraud reviews, credit checks, and drug tests are not enough to ensure the trustworthiness of employees for extremely sensitive job positions. Consider ethical hacking consultants who are paid to break into the networks of clients who request penetration tests. These employees have access to the keys to their clients' kingdom, and permission to storm the castle looking for valuables. Likewise, the leaders of an information security team and chief system administrators have access to all information stored on an organization's computers. For these highly sensitive positions, when possible, hire only people that you have known for at least 1 year. For these tasks, promote from within, or use people whose backgrounds you have personally witnessed for over a year to ensure you can trust them. Such a policy can obviously limit the speed of growth of your organization, but it is a good start in establishing the trustworthiness of the top of your IT and security groups.

ESTABLISH A MENTOR PROGRAM

One of the most effective things you can do to help detect suspicious activity by new employees in an IT organization is to develop a mentor program. After doing strong reference and background checks, assign every new employee a

Global –
Health Insurance

mentor who is a more senior, trusted member of staff. Each new hire should get a mentor for six to twelve months. Mentors are officially tasked as part of their job description with supporting new employees in their transition to the company.

In addition to helping the new employee, the mentor also acts as the eyes and ears of the company. The mentor can ensure that the new employee has the skills and attitude necessary to do the job, without exposing the company to risk. If mentors suspect that new hires have ill-will toward the company or are conducting insider attacks, they should report their concerns to management. This is not to say that mentors should be Big Brother, silently stalking every move of the new hire. However, mentors should have general knowledge of the activities of their assigned new hires. Not only can mentors help improve security through detecting and even preventing insider attacks, they can also be quite helpful in improving the productivity of new employees by getting them up to speed quickly.

WE ARE FROM THE GOVERNMENT, AND WE ARE HERE TO HELP

If you decide to hire ex-criminal hackers and you work for a U.S.-based company, you could benefit from a program established by the U.S. Department of Labor to help lower the financial risk companies face when hiring high-risk employees, such as ex-convicts. To encourage employers to hire such people, this federally funded Bonding Program is available to employers free of charge. The Department of Labor highlights the benefits of this program at its Web site as follows:[8]

> Jobseekers who have in the past committed a fraudulent or dishonest act, or who have demonstrated other past behavior which casts doubt upon their credibility or honesty, often experience a special barrier to gaining employment due to their personal backgrounds. Such persons are routinely classified as "at-risk" job applicants.
>
> These jobseekers, whose past life experience raises an obstacle to their future ability to secure employment, could benefit from the Federal Bonding Program. Created in 1966 by the U.S. Department of Labor, the Federal Bonding Program helps to alleviate employers concerns that at-risk job applicants would be untrustworthy workers by allowing them to purchase fidelity bonds to indemnify them for loss of money or property sustained through the dishonest acts of their employees...It is like a "guarantee" to the employer that the person hired will be an honest worker.

Keep in mind, however, that the bond only covers up to $5000 in damages. Admittedly, in a computer attack, $5000 in damages can occur in milliseconds. Still, this insurance program, which is operated for the Department of Labor by Travelers Property Casualty, may be helpful.

You can expand the coverage beyond $5000, but the additional coverage costs come out of your pockets, and not the taxpayers'. Additionally, if, instead of doing interviews, you are the one looking for a job and have a spotty record, you can get bonded yourself, to help assuage any concerns a potential employer may face.

BEYOND EMPLOYEE ISSUES: CONSULTANTS AND CONTRACTORS

A final but very important point to consider regarding the potential insider threat of ex-criminal hackers goes beyond the borders of your own organization. Sure, you would never hire someone who was widely known throughout the computer underground as "Death Kiddie" and served 5 years in prison for wreaking hacking havoc on another company, but what about the firms you hire for IT consulting or outsourcing? Contractors, consultants, or even temporary employees could easily be attacking your organization from the inside.

There have been cases where a temp gets a job with a particular organization for a few short weeks just for the purposes of installing backdoors and other hacking tools on the organization's internal systems. After the brief stint as a temp is over, the attacker covertly controls these hacking tools from the privacy of his own home. Furthermore, some of the world's largest information security consulting firms hire ex-criminal hackers or sub-contract their security business to ex-criminals. These people may be assigned to your ethical hacking exercises, firewall deployments, or security design tasks if you contract for consulting services from such companies. Do you trust these people? Do their hiring practices regarding ex-criminal hackers meet your own internal policies?

To deal with this problem, you need to be aware of the threat and require your contractors and temp agencies to carefully screen the applicants they send to your company. Similarly, before signing a contract for a project with a consulting company, ask about the consultant's hiring practices with respect to background checks and employing ex-criminal hackers. Make sure that your consultant's answer to this question lines up with your own company's philosophy and policies.

CONCLUSION

Most information security organizations do not pay much attention to the criminal backgrounds of their own employee base. You should carefully consider what impact such backgrounds should have on your hiring process, and coordinate your explicit policies with your Human Resources organization. Do not shun ex-criminal hackers for every job, but instead, carefully consider the particular job requirements and risks. By carefully structuring your

Global –
Health Insurance

own hiring program, as well as selecting contractors and consultants with a similar philosophy, you can make sure your organization is properly protected.

REFERENCES

1. Power, R. Computer Security Issues and Trends: 2002 CSI/ FBI Computer Crime and Security Survey, April **2002**, http:// www.gocsi.com/press/20020407.html.
2. Analysis of Recidivism Rates for Participants of the Academic/ Vocational/Transition Education Programs offered by the Virginia Department of Correctional Education, June 2000, http://www.easternlincs.org/correctional_education/ Hull.pdf.
3. *2600* Magazine, subscription information, http:// www.2600.org/magazine/.
4. Littman, J.; Brown, L. *The Watchman: The Twisted Life and Crimes of Serial Hacker Kevin Poulsen*, 1997.
5. The Fugitive Game: Online with Kevin Mitnick, Jonathan Littman, Little Brown, 1997.
6. Shimomura, T.; John Markoff, H. *Takedown*, 1996.
7. Ledford, J.L. Hiring Managers Face Challenges with "High-Risk" Candidates. Smart Pros. September **2001**, http:// finance.pro2net.com/x28047.xml.
8. Federal Bonding Program Information from the Department of Labor, http://wtw.doleta.gov/documents/ fedbonding.asp.

Global – Health Insurance

Hackers: Tools and Techniques

Ed Skoudis, CISSP
Senior Security Consultant, Intelguardians Network Intelligence, Howell, New Jersey, U.S.A.

Abstract
Many of the tools described in this entry have dual personalities; they can be used for good or evil. When used by malicious individuals, the tools allow a motivated attacker to gain access to a network, mask the fact that a compromise occurred, or even bring down service, thereby impacting large masses of users. When used by security practitioners with proper authorization, some tools can be used to measure the security stance of their own organizations, by conducting "ethical hacking" tests to find vulnerabilities before attackers do.

Recent headlines demonstrate that the latest crop of hacker tools and techniques can be highly damaging to an organization's sensitive information and reputation. With the rise of powerful, easy-to-use, and widely distributed hacker tools, many in the security industry have observed that today is the golden age of hacking. The purpose of this entry is to describe the tools in widespread use today for compromising computer and network security. Additionally, for each tool and technique described, the entry presents practical advice on defending against each type of attack.

The terminology applied to these tools and their users has caused some controversy, particularly in the computer underground. Traditionally, and particularly in the computer underground, the term "hacker" is a benign word, referring to an individual who is focused on determining how things work and devising innovative approaches to addressing computer problems. To differentiate these noble individuals from a nasty attacker, this school of thought labels malicious attackers as "crackers." While hackers are out to make the world a better place, crackers want to cause damage and mayhem. To avoid the confusion often associated with these terms, in this entry, the terms "system and security administrator" and "security practitioner" will be used to indicate an individual who has a legitimate and authorized purpose for running these tools. The term "attacker" will be used for those individuals who seek to cause damage to systems or who are not authorized to run such tools.

CAVEAT

The purpose of this entry is to explain the various computer underground tools in use today, and to discuss defensive techniques for addressing each type of tool. This entry is *not* designed to encourage attacks. Furthermore, the tools described below are for illustration purposes only, and mention in this entry is *not* an endorsement. If readers feel compelled to experiment with these tools, they should do so at their own risk, realizing that such tools frequently have viruses or other undocumented features that could damage networks and information systems. Curious readers who want to use these tools should conduct a thorough review of the source code, or at least install the tools on a separate, air-gapped network to protect sensitive production systems.

GENERAL TRENDS IN THE COMPUTER UNDERGROUND

The Smart Get Smarter, and the Rise of the Script Kiddie

The best and brightest minds in the computer underground are conducting probing research and finding new vulnerabilities and powerful, novel attacks on a daily basis. The ideas and deep research done by super-smart attackers and security practitioners are being implemented in software programs and scripts. Months of research into how a particular operating system implements its password scheme is being rendered in code, so even a clueless attacker (often called a "script kiddie") can conduct a highly sophisticated attack with just a point-and-click. Although the script kiddie may not understand the tools' true function and nuances, most of the attack is automated.

In this environment, security practitioners must be careful not to underestimate their adversaries' capabilities. Often, security and system administrators think of their potential attackers as mere teenage kids cruising the Internet looking for easy prey. While this assessment is sometimes accurate, it masks two major concerns. First, some of these teenage kids are amazingly intelligent, and

Encyclopedia of Information Assurance DOI: 10.1081/E-EIA-120046287
Copyright © 2011 by Taylor & Francis. All rights reserved.

Global – Health Insurance

can wreak havoc on a network. Second, attackers may not be just kids; organized crime, terrorists, and even foreign governments have taken to sponsoring cyberattacks.

Wide Distribution of High-Quality Tools

Another trend in the computing underground involves the widespread distribution of tools. In the past (a decade ago), powerful attack tools were limited to a core group of elites in the computer underground. Today, hundreds of Web sites are devoted to the sharing of tools for every attacker (and security practitioner) on the planet. FAQs abound describing how to penetrate any type of operating system. These overall trends converge in a world where smart attackers have detailed knowledge of undermining our systems, while the not-so-smart attackers grow more and more plentiful. To address this increasing threat, system administrators and security practitioners must understand these tools and how to defend against them. The remainder of this entry describes many of these very powerful tools in widespread use today, together with practical defensive tips for protecting one's network from each type of attack.

NETWORK MAPPING AND PORT SCANNING

When launching an attack across a TCP/IP network (such as the Internet or a corporate intranet), an attacker needs to know what addresses are active, how the network topology is constructed, and which services are available. A network mapper identifies systems that are connected to the target network. Given a network address range, the network mapper will send packets to each possible address to determine which addresses have machines.

By sending a simple Internet Control Message Protocol (ICMP) packet to a server (a "ping"), the mapping tool can discover if a server is connected to the network. For those networks that block incoming pings, many of the mapping tools available today can send a single SYN packet to attempt to open a connection to a server. If a server is listening, the SYN packet will trigger an ACK if the port is open, and potentially a "Port Unreachable" message if the port is closed. Regardless of whether the port is open or closed, the response indicates that the address has a machine listening. With this list of addresses, an attacker can refine the attack and focus on these listening systems.

A port scanner identifies open ports on a system. There are 65,535 TCP ports and 65,535 UDP ports, some of which are open on a system, but most of which are closed. Common services are associated with certain ports. For example, TCP Port 80 is most often used by Web servers, TCP Port 23 is used by Telnet daemons, and TCP Port 25 is used for server-to-server mail exchange across the Internet. By conducting a port scan, an attacker will send packets to each and every port. Essentially, ports are rather like doors on a machine. At any one of the thousands of doors available, common services will be listening. A port scanning tool allows an attacker to knock on every one of those doors to see who answers.

Some scanning tools include TCP fingerprinting capabilities. While the Internet Engineering Task Force (IETF) has carefully specified TCP and IP in various Requests for Comments (RFCs), not all packet options have standards associated with them. Without standards for how systems should respond to illegal packet formats, different vendors' TCP/IP stacks respond differently to illegal packets. By sending various combinations of illegal packet options (such as initiating a connection with an RST packet, or combining other odd and illegal TCP code bits), an attacker can determine what type of operating system is running on the target machine. For example, by conducting a TCP fingerprinting scan, an attacker can determine if a machine is running Cisco IOS, Sun Solaris, or Microsoft Windows 2000. In some cases, even the particular version or service pack level can be determined using this technique.

After utilizing network mapping tools and port scanners, an attacker will know which addresses on the target network have listening machines, which ports are open on those machines (and therefore which services are running), and which operating system platforms are in use. This treasure trove of information is useful to the attacker in refining the attack. With this data, the attacker can search for vulnerabilities on the particular services and systems to attempt to gain access.

Nmap, written by Fyodor, is one of the most full-featured mapping and scanning tools available today. Nmap, which supports network mapping, port scanning, and TCP fingerprinting, can be found at http://www.insecure.org/nmap.

Network Mapping and Port Scanning Defenses

To defend against network mapping and port scans, the administrator should remove all unnecessary systems and close all unused ports. To accomplish this, the administrator must disable and remove unneeded services from the machine. Only those services that have an absolute, defined business need should be running. A security administrator should also periodically scan the systems to determine if any unneeded ports are open. When discovered, these unneeded ports must be disabled.

VULNERABILITY SCANNING

Once the target systems are identified with a port scanner and network mapper, an attacker will search to determine if any vulnerabilities are present on the victim machines. Thousands of vulnerabilities have been discovered,

Global – Health Insurance

allowing a remote attacker to gain a toehold on a machine or to take complete administrative control. An attacker could try each of these vulnerabilities on each system by entering individual commands to test for every vulnerability, but conducting an exhaustive search could take years. To speed up the process, attackers use automated scanning tools to quickly search for vulnerabilities on the target.

These automated vulnerability scanning tools are essentially databases of well-known vulnerabilities with an engine that can read the database, connect to a machine, and check to see if it is vulnerable to the exploit. The effectiveness of the tool in discovering vulnerabilities depends on the quality and thoroughness of its vulnerability database. For this reason, the best vulnerability scanners support the rapid release and update of the vulnerability database and the ability to create new checks using a scripting language.

High-quality commercial vulnerability scanning tools are widely available, and are often used by security practitioners and attackers to search for vulnerabilities. On the freeware front, SATAN (the Security Administrator Tool for Analyzing Network) was one of the first widely distributed automated vulnerability scanners, introduced in 1995. More recently, Nessus has been introduced as a free, open-source vulnerability scanner available at http://www.nessus.org. The Nessus project, which is led by Renaud Deraison, provides a fullfeatured scanner for identifying vulnerabilities on remote systems. It includes source code and a scripting language for writing new vulnerability checks, allowing it to be highly customized by security practitioners and attackers alike.

While Nessus is a general-purpose vulnerability scanner, looking for holes in numerous types of systems and platforms, some vulnerability scanners are much more focused on particular types of systems. For example, Whisker is a full-feature vulnerability scanning tool focusing on Web server CGI scripts. Written by Rain Forest Puppy, Whisker can be found at http://www.wiretrip.net/rfp.

Vulnerability Scanning Defenses

As described above, the administrator must close unused ports. Additionally, to eliminate the vast majority of system vulnerabilities, system patches must be applied in a timely fashion. All organizations using computers should have a defined change control procedure that specifies when and how system patches will be kept up-to-date.

Security practitioners should also conduct periodic vulnerability scans of their own networks to find vulnerabilities before attackers do. These scans should be conducted on a regular basis (such as quarterly or even monthly for sensitive networks), or when major network changes are implemented. The discovered vulnerabilities must be addressed in a timely fashion by updating system configurations or applying patches.

WARDIALING

A cousin of the network mapper and scanner, a wardialing tool is used to discover target systems across a telephone network. Organizations often spend large amounts of money in securing their network from a full, frontal assault over the Internet by implementing a firewall, intrusion detection system, and secure DMZ. Unfortunately, many attackers avoid this route and instead look for other ways into the network. Modems left on users' desktops or old, forgotten machines often provide the simplest way into a target network.

Wardialers, also known as "demon dialers," dial a series of telephone numbers, attempting to locate modems on the victim network. An attacker will determine the telephone extensions associated with the target organization. This information is often gleaned from a Web site listing telephone contacts, employee newsgroup postings with telephone contact information in the signature line, or even general employee e-mail. Armed with one or a series of telephone numbers, the attacker will enter into the wardialing tool ranges of numbers associated with the original number (e.g., if an employee's telephone number in a newsgroup posting is listed as 555-1212, the attacker will dial 555-XXXX). The wardialer will automatically dial each number, listen for the familiar wail of a modem carrier tone, and make a list of all telephone numbers with modems listening.

With the list of modems generated by the wardialer, the attacker will dial each discovered modem using a terminal program or other client. Upon connecting to the modem, the attacker will attempt to identify the system based on its banner information and see if a password is required. Often, no password is required, because the modem was put in place by a clueless user requiring after-hours access and not wanting to bother using approved methods. If a password is required, the attacker will attempt to guess passwords commonly associated with the platform or company.

Some wardialing tools also support the capability of locating a repeat dial-tone, in addition to the ability to detect modems. The repeat dial-tone is a great find for the attacker, as it could allow for unrestricted dialing from a victim's PBX system to anywhere in the world. If an attacker finds a line on PBX supporting repeat dial-tone in the same local dialing exchange, the attacker can conduct international wardialing, with all phone bills paid for by the victim with the misconfigured PBX.

The most fully functional wardialing tool available today is distributed by The Hacker's Choice (THC) group. Known as THC-Scan, the tool was written by Van Hauser and can be found at http://inferno.tusculum.edu/thc. THC-Scan 2.0 supports many advanced features, including sequential or randomized dialing, dialing through a network out-dial, modem carrier and repeat dial-tone detection, and rudimentary detection avoidance capabilities.

Wardialing Defenses

The best defense against wardialing attacks is a strong modem policy that prohibits the use of modems and incoming lines without a defined business need. The policy should also require the registration of all modems with a business need in a centralized database only accessible by a security or system administrator.

Additionally, security personnel should conduct periodic wardialing exercises of their own networks to find the modems before the attackers do. When a phone number with an unregistered modem is discovered, the physical device must be located and deactivated. While finding such devices can be difficult, network defenses depend on finding these renegade modems before an attacker does.

NETWORK EXPLOITS: SNIFFING, SPOOFING, AND SESSION HIJACKING

TCP/IP, the underlying protocol suite that makes up the Internet, was not originally designed to provide security services. Likewise, the most common data-link type used with TCP/IP, Ethernet, is fundamentally unsecure. A whole series of attacks are possible given these vulnerabilities of the underlying protocols. The most widely used and potentially damaging attacks based on these network vulnerabilities are sniffing, spoofing, and session hijacking.

Sniffing

Sniffers are extremely useful tools for an attacker and are therefore a fundamental element of an attacker's toolchest. Sniffers allow an attacker to monitor data passing across a network. Given their capability to monitor network traffic, sniffers are also useful for security practitioners and network administrators in troubleshooting networks and conducting investigations. Sniffers exploit characteristics of several data-link technologies, including Token Ring and especially Ethernet.

Ethernet, the most common LAN technology, is essentially a broadcast technology. When Ethernet LANs are constructed using hubs, all machines connected to the LAN can monitor all data on the LAN segment. If userIDs, passwords, or other sensitive information are sent from one machine (e.g., a client) to another machine (e.g., a server or router) on the same LAN, all other systems connected to the LAN could monitor the data. A sniffer is a hardware or software tool that gathers all data on a LAN segment. When a sniffer is running on a machine gathering all network traffic that passes by the system, the Ethernet

interface and the machine itself are said to be in "promiscuous mode."

Many commonly used applications, such as Telnet, FTP, POP (the Post Office Protocol used for e-mail), and even some Web applications, transmit their passwords and sensitive data without any encryption. Any attacker on a broadcast Ethernet segment can use a sniffer to gather these passwords and data.

Attackers who take over a system often install a software sniffer on the compromised machine. This sniffer acts as a sentinel for the attacker, gathering sensitive data that moves by the compromised system. The sniffer gathers this data, including passwords, and stores it in a local file or transmits it to the attacker. The attacker then uses this information to compromise more and more systems. The attack methodology of installing a sniffer on one compromised machine, gathering data passing that machine, and using the sniffed information to take over other systems is referred to as an island-hopping attack.

Numerous sniffing tools are available across the Internet. The most fully functional sniffing tools include Sniffit (by Brecht Claerhout, available at http://reptile.rug.ac.be/~coder/sniffit/sniffit.html) and Snort (by Martin Roesch, available at http://www.clark.net/~roesch/security.html). Some operating systems ship with their own sniffers installed by default, notably Solaris (with the snoop tool) and some varieties of Linux (which ship with tcpdump). Other commercial sniffers are also available from a variety of vendors.

Sniffing defenses

The best defense against sniffing attacks is to encrypt the data in transit. Instead of sending passwords or other sensitive data in cleartext, the application or network should encrypt the data (SSH, secure Telnet, etc.).

Another defense against sniffers is to eliminate the broadcast nature of Ethernet. By utilizing a switch instead of a hub to create a LAN, the damage that can be done with a sniffer is limited. A switch can be configured so that only the required source and destination ports on the switch carry the traffic. Although they are on the same LAN, all other ports on the switch (and the machines connected to those ports) do not see this data. Therefore, if one system is compromised on a LAN, a sniffer installed on this machine will not be capable of seeing data exchanged between other machines on the LAN. Switches are therefore useful in improving security by minimizing the data a sniffer can gather, and also help to improve network performance.

IP Spoofing

Another network-based attack involves altering the source address of a computer to disguise the attacker and exploit weak authentication methods. IP address spoofing allows

Global – Health Insurance

an attacker to use the IP address of another machine to conduct an attack. If the target machines rely on the IP address to authenticate, IP spoofing can give an attacker access to the systems. Additionally, IP spoofing can make it very difficult to apprehend an attacker, because logs will contain decoy addresses and not the real source of the attack. Many of the tools described in other sections of this entry rely on IP spoofing to hide the true origin of the attack.

Spoofing defenses

Systems should not use IP addresses for authentication. Any functions or applications that rely solely on IP address for authentication should be disabled or replaced. In UNIX, the "**r**-commands" (**rlogin**, **rsh**, **rexec**, and **rcp**) are notoriously subject to IP spoofing attacks. UNIX trust relationships allow an administrator to manage systems using the **r**-commands without providing a password. Instead of a password, the IP address of the system is used for authentication. This major weakness should be avoided by replacing the **r**-commands with administration tools that utilize strong authentication. One such tool, secure shell (SSH), uses strong cryptography to replace the weak authentication of the **r**-commands. Similarly, all other applications that rely on IP addresses for critical security and administration functions should be replaced.

Additionally, an organization should deploy anti-spoof filters on its perimeter networks that connect the organization to the Internet and business partners. Anti-spoof filters drop all traffic coming from outside the network claiming to come from the inside. With this capability, such filters can prevent some types of spoofing attacks, and should be implemented on all perimeter network routers.

Session Hijacking

While sniffing allows an attacker to view data associated with network connections, a session hijack tool allows an attacker to take over network connections, kicking off the legitimate user or sharing a login. Session hijacking tools are used against services with persistent login sessions, such as Telnet, rlogin, or FTP. For any of these services, an attacker can hijack a session and cause a great deal of damage.

A common scenario illustrating session hijacking involves a machine, Alice, with a user logged in to remotely administer another system, Bob, using Telnet. Eve, the attacker, sits on a network segment between Alice and Bob (either Alice's LAN, Bob's LAN, or between any of the routers between Alice's and Bob's LANs). Fig. 1 illustrates this scenario in more detail.

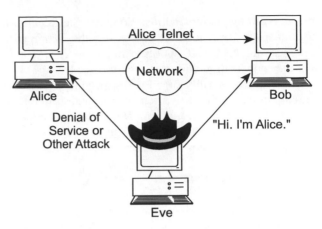

Fig. 1 Eve hijacks the session between Alice and Bob.

Using a session hijacking tool, Eve can do any of the following:

- *Monitor Alice's session.* Most session hijacking tools allow attackers to monitor all connections available on the network and select which connections they want to hijack.
- *Insert commands into the session.* An attacker may just need to add one or two commands into the stream to reconfigure Bob. In this type of hijack, the attacker never takes full control of the session. Instead, Alice's login session to Bob has a small number of commands inserted, which will be executed on Bob as though Alice had typed them.
- *Steal the session.* This feature of most session hijacking tools allows an attacker to grab the session from Alice, and directly control it. Essentially, the Telnet client control is shifted from Alice to Eve, without Bob's knowing.
- *Give the session back.* Some session hijacking tools allow the attacker to steal a session, interact with the server, and then smoothly give the session back to the user. While the session is stolen, Alice is put on hold while Eve controls the session. With Alice on hold, all commands typed by Alice are displayed on Eve's screen, but not transmitted to Bob. When Eve is finished making modifications on Bob, Eve transfers control back to Alice.

For a successful hijack to occur, the attacker must be on a LAN segment between Alice and Bob. A session hijacking tool monitors the connection using an integrate sniffer, observing the TCP sequence numbers of the packets going each direction. Each packet sent from Alice to Bob has a unique TCP sequence number used by Bob to verify that all packets are received and put in proper order. Likewise, all packets going back from Bob to Alice have sequence numbers. A session hijacking tool sniffs the packets to determine these sequence numbers. When a session is

Global –
Health Insurance

hijacked (through command insertion or session stealing), the hijacking tool automatically uses the appropriate sequence numbers and spoofs Alice's address, taking over the conversation with Bob where Alice left off.

One of the most fully functional session hijacking tool available today is Hunt, written by Kra and available at http://www.cri.cz/kra/index.html. Hunt allows an attacker to monitor and steal sessions, insert single commands, and even give a session back to the user.

Session hijacking defenses

The best defense against session hijacking is to avoid the use of insecure protocols and applications for sensitive sessions. Instead of using the easy-to-hijack (and easy-to-sniff) Telnet application, a more secure, encrypted session tool should be used. Because the attacker does not have the session encryption keys, an encrypted session cannot be hijacked. The attacker will simply see encrypted gibberish using Hunt, and will only be able to reset the connection, not take it over or insert commands.

Secure shell offers strong authentication and encrypted sessions, providing a highly secure alternative to Telnet and rlogin. Furthermore, ssh includes a secure file transfer capability (SCP) to replace traditional FTP. Other alternatives are available, including secure, encrypted Telnet or a virtual private network (VPN) established between the source and destination.

DENIAL-OF-SERVICE ATTACKS

Denial-of-service attacks are among the most common exploits available today. As their name implies, a denial-of-service attack prevents legitimate users from being able to access a system. With E-commerce applications constituting the lifeblood of many organizations and a growing piece of the world economy, a well-timed denial-of-service attack can cause a great deal of damage. By bringing down servers that control sensitive machinery or other functions, these attacks could also present a real physical threat to life and limb. An attacker could cause the service denial by flooding a system with bogus traffic, or even purposely causing the server to crash. Countless denial-of-service attacks are in widespread use today, and can be found at http://packetstorm.securify.com/exploits/DoS. The most often used network-based denial-of-service attacks fall into two categories: malformed packet attacks and packet floods.

Malformed Packet Attacks

This type of attack usually involves one or two packets that are formatted in an unexpected way. Many vendor product implementations do not take into account all variations of user entries or packet types. If the software handles such

errors poorly, the system may crash when it receives such packets. A classic example of this type of attack involves sending IP fragments to a system that overlap with each other (the fragment offset values are incorrectly set). Some unpatched Windows and Linux systems will crash when they encounter such packets. The teardrop attack is an example of a tool that exploits this IP fragmentation handling vulnerability. Other malformed packet attacks that exploit other weaknesses in TCP/IP implementations include the colorfully named WinNuke, Land, LaTierra, NewTear, Bonk, Boink, etc.

Packet Flood Attacks

Packet flood denial-of-service tools send a deluge of traffic to a system on the network, overwhelming its capability to respond to legitimate users. Attackers have devised numerous techniques for creating such floods, with the most popular being SYN floods, directed broadcast attacks, and distributed denial-of-service tools.

SYN flood tools initiate a large number of half-open connections with a system by sending a series of SYN packets. When any TCP connection is established, a three-way handshake occurs. The initiating system (usually the client) sends a SYN packet to the destination to establish a sequence number for all packets going from source to destination in that session. The destination responds with a SYN-ACK packet, which acknowledges the sequence number for packets going from source to destination, and establishes an initial sequence number for packets going the opposite direction. The source completes the three-way handshake by sending an ACK to the destination. The three-way handshake is completed, and communication (actual data transfer) can occur.

SYN floods take advantage of a weakness in TCP's three-way handshake. By sending only spoofed SYN packets and never responding to the SYN-ACK, an attacker can exhaust a server's ability to maintain state of all the initiated sessions. With a huge number of so-called half-open connections, a server cannot handle any new, legitimate traffic. Rather than filling up all of the pipe bandwidth to a server, only the server's capacity to handle session initiations needs to be overwhelmed (in most network configurations, a server's ability to handle SYNs is lower than the total bandwidth to the site). For this reason, SYN flooding is the most popular packet flood attack. Other tools are also available that flood systems with ICMP and UDP packets, but they merely consume bandwidth, so an attacker would require a bigger connection than the victim to cut off all service.

Another type of packet flood that allows attackers to amplify their bandwidth is the directed broadcast attack. Often called a smurf attack, named after the first tool to exploit this technique, directed broadcast attacks utilize a third-party's network as an amplifier for the packet flood. In a smurf attack, the attacker locates a network on the

Global –
Health Insurance

Internet that will respond to a broadcast ICMP message (essentially a ping to the network's broadcast address). If the network is configured to allow broadcast requests and responses, all machines on the network will send a response to the ping. By spoofing the ICMP request, the attacker can have all machines on the third-party network send responses to the victim. For example, if an organization has 30 hosts on a single DMZ network connected to the Internet, an attacker can send a spoofed network broadcast ping to the DMZ. All 30 hosts will send a response to the spoofed address, which would be the ultimate victim. By sending repeated messages to the broadcast network, the attacker has amplified bandwidth by a factor of 30. Even an attacker with only a 56-kbps dial-up line could fill up a T1 line (1.54 Mbps) with that level of amplification. Other directed broadcast attack tools include Fraggle and Papasmurf.

A final type of denial-of-service that has received considerable press is the distributed denial-of-service attack. Essentially based on standard packet flood concepts, distributed denial-of-service attacks were used to cripple many major Internet sites in February 2000. Tools such as Trin00, Tribe Flood Network 2000 (TFN2K), and Stacheldraht all support this type of attack. To conduct a distributed denial-of-service attack, an attacker must find numerous vulnerable systems on the Internet. Usually, a remote buffer overflow attack (described below) is used to take over a dozen, a hundred, or even thousands of machines. Simple daemon processes, called zombies, are installed on these machines taken over by the attacker. The attacker communicates with this network of zombies using a control program. The control program is used to send commands to the hundreds or thousands of zombies, requesting them to take uniform action simultaneously.

The most common action to be taken is to simultaneously launch a packet flood against a target. While a traditional SYN flood would deluge a target with packets from one host, a distributed denial-of-service attack would send packets from large numbers of zombies, rapidly exhausting the capacity of even very highbandwidth, well-designed sites. Many distributed denial-of-service attack tools support SYN, UDP, and ICMP flooding, smurf attacks, as well as some malformed packet attacks. Any one or all of these options can be selected by the attacker using the control program.

Denial-of-Service Attack Defenses

To defend against malformed packet attacks, system patches and security fixes must be regularly applied. Vendors frequently update their systems with patches to handle a new flavor of denial-of-service attack. An organization must have a program for monitoring vendor and industry security bulletins for security fixes, and a controlled method for implementing these fixes soon after they are announced and tested.

For packet flood attacks, critical systems should have underlying network architectures with multiple, redundant paths, eliminating a single point of failure. Furthermore, adequate bandwidth is a must. Also, some routers and firewalls support traffic flow control to help ease the burden of a SYN flood.

Finally, by configuring an Internet-accessible network appropriately, an organization can minimize the possibility that it will be used as a jumping-off point for smurf and distributed denial-of-service attacks. To prevent the possibility of being used as a smurf amplifier, the external router or firewall should be configured to drop all directed broadcast requests from the Internet. To lower the chance of being used in a distributed denial-of-service attack, an organization should implement anti-spoof filters on external routers and firewalls to make sure that all outgoing traffic has a source IP address of the site. This egress filtering prevents an attacker from sending spoofed packets from a zombie or other denial-of-service tool located on the network. Antispoof ingress filters, which drop all packets from the Internet claiming to come from one's internal network, are also useful in preventing some denial-of-service attacks.

STACK-BASED BUFFER OVERFLOWS

Stack-based buffer overflow attacks are commonly used by an attacker to take over a system remotely across a network. Additionally, buffer overflows can be employed by local malicious users to elevate their privileges and gain superuser access to a system. Stack-based buffer overflow attacks exploit the way many operating systems handle their stack, an internal data structure used by running programs to store data temporarily. When a function call is made, the current state of the executing program and variables to be passed to the function are pushed on the stack. New local variables used by the function are also allocated space on the stack. Additionally, the stack stores the return address of the code calling the function. This return address will be accessed from the stack once the function call is complete. The system uses this address to resume execution of the calling program at the appropriate place. Fig. 2 shows how a stack is constructed.

Most UNIX and all Windows systems have a stack that can hold data and executable code. Because local variables are stored on the stack when a function is called, poor code can be exploited to overrun the boundaries of these variables on the stack. If user input length is not examined by the code, a particular variable on the stack may exceed the memory allocated to it on the stack, overwriting all variables and even the return address for where execution should resume after the function is complete. This operation, called "smashing" the stack, allows an attacker to overflow the local variables to insert executable code and another return address on the stack. Fig. 2 also shows a stack that has been smashed with a buffer overflow.

Global – Health Insurance

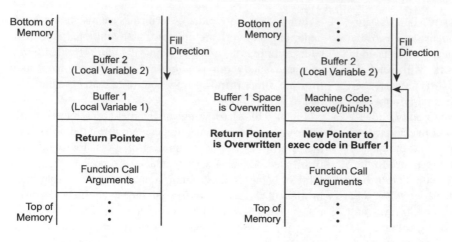

Normal Stack   Smashed Stack

Fig. 2 A normal stack and a stack with a buffer overflow.

The attacker will overflow the buffer on the stack with machine-specific bytecodes that consist of executable commands (usually a shell routine), and a return pointer to begin execution of these inserted commands. Therefore, with very carefully constructed binary code, the attacker can actually enter information as a user into a program that consists of executable code and a new return address. The buggy program will not analyze the length of this input, but will place it on the stack, and actually begin to execute the attacker's code. Such vulnerabilities allow an attacker to break out of the application code, and access any system components with the permissions of the broken program. If the broken program is running with superuser privileges (e.g., SUID root on a UNIX system), the attacker has taken over the machine with a buffer overflow.

Stack-Based Buffer Overflow Defenses

The most thorough defenses against buffer overflow attacks is to properly code software so that it cannot be used to smash the stack. All programs should validate all input from users and other programs, ensuring that it fits into allocated memory structures. Each variable should be checked (including user input, variables from other functions, input from other programs, and even environment variables) to ensure that allocated buffers are adequate to hold the data. Unfortunately, this ultimate solution is only available to individuals who write the programs and those with source code.

Additionally, security practitioners and system administrators should carefully control and minimize the number of SUID programs on a system that users can run and have permissions of other users (such as root). Only SUID programs with an explicit business need should be installed on sensitive systems.

Finally, many stack-based buffer overflow attacks can be avoided by configuring the systems to not execute code from the stack. Notably, Solaris and Linux offer this option. For example, to secure a Solaris system against stack-based buffer overflows, the following lines should be added:

```
/etc/system:

    set noexec_user_stack=1
    set noexec_user_stack_log=1
```

The first line will prevent execution on a stack, and the second line will log any attempt to do so. Unfortunately, some programs legitimately try to run code off the stack. Such programs will crash if this option is implemented. Generally, if the system is single purpose and needs to be secure (e.g., a Web server), this option should be used to prevent stack-based buffer overflow.

ART AND SCIENCE OF PASSWORD CRACKING

The vast majority of systems today authenticate users with a static password. When a user logs in, the password is transmitted to the system, which checks the password to make the decision whether to let the user log in. To make this decision, the system must have a mechanism to compare the user's input with the actual password. Of course, the system could just store all of the passwords locally and compare from this file. Such a file of cleartext passwords, however, would provide a very juicy target for an attacker. To make the target less useful for attackers, most modern operating systems use a one-way hash or encryption mechanism to protect the stored passswords. When a user types in a password, the system hashes the user's entry and compares it to the stored hash. If the two hashes match, the password is correct and the user can login.

Password cracking tools are used to attack this method of password protection. An attacker will use some exploit (often a buffer overflow) to gather the encrypted or hashed password file from a system (on a UNIX system without password shadowing, any user can read the hashed password file). After downloading the hashed password file, the attacker uses a password cracking tool to determine users' passwords. The cracking tool operates using a loop: it guesses a

Global – Health Insurance

password, hashes or encrypts the password, and compares it to the hashed password from the stolen file. If the hashes match, the attacker has the password. If the hashes do not match, the loop begins again with another password guess.

Password cracking tools base their password guesses on a dictionary or a complete brute-force attack, attempting every possible password. Dozens of dictionaries are available online, in a multitude of languages, including English, French, German, Klingon, etc.

Numerous password-cracking tools are available. The most popular and full-functional password crackers include:

- John-the-Ripper, by Solar Designer, focuses on cracking UNIX passwords, and is available at http://www.openwall.com/john/.
- L0phtCrack, used to crack Windows NT passwords, is available at http://www.l0pht.com.

Password Cracking Defenses

The first defense against password cracking is to minimize the exposure of the encrypted/hashed password file. On UNIX systems, shadow password files should be used, which allow only the superuser to read the password file. On Windows NT systems, the SYSKEY feature available in NT 4.0 SP 3 and later should be installed and enabled. Furthermore, all backups and system recovery disks should be stored in physically secured locations and possibly even encrypted.

A strong password policy is a crucial element in ensuring a secure network. A password policy should require password lengths greater than eight characters, require the use of alphanumeric *and* special characters in every password, and force users to have passwords with mixed-case letters. Users must be aware of the issue of weak passwords and be trained in creating memorable, yet difficult-to-guess passwords.

To ensure that passwords are secure and to identify weak passwords, security practitioners should check system passwords on a periodic basis using password cracking tools. When weak passwords are discovered, the security group should have a defined procedure for interacting with users whose passwords can be easily guessed.

Finally, several software packages are available that prevent users from setting their passwords to easily guessed values. When a user establishes a new password, these filtering programs check the password to make sure that it is sufficiently complex and is not just a variation of the user name or a dictionary word. With this kind of tool, users are simply unable to create passwords that are easily guessed, eliminating a significant security issue. For filtering software to be effective, it must be installed on all servers where users establish passwords, including UNIX servers, Windows NT Primary and Back-up Domain Controllers, and Novell servers.

BACKDOORS

Backdoors are programs that bypass traditional security checks on a system, allowing an attacker to gain access to a machine without providing a system password and getting logged. Attackers install backdoors on a machine (or dupe a user into installing one for them) to ensure they will be able to gain access to the system at a later time. Once installed, most backdoors listen on special ports for incoming connections from the attacker across the network. When the attacker connects to the backdoor listener, the traditional userID and password or other forms of authentication are bypassed. Instead, the attacker can gain access to the system without providing a password, or by using a special password used only to enter the backdoor.

Netcat is an incredibly flexible tool written for UNIX by Hobbit and for Windows NT by Weld Pond (both versions are available at http://www.l0pht.com/~weld/netcat/). Among its numerous other uses, Netcat can be used to create a backdoor listener with a superuser-level shell on any TCP or UDP port. For Windows systems, an enormous number of backdoor applications are available, including Back Orifice 2000 (called BO2K for short, and available at http://www.bo2k.com) and hack-a-tack (available at http://www.hack-atack.com).

Backdoor Defenses

The best defense against backdoor programs is for system and security administrators to know what is running on their machines, particularly sensitive systems storing critical information or processing high-value transactions. If a process suddenly appears running as the superuser listening on a port, the administrator needs to investigate. Backdoors listening on various ports can be discovered using the **netstat–na** command on UNIX and Windows NT systems.

Additionally, many backdoor programs (such as BO2K) can be discovered by an anti-virus program, which should be installed on all users' desktops, as well as on servers throughout an organization.

TROJAN HORSES AND ROOTKITS

Another fundamental element of an attacker's toolchest is the Trojan horse program. Like the Trojan horse of ancient Greece, these new Trojan horses appear to have some useful function, but in reality are just disguising some malicious activity. For example, a user may receive an executable birthday card program in electronic mail. When the unsuspecting user activates the birthday card program and watches birthday cakes dance across the screen, the program secretly installs a backdoor or perhaps deletes the users' hard drive. As illustrated in this example, Trojan horses rely on deception—they trick a user or system administrator into

Global – Health Insurance

running them for their (apparent) usefulness, but their true purpose is to attack the user's machine.

Traditional Trojan Horses

A traditional Trojan horse is simply an independent program that can be run by a user or administrator. Numerous traditional Trojan horse programs have been devised, including:

- The familiar birthday card or holiday greeting e-mail attachment described above.
- A software program that claims to be able to turn CD-ROM readers into CD writing devices. Although this feat is impossible to accomplish in software, many users have been duped into downloading this "tool," which promptly deletes their hard drives upon activation.
- A security vulnerability scanner, WinSATAN. This tool claims to provide a convenient security vulnerability scan for system and security administrators using a Windows NT system. Unfortunately, an unsuspecting user running this program will also have a deleted hard drive.

Countless other examples exist. While conceptually unglamorous, traditional Trojan horses can be a major problem if users are not careful and run untrusted programs on their machines.

RootKits

A RootKit takes the concept of a Trojan horse to a much more powerful level. Although the name implies otherwise, RootKits do not allow an attacker to gain "root" (superuser) access to a system. Instead, RootKits allow an attacker who already has superuser access to keep that access by foiling all attempts of an administrator to detect the invasion. RootKits consist of an entire suite of Trojan horse programs that replace or patch critical system programs. The various tools used by administrators to detect attackers on their machines are routinely undermined with RootKits.

Most RootKits include a Trojan horse backdoor program (in UNIX, the /bin/login routine). The attacker will install a new Trojan horse version of /bin/login, overwriting the previous version. The RootKit /bin/login routine includes a special backdoor userID and password so that the attacker can access the system at later times.

Additionally, RootKits include a sniffer and a program to hide the sniffer. An administrator can detect a sniffer on a system by running the **ifconfig** command. If a sniffer is running, the **ifconfig** output will contain the PROMISC flag, an indication that the Ethernet card is in promiscuous mode and therefore is sniffing. RootKit contains a Trojan horse version of **ifconfig** that does not display the PROMISC flag, allowing an attacker to avoid detection.

UNIX-based RootKits also replace other critical system executables, including **ps** and **du**. The **ps** command, emloyed by users and administrators to determine which processes are running, is modified so that an attacker can hide processes. The **du** command, which shows disk utilization, is altered so that the file space taken up by RootKit and the attacker's other programs can be masked.

By replacing programs like /bin/login, ifconfig, ps, du, and numerous others, these RootKit tools become part of the operating system itself. Therefore, RootKits are used to cover the eyes and ears of an administrator. They create a virtual world on the computer that appears benign to the system administrator, when in actuality, an attacker can log in and move around the system with impunity. RootKits have been developed for most major UNIX systems and Windows NT. A whole variety of UNIX RootKits can be found at http://packetstorm.securify.com/UNIX/penetration/rootkits, while an NT RootKit is available at http://www.rootkit.com.

A recent development in this arena is the release of kernel-level RootKits. These RootKits act at the most fundamental levels of an operating system. Rather than replacing application programs such as /bin/login and ifconfig, kernel-level RootKits actually patch the kernel to provide very low-level access to the system. These tools rely on the loadable kernel modules that many new UNIX variants support, including Linux and Solaris. Loadable kernel modules let an administrator add functionality to the kernel on-the-fly, without even rebooting the system. An attacker with superuser access can install a kernel-level RootKit that will allow for the remapping of execution of programs.

When an administrator tries to run a program, the Trojanized kernel will remap the execution request to the attacker's program, which could be a backdoor offering access or other Trojan horse. Because the kernel does the remapping of execution requests, this type of activity is very difficult to detect. If the administrator attempts to look at the remapped file or check its integrity, the program will appear unaltered, because the program's image *is* unaltered. However, when executed, the unaltered program is skipped, and a malicious program is substituted by the kernel. Knark, written by Creed, is a kernel-level RootKit that can be found at http://packetstorm.securify.com/UNIX/penetration/rootkits.

Trojan Horses and RootKit Defenses

To protect against traditional Trojan horses, user awareness is key. Users must understand the risks associated with downloading untrusted programs and running them. They must also be made aware of the problems of running executable attachments in e-mail from untrusted sources.

Additionally, some traditional Trojan horses can be detected and eliminated by antivirus programs. Every end-user computer system (and even servers) should have an effective and up-to-date antivirus program installed.

To defend against RootKits, system and security administrators must use integrity checking programs for critical system files. Numerous tools are available, including the

Global –
Health Insurance

venerable Tripwire, that generate a hash of the executables commonly altered when a RootKit is installed. The administrator should store these hashes on a protected medium (such as a write-protected floppy disk) and periodically check the veracity of the programs on the machine with the protected hashes. Commonly, this type of check is done at least weekly, depending on the sensitivity of the machine. The administrator must reconcile any changes discovered in these critical system files with recent patches. If system files have been altered, and no patches were installed by the administrator, a malicious user or outside attacker may have installed a RootKit. If a RootKit is detected, the safest way to ensure its complete removal is to rebuild the entire operating system and even critical applications.

Unfortunately, kernel-level RootKits cannot be detected with integrity check programs because the integrity checker relies on the underlying kernel to do its work. If the kernel lies to the integrity checker, the results will not show the RootKit installation. The best defense against the kernel-level RootKit is a monolithic kernel that does not support loadable kernel modules. On critical systems (such as firewalls, Internet Web servers, DNS servers, mail servers), administrators should build the systems with complete kernels without support for loadable kernel modules. With this configuration, the system will prevent an attacker from gaining root-level access and patching the kernel in real-time.

OVERALL DEFENSES: INTRUSION DETECTION AND INCIDENT RESPONSE PROCEDURES

Each of the defensive strategies described in this entry deals with particular tools and attacks. In addition to employing each of those strategies, organizations must also be capable of detecting and responding to an attack. These capabilities are realized through the deployment of intrusion detection systems (IDSs) and the implementation of incident response procedures.

IDSs act as burglar alarms on the network. With a database of known attack signatures, IDSs can determine when an attack is underway and alert security and system administration personnel. Acting as early warning systems, IDSs allow an organization to detect an attack in its early stages and minimize the damage that may be caused.

Perhaps even more important than IDSs, documented incident response procedures are among the most critical elements of an effective security program. Unfortunately, even with industry-best defenses, a sufficiently motivated attacker can penetrate the network. To address this possibility, an organization must have procedures defined in advance describing how the organization will react to the

attack. These incident response procedures should specify the roles of individuals in the organization during an attack. The chain of command and escalation procedures should be spelled out in advance. Creating these items during a crisis will lead to costly mistakes.

Truly effective incident response procedures should also be multidisciplinary, not focusing only on information technology. Instead, the roles, responsibilities, and communication channels for the Legal, Human Resources, Media Relations, Information Technology, and Security organizations should all be documented and communicated. Specific members of these organizations should be identified as the core of a Security Incident Response Team (SIRT), to be called together to address an incident when one occurs. Additionally, the SIRT should conduct periodic exercises of the incident response capability to ensure that team members are effective in their roles.

Additionally, with a large number of organizations outsourcing their information technology infrastructure by utilizing Web hosting, desktop management, e-mail, data storage, and other services, the extension of the incident response procedures to these outside organizations can be critical. The contract established with the outsourcing company should carefully state the obligations of the service provider in intrusion detection, incident notification, and participation in incident response. A specific service-level agreement for handling security incidents and the time needed to pull together members of the service company's staff in a SIRT should also be agreed upon.

CONCLUSIONS

While the number and power of these attack tools continues to escalate, system administrators and security personnel should not give up the fight. All of the defensive strategies discussed throughout this entry boil down to doing a thorough and professional job of administering systems: know what is running on the system, keep it patched, ensure appropriate bandwidth is available, utilize IDSs, and prepare a Security Incident Response Team. Although these activities are not easy and can involve a great deal of effort, through diligence, an organization can keep its systems secured and minimize the chance of an attack. By employing intrusion detection systems and sound incident response procedures, even those highly sophisticated attacks that do get through can be discovered and contained, minimizing the impact on the organization. By creating an effective security program with sound defensive strategies, critical systems and information can be protected.

Global – Health Insurance

Halon Fire Suppression Systems

Chris Hare, CISSP, CISA, CISM
Information Systems Auditor, Nortel, Dallas, Texas, U.S.A.

Abstract

Fire suppression in data centers and densely packed systems in wiring closets and network facilities is complicated by the use of wet fire-suppression systems that are used in the remainder of the facility. As is well understood, adding water to an environment packed with operating electrical equipment and possibly battery backup systems can result in as much damage to the systems as the fire itself. In both cases—the fire or the water damage caused by the suppression system—the result is the same: the loss of the devices and a service disruption affecting business operations. This entry discusses fire suppression methods focusing specifically on the history and operation of halon-based gaseous suppression systems.

NOT SIMPLY FIRE PROTECTION

Fire suppression systems are not only concerned with dealing with fire emergencies. This type of equipment and its associated contingency plans and personnel training constitute one component in an organization's business continuity plan. Being able to keep the business functioning and returning it to operation as quickly as possible after a fire event has occurred are primary goals of business continuity systems.

Fire suppression systems assist the organization in returning to operation as quickly as possible by assisting in the protection of personnel, equipment, assets, and records. The security professional, while having a working knowledge of fire suppression systems, should recognize the importance of fire suppression systems in the role of business continuity operations.

UNDERSTANDING FIRE

Before embarking on a discussion of fire suppression, a review of the characteristics associated with fire is necessary. According to the Merseyside Fire Liaison Panel, fire is "a process involving rapid oxidation at elevated temperatures accompanied by the evolution of heated gaseous products of combustion and the emission of visible and invisible radiation."[1]

The fire triangle/tetrahedron illustrated in Fig. 1[1] is a two-dimensional view of the elements necessary for fire to occur: fuel, heat, oxygen, and chemical reaction. Fire suppression systems operate by attempting to remove one or more of these elements, i.e., removing the fuel source or the specific material that is burning, lowering the heat level, removing oxygen from the surrounding air, or interrupting the chemical reaction itself.

The elements of fire did not initially include the chemical reaction that occurs during the fire. It was only after substantial research into the mechanics of fire that the chemical reaction aspect was fully understood: it is the nature of the chemical reaction that allows for the rapid oxidization of the combustible material. Temperatures in a fire can reach 1800°F in rare circumstances, although many fires will not reach 1000°F.[2] With an oxygen-rich environment and sufficient combustible material, a fire can spread quickly through a facility and destroy virtually everything.

CLASSIFYING FIRE

There are four classes of fires, each representing a different group of combustible materials. The use of the correct equipment is essential to suppressing the fire without injury to personnel, equipment, or the environment. The classes of fires are[3]

- Class A: Ordinary combustibles or fibrous material, such as wood, paper, cloth, rubber, and some plastics
- Class B: Flammable or combustible liquids such as gasoline, kerosene, paint, paint thinners, and propane
- Class C: Energized electrical equipment, such as appliances, switches, panel boxes, and power tools
- Class D: Certain combustible metals, such as magnesium, titanium, potassium, and sodium, which burn at high temperatures and give off sufficient oxygen to support combustion

Each fire suppression system has a fire rating or indicator identifying the types of fires the suppression equipment is effective against. Class A fires are extinguished by lowering the temperature of the combustible material below its ignition point using water or dry chemical. Some gas-based suppression systems can be dangerous

Encyclopedia of Information Assurance DOI: 10.1081/E-EIA-120046870

Copyright © 2011 by Taylor & Francis. All rights reserved.

Global –
Health Insurance

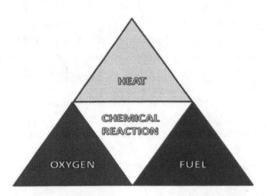

Fig. 1 The fire tetrahedron.
Source: From *Information About the Fire Triangle/Tetrahedron and Combustion*.[1]

when used only on this type of fire.[3] Class B fires, including flammable liquids like gasoline and kerosene, are extinguished using foam- or carbon dioxide-based suppression systems. Water-based systems are not only ineffective with this type of fire, but can efficiently spread the fire across a larger area.[3]

Class C fires involve energized electrical equipment, which fall into the category specifically targeted by halon-based suppression systems. To prevent damage to the equipment, the suppression agent must not be a conductor of electrical energy. It is most common to use dry chemical or gas-based suppression systems when working with this type of fire. The final class of fire, Class D, focuses on fires involving certain types of metals, including magnesium, titanium, potassium, and sodium. These fires require specialized suppression equipment because a by-product of the combustion process is oxygen, which can then reinforce the combustion process. Because of the highly specialized suppression equipment involved, the implementation cost is high. Consequently, additional precautions involving the use, storage, and handling of these metals are part of the protection regimen.

FIRE SUPPRESSION SYSTEMS

Modern facilities include fire suppression systems as required by national and local building codes to protect the facility and the safety of its occupants, as well as to reduce the risk to other structures. There are varieties of suppression systems available to fulfill these requirements:

- Water: Affects the fuel and heat
- Chemical: Affects the combustible material
- Gas: Interrupts the chemical reaction

The selection of any specific fire suppression system will be influenced directly by local and national building codes. Fire suppression systems, from portable fire extinguishers to more elaborate systems, are intended to handle one or more of the various fire classifications.

Water-based systems affect the heat and fuel of the fire. Many people are familiar with the traditional water-based sprinkler systems, which are found in most commercial buildings. These can be wet or dry systems, depending upon whether or not the water is already at the sprinkler head. A major disadvantage to wet sprinkler systems is the loss of a sprinkler head, even accidentally, which typically results in the system discharging its water whether or not it is needed.

Although suitable for most areas in a facility, water-based systems do not interact well with operational computer systems and other electrical equipment. Water, as a good electrical conductor, often results in system failures due to short circuits. Even if the water does not directly result in the destruction of the system, the time to dry it out and restore it to operation is extensive.

Chemical-based systems apply a coating of chemical to the combustible materials, interfering with the fire. They are best used on flammable liquids (Class B) and electrical fires (Class C), although they can be effectively used on Class A fires as well. Chemical-based systems are environmentally safe and commonly use sodium bicarbonate as the primary agent.[4]

Finally, the gas-based system can use a variety of gases including argon, carbon dioxide (CO_2), and halon. Gas-based systems work by affecting the oxygen levels within the environment and interrupting the chemical reaction. Because these suppression systems interrupt the chemical reaction, they can create personnel safety issues that must be addressed during the system design and implementation.

HALON-BASED FIRE SUPPRESSION

Halon has a long history of use as a fire suppression agent. Halon is a generic term referring to a collection of chlorofluorocarbons (CFC) or halocarbons. CFC chemicals were originally developed as refrigerants due to their unique chemical properties.[5] The first halon, known as Halon 104 or carbon tetrachloride was used before the twentieth century despite the toxic by-products from its use.[6] The United States National Library of Medicine Emergency Responder database provides an extensive description of the effects of this highly toxic substance, which can exist in liquid and gaseous forms. Carbon tetrachloride requires the use of extensive protective clothing and self-contained breathing equipment.[7]

Halon 122, or dichlorodifluoromethane, and Halon 1001, or methyl bromide, were discovered between 1900 and 1947. Like Halon 104, both of these chemicals have equally toxic side effects.[7] Halon 1211 is a liquid streaming agent chemically known as bromochlorodifluoromethane.[8] Halon 1211 has been widely used in managing airport and aviation fires.[9] It is less toxic than previous halons developed, but just as deadly from an

Global –
Health Insurance

ozone depletion perspective. However, when used in concentrations above 5%, it should be used only when portable breathing apparatus is used. Unlike the liquid properties of Halon 1211, Halon 1301 is a gas used to flood an area and interrupt the combustion. Halon 1301 is more commonly used in protecting enclosed areas with electrical equipment.

Halon is categorized by the National Fire Protection Association as a "clean agent," meaning it is an electrically non-conducting, volatile, or gaseous fire extinguishant that does not leave a residue upon evaporation.[6] A clean agent fire suppression system is desirable in situations where "live electrical or electronic circuits are in use, the area is normally occupied by personnel, and the protected area contains objects or processes highly susceptible to extensive damage or downtime."[10]

Clean agents are not only effective fire suppression agents, but they also do not leave a residue that could affect or damage the equipment being protected. Commonly used to protect expensive assets such as mainframe computer systems and telecommunications equipment, halon is effective as it does not leave any residue that could result in secondary damage to the equipment.

HALON DISTRIBUTION COMPONENTS

A halon distribution system consists of a number of pressurized cylinders to store the halon, a piping system to deliver the agent to the protection area, and nozzles that disperse the agent. The number of cylinders needed depends upon the size of the area to be protected. The larger the area, the more cylinders required. The piping system is a pressurized or "closed" system of a particular size to carry the agent to the nozzles. Because the system is under pressure, repairs or work around the pipe systems must be carefully conducted to prevent damage to the distribution systems.

With the transition away from halon to various replacements, companies with existing systems need to consult with a local authority on clean agent fire systems as the existing halon distribution system may not be compatible. Different requirements exist for the different halon replacement agents to ensure the proper distribution into the protected area.

REPLACING HALONS

In September 1987, the first of several landmark decisions to reduce and ultimately eliminate ozone depleting compounds was signed in Montreal, Canada. Known as the Montreal Protocol, it has been amended twice since its original signing and is part of the United Nations Environmental Program.[11] The Montreal Protocol defined a set of problem chemicals and identified their

removal from production and agreements to ban products that introduce ozone depleting chemicals into the atmosphere. The protocol set the production deadline at the end of 1993 for developed countries and 2010 for the developing countries.[12]

The Montreal Protocol focused primarily on reducing the use of chlorofluorocarbons (CFC), and the Kyoto Protocol aimed at specific reductions in global warming gases. Signed in December 1997, the fire protection industry was impacted as the Kyoto Protocol requires reductions in carbon dioxide and hydrofluorocarbons (HFC).[11]

The decision to reduce ozone depleting agents, such as halon, was made because both CFC and HFC chemicals have been shown to cause damage to the ozone layer through mishandling, transfers to application cylinders, and use in fire protection systems and other manufacturing processes. Their long atmospheric lifetime and their chemical interaction with ozone and the atmosphere continue for many years.

Given the requirements of the Montreal and Kyoto accords, new gas-based fire suppression systems cannot use any halon. Existing halon systems, if discharged, cannot be refilled with halon and will require modification to support a halon alternative. Organizations that have a national security link or can claim "critical use" may qualify for extensions to the accords. Typically, these installations are aircraft, military, petrochemical, and marine industries.

HALON ALTERNATIVES

Unfortunately, there is no direct "drop-in" replacement for existing systems. A number of alternatives exist, however, which will require changes to the existing distribution system, and possibly replacement. The only accurate method of establishing the replacement costs is to have your installation inspected by a qualified company that can provide specific recommendations for your needs. Aside from determining the changes needed to the distribution system, the company can provide advice on the best halon alternative.

Three halon alternatives are Inergen, Halotron I, carbon dioxide, and FM200. Like Halon 1301, Inergen is a gas and stored in cylinders similar to carbon dioxide. The gas is composed of nitrogen, argon, and carbon dioxide, which are three naturally occurring gases.[13] Unlike the halon systems, which deteriorate into toxic substances when released, Inergen does not interfere with human oxygen intake and does not decompose into toxic gases, eliminating personnel risk from the suppression agent.[14]

Like halon, Inergen affects the available oxygen in the protection area, reducing it to 15%, which is still capable of supporting human life, although the combustion

Global – Health Insurance

process is interrupted. An Inergen solution will require changes to existing halon systems, especially the distribution nozzles, to minimize air turbulence during the Inergen discharge.[15]

A second alternative to halon is Halotron I or II. Developed by American Pacific Corporation in the United States, Halotron is halocarbon based, but with very low ozone depletion, and is therefore allowed under current accords and legislation. Halotron I is a liquid streaming agent, and Halotron II is gaseous and can often be a direct replacement for Halon 1301.[16] The Halotron products have been extensively tested and approved for use in aircraft, portable fire extinguishers, marine systems, computer rooms, and military applications to name a few.[17]

The distribution system for Halotron is specific to the application. Aircraft or marine systems can be portable handheld units or mobile tanks with 500 pounds or more of Halotron. Fixed distribution systems consist of cylinders, piping, and nozzles to deliver the agent into the protected space. As mentioned previously, some halon installations can be easily converted to Halotron.

A third halon alternative is FM200, produced by DuPont. Like the other alternatives, FM200 can be used in situations where personnel are present with no risk of injury to them from the discharge.[18] FM200 distribution systems are somewhat different, as the agent is stored in liquid form and pressurized using nitrogen gas.[18] This method allows the use of much smaller storage cylinders than other methods, consequently using much less space. This makes FM200 invaluable in situations where space is severely limited.

FM200 has no halocarbon components and is not banned or controlled under the Montreal or Kyoto protocols. With the exception of Denmark and Switzerland, which carefully control the use of clean agents, FM200 is available for use in any country.[18] Like the other clean agent systems discussed, FM200 uses piping and nozzles to distribute the agent in the protected area. Although FM200 is stored in pressurized form as a liquid, releasing the agent transforms it to a gas that is dispersed through the protected space using existing air flow.

These are only a few of the halon alternatives available. Whether selecting a replacement for an existing halon system or preparing to install a new clean agent system, careful consultation with a reputable fire suppression company is necessary to ensure the installation is conducted according to your country's safety and fire standards.

CONCLUSION

This entry has examined the operation of halon-based fire suppression systems, including some of the available halon alternatives. The use of clean agent systems is widespread due to the massive amount of electrical and electronic components installed and both the large and small areas they occupy. As personal safety is paramount to all other concerns, selecting a clean agent system that will not create a dangerous environment for employees and emergency responders must be a critical factor in the selection and design of these systems.

REFERENCES

1. Fire Safety Advice Centre. Information about the fire triangle/ tetrahedron and combustion. 2007, http://www.firesafe.org.uk/ html/miscellaneous/firetria.htm (accessed December 2007).
2. American Institute of Steel Construction Inc. At what temperature does a typical fire burn?, 2008, http://www.aisc.org/ Template.cfm?Section=HOME&template=/CustomSource/ FAQContentDisplay.cfm&InterestCategoryID=402&FA-QID=2119 (accessed January 2008).
3. Riverdale Fire Department. Classifications of fire, 2007, http://www.riverdalevfd.org/index.php?option=com_content& task=view&id=33&Itemid=56 (accessed January 2008).
4. Illinois Fire and Safety Company. n.d. Fire suppression systems, http://www.illinoisfire.com/new/systems/drychemsystem.html (accessed January 2008).
5. Centre for Ecology and Hydrology. n.d. Chlorofluorocarbons (CFCs), http://www.apis.ac.uk/overview/pollutants/ overview_CFCs.htm (accessed January 2008).
6. H3R Clean Agents. What is halon and how does it work?, 2008, http://www.h3rcleanagents.com/support_ faq_2.htm (accessed January 2008).
7. United States National Library of Medicine. 10, January 2006. Methyl bromide, http://webwiser. nlm.nih.gov/getSubstanceData.do?substanceID=32&display SubstanceName=Halon+1001 (accessed January 2008).
8. International Labour Organization. Bromochloro-difluoromethane, 2000, http://www.ilo.org/public/english/ protection/safework/cis/products/icsc/dtasht/_icsc06/icsc0635. htm (accessed December 2007).
9. Federal Aviation Administration. Halon 1211: Alternative agents for airport fire fighting. 2007, http://www.airporttech. tc.faa.gov/safety/halon.asp (accessed January 2008).
10. UNEP. 1 2. Standards and codes of practice to eliminate dependency on halons.; United Nations Environment Programme: New York, 2001.
11. Gielle Srl. Halon 1301, Halon 2402, Halon 1211: replacing halon gas, 2003, http://www.fm200.biz/halon.htm (accessed April 2008).
12. The World Bank. Montreal protocol, 2008, http://go.world bank.org/KXM814CLA0 (accessed April 2008).
13. CJ Suppression Inc. n.d. Fire suppression dry/chemical, http://www.cjsuppression.com/fire_suppression.htm (accessed April 2008).
14. Fire Research–European Inergen Administration. n.d., http://www.inergen.dk/ (accessed April 2008).

Global – Health Insurance

15. Gielle Srl. n.d. Inergen fire suppression system, http://www.gielle.it/inergen_en.htm (accessed April 2008).

16. American Pacific Corporation. Clean fire extinguishing agents. 2007, http://www.halotron-inc.com/products.php (accessed April 2008).

17. American Pacific Corporation. Halotron applications. 2007, http://www.halotron-inc.com/applications.php (accessed April 2008).

18. DuPont. DuPont FM200, http://www2.dupont.com/FE/en_US/products/FM200.html (accessed April 2008).

BIBLIOGRAPHY

1. http://wiser.nlm.nih.gov/index.html.

Hash Algorithms

Keith Pasley, CISSP
PGP Security, Boonsboro, Maryland, U.S.A.

Abstract
Hash algorithms have existed in many forms at least since the 1950s. As a result of the increased value of data interactions and the increased motivation of attackers seeking to exploit electronic communications, the requirements for hash algorithms have changed. At one time, hashing was used to detect inadvertent errors generated by data processing equipment and poor communication lines. Now, secure hash algorithms are used to associate source of origin with data integrity, thus tightening the bonds of data and originator of data. So-called hashed message authentication codes (HMACs) facilitate this bonding through the use of public/ private cryptography. Protocols such as transport layer security (TLS) and Internet Protocal Security (IPSec) use HMACs extensively. Over time, weaknesses in algorithms have been discovered and hash algorithms have improved in reliability and speed. The present digital economy finds that hash algorithms are useful for creating message digests and digital signatures.

There are many information-sharing applications that are in use on modern networks today. Concurrently, there are a growing number of users sharing data of increasing value to both sender and recipient. As the value of data increases among users of information-sharing systems, the risks of unauthorized data modification, user identity theft, fraud, unauthorized access to data, data corruption, and a host of other business-related problems mainly dealing with data integrity and user authentication, are introduced. The issues of integrity and authentication play an important part in the economic systems of human society. Few would do business with companies and organizations that do not prove trustworthy or competent.

For example, the sentence "I owe Alice US$500" has a hash result of "gCWXVcL3fPV8VrJNajm8JKA==," while the sentence "I owe Alice US$5000" has a hash of "DSAy XRTza2bHLH46IPMrSq==." As can be seen, there is a big difference in hash results between the two sentences. If an attacker were trying to misappropriate the $4500 difference, hashing would allow detection.

WHY HASH ALGORITHMS ARE NEEDED AND THE PROBLEMS THEY SOLVE

- Is the e-mail you received really from who it says it is?
- Can you ensure the credit card details you submit are going to the site you expected?
- Can you be sure the latest anti-virus, firewall, or operating system software upgrade you install is really from the vendor?
- Do you know if the Web link you click on is genuine?
- Does the program hash the password when performing authentication or just passing it in the clear?

- Is there a way to know who you are really dealing with when disclosing your personal details over the Internet?
- Are you really you?
- Has someone modified a Web page or file without authorization?
- Can you verify that your routers are forwarding data only to authorized peer routers?
- Has any of the data been modified in route to its destination?
- Can hash algorithms help answer these questions?

WHAT ARE HASH ALGORITHMS?

A hash algorithm is a one-way mathematical function that is used to compress a large block of data into a smaller, fixed-size representation of that data.

To understand the concept of hash functions, it is helpful to review some underlying mathematical structures. One such structure is called a function. When hash functions were first introduced in the 1950s, the goal was to map a message into a smaller message called a message digest. This smaller message was used as a sort of shorthand of the original message. The digest was used originally for detection of random and unintended errors in processing and transmission by data processing equipment.

Functions

A function is a mathematical structure that takes one or more variables and outputs a variable. To illustrate how scientists think about functions, one can think of a function in terms of a machine (see Table 1). The machine in this illustration has

Encyclopedia of Information Assurance DOI: 10.1081/E-EIA-120046775
Copyright © 2011 by Taylor & Francis. All rights reserved.

Table 1 The hash function.

4 * 3	12
Drop the first digit (1) leaves	2
2 * next number (3)	6
6 * next number (7)	42
Drop the first digit (4) leaves	2
2 * next number (3)	6
6 * next number (8)	48
Drop the first digit (4)	8

Global –
Health Insurance

two openings. In this case the input opening is labeled x and the output opening is labeled y. These are considered traditional names for input and output. The following are the basic processing steps of mathematical functions:

1. A number goes in.
2. Something is done to it.
3. The resulting number is the output.

The same thing is done to every number input into the function machine. Step 2 above describes the actual mathematical transformation done to the input value, or hashed value, which yields the resulting output, or hash result. In this illustration, Step 2 can be described as a mathematical rule as follows: $x + 3 = y$. In the language of mathematics, if x is equal to 1, then y equals 4. Similarly, if x is equal to 2, then y equals 5. In this illustration the function, or mathematical structure, called an algorithm, is: for every number x, add 3 to the number. The result, y, is dependent on what is input, x.

As another example, suppose that, to indicate an internal company product shipment, the number 43,738 is exchanged. The hash function, or algorithm, is described as: multiply each number from left to right, and the first digit of any multiplied product above 9 is dropped. The hash function could be illustrated in mathematical notation as: $x *$ the number to the right $= y$ (see Table 1).

The input into a hash algorithm can be of variable length, but the output is usually of fixed length and somewhat shorter in length than the original message. The output of a hash function is called a message digest. In the case of the above, the hash input was of arbitrary (and variable) length; but the hash result, or message digest, was of a fixed length of 1 digit, 8. As can be seen, a hash function provides a shorthand representation of the original message. This is also the concept behind error checking (checksums) done on data transmitted across communications links. Checksums provide a non-secure method to check for message accuracy or message integrity. It is easy to see how the relatively weak mathematical functions described above could be manipulated by an intruder to change the hash output. Such weak algorithms could result in the successful alteration of message content leading to

inaccurate messages. If you can understand the concept of what a function is and does, you are on your way to understanding the basic concepts embodied in hash functions. Providing data integrity and authentication for such applications requires reliable, secure hash algorithms.

Secure Hash Algorithms

A hash algorithm was defined earlier as a one-way mathematical function that is used to compress a large block of data into a smaller, fixed size representation of that data. An early application for hashing was in detecting unintentional errors in data processing. However, due to the critical nature of their use in the high-security environments of today, hash algorithms must now also be resilient to deliberate and malicious attempts to break secure applications by highly motivated human attackers—more so than by erroneous data processing. The one-way nature of hash algorithms is one of the reasons they are used in public key cryptography. A oneway hash function processes a bit stream in a manner that makes it highly unlikely that the original message can be deduced by the output value. This property of a secure hash algorithm has significance in situations where there is zero tolerance for unauthorized data modification or if the identity of an object needs to be validated with a high assurance of accuracy. Applications such as user authentication and financial transactions are made more trustworthy by the use of hash algorithms.

Hash algorithms are called secure if they have the following properties:

- The hash result should not be predictable. It should be computationally impractical to recover the original message from the message digest (one-way property).
- No two different messages, over which a hash algorithm is applied, will result in the same digest (collision-free property).

Secure hash algorithms are designed so that any change to a message will have a high probability of resulting in a different message digest. As such, the message alteration can be detected by comparing hash results before and after hashing. The receiver can tell that a message has suspect validity by the fact that the message digest computed by the sender does not match the message digest computed by the receiver, assuming both parties are using the same hash algorithm. The most common hash algorithms as of this writing are based on Secure Hash Algorithm-1 (SHA-1) and Message Digest 5 (MD5).

Secure Hash Algorithm-1

SHA-1, part of the Secure Hash Standard (SHS), was one of the earliest hash algorithms specified for use by the U.S. federal government (see Table 2). SHA-1 was developed by NIST and the NSA. SHA-1 was published as a federal

Table 2 Output bit lengths.

Hash algorithm	Output bit length
SHA-1	160
SHA-256	256
SHA-384	384
SHA-512	512

government standard in 1995. SHA-1 was an update to the SHA, which was published in 1993.

How SHA-1 works. Think of SHA-1 as a hash machine that has two openings, input and output. The input value is called the hashed value, and the output is called the hash result. The hashed values are the bit streams that represent an electronic message or other data object. The SHA-1 hash function, or algorithm, transforms the hashed value by performing a mathematical operation on the input data. The length of the message is the same as the number of bits in the message. The SHA-1 algorithm processes blocks of 512 bits in sequence when computing the message digest. SHA-1 produces a 160-bit message digest. SHA-1 has a limitation on input message size of less than 18 quintillion (that is, 2^{64} or 18,446,744,073,709,551,616) bits in length.

SHA-1 has five steps to produce a message digest:

1. Append padding to make message length 64 bits less than a multiple of 512.
2. Append a 64-bit block representing the length of the message before padding out.
3. Initialize message digest buffer with five hexadecimal numbers. These numbers are specified in the FIPS 180-1 publication.
4. The message is processed in 512-bit blocks. This process consists of 80 steps of processing (four rounds of 20 operations), reusing four different hexadecimal constants, and some shifting and adding functions.
5. Output blocks are processed into a 160-bit message digest.

MD5

SHA was derived from the secure hash algorithms MD4 and MD5, developed by Professor Ronald L. Rivest of MIT in the early 1990s. As can be expected, SHA and MD5 work in a similar fashion. While SHA-1 yields a 160-bit message digest, MD5 yields a 128-bit message digest. SHA-1, with its longer message digest, is considered more secure than MD5 by modern cryptography experts, due in part to the longer output bit length and resulting increased collision resistance. However, MD5 is still in common use as of this writing.

Keyed Hash (HMAC)

Modern cryptographers have found the hash algorithms discussed above to be insufficient for extensive use in commercial cryptographic systems or in private electronic communications, digital signatures, electronic mail, electronic funds transfer, software distribution, data storage, and other applications that require data integrity assurance, data origin authentication, and the like. The use of asymmetric cryptography and, in some cases, symmetric cryptography, has extended the usefulness of hashing by associating identity with a hash result. The structure used to convey the property of identity (data origin) with a data object's integrity is hashed message authentication code (HMAC), or keyed hash.

For example, how does one know if the message and the message digest have not been tampered with? One way to provide a higher degree of assurance of identity and integrity is by incorporating a cryptographic key into the hash operation. This is the basis of the keyed hash or HMAC. The purpose of a message authentication code (MAC) is to provide verification of the source of a message and integrity of the message without using additional mechanisms. Other goals of HMAC are as follows:

- To use available cryptographic hash functions without modification
- To preserve the original performance of the selected hash without significant degradation
- To use and handle keys in a simple way
- To have a well-understood cryptographic analysis of the strength of the mechanism based on reasonable assumptions about the underlying hash function
- To enable easy replacement of the hash function in case a faster or stronger hash is found or required

To create an HMAC, an asymmetric (public/private) or a symmetric cryptographic key can be appended to a message and then processed through a hash function to derive the HMAC. In mathematical terms, if x = (key + message) and f = SHA-1, then f(x) = HMAC. Any hash function can be used, depending on the protocol defined, to compute the type of message digest called an HMAC. The two most common hash functions are based on MD5 and SHA. The message data and HMAC (message digest of a secret key and message) are sent to the receiver. The receiver processes the message and the HMAC using the shared key and the same hash function as that used by the originator. The receiver compares the results with the HMAC included with the message. If the two results match, then the receiver is assured that the message is authentic and came from a member of the community that shares the key.

Table 3 Other hash algorithms.

Hash algorithm	Output bit length	Country
RIPEMD (160,256,320)	160, 256, 320	Germany, Belgium
HAS-160	160	Korea
Tiger	128, 160, 192	United Kingdom

Other examples of HMAC usage include challenge–response authentication protocols such as Challenge Handshake Authentication Protocol (CHAP, RFC 1994). CHAP is defined as a peer entity authentication method for Point-to-Point Protocol (PPP), using a randomly generated challenge and requiring a matching response that depends on a cryptographic hash of the challenge and a secret key. Challenge–Response Authentication Mechanism (CRAM, RFC 2195), which specifies an HMAC using MD5, is a mechanism for authenticating Internet Mail Access Protocol (IMAP4) users. Digital signatures, used to authenticate data origin and integrity, employ HMAC functions as part of the "signing" process. A digital signature is created as follows:

1. A message (or some other data object) is input into a hash function (i.e., SHA-1, MD5, etc.).
2. The hash result is encrypted by the private key of the sender.

The result of these two steps yields what is called a *digital signature* of the message or data object. The properties of a cryptographic hash ensure that, if the data object is changed, the digital signature will no longer match it. There is a difference between a digital signature and an HMAC. An HMAC uses a shared secret key (symmetric cryptography) to "sign" the data object, whereas a digital signature is created by using a private key from a private/public key pair (asymmetric cryptography) to sign the data object. The strengths of digital signatures lend themselves to use in high-value applications that require protection against forgery and fraud.

See Table 3 for other hash algorithms.

HOW HASH ALGORITHMS ARE USED IN MODERN CRYPTOGRAPHIC SYSTEMS

In the past, hash algorithms were used for rudimentary data integrity and user authentication; today hash algorithms are incorporated into other protocols—digital signatures, virtual private network (VPN) protocols, software distribution and license control, Web page file modification detection, database file system integrity, and software update integrity verification are just a few. Hash algorithms used in hybrid cryptosystems discussed next.

Transport Layer Security

Transport layer security (TLS) is a network security protocol that is designed to provide data privacy and data integrity between two communicating applications. TLS was derived from the earlier Secure Sockets Layer (SSL) protocol developed by Netscape in the early 1990s. TLS is defined in IETF RFC 2246. TLS and SSL do not interoperate due to differences between the protocols. However, TLS 1.0 does have the ability to drop down to the SSL protocol during initial session negotiations with an SSL client. Deference is given to TLS by developers of most modern security applications. The security features designed into the TLS protocol include hashing.

The TLS protocol is composed of two layers:

1. The Record Protocol provides in-transit data privacy by specifying that symmetric cryptography be used in TLS connections. Connection reliability is accomplished by the Record Protocol through the use of HMACs.
2. TLS Handshake Protocol (really a suite of three subprotocols). The Handshake Protocol is encapsulated within the Record Protocol. The TLS Handshake Protocol handles connection parameter establishment. The Handshake Protocol also provides for peer identity verification in TLS through the use of asymmetric (public/private) cryptography.

There are several uses of keyed hash algorithms (HMAC) within the TLS protocol.

TLS uses HMAC in a conservative fashion. The TLS specification calls for the use of both HMAC MD5 and HMAC SHA-1 during the Handshake Protocol negotiation. Throughout the protocol, two hash algorithms are used to increase the security of various parameters:

- Pseudorandom number function
- Protect record payload data
- Protect symmetric cryptographic keys (used for bulk data encrypt/decrypt)
- Part of the mandatory cipher suite of TLS

If any of the above parameters were not protected by security mechanisms such as HMACs, an attacker could thwart the electronic transaction between two or more parties. The TLS protocol is the basis for most Web-based in-transit security schemes. As can be seen by this example, hash algorithms provide an intrinsic security value to applications that require secure in-transit communication using the TLS protocol.

IPSec

The Internet Protocol Security (IPSec) Protocol was designed as the packet-level security layer included in IPv6. IPv6 is a

Global – Health Insurance

replacement TCP/IP protocol suite for IPv4. IPSec itself is flexible and modular in design, which allows the protocol to be used in current IPv4 implementations. Unlike the session-level security of TLS, IPSec provides packet-level security. VPN applications such as intranet and remote access use IPSec for communications security.

Two protocols are used in IPSec operations, Authentication Header (AH) and Encapsulating Security Payload (ESP). Among other things, ESP is used to provide data origin authentication and connectionless integrity. Data origin authentication and connectionless integrity are joint services and are offered as an option in the implementation of the ESP. RFC 2406, which defines the ESP used in IPSec, states that either HMAC or oneway hash algorithms may be used in implementations. The authentication algorithms are used to create the integrity check value (ICV) used to authenticate an ESP packet of data. HMACs ensure the rapid detection and rejection of bogus or replayed packets. Also, because the authentication value is passed in the clear, HMACs are mandatory if the data authentication feature of ESP is used. If data authentication is used, the sender computes the integrity check value (ICV) over the ESP packet contents minus the authentication data. After receiving an IPSec data packet, the receiver computes and compares the ICV of the received datagrams. If they are the same, then the datagram is authentic; if not, then the data is not valid, it is discarded, and the event can be logged. MD5 and SHA-1 are the currently supported authentication algorithms.

The AH protocol provides data authentication for as much of the IP header as possible. Portions of the IP header are not authenticated due to changes to the fields that are made as a matter of routing the packet to its destination. The use of HMAC by the ESP has, according to IPSec VPN vendors, negated the need for AH.

Digital Signatures

Digital signatures serve a similar purpose as those of written signatures on paper—to prove the authenticity of a document. Unlike a pen-and-paper signature, a digital signature can also prove that a message has not been modified. HMACs play an important role in providing the property of integrity to electronic documents and transactions. Briefly, the process for creating a digital signature is very much like creating an HMAC. A message is created, and the message and the sender's private key (asymmetric cryptography) serve as inputs to a hash algorithm. The hash result is attached to the message. The sender creates a symmetric session encryption key to optionally encrypt the document. The sender then encrypts the session key with the sender's private key, reencrypts it with the receiver's public key to ensure that only the receiver can decrypt the session key, and attaches the signed session key to the document. The sender then sends the digital envelope (keyed hash value, encrypted session key, and the encrypted message) to the intended receiver. The receiver performs the entire process in reverse order. If the results match when the receiver decrypts the document and combines the sender's public key with the document through the specified hash algorithm, the receiver is assured that 1) the message came from the original sender and 2) the message has not been altered. The first case is due to use of the sender's private key as part of the hashed value. In asymmetric cryptography, a mathematical relationship exists between the public and private keys such that either can encrypt and decrypt; but the same key cannot both encrypt and decrypt the same item. The private key is known only to its owner. As such, only the owner of the private key could have used it to develop the HMAC.

Other Applications

HMACs are useful when there is a need to validate software that is downloaded from download sites. HMACs are used in logging onto various operating systems, including UNIX. When the user enters a password, the password is usually run through a hash algorithm; and the hashed result is compared to a user database or password file.

An interesting use of hash algorithms to prevent software piracy is in the Windows XP registration process. SHA-1 is used to develop the installation ID used to register the software with Microsoft.

During installation of Windows XP, the computer hardware is identified, reduced to binary representation, and hashed using MD5. The hardware hash is an eight-byte value that is created by running ten different pieces of information from the PC's hardware components through the MD5 algorithm. This means that the resultant hash value cannot be backward-calculated to determine the original values. Further, only a portion of the resulting hash value is used in the hardware hash to ensure complete anonymity.

Unauthorized file modification such as Web page defacement, system file modification, virus signature update, signing XML documents, and signing database keys are all applications for which various forms of hashing can increase security levels.

PROBLEMS WITH HASH ALGORITHMS

Flaws have been discovered in various hash algorithms. One such basic flaw is called the birthday attack.

Birthday Attack

This attack's name comes from the world of probability theory that out of any random group of 23 people, it is probable that at least two share a birthday. Finding two numbers that have the same hash result is known as the birthday attack. If hash function f maps into message digests of length 60 bits, then an attacker can find a collision using only 230 inputs

Global – Health Insurance

$(2^{f/2})$. Differential cryptanalysis has proven to be effective against one round of MD5. (There are four rounds of transformation defined in the MD5 algorithm.) When choosing a hash algorithm, speed of operation is often a priority. For example, in asymmetric (public/private) cryptography, a message may be hashed into a message digest as a data integrity enhancement. However, if the message is large, it can take some time to compute a hash result. In consideration of this, a review of speed benchmarks would give a basis for choosing one algorithm over another. Of course, implementation in hardware is usually faster than in a software-based algorithm.

LOOKING TO THE FUTURE

SHA-256, -384, and -512

In the summer of 2001, NIST published for public comment a proposed update to the SHS used by the U.S. government. Although SHA-1 appears to be still part of SHS, the update includes the recommendation to use hash algorithms with longer hash results. Longer hash results increase the work factor needed to break cryptographic hashing. This update of the Secure Hash Standard coincides with another NIST update—selection of the Rijndael symmetric cryptography algorithm for U.S. government use for encrypting data. According to NIST, it is thought that the cryptographic strength of Rijndael requires the higher strength of the new SHS algorithms. The new SHS algorithms feature similar functions but different structures. Newer and more secure algorithms, such as SHA-256, -384, and -512, may be integrated into the IPSec specification in the future to complement the Advanced Encryption Standard (AES), Rijndael. In May 2002, NIST announced that the Rijndael algorithm had been selected as the AES standard, FIPS 197.

SUMMARY

Hash algorithms have existed in many forms at least since the 1950s. As a result of the increased value of data interactions and the increased motivation of attackers seeking to exploit electronic communications, the requirements for hash algorithms have changed. At one time, hashing was used to detect inadvertent errors generated by data processing equipment and poor communication lines. Now, secure hash algorithms are used to associate source of origin with data integrity, thus tightening the bonds of data and originator of data. So-called hashed message authentication codes (HMACs) facilitate this bonding through the use of public/private cryptography. Protocols such as transport layer security (TLS) and Internet Protocal Security (IPSec) use HMACs extensively. Over time, weaknesses in algorithms have been discovered and hash algorithms have improved in reliability and speed. The present digital economy finds that hash algorithms are useful for creating message digests and digital signatures.

BIBLIOGRAPHY

1. http://www.deja.com/group/sci.crypt.

Health Insurance Portability and Accountability Act (HIPAA)

Lynda L. McGhie, CISSP, CISM
Information Security Officer (ISO)/Risk Manager, Private Client Services (PCS),
Wells Fargo Bank, Cameron Park, California, U.S.A.

Abstract

The most effective and defensible information security program is one that strictly adheres to a disciplined risk management methodology. Risk management is the critical first step leading to a successful and compliant implementation of the Health Insurance Portability and Accountability Act (HIPAA) Security Rule.

Security requirements imposed and mandated by the federal government have, for decades, resulted in requirements, recommendations, and guidelines that have proven over and over again to be practical baselines for legal and regulatory compliance. Implementations based on these standards will ensure the sound practice of risk management up front and throughout the security and compliance process. It is important to acknowledge that this guidance is practical and applicable to public and private enterprises, as well as government and commercial entities. It just makes good sense.

The most effective and defensible information security program is one that strictly adheres to a disciplined risk management methodology. Legal authorities warn that laws and regulations regarding information protection and privacy will continue to evolve over the next decade. These rules will continue to dictate how firms and government agencies protect and safeguard customer privacy information. The most effective and efficient way to guarantee compliance to these laws and regulations is through the adoption of risk management systems. Such a framework will provide a foundational information security management system leading to compliance and risk reduction and mitigation. Many functional areas within an organization practice risk management and deal with various aspects of risk management, including information security, business continuity planning (BCP), disaster recovery planning (DRP), insurance, finance, and internal auditing, to name a few. Risk management is the critical first step leading to a successful and compliant implementation of the Health Insurance Portability and Accountability Act (HIPAA) Security Rule.

Security requirements imposed and mandated by the federal government have, for decades, resulted in the development of guidance for agencies, contractors, suppliers, and customers. These requirements, recommendations, and guidelines have proven over and over again to be practical baselines for legal and regulatory compliance. An organization that follows the security and privacy roadmaps provided by the National Institute of Standards and Technology (NIST), Federal Information Processing Standards (FIPS), and International Standards Organization (ISO) 17799 will greatly enhance its ability to comply with existing and future legal and regulatory requirements, and that organization's information security and privacy programs will be compliant and sound. Additionally,

implementations based on these standards will ensure the sound practice of risk management up front and throughout the security and compliance process. It is important to acknowledge that this guidance is practical and applicable to public and private enterprises, as well as government and commercial entities. It just makes good sense.

A growing number of federal and state laws and regulations address information protection, privacy, management, and reporting practices, including data retention requirements. Many of these laws and regulations have common and similar requirements and controls. Many recommend or incorporate the audit and control methodologies of the Control Objectives for Information and Related Technology (COBIT) and Committee of Sponsoring Organizations (COSO), as well as other accepted information security standards and guidelines. Integration across these laws and regulations ensures synchronization and consistency of approach and controls. Additionally, a return on investment (ROI) can be demonstrated when one control or process satisfies multiple security requirements, laws, and regulations while streamlining and enhancing administration and technical processes. Additionally, automation and state-of-theart security tools can reduce overall costs for information security and compliance across the enterprise.

MANDATE

On August 21, 1996, President Clinton signed into law the HIPAA of 1996, Public Law 104–191. In so doing, the healthcare industry was given a farreaching and complex mandate that would impact every aspect of health care in the United States. After much debate and a major rewrite of the Notice of Proposed Rule Making (NPRM), the final

Encyclopedia of Information Assurance DOI: 10.1081/E-EIA-120046838
Copyright © 2011 by Taylor & Francis. All rights reserved.

Global –
Health Insurance

Security Rule was published in the *Federal Register* on February 20, 2003. Covered entities were required to implement reasonable administrative, physical, and technical safeguards to protect the confidentiality, integrity, and availability of electronic protected health information by April 20, 2005 (2006 for small health plans).

The HIPAA Security Rule specifically focuses on the safeguarding of electronic protected health information (ePHI). Only companies producing, utilizing, and storing ePHI are defined as "covered entities." Covered entities include health plans, healthcare clearinghouses, healthcare providers who transmit any electronic information in electronic form in connection with covered transactions, and Medicare prescription drug card sponsors. Although these companies are typically within the healthcare business, other entities such as the federal government and higher education may also utilize ePHI and would therefore also be required to comply with the HIPAA rule.

The HIPAA Security Rule specifically focuses on protecting the confidentiality, integrity, and availability of ePHI as defined and supported in the rule itself:

- *Confidentiality* is the property that data or information is not made available or disclosed to unauthorized persons or processes.
- *Integrity* is the property that data or information have not been altered or destroyed in an unauthorized manner.
- *Availability* is the property that data or information is accessible and useable upon demand by an authorized person.

The ePHI that a covered entity creates, receives, maintains, or transmits must be protected against reasonably anticipated threats, hazards, and impermissible uses or disclosures. Covered entities must also protect against reasonably anticipated uses or disclosures of such information that are not permitted by the Privacy Rule.

HIPAA SECURITY RULE OVERVIEW

The HIPAA Security Rule defines the standards in generic terms and provides little guidance on how to implement them. The security standards are based on three concepts:

- *Flexibility and scalability*—The standards must be applicable from the smallest provider to the largest health plan.
- *Comprehensiveness*—The standards must cover all aspects of security, behavioral as well as technical (process oriented).
- *Technology neutrality*—As technology changes, the standards remain constant.

It would be helpful to review and understand information security terminology prior to interpreting or seeking to understand the HIPAA Security Rule. The Security Rule is divided into six main sections, each of which includes standards and implementation specifications that a covered entity must address:

1. *Security standards general rules* include the general requirements that all covered entities must meet; establishes flexibility of approach; identifies standards and implementation specifications required and addressable; outlines decisions a covered entity must make regarding addressable implementation specifications; and requires maintenance of security measures to continue reasonable and appropriate protection of electronic protected health information.
2. *Administrative safeguards* are defined in the Security Rule as the administrative actions, policies, and procedures to manage the selection, development, implementation, and maintenance of security measures to protect electronic protected health information and to manage the conduct of the covered entity's workforce in relation to protection of that information.
3. *Physical safeguards* are defined as the physical measures, policies, and procedures to protect a covered entity's electronic information systems and related buildings and equipment from natural environmental hazards and unauthorized intrusion.
4. *Technical safeguards* are defined as the technology and the policies and procedures for its use that protect electronic protected health information and control access to it.
5. *Organizational requirements* include standards for business associate contracts and other arrangements, including memoranda of understanding between a covered entity and a business associate when both entities are government organizations, as well as requirements for group health plans.
6. *Policies and procedures and documentation requirements* require implementation of reasonable and appropriate policies and procedures to comply with the standards, implementation specifications, and other requirements of the Security Rule; maintenance of written (which may or may not be electronic) documentation or records that include policies, procedures, actions, activities, or assessments required by the Security Rule; and retention, availability, and update requirements for the documentation.

Each Security Rule section contains standards and implementation specifications. A covered entity is required to comply with all standards of the Security Rule with respect to all ePHI. Many of the standards also include implementation specifications. An implementation specification is a detailed description of the method or approach covered entities can use to meet a particular standard. Implementation specifications are either required or addressable; however, regardless of whether or not a standard includes

Table 1 HIPAA security rule standards and implementation specifications.

Standard	Section	Implementation Specifications (R = Required; A = Addressable)
Administrative Safeguards		
Security Management Process	164.308(a)(1)	Risk analysis (R) Sanction policy (R) Risk management (R) Activity information system activity review (R)
Assigned Security Responsibility	164.308(a)(2)	None
Workforce Security	164.308(a)(3)	Authorization and supervision (A) Workforce clearance procedures (A) Termination procedures (A)
Information Access Management	164.308 (a)(4)	Isolating healthcare clearinghouse (R) Access authorization (A) Access establishment and modifications (A)
Security Awareness and Training	164.308(a)(5)	Security reminders (A) Protection from malicious software (A) Log-in monitoring (A) Password management (A)
Security Incident Procedures	164.308(a)(6)	Response and reporting (R)
Contingency Plan	164.308(a)(7)	Data backup plan (R) Disaster recovery plan (R) Emergency mode operation plan (R) Testing and revision procedures (A) Applications and data criticality analysis (A)
Evaluation	164.308(a)(8)	None
Business Associate Contracts and Other Arrangements	164.308(b)(1)	Written contract or other arrangement (R)
Physical Safeguards		
Facility Access Controls	164.310(a)(1)	Contingency operations (A) Facility security plan (A) Access control and validation process (A) Maintenance records (A)
Workstation Use	164.310(b)	None
Device and Media Controls	164.310(d)(1)	Disposal (R) Media reuse (R) Accountability (A) Data backup and storage (A)
Technical Safeguards		
Access Control	164.312(a)(1)	Unique user identification (R) Emergency access procedure (R) Automatic log-off (A) Encryption and decryption (A)
Audit Controls	164.312(b)	None
Integrity	164.312(c)(1)	Mechanism to authenticate electronic protected health information (A)
Person or Entity Authentication	164.312(d)	None
Transmission Security	164.312(e)(1)	Integrity controls (A) Encryption (A)

implementation specifications, covered entities must comply with each standard.

- A *required* implementation specification is similar to a standard in that a covered entity must comply with it.

- For *addressable* implementation specifications, covered entities must perform an assessment to determine whether the implementation specification is a reasonable and appropriate safeguard for implementation in the covered entity's environment. In general, after performing the assessment, the organization can implement an equivalent alternative measure that allows the entity to comply with the standard, or it may not implement the addressable specification or any alternative measures if equivalent measures are not reasonable and appropriate within its environment. Covered entities are required to document these assessments and all decisions.

Table 1 lists the standards and implementation specifications within the Administrative, Physical, and Technical Safeguards sections of the Security Rule. The table is organized according to the categorization of standards within each of the safeguard sections in the Security Rule:

- Column 1 lists the Security Rule standards.
- Column 2 provides the regulatory citation to the appropriate section of the rule.
- Column 3 lists the implementation specifications associated with the standard, if any exist, and designates the specification as required or addressable.

Organizations must determine whether anyone within the company is qualified to interpret the HIPAA Security Rule or if this phase of the project should be outsourced. Perhaps an internal crossfunctional team could accomplish this critical initial task. Representatives from the legal, privacy, compliance, security, and technology departments should be able to research the HIPAA Security Rule and propose an interpretation and an implementation of the rule tailored to the organization. Many reference documents are available from the federal government and professional organizations to assist in this task. Many vendors and legal and accounting or audit firms sponsor information-sharing events regarding HIPAA compliance. Also, vertical industry focus groups have formed to share best practices and Security Rule interpretations.

It is absolutely fundamental to an organization's success to quickly gain consensus on interpretation of the rule and its application to the organization's unique healthcare environment. The quicker an organization can agree on an interpretation of the rule (what the rule is actually requiring the covered entity to do), the quicker the organization can document and solidify its approach, direction, and implementation plan for compliance. The plan should include only what is viable, practical, and required for that particular organization. This interpretation will allow the organization to establish the scope of the project and its compliance program.

It is critical that, when this interpretation and its resultant requirements and controls are identified and agreed upon, the project team *not* revisit, second guess, or continue to interpret the rule. When this foundational step is complete, the covered entity must not continue to debate the interpretation of the rule or the project requirements. It is important to document the process and the decisions

made during this phase. It is at this point in the process when the covered entity typically gets cold feet, as the scope of the project and the required resources for implementation become clear.

It is apparent that the required controls *must* be implemented, but what about the addressable controls? Of the 42 implementation specifications, 21 are considered to be addressable. To meet the addressable implementation specifications, a covered entity must first assess whether each implementation specification is a reasonable and appropriate safeguard in its environment. The analysis must take into consideration the likely contribution of each control to protecting the entity's electronic protected health information. Remember, organizations should implement a specification only if it is reasonable and appropriate for the covered entity. If implementing the specification is not reasonable and appropriate, the organization must document why and implement an equivalent alternative measure that is reasonable and appropriate.

CRITICAL COMPONENTS

A covered entity should very quickly establish a HIPAA compliance governance system with documented and supporting processes. The plan should identify executive sponsorship and define roles and responsibilities. The executives should be high up in the organization and preferably direct reports of the chief executive officer (CEO) or members of the board of directors. These individuals will not only provide governance and oversight but also determine financial allocations, project deliverables, and compliance variables. These same individuals may also be part of the executive advisory board or steering committee. Other functional and business area representatives may also be added to this advisory board, including the chief financial officer (CFO), chief legal representative, procurement officer, chief information officer (CIO), chief information security officer (CISO), chief privacy officer, chief compliance officer, and chief technology officer (CTO). It is suggested that the executive vice president for each business area also be included on the board. Each of these members should be allocated one vote, and majority rules for approvals and decision making. These key individuals are considered stakeholders in the success of the project as well as overall compliance to the HIPAA Security Rule. Key external stakeholders might include business partners or even customers.

In support of the advisory board and the governing process, the organization should define and initiate report, status, and metric processes. The board should meet at regular intervals, at least on a monthly basis, during peak activity such as project initiation, achievement of major milestones, project approvals, financial approvals, and problem resolution. Each meeting should follow a standard agenda with reports from functional areas and business areas. The business areas should report on progress and deliverables for their assigned areas of responsibility. The functional areas should report on the action items and tasks assigned to them. The board meeting should provide a forum not only for information sharing and reporting but also for decision making and approval. It will be the role of the project director to track and report on the progress of the project, to prepare the meeting materials, and to collect status and reporting information from the team. The project director will also be responsible for metrics and metrics tracking and reporting. Selection of the project director is critical to the success of the project.

CENTRALIZED AND DECENTRALIZED ROLES AND RESPONSIBILITIES

Separate companies within a corporation may be separate covered entities in certain situations, but the corporation itself is the highest level covered entity. Although the executive officers, board of directors, and CISO are all culpable for HIPAA Security Rule compliance, the HIPAA documentation set must clearly outline and define separate roles and responsibilities. Some corporations that have decentralized business units or companies that manage their own information systems may want to appoint decentralized security officials who will have a dotted line responsibility to the CISO for implementing HIPAA Security Rule compliance. This team will be responsible for implementing the enterprise information security program, defining and implementing the enterprise information security policies and procedures, and implementing technical and administrative controls for HIPAA Security Rule compliance.

IDENTIFY AND DEFINE THE PROJECT TEAM

Several approaches can be used to assemble a HIPAA Security Rule compliance and implementation team. Resources may be derived from existing staff or supplemented with external contractors or even compliance-type organizations. It is best to conduct an assessment of existing resources, conduct a gap analysis, and derive a staffing and resource plan. In general, team representatives should include at least legal, compliance, security, privacy, technology, and business personnel. Individual organizations may require additional representation such as human resources, finance, or audit. The business representatives may or may not be part of this core team. Two separate teams can meet specific to their areas of responsibilities and their roles in the project; the two teams would then join when issues of crossrepresentation arise.

As with any project or process, the smaller and more representative the team, the more efficient and cost-effective the team will be and hence the project outcome.

It is suggested that a small core team as well as a larger broader more representative team be identified. It is critical that roles and responsibilities be established and agreed to at the onset. The success of the project depends on achieving communication, understanding, and approval and buy-in throughout. Each organization will have to determine what existing tools and processes can be used to achieve these objectives and then define additive processes and tools for HIPAA Security Rule compliance. The main objective in the definition of these working teams is to ensure representation, to empower and enable the team, to streamline the process, and to eliminate bureaucracy to the extent feasible. Teams should adhere to strict project management and systems engineering processes.

DEVELOP AND IMPLEMENT A COMMUNICATION PLAN

A thorough, multifaceted, multimedia HIPAA Security Rule communication plan should be developed early on in the process. Tailored communications should be developed and deployed specific to each phase of the project with the goal of keeping all stakeholders, team members, vendors, contractors, customers, business partners, and workforce members well informed. Communications should include newsletters, regularly scheduled and distributed status reports, and informational Web sites with project and team information and other alerts and bulletins specific to the project. The Web site should include a question box, FAQs, and other ways for workforce members to ask questions and receive information regarding what is coming up and what is changing. The communication plan should adopt a sales and marketing approach to point out and illustrate the outcomes and benefits of the project and compliance. Communication should occur often and on a regular basis; it should be designed to share progress, metrics, achievement of major and minor supporting milestones and any and all ROI, cost–benefits, and other gains achieved through security improvements such as administration simplification.

DEFINE PROJECT SCOPE

It is critically important when initiating such a project to propose and agree on the scope of the project; for example, what relevant information systems fall within the scope of the project? In order to determine this, the covered entity must identify all information systems that store or transmit ePHI. This includes all hardware and software used to collect, store, process, and transmit ePHI. To accomplish this task, the project director and team should develop a survey or inventory matrix template. The template should be distributed to the business team members and the functional team members and will be used to define major

Table 2 Administrative safeguards.

Section	Standard	Implementation Specification	Required/ Addressable	Solution	Methodology
164.308(a)(1)	Security Management Process	Risk analysis	Required	Intrusion detection system (IDS)	Security risks come in many forms and can be both internal and external. IDS enables covered entities to monitor network activity to determine what exposures may be created. Supplemental scanning and vulnerability tools support discovery and provide input to remediation.

business units and functional units. The project director should assign responsibility for rolling up and summarizing the findings of the survey. This summary of the collected information will be included in a report presented to the project team and, following their concurrence, to the executive steering committee. The output of this process and this report will define the scope of the project and the systems, applications, network, storage, databases, etc. that house ePHI and therefore require compliant controls.

A companion process, or tool, that can assist in the definition of scope is an analysis of the organization's business functions. A common goal of such an analysis is definition of ownership and controls over these information systems. This information is critical to project initialization, defining project scope, project implementation, and ongoing compliance. At a minimum, policies, procedures, and processes should be implemented to ensure that this information is updated regularly and that the information is available for audit and compliance.

In addition to documentation and inventories of information, ePHI, and applications, system and network configurations should be documented, including internal and external connections. This is particularly critical for those systems processing ePHI. The reason why all systems should be documented, controlled, and managed is that over time it is difficult to isolate and control the flow of ePHI. To the extent possible, practical and affordable HIPAA Security Rule compliance should be integrated into the overall security system and program.

SECURITY RULE MATRIX

A Security Rule matrix should be mapped to HIPAA Security Rule requirements, policies, guidelines, actions, and ownership, including HIPAA Security Rule standards and implementation specifications. Our earlier discussion on the HIPAA Security Rule introduced the concept of addressable control mechanisms, including administrative, physical, and technical safeguards. Table 1 can be used to create the Security Rule matrix, which adds additional columns to specify controls and solutions. It can also be used to incorporate risk assessment questions and surveys. The benefit of building on information initiated from the HIPAA Security Rule interpretation and, further,

decomposition of its requirements is having a single data repository with supporting project documentation for audit and compliance verification. This baseline spreadsheet, as it evolves through each phase of the HIPAA security project, supplements project documentation. Subsequent phases can add additional columns, including risk questions, gap analysis findings, and administrative, technical, and physical controls that must be augmented, enhanced, or initiated for HIPAA compliance.

Table 2 is an example of how to build on previous tables and information collected as the HIPAA security project evolves. The previous spreadsheet (Table 1) included standards, citation sections, implementation specifications, and required/addressable categories. This spreadsheet adds a column for solutions and supporting methodologies for the solutions. An organization can create its own matrix or spreadsheet for this phase or can continue to build on this sample. Additional columns can be added that are specific to an organization's unique requirements, such as columns indicating existing controls and "to be" controls. Note that organizations should continue to build on this spreadsheet and matrix as risk assessment and gap analysis information is received, organized, and consolidated into meaningful data to be used to update the project plan.

RISK ASSESSMENT

Conducting a risk analysis is a required implementation specification of the HIPAA Security Rule. An entity must identify the risks to and vulnerabilities of the information in its care before it can take effective steps to eliminate or minimize those risks and vulnerabilities. As a first step, the organization must determine an approach and a methodology to set the course and provide a compass for its compliance initiatives. Following are some examples of existing security risk assessment frameworks:

- INFOSEC Assessment Methodology (IAM), from the National Security Agency (NSA)
- Operational Critical Threat, Asset, and Vulnerability Evaluation (OCTAVE), from Carnegie Mellon University Software Engineering Institute (SEI)
- NIST Special Publication 800-26 (*Security Self-Assessment Guide for Information Technology Systems*)

Global – Health Insurance

In 2004, draft NIST Special Publication 800-66 (*An Introductory Resource Guide for Implementing the Health Insurance Portability and Accountability Act [HIPAA] Security Rule*) was published. This document is intended to assist in identifying available NIST guidance that can serve as useful reference material in addressing the HIPAA security standards. In addition, it provides a cross-mapping among requirements to ensure that agencies do not do additional unnecessary work because many requirements overlap. The Centers for Medicare and Medicare Services (CMS), working with the Utilization Review Accreditation Committee (URAC), NIST, and the Workgroup for Electronic Data Interchange (WEDI) Strategic National Implementation Process (SNIP), will also be providing additional information on how to integrate NIST guidance into the HIPAA security compliance initiative. NIST guidance for risk assessment can be found in the following publications:

- NIST Special Publication 800-26 (*Security Self-Assessment Guide for Information Technology Systems*), http://csrc.nist.gov/publications/nistpubs/800-26/sp800-26.pdf.
- FIPS-199 (*Standards for Security Categorization of Federal Information and Information Systems*), http://csrc.nist.gov/publications/fips/fips199/FIPS-PUB-199-final.pdf.
- Administrative Safeguards, Section 164.308(a)(1)(ii)(A), Risk Analysis (Required), which requires covered entities to conduct an accurate and thorough assessment of the potential risks and vulnerabilities to the confidentiality, integrity, and availability of electronic protected health information held by the covered entity

Overall, the risks that must be assessed are the risks of non-compliance with the requirements of Section 164.306(a), General Rules, of the Security Rule: 1) ensure the confidentiality, integrity, and availability of all ePHI that the covered entity creates, receives, maintains, or transmits; 2) protect against any reasonably anticipated threats or hazards to the security or integrity of such information; 3) protect against any reasonably anticipated uses or disclosures of such information; and 4) ensure compliance with this subpart by its workforce. Risk management is the process of identifying and assessing risk and taking steps to reduce risk to an acceptable level. The risk assessment should identify potential risks and vulnerabilities with regard to the confidentiality, integrity, and availability of ePHI held by the covered entity. At a minimum, the risk assessment should determine the characteristics of the hardware, software, systems, interfaces, and information. It should include people, processes, and technology.

The next process or phase expands on information gathered in the previous phases, leading to further definition of the project scope, plan, schedule, resource requirements, and budget forecasting. Information from all inventories and surveys should be reviewed, analyzed, and summarized; this new knowledge should be utilized as input to the enterprisewide risk assessment. Enterprises or even individual business units that have recently completed risk assessments for any reason will be ahead of the game and have valuable input to the risk assessment process. Other inputs or sources of discovery might be audit reports and open audit findings; vendor reviews and contracts; statements of work (SOWs) and service level agreements (SLAs); external connection inventories; output from intrusion detection systems (IDSs); investigation and incident response systems; audit and monitoring systems; and scanning tools. The results and output from system- and application-level testing may also be of some value in putting together the risk assessment puzzle. Information on known project deliverables, life cycles, and known and identified problems should also be incorporated.

Many companies outsource their information technology (IT) services and support, either in their entirety or in smaller portions. Outsourcing partners or providers may be able to provide valuable information. Typically, SLAs are associated with these contracts, and metrics are reported and tracked. This information could also be of value to the risk assessment. A growing trend is to outsource security operations and management through security managed services. These companies constantly monitor a company's network and systems for security anomalies. Many map to known and permitted access and send an alert when violations or even suspected activities are detected. Vendors, managed service providers, and other sources can provide ongoing risk and vulnerability reporting and incident tracking.

Benchmarking within the industry and general security threat analysis information are also of value. This type of information could be specific to the healthcare industry, to security (e.g., Internet), or to compliance, or it could pertain to business operations in general. Such information could include virus alerts and occurrences, patches, code vulnerabilities, attack attempts, etc. If an organization already has a well-established information security program and has defined and implemented information security policies and procedures, then its risk assessment should map not only to the HIPAA Security Rule but also to existing security policies and procedures. The risk assessment must also consider compliance to physical and human resources security policies and procedures and should provide for consistent approaches and controls.

Other input can come from the areas of business continuity planning (BCP) and disaster recovery (DR). Risk assessments and impact analysis are the cornerstones of these functions, in addition to application inventories; defining critical applications; determining ownership of and classifying systems, data, and applications; and incident and crisis management.

Global – Health Insurance

Risk can never be totally eliminated. Compliance with the HIPAA Security Rule requires that appropriate and reasonable safeguards be implemented to protect the confidentiality, integrity, and availability of ePHI. In the context of HIPAA security, a covered entity may want to protect more than ePHI (e.g., employment, brand, patent, research and development, and financial information). In addition to integrating compliance with existing security policies and procedures during the risk assessment and inventory processes, it is helpful to ensure compliance to the technical security architecture, guidelines, and standard security configurations. The IT team should be assigned the responsibility to check all hardware and software to determine whether selected security settings are enabled. The output from this effort will provide input to the next process (gap analysis) and will assist in the determination of the effectiveness of current safeguards.

If organizations focus only on HIPAA security compliance, they leave themselves open to other risks. They must also assess change impact, people, business units, and technology. The risk assessment process is labor intensive and yields volumes of information. The team will need to have a predetermined plan for review, analysis, consolidation, interpretation, and summarization of the information gathered. Putting considerable thought into defining the risk analysis criteria, developing a useful assessment format, and determining the questions to ask will result in useful information (remember, "garbage in, garbage out"). Remember that the people filling out the risk assessment questionnaires and gathering the information may not be experts in IT, supporting business processes, or security. The process should include follow-up and information validation processes. The final outcome of the risk assessment process is the risk assessment report.

Covered entities should use a combination of qualitative and quantitative risk assessment methodologies. The process discussed above emphasizes qualitative risk assessment methodologies and processes. Although traditionally seen as subjective when compared to quantitative risk assessment, the resulting risk assessment report may be easier to defend when it is presented to the HIPAA Security Rule advisory board or steering committee.

Qualitative measurement is used to determine if a specific element qualifies. Qualitative analysis could be used to determine the scope of HIPAA security compliance by stating that if a system contains ePHI then it qualifies for inclusion in the risk assessment for the HIPAA Security Rule. Another use of qualitative assessment is for significance or strength. For example, qualitative evaluations such as low, moderate, or high may be used to determine the likelihood that a virus would be introduced to the organization's system via e-mail. Basically, qualitative analysis is used to determine "yes" or "no" with regard to including a specific element and is also used to determine the significance of something using non-numerical terminology. Qualitative analysis is subjective. The accuracy of

qualitative analysis determinations relies on subject matter expertise in the following areas:

- Operations and processes
- Workforce capabilities
- System capabilities
- Compliance program management
- System development lifecycle management

Quantitative measurement is used to determine characteristics in numerical terms, usually expressed in percentage, dollar amount, or number of times a specific event occurs in a stated period of time. If, during a qualitative analysis, it was determined that it was highly likely that a virus could be introduced to the system via e-mail, then the quantitative analysis might determine a probability of 99.99% that the system would have a virus introduced via e-mail.

Algorithm analysis is an example of quantitative analysis. Algorithm analysis can be used to quantify impact in a dollar amount by computing the annualized loss expectancy (ALE). ALE is computed as a function of the single loss expectancy (SLE) in dollars and the annualized rate of occurrence (ARO). The data that is used for the basis of these determinations vary. Usually the determinations are based on regional, national, or worldwide aggregated performance criteria of hardware and software configurations to security threats. Rarely does a covered entity have the capability to collect enough aggregated data to make these computations, so the use of algorithm quantitative analysis usually requires the expertise of vendors that specialize in this type (actuarial science) of risk assessment. Quantitative analysis is objective. The benefit of quantitative determinations relies on:

- Relevance of the data used in the computations
- Current accuracy of the data
- Ability to interpret the meaning of the numerical values
- Ability to translate determinations into risk mitigation

AS-IS STATE/GAP ANALYSIS

The risk assessment report provides a summarization of the as-is state of the existing information security program. It also highlights where the covered entity is relative to compliance with the HIPAA Security Rule. Utilizing the security rule matrix and the risk assessment report, the next project process or phase is to conduct an enterprisewide gap analysis to determine corrective action plans as well as updates to the compliance plan. It is important to determine gaps or vulnerabilities in the following areas: policy, procedures and processes, training and awareness, implementation or process integration, operational controls, and audit.

A critical and valuable tool in the gap analysis process is the gap analysis checklist, which is a list of the requirements of the HIPAA Security Rule as defined for the covered entity during the HIPAA Security Rule interpretation and in the Security Rule matrix. The checklist is written in a question format, is easy to understand and answer, and does not require specific technical or business process skills.

Project documentation is critical, particularly documentation leading to judgments and decisions. The documentation should be updated throughout each project phase or process. The auditor and accreditation authority will use this documentation to validate compliance initially and on an ongoing basis. A well-defined checklist will provide the auditor with a roadmap for review, leading to an organized list of recommendations for enhancements and remediation. Whether an organization designs or purchases a compliance checklist, the completed checklist will be used to draw up a task list for the remediation plan. The detailed checklist will serve as a tool to compare the organization's current as-is state to the Security Rule matrix. Determine whether or not current safeguards ensure the confidentiality, integrity, and availability of all ePHI. What technical and administrative safeguards are in place to protect and secure ePHI? Where are the gaps? This process allows the organization to easily identify the requirements that it is already meeting and those that still must be addressed within the project plan. The organization will also obtain critical additional information regarding the resources and timeline necessary for the HIPAA Security Rule compliance project.

ENHANCEMENTS AND IMPLEMENTATION OF ADMINISTRATIVE AND TECHNICAL CONTROLS

Although the Security Rule does not require purchasing any particular technology, additional hardware, software, or services may be needed to protect ePHI adequately. If additional technical controls are necessary, the organization should consider conducting a product evaluation in compliance with existing policies and procedures. A cost–benefit analysis should be conducted early on in the process to determine the reasonableness of the investment given the security risks identified. Administrative and manual processes may supplement or replace technology solutions. Members of the technical team should initiate the technology reviews utilizing requirements derived from the above processes or phases as well as ongoing input from the business and functional areas. Vendor presentations and demonstrations will be helpful for management, technical teams, and business functional areas. These will help inform, communicate, and gain concurrence throughout the process.

New technology or even new administrative controls should be integrated into the overall information security and technical architecture and its supporting processes to exploit and take advantage of existing investments. The

covered entity should have good security standards already in place that require only supplemental enhancement for HIPAA Security Rule compliance. It is advisable to closely monitor the introduction of new or additional technical and administrative controls to ensure security compliance without imposing undue burdens on the business and its operations.

Requirements and solutions at this stage of the process will come directly from the updated Security Control matrix. Activities will map to a combination of administrative and technical controls integrating this phase or process to both technical and administrative teams. Depending on the strategy that the covered entity has adopted, the focus here will be on centralized or decentralized solutions. Additionally, it may be necessary to look for automated technical solutions or administrative and manual solutions.

Some covered entities may also take a wait-and-see approach pending the outcome of future litigation and fines around HIPAA compliance. Another strategy might be to implement controls of the "lowhanging fruit" variety for initial compliance and then take a slower and longer approach to the hard and expensive solutions. In this case, it is important to document the reasoning in the project documentation management system and to have a solid and approved long-term project plan in place for audit and compliance. To the extent practical, the organization should stick with their major upfront decisions unless they are proven to be illogical or ill founded; they should not continue to second guess or revisit their rule interpretations, previous decisions and directions, or the project plan. Second guessing will cause the organization to lose credibility with its stakeholders and threaten its compliance plan and schedule.

TRAINING AND AWARENESS

Information security awareness training and regular security updates and reminders are required for all personnel who fall under HIPAA guidelines, including managers, agents, and contractors. A covered entity's HIPAA compliance training and awareness program should focus on the HIPAA Security Rule to ensure that the program framework meets and exceeds the requirements laid out in Section 142.308(12) regarding:

- Training on vulnerabilities of digital health information and how to protect that information
- Password maintenance
- Incident reporting
- Viruses
- Malicious code

As previously mentioned, a thorough and multimedia HIPAA Security Rule communication plan should be developed early on in the process. Tailored communications should be developed and deployed specific to each phase of the project, with a common goal of keeping all stakeholders, team members, vendors, contractors, customers, business partners, and workforce members well informed. The communication plan builds bridges to other enterprise communications and projects. It also works with the HIPAA Security Rule training and awareness program and the overall enterprise information security training and awareness program.

The primary goal of all Security Rule communication is to ensure that workforce members are well informed regarding executive management's position and direction on HIPAA Security Rule compliance and information security in general. The training course material provides a review of the HIPAA Security Rule specific to the covered entity's implementation and the enterprisewide information security policies and procedures. It establishes workforce member expectations and specifically informs them on new behavior expectations. It clearly outlines and explains what will change, what they need to do, and how they will do it.

The training should be ongoing and intermingled throughout the project, with an emphasis on the readiness of technical and administrative control mechanisms. For example, at project initiation some skill training for the project team may be conducted, in addition to training on how to interpret the HIPAA Security Rule, how to conduct a risk assessment and gap analysis, and how to evaluate the as-is state to determine what new administrative and technical controls might be necessary. Particular emphasis should be placed on training regarding policies, procedures, and technical and administrative tools and processes.

Security awareness and training should already be the cornerstones of an organization's information security program, and initial and annual HIPAA Security Rule training can be incorporated with these overall security training and awareness programs. Training may be tailored to the various roles and responsibilities within the enterprise—detailed training for security and privacy officials; briefer, more high-level training for senior executives and management; and, finally, more detailed training in tools, forms, and processes for those routinely handling and processing ePHI.

A search of the Internet will reveal a number of companies offering various types of HIPAA training, either standard or custom. An organization's training and awareness plan and supporting communication plan may require a combination of in-house and vendor HIPAA Security Rule training material.

IMPLEMENT AN ONGOING HIPAA COMPLIANCE ORGANIZATION AND INFRASTRUCTURE

Everyone has experienced the breakdown of an implemented project or infrastructure as interest in the project wanes over time and team members are reassigned or overcome by new projects and events. It is critical that the HIPAA Security Rule project sustain its momentum over time and that the ongoing organization structure, designated roles and responsibilities, and compliance infrastructure remain active and effective over time. This will be particularly critical when dealing with new laws and regulations. It is important to note that legal groups estimate that laws and regulations regarding personal privacy will continue to evolve over the next decade; consequently, covered entities must remain knowledgeable, informed, agile, and adaptive. A foundation must be established to quickly integrate new control requirements that are both administrative and technical. An ongoing risk assessment and gap analysis management process must be implemented to integrate controls for new and added risks and vulnerabilities that naturally occur within the business and within information technology.

The HIPAA Security Rule speaks to the need for external accreditation, and many vendors, as well as audit and accounting firms, are ramping up to conduct accreditations and certifications. A growing tendency is for companies to use compliance with laws and regulations (particularly if certified by external accreditation authorities) as a competitive advantage in their sales and marketing programs. Companies are also incorporating compliance certifications and accreditation into their annual reports, Securities and Exchange Commission (SEC) reports, and marketing and advertising.

As noted earlier, internal audit personnel are a critical component of the HIPAA Security Rule project team and not only have ongoing roles and responsibilities throughout the project but also have a critical role at the end of the project for certification of compliance. The documentation, checklists, and audit findings from the internal audit team will also serve as a guideline for external auditors, leading to a more efficient, effective, and compliant report.

It is important to allow enough time to do an in-depth preimplementation audit. The more information that can be acquired for developing task lists and project plans, the more efficient and effective the audit process will be. When the audit has been completed, representatives should meet with the auditors to summarize the results. These results can be transferred to task lists for remediation and corrective actions.

CHECKLIST FOR SUCCESS

- Do not over-react or panic, and do not overspend but leverage. Do *only* what is required to become compliant, and take the opportunity to enhance the organization's current security environment in the process.
- Be sure that the covered entity is protected against all reasonably anticipated threats or hazards to the security and integrity of ePHI. Interruption to business process and workflow should be avoided at all cost.
- Be sure business and technology converge to ensure compliance with the HIPAA Security Rule.

- Realize that there can only be one chief and that the governing and advisory boards are integral to the process.
- Understand that, although benchmarking and research are mandatory, the rule purposely and specifically provides guideline only, in recognition of each covered entity's individual risk, business imperative, and budget.

BIBLIOGRAPHY

1. CMS. 2002. *CMS Information Systems Threat Identification Resource*. Baltimore, MD: Center for Medicare and Medicaid Services (http://www.cms.hhs.gov/it/security/docs/Threat_ID_resource.pdf).
2. FIPS. 2004. *Standards for Security Categorization of Federal Information and Information Systems*, FIPS-199. Washington, DC: Federal Information Processing Standards (http://csrc.nist.gov/publications/fips/fips199/FIPS-PUB-199-final.pdf).
3. NIST. 2005. *An Introductory Resource Guide for Implementing the Health Insurance Portability and Accountability Act (HIPAA) Security Rule,* NIST Special Publication 800-66, Washington, DC: National Institute of Standards and Technology.
4. Parmigiani, J.; McGowan, B. *Risk Analysis: First Step in HIPAA Security.* Colts Neck, NJ: Blass Consulting; 2004 (http://www.complyassistant.com).

Global –
Health Insurance

Health Insurance Portability and Accountability Act (HIPAA): Requirements

Todd Fitzgerald, CISSP, CISA, CISM
*Director of Systems Security and Systems Security Officer, United Government Services, LLC,
Milwaukee, Wisconsin, U.S.A.*

Abstract

Health Insurance Portability and Accountability Act (HIPAA) should be viewed as an opportunity to address some areas that may not have received attention in the past due to other funding priorities. Protection of health information should be viewed as an opportunity—an opportunity to place some controls around health information such that new processes can be enabled. Technologies continue to emerge with exciting new possibilities, such as wireless access, personal digital assistants, digital photography advances, cell phone proliferation, and instant messaging, to name a few. These new technologies deliver new security challenges as well as new opportunities for collaboration. Creating the proper security foundation will enable these new uses to be exploited, increasing the availability and quality of healthcare, such as Internet health information lookup, while reducing some overhead costs, such as reducing staffing requirements (or providing more funds for increased quality) for customer service.

We are privileged to live in a society that values freedom and the individual rights of its citizens to have the opportunity to make choices that affect their own well-being. These freedoms are exercised on a daily basis without conscious thought and are many times taken for granted. For example, people make choices about where they will eat lunch, where they will have cars repaired, who will provide care for their children, where they will spend their money, what leisure activities they will participate in, and how they will use their time. One of the most important choices individuals make is the selection of healthcare. The choice of healthcare provider, be it a doctor, a hospital, or an integrated clinical system with a network of doctors and treatment facilities, is a personal choice based on many factors such as professional competence, practice location, specialty of the medicine, and trust in the ability of the medical professional. Selection of someone to provide medical attention is no small matter to be taken lightly; being able to trust the medical professional is arguably of the utmost importance.

In a generation where access to information is literally only seconds away, this trust is not blind. The Internet is used extensively by patients or concerned family members for researching medical ailments and then suggesting treatments or questioning the physician's recommended course of action. Even though a high level of trust may be invested with the physician, individuals still feel a need to find other sources of information that corroborate the recommended treatment. Due to this phenomenon, the patient is much more informed about treatment choices, medications, and potential outcomes. The Internet has accelerated this shift, which started as "Baby Boomers," also known as the "sandwich generation," needed to care simultaneously for their children and elderly parents, in addition to being concerned with the medical effects of their own aging.

Just as patients must be able to trust their medical professionals for their treatment, patients trust that they are using the medical health information, their personal medical health information, solely for the purposes of treatment, payment, or operations. They also trust that this information is kept private and that appropriate measures are taken to ensure that the information is not inadvertently disclosed, destroyed, or changed in a way that could adversely affect their treatment or create personal embarrassment. However, analogous to the trust that is placed in the medical professional, much more information is available today about privacy issues; thus people are also much more informed. The media has communicated countless examples such as hackers disclosing personal medical information by posting on the Internet, company e-mails inadvertently revealing patients using a particular medication, being solicited through someone having knowledge of personal medical history, or disclosure within an organization of psychological notes of other employees. People expect that their confidentiality will be maintained and the trust relationship between patient and provider is not compromised. Privacy issues address the rights of the individual with respect to this trust relationship, whereas security is the mechanism that ensures that this privacy is reasonably maintained throughout the system. True privacy of information cannot be achieved without adequate security controls. The Health Insurance Portability and Accountability Act (HIPAA) has several objectives, one of which is to ensure the appropriate security safeguards are in place to protect the privacy of health information.

Encyclopedia of Information Assurance DOI: 10.1081/E-EIA-120046839

Copyright © 2011 by Taylor & Francis. All rights reserved.

Global –
Health Insurance

HIPAA ARRIVES ON THE SCENE

The Health Insurance Portability and Accountability Act (HIPAA) of 1996 was enacted by Congress (Public Law 104–191) with two purposes in mind: 1) to reform health insurance to protect insurance coverage for workers and their families when they changed or lost their jobs, and 2) to simplify the administrative processes by adopting standards to improve the efficiency and effectiveness of the nation's healthcare system. Title I of HIPAA contains provisions to address health insurance reform. Title II addresses national standards for electronic transactions, unique health identifiers, privacy, and security. Title II is known as Administrative Simplification and is intended to reduce the costs of healthcare through the widespread use of electronic data interchange. Administrative Simplification was added to Title XI of the Social Security Act through subtitle F of Title II of the enacted HIPAA law.

Although the initial intent of Administrative Simplification was to reduce the administrative costs associated with processing healthcare transactions, Congress recognized that standardizing and electronically aggregating healthcare information would increase the risk of disclosure of confidential information, and the patient's privacy rights needed to be protected. Security provisions were needed not only to protect the confidentiality of information, but also to ensure that information retained the appropriate integrity. Consider the situation where the diagnosis or vital sign information is changed on a medical record, and subsequent treatment decisions are based on this information. The impact of not being able to rely on the information stored within the healthcare environment could have life-threatening consequences. Thus, privacy issues are primarily centered on the confidentiality of information to ensure that only the appropriate individuals have access to the information, whereas the security standards take on a larger scope to address issues of integrity and availability of information.

RULE-MAKING PROCESS

Each provision of Administrative Simplification must follow a rule-making process that is designed to achieve consensus within the Department of Health and Human Services (HHS) and other federal departments. When the rule is approved within the government, the public has the opportunity to comment on the proposal, and then these comments are evaluated in the determination of the final rule. Once the rules have gone through this process, they have the force of federal law. The Department of Health and Human Services implementation teams draft Notices of Proposed Rule Making (NPRMs), which are subsequently published in the Federal Register after being reviewed within the federal government, according

Table 1 Administrative simplification rule-making process.

1. HHS implementation team drafts Notice of Proposed Rule-Making (NPRM) for review
2. HHS Data Council Committee on Health Data Standards reviews
3. Advisors to HHS Secretary (division agency heads) agree
4. Office of Management and Budget (OMB) reviews
5. Proposed NPRM published in Federal Register
6. Public comments are solicited for 60 day period
7. Comments open for public view
8. Comments are analyzed and content summarized by implementation team
9. Final rule is published, standards become effective 24 months after adoption, 36 months for small health plans

to the process shown in Table 1. Once the NPRMs are published, they are available for a 60 day public comment period, which provides for input and for interested parties to influence the outcome of the final regulation. After the publication of the final rule, most large health plans, clearinghouses, and providers have 24 months to be in compliance, and smaller parties have 36 months.

The proposed security and electronic signature standards were originally published in the Federal Register on August 12, 1998. The Security Rule has been delayed on several occasions, as resources were committed to and focused on the proposed transaction and code set and Privacy Rules, both of which generated a large number of public comments. The number of public comments can be large, and each one must be reviewed. Over 17,000 public comments were received on the Transaction and Code Sets NPRM and several thousand on the Privacy Rule and on the proposed Security Rule. The transaction and code set compliance date was also delayed by 1 year, to October 16, 2003, as long as the covered entity filed an extension request by October 15, 2002. Additionally, the Security Rule was initiated during the Clinton administration and was carried over into the Bush administration, which created political challenges for expedient passage of the rule. As a result, the language was rewritten during 2002 to coincide with the Privacy Rule, which needed to go through the HHS clearance process prior to final rule publication. During 2002, the Centers for Medicare and Medicaid Services several times provided their best estimates of publication of the final rule, which passed through the clearance process and was submitted to the Office of Management and Budget (OMB) in early 2003 and was published in the Federal Register as 45 CFR Parts 160, 162, and 164 on February 20, 2003. The regulations became effective on April 21, 2003, and covered entities must comply with the requirements by April 21, 2005. Small health plans have until April 21, 2006, to comply with the rule.

THE SECURITY OBJECTIVES OF THE FINAL RULE DID NOT CHANGE SUBSTANTIALLY

Many organizations had been "waiting" for the final rule to be published before seriously embarking on security issues. Some started HIPAA security gap analysis efforts, but many were reluctant to invest large sums of money when there was the potential that the rules might change. The reality is that the rule embodies security practices that should be performed during the normal course of business to protect the information assets and should be initiated regardless of the rule. Waiting only shortens the time available to dedicate to reasonable security and can also have the negative effect of driving up costs at a later date. For example, if a new Web-based application is in the process of being designed and adequate attention to security is not taking place during early phases of the system development cycle, the costs of retrofitting security after implementation will be 10 to 20 times the cost. Reanalysis, rewriting of the applications, integrating technical security mechanisms, and retesting and implementing the system a second time all drive up the cost. There is also the business opportunity cost of deploying scarce information technology and business resources toward retrofitting the application vs. building new functionality.

Many of the security constructs remained in the rule, as these constructs are generally industry security practices necessary to secure information that have been applied successfully in other arenas requiring higher levels of security, such as the Department of Defense, financial institutions, and companies heavily engaged in E-commerce. The final HIPAA Security Rule recognizes the need to protect electronic health information with the appropriate administrative, physical, and technical safeguards that have been applied to other industries.

The final Security Rule was reoriented to support the final Privacy Rule, which was issued on December 28, 2000, and was last modified on August 14, 2002. The Privacy Rule compliance date for most covered entities was April 14, 2003. The proposed Security Rule focused on information maintained or transmitted by a covered entity in electronic form. The scope of the information now covered by the final Security Rule has been narrowed to health information addressed by the Privacy Rule. The Privacy Rule addresses individually identifiable health information known as protected health information (PHI) in all forms, including electronic and paper. The final Security Rule focuses only on the PHI that is in electronic form (e-PHI), in transit or in storage (data at rest); otherwise, the scope is the same as the Privacy Rule. This eliminates some of the confusion surrounding what information needed to be addressed by the Security Rule, which seemed to be in conflict with the Privacy Rule in the Security Rule NPRM.

In addition to the reorientation with the Privacy Rule, the final Security Rule changed the nomenclature of the "requirements" and "implementation features" and replaced these with "standards" and "implementation specifications," respectively. The implementation specifications were also categorized as "required" or "addressable." This was done to provide consistency with the Privacy Rule and the Transactions Rule and provide common terminology. The new approach is much cleaner, manageable, and easier to interpret. In making this change, the original 69 implementation features were reduced to 14 required implementation specifications to support the requirements, now referred to as the Security Standards.

There also appeared to be a change from a proscriptive approach to one that requires a covered entity to look at the risks and vulnerabilities to the protected health information that it transmits or maintains in electronic form and determine the reasonable and appropriate security measures to provide adequate protection of this information. The Administrative Simplification revisions to the Social Security Act required that that Secretary of HHS adopt standards that consider:

1. The technical capabilities of the record systems used to maintain the information
2. Costs of the security measures
3. Training needs for those who have access to health information
4. The value of audit trails in computerized record systems
5. The needs and capabilities of small health and rural health providers

Whereas these requirements apply to the broader topic of "health information," the final Security Rule has taken this approach with respect to electronic protected health information. Therefore, each organization must make the judgments as to what is "reasonable and appropriate" based on its size, complexity of systems, capabilities, cost of security measures, and probability and criticality of potential risks to e-PHI. Larger organizations are expected to provide more resources and have the financial ability to introduce more complex solutions.

Approximately 2350 comments were received on the initial Security Rule. These comments were assessed and taken into account with keeping the underlying goals of information protection in mind. Some of the proposed implementation specification changes were seen as resulting in standards that would be too difficult to understand or apply. Some comments proposed the expansion of applicability to all entities involved in healthcare, others sought clarification of their particular entity's requirements. Some comments demonstrated the confusion with understanding the requirements, or felt that the requirements were too granular or restrictive, or that the definitions needed further explanation. These comments were reviewed and considered in the final rule, with HHS providing changes to the rule based on industry practices, government regulations, and its mandate to produce a set of security standards.

PRIVACY RULE REQUIREMENTS FOR SECURITY

Even in the absence of the final Security Rule being available for most of the period that organizations were addressing Privacy Rule issues, the references in the Privacy Rule, which was originally published for public comment on November 11, 1999, and subsequently issued with a compliance date of April 14, 2003, as shown in Table 2, clearly indicated the need for a reasonable level of security practices to be in place. The safeguard standard contained within §164.530 of the Privacy Rule states:

> A covered entity must have in place appropriate administrative, technical, and physical safeguards to protect the privacy of protected health information.

This appears to suggest a linkage to the Security Rule requirements, which have a compliance date much further out (at least 2 years) from the compliance date of the Privacy Rule!

The implementation specification for safeguards in the final Privacy Rule continues this thought, by stating:

> A covered entity must reasonably safeguard protected health information from any intentional or unintentional use or disclosure that is in violation of the standards, implementation specifications or other requirements of this subpart.... A covered entity must reasonably safeguard protected health information to limit incidental uses or disclosures made pursuant to an otherwise permitted or required use or disclosure.

It is clear from these excerpts that "reasonable" security is expected to be implemented for the Privacy Rule to protect the privacy of health information. Moreover, the proposed Security Rule only applies to electronic information, whereas the Privacy Rule applies to all forms of protected health information. This creates a situation where the Privacy Rule assumes broader application in the form of protected information being addressed than the proposed Security Rule.

FINAL HIPAA SECURITY RULE

The Administrative Simplification (Part C of Title XI of the Social Security Act) provisions state that covered entities that maintain or transmit health information are required to:

> ...maintain reasonable and appropriate administrative, physical, and technical safeguards to ensure the integrity and confidentiality of the information and to protect against any reasonable anticipated threats or hazards to the security or integrity of the information and unauthorized use or disclosure of the information.

Because the final Security Rule was written to be consistent with the Privacy Rule, the focus of security standards applied to "health information" in support of the Administrative Simplification requirements were shifted to PHI and specifically to e-PHI. The applicability statement of the final Security Rule states:

> A covered entity must comply with the applicable standards, implementation specifications, and requirements of this subpart with respect to electronic protected health information.

Covered entities are defined as 1) a health plan, 2) a healthcare clearinghouse, and 3) a healthcare provider who transmits any health information in electronic form in connection with a transaction covered by Part 162 of Title 45 of the Code of Federal Regulations (CFR).

This is where the security standards become important. According to the Security Rule, these standards were written to "define the administrative, physical, and technical safeguards to protect the confidentiality, integrity, and

Global – Health Insurance

Table 2 Notice of proposed rule-making (NPRM) dates.

Proposed rule	NPRM date	Final date	Compliance date
Transaction and code sets	5/07/1998	8/17/2000[a]	10/16/2003[a]
Privacy	11/11/1999	March 2001[b]	4/14/2003[c]
Security	8/12/1998	2/20/2003	4/21/2005[d]
Employer ID	6/16/1998	3/31/2002	7/30/2004[e]

[a] Compliance date for Transaction and Code Sets was extended through legislation enacted on December 27, 2001, titled the Administrative Simplification Compliance Act, as long as providers submitted a request for extension by October 15, 2002. Modifications were made February 20, 2003, and corrected on March 10, 2003.

[b] Privacy rule changes were proposed March 27, 2002, and the final rule published August 14, 2002; however, the compliance date was not changed from the original date. Guidance was previously issued on July 6, 2001.

[c] Small health plans must be compliant by April 14, 2004.

[d] Small health plans must be compliant by April 21, 2006.

[e] Small health plans must be compliant by August 1, 2005.

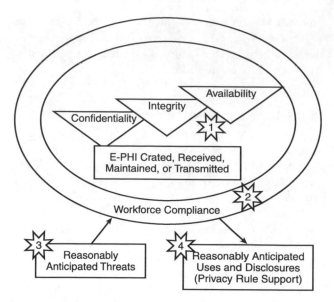

Fig. 1 Security rule general requirements.

availability of electronic protected health information." Therefore, by applying the security standards on electronic PHI as the scope, the objectives of Administrative Simplification will be satisfied. All of the security standards must be satisfied, some through required implementation specifications and some through addressable implementation specifications.

As shown in Fig. 1, protecting the confidentiality, integrity, and availability of electronic protected health information is at the core of the security requirements, while reasonably anticipated threats (security), uses, and disclosures (privacy) must also be protected and compliance of the workforce with the security standards ensured.

LET'S JUST BE REASONABLE

The definition of "reasonable" can vary from person to person. The final assessment appears to be headed for the courts and will be determined by case law as a result of lawsuits. Consider the case where an employer has installed a proximity card reader for 500 employees at a data center containing protected health information. Assume the facility has a guard during the daytime; however, during the evening hours the computer operators watch the surveillance cameras for suspicious activity. One evening, while the night operator went to the restroom, someone using an unreturned visitor's badge obtained during the day entered the building and removed three laptops. Were reasonable steps taken to prevent the theft? Was the fact that the operator left his station unattended unreasonable? Was it unreasonable that the unreturned visitor's badge still worked? Or, would a jury view this situation as one that could be reasonably expected to occur? Consider another example where patient information is

discovered after a Web server is hacked. If correct firewall configurations were set 99% of the time, except for one instance where the network engineer was upgrading the server and inadvertently opened some ports after a long, tiring weekend, was the information not reasonably protected? Is "most of the time" reasonable?

Different organizations make different security decisions based on the risk that they are willing to assume. Organizations take into account the costs, technical abilities, and the risk that they are willing to assume based on their business objectives. It is critical that companies assess the threats, vulnerabilities, and risks to electronic information and develop reasonable steps to address the risk. Each of these decisions and their rationale should be documented so that it can be understood at a later point in time why the decision was made. Documenting these decisions also forces the organization to really look at the decisions that are being made and whether or not they make sense. It is not uncommon to go through this process, only to find out that management team members were making different assumptions as to the level of risk and were accepting an unreasonable level of risk without being aware that they were.

SECURITY STANDARDS

The 1998 proposed Security Rule defined standards for the security of individual health information under the control of the covered entities (health plans, clearinghouses, and healthcare providers). The three safeguard categories of Administrative, Physical, and Technical contain a total of 18 security standards (vs. 24 requirements in the proposed rule) that must be addressed, as shown in Table 3. The standards are intended to be technology neutral so that advances in technology can be used to the best advantage as they evolve.

In support of the security standards, there are 14 required implementation specifications that address 7 of the 18 security standards, as some security standards are comprised of multiple required implementation specifications. For example, the Security Management Process security standard contains four required implementation specifications, including Risk Analysis, Risk Management, Sanction Policy, and Information System Activity Review.

The covered entity must decide, through executing the risk analysis, risk mitigation strategy, cost of implementation, and evaluating the security measures that are already in place, whether or not the "addressable implementation specification" is reasonable and appropriate and should be implemented. If the specification is viewed as not reasonable and appropriate, but for the standard to be met another security safeguard is necessary to be implemented, the entity may implement the safeguard using an alternative control as long as it accomplishes the same result as the

Global – Health Insurance

Table 3 HIPAA security standards and implementation specifications.

Security standard	Required implementation specification	Addressable implementation specification
Administrative Safeguards		
Security management process	Risk analysis Risk management Sanction policy Information system activity review	
Assigned security responsibility	Required (no implementation specification)	
Workforce security		Authorization and supervision Workforce clearance procedure Termination procedures
Information access management	Isolating healthcare clearinghouse function	Access authorization Access establishment and modification
Security awareness and training		Security reminders Protection from malicious software Log-in monitoring Password management
Security incident procedures	Response and reporting	
Contingency plan	Data backup plan Disaster recovery plan Emergency mode operation plan	Testing and revision procedure Applications and data criticality analysis
Evaluation	Required (no implementation specification)	
Business associate contracts and other arrangements	Written contract or other arrangement	
Physical Safeguards		
Facility access controls		Contingency operations Facility security plan Access control and validation procedures Maintenance records
Workstation use	Required (no implementation specification)	
Workstation security	Required (no implementation specification)	
Device and media controls	Disposal Media reuse	Accountability Data backup and storage
Technical Safeguards		
Access control	Unique user identification Emergency access procedure	Automatic log-off Encryption and decryption
Audit controls	Required (no implementation specification)	
Integrity		Mechanism to authenticate electronic protected health information
Person or entity authentication	Required (no implementation specification)	
Transmission security		Integrity controls Encryption

addressable implementation specification. In other words, an organization could select other controls as long as the security standard is met. In this case, the organization must document the decision not to implement the addressable implementation specification, the rationale behind it, and the alternative control that was implemented in its place. There are 22 addressable implementation specifications, which address nine of the Security Standards; four of the

Security Standards also contain required implementation specifications as well.

The six remaining Security Standards contain neither an addressable implementation specification nor a required implementation specification. In these cases it was felt that the definition of the standard itself was sufficient to understand the implementation required. For example, the Assigned Security Responsibility Standard is "identify the

Global –
Health Insurance

Global –
Health Insurance

security official who is responsible for the development and implementation of the policies and procedures required by this subpart [Security Rule] for the entity." Additional explanation is really not necessary to understand the standard; someone needs to be designated to fulfill this role to satisfy the standard.

To "meet the Security Standards," 36 required or addressable implementation specifications must be reviewed and complied with, either through the required implementation specification, the prescribed (addressable) implementation specification, or an alternative control; combined with six Security Standards without any implementation specification noted totals 42 areas that are required to be acted upon in some manner. Although some of these tasks can be completed quickly depending on the current security profile of the organization, this still represents a significant undertaking, requiring about two of these areas to be evaluated each and every month from now until the compliance date! If someone is not "charged with the security responsibility," this would be a great time to satisfy the Assigned Security Responsibility Security Standard and draft someone. In many organizations, the need was recognized and the positions filled during the attention to the Privacy Rule due to the requirements to "have in place appropriate administrative, technical, and physical safeguards to protect the privacy of protected health information."

CHANGES TO THE PROPOSED STANDARDS IN THE FINAL RULE

The following is a brief summary of the intent of each Security Standard, along with the changes from the proposed Security Rule. Each of the security standards descriptions contains references to addressable or required implementation specifications. The reader is referred to Table 3 for the specific implementation specification designation (required or addressable).

Administrative Safeguards

Administrative safeguards consist of the formal organizational practices that manage the selection and execution of security measures to protect data and the conduct of personnel in the protection of the data. It is important that these practices are documented in the form of policies, procedures, standards, or guidelines that are followed by the organization. Although there may be accepted practices that are followed within the organization, without proper documentation it is difficult to demonstrate that all employees are working with the same assumptions. Additionally, without the documented procedures new employees may not be adequately informed as to their security responsibilities.

Much of the detail of this section was removed and the requirements were generalized to be less proscriptive. The order of the previous requirements (alphabetical) was rearranged to be more logical, with the establishment of the security management process occurring first, as everything else within the security program should be built on this. The previous requirements for system configurations and for a formal mechanism for processing records were dropped from the final rule as they were seen as redundant, unnecessary, or ambiguous with other requirements for documentation and processes.

Security management process

Conduct risk analysis to assess vulnerabilities and risks to the confidentiality, integrity, and availability of e-PHI, risk management of the implemented security measures, apply appropriate sanctions to workforce members who fail to comply with the security policies and procedures, and implement procedures to regularly review records of information system activity (i.e., audit logs, access reports, security incident tracking reports). The specification of "Internal Audit" was changed from the proposed rule, as it was not intended to have a rigid, costly review process over the system activity related to security, but rather to ensure that appropriate attention to security continues to take place over time. Sanction policies were seen as necessary to meet the requirement of "ensuring" compliance of the officers and employees and that the introduction of negative consequences for non-compliance increases the chances that compliance will be achieved. It is a typical result that if employees know that something is being monitored and followed, they are less likely to be in non-compliance with the expectations.

Security management is an ongoing function with a continuous cycle of risk analysis, risk management, and issuance of security policies and their sanctions. Over time, attention to security within organizations tends to dissipate, which (unknowingly) increases the risk profile.

Assigned security responsibility

An individual must be identified who is responsible for the development and implementation of security policies and procedures. Many individuals may be involved in security for the organization, but there must be one individual named with the responsibility of protecting e-PHI. The proposed rule indicated an individual or organization could be named; however, this is no longer the case; it must be a single official. Multiple people are typically involved in the security function in larger organizations; however, someone must be named with accountability for the function to ensure that policies and procedures are developed and implemented as required by the rule. The individual and supporting organization utilize the security management processes to carry out the mission of the information security program.

Workforce security

Implement policies and procedures to ensure that every member of the workforce has appropriate access to e-PHI and prevent those who should not have access through authorization/supervision of workforce members, clearance procedures, and termination procedures. The specifications are all addressable because it will vary by organization as to whether or not they need to be formalized. Background checks are not required for all employees through the clearance specification; however, some form of screening needs to take place prior to permitting access to e-PHI. The detailed requirements of the termination procedures have been removed, again to be less proscriptive and allow flexibility for the specific environments. The intent is to ensure that when individuals with access to e-PHI are no longer associated with the entity, the exposure for potential damage is mitigated by removing their access. Small offices would most likely not require the formalized procedures that large organizations would require to meet the standard.

Information access management

Implement policies and procedures for establishing, authorizing, reviewing, documenting, and modifying a user's right to access a workstation, transaction, program, process, or other means of accessing e-PHI. This forms the basis of acceptable information security access management practices through 1) authorizing appropriate access, and then 2) establishing the access. This standard supports the minimum necessary requirements of the Privacy Rule, and as such, specific references to "role-based," "user-based," "context-based," discretionary/mandatory access control, and the distinctions between authorization and access control were omitted from the final rule. An added required implementation specification to isolate the clearinghouse functions from the larger organization through their own policies and procedures was added to this requirement.

Security awareness and training

Implement a security awareness and training program for all members of the workforce, including management, training on protection from malicious software (viruses, Trojan horses, worms, scripting, etc.), log-in monitoring, password management, and periodic security reminders. The end users are the key to successful security, and each member of the workforce must receive ongoing training. Flexibility is left up to the organization as to how this can be implemented through techniques such as face-to-face, pamphlets, new employee orientation, Web-based, etc. Many security practitioners feel that security awareness and training are the most effective areas to invest in security. These individuals represent the "security front line" and education here causes individuals to support the security program through awareness and preventing larger security issues. It does little good to implement a complex technical solution, such as implementing dynamic passwords utilizing RADIUS or TACACS+ authentication and token cards, if the user tapes a PIN to the back of the token card. Similarly, having policies that deal with the handling of confidential information would be ineffective if the users were not aware of the types of information considered confidential and needed extra measures to provide adequate protection. Training is a continual process that should focus on different aspects of information security.

Security incident procedures

Incident response and reporting procedures are required to mitigate the potential harmful effects of the incident and provide documentation of the incident and outcome. An incident is defined as the attempted or successful unauthorized access, use, disclosure, modification, or destruction of information or interference with system operations. Each organization must define what event would be considered a security incident and the internal/external reporting processes necessary to support the incident.

Formal, current, accurate, and documented procedures for the reporting and response to security incidents are necessary to ensure that violations are reported and handled promptly. Seemingly small incidents may be symptomatic of a larger problem and should be thoroughly investigated. Lack of attention to the small incidents also creates a culture that is desensitized to information security and creates a greater risk that a larger risk may occur. For example, if attention is not paid to the occasional laptop that is missing every few months because the information stored on the laptop was not seen as valuable, then the larger problem of laptop security awareness and the need for locking devices may be missed. Subsequently, a nurse's laptop containing health information or an executive's laptop containing confidential business strategic information may be compromised when it could have been prevented.

Contingency plan

In the aftermath of September 11, 2001, many organizations have increased their focus toward disaster recovery. The contingency plan provides the organizational readiness to respond to systems emergencies so that critical operations can be continued during an emergency. To meet the requirement, applications and data criticality analysis, data backup plans, disaster recovery plans, emergency-mode operation plans, and testing and revision procedures are included as required or addressable implementation specifications to support the Contingency Plan standard. Most large organizations have disaster recovery plans covering the mainframe environments as a result of the Y2K contingency planning that had previously taken place. However, infrastructure and staffing are constantly changing, and as a result, many of these plans need to be updated. Although most organizations tend to back up network environments on a regular schedule, these environments rarely have adequate disaster recovery plans or are tested on a regular basis. With the continuing shift to the network/server environment for mission-critical applications, increased attention will need to be paid to the contingency planning of these facilities.

Policies and procedures are to be implemented for responding to emergencies or other occurrences (i.e., fire, vandalism, system failure, natural disaster) that damage systems that contain e-PHI. This is accomplished through data backups, disaster recovery plans, emergency mode operation plans (ability to continue business during the crisis), testing and revision procedures, and applications and data criticality analysis. This standard was proposed and remained in the final rule as data becomes most vulnerable during crisis events because security controls are typically bypassed to bring the systems back into operation. e-PHI lost during these events impacts the availability and integrity of the information, exposing the data to confidentiality issues of improper use and disclosure.

Evaluation

Perform a periodic technical and non-technical evaluation based on the standards initially and also after environmental and operational changes affecting e-PHI. This evaluation can be performed internally or externally and replaces the certification requirement of the earlier rule. It can be expected that independent certification guides, secure software listings, and compliance guidelines will emerge from private enterprise. To form a meaningful evaluation, the risk-level acceptance of the organization should be understood prior to the evaluation, as the security measures chosen should be a result of the risk assessment decisions.

Evaluation processes, whether performed internally or externally, have the positive impact of documenting the security actions taken and obtaining management sign-off, which tends to create greater accountability beyond the security department for the implementation. It also tends to ensure that the agreed-upon security parameters in the design process are carried through to implementation.

Business associates and other arrangements

The final rule eliminated the chain-of-trust agreement and replaced it with the requirement for a covered entity to ensure that appropriate safeguards are assured by the business associate through inclusion of security requirements in written contracts. The scope is limited to e-PHI, as is the rest of the Security Rule. The business associate definitions are those that are utilized within the Privacy Rule. In the event that a covered entity is aware of a pattern or practice that the business associate is engaged in that is considered a violation of the business associate's obligation, the covered entity would be in non-compliance if it failed to take reasonable steps to end the violation. Other arrangements specify situations such as how the rules apply to government entities, other laws, terminations of contracts, etc.

Physical Safeguards

Protecting the covered entity's electronic information systems and the buildings that contain these systems from fire, natural and environmental hazards, and unauthorized intrusion are the focus of the Physical Safeguards. These controls support many of the administrative and technical controls defined in the other safeguard sections. Consider the situation where very tight logical access controls (Technical Safeguard Access Control Security Standard) are defined to support the Administrative Safeguard Standards For Information Access. Assume that a computer containing these controls is located in an area where other building tenants have unrestricted access. Even with two-factor authentication, encryption of files, and properly implemented access control facilities, if the physical server can be accessed, an alternate operating system could be loaded, or worse yet, the server could be stolen, thus providing the intruder with ample opportunity to decipher encrypted files. Unauthorized employees having physical access to the server creates unnecessary additional risk.

Two requirements of the proposed rule, assigned security responsibility and security awareness training, made much more sense in the Administrative Safeguards section, and they were moved to that section in the final Security Rule. Following is a discussion of the Physical Safeguard Standards and related implementation specifications.

Facility access controls

Focus on the facilities that provide physical access to the electronic information systems, the standard limits physical access through contingency operations (facility access in the event of an emergency), facility security plan (safeguard facility from unauthorized physical access, tampering, and theft), access control and validation procedures (validate access to facilities based on role, control access to programs for testing and revision), and maintenance records (document repairs to facility security components). The standards appear to be straightforward and permit the organization to review the risks and implement the appropriate controls, unlike the proposed rule, which appeared to require all of the implementation specifications without regard to the risk analysis. It is still the covered entity's responsibility to ensure the facilities where e-PHI is located and transmitted are secured properly, whether or not the facility is owned by the covered entity.

Global –
Health Insurance

Workstation use

For workstations that are allowed access to PHI, implement policies and procedures specifying proper functions and the manner in which those functions are to be performed (i.e., locking workstations, logging off, invoking screen-savers) and the physical attributes of the space surrounding the workstations. The workstation terminology is used to replace "terminal" and applies to the broad range of computing equipment with access to e-PHI (laptops, desktops, personal digital assistants, etc.) and is not limited to the desktop PC.

Workstation security

Implement physical safeguards for all workstations that access e-PHI, restricting access to authorized users, consistent with proposed rule. Contents displayed on the workstation, especially those in open areas such as nurses' stations, must be secured so that private information is not viewable by unauthorized persons. Workstations should also be secured so that only authorized personnel would have access to the workstation. In practice, some workstations need to be in open areas and approaches such as turning the monitor away from public viewing, logging off the workstation when unattended, utilizing screensavers, and ensuring that the workstation is protected from theft would appear to be reasonable.

Device and media controls

Implement policies and procedures governing the receipt and removal of hardware and software in and out of a facility and movement within a facility through disposal procedures, media reuse procedures, accountability (record of movements), and data backup and storage (in this case, this is related to the backup of e-PHI prior to the moving of equipment). Media reuse procedures were added to the rule to address reuse and recycling. There have been news stories of hard drives purchased on E-Bay that contained sensitive information, which subsequently was retrieved because it was not properly disposed of after final disposition.

Technical Safeguards

The technical security services (processes that protect, control, and monitor information access), and the technical security mechanisms (processes that prevent unauthorized access over a communications network) have been combined into the Technical Safeguards category. This is very logical, as many organizations viewed these as technical requirements. Data authentication was renamed to the standard security terminology of integrity. Following is a discussion of the Technical Safeguard Standards and related implementation specifications.

Access control

Implement technical policies and procedures for electronic information systems containing e-PHI to allow access only to those persons who have been granted access through the Information Access Management processes in the Administrative Safeguards. Unique user IDs are necessary to identify and track the individual's activity, emergency access procedures are required to support operations in an emergency situation, and implementation specifications of automatic log-off and the use of encryption can support the access security standards. There was much confusion around the requirements for role-based, context-based, mandatory access control, discretionary access control, etc., in the proposed rule. The new specification is much cleaner and affords the organization the ability to implement the appropriate rules based on the risk. For example, an organization may decide to encrypt highly sensitive e-PHI data-at-rest if there is an assessment that this information could be compromised, such as in the case of fraud investigation involving health information stored on a CD.

A procedure for emergency access during a crisis must be implemented. Consider the situation where a specialist is called in to perform an emergency procedure, but does not have access to needed health information from the local information system. The specialist needs a method to gain emergency access without "waiting for forms to be processed" by the security department.

Audit controls

Recording system activity is important so that the organization can identify suspect data access activities, assess the effectiveness of the security program, and respond to potential weaknesses. Implementation of hardware, software, and procedural mechanisms that record and examine activity in information systems containing e-PHI is necessary. Some organizations have assumed that the audit trails specified under this requirement would support the Privacy Rule. Typically, the types of information dealt with are different. Whereas the Privacy Rule is concerned with tracking of uses and disclosures, the Security Rule is concerned with tracking system activity, such as log-in attempts, access, and modification to records. Although similar, audit trails within the system context are typically not geared toward tracking the business-level information surrounding the use and disclosures, even though some records may provide supporting information. System audit trails are also not typically turned on to monitor read access to information due to the volume of information.

Integrity (formerly data authentication)

Implement policies and procedures to protect e-PHI from improper alteration or destruction through mechanisms that corroborate that the information has not been destroyed in an unauthorized manner. Techniques such as digital signatures, checksums, and error-correcting memory are all methods of ensuring data integrity. Again, the ability to assess risk, provide technology neutrality, and not be proscriptive enables the covered entity to determine the appropriate methods to ensure the integrity of the data.

Person or entity authentication (combined authentication requirements)

Implement procedures to verify that the person or entity seeking access to e-PHI is really the person or entity. The proposed rule was very proscriptive in suggesting biometrics, passwords, telephone callbacks, token systems, PINS, etc., where the rule now allows the implementation to be determined by the entity based on the risk assessment. The requirements for "irrefutable" entity authentication were removed in the final rule.

Transmission security

Implement technical security guarding against unauthorized access to e-PHI transmitted over an electronic communications network (vs. open network in the proposed rule). Integrity controls and encryption may be applied according to the risk level of the information. In cases such as dial-up lines or over a private network, encryption may not be necessary to achieve the standard's objectives; however, over the Internet the appropriate encryption levels to thwart brute-force cracking may be necessary. This is an area where technology is constantly changing, there are interoperability issues, and the feasibility of solutions may make this prohibitive for small providers.

Documentation and other related standards

To comply with the standards, implementation specifications, and any other requirements of the Security Rule, the covered entity must implement reasonable and appropriate policies and procedures in addition to the security standards specified in the Administrative, Technical, and Physical Safeguards. These must be documented and can be changed at any time. The covered entity can take into consideration the size, complexity, and capabilities of the covered entity; the technical infrastructure, hardware and software security capabilities, the costs of the security measures, and the probability and criticality of potential risks to the e-PHI.

Documentation of policies and procedures may seem to be such a logical practice that it may appear unnecessary to state it. However, many organizations operate without defined policies and procedures, and the work gets done. The difficulty is that many times it is done several different

ways, depending on the individual performing the activity. This increases the likelihood that inconsistencies will occur, increasing the potential for security incidents. Although the Security Rule does not specify a requirement to adopt ISO 9000-type standard processes, implementing procedures that follow this approach would further support that a "reasonable" approach was taken. This also permits the opportunity to review and discuss the processes across organizations and work toward improving the processes, thus increasing service delivery capabilities and reducing waste.

Consider as an example the practice of security configuration management changes. Security measures, practices, and procedures need to be documented and integrated with the other system configuration practices to ensure that routine changes to system hardware and software do not contribute to compromising the overall security. Security design efforts placed into new systems could easily be compromised and resources wasted without the appropriate level of security review for what appears to be a simple change. Security management is a continuous process. For example, a systems engineer who was upgrading a server unintentionally opened a security hole on the mail server that provided the capability to perform mail relays. This happened at 1:30 A.M., and the systems engineer discovered his error and closed the hole by 2:00 A.M. Unfortunately, within that timeframe a hacker discovered the open relay and used the mail server to send "get rich quick" e-mails to more than 2000 individuals. Each of the e-mail addresses included the mail header information, which showed that it was coming from the system engineer's organization. This demonstrates that clear, documented configurations and procedures for changing these configurations are necessary.

Many times, documentation is an afterthought. The more organizations get into the practice of seeing this as an important deliverable of the development process, the more efficient and effective the organization can become because the opportunity for future improvement becomes more visible.

PRAGMATIC APPROACH

At first glance, the 18 standards and their related implementation specifications can certainly seem daunting, presenting a case for the senior leadership, the Information Technology team, and the Information Security Officer to head for the emergency room!

The Security Rule was meant to be scalable such that small providers would not be burdened with excessive costs of implementation, and the large providers, health plans, and clearinghouses could take steps appropriate to their business environments. For example, backing up the data of a small provider may be a simple process of rotating the information to an offsite location on a weekly basis from one server, whereas a large operation may contract with a disaster recovery company or may employ electronic vaulting of the information. Decisions have to be made to reasonably protect the information, and document how the decisions were determined. Earlier it was recognized that security is always a risk-based decision, and it is sometimes difficult to determine what is "reasonable" under the circumstances.

A security plan for improvement is the most pragmatic way to move toward HIPAA compliance. Stepwise improvements in the security infrastructure, beginning with an understanding of what risks are being casually accepted within the environment, followed by targeting solutions to mitigate the critical risks, seems reasonable. Early in the process, someone needs to be assigned security responsibility to champion the security efforts. Management support should be obtained through articulation of the risks to the assets, not because "HIPAA requires that we become compliant." This approach only causes management to take a "wait and see" attitude until it is understood what other organizations are doing with the "HIPAA issue." Squarely explaining the risks and incrementally building support through successful delivery is the formula that will provide for longterm benefits for maintaining the security program. Selling the protection of assets as an ongoing activity provides the view that security is not "done" at the end of the HIPAA project. The idea should be generated that information is an asset that must be managed on an ongoing basis, just like the financial, human resources, and fixed assets of the organization. Although the temptation may be even stronger to use the "HIPAA Hammer" to pound the message into the organization now that the Final Security Rule has been published, the value of protecting the information assets, providing reduction in long-term "hidden" costs, and the opportunities enabled though secure systems, should be surfaced and promoted. A HIPAA project will have a beginning and an end, but the security program to continue protecting the information assets must survive as a fundamental business operation.

The first task in the plan should be to establish security responsibility, followed by formation of security policy and review committees, development of high-level policies, network assessments, and successive implementation of policies, procedures, and technical implementations to satisfy the various aspects of the HIPAA rule. The key is to get started, somewhere, and begin making progress. Individuals within the organization may already be working on efforts related to one of the security standards—use the opportunity to expand the scope and ensure that the security practices are formalized and documented and will meet the HIPAA security requirements.

RISK, RISK, RISK!

It should be very apparent at this point that much of the "proscriptive" nature of the Security Rule has been changed to an approach that places the emphasis on assessing the risk and determining the implementation choices that are "reasonable and appropriate." True, different organizations may look at the same risk information pertaining to e-PHI and evaluate it differently. This is to be expected, as management teams have different value systems, experiences, and views of criticality. As time goes on, industry best practices for various sizes of organizations, case law, civil suits, cost effective technology innovations, standards development, an increased focus on security and the efforts of local and national associations focused on healthcare and HIPAA will all contribute to the emergence of "*de facto* healthcare security practices." Some of these practices/standards currently exist and others will emerge prior to the compliance date, but this will be an evolutionary refinement process over time as organizations within this industry determine what security approaches support the business of healthcare. Security practices borrowed from other industries are excellent starting points for investigation. Risk assessment and risk management activities should proactively take into account the capabilities to ensure adequate protection of e-PHI.

The change away from the proscriptive nature of the Security Rule makes the rule much easier to read and understand. It also better supports the technology neutrality and scalability principles desired. Some may view the heavy reliance on the risk assessment as the lack of ability to make a "tough" standard. The more appropriate view is that each covered entity must meet the security standard, and the level to which they meet that standard must be consistent with the risk assessment results. In the case of large organizations, with the size, capabilities, and financial ability to implement the addressable specifications, they will most likely be expected to commit the resources. Taking the view that the standard does not need to be taken seriously because it is "addressable" is erroneous.

It is all about risk assessment, documenting the risks, and making good judgments as to the security measures that are reasonable and appropriate for the covered entity's individual situation.

CONCLUSION

Health Insurance Portability and Accountability Act (HIPAA) should be viewed as an opportunity to address some areas that may not have received attention in the past due to other funding priorities. Protection of health information should be viewed as an opportunity—an opportunity to place some controls around health information such that new processes can be enabled. Technologies continue to emerge with exciting new possibilities, such as wireless access, personal digital assistants, digital photography advances, cell phone proliferation, and instant messaging, to name a few. These new technologies deliver new security challenges as well as new opportunities for collaboration. Creating the proper security foundation will enable these new uses to be exploited, increasing the availability and quality of healthcare, such as Internet health information lookup, while reducing some overhead costs, such as reducing staffing requirements (or providing more funds for increased quality) for customer service.

In the short term, the struggle will continue to move toward compliance. By starting now, HIPAA decisions can be made with more planning and less reaction to the immediate security concern.

How can a covered entity possibly achieve compliance in less than 2 years (3 years for small health plans)? Disney World has the answer. Anyone that has been there knows that it is a magical place where fun things happen and the rest of life is temporarily forgotten. They also know that Disney World has an equally magical way of hiding the length of the lines to the amusements by snaking around one corner, and then the next, showing only a "manageable" line of people directly in front of you. This illusion makes the line seem shorter, as you can see only a little at a time.

Implementing the Security Standards is like Disney World in many ways. It is a very long line, with many dependencies. If we look at the whole line, we might just give up in frustration and decide to try again another day. If we view each security standard as a small line along the way to meeting our goal of protecting e-PHI, the effort does not seem quite so bad.

We are now at Disney World, we have been waiting to stand in line for the past several years, and now is our chance. There is the thrill of anticipation of getting to our destination, coupled with the fear of not getting there on time. But, we are in line now, and we need to celebrate our accomplishments . . . one turn at a time, and maybe, just maybe, have a little fun along the way.

BIBLIOGRAPHY

1. Health Insurance Reform: Security Standards; final rule, February 20, 2003, Federal Register 45 CFR Parts 160, 162 and 164, Department of Health and Human Services.
2. Security and Electronic Signature Standards—Proposed Rule, August 12, 1998, Federal Register 45 CFR Part 142, Department of Health and Human Services.
3. Health Insurance Portability and Accountability Act of 1996, August 21, 1996, Public Law 104–191.
4. The Health Insurance Portability and Accountability Act of 1996 (HIPAA), Centers for Medicare and Medicaid Services, http://cms.hhs.gov/hipaa.
5. HIPAA Administrative Simplification, Centers for Medicare and Medicaid Services, http://cms.hhs.gov/hipaa/ hipaa2.
6. Standards for Privacy of Individually Identifiable Health Information; final rule, August 14, 2002, Federal Register 45 CFR Parts 160 and 164, Department of Health and Human Services.

Health Insurance Portability and Accountability Act (HIPAA): Security Readiness

David MacLeod, Ph.D., CISSP
Chief Information Security Officer, The Regence Group, Portland, Oregon, U.S.A.

Brian T. Geffert, CISSP, CISA
Senior Manager, Deloitte & Touche Security Services Practice, San Francisco, California, U.S.A.

David Deckter, CISSP
Manager, Deloitte & Touche Enterprise Risk Services, Chicago, Illinois, U.S.A.

Abstract

Addressing health insurance portability and accountability act (HIPAA) security readiness may seem like an unmanageable task for most organizations. As outlined in this entry, by applying a framework approach to break down the task into manageable pieces, you should be able document your organization's current design, effectively identify your organization's gaps, develop an action plan to address those gaps, and execute that plan in an organized and systematic manner.

The Health Insurance Portability and Accountability Act (HIPAA) has presented numerous challenges for most healthcare organizations, but through using a framework approach we have been able to effectively identify gaps and develop plans to address those gaps in a timely and organized manner.

— *Wayne Haddad*
Chief Information Officer for The Regence Group

HIPAA SECURITY READINESS FRAMEWORK

Within the U.S. healthcare industry, increased attention is focusing on Health Insurance Portability and Accountability Act (HIPAA) readiness. For the past 5 years, healthcare organizations (HCOs) across the country have moved to prepare their environments for compliance with the proposed HIPAA security regulations. The past 5 years have also proved that HIPAA security readiness will not be a point-in-time activity for HCOs. Rather, organizations will need to ensure that HIPAA security readiness becomes a part of their operational processes that need to be maintained on a go-forward basis.

To incorporate HIPAA security readiness into your organization's operational processes, you must be able to functionally decompose your organization to ensure that you have effectively addressed all the areas within your organization. You must also be able to interpret the proposed HIPAA security regulations as they relate to your organization, identify any gaps, develop plans to address any gaps within your current organization, and monitor

your progress to ensure you are addressing the identified gaps. For most HCOs, the path to HIPAA security readiness will mean the development of a framework that will allow you to complete the tasks outlined in Fig. 1.

This entry guides you through the framework that will assist you in identifying and addressing your organization's HIPAA security readiness issues. In doing so, we assume that your organization has already established a HIPAA security team and developed a plan to apply the framework (e.g., Phase 0 activities). Finally, we do not address HIPAA's transactions, code sets, and identifiers (TCI) or privacy requirements, but you will need to consider both sets of requirements as you move through the phases of the framework.

PHASE 1: CURRENT DESIGN

The framework begins with the construction of a matrix that documents your organization's current design. The matrix captures the nuances of the environment (both physical and logical), its business processes, and the initiatives that make your HCO unique. It also lists the HIPAA security requirements and determines the applicability of the requirements to your organization's environment.

Functional Decomposition of the Organization

Organizations have typically approached HIPAA security readiness by starting with the HIPAA security requirements and applying those requirements to their information technology (IT) departments. By relying solely on this

Encyclopedia of Information Assurance DOI: 10.1081/E-EIA-120046840
Copyright © 2011 by Taylor & Francis. All rights reserved.

Global –
Health Insurance

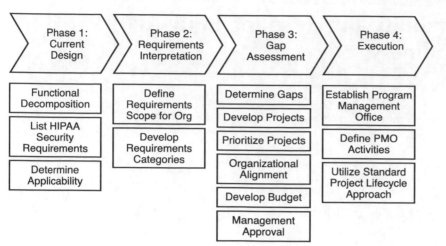

Fig. 1   HIPAA security readiness framework.

Global –
Health Insurance

approach, organizations have failed to recognize that security is cross-organizational, including business units and individual users alike. Today's Internet era is requiring ever more information sharing, further blurring the boundaries of internal access and external access. How then do you break down your organization to ensure you have adequately addressed all the areas of your organization concerning HIPAA security readiness?

Organizations can functionally decompose themselves in a number of ways, including IT environment, strategic initiatives, key business processes, or locations. To illustrate the idea of functionally decomposing your organization, we provide some examples of processes, applications, IT environment elements, strategic initiatives, and locations for a typical payer and provider in Table 1.

List HIPAA Security Requirements

The next step in building the matrix is to list the requirements for the five categories of the HIPAA security regulations as shown in Table 2. These include:

- Administrative procedures
- Physical safeguards
- Technical security services
- Technical security mechanisms
- Electronic signatures

Once you have completed the functional decomposition and listed the HIPAA security requirements, you will have created your organization's current design matrix.

Determine Applicability

The final step in the current design phase will be to determine the areas from the functional decomposition where the security requirements apply. The outcome of this exercise will be an initial list of areas on which to focus for developing the scope of the requirements. Table 3 illustrates a partial current design matrix for a typical payer organization.

PHASE 2: REQUIREMENTS INTERPRETATION

The HIPAA security requirements were designed to be used as guidelines, which means that each organization needs to interpret how it will implement them. In this section, we provide some context for defining the scope of each requirement as it applies to your organization, categorizing the practices for the security requirements, and developing the approach for meeting the security requirements based on the practices. In addition, we develop one of the security requirements as an example to support each of the steps in the process.

Define the Scope of the Security Requirements

The first step to define the scope of the security requirements is to understand the generally accepted practices and principles and where they apply for each of the requirements. To determine these generally accepted practices and their applications, you can use a number of different sources that are recognized as standards bodies for information security. The standards bodies typically fall into two categories: general practices and industryspecific practices. This is an important distinction because some industry-specific practices may be different from what is generally accepted across all industries (i.e., healthcare industry vs. automotive industry). Utilizing industry standards may be necessary when addressing a very specific area of risk for the organization. Table 4 provides a short list of standards bodies, although additional standards bodies can be located in the source listing of the HIPAA security regulations.

The next step is to evaluate the generally accepted practices against the description of each security requirement in the HIPAA security regulations, and then apply them to your environment to develop the scope of the requirements for your organization.

For our example, we use the certification requirement. Generally accepted practices for certification include the review of a system or application during its design to

Table 1 HCO functional decomposition.

Provider (Hospital and physician)	Payer
Processes	
Administration	Membership and enrollment
Financial	Claims administration
Scheduling	Contract management
Registration	Medical management
Admission, discharge, and	Underwriting and actuarial
transfer	Provider network management
Billing and A/R	Financial management
Insurance verification	Customer service
Practice management	
Applications	
AMR (EMR, CPR)	Enrollment
Laboratory	Billing and A/R
Radiology	Provider management
Pharmacy	Sales management
Order entry	Medical management
Nurse management	Claims
Financial	Financial
IT Environment	
Wireless	Wireless
WAN	WAN
LAN	LAN
Dial-up	Dial-up
Web	Web
Servers	Servers
Workstations	Workstations
Facilities	Facilities
Databases	Databases
Strategic Initiatives	
Integrating the healthcare	Customer relationship
enterprise (IHE)	management (CRM)
Electronic medical records	E-business
Web-enabling clinical	Electronic data interchange
applications	(EDI)
Electronic data interchange	
(EDI)	
Location	
Hospital	Headquarters
Outpatient clinic	Remote sales office
Off-site storage	Data center

ensure it meets certain security criteria. Once implemented, periodic reviews are conducted to ensure the system or application continues to meet those specified criteria. The certification requirement has been defined by the HIPAA security regulations as follows:

> The technical evaluation performed is part of, and in support of, the accreditation process that establishes the extent to which a particular computer system or network design and implementation meet a prespecified set of security requirements. This evaluation may be performed internally or by an external accrediting agency.

To define the scope based on this definition, we focus on two key sets of wording: *computer systems* and *network*. The term *computer system* is generally accepted to include operating systems, applications, databases, and middleware. The term *network* is generally accepted to include the architecture, design, and implementation of the components of the wide area network (WAN), extranet, dial-in, wireless, and the local area network (LAN); and it typically addresses such items as networking equipment (e.g., routers, switches, cabling, etc.). To summarize the scope of our example, we apply the certification requirement to the following areas:

- Network
- Operating systems
- Applications
- Databases
- Middleware

In addition, we document any assumptions made during the scoping process, because they will be important inputs to the solution design and as part of the final compliance assessment to understand why some areas were addressed and others were not. Finally, we store this information in each cell containing an X in our current design matrix from the applicability task in the current design phase as shown in Table 5.

Develop Requirements Categories

Developing categories for each of the security requirements assists organizations in understanding what needs to be implemented to meet the requirements. Most organizations develop security controls in a technology vacuum, meaning that they see and understand how the technology fits into their organizations, but do not understand the relationship of that technology to the policies, standards, procedures, or operations of their organizations and business. Using the technology-vacuum approach typically develops security solutions that will deteriorate over time because the solution does not have the supporting operational processes to appropriately maintain itself. We define operations as those areas that support and maintain the technology within the organization, such as assigning owners who are responsible and accountable for the technology and its supporting processes. By taking a more holistic approach that includes policies/standards, procedures, technology, and operations, you will develop security solutions to address your gaps that can be more rapidly implemented and maintained over time. Based on this approach, we typically use the following four categories for grouping the practices identified through defining the scope of requirements in the section above:

1. *Policies or standards.* Policies include senior management's directives to create a computer security

Table 2 HIPAA security requirements list.

Administrative Procedures	.308(a)(1)	Certification	
	.308(a)(2)	Chain of Trust Partner Agreement	
	.308(a)(3)	Contingency Plan	Applications and data criticality analysis
			Data backup plan
			Disaster recovery plan
			Emergency mode operation plan
			Testing and revision
	.308(a)(4)	Formal Mechanism for Processing Records	
	.308(a)(1)	Information Access Control	Access authorization
			Access establishment
			Access modification

function, establish goals for the function, and assign responsibilities for the function. Standards include specific security rules for particular information systems and practices.

2. *Procedures.* Procedures include the activities and tasks that dictate how the policies or supporting standards will be implemented in the organization's environment.

3. *Tools or infrastructure.* Tools or infrastructure includes the elements that are necessary to support implementation of the requirements within the organization such as process, organizational structure, network and system-related controls, and logging and monitoring devices.

4. *Operational.* Operational includes all the activities and supporting processes associated with maintaining the solution or system and ensuring it is running as intended. Typically, an owner is assigned to manage the execution of the activities and supporting processes. Examples of activities and supporting processes include maintenance, configuration management, technical documentation, backups, software support, and user support.

In addition, the categories will be used to monitor your progress with implementing the practices related to each requirement. To continue with our certification requirement example, we have identified some practices related to certification and placed them into categories as illustrated in Table 6.

Finally, we store this information in the current design matrix as illustrated in Table 7.

By completing your organization's current design matrix, you have developed your organization's to-be state, which includes a minimum set of practices for each area of your organization based on your interpretation of the HIPAA security requirements. You can now use this to-be state to conduct your gap assessment.

PHASE 3: GAP ASSESSMENT

With interpretation of the HIPAA security requirements complete, you are ready to conduct your HIPAA security readiness or gap assessment. The time it will take to conduct the assessment will vary greatly, depending on a number of factors that include, at a minimum, the size of the organization, the number of locations, the number of systems/applications, and current level of maturity of the security function within the organization. An example of a mature security organization is an organization with a defined security policy, an established enterprise security architecture (ESA), documented standards, procedures with defined roles and responsibilities that are followed, established metrics that measure the effectiveness of the security controls, and regular reporting to management.

The outcome of the assessment provides you with gaps based on your previously defined scope and practices for each of the security requirements. Because the identified gaps will pose certain risks to your organization, an important point to keep in mind, as your organization reviews the assessment gaps, is that your organization will not be able to address all the gaps due to limited time and resources. Typically, the gaps that you can translate into business risks need to be addressed, particularly the ones that will affect your organization's HIPAA TCI and privacy initiatives. One way of determining if a particular gap poses a business risk to the organization is to answer the question, "So what?" (by which we mean that, if we do not address this risk, how will it adversely impact our business?). For example, application security access controls are lacking on extranet-accessible applications, allowing for the compromise of sensitive health information and clearly having an adverse impact on your bottom line. If the gap does not adversely affect your business at this point in time, document the gap because it may become a business risk in the future. For example, consider an operating system that supports a non-sensitive application that has not been certified. The application, however, will be replaced in 30 days with a newer version that requires another operating system altogether. Therefore, there is no adverse impact on your bottom line. However, if the organization has resources available, then consider taking actions to mitigate the risk posed by the gap.

Global – Health Insurance

Table 3 Partial current design matrix.

	HIPAA security requirements	Processes				Locations			Applications			IT Environment		
		Claims/ Encounters	Customer service	Membership	Claims	Data center	Headquarters	Remote sales office	Claims	Sales management	Enrollment	Internet	WAN	LAN
Administrative Procedures .308(a)(1)	Certification								X	X	X	X	X	X
.308(a)(2)	Chain of Trust Partner Agreement			X										
.308(a)(3)	Contingency Plan													
	Applications and data criticality analysis					X	X	X	X	X	X	X	X	X
	Data backup plan	X	X	X	X				X	X	X			X
	Disaster recovery plan				X	X	X	X	X					
	Emergency mode operation plan	X	X	X	X	X	X	X	X					X
	Testing and revision	X	X	X	X	X	X	X	X	X	X			X
.308(a)(4)	Formal Mechanism for Processing Records	X	X	X	X				X	X	X			X
.308(a)(5)	Information Access Control													
	Access authorization								X	X	X	X	X	X
	Access establishment								X	X	X	X	X	X
	Access modification								X	X	X	X	X	X

Table 4 Generally accepted information security standards bodies.

Standards bodies	Category
United States Department of Commerce—National Institute of Standards and Technology (NIST)	General
System Administration, Networking, and Security (SANS) Institute	General
Critical Infrastructure Assurance Office (CIAO)	General
International Organization for Standardization (ISO) 17799	General
Health Care Financing Administration (HCFA)	Industry-specific: healthcare

Once you have completed your assessment and identified your gaps, you need to define a set of projects to remediate the issues. After you have defined these projects, you need to determine the resources and level of effort required to complete the projects, prioritize them, and develop a budget. In addition, you need to obtain organizational alignment around the projects. Finally, you need to get management approval for the projects.

Defining Projects

Gaps are identified based on analysis of prior requirements and then reevaluated against strategic initiatives to determine a project assignment. That is, some gaps are dealt with as stand-alone HIPAA security projects, and others are bundled or packaged within projects that more directly support strategic goals. A typical set of projects developed from an assessment includes the following:

- *High-risk mitigation.* Address high-risk vulnerabilities and exposures to your bottom line that were discovered as part of your assessment.
- *Security management.* Address the development of the core security plans and processes required to manage the day-to-day business operations at an acceptable level of risk, such as reporting and ownership, resources and skills, roles and responsibilities, risk management, data classification, operations, and maintenance for security management systems.
- *Policy development and implementation.* Address the development of security policies and standards with a supporting policy structure, a policy change management process, and a policy compliance function.
- *Education and awareness.* Address areas such as new employee orientation to meet legal and HR requirements, ongoing user and management awareness programs, and ongoing user training and education programs.
- *Security baseline.* Address development of an inventory of information assets, networking equipment, and entity connections to baseline your current environment.
- *Technical control architecture.* Address the development of a standards-based security strategy and architecture that is aligned with the organization's IT and business strategies and is applied across the organization.
- *Identity management solution.* Address the consistent use of authorization, authentication, and access controls for employees, customers, suppliers, and partners.
- *Physical safeguards.* Address physical access controls and safeguards.
- *Business continuity planning/disaster recovery planning.* Address an overall BCP/DRP program (backup and recovery plan, emergency mode operation plan, recovery plan, and restoration plan) to support the critical business functions.
- *Logging and monitoring.* Address monitoring, logging, and reporting requirements, as well as developing and implementing the monitoring architecture, policies, and standards
- *Policy compliance function.* Address the development of a policy compliance auditing and measurement process, which will also identify the process for coordinating with other compliance activities such as internal audit, regulatory, etc.
- *HIPAA security readiness support.* Address the management of the overall SRAP and supporting compliance assessment activities.

Once you have defined the projects, you have to estimate the resources and level of effort required to complete each of the projects. In addition, following management approval, further refinement of the estimate will be necessary during the scoping and planning phase of the project lifecycle.

Table 5 Certification scope and assumptions.

Scope	Network, operating systems, applications, databases, and middleware
Assumptions	None identified
Categories	Policy/standards
	Procedures
	Tools/infrastructure
	Operational

Table 6 Practice categories—certification.

Administrative Procedures—Certification	
Categories	**Practices**
Policies or standards	Written policy that identifies certification requirements
	Policy identifies individuals responsible for implementing that policy and defines what their duties are
	Policy identifies consequences of non-compliance
	Security standards for the configuration of networks, security services and mechanism, systems, applications, databases, and middleware
Procedures	Identifying certification need review
	Precertification review
	Certification readiness
	Periodic recertification review
Tools or infrastructure	Precertification readiness tool
	Certification criteria tool (standards)
	Certification compliance issue resolution tool
Operational	Operational when the following criteria are established:
	Owner
	Budget
	Charter
	Certification plan

Prioritizing Projects

For the identified projects, you need to prioritize them based on preselected criteria such as:

- *HIPAA interdependencies.* Does the project support HIPAA readiness for security, privacy, or TCI? For example, a project that includes the development of a data classification scheme can support both privacy and security.
- *Strategic initiatives.* Does the project support strategic initiatives for the organization? For example, a project that includes the development of a service to e-mail members' explanation of benefits (EOB) supports the strategic initiative to reduce paper-based transactions while facilitating HIPAA readiness for security and privacy.
- *Cost reduction.* Does the project help the organization reduce costs? For example, a project that includes the development of a VPN solution can support HIPAA security implementation requirements as well as support cost-reduction efforts related to migrating providers from extranet-based or dial-up access over the WAN to the Internet.
- *Improve customer service/experience.* Will the project improve customer service/experience? For example, implementing user provisioning and Web access

control solutions supports HIPAA security implementation requirements, as well as improves the customer experience by allowing for single sign-on (SSO) and the ability for end users to reset their own passwords with a challenge–response.

- *Foundation building.* Does the project facilitate the execution of future projects, or is it in the critical path of other necessary projects? For example, an organization will need to execute the project to develop and implement policies before executing a project to facilitate compliance.

Based on the prioritization, you can then arrange the projects into an initial order of completion or plan to present them for review by the organization.

Table 7 Certification categories.

Scope	Network, operating systems, applications, databases, and middleware
Assumptions	None identified
Categories	Policy/standards:

Policy/standards:

1. Written policy that identifies certification requirements
2. Policy identifies individuals responsible for implementing that policy and what their duties are
3. Policy identifies consequences of non-compliance
4. Security standards for the configuration of networks, security services, and mechanism, systems, applications, databases, and middleware

Procedures:

1. Identifying certification need review
2. Precertification review
3. Certification readiness
4. Periodic recertification review

Tools/infrastructure:

1. Precertification readiness tool
2. Certification criteria tool (standards)
3. Certification compliance issue resolution tool

Operational:

1. Operational when the following criteria are established:

   A. Owner, budget, charter, and certification plan

Develop Budget

Once you have the proposed plan developed, you need to develop an initial budget, which should include:

- Resources to be used to complete the project
- The duration of time needed to complete the project
- Hardware or software required to support the project's completion
- Training for new processes, and hardware or software additions
- Capitalization and accounting guidelines

Organizational Alignment and Management Approval

The plan you present to the organization will consist of the projects you have defined based on the gaps in your assessment, the resources and time needed to complete the projects, and the order of the projects' completion based on prioritization criteria. Based on input from the organization, you can modify your plan accordingly. The outcome of this activity will be to gain organizational buy-in and approval of your plan, which is especially critical when you require resources from outside of your organizational area to complete the projects.

PHASE 4: EXECUTION

Execution deals with both the management of projects and the reporting of completion status to the organization.

Program Management Office

Due to the sheer number of projects, the amount of work required to complete those projects, and the need to manage the issues arising from the projects, a formal program management office (PMO) and supporting structure will be required for the successful completion of your projects on time and within budget. You do not necessarily have to create your own security PMO, but instead you may wish to leverage an existing overall HIPAA or enterprise PMO to assist you with your project execution.

Define PMO Activities

Typically, a PMO performs the following activities:

- *Provides oversight for multiple projects.* Prioritize projects, manage project interdependencies and corresponding critical path items.
- *Manages the allocation of resources.* Deconflict resource constraints and shortages resulting from multiple project demands.
- *Manages budget.* Manage the budget for all related projects.
- *Resolves issues.* Facilitate resolution of issues both within projects and between cross-organizational departments.
- *Reports status.* Provide status reports on a periodic basis to oversight committees and management to report on the progress, issues, and challenges of the overall program.

Utilize a Standard Project Lifecycle Approach

Organizations should utilize a project lifecycle approach with a standard set of project documentation. Using a standard project lifecycle approach will streamline the design and implementation activities and support consistent, high-quality standards among different project teams and, potentially, different locations.

SUMMARY

Addressing HIPAA security readiness may seem like an unmanageable task for most organizations. As outlined in this entry, by applying a framework approach to break down the task into manageable pieces, you should be able document your organization's current design, effectively identify your organization's gaps, develop an action plan to address those gaps, and execute that plan in an organized and systematic manner.

ACKNOWLEDGMENT

Department of Health and Human Services (HHS) 45 CFR, Part 142—Security and Electronic Standards; Proposed Rule published in the Federal Register (August 12, 1998). Any reference to the HIPAA security regulations in this entry refer to the proposed HIPAA security regulations.

The framework can be used for any organization to address information security readiness by simply modifying, adding or changing the criteria (HIPAA security regulations, FDA regulations, ISO 17799, NIST, SANS, etc.).

BIBLIOGRAPHY

1. Guttman, B.; Roback, E.A. An introduction to computer security. *The NIST Handbook*; NIST Special Publication 800-12; U.S. Department of Commerce, Technology Administration, National Institute of Standards and Technology.

Global – Health Insurance

2. *Federal Register*, Part III, Department of Health and Human Services, 45 CFR Part 142—Security and Electronic Signature Standards; Proposed Rule, August 12, 1998.

3. Scholtz, T. *Global Networking Strategies — The Security Center of Excellence*; META Group: Stanford, CT; April 19, 2001.

4. *Practices for Securing Critical Information Assets*; Critical Infrastructure Assurance Office: Washington, DC, January 2000.

5. Rishel, W.; Frey, N. Strategic Analysis Report R-14-2030. *Integration Architecture for HIPAA Compliance: From "Getting It Done" to "Doing It Right,"* Gartner: Stanford, CT, August 23, 2001.

6. Guttman, B.; Swanson, M. *Generally Accepted Principles and Practices for Security Information Technology Systems*; NIST Special Publication 800-14; U.S. Department of Commerce, Technology Administration, National Institute of Standards and Technology.

Global –
Health Insurance

Health Insurance Portability and Accountability Act (HIPAA): Security Requirements

Brian T. Geffert, CISSP, CISA
Senior Manager, Deloitte & Touche Security Services Practice, San Francisco, California, U.S.A.

Abstract

With the requirements of the Health Insurance Portability and Accountability Act (HIPAA) and the growing concerns about security and privacy of all electronic personal information, organizations are now facing the reality of quickly and significantly changing the way they manage information. Thus, the gaps between current practices and the practices required for HIPAA security and privacy compliance related to personal health information present both risks and challenges to organizations. Nevertheless, these changes must be addressed and they must be implemented to meet the HIPAA security requirements.

OVERVIEW

One of the greatest challenges in any business is protecting information—in all forms—as it moves in, out, and through an organization. Because many of today's enterprise computing environments are ensembles of heterogeneous systems to which applications have been introduced one at a time, integration of each application into a cohesive system is complex. To compound the problem, paper-driven business processes tend to have makeshift origins tailored to the needs of the individual employees implementing the processes. These factors work against effective information management and protection in an organization.

MEETING HIPAA SECURITY REQUIREMENTS

For the past several years, organizations across the country have been implementing the Health Insurance Portability and Accountability Act (HIPAA) Privacy requirements while concurrently preparing their environments in anticipation of the final HIPAA Security requirements. Now that the Privacy regulations have become effective and the Security regulations have been finalized, organizations can begin to align their enterprises with the HIPAA requirements, both to ensure that HIPAA Security requirements are incorporated into their Enterprise Security Program and that the Enterprise Security Program is consistent with the Enterprise Privacy Program, Privacy Rules, and other regulatory compliance programs they have already implemented.

Enforcement of the HIPAA Security regulations will begin in April 2005. With this deadline looming, organizations must move quickly to develop and implement compliance plans. These plans should involve:

- Compiling an inventory of the individually identifiable electronic health information that the organization maintains, including "secondary networks" that are comprised of information kept on employees' personal computers and databases and are not necessarily supported by the organization's Information Technology (IT) department
- Conducting risk assessments to evaluate potential threats that could exploit the vulnerabilities to access protected health information within an organization's operating environment
- Developing tactical plans for addressing identified risks
- Reviewing existing information security policies to ensure they are current, consistent, and adequate to meet compliance requirements for security and privacy
- Developing new processes and policies and assigning responsibilities related to them
- Educating employees about the security and privacy policies
- Enforcement and penalties for violations
- Reviewing existing vendor contracts to ensure HIPAA compliance
- Developing flexible, scalable, viable solutions to address the security and privacy requirements

RISKS OF NON-COMPLIANCE

The security and privacy requirements of HIPAA compliance are potentially complex and costly to implement because they are broad in scope and will require ongoing attention to ensure compliance and awareness of regulatory updates, as well as incorporating the updates into security and privacy programs. There are also significant costs, risks, and criminal penalties associated with non-compliance, including:

Encyclopedia of Information Assurance DOI: 10.1081/E-EIA-120046542

Copyright © 2011 by Taylor & Francis. All rights reserved.

- *Impact on business arrangements.* Non-compliance may have an impact on business partner relationships that an organization maintains with third parties.
- *Damage to reputation.* Non-compliance can lead to bad publicity, lawsuits, and damage to an organization's brand and credibility.
- *Loss of employee trust.* If employees are concerned about unauthorized use of their health-related information, they are likely to be less candid in providing information and more inclined to mislead employers or health professionals seeking health information.
- *Penalties.* Penalties range from $25,000 to $250,000, and one to 10 years in prison for each offense.

Entities covered by HIPAA ("covered entity") are health plans, health-care clearinghouses, and health-care providers that conduct any of the HIPAA standard transactions. These "entities" include employers that sponsor health plans (with more than 50 covered employees); health, dental, vision, and prescription drug insurers; Health Maintenance Organizations (HMOs); Medicare; Medicaid; Medicare supplement insurers; and some long-term care insurers. Other entities that do business with a covered entity and have access to health information will be indirectly affected by HIPAA.

ENTERPRISE SECURITY AND HIPAA

HIPAA Privacy regulations apply to protected health information (PHI) in any form, whereas HIPAA Security regulations apply only to electronic PHI. Any approach to enterprise security affecting this information must include both, as shown in Fig. 1. Although the final HIPAA Security Standards apply only to electronic PHI (EPHI), organizations must begin their decision-making activities with a thorough understanding of the HIPAA Privacy regulations that became effective April 14, 2003.

An organization's approach to HIPAA Security regulations can effectively leverage the assessment information gathered and business processes developed during the implementation of HIPAA Privacy regulations to support a consistent enterprisewide approach to its enterprise security projects.

ROLE OF INDUSTRY STANDARDS

While an organization might be tempted to begin its security implementation by reviewing what the regulations require, most security experts agree that the organization should look first to industry standards and generally accepted practices to develop rational security solutions based on risk for the organization, and *then* evaluate whether HIPAA may require additional measures. As it turns out, the HIPAA Security Standards closely align with many generally accepted security standards (e.g., ISO 17799, National Institute of Standards and Technology [NIST], Common Criteria, and Centers for Medicare and Medicaid Services [CMS] standards). Moreover, organizations will be able to point to these industry standards as the basis for addressing their compliance with the HIPAA Security requirements. This same risk-based approach has proven successful with other industries and regulations (e.g., GLBA in Financial Services) and represents an opportunity for organizations to establish and implement the best solutions for their organizations.

HIPAA Security regulations allow significant flexibility as long as the organization documents, via a risk analysis, how its security program will meet the applicable HIPAA Security requirements. This flexible, risk-based approach provides organizations with the opportunity to select and implement safeguards that will support their specific operations and environment while also meeting the HIPAA Security Standards. To achieve this, the organization will need to develop consistent, structured, and documented processes (such as decision frameworks) for ensuring that its security measures continue to safeguard the organization's individually identifiable health information (IIHI) as required by HIPAA.

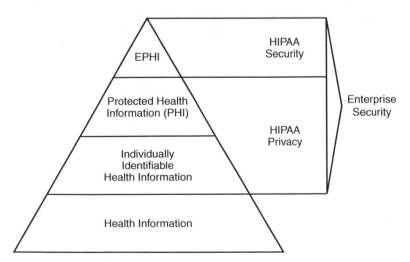

Fig. 1 Enterprise security.

Global – Health Insurance

A FLEXIBLE APPROACH: GOOD NEWS AND BAD NEWS

The final HIPAA security requirements describe what organizations should do to implement them, but not how to do it, thus providing organizations with flexibility in addressing the individual requirements or "specifications." This is good news for organizations because, with this flexibility, they can more easily balance the risks their particular organization faces with the costs of implementing the safeguards to address those risks.

The bad news about the flexible approach is that the regulation requires an organization to take a disciplined process-centric approach to understand and address the individual requirements.

To support this flexible and less prescriptive approach, the HIPAA Security regulations introduce two new concepts: 1) required implementation specifications and 2) addressable implementation specifications. Required implementation specifications must be implemented by all organizations subject to HIPAA Security regulations. Addressable implementation specifications must be evaluated by each organization to determine whether they are reasonable and appropriate for the organization's environment, therefore allowing organizations to make implementation decisions as they relate to their operating environment. Table 1 summarizes the required and addressable implementation specifications included in the final HIPAA Security regulations.

Table 1 HIPAA security requirements.

Standard	Implementation Specifications (R) = Required, (A) = Addressable
Administrative Safeguards	
Security management process	Risk analysis (R)
	Risk management (R)
	Sanction policy (R)
	Information system activity review (R)
Assigned security responsibility	Security official (R)
Workforce security	Authorization and/or supervision (A)
	Workforce clearance procedure (A)
	Termination procedures (A)
Information access management	Isolating health-care clearinghouse function (R)
	Access authorization (A)
	Access establishment and modification (A)
Security awareness and training	Security reminders (A)
	Protection from malicious software (A)
	Log-in monitoring (A)
	Password management (A)
Security incident procedures contingency plan	Response and reporting (R)
	Data backup plan (R)
	Disaster recovery plan (R)
	Emergency mode operation plan (R)
	Testing and revision procedure (A)
	Applications and data criticality analysis (A)
Evaluation	Replaces "certification" (R)
Business associate contracts and other arrangements	Written contract or other arrangement (R)
Physical Safeguards	
Facility access controls	Contingency operations (A)
	Facility security plan (A)
	Access control and validation procedures (A)
	Maintenance records (A)
Workstation use	(R)
Workstation security	(R)
Device and media controls	Disposal (R)
	Media re-use (R)
	Accountability A)
	Data backup and storage (A)
Technical Safeguards	
Access control	Unique user identification (R)
	Emergency access procedure (R)
	Automatic log-off (A)
	Encryption and decryption (A)
Audit controls	Mechanism to record and examine EPHI systems (R)
Integrity	Mechanism to authenticate electronic PHI (A)
Person or entity authentication	(R)
Transmission security	Integrity controls (A)
	Encryption (A)

RISK-BASED SOLUTIONS

Organizations should choose and implement the appropriate safeguards that work in their environment based on a thorough understanding of the risks the organization faces, and selection of the appropriate safeguards based on the identified risks. In addition, organizations must now document the decision-making process used to select the safeguards they intend to adopt.

Addressing individual implementation specifications in an effective and efficient manner will require the development of a *security decision* framework for making security decisions as it relates to each organization. The framework also enables an organization to methodically and consistently review the risks it faces in its environment and to select the appropriate safeguards.

BUILDING A SECURITY DECISION FRAMEWORK

A security decision framework through which the organization can effectively and consistently review both the HIPAA Security required and addressable implementation specifications can effectively be broken down into a four-step process, as shown in Table 2.

Step 1: Business Requirements Definition

The creation of a security decision framework starts with developing a business requirements definition that addresses reasonable and practical interpretations of HIPAA regulations as they apply to the specific organization. Generally accepted security standards and guidelines (such as ISO 17799, NIST, and CMS), which are readily available to organizations, can provide a context for interpreting the particular implementation specification and for understanding how certain implementation specifications have been interpreted by other groups.

For example, encrypting all the EPHI in an organization may seem an effective way to secure information, but it is probably not practical based on current encryption methods, and it will most likely degrade the performance of their systems as well as increase the costs associated with implementing such a solution.

Finally, the process of developing business requirements definitions needs to include working with both the business units and privacy program to avoid conflicts in business processes and policies. In addition, leveraging the information prepared as part of the HIPAA privacy readiness efforts (e.g., the assessment, policies, procedures, and processes) will assist most organizations in starting their efforts.

Step 2: Business Impact Analysis

The next step deals with understanding the organization's operating environment and developing a business impact analysis that addresses risks, costs, and the complexity of compliance activities in the organization's specific environment. A typical approach to HIPAA security readiness would be to apply HIPAA Security requirements to the IT department. This approach fails to address security as an enterprisewide function that affects all business units and all individual users alike. Also, today's Internet-driven environment is requiring ever more information sharing, even further blurring the boundaries of internal and external access. Thus, the HIPAA readiness team must segment the organization to ensure they have adequately addressed all the areas of concern for HIPAA Security readiness.

Certainly, the HIPAA readiness team can compartmentalize the organization any way it desires, such as IT, strategic initiatives, key business processes, or locations, as long as it segments it in a way that makes sense to both executive management and business unit leaders who will ultimately endorse or reject the HIPAA Security compliance approach.

Once the scope of the review has been defined, a risk analysis will identify the threats and the vulnerabilities faced by the organization. Gaining managerial agreement across the organization on the risks they face is important because, in the end, those managers will establish what areas are most valuable to the organization and prioritize that need to be protected. In addition, understanding what is important to the organization will help shape the Enterprise Security Program because it will allow a focus on resources in those areas. As with any risk analysis, key stakeholders should be closely involved in the process.

Table 2 Four-step process.

Framework steps	Key activities	Key issues
Business requirements definition	Security standards, privacy considerations	Develop reasonable and practical interpretations of HIPAA security rules
Business impact analysis	Document current environment, perform risk and safeguard analysis	Complexity, environment, risk, cost
Solution implementation	Compliance with strategy, define initiatives, define program management structure, plan projects	Develop actionable projects mapped to requirements
Compliance monitoring	Define monitoring and progress reporting, develop compliance plan and develop management reporting process	Place projects into overall plan to report progress and compliance

Global – Health Insurance

Finally, based on the identified risks and using the organization's interpretations of HIPAA Security regulations, the organization needs to conduct a safeguard analysis to select security measures that will account for the following factors:[1]

- The size, complexity, and capability of the organization
- The organization's technical infrastructure, hardware, and software capabilities
- The probability and criticality of the potential risk EPHI
- The cost of implementing security measures

Once appropriate security measures are identified, they should be organized into actionable projects for implementation.

Step 3: Solution Implementation

Developing actionable projects mapped to the HIPAA Security requirements defined in Step 1 is an essential building block in addressing HIPAA Security readiness. As the organization completes the projects, executive management and key stakeholders will require periodic status reports on HIPAA readiness progress and how they link to the original plan.

Finally, due to the sheer number of projects and the amount of resources required to implement them, a formal program management office (PMO) and supporting structure is often required to successfully complete the projects on time and within budget. The organization does not necessarily need to create a new PMO for this purpose, but should consider leveraging an existing organizational PMO to assist with project execution.

Step 4: Compliance Monitoring

Compliance monitoring involves ongoing measurement of the organization's conformity with HIPAA Security regulations using standard monitoring and reporting templates. The compliance monitoring strategy should be incorporated into the organization's overall compliance plan that also includes the organization's existing policies, such as Human Resources and Privacy policies.

DEPLOYING THE PEOPLE, PROCESSES, AND TECHNOLOGIES

Once the organization has developed its security decision framework for HIPAA Security, the focus of its efforts should be on the components (i.e., identified risks, projects, and interpretation of requirements) within the framework and incorporating them into their overall Enterprise Security Program (ESP) and operating environment. To accomplish that, companies should develop a "road map" for prioritizing steps, creating the timeline, and developing the plan for implementing the steps. The steps in the "road map" are tied to specific ongoing processes involved in HIPAA Security readiness. A sample road map is detailed further in this section.

MERGING HIPAA INTO AN ENTERPRISE SECURITY PROGRAM

New solutions and modifications that enable compliance with HIPAA requirements must be integrated into the operating environment and continuously maintained. One way to ensure this is to incorporate HIPAA Security requirements and other business requirements into an overall process-oriented ESP. This approach enables the organization to shift from an IT-centric to a business-centric security focus that more effectively manages risk and more closely aligns with the HIPAA Security risk-based approach.

Implementation of a program based on the proprietary Deloitte & Touche Enterprise Security Program Model shown in Fig. 2 helps organizations develop and maintain an enterprise security program that links all necessary organizational, technical, administrative, operational, and physical security controls. The model incorporates a strategic combination of business drivers, legal and regulatory requirements, and acceptable risk standards to ensure they are operationally integrated with the overall IT architecture, business processes, and business culture of the organization deploying the program.

The Deloitte & Touche model enables organizations to take a bottom-up or top-down approach, providing the flexibility to address security needs based on the maturity level of the organization's current enterprise security program and overall business priorities, through five key components:

1. *Strategic alignment.* Consensus on threats, vulnerabilities, and acceptable risks is established by leveraging ISO 17799, industry-specific standards, and strategic business drivers to create a desired risk profile to ensure that everyone is on the same page.
2. *Security effectiveness.* A user-friendly dashboard or portal is developed to enable management to monitor and report security performance effectiveness by measuring key performance indicators of core business processes, architectures, and business management processes.
3. *Business enablement.* Core business processes and architectures are defined, developed, and deployed in concert with the Core Security Operating Model and standards-based, risk tolerance-based criteria.
4. *Process enhancement.* Leveraging foundational blueprints, business management processes are refined and calibrated to efficiently integrate security standards and expertise throughout the system development life cycle and day-to-day operations.

5. *Security foundation.* Standards-based, risk tolerance-based foundational blueprints are used to define, develop, and implement an enterprise-level security architecture and business operating model—the Core Security Operating Model is established.

A majority of the HIPAA Security discussions fall into the "Strategic Alignment" area of the model. A desired risk profile and a business-driven security strategy are developed, in part, through facilitating management consensus on threats, vulnerabilities, and acceptable risks while maintaining links to the organization's strategic business objectives. This management consensus becomes a critical driver throughout the enterprise security program development and implementation as other important issues arise. Based on the results of these discussions and agreements, the organization can develop solutions and build the most effective implementation road map.

HIPAA AND A NEW LEVEL OF INFORMATION PROTECTION

HIPAA Security regulations are forcing many organizations to secure electronic individually identifiable health information. While developing a program to protect this information, organizations have an opportunity to improve their information management processes, thus increasing the security of all information. By developing a consistent, structured, and documented process to verify that HIPAA security measures are in place and working, organizations will have a foundation for compliance with other regulations. By integrating this into a process-oriented ESP that is linked with the organizations' privacy programs, organizations can maintain their level of readiness within a security program that aligns with the HIPAA Security risk-based approach, and provides effective, enterprisewide risk management.

Acknowledgment

Rena Mears, Ken DeJarnette, Bill Kobel, and Terrie Kreamer also contributed their support and expertise in developing this entry.

REFERENCE

1. 45 CFR Parts 160, 162, and 164; *Federal Register*, *68* (34); Feb 20, 2003, p. 8376, §164.306.

Healthcare Industry

Micki Krause, CISSP
Pacific Life Insurance Company, Newport Beach, California, U.S.A.

Abstract
Recently enacted government legislation, such as the Balanced Budget Act and the Health Insurance Portability and Accountability Act (HIPAA), are adding immense pressure to healthcare organizations, the majority of which have not yet adopted the generally accepted system-security principles common to other regulated industries.

INTRODUCTION

Proper management of the information security program addresses two very important areas: technological, because many of the controls we implement are technical security mechanisms, and people, because security is first and foremost a people issue. However, the information security manager in the healthcare industry is forced to heed another very important area: federal and state regulations.

This entry will address the following issues:

- History of healthcare information systems and the inherent lack of controls
- The challenges the healthcare organization faces, vis à vis its information systems
- The obstacles healthcare companies must overcome in order to implement consumer-centric systems in an environment of consumer distrust of both the healthcare industry and the technology
- The multitude of privacy laws proposed in the last 12 months
- E-commerce and the Internet
- An analysis of the Health Insurance Portability and Accountability Act (HIPAA) security standards

HISTORY OF HEALTHCARE INFORMATION SYSTEMS AND THE INHERENT LACK OF CONTROLS

The goal of today's healthcare organizations' information systems is open, interoperable, standards-compliant, and secure information systems. Unfortunately, this goal does not accurately reflect the state of healthcare's information systems today. We have some very real challenges to understand and overcome.

To begin, the healthcare industry has built information systems without the sufficient granularity required to adequately protect the information for which we are custodians. Many of the existing systems require no more than a three-character log-on ID; some have passwords that are shared by all users; and most have not implemented the appropriate classification of access controls for the jobs that users perform. One healthcare organization realized that their junior claims examiners were authorizing liposuction procedures, which ordinarily are not reimbursed. However, due to a lack of granularity, the junior examiners had the same privileges as the more senior personnel, and thus, the ability to perform inappropriate actions.

Because of this lack of appropriate controls, healthcare companies have recently come to the realization that they will have to invest in retrofitting security in order to be compliant with federal regulations. Not only will they be forced to expend incremental resources in this effort, but they lose the opportunity to utilize those resources for new application development.

Unfortunately, we don't see much of an improvement in many of the commercial product offerings on the market today. Consistently, from operating systems to off-the-shelf applications, too many new products lack sufficient controls. Products from large companies, with wide deployment, such as the Windows NT™ operating system or the Peoplesoft application, are not built to be compliant with best practices or generally accepted system-security principles. This is poor testimony to the quality of software today. In fact, many security practitioners find it unsettling to get blank stares from their vendor representatives when they ask whether the product has the most basic of controls. Worse yet is the null response security managers receive when they ask the vendor whether or not the manufacturers have a strategy for compliance with federal regulations.

There is no doubt that along with other industries, the healthcare industry must begin to collaborate with product vendors, to ensure that new products are built and implemented by default in a secure manner.

Encyclopedia of Information Assurance DOI: 10.1081/E-EIA-120046575

Copyright © 2011 by Taylor & Francis. All rights reserved.

CHALLENGES THE HEALTHCARE ORGANIZATION FACES, VIS À VIS ITS INFORMATION SYSTEMS

Another challenge facing organizations today is the pressure of keeping their networked resources open and closed at the same time, a security paradox of doing electronic commerce. Healthcare companies are forced to allow their insecure systems to be accessible to outside constituencies, trading partners, vendors, and members. In these situations, more robust authentication and access controls are mandatory, especially for those users who are not employees of the company. To exacerbate the challenge, the security manager has to reconcile decisions vis à vis the correct balance between access and security, especially with regard to requests for access to internal resources by external trading partners. Questions plaguing the healthcare organization include: "Should an employer have a right to see the patient-identifiable data on their employees?" For example, if a healthcare company is custodian of John Smith's medical records, and John drives a dynamite truck, should the health plan acquiesce to the employer if John's medical records indicate he has epileptic seizures? Should the employer only have this right if the safety of the public is at risk? Should the employer have access only with John's permission? The answers to these dilemmas are not clear today. Thus, health plans struggle with the overriding challenge of maintaining confidentiality of patient information, while providing reasonable access to it. Further, this balance of access and security has to be maintained across a broadly diverse infrastructure of disparate platforms and applications.

Also, there are other business partners that consistently request access to internal resources, e.g., fulfillment houses, marketing organizations, pharmacy companies. Where does it stop? How can it stop—when the competitive imperative for healthcare companies today is providing the ability to connect quickly and meaningfully with business partners and customers to improve the movement and quality of information and services?

Then, of course, there is the new frontier, the Internet, and the challenges that new technologies present. Organizations tread lightly at first, opening up their networks to the Internet by providing the ability for their employees to surf the Web. It wasn't long before they discovered that if an employee using a company computer on company premises downloads pornographic materials, another of their employees could sue the company for sexual harassment. Once the barn door is open, however, it's hard to get the horses back in. Health plans faced increasing demand to accommodate electronic commerce. Surprisingly, the industry that, until very recently, considered sending files on a diskette the definition for electronic data interchange, rapidly found that they were losing membership because employers' benefits administrators were refusing to do business with plans that could not support file transfers over the Internet.

Of course, when the healthcare organization reveals itself to the Internet, it introduces a multitude of threats to its internal network. Although most organizations implemented perimeter security with the installation of firewalls, business demands forced them to open holes in the defensive device, to allow certain types of inbound and outbound traffic. For example, one health plan encouraged its employees to enroll in courses offered on the Internet which required opening a specific port on the firewall and allowing traffic to and from the university's Internet address. In another instance, a health plan employee needed access to a non-profit entity's Web site in order to perform Webmaster activities. In order to accomplish this, the employee utilized a service through the Internet, requiring access through the firewall. Thus, the firewall slowly becomes like Swiss cheese, full of holes. Ergo, health plans have the challenge of engaging in business with external partners while *effectively* managing the firewall.

More challenging than managing external connectivity is the security manager's task of hiring security practitioners with the necessary skills and knowledge to effectively manage the firewall. These individuals must have experience managing UNIX® systems, since most firewalls are built on a UNIX operating system; must know how the Internet protocols such as file transfer protocol (FTP) work through the firewall; and must have the expertise to monitor network router devices and know how to write rules for those devices, in order to accommodate business requirements while protecting the enterprise. On the other hand, as healthcare organizations seek to outsource networked resources, for example, Web sites and firewalls, the security manager must be able to provide sufficient monitoring and security oversight, to ensure that the outsourcer is meeting its contractual obligations.

It's no wonder that insurance companies are offering a myriad of secure-systems insurance programs. Cigna Insurance, for example, recently developed a program to offer insurance policies of up to $25 million in liability per loss, reflecting the realization that companies are not only more reliant on information systems, but with the introduction of the Internet, the risk is that much greater.

OBSTACLES HEALTHCARE COMPANIES MUST OVERCOME IN ORDER TO IMPLEMENT CONSUMER-CENTRIC SYSTEMS IN AN ENVIRONMENT OF CONSUMER DISTRUST OF BOTH HEALTHCARE INDUSTRY AND TECHNOLOGY

In this competitive industry, the healthcare organization's mandate is to increase customer intimacy while decreasing operational costs; grant external access to internal data and applications, while most existing applications don't have the appropriate controls in place; and secure the new technologies, especially for third-party access. With all of these issues to resolve, health plans are turning toward Web-based solutions, utilizing public key encryption and digital certificate technologies. But even though health plans have the motivation to move into the Internet mainstream, there are obstacles to overcome that have, for now, slowed the adoption of Web technologies.

First, there are technological weaknesses in the Internet infrastructure. Most organizations have service-level agreements for their internal resources, which guarantee to their employees and customers a certain level of availability and response time. In the Internet space, no one entity is accountable for availability. Also, there are five major electronic junctions where the Internet is extremely vulnerable. When one junction is down, many customers feel the pain of not having reliable service. Since the Internet is not owned or operated by any one person or organization, by its very nature, it cannot be expected to provide the same reliability, availability, and security as a commercial network service provider can. For example, commercial telecommunications companies provide outsourced wide area networks and deploy state of the art communications and security technologies with multiple levels of redundancy and circuitry. The Internet is like a Thomas' English muffin—a maze of nooks and crannies that no one entity controls.

Next, all of the studies show that a large majority of physicians are not comfortable with computers, let alone the Internet. The doctors are ambivalent about adopting information technology, and since there is no control over the content of the information on the net, physicians have been slow to adopt electronic mail communications with their patients on the Internet. They have legitimate concern since there is no positive assurance that we can know exactly who we are communicating with on the Internet. Thus, the healthcare providers distrust the Internet.

They are not the only persons with doubts and concerns. The perception of a lack of security and privacy by consumers is a tremendous challenge for healthcare organizations. Moreover, the media promulgates the paranoia. It's no wonder that consumers are fearful of losing their privacy when publications offer headlines such as "Naked Before the World: Will your Medical Records be safe in a new National Databank?" (*Newsweek* magazine) or "The Death of Privacy: You Have No Secrets" (*Time* magazine).

Therefore, if healthcare organizations are to successfully deploy consumer-intimate Web-based applications, the biggest hurdle they have to overcome is consumer fear.

This consumer fear is not a new phenomenon. For many years, public polls have shown that consumers are increasingly distrustful of organizations that collect their private information. More disconcerting than this, from a healthcare perspective, is that this fear is manifesting itself in negative impacts to the quality of their personal health. More and more, consumers are going out of their local areas to obtain healthcare and lying or holding back information from their healthcare providers, primarily to maintain their sense of privacy and maintain some semblance of confidentiality. This reflects a real disconnect between the consumer and the custodians of the consumer data, the health plan and the doctor.

In early 1999, the Consumers Union, the largest consumer advocacy organization in the United States, sponsored a nationwide survey. They sampled 1000 adults in the United States and a separate 1000 adults in California. The survey asked people how willing they were to disclose their personal medical information.

In Fig. 1, we can see that the survey found that although people do concede that persons other than their immediate provider require access to their personal medical records, they display a very strong preference for restricting access. Only four of every ten asked were willing to disclose their medical information to health plans. Roughly six in ten would explicitly refuse to grant access to their information to a hospital, even if the hospital were to offer preventive

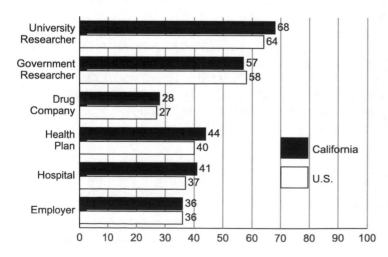

Fig. 1 Percentage of respondents willing to disclose to following parties.

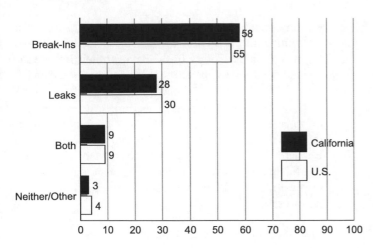

Fig. 2 Perceived threats to privacy.

care programs. Also, consumers are not happy having their employers or potential employers view their personal healthcare information. Most are not willing to offer their information to a potential employer who may be considering them for a job. Further, the drug companies are lowest on the totem pole because Americans do not want their medical data collected for the purposes of marketing new drugs.

In Fig. 2, we see another interesting finding from the survey: most people consider electronic piracy, that is hackers, the biggest threat to their privacy. This is counter to the real threat, which is the disclosure of information by medical personnel, health plans, or other authorized users, but it's not surprising that the average consumer would be very worried about hackers, when we consider how the media exploits attempts by teenagers to hack in to the Pentagon's computers. Moreover, the vendors exacerbate these fears by playing up the evil hacker as they attempt to sell products by instilling fear, uncertainty, and doubt in our hearts and minds.

Fig. 3 shows that most of the survey respondents perceive that if health plans and providers implement security provisions and information security management policies in order to protect medical information, it would make them more inclined to offer their personal information

when it was requested. Americans believe that three specific policies should be adopted to safeguard their medical privacy:

1. Impose fines and punishments for violations.
2. Require an individual's specific permission to release personal information.
3. Establish security systems with security technologies, such as passwords and encryption.

Further, the survey respondents were very favorable about sending a health plan's Chief Executive Officer to prison in the event of willful or intentional disclosure of medical information.

The Consumers' Union survey also revealed that consumers are aware—they know that their information is stored in computer databases, and they perceive computerization as the greatest threat to their privacy. In fact, more than one-half of the respondents think that the shift from paper records to electronic systems makes it *more* difficult to keep personal medical information private and confidential. This should be of interest to any information systems manager, since computerization really provides more of an opportunity to secure data. However,

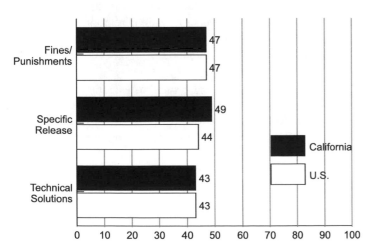

Fig. 3 Safeguards rated as very effective to protect privacy.

perception *is* reality. Therefore, the lesson from this survey is threefold:

- Consumers do not trust health plans or providers,
- Consumers do not trust computers, and
- Consumers will compromise the quality of their healthcare,

all in the name of privacy.

This lesson can be an opportunistic one for the health plan security manager. Healthcare can turn those consumer fears around, and win over the public by showing them that health plans take their obligation for due diligence very seriously, and protecting consumer privacy is in perfect alignment with healthcare organizations' internal values.

Case in point: In December 1998, more people purchased goods on the Internet than ever before. The question is why? Price Coopers, the accounting firm, completed a survey early in 1999 which found that the leading factor that would persuade fearful consumers to log on to the Internet was *an assurance of improved privacy protection*. Healthcare can leverage the capabilities of security to garner that public trust. Privacy is not an arcane or a technical issue. It is, however, a major issue with consumers, and there is heightened urgency around healthcare privacy and security today, more so than ever before.

HISTORY REPEATS ITSELF

In 1972, in a similar environment of public distrust, then Department of Health and Human Services (DHHS) Secretary Elliot Richardson appointed an advisory board to assist the federal government in identifying approaches to protect the privacy of information in an ever-evolving computer age. The board issued a report detailing a code of fair information principles, which became the National Privacy Act of 1974.

The act outlines five separate and distinct practices under "Fair Information Party Principles":

- "There must be a way ... to prevent information about a person that was obtained for one purpose from being used or made available for other purposes without that person's consent.
- There must be no personal data record-keeping systems whose very existence is secret.
- There must be a way for a person to correct or amend a record of identifiable information about that person.
- There must be a way for a person to find out what information about that person is in a record and how it is used.

- Any organization creating, maintaining, using, or disseminating records of identifiable personal data must ensure the reliability of the data for their intended use and must take steps to prevent misuse of the data."

Many bills and proposals concerning privacy of medical information have preceded the most prominent law, the (HIPAA), enacted in 1996. In 1995, Senator Robert Bennett (R-Utah) sponsored the Medical Records Confidentiality Act, designed to protect the privacy of medical records. Items addressed in the proposed legislation were:

1. Procedures for individuals to examine their medical records and the ability to correct any errors.
2. Identifying persons and entities with access to individually identifiable information as "health information trustees" and defines circumstances under which that information can be released, with or without patient authorization.
3. Establishing federal certification of health information services, which must meet certain requirements to protect identifiable information.
4. Providing both civil and criminal penalties, up to $500,000 and 10 years' imprisonment, for wrongful disclosure of protected information.

It is important to note that Bennett's bill would apply to medical information in any form, as compared to HIPAA legislation, which calls for the protection of *electronic* medical information. Bennett has indicated his resolve and declared his intention to reintroduce his bill, S.2609 in the 106th Congress in 1999.

Heightened interest in patient rights, sparked partially by tragic stories of individuals who died due to delays in medical treatment, led Senate Democratic Leader Tom Daschle to introduce the Patients' Bill of Rights in March of 1998. This law would guarantee patients greater access to information and necessary care, including access to needed specialists and emergency rooms, guarantee a fair appeals process when health plans deny care, expand choice, protect the doctor–patient relationship, and hold HMOs accountable for decisions that end up harming patients. Daschle's bill also:

- Requires plans and issuers to establish procedures to safeguard the privacy of any individually identifiable enrollee information.
- Maintains records and information in an accurate and timely manner.
- Assures the individual's timely access to such records and information.

Additionally, other organizations committed to strong privacy legislation, such as the Electronic Privacy

Information Center (EPIC), have proposed multiple versions of similar bills. Most call for stringent controls over medical records. Many go beyond and call for advanced technical controls, including encryption and audit trails which record every access to every individual.

MULTITUDE OF PRIVACY LAWS PROPOSED IN RECENT MONTHS

The federal government, very aware of its citizens' concerns, is answering their outcry with no less than a dozen healthcare privacy laws, proposed in recent congressional sessions. Some of the most publicized are:

- McDermott Bill, a.k.a. "Medical Privacy in the Age of New Technologies Act"—1997.
- Jeffords–Dodd Bill, a.k.a. "Health Care Personal Information Non-Disclosure Act"—1998.
- Senate Bill S.2609, a.k.a. the Bennett Bill. This proposed legislation is important to note because it addresses information in all media, whereas the other bills address the protection of information in electronic format only.
- Kennedy–Kassebaum Bill, a.k.a. the HIPAA—1996.

Electronic medical records can give us greater efficiency and lower cost. But those benefits must not come at the cost of loss of privacy. The proposals we are making today will help protect against one kind of threat—the vulnerability of information in electronic formats. Now we need to finish the bigger job and create broader legal protections for the privacy of those records.

—*The Honorable Donna E. Shalala, 1997*

Kennedy–Kassebaum Bill: Background

Several iterations of congressional hearings occurred where stories were told of citizens suddenly found to be uninsurable because they had changed jobs. These instances of insurance loss led to a plethora of tragic incidents, motivating Senators Edward M. Kennedy (D-Massachusetts) and Nancy Kassebaum (R-Kansas) to propose the legislation known as the Kennedy–Kassebaum Bill, also known as HIPAA. Because approximately two thirds of Americans are insured through their employers, the loss of a job often means the loss of health insurance—thus the justification for the term "portability," enabling individuals to port their health plan coverage to a new job. Legislators took this opportunity to incorporate privacy provisions into the bill, and thus, under HIPAA, the Health Care Financing Administration (HCFA) has issued a series of proposed rules that are designed to make healthcare plans operate securely and efficiently.

"For the Record": The Report

In 1997, the government-sponsored National Research Council report, "For the Record: Protecting Electronic Health Information," captured the essence of the status of security in the healthcare industry. The report came to several conclusions, which laid the foundation for the call from Congress and the Department of Health and Human Service, to define security standards for the healthcare industry. The report concluded:

1. Improving the quality of healthcare and lowering its cost will rely heavily on the effective and efficient use of information technology; therefore, it is incumbent on the industry to maintain the security, privacy, and confidentiality of medical information while making it available to those entities with a need.
2. Healthcare organizations, including health maintenance organizations (HMOs), insurance companies, and provider groups, must take immediate steps to establish safeguards for the protection of medical information.
3. Vendors have not offered products with inherent protective mechanisms because customers are not demanding them.
4. Individuals must take a more proactive role in demanding that their personally identifiable medical information is protected adequately.
5. Self-regulation has not proven successful; therefore, the state and federal governments must intercede and mandate legislation.
6. Medical information is subject to inadvertent or malicious abuse and disclosure, although the greatest threat to the security of patient healthcare data is the authorized insider.
7. Appropriate protection of sensitive healthcare data relies on both organizational policies and procedures as well as technological countermeasures.

Satisfying these important security and privacy considerations is the basis for the administrative simplification provisions of HIPAA. At last, the healthcare industry is being tasked to heed the cry that the citizenry has voiced for years, "Maintain my privacy and keep my personal, sensitive information private."

HIPAA ADMINISTRATIVE SIMPLIFICATION: SECURITY STANDARDS

The specific rules that apply to security standards that protect healthcare-related information (code set 6 HCPR 1317) were issued August 17, 1998, for public comment. The deadline for comment was October 13, 1998. According to HCFA, the volume of comments received was extraordinary.

Healthcare – Identity

Plans and providers cried that implementation of the standards would be onerous and cost-prohibitive. HCFA essentially replied that "security is a cost of doing business" and the deadlines will stand. Those deadlines include adoption of security standards by 2002. Moreover, HIPAA requires Congress to pass comprehensive privacy legislation to protect individual health information by August 1999. If lawmakers fail to meet that deadline, then the responsibility falls to the Secretary of DHHS to promulgate protections by February 2000.

Throwing her full support behind HIPAA security standards, Shalala stated, "When Americans give out their personal health information, they should feel like they're leaving it in good, safe hands.... Congress must pass a law that requires those who legally receive health information to take real steps to safeguard it."

President Bill Clinton has publicly supported privacy legislation for the healthcare industry since 1993. In a May 1997 speech at Morgan State University, the President reiterated that "technology should not be used to break down the wall of privacy and autonomy that [sic] free citizens are guaranteed in a free society."

Horror stories of inadvertent or malicious use or disclosure of medical information are held closely by healthcare organizations. No corporate officer wants to admit that information has "leaked" from his company. However, there are several publicized war stories in which sensitive patient healthcare information has been disclosed without proper authorization, resulting in misfortune and tragedy. For example, when former tennis star Arthur Ashe was admitted to a hospital due to chest pains, his HIV-positive status was discovered and leaked to the press, causing great embarrassment and strife not only to Ashe and his family, but to the medical institution as well.

In another instance, a claims processor brought her young teenager to work and sat her in front of a terminal to keep her occupied. The daughter accessed a database of patients who had been diagnosed with any number of maladies. The teenager concocted a game whereby she called several of the patients, pretended to be the provider, and misreported the diagnoses. One patient was told he had contracted AIDS. The man committed suicide before he could be told the report was the prank of a mischievous child.

In another instance, a healthcare maintenance employee, undergoing a nasty child custody battle with his wife's sister, gained access to his company's system, where he discovered some sensitive information about his sister-in-law, also covered by the health plan. He revealed this information in court in an attempt to discredit her. She sued the health plan for negligence and won the case.

These scenarios are not as rare as we would like to believe. The existing legal structure in healthcare does not provide for effective control of patient medical information. The federal government recognizes this and has attempted to forcefully impose stringent regulation over the protection of health information.

Under HIPAA, healthcare organizations must develop comprehensive security programs to protect patient-identifiable information or face severe penalties for non-compliance. Industry experts estimate that HIPAA will be the "next Y2K" in terms of resources and level of effort, and that annual healthcare expenditures for information security will increase from $2.2 million to $125 million over the next 3 years.

The HIPAA standards, designed to protect all electronic medical information from inadvertent or intentional improper use or disclosure, include provisions for the adoption of:

1. Organizational and administrative procedures.
2. Physical security safeguards.
3. Technological security measures.

Health plans have until early 2002 to adopt these requirements. Although the intent of the standards should be uniform and consistent across the healthcare industry, considerable interpretation might alter the implementation of the controls from one organization to another. The HIPAA security requirements are outlined below.

1. Organizational and Administrative Procedures

1. Ensure that organizational structures exist to develop and implement an information security program. This formal, senior management-sponsored and supported organizational structure is required so that the mechanisms needed to protect information and computing resources are not overridden by a senior manager from another function, for example, Operations or Development, with their own "agendas" in mind. This requirement also includes the assignment of a Chief Security Officer responsible for establishing and maintaining the information security program. This program's charter should ensure that a standard of due care and due diligence is applied throughout the enterprise to provide an adequate level of assurance for data security (integrity/reliability, privacy/confidentiality, and availability).

2. The Chief Security Officer is responsible for the development of policies to control access to and for the release of, individually identifiable patient healthcare information. The over-arching information security policy should declare the organization's intent to comply with regulations and protect and control the security of its information assets. Additional policies, standards, and procedures should define varying levels of granularity for the control of the sensitive information. For example, some of the policies may relate to data

classification, data destruction, disaster recovery, and business continuity planning.

One of the most important organizational moves that a healthcare organization must make for HIPAA compliance is in appointing a Chief Security Officer (CSO). This person should report at a sufficiently high level in the organization so as to be able to ensure compliance with regulations. Typically, the CSO reports to the Chief Information Officer (CIO) or higher. This function is tasked with establishing the information security program, implementing best practices management techniques, and satisfying legal and regulatory requirements. Healthcare organizations seeking qualified, experienced security officers prefer or require candidates to be certified information system security professionals (CISSPs). This certification is offered solely by the non-profit International Information Systems Security Certification Consortium (ISC²) in Massachusetts. More information about professional certification can be obtained from the organization's Web site at http://www.isc2.org.

3. The organization is required to establish a security certification review. This is an auditable, technical evaluation establishing the extent to which the system, application, or network meets specified security requirements. The certification should also include testing to ensure that the controls actually work as advertised. It is wise for the organization to define control requirements up front and ensure that they are integrated with the business requirements of a system, application, or network. The certification documentation should include details of those control requirements, as well as how the controls are implemented. HIPAA allows for the certification to be done internally, but, it can also be done by an external agency.

4. Establish policies and procedures for the receipt, storage, processing, and distribution of information. Realizing that information is not maintained solely within the walls of an individual organization, HIPAA calls for an assurance that the information is protected as it traverses outside. For example, an organization should develop a policy that mandates authorization by the business owner prior to sending specific data to a third-party business partner.

5. Develop a contractual agreement with all business partners, ensuring confidentiality and data integrity of exchanged information. This standard may manifest itself in the form of a confidentiality clause for all contractors and consultants, which will bind them to maintain the confidentiality of all information they encounter in the performance of their employment.

6. Ensure access controls that provide for an assurance that only those persons with a need can access specific information. A basic tenet of information

security is the "need to know." This standard requires that appropriate access is given only to that information an individual requires in order to perform his job. Organizations should establish procedures so that a business manager "owns" the responsibility for the integrity and confidentiality of the functional information, e.g., Claims, and that this manager authorizes approval for each employee to access said information.

7. Implement personnel security, including clearance policies and procedures. Several organizations have adopted human resources procedures that call for a background check of their employment candidates. This is a good practice and one that is recognized as an HIPAA standard. Employees, consultants, and contractors, who have authorized access to an organization's information assets, have an obligation to treat that information responsibly. A clearance of the employee can guarantee a higher degree of assurance that the organization can entrust that individual with sensitive information.

8. Perform security training for all personnel. Security education and awareness training is probably the most cost-effective security standard an organization can adopt. Information security analyses continually reflect that the greatest risk to the security of information is from the "insider threat."

9. Provide for disaster recovery and business resumption planning for critical systems, applications, and networks.

10. Document policies and procedures for the installation, networking, maintenance, and security testing of all hardware and software.

11. Establish system auditing policies and procedures.

12. Develop termination procedures which ensure that involuntarily terminated personnel are immediately removed from accessing systems and networks and voluntarily terminated personnel are removed from systems and networks in an expedient manner.

13. Document security violation reporting policies and procedures and sanctions for violations.

2. Physical Security Safeguards

1. Establish policies and procedures for the control of media (e.g., disks, tapes), including activity tracking and data backup, storage, and disposal.

2. Secure work stations and implement automatic logout after a specified period of non-use.

3. Technological Security Measures

1. Assure that sensitive information is altered or destroyed only by authorized personnel.

2. Provide the ability to properly identify and authenticate users.
3. Create audit records whenever users inquire or update records.
4. Provide for access controls that are either transaction-based, role-based, or user-based.
5. Implement controls to ensure that transmitted information has not been corrupted.
6. Implement message authentication to validate that a message is received unchanged.
7. Implement encryption or access controls, including audit trails, entity authentication, and mechanisms for detecting and reporting unauthorized activity in the network.

One of the biggest challenges facing the organizations that must comply with HIPAA security standards is the proper interpretation of the regulation. Some of the standards are hazy at this time, but the fines for non-compliance are well-defined. HIPAA enforcement provisions specify financial and criminal penalties for wrongful disclosure or willful misuse of individually identifiable information at $250,000 and 10 years of imprisonment per incident.

SUMMARY

The reader can see that the security manager in the healthcare industry has an ominous task, and federal regulations make that task an urgent one. However, with the adoption of generally accepted system-security principles and the implementation of best-security practices, it is possible to develop a security program that provides for a reasonable standard of due care, and one that is compliant with regulations.

High-Tech Trade Secrets

William C. Boni
Chief Information Security Officer, Motorola Information Protection Services, Bartlett, Illinois, U.S.A.

Abstract
Many thefts of sensitive proprietary information are preventable. Those that are not prevented can be detected earlier, thus minimizing potential losses. A well-designed protection program will enhance the organization's probability for successful prosecution and litigation.

As business organizations enter the twenty-first century, it is vital that the managers and executives who lead them understand that there is a wide array of dark new threats. These threats strike at the core of what is increasingly the organization's most critical assets—the information, intellectual property and unique "knowledge value" which has been acquired in designing, producing, and delivering products and services. Many of these threats arise from the digital properties now associated with forms of critical information. The methods and techniques of acquiring sensitive information, which were previously available only to the world's leading intelligence services, are now widely available to anyone willing to engage "retired" professionals or acquire sophisticated electronic equipment. These capabilities create a host of new vulnerabilities that extend far beyond the narrow focus on computers and networks. The risk to company information increases as both people and technology, honed in the Cold War, now move into collecting business and technology secrets. Information protection programs for leading organizations must move beyond the narrow focus of physical security and legal agreements, to a program that safeguards their proprietary rights. A new awareness derived from assessing security implications of operational practices and applying a counter-intelligence mindset are essential to protect the enterprises' critical information assets against sophisticated and determined adversaries.

The new opponents of an organization may range from disgruntled insiders seeking revenge, to unethical domestic competitors, to a foreign nation's intelligence services operating on behalf of their indigenous "national flag" industry participant. Such opponents will not be deterred or defeated by boilerplate legal documents nor minimum-wage security guards. Defeating these opponents requires a well-designed and carefully implemented program to deter, detect, and if necessary, actively neutralize efforts to obtain information about the organization's plans, products, processes, people, and facilities capabilities, intentions, or activities.

The fact is that few in business truly appreciate the arsenal now available to "The Dark Side," which is how many protection professionals refer to those who steal the fruits of other's hard work. Understanding how "technology bandits" operate, their methods, targets, capabilities, and limitations, is essential to allow the organization to design safeguards to protect its own critical information against the new dangers. It is also important that managers understand they have a responsibility to help level the global playing field by encouraging foreign and domestic competitors to conform to a common ethical standard. The common theme must be fair treatment of the intellectual property of others. When an organization detects an effort to improperly obtain its intellectual property and trade secrets, it must use the full sanctions of relevant laws. In the United States, companies now may benefit by seeking federal felony prosecutions under the Economic Espionage Act of 1996!

TRADE SECRET OVERVIEW AND IMPORTANCE

In any discussion of intellectual property and organizational information, it is first important to understand the distinction between trade secrets and patents. The United States (or any other national government) grants a patent to the inventor of a novel and useful product or process. In exchange for public disclosure of required information, the government grants the inventor exclusive benefits of ownership and profits derived from ownership for a period of time, commonly 17 years from date of issue or 20 years from date of application for a patent.

However, a business may decide that as a practical matter, it may ultimately derive more commercial advantages by maintaining as a "trade secret" the information, product, or process. The term "trade secret," for those from military or governmental backgrounds, is not the same as national security or "official" secrets. In identifying something as a trade secret, it qualifies as a special form of organizational property, which may be protected against theft or misappropriation. Essentially it means information, generally but not exclusively of a scientific or technical nature, which is held in confidence by the organization and

Encyclopedia of Information Assurance DOI: 10.1081/E-EIA-120046576
Copyright © 2011 by Taylor & Francis. All rights reserved.

which provides some sort of competitive advantage. The major advantage of protecting something as a trade secret rather than as a patent is that the company may, if it exercises appropriate oversight, continue to enjoy the profits of the "secret" indefinitely.

A practical example of a trade secret's potential for "unlimited" life is the closely guarded formula for Coca-Cola, which has been a carefully protected trade secret for over 80 years. However, there is a downside of protecting valuable discoveries as trade secrets. If the organization fails to take reasonable and prudent steps to protect the secret, they may lose some or all of the benefits of trade secret status for its information. This may allow another organization to profit from the originator's hard work!

Proprietary Information and Trade Secrets

As a practical matter, all of the information which a company generates or creates in the course of business operations and practices can be considered "proprietary." The dictionary defines proprietary as "used, made, or marketed by one having the exclusive legal rights" (*Webster's Collegiate*), which essentially means the company has an ownership right to its exclusive use. Although ALL trade secrets ARE proprietary information, not *all* proprietary information will meet the specific legal tests which are necessary to qualify them as trade secrets. Therefore, trade secrets are a specialized subset of proprietary information, which meet specific tests established in the law. Trade secrets statutes under U.S. laws provide the following three elements that must *all* be present for a specific piece or category of information to qualify for trade secret status:

- *The information MUST be a genuine, but not absolute or exclusive, "SECRET."* This means that an organization need not employ draconian protection measures and also that even though elements of the secret, indeed the secret itself, may be discoverable, through extraordinary (even legal means), it nonetheless is not generally apparent, and may thus qualify for trade secret status. The owner may even license the secret to others, and as long as appropriate legal and operational protections are applied, it remains a protected asset. It is also possible that a trade secret may be independently discoverable and usable by a competitor, and it can simultaneously be a trade secret for both developers!
- *It must provide the owner competitive or economic advantages.* This means the secret must have real (potential) business value to the holder/owner. A business secret that merely conceals inconsequential information from the general public cannot be protected as a trade secret.
- *The owner must take "reasonable" steps to protect the secret.* For those involved in both protection of an organization's trade secrets as well as those whose responsibility includes ferreting out the business strategies of competitors, *this* is the most crucial element in qualifying for trade secret status and attendant rights. Regrettably, neither courts nor legislatures have provided a convenient checklist of the minimum measures to qualify for the "reasonable" steps. Over the years, courts have applied the "reasonable" test and in a series of cases, defined commonly accepted minimum measures. In many cases the courts have ruled that a plaintiff's lack of a specific safeguard defeated their claim of trade secrets status for the information at issue. It is critical to understand that a court's decision as to what is necessary to protect an organization's trade secrets will depend on what is "reasonable" under the specific circumstances of a given situation, and therefore is extremely difficult to predict in advance of a trial. As a general standard, the protections that are "reasonable" will also reflect the common business practices of a particular industry.

Economic Espionage Act (EEA) of 1996

The single most significant development in trade secret protection in the United States was passage of the EEA in 1996. Title 18 USC sections 1831 and 1832 were added to the federal statutes after a series of disappointing cases became public which proved the need for new laws to deal with theft of technology and trade secrets. When President Clinton signed this act into law on October 11, 1996, American industry was given a strong weapon designed to combat the theft of trade secrets. The act created for the first time a *federal* law that criminalized the theft or misappropriation of organizational trade secrets, whether done by domestic or foreign competitors or by a foreign governmental entity. A key clause in the act defines trade secrets:

EEA definition of trade secrets

The term "trade secret" means all forms and types of financial, business, scientific, technical, economic, or engineering information, including patterns, plans, compilations, program devices, formulas, designs, prototypes, methods, techniques, processes, procedures, programs, or codes, whether tangible or intangible, and whether or how stored, compiled, or memorialized physically, electronically, graphically, photographically, or in writing if

1. the owner thereof has taken reasonable measures to keep such information secret; and
2. the information derives independent economic value, actual or potential, from not being generally known to, and not being readily ascertainable through proper means by, the public.

Value of Intellectual Property

In reviewing the definition as to what may qualify as a trade secret under the EEA, it seems that almost anything could be declared a trade secret. This seems to be a prudent approach because advanced business organizations in the developed world are largely based on the knowledge that such organizations have captured, for example, in their design, production, and operational systems. New and more advanced products and services derive from the aggregation of the learning organization knowledge, which is translated into "intellectual property" (abbreviated IP) to distinguish it from the tangible property of the organization. IP is generally considered to consist of the patents, copyrights, trademarks, and trade secrets of the organization, which are normally lumped into the overall category of "intangible assets" on the balance sheet. Although not reflected in traditional accounting practices, the IP of companies has increasingly become the source of competitive advantage. The significance of these assets is demonstrated by the fact that by some estimates over 50% or more of the market capitalization of a typical U.S. company is now subsumed under intangible assets, i.e., primarily intellectual property. Several industry segments are especially dependent on aggregating "knowledge" into their products in order to create valuable intellectual property.

Semiconductors

The most significant IP is not merely the designs (the specific masks or etchings) which are the road map of the chips, but also the exact assembly instructions. Although product lifecycles can be measured in months, the effort of thousands of highly educated engineers working in collaborative teams to design, debug, and manufacture leading-edge chips, should be measured in years. If a competitor has both the masks and the assembly instructions, they may anticipate the originator's target and "leap frog" over a current-generation product in price and performance. Alternatively they may merely join the originator in the market with a "me too" product. Such a strategy may be very attractive to an unethical competitor as it could allow them to remain competitive without investing as much time and resources in primary design as the originator.

Biotechnology and pharmaceutical products

Often developed over 5 to 7 years and costing hundreds of millions of dollars each, a successful product will represent the work of hundreds of highly trained scientists, engineers, medical experts, physicians, nurses, and others. This highly educated workforce generates a product, which in the end may only be protected by a "production process" patent. The pure science which provides the foundation for such drugs is often public, so the organization's return on investment may well ride on safeguarding the various unique processes associated with development, production, or delivery of a therapeutic drug. Once again a competitor, especially one from a country where intellectual property rights are not well established or respected, may derive significant advantages by misappropriating or stealing product information early in a product's lifecycle. With luck or planning, such thefts may allow development of a competitive alternative that could be produced at minimum cost to the competitor and marketed locally with the encouragement or support of the national government.

Software products

Without question, the rapid pace of information technology would not be as fast in the absence of sophisticated software products. Applications harness the raw horsepower of the silicon chip and deliver control to a user's business needs. Such tools benefit from highly skilled programmers working collaboratively to fashion new features and functionality. Their knowledge is captured in the product and becomes the source of an organization's ability to deliver new products.

Source code for new or unreleased software may be targeted by unscrupulous competitors or spirited away by employees lured away by better pay or working conditions. Too often, applications development staff will take with them copies of any new software they helped develop or to which they had access during their term of employment. This is an especially serious problem when contract programmers are employed, because by the nature of their assignments, they know their term is limited (e.g., Year 2000). Thus, they may be tempted to market a product developed for one client to another.

Sensitive Information Is Often Portable and Digital

Sensitive proprietary information and other valuable intellectual property including an organization's trade secrets are now often captured in some digital form. Critical trade secrets worth billions of dollars may be contained in CAD/CAM drawing files, a genetics database, or compiled source code for a breakthrough software application. This digital form creates a whole new class of problems that must be considered by protection professionals. Most new products owe their existence to the computers, networks, and users of those systems. However, in a digital state, and in a typical client-server-based systems environment, the "crown jewels" of organizational sensitive proprietary information are often poorly protected against unauthorized access. Such access may allow the hostile intruder or the malicious insider to purloin a duplicate of the original data, and perhaps corrupt or destroy the original. In a matter of seconds, a misappropriated copy of the corporate "crown jewels" can be sent to an exotic location on the other side of the planet. From there the thief may auction it off to the highest bidder or sell it to a competitor. This frightening possibility should, in and of itself, inspire the senior managers of leading companies to give increased priority to computer and network security. As we shall discuss a little later, it seems many organizations have not yet fully recognized the many risks to their intellectual property and trade secrets that poorly controlled systems and networks create.

Increased Potential for "Loss of Control"

As more organizations deploy network technology and as the IP crown jewels become more digital and portable, it's possible, perhaps even likely, that management will lose control of these key assets. Without constant attention, testing, and monitoring, the risk of a catastrophic loss of control and of the IP assets themselves is high.

Typical Confidential Information

Managers who apply themselves can quickly identify a list of the information about their organization that they consider confidential and which may be considered as sensitive and proprietary information that may also qualify for "trade secret" status. The difference between "confidential" and merely "proprietary" is often based on management's assessment of the competitive advantage that accrues to the organization by managing dissemination of the information. However, given the vast quantity of proprietary information created and stored by contemporary organizations, it is essential to stratify information. This essential step allows organization management to identify the truly critical proprietary information from items that are merely sensitive. Napoleon's maxim of war is appropriate to consider, "He who defends everything, defends nothing!" If an organization does not stratify or prioritize its information assets it is likely to spend too much time and money protecting the "crown jewels" (which typically also qualify as trade secrets), and mundane, low-value information equally. Alternatively, they may not invest sufficiently in protecting their core assets and lose considerable advantage when trade secrets and other critical information are compromised.

In a systematic and well-planned project, managers and corporate attorneys should consider what information, both by type and content, are of value and importance to the organization's business operations, capabilities, and intentions. From this list of valuable information the company should then identify those items or elements of information which are real sources of competitive advantage. Of this last group, the organization should determine which, if any, may qualify for trade secret status. Note that in this process it is likely that some very valuable and useful information will provide competitive advantage, but may not be protectable as a trade secret.

Unquestionably there will be trade secrets that have previously not been considered as such. The following list, while not all-inclusive, at least provides a point of departure for creating an organizational inventory which may be supplemented with industry and organization specific categories.

- Business plans and strategies
- Financial information
- Cost of research, development, and production
- New products: pricing, marketing plans, timing
- Customer lists, terms, pricing
- Research and development priorities, plans, activities
- Inventions and technology information
- Unique or exceptional manufacturing processes
- Facility blueprints, floor plans, layouts
- Employee records and human resources information

While any or all the above categories of information are likely to be considered "confidential," what does that really mean? Essentially "confidential" information if disclosed, modified, or destroyed, without appropriate controls or authorization, would likely have adverse consequences on the organization's business operations. However, any or all of the above information, plus any that is unique to your business could potentially be identified as a "trade secret" and benefit from additional legal protection providing it meets the previously discussed tests.

This "audit" or inventory procedure should then be taken to at least one more level of detail. In cooperation with the organization's information technology (IT) management and line managers, the specific documents, systems (servers, databases, work stations, document imaging/production, networks, etc.), file cabinets, and work areas (buildings) that contain the identified "trade secrets" and sensitive proprietary information should be identified. These environments should then be reviewed/inspected and the degree of compliance with trade secret protection requirements should be the standard for the inspection. At a minimum, all IT systems which contain trade secret and sensitive proprietary information must provide individual accountability for access to their contents and a secure audit trail of the access activity of specific users. Any systems, which do not provide at least these functions, should be upgraded to such functionality on a priority basis.

NEW THREATS TO SENSITIVE, PROPRIETARY INFORMATION

Threats to an organization's sensitive proprietary information have never been more formidable. Each of the following issues is significant and requires that any existing programs to safeguard the "crown jewels" be reassessed to ensure the risks have been appropriately managed.

Healthcare – Identity

Decline in Business Ethics and Loyalty

A recent newspaper headline declared "48% of Employees Lie, Cheat, Steal." However surprising such a statement may seem, the conclusions implied by the title were not fully justified in the supporting article—i.e., many employees engage in relatively innocuous acts of petty theft, such as office supplies. However, within the context of other studies, the conclusion is inescapable, there has been a substantial decline in employee loyalty and an increase in the range of actions that are considered acceptable business practices. As further proof of the overall change in business ethics, consider the story related by Staples' Chairman Thomas Stermberg in his book *Staples for Success*. In the book, the author describes how he asked his wife to apply for a job with arch rival Office Depot's Atlanta delivery-order center, apparently to gain insights concerning their training methods.

It's also important to appreciate the many changes in work force psychology, which grew out of the downsizing and outsourcing efforts of organizations in the late 1980s and early 1990s. Many workers and mid-level managers learned a harsh lesson: the organization will do without them, regardless of the consequences to the individuals. While such actions may have been necessary to survive in a global economy, many people drew the conclusion that the bond of loyalty between employer and employee had become a one-way street. As a consequence, some decided to do whatever they needed to survive. Once an individual reaches this point, it is easy to rationalize serious criminal behavior on the grounds that "everyone is doing it" or they are only getting their "fair share" before the organization eliminates their job. Although the U.S. economy now seems to have weathered the worst of this period, managers and executives must understand that the base of employee loyalty is often very shallow. Executives should consider the degree of employee loyalty as they design their protection measures, especially for the corporate crown jewels.

The Internet: Hacker Playground

One of the most remarkable changes in the late twentieth century has been the explosive growth in the use of the Internet. Until the late 1980s it was the playground for hackers and computer nerds. Since that time, tens of millions of individuals have obtained personal accounts and hundreds of thousands of organizations have established Internet connections. As the number of businesses using "the net" has exploded, so too has the reported rate of computer and network intrusions.

Without question, many network based "attacks" are not serious. However, the number and consequence of malicious activity are increasing. The 1997 Computer Security Institute/FBI Survey showed an increase of 36% in known instances of computer crime from the 1996 survey. The simple equation is increased network connectivity results in more computer crimes. Organizations that blindly hook up to the net without a well-thought-out protection plan place their sensitive intellectual property and trade secrets at serious risk.

The adverse impact on information protection of the global Internet and the rapid increases in Internet users should not be underestimated. Since the "net" now encompasses all continents and more than 100 countries, it is possible to reach anywhere from anywhere. The plans to circle the globe with low-orbiting satellites will increase both access and mobility. It is important to recognize that the Internet is essentially unregulated, and that there is NO central management or policing. When something happens, whether an attempted intrusion via the net or an unsolicited Spam storm, organizations often have few alternatives but to help themselves.

Growing Threat of Espionage

Perhaps the least appreciated new threat to organization information is the efforts by some companies and many countries to steal critical business information and trade secrets. Is this a real problem? According to the American Society of Industrial Security (ASIS), U.S. companies may have lost as much as $300 billion in trade secrets and other intellectual property in 1997.

A review of recent high-profile cases in the public domain shows that many well-known companies have been targets of industrial espionage and theft of technology and trade secrets. For example, a very short list would include:

- Intel®, whose Pentium™ chip designs were stolen by an employee and offered to AMD.
- Representatives of a Taiwanese company who were willing to bribe a corrupt scientist to steal the secrets of Bristol Myers Taxol® production process information.
- In the another recent case, Avery-Denison learned that one of their research scientists was selling company information to a foreign competitor.
- In the most famous case in recent times, a former high-ranking executive of General Motors was accused of stealing literally box loads of highly confidential documents and offering them to his new employer, Volkswagen.
- Other cases include a retired engineer who sold Kodak trade secrets and a contract programmer who offered to sell key information concerning Gillette's new shaving system.

These scenarios indicate that the theft of trade secrets is a thriving business. According to the FBI, they have literally hundreds of investigations under way. It's important to note that these represent only some of the cases which are publicly known, and do not include cases which are quietly investigated and resolved by organizations fearful

Healthcare – Identity

of the adverse publicity attendant to a litigation or prosecution. There are likely an even larger number of cases which go completely undetected and which may contribute to the potential failure of large and successful organizations.

Impact of Global Business Operations

Globalization of business operations is a major trend of the late twentieth century. It is now a fact that most business organizations operate and compete throughout the world. An important factor to consider in global operations is that the standards of business and ethics, which prevail in the heartland of the Midwest, are not necessarily those which exist in remote areas of the world. Nations such as China and various Southeast Asian nations are real challenges, as they do not, at present, honor intellectual property rights to the extent common in much of Europe and North America. Unrelenting competition for survival and success may create situations where theft of trade secrets seems to promise the beleaguered executive an easy way to remain in business without the need to invest as much in developing new products or improving his operations.

Threats from Networks, Computers and Phones

Generally it has been argued that advanced nations have reaped increased productivity through many benefits of sophisticated communication. With regard to protecting trade secrets, such technologies raise a host of questions. First, as they proliferate throughout the organization, WHERE are the organization's secrets? This is more than just a question of primary physical storage. To properly answer the question, the organization must consider both hard copy documents, individual desktop microcomputers, file servers, databases, backup files/media, as well as imaging/document management and other computer and networking systems.

The myriad of locations and variety of forms and formats which may contain sensitive proprietary information makes it very difficult, sometimes impossible, to know with certainty WHO has access to company secrets! And in cases where management believes they have adequate control over access to sensitive proprietary information, HOW do they really know? Too often managers rely on simple assertions from the Management Information Systems (MIS) and Information Technology (IT) staff that the system and network controls are adequate to protect the organizational crown jewels. Given the importance of the topic and complexity of the environments, senior management is well advised to verify actual conditions of the security and control measures on a periodic basis.

The advent of inter-organizational networks, typically dubbed "extra-nets," should cause managers concerned with safeguarding their crown jewels to take a hard look at the function and features of the environment. Without careful attention to the configuration and management, it is possible that outsiders will be able to gain access to organization information that extends well beyond the legitimate scope of the relationship.

WHAT MUST BE DONE?

Managers who appreciate the full nature and scope of the threat to sensitive proprietary information and trade secrets must implement protective measures to mitigate the most likely vulnerabilities of their organizations. With regard to protecting trade secrets, there are some measures which have been found to be essential. There are now many additional security measures, which are highly recommended, even though they have not yet been held to be essential.

Required Protection Measures for Protecting Trade Secret Information

Although the courts in the United States have not published any sort of handbook which describes required protective measures to safeguard intellectual property, review of various case decisions provides various examples where judges have ruled in such a way that clearly indicated the desirability of the security measure.

Visitor sign-in and escort

Common sense indicates all non-employees entering the company facility should be escorted by host employees, sign in at reception, and be retained until the host escort arrives. Too often, once inside the facility, host employees' excessive hospitality gives the visitor free reign of the site. In the absence of well-maintained internal perimeters, visitors may obtain accidental or deliberate access to sensitive areas, files, documents, and materials. Also, the unguarded conversations of co-workers unaware of the status of the listener may result in disclosure of sensitive information.

Identification badges

Distinctive badges with photo provide good control over egress and exit. These are also so inexpensive that organization management would appear foolish if they failed to implement some sort of badging system.

Facility access control system

Often tied into the photo-ID badge system used by the organization, facility access control systems provide convenient and automated authentication technology. In the past, card readers alone were sufficient. However, many sophisticated organizations with significant assets are implementing biometric (voice, hand geometry, or retina) systems. Such systems dramatically curtail the potential for abuse.

Healthcare – Identity

Confidentiality/Non-disclosure documents

These confidentiality and non-disclosure statements should specify invention assignments as well as an agreement to protect proprietary information.

Exit interviews with terminating employees

Remind employees that are leaving the company of their continuing obligation to protect any trade secrets to which they had access during the time of their employment.

Other "Reasonable" measures!

The courts have a remaining variable, which can be very important. They may decide, entirely after the fact, that a given organization did or did not act "reasonably" by implementing or failing to implement a specific protective measure. The important fact for protection professionals to consider is that the outcome of a particular ruling is not possible to predict in advance of a trial and a specific set of circumstances.

Recommended Protection Measures

Develop and disseminate policies and procedures

Although not strictly required, a policy that spells out the need for information protection and a procedural framework that addresses issues in both electronic and physical media is a useful tool.

Publication approval procedures

Disclosure of the trade secret information in publications will eliminate their trade secret status. Even if the proprietary information disclosed in an article, interview, or press release is not a trade secret, it may damage the company's competitive position. A publication screening procedure involving the company's patent staff or other knowledgeable attorneys, as well as other knowledgeable management, should consider not merely whether the content discloses trade secrets, but also whether it reveals competition-sensitive details. If available, the competitive intelligence group can render valuable service in advising on sensitivity. One must assume that the competitive intelligence analysts working for the most competent opponent will see the release/article and place it in appropriate context.

Contract language for vendors, suppliers, etc.

All vendors who provide products, services, even parts and supplies should be required to adhere to a basic confidentiality agreement concerning the nature and extent of the relationship with the company. Appropriate language should be inserted in the contract terms and conditions, specifying exactly how the vendor will act with regard to sensitive proprietary information to which they are granted access in the course of business. In the case of critical suppliers who provide unique or highly specialized elements which are essential to the company's success, it is appropriate to include a supplemental "security guidelines" document. This document should provide additional guidance and direction to the vendor describing (see example table of contents for a typical security guideline for a reprographic service provider).

1. Receipt
2. Storage
3. Handling
4. Work in process
5. Release of finished product
6. Destruction of overruns, QC failed copies, etc.
7. Reportable incidents

Train employees

Everyone who creates, processes, and handles company trade secrets and other sensitive proprietary information should be trained. This includes both regular (full-time) as well as contingent employees (temporaries, contractors, consultants, as well as part-time employees). They all need to know what is specifically considered trade secrets of the company, as well as what elements of information may not be trade secrets but are nonetheless considered critical and must not be disclosed outside the company without authorization from appropriate management. Training topics typically include the following:

- Identification of company trade secrets and sensitive proprietary information
- Marking
- Storage
- Physical transportation of hard copy documents and media
- Electronic transmission and storage of documents, materials
- Destruction of physical and electronic copies
- Reportable incidents

In addition a version of training should be tailored to the needs of the contingent employees, which commonly include temporary (clerical) staff as well as any on-site contractors, consultants, or vendor employees.

New-hire training classes

One of the best ways to help people in an organization to change is to indoctrinate the newly hired staff. This way you get your message to the new people before they develop bad habits. This will gradually create a critical mass of supporters for the organization's program to protect information, trade secrets, and other valuable intellectual property. This class and supporting documentation should instruct all employees in the value of trade secrets and company IP, as well as correct procedures for safeguarding these assets.

Develop incident response capability

Assume the worst and you will not be disappointed! There will come a time when the company knows or suspects trade secrets or other valuable intellectual property has been stolen or misappropriated. The statistics are very compelling: nearly 50% of high-technology companies experienced theft or misappropriation of trade secrets in a 1988 Institute of Justice study. Planning for that day is essential. Knowing who to call and what to do will maximize the company's chances for a successful prosecution or litigation.

Conduct audits, inspections, and tests

One of the best ways to know the risks is to conduct a formal trade secret audit or inspection. The process, which must always be conducted under attorney-client privilege, should be a comprehensive review of the company's current inventory of trade secrets, including how well they are managed and protected. A useful extension to the basic review is to conduct a "valuation estimate" for trade secrets and other critical intellectual property. Such estimates, conducted prior to any possible losses, are a useful guide to management. When estimated values of IP are presented in dollars and cents, it will allow a more rational allocation of investment in protecting what may have seemed previously unsubstantial assets.

CONCLUSION: DON'T RELY EXCLUSIVELY ON THE COURTS TO PROTECT YOUR SECRETS!

If the reader takes only one lesson from this entry it should be this: Although the legal system exists to provide redress for crimes and grievances through criminal prosecution and civil litigation, the process is laden with uncertainty and burdened with very high costs. It is estimated that General Motors spent millions of dollars pursuing Volkswagen and former executives for alleged theft of trade secrets. Even though in the end they prevailed, it was uncertain whether the German courts would find in favor of GM when the action was initiated. When the vagaries of international relations and politics are overlaid on top of the legal variables, it becomes obvious that prevention is a vastly preferable strategy.

Too often it seems that the organizations value more highly their capability to litigate and prosecute for theft or misappropriation of trade secrets. In the long run it is likely to be effective and more efficient to take reasonable steps to prevent incidents. It is important that management understand that a well-designed information protection program and aggressive, early intervention will often eliminate costly and uncertain legal conflicts. Of course, one could be cynical and assume that some attorneys relish the opportunity to showcase their awesome legal expertise on behalf of clients. There is the potential that such displays of capability will occur less frequently if organizations invest more in procedures and technologies designed to prevent and detect the attempts to steal sensitive proprietary information and trade secrets. However, it's more likely that many lawyers, the same as many executives, do not yet appreciate the vast scope of the problem and are merely applying their past experience.

In summary then, executive management should understand that:

1. Many thefts of sensitive proprietary information are preventable.
2. Those that are not prevented can be detected earlier, thus minimizing potential losses.
3. A well-designed protection program will enhance the organization's probability for successful prosecution and litigation.

Healthcare – Identity

Honeypots and Honeynets

Anton Chuvakin, Ph.D., GCIA, GCIH, GCFA
LogLogic, Inc., San Jose, California, U.S.A.

Abstract

This entry discusses honeypot (and honeynet) basics and definitions, and then outlines important implementation and setup guidelines. It also describes some of the security lessons, a company can derive from running a honeypot, based on this author's experience running a research honeypot. The chapter also provides insight on techniques of the attackers and concludes with considerations useful for answering the question, "Should your organization deploy a honeynet?"

OVERVIEW

This entry discusses honeypot (and honeynet) basics and definitions, and then outlines important implementation and setup guidelines. It also describes some of the security lessons a company can derive from running a honeypot, based on this author's experience running a research honeypot. The entry also provides insight on techniques of the attackers and concludes with considerations useful for answering the question, "Should your organization deploy a honeynet?"

INTRODUCTION TO HONEYPOTS

While known to security processionals for a long time, honeypots recently became a hot topic in information security. However, the amount of technical information available on their setup, configuration, and maintenance remains sparse, as are qualified people able to run them. In addition, higher-level guidelines (such as need and business case determination) are similarly absent.

This entry discusses some of the honeypot (and honeynet) basics and definitions and then outlines some important implementation issues. It also discusses security lessons a company can derive from running a research honeypot.

What is a honeypot? Lance Spitzner, a founder of Honeynet Project (http://www.honeynet.org), defines a honeypot as "a security resource whose value lies in being probed, attacked or compromised." The Project differentiates between research and production honeypots. The former focus on gaining intelligence information about attackers and their technologies and methods, while the latter aim to decrease the risk to a company's IT resources and provide advance warning about the incoming attacks on the network infrastructure. Honeypots of any kind are difficult to classify using the "prevention—detection—response" metaphor, but it is hoped that after reading this entry their value will become clearer.

This entry focuses on operating a research honeypot, or a "honeynet." The term "honeynet," as used in this entry, originated in the Honeynet Project and means a network of systems with fairly standard configurations connected to the Internet. The only difference between such a network and a regular production network is that all communication is recorded and analyzed, and no attacks targeted at third parties can escape the network. Sometimes, the system software is slightly modified to help deal with encrypted communication, often used by attackers. The systems are never "weakened" for easier hacking, but are often deployed in default configurations with a minimum of security patches. They might or might not have known security holes. The Honeynet Project defines such honeypots as "high-interaction" honeypots, meaning that attackers interact with a deception system exactly as they would with a real victim machine. On the other hand, various honeypot and deception daemons are "low-interaction" because they only provide an illusion to an attacker, and one that can hold their attention for a short time only. Such honeypots have value as an early attack indicator but do not yield in-depth information about the attackers.

Research honeypots are set up with no extra effort to lure attackers—blackhats locate and exploit systems on their own. It happens due to the widespread use of automatic hacking tools, such as fast multiple vulnerability scanners and automatic penetration scripts. For example, an attacker from our honeynet has attempted to scan 200,000 systems for a single FTP vulnerability in one night using such tools. Research honeypots are also unlikely to be used for prosecuting intruders; however, researchers are known to track hacker activities using various covert techniques for a long time after the intruder has broken into their honeypot. In addition, prosecution based on honeypot evidence has never been tested in a court of law. It is still wise to involve a company's legal team before setting up such a hacker study project.

Overall, the honeypot is the best tool for looking into the malicious hacker activity. The reason for that is simple: all

Encyclopedia of Information Assurance DOI: 10.1081/E-EIA-120046841
Copyright © 2011 by Taylor & Francis. All rights reserved.

Healthcare – Identity

communication to and from the honeynet is malicious by definition. No data filtering, no false positives, and no false negatives (the latter only if the data analysis is adequate) are obscuring the picture. Watching the honeypot provides insight into intruders' personalities and can be used to profile attackers. For example, in the recent past, the majority of penetrated Linux honeypots were hacked by Romanian attackers.

What are some of the common-sense prerequisites for running a honeynet? First, a honeypot is a sophisticated security project, and it makes sense to take care of security basics first. If your firewall crashes or your intrusion detection system misses attacks, you are clearly not yet ready for honeypot deployment. Running a honeypot also requires advanced knowledge in computer security. After running a honeynet for netForensics (http://www.netForensics.com), a member of Honeynet Research Alliance, I can state that operating a honeynet presents the ultimate challenge a security professional can face. The reason is simple: no "lock it down and maintain secure state" model is possible for such a deception network. It requires in-depth expertise in many security technologies and beyond.

Some of the technical requirements follow. Apparently, honeypot systems should not be allowed to attack other systems or, at least, such ability should be minimized. This requirement often conflicts with a desire to create a more realistic environment for malicious hackers to "feel at home" so that they manifest a full spectrum of their behavior. Related to the above is a need for the proper separation of a research honey network from company production machines. In addition to protecting innocent third parties, similar measures should be utilized to prevent attacks against your own systems from your honeypot. Honeypot systems should also have reliable out-of-band management. The main reason for having this capability is to be able to quickly cut off network access to and from the honeypot in case of emergency (and they do happen!) even if the main network connection is saturated by an attack. That sounds contradictory with the above statement about preventing outgoing attacks, but Murphy's law might play a trick or two and "human errors" can never be totally excluded.

The Honeynet Research Alliance (http://www.honeynet.org/alliance/) has guidelines on data control and data capture for the deployed honeynet. They distill the above ideas and guidelines into a wellwritten document entitled "Honeynet Definitions, Requirements, and Standards" (http://www.honeynet.org/alliance/requirements.html). This document establishes some "rules of the game," which have a direct influence on honeynet firewall rule sets and IDS policies.

Data control is a capability required to control the network traffic flow in and out of the honeynet in order to contain the blackhat actions within the defined policy. For example, rules such as "no outgoing connections," "limited number of outgoing connection per time unit," "only specific protocols or locations for outgoing connections," "limited bandwidth of outgoing connections," "attack string filtering in outgoing connections," or their combination can be used on a honeynet. Data control functionality should be multilayered, allow for manual and automatic intervention (such as remote disabling of the honeypot), and make every effort to protect innocent third parties from becoming victims of attacks launched from the honeynet (and launched they will be!).

Data capture defines the information that should be captured on the honeypot system for future analysis, data retention policies, and standardized data formats, which facilitate information sharing between the honeynets and cross-honeypot data processing. Cross-honeypot correlation is an extremely promising area of future research because it allows for the creation of an early warning system about new exploits and attacks. Data capture also covers the proper separation of honeypots from production networks to protect the attack data from being contaminated by regular network traffic. Another important aspect of data capture is the timely documentation of attacks and other incidents occurring in the honeypot. It is crucial for researchers to have a well-written log of malicious activities and configuration changes performed on the honeypot system.

RUNNING A HONEYPOT

Let us turn to the practical aspects of running a honeynet. Our example setup, a netForensics honeynet, consists of three hosts: a victim host, a firewall, and an IDS (intrusion detection system). This is the simplest configuration to maintain; however, a workable honeynet can even be set up on a single machine if a virtual environment (such as VMware or UML-Linux) is used. Combining IDS and firewall functionality using a gateway IDS (such as "snort-inline") allows one to reduce the requirement to just two machines. A gateway IDS is a host with two network cards that analyzes the traffic passing through it and can make packet-forwarding decisions (like a firewall) and send alerts based on network packet contents (like an IDS). Currently, the honeynet uses Linux on all systems, but various other UNIX flavors will be deployed as "victim" servers by the time this entry is published. Linux machines in default configurations are hacked often enough to provide a steady stream of data on blackhat activity. "Root"-level system penetration within hours of being deployed is not unheard of. UNIX also provides a safe choice for a victim system OS (operating system) due to its higher transparency and ease of reproducing a given configuration.

The honeypot is run on a separate network connection—always a good idea because the deception systems should not be seen as owned by your organization. A firewall (hardened Linux "iptables" stateful firewall) allows and logs all the inbound connections to the honeypot machines and limits the outgoing traffic, depending on the protocol (with full logging as well). It also blocks all IP spoofing attempts and fragmented packets, often used to conceal the

Healthcare – Identity

source of a connection or launch a denial-of-service attack. A firewall also protects the analysis network from attacks originating from the honeypot. In fact, in the above setup, an attacker must pierce two firewalls to get to the analysis network. The IDS machine is also firewalled, hardened, and runs no services accessible from the untrusted network. The part of the rule set relevant to protecting the analysis network is very simple: no connections are allowed from the untrusted LAN to an analysis network. The IDS (Snort from http://www.snort.org) records all network traffic to a database and a binary traffic file via a stealth IP-less interface, and also sends alerts on all known attacks detected by its wide signature base (approximately 1650 signatures as of July 2002). In addition, specially designed software is used to monitor the intruder's keystrokes and covertly send them to a monitoring station.

All data capture and data control functionality is duplicated as per Honeynet Project requirements. The 'tcpdump' tool is used as the secondary data capture facility, a bandwidth-limiting device serves as the second layer of data control, and the stealth kernel-level key logger backs up the keystroke recording. Numerous automated monitoring tools, some custom-designed for the environment, are watching the honeypot network for alerts and suspicious traffic patterns.

Data analysis is crucial for the honeypot environment. The evidence—in the form of system, firewall, and IDS log files, IDS alerts, keystroke captures, and full traffic captures—is generated in overwhelming amounts. Events are correlated and suspicious ones are analyzed using the full packet dumps. It is highly recommended to synchronize the time via the Network Time Protocol on all the honeypot servers for more reliable data correlation. netForensics software can be used to enable advanced data correlation and analysis, as well logging the compromises using the Incident Resolution Management system. Unlike in the production environment, having traffic data available in the honeypot is extremely helpful. It also allows for reliable recognition of new attacks. For example, a Solaris attack on the "dtspcd" daemon (TCP port 6112) was first captured in one of the Project's honeypots and then reported to CERT. Several new attacks against Linux sam servers were also detected recently. Samba is a Linux/UNIX implementation of a Microsoft Server Message Block (SMB) protocol.

The above setup has gone through many system compromises, several massive outbound denial-ofservice attacks (all blocked by the firewall!), major system vulnerability scanning, serving as an Internet Relay Chat server for Romanian hackers, and other exciting stuff. It passed with flying colors through all the above "adventures" and can be recommended for deployment.

LEARNING FROM HONEYPOTS

What insights have we gained about the attacking side from running the honeynet? It is true that most of the attackers "caught" in such honeynets are "script kiddies," that is, the less enlightened part of the hacker community. While famous early honeypot stories (such as those described in Bill Cheswick's "An Evening with Berferd" and Cliff Stolls' "Cuckoo's Nest") dealt with advanced attackers, most of your honeypot experience will probably be related to script kiddies. In opposition to common wisdom, companies do have something to fear from script kiddies. The number of scans and attacks aimed by the attackers at Internet-facing networks ensures that any minor mistake in network security configuration will be discovered fairly soon. Every unsecured server running a popular operating system (such as Solaris, Linux, or Windows) will be taken over fairly soon. Default configurations and bugs in services (UNIX/Linux ssh, bind, ftpd, and now even Apache Web server and Windows IIS are primary examples) are the reason. We have captured and analyzed multiple attack tools using the above flaws. For example, a fully automated scanner that looks for 25 common UNIX vulnerabilities, runs hundreds of attack threads simultaneously, and deploys a rootkit upon the system compromise is one such tool. The software can be set to choose a random A class (16 million hosts) and first scan it for a particular network service. Then, on second pass, the program collects FTP banners (such as "ftp.example.com FTP server [Version wu-2.6.1-16] ready") for target selection. On third pass, the servers that had the misfortune of running a particular vulnerable version of the FTP daemon, are attacked, exploited, and backdoored for convenience. The owner of such a tool can return in the morning to pick up a list of IP addresses that he now "owns" (meaning: has privileged access to).

In addition, malicious attackers are known to compile Internet-wide databases of available network services, complete with their versions, so that the hosts can be compromised quickly after the new software flaw is discovered. In fact, there is always a race between various groups to take over more systems. This advantage can come in handy in the case of a local denial-of-service war. While "our" attackers have not tried to draft the honeypot in their army of "zombie" bots, they did use it to launch old-fashioned point-to-point denial-of-service attacks (such as UDP and ping floods, and even the ancient modem hang-up ATH DoS).

The attacker's behavior seemed to indicate that they are used to operating with no resistance. One attacker's first action was to change the 'root' password on the system — clearly, an action that will be noticed the next time the system admin tries to log in. Not a single attacker bothered to check for the presence of the Tripwire integrity checking system, which is included by default in many Linux distributions. On the next Tripwire run, all the "hidden" files are easily discovered. One more attacker has created a directory for himself as "/his-hacker-handle," something that every system admin worth his or her salt will see immediately. The rootkits (i.e., hacker toolkits to maintain access to a system that include backdoors, Trojans, and common attack tools) now reach megabyte sizes and feature graphical installation interfaces suitable for novice blackhats. Research indicates that some of the script kiddies "own" networks consisting of hundreds of machines that can be used for DoS or other malicious purposes.

The exposed UNIX system is most often scanned for ports 111 (RPC services), 139 (SMB), 443 (OpenSSL), and 21 (FTP). Recent (2001 to 2003) remote "root" bugs in those services account for this phenomenon. The system with vulnerable Apache with SSL is compromised within several days.

Another benefit of running a honeypot is a better handle on Internet noise. Clearly, security professionals who run Internet-exposed networks are well aware of the common Internet noise (such as CodeRed, SQL, MSRPC worms, warez site FTP scans, etc.). A honeypot allows one to observe the minor oscillations of such noise. Sometimes, such changes are meaningful. In the recent case of the MS SQL worm, we detected a sharp increase in TCP port 1433 access attempts just before news of the worm became public. The same spike was seen when the RPC worms were released. The number of hits was similar to a well-researched CodeRed growth pattern. Thus, we concluded that a new worm was out.

An additional value of the honeypot is in its use as a security training platform. Using the honeypot, the company can bring up the level of incident response skills of the security team. Honeypot incidents can be investigated and then the answers verified by the honeypot's enhanced data collection capabilities. "What tool was used to attack?"—Here it is on the captured hard drive or extracted from network traffic. "What did they want?"—Look at their shell command history and know. One can quickly and effectively develop network and disk forensics skills, attacker tracking, log analysis, IDS tuning, and many other critical security skills in the controlled but realistic environment of the honeypot.

More advanced research uses of the honeypot include hacker profiling and tracking, statistical and anomaly analysis of incoming probes, capture of worms, and analysis of malicious code development. By adding some valuable resources (such as E-commerce systems and billing databases) and using the covert intelligence techniques to lure attackers, more sophisticated attackers can be attracted and studied. That will increase the operating risks.

ABUSE OF THE COMPROMISED SYSTEMS

The more recent OpenSSL incidents are more interesting because the attacker does not have root upon breaking into the system (such as, user "apache"). One might think that owning a system with no "root" access is useless, but we usually see active system use in these cases. Following are some of the things that such non-root attackers do on such compromised systems.

IRC Till You Drop

Installing an IRC bot or bouncer is a popular choice of such attackers. Several IRC channels dedicated entirely for communication of the servers compromised by a particular group were observed on several occasions. Running an IRC bot does not require additional privileges.

Local Exploit Bonanza

Throwing everything they have at the "Holy Grail" of root access seems common as well. Often, the attacker will try half a dozen different exploits, trying to elevate his privileges from mere "apache" to "root."

Evil Daemon

A secure shell daemon can be launched by a non-root user on a high numbered port. This was observed in several cases. In some of these cases, the intruder accepted the fact that he will not have root. He then started to make his new home on the net more comfortable by adding a backdoor and some other tools in "hidden" (".." and other non-printable names are common) directories in/tmp or /var/tmp.

Flood, Flood, Flood

While a spoofed DoS attack is more stealthy and more difficult to trace, many classic DoS attacks do not require root access. For example, ping floods and UDP floods can be initiated by non-root users. This capability is sometimes abused by the intruders, using the fact that even when the attack is traced, the only found source would be a compromised machine with no logs present.

More Boxes!

Similar to a root-owning intruder, those with non-root shells can use the compromised system for vulnerability scanning and widespread exploitation. Many of the scanners, such as openssl autorooter, recently discovered by us, do not need root to operate, but are still capable of discovering and exploiting a massive (thousands and more) system within a short time period. Such large networks can be used for devastating denial-of-service attacks (for example, such as recently warned by CERT).

CONCLUSION

As a conclusion we will try to answer the question: "Should you do it?" The precise answer depends on your

Healthcare – Identity

organization's mission and available security expertise. Again, the emphasis here is on research honeypots and not on "shield" or protection honeypots. If your organization has taken care of most routine security concerns, has a developed in-house security program (calling an outside consultant to investigate your honeypot incident does not qualify as a wise investment), and requires first-hand knowledge of attacker techniques and last-minute Internet threats—the answer tends toward a tentative "yes." Major security vendors and consultancies or universities with advanced computer security programs might fall into the category. If you are not happy with your existing security infrastructure and want to replace or supplement it with the new cutting-edge "honeypot technology"—the answer is a resounding "no." Research honeypots will not "directly" impact the safety of your organization. Moreover, honeypots have their own inherent dangers. They are analyzed in papers posted on the Honeynet Project Web site. The dangers include uncertain liability status, possible hacker retaliation, and others.

Host-Based Firewalls: Case Study

Jeffery J. Lowder, CISSP
Chief of Network Security Element, United States Air Force Academy, Westlake Village, California, U.S.A.

Abstract

Because hosts are exposed to a variety of threats, there is a growing need for organizations to deploy host-based firewalls across the enterprise. This entry outlines the ideal features of a host-based firewall—features that are typically not needed or present in a purely *personal* firewall software implementation on a privately owned PC. In addition, the author describes his own experiences with, and lessons learned from, deploying agent-based, host-based firewalls across an enterprise. The author concludes that host-based firewalls provide a valuable additional layer of security.

A SEMANTIC INTRODUCTION

Personal firewalls are often associated with (and were originally designed for) home PCs connected to "always-on" broadband Internet connections. Indeed, the term *personal firewall* is itself a vestige of the product's history: originally distinguished from *enterprise* firewalls, *personal* firewalls were initially viewed as a way to protect home PCs.[1] Over time, it was recognized that personal firewalls had other uses. The security community began to talk about using personal firewalls to protect notebooks that connect to the enterprise LAN via the Internet and eventually protecting notebooks that physically reside on the enterprise LAN.

Consistent with that trend—and consistent with the principle of defense-in-depth—it can be argued that the time has come for the potential usage of personal firewalls to be broadened once again. Personal firewalls should really be viewed as *host-based* firewalls. As soon as one makes the distinction between host-based and network-based firewalls, the additional use of a host-based firewall becomes obvious. Just as organizations deploy host-based *intrusion detection systems* (IDS) to provide an additional detection capability for critical servers, organizations should consider deploying host-based *firewalls* to provide an additional layer of access control for critical servers (e.g., exchange servers, domain controllers, print servers, etc.). Indeed, given that many host-based firewalls have an IDS capability built in, it is conceivable that, at least for some small organizations, host-based firewalls could even *replace* specialized host-based IDS software.

The idea of placing one firewall behind another is not new. For years, security professionals have talked about using so-called internal firewalls to protect especially sensitive back-office systems.[2] However, internal firewalls, like network-based firewalls in general, are still dedicated devices. (This applies to both firewall appliances such as Cisco's PIX and software-based firewalls such as Symantec's Raptor.) In contrast, host-based firewalls require no extra equipment. A host-based firewall is a firewall software package that runs on a preexisting server or client machine. Given that a host-based firewall runs on a server or client machine (and is responsible for protecting *only* that machine), host-based firewalls offer greater functionality than network-based firewalls, even including internal firewalls that are dedicated to protecting a single machine. Whereas both network- and host-based firewalls have the ability to filter inbound and outbound network connections, only host-based firewalls possess the *additional* capabilities of blocking network connections linked to specific programs and preventing the execution of mail attachments.

To put this into proper perspective, consider the network worm and Trojan horse program QAZ, widely suspected to be the exploit used in the November 2000 attack on Microsoft's internal network. QAZ works by hijacking the NOTEPAD.EXE program. From the end user's perspective, Notepad still appears to run normally; but each time Notepad is launched, QAZ sends an e-mail message (containing the IP address of the infected machine) to some address in China.[3] Meanwhile, in the background, the Trojan patiently waits for a connection on TCP port 7597, through which an intruder can upload and execute any applications.[4] Suppose QAZ were modified to run over TCP port 80 instead.[5] While all firewalls can block outbound connections on TCP port 80, implementing such a configuration would interfere with legitimate traffic. Only a host-based firewall can block an outbound connection on TCP port 80 associated with NOTEPAD.EXE and notify the user of the event. As Steve Riley notes, "Personal firewalls that monitor outbound connections will raise an alert; seeing a dialog with the notice 'Notepad is attempting to connect to the Internet' should arouse anyone's suspicions."[5]

Encyclopedia of Information Assurance DOI: 10.1081/E-EIA-120046369
Copyright © 2011 by Taylor & Francis. All rights reserved.

Healthcare – Identity

STAND-ALONE VS. AGENT-BASED FIREWALLS

Host-based firewalls can be divided into two categories: stand-alone and agent-based.[1] Stand-alone firewalls are independent of other network devices in the sense that their configuration is managed (and their logs are stored) on the machine itself. Examples of stand-alone firewalls include ZoneAlarm, Sygate Personal Firewall Pro, Network Associates' PGP Desktop Security, McAfee Personal Firewall [Although McAfee is (at the time this entry was written) currently in Beta testing with its own agent-based product, Personal Firewall 7.5, that product is not scheduled to ship until late March 2002][6] Norton Internet Security 2000, and Symantec Desktop Firewall.

In contrast, agent-based firewalls are not locally configured or monitored. Agent-based firewalls are configured from (and their logs are copied to) a centralized enterprise server. Examples of agent-based firewalls include ISS RealSecure Desktop Protector (formerly Network ICE's Black ICE Defender) and InfoExpress's CyberArmor Personal Firewall.

We chose to implement agent-based firewall software on our hosts. While stand-alone firewalls are often deployed as an enterprise solution, we wanted the agent-based ability to centrally administer and enforce a consistent access control list (ACL) across the enterprise. And as best practice dictates that the logs of network-based firewalls be reviewed on a regular basis, we wanted the ability to aggregate logs from host-based firewalls across the enterprise into a single source for regular review and analysis.

OUR PRODUCT SELECTION CRITERIA

Once we adopted an agent-based firewall model, our next step was to select a product. Again, as of the time this entry was written, our choices were RealSecure Desktop Protector or CyberArmor. We used the following criteria to select a product (cf. my discussion of network-based firewall criteria in Firewall Management and Internet Attacks in *Information Security Management Handbook*; 2000, 4th ed., pp. 118–119):

- *Effectiveness in blocking attacks.* The host-based firewall should effectively deny malicious inbound traffic. It should also at least be capable of effectively filtering outbound connections. As Steve Gibson argues, "Not only must our Internet connections be fortified to prevent *external intrusion,* they also [must] provide secure management of *internal extrusion.*"[7] By internal extrusion, Gibson is referring to outbound connections initiated by Trojan horses, viruses, and spyware. To effectively filter outbound connections, the host-based firewall must use cryptographic sums. The host-based firewall must first generate cryptographic sums for

each authorized application and then regenerate and compare that sum to the one stored in the database before any program (no matter what the filename) is allowed access. If the application does not maintain a database of cryptographic sums for all authorized applications (and instead only checks filenames or file paths), the host-based firewall may give an organization a false sense of security.

- *Centralized configuration.* Not only did we need the ability to centrally define the configuration of the host-based firewall, we also required the ability to *enforce* that configuration. In other words, we wanted the option to prevent end users from making security decisions about which applications or traffic to allow.

- *Transparency to end users.* Because the end users would not be making any configuration decisions, we wanted the product to be as transparent to them as possible. For example, we did not want users to have to "tell" the firewall how their laptops were connected (e.g., corporate LAN, home Internet connection, VPN, extranet, etc.) in order to get the right policy applied. In the absence of an attack, we wanted the firewall to run silently in the background without noticeably degrading performance. (Of course, in the event of an attack, we would want the user to receive an alert.)

- *Multiple platform support.* If we were only interested in personal firewalls, this would not have been a concern. (While Linux notebooks arguably might need personal firewall protection, we do not have such machines in our environment.) However, because we are interested in implementing host-based firewalls on our servers as well as our client PCs, support for multiple operating systems is a requirement.

- *Application support.* The firewall must be compatible with all authorized applications and the protocols used by those applications.

- *VPN support.* The host-based firewall must support our VPN implementation and client software. In addition, it must be able to detect and transparently adapt to VPN connections.

- *Firewall architecture.* There are many options for host-based firewalls, including packet filtering, application-level proxying, and stateful inspection.

- *IDS technology.* Likewise, there are several different approaches to IDS technology, each with its own strengths and weaknesses. The number of attacks detectable by a host-based firewall will clearly be relevant here.

- *Ease of use and installation.* As an enterprisewide solution, the product should support remote deployment and installation. In addition, the central administrative server should be (relatively) easy to use and configure.

- *Technical support.* Quality and availability are our prime concerns.

- *Scalability*. Although we are a small company, we do expect to grow. We need a robust product that can support a large number of agents.
- *Disk space*. We were concerned about the amount of disk space required on end-user machines as well as the centralized policy and logging server. For example, does the firewall count the number of times an attack occurs rather than log a single event for every occurrence of an attack?
- *Multiple policy groups*. Because we have diverse groups of end users, each with unique needs, we wanted the flexibility to enforce different policies on different groups. For example, we might want to allow SQL-Net traffic from our development desktops while denying such traffic for the rest of our employees.
- *Reporting*. As with similar enterprise solutions, an ideal reporting feature would include built-in reports for top intruders, targets, and attack methods over a given period of time (e.g., monthly, weekly, etc.).
- *Cost*. As a relatively small organization, we were especially concerned about the cost of selecting a high-end enterprise solution.

OUR TESTING METHODOLOGY

We eventually plan to install and evaluate both CyberArmor and RealSecure Desktop Protector by conducting a pilot study on each product with a small, representative sample of users. (At the time this entry was written, we were nearly finished with our evaluation of CyberArmor and about to begin our pilot study of ISS Real Secure.) While the method for evaluating both products according to most of our criteria is obvious, our method for testing one criterion deserves a detailed explanation: effectiveness in blocking attacks. We tested the effectiveness of each product in blocking unauthorized connections in several ways:

- *Remote Quick Scan from HackYourself.com*.[8] From a dial-up connection, we used HackYourself.com's Quick Scan to execute a simple and remote TCP and UDP port scan against a single IP address.
- *Nmap scan*. We used nmap to conduct two different scans. First, we performed an ACK scan to determine whether the firewall was performing stateful inspection or a simple packet filter. Second, we used nmap's operating system fingerprinting feature to determine whether the host-based firewall effectively blocked attempts to fingerprint target machines.
- *Gibson Research Corporation's LeakTest*. LeakTest determines a firewall product's ability to effectively filter *outbound* connections initiated by Trojans, viruses, and spyware.[9] This tool can test a firewall's ability to block LeakTest when it masquerades as a trusted program (OUTLOOK.EXE).
- *Steve Gibson's TooLeaky*. TooLeaky determines whether the firewall blocks unauthorized programs from controlling trusted programs. The TooLeaky executable tests whether this ability exists by spawning Internet Explorer to send a short, innocuous string to Steve Gibson's Web site, and then receiving a reply.[10]
- *Firehole*. Firehole relies on a modified dynamic link library (DLL) that is used by a trusted application (Internet Explorer). The test is whether the firewall allows the trusted application, under the influence of the malicious DLL, to send a small text message to a remote machine. The message contains the currently logged-on user's name, the name of the computer, and a message claiming victory over the firewall and the time the message was sent. (By default, this message is sent over TCP port 80 but this can be customised.)[11]

CONFIGURATION

One of our reasons for deploying host-based firewalls was to provide an additional layer of protection against Trojan horses, spyware, and other programs that initiate outbound network connections. While host-based firewalls are not designed to interfere with Trojan horses that do not send or receive network connections, they can be quite effective in blocking network traffic to or from an unauthorized application when configured properly. Indeed, in one sense, host-based firewalls have an advantage over antivirus software. Whereas anti-virus software can only detect Trojan horses that match a known *signature*, host-based firewalls can detect Trojan horses based on their network *behavior*. Host-based firewalls can detect, block, and even terminate any unauthorized application that attempts to initiate an outbound connection, even if that connection is on a well-known port like TCP 80 or even if the application causing that connection appears legitimate (NOTEPAD.EXE).

However, there are two well-known caveats to configuring a host-based firewall to block Trojan horses. First, the firewall must block all connections initiated by new applications *by default*. Second, the firewall must not be circumvented by end users who, for whatever reason, click "yes" whenever asked by the firewall if it should allow a new application to initiate outbound traffic. Taken together, these two caveats can cause the cost of ownership of host-based firewalls to quickly escalate. Indeed, other companies that have already implemented both caveats report large numbers of help desk calls from users wanting to get a specific application authorized.[12]

Given that we do not have a standard desktop image and given that we have a very small help desk staff, we decided to divide our pilot users into two different policy groups: pilot-tech-technical and pilot-normal-regular (see Fig. 1).

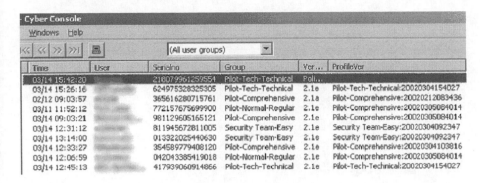

Fig. 1 CyberArmor policy groups.

The first configuration enabled users to decide whether to allow an application to initiate an outbound connection. This configuration was implemented only on the desktops of our IT staff. The user must choose whether to allow or deny the network connection requested by the connection. Once the user makes that choice, the host-based firewall generates a checksum and creates a rule reflecting the user's decision. (See Fig. 2 for a sample rule set in CyberArmor.)

The second configuration denied all applications by default and only allowed applications that had been specifically authorized. We applied this configuration on all laptops outside our IT organization, because we did not want to allow non-technical users to make decisions about the configuration of their host-based firewall.

LESSONS LEARNED

Although at the time this entry was finished we had not yet completed our pilot studies on both host-based firewall products, we had already learned several lessons about deploying agent-based, host-based firewalls across the enterprise. These lessons may be summarized as follows.

1. Our pilot study identified one laptop with a nonstandard and, indeed, unauthorized network configuration. For small organizations that do not enforce a standard desktop image, this should not be a surprise.

2. The ability to enforce different policies on different machines is paramount. This was evident from our experience with the host-based firewall to restrict outbound network connections. By having the ability to divide our users into two groups, those we would allow to make configuration decisions and those we would not, we were able to get both flexibility and security.

3. As is the case with network-based intrusion detection systems, our experience validated the need for well-crafted rule sets. Our configuration includes a rule that blocks inbound NetBIOS traffic. Given the amount of NetBIOS traffic present on both our internal network as well as external networks, this generated a significant amount of

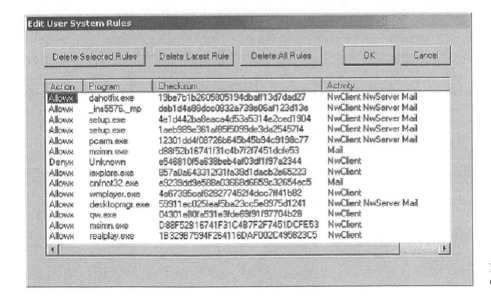

Fig. 2 Sample user-defined rules in CyberArmor.

Healthcare – Identity

Fig. 3 Sample CyberArmor alarm report.

alerts. This, in turn, underscored the need for finely tuned alerting rules.

4. As the author has found when implementing network-based firewalls, the process of constructing and then fine-tuning a host-based firewall rule set is time consuming. This is especially true if one decides to implement restrictions on outbound traffic (and not allow users or a portion of users to make configuration decisions of their own), because one then has to identify and locate the exact file path of each authorized application that has to initiate an outbound connection. While this is by no means an insurmountable problem, there was a definite investment of time in achieving that configuration.

5. We did not observe any significant performance degradation on end user machines caused by the firewall software. At the time this entry was written, however, we had not yet tested deploying host-based firewall software on critical servers.

6. Our sixth observation is product specific. We discovered that the built-in reporting tool provided by CyberArmor is primitive. There is no built-in support for graphical reports, and it is difficult to find information using the text reporting. For example, using the built-in text-reporting feature, one can obtain an "alarms" report. That report, presented in spreadsheet format, merely lists alarm messages and the number of occurrences. Source IP addresses, date, and time information are not included in the report. Moreover, the alarm messages are somewhat cryptic. (See Fig. 3 for a sample CyberArmor Alarm Report.) While CyberArmor is compatible with Crystal Reports, using Crystal Reports to produce useful reports requires extra software and time.

HOST-BASED FIREWALLS FOR UNIX®?

Host-based firewalls are often associated with Windows platforms, given the history and evolution of personal firewall software. However, there is no reason in theory why host-based firewalls cannot (or should not) be implemented on UNIX systems as well. To be sure, some UNIX packet filters already exist, including ipchains, iptables, and ipfw.[13–15] (I am grateful to an anonymous reviewer for suggesting I discuss these utilities in this entry.) Given that UNIX platforms have not been widely integrated into commercial host-based firewall products, these utilities may be very useful in an enterprisewide host-based firewall deployment. However, such tools generally have two limitations worth noting. First, unlike personal firewalls, those utilities are packet filters. As such, they do not have the capability to evaluate an outbound network connection according to the application that generated the connection. Second, the utilities are not agent based. Thus, as an enterprise solution, those tools might not be easily scalable. The lack of an agent-based architecture in such tools might also make it difficult to provide centralized reporting on events detected on UNIX systems.

CONCLUSIONS

While host-based firewalls are traditionally thought of as a way to protect corporate laptops and privately owned PCs, host-based firewalls can also provide a valuable layer of additional protection for servers. Similarly, while host-based firewalls are typically associated with Windows platforms, they can also be used to protect UNIX systems as well. Moreover, host-based firewalls can be an effective tool for interfering with the operation of Trojan horses and

Healthcare – Identity

similar applications. Finally, using an agent-based architecture can provide centralized management and reporting capability over all host-based firewalls in the enterprise.

ACKNOWLEDGMENTS

The author wishes to acknowledge Frank Aiello and Derek Conran for helpful suggestions. The author is also grateful to Lance Lahr, who proofread an earlier version of this entry.

REFERENCES

1. Michael, C. Personal firewalls block the inside threat. Gov. Comp. News **2000**, *19* (3), http://www.gcn.com/vol19_no7/reviews/1602-1.html (accessed February 2002).

2. William, R.C.; Steven, M. B. *Firewalls and Internet Security: Repelling the Wily Hacker*; Addison-Wesley: New York; 1994, 53–54.

3. F-Secure Computer Virus Information Pages, QAZ, January 2001, http://www.europe.f-secure.com/v-descs/qaz.shtml (accessed February 2002).

4. TROJ_QAZ.A – Technical Details, October 28, 2000, http://www.antivirus.com/vinfo/virusencyclo/default5.asp?VName=TROJ_QAZ.A&VSect=T (accessed February 2002).

5. Steve, R. Is Your Generic Port 80 Rule Safe Anymore? February 5, 2001, http://rr.sans.org/firewall/port80.php (accessed February 2002).

6. Douglas, H. The Evolving Threat, http://www.issadv.org/meetings/web/2002/08FEB02/McAfee%20ISSA-DV%20Meeting%20FEB02.pdf (accessed February 2002).

7. Gibson, S. LeakTest – Firewall Leakage Tester, January 24, 2002, http://grc.com/lt/leaktest.htm (accessed February 2002).

8. Hack Yourself Remote Computer Network Security Scan, 2000, http://hackyourself.com:4000/startdemo.dyn (accessed February 2002).

9. Leak Test—How to Use Version 1.x , November 3, 2001, http://grc.com/lt/howtouse.htm (accessed February 2002).

10. Gibson, S. Why Your Firewall Sucks, November 5, 2001, http://tooleaky.zensoft.com/ (accessed February 2002).

11. Robin, K. Firehole: How to Bypass Your Personal Firewall Outbound Detection, November 6, 2001, http://keir.net/firehole.html (accessed February 2002).

12. Brook, B.; Flaviani, A. Case Study of the Implementation of Symantec's Desktop Firewall Solution within a Large Enterprise, http://www.issadv.org/meetings/web/2002/08FEB02/Unisys%20ISSA-DV%20Meeting%20FEB02.pdf (accessed February 2002).

13. Russell, R. Linux IPCHAINS-HOWTO, July 4, 2000, http://www.linuxdoc.org/HOWTO/IPCHAINS-HOWTO.html (accessed March 2002).

14. Andreasson, O. Iptables Tutorial 1.1.9, 2001, http://people.unix-fu.org/andreasson/iptablestutorial/iptablestutorial.html (accessed March 2002).

15. Palmer, G.; Nash, A. Firewalls, 2001, http://www.freebsd.org/doc/en_US.ISO8859-1/books/handbook/firewalls.html (accessed March 2002).

Human Resources: Issues

Jeffrey H. Fenton, CBCP, CISSP
*Corporate IT Crisis Assurance/Mitigation Manager and Technical Lead for IT Risk Management,
Corporate Information Security Office, Lockheed Martin Corporation, Sunnyvale,
California, U.S.A.*

James M. Wolfe, MSM
Enterprise Virus Management Group, Lockheed Martin Corporation, Orlando, Florida, U.S.A.

Abstract

This entry focuses on roles and responsibilities for performing the job of information security. Roles and responsibilities are part of an operationally excellent environment, in which people and processes, along with technology, are integrated to sustain security on a consistent basis. *Separation of responsibilities*, requiring at least two persons with separate job duties to complete a transaction or process end-to-end, or avoiding a conflict of interest, is also introduced as part of organizing for success. This concept originated in accounting and financial management; for example, not having the same person who approves a purchase also able to write a check. The principle is applied to several roles in information technology (IT) development and operations, as well as the IT system development life cycle. All these principles support the overall management goal to protect and leverage the organization's information assets.

In a holistic view, information security is a triad of people, process, and technology. Appropriate technology must be combined with management support, understood requirements, clear policies, trained and aware users, and plans and processes for its use. While the perimeter is traditionally emphasized, threats from inside have received less attention. Insider threats are potentially more serious because an insider already has knowledge of the target systems. When dealing with insider threats, people and process issues are paramount. Also, too often, security measures are viewed as a box to install (technology) or a one-time review. Security is an ongoing process, never finished.

INFORMATION SECURITY ROLES AND RESPONSIBILITIES

This section introduces the functional components of information security, from a role and responsibility perspective, along with several other information technology (IT) and business functional roles. Information security is much more than a specialized function; it is everyone's responsibility in any organization.

Business Process Owner, Information Custodian, and End User

The *business process owner* is the manager responsible for a business process such as supply-chain management or payroll. This manager would be the focal point for one or more

IT applications and data supporting the processes. The process owner understands the business needs and the value of information assets to support them. The International Standard ISO 17799, *Information Security Management*, defines the role of the information asset owner responsible for maintaining the security of that asset.[1]

The *information custodian* is an organization, usually the internal IT function or an outsourced provider, responsible for operating and managing the IT systems and processes for a business owner on an ongoing basis. The business process owner is responsible for specifying the requirements for that operation, usually in the form of a service level agreement (SLA). While information security policy vests ultimate responsibility in business owners for risk management and compliance, the day-to-day operation of the compliance and risk mitigation measures is the responsibility of information custodians and end users.

End users interact with IT systems while executing business functional responsibilities. End users may be internal to the organization, or business partners, or end customers of an online business. End users are responsible for complying with information security policy, whether general, issue-specific, or specific to the applications they use. Educating end users on application usage, security policies, and best practices is essential to achieving compliance and quality.

In an era of budget challenges for the information security functions, the educated and committed end user is an information security force multiplier for defense-in-depth. John Weaver, in a recent essay, "Zen and Information Security,"[2]

Encyclopedia of Information Assurance DOI: 10.1081/E-EIA-120046577
Copyright © 2011 by Taylor & Francis. All rights reserved.

recommends turning people into assets. For training and awareness, this includes going beyond rules and alerts to make security "as second nature as being polite to customers," as Neal O'Farrell noted in his recent paper, "Employees: Your Best Defense, or Your Greatest Vulnerability?"[3] All users should be trained to recognize potential social engineering. Users should also watch the end results of the business processes they use. Accounting irregularities, sustained quality problems in manufacturing, or incorrect operation of critical automated temperature-control equipment could be due to many causes, including security breaches. When alert end users notice these problems and solve them in a results-oriented manner, they could identify signs of sabotage, fraud, or an internal hacker that technical information security tools might miss. End users who follow proper practices and alert management of suspicious conditions are as important as antivirus software, intrusion detection, and log monitoring. Users who learn this holistic view of security can also apply the concepts to their homes and families.[3]

In today's environment, users include an increasing proportion of *non-employee* users, including temporary or contract workers, consultants, outsourced provider personnel, and business-partner representatives. Two main issues with non-employee users are non-disclosure agreements (NDAs) and the process for issuing and deleting computer accounts. Non-employee users should be treated as business partners, or representatives of business partners, if they are given access to systems on the internal network. This should include a written, signed NDA describing their obligations to protect sensitive information. In contrast with employees, who go through a formal human resources (HR) hiring and separation process, non-employee users are often brought in by a purchasing group (for temporary labor or consulting services), or they are brought in by the program manager for a project or outsourced activity. While a formal HR information system (HRIS) can alert

system administrators to delete computer accounts when *employees* leave or transfer, *non-employees* who do not go through the HRIS would not generate this alert. Removing computer accounts for departed non-employees is an weak operational link in many organizations.

Information Security Functions

Information security functions fall into five main categories—policy/strategy/governance, engineering, disaster recovery/business continuity (DR/BC), crisis management and incident response/investigations, and administration/operations (see Fig. 1). In addition, information security functions have many interfaces with other business functions as well as with outsource providers, business partners, and other outside organizations.

Information security policy, strategy, and governance functions should be organized in an information security department or directorate, headed by an information security manager or director who may also be known as the chief information security officer (CISO). This individual directs, coordinates, plans, and organizes information security activities throughout the organization, as noted by Charles Cresson Wood.[4] The information security function must work with many other groups within and outside the organization, including physical security, risk management (usually an insurance-related group in larger companies), internal audit, legal, internal and external customers, industry peers, research groups, and law enforcement and regulatory agencies.

Within the information security function, policy and governance include the development and interpretation of written information security policies for the organization, an education and awareness program for all users, and a formal approval and waiver process. Any deviation from policy represents a risk above the acceptable level represented by compliance with policy. Such deviations should

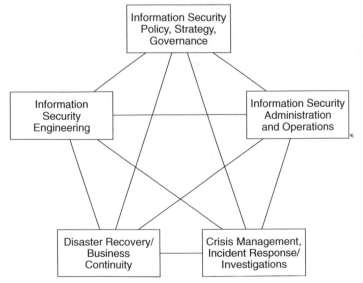

Fig. 1 Five information security roles.

Healthcare – Identity

be documented with a formal waiver approval, including the added risk and additional risk mitigation measures applied, a limited term, and a plan to achieve compliance. Ideally, all connections between the internal network and any outside entity should be consolidated as much as possible through one or a few gateways and demilitarized zones (DMZs), with a standard architecture and continuous monitoring. In very large organizations with decentralized business units, this might not be possible. When business units have unique requirements for external connectivity, those should be formally reviewed and approved by the information security group before implementation.

The security strategy role, also in the central information security group, includes the identification of long-term technology and risk trends driving the evolution of the organization's security architecture. The information security group should develop a security technology roadmap, planning for the next 5 years the organization's need for security technologies driven by risk management and business needs. Once the roadmap is identified, the security group would be responsible for identifying and integrating the products to support those capabilities. Evaluating new products is another part of this activity, and a formal test laboratory should be provided. In larger IT organizations, the security strategy function would work closely with an overall IT strategy function. The information security group should have project responsibility to execute all security initiatives that affect the entire organization.

Information security engineering is the function of identifying security requirements and bringing them to realization when a specific network or application environment is newly developed. While the information security group would set the policies as part of the policy and governance function, security engineers would assess the risks associated with a particular program [such as implementing a new enterprise resource planning (ERP) system], identify the applicable policies, and develop a system policy for the system or application environment. Working through the system development life cycle, engineers would identify requirements and specifications, develop the designs, and participate in the integration and testing of the final product. Engineering also includes developing the operational and change-control procedures needed to maintain security once the system is fielded. Information security engineering may be added to the central information security group, or it may be organized as a separate group (as part of an IT systems engineering function).

Disaster recovery/business continuity includes responding to and recovering from disruptive incidents. While DR involves the recovery of IT assets, BC is broader and includes recovery of the business functions (such as alternative office space or manufacturing facilities). While DR and BC began by focusing on physical risks to availability, especially natural disasters, both disciplines have broadened to consider typically non-physical events such as breaches of information confidentiality or integrity. Much of the planning component of DR/BC can utilize the same risk assessment methods as for information security risk assessments. In large organizations, the DR/BC group is often separate from the central information security group, and included in an operational IT function, because of DR's close relationship to computer operations and backup procedures. Because of the convergence of DR/BC applicability and methods with other information security disciplines, including DR/BC in the central information security group is a worthwhile option.

Crisis management is the overall discipline of planning for and responding to emergencies. Crisis management in IT began as a component of DR. With the broadening of the DR/BC viewpoint, crisis management needs to cover incident types beyond the traditional physical or natural disasters. For all types of incidents, similar principles can be applied to build a team, develop a plan, assess the incident at the onset and identify its severity, and match the response to the incident. In many organizations, the physical security and facilities functions have developed emergency plans, usually focusing on physical incidents or natural disasters, separate from the DR plans in IT. For this reason, an IT crisis management expert should ensure that IT emergency plans are integrated with other emergency plans in the organization. With the broadening of *crisis* to embrace non-physical information security incidents, the integrative role must also include coordinating the separate DR plans for various IT resources. During certain emergencies, while the emergency team is in action, it may be necessary to weigh information security risks along with other considerations (such as rapidly returning IT systems or networks to service). For this reason, as well as for coordinating the plans, the integrative crisis management role should be placed in the central information security group. Information security crisis management can also include working with the public relations, human resources, physical security, and legal functions as well as with suppliers, customers, and outside law enforcement agencies.

Incident response has already been noted as part of crisis management. Many information security incidents require special response procedures different from responding to a physical disaster. These procedures are closely tied to monitoring and notification, described in the next two paragraphs. An organization needs to plan for responding to various types of information security attacks and breaches, depending on their nature and severity. Investigation is closely related to incident response, because the response team must identify when an incident might require further investigation after service is restored. Investigation is fundamentally different in that it takes place after the immediate emergency is resolved, and it requires evidence collection and custody procedures that can withstand subsequent legal scrutiny. Along with this, however, the incident response must include the processes and technology to collect and preserve logs, alerts, and data for subsequent investigation. These provisions must be in place and operational before an incident happens. The investigation role may be centralized in the information security group, or decentralized in large organizations provided that common procedures are followed. If first-line investigation is decentralized to business units in a large corporation, there should be a central information security group specialist to set technical and process direction on incident response planning and investigation techniques. For all incidents and crises, the lessons learned must be documented—not to place blame but to prevent future incidents, improve the response, and help the central information security group update its risk assessment and strategy.

Information security administration and operations include account management, privilege management, security configuration management (on client systems, servers, and network devices), monitoring and notification, and malicious code and vulnerability management. These administrative and operational functions are diverse, not only in their content but also in who performs them, how they are performed, and where they reside organizationally. Account and privilege management include setting up and removing user accounts for all resources requiring access control, and defining and granting levels of privilege on those systems. These functions should be performed by a central security operations group, where possible, to leverage common processes and tools as well as to ensure that accounts are deleted promptly when users leave or transfer. In many organizations, however, individual system administrators perform these tasks. Security configuration management includes configuring computer operating systems and application software, and network devices such as routers and firewalls, with security functions and access rules. This activity actually implements much of the organization's security policy. While the central information security group owns the policy, configuration management is typically distributed among system administrators and telecommunication network administrators. This is consistent with enabling the central information security group to focus on its strategic, policy, and governance roles.

Monitoring and notification should also be part of a central security operations function, with the ability to "roll up" alerts and capture logs from systems and network devices across the enterprise. Intrusion detection systems (IDSs) would also be the responsibility of this group. In many large organizations, monitoring and notification are not well integrated, with some locally administered systems depending on their own system administrators who are often overworked with other duties. As noted earlier, monitoring and notification processes and tools must meet the needs of incident response. The additional challenges of providing 24/7 coverage are also noted below.

Malicious code and vulnerability management includes deploying and maintaining anti-virus software, isolating and remediating infected systems, and identifying and correcting security vulnerabilities (in operating systems, software applications, and network devices). These activities require centrally driven technical and process disciplines. It is not enough only to expect individual desktop users to keep anti-virus software updated and individual system administrators to apply patches. A central group should test and *push* anti-virus updates. The central group should also test patches on representative systems in a laboratory and provide a central repository of alerts and patches for system and network administrators to deploy. Malicious code management is also closely tied to incident response. With the advent of multifunctional worms, and exploits appearing quickly after vulnerabilities become known, an infection could easily occur before patches or antivirus signatures become available. In some cases, anomaly-based IDSs can detect unusual behavior before patches and signatures are deployed, bringing malicious code and vulnerability management into a closer relationship with monitoring. These central activities cross several functional boundaries in larger IT organizations, including e-mail/messaging operations, enterprise server operations, and telecommunications, as well as security operations. One approach is establishing a cross-functional team to coordinate these activities, with technical leadership in the central information security organization.

Distributed Information Security Support in Larger Organizations

Some of the challenges of providing security support in a large organization, especially a large corporation with multiple business units, have already been noted. Whether IT functions in general are centralized or distributed reflects the culture of the organization as well as its business needs and technology choices. In any organization, presenting the business value of the information security functions is challenging. Beyond simply preventing bad things from happening, security is an enabler for E-business. To make this case, the central information security group needs to partner with the business as its internal customer. Building a formal relationship with the business units in a large enterprise is strongly recommended.

This relationship can take the shape of a formal information protection council, with a representative from each division or business unit. The representative's role, which must be supported by business unit management, would include bringing the unique technical, process, and people concerns of security, as viewed by that business unit, to the information security group through two-way communication. The representatives can also assist in security training and awareness, helping to push the program to the user community. Representatives can also serve in a first-line role to assist their business units with the approval and waiver requests described earlier.

Healthcare – Identity

Information Security Options for Smaller Organizations

The most important information security problem in many smaller organizations is the lack of an information security function and program. Information security must have an individual (a manager, director, or CISO) with overall responsibility. Leaving it to individual system administrators, without policy and direction, will ensure failure. Once this need is met, the next challenge is to scale the function appropriately to the size and needs of the business. Some of the functions, which might be separate groups in a large enterprise, can be combined in a smaller organization. Security engineering and parts of security operations (account and privilege management, monitoring and notification, incident response, crisis management, and DR) could be combined with the policy, governance, and user awareness roles into the central information security group. The hands-on security configuration management of desktops, servers, and network devices should still be the separate responsibility of system and network administrators. In the earlier discussion, the role of an in-house test laboratory, especially for patches, was noted. Even in a smaller organization, it is strongly recommended that representative test systems be set aside and patches be tested by a system administrator before deployment.

For smaller organizations, there are special challenges in security strategy. In a smaller enterprise, the security technology roadmap is set by technology suppliers, as the enterprise depends on commercial off-the-shelf (COTS) vendors to supply all its products. Whatever the COTS vendors supply becomes the *de facto* security strategy for the enterprise. To a great extent, this is still true in large enterprises unless they have a business case to, and have or engage the expertise to, develop some of their own solutions. While a large enterprise can exert some influence over its suppliers, and should develop a formal technology strategy, smaller enterprises should not overlook this need. If a smaller enterprise cannot justify a strategy role on a full-time basis, it could consider engaging external consultants to assist with this function initially and on a periodic review basis. Consultants can also support DR plan development. As with any activity in information security, doing it once is not enough. The strategy or the DR plan must be maintained.

Internal and External Audit

The role of auditors is to provide an independent review of controls and compliance. The central information security group, and security operational roles, should not audit their own work. To do so would be a conflict of interest. Instead, auditors provide a crucial service because of their independence. The central information security group should partner with the internal audit organization to develop priorities for audit reviews based on risk, exchange views on the important risks to the enterprise, and develop corrective action plans based on the results of past audits. The audit organization can recognize risks based on what it sees in audit results. External auditors may be engaged to provide a second kind of independent review. For external engagements, it is very important to specify the scope of work, including the systems to be reviewed, attributes to be reviewed and tested, and processes and procedures for the review. These ground rules are especially important where vulnerability scanning or penetration testing is involved.

Outsourcing Providers

Outsourcing providers offer services for a variety of information security tasks, including firewall management and security monitoring. Some Internet service providers (ISPs) offer firewall and virtual private network management. Outsourcing firewall management can be considered if the organization's environment is relatively stable, with infrequent changes. If changes are frequent, an outsourcing provider's ability to respond quickly can be a limiting factor. In contrast, 24/7 monitoring of system logs and IDSs can be more promising as an outsource task. Staffing one seat 24/7 requires several people. This is out of reach for smaller organizations and a challenge in even the largest enterprises. An outsourcing provider for monitoring can leverage a staff across its customer base. Also, in contrast with the firewall, where the organization would trust the provider to have privileged access to firewalls, monitoring can be done with the provider having no interactive access to any of the customer's systems or network devices. In all consulting and outsourcing relationships, it is essential to have a written, signed NDA to protect the organization's sensitive information. Also, the contract must specify the obligations of the provider when the customer has an emergency. If an emergency affects many of the same provider's customers, how would priority be determined?

To Whom Should the Information Security Function Report?

Tom Peltier, in a report for the Computer Security Institute,[5] recommends that the central information security group report as high as possible in the organization, at least to the chief information officer (CIO). The group definitely should *not* be part of internal audit (due to the potential for conflict of interest) or part of an operational group in IT. If it were part of an operational group, conflict of interest could also result. Peltier noted that operational groups' top priority is maintaining maximum system uptime and production schedules. This emphasis can work against implementing and maintaining needed security controls. The central information security group should also never be part of an IT system development group because security controls are often viewed as an impediment or an extra cost add-on to development projects. A security engineer should be assigned

Healthcare –
Identity

from the security engineering group to support each development project.

There are several issues around having the central information security group as part of the physical security organization. This can help with investigations and crisis management. The drawbacks are technology incompatibility (physical security generally has little understanding of IT), being perceived *only* as preventing bad things from happening (contrast with the business enabler viewpoint noted earlier), and being part of a group that often suffers budget cuts during difficult times. Tracy Mayor[6] presented a successful experience with a single organization combining physical security and information security. Such an organization could be headed by a chief security officer (CSO), reporting to the chief executive officer (CEO), placing the combined group at the highest level. The combined group could also include the risk management function in large enterprises, an activity usually focused on insurance risks. This would recognize the emerging role of insurance for information security risks. The model can work but would require cultural compatibility, cross-training, management commitment, and a proactive partnership posture with customers. Another alternative, keeping information security and physical security separate, is to form a working partnership to address shared issues, with crisis management as a promising place to begin. Similarly, the CISO can partner with the risk management function.

Although the DR/BC function, as noted earlier, might be part of an operational group, DR/BC issues should be represented to upper management at a comparable level to the CISO. The CISO could consider making DR/BC a component of risk management in security strategy, and partnering with the head of the DR/BC group to ensure that issues are considered and presented at the highest level. Ed Devlin has recommended[7] that a BC officer, equal to the CISO, reports at the same high level.

FILLING THE ROLES: REMARKS ON HIRING INFORMATION SECURITY PROFESSIONALS

One of the most difficult aspects of information security management is finding the right people for the job. What should the job description say? Does someone necessarily need specific information security experience? What are the key points for choosing the best candidate? Answering these questions will provide a clearer picture of how to fill the role effectively.

Note: This section outlines several procedures for identifying and hiring job candidates. It is strongly recommended to review these procedures with your human resources team and legal advisors before implementing them in your environment.

Job Descriptions

A description of the position is the starting point in the process. This job description should contain the following:[8]

- The position title and functional reporting relationship
- The length of time the candidate search will be open
- A general statement about the position
- An explicit description of responsibilities, including any specific subject matter expertise required (such as a particular operating system or software application)
- The qualifications needed, including education
- The desired attributes wanted
- Job location (or telecommuting if allowed) and anticipated frequency of travel
- Start date
- A statement on required national security clearances (if any)
- A statement on requirements for U.S. citizenship or resident alien status, if the position is associated with a U.S. Government contract requiring such status
- A statement on the requirements for a background investigation and the organization's drug-free workplace policy

Other position attributes that could be included are:

- Salary range
- Supervisor name
- Etc.

The general statement should be two to three sentences, giving the applicant some insight into what the position is. It should be an outline of sorts for the responsibilities section. For example:

> **General:** The information security specialist (ISS) uses current computer science technologies to assist in the design, development, evaluation, and integration of computer systems and networks to maintain system security. Using various tools, the ISS will perform penetration and vulnerability analyses of corporate networks and will prepare reports that may be submitted to government regulatory agencies.

The most difficult part of the position description is the responsibilities section. To capture what is expected from the new employee, managers are encouraged to engage their current employees for input on the day-today activities of the position. This accomplishes two goals. First, it gives the manager a realistic view of what knowledge, skills, and abilities will be needed. Second, it involves the employees who will be working with the new candidate in the process. This can prevent some of the difficulties current employees encounter when trying to accept new employees. More importantly, it makes them feel a valued part of the process. Finally, this is more accurate than

Healthcare – Identity

reusing a previous job description or a standard job description provided by HR. HR groups often have difficulty describing highly technical jobs. An old job description may no longer match the needs of a changing environment. Most current employees are doing tasks not enumerated in the job descriptions when they were hired.

Using the above general statement, an example of responsibilities might be:

- Evaluate new information security products using a standard image of the corporate network and prepare reports for management.
- Represent information security in the design, development, and implementation of new customer secured networks.
- Assist in customer support issues.
- Using intrusion detection tools; test the corporation's network for vulnerabilities.
- Assist government auditors in regulatory compliance audits.

Relevant Experience

When hiring a new security professional, it is important to ensure that the person has the necessary experience to perform the job well. There are few professional training courses for information security professionals. Some certification programs, such as the Certified Information System Security Professional (CISSP),[9] require experience that would not be relevant for an entry-level position. In addition, Lee Kushner noted, "... while certification is indeed beneficial, it should be looked on as a valuable enhancement or add-on, as opposed to a prerequisite for hiring."[10] Several more considerations can help:

- Current information security professionals on the staff can describe the skills they feel are important and which might be overlooked.
- Some other backgrounds can help a person transition into an information security career:

  — Auditors are already trained in looking for minute inconsistencies.
  — Computer sales people are trained to know the features of computers and software. They also have good people skills and can help market the information security function.
  — Military experience can include thorough process discipline and hands-on expertise in a variety of system and network environments. Whether enlisted or officer grade, military personnel are often given much greater responsibility (in numbers supervised, value of assets, and criticality of missions) than civilians with comparable years of experience.

— A candidate might meet all qualifications except for having comparable experience on a different operating system, another software application in the same market space, or a different hardware platform. In many cases, the skills are easily transferable with some training for an eager candidate.

- A new employee might have gained years of relevant experience in college (or even in high school) in part-time work. An employee with experience on legacy systems may have critical skills difficult to find in the marketplace. Even if an employee with a legacy system background needs retraining, such an employee is often more likely to want to stay and grow with an organization. For a new college graduate, extracurricular activities that demonstrate leadership and discipline, such as competing in intercollegiate athletics while maintaining a good scholastic record, should also be considered.

Selection Process

Selecting the best candidate is often difficult. Current employees should help with interviewing the candidates. The potential candidates should speak to several, if not all, of the current employees. Most firms use interviews, yet the interview process is far from perfect. HR professionals, who have to interview candidates for many kinds of jobs, are not able to focus on the unique technical needs of information security. Any interview process can suffer from stereotypes, personal biases, and even the order in which the candidates are interviewed. Having current employees perform at least part of the interview can increase its validity.[8] Current employees can assess the candidate's knowledge with questions in their individual areas of expertise. Two additional recommendations are:

1. Making sure the interviews are structured with the same list of general questions for each candidate.
2. Using a candidate score sheet for interviewers to quantify their opinions about a candidate.

A good place to start is the required skills section and desired skills section of the position description. The required skills should be weighted about 70% of the score sheet, while the desired skills should be about 30%.

Filling an open position in information security can be difficult. Using tools like the position description[8] and the candidate score sheet (see Tables 1 and 2) can make selecting a new employee much easier. Having current employees involved throughout the hiring process is strongly recommended and will make choosing the right person even easier.

Because information security personnel play a critical and trusted role in the organization, criminal and financial

Healthcare –
Identity

Table 1 Sample position description.

Job Title: Information Security Specialist Associate

Pay Range: $40,000 to $50,000 per year

Application Date: 01/25/03–02/25/03

Business Unit: Data Security Assurance

Division: Computing Services

Location: Orlando, FL

Supervisor: John Smith

General:

The Information Security Specialist Associate uses current computer science technologies to assist in the design, development, evaluation, and integration of computer systems and networks to maintain system security. Using various tools, the information security specialist associate will perform penetration and vulnerability analyses of corporate networks and will prepare reports that may be submitted to government regulatory agencies.

Responsibilities:

- Evaluate new information security products using a standard image of the corporate network and prepare reports for management.
- Represent information security in the design, development, and implementation of new customer secured network.
- Assist in day-to-day customer support issues.
- Using intrusion detection tools, test the corporation's network for vulnerabilities.
- Provide security and integration services to internal and commercial customers.
- Build and maintain user data groups in the Win NT environment.
- Add and remove user Win NT accounts.
- Assist government auditors in regulatory compliance audits.

Required Education/Skills:

- Knowledge of Windows, UNIX, and Macintosh operating systems
- Understanding of current networking technologies, including TCP/IP and Banyan Vines
- Microsoft Certified Systems Engineer certification
- Bachelor's degree in computer science or relevant discipline

Desired Education/Skills:

- Two years of information security experience
- MBA
- CISSP certification

background checks are essential. Eric Shaw et al.[11] note that candidates should also be asked about past misuse of information resources. Resumes and references should be checked carefully. The same clearance procedures should apply to consultants, contractors, and temporary workers, depending on the access privileges they have. ISO 17799[1] also emphasizes the importance of these measures. Shaw and co-authors recommend working with HR to identify and intervene effectively when any employee (regardless of whether in information security) exhibits at-risk conduct. Schlossberg and Sarris[12] recommend repeating background checks annually for existing employees. HR and legal advisors must participate in developing and applying the background check procedures.

When Employees and Non-Employees Leave

The issue of deleting accounts promptly when users leave has already been emphasized. Several additional considerations apply, especially if employees are being laid off or any departure is on less than amicable terms. Anne Saita[13] recommends moving critical data to a separate database, to which the user(s) leaving does(do) not have access. Users leaving must be reminded of their NDA obligations. Saita further notes that the users' desktop computers could also contain backdoors and should be disconnected. Identifying at-risk behavior, as noted earlier, is even more important for the employees still working after a layoff who could be overworked or resentful.

Healthcare – Identity

Table 2 Candidate score sheet.

Candidate Name:	Fred Jones		
Date:	1/30/2003		
Position:	**Information Security Specialist Associate**		
Required skill	**Knowledge level**[a]	**Multiplier**	**Score**
OS knowledge	2	0.2	0.4
Networking knowledge	2	0.2	0.4
Bachelor's degree	3	0.2	0.6
MCSE	2	0.1	0.2
Desired skill			
InfoSec experience	0	0.1	0
MBA	2	0.1	0.2
CISSP	0	0.1	0
Total			1.8

Note: It is strongly recommended to review your procedures with your human resources team and legal advisors.
[a] Knowledge Level:
0—Does not meet requirement
1—Partially meets requirement
2—Meets requirement
3—Exceeds requirement
Knowledge level × Multiplier = Score

SEPARATION OF RESPONSIBILITIES

Separation of responsibilities, or segregation of duties, originated in financial internal control. The basic concept is that no single individual has complete control over a sequence of related transactions.[14] A 1977 U.S. federal law, the Foreign Corrupt Practices Act,[14] requires all corporations registering with the Securities and Exchange Commission to have effective internal accounting controls. Despite its name, this law applies even if an organization does no business outside the United States.[15] When separation of duties is enforced, it is more difficult to defraud the organization because two or more individuals must be involved and it is more likely that the conduct will be noticed.

In the IT environment, separation of duties applies to many tasks. Vallabhaneni[16] noted that computer operations should be separated from application programming, job scheduling, the tape library, the help desk, systems programming, database programming, information security, data entry, and users. Information security should be separate from database and application development and maintenance, system programming, telecommunications, data management or administration, and users. System programmers should never have access to application code, and application programmers should not have access to live production data. Kabay[17] noted that separation of duties should be applied throughout the development life cycle so that the person who codes a program would not also test it, test systems and production systems are separate, and operators cannot modify production programs. ISO 17799

emphasizes[1] that a program developer or tester with access to the production system could make unauthorized changes to the code or to production data. Conversely, compilers and other system utilities should also not be accessible from production systems. The earlier discussion of system administration and security operations noted that account and privilege management should be part of a central security operations group separate from local system administrators. In a small organization where the same person might perform both these functions, procedures should be in place (such as logging off and logging on with different privileges) to provide some separation.[18]

Several related administrative controls go along with separation of duties. One control is requiring mandatory vacations each year for certain job functions. When another person has to perform a job temporarily, a fraud perpetrated by the regular employee might be noticed. Job rotation has a similar effect.[15] Another approach is dual control, requiring two or more persons to perform an operation simultaneously, such as accessing emergency passwords.[17]

Separation of duties helps to implement the principle of *least privilege*.[19] Each user is given only the minimum access needed to perform the job, whether the access is logical or physical. Beyond IT positions, every position that has any access to sensitive information should be analyzed for sensitivity. Then the security requirements of each position can be specified, and appropriately controlled access to information can be provided. When each position at every level is specified in this fashion, HR can focus background checks and other safeguards on the positions that truly need them. Every worker with access to sensitive information has security responsibilities. Those responsibilities should be made part of the job description[20] and briefed to the user annually with written sign-off.

SUMMARY

This entry has presented several concepts on the human side of information security, including:

- Information security roles and responsibilities, including user responsibilities
- Information security relationships to other groups in the organization
- Options for organizing the information security functions
- Staffing the information security functions
- Separation of duties, job sensitivity, and least privilege

Security is a triad of people, process, and technology. This entry has emphasized the people issues, the importance of good processes, and the need to maintain security continuously. The information security function has unique human resources needs. Attention to the people issues throughout the enterprise helps to avoid or detect many potential security problems. Building processes based on separation of duties and least privilege helps build in controls organic to the organization, making security part of the culture while facilitating the business. Secure processes, when understood and made part of each person's business, are a powerful complement to technology. When the organization thinks and acts securely, the job of the information security professional becomes easier.

REFERENCES

1. British Standard 7799/ISO Standard 17799: *Information Security Management*; British Standards Institute: London, 1999; Section 4.1.3, Sections 6.1.1–2, Section 8.1.5.
2. Weaver, J. Zen and information security, http://www.info secnews.com/opinion/2001/12/19_03.htm.
3. O'Farrell, N. Employees: Your best defense, or your greatest vulnerability?. SearchSecurity.com, http://search security.techtarget.com/originalContent/0,289142,sid14_gci 771517,00.html.
4. Wood, C.C. *Information Security Roles & Responsibilities Made Easy*; PentaSafe: Houston, 2001; 72.
5. Peltier, T. Where should information protection report?. *Computer Security Institute editorial archive*, http://www.gocsi.com/infopro.htm.
6. Mayor, T. Someone to watch over you. *CIO*; March 1, **2001**.
7. Devlin, Ed. Business continuity programs, job levels need to change in the wake of Sept. 11 attacks. Disaster Recovery J. Winter **2002**.
8. Bernardin, H.J.; Russell, J. *Human Resource Management: An Experimental Approach*, 2nd ed.; McGraw-Hill: New York, 1998; 73–101, 161, 499–507.
9. International Information System Security Certification Consortium (ISC)^2, http://www.isc2.org/.
10. Rothke, B. The professional certification predicament. Comput. Security J. **2000**, *V.XVI* (2), 2.
11. Shaw, E.; Post, J.; Ruby, K. Managing the threat from within. Inf. Security, July **2000**; 70.
12. Schlossberg, B.J.; Sarris, S. Beyond the firewall: The enemy within. In Inf. Syst. Security Assoc. Password; January 2002.
13. Saita, A. The enemy within. Inf. Security; June **2001,** 20.
14. Walgenbach, P.H.; Dittrich, N.E.; Hanson, E.I. *Principles of Accounting*, 3rd ed.; Harcourt Brace Jovanovich: New York, 1984; 244, 260.
15. Horngren, C. T. *Cost Accounting: A Managerial Emphasis*, 5th ed.; Prentice Hall: Englewood Cliffs, NJ, 1982; 909, 914.
16. Vallabhaneni, S.R. *CISSP Examination Textbooks Vol. 1: Theory*; SRV Professional Publications. Schaumburg, IL, 2000; 142, 311–312.
17. Kabay, M.E. Personnel and security: separation of duties, *Network World Fusion*, http://www.nwfusion.com/news letters/sec/2000/0612sec2.html.
18. Russell, D.; Gangemi, G.T. Sr. *Computer Security Basics*; O'Reilly: Sebastopol, CA, 1991; 100–101.
19. Garfinkel, S.; Spafford, G. *Practical UNIX and Internet Security*; O'Reilly: Sebastopol, CA, 1996; 393.
20. Wood, C.C. Top 10 information security policies to help protect your organization against cyber-terrorism, p. 3, http://www.pentasafe.com/.

Identity Management

Lynda L. McGhie, CISSP, CISM
Information Security Officer (ISO)/Risk Manager, Private Client Services (PCS), Wells Fargo Bank, Cameron Park, California, U.S.A.

Abstract

Organizations finding themselves pushed further and further onto the Internet for electronic business are exposed to heightened risk to information security and have greater concerns for data protection and compliance with the ever-emerging and ever-evolving legislation and regulations regarding privacy, data protection, and security. Additionally, customer-facing portals and complex Web services architectures are adding a new complexity to information technology and making it more difficult to protect information. Managing access to information also becomes increasingly more difficult as security administrators struggle to keep up with new technology and integrate it into existing administrative functions. As organizations continue to pursue new business opportunities, move operations off-shore, and out-source day-to-day operations and development support, the "keys to the kingdom" and their information assets are increasingly at risk. No question, the business imperative supports accepting and mitigating this risk, thereby further enabling organizations to partner and team externally and electronically with business partners, customers, suppliers, vendors, etc.; however, if organizations wade into this environment blindly, without upgrading the existing information security infrastructure, technologies, tools, and processes, they may inadvertently put their organization at risk. Organizations that embark on identity management implementations, not just for compliance projects but as their core underlying security infrastructure, will ensure consistent, standard, and compliant security solutions for the enterprise.

WHY IS IDENTITY MANAGEMENT A SOLUTION?

The growing complexity of managing identities, authentication, and access rights to balance risks and access, as well as meet the organization's business goals and security requirements, is often forgotten in the haste to implement new and enhanced systems to maintain the competitive edge. An additional outgrowth of this trend has been a dramatic increase in access to information and new and expanded E-business infrastructures. As more and more new systems and applications are being added to existing information technology (IT) and business infrastructures, while legacy systems continue to be retrofitted, increasingly complex access roles (groups) are emerging to accommodate and manage access to information. Additionally, as more and more user IDs and passwords are added to support this new environment, they must be managed in an administrative environment that continues to grow more and more disjointed. Existing security administration and management systems and supporting processes cannot scale without new investment and the addition of new technology and automated processes.

Many organizations are looking toward advancements in identity management (IM) and identity and access management (IAM) products to solve the problems created by the increasing complexity of today's IT environments. Additionally, IM/IAM solutions enhance an organization's effectiveness in managing risks associated with the new technologies. These products have been around for some time, traditionally trying to solve the single sign-on (SSO) problem, but they have adapted and evolved to include other feature sets, such as account provisioning, password management, password self-service, advanced authentication and access management, and workflow. By implementing a well-planned and wel-thought-out IM or IAM strategy that provides cost-effective account management and enforceable security policies, organizations can actually recover investments in information security solutions and demonstrate a return on investment (ROI).

GETTING YOUR IM/IAM PROJECT STARTED

New and evolving legislation and regulations have been a double-edged sword for information security. In response to these laws and regulations, companies continue to launch separate and distinct compliance projects. Typically, these compliance projects are driven by organizations outside the corporate information security function, such as human resources, finance, legal, audit, compliance, privacy, or information technology. Often, these organizations are totally focused on compliance without knowing or understanding that the necessary technology and processes are already in place, or planned by the security team, to

Encyclopedia of Information Assurance DOI: 10.1081/E-EIA-120046288
Copyright © 2011 by Taylor & Francis. All rights reserved.

accommodate and manage the overall enterprise information security and risk posture.

The controls mandated by these laws and regulations are not new or unfamiliar to well-seasoned security professionals and are, in fact, part of the "security bibles" that we have been referencing, following, and complying with for decades (e.g., NIST, ISO 17799, COBIT, COSO). These guidelines and standards will be further discussed later in this entry as they relate to the components of an IM/IAM infrastructure, as well as ways in which they assist with the compliance task, secure the infrastructure, ensure identities and authentication, protect and grant access to information, and manage the administrative security process. The important point here is that the hype and fear surrounding the issue of compliance should not be the tail that wags the dog of a company's overall enterprise security program.

Initially, the information security team will be optimistic and look forward to security investments and enhancements to complement the existing information security program. Most frequently, however, this additional budget outlay will be met with grief by executive management and stakeholders, who will advocate taking the least expensive path to compliance. Security teams will be pressured to utilize existing tools and processes, even though they may be out of date or not up to the challenge of legal and regulatory compliance.

It is difficult to ensure that new compliance investments will complement and enhance existing solutions. Even though laws and regulations are driving the outlay of new funding for information security, the budgets of other projects of the security team may suffer. Another threat to the overall enterprise security posture is the loss of resources or attention to security and privacy as compliance dates come and go, with the result being an increased likelihood of failure, partially implemented technology or processes, the loss of management attention and business and technical resources, and the risk of non-compliance over time.

The information security program must continue to educate the organization and help them understand that information security is not a project but is an ongoing process. Additionally, security is embedded in all aspects of the business and IT infrastructure, with tentacles spreading to all projects and functional areas; therefore, it is essential to involve IT security in new and enhanced processes as well as to continue investing in new technology and process enhancements. Security alone is good business, and security embedded in new and enhanced technology and business processes is simply better business.

GETTING BUY-IN AND SUPPORT

It is important to gain enterprisewide concurrence with the organization's definition of identity management and what it means to the enterprise. Additionally, it is important to agree on what components of IM will be implemented and in what order and what the phased implementation plan and schedule will look like. Understanding the scope of a company's IM solution is important to defining the overall project objectives, meeting goals and timelines, and ensuring overall project success. The IM realm continues to evolve, and more companies offer products and technical solutions. Standards ensuring interoperability are also coalescing, and suites of products work together seamlessly to provide cost-effective IM solutions that can be sized and scoped to the needs of a particular organization. Being armed with a thorough understanding of IM is an asset to gathering support from stakeholders, team members, executive sponsors, and the business.

INITIAL THOUGHTS AND PLANNING

The primary motivation for embarking on an IM project may be to respond to new laws and regulations and the urgency of compliance. If this is the case, a company should assess its current risk and state of compliance and then determine what IM feature set or components will help achieve compliance. For IM projects designed to enhance the effectiveness of existing security administrative systems in order to streamline their effectiveness or improve time to market, the requirements and resultant approaches may differ. For a large, broad project that enhances a current enterprise IT security posture while complying with various new laws and regulations and incorporating IM into other IT infrastructure projects (Active Directory), the project will be a large and complicated one. The issue of who owns the project becomes uncertain. Additionally, the funding source could then span functional organizations and even separate business units within a single entity. Such issues add levels of complexity and potential points of failure throughout the project.

Having acknowledged that an IM project could have many drivers, such a project could also have any number of project sponsors, project owners, and funding sources. Some IM projects may be financially driven, such as Sarbanes–Oxley (SOX), and managed by the chief financial officer (CFO) or the controller's organization. Some IM projects may be driven by other IT enhancements, such as implementation of Microsoft's Active Directory system. Still others could be led by any combination of legal or human resources staffs, the compliance officer, or the chief privacy officer. Ideally, the IT security team is the owner of the IM project, and the executive sponsor is the chief information officer (CIO), coupled with executives from one of the functional areas listed above. Typically, the sponsoring executive would be the one in charge of and managing the project funding. A high-level enterprise executive steering committee can help to guide and govern an IM project while ensuring that its many bosses are served.

DEMONSTRATING IM RETURN ON INVESTMENT

Because information security is typically a cost center rather than a profit center, its function and resultant budget allocation are always in competition with other cost centers. This is particularly painful when competing for budget and resource allocations. Some functional organizations that typically have project overlap, synergies, and shared responsibilities include human resources (HR), finance, legal, compliance, risk management, insurance, and audit. Over the years, these organizations have been viewed as non-contributors to the company's revenue stream and have not fared well when cost-cutting and other reductions are being considered. Additionally, because information security most typically resides in the IT organization, its projects must also compete for resources and funding with other IT projects that are more frequently driven by operations where a return on investment can be easily identified, quantified, and supported.

Several years ago, Gartner, Inc. (Stamford, CT, U.S.A.) predicted that by 2005 help-desk costs associated with end-user password resets would be reduced by 70% through the implementation of self-service password management. The password management, self-service aspects of IM are frequently one of the first functional or module implementations and help build a ROI for the initial IM investment. Further, Gartner estimated that, by 2007, enterprisewide identity management solutions would demonstrate a net savings in total security administration costs (operations plus administration) of 21%. This savings can be realized through centralized provisioning and account management as well as workflow to automate and standardize security administration.

Gartner outlined the costs and projected savings for an average IM implementation including, password self-services, provisioning, and workflow. User provisioning software license costs for a 15,000-user enterprise can run as high as $700,000. Also, password reset and user ID problems represent 15% to 35% of help-desk call volume (at a typical cost per call of $10 to $31). It is no wonder that enterprises need, and want, to justify the cost of an identity management project. To do so, they typically consider three factors:

1. Head-count reduction of the help desk or security administration organization performing day-to-day activities such as password resets and user account management
2. Productivity savings for end users (they can reset their password faster than calling the help desk) and business management (for faster access-request approval processing)
3. Risk management, including electronic data processing audit management, best practices, and regulatory compliance

Other sources estimate that as many as 70% of the calls to the help desk are for password resets and password problems. As with any project, to best justify project approval and resources, it is necessary to understand the current environment and problems to be solved. Many organizations do not do this or really do not have an understanding of their current environment or the problems they are trying to solve. This is particularly true for security projects traditionally spanned by the FUD (fear, uncertainty, and doubt) principle. On the other hand, help-desk metrics are generally maintained and can be beneficial to building the case for an IM system. If the security administration group keeps metrics, supports a service level agreement (SLA), or even has an overall understanding of the turnaround time for processing user requests for account initiation and management, these will at least further justify such projects, in addition to password resets. Also, with regard to the account/user ID administration function, it is possible that supporting paperwork or authorizations are not being kept or cannot be produced for audits. IM can help with this problem through its workflow and reporting process. This is why IM is finding a new purpose in life with compliance projects. A clean IM implementation can also assist in providing integrity to the identification process through good passwords, good authentication, and password self-service. Other metrics to consider include other IT and functional organizations such as the help desk, security administration, HR, IT services, and contract management (for identifying the number of temporary workers, contractors, and consultants).

For identified cost savings and ROI, Gartner recommends the following four categories for metrics measurement and reporting:

1. Transaction volume
2. Access request process fulfillment
3. IT risk management
4. Security administration infrastructure

Another area to investigate is replacement of multiple online identities that users are required to know and administrators are required to maintain. In medium to large enterprises, these multiple identities result in a somewhat disjointed administrative environment, where one hand does not know what the other is doing with regard to granting and managing access. A valid IM goal, then, is to consolidate and reduce the numbers of online identities and credentials to be managed for each individual user. In larger organizations, these numbers get interesting very quickly.

According to RSA Security (Bedford, MA, U.S.A.), organizations can look for cost reductions and efficiencies through centralized, automated solutions that enable the elimination or reduction of costs stemming from deploying and managing disparate user management systems. Additionally, organizations can derive enhanced security, while differentiating themselves from the competition, by providing a more secure online E-business infrastructure. One example is enforcing privileges and implementing strong authentication, thereby reducing the likelihood that sensitive data may be accidentally exposed to the wrong users.

With an effective identity management solution in place, organizations can manage their business with a degree of flexibility, responsiveness, security, and economy that is simply unattainable with today's fragmented approaches to user management. By considering all of the factors mentioned here, organizations can set realistic ROI goals for identity management solutions and then deliver on plan and on schedule.

PROJECT MANAGEMENT CHALLENGES

As mentioned previously, different companies have different IM requirements and drivers. While IM projects will have aspects of commonality, they will also be unique and specific to a single entity. Because IM is evolving technically and functionally and standards are finally coalescing, solutions should have an eye toward being adaptive and agile. Additionally, because IM projects could include a variety of component parts, they should have a phased design and implementation structure.

As IM evolves within the organization and within the industry, companies will want to consider incorporating greater IM capabilities, including advanced features of identification, authentication, and authorization. A company can begin with a prototype environment utilizing representative systems from the overall project footprint. After proof of concept, more components can be added to the IM system, as this is where the company will realize greater cost savings and ROI. Also, the company should plan on continuing to enhance baseline system functionality and plan for such future enhancements as single sign-on (SSO), federated identity management, digital certificates, electronic signatures, centralized and decentralized management, provisioning, workflow, and integration with meta-directories and HR systems. These features are all discussed later in this entry.

The brief discussion here has indicated that an IM project has the potential of growing very quickly, evolving, and quickly becoming unwieldy and unmanageable. To be successful, adherence to a strict project management methodology and governance process is absolutely necessary. Remember, one size does not necessarily fit all, so it is important to seek the counsel of experts in the field, such as consulting firms; vendors; standards bodies; security organizations, such as SANS or Computer Emergency Response Team (CERT); and other professional security groups, such as Information Systems Security Association (ISSA), Computer Security Institute (CSI), or Information Systems Audit and Control Association (ISACA).

One final project goal and objective embedded in all laws and regulations, specified in all security standards and guidelines, and most likely already embedded in an organization's internal information security policies and procedures is the concept of confidentiality, integrity, and availability (CIA). CIA should be highest of the core and fundamental goals of all security projects and resultant and supporting technical infrastructures. The definitions below are universally accepted and have stood over time:

- *Confidentiality*—Data or information is not made available or disclosed to unauthorized persons or processes.
- *Integrity*—Data or information have not been altered or destroyed in an unauthorized manner.
- *Availability*—Data or information is accessible and useable upon demand by an authorized person.

MORE ON PLANNING

Companies that are already utilizing the Internet for business and those who already have electronic commerce and Web-based applications have most likely already considered compliance issues and security and are well vested relative to good security practices and compliance. The reality is that all companies will have to make some adjustment to comply with the barrage of legislation and regulations regarding privacy and the protection of information. Because security guidance has been available for some time within the government, across the industry, within universities and national laboratories, and from other research organizations and standards bodies, many organizations are considering implementing IM solutions or may have already consolidated administrative functions, implemented a workflow system for account/user ID management, or implemented other automated administrative processes.

All security and compliance projects should begin with identification and documentation of the "as is" state as a baseline. This typically requires a new and enterprisewide risk assessment. All existing risk assessments should also be used to provide input to defining the overall as-is state. As mentioned earlier, defining a solid set of project goals and objectives and the creation of a project plan and schedule are the most critical steps in the process. Getting upfront buy-in and approval is also critical, as is obtaining an experienced project manager who has managed enterprisewide IT and business projects.

The results of the risk assessment should be mapped to the controls prescribed in the organization's security policies and procedures and the laws and regulations being addressed. Also, other security feedback can serve as input to the planning process, such as results from vulnerability scans and disaster recovery testing or recent audit reports. The next step is a gap assessment, which will determine the controls to be implemented and project components.

The initial risk assessment must evaluate the entire IT environment, including data, networks, applications, and systems. Organizations will then have to determine what security policies and procedures must be written or augmented. It may be necessary to purchase or acquire new products or technology, in addition to enhancing or augmenting current products and technology. Additionally, it is possible that a simple restructuring of the security organization and a consolidation and centralization project could meet project needs and requirements. Outsourcing is another possibility. This could take many shapes and flavors, such as outsourcing part of security management or the entire security operation. The entire scope of people, processes, and technology should be considered for improvement, automation, and centralization. Remember that IM projects can get big very fast, and the best guidance is to keep it small initially by planning a proof-of-concept pilot and implementing a phased approach.

If it is necessary to acquire new technology or enhance existing technology, a thorough product evaluation should be performed. It should involve IT and business organizations according to the company's established processes of communication and partnership. Trusted vendors and business partners can be involved in the process. Working with vendors who have established themselves as experts in IM and IAM is recommended; do not be lured by new and unproven technology solutions. Products must be able to support heterogeneous and complex environments when necessary. It is important to look beyond systems and networks to large enterprise application support for products such as Oracle and SAP, for example.

Because IT and business training is also critical to the success of a project, vendors not only should be product experts but should also have a track record of supporting their products with ongoing service that includes training. Companies will want to partner with their vendors throughout their IM projects to exploit their experience with other companies and other implementations. Vendors who have well-established products and a significant marketshare will be able to offer a wealth of helpful advice and experience.

IDENTITY MANAGEMENT INFRASTRUCTURE

Underlying the need for organizations to establish and maintain a single integrated and authenticated identity management system is the establishment and implementation of a single, universally accessible, common IM infrastructure. Organizations should strive to achieve a centralized and decentralized IM implementation that eliminates the inefficiencies and vulnerabilities of independent decentralized approaches. A unified infrastructure will provide centralized, highly automated capabilities for creating and managing trusted user identities. It will allow administrators to define user access rights with a high degree of flexibility and granularity, in keeping with business goals and security policies. It will also validate identities and enforce rights and policies consistently across the enterprise, thereby further enhancing security and supporting compliance requirements. RSA defines identity and access management (IAM) as "an integrated system of business processes, policies, and technologies that enable organizations to facilitate and control users access to critical online applications and resources—while protecting confidential personal and business information from unauthorized users."

ADMINISTRATION, PROVISIONING, AND WORKFLOW

One of the biggest challenges to organizations is handling access to data, systems, applications, and networks when employees are hired, moved within the organization, or terminated. This challenge is compounded for external users, such as contractors, vendors, partners, and customers. The larger and more complex the organization is, the greater the challenge. By successfully managing this process from end to end, users will more quickly obtain system and application access, thereby becoming more effective and productive as quickly as possible. Good management represents a cost savings to the organization and can provide a demonstrated ROI. The challenge is even greater for organizations that are highly distributed with independent functions doing the granting and the management of account/user ID management. It is even more complex when parts of the administration function are centrally managed and other parts are decentrally managed. Another complexity is added when employees move from site to site or have access to multiple individual business units within one larger entity, such as company members of a larger corporation.

Provisioning provides automated capabilities for activating user accounts and establishing access privileges for those accounts across the entire enterprise. Many opinions and metrics exist regarding the time it takes to set up a user account initially, manage it over time, incorporate changes, and ultimately delete it. A variety of sources have estimated that it takes an average of 28 hours to set up an initial user account. In theory, then, every subsequent change to a user profile must also touch the same access databases, thereby potentially requiring another 28 hours per change. Some examples of changes include users changing positions or roles, thus requiring a change to access requirements or physically moving access to a different location.

Healthcare – Identity

One of the most important changes to an account or a user profile occurs upon termination. It is imperative that terminated employees be immediately removed from the system or, minimally, that their access be immediately terminated. In cases of suspension, after completion of file cleanup and fulfillment of delegated responsibilities and other administrative processes, actual deletion of the account/user ID should quickly follow. In highly decentralized and distributed organizations, supporting many applications and systems, it is important to coordinate the termination and account revocation process centrally and to automate this process to the extent feasible. It is also imperative to have an HR system interface to the IM system to compare the IM database to the HR database to highlight and react to changes. This functionality may be provided by another metadirectory such as Microsoft's Active Directory (AD) as long as it is the designated and established authoritative source.

If one considers this situation logically, there is no effective or manageable way to perform such tasks without automation and centralized management, tools, and processes, but organizations are continuing to fall behind in this process. As a result many systems have outdated user profiles or even "ghost accounts" (outdated accounts for users who are no longer working within the organization or have changed roles and obtained new accounts/user IDs).

An outdated but typical answer to this growing problem has been to add staff and manual processes in an effort to get a handle on the process of granting access, managing user IDs (accounts) and passwords, and granting access to objects within systems, such as data, databases, applications, systems, and networks. As more users are added, more profiles must be managed via a process that becomes increasingly burdensome and costly. Longer term support to sustain the IM system over time is threatened because of changes to the environment such as changes in sponsorship, budget allocations, IT and business priorities, or knowledgeable personnel. The IM team may over time find themselves left with an outdated system and support. Meanwhile, the function continues to expand and problems escalate, causing more risk to the organization.

When organizations struggle with such problems, they often look toward automation. Initially, an organization may think this automation can be achieved by writing programs and scripts. They may turn on other functionalities within operating systems, databases, or applications to make use of a number of utilities. Finally, they will look toward commercial off-the-shelf (COTS) products that integrate access control administration across heterogeneous platforms. Some organizations may be unable to make or support the case for purchasing additional products or technology due to poorly defined and supported cost–benefit analyses. These organizations must rely on efficiencies gained through streamlined manual processes and maximized implementation of each individual product and access control system.

It is this problem that IM products and technology are also trying to solve, in addition to addressing the legal and compliance issues surrounding ensuring that entities are who they claim to be. The administration aspects of granting and managing access greatly contribute to cost–benefit analyses and building a case for product and process improvements or investments in this area. The ROI is quantifiable and defendable, but it takes time to understand the current environment, envision an end state, conduct a gap analysis, and lay out an implementation plan for improvement. It should be noted that improvement involves not only faster access to systems, fewer errors in granting access, and compliance with company policies and procedures but also streamlined overall management and compliance.

Many IM or IAM products provide workflow front ends to automate and streamline the process of gaining access to systems, data, transactions, etc. As noted, this could be a complicated process, particularly for new employees and non-employees or for systems where the process is not centrally documented and managed. A typical employee requires access to as many as twenty separate applications and systems. The initial setup process can be frustrating and time consuming because often new employees must peel back the onion to figure out what access they may need just as a baseline to being successful.

Through process improvement, automation, workflow management tools, and new supporting infrastructures these processes can be consolidated and centralized. The ongoing goal continues to be finding the optimal blend of centralization and decentralization that will optimize the organization's efficiency. This contributes to the organization's business imperative and bottom line. This case must be made and defended and finally demonstrated throughout each phase of an IM/IAM implementation. Due to its universal reach and complexity, this is a project that can take some time.

During the initial stages of an IM project, organizations determine which systems will take part in the pilot and which systems will be included in the overall project scope, in addition to how systems will be added over time, what the project phases will look like, and how they will be managed. The initial project may envision an end state utilizing all the component parts of a robust IM system, or it may envision a system that provides only provisioning and password management. Done right the first time, the successful initial implementation of a centralized IM infrastructure could have the results promised in the old adage: "Build it and they will come." Minimally this should be the goal.

When users are added to the overall IM system, they reside in the core database and are managed from there out to the distributed environment. The IM system governs the relationship between decentralized systems and supporting administrative systems and underlying processes. No matter how it is decided to share and populate the core system

Healthcare – Identity

(master or system of record) and distributed systems (slaves), it is important to have these systems synchronized in real time. Synchronization is important not only for failover and recovery but also to ensuring that user profiles granting access are up to date and correct. Because this is configurable and can be tailored to each organization's particular needs, workflow and integrated centralized account management do not ever have to happen, or certainly not upfront in the process and within the initial phases of the project.

Workflow provides an automated front-end system that is Web enabled and forms based. It provides a mechanism for end users to communicate with the centralized and decentralized administration management system or IM/IAM system. Users access this system, complete forms, and are granted access. The forms automatically route for approvals and ultimately to the appropriate system administrator. In the best case scenario, users are added to the central database system with approved system access rights and roles during a single session. New profiles or modified profiles are instantly shared with the decentralized systems for which they have access or authenticated rights. This provides a single record of the process for granting and revoking access to systems and information. The system provides a centralized repository for documentation, as well as audit trail information and a central archive. Archive and retrieval are pivotal components of an IM implementation for compliance purposes and also for information security incident management and forensics. Access management reduces risk by ensuring that access privileges are accurately controlled, consistently enforced, and immediately revoked upon termination.

SELF-SERVICE PASSWORD MANAGEMENT

The password management features of IM are among the most attractive to organizations, and many enterprises are implementing third-party self-service password reset tools that enable users to change their own passwords upon expiration or to reset passwords when they have forgotten them and have locked themselves out of the system. With self-service password management, when users have forgotten their passwords they are required to authenticate themselves via an alternative method before being given access to the password reset function. In the case of a forgotten password, the tool requires the user to enter the answers to a predetermined set of questions (the answers have previously been provided during initial registration to the password reset facility).

The prompting question should not conflict with laws and regulations regarding the protection of customer information or privacy information; in other words, prompting for a customer account number or Social Security number is not allowed. Additionally, prompting for commonly known information such as name or mother's maiden name should be avoided. Exploiting such information is a fairly trivial matter for attackers familiar with social engineering or even database look ups. Controls should specify the number of times a user can enter an incorrect answer before alerting the system administrator for manual intervention. The answers must be kept secure and treated like sensitive information, with limited access and audit and monitoring enabled.

Third-party self-service password reset tools are attractive to enterprises in which a large percentage (e.g., 40%) of help-desk calls are for password resets. The tools not only reduce the cost of end-user support but also provide a more secure method for resetting a password, because user or requestor identity is authenticated through the prompting for private information, provided earlier by the user. Manual password changes to the help desk are frequently not authenticated without an automated password management process. This practice is not compliant and is heavily subjected to security compromise and error. This is of particular concern for contractors and other non-employees with access to a company's system. These users are usually not in the identity or HR official record databases.

AUTHENTICATION

Authentication establishes an identity owner, and the resultant single credential closely reflects the way identities are established and preserved in the offline world. The identity and supporting authentication system should be robust in detail, integrating data from a multitude of authoritative sources and pushing up-to-the-minute data back to those same sources. The technology and its supporting processes should reach out centrally to the decentralized technical and functional organizations, resulting in provisioning a trusted user with secure access to all the applications and resources that an individual needs to be productive in his or her relationship within the organization.

For years, user IDs and passwords have been adequately filling the bill for ensuring that persons or entities requesting access or service are who they say they are. This process is known as *authentication*. As information technology has evolved over the years, the password management process has improved. Many companies continue to rely on standard user IDs and passwords within their secure perimeter or within their company's protected and secured intranet. Many of these same companies do, however, have enhanced IM and authentication to accommodate increased threats and vulnerabilities or changes to trust models. Examples of enhanced risk and trust are remote access, wireless networking, traversing internal trust domains having differing trust levels, and accessing sensitive and high-risk systems and customer confidential data.

The previous discussion has addressed a perfectly acceptable and compliant IM that may be enhanced state-of-the-art user IDs and passwords with a compliant and well-managed administrative and technical support process (identity management or password management). As technology and business drivers have evolved to require employees to be more mobile to increase productivity and ROI, mobile technology has evolved to be cost effective and secure. Most companies today support a mobile work force and mobile computing or access from home for their employees. After assessing the risks associated with such access and the necessary control and process support requirements, a plan can be developed to enhance password management and authentication to include a higher level of authentication, typically migrating from single-factor authentication, passwords, and pins to higher level, more secure two-factor authentication. Single-factor authentication requires something the user knows. Two-factor authentication adds one more dimension, typically something that the user has. In this case, it is a token that generates a time-synchronized number when used in combination with a known password or PIN.

The evaluation and selection of a higher level authentication system and its ongoing management and operation can consume ever-increasing resources, which should be factored into the complexity of technical solutions. Companies should be leery of new, untested, and unproven technologies. An approved, compliant, and sound security strategy may revolve around simply building on the integrity and management of an existing user ID and password management system. Other forms of enhanced authentication are support through the use of USB port authenticators, public/private key encryption, Kerberos, digital certificates, smart cards, etc.

Two-factor authentication provides more integrity to the process, thereby ensuring that the person or entity is indeed who he or she is claiming to be. The authentication is innately stronger than standard user IDs and passwords (something that you know) and actually builds upon sound password management practices by adding an additional layer of authentication and security. Two-factor authentication improves the integrity of the authentication process by adding a second identifier (who the user is or what the user has). Over the years, for remote access the traditional two-factor authentication has been the user ID, standard password, PIN number, or a randomly generated authentication code generated by something the user has, which is typically a SecurID card. Biometric devices, such as those that read a fingerprint or iris pattern, are considered a stronger form of user authentication. When used alone, they are considered one-factor authentication; when combined with a PIN, password, or token, the solution is considered two-factor authentication; and when all three are used, the solution is considered three-factor authentication. Organizations can enhance security by requiring users to present multiple credentials or "factors." The more factors required, the greater the level of protection. Strong authentication validates an audit trail of user activity by requiring conclusive proof of identity before granting access to sensitive resources.

PASSWORD MANAGEMENT

One of the factors driving the growth of identity management solutions is widespread dissatisfaction with password protection. First invented in 1963, password-based authentication systems gained wide acceptance because they were easy to use, came free with various applications, and provided adequate security for most purposes. Equally important—with many organizations supporting dozens of distributed password systems—is the fact that passwords are costly to administer and a major security threat, due to their inherent vulnerability and the lax password practices of some users (such as attaching sticky notes with passwords and usernames to computers or using obvious passwords such as names and dates).

Although they are used widely, single-factor static passwords are the weakest form of authentication and are becoming weaker over time as new technology and hacker skills are finding ways to crack even the most secure password configurations. While six-character passwords combining alphanumerics with special characters have been recommended standards for decades, many companies are tightening up standard password management to enforce eight-character passwords that are a combination of upper- and lowercase letters, numerics, and special characters. In the past, this has been recommended but not necessarily enforced at the system configuration level. Most systems previously allowed those characters to be specified in the password string, but today it is becoming mandatory to include each of these elements in a password. If a company is certain that its password configuration or password management approach is sound, it can either eliminate or reduce its password cracking processes to check for good passwords. Most systems today feature secure password configuration and management as the first lines of defense.

Secure password configuration must be followed up with secure password management. If the help desk, security administrators, system administrators, and others with system administrative or security privileges can and do change passwords, it is important to ensure that the password change and management process is secure, up to date, and, most importantly, followed. This process should be monitored closely via ongoing and regular internal and external audits. Passwords should not be reset with telephone calls that do not ensure the identity of the caller or match to the account. Non-employees or contractors also should not be allowed to reset their passwords over the telephone without a process in place to ensure identity. Also, when non-employee accounts are suspended by the security group, they should not be allowed to be unsuspended by the help desk, only by the security organization or administrator with authorization from the sponsoring company manager.

Successfully authenticating a user establishes his or her identity, and all activity under that identity is tracked, thereby making the user accountable for the activity, thus the need for good management practices regarding authentication information. PINs or passwords are currently the standard user authentication solutions, both on the Internet and for internal applications. PINs typically control access to personal information (e.g., bank account information), and passwords are used to control access to personal information as well as shared information, such as sensitive or trade secret information contained in data files.

Following is a list of good password management practices; refer to ISO 17799, NIST and other guidance for additional password management standards and practices:

- The best line of defense for secure password management is up-to-date information security that addresses secure password management. By involving users in the process through a strong user awareness program, everyone understands the expectations of their role and the best practices imposed by the organization.
- Most organizations advocate not writing down passwords. Others acknowledge that passwords might need to be written down if users must memorize multiple passwords. Additionally, as organizations move to stronger password configurations or randomly generated passwords, it becomes increasingly more difficult to remember these passwords. Organizations acknowledging the need to write down passwords advocate storing them in a secure place.
- Security awareness programs and communications should warn users about the dangers of social engineering; for example, people posing as systems administrators or managers could request a user's password under the guise of eradicating a system problem.
- Today's acceptable password length is a minimum of eight characters with an enforced password configuration of a combination of upper- and lowercase alphabetic characters, numeric characters, and special characters.
- A default password should be assigned when the account is created and the users should be prompted to change the password upon initial log-on or account access.
- All administrative communications regarding user IDs and password initialization or account creation should be by separate communications—one communicating the user ID and a second separate communication regarding the initial one-time-only password.
- All passwords must be stored in a one-way encrypted format.
- All access to the authentication server must be strictly controlled.
- Passwords must never be displayed on the screen but should always be masked using dummy characters, such as an asterisk.

- Password history should be configured to ensure that users do not reuse the same password over a period of time.
- Passwords should be set to expire with a systemwide parameter within 60 days, minimum.
- Passwords for privileged accounts should be set to expire within 30 days.
- Screen savers or other software capabilities must be utilized to enforce automatic logoff for periods of inactivity greater than 15 minutes.
- Accounts should be locked out following three to five password attempts or guesses. Accounts should automatically be locked out and reenabled by the system administrator.

By tightening password management policies and supporting management systems, an organization can significantly reduce the vulnerabilities related to poor password practices.

SINGLE SIGN-ON

Single sign-on (SSO) enhances the integrity of the single credential or password. It is a productivity enhancer for both users and administrators. Users only have to remember one (or, more realistically, a smaller number of passwords). When their passwords expire, they only have to make the change to the central IM system, and the changes are automatically sent out to all decentralized systems registered to the core IM. SSO enhances the productivity of systems administrators because they do not have as many profiles and accounts to manage. They can install an account once, and it is populated out to all the systems the user is approved to access. This process becomes less expensive and faster as a single user accesses many systems and incurs some profile changes over time. Similarly, as illustrated previously, one of the greatest vulnerabilities to the system administration and account management processes is processing terminated users quickly and ensuring that the revocation process immediately follows termination or any change to a user's role within the organization. A user terminated from the master database is instantly denied all access to the decentralized systems simultaneously. By reducing the number of passwords a user must keep track of, SSO also reduces password-related help-desk costs.

For years, companies have sought to implement an SSO or other reduced sign-on solution to achieve economies of scale for end users as well as system and security administrators. Early solutions involved scripting and other hokey back-end or in some cases back-door interfaces to present front-end SSO type systems to the end user. The back-end processes then communicated with each system, sending cleartext passwords around the network from system to system. Highly vulnerable to man-in-the-middle attacks and password sniffing or even unintentional password compromise, these early systems introduced more risk than they tried to mitigate. The initial premise was that, as users were required to remember and manage a greater number of user IDs and passwords, the integrity of these user IDs and passwords would be lost over time, threatening the overall security and integrity of the system. In the early phases of SSO, passwords were the only real solid authentication technology that was technically stable and cost effective to implement, but compromises to a single password or even the entire password file in vulnerable pieced-together SSO systems introduced a vulnerability into an organization and its supporting IT infrastructure that most organizations were not willing to accept.

In an SSO environment, users only need to authenticate themselves once, after which they can directly access any application on the network for which they have permission. This eliminates the annoying stop-and-go user experience that results from multiple log-ins. Best of all, users no longer need to keep track of multiple passwords. Even in environments that continue to rely on a single password for authentication, SSO makes it much easier for users to follow secure practices. For example, with only one password to remember, it is more reasonable for a company to require users to employ strong passwords (ones that contain multiple non-alphabetical characters) and expect that they will not write them down.

FEDERATED IDENTITY MANAGEMENT

To do business in an online world electronically or further to exploit the productivity and financial gains associated with doing business on the Web with customer-facing portals and online transaction systems, an organization must be able to quickly grant access and the process must be as transparent and as easy as possible. Access should further be self-service, and user IDs, passwords, and other access rights must be easily managed internally and externally. External access typically comes from non-employees, such as customers, vendors, contractors, business partners, or suppliers. Organizations are challenged to maintain the security and integrity of their internal systems, while enabling external applications access into their internal trusted network. The challenge then becomes one of how an organization can authenticate users outside their own domain and across business boundaries to another organization. In order to capitalize on the business potential afforded by doing business across boundaries, organizations must be able to trust the electronic identities that access their Web-based applications across the Internet.

In business partnerships, applications may be shared across organizations that are in no other way connected, such as in the case of supplier networks for government contractors. Users must be able to navigate and move easily from application to application across domains. One way to do this is through federated identity management, which allows sharing trusted identities across the boundaries of the corporate network—with business partners, autonomous business units, and remote offices. Another example of a federated identity solution is a sales application that enables external users to log-in from an external-facing portal and easily navigate and click on links that lead to new product information at another hosted site or partner site without having to reauthenticate. In this scenario, business partners must be able to trust the identity of an externally hosted federated identity management provider.

An accepted definition of federated identity is "the agreements, standards, and technologies that make identity and entitlements portable across autonomous domains." Federated identity is analogous to a driver's license, where one state provides individuals with a credential that is trusted and accepted as proof of identity by other states. In the online world, this trust is established through a combination of two technologies that prove identity—strong authentication and access management—and the business and legal agreements that enterprises enter into to establish mutual responsibility and commitment concerning the sharing of trusted identities. The end result is that users can benefit from secure SSO access to multiple Web and non-Web applications and network resources, both internal and external to their own organization.

Federated environments facilitate secure collaborations across external networks among business partners, thus enhancing productivity and facilitating partnerships and agreements that otherwise could not happen in a closed networking environment or outside of established trust mechanisms. The federated identity provides and passes on details about the user, such as job title, company affiliation, and level of purchasing authority. These "attributes" travel with a user's identity and can be selectively exposed based on the user's preferences and the needs of participating organizations. The challenge for a federated identity is to provide access while simultaneously protecting the privacy of the user. Because these identities are authenticated across and among external "domains of trust," business partners are assured that their enterprise resources are protected from unauthorized users. The benefits to users include increased convenience and productivity, broader access to information and services, and control over what personal information is shared and with whom.

AUTHORIZATION

Following a successful implementation of IM including authentication, password management, password management self-service, and workflow, organizations will want to move into centralized or decentralized authorization and access control, or role-based access control (RBAC). This function is supported by product suites providing identity and access management. The functionality builds from the central baseline module core to most products and utilizes the central database and interfaces to central directory services such as LDAP or Microsoft Active Directory (AD), with real-time interfaces to human resources (HR) systems for implementing new access, managing access requirements change (organizational changes), and, most importantly, immediate revocation when users are terminated.

Authorization is based on the need to know or minimal access based on the user's role within the organization. It enables synchronization across the enterprise and the storing of not just a user's identity within a central data store but also the assignment of a role or a group within the organization, granting access to information, transactions, privileges, and capabilities across the enterprise. This is particularly important with regard to the instant removal of perimeter access and managing employee terminations, contractors, and disgruntled employees. Supporting processes must be automated to the extent possible and integrated with other HR, IT, and business processes, manual and electronic. It is also important to implement checks and balances in the form of reports and cross-checking. Solutions should be centrally managed and decentralized to accommodate local area networks (LANs) and distributed one-off applications.

LAWS AND REGULATIONS

Faced with a long and growing list of regulations affecting IT security, most organizations currently rank compliance among their top concerns. In a recent survey of 250 security executives—conducted for RSA by an independent firm—a large percentage of respondents said regulatory compliance had a greater impact on their company's awareness of security issues than actual security threats such as viruses, hacking, and identity theft. The new legislation and regulations hold organizations accountable for protecting the confidentiality and privacy of personal information entrusted to them by customers and business partners. Other measures require companies to document financial decisions and transactions, including who took part in related online activities. Still other directives govern the use of digital signatures as valid and binding substitutes for handwritten signatures, thereby eliminating paperwork and maintaining end-to-end electronic processes. More laws and regulations are being passed all the time, and the existing ones continue to evolve. Legal experts predict another decade of expanding, evolving, and fine-tuning of laws and regulations regarding the protection of information, customer and personal privacy, and accounting and financial practices, as well as other requirements for information security, protection, and privacy. While most laws do not specify the technologies that should be used to achieve compliance—preferring instead that organizations identify and adopt best

practices themselves—it is becoming increasingly clear that IM/IAM solutions provide a strong foundation for supporting compliance goals.

The primary applicable laws and regulations driving the need for IM are discussed later in this entry. These laws and regulations are forcing companies to invest heavily in information security and privacy solutions, particularly IM and IAM. Below are some definitions of the common legislation and regulation referenced in this entry:

- *Health Insurance Portability and Accountability Act (HIPAA)*—This broad legislation establishes privacy and security standards designed to protect patient identities and sensitive health and treatment information.
- *Gramm–Leach–Bliley*—This legislation applies to financial services firms operating in the United States and is designed to protect consumers' financial information from unauthorized access.
- *Sarbanes–Oxley Act (SOX)*—This legislation applies to all public companies in the United States; the Act sets forth auditing standards designed to ensure the integrity of the IT systems of publicly traded companies.
- *U.S. Patriot Act Customer Identification Program*—This program requires financial services firms operating in the United States to obtain, verify, and record information that identifies each individual or entity opening an account.

As a general guidance, security organizations should meet compliance needs by first documenting their security processes and controls using the ISO 17799 standard to baseline security best practices. Then, they must invest in four critical activities that align enterprise security needs and regulatory requirements:

- Enhance segregation of duties with identity and access management (IAM).
- Improve configuration and change management of regulated systems using security and configuration management tools.
- Increase activity auditing on key databases and applications, especially related to user access.
- Improve data security for personal information through encryption and content monitoring and filtering.

AVOID REGULATORY DISTRACTION

Regulatory compliance is mandatory, but companies should not allow it to derail their core security programs. Most organizations are using regulatory pressure to fund needed security projects and integrate security more tightly with business units. It is the excuse security professionals have been waiting for to force business integration. However, some organizations are distracted by reporting, ongoing audits, and putting out the fires of remediation. It is important for these companies to focus on *getting* secure first, then worry about *showing* that the organization is secure. Protect customer data and then document it. Most of the current regulatory burden is the result of increased reporting requirements and audit activities, particularly due to Sarbanes–Oxley, Section 404, and its extensive documentation and audits. In the case of a control deficiency, the company's CEO will not go to jail under Sarbanes–Oxley unless he or she perpetuated fraud by trying to cover up the problem.

Compliance changes priorities, but it should not reduce security. Security departments need to manage compliance reporting and remediation without losing focus on top security concerns. Not all auditors are experienced in IT and may make unreasonable requests, which should be discussed with their management. Company management should be notified when generating compliance reports interferes with core security operations and could hurt the business. Not every enterprise should implement all facets of a complete IM solution, such as self-service password reset, user provisioning, extranet access management, single sign-on, directory consolidation, and role management. The IM project team should be armed with the necessary facts by gathering the metrics that justify investment in and phasing implementation of the project.

Compliance with enterprise policies, as well as with regulations such as the Gramm–Leach–Bliley Financial Services Modernization Act of 1999, the U.S. Health Insurance Portability and Accountability Act (HIPAA), and the U.S. Public Company Accounting Reform and Investor Protection Act of 2002 (Sarbanes–Oxley), is bringing identity management practices to the forefront of many enterprises' information security agendas. Privacy enforcement, separation of duties, and need-to-know access policies are at the center of these regulations, although these are access-control best practices and are not considered to be new requirements for a mature information security program.

Another information security program best practice is to have a security administration review process that requires the production access-control infrastructure be reviewed quarterly, semiannually, or annually; therefore, companies should review their access-control policies to ensure that they have the appropriate policies (e.g., users must be uniquely identified to enterprise IT resources) and to determine the values (such as 30, 90, or 180 days) for policy compliance metrics (e.g., passwords that allow access to confidential information or applications that can affect the financial position of the enterprise must be changed every 30 days).

PRIVACY AND FRAUD

To add further complexity, the more extensive capture and use of identity information required for electronic authentication also raises customer privacy concerns. Gartner believes that new customer authentication requirements will continue to generate federal laws and regulations regarding new unanticipated risks for businesses. These risks include not only direct hits to an enterprise's bottom line, if the enterprise miscalculates the appropriate level of authentication required for new applications, but also a legal liability if certain customer identity information has not been adequately protected or if its use has not been authorized. Perhaps the biggest obstacles for enterprises are those that are most difficult to quantify: winning the confidence of customers so they share their identity information and engage in the significant types of transactions that harness the potential of E-business and make the online experience convenient enough to keep customers coming back.

Consumer mistrust contributes to the ongoing pursuit of IM solutions and infrastructures for organizations. While the growth tends to be slow and cautious, it continues to gain momentum throughout the industry. The technology is complex in that it must operate across large complex heterogeneous domains, but the implementation itself is also complex, for many reasons. Organizations typically fight against centralized corporate control. Separate business units within an entity or even further distributed administrative groups serving up a small application will not be able to establish an ROI for joining the enterprise-wide IM infrastructure.

Many organizations have established either a wait-and-see attitude or a proceed slowly approach to IM/IAM. Using IM for compliance to laws and regulations can establish consumer confidence and serve as a marketing and sales benefit for enterprises that are early adopters or who have automated the tools necessary for a successful IM implementation. Everyone today is aware of ongoing media accounts of the loss of personal information that was in the hands of trusted business partners or even employees. The issue of identity and privacy theft will continue to be core to decisions regarding investments and moving to E-business and IM/IAM.

In response to the growing online world, IM/IAM solutions must address the misuse of online identities to commit crimes. Weak and penetrable passwords offer the greatest risk for intrusion by impersonating legitimate users for the purpose of committing online crimes. Identity theft of information stored on corporate servers is a second area of vulnerability. Compromised confidential identity information has the potential to greatly harm an organization's financial solvency, as well as its branding. Information in this category includes Social Security numbers, birth dates, credit card numbers, etc. The individual whose identity has been compromised may suffer financial losses, ruined credit, loss of professional reputation, or even arrest and conviction for crimes someone else has committed. For an enterprise, the direct and indirect costs of such security breaches may include exposure of

Healthcare – Identity

high-value information and trade secrets, disruption of mission-critical business processes, adverse publicity, and the loss of customer and investor confidence.

CONCEPT AND VALUE OF TRUST RELATIONSHIPS

Enterprises must define customer identity protection standards, including how initial customer registration, verification, and enrollment should be conducted and how identity queries and issues should be handled. While password reset and identity verification are standard features of call center and contact center services, enterprises will need to reevaluate or include new customer identity management and protection procedures and training as new transactional capabilities and channels are introduced. Customer authentication and the collection, use, and access to customer identity information often occur outside the enterprise. Enterprises must ensure consistent authentication and customer identity protection standards for business affiliates that are responsible for part of the customer engagement or fulfillment process, as well as for other business partners and service providers. Enterprises should develop contracts that stipulate:

- How authentication technologies and supporting processes should be implemented and maintained
- How employees should or should not access applications and systems that contain customer identity information
- How identity information can be used or disclosed
- Non-compliance penalties

Contractual agreements that create obligations for the confidentiality and protection of customer information with business partners and service providers are required under recent privacy legislation, such as the Financial Modernization Act or HIPAA. Chains of trust can be created by ensuring that business partners and service providers adhere to authentication standards and the confidentiality of customer information via contracts. The integrity of the ongoing process with regard to other legislation and regulations, such as Sarbanes–Oxley, should be maintained by requiring business partners to provide SAS70 audit reports, at a minimum, annually.

ISO 17799 AS A BASELINE

For information security, ISO 17799 is a recognized global standard for best practices. Although it is not perfect, it is an excellent tool for benchmarking security programs and evaluating them over time for regulatory compliance. It is not possible to officially certify against the current ISO 17799 type 1; however, any reputable security consultant or auditor can measure a company's level of compliance and provide an official report. Type 2 provides certification but has not received final approval. Using ISO 17799 for internal self-audits allows a company to justify its choice of security policies to external auditors. Organizations with an effective security program should already be compliant with most, if not all, of ISO 17799. In some cases, they may have alternative security controls not included in the standard that provide equal or greater security. This is a good thing but nevertheless should be documented. Following security best practices and documenting and testing using ISO 17799 will allow a company to meet the majority of regulatory requirements for information security. IM/IAM covers many technologies related to user management, but two categories are most useful for compliance: User provisioning is used to document who has access to which systems and in what roles. Application-specific, role-based access control tools integrate with major applications such as SAP and dramatically enhance role analysis and access control enforcement. Although other areas of IM/IAM are useful and enhance information security, these two categories provide the most immediate compliance benefits while forming a foundation for future compliance needs. They help document rights with regard to systems which is useful for generating compliance reports and identifying segregation of duties. They can build audit logs of accesses and privilege changes, identify and disable inactive accounts, and adjust privileges and access as employees change job roles.

AUDITS AND MONITORING

While audits and monitoring are not recognized and advertised features of IM/IAM systems, the process certainly adds intrinsic value to security and compliance projects. Most laws and regulations require volumes of audit logs. This is a challenge for all organizations. It has been recognized and acknowledged for decades that process integrity can be demonstrated through the process of auditing and logging. Audits of security, administration, and system management functions will keenly scrutinize their audit and monitoring processes. Because the audit and monitoring process is fairly common to all security policies and programs, technologists, vendors, standards bodies, etc. have been working on this common challenge for some time. Many products and technologies are evolving for compliance and for good security practices.

Because the IM/IAM project provides a centralized authoritative source for the granting of access and privileges, it is a perfect place to audit the overall process. It is not enough to just collect the logs; companies actually have to do something with them. They need to develop and document supporting processes and, for today's emerging and evolving laws and regulations, must consider separation and segregation of duties; for example, your security administrator who is adding and managing accounts and user IDs should not be the one to audit reports of that process. Companies must also archive the logs and establish, document, and test a process for retrieval. This is particularly important for forensics and litigation purposes. Legal departments across industries are pondering this issue long and hard. What are the required retention periods for Sarbanes–Oxley? How about HIPAA? What about, in general, for compliance to internal security policies? What do the customers require? What is a company contractually obligated to do? What do the company's business partners require? What are the company's outsourcing partners obligated to provide? And the list of such questions continues.

With new audit and logging requirements as the driver, it is no surprise that new products are emerging to help address the problem. Middleware products are available that integrate with storage technology to actually ensure that a user can find the proverbial needle-in-the-haystack e-mail message for discovery and litigation.

CONCLUSION

Significant potential gains from implementing an enterprise-wide centralized and decentralized IM/IAM project can be expected. Many of the benefits are directly related to cost savings and process improvements. An additional benefit of an IM/IAM implementation is the compliance gains achieved from an enterprise IM/IAM that is already compliant with ISO 17799, HIPAA, or Sarbanes–Oxley, for example. Each successive application or project does not have to solve this problem time and again. A challenge is to ensure that the IM/IAM implementation remains compliant over time. Of course, a company's trusty auditors can help with that problem.

Healthcare – Identity

Identity Management Systems: Components

Kevin Castellow
Senior Technical Architect, AT&T, Marietta, Georgia, U.S.A.

Abstract

This entry defines five major components of an identity management (IdM) system. It introduces each part and describes what a scenario looks like when this option may be appropriate for the situation. From there, each component is described from a generic view of the market options that are available.

INTRODUCTION

This entry defines five major components of an identity management (IdM) system. It introduces each part and describes what a scenario looks like when this option may be appropriate for the situation. From there, each component is described from a generic view of the market options that are available. Table 1 displays common problems and the identity management approach to the solution for each problem.

These statements signal a need for expanding or implementing an identity management system. An IdM system is typically defined as the ability to create subjects, manage attributes of the subjects, and remove the subjects in a predefined flow. However, IdM has evolved to include more than add, modify, and delete capabilities of users or resources. In today's highly regulated environments, IdM also includes the need for other items like auditing, certification of users, and shared sessioning.

This entry will define IdM as the system that provides the foundation for subjects, whether a user or another system, to manage the addition, modification, and deletion process in a secure, repeatable flow while reducing data repetition throughout the system. The goal of a successful IdM system should allow existing and new applications a foundation of repeatable, easily accessible identity data appropriately controlled by access controls and auditing.

The five components are

1. A directory
2. Directory integration
3. Access control
4. Delegated administration
5. Provisioning

It is not necessary to have all five components for success. Each one has its own use and every enterprise is at a different state of need. In today's software market, some of these components bleed into other areas of functionality, which only makes the decision that much more difficult when determining a solution and the appropriate time to implement it.

FIRST COMPONENT

The directory is the first and likely the most important component in this system. It is not difficult to say that a directory is necessary because in most cases there are too many directories in place. This causes the staff to spend time managing directories that store the same data in multiple locations. What data does the directory store? The directory is the repository of data that describes the user of the system. Additionally, the directory may store metadata about the applications.

It is important to point out that in most technical discussions the term "directory" specifically describes an Lightweight Directory Access Protocol (LDAP) directory store. In this case, that is not completely accurate. Although it may be more common to use LDAP for user information, a relational database may also be utilized as the user directory. The tree structure of an LDAP was designed and optimized for fast lookups to find a user in a large system. However, relational databases were better for data that changed frequently and data that had to provide atomicity, consistency, isolation, and durability (ACID).

LDAP is typically deployed among many servers. The data structure within LDAP allows for data to be broken up into specific parts and distributed among many LDAP servers on a network. These servers can be dedicated for read requests or allocated specifically for update/write requests. All of the servers can then be replicated for maximum data availability. LDAP historically had advantages because it allowed for client interaction without the installation of additional driver software.

As mentioned earlier, versions of LDAP directories had a weakness of being very slow to handle an update request for data. This weakness has been corrected by dedicating one or multiple servers specifically for handling updates. This segregated the slower, more intensive requests to specific machines. This capability allowed architects to tune these specific machines further to handle the updates.

Encyclopedia of Information Assurance DOI: 10.1081/E-EIA-120046289

Copyright © 2011 by Taylor & Francis. All rights reserved.

Table 1 General indicators for identity management components.

Symptoms	Solution
Too many directories with the same user information.	Virtual directory or metadirectory
It is impossible to see who has access to which resources.	Delegated administration
End users complain of too many passwords.	SSO solution
Application development teams are forced to build new access controls for each application.	SSO solution
User information is stored in the same database as order information.	User directory
The IT Department can't keep up with requests to change permissions.	Delegated administration
There are accounts that are still enabled for people who no longer work at this company.	Delegated administration
It can take weeks to set up the permissions correctly for a new hire's account.	Provisioning
Users have no way to recover a lost password without calling the help desk.	Provisioning/delegated administration
Data owners do not want to give up control of their data to another group to manage.	Virtual directory

Today, many manufacturers are modifying the LDAP software to handle the updates better right from the beginning with no tuning or redesign necessary.

The second issue is the lack of ACID transactions. To reiterate, this issue was more of a problem in past versions of directory software, but it is important to mention. Whereas relational databases were designed to handle large amounts of updates quickly, it ensures that if one transaction updates three tables and one update fails, the entire transaction will fail and revert back to the original state. LDAP servers could leave information in a state where two of the three pieces of information were updated and the third failed. Depending on the manufacturer and version of the directory software, this should always be something to be aware of when working with LDAP. Additionally, the standard matured in this area to add greater atomic controls (refer specifically to RFC 4525, 4527, and 4528). Most of these RFCs were updated in 2006, and it should be expected that these capabilities would be present in any new version of LDAP software.

Relational databases can be used to store user information. Many projects already utilize the relational database capabilities because a database is almost always necessary for a transactional application to run. Once the database is in place, it seems logical to insert user data into its own table along with application data. This is generally why user data is found in a relational database that also stores the application data. It is convenient, the database administrator is already hired and in place, and the software for the relational database has already been purchased. Why not use it?

As mentioned earlier, a relational database does have its advantages. The database supports transactions that are guaranteed or else the entire request is rolled back. The speed can be easily tuned for different types of lookups and update requests. However, one drawback to the relational database is not necessarily related specifically to identity management, but the difference between relational tables and the tree structure of LDAP. If it was necessary to add a new column to a relational database, this could be difficult to modify. The difficulty could come from adding new

relationships to additional tables, possibly modifying the space allocation for the table. In general, the relational database is best managed if it is designed right from the beginning with very little changes to the design as it matures. LDAP has the ease of adding attributes, and they can be inherited without much issue to any other data.

Second, LDAP has a more natural way to break data apart. It is fairly easy to split data based on attribute values. As an example, all West Coast requests could be handled by referrals to the West Coast directory server. This is difficult for a relational database to handle without replicating the entire table between all servers.

Finally, when referring to the directory in an IdM project, do not assume that it is an LDAP server. A directory is the first step to an IdM system. It is not unusual to have many of these user directories across an enterprise because each application typically was responsible for signing up its own users and maintaining the user's ability to use the application.

The growth of these directories has now caused an enterprise problem where more components are created to handle the issue of having many directory stores with duplicate data or disparate data that needs to be combined and used in different combinations with newer applications.

SECOND COMPONENT

The growth of the user directories created the opportunity for metadirectories and virtual directories. These are the components that begin to tie together the disparate systems. Deciding which one is correct for each environment usually involves understanding the political landscape of the company.

Metadirectories (Fig. 1) are usually LDAP-compliant servers that provide a central hub for information to flow to and from. Typically, vendors build the metadirectories with their LDAP server as the underlying data store. It is important to understand that a metadirectory will create an additional directory in the enterprise. Metadirectories usually have the capabilities to synchronize data across

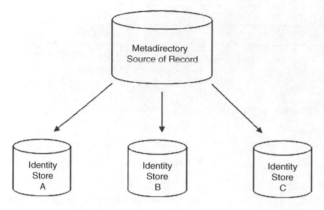

Fig. 1 The metadirectory acts as the synchronization device for all directories attached.

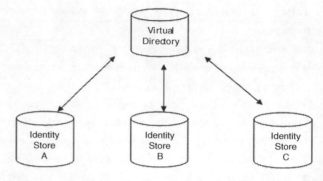

Fig. 2 The virtual directory provides an aggregated view of data for applications and maintains the original identity stores as the source of record for identity data.

multiple application repositories, as well as modifying the data as it is in transit. The metadirectory acts as the middleware piece for all directories and relational databases attached to it. Implementing a metadirectory requires knowledge of each downstream identity directory and its data. The work in the metadirectory is done first in the documentation of the data it will manage. If two different servers each store a user's address, but both servers have different information, it will be up to the rules defined in the metadirectory to decide which one has precedence. Defining the rules can be time consuming. Additionally, the downstream directory servers and relational databases are not replaced by the metadirectory. The metadirectory becomes the source for all changes and manages the data to make sure it stays in sync across the enterprise. The metadirectory can begin to add more rollback capabilities and error handling in case one server is down, but it needs to be updated. The metadirectory can try an update at a later point in case of an error or unscheduled downtime for the user directory.

The negative part of the metadirectory usually starts to materialize in the politics of the company. The metadirectory now controls the user data in any connected server. Existing applications and the management teams around those applications usually have trouble with another team managing the data they require for day-to-day operations. This is the politics of identity management. To implement a metadirectory for a large enterprise usually requires high-level support from management. Hopefully, all the integrating user directories will be required to participate. If one or two existing applications fail to participate or refuse to allow the connectivity, it can drastically reduce the value of the metadirectory. Imagine spending the money and the time to map the data, but still having rogue applications that refuse to provide their data to the metadirectory. Getting 100% participation and managing the data as new applications come online is critical to maintaining the value of the metadirectory to the enterprise.

Virtual directories (Fig. 2) are slightly different from metadirectories. They were created to work within the

political boundaries that are so often the cause of metadirectory problems. Virtual directories still make all the same connections and provide data manipulation of the data very similar to metadirectories. The main difference is the virtual directory holds no data. The data continues to reside in its original home with each application. The virtual directory provides mappings to the data and its location, but presents it as one identity directory to the requesting client. Virtual directories are not interested in replicating the data into one large set that then synchronizes across the enterprise. Instead, virtual directories are more like pointers to the data. This concept seems to ease the pain and allows for more cooperation from the data owners. They know they will still own their data and are responsible for the management of the same data. They will not lose the power they worked so hard to get in the first place. With the virtual directory, they probably gain more attention because more applications will now have access to the data that was previously reserved for applications that the department managed. That is the primary difference between virtual and metadirectories. It seems like a slight difference, but in the enterprise it is difficult to navigate around human emotions and politics. The virtual directory is typically an easier sell to participating groups than the metadirectory.

THIRD COMPONENT

The third component, which can exist without the use of a metadirectory or virtual directory, is the access control piece. Access controls depend on an identity directory to work. Access controls can be implemented with many different flavors. Some standard software-based access controls are basic authentication, digest authentication, and forms-based authentication. These access controls are based on username/password combinations.

Basic authentication is not secure and does not encrypt the username/password provided by the client to the server for authentication. The information is simply encoded for

Healthcare – Identity

transit. Typically, this type of control is not useful in today's highly regulated environments; although if it is combined with Secure Sockets Layer (SSL) communication, the username/password combo is protected while in transit.

Digest authentication is a variant of basic authentication. This process protects the username/password combination in transit without requiring the use of SSL. The username/password and a predefined realm are used to create a digest with a nonce provided by the server. The digest is passed from the client to the server, and each time, the server additionally numbers the sequence of messages further to prevent replay-type attacks.

Form-based authentication is a way for developers to customize their own look and feel for a log-in page. The page itself can use the logic provided by the developers. This has become more standardized with the adoption of predefined code snippets that are widely available in Java and .Net programming languages. In many instances, creating a form is as simple as dragging and dropping it onto a page.

Access controls can be based on hardware devices. Probably the most recognizable is the key fob with the six-digit random number generator. The key fob is synchronized with the server side management software. The username/password is combined with the random number to create a combination of something users have in their possession with something they know, like the password.

Other hardware-based access controls are based on smart cards, fingerprints, retina scans, or possibly, hand writing samples. They all work on the same principle of providing the important combination of something you possess with something only the user should know.

Although the previously mentioned options fall under the access control umbrella, there are many other options that exist as well. Single sign-on (SSO) systems are usually represented here and provide integration between applications and access control devices. Single sign-on is usually an option selected if the enterprise has problems managing the different types of access controls or wants to provide a more cohesive experience between different applications. SSO systems can be viewed from two perspectives. The first is how SSO is able to provide the single session experience between multiple applications. This is the benefit from the user perspective. The user is given a session after authentication is successful. A session token is usually placed in a cookie if the application is browser based. The cookie allows the user to move from application to application without the need for reauthentication. From the perspective of the user directories, SSO is able to provide some of the capabilities that a metadirectory or virtual directory may provide. However, it is usually not as flexible—generally having fewer options. The SSO server needs to know where to look or how to authorize the user for each URL that is requested. This data could be synchronized into a main SSO identity store or it may be provided in multiple locations that the SSO server is required to look up based on each request from the user. In any case, most SSO systems have caching, failover, shared session servers, and Web service based options. SSO is a mature design component and is essential to at least reducing the number of passwords a user may have to memorize even though the goal is to have a single password. Many times achieving the single password goal is just not practical because the enterprise wants to protect data at different levels. Some items may not require any authentication, some may require username/password, and the most secure may require a hardware token.

SSO systems provide a central location to create authentication and authorization rules. These rules can be centrally managed; generally, this is through a secure management system for the SSO environment. The ability to add and remove access from any application is a valuable time saver.

The value of SSO cannot be overlooked by an enterprise because it will provide valuable information on a user's complete session throughout all of the protected applications. This is the audit trail provided by the SSO environment. Because the SSO software is protecting the applications and providing the security session across all Web-based platforms, it allows for the audit trail to track a user throughout the entire session.

The SSO system provides a standard way for applications to rely on this framework for a consistent level of security throughout an enterprise. SSO may be one of the most valuable pieces in the identity management components because it is capable of taking all the parts and making them all appear to work together to the end user. It provides centralized access control for the administrators.

SSO can be used with virtual directories and metadirectories. Combining SSO is becoming more normal at this point whereas traditionally the SSO system would be pointed at one or more identity directories with no additional middleware in between.

Be careful with SSO systems because many vendors try to provide extra functionality at this level that can confuse some issues. Sometimes provisioning is provided by the same SSO software. This allows the users to create or delete users from the same software package. Although it may work well, it may be better to investigate other components that specialize in these peripheral areas.

Overall, access control is probably the area where there are the most choices and decisions in identity management. An architect always has to consider using simple username/password combinations or to opt for more secure options, like hardware tokens. If these options grow or the management of the environment becomes too tough, usually the SSO option is a good choice. SSO was developed to ease the pain of administrators by providing centralized control of rules, logs, and sessions. The developers can rely on SSO for a standardized system across all

Healthcare – Identity

applications, and it removes the need to develop a new authentication for each application. End users may not recognize an SSO system in use, but ideally they benefit as well by having to use fewer passwords.

FOURTH COMPONENT

The management of the user identity in the identity directory is an aspect that grows exponentially as users are added to the system, new applications are added, and new roles for the users to request are added or modified. Unless the enterprise is a small environment, it is impossible for one person to be the point of contact to make modifications to permissions or roles. It is not a good idea to put a person in charge of making changes to the directory if that person is unable to understand the request being made and whether or not it is appropriate. Imagine an employee in a remote office of a thousand-person company sending an e-mail to an administrator in the central office asking for delete permissions in the accounting application. How many e-mails would have to be sent to get clarification on whether or not this person is supposed to gain this access? How would the answer given be verified to be true? This scenario is the exact reason for delegated administration capabilities. The decisions to make modifications to a person's account should always be handled by people that directly know who that person is and what responsibilities that person should have within the company's applications. Delegated administration usually incorporates a workflow that defines an approval process. This is another example of an application that requires a strongly defined process flow. Enterprises that are still in growth mode that tend to change the process or poorly describe the process of granting rights within a system are not ideal candidates for a delegated administration system. This type of application works great when the process can be defined easily, and the workflow and approval processes can be mapped easily into the system. However, one could argue that any company with a poorly defined process for approvals is in great need of maturing their processes so that delegated administration does work for them. Thus, it would benefit the company by allowing growth that could be managed more easily.

Workflow is a component of delegated administration and is usually a necessary component. In some cases, the approval or denial can be a one-person decision or an automatic decision. If an application is strictly restricted to managers on the East Coast, any manager with an attribute of West Coast would automatically get denied. Delegated administration many times is associated with role-based access control (RBAC). Because RBAC has trouble scaling the delegated administration, it was created to force the decisions out of the IT administrator's hand and back into the lap of the business manager. As the workflow is designed, the key decision makers are mapped

out. Human Resources (HR) information should be used to make sure the workflow understands who needs to be notified once an event is triggered. There are many capabilities that include the ability to have multistep approvals. This is the opposite of the automatic approval process. In this scenario, an approval may be required by the direct manager and the next highest manager or any other combination. The delegated administration should provide the ability to log and verify who gave access and on what day. This is a powerful piece of information if it is discovered that an employee was given the wrong set of roles.

Recently, the addition of user certification has evolved as well in the delegated management arena. This requires managers to revisit who has access to their applications and certify that the list is correct. Sometimes users can move jobs, or stay in the same position but change their responsibilities. This is the instance where it is important to have the certification option implemented. Auditors always want this list to see who has access to what information. Being able to provide them a list that does not have hundreds of orphaned accounts or outdated access rights is always looked upon positively in the audit outcome.

The perfect time to implement delegated administration is always the sooner, the better for an enterprise. Be aware that some SSO applications will try to provide some level of delegated administration with the software. Although it may not have full workflow capabilities, it may suffice for the enterprise until a larger system can be purchased and designed. The SSO software usually offers it as a teaser for additional sales later as the needs grow and the enterprise matures with its processes.

The delegated administration can work for both internal and external users although the needs may be different. A typical issue for delegated administration manifests when the employees need to approve external entities roles. The issue arises because many times the delegated administration system is built with an internal view of the world from the beginning. The assumption is that external partners can have their own delegated administration system. It is easy to see the error in this discussion, but it does happen where the two systems are built separately and of course the needs change to have delegated administration in one system or at least two systems that are aware of each other. That creates more work and more costs as changing existing systems always do. It is best to try to make the delegated administration as flexible as possible and include the consideration that more processes will be dependent on outside systems or outside vendors or contractors participating in the complete process. Handling this concept drives the need for experienced vendors. When conducting this implementation, do not overlook the larger trends in computing, which is moving toward a more distributed workforce.

Healthcare – Identity

FIFTH COMPONENT

The last core component in an IdM system is the provisioning layer. The term "provisioning" is not new with identity management. It refers to the management of creating the user identity, and managing these identities throughout the entire life cycle of a user. This may sound somewhat similar to delegated administration. There are some similarities, and it could be said that provisioning will typically involve delegated administration and be carried out by a workflow process. The creation of a user is a perfect example of allowing the hiring manager to initiate the creation request for a user. The request will fall into a defined workflow that notifies IT, HR, and any other necessary core departments for the hiring of a new employee.

Provisioning is another component that could be added as a stand-alone piece of software or could be included as functionality within a metadirectory or delegated administration. Where it connects probably depends on the vendor's view of how to solve the issue of managing the user life cycle.

Also, the provisioning piece will probably come with additional "adapters." These pieces of software usually allow the provisioning system to hook into existing systems. The adapters are the pieces that allow a user account to be created on the internal network, an additional account on the mainframe, with a read-only account into the customer database. Each one of these databases, mainframes, or network directories could be provided by different software vendors and each is a completely different technology. It will not matter to the provisioning system. The availability of adapters may be an important decision in how to select a provisioning system. It is important to select a provisioning tool that has adapters provided which are useful right out of the box.

Once a user decides to move to another position, whether inside or outside of the company, the same provisioning tool that created the accounts on all of the remote systems can now disable the accounts through the same processes.

Although provisioning can appear to be a very small subset of features, it has become one of the more important because of the way systems are audited. Any user created should have proof of who initiated the creation. Users should be verified by at least one or more people with direct knowledge of the employee or into a separate container for customers. The audit will look for length of time since the privileges were reviewed. If there are ten thousand user accounts, but only five thousand employees on the payroll, the auditor will start looking for explanations. Provisioning software could monitor the length of time a user has been in the system. Certification periods should occur on the anniversary of the user's creation date if possible, sooner if the data or systems are considered more secure. If a user cannot be certified in time, the user will lose access to the system until the certification process can be completed. It is generally a best practice to disable accounts only and not to delete them totally. This again provides for some level of fact checking if a user's access rights are called into question.

Self-registration is a specific subset of provisioning. This is the ability for end users to register themselves to the application or network. In most cases, self-registration is excellent for customers. Asking them to register is the first step in the provisioning process. The customer information is collected and submitted, possibly for approval. Perhaps the account created is subject to a credit check, or possibly the account creation is set to automatic creation. Either way, self-registration gives flexibility to the entire process and enables customers or employees to make requests when the time is right for them.

Finally, do not overlook the provisioning aspect of identity management. It is important not to assume that delegated administration gives a company provisioning capabilities. Many times vendors have chosen to offer some of the capabilities as an incentive for the customer to purchase add-on capabilities at a later point in time. Provisioning is very much related and dependent upon delegated administration and workflow. It is a critical piece that will be checked in any environment subject to audits.

CONCLUSIONS

It is important to realize that the more components are added, the more mature the overall IdM system is for the enterprise. Maturity is a good thing in IdM systems because the larger savings are derived from the more advanced pieces. Maturity can be measured by the level of features an IdM system can provide (Fig. 3).

The components were presented in order from the lowest maturity to the highest. In describing the process, any enterprise would first need to have existing directories. Then, the pain of managing the directories sets in, and a

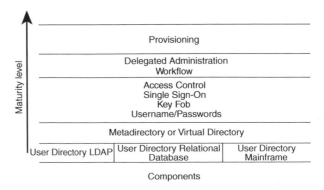

Fig. 3 Maturity can be measured by the level of features an IdM system can provide.

virtual or metadirectory is implemented to make the management easier.

The single sign-on is a close one because it could exist without a virtual directory or metadirectory. However, many vendors in the SSO space created architectures that replicated data into one main directory store. Only a very few allowed for data to reside where it was created. This may sound like a familiar difference. Again, it is the difference between the metadirectory and virtual directory. Implementing some SSO software actually forces you to choose a meta or virtual architecture. Additionally, the SSO software is considered part of access control. Access controls that exist on an individual application basis are not really grounds for saying an enterprise has passed a low level of IdM maturity. However, integrating the access controls that are managed by an SSO system are maturing to a higher level. This shows that there is centralized management and controls in place to create rules for access to multiple applications. It demonstrates an ability to audit access to multiple applications centrally.

Finally, the end user is provided a consistent security session across all types of applications that can ensure a level of protection which is consistent for applications that are part of the SSO security layer. After the SSO options, the delegated administration piece can be added. This is where quite a bit of data mapping will take place. The data that controls access to the systems which are being integrated into the workflow will need to have connectors. Rules that provide the decision-making logic during a data conflict get developed during this implementation. Delegated administration can provide the greatest impact across a company in speeding up requests for new privileges. This is a true enterprise asset because all employees and possibly customers will use it at some point. Adding the provisioning piece again adds more value to the delegated administration and strengthens the overall implementation. The workflow that is part of the delegated administration and provisioning adds information on status of in-process flows. Every process that is mapped into the system becomes easier to track and view at any point. This is one of the highest levels of IdM and provides a basis for the key components.

After these key components have been implemented, the enterprise now has the ability to go back and continue adding additional management pieces that may provide abilities like a public key infrastructure (PKI). Adding something like a PKI is typically considered very tough to manage, but if a delegated administration system with yearly certification of end users' access rights was already in place, adding additional public key issuing capabilities would easily fit as just another workflow in the delegated administration. Public key infrastructure was not mentioned as a key component because it is generally considered to be very expensive and tough to manage on a per-user basis. It is a perfect example of a technology that could benefit by having these processes in place.

Overall, the importance of an IdM system is critical to enterprises of all sizes. Only a very small enterprise can even exist without a user directory of some degree. Managing this directory data is important and critical to all processes within the enterprise. Building the infrastructure from the beginning for flexibility is important. Establishing the precedence for these types of processes and systems allows for faster, more manageable growth in the future.

Identity Theft

James S. Tiller, CISM, CISA, CISSP
Chief Security Officer and Managing Vice President of Security Services, International Network Services (INS), Raleigh, North Carolina, U.S.A.

Abstract
This entry discusses the elements of what identity is, its history, how it is used, exposures to theft, what thieves can accomplish, protection options, and what to do when a person's ID is stolen.

INTRODUCTION

According to the Federal Trade Commission's (FTC) identity (ID) theft survey conducted in late 2003, nearly 3.25 million Americans had reported their private information was illegally used to obtain credit cards, acquire loans, rent property, obtain medical care, and even used when perpetrating a crime. Over five million Americans fell victim to credit card fraud, where private information was used to acquire lines of credit. When combined with all forms of ID theft, the survey concludes that nearly ten million Americans discovered they were victims of ID theft. Finally, based on information accumulated over the past 5 years, over 25 million people have been victims of ID theft.

The FTC has categorized three severity levels of ID theft:

1. *New accounts and other frauds (NAF)*: considered the most severe form of ID theft; represents a criminal effectively assuming the entire identity of someone and creating new accounts and information.
2. *Misuse of existing non-credit card account or account number (MEA)*: represents the misuse of existing accounts and status.
3. *Misuse of existing credit card or card number (MEC)*: assigned as the least serious form of ID theft, it represents the misuse of credit cards specifically.

Based on three levels of severity, the survey states significant financial losses:

- $33 billion was lost due to NAF types of ID theft in the past year alone.
- Over $50 billion in losses are realized each year when all three types of attack are combined.
- Costs to the victims of NAF average $1200 per case, whereas victims of MEA and MEC average $500 per case, resulting in over $5 billion of expenses to victims. The bulk of personal costs ($3.8 billion) rests on the shoulders of NAF victims. (Note: The costs to victims are direct personal costs assuming that once fraud is proved, they were not liable for incurred expenses. Therefore, this number can be significantly higher considering interest and intangibles, such as the loss of jobs, reputation, and investments.)
- Victims of MEA and MEC, on average, spent 30 hours resolving their issues, while NAF victims averaged 60 hours. This results in nearly 300 million hours of people's time consumed in resolving ID theft.
- Interestingly, 15% of victims reported their ID was not used for financial gain, such as group memberships and the like. Additionally, 4% of victims reported their identity was misused in a crime, some resulting in warrants and arrests of the wrong person.

On average, it requires between one week and one month for someone to discover that he or she is the victim of ID theft. ID theft has also been known to be the result of poor information management occurring several years prior. A criminal can do a significant amount of damage when provided unfettered abuse for a week or more. Moreover, one must be cognizant of one's use of identifying materials as far back as 6 years. Makes you think about that Blockbuster account you opened while on vacation, does it not?

This entry discusses the elements of what identity is, its history, how it is used, exposures to theft, what thieves can accomplish, protection options, and what to do when a person's ID is stolen.

WHAT IS YOUR IDENTITY?

In the simplest definition, identity is one person's key to interacting with the rest of society. Within a social construct, it is fundamental for individuals to have the ability to signify their uniqueness and for governance to qualify that individual's participation.

For example, a person's identity provides membership to groups, counties, states, and countries, which in turn offer rights, benefits, and inclusion in the overall community. On the other hand, the governance of an entity uses

Encyclopedia of Information Assurance DOI: 10.1081/E-EIA-120046290
Copyright © 2011 by Taylor & Francis. All rights reserved.

the unique identity to authenticate that person's membership to allocate the rights (or costs) his or her role within the community stipulates.

A driver's license is a representation of membership that allows a person to operate a vehicle in a social framework, or highway system. The membership is based on a collection of prerequisites, such as a test, age requirement, vision specification, and legal considerations (i.e., do you live in that state, have you committed a felony, etc.). Once all the requirements are satisfied, a license is issued and the individual becomes part of the group and accepts all the responsibilities it demands.

Credit cards are a representation of an individual's participation in a financial agreement. Upon meeting the requirements of membership with a financial firm, a card is issued, providing a level of convenience in purchasing goods and services. Of course, this comes at a cost.

IDENTITY HISTORY

Long before cars and credit cards, social recognition was used to ensure one's place within the community. Ancient aboriginals in Australia used unique body painting and sprayed dye from their mouths to create hand marks on cave walls. Native Americans used face paintings, tattoos, and head dressings to signify their names, tribe, and even their role within that tribe. The ancient Egyptians mastered the art of symbolism that was pervasive throughout other cultures, such as Chinese and Mayan. Symbolism became more transferable and distinctive to a specific person with the proliferation of seals. Typically used in combination with wax, a seal would signify that the owner must have authenticated or approved the document or material for which the unique seal was applied.

As various societies grew, the use of a consistent and scalable schema began to evolve. Numerals replaced symbols as a common method of identification. Numerals are considered the purest form of language and are easily transferred between groups, countries, cultures, and languages.

Of course, today numerals are the de facto representation of the social element.

HIERARCHICAL FRAMEWORK

To understand the value attributed to identity information and the level of impact that can be realized when it is stolen, it is necessary to discuss the hierarchy (see Fig. 1) and the interdependencies of the data.

To demonstrate, consider the birth of a child. In the United States, as in most countries, a birth certificate is issued signifying that a baby was in fact born on a specific date, in a specific location, to two parents (for simplicity's sake, the baby was born to a living mother and father; U.S. citizens). The details of the birth are documented—names,

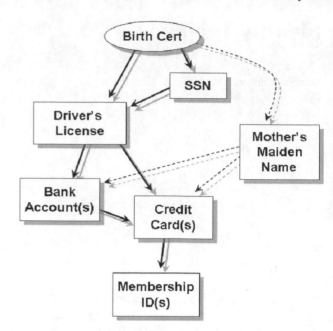

Fig. 1 Relationships and levels of identification.

dates, weight, city—and authenticated by the doctor, staff, or institution where the birth took place (interestingly, the document is typically certified with a seal). The birth certificate becomes the foundation of the hierarchical framework and is the first significant representation of identity in becoming a functioning part of society.

The birth certificate is then used to obtain a social security number (SSN). Established in the United States by the Social Security Act of 1932, the SSN was originally designed as a financial mechanism to build a social escrow for the betterment of the overall community. However, SSNs have become the root identifier, superceding the birth certificate. The basic reasoning for this evolution was the simple fact that it is easier to reference a number—something a person can remember, is transferable, and is easily organized—as opposed to a birth certificate. Seemingly overnight, the use of the SSN as the primary identifier became a reality for many institutions.

When the baby reaches adolescence and wants to drive a car, the birth certificate and SSN are used to validate his or her identity to issue a government document—a driver's license. Now we have an SSN and a government-issued driver's license that become the foundation for future identification. For example, both of these are typically needed to open a bank account or a line of credit. The financial institutions inherently trust the issuers of these documents. Then, of course, the credit card can be used as a form of identification to others.

What is interesting to note, and will be discussed in more detail later, is that the combination of these forms of identity are powerful in proving one's distinctiveness. However, how these are used, combined with the level of trust, the fragile underlying fabric, and hierarchical framework (i.e., inherent relationships), sets the stage for

Healthcare – Identity

someone else to steal that identity and use it for other, illegal purposes.

ISSUANCE AND USE

An important aspect of identity, and one of the many characteristics that have inadvertently supported identity theft, is the issuer of the documentation. In the above discussion, the issuer was an institution (birth certificate) and the government (SSN and driver's license). An established government has the necessary tools, processes, policy, and enforcement to act as a trusted entity. For example, a passport issued by Germany will have more legitimacy than one from a third-world, fragmented country. Therefore, government-provided documentation (e.g., SSN, driver's license, passport) is significant in proving one's identity and is inherently linked to the capability of that government to control and manage the issuance of those materials.

However, governments are not the only entities that will issue forms of identification. Private companies will provide documentation attesting to your identity, such as credit cards, membership cards, frequent flyer cards, certificates, and corporate badges. However, the value of these independent forms of identification—to you and a thief— is directly proportional to the level that other entities "trust" the independent issuer. Even in a post-9/11 world, it is simple to insert a frequent flyer card into a kiosk at the airport and print a boarding pass. What? You do not have a frequent flyer card? Use any major credit card and the flight number, and the ticket is provided. Therefore, this assumes that the airlines trust not only the membership cards they issue but the credit card issuers as well.

To summarize, identity is provided by unique representation issued by various entities with varying degrees of social and governmental trust, creating a hierarchy of trust and documentation—all of which is under attack.

THE INTERNET

Other than the industrial evolution and the telephone, surely the Internet has to be one of the most significant technical-to-social impacts humankind has experienced. Today, everything is online, interactive, flowing all around us instantly. One can approach an ATM just about anywhere in the world and draw funds from one's local bank. One can swipe a credit card in New York, immediately debiting one's account in Tampa.

Given the global economy and capability to access information and money from anywhere, it is only natural to see how ID theft becomes an attractive option for criminals.

The Internet presents two very fundamental challenges: 1) access to and 2) the presentation of information.

Access to Information

Adding to the ID theft malaise, private information about individuals is available on the Internet in several forms, in different places, and with varying degrees of security controls. Ask yourself how many times you have provided your name and address on an application. A lot? Consider the likelihood that your information was entered into a computer system. Then one has to speculate who was that information shared with or sold to. The point is clear: private information is collected in many ways and can have multiple occurrences (copies). Moreover, it is difficult for an individual to keep track of when he or she provided what information to whom. It is so common for companies to request private information that it has become an acceptable—forgettable—event in regular activities.

Each copy of private information exponentially increases the risk of someone obtaining that data without authorization. The potential for unauthorized disclosure is not only due to the fundamentals of numbers—more copies, more opportunities—but also no consistent application of security controls exists. Hacking into the Department of Motor Vehicles (DMV) to get a driver's license number is much more risky than giving $50 to the local Rent-A-Movie clerk for someone else's application.

The Internet provides potential access to all types of information from anywhere at anytime. The most prevalent attacks in recent history are hackers collecting credit card numbers by the thousands from insecure E-commerce sites. Hacking into American Express or Visa would seem more "profitable" from a hacker's perspective—the hacker would get more bang for the buck. However, one could rightly assume the security is substantially more sophisticated than that of an emerging online store.

However, to categorically conclude that gathering private information about someone requires advanced technical skills would be a gross overestimation of the attacker. The reality is that there are numerous sources of information easily accessible if one knows where to look. Add this to the realization that only a few pieces of information are required to wreak havoc, and it is no surprise that ID theft has nearly doubled in the past year.

Presentation of Information

With unsettling consistency, identity information is regularly requested without verification. More often than not, when I am asked to present my identity at the airport, the guard will look at the ID, look at the ticket or itinerary to make sure the names match, but never look at me to compare to the picture—the most fundamental factor for using the picture ID in the first place. Although this has very little to do with ID theft directly, it does demonstrate a flaw in the way identity materials are presented and accepted.

Healthcare – Identity

The presentation and acceptance flaw is most prevalent on the Internet where human interaction by the authenticator is nearly non-existent. For example, many states provide the online capability to renew a driver's license. Access the site, enter a birth date and current driver's license number (both easily obtainable by a foe) and authenticate the session with the last four digits of a SSN (granted, there are other implementations which vary by state). Once complete, one merely enters payment information and a shipping address and awaits delivery of a shiny new driver's license.

The acceptance of information, especially on the Internet, is founded on the concept that you *know* the information, as opposed to you are in possession of the document. To open a bank account, one never has to present a social security card—the fact that one knows the number typically will suffice (ID theft-aware organizations now require the document for photocopies, but this is not consistent or standard for all institutions). Therefore, a thief could simply have the necessary numbers on a scrap piece of paper and copy them onto an application. This practice is most damaging when the data is used to obtain root materials, such as birth certificates, social security cards, or driver's licenses.

As the type of identification materials and their utilization are placed under greater scrutiny, it is not difficult to find significant holes in the process, even when trying to fix it. For example, many people sign the back of a credit card and include the words "SEE ID" with the hope that if the card is stolen, the thief would be caught when the clerk asks for an ID. But how often are you asked for an ID, even when it is your own card? Finally, it is typical for clerks to compare signatures on the card and the one on the authorization receipt. So, are we to assume the clerk is an expert in forgery?

Armed with very little information and a predisposition for crime, it is easy to perform basic credit card fraud and begin the process of assuming someone's identity. Although each transaction by the thief is one more opportunity for the owner of the credit card to discover the illegal activities, it is, however, one more step for the thief in gaining more control over that ID. Therefore, discovering illicit activities early in the process is critical to stopping the attack before it gets much worse.

HOW IT HAPPENS

Thieves utilize tactics from varying elementary strategies to elaborate high-tech schemes. Following are some common scenarios:

- *Dumpster diving.* Thieves rummage through trashcans for pieces of non-shredded personal information that they can use or even sell. Maintaining awareness of what is discarded can go a long way toward protecting personal and potentially valuable information. Given that most people have some form of garbage collection, criminals can easily collect ample amounts of data many of us consider trash. Following are some common items that can be exploited to perform ID theft:

    — Credit card receipts
    — Phone, cell, cable, or power bills
    — Packaging (e.g., envelopes)
    — Tax forms and other documentation (e.g., investment reports, legal documents, group memberships, and healthcare data)

- *Mail theft.* The greatest level of threat of exposure of one's personal information is a thief getting it before you do. Just as someone would go through the trash in the middle of the night, criminals will search mailboxes for preapproved credit offers, bank statements, tax forms, or convenience checks. Mail theft is not limited only to incoming mail, but packages that have been left for postal carrier pick-up. The most significant barriers to mail theft are the level of prosecution if caught and the proximity to the target (mailboxes are usually close to the home). Thieves know that, if discovered, mail theft constitutes a serious crime with substantial penalties. Moreover, it is easier to go through the trash as opposed to someone's mailbox at their front door. Nevertheless, neither of these are strong deterrents, and the practice of stealing mail by criminals is at the top of the list of common tactics.

- *Other personal property theft.* Beyond taking trash and mail, there are other methods of obtaining personal information. Stolen purses and wallets usually contain a number of credit cards in addition to other personal documentation that can be very valuable (e.g., driver's license). Briefcases, laptops, planners, or anything that someone might take in a car are all treasure chests for identity thieves.

- *Inside sources.* An emerging trend in ID theft is brokering—the act of selling someone else's information to organized crime syndicates. A dishonest employee with privileged access to personal information can avoid the risk of assuming an identity and simply make a profit on the value of information to an ID theft ring. Unfortunately, there is very little an individual can do to mitigate this threat beyond trusting the organization to hire honest people who have access to private information.

- *Impostors.* People have fallen victim to an individual who fraudulently posed as someone who had a legitimate or legal reason to access the victim's personal information. Acting as a potential employer, bank representative, or landlord, a criminal can readily collect valuable information.

- *Online activities.* Returning to the Internet subject briefly, online activities greatly increase the exposure of personal information. For example:

  — Users enter private information on fraudulent Web sites that pose as legitimate companies.
  — Thieves purchase private information from online brokers.
  — Thieves track someone's activities online to gain information.

- *Documents in the home.* Unfortunately, there are identity thieves who can gain legitimate access to someone's home and personal information through household work, babysitting, healthcare, or by friends or roommates.

WHAT CRIMINALS WILL DO

Identity thieves know there is a race that starts the minute the first fraudulent transaction is completed. At this point they must make a decision: exact minimal damage through minor purchases, or completely consume your virtual existence; there is no middle ground. If they decide to take over your identity, they will do so very quickly, knowing that the more of your identity they own, the less power you have to stop them. In some extreme cases, the victim was decimated and was nearly incapable of reporting to authorities.

So, what do identity thieves actually do? Here are some common activities:

- They open a new credit card account, using your name, date of birth, and SSN. When they use the credit card and do not pay the bills, the delinquent account is reported on your credit report.
- They call your credit card issuer pretending to be you and ask to change the mailing address on your credit card account. The impostor then runs up charges on your card. Because bills are being sent to the new address, it may take some time before you realize there is a problem.
- They establish domestic services, such as phone, power, or wireless services in your name.
- They open a bank account in your name and write bad checks against the account, which will ultimately fill your mailbox and impact your credit report.
- Of the more sinister activities, they file for bankruptcy to avoid paying debts they have incurred under your name. This results in significant problems in proving that your identity was stolen.
- They buy cars and even houses by taking out loans in your name.
- They give your name to the police during an arrest. If they are released from police custody but do not show up for their court date, an arrest warrant is issued against you.

BASIC "DO"S AND "DON'T DO"S

Considering the plethora of threats to personal information and the impact that even the smallest amount of data exposure can have, there are some very basic practices everyone can do—and avoid. It should be noted that the examples given here are fundamental and relatively easy to do with minor personal disruption for everyday people, but they must be performed with tenacity and consistency.

Do:

- Shred all personal and financial information, such as bills, bank statements, ATM receipts, and credit card offers, before throwing them away. Although there are several very sophisticated and cheap methods for successfully reconstituting shredded data, it is effective for the average person. Additionally, a criminal rummaging through your trash at night will see the shredded paper and will more than likely move to your neighbor's bin. Of course, this assumes you are not being targeted. For those with greater concern and a knack for security and privacy, there are options:

  — *Double shredding.* Run documents through a shredder twice in two different directions.
  — *Tear shredder.* Although expensive, there are very aggressive shredders available that produce extremely small pieces of paper using a technique that exponentially increases the complexity of the reconstitution process.
  — *Disposal.* After shredding materials, the discarded paper can be taken to an incinerator or secure disposal site.
  — *Burning and chemicals.* It is not uncommon for people to burn or destroy documentation with chemicals. While effective, the act is typically illegal and potentially harmful to the environment. Therefore, this practice is strongly discouraged.

- Keep root, personal documentation (e.g., birth certificate, Social Security card) in a secure place, preferably in a safe deposit box.
- Regularly check your credit status through credit companies or organizations (e.g., Experian Information Solutions National Consumer Assistance Center, Equifax Information Service Center, Trans Union Consumer Disclosure Center) in an effort to see who is checking your credit and if there are any unknown activities.
- Contact the local post office if you are not receiving mail. A thief can forge your signature and have your mail forwarded to a P.O. Box for collection.
- Protect your personal identification numbers (PINs). Be aware of your surroundings when at an ATM,

grocery store, gas station, or any public place where private information is being entered.

- Report lost or stolen credit cards immediately. Moreover, cancel all inactive credit card accounts. Even when not being used, these accounts appear on your credit report, which is accessible to thieves.
- If you have applied for a credit card or any private documentation (e.g., birth certificate) and have not received it in a timely manner, immediately notify the appropriate institution.
- Sign all new credit cards upon receipt and seek credit cards that display personal photographs on the card.
- Avoid using your SSN. While this can become complicated and put you in an awkward situation, you gain more by making a concerted effort as opposed to blindly offering critical information. Unfortunately, most people avoid confrontations and do not challenge the establishment. Nevertheless, each person must make a decision on the potential risk of providing sensitive information.
- Seek options with organizations to avoid multiple exposure of your SSN. For example, many healthcare insurance cards have SSNs printed on the face of the card. Effectively, this is equivalent to having two SSN cards that require protection. However, many companies can offer cards without SSNs printed on them, if requested.

Don't Do:

- Never volunteer any personal information blindly. Always take a moment and consider the consequences before offering information. Not only does this apply to ID theft, but also it is a very sound practice for overall personal security. For example, you are at a restaurant celebrating your birthday and the table next to you politely asks how old you are and you tell them you turned 23 yesterday. In about ten seconds, they have your birth date, which may be all they need after they steal your credit card off the table. Game over.
- Do not give your SSN, credit card number, or any personal details over the phone unless you have initiated the call and know that the business that you are dealing with is reputable. In the event you receive a call from someone asking for information that appears to be legitimate, ask them some basic questions to help validate the call. For example, if you get a call from your bank, ask them the address of your local branch and they should respond with little hesitation. Moreover, if they ask you for the last four digits of your SSN to authenticate you (very common), ask them for the first three. In the latter example, the attacker can ask for the last four, you provide it, and then they say, "That does not match our records, what is your entire SSN so I can check again?" You give the whole number and they simply hang up.

- Do not leave receipts at ATMs, bank counters, or unattended gasoline pumps. Although many receipts do not display the credit card number, it is surprising how many do.
- Do not leave envelopes containing payments in your home mailbox for postal carrier pickup. Drop them off at a public mailbox or at your office when you get to work. Anything is better than at home. If there are no other alternatives, do not raise the little red flag on the mailbox, or anything that is designed to notify the postman you have mail to send. Postal carriers are not lemmings; if they open the box to insert mail, they will more than likely conclude that the envelopes already in the box are outgoing. The best practice is to avoid this altogether and simply drop your mail off for general pickup.
- Do not write any passwords, PINs, or your SSN on a piece of paper and keep in an insecure location. Memorize these kinds of information. If you cannot (for medical reasons), use a trusted entity, such as your lawyer (who has access to personal information anyway) or spouse, to be available via phone when in need of the information. Of course, you will have to write down the phone number.
- Do not freely enter personal information on Web sites. We discuss this in greater detail below. Nevertheless, one cannot assume authentication of a Web site because it looks good or familiar. Just because the correct URL was entered and the expected Web page was presented means absolutely nothing.

PROTECTING AGAINST IDENTITY THEFT ONLINE

The basics of ID theft, certainly in the physical world, have been discussed. Protecting information, not sharing private details, destroying sensitive documents, and just good, everyday practices are all steps in the right direction. Unfortunately, these practices have very little bearing when applied to the online world. The basic rules apply, but protection is employed differently.

The information contained within this section is not only for individuals using the Internet, but can be very helpful to those organizations providing online services.

The Web

Before peering into the idiosyncrasies of online security and protection against ID theft, there are some ground rules of which everyone should be aware. Apart from very specific situations, anything on the Internet can be impersonated, especially a Web site. While not a simple task, a hacker can recreate a fully functional Web site of a

Healthcare – Identity

legitimate organization and redirect the browser to the hacker's own site without the user's knowledge.

Cross-site scripting (also know as XSS) is an example of how links can be manipulated to gather information. Often, attackers will inject JavaScript, VBScript, ActiveX, HTML, or Flash into a vulnerable application to fool a user. Everything from account hijacking, changing of user settings, or cookie poisoning is possible. When combined with other attacks, such as DNS poisoning and vulnerabilities in common Web browsers, a user has very little chance of validating a Web site.

Therefore, one cannot assume that anything is what it appears to be on the Internet.

Policy Statement on Web Sites

One could correctly assume that if a hacker can duplicate an entire Web site to fool users, presenting an official-looking security policy or privacy statement is petty in comparison. However, a good policy or privacy statement will have a plethora of information, such as contact phone numbers, e-mail addresses, physical addresses, links to customer surveys and complaints, links to commerce information, and other characteristics that can be investigated. While not a foolproof solution, following some of the links provided can be helpful.

Secure Sockets Layer

Secure Sockets Layer (SSL) is a protocol supported by nearly every E-commerce site (at least the good ones) on the Internet. It provides authentication of the remote system for the user by way of certificates and establishes an encrypted session to protect information while in transit. Certificates are a security mechanism founded on trust and asymmetrical encryption for authentication.

A company will purchase a certificate from a root certificate vendor, such as VeriSign, Certisign, Entrust, and others to ensure users can validate their sites by way of the trust chain provided by the vendors. For example, Microsoft's Internet Explorer (IE) has several root and intermediate certificates preloaded into the application so the browser can validate the E-commerce company's certificate more readily (see Fig. 2). Given the expense and legal requirements for obtaining a root and signed certificate for a company Web site that supports SSL, the

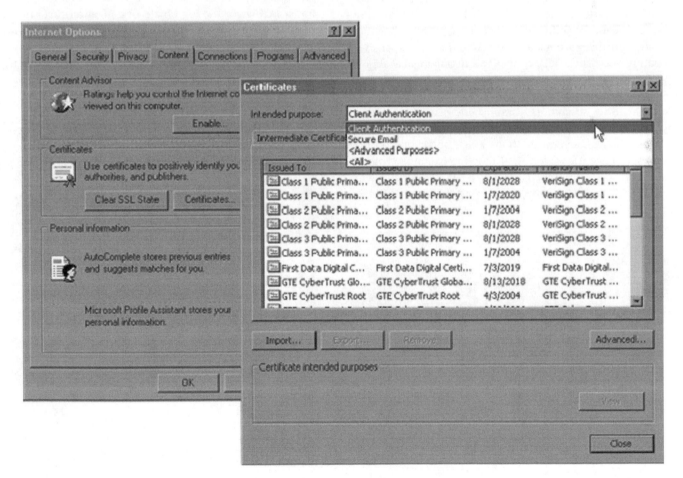

Fig. 2 IE root certificates. Data from 2003.

Fig. 3 IE lock icon signifying that SSL is active.

risks associated with a criminal making that investment is somewhat limited—but certainly not impossible or not practiced.

There are several validation tasks that can be exercised to help someone determine if the Web site is at least certified by an industry trusted organization. When connecting to a site to enter personal information, at a minimum some form of icon or notification should be visible showing that SSL is being employed (see Fig. 3).

However, there are cases where the browser does not have the root certificate associated with the company's Web site and the user is presented with information about the certificate and the option to continue the operation. As demonstrated in Fig. 4, basic security checks are performed on the certificate by the browser and the user is provided with the option to view any details about the certificate.

It is at this point in the process that the user must make a very critical decision: to trust the certificate or not. No other organization is supporting the trust, and an individual is left to his own devices. If there is the slightest doubt in the certificate's viability, do not continue. While obtaining a valid certificate from a trusted vendor may be expensive, creating a certificate takes only a few minutes and at almost no cost to the criminal.

If the certificate is trusted (or you are not prompted) and the SSL session is established, prior to entering information, take the time to investigate the validity of the certificate. Several methods exist, depending on the browser in use. However, the following example is based on Microsoft's Internet Explorer (IE). The "lock" will appear in the bottom corner signifying that SSL is

employed. By double-clicking on the icon, IE presents information about the certificate that was used to authenticate the session.

In the following example, American Express' Web site was accessed and a secured area was selected, initiating an SSL session. By picking the icon, a dialog box was presented to offer detailed information about American Express' certificate (see Fig. 5). Also provided is the option to install the certificate in the user's browser for future use and the ability to see an issuer statement (the latter being an effective opportunity to collect more information that is difficult to forge).

Earlier, the term "trust chain" was used to describe how trusted relationships between organizations are realized at the certificate level. At the top of the dialog in Fig. 5 there is a tab, "Certification Path," that presents the technical hierarchy of the certificates and issuing organizations. This particular security check is extraordinarily important. For example, a criminal can create a very official-looking certificate with many layers in the trust chain; but if the root certificate is questionable, the user can make an informed decision (it should be noted that most browsers do not include questionable root certificates off the shelf; therefore, the user would typically be prompted). The information presented in Fig. 5 is basic. However, as shown in Fig. 6, the legitimate organization that signed and approved the certificate is extremely difficult to fake. As one can see, American Express' Web site has a specific certificate that was signed and approved by one of VeriSign's intermediate certificate authorities.

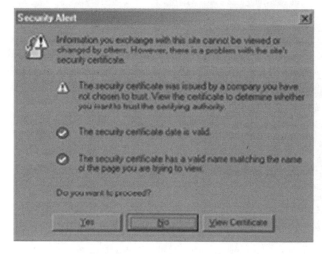

Fig. 4 IE certificate warning message.

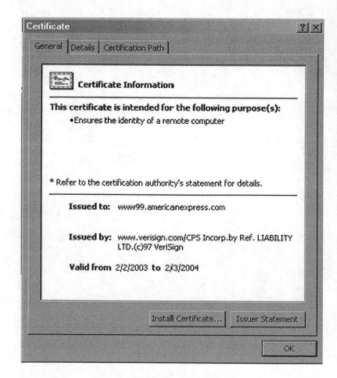

Fig. 5 Certificate information.

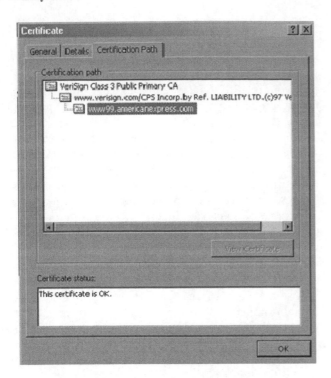

Fig. 6 Certificate trust chain.

Furthermore, the intermediate's certificate was signed by VeriSign's all-important root certificate, which with very little work can be found in the list of certificates built into the browser (see Fig. 2).

The entire process takes only a few seconds to perform and goes a long way in authenticating the site into which you are about to enter very sensitive information. The act of verifying even the most trusted of sites should be a common practice.

Data Input

Previously discussed were some of the security concerns and exposure of private information when on the Internet. The fact that a criminal can impersonate a Web site, redirect information, or even extract information from your computer are all fundamental concerns. However, even on trusted sites, one must reconsider entering an excessive amount of personal information.

As demonstrated, there is a hierarchy of identity information (such as SSN, driver's license, etc.). These, when used in combination, can be a very effective means of proving one's identity. In contrast, it can be exceedingly helpful for a criminal—a one-stop-shop for your information.

Red flags should be raised when buying something online or entering data into an application for credit, mortgage, loan, membership, or anything that asks for several forms of identity. It is common to enter credit card information on E-commerce Web sites (some specific options to avoid this common task are discussed later), but entering your SSN, driver's license number, or both should be avoided at all costs. If required, call the organization to reduce the risk of Internet-related exposures.

The best practice when dealing with private information online is to remove the unknown element—the Internet—and return to the physical world that offers more options for authentication with which most people are familiar.

Credit Cards

Comparatively speaking, credit card fraud is relatively insignificant in the realm of ID theft. However, credit cards are the launching point for thieves looking to steal someone's identity. It is also the proverbial training ground for criminals to advance to the next step—ID theft.

Today, using a credit card online is common practice and many people do not think twice about the transaction. Friends, the IT department at work, and "Is this safe?" links on Web sites typically state, "If there is a lock in the corner, you're fine." Of course, based on the discussion thus far, this may not be sound advice.

Given the proliferation of credit card use online, the endless exposures on the Internet, how criminals can use the data, and the cost to financial firms due to fraud, numerous security options, some very sophisticated, have been conceived to protect online users.

Codes

Early in the adoption of the Internet as a feasible foundation for business, the problem of authorizing credit cards without the merchant having the capability of physically validating the card became a serious challenge. The primary card vendors, such as Visa, American Express, and MasterCard, implemented a three- or four-digit code on the card to verify that the customer has a legitimate card in hand at the time of the order. The merchant asks the customer for the code and then sends it to the card issuer as part of the authorization request. The card issuer checks the code to determine its validity, then sends a result back to the merchant along with the authorization.

Following are some characteristics of each issuer:

- American Express (AMEX): AMEX's code is a four-digit number on the front of the card above the credit card number. The code will appear on either the right or the left side of the card.
- Visa: Visa's Card Verification Value (CVV) is a three-digit number on the back of the card. The full credit card number reprinted in the signature box and at the end of the number is the CVV.
- MasterCard: Card Validation Code (CVC) is a three-digit number on the back of the card. The full credit

number reprinted in the signature box and at the end of the number is the CVC.

Unfortunately, two problems prevail: 1) the process to create these numbers is not overly complicated and is easily duplicated, and 2) the lack of diversity (only three or four numbers, not alpha or special characters) makes for a limited number of permutations. It is important to understand that criminals are not without the technical means to perform complicated computer tasks (never underestimate your enemy). Nevertheless, every layer of security (defense-in-depth) adds one more obstacle to fraud.

Temporary Numbers

A recent advancement in credit card numbers was the introduction of temporary numbers. The concept is founded on the fact that criminals gain access to, or create card numbers and use them for some form of fraud. Therefore, some financial firms have provided for temporary numbers—exactly like credit card numbers—to be created on demand by the user. The temporary number can then be used online, significantly reducing the exposure of the user (and financial firm) because the thief would have only a short time to use the stolen number.

As a card-holding customer, you can generate temporary numbers online and associate them to one of your cards. Once the new number is obtained, it can be used online to make purchases. This provides for two basic forms of protection, assuming the number is stolen. First, the thief would have a limited timeframe in which to use the number for fraudulent purposes. Adding to this, the thief would be unaware that the number has a time limit and may not act quickly enough before it expires. Second, the use of the number can be uniquely tracked because the user knows when and where he used it, and that the number of transactions are minimal (unless you visit hundreds of sites during a spending frenzy). Moreover, the financial firm is more willing to work with the individual in credit disputes because the offered security measures were employed.

So, what is there to stop a criminal from creating the temporary number on the Web site? This is where we get back to usernames and passwords, not the most sophisticated method of authentication, but nevertheless a widely practiced one. For example, (let us stick with American Express) you have an American Express credit card and all that it implies (i.e., private information shared during the application, etc.). You can set up an online user account for bill payments and other tools for managing your card. This can be accomplished on the phone or online. Staying with the Internet, let us assume the account is created online. You must enter information that American Express either already knows or can

validate. Moreover, there are new pages presented and secured, adding to the complexity for an attacker. For example, the credit card number and code, your mother's maiden name, part of your SSN, your address, and a password (or PIN) you established early on in the application process over the phone is used to create the account.

Of course, this all comes down to a password for the account. It can be readily concluded that American Express has done as much as possible—online—to authenticate you. It is up to the customer, not American Express, to choose a secure password and not share it with others. Now you can log in, creating temporary numbers, and assign them to one of your cards, all of which is secured with SSL.

While employing a temporary number is not a total solution to protecting one's credit card and ID, it is, however, a significant step in a positive direction. (Note: American Express is *not* the only organization that provides this service and is only used herein for consistent demonstration purposes.)

Smart Cards

Computer chips are present in almost everything, from toys and cars to tools and people. One cannot look five feet ahead without seeing something that requires a computer chip. Over the past several years, credit card manufacturers have been integrating computer chips into cards, adding a new dimension to credit card authentication and use.

Companies put a surprising amount of authenticating data on microscopic chips embedded in cards—information, such as cryptographic keys and digital signatures, to small computer programs. Of course, to use a smart card there must be the ability to interface with the chip. No matter how sophisticated the information in the chip, the card swipe at the mall is not going to help. Naturally, the ability to use smart cards is increasing. For example, ATMs in metropolitan areas are being upgraded. When the card is inserted, not only is the magnetic strip read, but the card's chip is accessed to perform another level of authentication.

But ATMs have very little to do with using smart cards on the Internet—now comes the card reader. For a small price, a card reader can be attached to a home computer, along with some additional software from the card vendor that can be used to control the use of the card. Take, for example, that you want to buy a new book online and at checkout you are prompted to enter payment information. At this point, you insert your card into the reader and the system prompts you for a PIN to validate the user. Upon authentication, the software enters the payment data. When combined with temporary numbers, this makes for increased confidence in using your credit card online. Of course, with the existence of a number and magnetic strip on the card, it is still exposed to traditional fraud. However, as time progresses, the numbers and strip will no longer be necessary. (The only reason the numbers are embossed on cards to this day is to accommodate the very old process of imprinting.)

WHAT TO DO

Now you know what can happen and how to reduce the chances of someone stealing your ID or taking over your financial well-being, but what do you do if you suspect illegal activities?

Unfortunately, there is not a great deal at your disposal, at least not as much as one would hope to have. In a perfect world, one phone call to a central agency to freeze existing assets and gain new access to a pool of alternate funds for short-term support would be nice. But the reality is it can be an arduous task, consuming valuable time and resources while someone else is abusing your identity.

First Things First

You must get control over the financial exposure and promote awareness of the situation. Given that the majority (i.e., 85%) of ID theft is related to financial gain, aggressively limiting access to funds is essential. Moreover, every time the criminal spends money on your behalf, it inevitably results in some form of cost to you. So, the sooner you can stop it, the better.

Finally, alerting the financial industry to your situation is paramount in gaining an alliance early to support later financial disputes. Moreover, it will help stimulate the next step—if it goes far enough—in engaging with the Federal Bureau of Investigation (FBI), the government entity responsible for investigating ID theft.

To start the process, contact one (preferably all, but once the first is notified, the others are alerted) of the three major credit bureaus and instruct them to place "fraud alert" on your credit report. Additionally, have them send you a copy of your report. Typically, this will be done at no cost given the situation. Following are the three major credit bureaus:

1. *Equifax—http://www.equifax.com*—call 800-525-6285 and write to P.O. Box 740241, Atlanta, GA 30374-0241 (Hearing impaired call 1-800-255-0056 and ask the operator to call the Auto Disclosure Line at 1-800-685-1111 to request a copy of your report.)
2. *Experian—http://www.experian.com*—call 888-EXPERIAN (397-3742) and write to P.O. Box 9530, Allen, TX 75013 (TDD: 1-800-972-0322)
3. *Trans Union—http://www.transunion.com*—call 800-680-7289 and write to Fraud Victim Assistance Division, P.O. Box 6790, Fullerton, CA 92634 (TDD: 1-877-553-7803)

Shutting It Down

The next major step is to cancel credit cards, close accounts, or stop anything related to private information that is in progress, such as loan applications, requests for private information, legal elements, and the like.

In bad cases, where the criminal has had time to sink his or her teeth in and has created new accounts, it is typical to start the process to shut down an account only to find new ones in your name. In this case, you have to prepare for disputing fraudulent activities. Firms do not immediately assume you are not responsible for transactions you claim are not your own—that is the point of stealing your identity, to become you! Even if it is only assumed that the thief is creating new information on your behalf (assuming you are a New accounts and other frauds (NAF) victim), you should complete a Theft Affidavit, found at: http://www.ftc.gov/bcp/conline/pubs/credit/affidavit.pdf

Getting Law Enforcement Involved

After notifying credit bureaus, banks, and other potentially affected institutions, getting the police involved is the next step. Interestingly, this is more for procedure rather than "calling in the cavalry." No one is going to jump out of his seat to help you, but filing a report with your local police department is a necessary first step in getting law enforcement on your side of the equation.

The most important next step is to send copies of the police report to the major credit bureaus, your creditors, or anyone you suspect may be potentially involved in future dispute activity. Additionally, once the report is filed and your clone is caught stealing a car five states away, the odds of you being associated are greatly reduced.

Get Everyone Involved

As a victim, use the tools at your disposal with extreme prejudice. Once you start getting a handle on the situation and have a better understanding of the impact, file a complaint with the FTC. (Complaint form is found at: https://rn.ftc.gov/pls/dod/widtpubl$.startup?Z_ORG_CODE=PU03.)

The FTC serves as the federal clearinghouse for complaints from victims of identity theft. While the FTC does not resolve individual consumer problems, it can formally assist in investigating fraud, and can lead to broader law enforcement action. The FTC enters Internet, telemarketing, identity theft, and other fraud-related complaints into Consumer Sentinel (http://www.consumer.gov/sentinel/), a secure, online

Healthcare – Identity

database available to hundreds of civil and criminal law enforcement agencies worldwide.

Clean-up

Unfortunately, getting back to complete normalcy is not an option. The process for recovering from ID theft can be a painful experience and leave one feeling helpless.

Every ID theft case is different and therefore will require an assortment of tasks to get back to some point where one was before the attack. Institutions apply various policies and procedures for working with victims. The best hope for getting back as closely to one's original status as possible is to act quickly and to over communicate.

CONCLUSION

Although it is somewhat comforting to know there are tools, practices, and organizations out there willing to help, the sad reality is that there is very little consistency or extensive collaboration in the process, leaving many victims feeling as if they are being attacked on multiple fronts. The good news is that ID theft is firmly acknowledged as an epidemic, and government as well as private industry are providing more tools and assistance to help the innocent.

Nevertheless, the best method for surviving ID theft is prevention. One should practice common sense when sharing private information and remember that too much personal security is never enough.

Identity-Based Self-Defending Network: 5W Network

Samuel W. Chun, CISSP
Director of Information and Risk Assurance Services, TechTeam Global Government Solutions Inc., Burke, Virginia, U.S.A.

Abstract

This entry addresses this new emerging model of secure networking by discussing the five basic requirements of all networking systems: who, why, what, where, and when. The entry also provides a comparison between current networks found in most environments today with the new secure, identity-based, self-defending model (referred to by the author as the "5W Network" for brevity). The hypothetical architecture of a 5W Network in a large distributed medical setting follows a discussion of the various characteristics and components of the secure, identity-based, self-defending network. The entry concludes with a discussion of what the future holds for the 5W Network and in what environments it would be a likely fit.

INTRODUCTION

The amazing advances in networking and networking technologies over the last 25 years have come from a variety of different perspectives. Disparate groups such as government research labs, the military, universities, large corporations, and countless enterprising individuals have all played a part in advancing networking technologies at a breathtaking level; however, these individual and group innovations have rarely coordinated their efforts, resulting in various camps of advancement. Some, such as IBM, Banyan, Microsoft, and Novell, focused on the development of network and desktop operating systems (and directory service) while others, such as Synoptics, Alantec, 3Com, and Cisco Systems, put their primary research efforts on high-speed network infrastructures. In the early 1990s, the very first commercially available firewalls began to be offered to organizations by companies such as Check Point Software Technologies. Only within the last few years have enterprise-class intrusion detection and prevention systems finally become commonly available to those who have the resources to acquire and manage them.

Although technological advances in directory services, firewalls, switches, and routers have come at an astounding level, scant attention has been paid in the past to integrating these advances into a singular entity that serves as a critical asset for organizational productivity. The growing emphasis on the importance of information security has been accompanied by intense interest recently in technology *convergence* with the goal of developing a new model for a secure, identity-based, self-defending network.

THE FIVE "W"S OF SECURE NETWORKING

Even non-practitioners of information security will readily agree that access to an organization's private resources, regardless of what it is, should only be allowed when some very basic questions have been answered. Whether it is physical access to a building, use of a company directory, or connection to a server or network, it is essential to ask several questions before granting access, such as "Who are you?" "What are you going to do?" "Why are you here?" It is just common sense that access should only be allowed based on receiving appropriate answers to these simple questions.

That is why it is so surprising that even today the vast majority of networks fail to ask more than one question before granting access to a connection. For example, how many times has the reader been in a facility where the only requirement for network connectivity—Internet Protocol (IP) address via Dynamic Host Control Protocol (DHCP)—was physical access to a wall jack? In most environments today, connectivity (and the ability to do harm to the network and organization) is usually based on only one question: "Where?" (physical access). Where the user sits and where the user connects will almost always result in a connection appropriate for that location.

Network access, however, should be dependent on more. It is just not enough to rely on physical access to maintain the enterprise's network security. Ideally, five questions should be answered *before* being granting a network connection:

Identity: Who Are You?

Before anything else, the identity of the person or object attempting to connect to the network should be established. It is not enough simply to know the network jack, IP address, or message authentication code (MAC) when someone has connected to the wall jack to gain access to the network. It is important to establish true identity via some authentication system before granting a useful connection. Ideally, when a person plugs a laptop (could be

Encyclopedia of Information Assurance DOI: 10.1081/E-EIA-120046291
Copyright © 2011 by Taylor & Francis. All rights reserved.

wireless) into a network, access to the network resources should be denied unless an authentication challenge is met.

Role: Why Are You Here?

When the identity of the object has been verified via authentication, the network should know why the person or object requires access. The network infrastructure should know the role of the person or object within the organization (e.g., printer, network administrator, regular user). This is a function common in most network operating systems. Group-based access policies for server-based resources have been around for many years. Unfortunately, implementation of role-based access to the network infrastructure at OSI layers two and three is almost non-existent. It is very rare to find a network that requires authentication before granting port-level access to Transmission Control Protocol/Internet Protocol (TCP/IP) or other network services.

Appropriate Access: What Should You Have Access to?

Being cognizant of the identity and role of the requesting object or person should result in the network determining appropriate and inappropriate access. For example, a finance department employee on a roving laptop at a company should only have access to services (e.g., TCP/IP ports, servers, printers) that are appropriate to people working in the finance department, regardless of location. Conversely, the network should also be able to recognize inappropriate actions for particular roles. For example, if the same authenticated finance department employee attempts to perform a port scan or attempts a distributed denial of service (DDoS) attack on a server, the network should recognize that as inappropriate behavior and deny that action (e.g., port shutdown, connection reset).

Location: Where Should You Be?

Telecommunications advances have allowed organizations to grow beyond their geographical locations with impunity over the last 30 years. With inexpensive wide area solutions readily available, setting up remote offices with unfettered access to organizational information technology (IT) resources across the world has never been easier. The good news is that the question of where a person or object should have access has been thoroughly explored. Network segregation via routers (access control lists) and firewalls actually can be used (with considerable effort) to manage access based on location. The bad news is that doing so requires network segmentation (routing) and numerous configurations of routers and firewalls, which requires considerable effort to result in any type of success. It is accepted and very common practice for large organizations to have an "all locations, all access" network policy. The

overwhelming need for access regardless of location (and risk) has proliferated these types of networks. In many environments, it is possible (and often easy) to attack servers in data centers halfway across the world just by gaining physical access to a small remote field office. As a result of globalization, location is becoming less and less of a factor in access. This, unfortunately, allows intruders to target resources in an enterprise across the globe.

Time: When Can You Have Access?

Recent studies suggest that there is no real prime time for security incidents. Intrusions are just as likely to happen during the business day (an in-house event) as after hours; however, logical rhythms or cycles of access should not be ignored. Network access policy at the port level should be exercised with time constraints when available. For example, if a company's office is closed over the weekend with no need for user-level access, it would be ideal for all user network ports to be shut down with the exception of network management traffic (e.g., antivirus updates, OS updates and patches).

MODERN-DAY NETWORK: THE ONE "W" PONY

The need for fast access, not secure access, has been the primary motivator for the development of networking technologies over the last 25 years. From 2 Mbps Thinnet to 4/16 Mbps Token Ring to today's 10 Gbps Ethernet, networking vendors and consequently network implementations have focused on providing unparalleled access. From the pure networking perspective, the questions of who should have access, why they should have access, and where they should have access have been a function left up to the administrators that manage directory services and server-based resources. The serious problem with this is that authentication happens *after* network access. As shown in Fig. 1, when an intruder gains physical access to a network jack in any location (such as a field office), that intruder is free to perform malicious acts (e.g., DoS, Port Scan, malware, sending spam) on the entire network without ever having to authenticate to resources.

The single question that these common networks asks is "Where?" Where users plug in their PCs or laptops will determine what network address they will receive and what access they may be granted based on their connection point. In Fig. 1, the router that connects to two sites is a logical place for an Access Control List. Unfortunately, location is rarely used to limit access due to the trend of mobilization of the work place. From a networking perspective, it is difficult to use physical location as a means for controlling access when the users are moving around from one site to the next; consequently, it is easier to

Healthcare – Identity

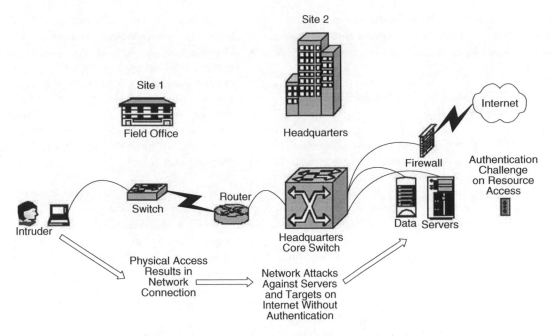

Fig. 1 A common modern-day network architecture.

provide a connection and full network access and then let authentication occur when the user attempts to connect to resources. This is most commonly done by asking the user to enter a username and password on the log-in screen; however, this is where serious trouble lurks. After connecting to a physical jack, an intruder can carry out network-based attacks without even attempting to access any of the server-based resources.

Characteristics

The most common characteristics of modern-day networks are easy and fast access. Wherever an employee goes within the company or around the world, that employee needs access to the company's network. The goal of modern-day networks is to provide such a connection with the least amount of effort. These networks tend to be simple and usually flat with little segmentation. Network traffic is generally switched with routers that only perform routing between wide area connections.

Common Components

The single most common component seen in modern-day networks is the Ethernet switch. The exponential advances in switching speed and technology have allowed organizations to deploy large unsegmented networks on an unprecedented scale. With switches that have system backplanes that can handle terabytes per second of information, entire campuses can be connected into a single network with automatic and instant assignment of network addresses.

Benefits

The benefits of these types of networks are clear. They are easy to deploy, manage, and administer because all the users have access to every network service they need. The network performs quickly because little overhead is wasted on such activities as verification of identity and monitoring. This type of solution also has the unfortunate appeal of requiring low capital investment.

Vulnerabilities

A fast, easy access network comes with many vulnerabilities and high risks. Allowing easy, unfettered network access for the end-user community also extends the same access to potentially malicious programs, intruders, and disgruntled internal employees. Reacting to security events, rather than preventing them, is likely to be normal for these types of networks. In addition, post-incident forensic analyses are hindered by the fact that attacks or incidents are likely only to be traceable by IP addresses, host names, and MAC addresses, yielding very little information about the identity of the intruder.

Future

Unfortunately, the vast majority of networks in existence, with the exception of highly secure government and defense environments, are configured and deployed in this manner. This pattern is not likely to change significantly due mainly to the ignorance of the risks posed by having these open access networks. In addition, the simplicity of this architecture coupled with the very low cost of

Healthcare – Identity

ownership ensures that these types of networks will be implemented well into the future by those that do not consider security a priority.

SECURE, IDENTITY-BASED, SELF-DEFENDING NETWORK (5W NETWORK)

In recent years, there has been intense interest in developing not only fast network access but secure access as well. Security breaches by hackers and improper acts performed by disgruntled insiders have resulted in several high-profile cases that have made the headlines in the last few years. Consider these following cases (excerpted from official press releases) from the U.S. Department of Justice Computer Crime and Intellectual Property Section (CCIPS):

- *United States v. Meydbray*—The U.S. Attorney's Office for the Northern District of California announced that the former Information Technology Manager of Creative Explosions, Inc., a Silicon Valley software firm, was indicted today by a federal grand jury on charges that he gained unauthorized access to the computer system of his former employer, reading e-mail of the company's president and damaging the company's computer network.
- *United States v. Smith*—The New Jersey man accused of unleashing the "Melissa" computer virus in 1999, causing millions of dollars in damage and infecting untold numbers of computers and computer networks, was sentenced today to 20 months in federal prison.
- *United States v. Dopps*—A San Dimas man pleaded guilty this afternoon to illegally accessing the computer system of his former employer and reading the e-mail messages of company executives for the purpose of gaining a commercial advantage at his new job at a competitor.

These examples are a small sample of the thousands of cases of computer-related crimes that are investigated by state, local, and federal authorities each year. It is not surprising that there has been a renewed interest in designing networks that are not just fast but also cognizant of the various threats they are likely to face.

An ideal network should do the following each and every time a person or object plugs into a jack:

- *Issue an immediate authentication challenge.* The network should establish who the person or object is before allowing any type of access to occur (i.e., it asks "Who or what are you?").
- *Grant appropriate access based on the identity.* The network should allow access to services (e.g., Web, network, database, FTP site) and resources (e.g., servers, printers, directories, files) based on identity, role,

or business policy of the organization (i.e., access is based on "What? Where? When?").
- *Monitor, react, and defend against inappropriate actions.* The network should monitor the connection granted for identity- or role-appropriate activity. If an authenticated user performs an action that is inappropriate for the role (e.g., port scan, multiple connections), the network should autonomously react in a predetermined manner (i.e., access is based on "Why are you here?").

A secure, identity-based, self-defending network (or 5W Network) is a network that asks five very important questions: Who? What? Where? When? Why? It then ensures that access is always granted based on the answers to these questions. After all, all organization should ask these questions when anyone enters their premises, so is it not reasonable to ask these same questions of users connecting to their networks?

CHARACTERISTICS: DESIGNING A 5W NETWORK

Designing a network architecture that grants, monitors, and ensures access based on functional roles is not a trivial or easy task. It requires the careful integration of different technologies that have traditionally evolved separately. No single manufacturer, technology, or product will result in a secure network. It is the *convergence* of these infused with good old-fashioned people-generated business policies that will ultimately result in a safe, secure network that is situationally aware. To accomplish this, we must first turn the paradigm of networking upside down: Authentication should happen *before* network access.

The only access that a network port should have enabled by default should be the ones that are required to verify identity. As shown in Fig. 2 (similar to Fig. 1), every time someone plugs a PC, printer, or laptop into a switch port, that person should be challenged for credentials. Only when appropriate credentials have been supplied is network access granted based on a combination of user identity, business policy, and business rules. Then, an automatic self-defense system [an intrusion detection system (IDS)] monitors the activity of the connection so it is ready to react if the connection deviates from identity-or role-appropriate behavior. For example, if the user makes sequential successive connections to other PCs (a sign of a virus) or begins to attempt to access servers that it should not (unauthorized access), the self-defense system should automatically issue reaction commands based on a predetermined incident management policy.

Based on preset rules, the self-defense system should be able to reset user connections, shut down ports, write logs, and send security event alerts. All of these actions should be performed autonomously so the network itself is

Healthcare –
Identity

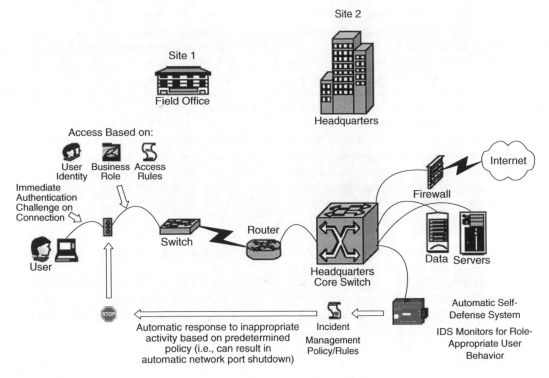

Fig. 2 5W Network architecture.

preventing and managing incidents. The security and network administrators are then freed from the mundane burden of chasing down problem cases, allowing more time for strategic activities such as reviewing policies and roles.

COMMON COMPONENTS: CONVERGENCE

A secure, identity-based, self-defending network is naturally complex. It requires not only the integration of several different technologies but also the definitions of user, group, and access policies that will be applied in granting network connectivity. The best-designed systems are almost always a result of combining the best technologies, hard work, and carefully considered policies. A truly secure network that is able to defend itself and its organization's most trusted assets is no exception. Five logical components of the 5W Network function together to protect the organization from internal and external threats. Each component can be a physically separate system but not necessarily so. Some manufacturers, such as Enterasys Networks, integrate some of these components and functions into their network equipment. Regardless of whether these components exist as separate systems or are integrated into a large chassis, they must always work together with the goal of security. These logical components are:

- *Authentication system*—The authentication system verifies the identity of the user and objects to the network. It requires that users (and objects) provide

credentials for any type of network access. Authentication systems are common in most network environments in the form of directory services. Some of the most commonly used authentication systems are Microsoft Active Directory, Novell eDirectory, and RADIUS. Other more advanced authentication systems, such as biometrics, can also be used for identity verification. This authentication system must be able to communicate in some form with the access control component of the network.

- *Access control system*—The access control component contains the specific user, group, and access policies of the network and serves as a gateway for network access. It takes the authenticated user information and reviews the individual and group rights to resources that the connection should have. It then issues commands to the network infrastructure equipment to grant specific access to the appropriate resources.

- *Network infrastructure*—The switches, routers, and firewalls should by default grant rights only to the services necessary to achieve authentication. Some of the competing protocols for transporting authentication data include Extensible Authentication Protocol (EAP), Protected EAP (PEAP), Lightweight and Efficient Application Protocol (LEAP), and Tunneled Transport Layer Security (TTLS). Whatever the method, the network infrastructure equipment should grant access to appropriate network services and resources only after successful authentication and access validation. The IEEE 802.1x standard—also known as EAPoL (EAP encapsulation over wired or wireless Ethernet), is commonly used to accomplish port-based network access control.

- *Intrusion detection and prevention systems*—Intrusion detection and prevention systems serve as the watch dogs of the network. They should, of course, monitor the network for suspicious traffic, but they should also serve the vital function of monitoring each connection to ensure that traffic on the connection is appropriate for the role determined by the access control system. If the network activity of a specific connection is questionable or contrary to the authenticated role, they should react based on predetermined incident policies. For example, an authenticated user who browses to a wrong server can result in an alert, but a "Ping of Death" from the same user can result in the IDS issuing a port shutdown command to the switch to which the user is connected.
- *User, group, access, and incident management policies*—Although the various systems in the 5W Network perform the mechanics of security policy enforcement on their own, the network still requires instructions on how to protect itself. These instructions come in the form of policies. The user, group, and access policies determine what role the requester plays in the organization and to what services they should have access. Incident management policies tell the network what it should do when there is activity that violates the role determined by the policies. In the 5W Network, the development of sound, effective policies is where the security practitioner can have the highest impact on the overall network security posture of an organization. Well-developed access and incident management policies, when applied objectively and evenly, reduce the total cost of owner-ship of a network by reducing the manual intervention required by the IT staff for security incidents.

BENEFITS

The benefits of a secure, identity-based, self-defending network are obvious. It achieves access without compromising security. The 5W Network provides objective (policy-based) access based on business role rather than physical location. It also has the ability to lower administration and security costs by being preventive and self-reacting, thus freeing up staff to perform more meaningful tasks.

DISADVANTAGES

Unfortunately, 5W Networks are not all that common. The convergence of the technologies necessary for true interoperability and the standards (such as 802.1x) that allow for the various components to work with each other are fairly new. Not very many networking vendors produce and market their equipment with secure, identity-based networking in mind. In addition, the complexity of the overall 5W solution, even though it achieves an unprecedented level of security, requires expertise in a variety of IT disciplines that is not always readily available. Cost is also a major factor as the 5W Network requires more equipment of a higher class, expert labor, and greater effort in creating effective policies, none of which is necessary to deploy a traditional switched, easy-access network.

FUTURE

Currently, a fully role-based, self-defending network is relatively rare. It is generally deployed in large environments that can afford the very best in technology or require such a network due to sensitive information. It is almost impossible to find these networks in small to mid-sized businesses, which cannot afford to invest in these new technologies. As the demand for secure access grows, however, so will the number of networks that integrate the various components described in the previous sections. Research and development efforts by various networking vendors are focusing on making integrative security an important feature of their products, in addition to performance. As of the writing of this entry, only one vendor, Enterasys Networks, offered a complete suite of networking equipment, including switches, routers, and IDSs, capable of integrating with existing authentication systems to offer true identity-based, self-defending capabilities. Other vendors, such as Cisco Systems, are not far behind in introducing products that have the same capability. As the demand increases and the technology matures, resulting in lower prices, it is expected that more organizations will choose to implement these networks.

APPLICATION OF THE 5W NETWORK: A SAMPLE ARCHITECTURE

Environments exist today that have invested in deploying a secure, identity-based, self-defending network. Unfortunately, these organizations are generally not amenable to sharing the details of their architecture to the public, fearing a compromise of a network they have invested so heavily in. So, instead of presenting a case study of an architecture that actually exists today, this section presents a theoretical application of a 5W Network in the setting of a large metropolitan hospital system.

Environment Overview

The MetroHealth Hospital System is a not-for-profit healthcare provider in the Washington, DC, Metro area. It operates four large hospitals in Virginia, Maryland, and

Healthcare – Identity

Washington, DC. Each hospital operates as a separate facility with its own administration that reports to a centralized executive structure of the overall MetroHealth System. In the hospitals, all of the patient care providers (doctors, nurses, and allied health professionals) need access to patient records, regardless of the facility or unit where they are working. A centralized medical record database stores all patient information in MetroHealth's administrative office building (which contains the hospital system's data center). Each hospital has an administration department that stores their own payroll, human resources, and operations information in servers that are dedicated to that hospital. The servers themselves are also located in MetroHealth's data center, but the administration staffs of the hospitals are mobile, working out of the administrative office building and their respective hospitals. All Internet access to the MetroHealth system, including Web browsing and e-mail, is provided through the datacenter in the administrative office building.

The MetroHealth enterprise network must provide the following functions:

- Limit access to anyone not authorized by the hospital.
- Provide access to patient records to healthcare providers regardless of the facility where they are working.
- Provide business-hours' access (Monday through Friday, 8:00 A.M. to 5:00 P.M.) to administrative staff to only resources and services dedicated to that particular hospital, regardless of the facility.
- Provide all administrative staff safe access to Internet and e-mail, but limit access to the medical records database, regardless of the facility.
- Prevent threats, including intruders and viruses, from spreading from one hospital to another or to the administrative office center.

Authentication System

An enterprise-wide authentication system should be implemented at MetroHealth (see Fig. 3). In this example, a single Microsoft Active Directory forest domain can be deployed, and each hospital and the administrative office center can be designated as an Organizational Unit (OU). Within each OU, user and role groups, such as doctors, nurses, allied health, payroll, human resources, and administration, can be created so a site-appropriate group is contained within each OU. Of course, redundant domain controllers will have to be deployed at each site to provide local authentication to resources in each hospital. In addition, Microsoft's implementation of RADIUS, an Internet Authentication Service (IAS), will need to be configured and running on the domain controllers so that an access control system can communicate with the authentication system.

Network Infrastructure

The network infrastructure, all of the switches, will have to support role-based networking at the port level. In this example, Enterasys Network's Matrix series will serve as the core, edge, and distribution layer switches for MetroHealth. Currently, Enterasys Networks is the only manufacturer that produces port-level security features (via their user private network [UPN] capability) embedded within their layer two and three devices. By default, all of the ports on the MetroHealth network will allow access to a single service—authentication. All other ports will be closed.

Access Control System

The logical access control system will be comprised of the Microsoft Active Directory Infrastructure (with RADIUS) working in conjunction with the embedded security features of the Matrix switches (UPN enabled) via the IEEE

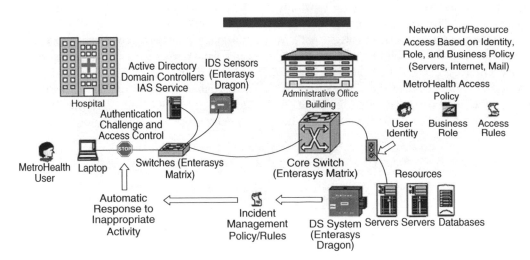

Fig. 3 MetroHealth's secure, self-defending network architecture.

802.1x communication standard. The 802.1x standard for port-level access control will be used to authenticate end users and provide policy-based networking access for the authenticated users. The Microsoft 802.1x Authentication Client will be used at all of the desktops and laptops at MetroHealth to provide for authentication challenge at connection. The peripheral authorization will occur via hardware MAC addresses so only devices that have been predefined within the MetroHealth network can gain network access. The logical access control system components will ensure that end-user, port-level access is consistent with predefined access policies that are assigned to each MetroHealth Active Directory role group. The access control system focuses on the prevention of unauthenticated and unauthorized access on the entire network.

Intrusion Detection and Prevention Systems

The Enterasys Dragon Intrusion Response system will serve as the intrusion detection and prevention system. The entire MetroHealth network will be monitored by Dragon sensors. These sensors will monitor the network for aberrant network traffic and abnormal end-user behavior by authenticated end users. If it detects any issues with a specific user or a port, such as scans or DDoS attack attempts, it can perform actions such as quarantine or port shutdown based on predefined incident management policies. This system will focus on the enforcement of network security policies on authenticated users and systems so the risk of incidents from trusted sources is also mitigated.

Access and Incident Management Policies

One of the most important aspects of designing a secure network is documenting access and incident management policies. With the help of business analysts who understand explicitly the requirements of the organization, access policies should be written so network access is only granted to services required by the functional group within the organization. For example, MetroHealth access policies should state that, regardless of which OU healthcare providers are members of, regardless of the facility they are in, they should have network access to the medical records system located in the administrative office building. In addition, they will need to be granted access to other

services (e-mail, Web access) when required. On the other hand, the access policies should restrict hospital- or OU-specific administrative users to their dedicated servers regardless of what facility they are logging in from. Access to the medical records system should only be granted to subgroups within administration, such as claims and billing, who use this information for their functional business roles. Because business roles play such a critical part in determining access, network architects need to work with business analysts carefully so the access policies assigned to groups within the Active Directory (or authentication systems) allow the appropriate level of access required for the role.

It is also important to document and implement incident management policies within the IDS that will minimize administrator intervention. Whether the response to the incident is user-level quarantine or immediate reset of a connection, the appropriate responses to events should be predetermined based on the level of seriousness of the incident. The IDS system should be preconfigured so it is enforcing a set of incident management rules rather than performing an alert. This will allow hospital engineering staff to focus on incident policies rather than incident response, which has a much greater value to the organization.

SUMMARY

This entry presented an emerging concept of networking based on business role and self defense. It provided a discussion of questions ("Who?" "What?" "Why?" "Where?" "When?") that should be asked before granting access to organizational resources, including networks. A brief introduction into the origins of modern-day networks was followed by a description of their features, benefits, and weaknesses, and they were compared against a new model of networking based on identity, role, and self-defense. This new model—the secure, identity-based, self-defending network (5W Network)—was discussed thoroughly with regard to its features, benefits, strengths, and weaknesses, as well as practical applications. It is expected that, as interest in security grows in enterprise environments, this type of networking, which balances access, security, and management, will become the standard for large organizations.

Healthcare–
Identity

Incident Response: Evidence Handling

Marcus Rogers, Ph.D., CISSP, CCCI
Chair, Cyber Forensics Program, Department of Computer and Information Technology, Purdue University, West Lafayette, Indiana, U.S.A.

Abstract
This entry gives a brief background on incident response and computer forensics, as well as the misperceptions that accompany those terms. The author discusses the incident response and cyber-forensics process models, as well as comparing the differences and similarities between them. The author also discusses the proper management and handling of digital evidence. This entry further stresses the importance of being proactive and prepared to conduct investigations at the enterprise level.

INTRODUCTION

Terms like "incident response" (IR) and "computer forensics" have become all too familiar in our modern technology-dependent society. Few if any organizations can claim immunity from the possible negative side eff ects of this dependence, namely misuse and abuse and other criminal behavior. Organizations today are paying more attention to protecting their information technology (IT) assets and the sensitive information that may be contained therein. The attention is directly translated into increased budgets, reallocation of resources (both personnel and equipment), and in some cases increased complexity of the enterprise-computing environment.

Regardless of the industry, there seems to be increasing statutory and regulatory compliance issues related to financial reporting controls (e.g., Sarbanes–Oxley, United States; CEO/CFO Certification, Canada), private information (e.g., Health Insurance Portability and Accountability Act), and financial information (e.g., Gramm–Leach–Bliley Act), to name just a few. The common element with these requirements is the ability to detect when a problem has occurred and the ability to respond in an eff ective and efficient manner. The consequence of not having these abilities is not only the danger of being in non-compliance and suffering financial or criminal consequences, but also includes the very real danger of never recovering and going out of business in less than a noble fashion. The risks faced today, other than regulatory compliance, stem from the increased frequency and prevalence of external and internal criminal activities. For various reasons that are beyond the scope of this entry, deviant computer behavior is on the rise and shows no sign of abating. Reported losses due to insider misuse and abuse have been estimated annually to be millions of dollars. Errors and omissions also account for a significant financial drain on organizations; these events can prove more costly than intentional abuse and misuse and often much harder to deal with, as the root cause can be difficult to ascertain. Wrongly configured systems can also endanger our personal safety (e.g., air traffic control systems and power grids) or create a very large national security risk.

There are other business considerations apart from the traditional information assurance and security risks. As the corporate world becomes increasingly more litigious, there is a corresponding increase in responding to requests for discovery for electronically stored information (ESI). An organization may have its house in order regarding compliance, information assurance, errors, and omissions and still be required to investigate, collect evidence, and provide reports in response to a request for discovery by another party who has or is anticipating filing a legal action against the organization.[1] The flip side is applicable as well. An organization may be in a position to initiate an action against another party and thereby be making the request for ESI in support of that action.

Those of us who have been in the information assurance and security field for a while recognize that incident management and response is the primary control strategy that organizations implement to meet the various risks that they face on a daily basis. However, what might not be readily apparent is the fact that the IR has evolved into a fairly mature systemic (enterprisewide) process. Owing to increased demand, organizations are becoming more comfortable in dealing with IT-related security incidents and the need to investigate negative events. The corollary to this increased need to respond to incidents in a formal manner is the requirement to collect digital evidence during the course of these incidents and investigations. Unfortunately the management and handling of digital evidence are not a process that most organizations are knowledgeable about or necessarily comfortable in dealing with. Digital evidence and how to deal with it appropriately is an extremely immature concept or process in most organizations.

Encyclopedia of Information Assurance DOI: 10.1081/E-EIA-120046842
Copyright © 2011 by Taylor & Francis. All rights reserved.

Incident –
Info Classification

The purpose of this entry is to assist with the understanding and comfort in dealing with digital evidence in the context of dealing with an incident. We begin by discussing some of the misperceptions surrounding the collection of digital evidence during an IR situation and then continue on by exploring the IR model. We will then look at the digital evidence management and handling methodology and focus on the similarities and differences between the two models. The entry concludes with an examination of how to combine the two process models to accentuate the strengths and reduce the inherent weaknesses and shortcomings of both.

MISPERCEPTIONS

Most discussions on digital evidence and IR ultimately touch on the perceived issues in combining these two models. Many business managers are very concerned with the possible negative impact that collecting evidence will have on the pressing need for business resumption.[1] Recall that one of the primary goals of IR is the timely resumption of business to minimize the economic impact of the event. In some industries, every minute that an organization is unable to use its information system translates into hundreds if not thousands of dollars of lost revenue (e.g., stock exchanges and e-commerce) or penalties (e.g., application service providers and telecommunications). Obviously, the loss of consumer or shareholder confidence has an economic impact as well.

The proper handling and management of digital evidence are commonly thought of as a process that interferes with or at the very least slows down the recovery and resumption of business operations. This is not necessarily the case. Even if it were, the failure to act in a reasonable manner that demonstrates due diligence may result in a larger impact than the cost of losing an hour or two. Businesses operating in an industry that falls under the various regulatory compliance requirements may face criminal or civil sanctions for failing to conduct a proper investigation that includes the proper handling of digital evidence.

A properly implemented and planned-out approach to combining digital evidence and IR should function in a manner that allows the two activities to occur in parallel, thus resulting in a minimal slowdown in time needed to recover (see Forensic Readiness). It also ensures that the resumption of business (recovery phase) is handled in a manner that does not place the organization in a more vulnerable position by rushing the recovery and placing the systems back online without being properly secured. Looking at the digital evidence allows the investigators and IR personnel to understand the full impact of the event and conduct a proper root-cause analysis. There are several documented cases in which businesses rushed the process and came back online only to be attacked again in the same or a similar manner. These businesses learned the hard way that patience really is a virtue.

INCIDENT RESPONSE PROCESS MODEL

The term "IR" can be defined in many ways. Several authors have focused on the incident handling aspect of the process, whereas others have dealt with the management and response capability.[2] Regardless of how we formally define the process, the ultimate goal is to respond in a manner that reduces the impact of the incident and allows the organization to recover appropriately so as not to be vulnerable to the same incident in the future. Specific goals of IR can be summed up as follows:

- Provide an effective and efficient means of dealing with the situation in a manner that reduces the potential impact to the organization.
- Provide management with sufficient information to decide on an appropriate course of action.
- Maintain or restore business continuity.
- Defend against future attacks.
- Deter attacks through investigation and prosecution.

The process assumes that prior planning has occurred, in the form of policies and procedures specific to IR management and handling, and that proactive (e.g., intrusion detection systems and intrusion prevention systems) as well as reactive controls (e.g., logs and monitoring) are in place.

The actual model used to conduct or implement an enterprisewide IR capability may vary from organization to organization in regard to minute details. However, at the conceptual level, the framework is usually based on a multiphase formal/methodical approach[1,2] (see Fig. 1).

Limitations on the size of this entry prohibit a detailed discussion of each phase, but readers interested in more details can refer to Schultz and Shumway or Rogers.[2,3]

It should be recognized that IR is a vital component of any organization's IT security posture. With the move toward a systemic or enterprise approach to information assurance and security, IR has now become part of the information security life cycle[3] (see Fig. 2). The information security life cycle begins with the detection of an event (incident) and encompasses the response to the incident and any countermeasures that are identified and implemented. The life cycle is dynamic and is a circular process that feeds back into itself.

This approach also places IR into the system development life cycle and thus IR considerations should be part of every project undertaken. The inclusion of IR in the system development life cycle allows IR to become a systemwide or enterprise-level event. Although there are numerous usages for the term "enterprise," for this discussion enterprise will refer to large-scale implementation across all business units and inclusive of all IT assets. It is important to have as broad a coverage as possible given that systemwide (enterprise) vulnerabilities and threats are a very real occurrence, thus risk must be dealt with at the enterprise level as opposed to the more "siloed" approach of dealing

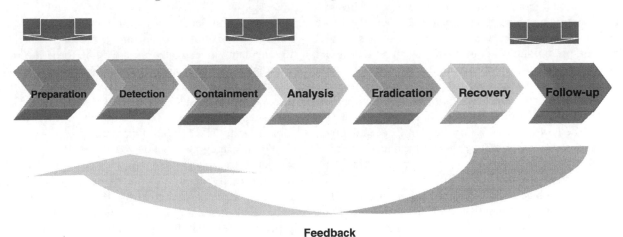

Fig. 1 Incident response process model.

with business units as unrelated entities. The days of IT risk management being purely a technology or an IT business unit problem are long gone.

CYBER-FORENSICS PROCESS MODEL

Let us turn our attention to cyber-forensics and digital evidence and examine a common approach or model. Before we jump into the model it is important that we properly define what is meant by "cyber-forensics" or "computer forensics." Cyber-forensics can be defined as follows:[2,4]

> The scientific examination and analysis of digital data in such a way that the information can be used as evidence in a court of law.

At first glance this definition appears somewhat simplistic, but upon deeper examination it becomes clear that by focusing on the modality of the evidence (digital), the definition overcomes the tendency to have multiple different terms depending upon the location of the evidence. In the past there have been many a heated debate regarding network forensics vs. computer forensics, or small-scale vs. large-scale device forensics. The common element in all these is in fact the nature of the evidence—it is digital. One could argue for the inclusion of an electronic evidence as well as a digital, but most electronic or analog materials are converted to digital for the analysis phase, so the argument is considered moot.

Although it is apparent that currently there are only emerging standards and protocols related to cyber-forensics, the underlying framework is rather generic and is derived from the fundamentals of forensic science or criminalistics. The framework focuses on the investigative nature of the activity and can be broken down into the following phases or steps:[1,2,5]

- Identification
- Collection
- Preservation
- Examination
- Analysis
- Documentation and report

Like the IR process model the cyber-forensics process model is an iterative process that follows a logical approach to dealing with both the crime scene and the durative evidence that is digital in nature.

INCIDENT RESPONSE VS. CYBER-FORENSICS

There have been numerous discussions and articles published on the topic of IR and cyberforensics. Some authors

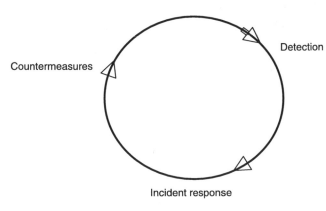

Fig. 2 Information security life cycle.

Incident –
Info Classification

take the view that these two terms are analogous, but this is incorrect. Granted, both IR and cyber-forensics are investigative in nature and both tend to deal with incidents in a reactive manner. However, the major difference lies in the standard of proof that is required. Cyber-forensics is a forensic science and by definition the admissibility of evidence is a major consideration with every task or phase. However, IR is concerned with the resumption of business and the return to a steady state—which, it is hoped, will be less vulnerable than before. IR does not by definition or convention deal with admissibility of evidence concerns, nor does it treat each event as having the potential to end in litigation.[4,6]

Although the objectives and standards of proof for IR and cyber-forensics are somewhat different, they are not mutually exclusive or contradictory activities; they are very complementary. In fact, exemplary IR programs integrate cyber-forensics into their response capacity. When an event triggers the IR process, care is taken to ensure that the admissibility of evidence, chain of custody of evidence, and ability to reproduce the "scene" are taken into consideration. In most cases, the IR and the cyber-forensics teams work in parallel and each team coordinates its actions with those of the other to ensure that nothing is overlooked. This symbiotic relationship has been recognized by the courts in many countries (e.g., the United States, Canada), with the passing of guidelines for determining the cost to the victim of the attack in criminal and civil cases. Here the value of the information and the cost to the organization to recover from and investigate the attack (e.g., prorated system administrator and IR team salary costs) are combined to arrive at an aggregate total loss for the victim (exceeding, it is hoped, the magic $5000 mark that has been established for some jurisdictions).

As indicated in Fig. 1, the introduction of cyber-forensics and the collection and preservation of digital evidence logically occur during different phases of the IR process model. What is very important to understand is that with digital evidence and cyber-forensics, once the evidence or scene has been contaminated, it cannot be decontaminated; there is no "do over" or "undo" button. Digital evidence and digital scenes are extremely fragile and volatile, and in some cases the evidence has a very short life span.

DIGITAL EVIDENCE

As was stated previously, when dealing with forensic investigations the primary concern is with evidence. Although the focus of this entry is on digital evidence, we cannot ignore physical evidence or physical crime scenes. In most instances, the digital evidence exists within a physical crime scene. Although we might be looking for spreadsheets, log files, pictures, etc. that are stored on a device, these devices exist in a physical space. The location of the system in a room, how the system or device was physically connected to the network, and what physical access points there were to the room may all be crucial to determining the context of what happened or who had or did not have exclusive opportunity. Although a majority of the incidents investigated are assumed to be the result of external attackers, the reality is that internal attacks are still the most predominant and costly events. With internal attacks, proving unauthorized access or exceeding account privileges may hinge on the physical evidence (e.g., closed-circuit TV and building access logs).

To truly integrate IR and cyber-forensics, it is necessary to reduce the process to its most basic element(s). In our case it is really all about digital evidence management and handling. If we assume that the IR process is fairly well understood and make an even larger assumption that the IR process is reasonably implemented and supported across the organization (i.e., enterprisewide), then the focus needs to be on the digital evidence.

Before moving on to a more detailed discussion of digital evidence management and handling, let us quickly discuss what digital evidence really is and place it within the context of the business environment. So what is really meant by the term digital evidence? One would think that defining digital evidence would be fairly straightforward, yet here again there has been some debate. Rather than getting caught up in semantics, let us turn to the physical domain and criminalistics, which has profited from its history of case law. Saferstein[7] defines physical evidence as follows:

> Physical objects that establish that a crime has been committed, can provide a link between a crime and its victim, or can provide a link between a crime and the perpetrator. (p. 34)

Using this well-established and accepted definition as a foundation, Carrier and Spafford (2003)[8] define digital evidence as follows:

> Digital data that establish that a crime has been committed, can provide a link between a crime and its victim, or can provide a link between a crime and the perpetrator (p. 6).

Within a business environment the digital evidence can encompass the actual data itself, contraband images, rootkits, log files, e-mails, etc. It is obvious that to list all possible examples or sources of digital evidence would be extremely time consuming. However, one of the most common sources or types of digital evidence is based on the concept of records.[3] As a quick aside, businesses now produce more electronic records than paper records. Records in our context can be subclassified into 1) computer stored, 2) computer generated, and 3) computer generated and stored in Ghosh.[9]

1. Computer stored pertains to such items as documents, e-mails, chat logs, and other "records" that

capture or record what has been created by a person. Here the technology is not an active entity in the creation of the content but is merely a passive receptacle.

2. Computer generated refers to records created without human intervention (non-human generated). These records rely on an automated process (this category is important when addressing the business exception to the hearsay problem). Examples here include output from computer programs, log files, event logs, and transaction records.

3. Computer generated and stored covers records that combine automated process and program outputs with human-generated input. Spreadsheets that contain calculations and formulas (computer) and manually entered data (human) are a good example.

EVIDENCE MANAGEMENT AND HANDLING

Regardless of whether the evidence is record based or not, there are some special considerations that one must be aware of when dealing with digital-based evidence. One of the most important considerations is the legal authority to actually collect the evidence. A number of countries are struggling with the balance between protecting the privacy of the individual, while at the same time allowing private organization and government entities to conduct investigations. Cyberspace has drastically changed the notion of what constitutes a reasonable expectation of privacy (REP); when does one's private space overlap with the public domain?

Reasonable Expectation of Privacy

The concept of REP is fundamental to most countries when defining what is an acceptable or unacceptable search and seizure of information/evidence. Businesses are not immune from these issues, as several jurisdictions have codified rules relating to the monitoring of employees and their activities, even when these individuals are using the technology belonging to the business. Investigators must be extremely careful to ensure that they both have a policy-based authority to take action and are legally allowed to. Corporate counsel should be consulted before taking any action. As a rule of thumb it is usually not a good idea to run afoul of the law when conducting an investigation! Even the most noble of intentions is not an excuse here and places the organization in the uncomfortable position of being open to criminal or civil redress.

Volatility

Digital evidence is very fragile (volatile) and in some cases has a very short life span [e.g., data in cache memory and random-access memory (RAM)]. Digital evidence can easily be modified or overwritten either as part of the normal system operation or during the identification and collection phase. Care must be taken to ensure that the evidence is handled in such a manner that any modifications are avoided or at least minimized. In the event that modifications occur (e.g., running programs for live memory analysis), detailed documentation must be made to explain the changes in the state of the scene or the evidence from its original state (state at which it was found by the investigator) and what impact this might have on evidence.[2,4,10]

Volume and Commingling

Given the sheer volume of data these days it should come as no surprise that often the data we are interested in (evidence) is commingled with other data that is of no evidentiary value or, in some cases, mixed in with information that is protected (e.g., lawyer–client and trade secret). Most desktop workstations these days have hard drives in excess of 300 GB and some are now being bundled with 1 terabyte (TB) of storage capacity. Business-class server farms routinely exceed 1 TB of data spread across several drives that may or may not reside in the same geographical location (e.g., grid computing). It is vital that an investigator be sensitive to potential commingling and be aware that it is functionally infeasible to expect to search every possible sector of storage for potential evidence. In response to these issues several jurisdictions have defined specific criteria for determining the scope of "discovery" and usually require a detailed investigative plan to ensure that the investigations are conducted in an efficient and effective manner. In an IR situation in which the authority to search is based on the ownership of the technology, commingling and volume of data are no less of a problem.

Integrity

Maintaining and demonstrating the integrity of the digital evidence is one of the integral in the consideration of admissibility of the evidence. Although the ultimate decision of what is admissible and what will be suppressed is up to a judge, precedent has provided guidance on the criteria that provide for the best chance of the evidence being admissible. The main method for demonstrating or proving that the evidence is an exact copy of the original, in the case of creating forensic copies, or that the data/evidence has not been altered from the original time of collection is through hash functions. These hash functions create a digital fingerprint of the data (128 bits in the case of MD5). The hash totals are extremely sensitive to bitwise changes. Most courts have accepted that if the hash totals match, the data has sufficient integrity.

Chain of Custody

The second most important consideration for evidence in general is the chain of custody. Simply put, the chain of custody deals with the who, what, when, where, and how of the collected evidence over its entire life span, from identification and collection to final disposition. If any part of the chain is broken or is doubtful, the evidence in question may be suppressed. At the very least a break in the chain of custody creates doubt in the minds of a judge, jury, arbitrator, etc., which can have serious ramifications if the evidence or its integrity is disputed.

Digital Evidence Life Cycle

Digital evidence management has a life cycle of its own. This life cycle starts with the initial design of systems to capture evidence and ends with determining the evidentiary "weight" of the data.[9] In between we have the production of records, the collection of evidence, the analysis and examination of the evidence, and the report or presentation.[9] This model highlights a key component for integrating computer forensics with IR, "design evidence." Design for evidence literally means that those individuals developing and designing systems and applications must understand digital evidence, its business life cycle, and the process model. Here again digital evidence management and handling, like IR, should be part of the system and software development life cycle. Systems across the enterprise must be forensically aware or, as Rowlingson[1] termed it, have forensic readiness. History has shown us that trying to retrofit something onto an already in production system or process is costly and usually ineffective.

FORENSIC READINESS

As was mentioned earlier, the forensic process needs to be conducted in parallel with any IR actions. To facilitate this, the typical approach of being reactive needs to be modified. Organizations need to be proactive and develop and implement policies, guidelines, and procedures that clearly articulate how the two processes will interact and who will be responsible for overseeing the combined approach and clearly define the so-called rules of engagement.[1,6] Waiting until one is engaged in the chaos of dealing with an incident is not a good time to start trying to institute this combined model or create policies, etc., literally on the fly; this ad hoc approach is doomed to failure for obvious reasons (numerous organizations bear witness to this fact).

Although it is beyond the scope of this entry to go into great detail as to how to prepare properly, it is necessary to at least touch on the higher-level concepts that must be considered. Apart from having policies and procedures in place as the National Institute of Standards and Technology (NIST)[6] recommends, it is actually necessary to have personnel trained in cyber-forensics. Remember, the skill sets for cyber-forensics are similar to, yet different from, IR skills. It is acceptable to have individuals cross-trained, but do not assume someone with IR training can perform an acceptable cyber-forensics investigation and vice versa. The cyber-forensics training, education, and

ongoing skill development will have costs associated with them. But, just as with the IR teams, these costs are marginal compared to the cost of properly dealing with an incident.

An excellent primer on considerations for implementing forensic readiness into the IR process is the NIST-SP800/86 Guideline.[6] In a nutshell the guideline recommends that organizations:

- Have a capability to perform cyber-forensics
- Determine a priori who is responsible for cyber-forensics
- Have incident handling teams with robust forensics capabilities
- Have many teams that can participate in forensics
- Have forensic considerations clearly addressed in policies, and
- Create and maintain guidelines and procedures for performing forensic tasks

Rowlingson[1] also provides a framework for implementing a "forensic readiness program" that is more focused on the private sector and corporate entities. The ten tasks he lists are similar to the recommendations by NIST but predate the formal publication of the NIST document:

- Define the business scenarios that require digital evidence.
- Identify available sources and different types of potential evidence.
- Determine the evidence collection requirement.
- Establish a capability for securely gathering legally admissible evidence to meet the requirement.
- Establish a policy for secure storage and handling of potential evidence.
- Ensure monitoring is targeted to detect and deter major incidents.
- Specify circumstances in which escalation to a full formal investigation (which may use the digital evidence) should be launched.
- Train staff in incident awareness, so that all those involved understand their role in the digital evidence process and the legal sensitivies of evidence.
- Document an evidence-based case describing the incident and its impact.
- Ensure legal review to facilitate action in response to the incident.

Although policy and procedures are important to ensure that IR and the management and handling of digital evidence interact properly, there are also some technical considerations to forensic readiness.[1,2,4,6] These considerations build on the technical capacity to collect meaningful and trustworthy digital evidence. Log and event files are probably the most common sources of information and evidence. But, if the system or network has been completely compromised, then how do we trust these sources of information? If proper care is not taken, then the data collected or the record is not trustworthy enough to be used as evidence, even if it can be trusted to help recover systems and resume business operations.

Given that there has not been a considerable amount of applied testing or implementation of forensic-ready technology at the enterprise network level, it is prudent to discuss this only at the research level. As NIST and Rowlingson[1] have indicated, the actual design and development of this technology stem from a thorough understanding of IR requirements and sound digital evidence or forensic practices. The current research in the area of forensic readiness of enterprise systems shows promise in several general areas:

- Kernel-level forensic capacity
- Distributed authenticated logging
- Digitally signed and encrypted logs
- Automated live forensic imaging of all affected systems

Hooking into the actual kernel level of an operating system to obtain valid and reliable information on what is being executed and by which process is extremely important. Those working in antivirus research have recognized the need to operate at the kernel level as opposed to any of the higher layers of abstraction; the same holds for obtaining information to be used as evidence.

Logs are a vital and rich source of information and potential evidence as to what transpired and the approximate timeline of events. However, we need to be able to trust the logs from these systems. This can lead to a conundrum: how do we trust logs from systems that we assume have been compromised and thus are now untrustworthy? A possible solution is to distribute the appropriate security and event logs to other systems not part of the primary network. These systems would require proper authentication not tied to any information that may be present on the potentially compromised systems. Although not foolproof, distributed authenticated logging would definitely increase the cost of the attack to the attacker and allow for greater trust of these logs.

Tied to the notion of distributed and authenticated logs is the integrity of the logs themselves. Even if we can show that the logs are trustworthy we need to demonstrate not only that they are a true and accurate recording of the events at the time of recording, but also that they have not been altered at any time from their creation to their presentation or use as evidence in a legal proceeding. A process that automatically signs the logs with a hash total that is stored in a trusted database and then encrypts the logs that are then stored in an authenticated and distributed manner would be beneficial. One could argue that the database hash totals could be altered and thus they must be signed, etc., until we collapse under the weight of the infinite loop of signing the signer. Fortunately, the courts have recognized that at some point it is necessary to trust a person unless evidence exists to the contrary. Thus, unless proved otherwise, the database administrator could testify that nothing was altered.

The ability to collect and analyze live systems and running memory is becoming increasingly more important. Large enterprise systems cannot be taken offline or shut down during the investigative process for business or technical reasons. Likewise, shutting down a system with 1–16 GB of RAM results in the loss of a great deal of potential evidence. However, how to collect the evidence with a live system in a forensically sound matter is difficult. To perform the collection one must load code or execute an operation on the suspected system, thus changing the state of the system and potentially overwriting evidence that may have been in memory. This is not a comfortable situation considering that forensics is concerned about the admissibility of any derived evidence. The ability to analyze the content of memory, etc., once collected is beyond the scope of this discussion but suffice to say it is rather difficult. The reality is that live system and memory collection and analysis will soon surpass the current approach of dealing with a powered-off (in a forensically sound manner, it is hoped) or "dead" analysis.

SUMMARY

The business environment is a seemingly constantly changing landscape. The demands placed on information security professionals is also changing to meet the new demands of business and technology. The ability to conduct effective and proper investigations is now a standard requirement for most organizations. This requirement has arisen due to various forces such as regulatory compliance, requests for discovery that include ESI, and the almost ubiquitous use of technology by businesses in general.

We are in a similar position today with cyber-forensics (digital evidence management and handling) that we were in about 5 years ago with IR. Organizations today are struggling with implementing digital forensic capabilities into their enterprise-level response processes and many are taking shortcuts and liberties with the management and handling of digital evidence. This is an extremely slippery slope that has some very serious and tangible consequences to businesses. Dealing with digital evidence occurs within the context of a forensic event and by its very nature carries the requirements and obligations related to the admissibility of evidence into a legal or quasi-legal arena. Criminal and civil liability considerations must be taken into account; this illustrates the fact that although cyber-forensics and IR are related processes they are not identical and must be treated as such.

Digital evidence has its unique characteristics and considerations that traditional physical evidence does not necessarily have, yet at the same time digital evidence resides in physical space. It is, therefore, important to understand the life cycle of digital evidence, its uniqueness, and where digital evidence management and handling fit into the IR process. IR and digital evidence management and handling are not mutually exclusive processes. Both models have considerable overlap and in some cases are mutually dependent upon each other. The key to combining these two investigative models or tools successfully is prior planning, such as developing policies, guidelines, and procedures that address both. IR and cyber-forensics teams as well as managers need to be properly cross-trained for everyone involved to understand the dependencies that each process has and the eff ect, if any, that certain actions may have on the other's primary goal.

Management needs to abandon the outdated notion that dealing with digital evidence will slow down or impair the time of recovery. With increased public and government scrutiny, speedy business resumption must be tempered with the proper mix of patience and strategic thinking. Knee-jerk reactions to incidents are no longer appropriate and are actually more costly in the long run. It seems plausible that attacks against our enterprise IT infrastructures from both external and internal sources will continue to grow before any type of plateau occurs. Thus, we must use and adapt security controls and tools to aid us in our eff ort to protect our systems and our information. The combining of process models and tools such as IR and digital evidence management and handling is a prime example of the synergistic activities that must continue if we are to deal eff ectively with the risk that we face today and will face tomorrow.

REFERENCES

1. Rowlingson, R. A ten step process for forensic readiness. International Journal of Digital Evidence **2004**, *2* (3).
2. Rogers, M. Law, regulations, investigations and compliance. In H. Tipton and K. Henry (Eds.). *Official (ISC)*^{2} *Guide to CISSP CBK* (pp. 683–718); 2007, Auerbach: Boca Raton, FL.
3. Schultz, E.; Shumway, R. *Incident Response: A Strategic Guide to Handling System and Network Security Breaches*; 2002, New Riders: Indianapolis, IN.
4. Mandia, K.; Prosise, C. *Incident Response: Investigating Computer Crime*; McGraw-Hill: New York, 2001.
5. Taylor, R.; Caeti, T.; Loper, D. K.; Fritsch, E.; Leiderbach, J. *Digital Crime and Digital Terrorism*; 2006, Pearson Prentice Hall: Upper Saddle River, NJ.
6. Kent, K.; Chevalier, S.; Grance, T.; Dang, H. *NIST SP800-86: Guide to Integrating Forensic Techniques into Incident Response*; McGraw-Hill: New York, 2006; 48–54, http://csrc.nist.gov/publications/nistpubs/800-86/SP800-86.pdf (accessed January 2007).
7. Saferstein, R. *Criminalistics: An Introduction to Forensic Science*; 2004, Pearson Education: Upper Saddle River, NJ.
8. Carrier, B.; Spafford, E. Getting physical with the digital investigation process. International Journal of Digital Evidence **2003**, *2* (2).
9. Ghosh, A. Paper presented at the APEC Telecommunications and Information Working Group: 29th Meeting. *Guidelines for the Management of IT Evidence*. 2004, http://unpan1.un.org/intradoc/groups/public/documents/APCITY/UNPAN016411.pdf (accessed November 2006).
10. Casey, E. Investigating sophisticated security breaches. Communications of the ACM **2006**, *49* (2), 48–54.

Incident Response: Exercises

Ken M. Shaurette, CISSP, CISA, CISM, IAM
Engagement Manager, Technology Risk Manager Services, Jefferson Wells, Inc., Madison, Wisconsin, U.S.A.

Thomas J. Schleppenbach
Senior Information Security Advisor and Security Solutions and Product Manager, Inacom Information Systems, Madison, Wisconsin, U.S.A.

Abstract
Several layers of defense are not always adequate regardless of how technically advanced or how cost effective they may be. A plan or procedure defined in advance with proper testing that can be quickly put into motion might be the last defense to protect the organization's assets. Any organization that does business using the Internet or private wide-area communications networks should have a security incident response program set up before an incident occurs. Having just access control, monitoring, and intrusion detection or prevention are not enough.

It was a quiet clear morning at about 2:26 A.M. I was sleeping soundly when I felt something on my leg. Whatever it was it was smaller than Holly, our cat, but bigger than a bug or a mouse. I quickly rolled over and, taking a swipe with my hand, knocked it off the bed. Without my glasses I could barely see anything, but I saw something run into the master bathroom. I thought to myself, "That sure looked like a small bunny rabbit."

I got up a bit apprehensive, put on my slippers, and found my glasses so I could focus better. Slowly I walked to the bathroom and, sure enough, there it was; something about the size of a softball, all brown and furry, crouching by the toilet. I had not turned the lights on, so it was still dark and hard to see. I stepped back quickly and closed the bathroom door. Gotcha. I had stopped the animal's activity by confining it to the master bathroom. Now what was I going to do? I walked over to the bed and tapped my wife on the shoulder. "What the heck is going on?" she asked, and I said, "I think there is a dangerous animal in our bathroom, it could be a rabbit." She said, "You're just having a bad dream, go back to sleep." I said, "No I can't, I saw it and felt it on my leg. I knocked it off and now I have it confined to the bathroom. I think it's a rabbit!" She said, "You've been stressed out lately, you're just having a dream, go back to bed." I said, "I don't think so; there is a rabbit in our bathroom." She followed with, "Are you sure? What are we going to do? We should call the Department of Natural Resources!" I said, "No, that won't work; the DNR isn't going to do anything at 2:30 in the morning." Suddenly, as quickly as she had doubted me, she asked, "Can we keep it?" I responded, "No, this is a wild rabbit; we need to get it out of here and figure out how it got in."

What was I to do? That thing could make a terrible mess in the bathroom, I thought, remembering that the kids had butterfly nets downstairs and that I had a pair of old leather gloves down on the counter in the kitchen that I had just used that afternoon. I gathered up my makeshift antirabbit tools and went back upstairs to the bathroom. I went in the bathroom and blocked the escape route by shutting the door behind me. I was now prepared to do battle. I could see it crouching motionless behind the toilet. I quickly determined that if I put the butterfly net on one side of the toilet, I could use the small bathroom garbage can to encourage the little beast to go toward the other side. I swiftly put my counter attack in motion. My hasty plan had worked; the critter ran out from under the toilet right into the net. I pounced on it, quickly grabbing the netting to trap a small rabbit—yes a bunny rabbit—in the net. I picked it up and carried it outside. Shortly, the bunny was released back into the wild.

As I put the battle tools away and walked back to the bedroom, I passed my fearless dog, a yellow lab, sleeping peacefully at the top of the stairs. I patted him and said, "Thanks a lot, where were you? That thing must have hopped right past your nose. Man's best friend indeed!" I walked back into the master bedroom and there was Holly, our fearless cat, rolled up in a cozy little ball in the corner. I thought to myself, "What about you? You didn't do your job either; you are supposed to protect me from undesirable events like what just happened." I got nothing from her but a little meow scolding me for the disturbance.

So now I am at work, a little bit tired from the whole experience and thinking, how did that rabbit get into our house? What measures can I take to better manage the risk

Encyclopedia of Information Assurance DOI: 10.1081/E-EIA-120046843
Copyright © 2011 by Taylor & Francis. All rights reserved.

Incident –
Info Classification

of losing another night's sleep in the future? Why did the protection measures—the door, the dog, the cat—not stop the event from occurring? Thank goodness I woke up and was able to put my makeshift response plan into effect.

INFORMATION SECURITY: LAYERED SECURITY

By now you have to be wondering what this story about a little bunny has to do with information security. This entire event brings to mind issues about intrusion detection, incident response procedures, testing, and overall security infrastructure as well as protecting evidence. It is really a great analogy covering several of these aspects. So we will evaluate the incident for comparisons to information security.

Start by asking a few basic questions such as: How secure is your perimeter? Has it been tested for vulnerabilities to undesirable entry? Are you prepared for a security incident? Are you prepared to respond?

We will respond to each question by comparing them to a typical environment.

How Secure Is Your Perimeter?

Is your firewall like the door of the house that let the bunny slip though? Was it just a small hole that allowed undesirable access to the internal environment? It did not take a very large hole to let the bunny into the house. I consciously opened the small porthole so I did not have to keep getting up to let the pets in or out. Does that sound familiar? "We just need one port open in order for this application to work."

Has It Been Tested for Vulnerabilities to Undesirable Entry?

I made sure that both my cat and dog were able to come and go using the small hole that I had opened. I did not consider what other, less-desirable creatures might take advantage of this opportunity. If I had only configured the hole a little differently, it could have kept out many of the other undesirables, including the bunny, and still have been functional for my pets to use.

Are You Prepared for a Security Incident? Are You Prepared to Respond?

I was not prepared. Who would have imagined a little bunny wanting to get into the house? There is nothing inside my house wild animals would want, why should I be concerned? Does your corporation have information someone might see as valuable, or perhaps a network that someone, like the bunny, might just be curious to check out? I was totally unprepared and did not expect the events

that occurred. How many times do you hear from users that they do not have access to anything that anyone else would want? I was on my last line of defense and just lucky to have the tools available to quarantine as well as to capture and remove the unwanted visitor.

Are you ready with the necessary tools to stop an intruder? Do you have a policy against normal users running hacker-type tools inside your environment? Does the policy allow for administrators to access similar tools to identify vulnerabilities and track incidents? After you stop an intruder, can you capture the necessary evidence to track any damage that may have been done? Is there an incident response plan in place that would have clearly instructed you on who to call and what to do to protect the evidence of an intrusion? Does your organization plan to prosecute for damages? Does a process exist to ensure that the evidence does not get damaged or tampered with and that a proper chain of custody is in place so the evidence retains its forensic quality and will hold up in court?

This entry will not attempt to answer all of these questions, but it should leave you with some ideas, points to ponder, and actions to consider.

An incident could be something as simple as an attacker (the bunny) spreading (hopping around the bedroom) the latest virus or worm ("rabbit raisins," poop, all over the room), or a more serious incident like using your e-mail server to send spam to other companies (the bunny biting one of your children) or maybe even penetrating through the external security architecture, the firewall (exterior doors), and getting inside the organization to disrupt services or steal intellectual property and confidential information (eating the dog and cat food or chewing on furniture).

Information security is all about defense-in-depth, layering protection so that the valuable assets of the organization are properly protected. In the bunny story I was essentially the last line of defense to protect my family and property from this rogue rabbit that had penetrated my exterior defenses.

What is the first thing you would do if you received a page from your Incident Response System or server system log paging software at 2:26 A.M. alerting you to the potential of a breach of external security?

On the other hand, perhaps the intrusion detection system generates so many alerts that system and network administrators have become numb to them and the messages are just ignored until the next day? Proper configuration of an intrusion detection solution so that it only sends message alerts for events that are considered issues is critical. Numerous alerts, such as every time the network is being "pinged," will cause numbness, resulting in a technician ignoring alerts and potentially missing the real thing.

Just having intrusion detection is inadequate protection. Without an incident response plan to react to the intrusion, just logging the event is not very effective. It is very

Table 1 Intrusion detection: Incident response questions.

- What actions are to be taken to identify that this is in fact an unwanted attacker who has penetrated the organization?
- Is there a call list for specific incidents?
- Can an automated action be taken to react to the alert, such as closing a port, or shutting down a service?
- Is it possible to identify the type of attack being used from the events logged and the intrusion detection information? (Refer to Table 2 for different types of attacks.)
- Would it be possible to determine where the attack is coming from or where it originated?
- Is this an organized attack against your organization and similar organizations in the same industry?
- What might an attacker want that the organization has, or what might be lost: reputation, public confidence, integrity, credibility?
- Is it possible to identify when the incident occurred along with all previous attempts that may or may not have failed?
- If there is real damage, would it be possible to get sufficient evidence to show damage, or evidence that can stand up to a court's scrutiny and meet forensic-level quality?

important to identify the steps to take beyond simply preparing for a long night (or day) by brewing another pot of strong coffee or getting a couple more liters of Code Red.

Most operating environments and network devices already produce volumes of logged activity. The availability of this data causes a need for answers to several more questions (refer to Table 1). Finding answers to the questions as outlined will help you select and configure effective intrusion detection as well as plan an organization's incident response system.

Preparing for an incident by planning and building the entire security program is essential. The security program becomes that defense-in-depth or layering of protection. Planning for security as well as selecting and testing intrusion detection and incident response is outlined in the remainder of this entry.

WHAT IS AN INFORMATION SECURITY OPERATIONS PLAN?

Every organization should have an Information Security Operations Plan (ISOP) as the starting point for layers of security. The plan establishes the components in an organization's security program. It ensures that an organization does not place too much emphasis on technology and not enough on people and process. It prioritizes the security activities that will be focused on during each year, helps set budget, and provides a status reports to management on the

state of all security activities. The plan should include functional areas defined by industry standards such as ISO17799. Before framing an incident response system, consider the components of an Information Security Operations Plan. The components of an effective security plan include:

- *Baseline*: This establishes where the company is at present. It is a high-level position statement of where security is at this point in time. It becomes an annual review to understand the current status of information security efforts in the organization. Each year it establishes what has been completed in the plan, areas of change, and new areas that have been added during the year.
- *Policies, Standards, and Procedures*: Policies, standards, and procedures are continuously changing. Information Security Policy provides the roadmap by which an organization identifies security philosophy and establishes the importance of security in the organization. Policy is the roadmap that defines appropriate handling of information in the business environment and sets the ground rules for building the information security architecture and technology. It helps determine the requirements for information security by setting expectations and requires management commitment and sign-off at the highest levels.
- *Architecture and Processes*: Designing security into the creation, selection, approval, and roll out of all technologies is vital. Security must be an integral part of building the data processing environment. Including information security early in the process of application and system development and selection will ensure that security issues can be addressed and that alternatives have sufficient lead time to be implemented within business deadlines. Secure architectures and the processes to support them are crucial to a secure environment.
- *Awareness and Training*: Every computer user in the organization must be made aware of company policy. An effective security program requires that everyone understands their personal responsibilities to protect the corporate information assets to help minimize organization liability.
- *Technologies and Products*: Technology is an important component of the security program. Although people and process make up potentially 70% of the security structure, technology alone accounts for probably 30% of the requirements to protect an organization. Technologies can range from simple system monitoring tools and access controls such as passwords and multiple factor authentication systems to virtual private networks (VPN) and data encryption or public key infrastructure (PKI) systems. Often, third-party

vendor products are required to support and monitor the operating environment.

- *Assessment and Monitoring*: To meet the needs and expectations of customers, auditors, and various levels of management, appropriate information must be collected so that reports can be created and distributed. Perimeter connections to the network and host system logs must also be monitored for unauthorized activities.
- *Compliance*: The mission of information security is to minimize security risks while maintaining the least possible impact on cost and schedules. To meet both company and customer expectations for information security, it is necessary to implement a process of continuous feedback so that business units can provide input to the improvement of information security planning.

The ISOP will frame out the organization's security program. The incident response program and procedures would be included as a component or subset of the overall information security program. In the next few paragraphs, we focus on incident response and preparedness.

WHAT ARE THE COMPONENTS OF AN INCIDENT RESPONSE PROGRAM?

An incident response program should include:

- Forming an incident response team
- Identifying a main contact (this must be a decision maker)
- Defining the monitoring or intrusion detection strategy
- Establishing an incident response flow
- Developing a set of basic required actions based on incident
- Preparing for recovery (business continuance)
- Knowing how and when to report an incident

There are several best-practice guidelines that are worth following, many of which can be found in books such as *Critical Incident Management* by Alan B. Sterneckert (Auerbach Publications, 2004).

As organizations develop their incident response program and associated procedures, they must take into consideration the specifics and details of their own unique networking and operating environment that only a person familiar with the inside workings of the organization would have. An important aspect in establishing intrusion detection and incident response is gaining an understanding of some of the typical attacker intrusion approaches.

ATTACK APPROACHES

To better understand intrusion activity and the process of identifying undesirable events, it is important to look at hacking approaches. Attacks can be separated into the following categories:[1]

- *Bomb*: This is a general synonym for crash, normally consisting of software or operating system failures.
- *Buffer Overflow*: This happens when more data is put into a buffer or holding area than the buffer can handle. It can be a result when there is a mismatch between processing rates of the producing and consuming processes. This can result in system crashes or the creation of a backdoor leading to system access.
- *Demon Dialer*: One name for a program that repeatedly calls the same telephone number is a demon dialer. This can be benign and legitimate for access to an authorized network or malicious when used as a denial-of-service attack.
- *Derf*: This is the name given to the act of exploiting a terminal which someone else has absentmindedly left logged on.
- *DNS (Domain Name Service) Spoofing*: The process of assuming the DNS name of another system by either corrupting the name service cache of a victim system or by compromising a domain name server to obtain a valid domain is called "spoofing."
- *Ethernet Sniffing*: This refers to the action of listening for packets or datagrams with software on the network looking at the Ethernet interface for packets that interest the user. Because Ethernet sends data by broadcasting all packets to all machines connected to the local network, it is trivial to receive packets that were intended for other machines. Ethernet interfaces support a feature commonly called "promiscuous mode," in which the interface listens to network traffic "promiscuously." That is, instead of dropping all packets that do not have the machine's Ethernet address in them, the interface processes all of the packets that it receives. When the software sees a packet that fits certain criteria, it logs it to a file. The most common criteria for an interesting packet are ones that contain words like log-in or password.
- *Fork Bomb*: Also known as Logic Bomb. Code that can be written in one line of code on any UNIX system; used to recursively spawn copies of itself; "explodes," eventually eating all the process table entries and effectively locks up the system.
- *IP Splicing/Hijacking*: The action caused when an active, established session is intercepted and co-opted by an unauthorized user. IP splicing attacks can occur after an authentication has been made, permitting the attacker to assume the role of an already authorized user. Primary protections against IP splicing rely on encryption at the session or network layer.

Incident –
Info Classification

- *IP Spoofing*: This type of attack occurs when the attacker causes one system to impersonate another system by using the system's IP network address without proper authorization. Essentially the attacker impersonates a different address than is normally assigned to him.

- *Keystroke Monitoring*: A specialized form of logging software, or a specially designed hardware device usually placed between the keyboard and the CPU. The device or software can record every keystroke a user makes. Properly used and secured, a legitimate use for this functionality is to capture forensicquality evidence for prosecuting illegal computer incidents. Improper use can result in an intruder capturing passwords and other personal information.

- *Leapfrog Attack*: The leapfrog attack results in the use of an illicitly obtained user ID and password gained from compromise of information on one host to compromise another host; for example, the act of TELNETing through one or more hosts to confuse attempts to trace the activity. This is a very common attacker activity used to make tracking undesirable activity back to the actual source more difficult.

- *Letter Bomb*: A piece of e-mail containing live data intended to do malicious things to the recipient's machine or terminal. In a UNIX environment, a letter bomb could try to get part of its contents interpreted as a shell command to the mailer. The results of this could range from silly to denial of service or complete system compromise.

- *Logic Bomb*: Also known as a Fork Bomb. A resident computer program which, when executed, checks for a particular condition or particular state of the system that, when satisfied, triggers the perpetration of an unauthorized act. These could be planted in the operating system software or coded into application code by an unscrupulous programmer.

- *Mail Bomb*: The mail sent to urge others to send massive amounts of e-mail to a single system or person, with the intent to crash the target recipient's system. Mail bombing is widely regarded as a serious offense. In more minor amounts or when not targeted to only one system, this is commonly known as spam.

- *Malicious Code*: This hardware, software, or firmware can be intentionally included in a system for an unauthorized purpose; e.g., a Trojan horse, virus, or any other code that might demonstrate nasty, undesirable behavior.

- *Mimicking*: This term is synonymous with impersonation, masquerading, or spoofing.

- *NAK Attack*: NAK stands for "negative acknowledgment." It is used as a penetration technique that capitalizes on a potential weakness in an operating system that does not handle asynchronous interrupts properly, and thus leaves the system in an unprotected state during such interrupts.

- *Network Weaving*: Another name for leapfrogging.

- *Phreaking*: This describes the art and science of cracking the telephone networks.

- *Replicator*: A program that copies itself is called a replicator program. Examples include a worm, a fork bomb, or virus. It is even claimed by some that UNIX and C are the symbiotic halves of an extremely successful replicator.

- *Retro-Virus*: A retro-virus is a form of malicious code that waits until all possible backup media are infected, so that it is not possible to restore the system to an uninfected state.

- *Rootkit*: The "rootkit" is a hacker security tool that provides that ability to capture passwords and message traffic to and from a computer. It is a collection of tools that allow a hacker to create a backdoor into a system, collect information on other systems on the network, mask the fact that the system is compromised, and much more. Rootkit is a classic example of Trojan horse software and is available for a wide range of operating systems. It gets its name from the name of the system administrative account in UNIX operating environments.

- *Smurfing*: Smurfing is an attack of a network by using spoofing of the source address to exploit Internet Protocol (IP) broadcast addressing and certain other aspects of Internet operation. Smurfing uses a program called Smurf and similar programs to cause the attacked part of a network to become inoperable, such as in a denial-of-service attack. The exploit of smurfing, as it has come to be known, takes advantage of certain known characteristics of the Internet Protocol (IP) and the Internet Control Message Protocol (ICMP). The ICMP is used by network nodes and their administrators to exchange information about the state of the network.

- *Spoofing*: Pretending to be someone else; also see mimicking. This is the deliberate inducement of a user or a resource to take an incorrect action. An attempt to gain access to a system by pretending to be an authorized user.

- *Subversion*: This intrusion act occurs when an intruder modifies the operation of the intrusion detector to force false-negatives to occur. The act can cause an intrusion detection system to send traffic that camouflages an attack.

- *SYN Flood*: The SYN flood attack sends TCP connection requests faster than a machine can process them. When the SYN queue is flooded, no new connection can be opened. The attacker creates a random source address for each packet. A SYN flood attack can be used as part of other attacks, such as disabling one side of a connection in TCP hijacking or by preventing authentication or logging between servers.

- *Terminal Hijacking*: This attack method allows an attacker, on a certain machine, to control any terminal session that is in progress. An attacker can send and receive terminal I/O while a user is on the terminal.

- *Trojan Horse*: The Trojan Horse can appear as an apparently useful and innocent program, but actually contains additional hidden code that allows the unauthorized collection, exploitation, falsification, or destruction of data. The actions can be activated by some other event such as on a specific date or when the deletion occurs of a specific account on a system.
- *Virus*: This is the common name assigned to many malicious programs that can "infect" other programs by modifying them to include a possibly evolved copy of itself.
- *Wardialer*: Made popular by the 1980s movie, *War Games,* this consists of a program that can dial a list or range of numbers and record those that answer with handshake tones, which might be entry points to computer or telecommunications systems. Handshake tones are "answer" tones given by a modem set to answer a request for connection.

Understanding the attack methods can be helpful in understanding why some features are important in selection of an intrusion detection system.

SELECTING INTRUSION DETECTION

Picking the proper intrusion detection (IDS) technology is an important step not to be taken lightly, and is not an easy task. An IDS should be easy to install and require minimal training, and should deploy in a "passive" or "parallel" mode, and not inline, which creates a potential bottleneck and failure point. To help with selection of an intrusion detection system, a capabilities matrix has been provided in Table 2.

Organizations must establish their internal requirements and priorities as they pertain to intrusion detection, to establish the components identified in Table 2 that are most important in a product.

Once the technology is chosen and deployed, just like a disaster recovery plan, it would be wise to periodically test it along with incident response plans.

INCIDENT RESPONSE EXERCISES

Incident response exercises are one method in helping reduce organizational risk and better prepare a company's staff to respond to intrusive behavior. Like war games, incident response exercises are designed to raise awareness to the security posture of an organization through the continuous testing of incident response procedures and network device and system configuration. The testing is followed by regular review

with experienced information security personnel and the organization's IS staff.

The goal is to raise security awareness with an organization's IS and management staff, and to verify and enforce proper and continual setup, configuration, and tuning of security and network systems while ensuring they are kept up to current patch levels.

The IS staff gets continuous exposure to real-world infiltration scenarios in a controlled environment, educating them to identify malicious behavior as well as having the organization's incident response procedures properly tested.

Incident response exercises generally work through continual footprinting of an organization's resources, and surprise infiltrations that are followed up with a meeting to discuss the "whats": what went right, what went wrong, and what could be done better?

If an organization is outsourcing the incident exercise service, the organization must be sure to check references and work with a credible company. Here are a few basic rules for selecting a security outsourcing vendor:

- Demand credentials and expertise, consider background checks
- Seek outside certifications
- Ensure vendor affiliations
- Talk to other customers and references
- Comparison shop
- Take small steps if unsure
- Know your escalation procedures
- Require standard inspections
- Know the rules with the vendor

MORAL OF THE STORY

We will go back to the story for a moment. The bunny entered a traditional, two-story house even though the doors were locked. It managed to get past the intrusion prevention system: a dog, which was deployed at the foot of the stairs that lead to the bedrooms. This is a dog that normally enjoys chasing small bunnies all over the backyard because they are invading his territory. The bunny climbed a flight of stairs, and found its way down the hall and into the master bedroom. It even managed to get past another line of defense, a very territorial house cat. The defense-in-depth failed in this case.

Doing a post mortem on the event, it would be necessary to consider the experience of a near-complete breach of security: getting past three layers of defense. Fortunately, the last defense—the owner—was able to react on the internal incident response procedure and take the appropriate actions to minimize damage and manage the risk. That action kept this attack from damaging property or causing terror for the inhabitants.

Table 2 Modern IDS capability comparison.

Modern IDS capability comparison	Product 1	Product 2	Product 3	Product 4
2.0 Detection				
2.1 Protocol anomaly detection				
2.2 DoS attack detection				
2.3 Network infrastructure attack detection				
2.4 Common application protocol detection				
2.5 Stateful signature detection				
2.6 Custom signature support				
2.7 Full protocol decode				
2.8 Evasion detection and resistance to IDS attack				
2.9 Full fragment reassembly				
2.10 Full multi-interface reassembly				
3.0 Analysis				
3.1 Third-party event integration				
3.2 Real-time event aggregation				
3.3 Real-time analysis				
3.4 Automated correlation and prioritization				
3.5 Cross-node event correlation				
3.6 Full packet capture				
3.7 Secure data store				
3.8 Duplicate suppression				
3.9 User tunable controls				
4.0 Response capabilities				
4.1 Automated policy-based response				
4.2 Alerting (SNMP, e-mail, console log)				
4.3 Session termination				
4.4 User-defined response actions				
4.5 Traffic recording and playback				
4.6 Remote threat tracing				
4.7 Peer network event notification				
4.8 Session blocking suggestions or integration				
5.0 Performance/Scalability				
5.1 Full 100 Mbps throughput (no packet loss)				
5.2 Full 1 Gbps throughput (no packet loss)				
5.3 Multiple 100 Mbps segment throughput (no packet loss)				
5.4 Handle 500,000 simultaneous TCP sessions				
5.5 Scales to hundreds of sensors				
5.6 Robust under edge conditions				
6.0 High availability				
6.1 Automatic failover and failback				
6.2 High-speed failover				
6.3 "Five nines" (99.999%) reliability				
6.4 Cost-effective high-availability deployment configurations				

(Continued)

**Incident –
Info Classification**

Table 2 Modern IDS capability comparison. *(Continued)*

Modern IDS capability comparison	Product 1	Product 2	Product 3	Product 4
7.0 Management				
7.1 Secure remote management				
7.2 Broad platform support for management				
7.3 Scalable information presentation				
7.4 Incident drill-down capability				
7.5 Additional reference data provided (CVE, BUGTRAQ, etc.)				
7.6 Cluster administration support				
7.7 Incident annotation/auditing				
8.0 Deployment				
8.1 Multiple interface support (Gigabit and Fast Ethernet)				
8.2 Sensor roaming in switched networks				
8.3 Easy to deploy and install				
8.4 Non-intrusive deployment (non-inline)				
8.5 VLAN-aware detection				
8.6 Minimal training requirements				
9.0 Reporting				
9.1 Integrated deep drill-down console reporting				
9.2 Web-based reporting				
9.3 SQL export				
10.0 Hardware requirements				
10.1 Multiple sensors per unit				
10.2 Multi-processor scalable				

The moral of the story is that several layers of defense are not always adequate regardless of how technically advanced or how cost effective they may be. A plan or procedure defined in advance with proper testing that can be quickly put into motion might be the last defense to protect the organization's assets. Any organization that does business using the Internet or private wide-area communications networks should have a security incident response program set up before an incident occurs. Having just access control, monitoring, and intrusion detection or prevention are not enough.

REFERENCE

1. Definitions come from the NSA's. *Glossary of Terms Used in Security and Intrusion Detection.*

Incident Response: Management

Alan B. Sterneckert, CISA, CISSP, CFE, CCCI
Owner and General Manager, Risk Management Associates, Salt Lake City, Utah, U.S.A.

Abstract

This entry discusses incident response management, which the author claims "is the most critical part of the enterprise risk management program." The entry discusses the importance of risk management and that it must be constantly reviewed to ensure that it is updated and able to do its job. The author recommends top-down risk management project planning and discusses key points to develop a comprehensive plan. The entry discusses the four key phases to developing a plan: assess the needs, plan, implement, and revise. The author further stresses the need to identify and categorize key assets within the company.

Incident response management is the most critical part of the enterprise risk management program. Frequently, organizations form asset protection strategies focused primarily on perceived rather than actual weaknesses, while failing to compare incident impact with continuing profitable operations. In the successful implementation of risk management programs, all possible contingencies must be considered, along with their impact on the enterprise and their chances of occurring.

By way of illustration, in the 1920s and 1930s, France spent millions of francs on the construction of the Maginot Line defenses, anticipating an invasion similar to the World War I German invasion. At that time, these fortifications were considered impregnable. During the 1940 German army invasion, they merely bypassed the Maginot Line, rendering these expensive fortifications ineffective. The Maginot planners failed to consider that invaders would take a route different than previous invasions, resulting in their defeat.

RISK MANAGEMENT PROJECT

Risk management is not a three-month project; it is not a project that, when completed, becomes shelved and never reviewed again. Rather, it is a continuous process requiring frequent review, testing, and revision. In the most basic terms, risk has two components: the probability of a harmful incident happening and the impact the incident will have on the enterprise.

TOP-DOWN RISK MANAGEMENT PROJECT PLANNING

Beginning at the end is a description of top-down planning. Information technology (IT) professionals must envision project results at the highest level by asking, what are my deliverables? Information risk management deliverables are simply defined: confidentiality, integrity, and availability (CIA). CIA, and the whole risk management process, must be first considered in the framework of the organization's strategic business plans. A formula for success is to move the risk management program forward with a clear vision of the business deliverables and their effect on the organization's business plans.

The concept of risk management is relatively simple. Imagine that the organization's e-mail service is not functioning or that critical data has been destroyed, pilfered, or altered. How long would the organization survive? If network restoration is achieved, what was the business loss during the restoration period? It is a situation in which one hopes for the best but expects the worst. Even the best risk management plan deals with numerous *what-if* scenarios. What if a denial-of-service (DoS) attacks our network? Or what if an employee steals our customer list? What if a critical incident happens—who is responsible and authorized to activate the incident response team?

In the world of risk management, the most desirable condition is one in which risks are avoided. And if risks cannot be avoided, can their frequency be increased and can their harmful effects be mitigated?

RISK MANAGEMENT KEY POINTS

These are general key points in developing a comprehensive risk management plan:

- Document the impact of an extended outage on profitable business operations in the form of a business impact analysis. Business impact analysis measures the effects of threats, vulnerabilities, and the frequency of their occurrence, against the organization's assets.

Encyclopedia of Information Assurance DOI: 10.1081/E-EIA-120046871
Copyright © 2011 by Taylor & Francis. All rights reserved.

Incident –
Info Classification

- Remember that risk management only considers risks at a given moment. These risks change as the business environment changes, necessitating the constantly evolving role of risk management.
- Complete a gap analysis, resulting in the measured difference between perceived and actual weaknesses and their effects on key assets.

OVERALL PROJECT PLANNING

Incident response planning is no different than other planning structures. There are four basic key phases:

1. Assess needs for asset protection within the organization's business plan
2. Plan
3. Implement
4. Revise

In assessing needs, representatives of the affected departments should participate in the initial stage and should form the core of the project team. Additional experts can be added to the project team on an ad hoc basis. This is also a good time to install the steering committee that has overall responsibility for the direction and guidance of the project team. The steering committee acts as a buffer between the project team and the various departmental executives. The early stage is the time for hard and direct questions to be asked by the project team members in detailing the business environment, corporate culture, and the minimum organizational infrastructure required for continuing profitable operations.

It becomes important to decide the project's owners at the outset. Project ownership and accountability are based on two levels: one is the line manager who oversees the project team, and the other is the executive who handles project oversight. This executive–owner is a member of the steering committee and has departmental liaison responsibilities. Project scope, success metrics, work schedules, and other issues should be decided by the project team. Project team managers, acting in cooperation with the steering committee, should keep the project focused, staffed, and progressing.

Planning is best conducted in an atmosphere of change control. The project team's direction will become lost if formal change control procedures are not instituted and followed. Change controls decide what changes may be made to the plan, who may approve changes, why these changes are being made, and the effect of these changes. It is critical that change controls require approvals from more than one authority, and that these changes are made part of any future auditing procedure. Once changes are proposed, approved, and adopted, they must be documented and incorporated as part of the plan.

With planning completed, implementation begins. Implementations do not usually fail because of poor planning; rather, they fail due to lack of accountability and ownership. Initial testing is conducted as part of the implementation phase. During the implementation step, any necessary modifications must be based on test results. Specific testing activities should include defining the test approach, structuring the test, conducting the test, analyzing the test results, and defining success metrics with modifications as required. In an organizational setting, the testing process should be executed in a quarantine environment, where the test is not connected to the work platforms and the data used for the test is not actual data. During testing, criteria should be documented so performance can be measured and a determination made as to where the test succeeded or failed.

With the implementation and testing completed, the project moves toward final adjustments that are often tuned to the changing business environment. Remember to maintain change controls in this phase also. More than one engineer has been surprised to find two identical hosts offering the same services with different configurations.

ENTERPRISE RISK

Risk is the possibility of harm or loss. Risk analysis often describes the two greatest sources of risk as human causes and natural causes. Before a risk can be managed, consideration must be given to the symptom as well as the result. Any risk statement must include what is causing the risk and the expected harmful results of that risk.

KEY ASSETS

Key assets are those enterprise assets required to ensure that profitable operations continue after a critical incident. Define, prioritize, and classify the organization's key assets into four general areas: personnel, data, equipment, and physical facilities. Schedule, in the form of a table, the priority of the organization's key assets and their associated threats and vulnerabilities. This table will serve the purpose of identifying security requirements associated with different priority levels of assets.

In developing asset values, the asset cost is multiplied by the asset exposure factor, with the resulting product being the single loss expectancy. The asset value is the replacement value of a particular asset, while the exposure factor is the measure of asset loss resulting from a specific harmful event. Multiplying this single loss expectancy by the annualized rate of occurrence will result in the annualized loss expectancy. An example of this equation is as follows: assume the replacement value of a server facility, complete with building, equipment, data, and software, is $10 million. This facility is located in a geographic area prone to hurricanes that have struck three times in the past 10 years and resulted in total facility losses. Annualized expectancy is the loss of the facility, data, and equipment once every 3 years, or 33% annually.

Step two of our four-step process is a threat assessment. Threats are simply defined as things that can possibly bring harm upon assets. Threats should be ranked by type, the impact they have on the specific asset, and their probability of occurrence. Even the most effective risk management plan cannot eliminate every threat; but with careful deliberation, most threats can be avoided or their effects minimized.

Identify vulnerabilities (weaknesses) in the security of the enterprise's key assets. Vulnerable areas include physical access, network access, application access, data control, policy, accountability, regulatory and legal requirements, operations, audit controls, and training. Risk levels should be expressed as a comparison of assets to threats and vulnerabilities. Create a column in the table (Table 1) providing a relative metric for threat frequency. Once completed, this table provides a measurement of the level of exposure for a particular key asset.

Avoidance and mitigation steps are processes by which analyses are put into action. Having identified the organization's key assets, threats to these assets, and potential vulnerabilities, there should be a final analytical step detailing how the specific risk can be avoided. If risk avoidance is not possible, then can the chance of its occurrence be extended?

From the outset it is recommended to include auditors. Audits must be scheduled and auditors' workpapers amended, assuring compliance with laws, regulations, policies, procedures, and operational standards.

RISK MANAGEMENT BEST PRACTICES DEVELOPMENT

As part of risk management best practices, there are three principle objectives: avoiding risk, reducing the probability of risk, and reducing the impact of the risk.

Initiate and foster an organizational culture that names every employee as a risk manager. Employee acceptance of responsibility and accountability pays short- and long-term dividends. In some circumstances, the creation of this risk manager culture is more important than developing and issuing extensive policies and procedures.

In a general sense, there are four key best practice areas that should be addressed: organizational needs, risk acceptance, risk management, and risk avoidance.

Organizational needs determine the requirement for more risk study and more information in ascertaining the characteristics of risk before taking preventive or remedial action.

Risk acceptance is defined in these terms: if these risks occur, can the organization profitably survive without further action?

Risk management is defined as efforts to mitigate the impact of the risk should it occur.

Risk avoidance includes the steps taken to avoid the risk from happening.

RISK CONTROLS

Avoidance controls are proactive in nature and attempt to remove, or at least minimize, the risk of accidental and intentional intrusions. Examples of these controls include encryption, authentication, network security architecture, policies, procedures, standards, and network services interruption prevention.

Table 1 Measurement of the level of exposure.

Asset	Threat	Frequency	Vulnerability	Impact
Name and Replacement Value	Type	Annualized	Type and Ranking: High, Medium, Low	Ranking: High, Medium, Low

Incident – Info Classification

Assurance controls are actions, such as compliance auditing, employed to ensure the continuous effectiveness of existing controls. Examples of these controls include application security testing, standards testing, and network penetration testing.

Detection controls are tools, procedures, and techniques employed to ensure early detection, interception, containment, and response to unauthorized intrusions. Examples of these controls include intrusion detection systems (IDSs) and remotely managed security systems.

Recovery controls involve response-related steps in rapidly restoring secure services and investigating the circumstances surrounding information security breaches. Included are legal steps taken in the criminal, civil, and administrative arenas to recover damages and punish offenders. Examples of these recovery controls include business continuity planning, crisis management, recovery planning, formation of a critical incident response team, and forensic investigative plans.

CRITICAL INCIDENT RESPONSE TEAM

A critical incident response team (CIRT) is a group of professionals assembled to address network risks. A CIRT forms the critical core component of the enterprise's information risk management plan. Successful teams include management personnel having the authority to act; technical personnel having the knowledge to prevent and repair network damage; and communications experts having the skills to handle internal and external inquiries. They act as a resource and participate in all risk management phases. CIRT membership should be composed of particular job titles rather than specifically named individuals. The time for forming a CIRT, creating an incident response plan, notification criteria, collecting tools, training, and executive-level support is not the morning after a critical incident. Rather, the CIRT must be ready for deployment before an incident happens. Rapidly activating the CIRT can mean the difference between an outage costing an organization its livelihood or being a mere annoyance.

Organizational procedures must be in place before an incident so the CIRT can be effective when deployed. This point is essential, because organizations fail to address critical incidents even when solid backup and recovery plans are in place. The problem is usually found to be that no one was responsible to activate the CIRT.

The CIRT plan must have clearly defined goals and objectives integrated in the organization's risk management plan. CIRT's mission objectives are planning and preparation, detection, containment, recovery, and critique. As part of its pre-incident planning, the CIRT will need: information flowcharts, hardware inventory, software inventory, personnel directories, emergency response checklists, hardware and software tools, configuration control documentation, systems documentation, outside resource contacts, organization chart, and CIRT activation and response plans. For example, when arriving on the scene, the CIRT should be able to review its documentation ascertaining information flow and relevant critical personnel of the organization's employee healthcare benefits processing unit.

Considering the nature, culture, and size of the organization, an informed decision must be made about when to activate the CIRT. What is the extent of the critical incident before the CIRT is activated? Who is authorized to make this declaration? Is it necessary for the whole CIRT to respond? Included in the CIRT activation plan should be the selection of team members needed for different types or levels of incidents.

If circumstances are sensitive or if they involve classified materials, then the CIRT activation plan must include out-of-band (OOB) communications. OOB communications take place outside the regular communications channels. Instead, these OOB communication methods include encrypted telephone calls, encrypted e-mail not transmitted through the organization's network, digital signatures, etc. The purpose of OOB communications is to ensure nothing is communicated through routine business channels that would alert someone having normal access to any unusual activity.

INCIDENT RESPONSE STEPS

The goals of incident response must serve a variety of interests, balancing the organization's business concerns with those of individual rights, corporate security, and law enforcement officials. An incident response plan will address the following baseline items:

- Determine if an incident has occurred and the extent of the incident.
- Select which CIRT members should respond.
- Assume control of the incident and involve appropriate personnel, as conditions require.
- Report to management for the decision on how to proceed.
- Begin interviews.
- Contain the incident before it spreads.
- Collect as much accurate and timely information as possible.
- Preserve evidence.
- Protect the rights of clients, employees, and others, as established by law, regulations, and policies.
- Establish controls for the proper collection and handling of evidence.
- Initiate a chain of custody of evidence.
- Minimize business interruptions within the organization.
- Document all actions and results.
- Restore the system.
- Conduct a post-incident critique.
- Revise response as required.

Table 2 Immediate actions to be taken by administrators to contain an incident.

1. Extinguish power to the affected systems. This is a drastic but effective decision in preventing any further loss or damage.

2. Disconnect the affected equipment from the network. There should be redundant systems so users will have access to their critical services.

3. Disable specific services being exploited.

4. Take all appropriate steps to preserve activity and event logs.

5. Document all symptoms and actions by administrators.

6. Notify system managers. If authorized, notify the CIRT for response.

Pre-incident preparation is vital in approaching critical incidents. Contingency plans that are tested and revised will be invaluable in handling incidents where a few minutes can make the difference between disaster and a complete restoration of key services. Network administrators should be trained to detect critical incidents and contact appropriate managers so a decision can be made relative to CIRT deployment. Some of the critical details that administrators should note are the current date and time, nature of the incident, who first noticed the incident, the hardware and software involved, symptoms, and results.

Suspected incidents will usually be detected through several processes, including IDSs, system monitors, and fire-walls. Managers should decide whether the administrators should attempt to isolate the affected systems from the rest of the network. Trained, experienced administrators can usually perform these preliminary steps, thereby preventing damage from spreading (see Table 2).

At the time of the initial response by the CIRT, no time should be lost looking for laptops, software, or tools. They should arrive at the scene with their plan, tools, and equipment in hand. CIRT members will begin interviews immediately in an effort to determine the nature and extent of any damage. It is important that they document these interviews for later action or as evidence. The CIRT will obtain and preserve the most volatile evidence immediately. After an initial investigation, the CIRT will formulate the best response and obtain management approval to proceed with further investigation and restoration steps.

CRITICAL INCIDENT INVESTIGATION

The goals of law enforcement officers and private investigators are basically the same. Both types of investigators want to collect evidence and preserve it for analysis and presentation at a later date. Evidence is simply defined as something physical and testimonial, material to an act. It is incumbent upon the CIRT to establish liaison with the appropriate levels of law enforcement to determine the best means of evidence collection, preservation, and delivery. If there are circumstances where law enforcement officers are not going to be involved, then the CIRT members should consider the wisdom of either developing forensic analysis skills or contracting others to perform these functions. Evidence collection and analysis are critical because incorrect crime scene processing and analysis can render evidence useless. Skilled technicians with specialized knowledge, tools, and equipment should accomplish collecting, processing, and analyzing evidence. Frequently, investigators want to be present during evidence collection and interviews; consequently, CIRT members should establish liaison with law enforcement and private investigators to establish protocols well in advance of a critical incident.

Evidence may be voluntarily surrendered, obtained through the execution of a search warrant, through a court order or summons, or through subpoenas. It is a common practice for investigators to provide a receipt for evidence that has been delivered to them. This receipt documents the transfer of items from one party to another and supports the chain of custody. It is important to note that only law enforcement investigators use search warrants and subpoenas to obtain evidence. Once received, the investigator will usually physically mark the evidence for later identification. Marking evidence typically consists of the receiving investigators placing the date and their initials on the item. In the case of electronic media, the item will be subjected to special software applications, causing a unique one-way identifier to be created and written to the media, thereby identifying any subsequent changes in the media's contents.

Does the investigator have the right to seize the computer and examine its contents? In corporate environments this right may be granted by policy. The enterprise should have a policy stating the ownership of equipment, data, and systems. It is a usual practice that organizations have policies requiring employees to waive any right to privacy as a condition of their employment. If the organization has such policies, it is important that its legal and human resources officers are consulted before any seizure takes place.

Under current U.S. law and the Fourth Amendment to the U.S. Constitution, the government must provide a judge or magistrate with an affidavit detailing the facts and circumstances surrounding the alleged crime. Search warrants are two-part documents. The first part is the search warrant, which bears a statutory description of the alleged crime, a description of the place to be searched, and the items or persons to be seized. At the conclusion of the search warrant execution, a copy of this search warrant document must be deposited at the premises, regardless of whether it was occupied. Affidavits are the second part of the search warrant and are statements where the officer or agent, known as the *affiant*, swears to the truth of the matter. The law does not require the affiant to have first-hand knowledge of the statement's details, merely that the affiant has reliable knowledge. Search warrants are granted based upon the establishment of probable cause. It is important to note that the affidavit must stand on its own; all relevant information must be contained within its borders.

Questions surrounding search warrants are these: is it probable that a crime has been committed, and is it probable that fruits, instrumentalities, or persons connected to that crime are located at a given location now? Unless there are unusual circumstances, search warrants may only be executed in daylight hours from 6 a.m. to 10 p.m. If unusual circumstances exist, then these must be submitted to the court. Such circumstances include the possibility of extreme danger to the officers or the likelihood of evidence destruction. Search warrants must be announced, and authorities must declare their purpose. At the completion of the search warrant, the officers are required to deposit a copy of the search warrant and an inventory of the items seized at the searched premises. Under special circumstances, the search warrant will be *sealed* by the issuing court. This means the sworn statement is not public record until unsealed by the issuing court. If the affidavit is not sealed, then it is a public document and retrievable from the court's office. At the conclusion of the search warrant, a return is completed and accompanied by an inventory of the seized items. This search warrant return is part of the original search warrant document and reflects the date, by whom, and where it was executed. Along with the search warrant return, an inventory of seized items is filed with the court, where it is available for public review. Law enforcement and non-law enforcement personnel, depending upon the nature of the investigation, may obtain court orders and summons. These documents are based upon applications made to the court of jurisdiction and may result in orders demanding evidence production by the judge or magistrate. Similar to search warrants, court orders are usually two-part documents with an application stating the reason the judge should issue an order to a party to produce items or testimony. The second part is the actual court order document. Court orders state the name of the case, the items to be brought before the court, the date the items are to be brought before the court, the location of the court, the name of the presiding judge, and the seal of the court. Summonses are similar to court orders and vary from jurisdiction to jurisdiction. Subpoenas are generally categorized as one of two types: one resulting from a grand jury investigation, and the second resulting from a trial or other judicial proceeding. Both documents carry the weight of the court—meaning these documents are demands that, if ignored, can result in contempt charges filed against persons or other entities. Grand juries are tasked with hearing testimony and reviewing evidence, hence their subpoenas are based upon investigative need. Their members are selected from the local community, and they are impaneled for periods of several months. Items or persons may be subpoenaed before a grand jury for examination. It is possible for a motion to quash the subpoena to be filed, causing the court to schedule a hearing where the subpoena's merits are heard. Different than grand jury subpoenas, judicial subpoenas are issued for witnesses and

evidence to be presented at trial or other hearings. Testimony is obtained through interviews, depositions, and judicial examinations. Interviewing someone is a conversation directed toward specific events. Interviews may be recorded in audio or video form, or the investigator may take carefully written notes. In the latter case, the interviewer's notes are reduced to a report of the interview. This report serves as the best recollection of the investigator and is not generally considered a verbatim transcript of the interview.

Depositions are more formal examinations and are attended by attorneys, witnesses, and persons who create a formal record of the proceedings. Usually, depositions are part of civil and administrative proceedings; however, in unusual circumstances they may be part of a criminal proceeding. Attorneys ask questions of the witnesses, with the plaintiff and defense attempting to ask questions that will cause the witness to provide an explanation favorable to their side. Judicial examinations are made before a judge or magistrate judge, and the witnesses are sworn to tell the whole truth while the proceedings are recorded.

It is important to note that providing mischaracterizations, lies, or withholding information during interviews may be considered grounds for criminal prosecution. In a similar vein, the CIRT and others must be very careful interviewing potential subjects and collecting evidence. If interviews are conducted or evidence is collected through coercion, these actions could be considered as intimidating and may be considered for charges.

FORENSIC EXAMINATION

There are several schools of thought in completing the forensic examination of evidence. Regardless, one rule remains steadfast—no examination should be conducted on original media; and the media, constituting evidence, must remain unchanged. There are several ways to obtain copies of media. There are forensic examination suites designed to perform exact bit-by-bit duplication; and there are specific software utilities used in duplicating media and hardware-copying devices that are convenient, but these are generally limited to the size and characteristics of the disks they can clone. There are also utilities that are part of some operating platforms that can produce bit-by-bit media duplications. It is important to remember that all forensic examination processes must be documented in the form of an activity log and, in the case of some very sensitive matters, witnessed by more than one examiner.

Forensic examiners must ensure that their media is not contaminated with unwanted data; so many have a policy that, before any evidence is copied, media will be cleansed with software utilities or a degaussing device designed for such purposes. In this fashion, the examiner can testify that appropriate precautions were taken to prevent cross-contamination from other sources.

As in the case of all evidence-handling practices, a chain of custody is prepared. Chain of custody is merely a schedule of the evidence, names, titles, reason for possession, places, times, and dates. From the time of the evidence seizure, the chain of custody is recorded and a copy attached to the evidence. The chain of custody documentation is maintained regardless of how the evidence was seized or whether the evidence is going to be introduced in criminal, civil, or administrative proceedings.

A covert search is one targeting a specific console or system involving real-time monitoring, and it is usually conducted discreetly. In a practical example, an organization may suspect one of its employees of downloading inappropriate materials in violation of its use policy. After examining logs, an exact workstation cannot be identified. There are two ways to conduct a covert search after authorization is obtained. One method copies the suspected hard drive and replaces it with the copy, with the original considered as evidence. The second method duplicates the suspect's hard drive while it remains in the computer. The duplicate is considered evidence and is duplicated again for examination. In either method it is important to ascertain that the organization has the right to access the equipment and that the suspect does not have any reasonable expectation of privacy. This topic must be fully addressed by the legal and human resources departments.

After having seized the evidence, the examiner decides to either conduct an analysis on the premises or take the media to another location. The advantage of having the examination take place where the evidence is seized is obvious. If there is something discovered requiring action, it can be addressed immediately. However, if the examination takes place in the calm of a laboratory, with all the tools available, then the quality of the examination is at its highest.

The CIRT and other investigators must consider the situation of sensitive or classified information that is resident on media destined for a courtroom. Sometimes, this consideration dissuades some entities from reporting criminal acts to the authorities. However, there are steps that can be legally pursued to mitigate the exposure of proprietary or sensitive information to the public.

CRIMINAL, FORFEITURE, AND CIVIL PROCESSES

Criminal acts are considered contrary to publicly acceptable behavior and are punished by confinement, financial fines, supervised probation, and restitution. Felonies are considered major crimes and are usually punished by periods of confinement for more than 1 year and fines of more than $1000. In some jurisdictions, those convicted of felonies suffer permanent loss of personal rights. Misdemeanors are minor crimes punishable by fines of less than $1000 and confinement of less than 1 year.

Sentencing may include confinement, fines, or a period of probation. The length of sentence, fines, and victim restitution depends upon the value of the crime. If proprietary information is stolen and valued at millions of dollars, then the sentence will be longer with greater fines than for an act of Web page defacement. There are other factors that can lengthen sentencing. Was the defendant directing the criminal actions of others? Was the defendant committing a crime when he committed this crime? Has the defendant been previously convicted of other crimes? Was the defendant influencing or intimidating potential witnesses? There are also factors that can reduce a sentence. Has the defendant expressed remorse? Has the defendant made financial restitution to the victim? Has the defendant cooperated against other possible defendants? Under the laws of the United States, the length of sentence, the type of sentence, and fines are determined in a series of weighted numerical calculations and are codified in the Federal Sentencing Guidelines. At the time of sentencing, a report is usually prepared and delivered to the sentencing judge detailing the nature of the crime and the extent of the damage. It is at the judge's discretion whether to order financial restitution to the victim; however, in recent times, more and more judges are inclined to order financial restitution as part of sentencing (see Table 3).

Frequently, organizations ask if there are statutory requirements for reports of criminal activities. Under the criminal codes of the United States, Title 18, Section 4, it states: "Whoever, having knowledge of the actual commission of a felony cognizable by a court of the United States, conceals and does not as soon as possible make known the same to some judge or other person in civil or military

Table 3 Partial list of applicable federal criminal statutes.

- 18 USC Section 1030: Fraud Activities with Computers
- 18 USC Section 2511: Unlawful Interception of Communications
- 18 USC Section 2701: Unlawful Access to Stored Electronic Communications
- 18 USC Section 2319: Criminal Copyright Infringement
- 18 USC Section 2320: Trafficking in Counterfeit Goods or Services
- 18 USC Section 1831: Economic Espionage
- 18 USC Section 1832: Theft of Trade Secrets
- 18 USC Section 1834: Criminal Asset Forfeiture
- 18 USC Section 1341: Mail Fraud
- 18 USC Section 1343: Wire Fraud
- 18 USC Sections 2251–2253: Sexual Exploitation of Children Act
- 18 USC Section 371: Criminal Conspiracy

authority under the United States, shall be fined under this title or imprisoned not more than 3 years or both." Many jurisdictions have similar statutes requiring the reporting of criminal activities.

Civil matters are disputes between parties that are resolved by the exchange of money or property. Civil suits may have actual, punitive, and statutory damages. In the case of actual damages, the plaintiff must prove to a preponderance of evidence (51%) that they suffered specific losses. Punitive damages are amounts that punish the defendant for harming the plaintiff. Statutory damages are those prescribed by law.

Many jurisdictions have laws allowing the simultaneous criminal prosecution of a defendant, a civil suit naming the same defendant, and allowing forfeiture proceedings to take place. This type of multifaceted prosecution is known as parallel-track prosecution.

Pursuant to criminal activities, many jurisdictions and the U.S. federal government, file concurrent forfeiture actions against offending entities. These proceedings also impact the relationship between CIRT members and the court system. Depending upon the specific jurisdiction, these actions may take the form of the criminal's assets being indicted, or civil suits filed against those assets, or those assets being administratively forfeited. An example of this type of parallel-track prosecution is illustrated with the person who unlawfully enters an organization's network and steals sensitive protected information that is subsequently sold to a competitor. Investigators conduct a thorough investigation, and the perpetrator is indicted. In this same case, a seizure warrant is obtained; and the defendant's computer equipment, software, and the crime's proceeds are seized. Depending upon the laws, the perpetrator may suffer confinement, loss of money resulting from the information sale, the forfeiture of his equipment or other items of value, restitution to the victim, and fines. It is also a reasonable and acceptable process that the subject is civilly sued for damages while he is criminally prosecuted and his assets forfeited.

USE OF MONITORING DEVICES

The enterprise must have policies governing the use of its system resources and the conduct of its employees. Pursuant to those policies, the CIRT may monitor network use by suspected employee offenders. The use of monitoring techniques is governed by the employees' reasonable expectation of privacy and is defined by both policy and law. Techniques used to monitor employee activities should be made part of audit and executive-level review processes to make certain these monitoring practices are not abused. Before implementing computer monitoring, it is wise to consult the organization's human resources and legal departments because, if these policies are not implemented correctly, computer monitoring can run afoul of

legal, policy, and ethical standards. Under federal statutes, network administrators are granted the ability to manage their systems. They may access and control all areas of their network and interact with other administrators in the performance of their duties. Because unauthorized system intruders do not have an expectation of privacy, their activities are not subject to such considerations. If administrators discover irregularities, fraud, or unauthorized software such as hacking tools on their systems, they are allowed to take corrective actions and report the offenders.

However, this is not the case for government agencies wanting access to network systems and electronic communications. Depending upon the state of the electronic communications, they may be required to obtain a court order, search warrant, or subpoena.

It is important to note that most jurisdictions do not allow retributive actions. For example, if a denial-of-service attack causes the organization to suffer losses, it may be considered unlawful for the organization to return a virus to the offender.

NATURE OF CRIMINAL INCIDENTS

Viruses and worms have been in existence for many years. Since the introduction of the Morris worm in 1988, managers and administrators have paid attention to their potential for harm. In years past, viruses and worms were ignored by law enforcement, and treated as merely a nuisance. However, in more recent times, following the outbreaks of Melissa and the Love Bug, persons responsible for their creation and proliferation are being investigated and prosecuted.

Insider attacks usually consist of employees or former employees gaining access to sensitive information. Because they are already located inside the network, it is possible they have already bypassed many access barriers; and, by elevating their privileges, they may gain access to the organization's most valuable information assets. Among the insiders are those who utilize the organization's information assets for their own purposes. Downloading files in violation of use policies wastes valuable resources and, depending upon their content, may be a violation of law.

Outsider attacks are more than an annoyance. A determined outsider may hammer at the target's systems until an entry is discovered. Attackers may be malicious or curious. Regardless, their efforts have the same results in that unauthorized entry is made. Often, their attacks cause serious damage to information systems and compromise sensitive data. Attackers do not need thorough systems knowledge because there are many Web sites that provide the necessary tools for intrusions and DoS attacks.

Unauthorized interception of communications may take place when an unauthorized intrusion takes place and software is installed allowing the intruder to monitor keystrokes and communications traffic. Because this activity

Incident –
Info Classification

is performed without the permission of the system owners, it may have the same net effect as an illegal wiretap.

DoS attacks gained significant negative publicity recently as unscrupulous persons targeted high-profile Web sites, forcing them offline. In some cases, perpetrators were unwitting participants, wherein their broadband assets were compromised by persons installing software executing distributed DoS attacks. These attacks flood their target systems with useless data launched from single or multiple sources, causing the target's network to crash.

CONCLUSION

Risk management consists of careful planning, implementation, testing, and revision. The most critical part of risk management is critical incident response. The principal purpose of risk management is avoidance and mitigation of harm. Incident response, with the development of a solid response strategy, outside liaison, and a well-trained CIRT, can make the difference between a manageable incident and a disaster costing the organization its future.

Incident Response: Managing

Michael Vangelos, CISSP
Information Security Officer, Federal Reserve Bank of Cleveland, Cleveland, Ohio, U.S.A.

Abstract

Management might believe that recovering from a security incident is a straightforward exercise that is part of an experienced system administrator's job. From a system administrator's perspective, that may be true in many instances. However, any incident may require expertise in a number of different areas and may require decisions to be made quickly based on factors unique to that incident. This entry discusses the nature of security incidents, describes how to assemble an incident response team (IRT), and explains the six phases of a comprehensive response to a serious computer security incident.

Organizations typically devote substantial information security resources to the prevention of attacks on computer systems. Strong authentication is used, with passphrases that change regularly, tokens, digital certificates, and biometrics. Information owners spend time assessing risk. Network components are kept in access-controlled areas. The least privilege model is used as a basis for access control. There are layers of software protecting against malicious code. Operating systems are hardened, unneeded services are disabled, and privileged accounts are kept to a minimum. Some systems undergo regular audits, vulnerability assessments, and penetration testing. Add it all up, and these activities represent a significant investment of time and money.

Management makes this investment despite full awareness that, in the real world, it is impossible to prevent the success of all attacks on computer systems. At some point in time, nearly every organization must respond to a serious computer security incident. Consequently, a well-written computer incident response plan is an extremely important piece of the information security management toolbox. Much like disaster recovery, an incident response plan is something to be fully developed and practiced—although one hopes that it will never be put into action.

GETTING STARTED

Why Have an Incident Response Plan?

All computer systems are vulnerable to attack. Attacks by internal users, attacks by outsiders, low-level probes, direct attacks on high-privilege accounts, and virus attacks are only some of the possibilities. Some attacks are merely annoying. Some can be automatically rejected by defenses built into a system. Others are more serious and require immediate attention. In this entry, incident response refers to handling of the latter group of attacks and is the vehicle for dealing with a situation that is a direct threat to an information system.

Some of the benefits of developing an incident response plan are:

- *Following a predefined plan of action can minimize damage to a network.* Discovery that a system has been compromised can easily result in a state of confusion, where people do not know what to do. Technical staff may scurry around gathering evidence, unsure of whether they should disable services or disconnect servers from the network. Another potential scenario is that system administrators become aggressive, believing their job is to "get the hacker," regardless of the effect their actions may have on the network's users. Neither of these scenarios is desirable. Better results can be attained through the use of a plan that guides the actions of management as well as technicians during the life of an incident. Without a plan, system administrators may spend precious time figuring out what logs are available, how to identify the device associated with a specific IP address, or perform other basic tasks. With a plan, indecision can be minimized and staff can act confidently as they respond to the incident.

- *Policy decisions can be made in advance.* An organization can make important policy decisions before they are needed, rather than in the heat of the moment during an actual incident. For example, how will decisions be made on whether gateways or servers will be taken down or users disconnected from the network? Will technicians be empowered to act on their own, or must management make those decisions? If management makes those decisions, what level of management? Who decides whether and when law enforcement is notified? If a system administrator finds an intruder with administrative access on a key server, should all user sessions be shut down immediately and log-ins

Encyclopedia of Information Assurance DOI: 10.1081/E-EIA-120046844
Copyright © 2011 by Taylor & Francis. All rights reserved.

prohibited? If major services are disrupted by an incident, how are they prioritized so that technicians understand the order in which they should be recovered? Invariably, these and other policy issues are best resolved well in advance of when they are needed.

- *Details likely to be overlooked can be documented in the plan.* Often, a seemingly unimportant event turns into a serious incident. A security administrator might notice something unusual and make a note of it. Over the next few days, other events might be observed. At some point, it might become clear that these events were related and constitute a potential intrusion. Unless the organization has an incident response plan, it would be easy for technical staff to treat the situation as simply another investigation into unusual activity. Some things may be overlooked, such as notifying internal audit, starting an official log of events pertaining to the incident, and ensuring that normal cleanup or routine activities do not destroy potential evidence. An incident response plan will provide a blueprint for action during an incident, minimizing the chance that important activities will fall through the cracks.

- *Non-technical business areas must also prepare for an incident.* Creation of an incident response plan and the act of performing walk-throughs or simulation exercises can prepare business functions for incident response situations. Business functions are typically not accustomed to dealing with computer issues and may be uncomfortable providing input or making decisions if "thrown into the fire" during an actual incident. For example, attorneys can be much better prepared to make legal decisions if they have some familiarity with the incident response process. Human resources and public relations may also be key players in an incident and will be better able to protect the organization after gaining an understanding of how they fit into the overall incident response plan.

- *A plan can communicate the potential consequences of an incident to senior management.* It is no secret that, over time, companies are becoming increasingly dependent on their networks for all aspects of business. The movement toward the ability to access all information from any place at any time is continuing. Senior executives may not have an appreciation for the extent to which automation systems are interconnected and the potential impact of a security breach on information assets. Information security management can use periodic exercises in which potential dollar losses and disruption of services in real-life situations are documented to articulate the gravity of a serious computer security incident.

Requirements for Successful Response to an Incident

There are some key characteristics of effective response to a computer security incident. They follow from effective preparation and the development of a plan that fits into an organization's structure and environment.

Key elements of a good incident response plan are

- *Senior management support.* Without it, every other project and task will drain resources necessary to develop and maintain a good plan.

- *A clear protocol for invoking the plan.* Everyone involved should understand where the authority lies to distinguish between a problem (e.g., a handful of workstations have been infected with a virus because users disabled anti-virus software) and an incident (e.g., a worm is being propagated to hundreds of workstations and an anti-virus signature does not exist for it). A threshold should be established as a guide for deciding when to mobilize the resources called for by the incident response plan.

- *Participation of all the right players.* Legal, audit, information security, information technology, human resources, protection (physical security), public relations, and internal communications should all be part of the plan. Legal, HR, and protection may play an important role, depending on the type of incident. For some organizations, public relations may be the most important function of all, ensuring that consistent messages are communicated to the outside world.

- *Clear establishment of one person to be the leader.* All activity related to the incident must be coordinated by one individual, typically from IT or information security. This person must have a thorough knowledge of the incident response plan, be technical enough to understand the nature of the incident and its impact, and have the ability to communicate to senior management as well as technical staff.

- *Attention to communication in all phases.* Depending on the nature of the incident, messages to users, customers, shareholders, senior management, law enforcement, and the press may be necessary. Bad incidents can easily become worse because employees are not kept informed and cautioned to refer all outside inquiries concerning the incident to public relations.

- *Periodic testing and updates.* The incident response plan should be revisited regularly. Many organizations test disaster recovery plans annually or more frequently. These tests identify existing weaknesses in the plan and uncover changes in the automation environment that require corresponding adjustments for disaster recovery. They also help participants become familiar with the plan. The same benefits will be derived from simulation exercises or structured walk-throughs of an incident response plan.

Defining an Incident

There is no single, universally accepted definition of incident. The Computer Emergency Response Team

Incident –
Info Classification

Coordination Center (CERT/CC) at Carnegie Mellon University defines incident as "the act of violating an explicit or implied security policy."[1] That may be a great way to describe all events that are bad for computer systems, but it is too broad to use as a basis for the implementation of an incident response plan. The installation of a packet sniffer without management authorization, for instance, may be a violation of policy but probably would not warrant the formality of invoking an incident response plan. However, the use of that sniffer to capture sensitive data such as passwords may be an incident for which the plan should be invoked. The Department of Energy's Computer Incident Advisory Capability (CIAC) uses this definition for *incident*:

> Any adverse event that threatens the security of information resources. Adverse events may include compromises of integrity, denial-of-service attacks, compromise of confidentiality, loss of accountability, or damage to any part of the system. Examples include the insertion of malicious code (e.g., viruses, Trojan horses, or backdoors), unauthorized scans or probes, successful and unsuccessful intrusions, and insider attacks.[2]

This, too, is a good definition and one that is better aligned with the goal of identifying events that should trigger implementation of an incident response plan. To make this definition more useful in the plan, it should be complemented by guidelines for assessing the potential severity of an incident and a threshold describing the level of severity that should trigger invocation of the plan. Responding to an incident, as described in this entry, involves focused, intense activity by multiple people in order to address a serious condition that may materially affect the health of an organization's information assets.

Therefore, as the incident response plan is developed, an organization should establish criteria for deciding whether to invoke the plan.

Developing an Incident Response Team

There is no singularly correct makeup of an incident response team (IRT). However, it is generally agreed that if the following functional units exist in an organization, they should be represented: information security, information technology, audit, legal, public relations, protection (physical security), and human resources. In an ideal situation, specific individuals (preferably a primary and secondary contact) from each of these areas are assigned to the IRT. They will be generally familiar with the incident response plan and have an understanding of what kinds of assistance they may be called upon to provide for any incident. Table 1 lists the participants and their respective roles.

Some organizations successfully manage incidents by effectively splitting an IRT into two distinct units. A technical team is made up of staff with responsibility for checking logs and other evidence, determining what damage if any has been done, taking steps to minimize damage if the incident is ongoing, and restoring systems to an appropriate state. A management team consists of representatives of the functional areas listed above and would act as a steering committee and decision-making body for the life of the incident. An individual leading the response to an incident would appoint leaders of each team or serve as chair of the management team. The two teams, of course, should be in frequent communication with each other, generally with the management team making decisions based on input from the technical team.

Table 1 Incident response team roles.

Function	Probable role
Information security	Often has responsibility for the plan and leads the response; probably leads the effort to put preventive controls in place during preparation phase; staff may also be involved in the technical response (reviewing logs, cleaning virus-infected workstations, reviewing user definitions and access rights, etc.)
Information technology	Performs most eradication and recovery activities; probably involved during detection phase; should be active during preparation phase
Audit	Independent observer who reports to highest level of the organization; can provide valuable input for improving incident response capability
Legal	May be a key participant if the incident was originated by an employee or agency hired by the victim organization; can also advise in situations where downstream liability may exist (e.g., there is evidence that a system was compromised and subsequently used to attack another company's network); may want to be involved any time a decision is made to contact law enforcement agencies; should have input to decisions on whether to prosecute criminal activity; would advise on any privacy issues
Public relations	Should coordinate all communication with the outside world; probably creates the messages that are used
Protection	May be necessary if the incident originated from within the organization and the response may involve confronting a potentially hostile employee or contractor; might also be the best entity to take custody of physical evidence
Human resources	Provides input on how to deal with a situation in which an employee caused the incident or is actively hacking the system

Table 2 Goal of each incident response phase.

Phase	Goal
Preparation	Adopt policies and procedures that enable effective incident response
Detection	Detect that an incident has occurred and make a preliminary assessment of its magnitude
Containment	Keep the incident from spreading
Eradication	Eliminate all effects of the incident
Recovery	Return the network to a production-ready status
Follow-up	Review the incident and improve incident-handling capabilities

SIX PHASES OF INCIDENT RESPONSE

It is generally accepted that there are six phases to the discipline of incident response, and the cycle begins well before an incident ever occurs. In any one incident, some of these phases will overlap. In particular, eradication and recovery often occur concurrently. The phases are:

1. Preparation
2. Detection
3. Containment
4. Eradication
5. Recovery
6. Follow-up

Table 2 briefly describes the goal of each phase.

Preparation Phase

If any one phase is more important than the others, it is the preparation phase. Before an incident occurs is the best time to secure the commitment of management at all levels to the development of an effective incident response capability. This is the time when a solid foundation for incident response is built. During this phase, an organization deploys preventive and detective controls and develops an incident response capability.

Management responsible for incident response should do the following:

- Name specific individuals (and alternates) as members of the IRT. Each functional area described in the preceding section of this entry (audit, legal, human resources, public relations, information security, information technology) should be represented by people with appropriate decision-making and problem-solving skills and authority.
- Ensure that there is an effective mechanism in place for contacting team members. Organizations have a

similar need for contacting specific people in a disaster recovery scenario. It may be possible to use the same process for incident response.
- Include guidelines for deciding when the incident response plan is invoked. One of the key areas of policy to be considered prior to an incident is answering the question, "What are the criteria for declaring an incident?"
- Specify the relative priority of goals during an incident. For example,

  - Protect human life and safety (this should always be first).
  - Protect classified systems and data.
  - Ensure the integrity of key operating systems and network components.
  - Protect critical data.

- Commit to conducting sessions to exercise the plan, simulating different types of incidents. Exercises should be as realistic as possible without actually staging an incident. An exercise may, for example, prompt legal, human resources, and protection to walk through their roles in a situation where an employee and contractor have conspired to compromise a network and are actively hacking the system while on company premises. Exercises should challenge IT and information security staff to identify the logs and other forensic data or tools that would be used to investigate specific types of incidents.
- Decide on the philosophy to be used in response to an intrusion. Should an attacker successfully hack in, does the victim organization want to get rid of the intruder as quickly as possible and get back to business (protect and proceed)? Or does the organization want to observe the intruder's movements and potentially gather data for prosecution (pursue and prosecute)?
- Ensure that there is a reasonable expectation that the skills necessary to perform the technical tasks of the incident response plan are present in the organization. Enough staff should understand the applicable network components, forensic tools, and the overall plan so that when an incident occurs, it can be investigated in a full and competent manner.
- Make adjustments to the plan based on test scenario exercises and reviews of the organization's response to actual incidents.
- Review the organization's security practices to ensure that intrusion detection systems are functional, logs are activated, sufficient backups are taken, and a program is in place for regularly identifying system vulnerabilities and addressing those vulnerabilities.

Detection Phase

The goal of the detection phase is to determine whether an incident has occurred. There are many symptoms of a security incident. Some common symptoms are

- New user accounts not created by authorized administrators
- Unusual activity by an account, such as an unexpected log-in while the user is known to be on vacation or use of the account during odd hours
- Unexpected changes in the lengths of timestamps of operating system files
- Unusually high network or server activity or poor system performance
- Probing activity such as port scans
- For Windows® Operating System, unexplained changes in registry settings
- Multiple attempts to log in as root or administrator

Various tools are available to help detect activity that could indicate a security incident. First, there are system logs. Systems should be configured so that logs capture events such as successful and failed log-ins of administrator-level accounts. In addition, failed log-ins of all accounts should be logged. Because log data is relatively worthless unless someone analyzes it, logs should be reviewed on a regular basis. For many systems, the amount of data captured in logs is so great that it is impossible to review it without a utility that searches for and reports those records that might be of interest.

Data integrity checkers exist for UNIX® and Windows platforms. These utilities typically keep a database of hash values for specified files, directories, and registry entries. Any time an integrity check is performed, the hash value for each object is computed and compared to its corresponding value in the database. Any discrepancy indicates that the object has changed since the previous integrity check. Integrity checkers can be good indications of an intrusion, but it can take a great deal of effort to configure the software to check only those objects that do not change due to normal system activity.

Intrusion detection systems (IDSs) claim to identify attacks on a network or host in real-time. IDSs basically come in two flavors—network based and host based. A network-based IDS examines traffic as it passes through the IDS sensor, comparing sequences of packets to a database of attack signatures. If it finds a match, the IDS reports an event, usually to a console. The IDS may also be able to send an e-mail or dial a pager as it detects specific events. In contrast, a host-based IDS examines log data from a specific host. As the system runs, the IDS looks at information written to logs in real-time and reports events based on policies set within the IDS.

Organizations become aware of security incidents in many ways. In one scenario, technical staff probably notices or is made aware of an unusual event and begins to investigate. After some initial analysis, it is determined that the event is a threat to the network, so the incident response plan is invoked. If so, the IRT is brought together and formal logging of all activity related to this incident begins. It should be noted that early detection of an incident could mean a huge difference in the amount of damage and cost to the organization. In particular, this is true of malicious code attacks as well as intrusions.

In this phase, the IRT is formally called into action. It is important that certain things occur at this time. Perhaps most importantly, one person should take charge of the process. A log of all applicable events should be initiated at this time and updated throughout the incident. Everyone involved in responding to the incident must be aware of the process. They should all be reminded that the incident will be handled in accordance with guidance provided by the plan, that technical staff should communicate all new developments as quickly as possible to the rest of the team, that everyone must remember to observe evidence chain-of-custody guidelines, and that all communication to employees as well as the outside world should flow through official channels. Some organizations will specify certain individuals who should always be notified when the incident response plan is invoked, even if they are not members of the IRT. For example, the highest internal audit official, COO, the highest information security official, or, in the case where each division of an organization has its own incident response capability, corporate information security may be notified.

Containment Phase

The goal of the containment phase is to keep the incident from spreading. At this time, actions are taken to limit the damage. If it is a malicious code incident, infected servers and workstations may be disconnected from the network. If there is an intruder on the network, the attacker may be limited to one network segment and most privileged accounts may be temporarily disabled. If the incident is a denial-of-service attack, the sources may be able to be identified and denied access to the target network. If one host has been compromised, communication to other hosts may be disabled.

There is much that can be done prior to an incident to make the job of containment easier. Putting critical servers on a separate subnet, for example, allows an administrator to quickly deny traffic to those servers from any other subnet or network known to be under attack.

It is prudent to consider certain situations in advance and determine how much risk to take if faced with those situations. Consider a situation where information security staff suspects that a rogue NT/2000 administrator with privileges at the top of the tree is logged in to the company's Active Directory (AD). In effect, the intruder is logged in to every Windows server defined to the AD. If staff cannot identify the workstation used by the intruder, it may be best to immediately disconnect all workstations from the network. On the other hand, such drastic action may not be warranted if the intrusion occurs on a less sensitive or less critical network segment. In another example, consider a devastating e-mail-borne worm spreading through an enterprise. At what point is the e-mail service disabled? The incident response plan should contain guidance for making this decision.

The containment phase is also the time when a message to users may be appropriate. Communication experts should craft the message, especially if it goes outside the organization.

Eradication Phase

Conceptually, eradication is simple—this is the phase in which the problem is eliminated. The methods and tools used will depend on the exact nature of the problem. For a virus incident, antivirus signatures may have to be developed and applied; and hard drives or e-mail systems may need to be scanned before access to infected systems is allowed to resume. For an intrusion, systems into which the intruder was logged must be identified and the intruder's active sessions must be disconnected. It may be possible to identify the device used by the intruder and either logically or physically separate it from the network. If the attack originated from outside the network, connections to the outside world can be disabled.

In addition to the immediate effects of the incident, such as an active intruder or virus, other unauthorized changes may have been made to systems as a result of the incident. Eradication includes the examination of network components that may have been compromised for changes to configuration files or registry settings, the appearance of Trojan horses or backdoors designed to facilitate a subsequent security breach, or new accounts that have been added to a system.

Recovery Phase

During the recovery phase, systems are returned to a normal state. In this phase, system administrators determine (as well as possible) the extent of the damage caused by the incident and use appropriate tools to recover. This is primarily a technical task, with the nature of the incident determining the specific steps taken to recover. For malicious code, antivirus software is the most common recovery mechanism. For denial-of-service attacks, there may not even be a recovery phase. An incident involving unauthorized use of an administrative-level account calls for a review of (at least) configuration files, registry settings, user definitions, and file permissions on any server or domain into which the intruder was logged. In addition, the integrity of critical user databases and files should be verified.

This is a phase where tough decisions may have to be made. Suppose, for example, the incident is an intrusion and an administrative account was compromised for a period of 2 days. The account has authority over many servers, such as in a Windows NT^{TM} domain. Unless one can account for every action taken by the intruder (maybe an impossible task in the real world), one can never be sure whether the intruder altered operating system files, updated data files, planted Trojan horses, defined accounts that do not show up in directory listings, or left time bombs. The only ways to be absolutely certain that a server has been recovered back to its preincident state is to restore from backup using backup tapes known to be taken before the intrusion started, or rebuild the server by installing the operating system from scratch. Such a process could consume a significant amount of time, especially if there are hundreds of servers that could have been compromised. So if a decision is made not to restore from tape or rebuild servers, an organization takes on more risk that the problem will not be fully eradicated and systems fully restored. The conditions under which an organization is willing to live with the added risk is a matter deserving of some attention during the preparation phase.

Follow-Up Phase

It should come as no surprise that after an incident has been detected, contained, eradicated, and all recovery activities have been completed, there is still work to do. In the follow-up phase, closure is brought to the matter with a thorough review of the entire incident.

Specific activities at this time include:

- Consolidate all documentation gathered during the incident.
- Calculate the cost.
- Examine the entire incident, analyzing the effectiveness of preparation, detection, containment, eradication, and recovery activities.
- Make appropriate adjustments to the incident response plan.

Documentation should be consolidated at this time. There may have been dozens of people involved during the incident, particularly in large, geographically dispersed organizations. If legal proceedings begin years later, it is highly unlikely that the documentation kept by each participant will still exist and be accessible when needed. Therefore, all documentation must be collected and archived immediately. There should be no question about the location of all information concerning this incident. Another potential benefit to consolidating all of the documentation is that a similar incident may occur in the future, and individuals handling the new incident should be able to review material from the earlier incident.

Table 3 Sample questions for postincident review.

Preparation

- Were controls applicable to the specific incident working properly?
- What conditions allowed the incident to occur?
- Could more education of users or administrators have prevented the incident?
- Were all of the people necessary to respond to the incident familiar with the incident response plan?
- Were any actions that required management approval clear to participants throughout the incident?

Detection

- How soon after the incident started did the organization detect it?
- Could different or better logging have enabled the organization to detect the incident sooner?
- Does the organization even know exactly when the incident started?
- How smooth was the process of invoking the incident response plan?
- Were appropriate individuals outside of the incident response team notified?
- How well did the organization follow the plan?
- Were the appropriate people available when the response team was called?
- Should there have been communication to inside and outside parties at this time; and if so, was it done?
- Did all communication flow from the appropriate source?

Containment

- How well was the incident contained?
- Did the available staff have sufficient skills to do an effective job of containment?
- If there were decisions on whether to disrupt service to internal or external customers, were they made by the appropriate people?
- Are there changes that could be made to the environment that would have made containment easier or faster?
- Did technical staff document all of their activities?

Eradication and recovery

- Was the recovery complete—was any data permanently lost?
- If the recovery involved multiple servers, users, networks, etc. how were decisions made on the relative priorities, and did the decision process follow the incident response plan?
- Were the technical processes used during these phases smooth?
- Was staff available with the necessary background and skills?
- Did technical staff document all of their activities?

The cost of the incident should be calculated, including direct costs due to data loss, loss of income due to the unavailability of any part of the network, legal costs, cost of recreating or restoring operating systems and data files, employee time spent reacting to the incident, and lost time of employees who could not access the network or specific services.

All aspects of the incident should be examined. Each phase of the plan should be reviewed, beginning with preparation. How did the incident occur—was there a preventable breakdown in controls, did the attacker take advantage of an old, unpatched vulnerability, was there a serious virus infection that may have been prevented with more security awareness? Table 3 shows questions that could apply at each phase of the incident.

Appropriate adjustments should be made to the incident response plan and to information security practices. No incident response plan is perfect. An organization may be

able to avoid future incidents, reduce the damage of future incidents, and get in a position to respond more effectively by applying knowledge gained from a postincident review. The review might indicate that changes should be made in any number of places, including the incident response plan, existing controls, the level of system monitoring, forensic skills of the technical staff, or the level of involvement of non-IT functions.

OTHER CONSIDERATIONS

Common Obstacles to Establishing an Effective Incident Response Plan

It may seem that any organization committed to establishing an incident response plan would be able to put one in place without much difficulty. However, there are many

Incident –
Info Classification

opportunities for failure as you address the issue of incident response. This section describes some of the obstacles that may arise during the effort.

- There is a tendency to think of serious computer security incidents primarily as IT issues to be handled on a technical level. They are not. Security incidents are primarily business issues that often have a technical component that needs prompt attention. Organizations that consider security incidents to be IT issues are more likely to make the mistake of including only IT and information security staff on the IRT.
- Technical staff with the skills to create and maintain an effective incident response plan may already be overworked simply trying to maintain and improve the existing infrastructure. There can be a tendency to have system administrators put together a plan in their spare time. Typically, these efforts lead to a lot of scurrying to get a plan thrown together in the last few days before a management-imposed deadline for its completion.
- It can be difficult to get senior management's attention unless a damaging incident has already occurred. Here is where it may help to draw parallels between business continuity/disaster recovery and incident response. By and large, executives recognize the benefits of investment in a good business continuity strategy. Pointing out the similarities, especially noting that both are vehicles for managing risk, can help overcome this obstacle.
- One can think of a hundred reasons *not* to conduct exercises of the plan. Too many people are involved; it is difficult to stage a realistic incident to test the plan; everybody is too busy; it will only scare people; etc. Lack of testing can very quickly render an incident response plan less than adequate. Good plans evolve over time and are constantly updated as the business and technical environments change. Without periodic testing and review, even a well-constructed incident response plan will become much less valuable over time.

Importance of Training

It is crucial that an organization conduct training exercises. No matter how good an incident response plan is, periodic simulations or walk-throughs will identify flaws in the plan and reveal where the plan has not kept pace with changes in the automation infrastructure. More importantly, it will keep IRT members aware of the general flow as an incident is reported and the organization responds. It will give technical staff an opportunity to utilize tools that may not be used normally. Each exercise is an opportunity to ensure that all of the tools that might be needed during an incident are still functioning as intended. Finally, it will serve to make key participants more comfortable and more confident during a real incident.

Benefits of a Structured Incident Response Methodology

As this entry describes, there is nothing trivial about preparing to respond to a serious computer security incident. Development and implementation of an incident response plan require significant resources and specialized skills. It is, however, well worth the effort for the following reasons.

- *An incident response plan provides structure to a response.* In the event of an incident, an organization would be extremely lucky if its technicians, managers, and users all do what they think best and those actions make for an effective response. On the other hand, the organization will almost always be better served if those people acted against the backdrop of a set of guidelines and procedures designed to take them through each step of the way.
- *Development of a plan allows an organization to identify actions and practices that should always be followed during an incident.* Examples are maintaining a log of activities, maintaining an evidentiary chain of custody, notifying specific entities of the incident, and referring all media inquiries to the public relations staff.
- *It is more likely that the organization will communicate effectively to employees if an incident response plan is in place.* If not, messages to management and staff will tend to be haphazard and may make the situation worse.
- *Handling unexpected events is easier if there is a framework that is familiar to all the participants.* Having critical people comfortable with the framework can make it easier to react to the twists and turns that sometimes occur during an incident.

Years ago, security practitioners and IT managers realized that a good business continuity plan was a sound investment. Like business continuity, a computer incident response plan has become an essential part of a good security program.

REFERENCES

1. CERT/CC. *Incident Reporting Guidelines*, http://www.cert.org/tech_tips/incident_reporting.html.
2. *CIAC Incident Reporting Procedures*, http://www.llnl.gov.

Incident Response: Privacy Breaches

Rebecca Herold, CISM, CISA, CISSP, FLMI
Information Privacy, Security and Compliance Consultant, Rebecca Herold and Associates LLC, Van Meter, Iowa, U.S.A.

Abstract

If you have not yet done so, and do not have it on your short to-do list, you need to plan to review the protection practices currently in place for your PII and how your organization would be impacted by a privacy breach. Or, perhaps your organization has already experienced one of the thousands of incidents that have already occurred and needs to re-examine, or create, your privacy breach incident response plan. Breaches happen and will continue to proliferate; businesses must be prepared.

DO YOU KNOW WHERE YOUR PERSONAL DATA IS?

On October 1, 2005, confidential health records originating from the Toronto Clinic dating back to 1992 were purposefully blown and scattered about the streets of Toronto, Ontario. The Clinic had given the Paper Disposal Company, which provided their shredding services, boxes containing health records. Reportedly due to a misunderstanding, the records were then given to a recycling company that subsequently sold the intact records to a film company that then used the records as props for a film about the immediate aftermath of the September 11, 2001, terrorist attacks on the World Trade Center. On October 31, 2005, Ontario's privacy commissioner found both the clinic and disposal company at fault and liable.

Do you know who is peeking at the personally identifiable information (PII) for which your organization is responsible? Do you know if that vendor to whom you have outsourced the processing of your PII has allowed your PII to get into the hands of a competitor or criminal without even knowing it? Do you know if they may have donated your unshredded confidential papers to the local public kindergarten to use as scrap paper? Do you have bells, whistles, and processes in place to notify you when PII is inappropriately used or accessed? Do you have tools implemented to notify you when someone is the inappropriately grabbing your PII? Have you even thought about these issues? Or, do you think someone else in your company has already taken care of all these possibilities? Or perhaps you think that such an incident is very unlikely and would have very little impact on your organization.

INCREASING INCIDENTS, INCREASING ANXIETY

The Privacy Rights Clearinghouse started keeping track of reported PII breaches within the United States on February 15, 2005, starting with the ChoicePoint incident, and by February 25, 2006, they had chronicled 129 breaches that had been reported in the news. These breaches cumulatively involved the information of at least 53.4 million people. Other sites are also keeping similar chronologies. Keep in mind that these are just the reported incidents.

I know at least four other organizations that experienced and addressed significant breaches during 2005 that did not get publicized or included within these accumulated statistics. And, yes, they contacted all their customers quickly. I am certain there have been many more organizations that have also quietly addressed breach incidents while working diligently to keep the incident from being reported. The types of breaches varied greatly and included such incidents as:

- Dishonest authorized insiders inappropriately using PII
- E-mail messages with confidential information sent or forwarded inappropriately
- Fraud activities perpetrated by outsiders, insiders, and combinations of both
- Hackers gaining unauthorized access to the information
- Information exposed online because of inadequate controls
- Lost or stolen backup media
- Confidential paper documents not being shredded and given to people outside the organization
- Password compromise
- Stolen or lost computing devices, such as laptops, PDAs, and so on

Encyclopedia of Information Assurance DOI: 10.1081/E-EIA-120046848

Copyright © 2011 by Taylor & Francis. All rights reserved.

INCREASING BREACHES, LOST CUSTOMERS

A Ponemon Lost Customer Information study released in November, 2005, sponsored by PGP Corporation (http://www.pgp.com), reveals that businesses suffer greater breach incident impact from lost customer confidence and business than what the actual breach itself costs. A survey of over 9000 people revealed:

- Close to 12% had been notified about a data breach by companies with whom they did business.
- Twenty percent of them said they immediately closed their accounts or stopped doing business with the company.
- Companies reported the percentages of all customers lost following incidents ranged from 2.5% to 11%.

Another study released in December, 2005, conducted in Canada by Leger Marketing and sponsored by Sun Microsystems of Canada, showed 58% of consumers said they would immediately stop doing business with a company that experienced a breach that put their personal information in jeopardy. This is significantly higher than the numbers found in the Ponemon study. The loss of customers will depend greatly on the type of breach, the service or product the company provides, how quickly the company contacts customers following a breach, and the history the customer has had with the company, along with the general reputation. The same survey reported 55% of companies indicate that the customer information for which they are responsible is not safe or secure. The study also indicated 14% of Canadian consumers believe they have already been identity theft victims.

INCREASING BREACHES, DECREASING REVENUES

Another Ponemon PGP Corporation–sponsored consumer breach study (http://www.pgp.com), also released in November, 2005, revealed that the average impact to each of the 14 companies studied following a security breach was $14 million. Actual costs included internal investigations, external legal fees, notification and call center costs, investor relations, promotions such as discounted services and products, lost personnel productivity, and the cost of lost customers. In fact, the costs to the organizations following a breach were more than the immediate costs of addressing a breach.

In addition to the costs identified within the Ponemon report, there can also be additional costs involved with breaches, such as when an organization's customers are other business organizations. For example, if you have customers that are companies that distribute your services or products to their employees or customers (such as if you provide group health insurance policies), then you will not only need to notify the individuals, but also demonstrate to the companies that are your customers what you are willing to do to keep their business. This will likely be pricey. You may need to fly representatives from the companies to your site to meet with your executives to discuss the situation, all on your dime.

Additional breach response costs are also involved for notifications to individuals who are located outside your country, such as the costs for resources to work with the applicable country privacy commissioners, costs for translation services, call centers with multilingual capabilities, and so on. And, depending upon your industry, locations, services, and products, there could be many other areas a breach could financially impact. It is worth periodically taking an afternoon to brainstorm the possible impacts to help you better prepare to respond to a breach. I created a privacy impact "calculator" (http://www.informationshield.com/privacybreachcalc.html) that organizations have used to demonstrate to their business leaders just how much a breach could cost when considering multiple possibilities and factors. Such an exercise is truly an eye-opener and gets the attention of the leaders who can relate best to information presented as profits and losses. It helps to get the resources to do the activities necessary to create a privacy breach incident response plan and implement the associated tools and procedures.

INCREASING LAWS, INCREASING LIABILITIES

In 2005, breach notification legislation was passed in at least 23 U.S. states. One of many sites listing these laws is http://www.pirg.org. All organizations must now effectively notify all affected U.S. residents for PII breaches. Trying to notify only those within the states that have notification laws would not only be impossible to manage, it would also be a very bad business decision from a public relations perspective, not to mention the fact that the number of states with such laws is increasing rapidly, and that doing so could still leave you open for civil suits.

With most of the U.S. states having passed privacy-breach notification legislation, and several federal breach notification bills of various flavors looming on the horizon, the issue of how to not only better protect personal information, but also respond to breaches of personal information, certainly should be on the radar of organizations. There was a spate of federal bill-writing activity during the summer of 2005, just before the August U.S. Congress recess, and personal information security was at the top of the agenda. Three different federal bills were proposed at that time addressing the protection of personal information. It is widely expected that a federal bill will be passed in 2006.

PRIVACY BREACHES SIGNIFICANTLY IMPACT BUSINESS

Privacy breaches have significant and long-lasting impact on business. Just a few examples of incidents and the resulting business impacts are given in Table 1.

NOW IS THE TIME TO BE PREPARED

The Ponemon Consumer Breach study highlights the importance of having an effective breach response plan in place to quickly notify customers. Companies that took longer to notify customers of a breach were four times as

Table 1 Examples of incidents and their business impacts.

Incident	Business Impact
October, 2005: Confidential health records originating from the Toronto Clinic dating back to 1992 were purposefully blown and scattered about the streets of Toronto, Ontario. The Clinic had given the Paper Disposal Company, which provided their shredding services, boxes containing health records. Reportedly due to a misunderstanding, the records were then given to a recycling company that subsequently sold the intact records to a film company that then used the records as props for a film about the immediate aftermath of the September 11, 2001 terrorist attacks on the World Trade Center	Ontario's privacy commissioner found both the clinic and disposal company at fault and liable and ordered the following • The Toronto Clinic to implement information practices, including proper training, to the security of personal health information in all forms; to use written contracts with any agent it retains to dispose of personal health information records, and to provide written confirmation through an attestation once secure disposal has been conducted • The Paper Disposal Company to implement a written contractual agreement with any health information custodian for whom it will shred personal health information and to provide an attestation of destruction; to ensure that any handling of personal health information by a third party company is documented within contracts; to implement procedures that prevent paper records containing personal health information designated for shredding from being mixed together with paper that is being disposed of through the recycling process • These requirements were identified by the commissioner as establishing the practice to be followed by all health information custodians and their agents in Ontario, with respect to the Commissioner's expectations for the secure disposal of health information records under Ontario's Health Information Privacy Law
June 2005: A network intruder exploiting network vulnerabilities stole information about 40 million credit card holders from CardSystems Solutions, Inc. This company had processed $15 billion annually in credit-card transactions for Visa, American Express, MasterCard, and Discover	• According to the FTC, the security breach resulted in millions of dollars in fraudulent purchases • VISA cancelled their contract with CardSystems • CardSystems, facing bankruptcy, sold their assets to Pay By Touch for $13 million • The FTC settlement requires CardSystems and Pay By Touch to implement a comprehensive information security program, including data protection education, and obtain audits by an independent third-party security professional every other year for 20 years • A class action suit was being tried in early 2006 against Card Systems, VISA and MASTERCARD in California
February 2005: Criminals posing as legitimate businesses accessed critical personal data stored by ChoicePoint, Inc., which maintains databases with personal information on virtually every U.S. citizen. 162,000 individuals have been impacted as of February 2006	• $1 billion in lost stock value $20 million loss in top-line revenue $3 million cost and counting for credit reporting, legal and other expenses Federal lawsuit for violation of the Fair Credit Reporting Act (FCRA) FTC investigation SEC lawsuit Shareholder lawsuit California state investigation for violation of SB 1386 Estimated personal damage: $500 per customer, not including loss of time Class action lawsuit filed in Los Angeles for $75,000 per victim

(Continued)

Table 1 Examples of incidents and their business impacts. *(Continued)*

Incident	Business Impact
June 2001: An Eli Lilly employee accidentally included clear text e-mail addresses of 669 Prozac patients in a message sent for its Prozaccom5 service	The FTC required Lilly to not make security misrepresentations; establish and maintain a four-stage information security program; designate appropriate personnel to coordinate and oversee the program; perform ongoing risk analysis; provide ongoing personnel training; implement intrusion detection mechanisms; conduct an annual written effectiveness review for at least 20 years; adjust the program according to the findings
	Eight states (California, Connecticut, Idaho, Iowa, Massachusetts, New Jersey, New York, and Vermont) filed lawsuits. To settle, Lilly agreed to install automated checks in its software systems to prevent a recurrence and to annually report to the states the results of their security evaluations

likely to lose customers than if the customers were notified quickly and consistently. A significant consideration determining customer retention was also the method of breach notification; the companies surveyed indicated they were three times more likely to lose customers if they notified them using a form letter or e-mail instead of calling them on the phone or sending them a personalized letter.

What steps should companies take to help stem the tide of PII breaches, and to be prepared in the event they still experience a breach? Even if organizations were not required by law to report breaches, it would still be wise for organizations to be prepared for how to handle PII breaches, not only to protect the individuals involved, but also to demonstrate due diligence, retain customers, and in turn help to reduce the negative financial impact that a breach could have upon the organization.

Preparing a privacy breach incident response plan as part of a solid information security management and privacy assurance program is, of course, no guarantee of avoiding bad publicity or having a negative impact to your business following a breach. However, performing the activities to prepare for a beach response will certainly help to mitigate and lessen the impact of a breach if and when one occurs, and it could very possibly help prevent the organization from going out of business. The more quickly, comprehensively, and efficiently an organization can respond to and resolve a breach incident, the less financial, brand, and likely legal impact and damage it will have on the organization. Remember, doing less following a breach will hurt an organization more in the long run.

PRIVACY INCIDENT RESPONSE PLAN PREPARATION

An information security and privacy program should include a privacy incident response plan that addresses privacy and security breaches and incidents including unauthorized access to or acquisition of PII. To ensure timely notice to affected individuals when appropriate, the following practices are among those that should be included in a privacy incident response plan:

1. *Define personally identifiable information.* Before you can determine if you have had a breach of PII, you need to specifically define what is considered as PII within your organization. Clearly define and document the information within your organization that is considered, or labeled, as PII.

Currently, there is no one existing list of what constitutes PII. Consider all applicable laws in all locations where you have consumers, employees, and business partners. Some countries include within their PII list information that is completely out of the consideration of most U.S. business leaders, such as IP addresses and serial numbers. You need to identify the privacy-related laws for the countries in which you do business and have offices, then compile a list of the items that are considered as PII within all of them.

Many organizations assume PII is just the types of information listed in HIPAA or California's SB 1386. Be very aware that numerous laws, not only U.S. federal and state level, but international, exist that define many other types of items as personal information. In 2004, I reviewed multiple data protection laws from around the world and identified at least 47 different items (see Table 2) specifically named as being legally considered as personal information, and some laws consider certain items when combined with other information, such as racial or ethnic origin, political and religious affiliations, and sexual activity information as being personal or sensitive information that organizations must protect.

Incident – Info Classification

Table 2 Items specifically stated within various data protection regulations as being personal information.

First Name or Initial	Last Name
Hospital dates of: birth, admission, discharge, death	Geographic subdivisions smaller than a state (street address)
Fax number	Telephone number
Social security number	E-mail address
Health plan beneficiary numbers	Medical records numbers
License and certificate numbers	Account numbers
Credit card numbers	Vehicle identifiers (e.g., license plate number)
California ID numbers	Debit card numbers
Internet URLs	Device identifiers (e.g., serial numbers)
Personnel files	Internet Protocol (IP) addresses
Unique identifiers that can be attributed to a specific individual	Full-face (and comparable) photographic images
Any identifier the FTC determines permits the contacting of a specific individual	Medical care information (e.g., organ donations, medications, disability info)
Biometric identifiers (such as DNA, finger, iris and voice prints)	Information concerning children
Employment history	Body identifiers (e.g., tattoos, scars)
Payment history	Income
Credit card purchases	Loan or deposit balances
Military history	Criminal charges, convictions and court records
Customer relationships	Credit reports and credit scores
Merchandise and product order history	Financial transaction information
Fraud alerts	Service subscription history
Video programming activity	"Black Box" data
Conversations (recorded or overheard)	Voting history
Education records	Descriptive consumer listings

Generally, some law or court may consider PII as being any information by which an individual may be identified.

When compiling your PII list, consider the information your organization handles and obtains from consumers, customers, employees, and business partners, as well as the information that may be purchased from data warehouses by some areas such as marketing, sales, or even government relations. Consider and include not only electronic information, but also information on paper, in voice mails, within faxes, and in other forms.

List all the items identified and convene a meeting with your business unit leaders and corporate area leaders, including information security, human relations, legal counsel, and physical security, and see if you have missed anything. If you already have an information security and/or privacy oversight board in place, this would be a great group to use. Discuss the information items, and come to consensus on the items your organization will consider and define as PII for the purposes necessary to meet legal and regulatory compliance, as well as compliance with your own posted privacy policy and your business partner contracts.

2. Locate PII within the organization. Create an inventory of all such PII items and where they are located, such as within specific systems, files, paper, CDs, backup tapes, and so on.

When considering where PII is located, consider where PII is colleted. In the course of a business day, organizations collect PII in a number of ways, such as when:

- Customers register their products
- Individuals respond to marketing campaigns or request product information
- Customers call for help or service for their products
- Individuals apply for and accept employment
- Employees enroll in benefits and other company-sponsored programs
- Entering into certain business agreements with third parties

This information resides within organizations in multiple forms, and widely spread locations. Much of this information is in the form of unstructured data, meaning it is basically under the complete control and whims of the end-user. Examples of unstructured data include e-mails, Word documents, spreadsheets, and so on.

Unstructured data, much of which likely includes PII in most organizations, multiplies at an amazing rate.

Incident –
Info Classification

According to a 2004 IDC study, unstructured data doubles every two months in large corporations. The ratio of unstructured data to structured is significant. A 2004 Goldman–Sachs study reported 90% of data within a corporation is unstructured data.

Locating and inventorying your PII will be no small task, but it is a critical task to accomplish to be able to identify when a breach occurs, not to mention knowing how to respond to customer questions and regulatory audits.

Be as comprehensive as possible identifying PII storage locations. Some of the most well-publicized and biggest-impact incidents have involved little-considered storage devices, such as handheld computer devices, backup media, and paper documents. Make sure you consider the following:

- File servers, application servers, mail servers
- Desktops, laptops, and notebooks
- PDAs, Blackberries, and other handheld computing devices
- Smart phones
- Voice mails
- Printed documents
- Fax machines and photocopiers
- Printers
- Backup tapes and media

And do not forget about those often-overlooked and even unsuspecting storage areas where massive amounts of PII could be hiding, such as:

- USB drives
- Scanners
- Telephones and camera phones
- Optical media
- CDs and diskettes
- Webservers
- DVDs
- iPods
- Employee-owned computers
- MP3 players
- Windows recycle bins

Once you have completed the important and necessary project to create your PII inventory, be diligent in keeping it up-to-date. This will not be nearly as hard as creating the initial inventory if you establish and implement procedures for reporting and cataloging all new PII and changes in existing PII. There are now many tools that make this job easier than it once was. Assign a role the responsibility for keeping the PII inventory up-to-date in a centralized location.

3. *Define a breach.* The term "breach," sometimes with "security" as a qualifier and sometimes with "privacy," has been published many times over the past few years. A significant vulnerability within many organizations is

that they have not defined a breach as it applies to their organization. Some assume it is just a hacking event. Others consider a breach only as being inappropriate access to a person's name and Social Security number. Organizations need to define what constitutes a breach within each of their own organizations based upon the industry, services, products, and geographic locations for not only where the offices are locates, but also where customers are located, in addition to the applicable laws and regulations.

When defining breach categories, consider this: generally, a privacy or security breach is defined as unauthorized access to information that compromises the security, confidentiality, or integrity of personal information collected or maintained by the organization. Good faith acquisition of personal information by an employee or agent of your company for business purposes is usually not considered a breach, provided that the personal information is not used or subject to further unauthorized disclosure.

Use the list of incidents at the beginning of this entry as examples of types of breaches that you can use to establish your own set of organizational breach definitions. Define a breach, and the different levels of severity, as they apply to the organization.

In determining whether unencrypted PII has been acquired, or is reasonably believed to have been acquired, by an unauthorized person, consider the following factors, among others:

- Indications that the information is in the physical possession and control of an unauthorized person, such as a lost or stolen computer or other device containing unencrypted notice-triggering information
- Indications that the information has been downloaded or copied
- Indications that the information was used by an unauthorized person, such as fraudulent accounts opened or instances of identity theft reported

4. *Create your breach identification and notification plan.* A 2005 Ponemon Institute survey of corporate privacy practices revealed only one-third of companies had a formal process in place to monitor and report security breaches. As more companies create breach monitoring and reporting procedures, and as companies improve upon them, there will be more incidents reported. Customer confidence will surely be impacted. Customer inquiries to companies demanding to know how their PII is protected will surely increase.

A June 2005 Conference Board survey reported 41% of customers are making fewer online purchases than in 2004 because of fears their personal information will not be adequately secured. This does not just impact companies with substandard security programs; it impacts all companies that offer services and products to customers.

Incident –
Info Classification

A privacy breach notification program and plan should include at a minimum the following components:

- Team member roles and clearly documented descriptions of the responsibilities for each; this is discussed in more detail in item 5.
- Definitions of breach categories; define when or if individual notifications must be made for each type of breach category.
- Documentation of the types of alerts that will be used for each of the breach categories.
- Forms and action checklists for each of the roles to use during the breach identification and response activities.
- A list of situations describing when individual notification is necessary.
- Procedures for making contacts with customers, credit card associations, business partners, legal staff, the board of directors, and other outside entities as applicable; this is discussed in more detail later.
- Directions for the information, actions and outcomes for each of the roles should clearly documented and logged.
- A report template for communicating to upper management a breach occurrence, how the breach was resolved, the impact to the business, subsequent changes made (or planned) to reduce the likelihood of a similar breach occurring again, and a breach follow-up time-table to identify any other unknown business impact that resulted three, six and twelve months following the breach resolution; a sample privacy breach incident report template is provided in Table 4.

Use clearly documented procedures to contain, control and correct all privacy and security incidents involve PII.

Require data custodians and anyone else who detects an information privacy or security incident, including business partners to whom you have entrusted your PII, to immediately notify the person responsible for incident response coordination upon the detection of any incident that may involve unauthorized access to systems or any type of media containing PII.

5. *Notification planning.* An international privacy principle, and a requirement within many data protection laws, is informing individuals about incidents such as privacy or security breaches that have caused their PII to be acquired, or likely acquired, by unauthorized persons. Notifying individuals of such incidents enables them to take actions to protect themselves against, or mitigate the damage from identity theft or other possible harm, as well as complies with legal requirements.

To ensure you can notify individuals in a timely and efficient manner, consider the taking the following actions:

- Collect contact information, such as postal mailing address, telephone number and e-mail address, from individuals when you collect their PII.

- If one of the ways you plan to contact impacted individuals is by e-mail, be sure to get the individuals' prior consent to use e-mail for that purpose, as required by various laws in the U.S. and worldwide. Do not depend solely upon e-mail notification, though, because many people may think such messages are phishing messages.
- Formally document the procedures for notifying individuals whose PII has been, or is reasonably believed to have been, acquired or accessed in unauthorized ways. Too many organizations depend upon ad-hoc notification; but to demonstrate due diligence as well as to consistently and efficiently provide such notifications, the procedures must be formally documented.
- Before sending individual notices, make reasonable efforts to include only those individuals whose PII was acquired. Undue notifications can have negative impacts. If you cannot identify the specific individuals whose PII was acquired, though, notify all those in the groups likely to have been effected, such as all whose information is stored in the files or on the media involved.
- Avoid sending notifications inappropriately. This can happen when the required notice of a PII breach is sent using a blanket approach to individuals who should not receive it because their PII was not involved with the breach.
- Notify impacted individuals in situations involving unauthorized acquisition of PII in any format, including computer printouts, storage media, and other forms where PII is located, as indicated within your breach definitions.
- Consider providing notice for breaches involving PII, even when if it is not "notice-triggering" information under applicable laws, but if you believe harm can come to the individual as a result. Notifying individuals will allow them to take action to protect themselves from possible harm.
- Implement procedures for determining who should get breach notifications and who should not. Document your process for determining inclusion in the group to be notified. Check the mailing list before sending the notice to be sure it is not over-inclusive.
- Notify impacted individuals as quickly as is reasonably possible after the discovery of an incident involving unauthorized access to notice-triggering information, unless law enforcement authorities indicate you cannot because it would impede their investigation. Law enforcement involvement is discussed at greater length in item 10.
- Follow a pre-planned documented procedure to contain and control the systems and files involved with the breach and have trained and qualified individuals conduct a preliminary internal assessment to determine the scope of the breach. Use computer forensic procedures to most effectively accomplish this.

Incident –
Info Classification

6. *Define roles.* Effectively responding to a breach requires participation from and coordination between virtually all areas of your company. Your breach notification team will have primary members who are involved continuously in the breach response process, and secondary members who will participate as needed based upon the type of breach. Members of your breach identification and notification team should include representatives from:

- Information security
- Privacy
- Public relations
- Law
- Human resources
- Customer relations
- Information technology operations
- Network architecture
- Operating system architecture
- Business services and applications
- Sales and marketing
- Internal auditing

Effectively responding to a breach requires participation from and coordination throughout all areas of the organization. Make the responsibilities for each role very clear and make sure your team members know and understand these roles. Make the responsibilities for each role very clear and make sure your team members know and understand these roles. Designate one individual, an incident response coordinator, to be responsible 24/7 for responding to and coordinating the privacy breach response activities.

Many organizations fail in their response efforts because the people involved either assumed someone else was performing a critical response activity, or multiple people were trying to perform the same activity and ended up at the least being inefficient by duplicating efforts, or even making the situation much worse by giving conflicting direction to personnel, or by sinking into political in-fighting and power struggles.

Collect 24/7 contact information for incident response team members and provide to team members. Each role should have backup personnel identified.

7. *Provide training to the breach identification and notification team members.* Require the team members to participate in regular response drills, perhaps once or twice a year, to ensure they fully understand what they need to do when a breach occurs. Provide training to the team members, and provide ongoing awareness messages so they stay up-to-date with incident response issues and news of incidents that have occurred at other organizations. Provide training to the breach identification and notification team members.

8. *Communicate the plan.* After investing all this work in creating a PII inventory and a breach identification and response plan, do not drop the ball by not communicating the plan throughout the organization. It is likely most, if not all, personnel handle or access some type of PII during the course of fulfilling their job responsibilities. Regularly train all personnel, including all new, temporary, and contract employees, in their roles and responsibilities in the incident response plan. Define key terms and activities within the incident response plan and identify responsible individuals.

Make sure you communicate to all personnel:

- The descriptions of the breach categories you have defined
- The items your organization considers as being PII
- An overview of the breach notification plan
- The names and contact information of the persons filling the primary privacy breach response team roles
- The potential impact a breach could have upon your organization

Regularly communicate information related to breaches and PII through a variety of awareness methods. Cover not only incidents within your own organization, but perhaps just as important for raising awareness, let your personnel know what has been happening within other organizations. Include this information within your yearly personnel information security and privacy training courses.

9. *Require third-party service providers and business partners to adopt and follow the privacy and security incident notification procedures.* When incidents happen with your business partners to whom you have entrusted personal information, it impacts your organization you must quickly be notified. You must ensure business partners have sound privacy breach identification and response procedures in place that at least match or exceed your organization's breach notification practices. Monitor and contractually enforce third-party compliance with the incident response procedures. Train key business partner contacts for their responsibilities for privacy breach response activities.

10. *Identify appropriate law enforcement contacts to notify on privacy or security incidents that may involve illegal activities.* Appropriate law enforcement agencies include your state's regional high-tech crimes task forces, the Federal Bureau of Investigation, the U.S. Secret Service, the National Infrastructure Protection Center, the local police or sheriff's department, the privacy commissioners within the countries where you do business, and so on.

Prepare a directory of privacy incident law enforcement contact information. Consider including within your response plan law enforcement with expertise in investigating high-technology crimes.

Contact your organization's legal counsel (who should be part of your response team) immediately to determine when law enforcement should contacted, especially if you believe that the incident may involve illegal activities.

When notifying law enforcement, inform the law enforcement official in charge of the investigation that you intend to notify affected individuals within ten business days, or sooner if possible. If the law enforcement official in charge tells you that giving notice within that time period would impede the criminal investigation, ask the official to inform you as soon as you can notify the affected individuals without impeding the criminal investigation. Typically, it should not be necessary for a law enforcement agency to complete an investigation before notification can be given.

Collect the following information and have it ready to provide to law enforcement if necessary:

- Description of the incident
- Date and time the incident occurred
- Date and time the incident was discovered
- Approximate number of impacted individuals
- Locations of impacted individuals

11. *Review and update.* Review the incident response plan at least annually and whenever there is a material change in your business practices that may reasonably impact the security of personal information. Test the plan at least annually, and whenever major changes are made:

- In the types of PII your organization handles
- In the systems and devices that process and store the PII
- When establishing a new business partner who will handle your PII in some manner
- When going through an acquisition, merger, divestiture or downsize

Implement a process to review and update the breach identification and notification program and plan:

- At the conclusion of an incident according to lessons learned
- To incorporate changes resulting from industry developments and new legal and regulatory requirements

12. *Communicate incidents.* Regularly communicate with your business leaders, partners, and personnel information related to breaches and PII using a variety of awareness methods. Cover not only incidents within the organization, but perhaps just as important for raising awareness, let them know what has been happening within other organizations. Include this information within yearly personnel information security and privacy training courses, as well as your ongoing awareness messages.

COORDINATION WITH CREDIT REPORTING AGENCIES

It is becoming standard practice for organizations to not only help the impacted individuals to get in touch with the consumer credit reporting agencies (Equifax, Experian, and TransUnion) following a breach, but also to pay for credit monitoring services for impacted individuals for anywhere from 2 to 5 years. Your can work with the consumer credit reporting agencies to help determine the best ways to tell impacted individuals how to contact the agencies.

If there are a large number of individuals involved, it could have a significant impact on the ability of the reporting agencies to respond efficiently if all the impacted individuals called them at once without prior notification. Contact the agencies before you send out notices, without causing the notices to be delayed, to more than 10,000 individuals.

Organizations can contact the consumer credit reporting agencies as follows:

- *Experian*: E-mail to BusinessRecordsVictimAssistance@experian.com.
- *Equifax*: Customer Services, Equifax Information Services, LLC, Customer Service: 1-800-685-5000; Cust.Serv@equifax.com.
- *TransUnion*: E-mail to fvad@transunion.com, with "Database Compromise" as subject.

BREACH NOTIFICATIONS

Organizations need to plan ahead the types of notifications that will be sent if a privacy breach occurs. See Table 3 for sample notification letters the State of California has created for organizations to use as models.

Notification Content

The following information should be included within your breach notification communications to impacted individuals:

1. A general description of what happened.
2. A general description of the types of personal information involved. Note: do not include the actual Social Security number or other actual items of information within the communications.
3. Actions taken since the incident to protect the individual's PII from further unauthorized access.
4. Actions the organization will take to assist individuals, including providing an internal contact telephone number, preferably toll-free, individuals can call for more information and assistance, providing information on the organization's website regarding the incident and what impacted individuals can do check for improper use of their PII, and so on.
5. Information describing what individuals can do to protect themselves from identity theft and other fraud. Include contact information for the three credit reporting agencies. Include contact information for the privacy commissioners of the applicable states or countries where individuals are located and/or the

Federal Trade Commission for additional information on protection against identity theft.

Make the communication easy to read and understand, using simple language and plenty of white space. Do not use condescending or flippant language. Do not use a standardized format, which could be result in the recipients thinking it is a form or marketing letter and throwing it away without reading. Do not combine the notification communication as part of another mailing.

Communication the Notifications

Here are some guidelines and considerations for sending the breach notifications:

1. Send individual notification communications to those impacted whenever possible.
2. Send the notifications by first class mail, not as bulk discount mailings.
3. Depending upon the nature and urgency of the breach, consider calling each impacted individual.
4. Use caution to send notifications by e-mail. Make sure you have received prior consent of the individuals for this type of notification. Consider if you normally communicate with the impacted individuals by e-mail; if you don't, the notifications will possibly be mistaken as being phishing messages.
5. California SB1386, and a few other state breach notification laws, indicate if more than 500,000 individuals are impacted, or if the cost of giving individual notice to impacted individuals is greater than $250,000, organizations can use all three of the following "substitute notice" procedures:

    *   Send the notice by e-mail to all affected parties whose e-mail address you have; AND
    *   Post the notice conspicuously on your web site; AND
    *   Notify major statewide media (television, radio, print).

However, consider carefully whether it will be good for your organization to notify ONLY in these substitute ways; doing so could alienate customers and possibly even result in civil suits. Most customers want organizations to contact them directly when a breach occurs. Consider the substitute notices to be used in addition to the first class mail as opposed to instead of first class mail.

ADDITIONAL RESOURCES

Here are some additional good resources you can use to help plan your privacy breach incident response and notification activities:

*   VISA paper, "What to Do if Compromised": http://usa.visa.com/download/business/accepting_visa/ops_risk_management/cisp_What_To_Do_If_Compromised.pdf?itZil, http://usa.visa.com/download/business/accepting_visa/ops_risk_management/cisp_tools_faq.html What %20To%20-Do%20If%20 Compromised
*   State of California recommended breach notification practices: http://www.privacy.ca.gov/recommendations/secbreach.pdf
*   Federal Trade Commission privacy initiatives: http://www.ftc.gov/privacy/index.html.

Table 3 Sample notice letters.

Sample Letter 1

Provided by the State of California Privacy Office
http://www.privacy.ca.gov
(Data Acquired: Credit card Number or Financial Account Number)

Dear:

I am writing to you because a recent incident may have exposed you to identity theft.

[*Describe what happened in general terms, what kind of personal information was involved, and what you are doing in response.*]

[*Name of your organization*] is writing to you so that you can take steps to protect yourself from the possibility of identity theft. We recommend that you immediately contact [credit card or financial account issuer] at [phone number] and close your account. Tell them that your account may have been compromised. If you want to open a new account, ask [name of account issuer] to give you a PIN or password. This will help control access to the account.

To further protect yourself, we recommend that you place a fraud alert on your credit file. A fraud alert lets creditors know to contact you before opening new accounts. Just call any one of the three credit reporting agencies at the number below. This will let you automatically place fraud alerts and order your credit report from all three.

*   Equifax: 800-525-6285
*   Experian: 888-397-3742
*   Trans Union: 800-680-7289

When you receive your credit reports, look them over carefully. Look for accounts you did not open. Look for inquiries from creditors that you did not initiate. And look for personal information, such as home address and Social Security number that is not accurate. If you see anything you do not understand, call the credit agency at the telephone number on the report.

If you do find suspicious activity on your credit reports, call your local police or sheriff's office and file a report of identity theft. [*Or, if appropriate, give contact number for law enforcement agency investigating the incident for you.*] Get a copy of the police report. You may need to give copies to creditors to clear up your records.

Incident – Info Classification

Even if you do not find any signs of fraud on your reports, the California Office of Privacy Protection recommends that you check your credit reports every three months for the next year. Just call one of the numbers above to order your reports and keep the fraud alert in place. For more information on identity theft, we suggest that you contact the Office of Privacy Protection. The toll-free number is 866-785-9663. Or you can visit their web site at http://www.privacy.ca.gov. If there is anything [name of your organization] can do to assist you, please call [*phone number, toll-free if possible*].

[*Closing*]

Sample Letter 2

Provided by the State of California Privacy Office
http://www.privacy.ca.gov
(Data Acquired: Driver's License or California ID Card Number)

Dear:

I am writing to you because a recent incident may have exposed you to identity theft.

[*Describe what happened in general terms, what kind of personal information was involved, and what you are doing in response.*]

[*Name of your organization*] is writing to you so that you can take steps to protect yourself from the possibility of identity theft. Since your Driver's License [or state Identification Card] number was involved, we recommend that you immediately contact your local DMV office to report the theft. Ask them to put a fraud alert on your license. This will cut off government access to your license record. Then call the toll-free DMV Fraud Hotline at 866-658-5758 for additional information.

To further protect yourself, we recommend that you place a fraud alert on your credit file. A fraud alert lets creditors know to contact you before opening new accounts. Just call any one of the three credit reporting agencies at the number below. This will let you automatically place fraud alerts and order your credit report from all three.

- Equifax: 800-525-6285
- Experian: 888-397-3742
- Trans Union: 800-680-7289

When you receive your credit reports, look them over carefully. Look for accounts you did not open. Look for inquiries from creditors that you did not initiate. And look for personal information, such as home address and Social Security number, which is not accurate. If you see anything you do not understand, call the credit agency at the telephone number on the report. If you do find suspicious activity on your credit reports, call your local police or sheriff's office and file a report of identity theft. [*Or, if appropriate, give contact number for law enforcement agency investigating the incident for you.*] Get a copy of the police report. You may need to give copies to creditors to clear up your records.

Even if you do not find any signs of fraud on your reports, the California Office of Privacy Protection recommends that you check your credit reports every three months for the next year.

Just call one of the numbers above to order your reports and keep the fraud alert in place. For more information on identity theft, we suggest that you contact the Office of Privacy Protection. The toll-free number is 866-785-9663. Or you can visit their web site at http://www.privacy.ca.gov. If there is anything [*name of your organization*] can do to assist you, please call [*phone number, toll-free if possible*].

[*Closing*]

Sample Letter 3

Provided by the State of California Privacy Office
http://www.privacy.ca.gov
(Data Acquired: Social Security Number)

Dear:

I am writing to you because a recent incident may have exposed you to identity theft.

[*Describe what happened in general terms, what kind of personal information was involved, and what you are doing in response.*]

[*Name of your organization*] is writing to you so that you can take steps to protect yourself from the possibility of identity theft. We recommend that you place a fraud alert on your credit file. A fraud alert lets creditors know to contact you before opening new accounts. Then call any one of the three credit reporting agencies at the number below. This will let you automatically place fraud alerts and order your credit report from all three.

- Equifax: 800-525-6285
- Experian: 888-397-3742
- Trans Union: 800-680-7289

When you receive your credit reports, look them over carefully. Look for accounts you did not open. Look for inquiries from creditors that you did not initiate. And look for personal information, such as home address and Social Security number, which is not accurate. If you see anything you do not understand, call the credit agency at the telephone number on the report.

If you do find suspicious activity on your credit reports, call your local police or sheriff's office and file a police report of identity theft. [*Or, if appropriate, give contact number for law enforcement agency investigating the incident for you.*] Get a copy of the police report. You may need to give copies of the police report to creditors to clear up your records.

Even if you do not find any signs of fraud on your reports, the California Office of Privacy Protection recommends that you check your credit report every three months for the next year. Just call one of the numbers above to order your reports and keep the fraud alert in place. For more information on identity theft we suggest that you contact the Office of Privacy Protection. The toll-free numbers is 866-785-9663. Or you can visit their web site at http://www.privacy.ca.gov. If there is anything [*name of your organization*] can do to assist you, please call [*phone number, toll-free if possible*].

[*Closing*]

Incident –
Info Classification

Table 4 Sample privacy incident breach report template for communication to organization leaders.

1. Executive Summary

   a. Date incident was discovered
   b. How the incident was discovered
   c. Date incident occurred
   d. Number of individuals involved
   e. Types of personal information involved
   f. Cost of the incident to the organization including:

   - Value of hardware and software lost
   - Notification costs (postage, calls, staff, website changes, etc.)
   - Lost customers
   - Legal costs
   - Public relations and advertising costs
   - Cost of additional staff to answer customer questions
   - Forensics costs
   - Fines and penalties
   - Cost to prevent the reoccurrence of a similar incident
   - Lost share value
   - Related ravel costs
   - Credit monitoring services for impacted individuals
   - Other related costs

   g. Cost to impacted individuals

   - Identified incidents of identity theft and fraud
   - Other

   h. If the incident within organization, or with a business partner
   i. Current status of incident resolution
   j. Changes made to prevent reoccurrence of the same type of incident
   k. Detail any public reports of the incident

2. Incident Details

   a. Who reported the incident or determined an incident had occurred?
   b. If someone outside the organization notified the company, what was that information told by the person within the company?
   c. Who was notified internally after the incident was discovered or reported?
   d. List the sequence events that happened from including:

   - Internal personnel involved and their assigned responsibilities
   - Time for each action
   - Meetings involved
   - Communications with news media
   - Outside persons or companies contacted to help

3. Incident Flow

   a. Diagram the movement and/or location of the impacted PII
   b. Include dates and times

4. Investigative Procedures

   a. Describe the forensic activities followed during the investigation
   b. List the forensic tools used during investigation

5. Findings

   a. Types of information compromised:

   - Name
   - Address
   - Birth date
   - Social Security number
   - Phone number
   - Medical information
   - Account number
   - Password
   - Credit card number
   - Other

   b. Number of accounts/individuals impacted
   c. Timeline of accounts/individuals at risk
   d. Timeline of compromise and source of compromise
   e. Data files compromised
   f. Were the PII data items encrypted?
   g. Were the PII data items taken on removable storage media? What kind? Has the media been recovered?
   h. Were PII data items accessed on computer systems through a network or remote access compromise? What kind of compromise?
   i. Provide details about the firewall, infrastructure, host, and personnel findings.
   j. Describe the hacking tools and utilities used.
   k. If no hacker utilities/tools were found, explain how the intrusion occurred, or could have occurred.
   l. Describe any third-party involvement with the incident, and the actions they have taken and plan to take.

6. Actions taken by compromised individuals

   a. Describe actions taken by notified individuals
   b. Include feedback from impacted individuals

7. Recommendations

   a. Procedural changes
   b. Contractual changes
   c. Technology changes
   d. Policy changes
   e. Business partner relationship changes
   f. Education activity changes
   g. Other

8. Contact information

   a. Contact information for persons participating in incident resolution
   b. Contact information or file locations for impacted individuals

Information Classification

Jim Appleyard
Senior Security Consultant, IBM Security and Privacy Services, Charlotte, North Carolina, U.S.A.

Abstract
Classifying corporate information based on business risk, data value, or other criteria (as discussed later in this entry), makes good business sense. Not all information has the same value or use, or is subject to the same risks. Therefore, protection mechanisms, recovery processes, etc., are—or should be—different, with differing costs associated with them. Data classification is intended to lower the cost of protecting data, and improve the overall quality of corporate decision making by helping ensure a higher quality of data upon which the decision makers depend.

INTRODUCTION

The benefits of an enterprisewide data classification program are realized at the corporate level, not the individual application or even departmental level. Some of the benefits to the organization include:

- Data confidentiality, integrity, and availability are improved because appropriate controls are used for all data across the enterprise.
- The organization gets the most for its information protection dollar because protection mechanisms are designed and implemented where they are needed most, and less costly controls can be put in place for non-critical information.
- The quality of decisions is improved because the quality of the data upon which the decisions are made has been improved.
- The company is provided with a process to review all business functions and informational requirements on a periodic basis to determine priorities and values of critical business functions and data.
- The implementation of an information security architecture is supported, which better positions the company for future acquisitions and mergers.

This entry will discuss the processes and techniques required to establish and maintain a corporate data classification program. There are costs associated with this process; however, most of these costs are front-end start-up costs. Once the program has been successfully implemented, the cost savings derived from the new security schemes, as well as the improved decision making, should more than offset the initial costs over the long haul, and certainly the benefits of the ongoing program outweigh the small, administrative costs associated with maintaining the data classification program.

Although not the only methodology that could be employed to develop and implement a data classification program, the one described here has been used and proved to work.

The following topics will be addressed:

- Getting started: questions to ask
- Policy
- Business Impact Analysis
- Establishing classifications
- Defining roles and responsibilities
- Identifying owners
- Classifying information and applications
- Ongoing monitoring

GETTING STARTED: QUESTIONS TO ASK

Before the actual implementation of the data classification program can begin, the Information Security Officer (ISO)—who, for the purposes of this discussion, is the assumed project manager—must ask some very important questions, and get the answers.

Is there an executive sponsor for this project?

Although not absolutely essential, obtaining an executive sponsor and champion for the project could be a critical success factor. Executive backing by someone well respected in the organization who can articulate the ISO's position to other executives and department heads will help remove barriers, and obtain much needed funding and buy-in from others across the corporation. Without an executive sponsor, the ISO will have a difficult time gaining access to executives or other influencers who can help sell the concept of data ownership and classification.

What are you trying to protect, and from what?

The ISO should develop a threat and risk analysis matrix to determine what the threats are to corporate information, the relative risks associated with those threats, and what data or

Encyclopedia of Information Assurance DOI: 10.1081/E-EIA-120046551
Copyright © 2011 by Taylor & Francis. All rights reserved.

Table 1 Threat/Risk analysis.

Application	Platform	Threat	Risk	Consequences of loss
Application				

information are subject to those threats. This matrix provides input to the business impact analysis, and forms the beginning of the plans for determining the actual classifications of data, as will be discussed later in this entry. (See Table 1 for an example of a Threat/Risk Analysis table).

Are there any regulatory requirements to consider?

Regulatory requirements will have an impact on any data classification scheme, if not on the classifications themselves, at least on the controls used to protect or provide access to regulated information. The ISO should be familiar with these laws and regulations, and use them as input to the business case justification for data classification, as well as input to the business impact analysis and other planning processes.

Has the business accepted ownership responsibilities for the data?

The business, not IT, owns the data. Decisions regarding who has what access, what classification the data should be assigned, etc. are decisions that rest solely with the business data owner. IT provides the technology and processes to implement the decisions of the data owners, but should not be involved in the decision-making process. The executive sponsor can be a tremendous help in selling this concept to the organization. Too many organizations still rely on IT for these types of decisions. The business manager must realize that the data is his data, not IT's; IT is merely the custodian of the data. Decisions regarding access, classification, ownership, etc. resides in the business units. This concept must be sold first, if data classification is to be successful.

Are adequate resources available to do the initial project?

Establishing the data classification processes and procedures, performing the business impact analysis, conducting training, etc. requires an up-front commitment of a team of people from across the organization if the project is to be successful. The ISO cannot and should not do it alone. Again, the executive sponsor can be of tremendous value in obtaining resources such as people and funding for this project that the ISO could not do. Establishing the processes, procedures, and tools to implement good, well-defined data classification processes takes time and dedicated people.

POLICY

A useful tool in establishing a data classification scheme is to have a corporate policy implemented stating that the data are an asset of the corporation and must be protected.

Within that same document, the policy should state that information will be classified based on data value, sensitivity, risk of loss or compromise, and legal and retention requirements. This provides the ISO the necessary authority to start the project, seek executive sponsorship, and obtain funding and other support for the effort.

If there is an Information Security Policy, these statements should be added if they are not already there. If no Information Security Policy exists, then the ISO should put the data classification project on hold, and develop an Information Security Policy for the organization. Without this policy, the ISO has no real authority or reason to pursue data classification. Information must first be recognized and treated as an asset of the company before efforts can be expended to protect it.

Assuming there is an Information Security Policy that mentions or states that data will be classified according to certain criteria, another policy—Data Management Policy—should be developed which establishes data classification as a process to protect information and provides:

- The definitions for each of the classifications
- The security criteria for each classification for both data and software
- The roles and responsibilities of each group of individuals charged with implementing the policy or using the data

Below is a sample Information Security Policy. Note that the policy is written at a very high level and is intended to describe the "what's" of information security. Processes, procedures, standards, and guidelines are the "hows" or implementation of the policy.

Sample Information Security Policy

All information, regardless of the form or format, which is created or used in support of company business activities is corporate information. Corporate information is a company asset and must be protected from its creation, through its useful life, and authorized disposal. It should be maintained in a secure, accurate, and reliable manner and be readily available for authorized use. Information will be classified based on its sensitivity, legal, and retention requirements, and type of access required by employees and other authorized personnel.

Information security is the protection of data against accidental or malicious disclosure, modification, or destruction. Information will be protected based on its value, confidentiality, and/or sensitivity to the company, and the risk of loss or compromise. At a minimum, information will be update-protected so that only authorized individuals can modify or erase the information.

The above policy is the minimum requirement to proceed with developing and implementing a data classification program. Additional policies may be required, such as an Information Management Policy, which supports the Information Security Policy. The ISO should consider developing this policy, and integrating it with the Information Security Policy. This policy would:

- Define information as an asset of the business unit
- Declare local business managers as the owners of information
- Establish Information Systems as the custodians of corporate information
- Clearly define roles and responsibilities of those involved in the ownership and classification of information
- Define the classifications and criteria that must be met for each
- Determine the minimum range of controls to be established for each classification

By defining these elements in a separate Information Management Policy, the groundwork is established for defining a corporate information architecture, the purpose of which is to build a framework for integrating all the strategic information in the company. This architecture can be used later in the enablement of larger, more strategic corporate applications.

The supporting processes, procedures, and standards required to implement the Information Security and Information Management policies must be defined at an operational level and be as seamless as possible. These are the "mechanical" portions of the policies, and represent the day-to-day activities that must take place to implement the policies. These include but are not limited to:

- The process to conduct a Business Impact Analysis
- Procedures to classify the information, both initially after the BIA has been completed, and to change the classification later, based on business need
- The process to communicate the classification to IS in a timely manner so the controls can be applied to the data and software for that classification
- The process to periodically review:

  — Current classification to determine if it is still valid
  — Current access rights of individuals and/or groups who have access to a particular resource
  — Controls in effect for a classification to determine their effectiveness
  — Training requirements for new data owners

- The procedures to notify custodians of any change in classification or access privileges of individuals or groups

The appropriate policies are required as a first step in the development of a Data Classification program. The policies provide the ISO with the necessary authority and mandate to develop and implement the program. Without it, the ISO will have an extremely difficult time obtaining the funding and necessary support to move forward. In addition to the policies, the ISO should solicit the assistance and support of both the Legal Department and Internal Audit. If a particular end-user department has some particularly sensitive data, their support would also provide some credibility to the effort.

BUSINESS IMPACT ANALYSIS

The next step in this process is to conduct a high-level business impact analysis on the major business functions within the company. Eventually this process should be carried out on all business functions, but initially it must be done on the business functions deemed most important to the organization.

A critical success factor in this effort is to obtain corporate sponsorship. An executive who supports the project, and may be willing to be the first whose area is analyzed, could help persuade others to participate, especially if the initial effort is highly successful and there is perceived value in the process.

A Study Team comprised of individuals from Information Security, Information Systems (application development and support), Business Continuity Planning, and Business Unit representatives should be formed to conduct the initial impact analysis. Others that may want to participate could include Internal Audit and Legal.

The Business Impact Analysis process is used by the team to:

- Identify major functional areas of information (i.e., human resources, financial, engineering, research and development, marketing, etc.).
- Analyze the threats associated with each major functional area. This could be as simple as identifying the risks associated with loss of confidentiality, integrity, or availability, or get into more detail with specific threats of computer virus infections, denial of service attacks, etc.
- Determine the risk associated with the threat (i.e., the threat could be disclosure of sensitive information, but the risk could be low because of the number of people who have access, and the controls that are imposed on the data).
- Determine the effect of loss of the information asset on the business (this could be financial, regulatory impacts, safety, etc.) for specific periods of unavailability—one hour, one day, two days, one week, a month.
- Build a table detailing the impact of loss of the information (as shown in Table 2).

Table 2 Business impact analysis.

Function	Application	Type loss (CIA)	Cost after 1 hour	Cost after 2 hours	Cost after 1 day	Cost after 1 week	Cost after 1 month
Human Resources	Payroll	Confidentiality					
		Integrity					
		Availability					
	Medical	Confidentiality					
		Integrity					
		Availability					

- Prepare a list of applications that directly support the business function (i.e., Human Resources could have personnel, medical, payroll files, skills inventory, employee stock purchase programs, etc.). This should be part of Table 2.

From the information gathered, the team can determine universal threats that cut across all business functional boundaries. This exercise can help place the applications in specific categories or classifications with a common set of controls to mitigate the common risks. In addition to the threats and their associated risks, sensitivity of the information, ease of recovery, and criticality must be considered when determining the classification of the information.

ESTABLISH CLASSIFICATIONS

Once all the risk assessment and classification criteria have been gathered and analyzed, the team must determine how many classifications are necessary and create the classification definitions, determine the controls necessary for each classification for the information and software, and begin to develop the roles and responsibilities for those who will be involved in the process. Relevant factors, including regulatory requirements, must be considered when establishing the classifications.

Too many classifications will be impractical to implement; most certainly will be confusing to the data owners and meet with resistance. The team must resist the urge for special cases to have their own data classifications. The danger is that too much granularity will cause the process to collapse under its own weight. It will be difficult to administer and costly to maintain.

On the other hand, too few classes could be perceived as not worth the administrative trouble to develop, implement, and maintain. A perception may be created that there is no value in the process, and indeed the critics may be right.

Each classification must have easily identifiable characteristics. There should be little or no overlap between the classes. The classifications should address how information and software are handled from their creation, through authorized disposal. See Table 3, Information/Software classification criteria.

Following is a sample of classification definitions that have been used in many organizations:

- **Public**—Information, that if disclosed outside the company, would not harm the organization, its employees, customers, or business partners.
- **Internal Use Only**—Information that is not sensitive to disclosure within the organization, but could harm the company if disclosed externally.
- **Company Confidential**—Sensitive information that requires "need to know" before access is given.

It is important to note that controls must be designed and implemented for both the information and software. It is not sufficient to classify and control the information alone. The software, and possibly the hardware on which the information and/or software resides, must also have proportionate controls for each classification the software manipulates. Below is a set of minimum controls for both information and software that should be considered.

Information—Minimum Controls

- **Encryption**—Data is encrypted with an encryption key so that the data is "scrambled." When the data is processed or viewed, it must be decrypted with the same key used to encrypt it. The encryption key must be kept secure and known only to those who are authorized to have access to the data. Public/private key algorithms could be considered for maximum security and ease of use.
- **Review and approve**—This is a procedural control, the intent of which is to ensure that any change to the

Table 3 Information/Software classification criteria.

Classification	Storage media	Minimum data controls	Minimum oftware ontrols	Transmission considerations	Destruction mechanisms
Application					

data is reviewed by someone technically knowledgeable to perform the task. The review and approval should be done by an authorized individual other than the person who developed the change.

- **Backup and recovery**—Depending on the criticality of the data and ease of recovery, plans should be developed and periodically tested to ensure the data is backed up properly, and can be fully recovered.
- **Separation of duties**—The intent of this control is to help ensure that no single person has total control over the data entry and validation process, which would enable someone to enter or conceal an error that is intended to defraud the organization or commit other harmful acts. An example would be not allowing the same individual to establish vendors to an Authorized Vendor File, then also be capable of authorizing payments to a vendor.
- **Universal access: none**—No one has access to the data unless given specific authority to read, update, etc. This type of control is generally provided by security access control software.
- **Universal access: read**—Everyone with access to the system can read data with the control applied; however, update authority must be granted to specific individuals, programs, or transactions. This type of control is provided by access control software.
- **Universal access: update**—Anyone with access to the system can update the data, but specific authority must be granted to delete the data. This control is provided by access control software.
- **Universal access: alter**—Anyone with access to the system can view, update, or delete the data. This is virtually no security.
- **Security access control software**—This software allows the administrator to establish security rules as to who has access rights to protected resources. Resources can include data, programs, transactions, individual computer IDs, and terminal IDs. Access control software can be set up to allow access by classes of users to classes of resources, or at any level of granularity required to any particular resource or group of resources.

Software—Minimum Controls

- **Review and approve**—The intent of this control is that any change to the software be reviewed by someone technically knowledgeable to perform this task. The review and approval should be an authorized individual other than the person who developed the change.
- **Review and Approve Test Plan and Results**—A test plan would be prepared, approved, documented, and followed.
- **Backup and recovery**—Procedures should be developed and periodically tested to ensure backups of the

software are performed in such a manner that the most recent production version is recoverable within a reasonable amount of time.

- **Audit/history**—Information documenting the software change such as the work request detailing the work to be performed, test plans, test results, corrective actions, approvals, who performed the work, and other pertinent documentation required by the business.
- **Version and configuration control**—Refers to maintaining control over the versions of software checked out for update, being loaded to staging or production libraries, etc. This would include the monitoring of error reports associated with this activity and taking appropriate corrective action.
- **Periodic testing**—Involves taking a test case and periodically running the system with known data that has predictable results. The intent is to ensure the system still performs as expected, and does not produce results that are inconsistent with the test case data. These tests could be conducted at random or on a regular schedule.
- **Random checking**—Production checking of defined data and results.
- **Separation of duties**—This procedural control is intended to meet certain regulatory and audit system requirements by helping ensure that one single individual does not have total control over a programming process without appropriate review points or requiring other individuals to perform certain tasks within the process prior to final user acceptance. For example, someone other than the original developer would be responsible for loading the program to the production environment from a staging library.
- **Access control of software**—In some applications, the coding techniques and other information contained within the program are sensitive to disclosure, or unauthorized access could have economic impact. Therefore, the source code must be protected from unauthorized access.
- **Virus checking**—All software destined for a PC platform, regardless of source, should be scanned by an authorized virus-scanning program for computer viruses before it is loaded into production on the PC or placed on a file server for distribution. Some applications would have periodic testing as part of a software quality assurance plan.

DEFINING ROLES AND RESPONSIBILITIES

To have an effective Information Classification program, roles and responsibilities of all participants must be clearly defined. An appropriate training program, developed and implemented, is an essential part of the program. The Study Team identified to conduct the Business Impact Analysis is a good starting point to develop these roles and responsibilities and identify training requirements. However, it should be noted that some members of the original team, such as Legal, Internal Audit, or Business Continuity Planning, most likely will not be interested in this phase. They should be replaced with representatives from the corporate organizational effectiveness group, training, and possibly corporate communications.

Not all of the roles defined in the sections that follow are applicable for all information classification schemes and many of the roles can be performed by the same individual. The key to this exercise is to identify which of the *roles* defined is appropriate for your particular organization, again keeping in mind that an individual may perform more than one of these when the process is fully functional.

- **Information owner**—Business executive or business manager who is responsible for a company business information asset. Responsibilities include, but are not limited to:

  - Assign initial information classification and periodically review the classification to ensure it still meets the business needs.
  - Ensure security controls are in place commensurate with the classification.
  - Review and ensure currency of the access rights associated with information assets they own.
  - Determine security requirements, access criteria, and backup requirements for the information assets they own.
  - Perform or delegate, if desired, the following:

    - Approval authority for access requests from other business units or assign a delegate in the same business unit as the executive or manager owner
    - Backup and recovery duties or assign to the custodian
    - Approval of the disclosure of information act on notifications received concerning security violations against their information assets

- **Information custodian**—The information custodian, usually an information systems person, is the delegate of the information owner with primary responsibilities for dealing with backup and recovery of the business information. Responsibilities include the following:

  - Perform backups according to the backup requirements established by the information owner.

  - When necessary, restore lost or corrupted information from backup media to return the application to production status.
  - Perform related tape and DASD management functions as required to ensure availability of the information to the business.
  - Ensure record retention requirements are met based on the information owner's analysis.

- **Application owner**—Manager of the business unit who is fully accountable for the performance of the business function served by the application. Responsibilities include the following:

  - Establish user access criteria and availability requirements for their applications.
  - Ensure the security controls associated with the application are commensurate with support for the highest level of information classification used by the application.
  - Perform or delegate the following:

    - Day-to-day security administration
    - Approval of exception access requests
    - Appropriate actions on security violations when notified by security administration
    - The review and approval of all changes to the application prior to being placed into the production environment
    - Verification of the currency of user access rights to the application

- **User manager**—The immediate manager or supervisor of an employee. They have ultimate responsibility for all user IDs and information assets owned by company employees. In the case of non-employee individuals such as contractors, consultants, this manager is responsible for the activity and for the company assets used by these individuals. This is usually the manager responsible for hiring the outside party. Responsibilities include the following:

  - Inform security administration of the termination of any employee so that the user ID owned by that individual can be revoked, suspended, or made inaccessible in a timely manner.
  - Inform security administration of the transfer of any employee if the transfer involves the change of access rights or privileges.
  - Report any security incident or suspected incident to Information Security.
  - Ensure the currency of user ID information such as the employee identification number and account information of the user ID owner.

— Receive and distribute initial passwords for newly created user IDs based on the manager's discretionary approval of the user having the user ID.
— Educate employees with regard to security policies, procedures, and standards to which they are accountable.

- **Security administrator**—Any company employee who owns a user ID that has been assigned attributes or privileges associated with access control systems, such as ACF2, Top Secret, or RACF. This user ID allows them to set system-wide security controls or administer user IDs and information resource access rights. These security administrators may report to either a business division or Information Security within Information Systems. Responsibilities include the following:

— Understand the different data environments and the impact of granting access to them.
— Ensure access requests are consistent with the information directions and security guidelines.
— Administer access rights according to criteria established by the Information Owners.
— Creat and remove user IDs as directed by the user manager.
— Administer the system within the scope of their job description and functional responsibilities.
— Distribute and follow up on security violation reports.
— Send passwords of newly created user IDs to the manager of the user ID owner only.

- **Security analyst**—Person responsible for determining the data security directions (strategies, procedures, guidelines) to ensure information is controlled and secured based on its value, risk of loss or compromise, and ease of recoverability. Duties include the following:

— Provide data security guidelines to the information management process.
— Develop basic understanding of the information to ensure proper controls are implemented.
— Provide data security design input, consulting and review.

- **Change control analyst**—Person responsible for analyzing requested changes to the IT infrastructure and determining the impact on applications. This function also analyzes the impact to the databases, data-related tools, application code, etc.
- **Data analyst**—This person analyzes the business requirements to design the data structures and

recommends data definition standards and physical platforms, and is responsible for applying certain data management standards. Responsibilities include the following:

— Design data structures to meet business needs.
— Design physical data base structure.
— Create and maintain logical data models based on business requirements.
— Provide technical assistance to data owner in developing data architectures.
— Record metadata in the data library.
— Creat, maintain, and use metadata to effectively manage database deployment.

- **Solution provider**—Person who participates in the solution (application) development and delivery processes in deploying business solutions; also referred to as an integrator, application provider/programmer, IT provider. Duties include the following:

— Work with the data analyst to ensure the application and data will work together to meet the business requirements.
— Give technical requirements to the data analyst to ensure performance and reporting requirements are met.

- **End user**—Any employees, contractors, or vendors of the company who use information systems resources as part of their job. Responsibilities include:

— Maintain confidentiality of log-on password(s).
— Ensure security of information entrusted to their care.
— Use company business assets and information resources for management approved purposes only.
— Adhere to all information security policies, procedures, standards, and guidelines.
— Promptly report security incidents to management.

- **Process owner**—This person is responsible for the management, implementation, and continuous improvement of a process that has been defined to meet a business need. This person:

— Ensures data requirements are defined to support the business process.
— Understands how the quality and availability affect the overall effectiveness of the process.
— Works with the data owners to define and champion the data quality program for data within the process.

Incident –
Info Classification

— Resolves data-related issues that span applications within the business processes.

- **Product line manager**—Person responsible for understanding business requirements and translating them into product requirements, working with the vendor/user area to ensure the product meets requirements, monitoring new releases, and working with the stakeholders when movement to a new release is required. This person:

— Ensures new releases of software are evaluated and upgrades are planned for and properly implemented.

— Ensures compliance with software license agreements.

— Monitors performance of production against business expectations.

— Analyzes product usage, trends, options, competitive sourcing, etc., to identify actions needed to meet project demands of the product.

IDENTIFYING OWNERS

The steps previously defined are required to establish the information classification infrastructure. With the classifications and their definitions defined, and roles and responsibilities of the participants articulated, it is time to execute the plan and begin the process of identifying the information owners. As stated previously, the information owners *must* be from the business units. It is the business unit that will be most greatly affected if the information becomes lost or corrupted; the data exists solely to satisfy a business requirement. The following criteria must be considered when identifying the proper owner for business data:

- Must be from the business; data ownership is *not* an IT responsibility.
- Senior management support is a key success factor.
- Data owners must be given (through policy, perhaps) the necessary authority commensurate with their responsibilities and accountabilities.
- For some business functions, a multilevel approach may be necessary.

A phased approach will most likely meet with less resistance than trying to identify all owners and classify all information at the same time. The Study Team formed to develop the roles and responsibilities should also develop the initial implementation plan. This plan should consider using a phased approach—first identifying from the risk assessment data those applications that are critical or most important by orders of magnitude to the

corporation (such as time-critical business functions first). Owners for these applications are more easily identified and probably are sensitized to the mission criticality of their information. Other owners and information can be identified later by business functions throughout the organization.

A training program must also be developed and be ready to implement as the information owners and their delegates are named. Any tools such as spreadsheets for recording application and information ownership and classification and reporting mechanisms should be developed ahead of time for use by the information owners. Once the owners have been identified, training should commence immediately so that it is delivered at the time it is needed.

CLASSIFY INFORMATION AND APPLICATIONS

The information owners, after completing their training, should begin collecting the meta data about their business functions and applications. A formal data collection process should be used to ensure a consistency in the methods and types of information gathered. This information should be stored in a central repository for future reference and analysis. Once the information has been collected, the information owners should review the definitions for the information classifications, and classify their data according to that criteria. The owners can use the following information in determining the appropriate controls for the classification:

- Audit information maintained: how much and where it is, and what controls are imposed on the audit data
- Separation of duties required: yes or no; if yes, how is it performed
- Encryption requirements
- Data protection mechanisms; access controls defined based on classification, sensitivity, etc.
- Universal access control assigned
- Backup and recovery processes documented
- Change control and review processes documented
- Confidence level in data accuracy
- Data retention requirements defined
- Location of documentation

The following application controls are required to complement the data controls, but care should be taken to ensure all controls (both data and software) are commensurate with the information classification and value of the information:

- Audit controls in place
- Develop and approve test plans
- Separation of duties practiced
- Change management processes in place

- Code tested, verified for accuracy
- Access control for code in place
- Version controls for code implemented
- Backup and recovery processes in place

ONGOING MONITORING

Once the information processes have been implemented and data classified, the ongoing monitoring processes should be implemented. The internal audit department should lead this effort to ensure compliance with policy and established procedures. Information Security, working with selected information owners, Legal, and other interested parties, should periodically review the information classifications themselves to ensure they still meet business requirements.

The information owners should periodically review the data to ensure that it is still appropriately classified. Also, access rights of individuals should be periodically reviewed to ensure these rights are still appropriate for the job requirements. The controls associated with each classification should also be reviewed to ensure they are still appropriate for the classification they define.

SUMMARY

Information and software classification is necessary to better manage information. If implemented correctly, classification can reduce the cost of protecting information because in today's environment, "one size fits all" will no longer work within the complexity of most corporation's heterogeneous platforms that make up the IT infrastructure. Information classification enhances the probability that controls will be placed on the data where they are needed the most, and not applied where they are not needed.

Classification security schemes enhance the usability of data by ensuring the confidentiality, integrity, and availability of information. By implementing a corporate-wide information classification program, good business practices are enhanced by providing a secure, cost-effective data platform that supports the company's business objectives. The key to the successful implementation of the information classification process is senior management support. The corporate information security policy should lay the groundwork for the classification process, and be the first step in obtaining management support and buy-in.

Index

design verification and testing,
503–504
functionally tested, 502
semiformally designed and tested,
502–503
semiformally verified design and
tested, 503
structurally tested, 502
white-box, black-box, and gray-box
testing, 503t
government and commercial use, 504
origins, 499–500
protection profiles and security targets,
500–501, 501f
sections, 500
security assurance classes, 501–502
security requirements, 501
and TCSEC levels, 502t
Common Criteria (CC), IT security
evaluation, 506
components of CC CEM, 509f
components of methodology, 509
CC, 510–513
CEM, 513
future of, 515
history, 506–508
purpose and intended use, 508–509
security functionality, 510
timeline of events leading to
development of, 507t
user community and stakeholders,
513–515
Common Criteria Implementation
Management Board (CCIMB), 515
Common criteria (ISO 15408), 1022
Common Criteria Recognition Agreement
(CCRA), 513
Common Criteria Testing Laboratories
(CCTL), 515
Common Data Security Architecture
(CDSA), 1768
Common Evaluation Criteria (CEM), 825t
Common Gateway Interface (CGI), 3098
Common Interface File System (CIFS), 2829
Common Object Request Broker
Architecture (CORBA), 3098
Common Open Policy Services (COPS),
3059
Commons, concept
emergent property, 1684–1685
oversight/individualized accountability,
problem, 1684
Common sense, 1055
Common Uniform Driver Architecture
(CUDA), 2065
Communication channel, 621
Communication protocol, classification
critical, 1867
emergency, 1867
informational, 1867
warning, 1867

Communication protocols and services,
517
protocols, 517–518
file transfer protocol (FTP), 519–520
hypertext transfer protocol (HTTP),
520
Internet Protocol, 518
Internet Protocol v6.0 (IPng), 518–519
point-to-point protocol (PPP), 520
serial line Internet protocol (SLIP),
520
Telnet, 519
transmission control protocol
(TCP), 519
user datagram protocol (UDP), 519
security protocols, 520
challenge handshake authentication
protocol (CHAP), 522
Internet security association key
management protocol
(ISAKMP), 522
layer 2 forwarding (L2F), 522
layer 2 tunneling protocol (L2TP), 522
password authentication protocol
(PAP), 522
point-to-point tunneling protocol
(PPTP), 521
secure electronic transaction
(SET), 521
secure file transfer protocol (S-FTP),
521
secure-HTTP (S-HTTP), 521
secure Internet protocol (Secure-IP or
IPSec), 522
secure socket layer (SSL), 520–521
services
Secure Shell (SSH 2), 522–523
Telnet, 522
Communications and data movement,
CRM, 731–733
Communications Assistance for Law
Enforcement Act (CALEA), 3054
Communications protocol, 29–30, 29f
Communications Security (COMSEC),
508
Communication surveillance, record
target of attack, 1635
target of fishing expeditions, 1635
Community, definition, 2722
Commwarrior virus, 1654
Compact Disk (CD), 1855
Company-to-customer interface, 2332
Comparative analysis, 385t
Comparison, 856
Compartmentalization, 1, 778, 839
Compensating controls
activity logs, review, 2087
monitoring, 2087
separation of duties, 2087
supervision, 2087

Competition-sensitive data; See
Confidential data
Competition-type arena, 2333
Competitive Local Exchange Carrier
(CLEC), 2256
Completed requirements matrix,
489–489t
Completeness, definition, 2698
Complex Adaptive Systems (CAS),
2015–2017, 2019
Complexity, 2848
Compliance, 1011
Compliance assurance, 524–525f
best practices, 529
control frameworks and standards, 526
definition, 524
11-Factor Security Compliance
Assurance Manifesto, 529–531
naming, 526–527
COBIT, 527
COSO, 527
FISCAM, 528
ISO 17799, 527
ITIL, 527
NIST, 528
technical control standards, 528
penalties for non-compliance,
528–529
regulations, 525–526
Compliance-checking activity, 1539
Composite application; See Mashup
application
Comprehensive security awareness
program, 2194
Compression-based images, MPEGand
JPEG, 2825
Computer-Aided Design (CAD), 2068
Computer-Aided Software Engineering
(CASE), 2032–2033
Computer and Internet Security (CIS), 731
Computer controls guideline questionnaire,
risk management, 2534t
Computer crime, 545; See also Computer
crime investigations
civil law, 1220
for financial restitution, 1220
compensatory damages, 1220
punitive damages, 1220
statutory damages, 1220
inpoundment order or writ of
possession, 1220
no jail sentence, 1220
search warrant, 1220
Committee of sponsoring organizations
(COSO), 545
concepts, 545
conspiracy, 546
destruction, 545–546
disruption, 546
fraud, 545
theft, 545

Transmission Control Protocol/Internet
 Protocol (TCP/IP), 1410
Transmission Control Protocol (TCP), 519,
 1826, 1845, 2776, 2903, 3063, 3120
Transmission method, 2360
Transmission methods security, 3116–3118
 CDMA, 3117–3118
 FDMA, 3116
 GSM, 3117
 TDMA, 3116–3117
Transmission security, 1320
Transparent connectivity, 2489
Transparent proxies, 2239
Transport Control Protocol/Internet
 Protocol (TCP/IP), 1673–1674, 2489,
 2491
Transport Control Protocol (TCP)
 connection-oriented protocol, 1674
 three-way handshake, 1674–1675
Transport Layer Security Protocol (TLSP),
 1965
Transport Layer Security (TLS), 916, 1296,
 1767, 2962–2968, 3030, 3060, 3067
 attacking TLS, 2966–2968
 encapsulating higher-level protocols,
 2967f
 man-in-the-middle attack, 2967f
 million-message attack, 2968
 timing cryptanalysis attack, 2967
 ensuring data integrity, 2963
 handling errors, 2966
 closure alerts, 2966
 error messages, 2966
 TLS error messages, 2967t
 Handshake Protocol, 2962
 IETF RFC 2246, 1296
 implementations, 2968
 parameters, 1296
 protecting data, 2962–2963
 DES, 2962
 IDEA, 2963
 RC2, 2963
 RC4, 2962
 Triple DES (3DES), 2963
 protocols, 2963
 certificates, 2965–2965t
 dissecting the handshake protocol,
 2964–2965
 handshake exchange, 2965f
 handshake protocol, 1296,
 2963–2964, 2964f
 record protocol, 1296, 2965–2966
 parameters, 2966t
 resuming an existing session, 2965
 security parameters, 2964t
 stack, 2963f
 Record Protocol, 2962
 Secure Sockets Layer (SSL), 1296
 use of, 1296, 2962
Transport Mode, 1722, 2838
Transposition cipher, 663

TransUnion, 1458
Trapdoors, 539–540
 detecting, 540–541
Trap-PDU, 2723
Trapping intruders, network security
 attributes, 1985
 benefit, 1983
 psychology at work, 1985
 qualities, good, 1983–1985
 accurate trigger, 1984
 attractive bait, 1983–1984
 combination, use, 1984
 entrapment, 1985
 hidden, 1983
 original, 1984
 strong snare, 1984
 threat, assessment, 1982–1983
 experimentation, 1982–1983
 firsthand experience, 1983
 911 emergency system, 1983
 measuring, 1983
 reading, 1982
 books, 1982
 mailing lists, 1982
 newsgroups, 1982
 newspaper articles, 1982
 technical articles, 1982
 trade journal articles, 1982
 surveys, 1983
Treadway Commission, 1525
Tree-structured directories/files, 2120
Trend Micro, 1839
Trends, enterprise risk management,
 2543–2544
Trends, VPN, 3003–3005
Trial and error method, 2018
Trigger, 1985
Trillian Professional client, 1629, 1633, 1637
Trinity Sinn Fein Web site, 1600
Tripartite model, 221–222
 affect, 221
 behavior, 221
 cognition, 222
Triple DES, 34, 37, 661, 843, 1757, 2713
 time line, 724f
Triple DES-112, 693
Tripwire, 2592–2593, 2725
Tripwire tool, 1858
Trival File Transfer Protocol (TFTP), 1967,
 3063
Trojan horse attack tool, 1711
Trojan horses, 536–537, 1484, 1562, 1957,
 2472–2473, 2480, 2483, 2592,
 2803–2804
 detecting and preventing attacks, 537
 and e-mail, 945
 and rootkits, 1285–1287
 defenses, 1286–1287
 anti-virus programs, 1286
 integrity checking programs, 1286
 monolithic kernel, 1287

rootkits, 1286
 /bin/login, 1286
 ifconfig command, 1286
 kernel-level RootKits, 1286
 ps and du command, 1286
 tools, 1286
 traditional Trojan horses, 1286
 programs, 1286
Trojan program, 2796
Trojans, VPN, 3003
Troubleshooting, 2489, 2491
Trouble tickets, 2220
TRU RADIUS Accountant, 3042
TruSecure, 2133
Trusted Computer System Evaluation
 Criteria (TCSEC), 1491
Trusted Computing Base (TCB), 138,
 1491
Trusted Computing Group (TCG), 977,
 2063, 2066
Trusted Computing Standards Evaluation
 Criteria, 2343
Trusted End System (TES), 988
Trusted network connect specification,
 977–980
 architecture, 977f
 architecture with provisioning and
 remediation layer, 979f
 layered , architecture levels, 978f
Trusted Network Connect (TNC), 977
 architecture, 977f
 layered , architecture levels, 978f
Trusted Network Connect (TNC) standard,
 2063
Trusted Network Interpretation, 1557
*Trusted Network Interpretation of the
 Trusted Computer System Evaluation
 Criteria*, 1557
Trusted Operating System (TOS), 1864
Trusted Platform Module (TPM),
 1481–1482, 2062
Trusted Solaris, 1864
Trusted Third Party (TTP), 1724
Trust relationships, 1388
"Try before you buy" program, 1646
TSA; *See* U.S. Transportation Security
 Authority (TSA)
TTLS; *See* Tunneled Transport Layer
 Security (TTLS)
TTP; *See* Trusted Third Party (TTP)
Tunneled Transport Layer Security
 (TTLS), 1413
Tunneling, 2832
Tunnel Mode, 2838
Tuple-level labeling, 2473
Turbo (LAN extensions), 3159
TurboTax database, 3006
Turnbull Report (1999), 1525
TVM; *See* Threat and Vulnerability
 Management (TVM)
Twinax cable, 1995